Graphical Drawing
- CDC
  - CClientDC
  - CMetaFileDC
  - CPaintDC
  - CWindowDC

Control Support
- CDockState
- CImageList

Graphical Drawing Objects
- CGdiObject
  - CBitmap
  - CBrush
  - CFont
  - CPalette
  - CPen
  - CRgn

Menus
- CMenu

Command Line
- CCommandLineInfo

ODBC Database Support
- CDatabase
- CRecordset
  - user recordsets
- CLongBinary

DAO Database Support
- CDaoDatabase
- CDaoQueryDef
- CDaoRecordset
- CDaoTableDef
- CDaoWorkspace

Synchronization
- CSyncObject
  - CCriticalSection
  - CEvent
  - CMutex
  - CSemaphore

Windows Sockets
- CAsyncSocket
  - CSocket

Arrays
- CArray (template)
- CByteArray
- CDWordArray
- CObArray
- CPtrArray
- CStringArray
- CUIntArray
- CWordArray
- arrays of user types

Lists
- CList (template)
- CPtrList
- CObList
- CStringList
- list of user types

Maps
- CMap (template)
- CMapWordToPtr
- CMapPtrToWord
- CMapPtrToPtr
- CMapWordToOb
- CMapStringToPtr
- CMapStringToOb
- CMapStringToString
- maps of user types

Internet Services
- CInternetSession
- CInternetConnection
  - CFtpConnection
  - CGopherConnection
  - CHttpConnection
- CFileFind
  - CFtpFileFind
  - CGopherFileFind
- CGopherLocator

Classes Not Derived from CObject

Internet Server API
- CHtmlStream
- CHttpFilter
- CHttpFilterContext
- CHttpServer
- CHttpServerContext

Run-Time Object Model Support
- CArchive
- CDumpContext
- CRuntimeClass

Simple Value Types
- CPoint
- CRect
- CSize
- CString
- CTime
- CTimeSpan

Structures
- CCreateContext
- CMemoryState
- COleSafeArray
- CPrintInfo

Support Classes
- CCmdUI
  - COleCmdUI
- CDaoFieldExchange
- CDataExchange
- CDBVariant
- CFieldExchange
- COleDataObject
- COleDispatchDriver
- CPropExchange
- CRectTracker
- CWaitCursor

Typed Template Collections
- CTypedPtrArray
- CTypedPtrList
- CTypedPtrMap

OLE Type Wrappers
- CFontHolder
- CPictureHolder

OLE Automation Types
- COleCurrency
- COleDateTime
- COleDateTimeSpan
- COleVariant

Synchronization
- CMultiLock
- CSingleLock

PROGRAMMING WINDOWS® WITH MFC

Second Edition

Jeff Prosise

Microsoft Press

PUBLISHED BY
Microsoft Press
A Division of Microsoft Corporation
One Microsoft Way
Redmond, Washington 98052-6399

Library of Congress Cataloging-in-Publication Data
Prosise, Jeff.
    Programming Windows with MFC / Jeff Prosise. -- 2nd ed.
       p.   cm.
    Rev. ed. of: Programming Windows 95 with MFC.
    ISBN 1-57231-695-0
    1. Microsoft Windows (Computer file)   2. Operating systems
(Computers) 3. Microsoft foundation class library. I. Prosise,
Jeff. Programming Windows 95 with MFC. II. Title.
    QA76.73.B3P77   1999
    005.265--dc21   99-13028
                                        CIP

Printed and bound in the United States of America.

1 2 3 4 5 6 7 8 9 WCWC 4 3 2 1 0 9

Distributed in Canada by ITP Nelson, a division of Thomson Canada Limited.

A CIP catalogue record for this book is available from the British Library.

Microsoft Press books are available through booksellers and distributors worldwide. For further information about international editions, contact your local Microsoft Corporation office, or contact Microsoft Press International directly at fax (425) 936-7329. Visit our Web site at mspress.microsoft.com.

Acquisitions Editor: Eric Stroo
Project Editor: Sally Stickney
Technical Editor: Marc Young

To Amy

Brief Contents

Contents

Contents

Contents

Contents

Contents

Contents

Part IV   COM, OLE, and Active X

Contents

Contents

Acknowledgments

The production of this book required the efforts of many people, but two in particular deserve to be singled out for their diligent, sustained, and unselfish efforts. Sally Stickney, the book's principal editor, navigated me through that minefield called the English language and contributed greatly to the book's readability. Marc Young, whose talents as a technical editor are nothing short of amazing, was relentless in tracking down bugs, testing sample code, and verifying facts. Sally, Marc: This book is immeasurably better because of you. Thanks.

Introduction

Like many of my colleagues in this industry, I learned Windows programming from Charles Petzold's *Programming Windows*—a classic programming text that is the bible to an entire generation of Windows programmers. When I set out to become an MFC programmer in 1994, I went shopping for an MFC equivalent to *Programming Windows*. After searching in vain for such a book and spending a year learning MFC the old-fashioned way, I decided to write one myself. It's the book you hold in your hands. And it's the book I would like to have had when I was learning to program Windows the MFC way.

MFC, as you probably already know, is Microsoft's C++ class library for Windows programming. *Programming Windows with MFC* isn't a book about C++; rather, it's a book about writing 32-bit Windows applications in C++ using MFC rather than the Windows API as the chief means of accessing the operating system's essential features and services. It was written with two kinds of people in mind:

- Windows API programmers who want to learn MFC

- Programmers who have never before programmed Windows

Whichever camp you fall into, I assume that you know the C++ programming language already and are comfortable with basic C++ idioms such as derived classes and virtual functions. If these assumptions are true, you're ready to begin climbing the hill that is MFC programming.

Even veteran Windows programmers frequently find MFC code confusing the first time they see it, in part because of the presence of code created by the MFC code-generating wizards in Visual C++ and in part because of the countless lines of code hidden away in MFC classes such as *CFrameWnd*, *CDocument*, and *CView*. That's why this book takes a rather unusual approach to teaching MFC. It begins by having you write MFC code by hand (without the wizards) and by utilizing MFC 1.0–style application architectures—that is, applications that use neither documents nor views. Only after you've mastered the fundamentals and become acquainted with basic MFC classes such as *CWnd* and *CWinApp* do I introduce the wizards and teach you how to take advantage of MFC's document/view architecture. Along the way, you build an understanding from the ground up of the message-oriented nature of Windows and of key components of Windows itself, such as the Graphics Device Interface (GDI). I believe that this approach makes learning MFC not only less intimidating but also more enjoyable. I think you'll agree once you've worked through the book and can look back on the learning experience from the standpoint of a knowledgeable Windows programmer.

Programming Windows with MFC is divided into four parts. Part I introduces the core tenets of MFC and Windows programming, beginning with a simple "Hello, MFC" application and introducing, one by one, menus, controls, dialog boxes, and other application building blocks. Part II builds on the foundation laid in Part I with a detailed look at the document/view architecture. In particular, Chapters 9, 10, and 11 reveal much of the "magic" behind documents and views and explain not only how to write basic document/view applications but also how to implement some not so basic features such as split-window views of a document and print previews. Part III covers some of the more advanced features of Windows and MFC—features such as color palettes, bitmap handling, and multiple threads of execution. In Part IV, you'll learn how MFC wraps its arms around COM, OLE, and ActiveX and how to write COM-enabled applications and software components. By the time you're finished with Chapter 21, you'll be well versed in the art of 32-bit Windows programming using MFC. And you'll have prodigious amounts of sample code to draw from when it's time to strike out on your own and write your first great Windows application.

WHAT'S NEW IN THE SECOND EDITION

Those of you who read the first edition of this book will notice two rather obvious changes in the second edition. First, this edition contains seven new chapters. One is devoted to the MFC view classes; another covers the MFC collection classes; one introduces MFC file I/O and serialization mechanisms; and four cover the relationship between MFC and COM. MFC is not the general-purpose COM framework that the Active Template Library (ATL) is, but MFC makes certain types of COM programming exceptionally easy. For example, MFC greatly simplifies the task of writing ActiveX controls, and it makes writing Automation servers—programs that use COM to expose their functionality to scripting clients—a breeze.

The second major change in this edition has to do with wizards. The first edition didn't cover the MFC wizards at all. The second edition uses hand-generated code in Chapters 1 through 3 but then shifts gears and begins using AppWizard and Class-Wizard in Chapter 4. Why the change of heart? I still believe that code-generating wizards are an impediment to learning and should be used only by knowledgeable programmers, but I've also come to realize that in the real world, MFC programmers use the wizards. For certain tasks—writing ActiveX controls, for example—it doesn't make sense *not* to use the wizards. So after much deliberation, I decided I would be remiss not to cover them.

Despite the new material regarding wizards, however, this is not—and never will be—a book about clicking buttons in AppWizard. After introducing a fundamental skill, such as how to write a message handler with ClassWizard, I thereafter let the source code do the talking and assume that you can figure out how the source code was created. Keep in mind that the wizards never do anything you can't do yourself, so it's perfectly feasible to type in every source code listing by hand if you'd like to.

The downside to using wizards in a book that teaches MFC programming is that the code they produce isn't fit to publish. The first edition of this book included printed listings for each and every source code file. This one does not. It contains printed copies of *relevant* source code files and provides the others on CD. Why? Because printing a source code file that's 50 percent meat and 50 percent fat adds bulk to a book without adding content. Some of the code produced by the MFC AppWizard in Visual C++ 6.0 won't even compile. (For details, see Chapter 4.) I'm not very proud of the parts of my book that the wizards created, because those portions are littered with arbitrary blank lines, comments that lack consistent style, and unnecessary functions. For someone who takes pride in writing concise, readable sample code, wizard output is a bitter pill to swallow.

Nevertheless, wizards represent the new world order in Windows programming, and they're something that you, I, and everyone else must get used to. It's a shame that the Visual C++ team won't give us real wizards to play with instead of the toys that they pass off as wizards today. Until they do, we must make do with what we have.

WHAT'S ON THE CD

The companion CD contains source code and executables for all the sample programs presented in the book. All samples were written and compiled with Visual C++ 6.0 and MFC 6.0 and tested on various Win32 platforms. Unless otherwise noted, all are compatible with Windows 98, Windows NT 4.0, and Windows 2000. Most are also compatible with Windows 95 and Windows NT 3.51.

You can copy the contents of the CD to your hard disk by running the setup program found in the CD's root directory, or you can retrieve the files directly from the CD's \Code directory. The \Code directory contains one subdirectory for each chapter of the book—Chap01, Chap02, and so on. Inside these subdirectories you'll find the sample programs. Each set of source code files is accompanied by a release-build EXE as well as a Visual C++ workspace (DSW) file that you can open with Visual C++'s Open Workspace command.

FROM ME TO YOU (AND YOU TO ME)

From the day in 1995 when I began writing the first edition of *Programming Windows with MFC*, my goal has been to provide C++ programmers with the same kind of timeless, irreplaceable resource that *Programming Windows* is to C programmers. Whether I've achieved that goal, I'll let you be the judge.

I want to know what you think about *Programming Windows with MFC*, and I particularly want to hear from you if you find mistakes. You can reach me by sending mail to *jeffpro@msn.com* or by visiting my Web site at *www.prosise.com*. At that site you'll find up-to-date information regarding the book, a list of errata, and information about other projects that I'm working on. Later this year, I plan to post a brand new chapter on MFC DLLs that you can read and comment on online.

Given the huge volume of computer books vying for buyers' attention in bookstores today, I know that you could have chosen any number of MFC books besides this one. I thank you for purchasing *Programming Windows with MFC*, and I sincerely hope you conclude that your money was well spent. Enjoy!

Jeff Prosise
March 12, 1999

Part I

Fundamentals of Windows and MFC

Chapter 1

Hello, MFC

A few short years ago, the person learning to program Microsoft Windows for the first time had a limited number of programming tools to choose from. C was the language spoken by the Windows Software Development Kit (SDK), and alternative Windows programming environments such as Microsoft Visual Basic hadn't arrived on the scene. Most Windows applications were written in C, and the fledgling Windows programmer faced the daunting task not only of learning the ins and outs of a new operating system but also of getting acquainted with the hundreds of different application programming interface (API) functions that Windows supports.

Today many Windows programs are still written in C. But the variety of Windows programming environments available means that commercial-quality Windows programs can be written in C, C++, Pascal, BASIC, and a number of other languages. Moreover, C++ has all but replaced C as the professional Windows programmer's language of choice because the sheer complexity of Windows, coupled with the wide-ranging scope of the Windows API, cries out for an object-oriented programming language. Many Windows programmers have concluded that C++ offers a compelling alternative to C that, combined with a class library that abstracts the API and encapsulates the basic behavior of windows and other objects in reusable classes, makes Windows programming simpler. And an overwhelming majority of C++ programmers have settled on the Microsoft Foundation Class library, better known by the acronym MFC, as their class library of choice. Other Windows class libraries are available, but only MFC was written by the company that writes the operating system. MFC is continually updated to incorporate the latest changes to Windows itself, and it provides a comprehensive set of classes representing everything from windows to ActiveX controls in order to make the job of writing Windows applications easier.

If you're coming to MFC from a traditional Windows programming environment such as C and the Windows SDK, you're already familiar with many of the concepts you need to know to understand Windows programming with MFC. But if you're coming from a character-oriented environment such as MS-DOS or UNIX, you'll find that Windows programming is fundamentally different from anything you've done before. This chapter begins with an overview of the Windows programming model and a peek under the hood at how Windows applications work. It continues with an introduction to MFC. After the preliminaries are out of the way, you'll develop your very first Windows application—one that uses MFC to create a resizeable window containing the message "Hello, MFC."

THE WINDOWS PROGRAMMING MODEL

Programs written for traditional operating environments use a procedural programming model in which programs execute from top to bottom in an orderly fashion. The path taken from start to finish may vary with each invocation of the program depending on the input it receives or the conditions under which it is run, but the path remains fairly predictable. In a C program, execution begins with the first line in the function named *main* and ends when *main* returns. In between, *main* might call other functions and these functions might call even more functions, but ultimately it is the program—not the operating system—that determines what gets called and when.

Windows programs operate differently. They use the event-driven programming model illustrated in Figure 1-1, in which applications respond to *events* by processing messages sent by the operating system. An event could be a keystroke, a mouse click, or a command for a window to repaint itself, among other things. The entry point for a Windows program is a function named *WinMain*, but most of the action takes place in a function known as the *window procedure*. The window procedure processes messages sent to the window. *WinMain* creates that window and then enters a *message loop,* alternately retrieving messages and dispatching them to the window procedure. Messages wait in a message queue until they are retrieved. A typical Windows application performs the bulk of its processing in response to the messages it receives, and in between messages, it does little except wait for the next message to arrive.

The message loop ends when a WM_QUIT message is retrieved from the message queue, signaling that it's time for the application to end. This message usually appears because the user selected Exit from the File menu, clicked the close button (the small button with an X in the window's upper right corner), or selected Close from the window's system menu. When the message loop ends, *WinMain* returns and the application terminates.

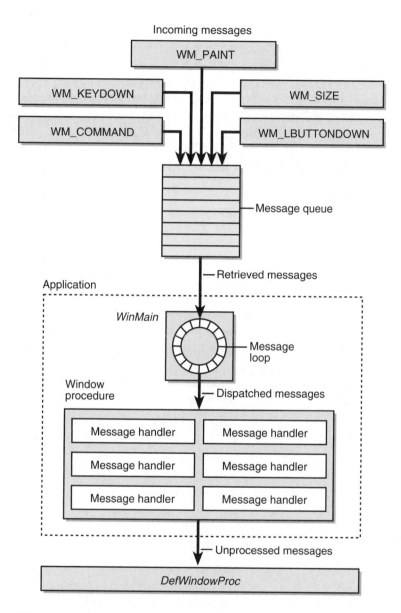

Figure 1-1. *The Windows programming model.*

The window procedure typically calls other functions to help process the messages it receives. It can call functions local to the application, or it can call API functions provided by Windows. API functions are contained in special modules known as *dynamic-link libraries,* or DLLs. The Win32 API includes hundreds of functions that an application can call to perform various tasks such as creating a window, drawing a line, and performing file input and output. In C, the window procedure is typically implemented as a monolithic function containing a large *switch* statement with cases for individual messages. The code provided to process a particular message is known as a *message handler*. Messages that an application doesn't process are passed on to an API function named *DefWindowProc*, which provides default responses to unprocessed messages.

Messages, Messages, and More Messages

Where do messages come from, and what kinds of information do they convey? Windows defines hundreds of different message types. Most messages have names that begin with the letters "WM" and an underscore, as in WM_CREATE and WM_PAINT. These messages can be classified in various ways, but for the moment classification is not nearly as important as realizing the critical role messages play in the operation of an application. The following table shows 10 of the most common messages. A window receives a WM_PAINT message, for example, when its interior needs repainting. One way to characterize a Windows program is to think of it as a collection of message handlers. To a large extent, it is a program's unique way of responding to messages that gives it its personality.

COMMON WINDOWS MESSAGES

Message	Sent When
WM_CHAR	A character is input from the keyboard.
WM_COMMAND	The user selects an item from a menu, or a control sends a notification to its parent.
WM_CREATE	A window is created.
WM_DESTROY	A window is destroyed.
WM_LBUTTONDOWN	The left mouse button is pressed.
WM_LBUTTONUP	The left mouse button is released.
WM_MOUSEMOVE	The mouse pointer is moved.
WM_PAINT	A window needs repainting.
WM_QUIT	The application is about to terminate.
WM_SIZE	A window is resized.

A message manifests itself in the form of a call to a window's window procedure. Bundled with the call are four input parameters: the handle of the window to which the message is directed, a message ID, and two 32-bit parameters known as *wParam* and *lParam*. The window handle is a 32-bit value that uniquely identifies a window. Internally, the value references a data structure in which Windows stores relevant information about the window such as its size, style, and location on the screen. The message ID is a numeric value that identifies the message type: WM_CREATE, WM_PAINT, and so on. *wParam* and *lParam* contain information specific to the message type. When a WM_LBUTTONDOWN message arrives, for example, *wParam* holds a series of bit flags identifying the state of the Ctrl and Shift keys and of the mouse buttons. *lParam* holds two 16-bit values identifying the location of the mouse pointer when the click occurred. Together, these parameters provide the window procedure with all the information it needs to process the WM_LBUTTONDOWN message.

Windows Programming, SDK-Style

If you haven't programmed Windows in C before, it's instructive to see what the source code for a simple program looks like. The program listed in Figure 1-2 creates a window and responds to WM_PAINT messages by drawing an ellipse in the window's upper left corner. This code is similar to the source code you'll find in books such as Charles Petzold's *Programming Windows* (1998, Microsoft Press) and other books that teach Windows programming in C.

```
#include <windows.h>

LONG WINAPI WndProc (HWND, UINT, WPARAM, LPARAM);

int WINAPI WinMain (HINSTANCE hInstance, HINSTANCE hPrevInstance,
    LPSTR lpszCmdLine, int nCmdShow)
{
    WNDCLASS wc;
    HWND hwnd;
    MSG msg;

    wc.style = 0;                                      // Class style
    wc.lpfnWndProc = (WNDPROC) WndProc;                // Window procedure address
    wc.cbClsExtra = 0;                                 // Class extra bytes
    wc.cbWndExtra = 0;                                 // Window extra bytes
    wc.hInstance = hInstance;                          // Instance handle
    wc.hIcon = LoadIcon (NULL, IDI_WINLOGO);           // Icon handle
    wc.hCursor = LoadCursor (NULL, IDC_ARROW);         // Cursor handle
    wc.hbrBackground = (HBRUSH) (COLOR_WINDOW + 1);    // Background color
    wc.lpszMenuName = NULL;                            // Menu name
    wc.lpszClassName = "MyWndClass";                   // WNDCLASS name

    RegisterClass (&wc);
```

Figure 1-2. *C source code for a simple Windows program.*

(continued)

Figure 1-2. *continued*

```
    hwnd = CreateWindow (
        "MyWndClass",               // WNDCLASS name
        "SDK Application",          // Window title
        WS_OVERLAPPEDWINDOW,        // Window style
        CW_USEDEFAULT,              // Horizontal position
        CW_USEDEFAULT,              // Vertical position
        CW_USEDEFAULT,              // Initial width
        CW_USEDEFAULT,              // Initial height
        HWND_DESKTOP,               // Handle of parent window
        NULL,                       // Menu handle
        hInstance,                  // Application's instance handle
        NULL                        // Window-creation data
    );

    ShowWindow (hwnd, nCmdShow);
    UpdateWindow (hwnd);

    while (GetMessage (&msg, NULL, 0, 0)) {
        TranslateMessage (&msg);
        DispatchMessage (&msg);
    }
    return msg.wParam;
}

LRESULT CALLBACK WndProc (HWND hwnd, UINT message, WPARAM wParam,
    LPARAM lParam)
{
    PAINTSTRUCT ps;
    HDC hdc;

    switch (message) {

    case WM_PAINT:
        hdc = BeginPaint (hwnd, &ps);
        Ellipse (hdc, 0, 0, 200, 100);
        EndPaint (hwnd, &ps);
        return 0;

    case WM_DESTROY:
        PostQuitMessage (0);
        return 0;
    }
    return DefWindowProc (hwnd, message, wParam, lParam);
}
```

WinMain begins by calling the API function *RegisterClass* to register a window class. The window class defines important characteristics of a window such as its window procedure address, its default background color, and its icon. These and other properties are defined by filling in the fields of a WNDCLASS structure, which is subsequently passed to *RegisterClass*. An application must specify a window class when it creates a window, and a class must be registered before it can be used. That's why *RegisterClass* is called at the outset of the program. Keep in mind that a WNDCLASS-type window class is not the same as a C++ window class. To avoid confusion, I'll use the term *WNDCLASS* throughout this book to refer to classes registered with *RegisterClass*. The term *window class* will refer to C++ classes derived from MFC's *CWnd* class.

Once the WNDCLASS is registered, *WinMain* calls the all-important *CreateWindow* function to create the application's window. The first parameter to *CreateWindow* is the name of the WNDCLASS from which the window will be created. The second parameter is the text that will appear in the window's title bar. The third specifies the window style. WS_OVERLAPPEDWINDOW is a commonly used style that creates a top-level window with a resizing border, a title bar, a system menu, and buttons for minimizing, maximizing, and closing the window.

The next four parameters specify the window's initial position and size. CW_USEDEFAULT tells Windows to use default values for both. The final four parameters specify, in order, the handle of the window's parent window (HWND-_DESKTOP for an application's main window); the handle of the menu associated with the window, if any; the application's instance handle (a value that lets the programmer differentiate between the program itself and the modules—that is, DLLs—that it loads); and a pointer to application-specific window-creation data. I could easily devote a section of this book to *CreateWindow* and its parameters, but as you'll see later, MFC hides much of this detail inside the class library. A typical MFC application doesn't have a *WinMain* function (at least not one you can see), and it doesn't call *RegisterClass* or *CreateWindow*.

The window that *CreateWindow* creates is not initially visible on the screen because it was not created with the WS_VISIBLE style. (Had it been used, WS_VISIBLE would have been combined with WS_OVERLAPPEDWINDOW in the call to *Create-Window*.) Therefore, *WinMain* follows *CreateWindow* with calls to *ShowWindow* and *UpdateWindow*, which make the window visible and ensure that its WM_PAINT handler is called immediately.

Next comes the message loop. In order to retrieve and dispatch messages, *WinMain* executes a simple *while* loop that calls the *GetMessage*, *TranslateMessage*, and *DispatchMessage* API functions repeatedly. *GetMessage* checks the message queue.

If a message is available, it is removed from the queue and copied to *msg*; otherwise, *GetMessage* blocks on the empty message queue until a message is available. *msg* is an instance of the structure MSG, whose fields contain pertinent message parameters such as the message ID and the time at which the message was placed in the queue. *TranslateMessage* converts a keyboard message denoting a character key to an easier-to-use WM_CHAR message, and *DispatchMessage* dispatches the message to the window procedure. The message loop executes until *GetMessage* returns 0, which happens only when a WM_QUIT message is retrieved from the message queue. When this occurs, *WinMain* ends and the program terminates.

Messages dispatched with *DispatchMessage* generate calls to the window procedure *WndProc*. The sample program in Figure 1-2 processes just two message types, WM_PAINT and WM_DESTROY; all other messages are passed to *DefWindowProc* for default processing. A *switch-case* block inspects the message ID passed in the *message* parameter and executes the appropriate message handler. The WM_PAINT handler calls the *BeginPaint* API function to obtain a device context handle before painting begins and the *EndPaint* API function to release the handle when painting is finished. In between, the *Ellipse* API function draws an ellipse that is 200 pixels wide and 100 pixels high. A device context handle is the "magic cookie" that permits a Windows application to draw on the screen. Without it, functions such as *Ellipse* won't work.

The WM_DESTROY handler calls the *PostQuitMessage* API function to post a WM_QUIT message to the message queue and ultimately cause the program to terminate. The WM_DESTROY message is sent to a window just before it is destroyed. A top-level window must call *PostQuitMessage* when it receives a WM_DESTROY message, or else the message loop will not fall through and the program will never end.

Hungarian Notation and Windows Data Types

Another aspect of Figure 1-2 that deserves mentioning is the variable naming convention that it uses. Veteran Windows programmers know it as *Hungarian notation,* in which each variable name begins with one or more lowercase characters identifying the variable's type: *h* for handle, *n* for integer, and so on. The table on the following page lists some of the commonly used Hungarian prefixes. Prefixes are often combined to form other prefixes, as when *p* and *sz* are joined to form *psz*, which stands for "pointer to zero-terminated string."

Many of the data types shown in this table aren't standard C/C++ data types but rather are "special" data types defined in the Windows header files. COLORREF, for example, is the Windows data type for 24-bit RGB color values. A BOOL is a Boolean data type that stores TRUE/FALSE values, while a DWORD is a 32-bit unsigned integer. Over time, you'll come to know these data types as well as you know your compiler's native data types.

COMMON HUNGARIAN NOTATION PREFIXES

Prefix	Data Type
b	BOOL
c or *ch*	char
clr	COLORREF
cx, cy	Horizontal or vertical distance
dw	DWORD
h	Handle
l	LONG
n	int
p	Pointer
sz	Zero-terminated string
w	WORD

Most MFC programmers use Hungarian notation, too. Glance through the source code for a typical MFC program and you'll see hundreds of *h*s and *lp*s and other familiar prefixes as well as prefixes representing MFC's own data types (for example, *wnd* for *CWnd* variables). It's also common to prefix member variables with *m_* so that it's obvious whether a variable is a member of a class. A temporary *CString* variable created on the stack might have the name *strWndClass*, but if it's a member variable it will probably be called *m_strWndClass*. You don't have to abide by these rules yourself, of course, but observing established naming conventions will make your code more readable to other programmers who do.

SDK Programming in Perspective

All this is a lot to digest if you've never programmed Windows before, but it brings to light a few very important concepts. First, Windows is an event-driven, message-based operating system. Messages are the key to everything that goes on in the system, and for an application, very few things happen that aren't the direct result of receiving a message. Second, there are many different API functions and many different message types, which complicates application development and makes it hard to predict all of the scenarios an application might encounter. Third, seeing how Windows programming is done the hard way provides a baseline for evaluating MFC and other class libraries. MFC is not the panacea some of its proponents would have you believe, but it undeniably makes certain aspects of Windows programming easier. And the higher order it lends to Windows programs frees programmers to spend more time developing the structural components of a program and less time worrying about the style bits passed to *CreateWindow* and other nuances of the API. If you haven't given

MFC a look, now is the time to consider it. Windows programming isn't getting any easier, and MFC lets you benefit from tens of thousands of lines of code already written and tested by Microsoft.

INTRODUCING MFC

MFC is the C++ class library Microsoft provides to place an object-oriented wrapper around the Windows API. Version 6 contains about 200 classes, some of which you'll use directly and others of which will serve primarily as base classes for classes of your own. Some MFC classes are exceedingly simple, such as the *CPoint* class that represents a point (a location defined by *x* and *y* coordinates). Others are more complex, such as the *CWnd* class that encapsulates the functionality of a window. In an MFC program, you don't often call the Windows API directly. Instead, you create objects from MFC classes and call member functions belonging to those objects. Many of the hundreds of member functions defined in the class library are thin wrappers around the Windows API and even have the same names as the corresponding API functions. An obvious benefit of this naming convention is that it speeds the transition for C programmers making the move to MFC. Want to move a window? A C programmer would probably call the *SetWindowPos* API function. Look up *SetWindowPos* in an MFC reference, and you'll find that MFC supports *SetWindowPos*, too. It's a member of the *CWnd* class, which makes sense when you think of a window as an object and *SetWindowPos* as an operation you might want to perform on that object.

MFC is also an *application framework*. More than merely a collection of classes, MFC helps define the structure of an application and handles many routine chores on the application's behalf. Starting with *CWinApp*, the class that represents the application itself, MFC encapsulates virtually every aspect of a program's operation. The framework supplies the *WinMain* function, and *WinMain* in turn calls the application object's member functions to make the program go. One of the *CWinApp* member functions called by *WinMain—Run—*provides the message loop that pumps messages to the application's window. The framework also provides abstractions that go above and beyond what the Windows API has to offer. For example, MFC's document/view architecture builds a powerful infrastructure on top of the API that separates a program's data from graphical representations, or views, of that data. Such abstractions are totally foreign to the API and don't exist outside the framework of MFC or a similar class library.

The Benefits of Using C++ and MFC

The fact that you're reading this book means you've probably already heard the traditional arguments in favor of using an object-oriented design methodology: reusability, tighter binding of code and data, and so on. And you should already be familiar with common object-oriented programming (OOP) terms such as *object, inheritance,* and *encapsulation,* particularly as they pertain to the C++ language. But without a good class library to serve as a starting point, OOP does little to reduce the amount of code you write.

That's where MFC comes in. Want to add a toolbar to your application—one that can be docked to different sides of a window or floated in a window of its own? No problem: MFC provides a *CToolBar* class that does the bulk of the work for you. Need a linked list or a resizeable array? That's easy, too: *CList, CArray,* and other MFC collection classes provide canned containers for your data. And don't forget about COM, OLE, and ActiveX. Few among us have the desire or the know-how to write an ActiveX control from scratch. MFC simplifies the development of ActiveX controls by providing the bulk of the code you need in classes such as *COleControl* and *COlePropertyPage.*

Another advantage to using MFC is that the framework uses a lot of tricks to make Windows objects such as windows, dialog boxes, and controls behave like C++ objects. Suppose you want to write a reusable list box class that displays a navigable list of drives and directories on the host PC. Unless you create a custom control to do the job, you can't implement such a list box in C because clicking an item in the list box sends a notification to the list box's parent (the window or the dialog box in which the list box appears), and it's up to the parent to process that notification. In other words, the list box control doesn't control its own destiny; it's the parent's job to update the list box's contents when a drive or a directory is changed.

Not so with MFC. In an MFC application, windows and dialog boxes reflect unprocessed notifications back to the controls that sent them. You can create a self-contained and highly reusable list box class that responds to its own click notifications by deriving your own list box class from *CListBox.* The resulting list box implements its own behavior and can be ported to another application with little more than a #include statement in a source code file. That's what reusability is all about.

The MFC Design Philosophy

When the programmers at Microsoft set out to create MFC, they had a vision of the future that included a pair of key design goals:

■   MFC should provide an object-oriented interface to the Windows operating system that supports reusability, self-containment, and other tenets of OOP.

■   It should do so without imposing undue overhead on the system or unnecessarily adding to an application's memory requirements.

The first goal was accomplished by writing classes to encapsulate windows, dialog boxes, and other objects and by including key virtual functions that can be overridden to alter the behavior of derived classes. The second goal required the architects of MFC to make some choices early on about how windows, menus, and other objects would be wrapped by MFC classes such as *CWnd* and *CMenu*. Efficient use of memory was important then and it's important today, because nobody likes a class library that produces bloated code.

One of the ways in which the designers of MFC minimized the overhead added by the class library is manifested in the relationship between MFC objects and Windows objects. In Windows, information about the characteristics and current state of a window is stored in memory owned by the operating system. This information is hidden from applications, which deal exclusively with window handles, or HWNDs. Rather than duplicate all the information associated with an HWND in the data members of the *CWnd* class, MFC wraps a window in a *CWnd* by storing the HWND in a public *CWnd* data member named *m_hWnd*. As a rule, if Windows exposes an object through a handle of some type, the corresponding MFC class will contain a data member for that handle. This knowledge can be useful if you want to call an API function that requires a handle but you have, say, a *CWnd* or *CWnd* pointer instead of an HWND.

The Document/View Architecture

The cornerstone of MFC's application framework is the document/view architecture, which defines a program structure that relies on document objects to hold an application's data and on view objects to render views of that data. MFC provides the infrastructure for documents and views in the classes *CDocument* and *CView*. *CWinApp*, *CFrameWnd*, and other classes work in conjunction with *CDocument* and *CView* to bind all the pieces together. It's a little early to discuss the details of the document/view architecture, but you should at least be familiar with the term *document/view* because it inevitably comes up in any discussion of MFC.

The reason documents and views are so important is that document/view applications derive the greatest benefit from the application framework. You can write MFC programs that don't use documents and views (and we'll do a lot of that in this book, especially in Chapters 1 through 8), but to get the most out of the framework and take advantage of some of MFC's most advanced features, you must use the document/view architecture. That's not as restricting as it sounds, because almost any program that relies on documents of some type can be cast in the document/view mold. Don't let the term *document* mislead you into thinking that the document/ view architecture is useful only for writing word processors and spreadsheet programs. A document is simply an abstract representation of a program's data. A document could just as easily be a byte array that stores board positions in a computerized game of chess as it could be a spreadsheet.

What kinds of support does MFC provide to document/view applications? Among other things, the document/view architecture vastly simplifies printing and print previewing, the mechanics of saving documents to disk and reading them back again, and converting applications into Active document servers whose documents can be opened in Microsoft Internet Explorer. You'll learn all about the document/ view architecture in Part II of this book, but only after you've done some programming without documents and views so that you can get to know MFC without having too much heaped on your plate at once.

The MFC Class Hierarchy

MFC provides a variety of classes designed to serve a wide range of needs. You'll find a handy diagram of the MFC 6.0 class hierarchy inside the front cover of this book.

The majority of MFC classes are derived, either directly or indirectly, from *CObject*. *CObject* provides three important features to classes that inherit from it:

■ Serialization support

■ Run-time class information support

■ Diagnostic and debugging support

Serialization is the process of streaming an object's persistent data to or from a storage medium such as a disk file. By using *CObject* as a base class, you can write serializable classes whose instances are easily saved and re-created. Run-time class information (RTCI) lets you retrieve an object's class name and other information about the object at run time. RTCI is implemented apart from the run-time type information (RTTI) mechanism in C++ because it predated RTTI by a number of years. Diagnostic and debugging support built into *CObject* let you perform validity checks on instances of *CObject*-derived classes and dump state information to a debugging window.

CObject provides other benefits to its derived classes as well. For example, it overloads the *new* and *delete* operators to provide protection against memory leaks. If you create an object from a *CObject*-derived class and fail to delete it before the application terminates, MFC will warn you by writing a message to the debug output window. The overarching importance of this most basic of MFC classes will become increasingly clear as you grow more familiar with MFC.

AFX Functions

Not all of the functions that MFC offers are members of classes. MFC provides an API of sorts all its own in the form of global functions whose names begin with *Afx*. Class member functions can be called only in the context of the objects to which they belong, but AFX functions are available anytime and anywhere.

The following table lists some of the more commonly used AFX functions. *AfxBeginThread* simplifies the process of creating threads of execution. *AfxMessageBox* is the global equivalent of the Windows *MessageBox* function and, unlike *CWnd::MessageBox*, can be called just as easily from a document class as from a window class. *AfxGetApp* and *AfxGetMainWnd* return pointers to the application object and the application's main window and are useful when you want to access a function or data member of those objects but don't have a pointer readily available. *AfxGetInstanceHandle* is handy when you need an instance handle to pass to a Windows API function. (Even MFC programs call API functions every now and then!)

COMMONLY USED AFX FUNCTIONS

Function Name	Description
AfxAbort	Unconditionally terminates an application; usually called when an unrecoverable error occurs
AfxBeginThread	Creates a new thread and begins executing it
AfxEndThread	Terminates the thread that is currently executing
AfxMessageBox	Displays a Windows message box
AfxGetApp	Returns a pointer to the application object
AfxGetAppName	Returns the name of the application
AfxGetMainWnd	Returns a pointer to the application's main window
AfxGetInstanceHandle	Returns a handle identifying the current application instance
AfxRegisterWndClass	Registers a custom WNDCLASS for an MFC application

YOUR FIRST MFC APPLICATION

It's time to build your first MFC application. And what better place to start than with one that displays "Hello, MFC" in a window? Based on the classic "Hello, world" program immortalized in Brian Kernighan and Dennis Ritchie's *The C Programming Language* (1988, Prentice-Hall), this very minimal program, which I'll call Hello, demonstrates the fundamental principles involved in using MFC to write a Windows application. Among other things, you'll get a close-up look at MFC's *CWinApp* and *CFrameWnd* classes and see firsthand how classes are derived from them and plugged into the application. You'll also learn about the all-important *CPaintDC* class, which serves as the conduit through which text and graphics are drawn in a window in response to WM_PAINT messages. Finally, you'll be introduced to *message mapping,* the mechanism MFC uses to correlate the messages your application receives with the member functions you provide to handle those messages.

Figure 1-3 lists the source code for Hello. Hello.h contains the declarations for two derived classes. Hello.cpp contains the implementations of those classes. Among C++ programmers, it's traditional to put class definitions in .h files and source code in .cpp files. We'll honor that tradition here and throughout the rest of this book. For large applications containing tens or perhaps hundreds of classes, it's also beneficial to put class declarations and implementations in separate source code files. That's overkill for the programs in the first few chapters of this book, but later on, when we begin working with documents and views, we'll give each class its own .h and .cpp files. On the CD in the back of the book, in the folder named Chap01, you'll find a folder with copies of Hello.h and Hello.cpp as well as a folder containing a copy of the compiled executable (Hello.exe).

Hello.h

```
class CMyApp : public CWinApp
{
public:
    virtual BOOL InitInstance ();
};

class CMainWindow : public CFrameWnd
{
public:
    CMainWindow ();

protected:
    afx_msg void OnPaint ();
    DECLARE_MESSAGE_MAP ()
};
```

Hello.cpp

```
#include <afxwin.h>
#include "Hello.h"

CMyApp myApp;

/////////////////////////////////////////////////////////////////////////////
// CMyApp member functions

BOOL CMyApp::InitInstance ()
{
    m_pMainWnd = new CMainWindow;
```

Figure 1-3. *The Hello application.*

(continued)

Figure 1-3. *continued*

```
    m_pMainWnd->ShowWindow (m_nCmdShow);
    m_pMainWnd->UpdateWindow ();
    return TRUE;
}


///////////////////////////////////////////////////////////////////////////
// CMainWindow message map and member functions

BEGIN_MESSAGE_MAP (CMainWindow, CFrameWnd)
    ON_WM_PAINT ()
END_MESSAGE_MAP ()

CMainWindow::CMainWindow ()
{
    Create (NULL, _T ("The Hello Application"));
}

void CMainWindow::OnPaint ()
{
    CPaintDC dc (this);

    CRect rect;
    GetClientRect (&rect);

    dc.DrawText (_T ("Hello, MFC"), -1, &rect,
        DT_SINGLELINE | DT_CENTER | DT_VCENTER);
}
```

Figure 1-4 shows the output from Hello. When you run the application, notice that the window is entirely functional; you can move it, resize it, minimize it, maximize it, and close it. And when the window is resized, "Hello, MFC" is redrawn in the center of the window.

Most of Hello's functionality comes from Windows. Windows, for example, draws the exterior, or *nonclient area,* of the window: the title bar, the buttons on the title bar, and the window's border. It's your responsibility to create the window and process WM_PAINT messages indicating that all or part of the window's interior, or *client area*, needs updating. Let's examine the source code to see how Hello works.

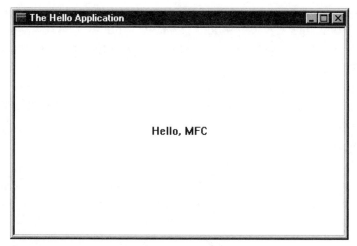

Figure 1-4. *The Hello window.*

The Application Object

The heart of an MFC application is an application object based on the *CWinApp* class. *CWinApp* provides the message loop that retrieves messages and dispatches them to the application's window. It also includes key virtual functions that can be overridden to customize the application's behavior. *CWinApp* and other MFC classes are brought into your application when you include the header file Afxwin.h. An MFC application can have one—and only one—application object, and that object must be declared with global scope so that it will be instantiated in memory at the very outset of the program.

Hello's application class is named *CMyApp*. It is instantiated in Hello.cpp with the statement

```
CMyApp myApp;
```

CMyApp's class declaration appears in Hello.h:

```
class CMyApp : public CWinApp
{
public:
    virtual BOOL InitInstance ();
};
```

CMyApp declares no data members and overrides just one function inherited from *CWinApp*. *InitInstance* is called early in the application's lifetime, right after the application starts running but before the window is created. In fact, unless *InitInstance* creates a window, the application doesn't *have* a window. That's why even a minimal MFC application must derive a class from *CWinApp* and override *CWinApp::InitInstance*.

The *InitInstance* Function

CWinApp::InitInstance is a virtual function whose default implementation contains just one statement:

```
return TRUE;
```

The purpose of *InitInstance* is to provide the application with the opportunity to initialize itself. The value returned by *InitInstance* determines what the framework does next. Returning FALSE from *InitInstance* shuts down the application. If initialization goes as planned, *InitInstance* should return TRUE in order to allow the program to proceed. *InitInstance* is the perfect place to perform initializations that need to be done each time the program starts. At the very least, this means creating the window that will represent the application on the screen.

CMyApp's implementation of *InitInstance*, which appears in Hello.cpp, creates the Hello window by instantiating Hello's *CMainWindow* class. The statement

```
m_pMainWnd = new CMainWindow;
```

constructs a *CMainWindow* object and copies its address to the application object's *m_pMainWnd* data member. After the window is created, *InitInstance* displays it—remember, a window is not initially visible unless it is created with a WS_VISIBLE attribute—by calling *ShowWindow* and *UpdateWindow* through the *CMainWindow* pointer:

```
m_pMainWnd->ShowWindow (m_nCmdShow);
m_pMainWnd->UpdateWindow ();
```

ShowWindow and *UpdateWindow* are *CWnd* member functions common to all window objects, including objects of the *CFrameWnd* class from which *CMainWindow* is derived. These functions are little more than wrappers around the API functions of the same name. To call a regular Windows API function from an MFC program, make it a practice to preface the function name with the global scope resolution operator ::, as in

```
::UpdateWindow (hwnd);
```

This notation will ensure that the API function is called even if the object that makes the call has a member function with the same name. In the remainder of this book, Windows API functions will be prefaced with :: to distinguish them from MFC member functions.

ShowWindow accepts just one parameter: an integer that specifies whether the window should initially be shown minimized, maximized, or neither minimized nor maximized. In accordance with Windows programming protocol, Hello passes *Show-Window* the value stored in the application object's *m_nCmdShow* variable, which holds the *nCmdShow* parameter passed to *WinMain*. The *m_nCmdShow* value is usually SW_SHOWNORMAL, indicating that the window should be displayed in its normal unmaximized and unminimized state. However, depending on how the user starts an application, Windows will occasionally slip in a value such as SW_SHOW-MAXIMIZED or SW_SHOWMINIMIZED. Unless there is a specific reason for it to do otherwise, *InitInstance* should always pass the *m_nCmdShow* variable instead of a hardcoded SW_ value to *ShowWindow*.

UpdateWindow completes the job that *ShowWindow* started by forcing an immediate repaint. Its work done, *InitInstance* returns TRUE to allow the application to proceed.

Other *CWinApp* Overridables

InitInstance is just one of several virtual *CWinApp* member functions you can override to customize the behavior of the application object. Look up the *CWinApp* overridables in your MFC documentation and you'll see a list of more than a dozen others with names such as *WinHelp* and *ProcessWndProcException*. Many of these functions are seldom overridden, but they're handy to have around nonetheless. For example, you can use *ExitInstance* to clean up when an application terminates. If you use *InitInstance* to allocate memory or other resources, *ExitInstance* is the perfect place to free those resources. The default implementation of *ExitInstance* performs some routine cleanup chores required by the framework, so you should be sure to call the base class version if you've overridden *ExitInstance*. Ultimately, the value returned by *ExitInstance* is the exit code returned by *WinMain*.

Other interesting *CWinApp* overridables include *OnIdle*, *Run*, and *PreTranslate-Message*. *OnIdle* is handy for performing background processing chores such as garbage collection. Because *OnIdle* is called when an application is "idle"—that is, when there are no messages waiting to be processed—it provides an excellent mechanism for performing low-priority background tasks without spawning a separate thread of execution. *OnIdle* is discussed at length in Chapter 14. You can override *Run* to customize the message loop, replacing it with a message loop of your own. If you just want to perform some specialized preprocessing on certain messages before they are dispatched, you can override *PreTranslateMessage* and save yourself the trouble of writing a whole new message loop.

How MFC Uses the Application Object

To someone who has never seen an MFC application's source code, one of the more remarkable aspects of Hello will be that it contains no executable code outside of the classes it defines. It has no *main* or *WinMain* function, for example; the only statement in the entire program that has global scope is the statement that instantiates the application object. So what actually starts the program running, and when does the application object come into the picture?

The best way to understand what goes on under the hood is to look at the framework's source code. One of the source code files provided with MFC—Winmain.cpp—contains an *AfxWinMain* function that is MFC's equivalent of *WinMain*. (That's right: when you purchase Visual C++, you get the source code for MFC, too.) *AfxWinMain* makes extensive use of the application object, which is why the application object must be declared globally. Global variables and objects are created before any code is executed, and the application object must be extant in memory before *AfxWinMain* starts.

Right after starting, *AfxWinMain* calls a function named *AfxWinInit* to initialize the framework and copy *hInstance*, *nCmdShow*, and other *AfxWinMain* function parameters to data members of the application object. Then it calls *InitApplication* and *InitInstance*. In 16-bit versions of MFC, *InitApplication* is called only if the *hPrevInstance* parameter passed to *AfxWinMain* is NULL, indicating that this is the only instance of the application currently running. In the Win32 environment, *hPrevInstance* is always NULL, so the framework doesn't bother to check it. A 32-bit application could just as easily use *InitApplication* to initialize itself as *InitInstance*, but *InitApplication* is provided for compatibility with previous versions of MFC and should not be used in 32-bit Windows applications. If *AfxWinInit*, *InitApplication*, or *InitInstance* returns 0, *AfxWinMain* terminates instead of proceeding further and the application is shut down.

Only if all of the aforementioned functions return nonzero values does *AfxWin-Main* perform the next critical step. The statement

```
pThread->Run();
```

calls the application object's *Run* function, which executes the message loop and begins pumping messages to the application's window. The message loop repeats until a WM_QUIT message is retrieved from the message queue, at which point *Run* breaks out of the loop, calls *ExitInstance*, and returns to *AfxWinMain*. After doing some last-minute cleaning up, *AfxWinMain* executes a *return* to end the application.

The Frame Window Object

MFC's *CWnd* class and its derivatives provide object-oriented interfaces to the window or windows an application creates. Hello's window class, *CMainWindow*, is derived from MFC's *CFrameWnd* class, which is derived from *CWnd*. *CFrameWnd* models the behavior of *frame windows*. For now, you can think of a frame window as a top-level window that serves as an application's primary interface to the outside world. In the greater context of the document/view architecture, frame windows play a larger role as intelligent containers for views, toolbars, status bars, and other user-interface (UI) objects.

An MFC application creates a window by creating a window object and calling its *Create* or *CreateEx* function. Hello creates a *CMainWindow* object in *CMyApp::InitInstance*. *CMainWindow*'s constructor creates the window you see on the screen:

```
Create (NULL, _T ("The Hello Application"));
```

_T is a macro that's used to make string literals character set neutral. It's discussed later in this chapter. *Create* is a *CMainWindow* member function that's inherited from *CFrameWnd*. It's one of approximately 20 member functions that *CFrameWnd* defines in addition to the functions it inherits from *CWnd*. *CFrameWnd::Create* is prototyped as follows:

```
BOOL Create (LPCTSTR lpszClassName,
    LPCTSTR lpszWindowName,
    DWORD dwStyle = WS_OVERLAPPEDWINDOW,
    const RECT& rect = rectDefault,
    CWnd* pParentWnd = NULL,
    LPCTSTR lpszMenuName = NULL,
    DWORD dwExStyle = 0,
    CCreateContext* pContext = NULL)
```

Default values are defined for six of the eight parameters *Create* accepts. Hello does the minimum amount of work required, specifying values for the function's first two parameters and accepting the defaults for the remaining six. The first parameter—*lpszClassName*—specifies the name of the WNDCLASS that the window is based on. Specifying NULL for this parameter creates a default frame window based on a WND-CLASS registered by the framework. The *lpszWindowName* parameter specifies the text that will appear in the window's title bar.

The *dwStyle* parameter specifies the window style. The default is WS_OVER-LAPPEDWINDOW. You can change the window style by specifying an alternative style or combination of styles in the call to *Create*. You'll find a complete list of window styles in the documentation for *CFrameWnd::Create*. Two of the styles frequently used with frame windows are WS_HSCROLL and WS_VSCROLL, which add horizontal and vertical scroll bars to the bottom and right edges of the window's client area. The statement

```
Create (NULL, _T ("Hello"), WS_OVERLAPPEDWINDOW | WS_VSCROLL);
```

creates an overlapped window that contains a vertical scroll bar. As this example illustrates, multiple styles may be combined using the C++ | operator. WS_OVER-LAPPEDWINDOW combines the WS_OVERLAPPED, WS_CAPTION, WS_SYSMENU, WS_MINIMIZEBOX, WS_MAXIMIZEBOX, and WS_THICKFRAME styles, so if you'd like to create a window that looks just like a WS_OVERLAPPEDWINDOW window but lacks the maximize button in the title bar, you could call *Create* this way:

```
Create (NULL, _T ("Hello"), WS_OVERLAPPED | WS_CAPTION |
    WS_SYSMENU | WS_MINIMIZEBOX | WS_THICKFRAME);
```

An alternative way to specify a window style is to override the virtual *PreCreate-Window* function that a window inherits from *CWnd* and modify the *style* field of the CREATESTRUCT structure passed to *PreCreateWindow*. This capability is handy to have when the framework creates your application's main window for you, as is frequently the case in document/view applications, but it's not necessary when your code calls *Create* directly and therefore controls the parameters passed to it. Later in this book, you'll see examples demonstrating when and how *PreCreateWindow* is used.

Additional window styles known as *extended styles* can be specified in *CFrame-Wnd::Create*'s *dwExStyle* parameter. Window styles are divided into standard and extended styles for a historical reason: Windows 3.1 added support for additional window styles by introducing the *::CreateWindowEx* API function. *::CreateWindowEx* is similar to *::CreateWindow*, but its argument list includes an additional parameter specifying the window's extended style. Windows 3.1 supported just five extended styles. More recent versions of Windows offer a much greater selection that includes the WS_EX_WINDOWEDGE and WS_EX_CLIENTEDGE styles, which give window borders a more pronounced 3D look. MFC automatically adds these two styles to frame windows for you, so you rarely need to specify them yourself.

After the *dwStyle* parameter comes *rect*, which is a C++ reference to a *CRect* object or a C-style RECT structure specifying the window's initial screen position and size. The default is *rectDefault*, which is a static member of the *CFrameWnd* class that simply tells Windows to choose the window's default initial position and size. If you want to, you can specify the initial position and size by initializing a *CRect* object with coordinates describing a rectangle on the screen and passing it to *Create*. The following statement creates a standard overlapped window whose upper left corner is located 32 pixels to the right of and 64 pixels down from the upper left corner of the screen and whose initial width and height are 320 and 240 pixels, respectively:

```
Create (NULL, _T ("Hello"), WS_OVERLAPPEDWINDOW,
    CRect (32, 64, 352, 304));
```

Note that the window's width and height are determined by the *difference* between the first and third parameters and the second and fourth parameters rather than by the absolute values of the third and fourth parameters. In other words, the *CRect* object specifies the rectangular region of the screen that the window will occupy. The four parameters passed to *CRect*'s constructor specify, in order, the rectangle's left, top, right, and bottom screen coordinates.

The *pParentWnd* parameter to *Create* identifies the window's parent or owner. Don't worry for now about parents and owners. This parameter is always NULL for top-level windows because top-level windows have neither parents nor owners. (Actually, specifying NULL for *pParentWnd* makes the desktop window—the window that forms the backdrop for the screen—the window's owner. But that's an implementation detail that matters only to Windows.)

Create's *lpszMenuName* parameter identifies the menu associated with the window. NULL indicates that the window has no menu. We'll begin using menus in Chapter 4.

The final parameter to *CFrameWnd::Create*, *pContext*, contains a pointer to a *CCreateContext* structure that is used by the framework when it initializes frame windows in document/view applications. Outside the document/view architecture, this parameter is meaningless and should be set to NULL.

Create offers a tremendous variety of options to the programmer. The number of choices might seem overwhelming at this early stage, especially if you haven't programmed for Windows before, but experience will teach you how and when to exercise the options available to you. Meanwhile, the class library's use of default function arguments hides much of the complexity when a standard *CFrameWnd*-type window is all you need. This is one example of the ways in which MFC makes Windows programming just a little bit easier.

Painting the Window

Hello doesn't draw to the screen just whenever it wants to. Instead, it draws in response to WM_PAINT messages from Windows signaling that it's time to update the window.

WM_PAINT messages can be generated for a variety of reasons. A WM_PAINT message might be sent because another window was moved, exposing a part of Hello's window that was previously obscured, or it could be sent because the window was resized. Whatever the stimulus, it is the application's responsibility to paint the client area of its window in response to WM_PAINT messages. Windows draws the nonclient area so that all applications will have a consistent look, but if the application doesn't implement its own drawing routines for the client area, the interior of the window will be blank.

In Hello, WM_PAINT messages are processed by *CMainWindow::OnPaint*, which is called anytime a WM_PAINT message arrives. *OnPaint*'s job is to draw "Hello, MFC" in the center of the window's client area. It begins by constructing a *CPaintDC* object named *dc*:

```
CPaintDC dc (this);
```

MFC's *CPaintDC* class is derived from MFC's more generic *CDC* class, which encapsulates a Windows device context and includes dozens of member functions for drawing to screens, printers, and other devices. In Windows, all graphical output is performed through device context objects that abstract the physical destinations for output. *CPaintDC* is a special case of *CDC* that is used only in WM_PAINT message handlers. Before drawing in response to a WM_PAINT message, an application must call the

Windows *::BeginPaint* API function to obtain a device context and prepare the device context for painting. When it's finished painting, the application must call *::EndPaint* to release the device context and inform Windows that painting is complete. If an application fails to call *::BeginPaint* and *::EndPaint* when it processes a WM_PAINT message, the message will not be removed from the message queue. Not surprisingly, *CPaintDC* calls *::BeginPaint* from its constructor and *::EndPaint* from its destructor to ensure that this doesn't happen.

In MFC, you'll always draw to the screen with a *CDC* object of some type, but you must use a *CPaintDC* object only inside *OnPaint* handlers. Furthermore, it's good practice to create *CPaintDC* objects on the stack so that their destructors will be called automatically when *OnPaint* ends. You can instantiate a *CPaintDC* object with the *new* operator if you want to, but then it becomes critical to delete that object before *OnPaint* ends. Otherwise, *::EndPaint* won't be called, and your application won't redraw properly.

After creating a *CPaintDC* object, *OnPaint* constructs a *CRect* object representing a rectangle and calls *CWnd::GetClientRect* to initialize the rectangle with the coordinates of the window's client area:

```
CRect rect;
GetClientRect (&rect);
```

OnPaint then calls *CDC::DrawText* to display "Hello, MFC" in the window's client area:

```
dc.DrawText (_T ("Hello, MFC"), -1, &rect,
    DT_SINGLELINE | DT_CENTER | DT_VCENTER);
```

DrawText is a powerful general-purpose function for outputting text. It accepts four parameters: a pointer to the string to display, the number of characters in the string (or −1 if the string is terminated with a NULL character), the address of a RECT structure or *CRect* object specifying the formatting rectangle (the rectangle in which the string is displayed), and flags specifying output options. In Hello, *CMainWindow::OnPaint* combines the DT_SINGLELINE, DT_CENTER, and DT_VCENTER flags to display a single line of text that is centered both horizontally and vertically in the formatting rectangle. *rect* describes the window's client area, so the resulting output is perfectly centered in the window.

Conspicuously missing from *DrawText*'s argument list are parameters specifying basic properties of the output such as the font and text color. These and other characteristics of the output are attributes of the device context and are controlled with *CDC* member functions such as *SelectObject* and *SetTextColor*. Because Hello didn't change any of the device context's attributes, the default font and default text color (black) were used. *DrawText* also fills a small rectangle surrounding the text it outputs with the device context's current background color. The default is white, so you don't see it if your system's default window background color also happens to be white. But change the window background color to gray and the white text background will stick out like a sore thumb.

In Chapter 2, you'll learn how to customize the output from *DrawText* and other *CDC* drawing functions by modifying device context attributes. Once you know how to do it, it's simple to change the text color or tell *DrawText* to paint the text background with "transparent" pixels.

The Message Map

How is it that a WM_PAINT message from Windows turns into a call to *CMainWindow::OnPaint*? The answer lies in the message map. A message map is a table that correlates messages and member functions. When Hello's frame window receives a message, MFC scans the window's message map, sees that a handler exists for WM_PAINT messages, and calls *OnPaint*. The message map is MFC's way of avoiding the lengthy vtables that would be required if every class had a virtual function for every possible message it might receive. Any class derived from *CCmdTarget* can contain a message map. What MFC does internally to implement message maps is hidden behind some rather complex macros, but *using* a message map is exceedingly simple. Here's all you have to do to add a message map to a class:

1. Declare the message map by adding a DECLARE_MESSAGE_MAP statement to the class declaration.

2. Implement the message map by placing macros identifying the messages that the class will handle between calls to BEGIN_MESSAGE_MAP and END_MESSAGE_MAP.

3. Add member functions to handle the messages.

Hello's *CMainWindow* class handles just one message type, WM_PAINT, so its message map is implemented as follows:

```
BEGIN_MESSAGE_MAP (CMainWindow, CFrameWnd)
    ON_WM_PAINT ()
END_MESSAGE_MAP ()
```

BEGIN_MESSAGE_MAP begins the message map and identifies both the class to which the message map belongs and the base class. (Message maps are passed by inheritance just as other class members are. The base class name is required so that the framework can find the base class's message map when necessary.) END_MESSAGE_MAP ends the message map. In between BEGIN_MESSAGE_MAP and END_MESSAGE_MAP are the message map entries. ON_WM_PAINT is a macro defined in the MFC header file Afxmsg_.h. It adds an entry for WM_PAINT messages to the message map. The macro accepts no parameters because it is hardcoded to link WM_PAINT messages to the class member function named *OnPaint*. MFC provides macros for more than 100 Windows messages, ranging from WM_ACTIVATE to WM_WININICHANGE. You can get the name of the message handler that corresponds to a given ON_WM macro from the MFC documentation, but it's fairly easy to deduce the name yourself by replacing WM_ with *On* and converting all the remaining letters except those at the beginning of the word to lowercase. Thus, WM_PAINT becomes *OnPaint*, WM_LBUTTONDOWN becomes *OnLButtonDown*, and so on.

You'll need to consult the MFC documentation to determine what kinds of arguments a message handler receives and what type of value it returns. *OnPaint* takes no arguments and returns no value, but *OnLButtonDown* is prototyped like this:

```
afx_msg void OnLButtonDown (UINT nFlags, CPoint point)
```

nFlags contains bit flags specifying the state of the mouse buttons and the Ctrl and Shift keys, and *point* identifies the location at which the click occurred. The arguments passed to a message handler come from the *wParam* and *lParam* parameters that accompanied the message. But whereas *wParam* and *lParam* are of necessity generic, the parameters passed to an MFC message handler are both specific and type-safe.

What happens if you want to process a message for which MFC doesn't provide a message-map macro? You can create an entry for the message using the generic ON_MESSAGE macro, which accepts two parameters: the message ID and the address of the corresponding class member function. The following statement maps WM_SETTEXT messages to a member function named *OnSetText*:

```
ON_MESSAGE (WM_SETTEXT, OnSetText)
```

OnSetText would be declared like this:

```
afx_msg LRESULT OnSetText (WPARAM wParam, LPARAM lParam);
```

Other special-purpose message-map macros provided by MFC include ON_COMMAND, which maps menu selections and other UI events to class member functions, and ON_UPDATE_COMMAND_UI, which connects menu items and other UI objects to "update handlers" that keep them in sync with the internal state of the application. You'll be introduced to these and other message-map macros in the chapters that follow.

Getting back to Hello for a moment, *CMainWindow*'s *OnPaint* function and message map are declared with the following statements in Hello.h:

```
afx_msg void OnPaint ();
DECLARE_MESSAGE_MAP ()
```

afx_msg is a visual reminder that *OnPaint* is a message handler. You can omit it if you'd like because it reduces to white space when compiled. The term *afx_msg* is meant to connote a function that behaves as if it were a virtual function but does so without requiring a vtable entry. DECLARE_MESSAGE_MAP is usually the final statement in the class declaration because it uses C++ keywords to specify the visibility of its members. You can follow DECLARE_MESSAGE_MAP with statements declaring other class members, but if you do, you should also lead off with a *public*, *protected*, or *private* keyword to ensure the visibility you want for those members.

How Message Maps Work

You can find out how message maps work by examining the DECLARE_MESSAGE_MAP, BEGIN_MESSAGE_MAP, and END_MESSAGE_MAP macros in Afxwin.h and the code for *CWnd::WindowProc* in Wincore.cpp. Here's a synopsis of what goes on under the hood when you use message-mapping macros in your code, and how the framework uses the code and data generated by the macros to convert messages into calls to corresponding class member functions.

MFC's DECLARE_MESSAGE_MAP macro adds three members to the class declaration: a private array of AFX_MSGMAP_ENTRY structures named *_messageEntries* that contains information correlating messages and message handlers; a static AFX_MSGMAP structure named *messageMap* that contains a pointer to the class's *_messageEntries* array and a pointer to the base class's *messageMap* structure; and a virtual function named *GetMessageMap* that returns *messageMap*'s address. (The macro implementation is slightly different for an MFC application that's dynamically rather than statically linked to MFC, but the principle is the same.) BEGIN_MESSAGE_MAP contains the implementation for the *GetMessageMap* function and code to initialize the *messageMap* structure. The macros that appear between BEGIN_MESSAGE_MAP and END_MESSAGE_MAP fill in the *_messageEntries* array, and END_MESSAGE_MAP marks the end of the array with a NULL entry. For the statements

```
// In the class declaration
DECLARE_MESSAGE_MAP ()

// In the class implementation
BEGIN_MESSAGE_MAP (CMainWindow, CFrameWnd)
    ON_WM_PAINT ()
END_MESSAGE_MAP ()
```

the compiler's preprocessor generates this:

```
// In the class declaration
private:
    static const AFX_MSGMAP_ENTRY _messageEntries[];
protected:
    static const AFX_MSGMAP messageMap;
    virtual const AFX_MSGMAP* GetMessageMap() const;
```

(continued)

29

```
// In the class implementation
const AFX_MSGMAP* CMainWindow::GetMessageMap() const
    { return &CMainWindow::messageMap; }

const AFX_MSGMAP CMainWindow::messageMap = {
    &CFrameWnd::messageMap,
    &CMainWindow::_messageEntries[0]
};

const AFX_MSGMAP_ENTRY CMainWindow::_messageEntries[] = {
    { WM_PAINT, 0, 0, 0, AfxSig_vv,
        (AFX_PMSG)(AFX_PMSGW)(void (CWnd::*)(void))OnPaint },
    {0, 0, 0, 0, AfxSig_end, (AFX_PMSG)0 }
};
```

With this infrastructure in place, the framework can call *GetMessageMap* to get a pointer to *CMainWindow*'s *messageMap* structure. It can then scan the *_messageEntries* array to see if *CMainWindow* has a handler for the message, and if necessary it can grab a pointer to *CFrameWnd*'s *messageMap* structure and scan the base class's message map, too.

That's a pretty good description of what happens when a message for *CMainWindow* arrives. To dispatch the message, the framework calls the virtual *WindowProc* function that *CMainWindow* inherits from *CWnd*. *WindowProc* calls *OnWndMsg*, which in turn calls *GetMessageMap* to get a pointer to *CMainWindow::messageMap* and searches *CMainWindow::_messageEntries* for an entry whose message ID matches the ID of the message that is currently awaiting processing. If the entry is found, the corresponding *CMainWindow* function (whose address is stored in the *_messageEntries* array along with the message ID) is called. Otherwise, *OnWndMsg* consults *CMainWindow::messageMap* for a pointer to *CFrameWnd::messageMap* and repeats the process for the base class. If the base class doesn't have a handler for the message, the framework ascends another level and consults the base class's base class, systematically working its way up the inheritance chain until it finds a message handler or passes the message to Windows for default processing. Figure 1-5 illustrates *CMainWindow*'s message map schematically and shows the route that the framework travels as it searches for a handler to match a given message ID, beginning with the message map entries for *CMainWindow*.

What MFC's message-mapping mechanism amounts to is a very efficient way of connecting messages to message handlers without using virtual functions. Virtual functions are not space-efficient because they require vtables, and vtables consume memory even if the functions in them are not overridden. The amount of

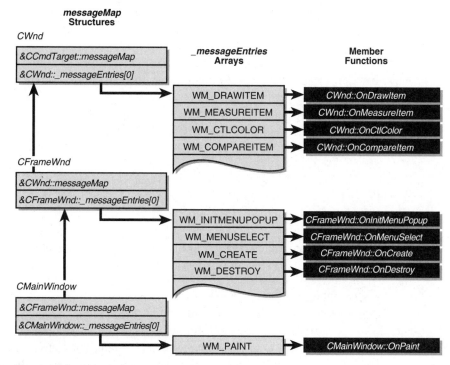

Figure 1-5. *Message-map processing.*

memory used by a message map, in contrast, is proportional to the number of entries it contains. Since it's extremely rare for a programmer to implement a window class that includes handlers for all of the different message types, message mapping conserves a few hundred bytes of memory just about every time a *CWnd* is wrapped around an HWND.

Windows, Character Sets, and the _T Macro

Microsoft Windows 98 and Microsoft Windows NT use two different character sets to form characters and strings. Windows 98 and its predecessors use the 8-bit ANSI character set, which is similar to the ASCII character set familiar to many programmers. Windows NT and Windows 2000 use the 16-bit Unicode character set, which is a superset of the ANSI character set. Unicode is ideal for applications sold in international markets because it contains a rich assortment of characters from non-U.S. alphabets. Programs compiled with ANSI characters will run on Windows NT and Windows 2000, but Unicode programs run slightly faster because Windows NT and Windows 2000 don't have to perform an ANSI-to-Unicode conversion on every character. Unicode applications won't run on Windows 98, period, unless *you* convert every character string passed to Windows from Unicode to ANSI format.

When an application is compiled, it is compiled to use either ANSI or Unicode characters. If your application will be deployed on both Windows 98 and Windows 2000, it may behoove you to make strings character set neutral. Then, by making a simple change to the project's build settings or adding a #define to a header file, you can tell the compiler whether to produce an ANSI build or a Unicode build. If you encode a string literal like this:

```
"Hello"
```

the compiler forms the string from ANSI characters. If you declare the string like this:

```
L"Hello"
```

the compiler uses Unicode characters. But if you use MFC's _T macro, like this:

```
_T ("Hello")
```

the compiler will emit Unicode characters if the preprocessor symbol _UNICODE is defined, and ANSI characters if it is not. If all your string literals are declared with _T macros, you can produce a special Windows NT–only build of your application by defining _UNICODE. Defining this symbol implicitly defines a related symbol named UNICODE (no underscore), which selects the Unicode versions of the numerous Windows API functions that come in both ANSI and Unicode versions. Of course, if you'd like the same executable to run on either platform and you're not concerned about the performance hit an ANSI application incurs under Windows NT, you can forget about the _T macro. I'll use _T throughout this book to make the sample code character set neutral.

Is wrapping string literals in _T macros sufficient to make an application completely agnostic with regard to character sets? Not quite. You must also do the following:

■   Declare characters to be of type TCHAR rather than char. If the _UNICODE symbol is defined, TCHAR evaluates to wchar_t, which is a 16-bit Unicode character. If _UNICODE is not defined, TCHAR becomes plain old char.

■   Don't use char* or wchar_t* to declare pointers to TCHAR strings. Instead, use TCHAR* or, better yet, the LPTSTR (pointer to TCHAR string) and LPCTSTR (pointer to const TCHAR string) data types.

■   Never assume that a character is only 8 bits wide. To convert a buffer length expressed in bytes to a buffer size in characters, divide the buffer length by sizeof(TCHAR).

■ Replace calls to string functions in the C run-time library (for example, *strcpy*) with the corresponding macros in the Windows header file Tchar.h (for example, *_tcscpy*).

Consider the following code snippet, which uses the ANSI character set:

```
char szMsg[256];
pWnd->GetWindowText (szMsg, sizeof (szMsg));
strcat (szMsg, " is the window title");
MessageBox (szMsg);
```

Here's what the same code would look like if it were revised to be character set neutral:

```
TCHAR szMsg[256];
pWnd->GetWindowText (szMsg, sizeof (szMsg) / sizeof (TCHAR));
_tcscat (szMsg, _T (" is the window title"));
MessageBox (szMsg);
```

The revised code uses the generic TCHAR data type, it makes no assumptions about the size of a character, and it uses the TCHAR-compatible string-concatenation function *_tcscat* in lieu of the more common but ANSI character set–dependent *strcat*.

There's more that could be said about ANSI/Unicode compatibility, but these are the essentials. For additional information, refer to the online documentation that comes with Visual C++ or to Jeffrey Richter's *Advanced Windows* (1997, Microsoft Press), which contains an excellent chapter on Unicode and a handy table listing the string macros defined in Tchar.h and their C run-time counterparts.

Building the Application

The CD in the back of this book contains everything you need to use the Hello program in Visual C++. The folder named \Chap01\Hello contains the program's source code as well as the files that make up a Visual C++ project. To open the project, simply select Open Workspace from Visual C++'s File menu and open Hello.dsw. If you modify the application and want to rebuild it, select Build Hello.exe from the Build menu.

You don't have to use the Hello files on the CD. If you'd prefer, you can create your own project and type in the source code. Here are step-by-step instructions for creating a new project in Visual C++ 6:

1. Select New from the Visual C++ File menu, and click the Projects tab to go to the Projects page.

2. Select Win32 Application, and enter a project name in the Project Name text box. If desired, you can change the path name—the drive and folder where the project and its source code will be stored—in the Location text box. Then click OK.

3.   In the Win32 Application window, select An Empty Project and then click Finish.

4.   Add source code files to the project. To enter a source code file from scratch, select New from the File menu, select the file type, and enter the file name. Be sure the Add To Project box is checked so that the file will be added to the project. Then click OK, and edit the file as you see fit. To add an existing source code file to a project, go to the Project menu, select Add To Project and then Files, and pick the file.

5.   Select Settings from the Project menu. In the Project Settings dialog box, be sure that the project name is selected in the left pane and then click the General tab if the General page isn't already displayed. Select Use MFC In A Shared DLL from the drop-down list labeled Microsoft Foundation Classes, and then click OK to register the change with Visual C++.

Choosing Use MFC In A Shared DLL minimizes your application's executable file size by allowing MFC to be accessed from a DLL. If you choose Use MFC In A Static Library instead, Visual C++ links MFC code into your application's EXE file and the file size grows considerably. Static linking uses disk space less efficiently than dynamic linking because a hard disk containing 10 statically linked MFC applications contains 10 copies of the same MFC library code. On the other hand, an application that is statically linked can be run on any PC, whether or not the MFC DLL is present. It's your call whether to link to MFC statically or dynamically, but remember that if you distribute a dynamically linked EXE, you'll need to distribute the DLL that houses MFC, too. For a release-build MFC application created with Visual C++ version 6, that DLL is named Mfc42.dll if the program uses ANSI characters and Mfc42u.dll if it uses Unicode characters.

The Big Picture

Before we move on, let's pause for a moment and review some of the important concepts learned from the Hello application. The very first thing that happens when the application is started is that a globally scoped application object is created. MFC's *AfxWinMain* function calls the application object's *InitInstance* function. *InitInstance* constructs a window object, and the window object's constructor creates the window that appears on the screen. After the window is created, *InitInstance* calls the window's *ShowWindow* function to make it visible and *UpdateWindow* to send it its first WM_PAINT message. Then *InitInstance* returns, and *AfxWinMain* calls the application object's *Run* function to start the message loop. WM_PAINT messages are converted by MFC's message-mapping mechanism into calls to *CMainWindow::OnPaint*, and *OnPaint* draws the text "Hello, MFC" in the window's client area by creating a *CPaintDC* object and calling its *DrawText* function.

If you're coming to MFC straight from the Windows SDK, this probably seems like a pretty strange way to do business. Two-step window creation? Application objects? No more *WinMain*? It's definitely different from the way Windows *used* to be programmed. But compare Hello's source code to the C program listing back in Figure 1-2, and you'll find that MFC undeniably simplifies things. MFC doesn't necessarily make the source code easier to understand—after all, Windows programming is still Windows programming—but by moving a lot of the boilerplate stuff out of the source code and into the class library, MFC reduces the amount of code you have to write. That, combined with the fact that you can modify the behavior of any MFC class by deriving from it a class of your own, makes MFC an effective tool for programming Windows. The benefits will really become apparent when you begin tapping into some of the more sophisticated features of Windows or building ActiveX controls and other Windows-based software components. With MFC, you can get an ActiveX control up and running in nothing flat. Without it—well, good luck.

Hello lacks many of the elements that characterize a full-blown Windows program, but it's still a good first step on the road to becoming an MFC programmer. In subsequent chapters, you'll learn about menus, dialog boxes, and other components of an application's user interface. You'll also see how Windows programs read input from the mouse and keyboard and learn more about drawing in a window. Chapter 2 leads off by introducing some additional *CDC* drawing functions and demonstrating how to add scroll bars to a frame window so that you can view a workspace larger than the window's client area. Both are essential next steps in building the knowledge base required to become a Windows programmer.

Chapter 2

Drawing in a Window

If you've been around PCs for a while, you probably remember what graphics programming was like before Microsoft Windows came along. If you were lucky, you had a decent graphics library with routines like *DrawLine* and *DrawCircle* to draw graphics primitives for you. If you weren't so lucky, you probably spent a lot of time writing your own output routines and tweaking them to shave off a few microseconds here and there. And whether it was your code or someone else's doing the drawing, you knew that when a new graphics standard emerged—in those days, that meant whenever IBM introduced a new graphics adapter like the EGA or the VGA— you'd be scrambling to support the latest hardware. That invariably meant buying an updated version of the graphics library, adding new code to your own routines, or writing a driver for the new video card. For the graphics programmer, the platform was a moving target that never seemed to stand still for very long. And even if you did manage to draw a bead on the video hardware, you still had plenty of work to do to adapt your code to work with printers and other output devices.

Windows changed all that by bringing to the PC platform something it sorely needed: a device-independent graphics output model. In Windows, the graphics code you write will work on any video adapter for which a Windows driver is available. These days, that's just about every adapter on the planet. And to a large extent, the same code that sends output to the screen will also work with printers and other hardcopy devices. This one-size-fits-all approach to graphics programming has a number of advantages, chief among them the fact that programmers can now spend their time developing code for their applications rather than code for the hardware their applications will run on. Moreover, you no longer need third-party graphics libraries in order to do your work because Windows provides a wide assortment of graphics API functions that do everything from draw lines to create complex clipping regions that serve as stencils for other output routines.

The part of Windows responsible for graphics output is the Graphics Device Interface, or GDI. The GDI provides a number of services that an application can call. Together, these services constitute a powerful and robust graphics programming language whose richness rivals that of some third-party graphics libraries. MFC works on top of the graphics API and codifies the interface with C++ classes that represent the various components of the Windows GDI.

Now that you know how to create a window, it's time to do something with that window. The Hello application in Chapter 1 used *CDC::DrawText* to output text to a window. *DrawText* is just one of many member functions that the *CDC* class provides for text and graphics output. This chapter looks at the *CDC* class and its derivative classes in more detail and introduces three of the most commonly used GDI primitives: pens, brushes, and fonts. It also demonstrates how to add scroll bars to a window.

THE WINDOWS GDI

In a single-tasking environment such as MS-DOS, the name of the game when it comes to screen output is "anything goes." A running application is free to do just about whatever it wants whenever it wants, whether that involves drawing a line on the screen, reprogramming the adapter's color palette, or switching to another video mode. In a windowed, multitasking environment such as Windows, programs can't be afforded such freedom because the output from program A must be protected from the output of program B. First and foremost, this means that each program's output must be restricted to its own window. The GDI uses a simple mechanism to make sure every program that draws in a window plays by the rules. That mechanism is the device context.

When a Windows program draws to a screen, a printer, or any other output device, it doesn't output pixels directly to the device. Instead, it draws to a logical "display surface" represented by a device context (DC). A device context is a data structure deep inside Windows that contains fields describing everything the GDI needs to know about the display surface, including the physical device with which it is associated and assorted state information. Before it draws anything on the screen, a Windows program acquires a device context handle from the GDI. It then passes that handle back to the GDI each time it calls a GDI output function. Without a valid device context handle, the GDI won't draw the first pixel. And through the device context, the

GDI can make sure that everything the program draws is clipped to a particular area of the screen. Device contexts play a huge role in making the GDI device-independent because, given a handle to a device context, the same GDI functions can be used to draw to a diverse assortment of output devices.

When you program Windows with MFC, the device context has even greater significance. In addition to serving as the key that unlocks the door to output devices, a device context object encapsulates the GDI functions that programs use to generate output. In MFC, you don't grab a handle to a device context and call GDI output functions, at least not directly; instead, you create a device context object and call its member functions to do your drawing. MFC's *CDC* class wraps a Windows device context and the GDI functions that require a device context handle into one convenient package, and *CDC*-derived classes such as *CPaintDC* and *CClientDC* represent the different types of device contexts that Windows applications use.

The MFC Device Context Classes

One way to get a device context in an MFC application is to call *CWnd::GetDC*, which returns a pointer to a *CDC* object representing a Windows device context. A device context pointer acquired with *CWnd::GetDC* should be released with *CWnd::ReleaseDC* when drawing is completed. The following code gets a *CDC* pointer from *GetDC*, does some drawing, and calls *ReleaseDC* to release the device context:

```
CDC* pDC = GetDC ();
// Do some drawing
ReleaseDC (pDC);
```

If the same code were to appear in an *OnPaint* handler, you would use *CWnd::BeginPaint* and *CWnd::EndPaint* in place of *GetDC* and *ReleaseDC* to ensure proper handling of the WM_PAINT message:

```
PAINTSTRUCT ps;
CDC* pDC = BeginPaint (&ps);
// Do some drawing
EndPaint (&ps);
```

The GDI also supports *metafiles,* which store sequences of GDI commands that can be "played back" to produce physical output. To acquire a device context for a metafile's output, you would use yet another set of functions to obtain and release the *CDC* pointer. And to acquire a *CDC* pointer for a device context that permits drawing anywhere in the window (as opposed to one that permits drawing only in the window's client area), you would call *CWnd::GetWindowDC* rather than *GetDC* and release the device context with *ReleaseDC*.

To save you the trouble of having to remember which functions to call to acquire and release a device context (and to help ensure that a device context is properly released when the message handler that uses the device context ends), MFC provides the *CDC*-derived classes listed in the following table.

SPECIAL-PURPOSE DEVICE CONTEXT CLASSES

Class Name	Description
CPaintDC	For drawing in a window's client area (*OnPaint* handlers only)
CClientDC	For drawing in a window's client area (anywhere but *OnPaint*)
CWindowDC	For drawing anywhere in a window, including the nonclient area
CMetaFileDC	For drawing to a GDI metafile

These classes are designed to be instantiated directly. Each class's constructor and destructor call the appropriate functions to get and release the device context so that using a device context is no more complicated than this:

```
CPaintDC dc (this);
// Do some drawing
```

The pointer passed to the class constructor identifies the window that the device context pertains to.

When a device context object is constructed on the stack, its destructor is called automatically when the object goes out of scope. And when the destructor is called, the device context is released back to Windows. The only time you need to be concerned about releasing one of these device contexts yourself is when (and if) you create a device context object on the heap with *new*, as shown here:

```
CPaintDC* pDC = new CPaintDC (this);
```

In this case, it's important to execute a

```
delete pDC;
```

statement before the function that created the device context ends so that the object's destructor will be called and the device context will be released. On some occasions, it's useful to create a device context on the heap rather than on the stack, but generally you're a lot better off creating device context objects on the stack and letting the compiler do the deleting for you.

The *CPaintDC* Class

MFC's *CPaintDC* class lets you paint in a window's client area in response to WM_PAINT messages. You should use it only in *OnPaint* handlers and never anywhere else. WM_PAINT messages are different from all other Windows messages in one very important respect: If the handler fails to call the Windows *::BeginPaint* and *::EndPaint* functions (or the MFC equivalents, *CWnd::BeginPaint* and *CWnd::EndPaint*), the message will not be removed from the message queue no matter how much drawing you do. Consequently, the application will get stuck processing the same WM_PAINT message over and over. *CPaintDC* virtually ensures that this won't happen by calling *::BeginPaint* and *::EndPaint* from its constructor and destructor, respectively.

The *CClientDC* and *CWindowDC* Classes

Windows programs don't always limit their painting to *OnPaint*. If you write an application that draws a circle on the screen whenever a mouse button is clicked, you'll probably want to paint the circle immediately—when you receive the button-click message—rather than wait for the next WM_PAINT message.

That's what MFC's *CClientDC* class is for. *CClientDC* creates a client-area device context that can be used outside *OnPaint*. The following message handler uses *CClientDC* and two *CDC* member functions to draw an X connecting the corners of the window's client area when the left mouse button is clicked:

```
void CMainWindow::OnLButtonDown (UINT nFlags, CPoint point)
{
    CRect rect;
    GetClientRect (&rect);

    CClientDC dc (this);
    dc.MoveTo (rect.left, rect.top);
    dc.LineTo (rect.right, rect.bottom);
    dc.MoveTo (rect.right, rect.top);
    dc.LineTo (rect.left, rect.bottom);
}
```

left, right, top, and *bottom* are public member variables defined in MFC's *CRect* class. They store the coordinates of the rectangle's four sides. *MoveTo* and *LineTo* are line-drawing functions that *CClientDC* inherits from *CDC*. You'll learn more about these two functions in a moment.

For the rare occasions on which you'd like to paint not only the window's client area but also the nonclient area (the title bar, the window border, and so on), MFC provides the *CWindowDC* class. *CWindowDC* is similar to *CClientDC*, but the device context it represents encompasses everything within the window's borders. Programmers sometimes use *CWindowDC* for unusual effects such as custom-drawn title bars and windows with rounded corners. In general, you won't need *CWindowDC* very often. If you do want to do your own painting in a window's nonclient area, you can trap WM_NCPAINT messages with an *OnNcPaint* handler to determine when the nonclient area needs to be painted. Unlike *OnPaint*, an *OnNcPaint* handler need not (and should not) call *BeginPaint* and *EndPaint*.

For the even rarer occasions on which a program requires access to the entire screen, you can create a *CClientDC* or *CWindowDC* object and pass its constructor a NULL pointer. The statements

```
CClientDC dc (NULL);
dc.Ellipse (0, 0, 100, 100);
```

draw a circle in the upper left corner of the screen. Screen capture programs frequently use full-screen DCs to access the whole screen. Needless to say, drawing outside your own window is a very unfriendly thing to do unless you have a specific reason for doing so.

Device Context Attributes

When you draw to the screen with *CDC* output functions, certain characteristics of the output aren't specified in the function call but are obtained from the device context itself. When you call *CDC::DrawText*, for example, you specify the text string and the rectangle in which the string will appear, but you don't specify the text color or the font because both are attributes of the device context. The following table lists some of the most useful device context attributes and the *CDC* functions used to access them.

KEY DEVICE CONTEXT ATTRIBUTES

Attribute	Default	Set with	Get with
Text color	Black	*CDC::SetTextColor*	*CDC::GetTextColor*
Background color	White	*CDC::SetBkColor*	*CDC::GetBkColor*
Background mode	OPAQUE	*CDC::SetBkMode*	*CDC::GetBkMode*
Mapping mode	MM_TEXT	*CDC::SetMapMode*	*CDC::GetMapMode*
Drawing mode	R2_COPYPEN	*CDC::SetROP2*	*CDC::GetROP2*
Current position	(0,0)	*CDC::MoveTo*	*CDC::GetCurrentPosition*
Current pen	BLACK_PEN	*CDC::SelectObject*	*CDC::SelectObject*
Current brush	WHITE_BRUSH	*CDC::SelectObject*	*CDC::SelectObject*
Current font	SYSTEM_FONT	*CDC::SelectObject*	*CDC::SelectObject*

Different *CDC* output functions use device context attributes in different ways. For example, when you draw a line with *LineTo*, the current pen determines the line's color, width, and style (solid, dotted, dashed, and so on). Similarly, when you draw a rectangle with the *Rectangle* function, the GDI borders the rectangle with the current pen and fills the rectangle with the current brush. All text output functions use the current font. The text color and the background color control the colors used when text is output. The text color determines the color of the characters, and the background color determines what color is used to fill behind them. The background color is also used to fill the gaps between line segments when dotted or dashed lines are drawn with the *LineTo* function and to fill the open areas between hatch marks painted by a hatch brush. If you'd like the background color to be ignored entirely, you can set the background mode to "transparent," like this:

```
dc.SetBkMode (TRANSPARENT);
```

Inserting this statement before the call to *DrawText* in Chapter 1's Hello program eliminates the white rectangle surrounding "Hello, MFC" that's visible when the window background color is nonwhite.

The *CDC* function you'll use more than any other to modify the attributes of a device context is *SelectObject*. The following six items are GDI objects that can be selected into a device context with *SelectObject*:

- Pens
- Brushes
- Fonts
- Bitmaps
- Palettes
- Regions

In MFC, pens, brushes, and fonts are represented by the classes *CPen*, *CBrush*, and *CFont*. (Bitmaps, palettes, and regions are discussed in Chapter 15.) Unless you call *SelectObject* to change the current pen, brush, or font, the GDI uses the device context's defaults. The default pen draws solid black lines 1 pixel wide. The default brush paints solid white. The default font is a rather plain proportional font with a height of roughly 12 points. You can create pens, brushes, and fonts of your own and select them into a device context to change the attributes of the output. To draw a solid red circle with a 10-pixel-wide black border, for example, you can create a black pen 10 pixels wide and a red brush and select them into the device context with *SelectObject* before calling *Ellipse*. If *pPen* is a pointer to a *CPen* object, *pBrush* is a pointer to a *CBrush* object, and *dc* represents a device context, the code might look like this:

```
dc.SelectObject (pPen);
dc.SelectObject (pBrush);
dc.Ellipse (0, 0, 100, 100);
```

SelectObject is overloaded to accept pointers to objects of various types. Its return value is a pointer to the object of the same type that was previously selected into the device context.

Each time you acquire a device context from Windows, its attributes are reset to the defaults. Consequently, if you want to use a red pen and a blue brush to paint your window in response to WM_PAINT messages, you must select them into the device context each time *OnPaint* is called and a new *CPaintDC* object is created. Otherwise, the default pen and brush will be used. If you'd like to avoid reinitializing a device context every time you use it, you can save its state with the *CDC::SaveDC* function and restore it the next time around with *CDC::RestoreDC*. Another option is to register a custom WNDCLASS that includes the CS_OWNDC style, which causes Windows to allocate to each instance of your application its own private device context that retains its settings. (A related but seldom used WNDCLASS style, CS_CLASSDC, allocates a "semiprivate" device context that is shared by all windows created from the same WNDCLASS.) If you select a red pen and a blue brush into a private device context, they remain selected until they're explicitly replaced.

The Drawing Mode

When the GDI outputs pixels to a logical display surface, it doesn't simply output pixel colors. Rather, it combines the colors of the pixels that it's outputting with the colors of the pixels at the destination using a combination of Boolean operations. The logic that's employed depends on the device context's current drawing mode, which you can change with *CDC::SetROP2* (short for "Set Raster Operation To"). The default drawing mode is R2_COPYPEN, which does, in fact, copy pixels to the display surface. But there are 15 other drawing modes to choose from, as shown in the table on the next page. Together, these drawing modes represent all the possible operations that can be performed by combining the Boolean primitives AND, OR, XOR, and NOT.

Why would you ever need to change the drawing mode? Suppose you want to draw a line not by copying pixels to the display surface but by inverting the colors of the pixels already there. It's easy to do; you just set the drawing mode to R2_NOT before drawing the line:

```
dc.SetROP2 (R2_NOT);
dc.MoveTo (0, 0);
dc.LineTo (100, 100);
```

This little trick might be more useful than you think, because it's a great way to rubber-band lines and rectangles. You'll see an example of what I mean in Chapter 3.

GDI Drawing Modes

Drawing Mode	Operation(s) Performed
R2_NOP	dest = dest
R2_NOT	dest = NOT dest
R2_BLACK	dest = BLACK
R2_WHITE	dest = WHITE
R2_COPYPEN	dest = src
R2_NOTCOPYPEN	dest = NOT src
R2_MERGEPENNOT	dest = (NOT dest) OR src
R2_MASKPENNOT	dest = (NOT dest) AND src
R2_MERGENOTPEN	dest = (NOT src) OR dest
R2_MASKNOTPEN	dest = (NOT src) AND dest
R2_MERGEPEN	dest = dest OR src
R2_NOTMERGEPEN	dest = NOT (dest OR src)
R2_MASKPEN	dest = dest AND src
R2_NOTMASKPEN	dest = NOT (dest AND src)
R2_XORPEN	dest = src XOR dest
R2_NOTXORPEN	dest = NOT (src XOR dest)

The Mapping Mode

Without a doubt, the aspect of GDI programming that new Windows programmers find the most confusing is the mapping mode. Simply put, the *mapping mode* is the attribute of the device context that governs how logical coordinates are translated into device coordinates. *Logical coordinates* are the coordinates you pass to *CDC* output functions. *Device coordinates* are the corresponding pixel positions within a window. When you call the *Rectangle* function like this:

```
dc.Rectangle (0, 0, 200, 100);
```

you're not necessarily telling the GDI to draw a rectangle that's 200 pixels wide and 100 pixels tall; you're telling it to draw a rectangle that's 200 units wide and 100 units tall. In the default mapping mode, MM_TEXT, it just so happens that 1 unit equals 1 pixel. But in other mapping modes, logical units are translated into device units differently. In the MM_LOENGLISH mapping mode, for example, 1 unit equals 1/100 of an inch. Therefore, drawing a rectangle that measures 200 units by 100 units in the MM_LOENGLISH mapping mode produces a 2-inch by 1-inch rectangle. Using a non-MM_TEXT mapping mode is a convenient way to scale your output so that sizes and distances are independent of the output device's physical resolution.

Windows supports eight different mapping modes. Their properties are summarized in the following table.

GDI MAPPING MODES

Mapping Mode	Distance Corresponding to One Logical Unit	Orientation of the x and y Axes
MM_TEXT	1 pixel	+x (right), +y (down)
MM_LOMETRIC	0.1 mm	+x (right), -y (down)
MM_HIMETRIC	0.01 mm	+x (right), -y (down)
MM_LOENGLISH	0.01 in.	+x (right), -y (down)
MM_HIENGLISH	0.001 in.	+x (right), -y (down)
MM_TWIPS	1/1440 in. (0.0007 in.)	+x (right), -y (down)
MM_ISOTROPIC	User-defined (x and y scale identically)	User-defined
MM_ANISOTROPIC	User-defined (x and y scale independently)	User-defined

When you draw in the MM_TEXT mapping mode, you're using the coordinate system shown in Figure 2-1. The origin is in the upper left corner of the window, the positive x axis points to the right, the positive y axis points downward, and 1 unit equals 1 pixel. If you switch to one of the "metric" mapping modes—MM_LOENGLISH, MM_HIENGLISH, MM_LOMETRIC, MM_HIMETRIC, or MM_TWIPS—the y axis flips so that positive y points upward and logical units are scaled to represent real distances rather than raw pixel counts. The origin, however, remains in the upper left corner. One thing to remember when using a metric mapping mode is that you must use negative y values if you want to see your output. The statement

```
dc.Rectangle (0, 0, 200, 100);
```

draws a 200-pixel by 100-pixel rectangle in the MM_TEXT mapping mode. The same statement produces no output in the MM_LOENGLISH mapping mode because positive y coordinates lie outside the visible part of the window. To make the rectangle visible, you must negate the y coordinates, as shown here:

```
dc.Rectangle (0, 0, 200, -100);
```

If you switch to a non-MM_TEXT mapping mode and suddenly your application's output is no longer visible, check the sign of your *y* coordinates. Positive *y* coordinates will be the problem almost every time.

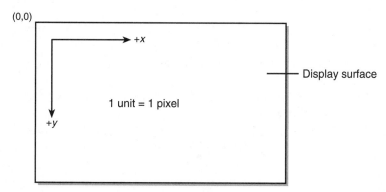

Figure 2-1. *The MM_TEXT coordinate system.*

The default mapping mode is MM_TEXT. If you want to use one of the other mapping modes, you must call *CDC::SetMapMode* to change the mapping mode. The following statements switch to the MM_LOMETRIC mapping mode and draw an ellipse whose major axis is 5 centimeters long and whose minor axis measures 3 centimeters:

```
dc.SetMapMode (MM_LOMETRIC);
dc.Ellipse (0, 0, 500, -300);
```

You can see that there's really nothing tricky about mapping modes. Things get slightly more complicated when you use the MM_ISOTROPIC and MM_ANISOTROPIC modes and when you do hit-testing on objects drawn in non-MM_TEXT mapping modes, but even that doesn't have to be difficult. The MM_ISOTROPIC and MM_ANISOTROPIC mapping modes are discussed in the next section.

One thing to keep in mind when you use the metric mapping modes is that on display screens, 1 logical inch usually doesn't equal 1 physical inch. In other words, if you draw a line that's 100 units long in the MM_LOENGLISH mapping mode, the line probably won't be exactly 1 inch long. The reason? Windows doesn't know the physical resolution of your monitor—the number of dots per inch (dpi) it's capable of displaying horizontally and vertically. (This might change in a future version of Windows.) The same is not true of printers and other hardcopy devices, however. The printer driver knows that a 600 dpi laser printer can print exactly 600 dots per inch, so a 100-unit line drawn in the MM_LOENGLISH mapping mode will measure exactly 1 inch on the printed page.

Programmable Mapping Modes

The MM_ISOTROPIC and MM_ANISOTROPIC mapping modes differ from the other mapping modes in one important respect: It's you, not Windows, who determines how logical coordinates are converted into device coordinates. For this reason, these mapping modes are sometimes called the "roll-your-own" or "programmable" mapping modes. Want a mapping mode in which 1 unit equals 1 centimeter? No problem: Just use the MM_ANISOTROPIC mapping mode and set its scaling parameters accordingly.

The most common use for the MM_ISOTROPIC and MM_ANISOTROPIC mapping modes is for drawing output that automatically scales to match the window size. The following code fragment uses the MM_ANISOTROPIC mapping mode to draw an ellipse that touches all four borders of the window in which it is drawn:

```
CRect rect;
GetClientRect (&rect);
dc.SetMapMode (MM_ANISOTROPIC);
dc.SetWindowExt (500, 500);
dc.SetViewportExt (rect.Width (), rect.Height ());
dc.Ellipse (0, 0, 500, 500);
```

See how it works? No matter what physical size the window is, you've told Windows that the window's *logical* size is 500 units by 500 units. Therefore, a bounding box that stretches from (0,0) to (500,500) encompasses the entire window. Initializing a device context in this way places the origin at the upper left corner of the window and orients the axes so that positive x points to the right and positive y points downward. If you'd rather have the y axis point upward (as it does in the metric mapping modes), you can reverse its direction by negating the y value passed to either *SetWindowExt* or *SetViewportExt*:

```
CRect rect;
GetClientRect (&rect);
dc.SetMapMode (MM_ANISOTROPIC);
dc.SetWindowExt (500, -500);
dc.SetViewportExt (rect.Width (), rect.Height ());
dc.Ellipse (0, 0, 500, -500);
```

Now you must use negative y coordinates to draw in the window. Only the MM_ISOTROPIC and MM_ANISOTROPIC mapping modes allow the directions of the x and y axes to be reversed. That's why the table in the previous section listed these two mapping modes' axis orientations as user defined.

The only difference between the MM_ISOTROPIC and MM_ANISOTROPIC mapping modes is that in the former, the scaling factors for the x and y directions are always the same. In other words, 100 horizontal units equals the same physical distance as 100 vertical units. Isotropic means "equal in all directions." The MM_ISOTROPIC mapping mode is ideal for drawing circles and squares. The following code draws a circle that spans the width or height of a window, whichever is smaller:

```
CRect rect;
GetClientRect (&rect);
dc.SetMapMode (MM_ISOTROPIC);
dc.SetWindowExt (500, 500);
dc.SetViewportExt (rect.Width (), rect.Height ());
dc.Ellipse (0, 0, 500, 500);
```

As far as Windows is concerned, the window's logical size is once again 500 units by 500 units. But now the GDI takes the output device's aspect ratio into consideration when converting logical units to device units. Chapter 14's Clock program uses the MM_ISOTROPIC mapping mode to draw a round clock face and to automatically scale the clock size to the window size. Without the MM_ISOTROPIC mapping mode, Clock would have to do all of the scaling manually.

Let's talk a bit about the *SetWindowExt* and *SetViewportExt* functions. Officially, *SetWindowExt* sets the "window extents" and *SetViewportExt* sets the "viewport extents." Think of a window as something whose size is measured in logical units and a viewport as something whose size is measured in device units, or pixels. When Windows converts between logical coordinates and device coordinates, it uses a pair of formulas that factor in the window's logical dimensions (the window extents) and its physical dimensions (the viewport extents) as well as the location of the origin. When you set the window extents and viewport extents, you're effectively programming in your own scaling parameters. Generally, the viewport extents are simply the size (in pixels) of the window you're drawing in and the window extents are the window's desired size in logical units.

One caveat regarding the use of *SetWindowExt* and *SetViewportExt* is that in the MM_ISOTROPIC mapping mode, you should call *SetWindowExt* first. Otherwise, a portion of the window's client area might fall outside the window's logical extents and become unusable. In the MM_ANISOTROPIC mapping mode, it doesn't matter which are set first—the window extents or the viewport extents.

Coordinate Conversions

You can translate logical coordinates to device coordinates using the *CDC::LPtoDP* function. Conversely, you can translate device coordinates to logical coordinates with *CDC::DPtoLP*.

Let's say you want to know where the center of a window is in device coordinates. All you have to do is halve the window's pixel width and height. *CWnd::GetClientRect* returns a window's pixel dimensions.

```
CRect rect;
GetClientRect (&rect);
CPoint point (rect.Width () / 2, rect.Height () / 2);
```

If you want to know where the center point is in MM_LOENGLISH units, however, you need *DPtoLP*:

```
CRect rect;
GetClientRect (&rect);
CPoint point (rect.Width () / 2, rect.Height () / 2);
CClientDC dc (this);
dc.SetMapMode (MM_LOENGLISH);
dc.DPtoLP (&point);
```

When *DPtoLP* returns, *point* holds the coordinates of the center point in logical (that is, MM_LOENGLISH) coordinates. If, on the other hand, you want to know the pixel coordinates of the point whose MM_LOENGLISH coordinates are (100,100), you use *LPtoDP*:

```
CPoint point (100, 100);
CClientDC dc (this);
dc.SetMapMode (MM_LOENGLISH);
dc.LPtoDP (&point);
```

One situation in which *LPtoDP* and *DPtoLP* are indispensable is when you're performing hit-testing in response to mouse clicks. Mouse clicks are always reported in device coordinates, so if you've drawn a rectangle in MM_LOENGLISH coordinates and you want to know whether a mouse click occurred inside that rectangle, you must either convert the rectangle's coordinates to device coordinates or convert the click coordinates to logical coordinates. Otherwise, you'll be comparing apples and oranges.

Moving the Origin

By default, a device context's origin is in the upper left corner of the display surface. Even if you change the mapping mode, the origin remains in the upper left corner. But just as you can change the mapping mode, you can also move the origin. MFC's *CDC* class provides two functions for moving the origin. *CDC::SetWindowOrg* moves the window origin, and *CDC::SetViewportOrg* moves the viewport origin. You'll normally use one but not both. Using both can be very confusing.

Suppose you'd like to move the origin to the center of the window so that you can center what you draw by centering your output around the point (0,0). Assuming that *dc* is a device context object, here's one way to do it:

```
CRect rect;
GetClientRect (&rect);
dc.SetViewportOrg (rect.Width () / 2, rect.Height () / 2);
```

Here's another way to accomplish the same thing, assuming that you're working in the MM_LOENGLISH mapping mode:

```
CRect rect;
GetClientRect (&rect);
CPoint point (rect.Width () / 2, rect.Height () / 2);
dc.SetMapMode (MM_LOENGLISH);
dc.DPtoLP (&point);
dc.SetWindowOrg (-point.x, -point.y);
```

It's easy to get *SetViewportOrg* and *SetWindowOrg* confused, but the distinction between them is actually quite clear. Changing the viewport origin to (x,y) with *SetViewportOrg* tells Windows to map the logical point $(0,0)$ to the device point (x,y). Changing the window origin to (x,y) with *SetWindowOrg* does essentially the reverse, telling Windows to map the logical point (x,y) to the device point $(0,0)$—the upper left corner of the display surface. In the MM_TEXT mapping mode, the only real difference between the two functions is the signs of x and y. In other mapping modes, there's more to it than that because *SetViewportOrg* deals in device coordinates and *SetWindowOrg* deals in logical coordinates. You'll see examples of how both functions are used later in this chapter.

As a final example, suppose you're drawing in the MM_HIMETRIC mapping mode, where 1 unit equals 1/100 of a millimeter, positive x points to the right, and positive y points upward, and you'd like to move the origin to the lower left corner of the window. Here's an easy way to do it:

```
CRect rect;
GetClientRect (&rect);
dc.SetViewportOrg (0, rect.Height ());
```

Now you can draw with positive x and y values using coordinates relative to the window's lower left corner.

A Final Word on Coordinate Systems

When you talk about mapping modes, window origins, viewport origins, and other idioms related to the GDI's handling of coordinates, it's easy to get tangled up in the terminology. Understanding the difference between the device coordinate system and the logical coordinate system might help clear some of the cobwebs.

In the device coordinate system, distances are measured in pixels. The device point $(0,0)$ is always in the upper left corner of the display surface, and the positive x and y axes always point right and downward. The logical coordinate system is altogether different. The origin can be placed anywhere, and both the orientation of the x and y axes and the scaling factor (the number of pixels that correspond to

1 logical unit) vary with the mapping mode. To be precise, they vary with the window extents and the viewport extents. You can change these extents in the MM_ISOTROPIC and MM_ANISOTROPIC mapping modes but not in the other mapping modes.

You'll sometimes hear Windows programmers talk about "client coordinates" and "screen coordinates." Client coordinates are simply device coordinates relative to the upper left corner of a window's client area. Screen coordinates are device co-ordinates relative to the upper left corner of the screen. You can convert from client coordinates to screen coordinates and vice versa using the *CWnd::ClientToScreen* and *CWnd::ScreenToClient* functions. Why these functions are useful will become apparent to you the first time you call a Windows function that returns screen coordinates and you pass them to a function that requires client coordinates, or vice versa.

Getting Information About a Device

Sometimes it's helpful to get information about a device before you send output to it. The *CDC::GetDeviceCaps* function lets you retrieve all kinds of information about a device, from the number of colors it supports to the number of pixels it can display horizontally and vertically. The following code initializes *cx* and *cy* to the width and height of the screen, in pixels:

```
CClientDC dc (this);
int cx = dc.GetDeviceCaps (HORZRES);
int cy = dc.GetDeviceCaps (VERTRES);
```

If the screen resolution is 1,024 by 768, *cx* and *cy* will be set to 1,024 and 768, re-spectively.

The table on the following page lists some of the parameters you can pass to *GetDeviceCaps* to acquire information about the physical output device associated with a device context. How you interpret the results depends somewhat on the device type. For example, calling *GetDeviceCaps* with a HORZRES parameter for a screen DC returns the screen width in pixels. Make the same call to a printer DC and you get back the width of the printable page, once more in pixels. As a rule, values that imply any kind of scaling (for example, LOGPIXELSX and LOGPIXELSY) return physi-cally correct values for printers and other hardcopy devices but not for screens. For a 600 dpi laser printer, both LOGPIXELSX and LOGPIXELSY return 600. For a screen, both will probably return 96, regardless of the physical screen size or resolution.

Interpreting the color information returned by the NUMCOLORS, BITSPIXEL, and PLANES parameters of *GetDeviceCaps* is a bit tricky. For a printer or a plotter, you can usually find out how many colors the device is capable of displaying from the NUMCOLORS parameter. For a monochrome printer, NUMCOLORS returns 2.

USEFUL *GETDEVICECAPS* PARAMETERS

Parameter	Returns
HORZRES	Width of the display surface in pixels
VERTRES	Height of the display surface in pixels
HORZSIZE	Width of the display surface in millimeters
VERTSIZE	Height of the display surface in millimeters
LOGPIXELSX	Number of pixels per logical inch horizontally
LOGPIXELSY	Number of pixels per logical inch vertically
NUMCOLORS	For a display device, the number of static colors; for a printer or plotter, the number of colors supported
BITSPIXEL	Number of bits per pixel
PLANES	Number of bit planes
RASTERCAPS	Bit flags detailing certain characteristics of the device, such as whether it is palettized and whether it can display bitmapped images
TECHNOLOGY	Bit flags identifying the device type—screen, printer, plotter, and so on

However, the color resolution of the screen (the number of colors that can be displayed onscreen simultaneously) is computed by multiplying BITSPIXEL and PLANES and raising 2 to the power of the result, as demonstrated here:

```
CClientDC dc (this);
int nPlanes = dc.GetDeviceCaps (PLANES);
int nBPP = dc.GetDeviceCaps (BITSPIXEL);
int nColors = 1 << (nPlanes * nBPP);
```

If this code is executed on a PC equipped with a 256-color video adapter, *nColors* equals 256. Calling *GetDeviceCaps* with a NUMCOLORS parameter, meanwhile, returns not 256 but 20—the number of "static colors" that Windows programs into the video adapter's color palette. I'll have more to say about the color characteristics of screens and video adapters and also about static colors in Chapter 15.

I'll use *GetDeviceCaps* several times in this book to adapt the sample programs' output to the physical attributes of the output device. The first use will come later in this chapter, when the screen's LOGPIXELSX and LOGPIXELSY parameters are used to draw rectangles 1 logical inch long and 1/4 logical inch tall in the MM_TEXT mapping mode.

DRAWING WITH THE GDI

Enough of the preliminaries. By now, you probably feel as if you asked for the time and got an explanation of watchmaking. Everything you've learned so far in this chapter will come in handy sooner or later—trust me. But now let's talk about functions for outputting pixels to the screen.

The functions discussed in the next several sections are by no means all of the available GDI output functions. A full treatment of every one would require a chapter much larger than this one. When you finish reading this chapter, look at the complete list of *CDC* member functions in your MFC documentation. Doing so will give you a better feel for the wide-ranging scope of the Windows GDI and let you know where to go when you need help.

Drawing Lines and Curves

MFC's *CDC* class includes a number of member functions that you can use to draw lines and curves. The following table lists the key functions. There are others, but these paint a pretty good picture of the range of available line-drawing and curve-drawing functions.

CDC FUNCTIONS FOR DRAWING LINES AND CURVES

Function	*Description*
MoveTo	Sets the current position in preparation for drawing
LineTo	Draws a line from the current position to a specified position and moves the current position to the end of the line
Polyline	Connects a set of points with line segments
PolylineTo	Connects a set of points with line segments beginning with the current position and moves the current position to the end of the polyline
Arc	Draws an arc
ArcTo	Draws an arc and moves the current position to the end of the arc
PolyBezier	Draws one or more Bézier splines
PolyBezierTo	Draws one or more Bézier splines and moves the current position to the end of the final spline
PolyDraw	Draws a series of line segments and Bézier splines through a set of points and moves the current position to the end of the final line segment or spline

Drawing a straight line is simple. You just set the current position to one end of the line and call *LineTo* with the coordinates of the other:

```
dc.MoveTo (0, 0);
dc.LineTo (0, 100);
```

To draw another line that's connected to the previous one, you call *LineTo* again. There's no need to call *MoveTo* a second time because the first call to *LineTo* sets the current position to the end of the line:

```
dc.MoveTo (0, 0);
dc.LineTo (0, 100);
dc.LineTo (100, 100);
```

You can draw several lines in one fell swoop using *Polyline* or *PolylineTo*. The only difference between the two is that *PolylineTo* uses the device context's current position and *Polyline* does not. The following statements draw a box that measures 100 units to a side from a set of points describing the box's vertices:

```
POINT aPoint[5] = { 0, 0, 0, 100, 100, 100, 100, 0, 0, 0 };
dc.Polyline (aPoint, 5);
```

These statements draw the same box using *PolylineTo*:

```
dc.MoveTo (0, 0);
POINT aPoint[4] = { 0, 100, 100, 100, 100, 0, 0, 0 };
dc.PolylineTo (aPoint, 4);
```

When *PolylineTo* returns, the current position is set to the endpoint of the final line segment—in this case, (0,0). If *Polyline* is used instead, the current position is not altered.

Charles Petzold's *Programming Windows* contains an excellent example showing how and why polylines can be useful. The following *OnPaint* function, which is basically just an MFC adaptation of Charles's code, uses *CDC::Polyline* to draw a sine wave that fills the interior of a window:

```
#include <math.h>
#define SEGMENTS 500
#define PI 3.1415926
    :
    :
void CMainWindow::OnPaint ()
{
    CRect rect;
    GetClientRect (&rect);
    int nWidth = rect.Width ();
    int nHeight = rect.Height ();

    CPaintDC dc (this);
    CPoint aPoint[SEGMENTS];
```

(continued)

```
for (int i=0; i<SEGMENTS; i++) {
    aPoint[i].x = (i * nWidth) / SEGMENTS;
    aPoint[i].y = (int) ((nHeight / 2) *
        (1 - (sin ((2 * PI * i) / SEGMENTS)))));
}
dc.Polyline (aPoint, SEGMENTS);
}
```

You can see the results for yourself by substituting this code for the *OnPaint* function in Chapter 1's Hello program. Note the use of the *CRect* functions *Width* and *Height* to compute the width and height of the window's client area.

An arc is a curve taken from the circumference of a circle or an ellipse. You can draw arcs quite easily with *CDC::Arc*. You just pass it a rectangle whose borders circumscribe the ellipse and a pair of points that specify the endpoints of two imaginary lines drawn outward from the center of the ellipse. The points at which the lines intersect the ellipse are the starting and ending points of the arc. (The lines must be long enough to at least touch the circumference of the ellipse; otherwise, the results won't be what you expect.) The following code draws an arc representing the upper left quadrant of an ellipse that is 200 units wide and 100 units high:

```
CRect rect (0, 0, 200, 100);
CPoint point1 (0, -500);
CPoint point2 (-500, 0);
dc.Arc (rect, point1, point2);
```

To reverse the arc and draw the upper right, lower right, and lower left quadrants of the ellipse, simply reverse the order in which *point1* and *point2* are passed to the *Arc* function. If you'd like to know where the arc ended (an item of information that's useful when using lines and arcs to draw three-dimensional pie charts), use *ArcTo* instead of *Arc* and then use *CDC::GetCurrentPosition* to locate the endpoint. Be careful, though. In addition to drawing the arc itself, *ArcTo* draws a line from the old current position to the arc's starting point. What's more, *ArcTo* is one of a handful of GDI functions that's not implemented in Windows 98. If you call it on a platform other than Windows NT or Windows 2000, nothing will be output.

If splines are more your style, the GDI can help out there, too. *CDC::PolyBezier* draws Bézier splines—smooth curves defined by two endpoints and two intermediate points that exert "pull." Originally devised to help engineers build mathematical models of car bodies, Bézier splines, or simply "Béziers," as they are more often known, are used today in everything from fonts to warhead designs. The following code fragment uses two Bézier splines to draw a figure that resembles the famous Nike "swoosh" symbol. (See Figure 2-2.)

```
POINT aPoint1[4] = { 120, 100, 120, 200, 250, 150, 500, 40 };
POINT aPoint2[4] = { 120, 100,  50, 350, 250, 200, 500, 40 };
dc.PolyBezier (aPoint1, 4);
dc.PolyBezier (aPoint2, 4);
```

The curves drawn here are independent splines that happen to join at the endpoints. To draw a continuous curve by joining two or more splines, add three points to the POINT array for each additional spline and increase the number of points specified in *PolyBezier*'s second parameter accordingly.

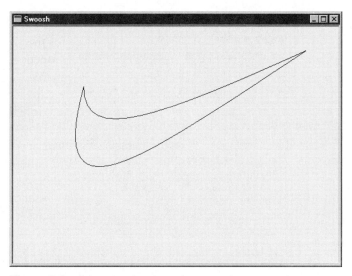

Figure 2-2. *A famous shoe logo drawn with Bézier splines.*

One peculiarity of all GDI line-drawing and curve-drawing functions is that the final pixel is never drawn. If you draw a line from (0,0) to (100,100) with the statements

```
dc.MoveTo (0, 0);
dc.LineTo (100, 100);
```

the pixel at (0,0) is set to the line color, as are the pixels at (1,1), (2,2), and so on. But the pixel at (100,100) is still the color it was before. If you want the line's final pixel to be drawn, too, you must draw it yourself. One way to do that is to use the *CDC::SetPixel* function, which sets a single pixel to the color you specify.

Drawing Ellipses, Polygons, and Other Shapes

The GDI doesn't limit you to simple lines and curves. It also lets you draw ellipses, rectangles, pie-shaped wedges, and other closed figures. MFC's *CDC* class wraps the associated GDI functions in handy class member functions that you can call on a device context object or through a pointer to a device context object. The following table lists a few of those functions.

CDC FUNCTIONS FOR DRAWING CLOSED FIGURES

Function	Description
Chord	Draws a closed figure bounded by the intersection of an ellipse and a line
Ellipse	Draws a circle or an ellipse
Pie	Draws a pie-shaped wedge
Polygon	Connects a set of points to form a polygon
Rectangle	Draws a rectangle with square corners
RoundRect	Draws a rectangle with rounded corners

GDI functions that draw closed figures take as a parameter the coordinates of a "bounding box." When you draw a circle with the *Ellipse* function, for example, you don't specify a center point and a radius; instead, you specify the circle's bounding box. You can pass the coordinates explicitly, like this:

```
dc.Ellipse (0, 0, 100, 100);
```

or pass them in a RECT structure or a *CRect* object, like this:

```
CRect rect (0, 0, 100, 100);
dc.Ellipse (rect);
```

When this circle is drawn, it touches the $x=0$ line at the left of the bounding box and the $y=0$ line at the top, but it falls 1 pixel short of the $x=100$ line at the right and 1 pixel short of the $y=100$ line at the bottom. In other words, figures are drawn from the left and upper limits of the bounding box up to (but not including) the right and lower limits. If you call the *CDC::Rectangle* function, like this:

```
dc.Rectangle (0, 0, 8, 4);
```

you get the output shown in Figure 2-3. Observe that the right and lower limits of the rectangle fall at $x=7$ and $y=3$, not $x=8$ and $y=4$.

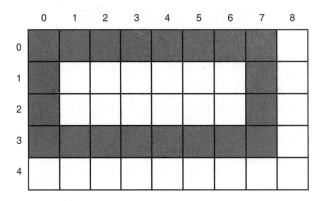

Figure 2-3. *A rectangle drawn with the statement dc.Rectangle (0, 0, 8, 4).*

Rectangle and *Ellipse* are about as straightforward as they come. You provide the bounding box, and Windows does the drawing. If you want to draw a rectangle that has rounded corners, use *RoundRect* instead of *Rectangle*.

The *Pie* and *Chord* functions merit closer scrutiny, however. Both are syntactically identical to the *Arc* function discussed in the previous section. The difference is in the output. (See Figure 2-4.) *Pie* draws a closed figure by drawing straight lines connecting the ends of the arc to the center of the ellipse. *Chord* closes the figure by connecting the arc's endpoints. The following *OnPaint* handler uses *Pie* to draw a pie chart that depicts four quarterly revenue values:

```
#include <math.h>
#define PI 3.1415926
    .
    .
    .
void CMainWindow::OnPaint ()
{
    CPaintDC dc (this);
    int nRevenues[4] = { 125, 376, 252, 184 };

    CRect rect;
    GetClientRect (&rect);
    dc.SetViewportOrg (rect.Width () / 2, rect.Height () / 2);

    int nTotal = 0;
    for (int i=0; i<4; i++)
        nTotal += nRevenues[i];

    int x1 = 0;
    int y1 = -1000;
    int nSum = 0;

    for (i=0; i<4; i++) {
        nSum += nRevenues[i];
        double rad = ((double) (nSum * 2 * PI) / (double) nTotal) + PI;
        int x2 = (int) (sin (rad) * 1000);
        int y2 = (int) (cos (rad) * 1000 * 3) / 4;
        dc.Pie (-200, -150, 200, 150, x1, y1, x2, y2);
        x1 = x2;
        y1 = y2;
    }
}
```

Note that the origin is moved to the center of the window with *SetViewportOrg* before any drawing takes place so that the chart will also be centered.

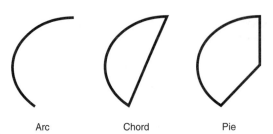

Arc   Chord   Pie

Figure 2-4. *Output from the Arc, Chord, and Pie functions.*

GDI Pens and the *CPen* Class

Windows uses the pen that is currently selected into the device context to draw lines and curves and also to border figures drawn with *Rectangle, Ellipse*, and other shape-drawing functions. The default pen draws solid black lines that are 1 pixel wide. To change the way lines are drawn, you must create a GDI pen and select it into the device context with *CDC::SelectObject.*

MFC represents GDI pens with the class *CPen*. The simplest way to create a pen is to construct a *CPen* object and pass it the parameters defining the pen:

```
CPen pen (PS_SOLID, 1, RGB (255, 0, 0));
```

A second way to create a GDI pen is to construct an uninitialized *CPen* object and call *CPen::CreatePen*:

```
CPen pen;
pen.CreatePen (PS_SOLID, 1, RGB (255, 0, 0));
```

Yet a third method is to construct an uninitialized *CPen* object, fill in a LOGPEN structure describing the pen, and then call *CPen::CreatePenIndirect* to create the pen:

```
CPen pen;
LOGPEN lp;
lp.lopnStyle = PS_SOLID;
lp.lopnWidth.x = 1;
lp.lopnColor = RGB (255, 0, 0);
pen.CreatePenIndirect (&lp);
```

LOGPEN's *lopnWidth* field is a POINT data structure. The structure's *x* data member specifies the pen width. The *y* data member is not used.

CreatePen and *CreatePenIndirect* return TRUE if a pen is successfully created, FALSE if it is not. If you allow *CPen*'s constructor to create the pen, an exception of type *CResourceException* is thrown if the pen can't be created. This should happen only if Windows is critically low on memory.

A pen has three defining characteristics: style, width, and color. The examples above create a pen whose style is PS_SOLID, whose width is 1, and whose color is bright red. The first of the three parameters passed to *CPen::CPen* and *CPen::CreatePen* specifies the pen style, which defines the type of line the pen draws. PS_SOLID creates a pen that draws solid, unbroken lines. Other pen styles are shown in Figure 2-5.

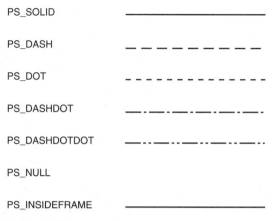

PS_SOLID

PS_DASH

PS_DOT

PS_DASHDOT

PS_DASHDOTDOT

PS_NULL

PS_INSIDEFRAME

Figure 2-5. *Pen styles.*

The special PS_INSIDEFRAME style draws solid lines that stay within the bounding rectangle, or "inside the frame," of the figure being drawn. If you use any of the other pen styles to draw a circle whose diameter is 100 units using a PS_SOLID pen that is 20 units wide, for example, the actual diameter of the circle, measured across the circle's outside edge, is 120 units, as shown in Figure 2-6. Why? Because the border drawn by the pen extends 10 units outward on either side of the theoretical circle. Draw the same circle with a PS_INSIDEFRAME pen, and the diameter is exactly 100 units. The PS_INSIDEFRAME style does not affect lines drawn with *LineTo* and other functions that don't use a bounding rectangle.

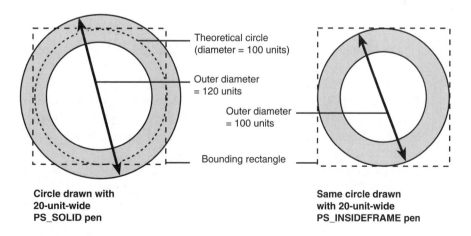

Theoretical circle
(diameter = 100 units)

Outer diameter
= 120 units

Outer diameter
= 100 units

Bounding rectangle

Circle drawn with
20-unit-wide
PS_SOLID pen

Same circle drawn
with 20-unit-wide
PS_INSIDEFRAME pen

Figure 2-6. *The PS_INSIDEFRAME pen style.*

The pen style PS_NULL creates what Windows programmers refer to as a "NULL pen." Why would you ever want to create a NULL pen? Believe it or not, there are times when a NULL pen can come in handy. Suppose, for example, that you want to draw a solid red circle with no border. If you draw the circle with MFC's *CDC::Ellipse* function, Windows automatically borders the circle with the pen currently selected into the device context. You can't tell the *Ellipse* function that you don't want a border, but you *can* select a NULL pen into the device context so that the circle will have no visible border. NULL brushes are used in a similar way. If you want the circle to have a border but want the interior of the circle to be transparent, you can select a NULL brush into the device context before you draw.

The second parameter passed to *CPen*'s pen-create functions specifies the width of the lines drawn with the pen. Pen widths are specified in logical units whose physical meanings depend on the current mapping mode. You can create PS_SOLID, PS_NULL, and PS_INSIDEFRAME pens of any logical width, but PS_DASH, PS_DOT, PS_DASHDOT, and PS_DASHDOTDOT pens must be 1 logical unit wide. Specifying a pen width of 0 in any style creates a pen that is 1 pixel wide, no matter what the mapping mode.

The third and final parameter specified when a pen is created is the pen's color. Windows uses a 24-bit RGB color model in which each possible color is defined by red, green, and blue color values from 0 through 255. The higher the value, the brighter the corresponding color component. The RGB macro combines values that specify the three independent color components into one COLORREF value that can be passed to the GDI. The statement

```
CPen pen (PS_SOLID, 1, RGB (255, 0, 0));
```

creates a bright red pen, and the statement

```
CPen pen (PS_SOLID, 1, RGB (255, 255, 0));
```

creates a bright yellow pen by combining red and green. If the display adapter doesn't support 24-bit color, Windows compensates by dithering colors that it can't display directly. Be aware, however, that only PS_INSIDEFRAME pens greater than 1 logical unit in width can use dithered colors. For the other pen styles, Windows maps the color of the pen to the nearest solid color that can be displayed. You can be reasonably certain of getting the exact color you want on all adapters by sticking to the "primary" colors shown in the table on the following page. These colors are part of the basic palette that Windows programs into the color registers of every video adapter to ensure that a common subset of colors is available to all programs.

PRIMARY GDI COLORS

Color	*R*	*G*	*B*	*Color*	*R*	*G*	*B*
Black	0	0	0	Light gray	192	192	192
Blue	0	0	192	Bright blue	0	0	255
Green	0	192	0	Bright green	0	255	0
Cyan	0	192	192	Bright cyan	0	255	255
Red	192	0	0	Bright red	255	0	0
Magenta	192	0	192	Bright magenta	255	0	255
Yellow	192	192	0	Bright yellow	255	255	0
Dark gray	128	128	128	White	255	255	255

How do you use a pen once it's created? Simple: You select it into a device context. The following code snippet creates a red pen that's 10 units wide and draws an ellipse with it:

```
CPen pen (PS_SOLID, 10, RGB (255, 0, 0));
CPen* pOldPen = dc.SelectObject (&pen);
dc.Ellipse (0, 0, 100, 100);
```

The ellipse is filled with the color or pattern of the current brush, which defaults to white. To change the default, you need to create a GDI brush and select it into the device context before calling *Ellipse*. I'll demonstrate how to do that in just a moment.

Extended Pens

If none of the basic pen styles suits your needs, you can use a separate class of pens known as "extended" pens, which the Windows GDI and MFC's *CPen* class support. These pens offer a greater variety of output options. For example, you can create an extended pen that draws a pattern described by a bitmap image or uses a dithered color. You can also exercise precise control over endpoints and joins by specifying the end cap style (flat, round, or square) and join style (beveled, mitered, or rounded). The following code creates an extended pen 16 units wide that draws solid green lines with flat ends. Where two lines meet, the adjoining ends are rounded to form a smooth intersection:

```
LOGBRUSH lb;
lb.lbStyle = BS_SOLID;
lb.lbColor = RGB (0, 255, 0);
CPen pen (PS_GEOMETRIC | PS_SOLID | PS_ENDCAP_FLAT |
    PS_JOIN_ROUND, 16, &lb);
```

Windows places several restrictions on the use of extended pens, not the least of which is that endpoint joins will work only if the figure is first drawn as a "path" and is then rendered with *CDC::StrokePath* or a related function. You define a path by enclosing drawing commands between calls to *CDC::BeginPath* and *CDC::EndPath*, as shown here:

```
dc.BeginPath ();        // Begin the path definition
dc.MoveTo (0, 0);       // Create a triangular path
dc.LineTo (100, 200);
dc.LineTo (200, 100);
dc.CloseFigure ();
dc.EndPath ();          // End the path definition
dc.StrokePath ();       // Draw the triangle
```

Paths are a powerful feature of the GDI that you can use to create all sorts of interesting effects. We'll look more closely at paths—and at the *CDC* functions that use them—in Chapter 15.

GDI Brushes and the *CBrush* Class

By default, closed figures drawn with *Rectangle, Ellipse,* and other *CDC* output functions are filled with white pixels. You can change the fill color by creating a GDI brush and selecting it into the device context prior to drawing.

MFC's *CBrush* class encapsulates GDI brushes. Brushes come in three basic varieties: solid, hatch, and pattern. Solid brushes paint with solid colors. If the display hardware won't allow a solid brush color to be displayed directly, Windows simulates the color by dithering colors that *can* be displayed. A hatch brush paints with one of six predefined crosshatch patterns that are similar to ones commonly found in engineering and architectural drawings. A pattern brush paints with a bitmap. The *CBrush* class provides a constructor for each different brush style.

You can create a solid brush in one step by passing a COLORREF value to the *CBrush* constructor:

```
CBrush brush (RGB (255, 0, 0));
```

Or you can create a solid brush in two steps by creating an uninitialized *CBrush* object and calling *CBrush::CreateSolidBrush*:

```
CBrush brush;
brush.CreateSolidBrush (RGB (255, 0, 0));
```

Both examples create a solid brush that paints in bright red. You can also create a brush by initializing a LOGBRUSH structure and calling *CBrush::CreateBrushIndirect*. As with *CPen* constructors, all *CBrush* constructors that create a brush for you throw a resource exception if the GDI is low on memory and a brush can't be created.

Hatch brushes are created by passing *CBrush*'s constructor both a hatch index and a COLORREF value or by calling *CBrush::CreateHatchBrush*. The statement

```
CBrush brush (HS_DIAGCROSS, RGB (255, 0, 0));
```

creates a hatch brush that paints perpendicular crosshatch lines oriented at 45-degree angles, as do these statements:

```
CBrush brush;
brush.CreateHatchBrush (HS_DIAGCROSS, RGB (255, 0, 0));
```

HS_DIAGCROSS is one of six hatch styles you can choose from. (See Figure 2-7.) When you paint with a hatch brush, Windows fills the space between hatch lines with the default background color (white) unless you change the device context's current background color with *CDC::SetBkColor* or turn off background fills by changing the background mode from OPAQUE to TRANSPARENT with *CDC::SetBkMode*. The statements

```
CBrush brush (HS_DIAGCROSS, RGB (255, 255, 255));
dc.SelectObject (&brush);
dc.SetBkColor (RGB (192, 192, 192));
dc.Rectangle (0, 0, 100, 100);
```

draw a rectangle 100 units square and fill it with white crosshatch lines drawn against a light gray background. The statements

```
CBrush brush (HS_DIAGCROSS, RGB (0, 0, 0));
dc.SelectObject (&brush);
dc.SetBkMode (TRANSPARENT);
dc.Rectangle (0, 0, 100, 100);
```

draw a black crosshatched rectangle against the existing background.

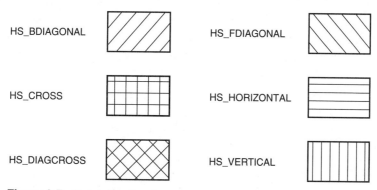

Figure 2-7. *Hatch brush styles.*

The Brush Origin

One attribute of a device context that you should be aware of when using dithered brush colors or hatch brushes is the brush origin. When Windows fills an area with a hatched or dithered brush pattern, it tiles an 8-pixel by 8-pixel pattern horizontally and vertically within the affected area. By default, the origin for this pattern, better known as the *brush origin,* is the device point (0,0)—the screen pixel in the upper left corner of the window. This means that a pattern drawn in a rectangle that begins 100 pixels to the right of and below the origin will be aligned somewhat differently with respect to the rectangle's border than a pattern drawn in a rectangle positioned a few pixels to the left or right, as shown in Figure 2-8. In many applications, it doesn't matter; the user isn't likely to notice minute differences in brush alignment. However, in some situations it matters a great deal.

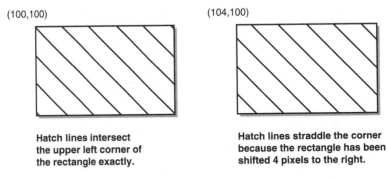

(100,100)

(104,100)

Hatch lines intersect the upper left corner of the rectangle exactly.

Hatch lines straddle the corner because the rectangle has been shifted 4 pixels to the right.

Figure 2-8. *Brush alignment.*

Suppose you're using a hatch brush to fill a rectangle and you're animating the motion of that rectangle by repeatedly erasing it and redrawing it 1 pixel to the right or the left. If you don't reset the brush origin to a point that stays in the same position relative to the rectangle before each redraw, the hatch pattern will "walk" as the rectangle moves.

The solution? Before selecting the brush into the device context and drawing the rectangle, call *CGdiObject::UnrealizeObject* on the brush object to permit the brush origin to be moved. Then call *CDC::SetBrushOrg* to align the brush origin with the rectangle's upper left corner, as shown here:

```
CPoint point (x1, y1);
dc.LPtoDP (&point);
point.x %= 8;
point.y %= 8;
brush.UnrealizeObject ();
dc.SetBrushOrg (point);
dc.SelectObject (&brush);
dc.Rectangle (x1, y1, x2, y2);
```

In this example, *point* is a *CPoint* object that holds the logical coordinates of the rectangle's upper left corner. *LPtoDP* is called to convert logical coordinates into device coordinates (brush origins are always specified in device coordinates), and a modulo-8 operation is performed on the resulting values because coordinates passed to *SetBrushOrg* should fall within the range 0 through 7. Now the hatch pattern will be aligned consistently no matter where in the window the rectangle is drawn.

Drawing Text

You've already seen one way to output text to a window. The *CDC::DrawText* function writes a string of text to a display surface. You tell *DrawText* where to draw its output by specifying both a formatting rectangle and a series of option flags indicating how the text is to be positioned within the rectangle. In Chapter 1's Hello program, the statement

```
dc.DrawText (_T ("Hello, MFC"), -1, &rect,
    DT_SINGLELINE | DT_CENTER | DT_VCENTER);
```

drew "Hello, MFC" so that it was centered in the window. *rect* was a rectangle object initialized with the coordinates of the window's client area, and the DT_CENTER and DT_VCENTER flags told *DrawText* to center its output in the rectangle both horizontally and vertically.

DrawText is one of several text-related functions that are members of MFC's *CDC* class. Some of the others are listed in the table on the next page. One of the most useful is *TextOut*, which outputs text like *DrawText* but accepts an *x-y* coordinate pair that specifies where the text will be output and also uses the current position if it is asked to. The statement

```
dc.TextOut (0, 0, CString (_T ("Hello, MFC")));
```

writes "Hello, MFC" to the upper left of the display surface represented by *dc*. A related function named *TabbedTextOut* works just like *TextOut* except that it expands tab characters into white space. (If a string passed to *TextOut* contains tabs, the characters show up as rectangles in most fonts.) Tab positions are specified in the call to *TabbedTextOut*. A related function named *ExtTextOut* gives you the added option of filling a rectangle surrounding the output text with an opaque background color. It also gives the programmer precise control over intercharacter spacing.

By default, the coordinates passed to *TextOut*, *TabbedTextOut*, and *ExtTextOut* specify the location of the upper left corner of the text's leftmost character cell. However, the relationship between the coordinates passed to *TextOut* and the characters in the output string, a property known as the *text alignment*, is an attribute of the device context. You can change it with *CDC::SetTextAlign*. For example, after a

```
dc.SetTextAlign (TA_RIGHT);
```

statement is executed, the *x* coordinate passed to *TextOut* specifies the rightmost position in the character cell—perfect for drawing right-aligned text.

You can also call *SetTextAlign* with a TA_UPDATECP flag to instruct *TextOut* to ignore the *x* and *y* arguments passed to it and use the device context's current position instead. When the text alignment includes TA_UPDATECP, *TextOut* updates the *x* component of the current position each time a string is output. One use for this feature is to achieve proper spacing between two or more character strings that are output on the same line.

CDC TEXT FUNCTIONS

Function	Description
DrawText	Draws text in a formatting rectangle
TextOut	Outputs a line of text at the current or specified position
TabbedTextOut	Outputs a line of text that includes tabs
ExtTextOut	Outputs a line of text and optionally fills a rectangle with a background color or varies the intercharacter spacing
GetTextExtent	Computes the width of a string in the current font
GetTabbedTextExtent	Computes the width of a string with tabs in the current font
GetTextMetrics	Returns font metrics (character height, average character width, and so on) for the current font
SetTextAlign	Sets alignment parameters for *TextOut* and other output functions
SetTextJustification	Specifies the added width that is needed to justify a string of text
SetTextColor	Sets the device context's text output color
SetBkColor	Sets the device context's background color, which determines the fill color used behind characters that are output to a display surface

Two functions—*GetTextMetrics* and *GetTextExtent*—let you retrieve information about the font that is currently selected into the device context. *GetTextMetrics* fills a TEXTMETRIC structure with information on the characters that make up the font. *GetTextExtent* returns the width of a given string, in logical units, rendered in that font. (Use *GetTabbedTextExtent* if the string contains tab characters.) One use for *GetTextExtent* is to gauge the width of a string prior to outputting it in order to compute how much space is needed between words to fully justify the text. If *nWidth* is the distance between left and right margins, the following code outputs the text "Now is the time" and justifies the output to both margins:

```
CString string = _T ("Now is the time");
CSize size = dc.GetTextExtent (string);
dc.SetTextJustification (nWidth - size.cx, 3);
dc.TextOut (0, y, string);
```

The second parameter passed to *SetTextJustification* specifies the number of break characters in the string. The default break character is the space character. After *SetTextJustification* is called, subsequent calls to *TextOut* and related text output functions distribute the space specified in the *SetTextJustification*'s first parameter evenly between all the break characters.

GDI Fonts and the *CFont* Class

All *CDC* text functions use the font that is currently selected into the device context. A *font* is a group of characters of a particular size (height) and typeface that share common attributes such as character weight—for example, normal or boldface. In classical typography, font sizes are measured in units called *points*. One point equals about 1/72 inch. Each character in a 12-point font is nominally 1/6 inch tall, but in Windows, the actual height can vary somewhat depending on the physical characteristics of the output device. The term *typeface* describes a font's basic style. Times New Roman is one example of a typeface; Courier New is another.

A font is a GDI object, just as a pen or a brush is. In MFC, fonts are represented by objects of the *CFont* class. Once a *CFont* object is constructed, you create the underlying GDI font by calling the *CFont* object's *CreateFont*, *CreateFontIndirect*, *CreatePointFont*, or *CreatePointFontIndirect* function. Use *CreateFont* or *CreateFontIndirect* if you want to specify the font size in pixels, and use *CreatePointFont* and *CreatePointFontIndirect* to specify the font size in points. Creating a 12-point Times New Roman screen font with *CreatePointFont* requires just two lines of code:

```
CFont font;
font.CreatePointFont (120, _T ("Times New Roman"));
```

Doing the same with *CreateFont* requires you to query the device context for the logical number of pixels per inch in the vertical direction and to convert points to pixels:

```
CClientDC dc (this);
int nHeight = -((dc.GetDeviceCaps (LOGPIXELSY) * 12) / 72);
CFont font;
font.CreateFont (nHeight, 0, 0, 0, FW_NORMAL, 0, 0, 0,
    DEFAULT_CHARSET, OUT_CHARACTER_PRECIS, CLIP_CHARACTER_PRECIS,
    DEFAULT_QUALITY, DEFAULT_PITCH | FF_DONTCARE,
    _T ("Times New Roman"));
```

Incidentally, the numeric value passed to *CreatePointFont* is the desired point size *times 10*. This allows you to control the font size down to 1/10 point—plenty accurate enough for most applications, considering the relatively low resolution of most screens and other commonly used output devices.

The many parameters passed to *CreateFont* specify, among other things, the font weight and whether characters in the font are italicized. You can't create a bold, italic font with *CreatePointFont*, but you can with *CreatePointFontIndirect*. The following code creates a 12-point bold, italic Times New Roman font using *CreatePointFontIndirect*.

```
LOGFONT lf;
::ZeroMemory (&lf, sizeof (lf));
lf.lfHeight = 120;
lf.lfWeight = FW_BOLD;
lf.lfItalic = TRUE;
::lstrcpy (lf.lfFaceName, _T ("Times New Roman"));

CFont font;
font.CreatePointFontIndirect (&lf);
```

LOGFONT is a structure whose fields define all the characteristics of a font. *::ZeroMemory* is an API function that zeroes a block of memory, and *::lstrcpy* is an API function that copies a text string from one memory location to another. You can use the C run time's *memset* and *strcpy* functions instead (actually, you should use *_tcscpy* in lieu of *strcpy* so the call will work with ANSI or Unicode characters), but using Windows API functions frequently makes an executable smaller by reducing the amount of statically linked code.

After creating a font, you can select it into a device context and draw with it using *DrawText*, *TextOut*, and other *CDC* text functions. The following *OnPaint* handler draws "Hello, MFC" in the center of a window. But this time the text is drawn using a 72-point Arial typeface, complete with drop shadows. (See Figure 2-9.)

```
void CMainWindow::OnPaint ()
{
    CRect rect;
    GetClientRect (&rect);

    CFont font;
    font.CreatePointFont (720, _T ("Arial"));

    CPaintDC dc (this);
    dc.SelectObject (&font);
    dc.SetBkMode (TRANSPARENT);

    CString string = _T ("Hello, MFC");

    rect.OffsetRect (16, 16);
    dc.SetTextColor (RGB (192, 192, 192));
    dc.DrawText (string, &rect, DT_SINGLELINE |
        DT_CENTER | DT_VCENTER);

    rect.OffsetRect (-16, -16);
    dc.SetTextColor (RGB (0, 0, 0));
    dc.DrawText (string, &rect, DT_SINGLELINE |
        DT_CENTER | DT_VCENTER);
}
```

Figure 2-9. *"Hello, MFC" rendered in 72-point Arial with drop shadows.*

The shadow effect is achieved by drawing the text string twice—once a few pixels to the right of and below the center of the window, and once in the center. MFC's *CRect::OffsetRect* function makes it a snap to "move" rectangles by offsetting them a specified distance in the *x* and *y* directions.

What happens if you try to create, say, a Times New Roman font on a system that doesn't have Times New Roman installed? Rather than fail the call, the GDI will pick a similar typeface that *is* installed. An internal font-mapping algorithm is called to pick the best match, and the results aren't always what one might expect. But at least your application won't output text just fine on one system and mysteriously output nothing on another.

Raster Fonts vs. TrueType Fonts

Most GDI fonts fall into one of two categories: raster fonts and TrueType fonts. Raster fonts are stored as bitmaps and look best when they're displayed in their native sizes. One of the most useful raster fonts provided with Windows is MS Sans Serif, which is commonly used (in its 8-point size) on push buttons, radio buttons, and other dialog box controls. Windows can scale raster fonts by duplicating rows and columns of pixels, but the results are rarely pleasing to the eye due to stair-stepping effects.

The best fonts are TrueType fonts because they scale well to virtually any size. Like PostScript fonts, TrueType fonts store character outlines as mathematical formulas. They also include "hint" information that's used by the GDI's TrueType font rasterizer to enhance scalability. You can pretty much bank on the fact that any system your application runs on will have the following TrueType fonts installed, because all four are provided with Windows:

- Times New Roman
- Arial
- Courier New
- Symbol

In Chapter 7, you'll learn how to query the system for font information and how to enumerate the fonts that are installed. Such information can be useful if your application requires precise character output or if you want to present a list of installed fonts to the user.

Rotated Text

One question that's frequently asked about GDI text output is "How do I display rotated text?" There are two ways to do it, one of which works only in Microsoft Windows NT and Windows 2000. The other method is compatible with all 32-bit versions of Windows, so it's the one I'll describe here.

The secret is to create a font with *CFont::CreateFontIndirect* or *CFont::Create-PointFontIndirect* and to specify the desired rotation angle (in degrees) times 10 in the LOGFONT structure's *lfEscapement* and *lfOrientation* fields. Then you output the text in the normal manner—for example, using *CDC::TextOut*. Conventional text has an escapement and orientation of 0; that is, it has no slant and is drawn on a horizontal. Setting these values to 450 rotates the text counterclockwise 45 degrees. The following *OnPaint* handler increments *lfEscapement* and *lfOrientation* in units of 15 degrees and uses the resulting fonts to draw the radial text array shown in Figure 2-10:

```
void CMainWindow::OnPaint ()
{
    CRect rect;
    GetClientRect (&rect);

    CPaintDC dc (this);
    dc.SetViewportOrg (rect.Width () / 2, rect.Height () / 2);
    dc.SetBkMode (TRANSPARENT);

    for (int i=0; i<3600; i+=150) {
        LOGFONT lf;
        ::ZeroMemory (&lf, sizeof (lf));
        lf.lfHeight = 160;
        lf.lfWeight = FW_BOLD;
        lf.lfEscapement = i;
```

```
        lf.lfOrientation = i;
        ::lstrcpy (lf.lfFaceName, _T ("Arial"));

        CFont font;
        font.CreatePointFontIndirect (&lf);

        CFont* pOldFont = dc.SelectObject (&font);
        dc.TextOut (0, 0, CString (_T ("          Hello, MFC")));
        dc.SelectObject (pOldFont);
    }
}
```

This technique works great with TrueType fonts, but it doesn't work at all with raster fonts.

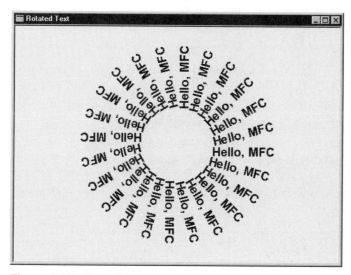

Figure 2-10. *Rotated text.*

Stock Objects

Windows predefines a handful of pens, brushes, fonts, and other GDI objects that can be used without being explicitly created. Called *stock objects*, these GDI objects can be selected into a device context with the *CDC::SelectStockObject* function or assigned to an existing *CPen*, *CBrush*, or other object with *CGdiObject::CreateStock-Object*. *CGdiObject* is the base class for *CPen*, *CBrush*, *CFont*, and other MFC classes that represent GDI objects.

The following table shows a partial list of the available stock objects. Stock pens go by the names WHITE_PEN, BLACK_PEN, and NULL_PEN. WHITE_PEN and BLACK_PEN draw solid lines that are 1 pixel wide. NULL_PEN draws nothing. The stock brushes include one white brush, one black brush, and three shades of gray.

HOLLOW_BRUSH and NULL_BRUSH are two different ways of referring to the same thing—a brush that paints nothing. SYSTEM_FONT is the font that's selected into every device context by default.

COMMONLY USED STOCK OBJECTS

Object	Description
NULL_PEN	Pen that draws nothing
BLACK_PEN	Black pen that draws solid lines 1 pixel wide
WHITE_PEN	White pen that draws solid lines 1 pixel wide
NULL_BRUSH	Brush that draws nothing
HOLLOW_BRUSH	Brush that draws nothing (same as NULL_BRUSH)
BLACK_BRUSH	Black brush
DKGRAY_BRUSH	Dark gray brush
GRAY_BRUSH	Medium gray brush
LTGRAY_BRUSH	Light gray brush
WHITE_BRUSH	White brush
ANSI_FIXED_FONT	Fixed-pitch ANSI font
ANSI_VAR_FONT	Variable-pitch ANSI font
SYSTEM_FONT	Variable-pitch system font
SYSTEM_FIXED_FONT	Fixed-pitch system font

Suppose you want to draw a light gray circle with no border. How do you do it? Here's one way:

```
CPen pen (PS_NULL, 0, (RGB (0, 0, 0)));
dc.SelectObject (&pen);
CBrush brush (RGB (192, 192, 192));
dc.SelectObject (&brush);
dc.Ellipse (0, 0, 100, 100);
```

But since NULL pens and light gray brushes are stock objects, here's a better way:

```
dc.SelectStockObject (NULL_PEN);
dc.SelectStockObject (LTGRAY_BRUSH);
dc.Ellipse (0, 0, 100, 100);
```

The following code demonstrates a third way to draw the circle. This time the stock objects are assigned to a *CPen* and a *CBrush* rather than selected into the device context directly:

```
CPen pen;
pen.CreateStockObject (NULL_PEN);
dc.SelectObject (&pen);
```

```
CBrush brush;
brush.CreateStockObject (LTGRAY_BRUSH);
dc.SelectObject (&brush);

dc.Ellipse (0, 0, 100, 100);
```

Which of the three methods you use is up to you. The second method is the shortest, and it's the only one that's guaranteed not to throw an exception since it doesn't create any GDI objects.

Deleting GDI Objects

Pens, brushes, and other objects created from *CGdiObject*-derived classes are resources that consume space in memory, so it's important to delete them when you no longer need them. If you create a *CPen*, *CBrush*, *CFont*, or other *CGdiObject* on the stack, the associated GDI object is automatically deleted when *CGdiObject* goes out of scope. If you create a *CGdiObject* on the heap with *new*, be sure to delete it at some point so that its destructor will be called. The GDI object associated with a *CGdiObject* can be explicitly deleted by calling *CGdiObject::DeleteObject*. You never need to delete stock objects, even if they are "created" with *CreateStockObject*.

In 16-bit Windows, GDI objects frequently contributed to the problem of resource leakage, in which the Free System Resources figure reported by Program Manager gradually decreased as applications were started and terminated because some programs failed to delete the GDI objects they created. All 32-bit versions of Windows track the resources a program allocates and deletes them when the program ends. However, it's *still* important to delete GDI objects when they're no longer needed so that the GDI doesn't run out of memory while a program is running. Imagine an *OnPaint* handler that creates 10 pens and brushes every time it's called but neglects to delete them. Over time, *OnPaint* might create thousands of GDI objects that occupy space in system memory owned by the Windows GDI. Pretty soon, calls to create pens and brushes will fail, and the application's *OnPaint* handler will mysteriously stop working.

In Visual C++, there's an easy way to tell whether you're failing to delete pens, brushes, and other resources: Simply run a debug build of your application in debugging mode. When the application terminates, resources that weren't freed will be listed in the debugging window. MFC tracks memory allocations for *CPen*, *CBrush*, and other *CObject*-derived classes so that it can notify you when an object hasn't been deleted. If you have difficulty ascertaining from the debug messages which objects weren't deleted, add the statement

```
#define new DEBUG_NEW
```

to your application's source code files after the statement that includes Afxwin.h. (In AppWizard-generated applications, this statement is included automatically.)

Debug messages for unfreed objects will then include line numbers and file names to help you pinpoint leaks.

Deselecting GDI Objects

It's important to delete the GDI objects you create, but it's equally important to never delete a GDI object while it's selected into a device context. Code that attempts to paint with a deleted object is buggy code. The only reason it doesn't crash is that the Windows GDI is sprinkled with error-checking code to prevent such crashes from occurring.

Abiding by this rule isn't as easy as it sounds. The following *OnPaint* handler allows a brush to be deleted while it's selected into a device context. Can you figure out why?

```
void CMainWindow::OnPaint ()
{
    CPaintDC dc (this);
    CBrush brush (RGB (255, 0, 0));
    dc.SelectObject (&brush);
    dc.Ellipse (0, 0, 200, 100);
}
```

Here's the problem. A *CPaintDC* object and a *CBrush* object are created on the stack. Since the *CBrush* is created second, its destructor gets called first. Consequently, the associated GDI brush is deleted before *dc* goes out of scope. You could fix this by creating the brush first and the DC second, but code whose robustness relies on stack variables being created in a particular order is bad code indeed. As far as maintainability goes, it's a nightmare.

The solution is to select the *CBrush* out of the device context before the *CPaintDC* object goes out of scope. There is no *UnselectObject* function, but you can select an object out of a device context by selecting in another object. Most Windows programmers make it a practice to save the pointer returned by the first call to *SelectObject* for each object type and then use that pointer to reselect the default object. An equally viable approach is to select stock objects into the device context to replace the objects that are currently selected in. The first of these two methods is illustrated by the following code:

```
CPen pen (PS_SOLID, 1, RGB (255, 0, 0));
CPen* pOldPen = dc.SelectObject (&pen);
CBrush brush (RGB (0, 0, 255));
CBrush* pOldBrush = dc.SelectObject (&brush);
    .
    .
    .
dc.SelectObject (pOldPen);
```

```
dc.SelectObject (pOldBrush);
```

The second method works like this:

```
CPen pen (PS_SOLID, 1, RGB (255, 0, 0));
dc.SelectObject (&pen);
CBrush brush (RGB (0, 0, 255));
dc.SelectObject (&brush);
    .
    .
    .
dc.SelectStockObject (BLACK_PEN);
dc.SelectStockObject (WHITE_BRUSH);
```

The big question is why this is necessary. The simple truth is that it's not. In modern versions of Windows, there's no harm in allowing a GDI object to be deleted a split second before a device context is released, especially if you're absolutely sure that no drawing will be done in the interim. Still, cleaning up a device context by deselecting the GDI objects you selected in is a common practice in Windows programming. It's also considered good form, so it's something I'll do throughout this book.

Incidentally, GDI objects are occasionally created on the heap, like this:

```
CPen* pPen = new CPen (PS_SOLID, 1, RGB (255, 0, 0));
CPen* pOldPen = dc.SelectObject (pPen);
```

At some point, the pen must be selected out of the device context and deleted. The code to do it might look like this:

```
dc.SelectObject (pOldPen);
delete pPen;
```

Since the *SelectObject* function returns a pointer to the object selected out of the device context, it might be tempting to try to deselect the pen and delete it in one step:

```
delete dc.SelectObject (pOldPen);
```

But don't do this. It works fine with pens, but it might not work with brushes. Why? Because if you create two identical *CBrush*es, 32-bit Windows conserves memory by creating just one GDI brush and you'll wind up with two *CBrush* pointers that reference the same HBRUSH. (An HBRUSH is a handle that uniquely identifies a GDI brush, just as an HWND identifies a window and an HDC identifies a device context. A *CBrush* wraps an HBRUSH and stores the HBRUSH handle in its *m_hObject* data member.) Because *CDC::SelectObject* uses an internal table maintained by MFC to convert the HBRUSH handle returned by *SelectObject* to a *CBrush* pointer and because that table assumes a one-to-one mapping between HBRUSHes and *CBrush*es, the *CBrush* pointer you get back might not match the *CBrush* pointer returned by *new*. Be sure you pass *delete* the pointer returned by *new*. Then both the GDI object and the C++ object will be properly destroyed.

The Ruler Application

The best way to get acquainted with the GDI and the MFC classes that encapsulate it is to write code. Let's start with a very simple application. Figure 2-12 contains the source code for Ruler, a program that draws a 12-inch ruler on the screen. Ruler's output is shown in Figure 2-11.

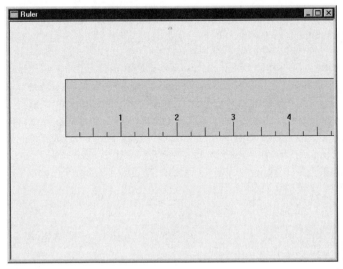

Figure 2-11. *The Ruler window.*

Ruler.h

```
class CMyApp : public CWinApp
{
public:
    virtual BOOL InitInstance ();
};

class CMainWindow : public CFrameWnd
{
public:
    CMainWindow ();

protected:
    afx_msg void OnPaint ();
    DECLARE_MESSAGE_MAP ()
};
```

Figure 2-12. *The Ruler application.*

Ruler.cpp

```cpp
#include <afxwin.h>
#include "Ruler.h"

CMyApp myApp;

///////////////////////////////////////////////////////////////////////
// CMyApp member functions

BOOL CMyApp::InitInstance ()
{
    m_pMainWnd = new CMainWindow;
    m_pMainWnd->ShowWindow (m_nCmdShow);
    m_pMainWnd->UpdateWindow ();
    return TRUE;
}

///////////////////////////////////////////////////////////////////////
// CMainWindow message map and member functions

BEGIN_MESSAGE_MAP (CMainWindow, CFrameWnd)
    ON_WM_PAINT ()
END_MESSAGE_MAP ()

CMainWindow::CMainWindow ()
{
    Create (NULL, _T ("Ruler"));
}

void CMainWindow::OnPaint ()
{
    CPaintDC dc (this);

    //
    // Initialize the device context.
    //
    dc.SetMapMode (MM_LOENGLISH);
    dc.SetTextAlign (TA_CENTER | TA_BOTTOM);
    dc.SetBkMode (TRANSPARENT);

    //
    // Draw the body of the ruler.
    //
```

(continued)

Figure 2-12. *continued*

```
CBrush brush (RGB (255, 255, 0));
CBrush* pOldBrush = dc.SelectObject (&brush);
dc.Rectangle (100, -100, 1300, -200);
dc.SelectObject (pOldBrush);

//
// Draw the tick marks and labels.
//
for (int i=125; i<1300; i+=25) {
    dc.MoveTo (i, -192);
    dc.LineTo (i, -200);
}

for (i=150; i<1300; i+=50) {
    dc.MoveTo (i, -184);
    dc.LineTo (i, -200);
}

for (i=200; i<1300; i+=100) {
    dc.MoveTo (i, -175);
    dc.LineTo (i, -200);

    CString string;
    string.Format (_T ("%d"), (i / 100) - 1);
    dc.TextOut (i, -175, string);
}
}
```

The structure of Ruler is similar to that of the Hello application presented in Chapter 1. The *CMyApp* class represents the application itself. *CMyApp::InitInstance* creates a frame window by constructing a *CMainWindow* object, and *CMainWindow*'s constructor calls *Create* to create the window you see on the screen. *CMainWindow::OnPaint* handles all the drawing. The body of the ruler is drawn with *CDC::Rectangle,* and the hash marks are drawn with *CDC::LineTo* and *CDC::MoveTo*. Before the rectangle is drawn, a yellow brush is selected into the device context so that the body of the ruler will be painted yellow. Numeric labels are drawn with *CDC::TextOut* and positioned over the tick marks by calling *SetTextAlign* with TA_CENTER and TA_BOTTOM flags and passing *TextOut* the coordinates of the top of each tick mark. Before *TextOut* is called for the first time, the device context's background mode is set to TRANSPARENT. Otherwise, the numbers on the face of the ruler would be drawn with white backgrounds.

Rather than hardcode the strings passed to *TextOut*, Ruler uses *CString::Format* to generate text on the fly. *CString* is the MFC class that represents text strings.

CString::Format works like C's *printf* function, converting numeric values to text and substituting them for placeholders in a formatting string. Windows programmers who work in C frequently use the *::wsprintf* API function for text formatting. *Format* does the same thing for *CString* objects without requiring an external function call. And unlike *::wsprintf*, *Format* supports the full range of *printf* formatting codes, including codes for floating-point and string variable types.

Ruler uses the MM_LOENGLISH mapping mode to scale its output so that 1 inch on the ruler corresponds to 1 logical inch on the screen. Hold a real ruler up to the screen and on most PCs you'll find that 1 logical inch equals a little more than 1 physical inch. If the ruler is output to a printer instead, logical inches and physical inches will match exactly.

SEEING WHAT YOU'VE DRAWN

Unfortunately, there is one small problem with Ruler's output: Unless you're running the program on a very high resolution video adapter, you can't see everything it draws. Even on a 1,280-pixel by 1,204-pixel screen, the window can't be stretched wide enough to make all the output visible. What doesn't fit inside the window's client area is clipped by the GDI. You could modify the sample program to make the ruler shorter, but that still wouldn't do much for someone running Windows on a 640-by-480 screen. No, there's a better solution, one that's entirely independent of the screen resolution. That solution is a scroll bar.

Adding a Scroll Bar to a Window

A scroll bar is a window with an arrow at each end and a traveling "thumb" in between that can be dragged with the mouse. Scroll bars can be oriented horizontally or vertically, but never at an angle. When the user clicks one of the scroll bar arrows, moves the thumb, or clicks the scroll bar shaft, the scroll bar informs the window it's attached to by sending it a message. It's up to the window to decide what, if anything, to do with that message because a scroll bar does very little on its own. It doesn't, for example, magically scroll the window's contents. What it does do is provide a very intuitive and universally recognized mechanism for scrolling backward and forward over a virtual landscape that's too large to fit within the physical confines of a window.

Adding a scroll bar to a window is one of the easiest things you'll ever do in a Windows program. To add a vertical scroll bar, create the window with the WS_VSCROLL style. To add a horizontal scroll bar, use the WS_HSCROLL style. To add horizontal and vertical scroll bars, use both WS_VSCROLL and WS_HSCROLL. Recall from Chapter 1 that the third parameter passed to *CFrameWnd::Create* is the window style, and that the default is WS_OVERLAPPEDWINDOW. An application that creates a conventional frame window with the statement

```
Create (NULL, _T ("My Application"));
```

can create a frame window containing a vertical scroll bar with the statement

```
Create (NULL, _T ("My Application"), WS_OVERLAPPEDWINDOW | WS_VSCROLL);
```

Accordingly, Windows provides a scroll bar that extends the height of the window's client area from top to bottom on the right side. If you'd rather have the scroll bar appear on the left, include a WS_EX_LEFTSCROLLBAR flag in *Create*'s optional *dwExStyle* (seventh) parameter.

Setting a Scroll Bar's Range, Position, and Page Size

After you create a scroll bar, you should initialize it with a range, position, and page size. The *range* is a pair of integers that define the upper and lower limits of the scroll bar's travel. The *position* is an integer value that specifies the current location within that range; its value is reflected in the position of the scroll bar thumb. The *page size* sets the size of the thumb to provide a visual representation of the relationship between the size of the window and the size of the scrollable view. For example, if the scroll bar range is 0 to 100 and the page size is 50, the thumb size is half the scroll bar length. If you don't set the page size, Windows picks a default, nonproportional thumb size for you.

One way to set a scroll bar's range and position is with the *CWnd::SetScrollRange* and *CWnd::SetScrollPos* functions. The statement

```
SetScrollRange (SB_VERT, 0, 100, TRUE);
```

sets a vertical scroll bar's range to 0 through 100, while the statement

```
SetScrollPos (SB_VERT, 50, TRUE);
```

sets the current position to 50 and consequently moves the thumb to the middle of the scroll bar. (For horizontal scroll bars, use SB_HORZ instead of SB_VERT.) A scroll bar maintains a record of its current range and position internally. You can query for those values at any time with *CWnd::GetScrollRange* and *CWnd::GetScrollPos*.

The TRUE parameter passed to *SetScrollRange* and *SetScrollPos* specifies that the scroll bar should be redrawn to reflect the change. You can prevent redraws by specifying FALSE. If you specify neither TRUE nor FALSE, both *SetScrollRange* and *SetScrollPos* default to TRUE. You generally want a scroll bar to redraw itself after one of these functions is called, but not if both are called in quick succession. Redrawing a scroll bar twice in a very short period of time produces an undesirable flashing effect. If you're setting the range and the position together, do it like this:

```
SetScrollRange (SB_VERT, 0, 100, FALSE);
SetScrollPos (SB_VERT, 50, TRUE);
```

SetScrollPos and *SetScrollRange* date back to the very first version of Windows. In today's versions, the preferred way to set a scroll bar's range and position is with the *CWnd::SetScrollInfo* function. In addition to allowing the range and the position to be set with a single function call, *SetScrollInfo* also provides a means—the *only* means, as it turns out—for setting the page size. *SetScrollInfo* accepts three parameters:

■ An SB_VERT or SB_HORZ parameter that specifies whether the scroll bar is vertical or horizontal (or SB_BOTH if you want to initialize two scroll bars at once)

■ A pointer to a SCROLLINFO structure

■ A BOOL value (TRUE or FALSE) that specifies whether the scroll bar should be redrawn

SCROLLINFO is defined as follows in Winuser.h:

```
typedef struct tagSCROLLINFO
{
    UINT    cbSize;
    UINT    fMask;
    int     nMin;
    int     nMax;
    UINT    nPage;
    int     nPos;
    int     nTrackPos;
} SCROLLINFO, FAR *LPSCROLLINFO;
```

cbSize specifies the size of the structure, *nMin* and *nMax* specify the scroll bar range, *nPage* specifies the page size, and *nPos* specifies the position. *nTrackPos* is not used in calls to *SetScrollInfo*, but it returns the scroll bar's thumb position when the complementary *GetScrollInfo* function is called to retrieve information about the scroll bar while the thumb is being dragged. The *fMask* field holds a combination of one or more of the following bit flags:

■ SIF_DISABLENOSCROLL, which disables the scroll bar

■ SIF_PAGE, which indicates that *nPage* holds the page size

■   SIF_POS, which indicates that *nPos* holds the scroll bar position

■   SIF_RANGE, which indicates that *nMin* and *nMax* hold the scroll bar range

■   SIF_ALL, which is equivalent to SIF_PAGE ¦ SIF_POS ¦ SIF_RANGE.

SetScrollInfo ignores fields for which bit flags are not specified. The statements

```
SCROLLINFO si;
si.fMask = SIF_POS;
si.nPos = 50;
SetScrollInfo (SB_VERT, &si, TRUE);
```

set the position while leaving the range and page size unaffected, and

```
SCROLLINFO si;
si.fMask = SIF_RANGE ¦ SIF_POS ¦ SIF_PAGE;  // Or SIF_ALL
si.nMin = 0;
si.nMax = 99;
si.nPage = 25;
si.nPos = 50;
SetScrollInfo (SB_VERT, &si, TRUE);
```

sets the range, page size, and position in one operation. You don't need to initialize *cbSize* before calling *SetScrollInfo* or *GetScrollInfo* because MFC initializes it for you.

You can make a scroll bar disappear by setting the upper limit of its range equal to the lower limit. The scroll bar doesn't go away entirely; it's still there, even though you can't see it, and—more important—you can bring it back by making the range upper and lower limits different again. This turns out to be quite a useful trick if you want to hide the scroll bar because the window has been enlarged to the point that a scroll bar is no longer required. *SetScrollInfo*'s SIF_DISABLENOSCROLL flag prevents a scroll bar from accepting further input, but it doesn't make the scroll bar disappear. Having a disabled scroll bar visible inside a window can be confusing to users, who are apt to wonder why the scroll bar is there if it can't be used.

When you set a scroll bar's range, page size, and position, here's a convenient model to keep in mind. Suppose your window's client area is 100 units high and the workspace you want to cover with a vertical scroll bar is 400 units high. Set the scroll bar range to 0-399 and the page size to 100. Accordingly, Windows will draw the scroll bar thumb so that it is one-fourth the height of the scroll bar. When the scroll bar position is 0, the thumb is positioned at the top of the scroll bar. As the thumb is scrolled down, scroll the contents of your window up an amount proportional to the distance the thumb was moved. If you limit the scroll bar's maximum position to 300 (the difference between the magnitude of the scroll bar range and the page size), the bottom of the thumb will reach the bottom of the scroll bar at the same time that the bottom of the workspace scrolls into view at the bottom of the window.

Synchronizing the Thumb Size and the Window Size

Since a scroll bar's thumb size reflects the relative size of the window compared to the width or the height of the virtual workspace, you should update the thumb size when the window size changes. It's easy to do: Just call *SetScrollInfo* with an SIF_PAGE flag each time your window receives a WM_SIZE message. The first WM_SIZE message comes when a window is created. Subsequent WM_SIZE messages arrive whenever the window's size changes. In MFC, an ON_WM_SIZE entry in a class's message map directs WM_SIZE messages to a handler named *OnSize*. The handler is prototyped as follows:

```
afx_msg void OnSize (UINT nType, int cx, int cy)
```

The *nType* parameter informs the window whether it has been minimized, maximized, or simply resized by using the code SIZE_MINIMIZED, SIZE_MAXIMIZED, or SIZE_RESTORED, respectively. *cx* and *cy* are the client area's new width and height in pixels. If you know the dimensions of your application's virtual workspace, you can set the thumb size accordingly.

Processing Scroll Bar Messages

A scroll bar notifies its owner (the window to which it is attached) of scroll bar events by sending messages. A horizontal scroll bar sends WM_HSCROLL messages, and a vertical scroll bar sends WM_VSCROLL messages. In MFC, these messages are directed to a window's *OnHScroll* and *OnVScroll* functions by ON_WM_HSCROLL and ON_WM_VSCROLL entries in the window's message map. Scroll bar message handlers are prototyped like this:

```
afx_msg void OnHScroll (UINT nCode, UINT nPos, CScrollBar* pScrollBar)
afx_msg void OnVScroll (UINT nCode, UINT nPos, CScrollBar* pScrollBar)
```

nCode identifies the type of event that precipitated the message; *nPos* contains the latest thumb position if the thumb is being dragged or was just dragged and released; and, for a scroll bar that was created by adding a WS_HSCROLL or WS_VSCROLL style bit to a window, *pScrollBar* is NULL.

There are seven different event notifications that an application might receive in *OnVScroll*'s *nCode* parameter, as shown in the table on the following page.

Event Code	Sent When
SB_LINEUP	The arrow at the top of the scroll bar is clicked.
SB_LINEDOWN	The arrow at the bottom of the scroll bar is clicked.
SB_PAGEUP	The scroll bar shaft is clicked between the up arrow and the thumb.
SB_PAGEDOWN	The scroll bar shaft is clicked between the thumb and down arrow.
SB_ENDSCROLL	The mouse button is released, and no more SB_LINEUP, SB_LINEDOWN, SB_PAGEUP, or SB_PAGEDOWN notifications are forthcoming.
SB_THUMBTRACK	The scroll bar thumb is dragged.
SB_THUMBPOSITION	The thumb is released after being dragged.

Horizontal scroll bars send the same notifications as vertical scroll bars, but the notifications have slightly different meanings. For a horizontal scroll bar, SB_LINEUP signifies that the left arrow was clicked, SB_LINEDOWN means the right arrow was clicked, SB_PAGEUP means the scroll bar was clicked between the left arrow and the thumb, and SB_PAGEDOWN means the scroll bar was clicked between the thumb and the right arrow. If you prefer, you can use SB_LINELEFT, SB_LINERIGHT, SB_PAGELEFT, and SB_PAGERIGHT rather than SB_LINEUP, SB_LINEDOWN, SB_PAGEUP, and SB_PAGEDOWN. The discussions in the remainder of this chapter deal exclusively with vertical scroll bars, but keep in mind that anything said about vertical scroll bars also applies to horizontal scroll bars.

If the user clicks a scroll bar or scroll bar arrow and leaves the mouse button pressed, a series of SB_LINEUP, SB_LINEDOWN, SB_PAGEUP, or SB_PAGEDOWN notifications will arrive in rapid succession—similar to the stream of typematic key codes generated when a key is held down. SB_ENDSCROLL terminates a stream of UP or DOWN notifications and indicates that the mouse button has been released. Even a single click of a scroll bar or scroll bar arrow generates an UP or a DOWN notification followed by an SB_ENDSCROLL notification. Similarly, a window is bombarded with SB_THUMBTRACK notifications that report new thumb positions as a scroll bar thumb is dragged, and it receives an SB_THUMBPOSITION notification when the thumb is released. When an SB_THUMBTRACK or SB_THUMBPOSITION notification arrives, the message's *nPos* parameter holds the latest thumb position. For other event codes, the value of *nPos* is undefined.

How your program responds to scroll bar event messages is up to you. Most programs that use scroll bars disregard SB_ENDSCROLL messages and respond to SB_LINEUP, SB_LINEDOWN, SB_PAGEUP, and SB_PAGEDOWN messages instead. A typical response to SB_LINEUP and SB_LINEDOWN messages is to scroll the contents of the window up or down one line and call *SetScrollPos* or *SetScrollInfo* to set the new scroll bar position and update the thumb location. "Line" can have whatever physical meaning you want it to have; it might mean 1 pixel, or it might mean the height of one line of text. Similarly, the usual response to SB_PAGEUP and SB_PAGEDOWN messages is to scroll up or down a distance equal to or slightly less than one "page," which is typically defined as the height of the window's client area or slightly less, and to call *SetScrollInfo* to set the new scroll position. In any event, it's your responsibility to update the scroll bar position. The scroll bar doesn't do that by itself.

Another, though less common, approach to processing UP and DOWN notifications is to continually move the scroll bar thumb by calling *SetScrollPos* or *SetScrollInfo* but to defer scrolling the window until an SB_ENDSCROLL notification arrives. I once used this technique in a multimedia application that was relatively slow to respond to positional changes so that the latency of commands sent to a CD-ROM drive wouldn't impede the smooth movement of the scroll bar thumb.

SB_THUMBTRACK and SB_THUMBPOSITION notifications are handled a little differently. Since SB_THUMBTRACK notifications are liable to come fast and furious when the thumb is dragged, some Windows applications ignore SB_THUMBTRACK notifications and respond only to SB_THUMBPOSITION notifications. In this case, the window doesn't scroll until the thumb is released. If you can scroll the contents of your window quickly enough to keep up with SB_THUMBTRACK notifications, you can make your program more responsive to user input by scrolling as the thumb is dragged. It's still up to you to update the scroll bar position each time you scroll the window. Windows animates the movement of the scroll bar thumb as it's dragged up and down, but if you fail to call *SetScrollPos* or *SetScrollInfo* in response to SB_THUMBTRACK or SB_THUMBPOSITION notifications, the thumb will snap back to its original position the moment it's released.

Scrolling a Window

Now that you understand how a scroll bar works, it's time to think about how to scroll the contents of a window in response to scroll bar messages.

The simplest approach is to change the scroll bar position each time a scroll bar message arrives and to call *CWnd::Invalidate* to force a repaint. The window's *OnPaint* handler can query the scroll bar for its current position and factor that information into its output. Unfortunately, scrolling a window this way is slow—*very* slow, for that matter. If the user clicks the up arrow to scroll the window contents up one line, it's wasteful to redraw the entire window because most of the information you want to display is already there, albeit in the wrong location. A more efficient approach to processing SB_LINEUP messages is to copy everything currently displayed in the window down one line using a fast block copy and then to draw just the new top line. That's what *CWnd::ScrollWindow* is for.

ScrollWindow scrolls the contents of a window's client area—in whole or in part—up or down, left or right, by 1 or more pixels using a fast block pixel transfer. Moreover, it invalidates only the part of the window contents that is "uncovered" by the scrolling operation so that the next WM_PAINT message doesn't have to repaint the entire window. If *ScrollWindow* is called to scroll a window downward by 10 pixels, it performs the scroll by doing a block copy. Then it invalidates the window's top 10 rows. This activates *OnPaint* and causes only the top 10 rows to be redrawn. Even if *OnPaint* tries to redraw the contents of the entire client area, performance is improved because most of the output is clipped. A smart *OnPaint* handler can further boost performance by restricting its GDI calls to those that affect pixels in the window's invalid rectangle. You'll see sample programs in Chapters 10 and 13 that use this technique to optimize scrolling performance.

ScrollWindow accepts four parameters. Two are required and two are optional. The function is prototyped as follows:

```
void ScrollWindow (int xAmount, int yAmount,
    LPCRECT lpRect = NULL, LPCRECT lpClipRect = NULL)
```

xAmount and *yAmount* are signed integers that specify the number of pixels to scroll horizontally and vertically. Negative values scroll left and up, while positive values scroll right and down. *lpRect* points to a *CRect* object or a RECT structure that specifies the part of the client area to scroll, and *lpClipRect* points to a *CRect* object or a RECT structure that specifies a clipping rectangle. Specifying NULL for *lpRect* and *lpClipRect* scrolls the contents of the entire client area. The statement

```
ScrollWindow (0, 10);
```

scrolls everything in a window's client area downward by 10 pixels and prompts a redraw of the first 10 rows.

You can use *ScrollWindow* whether your application displays text, graphics, or both. In Windows all things are graphical—including text.

The Accel Application

Let's put this newfound knowledge to work by writing an application that scrolls. Accel draws a window that resembles Microsoft Excel. (See Figure 2-13.) The spreadsheet depicted in the window is 26 columns wide and 99 rows high—much too large to be displayed all at once. However, scroll bars allow the user to view all parts of the spreadsheet. In addition to providing a hands-on look at the principles discussed in the preceding sections, Accel demonstrates another way that a program can scale its output. Rather than use a non-MM_TEXT mapping mode, it uses *CDC::GetDeviceCaps* to query the display device for the number of pixels per inch displayed horizontally and vertically. Then it draws each spreadsheet cell so that it's 1 inch wide and ¼ inch tall using raw pixel counts.

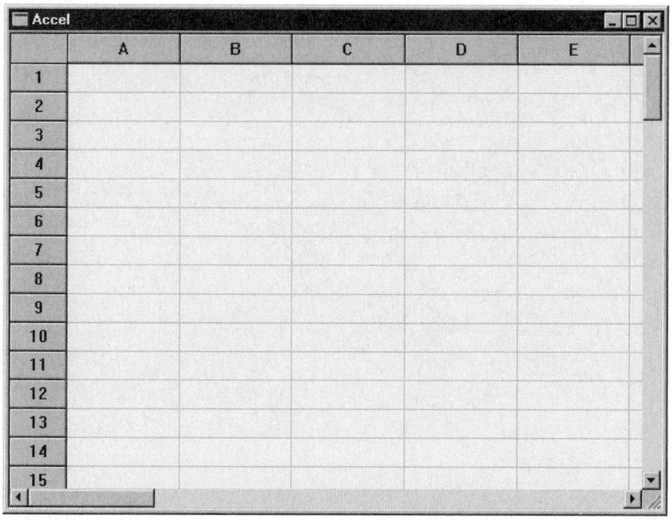

Figure 2-13. *The Accel window.*

Accel.h

```
#define LINESIZE 8

class CMyApp : public CWinApp
{
public:
    virtual BOOL InitInstance ();
};

class CMainWindow : public CFrameWnd
{
protected:
    int m_nCellWidth;    // Cell width in pixels
    int m_nCellHeight;   // Cell height in pixels
    int m_nRibbonWidth;  // Ribbon width in pixels
    int m_nViewWidth;    // Workspace width in pixels
    int m_nViewHeight;   // Workspace height in pixels
    int m_nHScrollPos;   // Horizontal scroll position
    int m_nVScrollPos;   // Vertical scroll position
    int m_nHPageSize;    // Horizontal page size
    int m_nVPageSize;    // Vertical page size
```

Figure 2-14. *The Accel application.*

(continued)

Figure 2-14. *continued*

```
public:
    CMainWindow ();
protected:
    afx_msg void OnPaint ();
    afx_msg int OnCreate (LPCREATESTRUCT lpCreateStruct);
    afx_msg void OnSize (UINT nType, int cx, int cy);
    afx_msg void OnHScroll (UINT nCode, UINT nPos,
        CScrollBar* pScrollBar);
    afx_msg void OnVScroll (UINT nCode, UINT nPos,
        CScrollBar* pScrollBar);

    DECLARE_MESSAGE_MAP ()
};
```

Accel.cpp

```
#include <afxwin.h>
#include "Accel.h"

CMyApp myApp;

///////////////////////////////////////////////////////////////////////
// CMyApp member functions

BOOL CMyApp::InitInstance ()
{
    m_pMainWnd = new CMainWindow;
    m_pMainWnd->ShowWindow (m_nCmdShow);
    m_pMainWnd->UpdateWindow ();
    return TRUE;
}

///////////////////////////////////////////////////////////////////////
// CMainWindow message map and member functions

BEGIN_MESSAGE_MAP (CMainWindow, CFrameWnd)
    ON_WM_CREATE ()
    ON_WM_SIZE ()
    ON_WM_PAINT ()
    ON_WM_HSCROLL ()
    ON_WM_VSCROLL ()
END_MESSAGE_MAP ()

CMainWindow::CMainWindow ()
```

```
{
    Create (NULL, _T ("Accel"),
        WS_OVERLAPPEDWINDOW | WS_HSCROLL | WS_VSCROLL);
}

int CMainWindow::OnCreate (LPCREATESTRUCT lpCreateStruct)
{
    if (CFrameWnd::OnCreate (lpCreateStruct) == -1)
        return -1;

    CClientDC dc (this);
    m_nCellWidth = dc.GetDeviceCaps (LOGPIXELSX);
    m_nCellHeight = dc.GetDeviceCaps (LOGPIXELSY) / 4;
    m_nRibbonWidth = m_nCellWidth / 2;
    m_nViewWidth = (26 * m_nCellWidth) + m_nRibbonWidth;
    m_nViewHeight = m_nCellHeight * 100;
    return 0;
}

void CMainWindow::OnSize (UINT nType, int cx, int cy)
{
    CFrameWnd::OnSize (nType, cx, cy);

    //
    // Set the horizontal scrolling parameters.
    //
    int nHScrollMax = 0;
    m_nHScrollPos = m_nHPageSize = 0;

    if (cx < m_nViewWidth) {
        nHScrollMax = m_nViewWidth - 1;
        m_nHPageSize = cx;
        m_nHScrollPos = min (m_nHScrollPos, m_nViewWidth -
            m_nHPageSize - 1);
    }

    SCROLLINFO si;
    si.fMask = SIF_PAGE | SIF_RANGE | SIF_POS;
    si.nMin = 0;
    si.nMax = nHScrollMax;
    si.nPos = m_nHScrollPos;
    si.nPage = m_nHPageSize;

    SetScrollInfo (SB_HORZ, &si, TRUE);
```

(continued)

Figure 2-14. *continued*

```
    //
    // Set the vertical scrolling parameters.
    //
    int nVScrollMax = 0;
    m_nVScrollPos = m_nVPageSize = 0;

    if (cy < m_nViewHeight) {
        nVScrollMax = m_nViewHeight - 1;
        m_nVPageSize = cy;
        m_nVScrollPos = min (m_nVScrollPos, m_nViewHeight -
            m_nVPageSize - 1);
    }

    si.fMask = SIF_PAGE | SIF_RANGE | SIF_POS;
    si.nMin = 0;
    si.nMax = nVScrollMax;
    si.nPos = m_nVScrollPos;
    si.nPage = m_nVPageSize;

    SetScrollInfo (SB_VERT, &si, TRUE);
}

void CMainWindow::OnPaint ()
{
    CPaintDC dc (this);

    //
    // Set the window origin to reflect the current scroll positions.
    //
    dc.SetWindowOrg (m_nHScrollPos, m_nVScrollPos);

    //
    // Draw the grid lines.
    //
    CPen pen (PS_SOLID, 0, RGB (192, 192, 192));
    CPen* pOldPen = dc.SelectObject (&pen);

    for (int i=0; i<99; i++) {
        int y = (i * m_nCellHeight) + m_nCellHeight;
        dc.MoveTo (0, y);
        dc.LineTo (m_nViewWidth, y);
    }

    for (int j=0; j<26; j++) {
        int x = (j * m_nCellWidth) + m_nRibbonWidth;
        dc.MoveTo (x, 0);
```

```
        dc.LineTo (x, m_nViewHeight);
    }

    dc.SelectObject (pOldPen);

    //
    // Draw the bodies of the rows and the column headers.
    //
    CBrush brush;
    brush.CreateStockObject (LTGRAY_BRUSH);

    CRect rcTop (0, 0, m_nViewWidth, m_nCellHeight);
    dc.FillRect (rcTop, &brush);
    CRect rcLeft (0, 0, m_nRibbonWidth, m_nViewHeight);
    dc.FillRect (rcLeft, &brush);

    dc.MoveTo (0, m_nCellHeight);
    dc.LineTo (m_nViewWidth, m_nCellHeight);
    dc.MoveTo (m_nRibbonWidth, 0);
    dc.LineTo (m_nRibbonWidth, m_nViewHeight);

    dc.SetBkMode (TRANSPARENT);

    //
    // Add numbers and button outlines to the row headers.
    //
    for (i=0; i<99; i++) {
        int y = (i * m_nCellHeight) + m_nCellHeight;
        dc.MoveTo (0, y);
        dc.LineTo (m_nRibbonWidth, y);

        CString string;
        string.Format (_T ("%d"), i + 1);

        CRect rect (0, y, m_nRibbonWidth, y + m_nCellHeight);
        dc.DrawText (string, &rect, DT_SINGLELINE |
            DT_CENTER | DT_VCENTER);

        rect.top++;
        dc.Draw3dRect (rect, RGB (255, 255, 255),
            RGB (128, 128, 128));
    }

    //
    // Add letters and button outlines to the column headers.
    //
```

(continued)

Figure 2-14. *continued*

```
    for (j=0; j<26; j++) {
        int x = (j * m_nCellWidth) + m_nRibbonWidth;
        dc.MoveTo (x, 0);
        dc.LineTo (x, m_nCellHeight);

        CString string;
        string.Format (_T ("%c"), j + 'A');

        CRect rect (x, 0, x + m_nCellWidth, m_nCellHeight);
        dc.DrawText (string, &rect, DT_SINGLELINE |
            DT_CENTER | DT_VCENTER);

        rect.left++;
        dc.Draw3dRect (rect, RGB (255, 255, 255),
            RGB (128, 128, 128));
    }
}

void CMainWindow::OnHScroll (UINT nCode, UINT nPos, CScrollBar* pScrollBar)
{
    int nDelta;

    switch (nCode) {

    case SB_LINELEFT:
        nDelta = -LINESIZE;
        break;

    case SB_PAGELEFT:
        nDelta = -m_nHPageSize;
        break;

    case SB_THUMBTRACK:
        nDelta = (int) nPos - m_nHScrollPos;
        break;

    case SB_PAGERIGHT:
        nDelta = m_nHPageSize;
        break;

    case SB_LINERIGHT:
        nDelta = LINESIZE;
        break;
```

```
    default: // Ignore other scroll bar messages
        return;
    }

    int nScrollPos = m_nHScrollPos + nDelta;
    int nMaxPos = m_nViewWidth - m_nHPageSize;

    if (nScrollPos < 0)
        nDelta = -m_nHScrollPos;
    else if (nScrollPos > nMaxPos)
        nDelta = nMaxPos - m_nHScrollPos;

    if (nDelta != 0) {
        m_nHScrollPos += nDelta;
        SetScrollPos (SB_HORZ, m_nHScrollPos, TRUE);
        ScrollWindow (-nDelta, 0);
    }
}

void CMainWindow::OnVScroll (UINT nCode, UINT nPos, CScrollBar* pScrollBar)
{
    int nDelta;

    switch (nCode) {

    case SB_LINEUP:
        nDelta = -LINESIZE;
        break;

    case SB_PAGEUP:
        nDelta = -m_nVPageSize;
        break;

    case SB_THUMBTRACK:
        nDelta = (int) nPos - m_nVScrollPos;
        break;

    case SB_PAGEDOWN:
        nDelta = m_nVPageSize;
        break;

    case SB_LINEDOWN:
        nDelta = LINESIZE;
        break;
```

(continued)

Figure 2-14. *continued*

```
default: // Ignore other scroll bar messages
    return;
}

int nScrollPos = m_nVScrollPos + nDelta;
int nMaxPos = m_nViewHeight - m_nVPageSize;

if (nScrollPos < 0)
    nDelta = -m_nVScrollPos;
else if (nScrollPos > nMaxPos)
    nDelta = nMaxPos - m_nVScrollPos;

if (nDelta != 0) {
    m_nVScrollPos += nDelta;
    SetScrollPos (SB_VERT, m_nVScrollPos, TRUE);
    ScrollWindow (0, -nDelta);
}
}
```

GetDeviceCaps is called from *CMainWindow*'s *OnCreate* handler, which is called upon receipt of a WM_CREATE message. WM_CREATE is the first message a window receives. It is sent just once, and it arrives very early in the window's lifetime—before the window is even visible on the screen. An ON_WM_CREATE entry in the window's message map connects WM_CREATE messages to the member function named *OnCreate*. *OnCreate* is the ideal place to initialize member variables whose values can only be determined at run time. It is prototyped as follows:

```
afx_msg int OnCreate (LPCREATESTRUCT lpCreateStruct)
```

lpCreateStruct is a pointer to a structure of type CREATESTRUCT, which contains useful information about a window such as its initial size and location on the screen. The value returned by *OnCreate* determines what Windows does next. If all goes as planned, *OnCreate* returns 0, signaling to Windows that the window was properly initialized. If *OnCreate* returns -1, Windows fails the attempt to create the window. A prototype *OnCreate* handler looks like this:

```
int CMainWindow::OnCreate (LPCREATESTRUCT lpCreateStruct)
{
    if (CFrameWnd::OnCreate (lpCreateStruct) == -1)
        return -1;
      .
      .
      .
    return 0;
}
```

OnCreate should always call the base class's *OnCreate* handler to give the framework the opportunity to execute its own window-creation code. This is especially important when you write document/view applications, because it is a function called by *CFrameWnd::OnCreate* that creates the view that goes inside a frame window.

You'll find the code that does the scrolling in the window's *OnHScroll* and *OnVScroll* handlers. *switch-case* logic converts the notification code passed in *nCode* into a signed *nDelta* value that represents the number of pixels the window should be scrolled. Once *nDelta* is computed, the scroll position is adjusted by *nDelta* pixels and the window is scrolled with the statements

```
m_nVScrollPos += nDelta;
SetScrollPos (SB_VERT, m_nVScrollPos, TRUE);
ScrollWindow (0, -nDelta);
```

for the vertical scroll bar and

```
m_nHScrollPos += nDelta;
SetScrollPos (SB_HORZ, m_nHScrollPos, TRUE);
ScrollWindow (-nDelta, 0);
```

for the horizontal scroll bar.

How are the scroll positions stored in *m_nHScrollPos* and *m_nVScrollPos* factored into the program's output? When *OnPaint* is called to paint the part of the workspace that was exposed by the scrolling operation, it repositions the window origin with the statement

```
dc.SetWindowOrg (m_nHScrollPos, m_nVScrollPos);
```

Recall that *CDC::SetWindowOrg* tells Windows to map the logical point (x,y) to the device point $(0,0)$, which, for a client-area device context, corresponds to the upper left corner of the window's client area. The statement above moves the origin of the coordinate system left *m_nHScrollPos* pixels and upward *m_nVScrollPos* pixels. If *OnPaint* tries to paint the pixel at $(0,0)$, the coordinate pair is transparently transformed by the GDI into $(-m\_nHScrollPos,-m\_nVScrollPos)$. If the scroll position is $(0,100)$, the first 100 rows of pixels are clipped from the program's output and the *real* output—the output the user can see—begins with the 101st row. Repositioning the origin in this manner is a simple and effective way to move a scrollable window over a virtual display surface.

If you could enlarge the window enough to see the entire spreadsheet, you would see the scroll bars disappear. That's because *CMainWindow::OnSize* sets the scroll bar range to 0 if the window size equals or exceeds the size of the virtual workspace. The *OnSize* handler also updates the scrolling parameters whenever the window size changes so that the thumb size accurately reflects the relative proportions of the window and the virtual workspace.

And with that, all the pieces are in place. The user clicks a scroll bar or drags a scroll bar thumb; *OnHScroll* or *OnVScroll* receives the message and responds by updating the scroll position and scrolling the window; and *OnPaint* redraws the window, using *SetWindowOrg* to move the drawing origin an amount that equals the current scroll position. The program's entire workspace is now accessible, despite the physical limitations that the window size imposes on the output. And all for less than 100 additional lines of code. How could it be any easier?

Funny you should ask. Because that's exactly what MFC's *CScrollView* class is for: to make scrolling easier. *CScrollView* is an MFC class that encapsulates the behavior of a scrolling window. You tell *CScrollView* how large a landscape you wish to view, and it handles everything else. Among other things, *CScrollView* processes WM_VSCROLL and WM_HSCROLL messages for you, scrolls the window in response to scroll bar events, and updates the thumb size when the window size changes.

While it's perfectly possible to wire a *CScrollView* into an application like Accel, *CScrollView* was designed primarily for document/view applications. Chapter 10 examines *CScrollView* more closely and also introduces some of the other view classes that MFC provides.

LOOSE ENDS

Before we close out the chapter, we need to tie up one loose end. All the programs presented thus far have created a window with the statement

```
m_pMainWnd = new CMainWindow;
```

in *InitInstance*. Since the object is instantiated with *new*, it remains in memory after *InitInstance* ends and, in fact, will not go away until it is deleted with a *delete* statement. Yet nowhere in the programs' source code will you find such a statement. On the surface, this would seem to be a problem. After all, every C++ programmer knows that every *new* must be countered with a *delete* or objects will be left behind in memory. So what gives?

As you probably suspected, the class library deletes the object for you. To be more precise, the object deletes itself. The key to this little trick is that the very last message a window receives before it goes away for good is WM_NCDESTROY. If you look at the source code for *CWnd::OnNcDestroy*, you'll see that it calls a virtual function named *PostNcDestroy*. *CFrameWnd* overrides *PostNcDestroy* and executes a

```
delete this;
```

statement. Therefore, when a frame window is destroyed, the object associated with that window is automatically deleted, too. A frame window is destroyed when the user closes the application.

It's worth noting that *CWnd*'s own implementation of *PostNcDestroy* does not delete the associated window object. Therefore, if you derive your own window class directly from *CWnd*, you also need to override *PostNcDestroy* in the derived class and execute a *delete this* statement. Otherwise, the *CWnd* object will not be properly deleted. You'll see what I mean in the next chapter.

Chapter 3

The Mouse
and the Keyboard

If life were like the movies, traditional input devices would have given way long ago to speech-recognition units, 3D headsets, and other human-machine interface gadgets. At present, however, the two most common input devices remain the mouse and the keyboard. Microsoft Windows handles some mouse and keyboard input itself, automatically dropping down a menu, for example, when the user clicks an item on the menu bar, and sending the application a WM_COMMAND message when an item is selected from the menu. It's entirely possible to write a full-featured Windows program that processes no mouse or keyboard input directly, but as an application developer, you'll eventually discover the need to read input from the mouse and keyboard directly. And when you do, you'll need to know about the mouse and keyboard interfaces that Windows provides.

Not surprisingly, mouse and keyboard input comes in the form of messages. Device drivers process mouse and keyboard interrupts and place the resultant event notifications in a systemwide queue known as the *raw input queue*. Entries in the raw input queue have WM_ message identifiers just as conventional messages do, but the data in them requires further processing before it is meaningful to an application. A dedicated thread owned by the operating system monitors the raw input queue and transfers each message that shows up there to the appropriate thread message queue. The "cooking" of the message data is performed later, in the context of the receiving application, and the message is ultimately retrieved and dispatched just as any other message is.

This input model differs from that of 16-bit Windows, which stored mouse and keyboard messages in a single systemwide input queue until they were retrieved by an application. This arrangement proved to be an Achilles' heel of sorts because it meant that an application that failed to dispose of input messages in a timely manner could prevent other applications from doing the same. Win32's asynchronous input model solves this problem by using the raw input queue as a temporary holding buffer and moving input messages to thread message queues at the earliest opportunity. (In 32-bit Windows, each thread that calls certain Windows API functions is given its own message queue, so a multithreaded application can have not one, but many, message queues.) A 32-bit application that goes too long without checking the message queue responds sluggishly to user input, but it doesn't affect the responsiveness of other applications running on the system.

Learning to respond to mouse and keyboard input in a Windows application is largely a matter of learning about which messages to process. This chapter introduces mouse and keyboard messages and the various functions, both in MFC and the API, that are useful for processing them. We'll apply the concepts presented here to the real world by developing three sample applications:

- TicTac, a tic-tac-toe game that demonstrates how to respond to mouse clicks

- MouseCap, a simple drawing program that demonstrates how mouse capturing works and how nonclient-area mouse messages are processed

- VisualKB, a typing program that brings mouse and keyboard handlers together under one roof and lists the keyboard messages it receives

We have a lot of ground to cover, so let's get started.

GETTING INPUT FROM THE MOUSE

Windows uses a number of different messages—more than 20 in all—to report input events involving the mouse. These messages fall into two rather broad categories: client-area mouse messages, which report events that occur in a window's client area, and nonclient-area mouse messages, which pertain to events in a window's nonclient area. An "event" can be any of the following:

- The press or release of a mouse button

- The double click of a mouse button

- The movement of the mouse

You'll typically ignore events in the nonclient area of your window and allow Windows to handle them. If your program processes mouse input, it's client-area mouse messages you'll probably be concerned with.

Client-Area Mouse Messages

Windows reports mouse events in a window's client area using the messages shown in the following table.

CLIENT-AREA MOUSE MESSAGES

Message	*Sent When*
WM_LBUTTONDOWN	The left mouse button is pressed.
WM_LBUTTONUP	The left mouse button is released.
WM_LBUTTONDBLCLK	The left mouse button is double-clicked.
WM_MBUTTONDOWN	The middle mouse button is pressed.
WM_MBUTTONUP	The middle mouse button is released.
WM_MBUTTONDBLCLK	The middle mouse button is double-clicked.
WM_RBUTTONDOWN	The right mouse button is pressed.
WM_RBUTTONUP	The right mouse button is released.
WM_RBUTTONDBLCLK	The right mouse button is double-clicked.
WM_MOUSEMOVE	The cursor is moved over the window's client area.

Messages that begin with WM_LBUTTON pertain to the left mouse button, WM_MBUTTON messages to the middle mouse button, and WM_RBUTTON messages to the right mouse button. An application won't receive WM_MBUTTON messages if the mouse has only two buttons. (This rule has one important exception: mice that have mouse wheels. Mouse wheels are discussed later in this chapter.) An application won't receive WM_RBUTTON messages if the mouse has just one button. The vast majority of PCs running Windows have two-button mice, so it's reasonably safe to assume that the right mouse button exists. However, if you'd like to be certain (or if you'd like to determine whether there is a third button, too), you can use the Windows *::GetSystemMetrics* API function:

```
int nButtonCount = ::GetSystemMetrics (SM_CMOUSEBUTTONS);
```

The return value is the number of mouse buttons, or it is 0 in the unlikely event that a mouse is not installed.

WM_*x*BUTTONDOWN and WM_*x*BUTTONUP messages report button presses and releases. A WM_LBUTTONDOWN message is normally followed by a WM_LBUTTONUP message, but don't count on that being the case. Mouse messages go to the window under the cursor (the Windows term for the mouse pointer), so if the user clicks the left mouse button over a window's client area and then moves the cursor outside the window before releasing the button, the window receives a WM_LBUT-TONDOWN message but not a WM_LBUTTONUP message. Many programs react only to button-down messages and ignore button-up messages, in which case the pairing of the two isn't important. If pairing is essential, a program can "capture" the mouse on receipt of a button-down message and release it when a button-up message arrives. In between, all mouse messages, even those pertaining to events outside the window, are directed to the window that performed the capture. This ensures that a button-up message is received no matter where the cursor is when the button is released. Mouse capturing is discussed later in this chapter.

When two clicks of the same button occur within a very short period of time, the second button-down message is replaced by a WM_xBUTTONDBLCLK message. Significantly, this happens only if the window's WNDCLASS includes the class style CS_DBLCLKS. The default WNDCLASS that MFC registers for frame windows has this style, so frame windows receive double-click messages by default. For a CS_DBLCLKS-style window, two rapid clicks of the left mouse button over the window's client area produce the following sequence of messages:

```
WM_LBUTTONDOWN
WM_LBUTTONUP
WM_LBUTTONDBLCLK
WM_LBUTTONUP
```

If the window is not registered to be notified of double clicks, however, the same two button clicks produce the following sequence of messages:

```
WM_LBUTTONDOWN
WM_LBUTTONUP
WM_LBUTTONDOWN
WM_LBUTTONUP
```

How your application responds to these messages—or whether it responds to them at all—is up to you. You should, however, steer away from having clicks and double clicks of the same mouse button carry out two unrelated tasks. A double-click message is always preceded by a single-click message, so the actions that generate the two messages are not easily divorced. Applications that process single and double clicks of the same button typically select an object on the first click and take some action upon that object on the second click. When you double-click a folder in the right pane of the Windows Explorer, for example, the first click selects the folder and the second click opens it.

WM_MOUSEMOVE messages report that the cursor has moved within the window's client area. As the mouse is moved, the window under the cursor receives a flurry of WM_MOUSEMOVE messages reporting the latest cursor position. Windows has an interesting way of delivering WM_MOUSEMOVE messages that prevents slow applications from being overwhelmed by messages reporting every position in the cursor's path. Rather than stuff a WM_MOUSEMOVE message into the message queue each time the mouse is moved, Windows simply sets a flag in an internal data structure. The next time the application retrieves a message, Windows, seeing that the flag is set, manufactures a WM_MOUSEMOVE message with the current cursor coordinates. Therefore, an application receives WM_MOUSEMOVE messages only as often as it can handle them. If the cursor is moved very slowly, every point in its journey is reported unless the application is busy doing other things. But if the cursor is whisked very rapidly across the screen, most applications receive only a handful of WM_MOUSEMOVE messages.

In an MFC program, message-map entries route mouse messages to class member functions that are provided to handle those messages. The following table lists the message-map macros and message handler names for client-area mouse messages.

MESSAGE-MAP MACROS AND MESSAGE HANDLERS FOR CLIENT-AREA MOUSE MESSAGES

Message	*Message-Map Macro*	*Handling Function*
WM_LBUTTONDOWN	ON_WM_LBUTTONDOWN	*OnLButtonDown*
WM_LBUTTONUP	ON_WM_LBUTTONUP	*OnLButtonUp*
WM_LBUTTONDBLCLK	ON_WM_LBUTTONDBLCLK	*OnLButtonDblClk*
WM_MBUTTONDOWN	ON_WM_MBUTTONDOWN	*OnMButtonDown*
WM_MBUTTONUP	ON_WM_MBUTTONUP	*OnMButtonUp*
WM_MBUTTONDBLCLK	ON_WM_MBUTTONDBLCLK	*OnMButtonDblClk*
WM_RBUTTONDOWN	ON_WM_RBUTTONDOWN	*OnRButtonDown*
WM_RBUTTONUP	ON_WM_RBUTTONUP	*OnRButtonUp*
WM_RBUTTONDBLCLK	ON_WM_RBUTTONDBLCLK	*OnRButtonDblClk*
WM_MOUSEMOVE	ON_WM_MOUSEMOVE	*OnMouseMove*

OnLButtonDown and other client-area mouse message handlers are prototyped as follows:

```
afx_msg void OnMsgName (UINT nFlags, CPoint point)
```

point identifies the location of the cursor. In WM_*x*BUTTONDOWN and WM_*x*BUTTONDBLCLK messages, *point* specifies the location of the cursor when the button was pressed. In WM_*x*BUTTONUP messages, *point* specifies the location of the cursor when the button was released. And in WM_MOUSEMOVE messages, *point* specifies the latest cursor position. In all cases, positions are reported in device coordinates relative to the upper left corner of the window's client area. A WM_LBUTTONDOWN message with *point.x* equal to 32 and *point.y* equal to 64 means the left mouse button was clicked 32 pixels to the right of and 64 pixels below the client area's upper left corner. If necessary, these coordinates can be converted to logical coordinates using MFC's *CDC::DPtoLP* function.

The *nFlags* parameter specifies the state of the mouse buttons and of the Shift and Ctrl keys at the time the message was generated. You can find out from this parameter whether a particular button or key is up or down by testing for the bit flags listed in the following table.

THE *nFLAGS* PARAMETER

Mask	*Meaning If Set*
MK_LBUTTON	The left mouse button is pressed.
MK_MBUTTON	The middle mouse button is pressed.
MK_RBUTTON	The right mouse button is pressed.
MK_CONTROL	The Ctrl key is pressed.
MK_SHIFT	The Shift key is pressed.

The expression

```
nFlags & MK_LBUTTON
```

is nonzero if and only if the left mouse button is pressed, while

```
nFlags & MK_CONTROL
```

is nonzero if the Ctrl key was held down when the event occurred. Some programs respond differently to mouse events if the Shift or Ctrl key is held down. For example, a drawing program might constrain the user to drawing only horizontal or vertical lines if the Ctrl key is pressed as the mouse is moved by checking the MK_CONTROL bit in the *nFlags* parameter accompanying WM_MOUSEMOVE messages. At the conclusion of a drag-and-drop operation, the Windows shell interprets the MK_CONTROL bit to mean that the objects involved in the drop should be copied rather than moved.

The TicTac Application

To show how easy it is to process mouse messages, let's look at a sample application that takes input from the mouse. TicTac, whose output is shown in Figure 3-1, is a tic-tac-toe program that responds to three types of client-area mouse events: left button clicks, right button clicks, and left button double clicks. Clicking the left mouse button over an empty square places an X in that square. Clicking the right mouse button places an O in an empty square. (The program prevents cheating by making sure that Xs and Os are alternated.) Double-clicking the left mouse button over the thick black lines that separate the squares clears the playing grid and starts a new game. After each X or O is placed, the program checks to see if there's a winner or the game

Figure 3-1. *The TicTac window.*

has been played to a draw. A draw is declared when all nine squares are filled and neither player has managed to claim three squares in a row horizontally, vertically, or diagonally.

In addition to providing a hands-on demonstration of mouse-message processing, TicTac also introduces some handy new MFC functions such as *CWnd::Message-Box*, which displays a message box window, and *CRect::PtInRect*, which quickly tells you whether a point lies inside a rectangle represented by a *CRect* object. TicTac's source code appears in Figure 3-2.

TicTac.h

```
#define EX 1
#define OH 2

class CMyApp : public CWinApp
{
public:
    virtual BOOL InitInstance ();
};

class CMainWindow : public CWnd
{
protected:
    static const CRect m_rcSquares[9];    // Grid coordinates
    int m_nGameGrid[9];                   // Grid contents
    int m_nNextChar;                      // Next character (EX or OH)
```

Figure 3-2. *The TicTac application.*   *(continued)*

Figure 3-2. *continued*

```
    int GetRectID (CPoint point);
    void DrawBoard (CDC* pDC);
    void DrawX (CDC* pDC, int nPos);
    void DrawO (CDC* pDC, int nPos);
    void ResetGame ();
    void CheckForGameOver ();
    int IsWinner ();
    BOOL IsDraw ();

public:
    CMainWindow ();

protected:
    virtual void PostNcDestroy ();

    afx_msg void OnPaint ();
    afx_msg void OnLButtonDown (UINT nFlags, CPoint point);
    afx_msg void OnLButtonDblClk (UINT nFlags, CPoint point);
    afx_msg void OnRButtonDown (UINT nFlags, CPoint point);

    DECLARE_MESSAGE_MAP ()
};
```

TicTac.cpp

```
#include <afxwin.h>
#include "TicTac.h"

CMyApp myApp;

/////////////////////////////////////////////////////////////////////////
// CMyApp member functions

BOOL CMyApp::InitInstance ()
{
    m_pMainWnd = new CMainWindow;
    m_pMainWnd->ShowWindow (m_nCmdShow);
    m_pMainWnd->UpdateWindow ();
    return TRUE;
}


/////////////////////////////////////////////////////////////////////////
// CMainWindow message map and member functions

BEGIN_MESSAGE_MAP (CMainWindow, CWnd)
```

```
    ON_WM_PAINT ()
    ON_WM_LBUTTONDOWN ()
    ON_WM_LBUTTONDBLCLK ()
    ON_WM_RBUTTONDOWN ()
END_MESSAGE_MAP ()

const CRect CMainWindow::m_rcSquares[9] = {
    CRect ( 16,  16, 112, 112),
    CRect (128,  16, 224, 112),
    CRect (240,  16, 336, 112),
    CRect ( 16, 128, 112, 224),
    CRect (128, 128, 224, 224),
    CRect (240, 128, 336, 224),
    CRect ( 16, 240, 112, 336),
    CRect (128, 240, 224, 336),
    CRect (240, 240, 336, 336)
};

CMainWindow::CMainWindow ()
{
    m_nNextChar = EX;
    ::ZeroMemory (m_nGameGrid, 9 * sizeof (int));

    //
    // Register a WNDCLASS.
    //
    CString strWndClass = AfxRegisterWndClass (
        CS_DBLCLKS,                                     // Class style
        AfxGetApp ()->LoadStandardCursor (IDC_ARROW),   // Class cursor
        (HBRUSH) (COLOR_3DFACE + 1),                    // Background brush
        AfxGetApp ()->LoadStandardIcon (IDI_WINLOGO)    // Class icon
    );

    //
    // Create a window.
    //
    CreateEx (0, strWndClass, _T ("Tic-Tac-Toe"),
        WS_OVERLAPPED | WS_SYSMENU | WS_CAPTION | WS_MINIMIZEBOX,
        CW_USEDEFAULT, CW_USEDEFAULT, CW_USEDEFAULT, CW_USEDEFAULT,
        NULL, NULL);

    //
    // Size the window.
    //
    CRect rect (0, 0, 352, 352);
    CalcWindowRect (&rect);
```

(continued)

Figure 3-2. *continued*

```
    SetWindowPos (NULL, 0, 0, rect.Width (), rect.Height (),
        SWP_NOZORDER ¦ SWP_NOMOVE ¦ SWP_NOREDRAW);
}

void CMainWindow::PostNcDestroy ()
{
    delete this;
}

void CMainWindow::OnPaint ()
{
    CPaintDC dc (this);
    DrawBoard (&dc);
}

void CMainWindow::OnLButtonDown (UINT nFlags, CPoint point)
{
    //
    // Do nothing if it's O's turn, if the click occurred outside the
    // tic-tac-toe grid, or if a nonempty square was clicked.
    //
    if (m_nNextChar != EX)
        return;

    int nPos = GetRectID (point);
    if ((nPos == -1) ¦¦ (m_nGameGrid[nPos] != 0))
        return;

    //
    // Add an X to the game grid and toggle m_nNextChar.
    //
    m_nGameGrid[nPos] = EX;
    m_nNextChar = OH;

    //
    // Draw an X on the screen and see if either player has won.
    //
    CClientDC dc (this);
    DrawX (&dc, nPos);
    CheckForGameOver ();
}

void CMainWindow::OnRButtonDown (UINT nFlags, CPoint point)
{
    //
    // Do nothing if it's X's turn, if the click occurred outside the
```

```
        // tic-tac-toe grid, or if a nonempty square was clicked.
        //
        if (m_nNextChar != OH)
            return;

        int nPos = GetRectID (point);
        if ((nPos == -1) || (m_nGameGrid[nPos] != 0))
            return;

        //
        // Add an O to the game grid and toggle m_nNextChar.
        //
        m_nGameGrid[nPos] = OH;
        m_nNextChar = EX;

        //
        // Draw an O on the screen and see if either player has won.
        //
        CClientDC dc (this);
        DrawO (&dc, nPos);
        CheckForGameOver ();
}

void CMainWindow::OnLButtonDblClk (UINT nFlags, CPoint point)
{
        //
        // Reset the game if one of the thick black lines defining the game
        // grid is double-clicked with the left mouse button.
        //
        CClientDC dc (this);
        if (dc.GetPixel (point) == RGB (0, 0, 0))
            ResetGame ();
}

int CMainWindow::GetRectID (CPoint point)
{
        //
        // Hit-test each of the grid's nine squares and return a rectangle ID
        // (0-8) if (point.x, point.y) lies inside a square.
        //
        for (int i=0; i<9; i++) {
            if (m_rcSquares[i].PtInRect (point))
                return i;
        }
        return -1;
}
```

(continued)

Figure 3-2. *continued*

```
void CMainWindow::DrawBoard (CDC* pDC)
{
    //
    // Draw the lines that define the tic-tac-toe grid.
    //
    CPen pen (PS_SOLID, 16, RGB (0, 0, 0));
    CPen* pOldPen = pDC->SelectObject (&pen);

    pDC->MoveTo (120, 16);
    pDC->LineTo (120, 336);

    pDC->MoveTo (232, 16);
    pDC->LineTo (232, 336);

    pDC->MoveTo (16, 120);
    pDC->LineTo (336, 120);

    pDC->MoveTo (16, 232);
    pDC->LineTo (336, 232);

    //
    // Draw the Xs and Os.
    //
    for (int i=0; i<9; i++) {
        if (m_nGameGrid[i] == EX)
            DrawX (pDC, i);
        else if (m_nGameGrid[i] == OH)
            DrawO (pDC, i);
    }
    pDC->SelectObject (pOldPen);
}

void CMainWindow::DrawX (CDC* pDC, int nPos)
{
    CPen pen (PS_SOLID, 16, RGB (255, 0, 0));
    CPen* pOldPen = pDC->SelectObject (&pen);

    CRect rect = m_rcSquares[nPos];
    rect.DeflateRect (16, 16);
    pDC->MoveTo (rect.left, rect.top);
    pDC->LineTo (rect.right, rect.bottom);
    pDC->MoveTo (rect.left, rect.bottom);
    pDC->LineTo (rect.right, rect.top);

    pDC->SelectObject (pOldPen);
}
```

```
void CMainWindow::DrawO (CDC* pDC, int nPos)
{
    CPen pen (PS_SOLID, 16, RGB (0, 0, 255));
    CPen* pOldPen = pDC->SelectObject (&pen);
    pDC->SelectStockObject (NULL_BRUSH);

    CRect rect = m_rcSquares[nPos];
    rect.DeflateRect (16, 16);
    pDC->Ellipse (rect);

    pDC->SelectObject (pOldPen);
}

void CMainWindow::CheckForGameOver ()
{
    int nWinner;

    //
    // If the grid contains three consecutive Xs or Os, declare a winner
    // and start a new game.
    //
    if (nWinner = IsWinner ()) {
        CString string = (nWinner == EX) ?
            _T ("X wins!") : _T ("O wins!");
        MessageBox (string, _T ("Game Over"), MB_ICONEXCLAMATION | MB_OK);
        ResetGame ();
    }

    //
    // If the grid is full, declare a draw and start a new game.
    //
    else if (IsDraw ()) {
        MessageBox (_T ("It's a draw!"), _T ("Game Over"),
            MB_ICONEXCLAMATION | MB_OK);
        ResetGame ();
    }
}

int CMainWindow::IsWinner ()
{
    static int nPattern[8][3] = {
        0, 1, 2,
        3, 4, 5,
        6, 7, 8,
        0, 3, 6,
        1, 4, 7,
```

(continued)

113

Figure 3-2. *continued*

```
        2, 5, 8,
        0, 4, 8,
        2, 4, 6
    };

    for (int i=0; i<8; i++) {
        if ((m_nGameGrid[nPattern[i][0]] == EX) &&
            (m_nGameGrid[nPattern[i][1]] == EX) &&
            (m_nGameGrid[nPattern[i][2]] == EX))
            return EX;

        if ((m_nGameGrid[nPattern[i][0]] == OH) &&
            (m_nGameGrid[nPattern[i][1]] == OH) &&
            (m_nGameGrid[nPattern[i][2]] == OH))
            return OH;
    }
    return 0;
}

BOOL CMainWindow::IsDraw ()
{
    for (int i=0; i<9; i++) {
        if (m_nGameGrid[i] == 0)
            return FALSE;
    }
    return TRUE;
}

void CMainWindow::ResetGame ()
{
    m_nNextChar = EX;
    ::ZeroMemory (m_nGameGrid, 9 * sizeof (int));
    Invalidate ();
}
```

The first step in processing mouse input is to add entries for the messages you want to handle to the message map. *CMainWindow*'s message map in TicTac.cpp contains the following message-map entries:

```
ON_WM_LBUTTONDOWN ()
ON_WM_LBUTTONDBLCLK ()
ON_WM_RBUTTONDOWN ()
```

These three statements correlate WM_LBUTTONDOWN, WM_LBUTTONDBLCLK, and WM_RBUTTONDOWN messages to the *CMainWindow* member functions *OnLButton-Down*, *OnLButtonDblClk*, and *OnRButtonDown*. When the messages start arriving, the fun begins.

The *OnLButtonDown* handler processes clicks of the left mouse button in *CMainWindow*'s client area. After checking *m_nNextChar* to verify that it's X's turn and not O's (and returning without doing anything if it's not), *OnLButtonDown* calls the protected member function *GetRectID* to determine whether the click occurred in one of the nine rectangles corresponding to squares in the tic-tac-toe grid. The rectangles' coordinates are stored in the static array of *CRect* objects named *CMainWindow::m_rcSquares*. *GetRectID* uses a *for* loop to determine whether the cursor location passed to it by the message handler lies inside any of the squares:

```
for (int i=0; i<9; i++) {
    if (m_rcSquares[i].PtInRect (point))
        return i;
}
return -1;
```

CRect::PtInRect returns a nonzero value if the point passed to it lies within the rectangle represented by the *CRect* object, or 0 if it does not. If *PtInRect* returns nonzero for any of the rectangles in the *m_rcSquares* array, *GetRectID* returns the rectangle ID. The ID is an integer from 0 through 8, with 0 representing the square in the upper left corner of the grid, 1 the square to its right, 2 the square in the upper right corner, 3 the leftmost square in the second row, and so on. Each square has a corresponding element in the *m_nGameGrid* array, which initially holds all zeros representing empty squares. If none of the calls to *PtInRect* returns TRUE, *GetRectID* returns -1 to indicate that the click occurred outside the squares and *OnLButtonDown* ignores the mouse click. If, however, *GetRectID* returns a valid ID and the corresponding square is empty, *OnLButtonDown* records the X in the *m_nGameGrid* array and calls *CMainWindow::DrawX* to draw an X in the square. *DrawX* creates a red pen 16 pixels wide and draws two perpendicular lines oriented at 45-degree angles.

OnRButtonDown works in much the same way as *OnLButtonDown*, except that it draws an O instead of an X. The routine that does the drawing is *CMainWindow::DrawO*. Before it draws an O with the *CDC::Ellipse* function, *DrawO* selects a NULL brush into the device context:

```
pDC->SelectStockObject (NULL_BRUSH);
```

This prevents the interior of the O from being filled with the device context's default white brush. (As an alternative, we could have created a brush whose color matched the window's background color and selected it into the device context. But drawing with a NULL brush is slightly faster because it produces no physical screen output.) The O is then drawn with the statements

```
CRect rect = m_rcSquares[nPos];
rect.DeflateRect (16, 16);
pDC->Ellipse (rect);
```

The first statement copies the rectangle representing the grid square to a local *CRect* object named *rect*; the second uses *CRect::DeflateRect* to "deflate" the rectangle by 16 pixels in each direction and form the circle's bounding box; and the third draws the circle. The result is a nicely formed O that's centered in the square in which it is drawn.

Double-clicking the grid lines separating the squares clears the Xs and Os and begins a new game. While this is admittedly a poor way to design a user interface, it does provide an excuse to write a double-click handler. (A better solution would be a push button control with the words *New Game* stamped on it or a New Game menu item, but since we haven't covered menus and controls yet, the perfect user interface will just have to wait.) Left mouse button double clicks are processed by *CMainWindow::OnLButtonDblClk*, which contains these simple statements:

```
CClientDC dc (this);
if (dc.GetPixel (point) == RGB (0, 0, 0))
    ResetGame ();
```

To determine whether the double click occurred over the thick black strokes separating the squares in the playing grid, *OnLButtonDblClk* calls *CDC::GetPixel* to get the color of the pixel under the cursor and compares it to black (RGB (0, 0, 0)). If there's a match, *ResetGame* is called to reset the game. Otherwise, *OnLButtonDblClk* returns and the double click is ignored. Testing the color of the pixel under the cursor is an effective technique for hit-testing irregularly shaped areas, but be wary of using nonprimary colors that a display driver is likely to dither. Pure black (RGB (0, 0, 0)) and pure white (RGB (255, 255, 255)) are supported on every PC that runs Windows, so you can safely assume that neither of these colors will be dithered.

To be consistent with published user interface guidelines, applications should not use the right mouse button to carry out application-specific tasks as TicTac does. Instead, they should respond to right mouse clicks by popping up context menus. When a WM_RBUTTONUP message is passed to the system for default processing, Windows places a WM_CONTEXTMENU message in the message queue. You'll learn more about this feature of the operating system in the next chapter.

Message Boxes

Before returning, TicTac's *OnLButtonDown* and *OnRButtonDown* handlers call *CMainWindow::CheckForGameOver* to find out if the game has been won or played to a draw. If either player has managed to align three Xs or Os in a row or if no empty squares remain, *CheckForGameOver* calls *CMainWindow*'s *MessageBox* function to display a message box announcing the outcome, as shown in Figure 3-3. *MessageBox* is a function that all window classes inherit from *CWnd*. It is an extraordinarily useful

Figure 3-3. *A Windows message box.*

tool to have at your disposal because it provides a one-step means for displaying a message on the screen and optionally obtaining a response.

CWnd::MessageBox is prototyped as follows:

```
int MessageBox (LPCTSTR lpszText, LPCTSTR lpszCaption = NULL,
    UINT nType = MB_OK)
```

lpszText specifies the text in the body of the message box, *lpszCaption* specifies the caption for the message box's title bar, and *nType* contains one or more bit flags defining the message box's style. The return value identifies the button that was clicked to dismiss the message box. *lpszText* and *lpszCaption* can be *CString* objects or pointers to conventional text strings. (Because the *CString* class overloads the LPCTSTR operator, you can always pass a *CString* to a function that accepts an LPCTSTR data type.) A NULL *lpszCaption* value displays the caption "Error" in the title bar.

The simplest use for *MessageBox* is to display a message and pause until the user clicks the message box's OK button:

```
MessageBox (_T ("Click OK to continue"), _T ("My Application"));
```

Accepting the default value for *nType* (MB_OK) means the message box will have an OK button but no other buttons. Consequently, the only possible return value is IDOK. But if you want to use a message box to ask the user whether to save a file before exiting the application, you can use the MB_YESNOCANCEL style:

```
MessageBox (_T ("Your document contains unsaved data. Save it?"),
    _T ("My Application"), MB_YESNOCANCEL);
```

Now the message box contains three buttons—Yes, No, and Cancel—and the value returned from the *MessageBox* function is IDYES, IDNO, or IDCANCEL. The program can then test the return value and save the data before closing (IDYES), close without saving (IDNO), or return to the application without shutting down (IDCANCEL). The table on the following page lists the six message box types and the corresponding return values, with the default push button—the one that's "clicked" if the user presses the Enter key—highlighted in boldface type.

MESSAGE BOX TYPES

Type	Buttons	Possible Return Codes
MB_ABORTRETRYIGNORE	**Abort**, Retry, Ignore	IDABORT, IDRETRY, IDIGNORE
MB_OK	**OK**	IDOK
MB_OKCANCEL	**OK**, Cancel	IDOK, IDCANCEL
MB_RETRYCANCEL	**Retry**, Cancel	IDRETRY, IDCANCEL
MB_YESNO	**Yes**, No	IDYES, IDNO
MB_YESNOCANCEL	**Yes**, No, Cancel	IDYES, IDNO, IDCANCEL

In message boxes with multiple buttons, the first (leftmost) button is normally the default push button. You can make the second or third button the default by ORing MB_DEFBUTTON2 or MB_DEFBUTTON3 into the value that specifies the message box type. The statement

```
MessageBox (_T ("Your document contains unsaved data. Save it?"),
    _T ("My Application"), MB_YESNOCANCEL ¦ MB_DEFBUTTON3);
```

displays the same message box as before but makes Cancel the default action.

By default, message boxes are application modal, which means the application that called the *MessageBox* function is disabled until the message box is dismissed. You can add MB_SYSTEMMODAL to the *nType* parameter and make the message box system modal. In 16-bit Windows, system-modal means that input to *all* applications is suspended until the message box is dismissed. In the Win32 environment, Windows makes the message box a topmost window that stays on top of other windows, but the user is still free to switch to other applications. System-modal message boxes should be used only for serious errors that demand immediate attention.

You can add an artistic touch to your message boxes by using MB_ICON identifiers. MB_ICONINFORMATION displays a small text balloon with an "i" for "information" in it in the upper left corner of the message box. The "i" is generally used when information is provided to the user but no questions are being asked, as in

```
MessageBox (_T ("No errors found. Click OK to continue"),
    _T ("My Application"), MB_ICONINFORMATION ¦ MB_OK);
```

MB_ICONQUESTION displays a question mark instead of an "i" and is normally used for queries such as "Save before closing?" MB_ICONSTOP displays a red circle with an X and usually indicates that an unrecoverable error has occurred—for example, an out-of-memory error is forcing the program to terminate prematurely. Finally, MB_ICONEXCLAMATION displays a yellow triangle containing an exclamation mark. (See Figure 3-3.)

MFC provides an alternative to *CWnd::MessageBox* in the form of the global *AfxMessageBox* function. The two are similar, but *AfxMessageBox* can be called from application classes, document classes, and other non-window classes. One situation in which *AfxMessageBox* is irreplaceable is when you want to report an error in the application object's *InitInstance* function. *MessageBox* requires a valid *CWnd* pointer and therefore can't be called until after a window is created. *AfxMessageBox*, on the other hand, can be called at any time.

What? No Frame Window?

TicTac differs from the sample programs in Chapters 1 and 2 in one important respect: Rather than using a frame window for its main window, it derives its own window class from *CWnd*. It's not that a *CFrameWnd* wouldn't work; it's that *CWnd* has everything TicTac needs and more. *CWnd* is the root of all window classes in MFC. Depending on what kinds of applications you write, deriving from *CWnd* is something you might need to do often or not at all. Still, it's something every MFC programmer should know *how* to do, and seeing a window class derived from *CWnd* also helps to underscore the point that MFC programs don't have to use frame windows.

Creating your own *CWnd*-derived window class is simple. For starters, you derive the window class from *CWnd* instead of from *CFrameWnd*. In the BEGIN_MESSAGE_MAP macro, be sure to specify *CWnd*, not *CFrameWnd*, as the base class. Then, in the window's constructor, use *AfxRegisterWndClass* to register a WNDCLASS and call *CWnd::CreateEx* to create the window. Remember the beginning of Chapter 1, where we looked at the C source code for an SDK-style Windows application? Before creating a window, *WinMain* initialized a WNDCLASS structure with values describing the window's class attributes and then called *::RegisterClass* to register the WNDCLASS. Normally you don't register a WNDCLASS in an MFC program because MFC registers one for you. Specifying NULL in the first parameter to *CFrameWnd::Create* accepts the default WNDCLASS. When you derive from *CWnd*, however, you must register your own WNDCLASS because *CWnd::CreateEx* does not accept a NULL WNDCLASS name.

The *AfxRegisterWndClass* Function

MFC makes WNDCLASS registration easy with its global *AfxRegisterWndClass* function. If you use *::RegisterClass* or MFC's *AfxRegisterClass* to register a WNDCLASS, you must initialize every field in the WNDCLASS structure. But *AfxRegisterWndClass* fills in most of the fields for you, leaving you to specify values for just the four that MFC applications are typically concerned with. *AfxRegisterWndClass* is prototyped as follows:

```
LPCTSTR AfxRegisterWndClass (UINT nClassStyle, HCURSOR hCursor = 0,
    HBRUSH hbrBackground = 0, HICON hIcon = 0)
```

The value returned by *AfxRegisterWndClass* is a pointer to a null-terminated string containing the WNDCLASS name. Before seeing how TicTac uses *AfxRegisterWndClass*, let's take a closer look at the function itself and the parameters it accepts.

nClassStyle specifies the class style, which defines certain behavioral characteristics of a window. *nClassStyle* is a combination of zero or more of the bit flags shown in the following table.

WNDCLASS STYLE FLAGS

Class Style	Description
CS_BYTEALIGNCLIENT	Ensures that a window's client area is always aligned on a byte boundary in the video buffer to speed drawing operations.
CS_BYTEALIGNWINDOW	Ensures that the window itself is always aligned on a byte boundary in the video buffer to speed moving and resizing operations.
CS_CLASSDC	Specifies that the window should share a device context with other windows created from the same WNDCLASS.
CS_DBLCLKS	Specifies that the window should be notified of double clicks with WM_*x*BUTTONDBLCLK messages.
CS_GLOBALCLASS	Registers the WNDCLASS globally so that all applications can use it. (By default, only the application that registers a WNDCLASS can create windows from it.) Used primarily for child window controls.
CS_HREDRAW	Specifies that the entire client area should be invalidated when the window is resized horizontally.
CS_NOCLOSE	Disables the Close command on the system menu and the close button on the title bar.
CS_OWNDC	Specifies that each window created from this WNDCLASS should have its own device context. Helpful when optimizing repaint performance because an application doesn't have to reinitialize a private device context each time the device context is acquired.
CS_PARENTDC	Specifies that a child window should inherit the device context of its parent.
CS_SAVEBITS	Specifies that areas of the screen covered by windows created from this WNDCLASS should be saved in bitmap form for quick repainting. Used primarily for menus and other windows with short life spans.
CS_VREDRAW	Specifies that the entire client area should be invalidated when the window is resized vertically.

The CS_BYTEALIGNCLIENT and CS_BYTEALIGNWINDOW styles were useful back in the days of dumb frame buffers and monochrome video systems, but they are largely obsolete today. CS_CLASSDC, CS_OWNDC, and CS_PARENTDC are used to implement special handling of device contexts. You'll probably use CS_GLOBAL-CLASS only if you write custom controls to complement list boxes, push buttons, and other built-in control types. The CS_HREDRAW and CS_VREDRAW styles are useful for creating resizeable windows whose content scales with the window size.

hCursor identifies the "class cursor" for windows created from this WNDCLASS. When the cursor moves over a window's client area, Windows retrieves the class cursor's handle from the window's WNDCLASS and uses it to draw the cursor image. You can create custom cursors using an icon editor, or you can use the predefined system cursors that Windows provides. *CWinApp::LoadStandardCursor* loads a system cursor. The statement

```
AfxGetApp ()->LoadStandardCursor (IDC_ARROW);
```

returns the handle of the arrow cursor that most Windows applications use. For a complete list of system cursors, see the documentation for *CWinApp::LoadStandard-Cursor* or the *::LoadCursor* API function. Generally speaking, only the IDC_ARROW, IDC_IBEAM, and IDC_CROSS cursors are useful as class cursors.

The *hbrBackground* parameter passed to *AfxRegisterWndClass* defines the window's default background color. Specifically, *hbrBackground* identifies the GDI brush that is used to erase the window's interior each time a WM_ERASEBKGND message arrives. A window receives a WM_ERASEBKGND message when it calls *::BeginPaint* in response to a WM_PAINT message. If you don't process WM_ERASE-BKGND messages yourself, Windows processes them for you by retrieving the class background brush and using it to fill the window's client area. (You can create custom window backgrounds—for example, backgrounds formed from bitmap images—by processing WM_ERASEBKGND messages yourself and returning a nonzero value. The nonzero return prevents Windows from painting the background and overwriting what you wrote.) You can either provide a brush handle for *hbrBackground* or specify one of the predefined Windows system colors with the value 1 added to it, as in COLOR_WINDOW+1 or COLOR_APPWORKSPACE+1. See the documentation for the *::GetSysColor* API function for a complete list of system colors.

The final *AfxRegisterWndClass* parameter, *hIcon*, specifies the handle of the icon that Windows uses to represent the application on the desktop, in the taskbar, and elsewhere. You can create a custom icon for your application and load it with *CWinApp::LoadIcon*, or you can load a predefined system icon with *CWinApp::Load-StandardIcon*. You can even load icons from other executable files using the *::Extract-Icon* API function.

Here's what the code to register a custom WNDCLASS looks like in TicTac.cpp:

```
CString strWndClass = AfxRegisterWndClass (
    CS_DBLCLKS,
    AfxGetApp ()->LoadStandardCursor (IDC_ARROW),
    (HBRUSH) (COLOR_3DFACE + 1),
    AfxGetApp ()->LoadStandardIcon (IDI_WINLOGO)
);
```

The class style CS_DBLCLKS registers the TicTac window to receive double-click messages. IDC_ARROW tells Windows to display the standard arrow when the cursor is over the TicTac window, and IDI_WINLOGO is one of the standard icons that Windows makes available to all applications. COLOR_3DFACE+1 assigns the TicTac window the same background color as push buttons, dialog boxes, and other 3D display elements. COLOR_3DFACE defaults to light gray, but you can change the color by using the system's Display Properties property sheet. Using COLOR_3DFACE for the background color gives your window the same 3D look as a dialog box or message box *and* enables it to adapt to changes in the Windows color scheme.

AfxRegisterWndClass and Frame Windows

The *AfxRegisterWndClass* function isn't only for applications that derive window classes from *CWnd;* you can also use it to register custom WNDCLASSes for frame windows. The default WNDCLASS that MFC registers for frame windows has the following attributes:

- *nClassStyle* = CS_DBLCLKS ¦ CS_HREDRAW ¦ CS_VREDRAW

- *hCursor* = The handle of the predefined cursor IDC_ARROW

- *hbrBackground* = COLOR_WINDOW+1

- *hIcon* = The handle of the icon whose resource ID is AFX_IDI_STD_FRAME or AFX_IDI_STD_MDIFRAME, or the system icon ID IDI_APPLICATION if no such resource is defined

Suppose you want to create a *CFrameWnd* frame window that lacks the CS_DBL-CLKS style, that uses the IDI_WINLOGO icon, and that uses COLOR_APPWORKSPACE as its default background color. Here's how to create a frame window that meets these qualifications:

```
CString strWndClass = AfxRegisterWndClass (
    CS_HREDRAW ¦ CS_VREDRAW,
    AfxGetApp ()->LoadStandardCursor (IDC_ARROW),
    (HBRUSH) (COLOR_APPWORKSPACE + 1),
    AfxGetApp ()->LoadStandardIcon (IDI_WINLOGO)
);
```

```
Create (strWndClass, _T ("My Frame Window"));
```

These statements replace the

```
Create (NULL, _T ("My Frame Window"));
```

statement that normally appears in a frame window's constructor.

More About the TicTac Window

After registering a WNDCLASS, TicTac creates its main window with a call to *CWnd-::CreateEx*:

```
CreateEx (0, strWndClass, _T ("Tic-Tac-Toe"),
    WS_OVERLAPPED | WS_SYSMENU | WS_CAPTION | WS_MINIMIZEBOX,
    CW_USEDEFAULT, CW_USEDEFAULT, CW_USEDEFAULT, CW_USEDEFAULT,
    NULL, NULL);
```

The first parameter specifies the extended window style and is a combination of zero or more WS_EX flags. TicTac requires no extended window styles, so this parameter is 0. The second parameter is the WNDCLASS name returned by *AfxRegisterWndClass*, and the third is the window title. The fourth is the window style. The combination of WS_OVERLAPPED, WS_SYSMENU, WS_CAPTION, and WS_MINIMIZEBOX creates a window that resembles a WS_OVERLAPPEDWINDOW-style window but lacks a maximize button and can't be resized. What is it about the window that makes it nonresizeable? Look up the definition of WS_OVERLAPPEDWINDOW in Winuser.h (one of several large header files that comes with Visual C++), and you'll see something like this:

```
#define WS_OVERLAPPEDWINDOW (WS_OVERLAPPED | WS_CAPTION | \
    WS_SYSMENU | WS_THICKFRAME | WS_MINIMIZE | WS_MAXIMIZE)
```

The WS_THICKFRAME style adds a resizing border whose edges and corners can be grabbed and dragged with the mouse. TicTac's window lacks this style, so the user can't resize it.

The next four parameters passed to *CWnd::CreateEx* specify the window's initial position and size. TicTac uses CW_USEDEFAULT for all four so that Windows will pick the initial position and size. Yet clearly the TicTac window is not arbitrarily sized; it is sized to match the playing grid. But how? The statements following the call to *CreateEx* hold the answer:

```
CRect rect (0, 0, 352, 352);
CalcWindowRect (&rect);

SetWindowPos (NULL, 0, 0, rect.Width (), rect.Height (),
    SWP_NOZORDER | SWP_NOMOVE | SWP_NOREDRAW);
```

The first of these statements creates a *CRect* object that holds the desired size of the window's client area—352 by 352 pixels. It wouldn't do to pass these values directly to *CreateEx* because *CreateEx*'s sizing parameters specify the size of the entire window, not just its client area. Since the sizes of the various elements in the window's nonclient area (for example, the height of the title bar) vary with different video drivers and display resolutions, we must calculate the size of the window rectangle from the client rectangle and then size the window to fit.

MFC's *CWnd::CalcWindowRect* is the perfect tool for the job. Given a pointer to a *CRect* object containing the coordinates of a window's client area, *CalcWindowRect* calculates the corresponding window rectangle. The width and height of that rectangle can then be passed to *CWnd::SetWindowPos* to effect the proper window size. The only catch is that *CalcWindowRect* must be called *after* the window is created so that it can factor in the dimensions of the window's nonclient area.

The *PostNcDestroy* Function

Something you must consider when you derive your own window class from *CWnd* is that once created, the window object must somehow be deleted. As described in Chapter 2, the last message a window receives before it is destroyed is WM_NC-DESTROY. MFC's *CWnd* class includes a default *OnNcDestroy* handler that performs some routine cleanup chores and then, as its very last act, calls a virtual function named *PostNcDestroy*. *CFrameWnd* objects delete themselves when the windows they are attached to are destroyed; they do this by overriding *PostNcDestroy* and executing a *delete this* statement. *CWnd::PostNcDestroy* does not perform a *delete this*, so a class derived from *CWnd* should provide its own version of *PostNcDestroy* that does. TicTac includes a trivial *PostNcDestroy* function that destroys the *CMainWindow* object just before the program terminates:

```
void CMainWindow::PostNcDestroy ()
{
    delete this;
}
```

The question of "who deletes it" is something you should think about whenever you derive a window class from *CWnd*. One alternative to overriding *CWnd::Post-NcDestroy* is to override *CWinApp::ExitInstance* and call *delete* on the pointer stored in *m_pMainWnd*.

Nonclient-Area Mouse Messages

When the mouse is clicked inside or moved over a window's nonclient area, Windows sends the window a nonclient-area mouse message. The following table lists the nonclient-area mouse messages.

NONCLIENT-AREA MOUSE MESSAGES

Message	*Sent When*
WM_NCLBUTTONDOWN	The left mouse button is pressed.
WM_NCLBUTTONUP	The left mouse button is released.
WM_NCLBUTTONDBLCLK	The left mouse button is double-clicked.
WM_NCMBUTTONDOWN	The middle mouse button is pressed.
WM_NCMBUTTONUP	The middle mouse button is released.
WM_NCMBUTTONDBLCLK	The middle mouse button is double-clicked.
WM_NCRBUTTONDOWN	The right mouse button is pressed.
WM_NCRBUTTONUP	The right mouse button is released.
WM_NCRBUTTONDBLCLK	The right mouse button is double-clicked.
WM_NCMOUSEMOVE	The cursor is moved over the window's nonclient area.

Notice the parallelism between the client-area mouse messages shown in the table on page 103 and the nonclient-area mouse messages; the only difference is the letters *NC* in the message ID. Unlike double-click messages in a window's client area, WM_NC*x*BUTTONDBLCLK messages are transmitted regardless of whether the window was registered with the CS_DBLCLKS style.

As with client-area mouse messages, message-map entries route messages to the appropriate class member functions. The following table lists the message-map macros and message handlers for nonclient-area mouse messages.

MESSAGE-MAP MACROS AND MESSAGE HANDLERS FOR NONCLIENT-AREA MOUSE MESSAGES

Message	*Message-Map Macro*	*Handling Function*
WM_NCLBUTTONDOWN	ON_WM_NCLBUTTONDOWN	*OnNcLButtonDown*
WM_NCLBUTTONUP	ON_WM_NCLBUTTONUP	*OnNcLButtonUp*
WM_NCLBUTTONDBLCLK	ON_WM_NCLBUTTONDBLCLK	*OnNcLButtonDblClk*
WM_NCMBUTTONDOWN	ON_WM_NCMBUTTONDOWN	*OnNcMButtonDown*
WM_NCMBUTTONUP	ON_WM_NCMBUTTONUP	*OnNcMButtonUp*
WM_NCMBUTTONDBLCLK	ON_WM_NCMBUTTONDBLCLK	*OnNcMButtonDblClk*
WM_NCRBUTTONDOWN	ON_WM_NCRBUTTONDOWN	*OnNcRButtonDown*
WM_NCRBUTTONUP	ON_WM_NCRBUTTONUP	*OnNcRButtonUp*
WM_NCRBUTTONDBLCLK	ON_WM_NCRBUTTONDBLCLK	*OnNcRButtonDblClk*
WM_NCMOUSEMOVE	ON_WM_NCMOUSEMOVE	*OnNcMouseMove*

Message handlers for nonclient-area mouse messages are prototyped this way:

```
afx_msg void OnMsgName (UINT nHitTest, CPoint point)
```

Once again, the *point* parameter specifies the location in the window at which the event occurred. But for nonclient-area mouse messages, *point.x* and *point.y* contain screen coordinates rather than client coordinates. In screen coordinates, (0,0) corresponds to the upper left corner of the screen, the positive *x* and *y* axes point to the right and down, and one unit in any direction equals one pixel. If you want, you can convert screen coordinates to client coordinates with *CWnd::ScreenToClient*. The *nHitTest* parameter contains a hit-test code that identifies where in the window's nonclient area the event occurred. Some of the most interesting hit-test codes are shown in the following table. You'll find a complete list of hit-test codes in the documentation for WM_NCHITTEST or *CWnd::OnNcHitTest*.

COMMONLY USED HIT-TEST CODES

Value	Corresponding Location
HTCAPTION	The title bar
HTCLOSE	The close button
HTGROWBOX	The restore button (same as HTSIZE)
HTHSCROLL	The window's horizontal scroll bar
HTMENU	The menu bar
HTREDUCE	The minimize button
HTSIZE	The restore button (same as HTGROWBOX)
HTSYSMENU	The system menu box
HTVSCROLL	The window's vertical scroll bar
HTZOOM	The maximize button

Programs don't usually process nonclient-area mouse messages; they allow Windows to process them instead. Windows provides appropriate default responses that frequently result in still more messages being sent to the window. For example, when Windows processes a WM_NCLBUTTONDBLCLK message with a hit-test value equal to HTCAPTION, it sends the window a WM_SYSCOMMAND message with *wParam* equal to SC_MAXIMIZE or SC_RESTORE to maximize or unmaximize the window. You can prevent double clicks on a title bar from affecting a window by including the following message handler in the window class:

```
// In CMainWindow's message map
ON_WM_NCLBUTTONDBLCLK ()
    :
    :

void CMainWindow::OnNcLButtonDblClk (UINT nHitTest, CPoint point)
```

```
{
    if (nHitTest != HTCAPTION)
        CWnd::OnNcLButtonDblClk (nHitTest, point);
}
```

Calling the base class's *OnNcLButtonDblClk* handler passes the message to Windows and allows default processing to take place. Returning without calling the base class prevents Windows from knowing that the double click occurred. You can use other hit-test values to customize the window's response to other nonclient-area mouse events.

The WM_NCHITTEST Message

Before a window receives a client-area or nonclient-area mouse message, it receives a WM_NCHITTEST message accompanied by the cursor's screen coordinates. Most applications don't process WM_NCHITTEST messages, instead electing to let Windows process them. When Windows processes a WM_NCHITTEST message, it uses the cursor coordinates to determine what part of the window the cursor is over and then generates either a client-area or nonclient-area mouse message.

One clever use of an *OnNcHitTest* handler is for substituting the HTCAPTION hit-test code for HTCLIENT, which creates a window that can be dragged by its client area:

```
// In CMainWindow's message map
ON_WM_NCHITTEST ()
    :

UINT CMainWindow::OnNcHitTest (CPoint point)
{
    UINT nHitTest = CFrameWnd::OnNcHitTest (point);
    if (nHitTest == HTCLIENT)
        nHitTest = HTCAPTION;
    return nHitTest;
}
```

As this example demonstrates, WM_NCHITTEST messages that you don't process yourself should be forwarded to the base class so that other aspects of the program's operation aren't affected.

The WM_MOUSELEAVE and WM_MOUSEHOVER Messages

It's easy to tell when the cursor enters a window or moves over it because the window receives WM_MOUSEMOVE messages. The *::TrackMouseEvent* function, which debuted in Windows NT 4.0 and is also supported in Windows 98, makes it equally easy to determine when the cursor leaves a window or hovers motionlessly over the top of it. With *::TrackMouseEvent*, an application can register to receive WM_MOUSELEAVE messages when the cursor leaves a window and WM_MOUSEHOVER messages when the cursor hovers over a window.

::TrackMouseEvent accepts just one parameter: a pointer to a TRACKMOUSE-EVENT structure. The structure is defined this way in Winuser.h:

```
typedef struct tagTRACKMOUSEEVENT {
    DWORD cbSize;
    DWORD dwFlags;
    HWND  hwndTrack;
    DWORD dwHoverTime;
} TRACKMOUSEEVENT;
```

cbSize holds the size of the structure. *dwFlags* holds bit flags specifying what the caller wants to do: register to receive WM_MOUSELEAVE messages (TME_LEAVE), register to receive WM_MOUSEHOVER messages (TME_HOVER), cancel WM_MOUSELEAVE and WM_MOUSEHOVER messages (TME_CANCEL), or have the system fill the TRACKMOUSEEVENT structure with the current *::TrackMouseEvent* settings (TME_QUERY). *hwndTrack* is the handle of the window for which WM_MOUSELEAVE and WM_MOUSEHOVER messages are generated. *dwHoverTime* is the length of time in milliseconds that the cursor must pause before a WM_MOUSEHOVER message is sent to the underlying window. You can accept the system default of 400 milliseconds by setting *dwHoverTime* equal to HOVER_DEFAULT.

The cursor doesn't have to be perfectly still for the system to generate a WM_MOUSEHOVER message. If the cursor stays within a rectangle whose width and height equal the values returned by *::SystemParametersInfo* when it's called with SPI_GETMOUSEHOVERWIDTH and SPI_GETMOUSEHOVERHEIGHT values, and if it stays there for the number of milliseconds returned by *::SystemParametersInfo* when it's called with an SPI_GETMOUSEHOVERTIME value, a WM_MOUSEHOVER message ensues. If you want, you can change these parameters by calling *::System-ParametersInfo* with SPI_SETMOUSEHOVERWIDTH, SPI_SETMOUSEHOVERHEIGHT, and SPI_SETMOUSEHOVERTIME values.

One of the more interesting aspects of *::TrackMouseEvent* is that its effects are cancelled when a WM_MOUSELEAVE or WM_MOUSEHOVER message is generated. This means that if you want to receive these message anytime the cursor exits or pauses over a window, you must call *::TrackMouseEvent* again whenever a WM_MOUSE-LEAVE or WM_MOUSEHOVER message is received. To illustrate, the following code snippet writes "Mouse enter," "Mouse leave," or "Mouse hover" to the debug output window anytime the mouse enters, leaves, or pauses over a window. *m_bMouseOver* is a BOOL *CMainWindow* member variable. It should be set to FALSE in the class constructor:

```
// In the message map
ON_WM_MOUSEMOVE ()
ON_MESSAGE (WM_MOUSELEAVE, OnMouseLeave)
ON_MESSAGE (WM_MOUSEHOVER, OnMouseHover)
    :
    :
```

```
void CMainWindow::OnMouseMove (UINT nFlags, CPoint point)
{
    if (!m_bMouseOver) {
        TRACE (_T ("Mouse enter\n"));
        m_bMouseOver = TRUE;

        TRACKMOUSEEVENT tme;
        tme.cbSize = sizeof (tme);
        tme.dwFlags = TME_HOVER | TME_LEAVE;
        tme.hwndTrack = m_hWnd;
        tme.dwHoverTime = HOVER_DEFAULT;
        ::TrackMouseEvent (&tme);
    }
}

LRESULT CMainWindow::OnMouseLeave (WPARAM wParam, LPARAM lParam)
{
    TRACE (_T ("Mouse leave\n"));
    m_bMouseOver = FALSE;
    return 0;
}

LRESULT CMainWindow::OnMouseHover (WPARAM wParam, LPARAM lParam)
{
    TRACE (_T ("Mouse hover (x=%d, y=%d)\n"),
        LOWORD (lParam), HIWORD (lParam));

    TRACKMOUSEEVENT tme;
    tme.cbSize = sizeof (tme);
    tme.dwFlags = TME_HOVER | TME_LEAVE;
    tme.hwndTrack = m_hWnd;
    tme.dwHoverTime = HOVER_DEFAULT;
    ::TrackMouseEvent (&tme);
    return 0;
}
```

MFC doesn't provide type-specific message-mapping macros for WM_MOUSE-LEAVE and WM_MOUSEHOVER messages, so as this example demonstrates, you must use the ON_MESSAGE macro to link these messages to class member functions. The *lParam* value accompanying a WM_MOUSEHOVER message holds the cursor's *x* coordinate in its low word and the cursor's *y* coordinate in its high word. *wParam* is unused. Both *wParam* and *lParam* are unused in WM_MOUSELEAVE messages.

One final note regarding *::TrackMouseEvent*: In order to use it, you must include the following #define in your source code:

```
#define _WIN32_WINNT 0x0400
```

Be sure to include this line before the line that #includes Afxwin.h. Otherwise, it will have no effect.

The Mouse Wheel

Many of the mice used with Windows today include a wheel that can be used to scroll a window without clicking the scroll bar. When the wheel is rolled, the window with the input focus receives WM_MOUSEWHEEL messages. MFC's *CScrollView* class provides a default handler for these messages that automatically scrolls the window, but if you want mouse wheel messages to scroll a non-*CScrollView* window, you must process WM_MOUSEWHEEL messages yourself.

MFC's ON_WM_MOUSEWHEEL macro maps WM_MOUSEWHEEL messages to the message handler *OnMouseWheel*. *OnMouseWheel* is prototyped like this:

```
BOOL OnMouseWheel (UINT nFlags, short zDelta, CPoint point)
```

The *nFlags* and *point* parameters are identical to those passed to *OnLButtonDown*. *zDelta* is the distance the wheel was rotated. A *zDelta* equal to WHEEL_DELTA (120) means the wheel was rotated forward one increment, or *notch*, and –WHEEL-_DELTA means the wheel was rotated backward one notch. If the wheel is rotated forward five notches, the window will receive five WM_MOUSEWHEEL messages, each with a *zDelta* of WHEEL_DELTA. *OnMouseWheel* should return a nonzero value if it scrolled the window, or zero if it did not.

A simple way to respond to a WM_MOUSEWHEEL message is to scroll the window one line up (if *zDelta* is positive) or one line down (if *zDelta* is negative) for every WHEEL_DELTA unit. The recommended approach, however, is slightly more involved. First you ask the system for the number of lines that corresponds to WHEEL_DELTA units. In Windows NT 4.0 and higher and in Windows 98, you can get this value by calling *::SystemParametersInfo* with a first parameter equal to SPI_GETWHEELSCROLLLINES. Then you multiply the result by *zDelta* and divide by WHEEL_DELTA to determine how many lines to scroll. You can modify the Accel program presented in Chapter 2 to respond to WM_MOUSEWHEEL messages in this manner by adding the following message-map entry and message handler to *CMainWindow*:

```
// In the message map
ON_WM_MOUSEWHEEL ()

   :
   :

BOOL CMainWindow::OnMouseWheel (UINT nFlags, short zDelta, CPoint point)
{
    BOOL bUp = TRUE;
    int nDelta = zDelta;

    if (zDelta < 0) {
        bUp = FALSE;
        nDelta = -nDelta;
    }
```

```
UINT nWheelScrollLines;
::SystemParametersInfo (SPI_GETWHEELSCROLLLINES, 0,
    &nWheelScrollLines, 0);

if (nWheelScrollLines == WHEEL_PAGESCROLL) {
    SendMessage (WM_VSCROLL,
        MAKEWPARAM (bUp ? SB_PAGEUP : SB_PAGEDOWN, 0), 0);
}
else {
    int nLines = (nDelta * nWheelScrollLines) / WHEEL_DELTA;
    while (nLines--)
        SendMessage (WM_VSCROLL,
            MAKEWPARAM (bUp ? SB_LINEUP : SB_LINEDOWN, 0), 0);
}
return TRUE;
}
```

Dividing *zDelta* by WHEEL_DELTA ensures that the application won't scroll too quickly if, in the future, it's used with a mouse that has a wheel granularity less than 120 units. WHEEL_PAGESCROLL is a special value that indicates the application should simulate a click of the scroll bar shaft—in other words, perform a page-up or page-down. Both WHEEL_DELTA and WHEEL_PAGESCROLL are defined in Winuser.h.

One issue to be aware of regarding this code sample is that it's not compatible with Windows 95. Why? Because calling *::SystemParametersInfo* with an SPI_GET-WHEELSCROLLLINES value does nothing in Windows 95. If you want to support Windows 95, you can either assume that *::SystemParametersInfo* would return 3 (the default) or resort to more elaborate means to obtain the user's preference. MFC uses an internal function named *_AfxGetMouseScrollLines* to get this value. *_AfxGetMouseScrollLines* is platform-neutral; it uses various methods to attempt to obtain a scroll line count and defaults to 3 if none of those methods work. See the MFC source code file Viewscrl.cpp if you'd like to mimic that behavior in your code.

If the mouse wheel is clicked rather than rotated, the window under the cursor generally receives middle-button mouse messages—WM_MBUTTONDOWN messages when the wheel is pressed, WM_MBUTTONUP messages when the wheel is released. (I say "generally" because this is the default behavior; it can be changed through the Control Panel.) Some applications respond to wheel clicks in a special way. Microsoft Word 97, for example, scrolls the currently displayed document when it receives WM_MOUSEMOVE messages with the wheel held down. Knowing that the mouse wheel produces middle-button messages, you can customize your applications to respond to mouse wheel events any way you see fit.

Capturing the Mouse

One problem that frequently crops up in programs that process mouse messages is that the receipt of a button-down message doesn't necessarily mean that a button-up message will follow. Suppose you've written a drawing program that saves the *point* parameter passed to *OnLButtonDown* and uses it as an anchor point to draw a line whose other endpoint follows the cursor—an action known as "rubber-banding" a line. When a WM_LBUTTONUP message arrives, the application erases the rubber-band line and draws a real line in its place. But what happens if the user moves the mouse outside the window's client area before releasing the mouse button? The application never gets that WM_LBUTTONUP message, so the rubber-band line is left hanging in limbo and the real line isn't drawn.

Windows provides an elegant solution to this problem by allowing an application to "capture" the mouse upon receiving a button-down message and to continue receiving mouse messages no matter where the cursor goes on the screen until the button is released or the capture is canceled. (In the Win32 environment, to prevent applications from monopolizing the mouse, the system stops sending mouse messages to a window that owns the capture if the button is released.) The mouse is captured with *CWnd::SetCapture* and released with *::ReleaseCapture*. Calls to these functions are normally paired in button-down and button-up handlers, as shown here:

```
// In CMainWindow's message map
ON_WM_LBUTTONDOWN ()
ON_WM_LBUTTONUP ()
    :
    :
void CMainWindow::OnLButtonDown (UINT nFlags, CPoint point)
{
    SetCapture ();
}

void CMainWindow::OnLButtonUp (UINT nFlags, CPoint point)
{
    ::ReleaseCapture ();
}
```

In between, *CMainWindow* receives WM_MOUSEMOVE messages that report the cursor position even if the cursor leaves it. Client-area mouse messages continue to report cursor positions in client coordinates, but coordinates can now go negative and can also exceed the dimensions of the window's client area.

A related function, *CWnd::GetCapture*, returns a *CWnd* pointer to the window that owns the capture. In the Win32 environment, *GetCapture* returns NULL if the mouse is not captured or if it's captured by a window belonging to another thread.

The most common use of *GetCapture* is for determining whether your own window has captured the mouse. The statement

```
if (GetCapture () == this)
```

is true if and only if the window identified by *this* currently has the mouse captured.

How does capturing the mouse solve the problem with the rubber-banded line? By capturing the mouse in response to a WM_LBUTTONDOWN message and releasing it when a WM_LBUTTONUP message arrives, you're guaranteed to get the WM_LBUTTONUP message when the mouse button is released. The sample program in the next section illustrates the practical effect of this technique.

Mouse Capturing in Action

The MouseCap application shown in Figure 3-4 is a rudimentary paint program that lets the user draw lines with the mouse. To draw a line, press the left mouse button anywhere in the window's client area and drag the cursor with the button held down. As the mouse is moved, a thin line is rubber-banded between the anchor point and the cursor. When the mouse button is released, the rubber-band line is erased and a red line 16 pixels wide is drawn in its place. Because the mouse is captured while the button is depressed, rubber-banding works even if the mouse is moved outside the window. And no matter where the cursor is when the mouse button is released, a red line is drawn between the anchor point and the endpoint. MouseCap's source code appears in Figure 3-5.

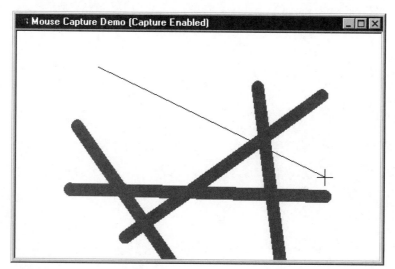

Figure 3-4. *The MouseCap window.*

MouseCap.h

```
class CMyApp : public CWinApp
{
public:
    virtual BOOL InitInstance ();
};

class CMainWindow : public CFrameWnd
{
protected:
    BOOL m_bTracking;              // TRUE if rubber banding
    BOOL m_bCaptureEnabled;        // TRUE if capture enabled
    CPoint m_ptFrom;               // "From" point for rubber banding
    CPoint m_ptTo;                 // "To" point for rubber banding

    void InvertLine (CDC* pDC, CPoint ptFrom, CPoint ptTo);

public:
    CMainWindow ();

protected:
    afx_msg void OnLButtonDown (UINT nFlags, CPoint point);
    afx_msg void OnLButtonUp (UINT nFlags, CPoint point);
    afx_msg void OnMouseMove (UINT nFlags, CPoint point);
    afx_msg void OnNcLButtonDown (UINT nHitTest, CPoint point);
    DECLARE_MESSAGE_MAP ()
};
```

MouseCap.cpp

```
#include <afxwin.h>
#include "MouseCap.h"

CMyApp myApp;

///////////////////////////////////////////////////////////////////////
// CMyApp member functions

BOOL CMyApp::InitInstance ()
{
    m_pMainWnd = new CMainWindow;
    m_pMainWnd->ShowWindow (m_nCmdShow);
```

Figure 3-5. *The MouseCap application.*

```
        m_pMainWnd->UpdateWindow ();
        return TRUE;
}


/////////////////////////////////////////////////////////////////////////
// CMainWindow message map and member functions

BEGIN_MESSAGE_MAP (CMainWindow, CFrameWnd)
    ON_WM_LBUTTONDOWN ()
    ON_WM_LBUTTONUP ()
    ON_WM_MOUSEMOVE ()
    ON_WM_NCLBUTTONDOWN ()
END_MESSAGE_MAP ()

CMainWindow::CMainWindow ()
{
    m_bTracking = FALSE;
    m_bCaptureEnabled = TRUE;

    //
    // Register a WNDCLASS.
    //

    CString strWndClass = AfxRegisterWndClass (
        0,
        AfxGetApp ()->LoadStandardCursor (IDC_CROSS),
        (HBRUSH) (COLOR_WINDOW + 1),
        AfxGetApp ()->LoadStandardIcon (IDI_WINLOGO)
    );

    //
    // Create a window.
    //
    Create (strWndClass, _T ("Mouse Capture Demo (Capture Enabled)"));
}

void CMainWindow::OnLButtonDown (UINT nFlags, CPoint point)
{
    //
    // Record the anchor point and set the tracking flag.
    //
    m_ptFrom = point;
    m_ptTo = point;
    m_bTracking = TRUE;
```

(continued)

Figure 3-5. *continued*

```
    //
    // If capture is enabled, capture the mouse.
    //
    if (m_bCaptureEnabled)
        SetCapture ();
}

void CMainWindow::OnMouseMove (UINT nFlags, CPoint point)
{
    //
    // If the mouse is moved while we're "tracking" (that is, while a
    // line is being rubber-banded), erase the old rubber-band line and
    // draw a new one.
    //
    if (m_bTracking) {
        CClientDC dc (this);
        InvertLine (&dc, m_ptFrom, m_ptTo);
        InvertLine (&dc, m_ptFrom, point);
        m_ptTo = point;
    }
}

void CMainWindow::OnLButtonUp (UINT nFlags, CPoint point)
{
    //
    // If the left mouse button is released while we're tracking, release
    // the mouse if it's currently captured, erase the last rubber-band
    // line, and draw a thick red line in its place.
    //
    if (m_bTracking) {
        m_bTracking = FALSE;
        if (GetCapture () == this)
            ::ReleaseCapture ();

        CClientDC dc (this);
        InvertLine (&dc, m_ptFrom, m_ptTo);

        CPen pen (PS_SOLID, 16, RGB (255, 0, 0));
        dc.SelectObject (&pen);

        dc.MoveTo (m_ptFrom);
        dc.LineTo (point);
    }
}
```

```
void CMainWindow::OnNcLButtonDown (UINT nHitTest, CPoint point)
{
    //
    // When the window's title bar is clicked with the left mouse button,
    // toggle the capture flag on or off and update the window title.
    //
    if (nHitTest == HTCAPTION) {
        m_bCaptureEnabled = m_bCaptureEnabled ? FALSE : TRUE;
        SetWindowText (m_bCaptureEnabled ?
            _T ("Mouse Capture Demo (Capture Enabled)") :
            _T ("Mouse Capture Demo (Capture Disabled)"));
    }
    CFrameWnd::OnNcLButtonDown (nHitTest, point);
}

void CMainWindow::InvertLine (CDC* pDC, CPoint ptFrom, CPoint ptTo)
{
    //
    //Invert a line of pixels by drawing a line in the R2_NOT drawing mode.
    //
    int nOldMode = pDC->SetROP2 (R2_NOT);
    pDC->MoveTo (ptFrom);
    pDC->LineTo (ptTo);

    pDC->SetROP2 (nOldMode);
}
```

Most of the action takes place in the program's *OnLButtonDown*, *OnMouseMove*, and *OnLButtonUp* handlers. *OnLButtonDown* starts the drawing process by initializing a trio of variables that are members of the *CMainWindow* class:

```
m_ptFrom = point;
m_ptTo = point;
m_bTracking = TRUE;
```

m_ptFrom and *m_ptTo* are the starting and ending points for the rubber-band line. *m_ptTo* is continually updated by the *OnMouseMove* handler as the mouse is moved. *m_bTracking*, which is TRUE when the left button is down and FALSE when it is not, is a flag that tells *OnMouseMove* and *OnLButtonUp* whether a line is being rubber-banded. *OnLButtonDown*'s only other action is to capture the mouse if *m_bCaptureEnabled* is TRUE:

```
if (m_bCaptureEnabled)
    SetCapture ();
```

m_bCaptureEnabled is initialized to TRUE by *CMainWindow*'s constructor. It is toggled by the window's *OnNcLButtonDown* handler so that you can turn mouse capturing on and off and see the effect that mouse capturing has on the program's operation. (More on this in a moment.)

OnMouseMove's job is to move the rubber-band line and update *m_ptTo* with the new cursor position whenever the mouse is moved. The statement

```
InvertLine (&dc, m_ptFrom, m_ptTo);
```

erases the previously drawn rubber-band line, and

```
InvertLine (&dc, m_ptFrom, point);
```

draws a new one. *InvertLine* is a member of *CMainWindow*. It draws a line not by setting each pixel to a certain color, but by inverting the existing pixel colors. This ensures that the line can be seen no matter what background it is drawn against and that drawing the line again in the same location will erase it by restoring the original screen colors. The inversion is accomplished by setting the device context's drawing mode to R2_NOT with the statement

```
int nOldMode = pDC->SetROP2 (R2_NOT);
```

See Chapter 2 for a discussion of R2_NOT and other drawing modes.

When the left mouse button is released, *CMainWindow::OnLButtonUp* is called. After setting *m_bTracking* to FALSE and releasing the mouse, it erases the rubber-band line drawn by the last call to *OnMouseMove*:

```
CClientDC dc (this);
InvertLine (&dc, m_ptFrom, m_ptTo);
```

OnLButtonUp then creates a solid red pen 16 pixels wide, selects it into the device context, and draws a thick red line:

```
CPen pen (PS_SOLID, 16, RGB (255, 0, 0));
dc.SelectObject (&pen);

dc.MoveTo (m_ptFrom);
dc.LineTo (point);
```

Its work done, *OnLButtonUp* returns, and the drawing operation is complete. Figure 3-4 on page 133 shows what the MouseCap window looks like after a few lines have been drawn and as a new line is rubber-banded.

After you've played around with the program a bit, click the title bar to activate the *OnNcLButtonDown* handler and toggle the *m_bCaptureEnabled* flag from TRUE to FALSE. The window title should change from "Mouse Capture Demo (Capture Enabled)" to "Mouse Capture Demo (Capture Disabled)." *OnNcLButtonDown* processes left button clicks in the nonclient area and uses *CWnd::SetWindowText* to change the window title if the hit-test code in *nHitTest* is equal to HTCAPTION, indicating that the click occurred in the title bar.

Now draw a few lines with mouse capturing disabled. Observe that if you move the mouse outside the window while rubber-banding, the line freezes until the mouse reenters the client area, and that if you release the mouse button outside the window, the program gets out of sync. The rubber-band line follows the mouse when you move it back to the interior of the window (even though the mouse button is no longer pressed), and it never gets erased. Click the title bar once again to reenable mouse capturing, and the program will revert to its normal self.

The Cursor

Rather than use the arrow-shaped cursor you see in most Windows applications, MouseCap uses a crosshair cursor. Arrows and crosshairs are just two of several predefined cursor types that Windows places at your disposal, and if none of the predefined cursors fits the bill, you can always create your own. As usual, Windows gives programmers a great deal of latitude in this area.

First, a bit of background on how cursors work. As you know, every window has a corresponding WNDCLASS whose characteristics are defined in a WNDCLASS structure. One of the fields of the WNDCLASS structure is *hCursor*, which holds the handle of the class cursor—the image displayed when the cursor is over a window's client area. When the mouse is moved, Windows erases the cursor from its old location by redrawing the background behind it. Then it sends the window under the cursor a WM_SETCURSOR message containing a hit-test code. The system's default response to this message is to call *::SetCursor* to display the class cursor if the hit-test code is HTCLIENT or to display an arrow if the hit-test code indicates that the cursor is outside the client area. As a result, the cursor is automatically updated as it is moved about the screen. When you move the cursor into an edit control, for example, it changes into a vertical bar or "I-beam" cursor. This happens because Windows registers a special WNDCLASS for edit controls and specifies the I-beam cursor as the class cursor.

It follows that one way to change the cursor's appearance is to register a WND-CLASS and specify the desired cursor type as the class cursor. In MouseCap, *CMainWindow*'s constructor registers a WNDCLASS whose class cursor is IDC_CROSS and passes the WNDCLASS name to *CFrameWnd::Create*:

```
CString strWndClass = AfxRegisterWndClass (
    0,
    AfxGetApp ()->LoadStandardCursor (IDC_CROSS),
    (HBRUSH) (COLOR_WINDOW + 1),
    AfxGetApp ()->LoadStandardIcon (IDI_WINLOGO)
);
```

```
Create (strWndClass, _T ("Mouse Capture Demo (Capture Enabled)"));
```

Windows then displays a crosshair cursor anytime the mouse pointer is positioned in *CMainWindow*'s client area.

A second way to customize the cursor is to call the API function *::SetCursor* in response to WM_SETCURSOR messages. The following *OnSetCursor* function displays the cursor whose handle is stored in *CMainWindow::m_hCursor* when the cursor is over *CMainWindow*'s client area:

```
// In CMainWindow's message map
ON_WM_SETCURSOR ()
      ⋮
BOOL CMainWindow::OnSetCursor (CWnd* pWnd, UINT nHitTest,
    UINT message)
{
    if (nHitTest == HTCLIENT) {
        ::SetCursor (m_hCursor);
        return TRUE;
    }
    return CFrameWnd::OnSetCursor (pWnd, nHitTest, message);
}
```

Returning TRUE after calling *::SetCursor* tells Windows that the cursor has been set. WM_SETCURSOR messages generated outside the window's client area are passed to the base class so that the default cursor is displayed. The class cursor is ignored because *OnSetCursor* never gives Windows the opportunity to display it.

Why would you want to use *OnSetCursor* rather than just registering *m_hCursor* as the class cursor? Suppose you want to display an arrow cursor when the cursor is in the top half of the window and an I-beam cursor when the cursor is in the bottom half. A class cursor won't suffice in this case, but *OnSetCursor* will do the job quite nicely. The following *OnSetCursor* handler sets the cursor to either *m_hCursorArrow* or *m_hCursorIBeam* when the cursor is in *CMainWindow*'s client area:

```
BOOL CMainWindow::OnSetCursor (CWnd* pWnd, UINT nHitTest,
    UINT message)
{
    if (nHitTest == HTCLIENT) {
        DWORD dwPos = ::GetMessagePos ();
        CPoint point (LOWORD (dwPos), HIWORD (dwPos));
        ScreenToClient (&point);
        CRect rect;
        GetClientRect (&rect);
        ::SetCursor ((point.y < rect.Height () / 2) ?
            m_hCursorArrow : m_hCursorIBeam);
        return TRUE;
    }
    return CFrameWnd::OnSetCursor (pWnd, nHitTest, message);
}
```

::GetMessagePos returns a DWORD value containing the cursor's *x* and *y* screen coordinates at the moment the WM_SETCURSOR message was retrieved from the mes-

sage queue. *CWnd::ScreenToClient* converts screen coordinates to client coordinates. If the converted point's *y* coordinate is less than half the height of the window's client area, the cursor is set to *m_hCursorArrow*. But if *y* is greater than or equal to half the client area height, the cursor is set to *m_hCursorIBeam* instead. The VisualKB application presented later in this chapter uses a similar technique to change the cursor to an I-beam when it enters a rectangle surrounding a text-entry field.

Should the need ever arise, you can hide the cursor with the statement

```
::ShowCursor (FALSE);
```

and display it again with

```
::ShowCursor (TRUE);
```

Internally, Windows maintains a display count that's incremented each time *::ShowCursor (TRUE)* is called and decremented by each call to *::ShowCursor (FALSE)*. The count is initially set to 0 if a mouse is installed and to -1 if no mouse is present, and the cursor is displayed whenever the count is greater than or equal to 0. Thus, if you call *::ShowCursor (FALSE)* twice to hide the cursor, you must call *::ShowCursor (TRUE)* twice to display it again.

The Hourglass Cursor

When an application responds to a message by undertaking a lengthy processing task, it's customary to change the cursor to an hourglass to remind the user that the application is "busy." (While a message handler executes, no further messages are retrieved from the message queue and the program is frozen to input. In Chapter 17, you'll learn about ways to perform background processing tasks while continuing to retrieve and dispatch messages.)

Windows provides the hourglass cursor for you; its identifier is IDC_WAIT. An easy way to display an hourglass cursor is to declare a *CWaitCursor* variable on the stack, like this:

```
CWaitCursor wait;
```

CWaitCursor's constructor displays an hourglass cursor, and its destructor restores the original cursor. If you'd like to restore the cursor before the variable goes out of scope, simply call *CWaitCursor::Restore*:

```
wait.Restore ();
```

You should call *Restore* before taking any action that would allow a WM_SETCURSOR message to seep through and destroy the hourglass—for example, before displaying a message box or a dialog box.

You can change the cursor displayed by *CWaitCursor::CWaitCursor* and *BeginWaitCursor* by overriding *CWinApp*'s virtual *DoWaitCursor* function. Use the default implementation of *CWinApp::DoWaitCursor* found in the MFC source code file Appui.cpp as a model for your own implementations.

Mouse Miscellanea

As mentioned earlier, calling the *::GetSystemMetrics* API function with an SM_CMOUSE-BUTTONS argument queries the system for the number of mouse buttons. (There is no MFC equivalent to *::GetSystemMetrics*, so you must call it directly.) The usual return value is 1, 2, or 3, but a 0 return means no mouse is attached. You can also find out whether a mouse is present by calling *::GetSystemMetrics* this way:

```
::GetSystemMetrics (SM_MOUSEPRESENT)
```

The return value is nonzero if there is a mouse attached, 0 if there is not. In the early days of Windows, programmers had to consider the possibility that someone might be using Windows without a mouse. Today that's rarely a concern, and a program that queries the system to determine whether a mouse is present is a rare program indeed.

Other mouse-related *::GetSystemMetrics* parameters include SM_CXDOUBLECLK and SM_CYDOUBLECLK, which specify the maximum horizontal and vertical distances (in pixels) that can separate the two halves of a double click, and SM_SWAPBUTTON, which returns a nonzero value if the user has swapped the left and right mouse buttons using the Control Panel. When the mouse buttons are swapped, the left mouse button generates WM_RBUTTON messages and the right mouse button generates WM_LBUTTON messages. Generally you don't need to be concerned about this, but if for some reason your application wants to be sure that the left mouse button *really* means the left mouse button, it can use *::GetSystemMetrics* to determine whether the buttons have been swapped.

The API functions *::SetDoubleClickTime* and *::GetDoubleClickTime* enable an application to set and retrieve the mouse double-click time—the maximum amount of time permitted between clicks when a mouse button is double-clicked. The expression

```
::GetDoubleClickTime ()
```

returns the double-click time in milliseconds, while the statement

```
::SetDoubleClickTime (250);
```

sets the double-click time to 250 milliseconds, or one quarter of a second. When the same mouse button is clicked twice in succession, Windows uses both the double-click time and the SM_CXDOUBLECLK and SM_CYDOUBLECLK values returned by *::GetSystemMetrics* to determine whether to report the second of the two clicks as a double click.

A function that processes mouse messages can determine which, if any, mouse buttons are pressed by checking the *nFlags* parameter passed to the message handler. It's also possible to query the state of a mouse button outside a mouse message handler by calling *::GetKeyState* or *::GetAsyncKeyState* with a VK_LBUTTON, VK_M-

BUTTON, or VK_RBUTTON parameter. *::GetKeyState* should be called only from a keyboard message handler because it returns the state of the specified mouse button at the time the keyboard message was generated. *::GetAsyncKeyState* can be called anywhere, anytime. It works in real time, returning the state of the button at the moment the function is called. A negative return value from

```
::GetKeyState (VK_LBUTTON)
```

or

```
::GetAsyncKeyState (VK_LBUTTON)
```

indicates that the left mouse button is pressed. Swapping the mouse buttons does not affect *::GetAsyncKeyState*, so if you use this function, you should also use *::GetSystemMetrics* to determine whether the buttons have been swapped. The expression

```
::GetAsyncKeyState (::GetSystemMetrics (SM_SWAPBUTTON) ?
    VK_RBUTTON : VK_LBUTTON)
```

checks the state of the left mouse button asynchronously and automatically queries the right mouse button instead if the buttons have been swapped.

Windows provides a pair of API functions named *::GetCursorPos* and *::SetCursorPos* for getting and setting the cursor position manually. *::GetCursorPos* copies the cursor coordinates to a POINT structure. A related function named *::GetMessagePos* returns a DWORD value containing a pair of 16-bit coordinates specifying where the cursor was when the last message was retrieved from the message queue. You can extract those coordinates using the Windows LOWORD and HIWORD macros:

```
DWORD dwPos = ::GetMessagePos ();
int x = LOWORD (dwPos);
int y = HIWORD (dwPos);
```

::GetCursorPos and *::GetMessagePos* both report the cursor position in screen coordinates. Screen coordinates can be converted to client coordinates by calling a window's *ClientToScreen* function.

Windows also provides a function named *::ClipCursor* that restricts the cursor to a particular area of the screen. *::ClipCursor* accepts a pointer to a RECT structure that describes, in screen coordinates, the clipping rectangle. Since the cursor is a global resource shared by all applications, an application that uses *::ClipCursor* must free the cursor by calling

```
::ClipCursor (NULL);
```

before terminating, or else the cursor will remain locked into the clipping rectangle indefinitely.

GETTING INPUT FROM THE KEYBOARD

A Windows application learns of keyboard events the same way it learns about mouse events: through messages. A program receives a message whenever a key is pressed or released. If you want to know when the Page Up or Page Down key is pressed so that your application can react accordingly, you process WM_KEYDOWN messages and check for key codes identifying the Page Up or Page Down key. If you'd rather know when a key is released, you process WM_KEYUP messages instead. For keys that produce printable characters, you can ignore key-down and key-up messages and process WM_CHAR messages that denote characters typed at the keyboard. Relying on WM_CHAR messages instead of WM_KEYUP/DOWN messages simplifies character processing by enabling Windows to factor in events and circumstances surrounding the keystroke, such as whether the Shift key is pressed, whether Caps Lock is on or off, and differences in keyboard layouts.

The Input Focus

Like the mouse, the keyboard is a global hardware resource shared by all applications. Windows decides which window to send mouse messages to by identifying the window under the cursor. Keyboard messages are targeted differently. Windows directs keyboard messages to the window with the "input focus." At any given time, no more than one window has the input focus. Often the window with the input focus is the main window of the active application. However, the input focus might belong to a child of the main window or to a control in a dialog box. Regardless, Windows *always* sends keyboard messages to the window that owns the focus. If your application's window has no child windows, keyboard processing is relatively straightforward: When your application is active, its main window receives keyboard messages. If the focus shifts to a child window, keyboard messages go to the child window instead and the flow of messages to the main window ceases.

Windows notifies a window that it is about to receive or lose the input focus with WM_SETFOCUS and WM_KILLFOCUS messages, which MFC programs process as shown here:

```
// In CMainWindow's message map
ON_WM_SETFOCUS ()
ON_WM_KILLFOCUS ()
    :
    :

void CMainWindow::OnSetFocus (CWnd* pOldWnd)
```

```
{
    // CMainWindow now has the input focus. pOldWnd
    // identifies the window that lost the input focus.
    // pOldWnd will be NULL if the window that lost the
    // focus was created by another thread.
}

void CMainWindow::OnKillFocus (CWnd* pNewWnd)
{
    // CMainWindow is about to lose the input focus.
    // pNewWnd identifies the window that will receive
    // the input focus. pNewWnd will be NULL if the
    // window that's receiving the focus is owned by
    // another thread.
}
```

An application can shift the input focus to another window with *CWnd::SetFocus*:

```
pWnd->SetFocus ();
```

Or it can use the static *CWnd::GetFocus* function to find out who currently has the input focus:

```
CWnd* pFocusWnd = CWnd::GetFocus ();
```

In the Win32 environment, *GetFocus* returns NULL if the window that owns the focus was not created by the calling thread. You can't use *GetFocus* to get a pointer to a window created by another application, but you *can* use it to identify windows that belong to your application.

Keystroke Messages

Windows reports key presses and releases by sending WM_KEYDOWN and WM_KEY-UP messages to the window with the input focus. These messages are commonly referred to as *keystroke messages*. When a key is pressed, the window with the input focus receives a WM_KEYDOWN message with a virtual key code identifying the key. When the key is released, the window receives a WM_KEYUP message. If other keys are pressed and released while the key is held down, the resultant WM_KEYDOWN and WM_KEYUP messages separate the WM_KEYDOWN and WM_KEYUP messages generated by the key that's held down. Windows reports keyboard events as they happen in the order in which they happen, so by examining the stream of keystroke messages coming into your application, you can tell exactly what was typed and when.

All keys but two generate WM_KEYDOWN and WM_KEYUP messages. The two exceptions are Alt and F10, which are "system" keys that have a special meaning to Windows. When either of these keys is pressed and released, a window receives a WM_SYSKEYDOWN message followed by a WM_SYSKEYUP message. If other keys are pressed while the Alt key is held down, they, too, generate WM_SYSKEYDOWN and WM_SYSKEYUP messages instead of WM_KEYDOWN and WM_KEYUP messages. Pressing F10 puts Windows in a special modal state that treats the next keypress as a menu shortcut. Pressing F10 followed by the F key, for example, pulls down the File menu in most applications.

An application processes keystroke messages by providing message-map entries and message handling functions for the messages it is interested in. WM_KEYDOWN, WM_KEYUP, WM_SYSKEYDOWN, and WM_SYSKEYUP messages are processed by a class's *OnKeyDown*, *OnKeyUp*, *OnSysKeyDown*, and *OnSysKeyUp* member functions, respectively. The corresponding message-map macros are ON_WM_KEYDOWN, ON_WM_KEYUP, ON_WM_SYSKEYDOWN, and ON_WM_SYSKEYUP. When activated, a keystroke handler receives a wealth of information about the keystroke, including a code identifying the key that was pressed or released.

Keystroke message handlers are prototyped as follows:

```
afx_msg void OnMsgName (UINT nChar, UINT nRepCnt, UINT nFlags)
```

nChar is the virtual key code of the key that was pressed or released. *nRepCnt* is the repeat count—the number of keystrokes encoded in the message. *nRepCnt* is usually equal to 1 for WM_KEYDOWN or WM_SYSKEYDOWN messages and is always 1 for WM_KEYUP or WM_SYSKEYUP messages. If key-down messages arrive so fast that your application can't keep up, Windows combines two or more WM_KEYDOWN or WM_SYSKEYDOWN messages into one and increases the repeat count accordingly. Most programs ignore the repeat count and treat combinatorial key-down messages (messages in which *nRepCnt* is greater than 1) as a single keystroke to prevent overruns—situations in which a program continues to scroll or otherwise respond to keystroke messages after the user's finger has released the key. In contrast to the PC's keyboard BIOS, which buffers incoming keystrokes and reports each one individually, the Windows method of reporting consecutive presses of the same key to your application provides a built-in hedge against keyboard overruns.

The *nFlags* parameter contains the key's scan code and zero or more of the bit flags described here:

Bit(s)	Meaning	Description
0–7	OEM scan code	8-bit OEM scan code
8	Extended key flag	1 if the key is an extended key, 0 if it is not
9–12	Reserved	N/A
13	Context code	1 if the Alt key is pressed, 0 if it is not
14	Previous key state	1 if the key was previously pressed, 0 if it was up
15	Transition state	0 if the key is being pressed, 1 if it is being released

The extended key flag allows an application to differentiate between the duplicate keys that appear on most keyboards. On the 101-key and 102-key keyboards used with the majority of IBM-compatible PCs, the extended key flag is set for the Ctrl and Alt keys on the right side of the keyboard; the Home, End, Insert, Delete, Page Up, Page Down, and arrow keys that are clustered between the main part of the keyboard and the numeric keypad; and the keypad's Enter and forward-slash (/) keys. For all other keys, the extended key flag is 0. The OEM scan code is an 8-bit value that identifies the key to the keyboard BIOS. Most Windows applications ignore this field because it is inherently hardware dependent. (If needed, scan codes can be translated into virtual key codes with the *::MapVirtualKey* API function.) The transition state, previous key state, and context code are generally disregarded too, but they are occasionally useful. A previous key state value equal to 1 identifies *typematic keystrokes*—keystrokes generated when a key is pressed and held down for some length of time. Holding down the Shift key for a second or so, for instance, generates the following sequence of messages:

Message	*Virtual Key Code*	*Previous Key State*
WM_KEYDOWN	VK_SHIFT	0
WM_KEYDOWN	VK_SHIFT	1
WM_KEYDOWN	VK_SHIFT	1
WM_KEYDOWN	VK_SHIFT	1
WM_KEYDOWN	VK_SHIFT	1
WM_KEYDOWN	VK_SHIFT	1
WM_KEYDOWN	VK_SHIFT	1
WM_KEYDOWN	VK_SHIFT	1
WM_KEYDOWN	VK_SHIFT	1
WM_KEYUP	VK_SHIFT	1

If you want your application to disregard keystrokes generated as a result of typematic action, simply have it ignore WM_KEYDOWN messages with previous key state values equal to 1. The transition state value is 0 for WM_KEYDOWN and WM_SYSKEYDOWN messages and 1 for WM_KEYUP and WM_SYSKEYUP messages. Finally, the context code indicates whether the Alt key was pressed when the message was generated. With certain (usually unimportant) exceptions, the code is 1 for WM_SYSKEYDOWN and WM_SYSKEYUP messages and 0 for WM_KEYDOWN and WM_KEYUP messages.

In general, applications shouldn't process WM_SYSKEYDOWN and WM_SYS-KEYUP messages; they should let Windows process them instead. If these messages don't eventually find their way to *::DefWindowProc*, system keyboard commands such as Alt-Tab and Alt-Esc will stop working. Windows puts a tremendous amount of power in your hands by routing all mouse and keyboard messages through your application first, even though many of these messages are meaningful first and foremost to the operating system. As with nonclient-area mouse messages, the improper handling of system keystroke messages—in particular, the failure to pass these messages on to the operating system—can result in all sorts of quirky behavior.

Virtual Key Codes

The most important value by far that gets passed to a keystroke message handler is the *nChar* value identifying the key that was pressed or released. Windows identifies keys with the virtual key codes shown in the table on the following page so that applications won't have to rely on hardcoded values or OEM scan codes that might differ from keyboard to keyboard.

Conspicuously missing from this table are virtual key codes for the letters A through Z and a through z and for the numerals 0 through 9. The virtual key codes for these keys are the same as the corresponding characters' ANSI codes: 0x41 through 0x5A for A through Z, 0x61 through 0x7A for a through z, and 0x30 through 0x39 for 0 through 9.

If you look inside Winuser.h, where the virtual key codes are defined, you'll find a few key codes that aren't listed in the following table, including VK_SELECT, VK_EXECUTE, and VK_F13 through VK_F24. These codes are provided for use on other platforms and can't be generated on conventional IBM keyboards. Nonletter and nonnumeric keys for which Windows does not provide virtual key codes—for example, the semicolon (;) and square bracket ([]) keys—are best avoided when processing key-down and key-up messages because their IDs can vary on international keyboards. This doesn't mean that your program can't process punctuation symbols and other characters for which no VK_ identifiers exist; it simply means that there's a better way to do it than relying on key-up and key-down messages. That "better way" is WM_CHAR messages, which we'll discuss in a moment.

VIRTUAL KEY CODES

Virtual Key Code(s)	*Corresponding Key(s)*
VK_F1–VK_F12	Function keys F1–F12
VK_NUMPAD0–VK_NUMPAD9	Numeric keypad 0–9 with Num Lock on
VK_CANCEL	Ctrl-Break
VK_RETURN	Enter
VK_BACK	Backspace
VK_TAB	Tab
VK_CLEAR	Numeric keypad 5 with Num Lock off
VK_SHIFT	Shift
VK_CONTROL	Ctrl
VK_MENU	Alt
VK_PAUSE	Pause
VK_ESCAPE	Esc
VK_SPACE	Spacebar
VK_PRIOR	Page Up and PgUp
VK_NEXT	Page Down and PgDn
VK_END	End
VK_HOME	Home
VK_LEFT	Left arrow
VK_UP	Up arrow
VK_RIGHT	Right arrow
VK_DOWN	Down arrow
VK_SNAPSHOT	Print Screen
VK_INSERT	Insert and Ins
VK_DELETE	Delete and Del
VK_MULTIPLY	Numeric keypad *
VK_ADD	Numeric keypad +
VK_SUBTRACT	Numeric keypad -
VK_DECIMAL	Numeric keypad .
VK_DIVIDE	Numeric keypad /
VK_CAPITAL	Caps Lock
VK_NUMLOCK	Num Lock
VK_SCROLL	Scroll Lock
VK_LWIN	Left Windows key (⊞)
VK_RWIN	Right Windows key (⊞)
VK_APPS	Menu key (▤)

Shift States and Toggles

When you write handlers for WM_KEYDOWN, WM_KEYUP, WM_SYSKEYDOWN, or WM_SYSKEYUP messages, you might need to know whether the Shift, Ctrl, or Alt key is held down before deciding what to do. Information about the shift states of the Shift and Ctrl keys is not encoded in keyboard messages as it is in mouse messages, so Windows provides the *::GetKeyState* function. Given a virtual key code, *::GetKeyState* reports whether the key in question is held down. The expression

```
::GetKeyState (VK_SHIFT)
```

returns a negative value if the Shift key is held down or a nonnegative value if it is not. Similarly, the expression

```
::GetKeyState (VK_CONTROL)
```

returns a negative value if the Ctrl key is held down. Thus, the bracketed statements in the following code fragment taken from an *OnKeyDown* handler are executed only when Ctrl-Left (the left arrow key in combination with the Ctrl key) is pressed:

```
if ((nChar == VK_LEFT) && (::GetKeyState (VK_CONTROL) < 0)) {
    :
    :
}
```

To inquire about the Alt key, you can call *::GetKeyState* with a VK_MENU parameter or simply check the context code bit in the *nFlags* parameter. Usually even that amount of effort isn't necessary because if the Alt key is pressed, your window will receive a WM_SYSKEYDOWN or WM_SYSKEYUP message instead of a WM_KEYDOWN or WM_KEYUP message. In other words, the message ID generally tells you all you need to know about the Alt key. As a bonus, you can use the identifiers VK_LBUTTON, VK_MBUTTON, and VK_RBUTTON in conjunction with *::GetKeyState* to determine if any of the mouse buttons is held down.

An application can also use *::GetKeyState* to determine whether Num Lock, Caps Lock, and Scroll Lock are on or off. While the high bit of the return code indicates whether a key is currently pressed (yielding a negative number when the high bit is 1), the low bit—bit 0—indicates the state of the toggle. The expression

```
::GetKeyState (VK_NUMLOCK) & 0x01
```

evaluates to nonzero if Num Lock is on and evaluates to 0 if it is not. The same technique works for the VK_CAPITAL (Caps Lock) and VK_SCROLL (Scroll Lock) keys. It's important to mask off all but the lowest bit of the return code before testing because the high bit still indicates whether the key itself is up or down.

In all cases, *::GetKeyState* reports the state of the key or the mouse button *at the time the keyboard message was generated,* not at the precise moment that the function is called. This is a feature, not a bug, because it means you don't have to worry about a key being released before your message handler gets around to inquiring about the key state. The *::GetKeyState* function should never be called outside a keyboard message handler because the information it returns is valid only after a keyboard message has been retrieved from the message queue. If you really need to know the current state of a key or a mouse button, or if you want to check a key or a mouse button outside a keyboard message handler, use *::GetAsyncKeyState* instead.

Character Messages

One problem you'll encounter if you rely exclusively on key-up and key-down messages for keyboard input is shown in the following scenario. Suppose you're writing a text editor that turns messages reporting presses of the character keys into characters on the screen. The A key is pressed, and a WM_KEYDOWN message arrives with a virtual key code equal to 0x41. Before you put an A on the screen, you call *::GetKeyState* to determine whether the Shift key is held down. If it is, you output an uppercase "A"; otherwise, you output a lowercase "a." So far, so good. But what if Caps Lock is enabled too? Caps Lock undoes the effect of the Shift key, converting "A" to "a" and "a" to "A." Now you have four different permutations of the letter A to consider:

Virtual Key Code	VK_SHIFT	Caps Lock	Result
0x41	No	Off	a
0x41	Yes	Off	A
0x41	No	On	A
0x41	Yes	On	a

While you might reasonably expect to overcome this problem by writing code to sense all the possible shift and toggle states, your work is complicated by the fact that the user might also have the Ctrl key held down. And the problem is only compounded when your application is run outside the United States, where keyboard layouts typically differ from the U.S. keyboard layout. A U.S. user presses Shift-0 to enter a right parenthesis symbol. But Shift-0 produces an equal sign on most international keyboards and an apostrophe on Dutch keyboards. Users won't appreciate it much if the characters your program displays don't match the characters they type.

That's why Windows provides the *::TranslateMessage* API function. *::TranslateMessage* converts keystroke messages involving character keys into WM_CHAR messages. The message loop provided by MFC calls *::TranslateMessage* for you, so in an MFC application you don't have to do anything special to translate keystroke messages into WM_CHAR messages. When you use WM_CHAR messages for keyboard input, you needn't worry about virtual key codes and shift states because each WM_CHAR message includes a character code that maps directly to a symbol in the ANSI character set (Windows 98) or Unicode character set (Windows 2000). Assuming that Caps Lock is not turned on, pressing Shift-A produces the following sequence of messages:

Message	Virtual Key Code	Character Code
WM_KEYDOWN	VK_SHIFT	
WM_KEYDOWN	0x41	
WM_CHAR		0x41 ("A")
WM_KEYUP	0x41	
WM_KEYUP	VK_SHIFT	

Now you can safely ignore key-up and key-down messages because everything you need to know about the keystroke is encoded in the WM_CHAR message. If the Alt key had been held down while Shift-A was pressed, your application would have received a WM_SYSCHAR message instead:

Message	Virtual Key Code	Character Code
WM_SYSKEYDOWN	VK_SHIFT	
WM_SYSKEYDOWN	0x41	
WM_SYSCHAR		0x41 ("A")
WM_SYSKEYUP	0x41	
WM_SYSKEYUP	VK_SHIFT	

Since Alt-key combinations are generally used for special purposes, most applications ignore WM_SYSCHAR messages and process WM_CHAR messages instead.

Figure 3-6 shows the characters in the ANSI character set. Since ANSI codes are only 8 bits wide, there are only 256 possible characters. Unicode uses 16-bit character codes, expanding the possible character count to 65,536. Fortunately, the first 256 characters in the Unicode character set and the 256 characters in the ANSI character set are identical. Thus, code like this:

```
case _T ('a'):
case _T ('A'):
```

works fine with either character set.

```
      0  1  2  3  4  5  6  7  8  9  A  B  C  D  E  F
00:   ■  ■  ■  ■  ■  ■  ■  ■  ■  ■  ■  ■  ■  ■  ■  ■
10:   ■  ■  ■  ■  ■  ■  ■  ■  ■  ■  ■  ■  ■  ■  ■  ■
20:      !  "  #  $  %  &  '  (  )  *  +  ,  -  .  /
30:   0  1  2  3  4  5  6  7  8  9  :  ;  <  =  >  ?
40:   @  A  B  C  D  E  F  G  H  I  J  K  L  M  N  O
50:   P  Q  R  S  T  U  V  W  X  Y  Z  [  \  ]  ^  _
60:   `  a  b  c  d  e  f  g  h  i  j  k  l  m  n  o
70:   p  q  r  s  t  u  v  w  x  y  z  {  |  }  ~  ■
80:   ■  ■  ■  ■  ■  ■  ■  ■  ■  ■  ■  ■  ■  ■  ■  ■
90:   ■  '  '  ■  ■  ■  ■  ■  ■  ■  ■  ■  ■  ■  ■  ■
A0:      ¡  ¢  £  ¤  ¥  ¦  §  ¨  ©  ª  «  ¬  -  ®  ‾
B0:   °  ±  ²  ³  ´  µ  ¶  ·  ¸  ¹  º  »  ¼  ½  ¾  ¿
C0:   À  Á  Â  Ã  Ä  Å  Æ  Ç  È  É  Ê  Ë  Ì  Í  Î  Ï
D0:   Ð  Ñ  Ò  Ó  Ô  Õ  Ö  ×  Ø  Ù  Ú  Û  Ü  Ý  Þ  ß
E0:   à  á  â  ã  ä  å  æ  ç  è  é  ê  ë  ì  í  î  ï
F0:   ð  ñ  ò  ó  ô  õ  ö  ÷  ø  ù  ú  û  ü  ý  þ  ÿ
```

Figure 3-6. *The ANSI character set.*

An ON_WM_CHAR entry in a class's message map routes WM_CHAR messages to the member function *OnChar*, which is prototyped as follows:

```
afx_msg void OnChar (UINT nChar, UINT nRepCnt, UINT nFlags)
```

nRepCnt and *nFlags* have the same meanings that they have in keystroke messages. *nChar* holds an ANSI or Unicode character code. The following code fragment traps presses of the letter keys, the Enter key, and the Backspace key, all of which produce WM_CHAR messages:

```
// In CMainWindow's message map
ON_WM_CHAR ()
    :
    :
void CMainWindow::OnChar (UINT nChar, UINT nRepCnt, UINT nFlags)
```

(continued)

```
{
    if (((nChar >= _T ('A')) && (nChar <= _T ('Z'))) ||
        ((nChar >= _T ('a')) && (nChar <= _T ('z')))) {
        // Display the character
    }
    else if (nChar == VK_RETURN) {
        // Process the Enter key
    }
    else if (nChar == VK_BACK) {
        // Process the Backspace key
    }
}
```

If it's unclear to you whether a particular key produces a WM_CHAR message, there's an easy way to find out. Simply run the VisualKB application that comes with this book and press the key. If the key produces a WM_CHAR message, the message will appear in VisualKB's window.

Dead-Key Messages

There are two keyboard messages I didn't mention because they are rarely used by application programs. Many international keyboard drivers allow users to enter a character accented with a diacritic by typing a "dead key" representing the diacritic and then typing the character itself. *::TranslateMessage* translates WM_KEYUP messages corresponding to dead keys into WM_DEADCHAR messages, and it translates WM_SYSKEYUP messages generated by dead keys into WM_SYSDEADCHAR messages. Windows provides the logic that combines these messages with character messages to produce accented characters, so dead-key messages are usually passed on for default processing. Some applications go the extra mile by intercepting dead-key messages and displaying the corresponding diacritics. The keystroke following the dead key then replaces the diacritic with an accented character. This provides visual feedback to the user and prevents dead keys from having to be typed "blind."

You can process dead-key messages in an MFC application by including an ON_WM_DEADCHAR or ON_WM_SYSDEADCHAR entry in a message map and supplying handling functions named *OnDeadChar* and *OnSysDeadChar*. You'll find descriptions of these functions in the MFC documentation.

The Caret

The flashing vertical bar that word processors and other Windows applications use to mark the point where the next character will be inserted is called the *caret*. The caret serves the same purpose in a Windows application that the blinking underscore cursor does in a character-mode application. MFC's *CWnd* class provides the seven caret-handling functions shown below. The one essential function missing from this table, *::DestroyCaret*, must be called directly from the Windows API because there is no MFC equivalent.

CWND CARET HANDLING FUNCTIONS

Function	Description
CreateCaret	Creates a caret from a bitmap
CreateSolidCaret	Creates a solid line caret or a block caret
CreateGrayCaret	Creates a gray line caret or a block caret
GetCaretPos	Retrieves the current caret position
SetCaretPos	Sets the caret position
ShowCaret	Displays the caret
HideCaret	Hides the caret

The caret, like the mouse cursor, is a shared resource. However, unlike the cursor, which is a global resource shared by everyone, the caret is a per-thread resource that's shared by all windows running on the same thread. To ensure proper handling, applications that use the caret should follow these simple rules:

■ A window that uses the caret should "create" a caret when it receives the input focus and should "destroy" the caret when it loses the input focus. A caret is created with *CreateCaret*, *CreateSolidCaret*, or *CreateGrayCaret* and is destroyed with *::DestroyCaret*.

■ Once a caret is created, it isn't visible until *ShowCaret* is called to make it visible. The caret can be hidden again with a call to *HideCaret*. If calls to *HideCaret* are nested—that is, if *HideCaret* is called twice or more in succession—*ShowCaret* must be called an equal number of times to make the caret visible again.

■ When you draw in the area of a window that contains the caret outside an *OnPaint* handler, you should hide the caret to avoid corrupting the display. You can redisplay the caret after drawing is complete. You don't need to hide and redisplay the caret in an *OnPaint* handler because *::BeginPaint* and *::EndPaint* do that for you.

■ A program moves the caret by calling *SetCaretPos*. Windows doesn't move the caret for you; it's your program's job to process incoming keyboard messages (and perhaps mouse messages) and manipulate the caret accordingly. *GetCaretPos* can be called to retrieve the caret's current position.

As you know, a window receives a WM_SETFOCUS message when it receives the input focus and a WM_KILLFOCUS message when it loses the input focus. The following WM_SETFOCUS handler creates a caret, positions it, and displays it when a window gains the input focus:

```
void CMainWindow::OnSetFocus (CWnd* pWnd)
{
    CreateSolidCaret (2, m_cyChar);
    SetCaretPos (m_ptCaretPos);
    ShowCaret ();
}
```

And this WM_KILLFOCUS handler saves the caret position and hides and destroys the caret when the input focus is lost:

```
void CMainWindow::OnKillFocus (CWnd* pWnd)
{
    HideCaret ();
    m_ptCaretPos = GetCaretPos ();
    ::DestroyCaret ();
}
```

In these examples, *m_cyChar* holds the caret height and *m_ptCaretPos* holds the caret position. The caret position is saved when the focus is lost, and it is restored when the focus is regained. Since only one window can have the input focus at a time and keyboard messages are directed to the window with the input focus, this approach to caret handling ensures that the window that "owns" the keyboard also owns the caret.

The caret-create functions serve two purposes: defining the look of the caret and claiming ownership of the caret. The caret is actually a bitmap, so you can customize its appearance by supplying a bitmap to *CWnd::CreateCaret*. But more often than not you'll find that the easier-to-use *CreateSolidCaret* function (it's easier to use because it doesn't require a bitmap) does the job nicely. *CreateSolidCaret* creates a solid block caret that, depending on how you shape it, can look like a rectangle, a horizontal or vertical line, or something in between. In the *OnSetFocus* example above, the statement

```
CreateSolidCaret (2, m_cyChar);
```

creates a vertical-line caret 2 pixels wide whose height equals the character height of the current font (*m_cyChar*). This is the traditional way of creating a caret for use with a proportional font, although some programs key the width of the caret to the width of a window border. You can obtain the border width by calling *::GetSystem-Metrics* with the value SM_CXBORDER. For fixed-pitch fonts, you might prefer to use a block caret whose width and height equal the width and height of one character, as in

```
CreateSolidCaret (m_cxChar, m_cyChar);
```

A block caret doesn't make sense for a proportionally spaced font because of the varying character widths. *CWnd*'s *CreateGrayCaret* function works just as *CreateSolidCaret* does except that it creates a gray caret rather than a solid black caret. Caret dimensions are expressed in logical units, so if you change the mapping mode before creating a caret, the dimensions you specify will be transformed accordingly.

As mentioned above, it's your job to move the caret. *CWnd::SetCaretPos* repositions the caret, accepting a *CPoint* object that contains the *x* and *y* client-area coordinates of the new cursor position. Positioning the caret in a string of text is fairly straightforward if you're using a fixed-pitch font because you can calculate a new *x* offset into the string by multiplying the character position by the character width. If the font is proportionally spaced, you'll have to do a little more work. MFC's *CDC::GetTextExtent* and *CDC::GetTabbedTextExtent* functions enable an application to determine the width, in logical units, of a string of characters rendered in a proportional font. (Use *GetTabbedTextExtent* if the string contains tab characters.) Given a character position *n*, you can compute the corresponding caret position by calling *GetTextExtent* or *GetTabbedTextExtent* to find the cumulative width of the first *n* characters. If the string "Hello, world" is displayed at the position specified by a *CPoint* object named *point* and *dc* is a device context object, the following statements position the caret between the "w" and "o" in "world":

```
CSize size = dc.GetTextExtent (_T ("Hello, w"), 8);
SetCaretPos (CPoint (point.x + size.cx, point.y));
```

GetTextExtent returns a *CSize* object whose *cx* and *cy* members reflect the string's width and height.

Caret positioning gets slightly more complicated if you're using a proportional font and don't have a character offset to work with, which is exactly the situation you'll find yourself in when you write an *OnLButtonDown* handler that repositions the caret when the left mouse button is clicked. Suppose your application maintains a variable named *m_nCurrentPos* that denotes the current character position—the position within a string at which the next typed character will be inserted. It's easy to calculate the new caret position when the left or right arrow key is pressed: You just decrement or increment *m_nCurrentPos* and call *GetTextExtent* or *GetTabbedText-Extent* with the new character position to compute a new offset. But what if the left mouse button is clicked at some arbitrary location in the string? There is no relationship between where the mouse click occurred and *m_nCurrentPos*, so you must use the horizontal difference between the cursor position and the beginning of the string to work backward to a character position, and *then* calculate the final caret position. This inevitably involves some iteration since there is neither a Windows API function nor an MFC class member function that accepts a string and a pixel offset and returns the character at that offset. Fortunately, it's not terribly difficult to write that function yourself. You'll see how it's done in the next section.

The VisualKB Application

Let's put together everything we've learned in this chapter by developing a sample application that accepts text input from the keyboard, displays the text in a window, and lets the user perform simple text-editing functions that include moving the caret with the arrow keys and the mouse. For educational purposes, let's add a scrolling display of the keyboard messages that the program receives and the parameters bundled with those messages, similar to the KEYLOOK program featured in Charles Petzold's *Programming Windows*. In addition to providing a hands-on lesson in mouse and keyboard handling, the program, which I've called VisualKB, demonstrates some techniques for handling proportionally spaced text. VisualKB also provides a handy tool for examining the stream of messages coming from the keyboard and experimenting to see what messages result from specific keystrokes and key combinations.

Figure 3-7 shows how VisualKB looks right after it's started and the letters "MFC" are typed. The typed characters appear in the text-entry rectangle (the "text box") at the top of the window, and keyboard messages are displayed in the rectangle below (the "message list"). The first and final messages were generated when the Shift key was pressed and released. In between, you see the WM_KEYDOWN, WM_CHAR, and WM_KEYUP messages generated by the M, F, and C keystrokes. To the right of each message name, VisualKB displays the message parameters. "Char" is the virtual key code or character code passed to the message handler in *nChar*. "Rep" is the repeat count in *nRepCnt*. "Scan" is the OEM scan code stored in bits 0 through 7 of the *nFlags* parameter, and "Ext," "Con," "Prv," and "Tran" represent the extended key flag, context code, previous key state, and transition state values. VisualKB also displays WM_SYSKEYDOWN, WM_SYSCHAR, and WM_SYSKEYUP messages, which you can verify by pressing an Alt key combination such as Alt-S.

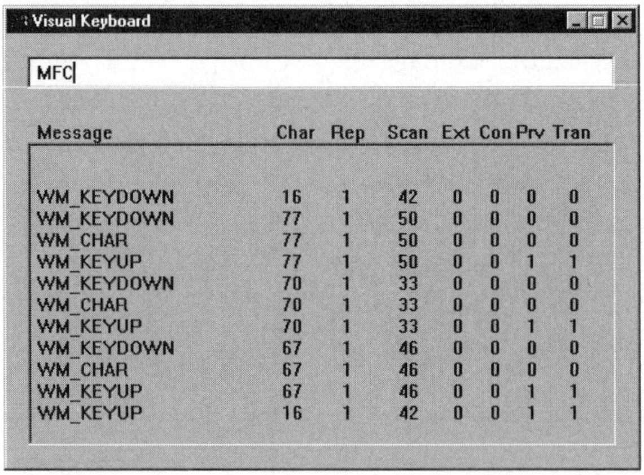

Figure 3-7. *The VisualKB window after the letters MFC are typed.*

Take a moment to play with VisualKB and see what happens when you press various keys and combinations of keys. In addition to typing in text, you can use the following editing keys:

- The left and right arrow keys move the caret one character to the left and right. Home and End move the caret to the beginning and end of the line. The caret can also be moved with mouse clicks.

- The Backspace key deletes the character to the left of the caret and moves the caret one position to the left.

- The Esc and Enter keys clear the text and reset the caret to the beginning of the line.

Typed characters are entered in overstrike mode, so if the caret isn't at the end of the line, the next character you type will replace the character to the right. If you type beyond the end of the line (about one character position to the left of the far right end of the text box), the text is automatically cleared. I resisted the urge to add features such as horizontal scrolling and insert mode to keep the program from becoming unnecessarily complicated. Besides, in the real world you can avoid writing a lot of the code for a program like this one by using an edit control, which provides similar text-entry capabilities and includes support for cutting and pasting, scrolling, and much more. Unless you're writing the world's next great word processor, an edit control probably has everything you need. Still, it's useful to see how text entry is done the hard way, not only because it's instructive but also because you'll get a feel for what's happening inside Windows when you start using edit controls.

There is much to be learned from VisualKB's source code, which is reproduced in Figure 3-8. The following sections point out a few of the highlights.

VisualKB.h

```
#define MAX_STRINGS 12

class CMyApp : public CWinApp
{
public:
    virtual BOOL InitInstance ();
};
```

Figure 3-8. *The VisualKB application.*

(continued)

Figure 3-8. *continued*

```
class CMainWindow : public CWnd
{
protected:
    int m_cxChar;                   // Average character width
    int m_cyChar;                   // Character height
    int m_cyLine;                   // Vertical line spacing in message box
    int m_nTextPos;                 // Index of current character in text box
    int m_nTabStops[7];             // Tab stop locations for tabbed output
    int m_nTextLimit;               // Maximum width of text in text box
    int m_nMsgPos;                  // Current position in m_strMessages array

    HCURSOR m_hCursorArrow;         // Handle of arrow cursor
    HCURSOR m_hCursorIBeam;         // Handle of I-beam cursor

    CPoint m_ptTextOrigin;          // Origin for drawing input text
    CPoint m_ptHeaderOrigin;        // Origin for drawing header text
    CPoint m_ptUpperMsgOrigin;      // Origin of first line in message box
    CPoint m_ptLowerMsgOrigin;      // Origin of last line in message box
    CPoint m_ptCaretPos;            // Current caret position

    CRect m_rcTextBox;              // Coordinates of text box
    CRect m_rcTextBoxBorder;        // Coordinates of text box border
    CRect m_rcMsgBoxBorder;         // Coordinates of message box border
    CRect m_rcScroll;               // Coordinates of scroll rectangle

    CString m_strInputText;                    // Input text
    CString m_strMessages[MAX_STRINGS];        // Array of message strings

public:
    CMainWindow ();

protected:
    int GetNearestPos (CPoint point);
    void PositionCaret (CDC* pDC = NULL);
    void DrawInputText (CDC* pDC);
    void ShowMessage (LPCTSTR pszMessage, UINT nChar, UINT nRepCnt,
        UINT nFlags);
    void DrawMessageHeader (CDC* pDC);
    void DrawMessages (CDC* pDC);

protected:
    virtual void PostNcDestroy ();

    afx_msg int OnCreate (LPCREATESTRUCT lpCreateStruct);
    afx_msg void OnPaint ();
    afx_msg void OnSetFocus (CWnd* pWnd);
```

```
    afx_msg void OnKillFocus (CWnd* pWnd);
    afx_msg BOOL OnSetCursor (CWnd* pWnd, UINT nHitTest, UINT message);
    afx_msg void OnLButtonDown (UINT nFlags, CPoint point);
    afx_msg void OnKeyDown (UINT nChar, UINT nRepCnt, UINT nFlags);
    afx_msg void OnKeyUp (UINT nChar, UINT nRepCnt, UINT nFlags);
    afx_msg void OnSysKeyDown (UINT nChar, UINT nRepCnt, UINT nFlags);
    afx_msg void OnSysKeyUp (UINT nChar, UINT nRepCnt, UINT nFlags);
    afx_msg void OnChar (UINT nChar, UINT nRepCnt, UINT nFlags);
    afx_msg void OnSysChar (UINT nChar, UINT nRepCnt, UINT nFlags);

    DECLARE_MESSAGE_MAP ()
};
```

VisualKB.cpp

```
#include <afxwin.h>
#include "VisualKB.h"

CMyApp myApp;

///////////////////////////////////////////////////////////////////////
// CMyApp member functions

BOOL CMyApp::InitInstance ()
{
    m_pMainWnd = new CMainWindow;
    m_pMainWnd->ShowWindow (m_nCmdShow);
    m_pMainWnd->UpdateWindow ();
    return TRUE;
}

///////////////////////////////////////////////////////////////////////
// CMainWindow message map and member functions

BEGIN_MESSAGE_MAP (CMainWindow, CWnd)
    ON_WM_CREATE ()
    ON_WM_PAINT ()
    ON_WM_SETFOCUS ()
    ON_WM_KILLFOCUS ()
    ON_WM_SETCURSOR ()
    ON_WM_LBUTTONDOWN ()
    ON_WM_KEYDOWN ()
    ON_WM_KEYUP ()
    ON_WM_SYSKEYDOWN ()
```

(continued)

Figure 3-8. *continued*

```
    ON_WM_SYSKEYUP ()
    ON_WM_CHAR ()
    ON_WM_SYSCHAR ()
END_MESSAGE_MAP ()

CMainWindow::CMainWindow ()
{
    m_nTextPos = 0;
    m_nMsgPos = 0;

    //
    // Load the arrow cursor and the I-beam cursor and save their handles.
    //
    m_hCursorArrow = AfxGetApp ()->LoadStandardCursor (IDC_ARROW);
    m_hCursorIBeam = AfxGetApp ()->LoadStandardCursor (IDC_IBEAM);

    //
    // Register a WNDCLASS.
    //
    CString strWndClass = AfxRegisterWndClass (
        0,
        NULL,
        (HBRUSH) (COLOR_3DFACE + 1),
        AfxGetApp ()->LoadStandardIcon (IDI_WINLOGO)
    );

    //
    // Create a window.
    //
    CreateEx (0, strWndClass, _T ("Visual Keyboard"),
        WS_OVERLAPPED | WS_SYSMENU | WS_CAPTION | WS_MINIMIZEBOX,
        CW_USEDEFAULT, CW_USEDEFAULT, CW_USEDEFAULT, CW_USEDEFAULT,
        NULL, NULL);
}

int CMainWindow::OnCreate (LPCREATESTRUCT lpCreateStruct)
{
    if (CWnd::OnCreate (lpCreateStruct) == -1)
        return -1;

    //
    // Initialize member variables whose values are dependent upon screen
    // metrics.
    //
    CClientDC dc (this);
```

```
TEXTMETRIC tm;
dc.GetTextMetrics (&tm);
m_cxChar = tm.tmAveCharWidth;
m_cyChar = tm.tmHeight;
m_cyLine = tm.tmHeight + tm.tmExternalLeading;

m_rcTextBoxBorder.SetRect (16, 16, (m_cxChar * 64) + 16,
    ((m_cyChar * 3) / 2) + 16);

m_rcTextBox = m_rcTextBoxBorder;
m_rcTextBox.InflateRect (-2, -2);

m_rcMsgBoxBorder.SetRect (16, (m_cyChar * 4) + 16,
    (m_cxChar * 64) + 16, (m_cyLine * MAX_STRINGS) +
    (m_cyChar * 6) + 16);

m_rcScroll.SetRect (m_cxChar + 16, (m_cyChar * 6) + 16,
    (m_cxChar * 63) + 16, (m_cyLine * MAX_STRINGS) +
    (m_cyChar * 5) + 16);

m_ptTextOrigin.x = m_cxChar + 16;
m_ptTextOrigin.y = (m_cyChar / 4) + 16;
m_ptCaretPos = m_ptTextOrigin;
m_nTextLimit = (m_cxChar * 63) + 16;

m_ptHeaderOrigin.x = m_cxChar + 16;
m_ptHeaderOrigin.y = (m_cyChar * 3) + 16;

m_ptUpperMsgOrigin.x = m_cxChar + 16;
m_ptUpperMsgOrigin.y = (m_cyChar * 5) + 16;

m_ptLowerMsgOrigin.x = m_cxChar + 16;
m_ptLowerMsgOrigin.y = (m_cyChar * 5) +
    (m_cyLine * (MAX_STRINGS - 1)) + 16;

m_nTabStops[0] = (m_cxChar * 24) + 16;
m_nTabStops[1] = (m_cxChar * 30) + 16;
m_nTabStops[2] = (m_cxChar * 36) + 16;
m_nTabStops[3] = (m_cxChar * 42) + 16;
m_nTabStops[4] = (m_cxChar * 46) + 16;
m_nTabStops[5] = (m_cxChar * 50) + 16;
m_nTabStops[6] = (m_cxChar * 54) + 16;

//
// Size the window.
//
```

(continued)

Figure 3-8. *continued*

```
    CRect rect (0, 0, m_rcMsgBoxBorder.right + 16,
        m_rcMsgBoxBorder.bottom + 16);
    CalcWindowRect (&rect);

    SetWindowPos (NULL, 0, 0, rect.Width (), rect.Height (),
        SWP_NOZORDER | SWP_NOMOVE | SWP_NOREDRAW);
    return 0;
}

void CMainWindow::PostNcDestroy ()
{
    delete this;
}

void CMainWindow::OnPaint ()
{
    CPaintDC dc (this);

    //
    // Draw the rectangles surrounding the text box and the message list.
    //
    dc.DrawEdge (m_rcTextBoxBorder, EDGE_SUNKEN, BF_RECT);
    dc.DrawEdge (m_rcMsgBoxBorder, EDGE_SUNKEN, BF_RECT);

    //
    // Draw all the text that appears in the window.
    //
    DrawInputText (&dc);
    DrawMessageHeader (&dc);
    DrawMessages (&dc);
}

void CMainWindow::OnSetFocus (CWnd* pWnd)
{
    //
    // Show the caret when the VisualKB window receives the input focus.
    //
    CreateSolidCaret (max (2, ::GetSystemMetrics (SM_CXBORDER)),
        m_cyChar);
    SetCaretPos (m_ptCaretPos);
    ShowCaret ();
}

void CMainWindow::OnKillFocus (CWnd* pWnd)
{
```

```
    //
    // Hide the caret when the VisualKB window loses the input focus.
    //
    HideCaret ();
    m_ptCaretPos = GetCaretPos ();
    ::DestroyCaret ();
}

BOOL CMainWindow::OnSetCursor (CWnd* pWnd, UINT nHitTest, UINT message)
{
    //
    // Change the cursor to an I-beam if it's currently over the text box,
    // or to an arrow if it's positioned anywhere else.
    //
    if (nHitTest == HTCLIENT) {
        DWORD dwPos = ::GetMessagePos ();
        CPoint point (LOWORD (dwPos), HIWORD (dwPos));
        ScreenToClient (&point);
        ::SetCursor (m_rcTextBox.PtInRect (point) ?
            m_hCursorIBeam : m_hCursorArrow);
        return TRUE;
    }
    return CWnd::OnSetCursor (pWnd, nHitTest, message);
}

void CMainWindow::OnLButtonDown (UINT nFlags, CPoint point)

{
    //
    / Move the caret if the text box is clicked with the left mouse button.
    //
    if (m_rcTextBox.PtInRect (point)) {
        m_nTextPos = GetNearestPos (point);
        PositionCaret ();
    }
}

void CMainWindow::OnKeyDown (UINT nChar, UINT nRepCnt, UINT nFlags)
{
    ShowMessage (_T ("WM_KEYDOWN"), nChar, nRepCnt, nFlags);

    //
    // Move the caret when the left, right, Home, or End key is pressed.
    //
    switch (nChar) {
```

(continued)

Figure 3-8. *continued*

```
    case VK_LEFT:
        if (m_nTextPos != 0) {
            m_nTextPos--;
            PositionCaret ();
        }
        break;

    case VK_RIGHT:
        if (m_nTextPos != m_strInputText.GetLength ()) {
            m_nTextPos++;
            PositionCaret ();
        }
        break;

    case VK_HOME:
        m_nTextPos = 0;
        PositionCaret ();
        break;

    case VK_END:
        m_nTextPos = m_strInputText.GetLength ();
        PositionCaret ();
        break;
    }
}

void CMainWindow::OnChar (UINT nChar, UINT nRepCnt, UINT nFlags)
{
    ShowMessage (_T ("WM_CHAR"), nChar, nRepCnt, nFlags);

    CClientDC dc (this);

    //
    // Determine which character was just input from the keyboard.
    //
    switch (nChar) {

    case VK_ESCAPE:
    case VK_RETURN:
        m_strInputText.Empty ();
        m_nTextPos = 0;
        break;

    case VK_BACK:
        if (m_nTextPos != 0) {
            m_strInputText = m_strInputText.Left (m_nTextPos - 1) +
```

```
                    m_strInputText.Right (m_strInputText.GetLength () -
                        m_nTextPos);
                    m_nTextPos--;
            }
            break;

        default:
            if ((nChar >= 0) && (nChar <= 31))
                return;

            if (m_nTextPos == m_strInputText.GetLength ()) {
                m_strInputText += nChar;
                m_nTextPos++;
            }
            else
                m_strInputText.SetAt (m_nTextPos++, nChar);

            CSize size = dc.GetTextExtent (m_strInputText,
                m_strInputText.GetLength ());

            if ((m_ptTextOrigin.x + size.cx) > m_nTextLimit) {
                m_strInputText = nChar;
                m_nTextPos = 1;
            }
            break;
    }

    //
    // Update the contents of the text box.
    //
    HideCaret ();
    DrawInputText (&dc);
    PositionCaret (&dc);
    ShowCaret ();
}

void CMainWindow::OnKeyUp (UINT nChar, UINT nRepCnt, UINT nFlags)
{
    ShowMessage (_T ("WM_KEYUP"), nChar, nRepCnt, nFlags);
    CWnd::OnKeyUp (nChar, nRepCnt, nFlags);
}

void CMainWindow::OnSysKeyDown (UINT nChar, UINT nRepCnt, UINT nFlags)
{
    ShowMessage (_T ("WM_SYSKEYDOWN"), nChar, nRepCnt, nFlags);
    CWnd::OnSysKeyDown (nChar, nRepCnt, nFlags);
}
```

(continued)

Figure 3-8. *continued*

```
void CMainWindow::OnSysChar (UINT nChar, UINT nRepCnt, UINT nFlags)
{
    ShowMessage (_T ("WM_SYSCHAR"), nChar, nRepCnt, nFlags);
    CWnd::OnSysChar (nChar, nRepCnt, nFlags);
}

void CMainWindow::OnSysKeyUp (UINT nChar, UINT nRepCnt, UINT nFlags)
{
    ShowMessage (_T ("WM_SYSKEYUP"), nChar, nRepCnt, nFlags);
    CWnd::OnSysKeyUp (nChar, nRepCnt, nFlags);
}

void CMainWindow::PositionCaret (CDC* pDC)
{
    BOOL bRelease = FALSE;

    //
    // Create a device context if pDC is NULL.
    //
    if (pDC == NULL) {
        pDC = GetDC ();
        bRelease = TRUE;
    }

    //
    // Position the caret just right of the character whose 0-based
    // index is stored in m_nTextPos.
    //
    CPoint point = m_ptTextOrigin;
    CString string = m_strInputText.Left (m_nTextPos);
    point.x += (pDC->GetTextExtent (string, string.GetLength ())).cx;
    SetCaretPos (point);

    //
    // Release the device context if it was created inside this function.
    //
    if (bRelease)
        ReleaseDC (pDC);
}

int CMainWindow::GetNearestPos (CPoint point)
{
    //
    // Return 0 if (point.x, point.y) lies to the left of the text in
    // the text box.
```

```
    //
    if (point.x <= m_ptTextOrigin.x)
        return 0;

    //
    // Return the string length if (point.x, point.y) lies to the right
    // of the text in the text box.
    //
    CClientDC dc (this);
    int nLen = m_strInputText.GetLength ();
    if (point.x >= (m_ptTextOrigin.x +
        (dc.GetTextExtent (m_strInputText, nLen)).cx))
        return nLen;

    //
    // Knowing that (point.x, point.y) lies somewhere within the text
    // in the text box, convert the coordinates into a character index.
    //
    int i = 0;
    int nPrevChar = m_ptTextOrigin.x;
    int nNextChar = m_ptTextOrigin.x;

    while (nNextChar < point.x) {
        i++;
        nPrevChar = nNextChar;
        nNextChar = m_ptTextOrigin.x +
            (dc.GetTextExtent (m_strInputText.Left (i), i)).cx;
    }
    return ((point.x - nPrevChar) < (nNextChar - point.x)) ? i - 1: i;
}

void CMainWindow::DrawInputText (CDC* pDC)
{
    pDC->ExtTextOut (m_ptTextOrigin.x, m_ptTextOrigin.y,
        ETO_OPAQUE, m_rcTextBox, m_strInputText, NULL);
}

void CMainWindow::ShowMessage (LPCTSTR pszMessage, UINT nChar,
    UINT nRepCnt, UINT nFlags)
{
    //
    // Formulate a message string.
    //
    CString string;
    string.Format (_T ("%s\t %u\t  %u\t  %u\t  %u\t  %u\t  %u\t   %u"),
        pszMessage, nChar, nRepCnt, nFlags & 0xFF,
        (nFlags >> 8) & 0x01,
```

(continued)

Figure 3-8. *continued*

```
        (nFlags >> 13) & 0x01,
        (nFlags >> 14) & 0x01,
        (nFlags >> 15) & 0x01);

    //
    // Scroll the other message strings up and validate the scroll
    // rectangle to prevent OnPaint from being called.
    //
    ScrollWindow (0, -m_cyLine, &m_rcScroll);
    ValidateRect (m_rcScroll);

    //
    // Record the new message string and display it in the window.
    //
    CClientDC dc (this);
    dc.SetBkColor ((COLORREF) ::GetSysColor (COLOR_3DFACE));

    m_strMessages[m_nMsgPos] = string;
    dc.TabbedTextOut (m_ptLowerMsgOrigin.x, m_ptLowerMsgOrigin.y,
        m_strMessages[m_nMsgPos], m_strMessages[m_nMsgPos].GetLength (),
        sizeof (m_nTabStops), m_nTabStops, m_ptLowerMsgOrigin.x);

    //
    // Update the array index that specifies where the next message
    // string will be stored.
    //
    if (++m_nMsgPos == MAX_STRINGS)
        m_nMsgPos = 0;
}

void CMainWindow::DrawMessageHeader (CDC* pDC)
{
    static CString string =
        _T ("Message\tChar\tRep\tScan\tExt\tCon\tPrv\tTran");

    pDC->SetBkColor ((COLORREF) ::GetSysColor (COLOR_3DFACE));
    pDC->TabbedTextOut (m_ptHeaderOrigin.x, m_ptHeaderOrigin.y,
        string, string.GetLength (), sizeof (m_nTabStops), m_nTabStops,
        m_ptHeaderOrigin.x);
}

void CMainWindow::DrawMessages (CDC* pDC)
{
    int nPos = m_nMsgPos;
    pDC->SetBkColor ((COLORREF) ::GetSysColor (COLOR_3DFACE));
```

```
    for (int i=0; i<MAX_STRINGS; i++) {
        pDC->TabbedTextOut (m_ptUpperMsgOrigin.x,
            m_ptUpperMsgOrigin.y + (m_cyLine * i),
            m_strMessages[nPos], m_strMessages[nPos].GetLength (),
            sizeof (m_nTabStops), m_nTabStops, m_ptUpperMsgOrigin.x);

        if (++nPos == MAX_STRINGS)
            nPos = 0;
    }
}
```

Handling the Caret

CMainWindow's *OnSetFocus* and *OnKillFocus* handlers create a caret when the VisualKB window receives the input focus and destroy the caret when the focus goes away. *OnSetFocus* sets the caret width to 2 or the SM_CXBORDER value returned by *::GetSystemMetrics*, whichever is greater, so that the caret is visible even on very high resolution displays:

```
void CMainWindow::OnSetFocus (CWnd* pWnd)
{
    CreateSolidCaret (max (2, ::GetSystemMetrics (SM_CXBORDER)),
        m_cyChar);
    SetCaretPos (m_ptCaretPos);
    ShowCaret ();
}
```

OnKillFocus hides the caret, saves the current caret position so that it can be restored the next time *OnSetFocus* is called, and then destroys the caret:

```
void CMainWindow::OnKillFocus (CWnd* pWnd)
{
    HideCaret ();
    m_ptCaretPos = GetCaretPos ();
    ::DestroyCaret ();
}
```

m_ptCaretPos is initialized with the coordinates of the leftmost character cell in *CMainWindow::OnCreate*. It is reinitialized with the current caret position whenever the window loses the input focus. Therefore, the call to *SetCaretPos* in *OnSetFocus* sets the caret to the beginning of the text box when the program is first activated and restores the caret to the position it previously occupied in subsequent invocations.

The *OnKeyDown* handler moves the caret when the left arrow, right arrow, Home key, or End key is pressed. None of these keys generates WM_CHAR messages, so VisualKB processes WM_KEYDOWN messages instead. A *switch-case* block executes the appropriate handling routine based on the virtual key code in *nChar*. The handler for the left arrow key (whose virtual key code is VK_LEFT) consists of the following statements:

```
case VK_LEFT:
    if (m_nTextPos != 0) {
        m_nTextPos--;
        PositionCaret ();
    }
    break;
```

m_nTextPos is the position at which the next character will be inserted into the text string. The text string itself is stored in the *CString* object *m_strInputText*. *Position-Caret* is a protected *CMainWindow* member function that uses *GetTextExtent* to find the pixel position in the text string that corresponds to the character position stored in *m_nTextPos* and then moves the caret to that position with *SetCaretPos*. After checking *m_nTextPos* to make sure it hasn't run out of room to move the caret further left, the VK_LEFT handler decrements *m_nTextPos* and calls *PositionCaret* to move the caret. If *m_nTextPos* is 0, which indicates that the caret is already positioned at the left end of the entry field, the keystroke is ignored. The other VK_ handlers are similarly straightforward. The VK_END handler, for example, moves the caret to the end of the text string with the statements

```
m_nTextPos = m_strInputText.GetLength ();
PositionCaret ();
```

GetLength is a *CString* member function that returns the number of characters in the string. The use of a *CString* object to hold the text entered into VisualKB makes text handling much simpler than it would be if strings were handled simply as arrays of characters. For example, all the *OnChar* handler has to do to add a new character to the end of the string is

```
m_strInputText += nChar;
```

When it comes to string handling, it doesn't get much easier than that. Browse through VisualKB.cpp and you'll see several *CString* member functions and operators, including *CString::Left*, which returns a *CString* object containing the string's left *n* characters; *CString::Right*, which returns the rightmost *n* characters; and *CString::Format*, which performs *printf*-like string formatting.

It seemed a shame not to have VisualKB do anything with the mouse when half of this chapter is devoted to mouse input, so I added an *OnLButtonDown* handler, which allows the caret to be moved with a click of the left mouse button in the text box. In addition to adding a nice feature to the program, the *OnLButtonDown* handler also lets us examine a function that takes the point at which a mouse click occurred and returns the corresponding character position within a text string. The button handler itself is exceedingly simple:

```
void CMainWindow::OnLButtonDown (UINT nFlags, CPoint point)
{
    if (m_rcTextBox.PtInRect (point)) {
        m_nTextPos = GetNearestPos (point);
        PositionCaret ();
    }
}
```

m_rcTextBox is the rectangle that bounds the text box. After calling *CRect::PtInRect* to determine whether the click occurred inside the rectangle (and returning without doing anything if it didn't), *OnLButtonDown* computes a new value for *m_nTextPos* with *CMainWindow::GetNearestPos* and calls *PositionCaret* to reposition the caret. *GetNearestPos* first checks to see if the mouse was clicked to the left of the character string and returns 0 for the new character position if it was:

```
if (point.x <= m_ptTextOrigin.x)
    return 0;
```

m_ptTextOrigin holds the coordinates of the character string's upper left corner. *GetNearestPos* then returns an integer value that equals the string length if the mouse was clicked beyond the string's rightmost extent:

```
CClientDC dc (this);
int nLen = m_strInputText.GetLength ();
if (point.x >= (m_ptTextOrigin.x +
    (dc.GetTextExtent (m_strInputText, nLen)).cx))
    return nLen;
```

The result? If the mouse was clicked inside the text rectangle but to the right of the rightmost character, the caret is moved to the end of the string.

If *GetNearestPos* makes it beyond the *return nLen* statement, we can conclude that the cursor was clicked inside the text box somewhere between the character string's left and right extents. *GetNearestPos* next initializes three variables and executes a *while* loop that calls *GetTextExtent* repeatedly until *nPrevChar* and *nNextChar* hold values that bracket the *x* coordinate of the point at which the click occurred:

```
while (nNextChar < point.x) {
    i++;
    nPrevChar = nNextChar;
    nNextChar = m_ptTextOrigin.x +
        (dc.GetTextExtent (m_strInputText.Left (i), i)).cx;
}
```

When the loop falls through, *i* holds the number of the character position to the right of where the click occurred, and *i*-1 identifies the character position to the left. Finding the character position is a simple matter of finding out whether *point.x* is closer to *nNextChar* or *nPrevChar* and returning *i* or *i-1*. This is accomplished with the following one-liner:

```
return ((point.x - nPrevChar) < (nNextChar - point.x)) ? i - 1: i;
```

That's it; given an arbitrary point in the window's client area, *GetNearestPos* returns a matching character position in the string *m_strInputText*. A small amount of inefficiency is built into this process because the farther to the right the point lies, the more times *GetTextExtent* is called. (The *while* loop starts with the leftmost character in the string and moves right one character at a time until it finds the character just to the right of the point at which the click occurred.) A really smart implementation of *GetNearestPos* could do better by using a binary-halving approach, starting in the middle of the string and iterating to the left or right by a number of characters equal to half the area that hasn't already been covered until it zeroes in on the characters to the left and right of the point at which the click occurred. A character position in a string 128 characters long could then be located with no more than 8 calls to *GetTextExtent*. The brute force technique employed by *GetNearestPos* could require as many as 127 calls.

Entering and Editing Text

The logic for entering and editing text is found in *CMainWindow::OnChar*. *OnChar*'s processing strategy can be summarized in this way:

1. Echo the message to the screen.

2. Modify the text string using the character code in *nChar*.

3. Draw the modified text string on the screen.

4. Reposition the caret.

Step 1 is accomplished by calling *CMainWindow::ShowMessage*, which is discussed in the next section. How the text string is modified in step 2 depends on what the character code in *nChar* is. If the character is an escape or a return (VK_ESCAPE or VK_RETURN), *m_strInputText* is cleared by a call to *CString::Empty* (another handy member of the *CString* class) and *m_nTextPos* is set to 0. If the character is a backspace (VK_BACK) and *m_nTextPos* isn't 0, the character at *m_nTextPos-1* is deleted and *m_nTextPos* is decremented. If the character is any other value between 0 and 31, inclusive, it is ignored. If *nChar* represents any other character, it is added to *m_strInputText* at the current character position and *m_nTextPos* is incremented accordingly.

With the character that was just entered now added to *m_strInputText*, *OnChar* hides the caret and proceeds to step 3. The modified string is output to the screen with *CMainWindow::DrawInputText*, which in turn relies on *CDC::ExtTextOut* to do its text output. *ExtTextOut* is similar to *TextOut*, but it offers a few options that *TextOut* doesn't. One of those options is an ETO_OPAQUE flag that fills a rectangle surrounding the text with the device context's current background color. Repainting the entire rectangle erases artifacts left over from the previous text-output operation if the string's new width is less than its previous width. The border around the text box (and the border around the message list) is drawn with the *CDC::DrawEdge* function, which calls through to the *::DrawEdge* API function. *DrawEdge* is the easy way to draw 3D borders that conform to the specifications prescribed in the Windows interface guidelines and that automatically adapt to changes in the system colors used for highlights and shadows. You can use a related *CDC* function, *Draw3dRect*, to draw simple 3D rectangles in your choice of colors.

    OnChar finishes up by calling *PositionCaret* to reposition the caret using the value in *m_nTextPos* and then *ShowCaret* to redisplay the caret. As an experiment, comment out *OnChar*'s calls to *HideCaret* and *ShowCaret*, recompile the program, and type a few characters into the text-entry field. This simple exercise will make clear why it's important to hide the caret before painting text behind it.

Other Points of Interest

As you move the cursor around inside the VisualKB window, notice that it changes from an arrow when it's outside the text box to an I-beam when it's inside. *CMainWindow*'s constructor registers a WNDCLASS with a NULL class cursor and stores the handles for the system's arrow and I-beam cursors in the member variables *m_hCursorArrow* and *m_hCursorIBeam*. Each time *CMainWindow* receives a WM_SET-CURSOR message, its *OnSetCursor* handler checks the current cursor location and calls *::SetCursor* to display the appropriate cursor.

    VisualKB echoes keyboard messages to the screen by calling *CMainWindow::ShowMessage* each time a message is received. *ShowMessage* formulates a new output string with help from *CString::Format*, copies the result to the least recently used entry in the *m_strMessages* array, scrolls the message list up one line, and calls *CDC::TabbedTextOut* to display the new message string on the bottom line. *Tabbed-TextOut* is used in lieu of *TextOut* so that columns will be properly aligned in the output. (Without tab characters, it's virtually impossible to get characters in a proportionally spaced font to line up in columnar format.) The tab stop settings are initialized in *OnCreate* using values based on the default font's average character width and stored in the *m_nTabStops* array. Message strings are saved in the *m_strMessages* array so the *OnPaint* handler can repaint the message display when necessary. The *CMainWindow* data member *m_nMsgPos* marks the current position in the array—the index of the array element that the next string will be copied to. *m_nMsgPos* is incremented each time *ShowMessage* is called and wrapped around to 0 when it reaches the array limit so that *m_strMessages* can maintain a record of the last 12 keyboard messages received.

VisualKB's *CMainWindow* class includes *OnKeyUp*, *OnSysKeyDown*, *OnSysKeyUp*, and *OnSysChar* handlers whose only purpose is to echo keyboard messages to the screen. Each message handler is careful to call the corresponding message handler in the base class before returning, as shown here:

```
void CMainWindow::OnSysKeyDown (UINT nChar, UINT nRepCnt, UINT nFlags)
{
        :
        :

    CWnd::OnSysKeyDown (nChar, nRepCnt, nFlags);
}
```

Nonclient-area mouse messages and system keyboard messages are frequently catalysts for other messages, so it's important to forward them to the base class to permit default processing to take place.

Chapter 4

Menus

Up to now, the programs we've developed have lacked an important feature found in nearly every Microsoft Windows application: a menu. It's time to remedy that omission by learning how to incorporate menus into our code.

Drop-down menus may be the most widely recognized user interface element in the world. Nearly everyone who sits down in front of a computer and sees a menu knows that clicking an item in the menu bar displays a drop-down list of commands. Even novice computer users quickly catch on once they see menus demonstrated a time or two. Many computer users remember what it was like to use a new MS-DOS application—learning unintuitive key combinations and memorizing obscure commands to carry out basic tasks. Menus, which sprang out of research at Xerox's famed Palo Alto Research Center (PARC) in the 1970s and were popularized by the Apple Macintosh in the 1980s, make computers vastly more approachable by making concise lists of commands readily available and allowing users to select those commands through the simple act of pointing and clicking. Menus aren't required in Windows programs, but they contribute to ease of use. The more complicated the program and its command structure, the more likely it is to benefit from a menu-based user interface.

Because menus are such an important part of the user interface, Windows provides a great deal of support to applications that use them. The operating system does the bulk of the work involved in managing menus, including displaying the menu bar, dropping down a menu when an item on the menu bar is clicked, and notifying the application when a menu item is selected. MFC further enhances the menu processing model by routing menu item commands to designated class member functions, providing an update mechanism for keeping menu items in sync with the state of the application, and more.

We'll begin this chapter by reviewing the fundamentals of menu handling and building a rudimentary program that features a menu. Then we'll move on to more advanced topics and build a second application, one that offers a few bells and whistles.

MENU BASICS

Let's start by defining a few terms. The menu bar that appears at the top of a window is an application's *top-level menu,* and the commands in it are called *top-level menu items.* The menu that appears when a top-level menu item is clicked is a *drop-down menu,* and items in that menu are referred to as *menu items.* Menu items are identified by integer values called *menu item IDs* or *command IDs.* Windows also supports *popup menus* that look like drop-down menus but can be popped up anywhere on the screen. The context menu that appears when you right-click an object in the Windows shell is an example of a popup menu. Drop-down menus are actually popup menus that are submenus of an application's top-level menu.

Most top-level windows also feature a *system menu* containing commands for restoring, moving, sizing, minimizing, maximizing, and closing the window. Windows provides this menu, which you display by clicking the left mouse button on the small icon in the window's title bar, clicking the right mouse button in the body of the title bar, or pressing Alt-Spacebar.

MFC encapsulates menus and the actions that can be performed on them in the *CMenu* class. *CMenu* contains one public data member—an HMENU named *m_hMenu* that holds the handle of the corresponding menu—and several member functions that provide object-oriented wrappers around functions in the Windows API. *CMenu::TrackPopupMenu,* for example, displays a context menu, and *CMenu::EnableMenuItem* enables or disables a menu item. *CMenu* also contains a pair of virtual functions named *DrawItem* and *MeasureItem* that you can override if you want to create stylized menu items containing bitmaps and other graphical user interface elements.

You can create a menu in an MFC application in three ways:

■ You can create a menu programmatically, piecing it together using *CreateMenu*, *InsertMenu*, and other *CMenu* functions.

■ You can initialize a series of data structures defining the menu's contents and create the menu with *CMenu::LoadMenuIndirect*.

■ You can create a menu resource and load the resulting menu into the application at run time.

The third method is far and away the most common because it allows you to define a menu off line using a resource editor or, if you'd prefer, a simple text editor. We'll focus on this method in the first half of the chapter.

Creating a Menu

The easiest way to create a menu is to add a menu template to your application's resource file. A *resource file* is a scriptlike text file that defines an application's resources; by convention, it is assigned the file name extension .rc and hence is often referred to as an RC file. A *resource* is a binary object such as a menu or an icon. Windows supports several types of resources, including (but not limited to) menus, icons, bitmaps, and strings. The resource compiler Rc.exe, which is provided with the Windows Software Development Kit (SDK) and is also part of Microsoft Visual C++, compiles the statements in an RC file and links the resulting resources into the application's EXE file. Every resource is identified by a string or an integer ID such as "MyMenu" (string) or IDR_MYMENU (integer). Integer resource IDs are given human-readable names such as IDR_MYMENU by means of #define statements in a header file. Once a resource is compiled and linked into an EXE, it can be loaded with a simple function call.

A menu template contains all the information the resource compiler needs to create a menu resource, including the menu's resource ID, the names of the menu items, and the IDs of the menu items. The menu template in Figure 4-1 comes from a project created by Visual C++'s MFC AppWizard. It defines a single menu resource consisting of a top-level menu and four submenus—File, Edit, View, and Help. IDR_MAINFRAME is the menu's resource ID. PRELOAD and DISCARDABLE are resource attributes. PRELOAD tells Windows to load the menu resource into memory when the application starts. DISCARDABLE allows Windows to discard the resource if the memory it occupies is needed for other purposes. (If it's needed again, a discarded resource can be reloaded from the application's EXE file.) PRELOAD and DISCARDABLE are both artifacts of 16-bit Windows and have no impact on either the performance or behavior of 32-bit applications.

```
IDR_MAINFRAME MENU PRELOAD DISCARDABLE
BEGIN
    POPUP "&File"
    BEGIN
        MENUITEM "&New\tCtrl+N",          ID_FILE_NEW
        MENUITEM "&Open...\tCtrl+O",       ID_FILE_OPEN
        MENUITEM "&Save\tCtrl+S",          ID_FILE_SAVE
        MENUITEM "Save &As...",            ID_FILE_SAVE_AS
        MENUITEM SEPARATOR
        MENUITEM "Recent File",            ID_FILE_MRU_FILE1,GRAYED
        MENUITEM SEPARATOR
        MENUITEM "E&xit",                  ID_APP_EXIT
    END
```

Figure 4-1. *A menu template generated by the MFC AppWizard.*   *(continued)*

Figure 4-1. *continued*

```
    POPUP "&Edit"
    BEGIN
        MENUITEM "&Undo\tCtrl+Z",        ID_EDIT_UNDO
        MENUITEM SEPARATOR
        MENUITEM "Cu&t\tCtrl+X",          ID_EDIT_CUT
        MENUITEM "&Copy\tCtrl+C",         ID_EDIT_COPY
        MENUITEM "&Paste\tCtrl+V",        ID_EDIT_PASTE
    END
    POPUP "&View"
    BEGIN
        MENUITEM "&Toolbar",              ID_VIEW_TOOLBAR
        MENUITEM "&Status Bar",           ID_VIEW_STATUS_BAR
    END
    POPUP "&Help"
    BEGIN
        MENUITEM "&About MyApp...",       ID_APP_ABOUT
    END
END
```

The statements between the opening and closing BEGIN and END statements define the contents of the menu, with POPUP statements defining top-level menu items and the associated submenus. The BEGIN and END statements following POPUP statements bracket MENUITEM statements defining the items in the submenus. The special MENUITEM SEPARATOR statement adds a thin horizontal line to the menu; it's used to provide visual separation between groups of menu items. The ampersands in the text of the menu items identify shortcut keys the user can press in combination with the Alt key to display submenus and select items from submenus. In this example, the File-Exit command can be selected by pressing Alt-F and then X. Windows underlines the F in "File" and the x in "Exit" so that they're easily identifiable as shortcut keys. If two or more items in the same menu are assigned the same shortcut key, the shortcut cycles among the menu items and no selection is made until the Enter key is pressed.

An ellipsis (...) in the text of a menu item indicates that further input is required after the item is selected. If the user selects Save, the document is saved immediately. But if the user selects Save As, a dialog box is displayed instead. To be consistent with other Windows applications, use an ellipsis for any menu item whose action is deferred until subsequent input is received from the user. If an item in the top-level menu executes a command instead of displaying a submenu, the text of the item should be followed with an exclamation mark, as in

```
IDR_MAINFRAME MENU PRELOAD DISCARDABLE
BEGIN
    POPUP "&File"
```

```
        [...]
    POPUP "&Edit"
        [...]
    POPUP "&View"
        [...]
    POPUP "&Help"
        [...]
    MENUITEM "E&xit!",         ID_APP_EXIT
END
```

It's legal to include MENUITEM statements in top-level menus this way, but these days it's considered bad form. And it's likely to surprise your users, most of whom are accustomed to seeing top-level menu items display submenus rather than take action themselves.

The ID_ values following the menu item names in the MENUITEM statements are command IDs. Every menu item should be assigned a unique command ID because it is this value that identifies the menu item to your application when the user makes a selection. By convention, IDs are defined with #define statements, and each is given the name ID_ or IDM_ followed by an item name spelled in capital letters. MFC's Afxres.h header file defines ID_ values for commonly used commands such as File-New and Edit-Paste. When you write document/view applications, using the predefined IDs automatically connects certain menu items to handling functions the framework provides. In nondocument/view applications, use of the predefined IDs is optional.

Valid values for menu item IDs range from 1 through 0xEFFF, but MFC Technical Note #20 recommends restricting the range to 0x8000 through 0xDFFF. IDs equal to 0xF000 and higher are reserved for Windows—specifically, for items in the system menu. The range 0xE000 to 0xEFFF is reserved for MFC. In practice, it's perfectly safe to use values lower than 0x8000, and in fact, restricting item IDs to the range 1 through 0x7FFF sidesteps a nasty bug in Windows 95 that affects owner-draw menu items. This bug is explained—and work-arounds are presented—later in this chapter.

The text following the tab character in some of the menu items (for example, the "Ctrl+O" in "Open...\tCtrl+O") identifies an accelerator. An *accelerator* is a key or combination of keys that, when pressed, has the same effect as selecting a menu item. Commonly used accelerators include Ctrl-X for Edit-Cut, Ctrl-C for Edit-Copy, and Ctrl-V for Edit-Paste. Text strings denoting accelerator keys are preceded by tab characters for alignment purposes. The default font used in menus is proportionally spaced, so it's futile to try to align menu text with spaces.

When you define a menu item with MENUITEM, you also have the option of specifying the item's initial state. The GRAYED keyword accompanying the File-Recent File command in Figure 4-1 disables the menu item so that it can't be selected. A disabled item is "grayed out" as a visual reminder that it is disabled. Grayed menu text is displayed in the system color COLOR_GRAYTEXT, which defaults to gray, with a thin border added to provide a three-dimensional look. Another optional keyword is CHECKED, which places a check mark beside a menu item. Although common in Windows applications written in C using the SDK, menu item state specifiers are rarely used in MFC applications because the framework provides a powerful mechanism for updating menu items programmatically. You'll learn more about this mechanism shortly.

Loading and Displaying a Menu

At run time, a menu resource needs to be loaded and attached to a window. When the window is displayed, the menu will also be displayed.

One way to attach a menu to a window is to pass the menu's resource ID to *CFrameWnd::Create*. The following statement creates a frame window and attaches the menu whose resource ID is IDR_MAINFRAME:

```
Create (NULL, _T ("My Application"), WS_OVERLAPPEDWINDOW,
    rectDefault, NULL, MAKEINTRESOURCE (IDR_MAINFRAME));
```

The sixth argument to *Create* identifies the menu resource. The MAKEINTRESOURCE macro converts an integer resource ID to an LPTSTR data type ID compatible with functions that expect string-based resource IDs. When the window appears on the screen, the menu will be visible just below the title bar.

A second method involves the *CFrameWnd::LoadFrame* function. Given a resource ID, *LoadFrame* creates a frame window and attaches a menu, much like *Create*. The statement

```
LoadFrame (IDR_MAINFRAME, WS_OVERLAPPEDWINDOW, NULL, NULL);
```

creates a window and attaches the menu IDR_MAINFRAME. Some MFC programs— particularly wizard-generated applications—use *LoadFrame* instead of *Create* because *LoadFrame* will load icons and other resources, too. MAKEINTRESOURCE isn't required in this example because it's built into *LoadFrame*.

Yet another method for loading a top-level menu and attaching it to a window is to construct a *CMenu* object, call *CMenu::LoadMenu* to load the menu resource, and call *CWnd::SetMenu*, like this:

```
CMenu menu;
menu.LoadMenu (IDR_MAINFRAME);
SetMenu (&menu);
menu.Detach ();
```

In this example, *CMenu::Detach* is called to detach the menu from the *CMenu* object so that the menu won't be destroyed prematurely when *menu* goes out of scope. The *CMenu* class helps guard against resource leaks by calling *CMenu::DestroyMenu* from its destructor. As a rule, a menu loaded with *LoadMenu* should be destroyed with *DestroyMenu* before the application that loaded the menu terminates. However, a menu attached to a window is automatically destroyed when the window is destroyed, so detaching a menu from a *CMenu* object after attaching it to a window won't cause a resource leak unless the menu is later detached from the window without a subsequent call to *DestroyMenu*.

The *SetMenu* technique offers no advantage over simply passing the menu ID to *Create* or *LoadFrame* when a program contains just one menu, but it's very useful in programs that contain two or more menus. Suppose you want to write an application that allows the user to choose short or long menus. Here's one way to go about it. First, create two menu resources—one for the short menus, another for the long. At startup, load the menu resources into *CMenu* data members named *m_menuLong* and *m_menuShort*. Then choose the menu type based on the value of a BOOL data member named *m_bShortMenu*, which is TRUE if short menus are selected and FALSE if they're not. Here's what the window's constructor might look like:

```
Create (NULL, _T ("My Application"));
m_menuLong.LoadMenu (IDR_LONGMENU);
m_menuShort.LoadMenu (IDR_SHORTMENU);
SetMenu (m_bShortMenu ? &m_menuShort : &m_menuLong);
```

In response to a command from the user, the following code would switch from long menus to short menus:

```
m_bShortMenu = TRUE;
SetMenu (&m_menuShort);
DrawMenuBar ();
```

And these statements would switch back to long menus:

```
m_bShortMenu = FALSE;
SetMenu (&m_menuLong);
DrawMenuBar ();
```

CWnd::DrawMenuBar redraws the menu bar to reflect the change. You should always follow calls to *SetMenu* with calls to *DrawMenuBar* unless the window isn't visible on the screen.

What about code to delete the menus, since only one will be attached to a window when the application ends? If *m_menuLong* and *m_menuShort* are data members of the frame window class, their destructors will be called when the frame window is destroyed and the menus associated with them will also be deleted. Therefore, explicit calls to *DestroyMenu* aren't required.

Responding to Menu Commands

When the user pulls down a menu, the window to which the menu is attached receives a series of messages. Among the first to arrive is a WM_INITMENU message notifying the window that a top-level menu item was selected. Before a submenu is displayed, the window receives a WM_INITMENUPOPUP message. Windows programs sometimes take this opportunity to update the submenu's menu items—for example, putting a check mark next to the Toolbar item in the View menu if the application's toolbar is displayed or unchecking the menu item if the toolbar is currently hidden. As the highlight travels up and down the menu, the window receives WM_MENU-SELECT messages reporting the latest position in the menu. In SDK-style programs, WM_MENUSELECT messages are sometimes used to display context-sensitive menu help in a status bar.

The most important message of all is the WM_COMMAND message sent when the user selects an item from the menu. The low word of the message's *wParam* parameter holds the item's command ID. SDK programmers often use *switch-case* logic to vector execution to the appropriate handling routine, but MFC provides a better way. An ON_COMMAND statement in the message map links WM_COMMAND messages referencing a particular menu item to the class member function, or *command handler,* of your choice. The following message-map entry tells MFC to call *OnFileSave* when the ID_FILE_SAVE menu item is selected:

```
ON_COMMAND (ID_FILE_SAVE, OnFileSave)
```

Other items in the File menu might be mapped like this:

```
ON_COMMAND (ID_FILE_NEW, OnFileNew)
ON_COMMAND (ID_FILE_OPEN, OnFileOpen)
ON_COMMAND (ID_FILE_SAVE, OnFileSave)
ON_COMMAND (ID_FILE_SAVE_AS, OnFileSaveAs)
ON_COMMAND (ID_FILE_EXIT, OnFileExit)
```

Now *OnFileNew* will be activated when File-New is selected, *OnFileOpen* will be called when File-Open is selected, and so on.

Command handlers take no arguments and return no values. The *OnFileExit* function, for example, is typically implemented like this:

```
void CMainWindow::OnFileExit ()
{
    PostMessage (WM_CLOSE, 0, 0);
}
```

This command handler terminates the application by posting a WM_CLOSE message to the application's main window. This message ultimately ends the application by causing a WM_QUIT message to appear in the application's message queue.

You can name command handlers whatever you like. There are no naming criteria as there are for WM_ message handlers. Handlers for WM_PAINT and WM_CREATE must be named *OnPaint* and *OnCreate* unless you care to rewrite MFC's ON_WM_PAINT and ON_WM_CREATE macros. But you could just as easily have written the message-map entries for our File menu like this:

```
ON_COMMAND (ID_FILE_NEW, CreateMeAFile)
ON_COMMAND (ID_FILE_OPEN, OpenMeAFile)
ON_COMMAND (ID_FILE_SAVE, SaveThisFile)
ON_COMMAND (ID_FILE_SAVE_AS, SaveThisFileUnderAnotherName)
ON_COMMAND (ID_FILE_EXIT, KillThisAppAndDoItNow)
```

Command Ranges

Sometimes it's more efficient to process a group of menu item IDs with a single command handler than to provide a separate member function for each ID. Consider a drawing application that contains a Color menu from which the user can choose red, green, or blue. Selecting a color from the menu sets a member variable named *m_nCurrentColor* to 0, 1, or 2 and subsequently changes the color of what the user draws on the screen. The message-map entries and command handlers for these menu items might be implemented as follows:

```
// In CMainWindow's message map
ON_COMMAND (ID_COLOR_RED, OnColorRed)
ON_COMMAND (ID_COLOR_GREEN, OnColorGreen)
ON_COMMAND (ID_COLOR_BLUE, OnColorBlue)
    .
    .
    .
void CMainWindow::OnColorRed ()
{
    m_nCurrentColor = 0;
}

void CMainWindow::OnColorGreen ()
{
    m_nCurrentColor = 1;
}

void CMainWindow::OnColorBlue ()
{
    m_nCurrentColor = 2;
}
```

This isn't a terribly efficient way to process messages from the Color menu because each message handler does essentially the same thing. And the inefficiency would be compounded if the menu contained 10 or 20 different colors rather than just 3.

One way to reduce the redundancy in the command handlers for the Color menu is to map all three items to the same *CMainWindow* member function and retrieve the menu item ID with *CWnd::GetCurrentMessage*, as shown on the following page.

```
// In CMainWindow's message map
ON_COMMAND (ID_COLOR_RED, OnColor)
ON_COMMAND (ID_COLOR_GREEN, OnColor)
ON_COMMAND (ID_COLOR_BLUE, OnColor)
    :
    :
void CMainWindow::OnColor ()
{
    UINT nID = (UINT) LOWORD (GetCurrentMessage ()->wParam);
    m_nCurrentColor = nID - ID_COLOR_RED;
}
```

This approach works just fine as long as the command IDs constitute a contiguous range beginning with ID_COLOR_RED, but it's an imperfect solution because it relies on the value of *wParam*. If the meaning of the *wParam* parameter accompanying WM_COMMAND messages changes in a future release of Windows (as it did between Windows 3.1 and Windows 95), you might have to modify this code to get it to work properly. And even though you've reduced the number of command handlers from three to one, you're still adding three separate entries to the class's message map at a cost of 24 bytes each.

A better solution is the MFC ON_COMMAND_RANGE macro, which maps a range of contiguous command IDs to a common handling function. Assuming ID_COLOR_RED is the lowest value in the range and ID_COLOR_BLUE is the highest, ON_COM-MAND_RANGE allows you to rewrite the code for the Color menu like this:

```
// In CMainWindow's message map
ON_COMMAND_RANGE (ID_COLOR_RED, ID_COLOR_BLUE, OnColor)
    :
    :
void CMainWindow::OnColor (UINT nID)
{
    m_nCurrentColor = nID - ID_COLOR_RED;
}
```

When *OnColor* is called because the user chose an item from the Color menu, *nID* contains ID_COLOR_RED, ID_COLOR_GREEN, or ID_COLOR_BLUE. One simple statement sets *m_nCurrentColor* to the proper value, no matter which menu item was selected.

Updating the Items in a Menu

In many applications, menu items must be constantly updated to reflect internal states of the application or its data. When a color is selected from a Color menu, for example, the corresponding menu item should be checked or bulleted to indicate which color is currently selected. An application that features an Edit menu with Cut, Copy, and Paste commands should disable the Cut and Copy menu items when nothing is selected and disable the Paste menu item when the clipboard is empty. Menus are more than just lists of commands. Deployed properly, they provide visual feedback to the user about the current state of the application and make clear what commands are (and are not) available at any given moment.

Windows programmers have traditionally taken one of two approaches to keeping menu items up to date. The first approach is illustrated by the following code sample, which is a modified version of the *OnColor* function presented in the previous section:

```
void CMainWindow::OnColor (UINT nID)
{
    CMenu* pMenu = GetMenu ();
    pMenu->CheckMenuItem (m_nCurrentColor + ID_COLOR_RED, MF_UNCHECKED);
    pMenu->CheckMenuItem (nID, MF_CHECKED);
    m_nCurrentColor = nID - ID_COLOR_RED;
}
```

In this example, the Color menu is updated the moment an item is selected. First *CMenu::CheckMenuItem* is called with an MF_UNCHECKED flag to uncheck the item that's currently checked. Then *CheckMenuItem* is called with an MF_CHECKED flag to place a check mark by the item that was just selected. The next time the Color menu is pulled down, the check mark will identify the current color.

The second approach is to move the code that updates the menu to an *OnInitMenuPopup* handler that's activated in response to WM_INITMENUPOPUP messages. This strategy positions the check mark each time the Color menu is pulled down, *just before* the menu is actually displayed. *OnInitMenuPopup* receives three parameters: a *CMenu* pointer referencing the submenu that's about to be displayed, a UINT value holding the submenu's 0-based index in the top-level menu, and a BOOL value that's nonzero if the message pertains to the system menu instead of a submenu. Here's what an *OnInitMenuPopup* handler for the Color menu might look like. COLOR_MENU_INDEX is an index specifying the Color menu's position in the top-level menu:

```
// In CMainWindow's message map
ON_WM_INITMENUPOPUP ()
    :

void CMainWindow::OnInitMenuPopup (CMenu* pPopupMenu, UINT nIndex,
    BOOL bSysMenu)
{
    if (!bSysMenu && (nIndex == COLOR_MENU_INDEX)) {
        pPopupMenu->CheckMenuItem (ID_COLOR_RED, MF_UNCHECKED);
        pPopupMenu->CheckMenuItem (ID_COLOR_GREEN, MF_UNCHECKED);
        pPopupMenu->CheckMenuItem (ID_COLOR_BLUE, MF_UNCHECKED);
```

(continued)

```
    pPopupMenu->CheckMenuItem (m_nCurrentColor + ID_COLOR_RED,
        MF_CHECKED);
    }
}
```

This method is more robust than the first because it decouples the code that processes commands from the code that updates the menu. Now any function anywhere in the application can change the drawing color, and the menu will be updated automatically the next time it's displayed.

MFC provides a similar but more convenient mechanism for keeping menu items updated. Through ON_UPDATE_COMMAND_UI macros in the message map, you can designate selected member functions to serve as *update handlers* for individual menu items. When the user pulls down a menu, MFC traps the ensuing WM_INITMENUPOPUP message and calls the update handlers for all the items in the menu. Each update handler is passed a pointer to a *CCmdUI* object whose member functions can be used to modify the menu item. And because the *CCmdUI* class isn't specific to any particular type of user interface (UI) element, the same update handler that serves a menu item can serve toolbar buttons and other UI objects, too. Abstracting UI updates in this way simplifies the program logic and helps make an application independent of the operating system it's written for.

Here's how to rewrite the code for the Color menu to take advantage of update handlers:

```
// In CMainWindow's message map
ON_COMMAND_RANGE (ID_COLOR_RED, ID_COLOR_BLUE, OnColor)
ON_UPDATE_COMMAND_UI (ID_COLOR_RED, OnUpdateColorRed)
ON_UPDATE_COMMAND_UI (ID_COLOR_GREEN, OnUpdateColorGreen)
ON_UPDATE_COMMAND_UI (ID_COLOR_BLUE, OnUpdateColorBlue)
     :
     :

void CMainWindow::OnColor (UINT nID)
{
    m_nCurrentColor = nID - ID_COLOR_RED;
}

void CMainWindow::OnUpdateColorRed (CCmdUI* pCmdUI)
{
    pCmdUI->SetCheck (m_nCurrentColor == 0);
}

void CMainWindow::OnUpdateColorGreen (CCmdUI* pCmdUI)
{
    pCmdUI->SetCheck (m_nCurrentColor == 1);
}

void CMainWindow::OnUpdateColorBlue (CCmdUI* pCmdUI)
```

```
{
    pCmdUI->SetCheck (m_nCurrentColor == 2);
}
```

ON_UPDATE_COMMAND_UI connects menu items to update handlers just as ON-_COMMAND connects menu items to command handlers. Now selecting a color from the Color menu will activate *CMainWindow::OnColor*, and before the Color menu is displayed, each item's update handler will be called. The handlers shown here do their updating by calling *CCmdUI::SetCheck* to check or uncheck the corresponding menu item. Called with a nonzero value, *SetCheck* adds a check mark to the corresponding menu item; called with a 0, it displays no check mark.

SetCheck is just one of the *CCmdUI* methods that you can use to update a menu item. The following table shows a complete list, along with a description of each function's effect on a menu item.

Function	*Description*
CCmdUI::Enable	Enables or disables a menu item
CCmdUI::SetCheck	Checks or unchecks a menu item
CCmdUI::SetRadio	Bullets or unbullets a menu item
CCmdUI::SetText	Changes the text of a menu item

SetRadio works like *SetCheck* but adds or removes a bullet instead of a check mark. *SetRadio* is one of those MFC functions that doesn't have a direct counterpart in the Windows API; the framework does some work behind the scenes to allow menu items to be bulleted rather than checked. Ideally, you'd use a bullet to indicate which item in a group of mutually exclusive menu items is currently selected and a check mark to indicate whether a feature is on or off. (In practice, check marks are frequently used for both.) *Enable* enables or disables a menu item, and *SetText* allows you to change the text of the menu item on the fly.

Update Ranges

For updating groups of menu items with a single update handler, MFC provides the ON_UPDATE_COMMAND_UI_RANGE macro, which is to ON_COMMAND_RANGE as ON_UPDATE_COMMAND_UI is to ON_COMMAND. To understand how ON_UP-DATE_COMMAND_UI_RANGE is used, let's revisit the Color menu and assume that it contains eight color choices: black, blue, green, cyan, red, magenta, yellow, and white, in that order. The corresponding menu item IDs are ID_COLOR_BLACK through ID_COLOR_WHITE. Let's also assume that we want to put a bullet by the current color. Here's the most concise way to do it.

```
// In CMainWindow's message map
ON_COMMAND_RANGE (ID_COLOR_BLACK, ID_COLOR_WHITE, OnColor)
ON_UPDATE_COMMAND_UI_RANGE (ID_COLOR_BLACK, ID_COLOR_WHITE,
    OnUpdateColorUI)
    :
    :
void CMainWindow::OnColor (UINT nID)
{
    m_nCurrentColor = nID - ID_COLOR_BLACK;
}

void CMainWindow::OnUpdateColorUI (CCmdUI* pCmdUI)
{
    pCmdUI->SetRadio (pCmdUI->m_nID - ID_COLOR_BLACK ==
        m_nCurrentColor);
}
```

m_nID is a public data member of *CCmdUI* that holds the ID of the menu item for which the update handler was called. By comparing *m_nID* minus ID_COLOR_BLACK to *m_nCurrentColor* and passing the result to *SetRadio*, you can ensure that only the current color is bulleted.

Just how useful is MFC's command-update mechanism? Later in this chapter, we'll develop a sample program that uses two identical Color menus—one that's invoked from a top-level menu and another that's invoked from a right-click context menu. The same command and update handler will serve both menus, and no matter how a color is selected, both menus will be updated to match—with *one line of code* no less. It's hard to imagine how updating menu items could be any easier.

Keyboard Accelerators

As you design your application's menus, you have the option of using keyboard accelerators to assign shortcut keys to any or all of the menu items. An accelerator produces a WM_COMMAND message just as making a menu selection does. Adding keyboard accelerators to your application is simplicity itself. You create an accelerator table resource—a special resource that correlates menu item IDs to keys or combinations of keys—and load the resource into your program with a function call. If the application's main window is a frame window, Windows and the framework do the rest, automatically trapping presses of accelerator keys and notifying your application with WM_COMMAND messages.

An accelerator table resource is defined by an ACCELERATORS block in an RC file. Here is the general format:

```
ResourceID ACCELERATORS
BEGIN
    .
    .
    .
END
```

ResourceID is the accelerator table's resource ID. The statements between BEGIN and END identify the accelerator keys and the corresponding menu item IDs. The MFC AppWizard generates accelerator tables using the following format:

```
IDR_MAINFRAME ACCELERATORS PRELOAD MOVEABLE
BEGIN
    "N",            ID_FILE_NEW,        VIRTKEY,CONTROL
    "O",            ID_FILE_OPEN,       VIRTKEY,CONTROL
    "S",            ID_FILE_SAVE,       VIRTKEY,CONTROL
    "Z",            ID_EDIT_UNDO,       VIRTKEY,CONTROL
    "X",            ID_EDIT_CUT,        VIRTKEY,CONTROL
    "C",            ID_EDIT_COPY,       VIRTKEY,CONTROL
    "V",            ID_EDIT_PASTE,      VIRTKEY,CONTROL
    VK_BACK,        ID_EDIT_UNDO,       VIRTKEY,ALT
    VK_DELETE,      ID_EDIT_CUT,        VIRTKEY,SHIFT
    VK_INSERT,      ID_EDIT_COPY,       VIRTKEY,CONTROL
    VK_INSERT,      ID_EDIT_PASTE,      VIRTKEY,SHIFT
END
```

In this example, IDR_MAINFRAME is the accelerator table's resource ID. PRELOAD and MOVEABLE are load options that, like the equivalent keywords in MENU statements, have no effect in the Win32 environment. Each line in the table defines one accelerator. The first entry in each line defines the accelerator key, and the second identifies the corresponding menu item. The VIRTKEY keyword tells the resource compiler that the first entry is a virtual key code, and the keyword following it— CONTROL, ALT, or SHIFT—identifies an optional modifier key. In this example, Ctrl-N is an accelerator for File-New, Ctrl-O is an accelerator for File-Open, and so on. The Edit menu's Undo, Cut, Copy, and Paste functions each have two accelerators defined: Ctrl-Z and Alt-Backspace for Undo, Ctrl-X and Shift-Del for Cut, Ctrl-C and Ctrl-Ins for Copy, and Ctrl-V and Shift-Ins for Paste.

Like menus, keyboard accelerators must be loaded and attached to a window before they'll do anything. For a frame window, *LoadAccelTable* does the loading and attaching in one step:

```
LoadAccelTable (MAKEINTRESOURCE (IDR_MAINFRAME));
```

LoadFrame also does the job nicely. In fact, the same function call that loads the menu also loads the accelerator table if the two resources share the same ID:

```
LoadFrame (IDR_MAINFRAME, WS_OVERLAPPEDWINDOW, NULL, NULL);
```

For accelerators to work, the message loop must include a call to the API function *::TranslateAccelerator*, as shown here:

```
while (GetMessage (&msg, NULL, 0, 0)) {
    if (!TranslateAccelerator (hwnd, hAccel, &msg)) {
        TranslateMessage (&msg);
        DispatchMessage (&msg);
    }
}
```

MFC's *CFrameWnd* class handles this part for you. Specifically, it overrides the virtual *PreTranslateMessage* function that it inherits from *CWnd* and calls *::TranslateAccelerator* if it sees an accelerator table has been loaded—that is, if the frame window's *m_hAccelTable* data member contains a non-NULL accelerator table handle. Not surprisingly, *LoadAccelTable* loads an accelerator resource and copies the handle to *m_hAccelTable*. *LoadFrame* does the same by calling *LoadAccelTable*.

Accelerators must be handled differently when loaded for nonframe windows that lack the accelerator support in *CFrameWnd*. Suppose you derive a custom window class from *CWnd* and want to use accelerators, too. Here's how you'd go about it:

1. Add an *m_hAccelTable* data member (type HACCEL) to the derived class.

2. Early in your application's lifetime, use the API function *::LoadAccelerators* to load the accelerator table. Copy the handle returned by *::LoadAccelerators* to *m_hAccelTable*.

3. In the window class, override *PreTranslateMessage* and call *::TranslateAccelerator* with the handle stored in *m_hAccelTable*. Use the value returned by *::TranslateAccelerator* as the return value for *PreTranslateMessage* so that the message won't be translated and dispatched if *::TranslateAccelerator* has dispatched it already.

Here's how it looks in code:

```
// In CMainWindow's constructor
m_hAccelTable = ::LoadAccelerators (AfxGetInstanceHandle (),
    MAKEINTRESOURCE (IDR_ACCELERATORS));

// PreTranslateMessage override
BOOL CMainWindow::PreTranslateMessage (MSG* pMsg)
{
    if (CWnd::PreTranslateMessage (pMsg))
        return TRUE;
    return ((m_hAccelTable != NULL) &&
        ::TranslateAccelerator (m_hWnd, m_hAccelTable, pMsg));
}
```

With this framework in place, a *CWnd*-type window will use accelerators just as a frame window does. Note that accelerators loaded with *::LoadAccelerators* (or *LoadAccelTable*) don't need to be deleted before termination because Windows deletes them automatically.

Using accelerators to provide shortcuts for commonly used menu commands is preferable to processing keystroke messages manually for two reasons. The first is that accelerators simplify the programming logic. Why write WM_KEYDOWN and WM_CHAR handlers if you don't have to? The second is that if your application's window contains child windows and a child window has the input focus, keyboard messages will go to the child window instead of the main window. (Child windows are discussed in Chapter 7.) As you learned in Chapter 3, keyboard messages always go to the window with the input focus. But when an accelerator is pressed, Windows makes sure the resulting WM_COMMAND message goes to the main window even if one of its children has the input focus.

Accelerators are so useful for trapping keystrokes that they're sometimes used apart from menus. If you want to be notified any time the Ctrl-Shift-F12 combination is pressed, for example, simply create an accelerator for that key combination with a statement like this one:

```
VK_F12, ID_CTRL_SHIFT_F12, VIRTKEY, CONTROL, SHIFT
```

Then map the accelerator to a class member function by adding an

```
ON_COMMAND (ID_CTRL_SHIFT_F12, OnCtrlShiftF12)
```

entry to the message map. Presses of Ctrl-Shift-F12 will thereafter activate *OnCtrl-ShiftF12*, even if no menu item is assigned the ID ID_CTRL_SHIFT_F12.

THE SHAPES APPLICATION

Let's put what we've learned so far to work by building an application that uses menus and accelerators and also uses MFC's UI update mechanism to keep menu items in sync with data members whose values reflect internal application states. For the first time, we'll use AppWizard to generate the initial source code for the application and ClassWizard to write message handlers. We'll also use ClassWizard to write command handlers and update handlers for the application's menu items. AppWizard and ClassWizard are MFC code generators that conserve development time by reducing the amount of code you have to write.

The application, which is named Shapes, is shown in Figure 4-2. Shapes displays a polygon in the center of a frame window. You can change the polygon's shape by selecting a command from the Shape menu (Circle, Triangle, or Square) or pressing the corresponding keyboard accelerator key (F7, F8, or F9).

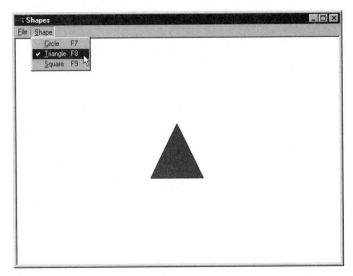

Figure 4-2. *The Shapes window.*

The program's source code is reproduced in Figure 4-3. When you write an application using the wizards, however, the source code doesn't tell the whole story; it's just as important to understand *how* the source code was created, and by whom. Therefore, I'll begin with a step-by-step description of how to create the initial source code for Shapes with the MFC AppWizard. Then we'll pause to examine what App-Wizard has wrought.

Shapes.h

```
// Shapes.h : main header file for the SHAPES application
//

#if !defined(AFX_SHAPES_H__437C8B37_5C45_11D2_8E53_006008A82731__INCLUDED_)
#define AFX_SHAPES_H__437C8B37_5C45_11D2_8E53_006008A82731__INCLUDED_

#if _MSC_VER > 1000
#pragma once
#endif // _MSC_VER > 1000

#ifndef __AFXWIN_H__
        #error include 'stdafx.h' before including this file for PCH
#endif

#include "resource.h"        // main symbols
```

Figure 4-3. *The Shapes program.*

```
///////////////////////////////////////////////////////////////////////
// CShapesApp:
// See Shapes.cpp for the implementation of this class
//

class CShapesApp : public CWinApp
{
public:
        CShapesApp();

// Overrides
        // ClassWizard generated virtual function overrides
        //{{AFX_VIRTUAL(CShapesApp)
        public:
        virtual BOOL InitInstance();
        //}}AFX_VIRTUAL

// Implementation

public:
        //{{AFX_MSG(CShapesApp)
        afx_msg void OnAppAbout();
        //}}AFX_MSG
        DECLARE_MESSAGE_MAP()
};


///////////////////////////////////////////////////////////////////////

//{{AFX_INSERT_LOCATION}}
// Microsoft Visual C++ will insert additional declarations immediately
// before the previous line.

#endif
// !defined(AFX_SHAPES_H__437C8B37_5C45_11D2_8E53_006008A82731__INCLUDED_)
```

Shapes.cpp

```
// Shapes.cpp : Defines the class behaviors for the application.
//
#include "stdafx.h"
"#include "Shapes.h"

#include "MainFrm.h"
```

(continued)

Figure 4-3. *continued*

```
#ifdef _DEBUG
#define new DEBUG_NEW
#undef THIS_FILE
static char THIS_FILE[] = __FILE__;
#endif

//////////////////////////////////////////////////////////////////////
// CShapesApp

BEGIN_MESSAGE_MAP(CShapesApp, CWinApp)
        //{{AFX_MSG_MAP(CShapesApp)
        ON_COMMAND(ID_APP_ABOUT, OnAppAbout)
        //}}AFX_MSG_MAP
END_MESSAGE_MAP()

//////////////////////////////////////////////////////////////////////
// CShapesApp construction

CShapesApp::CShapesApp()
{
}

//////////////////////////////////////////////////////////////////////
// The one and only CShapesApp object

CShapesApp theApp;

//////////////////////////////////////////////////////////////////////
// CShapesApp initialization

BOOL CShapesApp::InitInstance()
{
        // Standard initialization

        // Change the registry key under which our settings are stored.
        SetRegistryKey(_T("Local AppWizard-Generated Applications"));

        CMainFrame* pFrame = new CMainFrame;
        m_pMainWnd = pFrame;

        // create and load the frame with its resources

        pFrame->LoadFrame(IDR_MAINFRAME,
                WS_OVERLAPPEDWINDOW | FWS_ADDTOTITLE, NULL,
                NULL);
```

```
        pFrame->ShowWindow(SW_SHOW);
        pFrame->UpdateWindow();

        return TRUE;
}

/////////////////////////////////////////////////////////////////////////
// CShapesApp message handlers




/////////////////////////////////////////////////////////////////////////
// CAboutDlg dialog used for App About

class CAboutDlg : public CDialog
{
public:
        CAboutDlg();

// Dialog Data
        //{{AFX_DATA(CAboutDlg)
        enum { IDD = IDD_ABOUTBOX };
        //}}AFX_DATA

        // ClassWizard generated virtual function overrides
        //{{AFX_VIRTUAL(CAboutDlg)
        protected:
        virtual void DoDataExchange(CDataExchange* pDX);  // DDX/DDV support
        //}}AFX_VIRTUAL

// Implementation
protected:
        //{{AFX_MSG(CAboutDlg)
                // No message handlers
        //}}AFX_MSG
        DECLARE_MESSAGE_MAP()
};

CAboutDlg::CAboutDlg() : CDialog(CAboutDlg::IDD)
{
        //{{AFX_DATA_INIT(CAboutDlg)
        //}}AFX_DATA_INIT
}
```

(continued)

Figure 4-3. *continued*

```
void CAboutDlg::DoDataExchange(CDataExchange* pDX)
{
        CDialog::DoDataExchange(pDX);
        //{{AFX_DATA_MAP(CAboutDlg)
        //}}AFX_DATA_MAP
}

BEGIN_MESSAGE_MAP(CAboutDlg, CDialog)
        //{{AFX_MSG_MAP(CAboutDlg)
                // No message handlers
        //}}AFX_MSG_MAP
END_MESSAGE_MAP()

// App command to run the dialog
void CShapesApp::OnAppAbout()
{
        CAboutDlg aboutDlg;
        aboutDlg.DoModal();
}

/////////////////////////////////////////////////////////////////////
// CShapesApp message handlers
```

MainFrm.h

```
// MainFrm.h : interface of the CMainFrame class
//
/////////////////////////////////////////////////////////////////////////////

#if !defined(AFX_MAINFRM_H__437C8B3B_5C45_11D2_8E53_006008A82731__INCLUDED_)
#define AFX_MAINFRM_H__437C8B3B_5C45_11D2_8E53_006008A82731__INCLUDED_

#if _MSC_VER > 1000
#pragma once
#endif // _MSC_VER > 1000

#include "ChildView.h"

class CMainFrame : public CFrameWnd
{

public:
    CMainFrame();
```

```
protected:
    DECLARE_DYNAMIC(CMainFrame)

// Attributes
public:

// Operations
public:

// Overrides
    // ClassWizard generated virtual function overrides
    //{{AFX_VIRTUAL(CMainFrame)
    virtual BOOL PreCreateWindow(CREATESTRUCT& cs);
    virtual BOOL OnCmdMsg(UINT nID, int nCode, void* pExtra,
        AFX_CMDHANDLERINFO* pHandlerInfo);
    //}}AFX_VIRTUAL

// Implementation
public:
    virtual ~CMainFrame();
#ifdef _DEBUG
    virtual void AssertValid() const;
    virtual void Dump(CDumpContext& dc) const;
#endif
    CChildView    m_wndView;

// Generated message map functions
protected:
    //{{AFX_MSG(CMainFrame)
    afx_msg void OnSetFocus(CWnd *pOldWnd);
    afx_msg int OnCreate(LPCREATESTRUCT lpCreateStruct);
    //}}AFX_MSG
    DECLARE_MESSAGE_MAP()
};
/////////////////////////////////////////////////////////////////////////////

//{{AFX_INSERT_LOCATION}}
// Microsoft Visual C++ will insert additional declarations immediately
// before the previous line.

#endif
// !defined(AFX_MAINFRM_H__437C8B3B_5C45_11D2_8E53_006008A82731__INCLUDED_)
```

(continued)

Figure 4-3. *continued*

MainFrm.cpp

```cpp
// MainFrm.cpp : implementation of the CMainFrame class
//

#include "stdafx.h"
#include "Shapes.h"

#include "MainFrm.h"

#ifdef _DEBUG
#define new DEBUG_NEW
#undef THIS_FILE
static char THIS_FILE[] = __FILE__;
#endif

/////////////////////////////////////////////////////////////////////////////
// CMainFrame

IMPLEMENT_DYNAMIC(CMainFrame, CFrameWnd)

BEGIN_MESSAGE_MAP(CMainFrame, CFrameWnd)
    //{{AFX_MSG_MAP(CMainFrame)
    ON_WM_SETFOCUS()
    ON_WM_CREATE()
    //}}AFX_MSG_MAP
END_MESSAGE_MAP()

/////////////////////////////////////////////////////////////////////////////
// CMainFrame construction/destruction

CMainFrame::CMainFrame()
{
}

CMainFrame::~CMainFrame()
{
}

BOOL CMainFrame::PreCreateWindow(CREATESTRUCT& cs)
{
    if( !CFrameWnd::PreCreateWindow(cs) )
        return FALSE;
    cs.dwExStyle &= ~WS_EX_CLIENTEDGE;
```

```
        cs.lpszClass = AfxRegisterWndClass(0);
        return TRUE;
}
/////////////////////////////////////////////////////////////////////////
// CMainFrame diagnostics

#ifdef _DEBUG
void CMainFrame::AssertValid() const
{
        CFrameWnd::AssertValid();
}

void CMainFrame::Dump(CDumpContext& dc) const
{
        CFrameWnd::Dump(dc);
}

#endif //_DEBUG

/////////////////////////////////////////////////////////////////////////
// CMainFrame message handlers
void CMainFrame::OnSetFocus(CWnd* pOldWnd)
{
        // forward focus to the view window
        m_wndView.SetFocus();
}

BOOL CMainFrame::OnCmdMsg(UINT nID, int nCode, void* pExtra,
        AFX_CMDHANDLERINFO* pHandlerInfo)
{
        // let the view have first crack at the command
        if (m_wndView.OnCmdMsg(nID, nCode, pExtra, pHandlerInfo))
            return TRUE;

        // otherwise, do default handling
        return CFrameWnd::OnCmdMsg(nID, nCode, pExtra, pHandlerInfo);
}


int CMainFrame::OnCreate(LPCREATESTRUCT lpCreateStruct)
{
        if (CFrameWnd::OnCreate(lpCreateStruct) == -1)
            return -1;
```

(continued)

Figure 4-3. *continued*

```
    if (!m_wndView.Create(NULL, NULL, AFX_WS_DEFAULT_VIEW,
        CRect(0, 0, 0, 0), this, AFX_IDW_PANE_FIRST, NULL))
    {
        TRACE0("Failed to create view window\n");
        return -1;
    }
    return 0;
}
```

ChildView.h

```
// ChildView.h : interface of the CChildView class
//
/////////////////////////////////////////////////////////////////////////////

#if !defined(AFX_CHILDVIEW_H__437C8B3D_5C45_11D2_8E53_006008A82731__INCLUDED_)
#define AFX_CHILDVIEW_H__437C8B3D_5C45_11D2_8E53_006008A82731__INCLUDED_

#if _MSC_VER > 1000
#pragma once
#endif // _MSC_VER > 1000


/////////////////////////////////////////////////////////////////////////////
// CChildView window

class CChildView : public CWnd
{
// Construction
public:
    CChildView();

// Attributes
public:

// Operations
public:

// Overrides
    // ClassWizard generated virtual function overrides
    //{{AFX_VIRTUAL(CChildView)
    protected:
    virtual BOOL PreCreateWindow(CREATESTRUCT& cs);
    //}}AFX_VIRTUAL
```

```
// Implementation
public:
    virtual ~CChildView();

    // Generated message map functions
protected:
    int m_nShape;
    //{{AFX_MSG(CChildView)
    afx_msg void OnPaint();
    afx_msg void OnShapeCircle();
    afx_msg void OnShapeTriangle();
    afx_msg void OnShapeSquare();
    afx_msg void OnUpdateShapeCircle(CCmdUI* pCmdUI);
    afx_msg void OnUpdateShapeTriangle(CCmdUI* pCmdUI);
    afx_msg void OnUpdateShapeSquare(CCmdUI* pCmdUI);
    //}}AFX_MSG
    DECLARE_MESSAGE_MAP()
};


/////////////////////////////////////////////////////////////////////////

//{{AFX_INSERT_LOCATION}}
// Microsoft Visual C++ will insert additional declarations immediately
// before the previous line.

#endif
// !defined(AFX_CHILDVIEW_H__437C8B3D_5C45_11D2_8E53_006008A82731__INCLUDED_)
```

ChildView.cpp

```
// ChildView.cpp : implementation of the CChildView class
//

#include "stdafx.h"
#include "Shapes.h"
#include "ChildView.h"

#ifdef _DEBUG
#define new DEBUG_NEW
#undef THIS_FILE
static char THIS_FILE[] = __FILE__;
#endif


/////////////////////////////////////////////////////////////////////////
// CChildView

CChildView::CChildView()
```

(continued)

Figure 4-3. *continued*

```
{
    m_nShape = 1; // Triangle
}


CChildView::~CChildView()
{
}


BEGIN_MESSAGE_MAP(CChildView,CWnd )
    //{{AFX_MSG_MAP(CChildView)
    ON_WM_PAINT()
    ON_COMMAND(ID_SHAPE_CIRCLE, OnShapeCircle)
    ON_COMMAND(ID_SHAPE_TRIANGLE, OnShapeTriangle)
    ON_COMMAND(ID_SHAPE_SQUARE, OnShapeSquare)
    ON_UPDATE_COMMAND_UI(ID_SHAPE_CIRCLE, OnUpdateShapeCircle)
    ON_UPDATE_COMMAND_UI(ID_SHAPE_TRIANGLE, OnUpdateShapeTriangle)
    ON_UPDATE_COMMAND_UI(ID_SHAPE_SQUARE, OnUpdateShapeSquare)
    //}}AFX_MSG_MAP
END_MESSAGE_MAP()


/////////////////////////////////////////////////////////////////////////////
// CChildView message handlers

BOOL CChildView::PreCreateWindow(CREATESTRUCT& cs)
{
    if (!CWnd::PreCreateWindow(cs))
        return FALSE;

    cs.dwExStyle |= WS_EX_CLIENTEDGE;
    cs.style &= ~WS_BORDER;
    cs.lpszClass = AfxRegisterWndClass(CS_HREDRAW|CS_VREDRAW|CS_DBLCLKS,
        ::LoadCursor(NULL, IDC_ARROW), HBRUSH(COLOR_WINDOW+1), NULL);

    return TRUE;
}


void CChildView::OnPaint()
{
    CPoint points[3];
    CPaintDC dc(this);

    CRect rcClient;
    GetClientRect (&rcClient);
```

```
    int cx = rcClient.Width () / 2;
    int cy = rcClient.Height () / 2;
    CRect rcShape (cx - 45, cy - 45, cx + 45, cy + 45);

    CBrush brush (RGB (255, 0, 0));
    CBrush* pOldBrush = dc.SelectObject (&brush);

    switch (m_nShape) {

    case 0: // Circle
        dc.Ellipse (rcShape);
        break;

    case 1: // Triangle
        points[0].x = cx - 45;
        points[0].y = cy + 45;
        points[1].x = cx;
        points[1].y = cy - 45;
        points[2].x = cx + 45;
        points[2].y = cy + 45;
        dc.Polygon (points, 3);
        break;

    case 2: // Square
        dc.Rectangle (rcShape);
        break;
    }
    dc.SelectObject (pOldBrush);
}

void CChildView::OnShapeCircle()
{
    m_nShape = 0;
    Invalidate ();
}

void CChildView::OnShapeTriangle()
{
    m_nShape = 1;
    Invalidate ();
}
```

(continued)

Figure 4-3. *continued*

```
void CChildView::OnShapeSquare()
{
    m_nShape = 2;
    Invalidate ();
}

void CChildView::OnUpdateShapeCircle(CCmdUI* pCmdUI)
{
    pCmdUI->SetCheck (m_nShape == 0);
}

void CChildView::OnUpdateShapeTriangle(CCmdUI* pCmdUI)
{
    pCmdUI->SetCheck (m_nShape == 1);
}

void CChildView::OnUpdateShapeSquare(CCmdUI* pCmdUI)
{
    pCmdUI->SetCheck (m_nShape == 2);
}
```

Resource.h

```
//{{NO_DEPENDENCIES}}
// Microsoft Developer Studio generated include file.
// Used by Shapes.rc
//
#define IDD_ABOUTBOX                    100
#define IDR_MAINFRAME                   128
#define IDR_SHAPESTYPE                  129
#define ID_SHAPE_CIRCLE                 32771
#define ID_SHAPE_TRIANGLE               32772
#define ID_SHAPE_SQUARE                 32773

// Next default values for new objects
//
#ifdef APSTUDIO_INVOKED
#ifndef APSTUDIO_READONLY_SYMBOLS
#define _APS_NEXT_RESOURCE_VALUE        130
#define _APS_NEXT_COMMAND_VALUE         32774
#define _APS_NEXT_CONTROL_VALUE         1000
#define _APS_NEXT_SYMED_VALUE           101
#endif
#endif
```

Shapes.rc

```
//Microsoft Developer Studio generated resource script.
//
#include "resource.h"

#define APSTUDIO_READONLY_SYMBOLS
/////////////////////////////////////////////////////////////////////////////
//
// Generated from the TEXTINCLUDE 2 resource.
//
#include "afxres.h"


/////////////////////////////////////////////////////////////////////////////
#undef APSTUDIO_READONLY_SYMBOLS


/////////////////////////////////////////////////////////////////////////////
// English (U.S.) resources

#if !defined(AFX_RESOURCE_DLL) || defined(AFX_TARG_ENU)
#ifdef _WIN32
LANGUAGE LANG_ENGLISH, SUBLANG_ENGLISH_US
#pragma code_page(1252)
#endif //_WIN32

#ifdef APSTUDIO_INVOKED
/////////////////////////////////////////////////////////////////////////////
//
// TEXTINCLUDE
//

1 TEXTINCLUDE DISCARDABLE
BEGIN
    "resource.h\0"
END

2 TEXTINCLUDE DISCARDABLE
BEGIN
    "#include ""afxres.h""\r\n"
    "\0"
END

3 TEXTINCLUDE DISCARDABLE
BEGIN
    "#define _AFX_NO_SPLITTER_RESOURCES\r\n"
    "#define _AFX_NO_OLE_RESOURCES\r\n"
    "#define _AFX_NO_TRACKER_RESOURCES\r\n"
```

(continued)

Figure 4-3. *continued*

```
    "#define _AFX_NO_PROPERTY_RESOURCES\r\n"
    "\r\n"
    "#if !defined(AFX_RESOURCE_DLL) || defined(AFX_TARG_ENU)\r\n"
    "#ifdef _WIN32\r\n"
    "LANGUAGE 9, 1\r\n"
    "#pragma code_page(1252)\r\n"
    "#endif //_WIN32\r\n"
    "#include ""res\\Shapes.rc2"
    "   // non-Microsoft Visual C++ edited resources\r\n"
    "#include ""afxres.rc""          // Standard components\r\n"
    "#endif\r\n"
    "\0"
END


#endif    // APSTUDIO_INVOKED


/////////////////////////////////////////////////////////////////////////////
//
// Icon
//

// Icon with lowest ID value placed first to ensure application icon
// remains consistent on all systems.
IDR_MAINFRAME           ICON    DISCARDABLE     "res\\Shapes.ico"


/////////////////////////////////////////////////////////////////////////////
//
// Menu
//

IDR_MAINFRAME MENU PRELOAD DISCARDABLE
BEGIN
    POPUP "&File"
    BEGIN
        MENUITEM "E&xit",                       ID_APP_EXIT
    END
    POPUP "&Shape"
    BEGIN
        MENUITEM "&Circle\tF7",                 ID_SHAPE_CIRCLE
        MENUITEM "&Triangle\tF8",               ID_SHAPE_TRIANGLE
        MENUITEM "&Square\tF9",                 ID_SHAPE_SQUARE
    END
END
```

```
///////////////////////////////////////////////////////////////////////
//
// Accelerator
//

IDR_MAINFRAME ACCELERATORS PRELOAD MOVEABLE PURE
BEGIN
    VK_F7,          ID_SHAPE_CIRCLE,        VIRTKEY, NOINVERT
    VK_F8,          ID_SHAPE_TRIANGLE,      VIRTKEY, NOINVERT
    VK_F9,          ID_SHAPE_SQUARE,        VIRTKEY, NOINVERT
END


///////////////////////////////////////////////////////////////////////
//
// Dialog
//

IDD_ABOUTBOX DIALOG DISCARDABLE  0, 0, 235, 55
STYLE DS_MODALFRAME | WS_POPUP | WS_CAPTION | WS_SYSMENU
CAPTION "About Shapes"
FONT 8, "MS Sans Serif"
BEGIN
    ICON            IDR_MAINFRAME,IDC_STATIC,11,17,20,20
    LTEXT           "Shapes Version 1.0",IDC_STATIC,40,10,119,8,SS_NOPREFIX
    LTEXT           "Copyright (C) 1998",IDC_STATIC,40,25,119,8
    DEFPUSHBUTTON   "OK",IDOK,178,7,50,14,WS_GROUP
END


#ifndef _MAC
///////////////////////////////////////////////////////////////////////
//
// Version
//

VS_VERSION_INFO VERSIONINFO
    FILEVERSION 1,0,0,1
    PRODUCTVERSION 1,0,0,1
    FILEFLAGSMASK 0x3fL
#ifdef _DEBUG
    FILEFLAGS 0x1L
#else
    FILEFLAGS 0x0L
#endif
```

(continued)

Figure 4-3. *continued*

```
    FILEOS 0x4L
    FILETYPE 0x1L
    FILESUBTYPE 0x0L
BEGIN
    BLOCK "StringFileInfo"
    BEGIN
        BLOCK "040904B0"
        BEGIN
            VALUE "CompanyName", "\0"
            VALUE "FileDescription", "Shapes MFC Application\0"
            VALUE "FileVersion", "1, 0, 0, 1\0"
            VALUE "InternalName", "Shapes\0"
            VALUE "LegalCopyright", "Copyright (C) 1998\0"
            VALUE "LegalTrademarks", "\0"
            VALUE "OriginalFilename", "Shapes.EXE\0"
            VALUE "ProductName", "Shapes Application\0"
            VALUE "ProductVersion", "1, 0, 0, 1\0"
        END
    END
    BLOCK "VarFileInfo"
    BEGIN
        VALUE "Translation", 0x409, 1200
    END
END

#endif    // !_MAC


/////////////////////////////////////////////////////////////////////////////
//
// DESIGNINFO
//

#ifdef APSTUDIO_INVOKED
GUIDELINES DESIGNINFO DISCARDABLE
BEGIN
    IDD_ABOUTBOX, DIALOG
    BEGIN
        LEFTMARGIN, 7
        RIGHTMARGIN, 228
        TOPMARGIN, 7
        BOTTOMMARGIN, 48
    END
END
#endif    // APSTUDIO_INVOKED
```

```
//////////////////////////////////////////////////////////////////////////
/
//
// String Table
//

STRINGTABLE PRELOAD DISCARDABLE
BEGIN
    IDR_MAINFRAME            "Shapes"
END

STRINGTABLE PRELOAD DISCARDABLE
BEGIN
    AFX_IDS_APP_TITLE        "Shapes"
    AFX_IDS_IDLEMESSAGE      "Ready"
END

STRINGTABLE DISCARDABLE
BEGIN
    ID_INDICATOR_EXT         "EXT"
    ID_INDICATOR_CAPS        "CAP"
    ID_INDICATOR_NUM         "NUM"
    ID_INDICATOR_SCRL        "SCRL"
    ID_INDICATOR_OVR         "OVR"
    ID_INDICATOR_REC         "REC"
END

STRINGTABLE DISCARDABLE
BEGIN
    ID_APP_ABOUT          "Display program information, version number and copyright\nAbout"
    ID_APP_EXIT              "Quit the application; prompts to save documents\nExit"
END

STRINGTABLE DISCARDABLE
BEGIN
    ID_NEXT_PANE             "Switch to the next window pane\nNext Pane"
    ID_PREV_PANE          "Switch back to the previous window pane\nPrevious Pane"
END

STRINGTABLE DISCARDABLE
BEGIN
    ID_WINDOW_SPLIT          "Split the active window into panes\nSplit"
END
```

(continued)

Figure 4-3. *continued*

```
STRINGTABLE DISCARDABLE
BEGIN
    ID_EDIT_CLEAR              "Erase the selection\nErase"
    ID_EDIT_CLEAR_ALL          "Erase everything\nErase All"
    ID_EDIT_COPY              "Copy the selection and put it on the Clipboard\nCopy"
    ID_EDIT_CUT               "Cut the selection and put it on the Clipboard\nCut"
    ID_EDIT_FIND               "Find the specified text\nFind"
    ID_EDIT_PASTE              "Insert Clipboard contents\nPaste"
    ID_EDIT_REPEAT             "Repeat the last action\nRepeat"
    ID_EDIT_REPLACE            "Replace specific text with different text\nReplace"
    ID_EDIT_SELECT_ALL         "Select the entire document\nSelect All"
    ID_EDIT_UNDO               "Undo the last action\nUndo"
    ID_EDIT_REDO               "Redo the previously undone action\nRedo"
END

STRINGTABLE DISCARDABLE
BEGIN
    AFX_IDS_SCSIZE             "Change the window size"
    AFX_IDS_SCMOVE             "Change the window position"
    AFX_IDS_SCMINIMIZE         "Reduce the window to an icon"
    AFX_IDS_SCMAXIMIZE         "Enlarge the window to full size"
    AFX_IDS_SCNEXTWINDOW       "Switch to the next document window"
    AFX_IDS_SCPREVWINDOW       "Switch to the previous document window"
    AFX_IDS_SCCLOSE          "Close the active window and prompts to save the documents"
END

STRINGTABLE DISCARDABLE
BEGIN
    AFX_IDS_SCRESTORE          "Restore the window to normal size"
    AFX_IDS_SCTASKLIST         "Activate Task List"
END

#endif    // English (U.S.) resources
/////////////////////////////////////////////////////////////////////////////
//


#ifndef APSTUDIO_INVOKED
/////////////////////////////////////////////////////////////////////////////
//
//
// Generated from the TEXTINCLUDE 3 resource.
//
```

```
#define _AFX_NO_SPLITTER_RESOURCES
#define _AFX_NO_OLE_RESOURCES
#define _AFX_NO_TRACKER_RESOURCES
#define _AFX_NO_PROPERTY_RESOURCES

#if !defined(AFX_RESOURCE_DLL) || defined(AFX_TARG_ENU)
#ifdef _WIN32
LANGUAGE 9, 1
#pragma code_page(1252)
#endif //_WIN32
#include "res\Shapes.rc2"  // non-Microsoft Visual C++ edited resources
#include "afxres.rc"       // Standard components
#endif

/////////////////////////////////////////////////////////////////////////////
#endif    // not APSTUDIO_INVOKED
```

Running the MFC AppWizard

Shapes' source code is a combination of wizard-generated code and handwritten code. The first step in creating it is to run the MFC AppWizard. Here's how to get started:

1. Create a new Visual C++ project named Shapes. Select MFC AppWizard (Exe) as the application type, as shown in Figure 4-4. This will start App-Wizard, which will ask you a series of questions before generating the project.

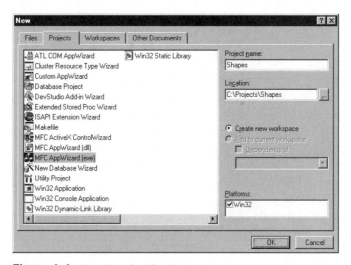

Figure 4-4. *Creating the Shapes project.*

2. In AppWizard's Step 1 dialog box, select Single Document as the application type and uncheck the box labeled Document/View Architecture Support, as shown in Figure 4-5. The latter is a new option in Visual C++ 6; it prevents AppWizard from generating an MFC document/view application. The meaning of Single Document is discussed in Chapter 8.

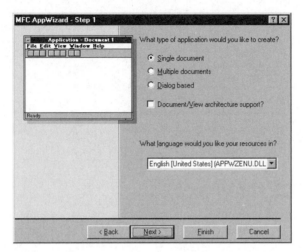

Figure 4-5. *AppWizard's Step 1 dialog box.*

3. In AppWizard's Step 2 dialog box, accept the defaults.

4. In AppWizard's Step 3 dialog box, uncheck the ActiveX Controls box. When checked, this option adds infrastructure that allows MFC windows to host ActiveX controls—a subject that we'll cover in Chapter 21.

5. In AppWizard's Step 4 dialog box, uncheck the Docking Toolbar, Initial Status Bar, and 3D Controls check boxes, as shown in Figure 4-6. Accept the defaults elsewhere in this dialog box.

6. Accept the defaults in the remaining AppWizard dialog boxes, and allow AppWizard to create the project. You don't even have to see the Step 5 and Step 6 dialog boxes to accept the defaults in them; just click the Finish button in the Step 4 dialog box.

After you click Finish, AppWizard will display a summary of the code it is about to create. Click OK to affirm or click Cancel and then use the Back and Next buttons to move backward and forward through the dialog boxes, making changes as needed.

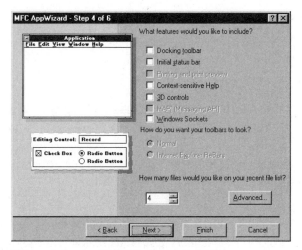

Figure 4-6. *AppWizard's Step 4 dialog box.*

NOTE Because of a bug in Visual C++ 6.0, the most important part of *CMain-Frame* might not appear in your source code if you follow the steps prescribed above. One of the frame window's most important tasks is to create the view window. It's supposed to do so with the following WM_CREATE handler:

```
int CMainFrame::OnCreate(LPCREATESTRUCT lpCreateStruct)
{
    if (CFrameWnd::OnCreate(lpCreateStruct) == -1)
        return -1;

    if (!m_wndView.Create(NULL, NULL, AFX_WS_DEFAULT_VIEW,
        CRect(0, 0, 0, 0), this, AFX_IDW_PANE_FIRST, NULL))
    {
        TRACE0("Failed to create view window\n");
        return -1;
    }
    return 0;
}
```

Unfortunately, the Visual C++ 6.0 AppWizard erroneously omits this handler when the toolbar and status bar options are turned off in the Step 4 dialog box. Therefore, you must add it yourself. Don't forget to add an ON_WM_CREATE statement to the message map, too.

Analyzing AppWizard's Output

So what exactly did AppWizard do? First, it created a new project that includes all the build settings required for an MFC application. Second, it derived several classes from MFC base classes and inserted them into the project. Third, it created a set of resources for the application to use and inserted them into the project, too. A good way to familiarize yourself with AppWizard's output is to look at the files that it generated. Note that this output can vary widely depending on what options you selected in the AppWizard dialog boxes. The following sections provide a quick tour of the source code files that AppWizard generated for the Shapes application and a brief look at some of the important program elements found inside them.

StdAfx.h and StdAfx.cpp

AppWizard-generated projects speed program builds by taking advantage of a feature of Visual C++ known as *precompiled headers*. As a result of build settings implemented by AppWizard, all header files that are #included in StdAfx.h are precompiled into files named *projectname*.pch and StdAfx.obj so that once compiled, they don't have to be compiled again. AppWizard #includes StdAfx.h in the CPP files that it generates, and inside StdAfx.h, it adds #includes for core MFC header files such as Afxwin.h. You can add #includes of your own for other MFC header files, for C run-time header files, and for static header files of other types. Do not #include header files that are subject to change as the application is being developed, or you'll lose the benefits of using precompiled headers.

An interesting aside to a discussion of precompiled headers is the fact that Visual C++ effectively ignores statements that appear in a source code file *before* the statement that #includes StdAfx.h. That means code like this will compile just fine:

```
kjasdfj;oai4efj
#include "Stdafx.h"
```

Why is this fact important? Because more than one MFC programmer has been bitten by code like this:

```
#include <math.h>
#include "Stdafx.h"
```

Put the #include for Math.h *after* the #include for StdAfx.h (or better yet, put it inside StdAfx.h) to avoid this kind of error.

Resource.h and Shapes.rc

Among the source code files that AppWizard generates are an RC file containing definitions for all the application's resources and a header file (Resource.h) containing #defines for the command IDs and other symbols the RC file uses. Look inside the RC file and you'll find, among other things, a menu template and an accelerator table. Rather than edit these resources by hand, you can use Visual C++'s resource editor, which allows you to edit menus, accelerators, icons, and other resources visually and then applies your changes to the RC file. To see the menu editor firsthand, click the ResourceView tab in Visual C++'s workspace window and then double-click the menu resource IDR_MAINFRAME. This will open the menu in the menu editor, where making changes is as simple as pointing and clicking and typing information into dialog boxes. You can also edit the RC file directly, but if you decide to do this, be sure to use the Open dialog box's Open As Text option to open the file as if it were an ordinary text file.

Shapes.h and Shapes.cpp

You already know that every MFC application contains a global instance of a *CWinApp*-derived class representing the application itself. AppWizard has already derived an application class named *CShapesApp* and placed the source code in Shapes.h and Shapes.cpp. It has also declared a global instance of the class by including the statement

```
CShapesApp theApp;
```

in Shapes.cpp.

CShapesApp::InitInstance looks a little different than the *InitInstance* functions in Chapters 1, 2, and 3. It creates a frame window by instantiating a class named *CMainFrame* and calling *LoadFrame* on the resulting object:

```
CMainFrame* pFrame = new CMainFrame;
m_pMainWnd = pFrame;
   .
   .
   .
pFrame->LoadFrame(IDR_MAINFRAME,
    WS_OVERLAPPEDWINDOW | FWS_ADDTOTITLE, NULL,
    NULL);
```

CMainFrame is another AppWizard-generated class, one that represents the application's top-level window. Like the *CMainWindow* class featured in previous chapters, *CMainFrame*'s base class is *CFrameWnd*. Unlike *CMainWindow*, *CMainFrame*'s constructor doesn't call *Create*. Therefore, it's up to *InitInstance* to create the frame window object and the frame window that goes with it.

AppWizard's *CShapesApp* class also includes a command handler named *OnAppAbout*:

```
// In the message map
ON_COMMAND(ID_APP_ABOUT, OnAppAbout)
   .
   .
   .
void CShapesApp::OnAppAbout()
{
    CAboutDlg aboutDlg;
    aboutDlg.DoModal();
}
```

This code will make more sense to you after you read about dialog boxes in Chapter 8. Its purpose is to display an "About box"—a dialog box containing information about the program, such as its author and copyright. *CAboutDlg* is the class that represents the About box; its source code is also found in Shapes.h and Shapes.cpp. AppWizard inserts an About Shapes command (ID=ID_APP_ABOUT) into the application's Help menu in support of this feature. Selecting the Help-About Shapes command executes *CShapesApp::OnAppAbout* and displays a simple About box.

ChildView.h and ChildView.cpp

The greatest difference between the AppWizard-generated Shapes application and the applications we built by hand in earlier chapters is the addition of a new class named *CChildView*. *CChildView* is a *CWnd* derivative that represents the application's "view"—a special window that is sized to fit the client area of the application's frame window and then placed neatly over the top of it. What appears to be the frame window's client area is actually the view window, which means that we'll write our WM_PAINT handler in *CChildView*, not *CMainFrame*. In fact, AppWizard has already included a do-nothing *OnPaint* function in *CChildView*. It has also overridden *CWnd::Pre-CreateWindow* and, in the override, included code that registers a special WND-CLASS for the view and adds WS_EX_CLIENTEDGE to the view's window style. WS_EX_CLIENTEDGE gives the window a three-dimensional look by making the view appear to be recessed inside the frame window. MFC's *CFrameWnd* class includes code that keeps the view glued to the frame window by automatically resizing the view window whenever the frame window is resized.

In effect, AppWizard has created an application that uses a view in much the same way that a document/view application uses a view. The question is, Why? Is this an inherently better way to architect an application? The primary reason AppWizard inserts a view is that a view-based architecture simplifies the task of managing space inside a frame window that hosts toolbars and other UI objects. If you were to draw directly to the client area of a frame window that contains a toolbar, you'd have to subtract the toolbar rectangle from the frame window's client-area rectangle to compute an "effective" client area every time you called *GetClientRect*. Such shenanigans aren't necessary in view-based applications because MFC resizes the view to fit the frame window's effective client area whenever the frame window's size changes or a change occurs in the size, position, or visibility of a toolbar or status bar. Call *GetClient-Rect* in a view class and you get a precise measure of the space available to you.

The effect that a view-based application architecture will have on the code that you write can be summarized as follows:

■   WM_PAINT messages should be processed in the view, not in the frame window.

■ Client-area mouse messages should be processed in the view, not in the frame window. Because the view completely obscures the frame window's client area, the frame window won't receive any client-area mouse messages.

■ Keyboard message handlers, too, should be processed in the view, not in the frame window.

Writing view-based applications now will help prepare you to write full-blown document/view MFC applications beginning in Chapter 9.

MainFrm.h and MainFrm.cpp

These files contain the source code for the AppWizard-generated frame window class named *CMainFrame*. This frame window class differs from the *CMainWindow* class we've been using in several respects:

■ It overrides *CFrameWnd::PreCreateWindow*. Because *CMainFrame* doesn't create a window in its class constructor, overriding *PreCreateWindow* is the only way it can exercise control over the window style and other window characteristics.

■ It overrides *AssertValid* and *Dump*, two *CObject* functions used for diagnostic testing.

■ It includes a *CChildView* member variable named *m_wndView* that represents the view window.

■ It includes a WM_SETFOCUS handler that shifts the input focus to the view anytime the frame window receives the input focus. This transfer is important because it is the view, not the frame window, that is the primary source of mouse and keyboard input. If the input focus were given to the frame window and not transferred to the view, keyboard message handlers in the view class wouldn't work.

■ It overrides *CFrameWnd::OnCmdMsg* and routes commands to the view and (indirectly) to the application object using a simplified form of the command routing architecture used in document/view applications. The practical effect is that command handlers and update handlers for the program's menu items can be placed in the frame window class, the view class, or the application class. Without *OnCmdMsg*, command and update handlers would be restricted to the frame window. Command routing is discussed in Chapters 9 and 11.

Beyond AppWizard

AppWizard generates a generic application skeleton. Once AppWizard has run its course, it's up to you to write the code that makes your application different from all the rest. You don't have to write all that code by hand; you can use ClassWizard to perform basic tasks such as adding message handlers, command handlers, and update handlers. In effect, ClassWizard writes the mundane code, so you can concentrate on the application-specific code. With that thought in mind, here are the steps required to duplicate the source code presented in Figure 4-3:

1. With the Shapes project open in Visual C++, add a protected int member variable named *m_nShape* to the *CChildView* class. You can add this member variable manually, or you can add it visually. To add it visually, click the ClassView tab in the workspace window, right-click *CChildView* in ClassView, select Add Member Variable from the context menu, and fill in the Add Member Variable dialog box as shown in Figure 4-7.

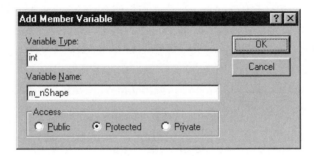

Figure 4-7. *The Add Member Variable dialog box.*

2. Initialize *m_nShape* to 1 by adding the following statement to *CChildView*'s constructor:

   ```
   m_nShape = 1; // Triangle
   ```

   m_nShape will hold 0, 1, or 2, indicating that the shape drawn in the view is a circle, a triangle, or a square, respectively. Initializing *m_nShape* to 1 makes a triangle the default.

3. Modify the view's *OnPaint* handler so that it looks like the one in Figure 4-3. AppWizard has already added an empty *OnPaint* handler to the view class; all you have to do is edit it.

4. Click the ResourceView tab at the bottom of the workspace window to see a list of the resources that AppWizard created. Double-click the IDR_MAINFRAME menu resource to open it for editing, and delete the Edit

and Help menus. Then add a Shape menu to the right of the File menu, and add these three items to the Shape menu:

Menu Item Text	Command ID
&Circle\tF7	ID_SHAPE_CIRCLE
&Triangle\tF8	ID_SHAPE_TRIANGLE
&Square\tF9	ID_SHAPE_SQUARE

To delete an item from a menu, click the item once to select it and then press the Delete key. To add an item, double-click the empty rectangle that appears in the menu and type the menu item text and command ID into the Menu Item Properties dialog box. (See Figure 4-8.) Top-level menu items don't need command IDs, so for them the ID box is disabled. For other menu items, you can type in the command ID or let Visual C++ choose one for you. If you dismiss the Menu Item Properties dialog box and the ID box is blank, Visual C++ will generate a command ID of the form ID_*top*_*item*, where *top* is the top-level menu item name and *item* is the text assigned to the menu item. Regardless of how the command ID is generated, Visual C++ adds a #define statement to Resource.h assigning the ID a numeric value. The completed Shape menu is shown in Figure 4-9.

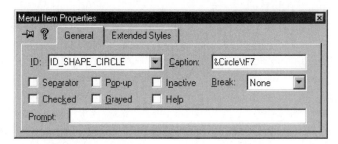

Figure 4-8. *The Menu Item Properties dialog box.*

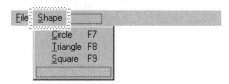

Figure 4-9. *The Shape menu.*

5. Add command handlers to the view class for the Circle, Triangle, and Square commands. Here's the finished code:

```
// In CChildView's message map
ON_COMMAND(ID_SHAPE_CIRCLE, OnShapeCircle)
ON_COMMAND(ID_SHAPE_TRIANGLE, OnShapeTriangle)
ON_COMMAND(ID_SHAPE_SQUARE, OnShapeSquare)
    .
    .
    .
void CChildView::OnShapeCircle()
{
    m_nShape = 0;
    Invalidate ();
}

void CChildView::OnShapeTriangle()
{
    m_nShape = 1;
    Invalidate ();
}

void CChildView::OnShapeSquare()
{
    m_nShape = 2;
    Invalidate ();
}
```

You can add these command handlers by hand, or you can let ClassWizard add them for you. To use ClassWizard to add a command handler for the Circle command, click the ClassView tab at the bottom of the workspace window, right-click *CChildView* in ClassView, and select Add Windows Message Handler from the context menu to display the New Windows Message And Event Handlers dialog box. (See Figure 4-10.) Find ID_SHAPE_CIRCLE in the Class Or Object To Handle list box, and click it. Then double-click COMMAND in the New Windows Messages/Events list box. When ClassWizard asks you for a function name, accept the default—*OnShapeCircle*. COMMAND will move to the Existing Message/Event Handlers list box, indicating that a command handler now exists for the ID_SHAPE_CIRCLE menu item. Finish up by clicking the Edit Existing button to go to the empty command handler and adding the statements

```
m_nShape = 0;
Invalidate ();
```

to the function body. Repeat this process to write command handlers for the Triangle and Square commands, but set *m_nShape* to 1 and 2, respectively, in their function bodies.

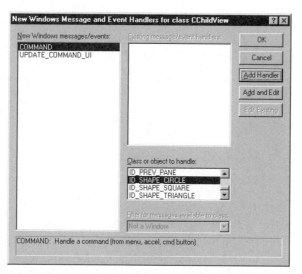

Figure 4-10. *The New Windows Message And Event Handlers dialog box.*

6. Add update handlers to the view class for the Circle, Triangle, and Square commands. Here's the completed code:

```
ON_UPDATE_COMMAND_UI(ID_SHAPE_CIRCLE, OnUpdateShapeCircle)
ON_UPDATE_COMMAND_UI(ID_SHAPE_TRIANGLE, OnUpdateShapeTriangle)
ON_UPDATE_COMMAND_UI(ID_SHAPE_SQUARE, OnUpdateShapeSquare)
    .
    .
    .
void CChildView::OnUpdateShapeCircle(CCmdUI* pCmdUI)
{
    pCmdUI->SetCheck (m_nShape == 0);
}

void CChildView::OnUpdateShapeTriangle(CCmdUI* pCmdUI)
{
    pCmdUI->SetCheck (m_nShape == 1);
}

void CChildView::OnUpdateShapeSquare(CCmdUI* pCmdUI)
{
    pCmdUI->SetCheck (m_nShape == 2);
}
```

Once more, you can add these handlers by hand or you can add them with ClassWizard. To write an update handler with ClassWizard, follow the same procedure used to write a command handler, but double-click UPDATE_COMMAND_UI rather than COMMAND in the New Windows Messages/Events list box.

7. Click the ResourceView tab in the workspace window, and open the accelerator resource IDR_MAINFRAME for editing. Add the following accelerators to serve as shortcuts for the items in the Shape menu:

Shortcut Key	Command ID
F7	ID_SHAPE_CIRCLE
F8	ID_SHAPE_TRIANGLE
F9	ID_SHAPE_SQUARE

To add an accelerator, double-click the empty rectangle at the bottom of the edit window and define the accelerator in the Accel Properties dialog box. (See Figure 4-11.) If you don't carry virtual key codes around in your head, you can click the Next Key Typed button and press the shortcut key rather than type the key code into the Key combo box. While you're at it, delete the other accelerators (the ones that AppWizard created) since Shapes doesn't use them. To delete an accelerator, simply click it once to select it and press the Delete key.

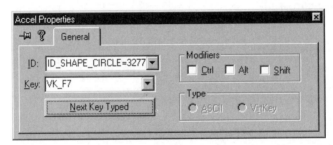

Figure 4-11. *The Accel Properties dialog box.*

8. If *CMainFrame* doesn't include the *OnCreate* handler discussed in the note on page 215, add it now. Rather than add the message handler by hand, you can add it with ClassWizard. How? Right-click *CMainFrame* in the ClassView window, select Add Windows Message Handler, double-click WM_CREATE, and click Edit Existing. You'll find yourself in the empty message handler body, poised to type in the finished code. ClassWizard has already done everything else, including adding an ON_WM_CREATE entry to the message map.

With that, you've successfully built the Shapes application depicted in Figure 4-2. It's a simple application whose *OnPaint* handler examines a member variable (*m_nShape*) and draws a circle, a triangle, or a square. Command handlers for the items in the Shape menu set *m_nShape* to 0, 1, or 2 and force a repaint by calling *CWnd::Invalidate*. Update handlers place a check mark by the shape that is currently selected. All painting and processing of menu commands is done in the view class, which serves as a proxy of sorts for the frame window's client area. The function keys F7, F8, and F9 provide shortcuts for the Circle, Triangle, and Square commands by virtue of the accelerators that you added. Given this basis to work from, you should be able to add menu items to any application and write command and update handlers for them.

An interesting point to ponder regarding Shapes is that the File-Exit command closes the application, yet nowhere in the program's source code will you find a command handler for File-Exit. The secret is the following statement in *CWinApp*'s message map, which is found in the MFC source code file Appcore.cpp:

```
ON_COMMAND(ID_APP_EXIT, OnAppExit)
```

Remember that message maps are passed to derived classes by inheritance just like function and data members. Even though this entry doesn't appear in *CShapesApp*'s message map, it's there implicitly because *CShapesApp* derives from *CWinApp*. Because AppWizard assigned the Exit command the ID ID_APP_EXIT, selecting the command invokes *OnAppExit*, which also comes to *CShapesApp* via inheritance. *OnAppExit* sends a WM_CLOSE message to the application's main window. You can view its source code in Appui.cpp.

The Process in Review

Building an application with AppWizard and ClassWizard is altogether different than building an application by hand. It's important to realize that the wizards do nothing you can't do yourself; they're simply code-generating tools that make the development process more efficient. It makes sense to use the wizards if you understand the code that they generate. That's why the first three chapters of this book didn't use the wizards—to help build your fundamental knowledge of MFC. As the applications that you build become more complex, the code that the wizards generate will become more complex, too. You'll see what I mean in the last few chapters of this book, when we use MFC to build COM-enabled applications and a few button clicks with the wizards will touch not just one or two source code files, but several. The wizards *never* do anything you can't do yourself, but they can save you a lot of time and effort that you'd otherwise spend re-creating the basic plumbing common to all Windows applications.

MENU MAGIC

The first half of this chapter covered probably 80 percent of everything you'll ever need to know about menus. Occasionally, however, you'll need to go beyond the basics and do something extra. The following "something extras" are discussed in the second half of the chapter:

■ Techniques for creating and modifying menus on the fly

■ The system menu and methods for customizing it

■ Menus that display graphics instead of text (owner-draw menus)

■ Cascading menus

■ Context menus

We'll close out this chapter by revising the Shapes application to include both an owner-draw Color menu and a right-click context menu.

Creating Menus Programmatically

Loading a menu resource from your application's EXE file isn't the only way to create a menu. You can also do it programmatically using MFC's *CMenu* class and its member functions. We've yet to explore *CMenu* in any depth because basic menu support doesn't require a *CMenu*. *CMenu* comes in handy when you want to create a menu on the fly, perhaps from information that isn't available until run time, or when you want to modify an existing menu (a subject we'll cover in the next section). In situations such as these, *CMenu* will be your best friend.

You create menus programmatically using a combination of *CMenu::CreateMenu*, *CMenu::CreatePopupMenu*, and *CMenu::AppendMenu*. You build a top-level menu and its submenus by creating a menu with *CreateMenu*, creating the submenus with *CreatePopupMenu*, and attaching the submenus to the top-level menu with *Append-Menu*. The following program listing creates a menu identical to the one featured in the Shapes application and attaches it to the frame window. The only difference is that the application, not the resource editor, creates this menu:

```
CMenu menuMain;
menuMain.CreateMenu ();

CMenu menuPopup;
menuPopup.CreatePopupMenu ();
menuPopup.AppendMenu (MF_STRING, ID_FILE_EXIT, "E&xit");
menuMain.AppendMenu (MF_POPUP, (UINT) menuPopup.Detach (), "&File");
```

```
menuPopup.CreatePopupMenu ();
menuPopup.AppendMenu (MF_STRING, ID_SHAPE_CIRCLE, "&Circle\tF7");
menuPopup.AppendMenu (MF_STRING, ID_SHAPE_TRIANGLE, "&Triangle\tF8");
menuPopup.AppendMenu (MF_STRING, ID_SHAPE_SQUARE, "&Square\tF9");
menuMain.AppendMenu (MF_POPUP, (UINT) menuPopup.Detach (), "&Shape");

SetMenu (&menuMain);
menuMain.Detach ();
```

The first two statements create a *CMenu* object named *menuMain* that represents an empty top-level menu. The next block of statements creates the File menu and attaches it to the top-level menu. The MF_POPUP parameter passed to *AppendMenu* tells Windows that the second parameter is a menu handle, not a menu item ID, and *Detach* both detaches the menu from the *menuPopup* object and retrieves the menu handle. The third statement block creates the Shape menu and attaches it to the top-level menu. Finally, the call to *SetMenu* attaches the newly formed menu to the frame window, and *Detach* disassociates the top-level menu and *menuMain* so the top-level menu won't be destroyed as soon as the function ends. If the window is visible when *SetMenu* is called, *DrawMenuBar* should also be called to paint the menu on the screen.

Modifying Menus Programmatically

In addition to creating menus dynamically, you can modify existing menus. The following table lists the *CMenu* member functions used to add, modify, and delete menu items.

Function	*Description*
AppendMenu	Adds an item to the end of a menu
InsertMenu	Inserts an item into a menu at a specified location
ModifyMenu	Changes the command ID, text, or other characteristics of a menu item
DeleteMenu	Deletes a menu item and the submenu associated with it, if any
RemoveMenu	Deletes a menu item

The difference between *RemoveMenu* and *DeleteMenu* is that if the item being removed has a submenu, *DeleteMenu* removes the item and destroys the submenu, too. *RemoveMenu* removes the item but leaves the submenu extant in memory. *DeleteMenu* is the one you'll usually want to use, but *RemoveMenu* is useful if you want to preserve the submenu for later use.

Before you can modify a menu by adding, changing, or deleting menu items, you need a *CMenu* pointer referencing the menu. MFC's *CWnd::GetMenu* function returns a *CMenu* pointer for a window's top-level menu or NULL if the window doesn't have a top-level menu. Let's say you want to delete the Shapes application's Shape menu at run time. Here's the code to do it:

```
CMenu* pMenu = GetMenu ();
pMenu->DeleteMenu (1, MF_BYPOSITION);
```

The 1 passed to *DeleteMenu* is the Shape menu's 0-based index. The File menu occupies position 0, the Shape menu position 1. MF_BYPOSITION tells *DeleteMenu* that the first parameter is a positional index and not a menu item ID. In this case, your only choice is to identify the menu item by position because Shape is a submenu that has no menu item ID.

To apply *DeleteMenu* and other *CMenu* functions to items in a submenu, you need a pointer either to the main menu or to the submenu. *CMenu::GetSubMenu* returns a pointer to a submenu. The following code fragment uses *GetMenu* to get a pointer to the main menu and *GetSubMenu* to get a pointer to the Shape menu. It then deletes the Square and Circle commands.

```
CMenu* pMenu = GetMenu ()->GetSubMenu (1);
pMenu->DeleteMenu (2, MF_BYPOSITION);                    // Delete Square
pMenu->DeleteMenu (ID_SHAPE_CIRCLE, MF_BYCOMMAND); // Delete Circle
```

The first call to *DeleteMenu* identifies the menu item by its position in the menu; the second identifies it by its command ID. The MF_BYPOSITION and MF_BYCOMMAND flags tell Windows which means of identification you're using. If you specify neither, the default is MF_BYCOMMAND. The lone parameter passed to *GetSubMenu* is the 0-based index of the submenu. Because you identified Circle by ID and not by position, you could also delete it by calling *DeleteMenu* through the pointer to the main menu, like this:

```
CMenu* pMenu = GetMenu ();
pMenu->DeleteMenu (ID_SHAPE_CIRCLE, MF_BYCOMMAND);
```

As long as a menu item is identified by ID, you can access it through a pointer to the menu in which it appears or a pointer to any higher-level menu. Don't try to use MF_BYPOSITION to delete an item in a submenu with the pointer returned by *GetMenu*—you might delete a submenu by mistake.

To change the characteristics of an existing menu item, use *CMenu::ModifyMenu*. If *pMenu* refers to the Shape menu, the statements

```
pMenu->ModifyMenu (ID_SHAPE_TRIANGLE, MF_STRING | MF_BYCOMMAND,
    ID_SHAPE_TRIANGLE, "&Three-Sided Polygon");
pMenu->ModifyMenu (2, MF_STRING | MF_BYPOSITION,
    ID_SHAPE_SQUARE, "&Four-Sided Polygon");
```

modify the Triangle and Square commands to read "Three-Sided Polygon" and "Four-Sided Polygon," respectively. The third parameter passed to the *ModifyMenu* function is the menu item's new command ID, which should be the same as the original if you don't want to change it. If the item you're changing represents a submenu rather than an ordinary menu item, the third parameter holds the menu handle instead of a menu item ID. Given a *CMenu* pointer to a submenu, you can always get the menu handle from the object's *m_bMenu* data member.

The System Menu

Just as a window can call *CWnd::GetMenu* to obtain a *CMenu* pointer to its top-level menu, it can call *CWnd::GetSystemMenu* to obtain a pointer to its system menu. Most applications are content to let Windows manage the system menu, but every now and then the need to do something special arises, such as adding an item of your own to the system menu or changing the behavior of an existing item.

Suppose you want to add an About MyApp menu item to your application's system menu. About commands are normally placed in the Help menu, but maybe your application doesn't have a Help menu. Or maybe your application is a small utility program that doesn't have any menus at all, in which case adding About MyApp to the system menu is more efficient than loading an entire menu for the benefit of just one command.

The first step is to get a pointer to the system menu, like this:

```
CMenu* pSystemMenu = GetSystemMenu (FALSE);
```

The FALSE parameter tells *GetSystemMenu* that you want a pointer to a copy of the system menu that you can modify. (TRUE resets the system menu to its default state.)

The second step is to add "About MyApp" to the system menu:

```
pSystemMenu->AppendMenu (MF_SEPARATOR);
pSystemMenu->AppendMenu (MF_STRING, ID_SYSMENU_ABOUT,
    _T ("&About MyApp"));
```

The first call to *AppendMenu* adds a menu item separator to set your menu item apart from other items in the system menu; the second adds "About MyApp," whose ID is ID_SYSMENU_ABOUT. A good place to put this code is in the main window's *OnCreate* handler. Be aware that items added to the system menu should be assigned IDs that are multiples of 16 (16, 32, 48, and so on). Windows uses the lower four bits of the system menu's command IDs for its own purposes, so if you use any of those bits, you could receive some unexpected results.

As it stands now, the new item will show up in the system menu but it won't do anything. When the user picks an item from the system menu, the window receives a

WM_SYSCOMMAND message with *wParam* equal to the menu item ID. The following *OnSysCommand* handler inspects the menu item ID and displays an About box if the ID equals ID_SYSMENU_ABOUT:

```
// In CMainWindow's message map
ON_WM_SYSCOMMAND ()
   .
   .
   .
void CMainWindow::OnSysCommand (UINT nID, LPARAM lParam)
{
    if ((nID & 0xFFF0) == ID_SYSMENU_ABOUT) {
        // Display the About box.
        return;
    }
    CFrameWnd::OnSysCommand (nID, lParam);
}
```

An *nID* value equal to ID_SYSMENU_ABOUT means that "About MyApp" was selected. If *nID* equals anything else, you must call the base class's *OnSysCommand* handler or else the system menu (and other parts of the program, too) will cease to function. Before you test the *nID* value passed to *OnSysCommand*, be sure to AND it with 0xFFF0 to strip any bits added by Windows.

You can also use *OnSysCommand* to modify the behavior of items Windows places in the system menu. The following message handler disables the system menu's Close command in a frame window:

```
void CMainWindow::OnSysCommand (UINT nID, LPARAM lParam)
{
    if ((nID & 0xFFF0) != SC_CLOSE)
        CFrameWnd::OnSysCommand (nID, lParam);
}
```

This version of *OnSysCommand* tests *nID* and passes the message to *CFrameWnd* only if *nID* represents an item other than Close. Alternatives to disabling Close with an *OnSysCommand* handler include disabling the menu item with *CMenu::EnableMenuItem* or deleting it altogether with *CMenu::DeleteMenu*, as shown here:

```
CMenu* pSystemMenu = GetSystemMenu (FALSE);
pSystemMenu->EnableMenuItem (SC_CLOSE,                   // Disable it.
    MF_BYCOMMAND | MF_DISABLED);
pSystemMenu->DeleteMenu (SC_CLOSE, MF_BYCOMMAND);       // Delete it.
```

The command IDs for Close and other system menu items are listed in the documentation for *OnSysCommand*.

Owner-Draw Menus

Menus that display strings of text are fine for most applications, but some menus cry out for pictures instead of text. One example is a Color menu containing Cyan and Magenta commands. Many users won't know that cyan is a 50-50 mix of blue and green, or that magenta is a mix of equal parts red and blue. But if the menu contained color swatches instead of text, the meanings of the menu items would be crystal clear. Graphical menus are a little more work to put together than text menus, but the reward can be well worth the effort.

The easiest way to do graphical menus is to create bitmaps depicting the menu items and use them in calls to *CMenu::AppendMenu*. MFC represents bitmapped images with the class *CBitmap*, and one form of *AppendMenu* accepts a pointer to a *CBitmap* object whose image then becomes the menu item. Once a *CBitmap* object is appended to the menu, Windows displays the bitmap when the menu is displayed. The drawback to using bitmaps is that they're fixed in size and not easily adapted to changes in screen metrics.

A more flexible way to replace text with graphics in a menu is to use *owner-draw* menu items. When a menu containing an owner-draw item is displayed, Windows sends the menu's owner (the window to which the menu is attached) a WM_DRAWITEM message saying, "It's time to draw the menu item, and here's where I want you to draw it." Windows even supplies a device context in which to do the drawing. The WM_DRAWITEM handler might display a bitmap, or it could use GDI functions to draw the menu item at the specified location. Before a menu containing an owner-draw menu item is displayed for the first time, Windows sends the menu's owner a WM_MEASUREITEM message to inquire about the menu item's dimensions. If a submenu contains, say, five owner-draw menu items, the window that the menu is attached to will receive five WM_MEASUREITEM messages and five WM_DRAWITEM messages the first time the submenu is displayed. Each time the submenu is displayed thereafter, the window will receive five WM_DRAWITEM messages but no further WM_MEASUREITEM messages.

The first step in implementing an owner-draw menu is to stamp all the owner-draw items with the label MF_OWNERDRAW. Unfortunately, MF_OWNERDRAW can't be specified in a MENU template unless the template is manually changed to a MENUEX resource, and the Visual C++ resource editor doesn't support the owner-draw style, anyway. Therefore, the best way to create MF_OWNERDRAW items in an MFC application is to convert conventional items into owner-draw items programmatically using *CMenu::ModifyMenu*.

The second step is adding an *OnMeasureItem* handler and associated message-map entry to respond to WM_MEASUREITEM messages. *OnMeasureItem* is prototyped as follows:

```
afx_msg void OnMeasureItem (int nIDCtl, LPMEASUREITEMSTRUCT lpmis)
```

nIDCtl contains a control ID identifying the control to which the message pertains and is meaningless for owner-draw menus. (WM_MEASUREITEM messages are used for owner-draw controls as well as owner-draw menus. When *OnMeasureItem* is called for a control, *nIDCtl* identifies the control.) *lpmis* points to a structure of type MEASUREITEMSTRUCT, which has the following form:

```
typedef struct tagMEASUREITEMSTRUCT {
    UINT    CtlType;
    UINT    CtlID;
    UINT    itemID;
    UINT    itemWidth;
    UINT    itemHeight;
    DWORD   itemData;
} MEASUREITEMSTRUCT;
```

OnMeasureItem's job is to fill in the *itemWidth* and *itemHeight* fields, informing Windows of the menu item's horizontal and vertical dimensions, in pixels. An *OnMeasureItem* handler can be as simple as this:

```
lpmis->itemWidth = 64;
lpmis->itemHeight = 16;
```

To compensate for differing video resolutions, a better approach is to base the width and height of items in an owner-draw menu on some standard such as the SM_CYMENU value returned by *::GetSystemMetrics*:

```
lpmis->itemWidth = ::GetSystemMetrics (SM_CYMENU) * 4;
lpmis->itemHeight = ::GetSystemMetrics (SM_CYMENU);
```

SM_CYMENU is the height of the menu bars the system draws for top-level menus. By basing the height of owner-draw menu items on this value and scaling the width accordingly, you can ensure that owner-draw items have roughly the same proportions as menu items drawn by Windows.

The *CtlType* field of the MEASUREITEMSTRUCT structure is set to ODT_MENU if the message pertains to an owner-draw menu and is used to differentiate between owner-draw UI elements if a window contains owner-draw controls as well as owner-draw menu items. *CtlID* and *itemData* are not used for menus, but *itemID* contains the menu item ID. If the owner-draw menu items your application creates are of different heights and widths, you can use this field to determine which menu item *OnMeasureItem* was called for.

The third and final step in implementing owner-draw menu items is to provide an *OnDrawItem* handler for WM_DRAWITEM messages. The actual drawing is done inside *OnDrawItem*. The function is prototyped as follows:

```
afx_msg void OnDrawItem (int nIDCtl, LPDRAWITEMSTRUCT lpdis)
```

Once again, *nIDCtl* is undefined for owner-draw menu items. *lpdis* points to a DRAWITEMSTRUCT structure, which contains the following members:

```
typedef struct tagDRAWITEMSTRUCT {
    UINT    CtlType;
    UINT    CtlID;
    UINT    itemID;
    UINT    itemAction;
    UINT    itemState;
    HWND    hwndItem;
    HDC     hDC;
    RECT    rcItem;
    DWORD   itemData;
} DRAWITEMSTRUCT;
```

As in MEASUREITEMSTRUCT, *CtlType* is set to ODT_MENU if the message pertains to an owner-draw menu item, *itemID* holds the menu item ID, and *CtlID* and *itemData* are unused. *hDC* holds the handle of the device context in which the menu item is drawn, and *rcItem* is a RECT structure containing the coordinates of the rectangle in which the item appears. The size of the rectangle described by *rcItem* is based on the dimensions you provided to Windows in response to the WM_MEASUREITEM message for this particular menu item. Windows doesn't clip what you draw to the rectangle but instead relies on your code to be "well-behaved" and stay within the bounds described by *rcItem*. *hwndItem* holds the handle of the menu to which the menu item belongs. This value isn't often used because the other fields provide most or all of the information that's needed.

DRAWITEMSTRUCT's *itemAction* and *itemState* fields describe the drawing action required and the current state of the menu item—checked or unchecked, enabled or disabled, and so on. For an owner-draw item, *itemAction* contains one of two values: ODA_DRAWENTIRE means that you should draw the entire item, and ODA_SELECT means that you can optionally redraw just the part of the item that changes when the item is highlighted or unhighlighted. When the highlight bar is moved from one owner-draw menu item to another, the menu's owner receives a WM_DRAWITEM message without the ODA_SELECT flag for the item that's losing the highlight and another WM_DRAWITEM message with an ODA_SELECT flag for the item that's becoming highlighted. Programs that use owner-draw menus often ignore the value in *itemAction* and redraw the menu item in its entirety no matter what the value of *itemAction*, using *itemState* to decide whether the item should be drawn with or without highlighting.

itemState contains zero or more of the bit flags shown in the following table specifying the menu item's current state.

Value	Meaning
ODS_CHECKED	The menu item is currently checked.
ODS_DISABLED	The menu item is currently disabled.
ODS_GRAYED	The menu item is currently grayed out.
ODS_SELECTED	The menu item is currently selected.

This state information is important because it tells you how you should draw the menu item. Which of the bit flags you examine depends on which states you allow the menu item to assume. You should always check the ODS_SELECTED flag and highlight the menu item if the flag is set. If your application includes code to check and uncheck owner-draw menu items, you should look for ODS_CHECKED and draw a check mark next to the menu item if the flag is set. Similarly, if you allow the item to be enabled and disabled, look for an ODS_DISABLED flag and draw accordingly. By default, MFC disables a menu item if you provide neither an ON_COMMAND handler nor an ON_UPDATE_COMMAND_UI handler for it, so it's possible for menu items to become disabled even though your application didn't explicitly disable them. You can disable this feature of MFC for frame windows by setting *CFrameWnd::m_bAutoMenuEnable* to FALSE.

An alternative method for implementing owner-draw menus is to attach the menu to a *CMenu* object and override *CMenu*'s virtual *MeasureItem* and *DrawItem* functions to do the drawing. This technique is useful for creating self-contained menu objects that do their own drawing rather than rely on their owners to do it for them. For cases in which a menu is loaded from a resource and attached to a window without using a *CMenu* object as an intermediary, however, it's just as easy to let the window that owns the menu draw the menu items as well. That's the approach we'll use when we modify Shapes to include an owner-draw Color menu.

OnMenuChar Processing

One drawback to using owner-draw menus is that Windows doesn't provide keyboard shortcuts such as Alt-C-R for Color-Red. Even if you define the menu item text as "&Red" before using *ModifyMenu* to change the menu item to MF_OWNERDRAW, Alt-C-R will no longer work. Alt-C will still pull down the Color menu, but the R key will do nothing.

Windows provides a solution to this problem in the form of WM_MENUCHAR messages. A window receives a WM_MENUCHAR message when a menu is displayed and a key that doesn't correspond to a menu item is pressed. By processing WM_MENU-CHAR messages, you can add keyboard shortcuts to owner-draw menu items. MFC's *CWnd::OnMenuChar* function is prototyped as follows:

```
afx_msg LRESULT OnMenuChar (UINT nChar, UINT nFlags, CMenu* pMenu)
```

When *OnMenuChar* is called, *nChar* contains the ANSI or Unicode character code of the key that was pressed, *nFlags* contains an MF_POPUP flag if the menu to which the message pertains is a submenu, and *pMenu* identifies the menu itself. The pointer stored in *pMenu* might be a temporary one created by the framework and shouldn't be saved for later use.

The value returned by *OnMenuChar* tells Windows how to respond to the keystroke. The high word of the return value should be set to one of the following values:

- 0 if Windows should ignore the keystroke

- 1 if Windows should close the menu

- 2 if Windows should select one of the items displayed in the menu

If the high word of the return value is 2, the low word should hold the ID of the corresponding menu item. Windows provides a MAKELRESULT macro for setting the high and low words of an LRESULT value. The following statement sets the high word of an LRESULT value to 2 and the low word to ID_COLOR_RED:

```
LRESULT lResult = MAKELRESULT (ID_COLOR_RED, 2);
```

Of course, you can always rely on keyboard accelerators instead of keyboard shortcuts. They work just fine with owner-draw menu items. But thanks to WM_MENU-CHAR messages, you have the option of providing conventional keyboard shortcuts as well.

Cascading Menus

When you click the Start button in the taskbar, a popup menu appears listing the various options for starting applications, opening documents, changing system settings, and so on. Some of the menu items have arrows next to them indicating that clicking invokes another menu. And in some cases, these menus are nested several levels deep. Click Start-Programs-Accessories-Games, for example, and the Games menu is the fourth in a series of menus cascaded across the screen. This multitiered menu structure permits items in the Start menu to be organized hierarchically and prevents individual menus from being so cluttered that they become practically useless.

Cascading menus aren't the sole property of the operating system; application programs can use them, too. Creating a cascading menu is as simple as inserting one menu into another as if it were a menu item. Windows sweats the details, which include drawing the arrow next to the item name and displaying the cascaded menu without a button click if the cursor pauses over the item. Here's how Shapes' top-level menu would be defined if the Shape menu was nested inside an Options menu.

```
IDR_MAINFRAME MENU PRELOAD DISCARDABLE
BEGIN
    POPUP "&File"
    BEGIN
        MENUITEM "E&xit",                   ID_APP_EXIT
    END
    POPUP "&Options"
    BEGIN
        POPUP "&Shape"
        BEGIN
            MENUITEM "&Circle\tF7",         ID_SHAPE_CIRCLE
            MENUITEM "&Triangle\tF8",       ID_SHAPE_TRIANGLE
            MENUITEM "&Square\tF9",         ID_SHAPE_SQUARE
        END
        MENUITEM "&Color…",                 ID_OPTIONS_COLOR
        MENUITEM "Si&ze…",                  ID_OPTIONS_SIZE
    END
END
```

Figure 4-12 shows how the resulting menu would look. Selecting Shape from the Options menu displays a cascading menu. Moreover, the remainder of the program works as it did before, so the command and update handlers associated with the items in the Shape menu needn't change.

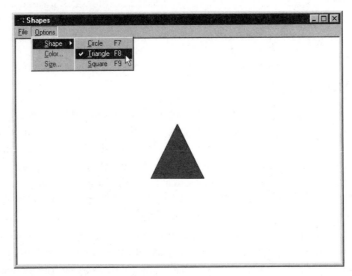

Figure 4-12. *Cascading menus.*

You don't have to edit menu resources by hand to create cascading menus. Instead, you can create a nested menu in Visual C++'s menu editor by checking the Pop-up check box in the Menu Item Properties dialog box, as shown in Figure 4-13.

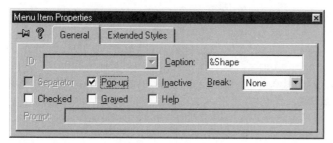

Figure 4-13. *Creating a nested menu.*

Context Menus

Windows uses right-click context menus extensively to make objects displayed by the shell easier to manipulate. Right-clicking the My Computer icon on the desktop, for example, displays a context menu containing a concise list of actions that can be performed on My Computer: Explore, Rename, Map Network Drive, and so on. Right-clicking the desktop produces an entirely different context menu. Developers are encouraged to build context menus into their applications to be consistent with the shell and to reinforce the object-oriented UI paradigm. Windows makes it easy by sending your application a WM_CONTEXTMENU message when the right mouse button is clicked in a window and the resulting right-button message isn't processed.

A context menu is nothing more than a submenu that isn't attached to a top-level menu. MFC's *CMenu::TrackPopupMenu* function displays such a menu. Here's the function prototype:

```
BOOL TrackPopupMenu (UINT nFlags, int x, int y, CWnd* pWnd,
    LPCRECT lpRect = NULL)
```

x and *y* identify the location on the screen (in screen coordinates) at which the menu will appear. *nFlags* contains bit flags specifying the menu's horizontal alignment relative to *x* and which mouse button (or buttons) can be used to select items from the menu. The alignment flags TPM_LEFTALIGN, TPM_CENTERALIGN, and TPM_RIGHTALIGN tell Windows that *x* specifies the location of the menu's left edge, center, and right edge, respectively, and the TPM_LEFTBUTTON and TPM_RIGHTBUTTON flags specify whether menu selections will be made with the left or the right mouse button. Only one of the alignment flags can be specified, but either or both of the button flags can be used. *pWnd* identifies the window that will receive messages emanating from actions in the menu, and *lpRect* points to a *CRect* object or RECT structure containing the screen coordinates of the rectangle within which the user can click without dismissing the menu. If *lpRect* is NULL, clicking outside the menu dismisses it. Assuming *pMenu* is a *CMenu* pointer that references a submenu, the statement

```
pMenu->TrackPopupMenu (TPM_LEFTALIGN ¦ TPM_LEFTBUTTON ¦
    TPM_RIGHTBUTTON, 32, 64, AfxGetMainWnd ());
```

displays the menu whose upper left corner is positioned 32 pixels right and 64 pixels down from the upper left corner of the screen. The user can make selections from the menu with either the left or the right mouse button. While the menu is displayed, the application's main window receives messages just as if the menu were part of a top-level menu. Once the menu is dismissed, the messages will cease until the menu is displayed again.

TrackPopupMenu is typically called in response to WM_CONTEXTMENU messages. MFC's ON_WM_CONTEXTMENU macro maps WM_CONTEXTMENU messages to the message handler *OnContextMenu*. *OnContextMenu* receives two parameters: a *CWnd* pointer identifying the window in which the click occurred and a *CPoint* containing the cursor's screen coordinates:

```
afx_msg void OnContextMenu (CWnd* pWnd, CPoint point)
```

If necessary, you can translate the screen coordinates passed in *point* into client coordinates with *CWnd::ScreenToClient*. It might seem curious that *OnContextMenu* receives a pointer identifying a window since mouse messages go to the window under the cursor. However, there's a reason. Unlike other messages, WM_CONTEXTMENU messages percolate upward through the window hierarchy if a right-click occurs in a child window (for example, a push button control) and the child window doesn't process the message. Therefore, if a window contains child windows, it could receive WM_CONTEXTMENU messages with *pWnd* containing a pointer to one of its children.

It's important for an *OnContextMenu* handler to call the base class's *OnContextMenu* handler if it examines *pWnd* or *point* and decides not to process the message. Otherwise, WM_CONTEXTMENU messages won't percolate upward. Worse, right-clicking the window's title bar will no longer display the system menu. The following *OnContextMenu* handler displays the context menu referenced by *pContextMenu* if the button click occurs in the upper half of the window and passes it to the base class if the click occurs elsewhere:

```
void CChildView::OnContextMenu (CWnd* pWnd, CPoint point)
{
    CPoint pos = point;
    ScreenToClient (&pos);

    CRect rect;
    GetClientRect (&rect);
    rect.bottom /= 2; // Divide the height by 2.

    if (rect.PtInRect (pos)) {
        pContextMenu->TrackPopupMenu (TPM_LEFTALIGN |
            TPM_LEFTBUTTON | TPM_RIGHTBUTTON, point.x, point.y,
```

```
            AfxGetMainWnd ());
        return;
    }
    CWnd::OnContextMenu (pWnd, point);
}
```

In a view-based application like Shapes, the WM_CONTEXTMENU handler is typically placed in the view class because that's where the objects that are subject to right clicks are displayed.

How do you get a pointer to a context menu in order to display it? One method is to construct a *CMenu* object and build the menu with *CMenu* member functions. Another is to load the menu from a resource in the same way that a top-level menu is loaded. The following menu template defines a menu that contains one submenu:

```
IDR_CONTEXTMENU MENU
BEGIN
    POPUP ""
    BEGIN
        MENUITEM "&Copy",        ID_CONTEXT_COPY
        MENUITEM "&Rename",       ID_CONTEXT_RENAME
        MENUITEM "&Delete",       ID_CONTEXT_DELETE
    END
END
```

The following statements load the menu into a *CMenu* object and display it as a context menu:

```
CMenu menu;
menu.LoadMenu (IDR_CONTEXTMENU);
CMenu* pContextMenu = menu.GetSubMenu (0);
pContextMenu->TrackPopupMenu (TPM_LEFTALIGN ¦
    TPM_LEFTBUTTON ¦ TPM_RIGHTBUTTON, point.x, point.y,
    AfxGetMainWnd ());
```

If your application uses several context menus, you can define each context menu as a separate submenu of IDR_CONTEXTMENU and retrieve *CMenu* pointers by varying the index passed to *GetSubMenu*. Or you can define each one as a separate menu resource. In any event, attaching the context menu to a *CMenu* object that resides on the stack ensures that the menu will be destroyed when the object goes out of scope. The menu is no longer needed after *TrackPopupMenu* returns, so deleting it frees up memory that can be put to other uses.

The TPM_RETURNCMD Flag

How do you process context menu commands? The same way you process commands from conventional menus: by writing command handlers. You can write update handlers for commands in a context menu, too. In fact, it's perfectly legal to assign a command in a conventional menu and a command in a context menu the same command ID and let one command handler (and, if you'd like, one update handler) service both of them.

Occasionally, you'll want to get a return value from *TrackPopupMenu* indicating which, if any, menu item was selected and to process the command on the spot rather than delegate to a command handler. That's why TPM_RETURNCMD exists. Passed a TPM_RETURNCMD flag in its first parameter, *TrackPopupMenu* returns the command ID of the item selected from the menu. A 0 return means that the menu was dismissed with no selection. Assuming *pContextMenu* references the context menu used in the example in the previous section, the following statements demonstrate how to display the menu and act immediately on the user's selection:

```
int nCmd = (int) pContextMenu->TrackPopupMenu (TPM_LEFTALIGN |
    TPM_LEFTBUTTON | TPM_RIGHTBUTTON | TPM_RETURNCMD,
    point.x, point.y, AfxGetMainWnd ());

switch (nCmd) {
case ID_CONTEXT_COPY:
    // Copy the object.
    break;
case ID_CONTEXT_RENAME:
    // Rename the object.
    break;
case ID_CONTEXT_DELETE:
    // Delete the object.
    break;
}
```

A menu displayed this way still generates a WM_COMMAND message when an item is selected. That's normally not a problem, because if you don't provide a command handler for the item, the message is passed harmlessly on to Windows. But suppose you'd like to suppress such messages, perhaps because you've used the same ID for an item in a conventional menu and an item in a context menu and you want the item in the context menu to behave differently than the one in the conventional menu. To do it, simply include a TPM_NONOTIFY flag in the call to *TrackPopupMenu*.

Don't forget that by default, MFC disables menu items for which no command and update handlers are provided. Therefore, if you use the TPM_RETURNCMD flag, you'll probably find it necessary to set *m_bAutoMenuEnable* to FALSE in your frame window.

THE COLORS APPLICATION

Let's close out this chapter by writing an application that uses owner-draw menus and context menus. Colors is a souped-up version of Shapes that features an owner-draw Color menu and a context menu from which the user can select both shapes and colors. The items in the context menu are functional duplicates of the items in the Shape and Color menus and even share command and update handlers. The context menu appears when the user clicks the shape in the middle of the window with the right mouse button, as seen in Figure 4-14.

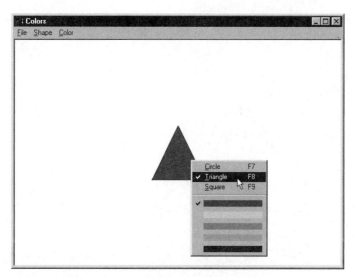

Figure 4-14. *The Colors window.*

Colors' source code appears in Figure 4-15. To generate the source code, I used AppWizard to create a new project named Colors and then proceeded as if I were writing Shapes all over again by implementing *OnPaint*, adding the Shape menu, writing command and update handlers, and so on. I then added the Color menu. Even though the menu items are assigned text strings such as "&Red" and "&Blue," those strings are never seen because the menu is owner-draw. The code that converts the items in the menu into owner-draw items is found in *InitInstance*:

```
CMenu* pMenu = pFrame->GetMenu ();
ASSERT (pMenu != NULL);

for (int i=0; i<5; i++)
    pMenu->ModifyMenu (ID_COLOR_RED + i, MF_OWNERDRAW,
        ID_COLOR_RED + i);
```

The first statement initializes *pMenu* with a pointer to a *CMenu* object representing the main menu. *ModifyMenu* is then called five times in succession to tag the items in the Color menu with the flag MF_OWNERDRAW.

Colors.h

```
// Colors.h : main header file for the COLORS application
//

#if !defined(AFX_COLORS_H__1B036BE8_5C6F_11D2_8E53_006008A82731__INCLUDED_)
#define AFX_COLORS_H__1B036BE8_5C6F_11D2_8E53_006008A82731__INCLUDED_

#if _MSC_VER > 1000
#pragma once
#endif // _MSC_VER > 1000

#ifndef __AFXWIN_H__
    #error include 'stdafx.h' before including this file for PCH
#endif

#include "resource.h"        // main symbols

/////////////////////////////////////////////////////////////////////////////
// CColorsApp:
// See Colors.cpp for the implementation of this class
//

class CColorsApp : public CWinApp
{
public:
    CColorsApp();

// Overrides
    // ClassWizard generated virtual function overrides
    //{{AFX_VIRTUAL(CColorsApp)
    public:
    virtual BOOL InitInstance();
    //}}AFX_VIRTUAL

// Implementation

public:
    //{{AFX_MSG(CColorsApp)
    afx_msg void OnAppAbout();
    //}}AFX_MSG
    DECLARE_MESSAGE_MAP()
};
```

Figure 4-15. *The Colors program.*

```
///////////////////////////////////////////////////////////////////////

//{{AFX_INSERT_LOCATION}}
// Microsoft Visual C++ will insert additional declarations immediately
// before the previous line.

#endif
// !defined(AFX_COLORS_H__1B036BE8_5C6F_11D2_8E53_006008A82731__INCLUDED_)
```

Colors.cpp

```
// Colors.cpp : Defines the class behaviors for the application.
//

#include "stdafx.h"
#include "Colors.h"

#include "MainFrm.h"

#ifdef _DEBUG
#define new DEBUG_NEW
#undef THIS_FILE
static char THIS_FILE[] = __FILE__;
#endif

///////////////////////////////////////////////////////////////////////
// CColorsApp

BEGIN_MESSAGE_MAP(CColorsApp, CWinApp)
    //{{AFX_MSG_MAP(CColorsApp)
    ON_COMMAND(ID_APP_ABOUT, OnAppAbout)
    //}}AFX_MSG_MAP
END_MESSAGE_MAP()

///////////////////////////////////////////////////////////////////////
// CColorsApp construction

CColorsApp::CColorsApp()
{
}
```

(continued)

Figure 4-15. *continued*

```
//////////////////////////////////////////////////////////////////////
// The one and only CColorsApp object

CColorsApp theApp;

//////////////////////////////////////////////////////////////////////
// CColorsApp initialization

BOOL CColorsApp::InitInstance()
{
    // Standard initialization

    // Change the registry key under which our settings are stored.
    SetRegistryKey(_T("Local AppWizard-Generated Applications"));

    CMainFrame* pFrame = new CMainFrame;
    m_pMainWnd = pFrame;

    // create and load the frame with its resources

    pFrame->LoadFrame(IDR_MAINFRAME,
        WS_OVERLAPPEDWINDOW | FWS_ADDTOTITLE, NULL,
        NULL);

    pFrame->ShowWindow(SW_SHOW);
    pFrame->UpdateWindow();

    //
    // Convert the items in the Color menu to owner-draw.
    //
    CMenu* pMenu = pFrame->GetMenu ();
    ASSERT (pMenu != NULL);

    for (int i=0; i<5; i++)
        pMenu->ModifyMenu (ID_COLOR_RED + i, MF_OWNERDRAW,
            ID_COLOR_RED + i);

    return TRUE;
}

//////////////////////////////////////////////////////////////////////
// CColorsApp message handlers
```

```
/////////////////////////////////////////////////////////////////////////
// CAboutDlg dialog used for App About

class CAboutDlg : public CDialog
{
public:
    CAboutDlg();

// Dialog Data
    //{{AFX_DATA(CAboutDlg)
    enum { IDD = IDD_ABOUTBOX };
    //}}AFX_DATA

    // ClassWizard generated virtual function overrides
    //{{AFX_VIRTUAL(CAboutDlg)
    protected:
    virtual void DoDataExchange(CDataExchange* pDX);     // DDX/DDV support
    //}}AFX_VIRTUAL

// Implementation
protected:
    //{{AFX_MSG(CAboutDlg)
        // No message handlers
    //}}AFX_MSG
    DECLARE_MESSAGE_MAP()
};

CAboutDlg::CAboutDlg() : CDialog(CAboutDlg::IDD)
{
    //{{AFX_DATA_INIT(CAboutDlg)
    //}}AFX_DATA_INIT
}

void CAboutDlg::DoDataExchange(CDataExchange* pDX)
{
    CDialog::DoDataExchange(pDX);
    //{{AFX_DATA_MAP(CAboutDlg)
    //}}AFX_DATA_MAP
}

BEGIN_MESSAGE_MAP(CAboutDlg, CDialog)
    //{{AFX_MSG_MAP(CAboutDlg)
        // No message handlers
    //}}AFX_MSG_MAP
END_MESSAGE_MAP()
```

(continued)

Figure 4-15. *continued*

```
// App command to run the dialog
void CColorsApp::OnAppAbout()
{
    CAboutDlg aboutDlg;
    aboutDlg.DoModal();
}


/////////////////////////////////////////////////////////////////////////////
// CColorsApp message handlers
```

MainFrm.h

```
// MainFrm.h : interface of the CMainFrame class
//
/////////////////////////////////////////////////////////////////////////////

#if !defined(AFX_MAINFRM_H__1B036BEC_5C6F_11D2_8E53_006008A82731__INCLUDED_)
#define AFX_MAINFRM_H__1B036BEC_5C6F_11D2_8E53_006008A82731__INCLUDED_

#if _MSC_VER > 1000
#pragma once
#endif // _MSC_VER > 1000

#include "ChildView.h"

class CMainFrame : public CFrameWnd
{

public:
    CMainFrame();
protected:
    DECLARE_DYNAMIC(CMainFrame)

// Attributes
public:

// Operations
public:

// Overrides
    // ClassWizard generated virtual function overrides
    //{{AFX_VIRTUAL(CMainFrame)
    virtual BOOL PreCreateWindow(CREATESTRUCT& cs);
    virtual BOOL OnCmdMsg(UINT nID, int nCode, void* pExtra,
```

```
        AFX_CMDHANDLERINFO* pHandlerInfo);
    //}}AFX_VIRTUAL

// Implementation
public:
    virtual ~CMainFrame();
#ifdef _DEBUG
    virtual void AssertValid() const;
    virtual void Dump(CDumpContext& dc) const;
#endif
    CChildView      m_wndView;

// Generated message map functions
protected:
    //{{AFX_MSG(CMainFrame)
    afx_msg void OnSetFocus(CWnd *pOldWnd);
    afx_msg int OnCreate(LPCREATESTRUCT lpCreateStruct);
    //}}AFX_MSG
    afx_msg void OnMeasureItem (int nIDCtl, LPMEASUREITEMSTRUCT lpmis);
    afx_msg void OnDrawItem (int nIDCtl, LPDRAWITEMSTRUCT lpdis);
    DECLARE_MESSAGE_MAP()
};

/////////////////////////////////////////////////////////////////////////////

//{{AFX_INSERT_LOCATION}}
// Microsoft Visual C++ will insert additional declarations immediately
// before the previous line.

#endif
// !defined(AFX_MAINFRM_H__1B036BEC_5C6F_11D2_8E53_006008A82731__INCLUDED_)
```

MainFrm.cpp

```
// MainFrm.cpp : implementation of the CMainFrame class
//

#include "stdafx.h"
#include "Colors.h"

#include "MainFrm.h"

#ifdef _DEBUG
#define new DEBUG_NEW
#undef THIS_FILE
```

(continued)

Figure 4-15. *continued*

```
static char THIS_FILE[] = __FILE__;
#endif


/////////////////////////////////////////////////////////////////////////////
// CMainFrame

IMPLEMENT_DYNAMIC(CMainFrame, CFrameWnd)

BEGIN_MESSAGE_MAP(CMainFrame, CFrameWnd)
    //{{AFX_MSG_MAP(CMainFrame)
    ON_WM_SETFOCUS()
    ON_WM_CREATE()
    //}}AFX_MSG_MAP
    ON_WM_MEASUREITEM ()
    ON_WM_DRAWITEM ()
END_MESSAGE_MAP()


/////////////////////////////////////////////////////////////////////////////
// CMainFrame construction/destruction

CMainFrame::CMainFrame()
{
}


CMainFrame::~CMainFrame()
{
}


BOOL CMainFrame::PreCreateWindow(CREATESTRUCT& cs)
{
    if( !CFrameWnd::PreCreateWindow(cs) )
        return FALSE;
    cs.dwExStyle &= ~WS_EX_CLIENTEDGE;
    cs.lpszClass = AfxRegisterWndClass(0);
    return TRUE;
}


/////////////////////////////////////////////////////////////////////////////
// CMainFrame diagnostics

#ifdef _DEBUG
void CMainFrame::AssertValid() const
{
    CFrameWnd::AssertValid();
}
```

```
void CMainFrame::Dump(CDumpContext& dc) const
{
    CFrameWnd::Dump(dc);
}


#endif //_DEBUG


//////////////////////////////////////////////////////////////////////////
// CMainFrame message handlers
void CMainFrame::OnSetFocus(CWnd* pOldWnd)
{
    // forward focus to the view window
    m_wndView.SetFocus();
}

BOOL CMainFrame::OnCmdMsg(UINT nID, int nCode, void* pExtra,
    AFX_CMDHANDLERINFO* pHandlerInfo)
{
    // let the view have first crack at the command
    if (m_wndView.OnCmdMsg(nID, nCode, pExtra, pHandlerInfo))
        return TRUE;

    // otherwise, do default handling
    return CFrameWnd::OnCmdMsg(nID, nCode, pExtra, pHandlerInfo);
}


int CMainFrame::OnCreate(LPCREATESTRUCT lpCreateStruct)
{
    if (CFrameWnd::OnCreate(lpCreateStruct) == -1)
        return -1;

    if (!m_wndView.Create(NULL, NULL, AFX_WS_DEFAULT_VIEW,
        CRect(0, 0, 0, 0), this, AFX_IDW_PANE_FIRST, NULL))
    {
        TRACE0("Failed to create view window\n");
        return -1;
    }
    return 0;
}

void CMainFrame::OnMeasureItem (int nIDCtl, LPMEASUREITEMSTRUCT lpmis)
{
    lpmis->itemWidth = ::GetSystemMetrics (SM_CYMENU) * 4;
    lpmis->itemHeight = ::GetSystemMetrics (SM_CYMENU);
}
```

(continued)

Figure 4-15. *continued*

```
void CMainFrame::OnDrawItem (int nIDCtl, LPDRAWITEMSTRUCT lpdis)
{
    BITMAP bm;
    CBitmap bitmap;
    bitmap.LoadOEMBitmap (OBM_CHECK);
    bitmap.GetObject (sizeof (bm), &bm);

    CDC dc;
    dc.Attach (lpdis->hDC);

    CBrush* pBrush = new CBrush (::GetSysColor ((lpdis->itemState &
        ODS_SELECTED) ? COLOR_HIGHLIGHT : COLOR_MENU));
    dc.FrameRect (&(lpdis->rcItem), pBrush);
    delete pBrush;

    if (lpdis->itemState & ODS_CHECKED) {
        CDC dcMem;
        dcMem.CreateCompatibleDC (&dc);
        CBitmap* pOldBitmap = dcMem.SelectObject (&bitmap);

        dc.BitBlt (lpdis->rcItem.left + 4, lpdis->rcItem.top +
            (((lpdis->rcItem.bottom - lpdis->rcItem.top) -
            bm.bmHeight) / 2), bm.bmWidth, bm.bmHeight, &dcMem,
            0, 0, SRCCOPY);

        dcMem.SelectObject (pOldBitmap);
    }

    UINT itemID = lpdis->itemID & 0xFFFF; // Fix for Win95 bug.
    pBrush = new CBrush (m_wndView.m_clrColors[itemID - ID_COLOR_RED]);
    CRect rect = lpdis->rcItem;
    rect.DeflateRect (6, 4);
    rect.left += bm.bmWidth;
    dc.FillRect (rect, pBrush);
    delete pBrush;

    dc.Detach ();
}
```

ChildView.h

```
// ChildView.h : interface of the CChildView class
//
/////////////////////////////////////////////////////////////////////////////
```

```
#if !defined(AFX_CHILDVIEW_H__1B036BEE_5C6F_11D2_8E53_006008A82731__INCLUDED_)
#define AFX_CHILDVIEW_H__1B036BEE_5C6F_11D2_8E53_006008A82731__INCLUDED_

#if _MSC_VER > 1000
#pragma once
#endif // _MSC_VER > 1000

/////////////////////////////////////////////////////////////////////////////
// CChildView window

class CChildView : public CWnd
{
// Construction
public:
    CChildView();

// Attributes
public:
    static const COLORREF m_clrColors[5];

// Operations
public:

// Overrides
    // ClassWizard generated virtual function overrides
    //{{AFX_VIRTUAL(CChildView)
    protected:
    virtual BOOL PreCreateWindow(CREATESTRUCT& cs);
    //}}AFX_VIRTUAL

// Implementation
public:
    virtual ~CChildView();

    // Generated message map functions
protected:
    int m_nColor;
    int m_nShape;
    //{{AFX_MSG(CChildView)
    afx_msg void OnPaint();
    afx_msg void OnShapeCircle();
    afx_msg void OnShapeTriangle();
    afx_msg void OnShapeSquare();
    afx_msg void OnUpdateShapeCircle(CCmdUI* pCmdUI);
    afx_msg void OnUpdateShapeTriangle(CCmdUI* pCmdUI);
    afx_msg void OnUpdateShapeSquare(CCmdUI* pCmdUI);
```

(continued)

Figure 4-15. *continued*

```
    afx_msg void OnContextMenu(CWnd* pWnd, CPoint point);
    //}}AFX_MSG
    afx_msg void OnColor (UINT nID);
    afx_msg void OnUpdateColor (CCmdUI* pCmdUI);
    DECLARE_MESSAGE_MAP()
};


/////////////////////////////////////////////////////////////////////////////

//{{AFX_INSERT_LOCATION}}
// Microsoft Visual C++ will insert additional declarations immediately
// before the previous line.

#endif
//!defined(AFX_CHILDVIEW_H__1B036BEE_5C6F_11D2_8E53_006008A82731__INCLUDED_)
```

ChildView.cpp

```
// ChildView.cpp : implementation of the CChildView class
//

#include "stdafx.h"
#include "Colors.h"
#include "ChildView.h"

#ifdef _DEBUG
#define new DEBUG_NEW
#undef THIS_FILE
static char THIS_FILE[] = __FILE__;
#endif

/////////////////////////////////////////////////////////////////////////////
// CChildView

CChildView::CChildView()
{
    m_nShape = 1; // Triangle
    m_nColor = 0; // Red
}

CChildView::~CChildView()
{
}
```

```
BEGIN_MESSAGE_MAP(CChildView,CWnd )
    //{{AFX_MSG_MAP(CChildView)
    ON_WM_PAINT()
    ON_COMMAND(ID_SHAPE_CIRCLE, OnShapeCircle)
    ON_COMMAND(ID_SHAPE_TRIANGLE, OnShapeTriangle)
    ON_COMMAND(ID_SHAPE_SQUARE, OnShapeSquare)
    ON_UPDATE_COMMAND_UI(ID_SHAPE_CIRCLE, OnUpdateShapeCircle)
    ON_UPDATE_COMMAND_UI(ID_SHAPE_TRIANGLE, OnUpdateShapeTriangle)
    ON_UPDATE_COMMAND_UI(ID_SHAPE_SQUARE, OnUpdateShapeSquare)
    ON_WM_CONTEXTMENU()
    //}}AFX_MSG_MAP
    ON_COMMAND_RANGE (ID_COLOR_RED, ID_COLOR_BLUE, OnColor)
    ON_UPDATE_COMMAND_UI_RANGE (ID_COLOR_RED, ID_COLOR_BLUE, OnUpdateColor)
END_MESSAGE_MAP()

const COLORREF CChildView::m_clrColors[5] = {
    RGB ( 255,   0,   0), // Red
    RGB ( 255, 255,   0), // Yellow
    RGB (   0, 255,   0), // Green
    RGB (   0, 255, 255), // Cyan
    RGB (   0,   0, 255)  // Blue
};


/////////////////////////////////////////////////////////////////////////
// CChildView message handlers

BOOL CChildView::PreCreateWindow(CREATESTRUCT& cs)
{
    if (!CWnd::PreCreateWindow(cs))
        return FALSE;

    cs.dwExStyle |= WS_EX_CLIENTEDGE;
    cs.style &= ~WS_BORDER;
    cs.lpszClass = AfxRegisterWndClass(CS_HREDRAW|CS_VREDRAW|CS_DBLCLKS,
        ::LoadCursor(NULL, IDC_ARROW), HBRUSH(COLOR_WINDOW+1), NULL);

    return TRUE;
}


void CChildView::OnPaint()
{
    CPoint points[3];
    CPaintDC dc(this);

    CRect rcClient;
    GetClientRect (&rcClient);
```

(continued)

Figure 4-15. *continued*

```
    int cx = rcClient.Width () / 2;
    int cy = rcClient.Height () / 2;
    CRect rcShape (cx - 45, cy - 45, cx + 45, cy + 45);

    CBrush brush (m_clrColors[m_nColor]);
    CBrush* pOldBrush = dc.SelectObject (&brush);

    switch (m_nShape) {

    case 0: // Circle
        dc.Ellipse (rcShape);
        break;

    case 1: // Triangle
        points[0].x = cx - 45;
        points[0].y = cy + 45;
        points[1].x = cx;
        points[1].y = cy - 45;
        points[2].x = cx + 45;
        points[2].y = cy + 45;
        dc.Polygon (points, 3);
        break;

    case 2: // Square
        dc.Rectangle (rcShape);
        break;
    }
    dc.SelectObject (pOldBrush);
}

void CChildView::OnShapeCircle()
{
    m_nShape = 0;
    Invalidate ();
}

void CChildView::OnShapeTriangle()
{
    m_nShape = 1;
    Invalidate ();
}

void CChildView::OnShapeSquare()
{
    m_nShape = 2;
    Invalidate ();
}
```

```
void CChildView::OnUpdateShapeCircle(CCmdUI* pCmdUI)
{
    pCmdUI->SetCheck (m_nShape == 0);
}

void CChildView::OnUpdateShapeTriangle(CCmdUI* pCmdUI)
{
    pCmdUI->SetCheck (m_nShape == 1);
}

void CChildView::OnUpdateShapeSquare(CCmdUI* pCmdUI)
{
    pCmdUI->SetCheck (m_nShape == 2);
}

void CChildView::OnColor (UINT nID)
{
    m_nColor = nID - ID_COLOR_RED;
    Invalidate ();
}

void CChildView::OnUpdateColor (CCmdUI* pCmdUI)
{
    pCmdUI->SetCheck ((int) pCmdUI->m_nID - ID_COLOR_RED == m_nColor);
}

void CChildView::OnContextMenu(CWnd* pWnd, CPoint point)
{
    CRect rcClient;
    GetClientRect (&rcClient);

    int cx = rcClient.Width () / 2;
    int cy = rcClient.Height () / 2;
    CRect rcShape (cx - 45, cy - 45, cx + 45, cy + 45);

    CPoint pos = point;
    ScreenToClient (&pos);

    CPoint points[3];
    BOOL bShapeClicked = FALSE;
    int dx, dy;

    //
    // Hit test the shape.
    //
    switch (m_nShape) {
```

(continued)

Figure 4-15. *continued*

```
    case 0: // Circle
        dx = pos.x - cx;
        dy = pos.y - cy;
        if ((dx * dx) + (dy * dy) <= (45 * 45))
            bShapeClicked = TRUE;
        break;

    case 1: // Triangle
        if (rcShape.PtInRect (pos)) {
            dx = min (pos.x - rcShape.left, rcShape.right - pos.x);
            if ((rcShape.bottom - pos.y) < (2 * dx))
                bShapeClicked = TRUE;
        }
        break;

    case 2: // Square
        if (rcShape.PtInRect (pos))
            bShapeClicked = TRUE;
        break;
    }

    //
    // Display a context menu if the shape was clicked.
    //
    if (bShapeClicked) {
        CMenu menu;
        menu.LoadMenu (IDR_CONTEXTMENU);
        CMenu* pContextMenu = menu.GetSubMenu (0);

        for (int i=0; i<5; i++)
            pContextMenu->ModifyMenu (ID_COLOR_RED + i,
                MF_BYCOMMAND | MF_OWNERDRAW, ID_COLOR_RED + i);

        pContextMenu->TrackPopupMenu (TPM_LEFTALIGN | TPM_LEFTBUTTON |
            TPM_RIGHTBUTTON, point.x, point.y, AfxGetMainWnd ());
        return;
    }

    //
    // Call the base class if the shape was not clicked.
    //
    CWnd::OnContextMenu (pWnd, point);
}
```

Resource.h

```
//{{NO_DEPENDENCIES}}
// Microsoft Developer Studio generated include file.
// Used by Colors.rc
//
#define IDD_ABOUTBOX                    100
#define IDR_MAINFRAME                   128
#define IDR_COLORSTYPE                  129
#define IDR_CONTEXTMENU                 130
#define ID_SHAPE_CIRCLE                 32771
#define ID_SHAPE_TRIANGLE               32772
#define ID_SHAPE_SQUARE                 32773
#define ID_COLOR_RED                    32774
#define ID_COLOR_YELLOW                 32775
#define ID_COLOR_GREEN                  32776
#define ID_COLOR_CYAN                   32777
#define ID_COLOR_BLUE                   32778


// Next default values for new objects
//
#ifdef APSTUDIO_INVOKED
#ifndef APSTUDIO_READONLY_SYMBOLS
#define _APS_NEXT_RESOURCE_VALUE        131
#define _APS_NEXT_COMMAND_VALUE         32779
#define _APS_NEXT_CONTROL_VALUE         1000
#define _APS_NEXT_SYMED_VALUE           101
#endif
#endif
```

Colors.rc

```
//Microsoft Developer Studio generated resource script.

//
#include "resource.h"

#define APSTUDIO_READONLY_SYMBOLS
/////////////////////////////////////////////////////////////////////////////
//
// Generated from the TEXTINCLUDE 2 resource.
//
#include "afxres.h"
```

(continued)

Figure 4-15. *continued*

```
///////////////////////////////////////////////////////////////////////////
#undef APSTUDIO_READONLY_SYMBOLS

///////////////////////////////////////////////////////////////////////////
// English (U.S.) resources

#if !defined(AFX_RESOURCE_DLL) || defined(AFX_TARG_ENU)
#ifdef _WIN32
LANGUAGE LANG_ENGLISH, SUBLANG_ENGLISH_US
#pragma code_page(1252)
#endif //_WIN32

#ifdef APSTUDIO_INVOKED
///////////////////////////////////////////////////////////////////////////
//
// TEXTINCLUDE
//

1 TEXTINCLUDE DISCARDABLE
BEGIN
    "resource.h\0"
END

2 TEXTINCLUDE DISCARDABLE
BEGIN
    "#include ""afxres.h""\r\n"
    "\0"
END

3 TEXTINCLUDE DISCARDABLE
BEGIN
    "#define _AFX_NO_SPLITTER_RESOURCES\r\n"
    "#define _AFX_NO_OLE_RESOURCES\r\n"
    "#define _AFX_NO_TRACKER_RESOURCES\r\n"
    "#define _AFX_NO_PROPERTY_RESOURCES\r\n"
    "\r\n"
    "#if !defined(AFX_RESOURCE_DLL) || defined(AFX_TARG_ENU)\r\n"
    "#ifdef _WIN32\r\n"
    "LANGUAGE 9, 1\r\n"
    "#pragma code_page(1252)\r\n"
    "#endif //_WIN32\r\n"
    "#include ""res\\Colors.rc2"
    "   // non-Microsoft Visual C++ edited resources\r\n"
    "#include ""afxres.rc""         // Standard components\r\n"
```

```
        "#endif\r\n"
        "\0"
END

#endif    // APSTUDIO_INVOKED


/////////////////////////////////////////////////////////////////////////////
//
// Icon
//

// Icon with lowest ID value placed first to ensure application icon
// remains consistent on all systems.
IDR_MAINFRAME              ICON    DISCARDABLE     "res\\Colors.ico"

/////////////////////////////////////////////////////////////////////////////
//
// Menu
//

IDR_MAINFRAME MENU PRELOAD DISCARDABLE
BEGIN
    POPUP "&File"
    BEGIN
        MENUITEM "E&xit",                   ID_APP_EXIT
    END
    POPUP "&Shape"
    BEGIN
        MENUITEM "&Circle\tF7",             ID_SHAPE_CIRCLE
        MENUITEM "&Triangle\tF8",           ID_SHAPE_TRIANGLE
        MENUITEM "&Square\tF9",             ID_SHAPE_SQUARE
    END
    POPUP "&Color"
    BEGIN
        MENUITEM "&Red",                    ID_COLOR_RED
        MENUITEM "&Yellow",                 ID_COLOR_YELLOW
        MENUITEM "&Green",                  ID_COLOR_GREEN
        MENUITEM "&Cyan",                   ID_COLOR_CYAN
        MENUITEM "&Blue",                   ID_COLOR_BLUE
    END
END
```

(continued)

Figure 4-15. *continued*

```
IDR_CONTEXTMENU MENU DISCARDABLE
BEGIN
    POPUP "Top"
    BEGIN
        MENUITEM "&Circle\tF7",              ID_SHAPE_CIRCLE
        MENUITEM "&Triangle\tF8",            ID_SHAPE_TRIANGLE
        MENUITEM "&Square\tF9",              ID_SHAPE_SQUARE
        MENUITEM SEPARATOR
        MENUITEM "&Red",                     ID_COLOR_RED
        MENUITEM "&Yellow",                  ID_COLOR_YELLOW
        MENUITEM "&Green",                   ID_COLOR_GREEN
        MENUITEM "&Cyan",                    ID_COLOR_CYAN
        MENUITEM "&Blue",                    ID_COLOR_BLUE
    END
END


/////////////////////////////////////////////////////////////////////////
//
// Accelerator
//

IDR_MAINFRAME ACCELERATORS PRELOAD MOVEABLE PURE
BEGIN
    "B",            ID_COLOR_BLUE,      VIRTKEY, CONTROL, NOINVERT
    "C",            ID_COLOR_CYAN,      VIRTKEY, CONTROL, NOINVERT
    "G",            ID_COLOR_GREEN,     VIRTKEY, CONTROL, NOINVERT
    "R",            ID_COLOR_RED,       VIRTKEY, CONTROL, NOINVERT
    VK_F7,          ID_SHAPE_CIRCLE,    VIRTKEY, NOINVERT
    VK_F8,          ID_SHAPE_TRIANGLE,  VIRTKEY, NOINVERT
    VK_F9,          ID_SHAPE_SQUARE,    VIRTKEY, NOINVERT
    "Y",            ID_COLOR_YELLOW,    VIRTKEY, CONTROL, NOINVERT
END


/////////////////////////////////////////////////////////////////////////
//
// Dialog
//

IDD_ABOUTBOX DIALOG DISCARDABLE  0, 0, 235, 55
STYLE DS_MODALFRAME | WS_POPUP | WS_CAPTION | WS_SYSMENU
CAPTION "About Colors"
FONT 8, "MS Sans Serif"
BEGIN
    ICON            IDR_MAINFRAME,IDC_STATIC,11,17,20,20
    LTEXT           "Colors Version 1.0",IDC_STATIC,40,10,119,8,SS_NOPREFIX
```

```
    LTEXT           "Copyright (C) 1998",IDC_STATIC,40,25,119,8
    DEFPUSHBUTTON   "OK",IDOK,178,7,50,14,WS_GROUP
END


#ifndef _MAC
/////////////////////////////////////////////////////////////////////////////
//
// Version
//

VS_VERSION_INFO VERSIONINFO
 FILEVERSION 1,0,0,1
 PRODUCTVERSION 1,0,0,1
 FILEFLAGSMASK 0x3fL
#ifdef _DEBUG
 FILEFLAGS 0x1L
#else
 FILEFLAGS 0x0L
#endif
 FILEOS 0x4L
 FILETYPE 0x1L
 FILESUBTYPE 0x0L
BEGIN
    BLOCK "StringFileInfo"
    BEGIN
        BLOCK "040904B0"
        BEGIN
            VALUE "CompanyName", "\0"
            VALUE "FileDescription", "Colors MFC Application\0"
            VALUE "FileVersion", "1, 0, 0, 1\0"
            VALUE "InternalName", "Colors\0"
            VALUE "LegalCopyright", "Copyright (C) 1998\0"
            VALUE "LegalTrademarks", "\0"
            VALUE "OriginalFilename", "Colors.EXE\0"
            VALUE "ProductName", "Colors Application\0"
            VALUE "ProductVersion", "1, 0, 0, 1\0"
        END
    END
    BLOCK "VarFileInfo"
    BEGIN
        VALUE "Translation", 0x409, 1200
    END
END

#endif    // !_MAC
```

(continued)

Figure 4-15. *continued*

```
/////////////////////////////////////////////////////////////////////////////
//
// DESIGNINFO
//

#ifdef APSTUDIO_INVOKED
GUIDELINES DESIGNINFO DISCARDABLE
BEGIN
    IDD_ABOUTBOX, DIALOG
    BEGIN
        LEFTMARGIN, 7
        RIGHTMARGIN, 228
        TOPMARGIN, 7
        BOTTOMMARGIN, 48
    END
END
#endif    // APSTUDIO_INVOKED


/////////////////////////////////////////////////////////////////////////////
//
// String Table
//

STRINGTABLE PRELOAD DISCARDABLE
BEGIN
    IDR_MAINFRAME           "Colors"
END

STRINGTABLE PRELOAD DISCARDABLE
BEGIN
    AFX_IDS_APP_TITLE       "Colors"
    AFX_IDS_IDLEMESSAGE     "Ready"
END

STRINGTABLE DISCARDABLE
BEGIN
    ID_INDICATOR_EXT        "EXT"
    ID_INDICATOR_CAPS       "CAP"
    ID_INDICATOR_NUM        "NUM"
    ID_INDICATOR_SCRL       "SCRL"
    ID_INDICATOR_OVR        "OVR"
    ID_INDICATOR_REC        "REC"
END
```

```
STRINGTABLE DISCARDABLE
BEGIN
    ID_APP_ABOUT            "Display program information, version number and copyright\nAbout"
    ID_APP_EXIT             "Quit the application; prompts to save documents\nExit"
END

STRINGTABLE DISCARDABLE
BEGIN
    ID_NEXT_PANE            "Switch to the next window pane\nNext Pane"
    ID_PREV_PANE            "Switch back to the previous window pane\nPrevious Pane"
END

STRINGTABLE DISCARDABLE
BEGIN
    ID_WINDOW_SPLIT         "Split the active window into panes\nSplit"
END

STRINGTABLE DISCARDABLE
BEGIN
    ID_EDIT_CLEAR           "Erase the selection\nErase"
    ID_EDIT_CLEAR_ALL       "Erase everything\nErase All"
    ID_EDIT_COPY            "Copy the selection and put it on the Clipboard\nCopy"
    ID_EDIT_CUT             "Cut the selection and put it on the Clipboard\nCut"
    ID_EDIT_FIND            "Find the specified text\nFind"
    ID_EDIT_PASTE           "Insert Clipboard contents\nPaste"
    ID_EDIT_REPEAT          "Repeat the last action\nRepeat"
    ID_EDIT_REPLACE         "Replace specific text with different text\nReplace"
    ID_EDIT_SELECT_ALL      "Select the entire document\nSelect All"
    ID_EDIT_UNDO            "Undo the last action\nUndo"
    ID_EDIT_REDO            "Redo the previously undone action\nRedo"
END

STRINGTABLE DISCARDABLE
BEGIN
    AFX_IDS_SCSIZE          "Change the window size"
    AFX_IDS_SCMOVE          "Change the window position"
    AFX_IDS_SCMINIMIZE      "Reduce the window to an icon"
    AFX_IDS_SCMAXIMIZE      "Enlarge the window to full size"
    AFX_IDS_SCNEXTWINDOW    "Switch to the next document window"
    AFX_IDS_SCPREVWINDOW    "Switch to the previous document window"
    AFX_IDS_SCCLOSE         "Close the active window and prompts to save the documents"
END
```

(continued)

Figure 4-15. *continued*

```
STRINGTABLE DISCARDABLE
BEGIN
    AFX_IDS_SCRESTORE        "Restore the window to normal size"
    AFX_IDS_SCTASKLIST       "Activate Task List"
END


#endif    // English (U.S.) resources
/////////////////////////////////////////////////////////////////////////////



#ifndef APSTUDIO_INVOKED
/////////////////////////////////////////////////////////////////////////////
//
// Generated from the TEXTINCLUDE 3 resource.
//
#define _AFX_NO_SPLITTER_RESOURCES
#define _AFX_NO_OLE_RESOURCES
#define _AFX_NO_TRACKER_RESOURCES
#define _AFX_NO_PROPERTY_RESOURCES

#if !defined(AFX_RESOURCE_DLL) || defined(AFX_TARG_ENU)
#ifdef _WIN32
LANGUAGE 9, 1
#pragma code_page(1252)
#endif //_WIN32
#include "res\Colors.rc2"  // non-Microsoft Visual C++ edited resources
#include "afxres.rc"        // Standard components
#endif


/////////////////////////////////////////////////////////////////////////////
#endif    // not APSTUDIO_INVOKED
```

Because the frame window is the menu's owner, the frame window receives the WM_MEASUREITEM and WM_DRAWITEM messages that the owner-draw items generate. Therefore, the message handlers appear in the frame window class. *CMainFrame::OnMeasureItem* contains just two statements: one specifying the height of each menu item (the SM_CYMENU value returned by *::GetSystemMetrics*), the other specifying the width (SM_CYMENU*4). *CMainFrame::OnDrawItem* is a bit more complicated because it's responsible for doing the actual drawing. After doing some preliminary work involving a *CBitmap* object that we'll discuss in a moment, *OnDrawItem* constructs an empty *CDC* object and attaches to it the device context handle provided in the DRAWITEMSTRUCT structure using *CDC::Attach*:

```
CDC dc;
dc.Attach (lpdis->hDC);
```

This converts *dc* into a valid device context object that wraps the Windows-provided device context. That device context should be returned to Windows in the same state in which it was received. Objects selected into the device context should be selected back out, and any changes made to the state of the device context (for example, to the background mode or the text color) should be undone before *OnDrawItem* ends.

Next, *OnDrawItem* creates a brush whose color is either COLOR_MENU or COLOR_HIGHLIGHT, depending on whether the ODS_SELECTED bit in the *itemState* field is set. Then it outlines the menu item with a rectangle by calling *CDC::FrameRect* with a pointer to the brush:

```
CBrush* pBrush = new CBrush (::GetSysColor ((lpdis->itemState &
    ODS_SELECTED) ? COLOR_HIGHLIGHT : COLOR_MENU));
dc.FrameRect (&(lpdis->rcItem), pBrush);
delete pBrush;
```

COLOR_MENU is the default menu background color; COLOR_HIGHLIGHT is the color of a menu's highlight bar. *CDC::FrameRect* uses the specified brush to draw a rectangle with lines 1 pixel wide. The code above draws a rectangle around the menu item in the background color if the item isn't selected or in the highlight color if it is. This is the rectangle you see when you pull down the Color menu and move the mouse up and down. Drawing the rectangle in the background color if the ODS_SELECTED bit is clear erases the selection rectangle when the highlight passes from one item to another.

OnDrawItem's next task is to draw a check mark next to the menu item if the ODS_CHECKED bit is set. Unfortunately, drawing check marks is a detail you have to take care of yourself when you use owner-draw menus. More unfortunate still, neither MFC nor the Windows API has a *DrawCheckMark* function that would make drawing a check mark easy. The alternative is to create a bitmap depicting the check mark and use *CDC::BitBlt* to "blit" the check mark to the screen. Blitting is discussed in detail in Chapter 15, but even without that background preparation, the *OnDrawItem* code that draws a check mark if ODS_CHECKED is set is relatively easy to understand:

```
CDC dcMem;
dcMem.CreateCompatibleDC (&dc);
CBitmap* pOldBitmap = dcMem.SelectObject (&bitmap);

dc.BitBlt (lpdis->rcItem.left + 4, lpdis->rcItem.top +
    (((lpdis->rcItem.bottom - lpdis->rcItem.top) -
    bm.bmHeight) / 2), bm.bmWidth, bm.bmHeight, &dcMem,
    0, 0, SRCCOPY);

dcMem.SelectObject (pOldBitmap);
```

dcMem represents a memory device context (DC)—a virtual display surface in memory that can be drawn to as if it were a screen or other output device. *CreateCompatibleDC* creates a memory DC. Windows doesn't let you blit bitmaps directly to a display surface, so instead you must select the bitmap into a memory DC and copy it to the screen DC. In this example, *BitBlt* copies the bitmap from the memory DC to a location near the left end of the rectangle described by *lpdis->rcItem* in the screen DC. When *BitBlt* returns, the bitmap is selected out of the memory DC in preparation for the memory DC to be destroyed when *dcMem* goes out of scope.

Where does the bitmap come from? The first four statements in *OnDrawItem* create an empty *CBitmap* object, initialize it with the bitmap that Windows uses to draw menu check marks, and copy information about the bitmap (including its width and height) to a BITMAP structure:

```
BITMAP bm;
CBitmap bitmap;
bitmap.LoadOEMBitmap (OBM_CHECK);
bitmap.GetObject (sizeof (bm), &bm);
```

OBM_CHECK is the bitmap ID; *CBitmap::LoadOEMBitmap* copies the bitmap to a *CBitmap* object. *CBitmap::GetObject* copies information about the bitmap to a BITMAP structure, and the width and height values stored in the structure's *bmWidth* and *bmHeight* fields are used in the call to *BitBlt*. *bmWidth* is used again toward the end of *OnDrawItem* to indent the left end of each color swatch by an amount that equals the width of the check mark. For OBM_CHECK to be recognized, the statement

```
#define OEMRESOURCE
```

must appear before the statement that includes Afxwin.h. In Colors, you'll find the #define in StdAfx.h.

After the selection rectangle is drawn or erased and the check mark is drawn if the ODS_CHECKED bit is set, *OnDrawItem* draws the colored rectangle representing the menu item itself. To do so, it creates a solid brush, creates a *CRect* object from the *rcItem* structure passed in DRAWITEMSTRUCT, shrinks the rectangle a few pixels, and paints the rectangle using *CDC::FillRect*:

```
UINT itemID = lpdis->itemID & 0xFFFF; // Fix for Win95 bug.
pBrush = new CBrush (m_wndView.m_clrColors[itemID - ID_COLOR_RED]);
CRect rect = lpdis->rcItem;
rect.DeflateRect (6, 4);
rect.left += bm.bmWidth;
dc.FillRect (rect, pBrush);
delete pBrush;
```

CDC::FillRect is yet another *CDC* rectangle function. It fills the interior of the rectangle with a specified brush rather than with the brush selected into the device context, and it doesn't outline the rectangle with the current pen. Using *FillRect* rather than

Rectangle prevents us from having to select a pen and a brush into the device context and select them back out again when we're done. The color of the brush passed to *FillRect* is determined by subtracting ID_COLOR_RED from the menu item ID supplied in *lpdis->itemID* and using the result as an index into the view object's *m_clrColors* array.

Speaking of *lpdis->itemID*: Observe that the code fragment in the previous paragraph ANDs the item ID with 0xFFFF. This is done to work around a bug in Windows 95. If you assign an owner-draw menu item an ID equal to 0x8000 or higher, Windows 95 unwittingly sign-extends the value when passing it between the 16-bit and 32-bit halves of USER. The result? The command ID 0x8000 becomes 0xFFFF8000, 0x8001 becomes 0xFFFF8001, and so on, and *OnDrawItem* won't recognize its own command IDs unless it masks off the upper 16 bits. Using ID values lower than 0x8000 fixes this problem by eliminating the 1 in the upper bit, but it just so happens that when you allow Visual C++ to pick your command IDs, it uses values greater than 0x8000. Rather than manually change the IDs, I chose to strip the bits instead. This problem doesn't exist in Windows NT and is fixed in Windows 98.

OnDrawItem's final act is to detach *dc* from the device context handle obtained from DRAWITEMSTRUCT. This final step is important because it prevents *dc*'s destructor from deleting the device context when *OnDrawItem* ends. Normally you *want* a device context to be deleted when a message handler returns, but because this device context was borrowed from Windows, only Windows should delete it. *CDC::Detach* disassociates a *CDC* object and its device context so that the object can safely go out of scope.

The Context Menu

Colors' context menu comes from the menu resource IDR_CONTEXTMENU. The menu resource is defined as follows in Colors.rc:

```
IDR_CONTEXTMENU MENU DISCARDABLE
BEGIN
    POPUP "Top"
    BEGIN
        MENUITEM "&Circle\tF7",             ID_SHAPE_CIRCLE
        MENUITEM "&Triangle\tF8",           ID_SHAPE_TRIANGLE
        MENUITEM "&Square\tF9",             ID_SHAPE_SQUARE
        MENUITEM SEPARATOR
        MENUITEM "&Red",                    ID_COLOR_RED
        MENUITEM "&Yellow",                 ID_COLOR_YELLOW
        MENUITEM "&Green",                  ID_COLOR_GREEN
        MENUITEM "&Cyan",                   ID_COLOR_CYAN
        MENUITEM "&Blue",                   ID_COLOR_BLUE
    END
END
```

I created it by inserting a new menu resource into the application with Visual C++'s Insert-Resource command. I added items using the menu editor.

When the right mouse button is clicked in the view, the context menu is loaded and displayed by *CChildView::OnContextMenu*. Before loading the menu, *OnContextMenu* hit-tests the shape in the window and passes the WM_CONTEXTMENU message to the base class if the click occurred outside the shape. If it determines that the click occurred over the circle, the triangle, or the square, *OnContextMenu* loads the menu and converts the items in it to owner-draw items before calling *TrackPopupMenu*:

```
if (bShapeClicked) {
    CMenu menu;
    menu.LoadMenu (IDR_CONTEXTMENU);
    CMenu* pContextMenu = menu.GetSubMenu (0);

    for (int i=0; i<5; i++)
        pContextMenu->ModifyMenu (ID_COLOR_RED + i,
            MF_BYCOMMAND | MF_OWNERDRAW, ID_COLOR_RED + i);

    pContextMenu->TrackPopupMenu (TPM_LEFTALIGN | TPM_LEFTBUTTON |
        TPM_RIGHTBUTTON, point.x, point.y, AfxGetMainWnd ());
    return;
}
```

The owner-draw conversion must be performed each time the menu is loaded because when *menu* goes out of scope, the menu is destroyed and the modifications made to it are lost.

The colors in the Color menu and the context menu are linked to the command handler *OnColor* and the update handler *OnUpdateColor* by the following entries in *CChildView*'s message map:

```
ON_COMMAND_RANGE (ID_COLOR_RED, ID_COLOR_BLUE, OnColor)
ON_UPDATE_COMMAND_UI_RANGE (ID_COLOR_RED, ID_COLOR_BLUE, OnUpdateColor)
```

I added these entries to the source code manually because ClassWizard doesn't support either ON_COMMAND_RANGE or ON_UPDATE_COMMAND_UI_RANGE. ClassWizard's lack of support for these macros is one very important reason why MFC programmers shouldn't become too reliant on code-generating wizards. The wizards are useful, but they support only a subset of MFC's functionality. I could have used ClassWizard to write separate command and update handlers for every command, but hand-coding RANGE macros into the message map is more efficient because it reduces what would have been 10 separate command and update handlers to just 2. Note that entries added to a message map manually should be added *outside* the AFX_MSG_MAP comments generated by AppWizard. The portion of the message map that lies between these comments belongs to ClassWizard.

For these RANGE macros to work, the items in the Color menu must be assigned contiguous command IDs, with ID_COLOR_RED and ID_COLOR_BLUE bracketing the low and high ends of the range, respectively. To ensure that these conditions are met, you should either specify the command IDs explicitly when creating the menu items in the menu editor or edit them after the fact. You can specify a numeric command ID when creating or editing a menu item by appending "=*value*" to the command ID typed into the Menu Item Properties dialog box's ID combo box, as shown in Figure 4-16. Or you can edit Resource.h instead. I used the values 32774 through 32778 for ID_COLOR_RED through ID_COLOR_BLUE.

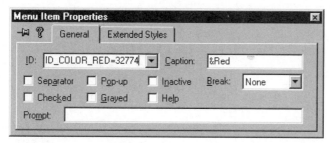

Figure 4-16. *Assigning a numeric value to a menu item ID.*

On Your Own

Here's an exercise you can try on your own. Go to ResourceView and edit the icon resource IDR_MAINFRAME. This resource, which was created by AppWizard, defines the application icon. The icon contains two images: a large (32 by 32) image and a small (16 by 16) image. You should edit both of them before you ship an application so that your application will have a unique icon. You can pick the one you want to edit by selecting Standard or Small from the icon editor's Device drop-down list. You can see the large icon in the operating system shell if you navigate to the folder containing Colors.exe and select Large Icons as the view type. If you have Small Icons, List, or Details selected instead, you'll see the small icon. The small icon also appears in the frame window's title bar, thanks to some code in *CFrameWnd::LoadFrame* that loads the icon resource and associates it with the window.

Chapter 5

The MFC Collection Classes

Many C++ programmers use the Standard Template Library (STL) because of its convenient implementations of arrays, linked lists, maps, and other containers. In the language of STL, a *container* is an object that stores collections of data. But before there was STL, there was MFC. MFC provides its own implementations of arrays, linked lists, and maps in a family of classes known as the *MFC collection classes*. Even though it's perfectly safe to use STL classes in MFC applications, many MFC programmers prefer MFC's collection classes to STL's, either because they're more familiar with MFC's or because they don't want to increase their applications' EXE size by linking to two separate class libraries.

   With the MFC collection classes to lend a hand, you might never have to write a linked list from scratch again. This chapter introduces the MFC collection classes and provides provides key insights into their use and operation.

ARRAYS

One of the greatest weaknesses of C and C++ is that arrays are not bounds-checked. Consider the following code, which reflects one of the most common bugs found in C and C++ applications:

```
int array[10];
for (int i=0; i<=10; i++)
    array[i] = i + 1;
```

This code is buggy because the final iteration of the *for* loop writes past the end of the array. When executed, it will cause an access violation.

C++ programmers frequently combat such problems by writing array classes that perform internal bounds checks. The following array class features *Get* and *Set* functions that check the array indexes passed to them and assert when passed an invalid index:

```
class CArray
{
protected:
    int m_nSize;      // Number of elements in the array.
    int* m_pData;     // Where the array's elements are stored.

public:
    CArray (int nSize)
    {
        m_nSize = nSize;
        m_pData = new int[nSize];
    }
    ~CArray ()
    {
        m_nSize = 0;
        if (m_pData != NULL) {
            delete[] m_pData;
            m_pData = NULL;
        }
    }
    int Get (int nIndex)
    {
        assert (nIndex >= 0 && nIndex < m_nSize);
        return m_pData[nIndex];
    }
    void Set (int nIndex, int nVal)
    {
        assert (nIndex >= 0 && nIndex < m_nSize);
        m_pData[nIndex] = nVal;
    }
};
```

With this simple class serving as a container for an array of integers, the following code will assert when *Set* is called for the final time:

```
CArray array (10);
for (int i=0; i<=10; i++)
    array.Set (i, i + 1); // Asserts when i == 10.
```

Now the error will be caught before an access violation occurs.

The MFC Array Classes

You don't have to write array classes yourself because MFC provides an assortment of them for you. First there's the generic *CArray* class, which is actually a template class from which you can create type-safe arrays for data of any type. *CArray* is defined in the header file Afxtempl.h. Then there are the nontemplatized array classes, each of which is designed to hold a particular type of data. These classes are defined in Afxcoll.h. The following table lists the nontemplatized MFC array classes and the types of data that they store.

TYPE-SPECIFIC MFC ARRAY CLASSES

Class Name	Data Type
CByteArray	8-bit bytes (BYTEs)
CWordArray	16-bit words (WORDs)
CDWordArray	32-bit double words (DWORDs)
CUIntArray	Unsigned integers (UINTs)
CStringArray	*CStrings*
CPtrArray	void pointers
CObArray	*CObject* pointers

Once you learn to use one of these array classes, you can use the others too, because all share a common set of member functions. The following example declares an array of 10 UINTs and initializes it with the numbers 1 through 10:

```
CUIntArray array;
array.SetSize (10);
for (int i=0; i<10; i++)
    array[i] = i + 1;
```

You can use the same approach to declare an array of *CStrings* and initialize it with textual representations of the integers 1 through 10:

```
CStringArray array;
array.SetSize (10);
for (int i=0; i<10; i++) {
    CString string;
    string.Format (_T ("%d"), i);
    array[i] = string;
}
```

In both cases, *SetSize* sizes the array to hold 10 elements. In both cases, the overloaded [] operator calls the array's *SetAt* function, which copies a value to an element at a specified location in the array. And in both cases, the code asserts if the array's bounds are violated. The bounds check is built into the code for *SetAt*:

```
ASSERT(nIndex >= 0 && nIndex < m_nSize);
```

You can see this code for yourself in the MFC source code file Afxcoll.inl.

You can insert items into an array without overwriting the items that are already there by using the *InsertAt* function. Unlike *SetAt*, which simply assigns a value to an existing array element, *InsertAt* makes room for the new element by moving elements above the insertion point upward in the array. The following statements initialize an array with the numbers 1 through 4 and 6 through 10, and then insert a 5 between the 4 and the 6:

```
CUIntArray array;
array.SetSize (9);
for (int i=0; i<4; i++)
    array[i] = i + 1;
for (i=4; i<9; i++)
    array[i] = i + 2;
array.InsertAt (4, 5); // Insert a 5 at index 4.
```

You can also pass a third parameter to *InsertAt* specifying the number of times the item should be inserted or pass a pointer to another array object in parameter 2 to insert an entire array. Note that this example sets the array size to 9, not 10, yet no assertion occurs when *InsertAt* is called. That's because *InsertAt* is one of a handful of array functions that automatically grow the array as new items are added. Dynamically sized arrays are discussed in the next section.

Values can be retrieved from an MFC array using standard array addressing syntax. The following example reads back the UINTs written to the *CUIntArray* in the previous example:

```
for (int i=0; i<10; i++)
    UINT nVal = array[i];
```

Used this way, the [] operator calls the array's *GetAt* function, which retrieves a value from a specified position in the array—with bounds checking, of course. If you'd prefer, you can call *GetAt* directly rather than use the [] operator.

To find out how many elements an array contains, call the array's *GetSize* function. You can also call *GetUpperBound*, which returns the 0-based index of the array's upper bound—the number of elements in the array minus 1.

MFC's array classes provide two functions for removing elements from an array: *RemoveAt* and *RemoveAll*. *RemoveAt* removes one or more items from the array and shifts down any items above the ones that were removed. *RemoveAll* empties the array.

Both functions adjust the array's upper bounds to reflect the number of items that were removed, as the following example demonstrates:

```
// Add 10 items.
CUIntArray array;
array.SetSize (10);
for (int i=0; i<10; i++)
    array[i] = i + 1;

// Remove the item at index 0.
array.RemoveAt (0);
TRACE (_T ("Count = %d\n"), array.GetSize ()); // 9 left.

// Remove items 0, 1, and 2.
array.RemoveAt (0, 3);
TRACE (_T ("Count = %d\n"), array.GetSize ()); // 6 left.

// Empty the array.
array.RemoveAll ();
TRACE (_T ("Count = %d\n"), array.GetSize ()); // 0 left.
```

The *Remove* functions delete elements, but they don't delete the objects that the elements point to if the elements are pointers. If *array* is a *CPtrArray* or a *CObArray* and you want to empty the array *and* delete the objects referenced by the deleted pointers, rather than write

```
array.RemoveAll ();
```

you should write this:

```
int nSize = array.GetSize ();
for (int i=0; i<nSize; i++)
    delete array[i];
array.RemoveAll ();
```

Failure to delete the objects whose addresses are stored in a pointer array will result in memory leaks. The same is true of MFC lists and maps that store pointers.

Dynamic Array Sizing

Besides being bounds-checked, the MFC array classes also support dynamic sizing. You don't have to predict ahead of time how many elements a dynamically sized array should have because the memory set aside to store array elements can be grown as elements are added and shrunk as elements are removed.

One way to dynamically grow an MFC array is to call *SetSize*. You can call *SetSize* as often as needed to allocate additional memory for storage. Suppose you initially size an array to hold 10 items but later find that it needs to hold 20. Simply call *SetSize* a second time to make room for the additional items:

```
// Add 10 items.
CUIntArray array;
array.SetSize (10);
for (int i=0; i<10; i++)
    array[i] = i + 1;
        .
        .
        .
// Add 10 more.
array.SetSize (20);
for (i=10; i<20; i++)
    array[i] = i + 1;
```

When an array is resized this way, the original items retain their values. Thus, only the new items require explicit initialization following a call to *SetSize*.

Another way to grow an array is to use *SetAtGrow* instead of *SetAt* to add items. For example, the following code attempts to use *SetAt* to add 10 items to an array of UINTs:

```
CUIntArray array;
for (int i=0; i<10; i++)
    array.SetAt (i, i + 1);
```

This code will assert the first time *SetAt* is called. Why? Because the array's size is 0 (note the absence of a call to *SetSize*), and *SetAt* doesn't automatically grow the array to accommodate new elements. Change *SetAt* to *SetAtGrow*, however, and the code works just fine:

```
CUIntArray array;
for (int i=0; i<10; i++)
    array.SetAtGrow (i, i + 1);
```

Unlike *SetAt*, *SetAtGrow* automatically grows the array's memory allocation if necessary. So does *Add*, which adds an item to the end of the array. The next example is functionally identical to the previous one, but it uses *Add* instead of *SetAtGrow* to add elements to the array:

```
CUIntArray array;
for (int i=0; i<10; i++)
    array.Add (i + 1);
```

Other functions that automatically grow an array to accommodate new items include *InsertAt*, *Append* (which appends one array to another), and *Copy*, which, as the name implies, copies one array to another.

MFC grows an array by allocating a new memory buffer and copying items from the old buffer to the new one. If a grow operation fails because of insufficient memory,

MFC throws an exception. To trap such errors when they occur, wrap calls that grow an array in a *try* block accompanied by a *catch* handler for *CMemoryException*s:

```
try {
    CUIntArray array;
    array.SetSize (1000); // Might throw a CMemoryException.
        .
        .
        .
}
catch (CMemoryException* e) {
    AfxMessageBox (_T ("Error: Insufficient memory"));
    e->Delete (); // Delete the exception object.
}
```

This *catch* handler displays an error message warning the user that the system is low on memory. In real life, more extensive measures might be required to recover gracefully from out-of-memory situations.

Because a new memory allocation is performed every time an array's size is increased, growing an array too frequently can adversely impact performance and can also lead to memory fragmentation. Consider the following code fragment:

```
CUIntArray array;
for (int i=0; i<100000; i++)
    array.Add (i + 1);
```

These statements look innocent enough, but they're inefficient because they require thousands of separate memory allocations. That's why MFC lets you specify a *grow size* in *SetSize*'s optional second parameter. The following code initializes the array more efficiently because it tells MFC to allocate space for 10,000 new UINTs whenever more memory is required:

```
CUIntArray array;
array.SetSize (0, 10000);
for (int i=0; i<100000; i++)
    array.Add (i + 1);
```

Of course, this code would be even better if it allocated room for 100,000 items up front. But very often it's impossible to predict in advance how many elements the array will be asked to hold. Large grow sizes are beneficial if you anticipate adding many items to an array but can't determine just how big the number will be up front.

If you don't specify a grow size, MFC picks one for you using a simple formula based on the array size. The larger the array, the larger the grow size. If you specify 0 as the array size or don't call *SetSize* at all, the default grow size is 4 items. In the first of the two examples in the previous paragraph, the *for* loop causes memory to be allocated and reallocated no less than 25,000 times. Setting the grow size to 10,000 reduces the allocation count to just 10.

The same *SetSize* function used to grow an array can also be used to reduce the number of array elements. When it downsizes an array, however, *SetSize* doesn't automatically shrink the buffer in which the array's data is stored. No memory is freed until you call the array's *FreeExtra* function, as demonstrated here:

```
array.SetSize (50);      // Allocate room for 50 elements.
array.SetSize (30);      // Shrink the array size to 30 elements.
array.FreeExtra ();      // Shrink the buffer to fit exactly 30 elements.
```

You should also call *FreeExtra* after *RemoveAt* and *RemoveAll* if you want to shrink the array to the minimum size necessary to hold the remaining elements.

Creating Type-Safe Array Classes with *CArray*

CUIntArray, *CStringArray*, and other MFC array classes work with specific data types. But suppose you need an array for another data type—say, *CPoint* objects. Because there is no *CPointArray* class, you must create your own from MFC's *CArray* class. *CArray* is a template class used to build type-safe array classes for arbitrary data types.

To illustrate, the following code sample declares a type-safe array class for *CPoint* objects and then instantiates the class and initializes it with an array of *CPoint*s describing a line:

```
CArray<CPoint, CPoint&> array;

// Populate the array, growing it as needed.
for (int i=0; i<10; i++)
    array.SetAtGrow (i, CPoint (i*10, 0));

// Enumerate the items in the array.
int nCount = array.GetSize ();
for (i=0; i<nCount; i++) {
    CPoint point = array[i];
    TRACE (_T ("x=%d, y=%d\n"), point.x, point.y);
}
```

The first *CArray* template parameter specifies the type of data stored in the array; the second specifies how the type is represented in parameter lists. You could use *CPoint*s instead of *CPoint* references, but references are more efficient when the size of the item exceeds the size of a pointer.

You can use data of any kind—even classes of your own creation—in *CArray*'s template parameters. The following example declares a class that represents points in three-dimensional space and fills an array with 10 class instances:

```
class CPoint3D
{
public:
    CPoint3D ()
```

```
    {
        x = y = z = 0;
    }
    CPoint3D (int xPos, int yPos, int zPos)
    {
        x = xPos;
        y = yPos;
        z = zPos;
    }
    int x, y, z;
};

CArray<CPoint3D, CPoint3D&> array;

// Populate the array, growing it as needed.
for (int i=0; i<10; i++)
    array.SetAtGrow (i, CPoint3D (i*10, 0, 0));

// Enumerate the items in the array.
int nCount = array.GetSize ();
for (i=0; i<nCount; i++) {
    CPoint3D point = array[i];
    TRACE (_T ("x=%d, y=%d, z=%d\n"), point.x, point.y, point.z);
}
```

It's important to include default constructors in classes you use with *CArray* and other template-based MFC collection classes because MFC uses a class's default constructor to create new items when functions such as *InsertAt* are called.

   With *CArray* at your disposal, you can, if you want to, do without the older (and nontemplatized) MFC array classes such as *CUIntArray* and use templates exclusively. The following *typedef* declares a *CUIntArray* data type that is functionally equivalent to MFC's *CUIntArray*:

```
typedef CArray<UINT, UINT> CUIntArray;
```

Ultimately, the choice of which *CUIntArray* class to use is up to you. However, the MFC documentation recommends that you use the template classes whenever possible, in part because doing so is more in keeping with modern C++ programming practices.

LISTS

The *InsertAt* and *RemoveAt* functions make it easy to add items to an array and to take them away. But the ease with which items are inserted and removed comes at a cost: when items are inserted or removed in the middle of an array, items higher in the array must be shifted upward or downward in memory. The performance penalty incurred when manipulating large arrays in this manner can be quite expensive.

A classic solution to the problem of maintaining ordered lists that support fast item insertion and removal is the linked list. A *linked list* is a collection of items that contain pointers to other items. In a singly linked list, each item contains a pointer to the next item in the list. Moving forward through a singly linked list is fast because moving to the next item is a simple matter of extracting that item's address from the current item. To support fast forward and backward traversal, many lists are doubly linked—that is, each item contains a pointer to the previous item in the list as well as to the next item. Given the address of the first item in the list (the *head*), it's a simple matter to enumerate the items in the list using code like this:

```
item* pItem = GetHead ();
while (pItem != NULL)
    pItem = pItem->pNextItem;
```

Conversely, given the address of the final item in the list (the *tail*), a doubly linked list can be traversed in reverse order, like this:

```
item* pItem = GetTail ();
while (pItem != NULL)
    pItem = pItem->pPrevItem;
```

These examples assume that the list doesn't wrap around on itself—that is, that the *pNextItem* pointer in the final item and the *pPrevItem* pointer in the first item are equal to NULL. Some linked lists form a circular chain of items by connecting the first and last items.

How do linked lists solve the problem of fast item insertion and removal? Inserting an item midway through the list doesn't require any items to be shifted upward in memory; it simply requires that the pointers stored in the items before and after the insertion point be adjusted to reference the new item. Removing an item is equally efficient, requiring nothing more than the adjustment of two pointers. Compare this to inserting an item into the middle of an array, which could require a *memcpy* involving tens, hundreds, or perhaps thousands of items to make room for one new item, and the benefits should be obvious.

Nearly every programmer has, at some point in his or her career, implemented a linked list. Everyone should do it once, but no one should have to do it more than once. Fortunately, many class libraries, including MFC, provide canned implementations of linked lists. As an MFC programmer, you can sleep well tonight knowing that you'll probably never have to write a linked list from scratch again.

The MFC List Classes

The MFC template class *CList* implements a generic linked list that can be customized to work with any data type. MFC also provides the following nontemplatized list classes to deal with specific data types. These classes are provided primarily for compatibility with older versions of MFC and aren't used very often in modern MFC applications.

TYPE-SPECIFIC MFC LIST CLASSES

Class Name	Data Type
CObList	*CObject* pointers
CPtrList	void pointers
CStringList	*CStrings*

MFC lists are doubly linked for fast forward and backward traversal. Positions in the list are identified by abstract values called POSITIONs. For a list, a POSITION is actually a pointer to a *CNode* data structure representing one item in the list. *CNode* contains three fields: a pointer to the next *CNode* structure in the list, a pointer to the previous *CNode* structure, and a pointer to the item data. Insertions at the head of the list, the tail, or at a specified POSITION are fast and efficient. Lists can also be searched, but because searches are performed by traversing the list sequentially and examining its items one by one, they can be time-consuming if the list is long.

I'll use *CStringList* to demonstrate how the list classes are used, but keep in mind that the principles demonstrated here apply to the other list classes as well. The following example creates a *CStringList* object and adds 10 strings to it:

```
// Schools of the Southeastern Conference
const TCHAR szSchools[][20] = {
    _T ("Alabama"),
    _T ("Arkansas"),
    _T ("Florida"),
    _T ("Georgia"),
    _T ("Kentucky"),
    _T ("Mississippi"),
    _T ("Mississippi State"),
    _T ("South Carolina"),
    _T ("Tennessee"),
    _T ("Vanderbilt"),
};

CStringList list;
for (int i=0; i<10; i++)
    list.AddTail (szSchools[i]);
```

The *AddTail* function adds an item (or all the items in another linked list) to the end of the list. To add items to the head of the list, use the *AddHead* function instead. Removing an item from the head or tail is as simple as calling *RemoveHead* or *Remove-Tail*. The *RemoveAll* function removes all the items in one fell swoop.

Each time a string is added to a *CStringList*, MFC copies the string to a *CString* and stores it in the corresponding *CNode* structure. Therefore, it's perfectly accept-able to allow the strings that you initialize a list with to go out of scope once the list is built.

Once a list is created, you can iterate through it forward and backward using the *GetNext* and *GetPrev* functions. Both accept a POSITION value identifying the current position in the list and return the item at that position. Each also updates the POSITION value to reference the next or previous item. You can retrieve the POSI-TION of the first or last item in the list with *GetHeadPosition* or *GetTailPosition*. The following statements enumerate the items in the list from first to last, writing each string retrieved from the list to the debug output window using MFC's TRACE macro:

```
POSITION pos = list.GetHeadPosition ();
while (pos != NULL) {
    CString string = list.GetNext (pos);
    TRACE (_T ("%s\n"), string);
}
```

Walking the list backward is equally simple:

```
POSITION pos = list.GetTailPosition ();
while (pos != NULL) {
    CString string = list.GetPrev (pos);
    TRACE (_T ("%s\n"), string);
}
```

If you simply want to retrieve the first or last item in the list, you can use the list's *GetHead* or *GetTail* function. Neither requires a POSITION value as input because the position is implied in the call.

Given a POSITION value *pos* identifying a particular item, you can use the list's *At* functions to retrieve, modify, or delete the item:

```
CString string = list.GetAt (pos);        // Retrieve the item.
list.SetAt (pos, _T ("Florida State"));   // Change it.
list.RemoveAt (pos);                       // Delete it.
```

You can also use *InsertBefore* or *InsertAfter* to insert items into the list:

```
list.InsertBefore (pos, _T ("Florida State"));  // Insert at pos.
list.InsertAfter (pos, _T ("Florida State"));   // Insert after pos.
```

Because of the nature of linked lists, insertions and removals performed this way are fast.

MFC's list classes include two member functions that you can use to perform searches. *FindIndex* accepts a 0-based index and returns the POSITION of the item at the corresponding location in the list. *Find* searches the list for an item matching an input you specify and returns its POSITION. For string lists, *Find* compares strings. For pointer lists, it compares pointers; it does *not* dereference the pointers and compare the items that they point to. Searching a string list for "Tennessee" requires just one function call:

```
POSITION pos = list.Find (_T ("Tennessee"));
```

By default, *Find* searches the list from beginning to end. If you'd like, you can specify an alternate starting point in the function's second parameter. But be aware that if the item you're looking for occurs before the starting POSITION, *Find* won't find it because searches don't wrap around to the beginning of the list.

You can find out how many elements a list contains with the *GetCount* function. If *GetCount* returns 0, the list is empty. A quick way to test for an empty list is to call *IsEmpty*.

Creating Type-Safe List Classes with *CList*

You can create type-safe list classes for the data types of your choice from MFC's *CList* class. Here's an example involving a linked list of *CPoint* objects:

```
CList<CPoint, CPoint&> list;

// Populate the list.
for (int i=0; i<10; i++)
    list.AddTail (CPoint (i*10, 0));

// Enumerate the items in the list.
POSITION pos = list.GetHeadPosition ();
while (pos != NULL) {
    CPoint point = list.GetNext (pos);
    TRACE (_T ("x=%d, y=%d\n"), point.x, point.y);
}
```

As with *CArray*, the first template parameter specifies the data type (*CPoint* objects) and the second specifies how items are passed in parameter lists (by reference).

If you use classes rather than primitive data types in a *CList* and you call the list's *Find* function, your code won't compile unless one of the following conditions is true:

- The class has an overloaded == operator that performs a comparison to a like object.

- You override the template function *CompareElements* with a type-specific version that compares two instances of the class.

The first method—overloading the == operator—is the more common of the two and has already been done for you in MFC classes such as *CPoint* and *CString*. If you write a class yourself, you must do the operator overloading. Here's a modified version of *CPoint3D* that overloads the comparison operator for compatibility with *CList::Find*:

```
class CPoint3D
{
public:
    CPoint3D ()
    {
        x = y = z = 0;
    }
    CPoint3D (int xPos, int yPos, int zPos)
    {
        x = xPos;
        y = yPos;
        z = zPos;
    }
    operator== (CPoint3D point) const
    {
        return (x == point.x && y == point.y && z == point.z);
    }
    int x, y, z;
};
```

The alternative to overloading the comparison operator is to override the global *CompareElements* function, as demonstrated here:

```
class CPoint3D
{
public:
    CPoint3D ()
    {
        x = y = z = 0;
    }
    CPoint3D (int xPos, int yPos, int zPos)
    {
        x = xPos;
        y = yPos;
        z = zPos;
    }
    // Note: No operator==
    int x, y, z;
};

BOOL AFXAPI CompareElements (const CPoint3D* p1, const CPoint3D* p2)
{
    return (p1->x == p2->x && p1->y == p2->y && p1->z == p2->z);
}
```

Overriding *CompareElements* eliminates the need for operator overloading because the default implementation of *CompareElements*, which is called by *CList::Find*, compares items using the comparison operator. If you override *CompareElements* and don't use == in the override, you don't need to overload the == operator either.

MAPS

Of all the MFC collection types, maps might be the most interesting. A *map*, also known as a *dictionary*, is a table of items keyed by other items. A simple example of a map is a list of the 50 states keyed by each state's two-letter abbreviation. Given a key such as CA, the corresponding state name (California) can be retrieved with a simple function call. Maps are designed so that given a key, the corresponding item can be found in the table very quickly—often with just one lookup. Maps are ideal containers for large amounts of data when lookup performance is of paramount importance. MFC uses maps to implement handle maps (tables that correlate HWNDs to *CWnds*, HPENs to *CPens*, and so on) and other internal data structures. It also makes its map classes public, so you can use them to create maps of your own.

The MFC Map Classes

In addition to the template-based map class *CMap*, which can be specialized to handle specific data types, MFC provides the following type-specific (and non-template-based) map classes. Each class includes member functions for adding and removing items, retrieving items by key, and enumerating all the items in the map.

TYPE-SPECIFIC MFC MAP CLASSES

Class Name	*Description*
CMapWordToPtr	Stores void pointers keyed by WORDs
CMapPtrToWord	Stores WORDs keyed by void pointers
CMapPtrToPtr	Stores void pointers keyed by other void pointers
CMapWordToOb	Stores *CObject* pointers keyed by WORDs
CMapStringToOb	Stores *CObject* pointers keyed by strings
CMapStringToPtr	Stores void pointers keyed by strings
CMapStringToString	Stores strings keyed by other strings

To demonstrate the semantics of map usage, let's use *CMapStringToString* to build a simple English-French dictionary containing the names of the days in the week. The following statements build the map.

```
CMapStringToString map;
map[_T ("Sunday")]    = _T ("Dimanche");
map[_T ("Monday")]    = _T ("Lundi");
map[_T ("Tuesday")]   = _T ("Mardi");
map[_T ("Wednesday")] = _T ("Mercredi");
map[_T ("Thursday")]  = _T ("Jeudi");
map[_T ("Friday")]    = _T ("Vendredi");
map[_T ("Saturday")]  = _T ("Samedi");
```

In this example, the items stored in the map are the French names for the days of the week. Each item is keyed by a string specifying its English-language equivalent. The [] operator inserts an item and its key into the map. Because *CMapStringToString* stores keys and items in *CString* objects, inserting an item copies both its text and the key text to *CStrings*.

With the map initialized like this, a simple lookup retrieves the French word for Thursday. You perform lookups by calling the map's *Lookup* function and specifying the key:

```
CString string;
if (map.Lookup (_T ("Thursday"), string))
    TRACE (_T ("Thursday in English = %s in French\n"), string);
```

A nonzero return from *Lookup* indicates that the item was successfully retrieved. A 0 return means that no such item exists—that is, that no item is keyed by the key specified in *Lookup*'s first parameter.

You can remove items from a map with *RemoveKey* and *RemoveAll*. *GetCount* returns the number of items in the map, and *IsEmpty* indicates whether the map contains any items at all. *GetStartPosition* and *GetNextAssoc* permit you to enumerate the map's contents item by item:

```
POSITION pos = map.GetStartPosition ();
while (pos != NULL) {
    CString strKey, strItem;
    map.GetNextAssoc (pos, strKey, strItem);
    TRACE (_T ("Key=%s, Item=%s\n"), strKey, strItem);
}
```

Run on the *CMapStringToString* object shown above, this code produces the following output:

```
Key=Tuesday, Item=Mardi
Key=Saturday, Item=Samedi
Key=Wednesday, Item=Mercredi
Key=Thursday, Item=Jeudi
Key=Friday, Item=Vendredi
Key=Monday, Item=Lundi
Key=Sunday, Item=Dimanche
```

As this listing shows, items aren't necessarily stored in the order in which they are added. This is a natural consequence of the fact that maps are not designed to preserve order, but to enable items to be retrieved as quickly as possible. Map architecture is described in the next section.

Incidentally, if you insert an item into a map and that item has the same key as an item that was previously inserted, the new item will replace the old one. It's not possible for an MFC map to contain two or more items identified by the same key.

How Maps Work

Maps wouldn't be very remarkable if it weren't for the fact that lookups are so fast. The key to maximizing performance is minimizing the number of items examined during the search. Sequential searches are the worst, because if the map contains n items, up to n individual lookups could be required. Binary searches are better but require ordered items. The best algorithm is one that can go directly to the requested item without having to do any searching, regardless of the number of items present. Sounds impossible? It's not. If a map is set up properly, MFC's *Lookup* function can normally find any item with a single lookup. Rarely, in fact, are more than two or three lookups required. Here's why.

Soon after a map is created (usually at the moment the first item is added, but occasionally before), it allocates memory for a hash table, which is actually an array of pointers to *CAssoc* structures. MFC uses *CAssoc* structures to represent the items (and keys) that you add to a map. *CAssoc* is defined this way for *CMapStringToString*:

```
struct CAssoc
{
    CAssoc* pNext;
    UINT nHashValue;
    CString key;
    CString value;
};
```

Whenever an item is added to the map, a new *CAssoc* structure is created, a hash value is computed from the item's key, and a pointer to the *CAssoc* structure is copied to the hash table at index *i*, where *i* is computed using the following formula:

```
i = nHashValue % nHashTableSize
```

nHashValue is the hash value computed from the key; *nHashTableSize* is the number of elements in the hash table. The default hash table size is 17 entries; I'll discuss how (and why) you change the size in just a moment. If perchance the element at index *i* already holds a *CAssoc* pointer, MFC builds a singly linked list of *CAssoc* structures. The address of the first *CAssoc* structure in the list is stored in the hash table. The address of the second *CAssoc* structure is stored in the first *CAssoc* structure's *pNext* field, and so on. Figure 5-1 illustrates how the hash table might look after 10 items are added. In this example, five of the items' addresses are stored at unique locations in the hash table, and five others are split between two linked lists whose lengths are 2 and 3, respectively.

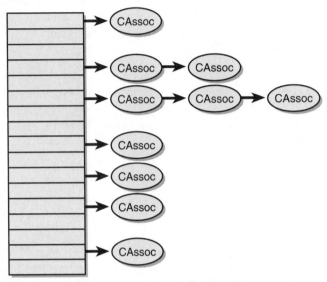

Figure 5-1. *A hash table containing a combination of unique items and linked lists.*

When a map's *Lookup* function is called, MFC computes a hash value from the input key, converts the hash into an index into the hash table using the formula described in the previous paragraph, and retrieves the *CAssoc* pointer from the corresponding location in the hash table. Under ideal conditions, there is just one *CAssoc* pointer at that location, and not a linked list of *CAssoc* pointers. If that's the case, the item has been found with just one lookup in the map, and its value is retrieved from the *CAssoc* object. If the *CAssoc* pointer retrieved from the hash table is the head of a linked list, MFC walks the list until it finds the key it's looking for. A properly built map will never have more than two or three items in a list of *CAssoc* structures, which means a lookup should never require more than two or three items to be examined.

Optimizing Lookup Efficiency

The efficiency with which lookups are performed depends on two factors:

- The size of the hash table
- The hashing algorithm's ability to generate unique hash values from arbitrary (and possibly similar) input keys

The hash table size is important. If a map contains 1,000 items but the hash table has room for only 17 *CAssoc* pointers, the best case is that each entry in the hash table stores the address of the first *CAssoc* structure in a linked list of 58 or 59 *CAssoc* structures. This arrangement greatly impedes lookup performance. The hashing algorithm is important too, because no matter how many *CAssoc* pointers the hash table can hold, if the hashing algorithm generates only a handful of different hash values (and therefore a handful of different hash table indexes), lookup performance is similarly diminished.

The best way to optimize lookup efficiency is to make the hash table as large as possible to minimize the number of collisions. A collision occurs when dissimilar input keys yield the same hash table index. Microsoft recommends setting the hash table size to a value 10 to 20 percent larger than the number of items in the map to strike a reasonable balance between memory consumption and lookup efficiency. To specify the hash table size, call the map's *InitHashTable* function:

```
// Assume the map will hold about 1,000 items.
map.InitHashTable (1200); // 1200 = 1000 + 20 percent
```

For statistical reasons, using a prime number for the hash table size also helps to minimize collisions. Therefore, an even better way to initialize a hash table for 1,000 items is to call *InitHashTable* this way:

```
map.InitHashTable (1201);
```

You should call *InitHashTable* before adding any items to the map. Attempting to resize the hash table when the map contains one or more items causes an assertion error.

Although the algorithms that MFC uses to generate hash values are adequate for most purposes, you can replace them with your own if you want to. To hash an input key, MFC calls a global template function named *HashKey*. For most data types, *HashKey* is implemented this way:

```
AFX_INLINE UINT AFXAPI HashKey(ARG_KEY key)
{
    // default identity hash - works for most primitive values
    return ((UINT)(void*)(DWORD)key) >> 4;
}
```

For strings, however, it's implemented this way:

```
UINT AFXAPI HashKey(LPCWSTR key) // Unicode strings
{
    UINT nHash = 0;
    while (*key)
        nHash = (nHash<<5) + nHash + *key++;
    return nHash;
}
```

(continued)

```
UINT AFXAPI HashKey(LPCSTR key) // ANSI strings
{
    UINT nHash = 0;
    while (*key)
        nHash = (nHash<<5) + nHash + *key++;
    return nHash;
}
```

To implement your own algorithm for a particular data type, simply write a type-specific *HashKey* function. You can use the string versions of *HashKey* shown above as a model.

Creating Type-Safe Map Classes with *CMap*

As you probably suspected, you can use MFC's *CMap* template class to create maps for data types that aren't supported by the type-specific map classes. The following example creates a collection of *CPoint* objects keyed by *CStrings* and then performs a lookup:

```
CMap<CString, CString&, CPoint, CPoint&> map;
map[CString (_T ("Vertex1"))] = CPoint (  0,   0);
map[CString (_T ("Vertex2"))] = CPoint (100,   0);
map[CString (_T ("Vertex3"))] = CPoint (100, 100);
map[CString (_T ("Vertex4"))] = CPoint (  0, 100);

CPoint point;
if (map.Lookup (CString (_T ("Vertex3")), point))
    TRACE (_T ("Vertex 3 = (%d,%d)\n"), point.x, point.y);
```

Because *CString* is used as a key, this code won't compile unless you override *HashKey* with a version that is specifically designed to hash *CStrings*. Here's one possibility:

```
UINT AFXAPI HashKey(CString& string)
{
    LPCTSTR key = (LPCTSTR) string;
    UINT nHash = 0;
    while (*key)
        nHash = (nHash<<5) + nHash + *key++;
    return nHash;
}
```

After converting the *CString* reference into a conventional string pointer, this code hashes the string the same way MFC's LPCSTR/LPCWSTR *HashKey* functions hash a string.

Like the *CList* class's *Find* function, *CMap::Lookup* uses the *CompareElements* template function to compare elements. Because *CompareElements* uses the ==

operator to perform comparisons, the default implementation is fine for primitive data types and classes that overload the == operator. If you use classes of your own devising as keys in a map, however, you must either overload the == operator in those classes or override *CompareElements* for individual data types. Refer to the section "Creating Type-Safe List Classes with *CList*" earlier in this chapter for examples of how to do both.

THE TYPED POINTER CLASSES

The MFC collection classes with *Ptr* and *Ob* in their names (the "Ptr" and "Ob" classes) provide convenient implementations of containers that store generic (void) pointers and containers that store pointers to MFC objects—that is, objects created from classes derived from *CObject*. The problem with the *Ptr* and *Ob* classes is that they're *too* generic. Using them typically requires lots of type casting, which is anathema to many C++ programmers and poor programming practice besides.

MFC's *typed pointer classes*—a set of three template classes designed to handle collections of pointers in a type-safe manner—offer a convenient solution to the problem of storing pointers without compromising type safety. The typed pointer classes are listed in the following table.

COLLECTION CLASSES FOR POINTERS

Class Name	*Description*
CTypedPtrArray	Manages arrays of pointers
CTypedPtrList	Manages linked lists of pointers
CTypedPtrMap	Manages maps that use pointers as items or keys

Suppose you're writing a drawing program and you've written a class named *CLine* that represents lines drawn on the screen. Each time the user draws a line, you create a new *CLine* object. You need somewhere to store *CLine* pointers, and because you want to be able to add and delete pointers anywhere in the collection without incurring a performance hit, you decide to use a linked list. Because you derived *CLine* from *CObject*, *CObList* would seem a natural fit.

CObList will do the job, but every time you retrieve a *CLine* pointer from the list, you must cast it to *CLine** because *CObList* returns *CObject* pointers. *CTypedPtrList* offers a clean alternative that requires no casting. Here's a code sample that demonstrates this point:

```
CTypedPtrList<CObList, CLine*> list;

// Populate the list.
for (int i=0; i<10; i++) {
```

(continued)

```
    int x = i * 10;
    CLine* pLine = new CLine (x, 0, x, 100);
    list.AddTail (pLine);
}


// Enumerate the items in the list.
POSITION pos = list.GetHeadPosition ();
while (pos != NULL)
    CLine* pLine = list.GetNext (pos); // No casting!
```

When you retrieve a *CLine* pointer with *GetNext*, you get back a *CLine* pointer that requires no casting. That's type safety.

CTypedPtrList and the other typed pointer classes work by deriving from the class whose name is specified in the first template parameter. Inside the derived class are type-safe member functions that wrap the corresponding member functions in the base class. You can call any of the functions in the base class or in the derived class, but where they overlap, you'll normally use the type-safe versions instead. In general, you should use *Ob* classes as base classes for collections that hold pointers to objects derived from *CObject*, and *Ptr* classes as base classes for collections that hold pointers to other types of objects.

As is true of all MFC collection classes that store pointers, deleting pointers from an array, a list, or a map doesn't delete the items that the pointers point to. Therefore, before emptying a list of *CLine* pointers, you'll probably find it necessary to delete the *CLines*, too:

```
POSITION pos = list.GetHeadPosition ();
while (pos != NULL)
    delete list.GetNext (pos);
list.RemoveAll ();
```

Remember: If you don't delete the *CLines*, nobody will. Don't assume that the collection classes will delete them for you.

Chapter 6

File I/O and Serialization

File input and output (I/O) services are a staple of any operating system. Not surprisingly, Microsoft Windows provides an assortment of API functions for reading, writing, and manipulating disk files. MFC casts these functions in an object-oriented mold with its *CFile* class, which lets files be viewed as objects that are operated on with *CFile* member functions such as *Read* and *Write*. *CFile* has all the tools the MFC programmer needs to perform low-level file I/O.

The most common reason for writing file I/O code is to support document saving and loading. Although there's nothing wrong with using *CFile* objects to write documents to disk and read them back, most MFC applications don't do it that way; they use *CArchive* objects instead. Thanks to some strategic operator overloading performed by MFC, most data can be serialized—that is, output as a byte stream— to a *CArchive* or deserialized from a *CArchive* with syntactical ease. Moreover, if a *CArchive* object is attached to a *CFile* object, data that is serialized to the *CArchive* is transparently written to disk. You can later reconstitute data archived in this manner by deserializing it from a *CArchive* associated with the same file.

The ability to save and load documents by serializing them to or from a *CArchive* is one of the fundamental building blocks of MFC's document/view architecture. Although knowledge of *CArchive* is of limited use for now, rest assured that it will come in exceedingly handy when we begin writing document/view applications in Chapter 9.

THE *CFILE* CLASS

CFile is a relatively simple class that encapsulates the portion of the Win32 API that deals with file I/O. Among its 25-plus member functions are functions for opening and closing files, reading and writing file data, deleting and renaming files, and retrieving file information. Its one public data member, *m_hFile*, holds the handle of the file associated with a *CFile* object. A protected *CString* data member named *m_strFileName* holds the file name. The member functions *GetFilePath*, *GetFileName*, and *GetFileTitle* can be used to extract the file name, in whole or in part. For example, if the full file name, path name included, is C:\Personal\File.txt, *GetFilePath* returns the entire string, *GetFileName* returns "File.txt," and *GetFileTitle* returns "File."

But to dwell on these functions is to disregard the features of *CFile* that are the most important to programmers—that is, the functions used to write data to disk and read it back. The next several sections offer a brief tutorial in the use of *CFile* and its rather peculiar way of letting you know when an error occurs. (*Hint*: If you've never used C++ exception handling, now is a good time to dust off the manual and brush up on it.)

Opening, Closing, and Creating Files

Files can be opened with *CFile* in either of two ways. The first option is to construct an uninitialized *CFile* object and call *CFile::Open*. The following code fragment uses this technique to open a file named File.txt with read/write access. Because no path name is provided in the function's first parameter, *Open* will fail unless the file is located in the current directory:

```
CFile file;
file.Open (_T ("File.txt"), CFile::modeReadWrite);
```

CFile::Open returns a BOOL indicating whether the operation was successful. The following example uses that return value to verify that the file was successfully opened:

```
CFile file;
if (file.Open (_T ("File.txt"), CFile::modeReadWrite)) {
    // It worked!
        :
        :
}
```

A nonzero return value means the file was opened; 0 means it wasn't. If *CFile::Open* returns 0 and you want to know *why* the call failed, create a *CFileException* object and pass its address to *Open* in the third parameter:

```
CFile file;
CFileException e;
if (file.Open (_T ("File.txt"), CFile::modeReadWrite, &e)) {
    // It worked!
        .
        .
        .
}
else {
    // Open failed. Tell the user why.
    e.ReportError ();
}
```

If *Open* fails, it initializes the *CFileException* object with information describing the nature of the failure. *ReportError* displays an error message based on that information. You can find out what caused the failure by examining the *CFileException*'s public *m_cause* data member. The documentation for *CFileException* contains a complete list of error codes.

The second option is to open the file using *CFile*'s constructor. Rather than construct an empty *CFile* object and call *Open*, you can create a *CFile* object and open a file in one step like this:

```
CFile file (_T ("File.txt"), CFile::modeReadWrite);
```

If the file can't be opened, *CFile*'s constructor throws a *CFileException*. Therefore, code that opens files using *CFile::CFile* normally uses *try* and *catch* blocks to trap errors:

```
try {
    CFile file (_T ("File.txt"), CFile::modeReadWrite);
        .
        .
        .
}
catch (CFileException* e) {
    // Something went wrong.
    e->ReportError ();
    e->Delete ();
}
```

It's up to you to delete the *CFileException* objects MFC throws to you. That's why this example calls *Delete* on the exception object after processing the exception. The only time you don't want to call *Delete* is the rare occasion when you use *throw* to rethrow the exception.

To create a new file rather than open an existing one, include a *CFile::modeCreate* flag in the second parameter to *CFile::Open* or the *CFile* constructor:

```
CFile file (_T ("File.txt"), CFile::modeReadWrite | CFile::modeCreate);
```

If a file created this way already exists, its length is truncated to 0. To create the file if it doesn't exist or to open it without truncating it if it does exist, include a *CFile-::modeNoTruncate* flag as well:

```
CFile file (_T ("File.txt"), CFile::modeReadWrite | CFile::modeCreate |
    CFile::modeNoTruncate);
```

An open performed this way almost always succeeds because the file is automatically created for you if it doesn't already exist.

By default, a file opened with *CFile::Open* or *CFile::CFile* is opened for exclusive access, which means that no one else can open the file. If desired, you can specify a sharing mode when opening the file to explicitly grant others permission to access the file, too. Here are the four sharing modes that you can choose from:

Sharing Mode	Description
CFile::shareDenyNone	Opens the file nonexclusively
CFile::shareDenyRead	Denies read access to other parties
CFile::shareDenyWrite	Denies write access to other parties
CFile::shareExclusive	Denies both read and write access to other parties (default)

In addition, you can specify any one of the following three types of read/write access:

Access Mode	Description
CFile::modeReadWrite	Requests read and write access
CFile::modeRead	Requests read access only
CFile::modeWrite	Requests write access only

A common use for these options is to allow any number of clients to open a file for reading but to deny any client the ability to write to it:

```
CFile file (_T ("File.txt"), CFile::modeRead | CFile::shareDenyWrite);
```

If the file is already open for writing when this statement is executed, the call will fail and *CFile* will throw a *CFileException* with *m_cause* equal to *CFileException::sharing-Violation*.

An open file can be closed in two ways. To close a file explicitly, call *CFile::Close* on the corresponding *CFile* object:

```
file.Close ();
```

If you'd prefer, you can let *CFile*'s destructor close the file for you. The class destructor calls *Close* if the file hasn't been closed already. This means that a *CFile* object created on the stack will be closed automatically when it goes out of scope. In the following example, the file is closed the moment the brace marking the end of the *try* block is reached:

```
try {
    CFile file (_T ("File.txt"), CFile::modeReadWrite);
        :
        :
    // CFile::~CFile closes the file.
}
```

One reason programmers sometimes call *Close* explicitly is to close the file that is currently open so that they can open another file using the same *CFile* object.

Reading and Writing

A file opened with read access can be read using *CFile::Read*. A file opened with write access can be written with *CFile::Write*. The following example allocates a 4-KB file I/O buffer and reads the file 4 KB at a time. Error checking is omitted for clarity.

```
BYTE buffer[0x1000];
CFile file (_T ("File.txt"), CFile::modeRead);
DWORD dwBytesRemaining = file.GetLength ();

while (dwBytesRemaining) {
    UINT nBytesRead = file.Read (buffer, sizeof (buffer));
    dwBytesRemaining -= nBytesRead;
}
```

A count of bytes remaining to be read is maintained in *dwBytesRemaining*, which is initialized with the file size returned by *CFile::GetLength*. After each call to *Read*, the number of bytes read from the file (*nBytesRead*) is subtracted from *dwBytesRemaining*. The *while* loop executes until *dwBytesRemaining* reaches 0.

The following example builds on the code in the previous paragraph by using *::CharLowerBuff* to convert all the uppercase characters read from the file to lowercase and using *CFile::Write* to write the converted text back to the file. Once again, error checking is omitted for clarity.

```
BYTE buffer[0x1000];
CFile file (_T ("File.txt"), CFile::modeReadWrite);
DWORD dwBytesRemaining = file.GetLength ();

while (dwBytesRemaining) {
    DWORD dwPosition = file.GetPosition ();
    UINT nBytesRead = file.Read (buffer, sizeof (buffer));
```

(continued)

```
    ::CharLowerBuff ((LPTSTR)buffer, nBytesRead);
    file.Seek (dwPosition, CFile::begin);
    file.Write (buffer, nBytesRead);
    dwBytesRemaining -= nBytesRead;
}
```

This example uses the *CFile* functions *GetPosition* and *Seek* to manipulate the file pointer—the offset into the file at which the next read or write is performed—so that the modified data is written over the top of the original. *Seek*'s second parameter specifies whether the byte offset passed in the first parameter is relative to the beginning of the file (*CFile::begin*), the end of the file (*CFile::end*), or the current position (*CFile::current*). To quickly seek to the beginning or end of a file, use *CFile::SeekToBegin* or *CFile::SeekToEnd*.

Read, *Write*, and other *CFile* functions throw a *CFileException* if an error occurs during a file I/O operation. *CFileException::m_cause* tells you why the error occurred. For example, attempting to write to a disk that is full throws a *CFileException* with *m_cause* equal to *CFileException::diskFull*. Attempting to read beyond the end of a file throws a *CFileException* with *m_cause* equal to *CFileException::endOfFile*. Here's how the routine that converts all the lowercase text in a file to uppercase might look with error checking code included:

```
BYTE buffer[0x1000];
try {
    CFile file (_T ("File.txt"), CFile::modeReadWrite);
    DWORD dwBytesRemaining = file.GetLength ();
    while (dwBytesRemaining) {
        DWORD dwPosition = file.GetPosition ();
        UINT nBytesRead = file.Read (buffer, sizeof (buffer));
        ::CharLowerBuff ((LPTSTR)buffer, nBytesRead);
        file.Seek (dwPosition, CFile::begin);
        file.Write (buffer, nBytesRead);
        dwBytesRemaining -= nBytesRead;
    }
}
catch (CFileException* e) {
    e->ReportError ();
    e->Delete ();
}
```

If you don't catch exceptions thrown by *CFile* member functions, MFC will catch them for you. MFC's default handler for unprocessed exceptions uses *ReportError* to display a descriptive error message. Normally, however, it's in your best interest to catch file I/O exceptions to prevent critical sections of code from being skipped.

CFile Derivatives

CFile is the root class for an entire family of MFC classes. The members of this family and the relationships that they share with one another are shown in Figure 6-1.

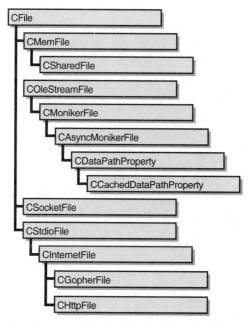

Figure 6-1. *The* CFile *family.*

Some members of the *CFile* family exist solely to provide filelike interfaces to nonfile media. For example, *CMemFile* and *CSharedFile* let blocks of memory be read and written as if they were files. MFC's *COleDataObject::GetFileData* function, which is discussed in Chapter 19, uses this handy abstraction to allow OLE drop targets and users of the OLE clipboard to retrieve data from memory with *CFile::Read*. *CSocketFile* provides a similar abstraction for TCP/IP sockets. MFC programmers sometimes place a *CSocketFile* object between a *CSocket* object and a *CArchive* object so that C++'s insertion and extraction operators can be used to write to and read from an open socket. *COleStreamFile* makes a stream object—a COM object that represents a byte stream—look like an ordinary file. It plays an important role in MFC applications that support object linking and embedding (OLE).

CStdioFile simplifies the programmatic interface to text files. It adds just two member functions to those it inherits from *CFile*: a *ReadString* function for reading lines of text and a *WriteString* function for outputting lines of text. In *CStdioFile*-speak, a line of text is a string of characters delimited by a carriage return and line feed pair (0x0D and 0x0A). *ReadString* reads everything from the current file position up to, and optionally including, the next carriage return. *WriteString* outputs a text string and writes a carriage return and line feed to the file, too. The following code fragment opens a text file named File.txt and dumps its contents to the debug output window:

```
try {
    CString string;
    CStdioFile file (_T ("File.txt"), CFile::modeRead);
    while (file.ReadString (string))
        TRACE (_T ("%s\n"), string);
}
catch (CFileException* e) {
    e->ReportError ();
    e->Delete ();
}
```

Like *Read* and *Write*, *ReadString* and *WriteString* throw exceptions if an error prevents them from carrying out their missions.

Enumerating Files and Folders

CFile includes a pair of static member functions named *Rename* and *Remove* that can be used to rename and delete files. It doesn't, however, include functions for enumerating files and folders. For that, you must resort to the Windows API.

The key to enumerating files and folders is a pair of API functions named *::FindFirstFile* and *::FindNextFile*. Given an absolute or relative file name specification (for example, "C:*.*" or "*.*"), *::FindFirstFile* opens a *find handle* and returns it to the caller. *::FindNextFile* uses that handle to enumerate file system objects. The general strategy is to call *::FindFirstFile* once to begin an enumeration and then to call *::FindNextFile* repeatedly until the enumeration is exhausted. Each successful call to *::FindFirstFile* or *::FindNextFile*—that is, a call to *::FindFirstFile* that returns any value other than INVALID_HANDLE_VALUE or a call to *::FindNextFile* that returns a non-NULL value—fills a WIN32_FIND_DATA structure with information about one file or directory. WIN32_FIND_DATA is defined this way in ANSI code builds:

```
typedef struct _WIN32_FIND_DATAA {
    DWORD dwFileAttributes;
    FILETIME ftCreationTime;
    FILETIME ftLastAccessTime;
    FILETIME ftLastWriteTime;
    DWORD nFileSizeHigh;
    DWORD nFileSizeLow;
    DWORD dwReserved0;
    DWORD dwReserved1;
```

```
    CHAR    cFileName[ MAX_PATH ];
    CHAR    cAlternateFileName[ 14 ];
} WIN32_FIND_DATAA;

typedef WIN32_FIND_DATAA WIN32_FIND_DATA;
```

To determine whether the item represented by the WIN32_FIND_DATA structure is a file or a directory, test the *dwFileAttributes* field for a FILE_ATTRIBUTE_DIRECTORY flag:

```
if (fd.dwFileAttributes & FILE_ATTRIBUTE_DIRECTORY) {
    // It's a directory.
}
else {
    // It's a file.
}
```

The *cFileName* and *cAlternateFileName* fields hold the file or directory name. *cFile-Name* contains the long name; *cAlternateFileName* contains the short (8.3 format) name. When the enumeration is complete, you should close any handles returned by *::FindFirstFile* with *::FindClose*.

To demonstrate, the following routine enumerates all the files in the current directory and writes their names to the debug output window:

```
WIN32_FIND_DATA fd;
HANDLE hFind = ::FindFirstFile (_T ("*.*"), &fd);

if (hFind != INVALID_HANDLE_VALUE) {
    do {
        if (!(fd.dwFileAttributes & FILE_ATTRIBUTE_DIRECTORY))
            TRACE (_T ("%s\n"), fd.cFileName);
    } while (::FindNextFile (hFind, &fd));
    ::FindClose (hFind);
}
```

Enumerating all the subdirectories in the current directory requires just one simple change:

```
WIN32_FIND_DATA fd;
HANDLE hFind = ::FindFirstFile (_T ("*.*"), &fd);

if (hFind != INVALID_HANDLE_VALUE) {
    do {
        if (fd.dwFileAttributes & FILE_ATTRIBUTE_DIRECTORY)
            TRACE (_T ("%s\n"), fd.cFileName);
    } while (::FindNextFile (hFind, &fd));
    ::FindClose (hFind);
}
```

The more interesting case is how you can enumerate all the directories in a given directory *and its subdirectories*. The following function enumerates all the directories in the current directory and its descendants, writing the name of each directory to the debug output window. The secret? Whenever it encounters a directory, *EnumerateFolders* descends into that directory and calls itself recursively.

```
void EnumerateFolders ()
{
    WIN32_FIND_DATA fd;
    HANDLE hFind = ::FindFirstFile (_T ("*.*"), &fd);

    if (hFind != INVALID_HANDLE_VALUE) {
        do {
            if (fd.dwFileAttributes & FILE_ATTRIBUTE_DIRECTORY) {
                CString name = fd.cFileName;
                if (name != _T (".") && name != _T ("..")) {
                    TRACE (_T ("%s\n"), fd.cFileName);
                    ::SetCurrentDirectory (fd.cFileName);
                    EnumerateFolders ();
                    ::SetCurrentDirectory (_T (".."));
                }
            }
        } while (::FindNextFile (hFind, &fd));
        ::FindClose (hFind);
    }
}
```

To use this function, navigate to the directory in which you want the enumeration to begin and call *EnumerateFolders*. The following statements enumerate all the directories on drive C:

```
::SetCurrentDirectory (_T ("C:\\"));
EnumerateFolders ();
```

We'll use a similar technique in Chapter 10 to populate a tree view with items representing all the folders on a drive.

SERIALIZATION AND THE *CARCHIVE* CLASS

Although MFC's *CFile* class makes reading and writing file data rather easy, most MFC applications don't interact with *CFile* objects directly. Instead, they do their reading and writing through *CArchive* objects that in turn use *CFile* functions to perform file I/O. MFC overloads the << and >> operators used with *CArchive* to make serializing data to or from a *CArchive* simple. The most common reason for serializing to or from an archive is to save an application's persistent data to disk or to read it back again.

Serialization is an important concept in MFC programming because it is the basis for MFC's ability to open and save documents in document/view applications. As you'll learn in Chapter 9, when someone using a document/view application selects Open or Save from the application's File menu, MFC opens the file for reading or writing and passes the application a reference to a *CArchive* object. The application, in turn, serializes its persistent data to or from the archive and, by so doing, saves a complete document to disk or reads it back again. A document whose persistent data consists entirely of primitive data types or serializable objects can often be serialized with just a few lines of code. This is in contrast to the hundreds of lines that might be required if the application were to query the user for a file name, open the file, and do all the file I/O itself.

Serialization Basics

Assume that a *CFile* object named *file* represents an open file, that the file was opened with write access, and that you want to write a pair of integers named *a* and *b* to that file. One way to accomplish this is to call *CFile::Write* once for each integer:

```
file.Write (&a, sizeof (a));
file.Write (&b, sizeof (b));
```

An alternative method is to create a *CArchive* object, associate it with the *CFile* object, and use the << operator to serialize the integers into the archive:

```
CArchive ar (&file, CArchive::store);
ar << a << b;
```

CArchive objects can be used for reading, too. Assuming *file* once again represents an open file and that the file is open with read access, the following code snippet attaches a *CArchive* object to the file and reads, or *deserializes*, the integers from the file:

```
CArchive ar (&file, CArchive::load);
ar >> a >> b;
```

MFC allows a wide variety of primitive data types to be serialized this way, including BYTEs, WORDs, LONGs, DWORDs, floats, doubles, ints, unsigned ints, shorts, and chars.

MFC also overrides the << and >> operators so that *CString*s and certain other nonprimitive data types represented by MFC classes can be serialized to or from an archive. If *string* is a *CString* object and *ar* is a *CArchive* object, writing the string to the archive is as simple as this:

```
ar << string;
```

Turning the operator around reads the string from the archive:

```
ar >> string;
```

Classes that can be serialized this way include *CString*, *CTime*, *CTimeSpan*, *COleVariant*, *COleCurrency*, *COleDateTime*, *COleDateTimeSpan*, *CSize*, *CPoint*, and *CRect*. Structures of type SIZE, POINT, and RECT can be serialized, too.

Perhaps the most powerful aspect of MFC's serialization mechanism is the fact that you can create serializable classes of your own that work with *CArchive*'s insertion and extraction operators. And you don't have to do any operator overloading of your own to make it work. Why? Because MFC overloads the << and >> operators for pointers to instances of classes derived from *CObject*.

To demonstrate, suppose you've written a drawing program that represents lines drawn by the user with instances of a class named *CLine*. Also suppose that *CLine* is a serializable class that derives, either directly or indirectly, from *CObject*. If *pLines* is an array of *CLine* pointers, *nCount* is an integer that holds the number of pointers in the array, and *ar* is a *CArchive* object, you could archive each and every *CLine* along with a count of the number of *CLine*s like this:

```
ar << nCount;
for (int i=0; i<nCount; i++)
    ar << pLines[i];
```

Conversely, you could re-create the *CLine*s from the information in the archive and initialize *pLines* with *CLine* pointers with the statements

```
ar >> nCount;
for (int i=0; i<nCount; i++)
    ar >> pLines[i];
```

How do you write serializable classes like *CLine*? It's easy; the next section describes how.

If an error occurs as data is serialized to or from an archive, MFC throws an exception. The type of exception that's thrown depends on the nature of the error. If a serialization request fails because of a lack of memory (for example, if there's too little memory to create an instance of an object that's being deserialized from an archive), MFC throws a *CMemoryException*. If a request fails because of a file I/O error, MFC throws a *CFileException*. If any other error occurs, MFC throws a *CArchiveException*. If you'd like, you can supply *catch* handlers for exceptions of these types to enact your own special processing regimen if and when errors occur.

Writing Serializable Classes

For an object to support serialization, it must be an instance of a serializable class. You can write a serializable class by following these five steps:

1. Derive the class, either directly or indirectly, from *CObject*.

2. Include MFC's DECLARE_SERIAL macro in the class declaration. DECLARE-_SERIAL accepts just one parameter: your class's name.

3. Override the base class's *Serialize* function, and serialize the derived class's data members.

4. If the derived class doesn't have a default constructor (one that takes no arguments), add one. This step is necessary because when an object is deserialized, MFC creates it on the fly using the default constructor and initializes the object's data members with values retrieved from the archive.

5. In the class implementation, include MFC's IMPLEMENT_SERIAL macro. The IMPLEMENT_SERIAL macro takes three parameters: the class name, the name of the base class, and a schema number. The *schema number* is an integer value that amounts to a version number. You should change the schema number any time you modify the class's serialized data format. Versioning of serializable classes is discussed in the next section.

Suppose you've written a simple class named *CLine* to represent lines. The class has two *CPoint* data members that store the line's endpoints, and you'd like to add serialization support. Originally, the class declaration looks like this:

```
class CLine
{
protected:
    CPoint m_ptFrom;
    CPoint m_ptTo;

public:
    CLine (CPoint from, CPoint to) { m_ptFrom = from; m_ptTo = to; }
};
```

It's easy to make this class serializable. Here's how it looks after serialization support is added:

```
class CLine : public CObject
{
DECLARE_SERIAL (CLine)

protected:
    CPoint m_ptFrom;
    CPoint m_ptTo;

public:
    CLine () {} // Required!
    CLine (CPoint from, CPoint to) { m_ptFrom = from; m_ptTo = to; }
    void Serialize (CArchive& ar);
};
```

The *Serialize* function looks like this:

```
void CLine::Serialize (CArchive& ar)
{
    CObject::Serialize (ar);
    if (ar.IsStoring ())
        ar << m_ptFrom << m_ptTo;
    else // Loading, not storing
        ar >> m_ptFrom >> m_ptTo;
}
```

And somewhere in the class implementation the statement

```
IMPLEMENT_SERIAL (CLine, CObject, 1)
```

appears. With these modifications, the class is fully serializable. The schema number is 1, so if you later add a persistent data member to *CLine*, you should bump the schema number up to 2 so that the framework can distinguish between *CLine* objects serialized to disk by different versions of your program. Otherwise, a version 1 *CLine* on disk could be read into a version 2 *CLine* in memory, with possibly disastrous consequences.

When an instance of this class is asked to serialize or deserialize itself, MFC calls the instance's *CLine::Serialize* function. Before serializing its own data members, *CLine::Serialize* calls *CObject::Serialize* to serialize the base class's data members. In this example, the base class's *Serialize* function doesn't do anything, but that might not be the case if the class you're writing derives indirectly from *CObject*. After the call to the base class returns, *CLine::Serialize* calls *CArchive::IsStoring* to determine the direction of data flow. A nonzero return means data is being serialized into the archive; 0 means data is being serialized out. *CLine::Serialize* uses the return value to decide whether to write to the archive with the << operator or to read from it using the >> operator.

Versioning Serializable Classes: Versionable Schemas

When you write a serializable class, MFC uses the schema number that you assign to enact a crude form of version control. MFC tags instances of the class with the schema number when it writes them to the archive, and when it reads them back, it compares the schema number recorded in the archive to the schema number of the objects of that type in use within the application. If the two numbers don't match, MFC throws a *CArchiveException* with *m_cause* equal to *CArchiveException::badSchema*. An unhandled exception of this type prompts MFC to display a message box with the warning "Unexpected file format." By incrementing the schema number each time you revise an object's serialized storage format, you create an effective safeguard against inadvertent attempts to read an old version of an object stored on disk into a new version that resides in memory.

One problem that frequently crops up in applications that use serializable classes is one of backward compatibility—that is, deserializing objects that were created with older versions of the application. If an object's persistent storage format changes from one version of the application to the next, you'll probably want the new version to be able to read both formats. But as soon as MFC sees the mismatched schema numbers, it throws an exception. Because of the way MFC is architected, there's no good way to handle the exception other than to do as MFC does and abort the serialization process.

That's where versionable schemas come in. A versionable schema is simply a schema number that includes a VERSIONABLE_SCHEMA flag. This flag tells MFC that the application can handle multiple serialized data formats for a given class. It suppresses the *CArchiveException* and allows an application to respond intelligently to different schema numbers. An application that uses versionable schemas can provide the backward compatibility that users expect.

Writing a serializable class that takes advantage of MFC's versionable schema support involves two steps:

1. OR the value VERSIONABLE_SCHEMA into the schema number in the IMPLEMENT_SERIAL macro.

2. Modify the class's *Serialize* function to call *CArchive::GetObjectSchema* when loading an object from an archive and adapt its deserialization routine accordingly. *GetObjectSchema* returns the schema number of the object that's about to be deserialized.

You need to be aware of a few rules when you use *GetObjectSchema*. First, it should be called only when an object is being deserialized. Second, it should be called before any of the object's data members are read from the archive. And third, it should be called only once. If called a second time in the context of the same call to *Serialize, GetObjectSchema* returns −1.

Let's say that in version 2 of your application, you decide to modify the *CLine* class by adding a member variable to hold a line color. Here's the revised class declaration:

```
class CLine : public CObject
{
DECLARE_SERIAL (CLine)

protected:
    CPoint m_ptFrom;
    CPoint m_ptTo;
    COLORREF m_clrLine; // Line color (new in version 2)
```

(continued)

```
public:
    CLine () {}
    CLine (CPoint from, CPoint to, COLORREF color)
        { m_ptFrom = from; m_ptTo = to; m_clrLine = color }
    void Serialize (CArchive& ar);
};
```

Because the line color is a persistent property (that is, a red line saved to an archive should still be red when it is read back), you want to modify *CLine::Serialize* to serialize *m_clrLine* in addition to *m_ptFrom* and *m_ptTo*. That means you should bump up *CLine*'s schema number to 2. The original class implementation invoked MFC's IMPLEMENT_SERIAL macro like this:

```
IMPLEMENT_SERIAL (CLine, CObject, 1)
```

In the revised class, however, IMPLEMENT_SERIAL should be called like this:

```
IMPLEMENT_SERIAL (CLine, CObject, 2 | VERSIONABLE_SCHEMA)
```

When the updated program reads a *CLine* object whose schema number is 1, MFC won't throw a *CArchive* exception because of the VERSIONABLE_SCHEMA flag in the schema number. But it will know that the two schemas are different because the base schema number was increased from 1 to 2.

You're halfway there. The final step is to modify *CLine::Serialize* so that it deserializes a *CLine* differently depending on the value returned by *GetObjectSchema*. The original *Serialize* function looked like this:

```
void CLine::Serialize (CArchive& ar)
{
    CObject::Serialize (ar);
    if (ar.IsStoring ())
        ar << m_ptFrom << m_ptTo;
    else // Loading, not storing
        ar >> m_ptFrom >> m_ptTo;
}
```

You should implement the new one like this:

```
void CLine::Serialize (CArchive& ar)
{
    CObject::Serialize (ar);
    if (ar.IsStoring ())
        ar << m_ptFrom << m_ptTo << m_clrLine;
    else {
        UINT nSchema = ar.GetObjectSchema ();
        switch (nSchema) {
        case 1: // Version 1 CLine
            ar >> m_ptFrom >> m_ptTo;
```

```
            m_clrLine = RGB (0, 0, 0); // Default color
            break;
        case 2: // Version 2 CLine
            ar >> m_ptFrom >> m_ptTo >> m_clrLine;
            break;
        default: // Unknown version
            AfxThrowArchiveException (CArchiveException::badSchema);
            break;
        }
    }
}
```

See how it works? When a *CLine* object is written *to* the archive, it's always formatted as a version 2 *CLine*. But when a *CLine* is read *from* the archive, it's treated as a version 1 *CLine* or a version 2 *CLine*, depending on the value returned by *GetObjectSchema*. If the schema number is 1, the object is read the old way and *m_clrLine* is set to a sensible default. If the schema number is 2, all of the object's data members, including *m_clrLine*, are read from the archive. Any other schema number results in a *CArchive-Exception* indicating that the version number is unrecognized. (If this occurs, you're probably dealing with buggy code or a corrupted archive.) If, in the future, you revise *CLine* again, you can bump the schema number up to 3 and add a *case* block for the new schema.

How Serialization Works

Looking under the hood to see what happens when data is serialized to or from an archive provides a revealing glimpse into both the operation and the architecture of MFC. MFC serializes primitive data types such as ints and DWORDs by copying them directly to the archive. To illustrate, here's an excerpt from the MFC source code file Arccore.cpp showing how the *CArchive* insertion operator for DWORDs is implemented:

```
CArchive& CArchive::operator<<(DWORD dw)
{
    if (m_lpBufCur + sizeof(DWORD) > m_lpBufMax)
        Flush();

    if (!(m_nMode & bNoByteSwap))
        _AfxByteSwap(dw, m_lpBufCur);
    else
        *(DWORD*)m_lpBufCur = dw;

    m_lpBufCur += sizeof(DWORD);
    return *this;
}
```

For performance reasons, *CArchive* objects store the data that is written to them in an internal buffer. *m_lpBufCur* points to the current location in that buffer. If the buffer is too full to hold another DWORD, it is flushed before the DWORD is copied to it. For a *CArchive* object that's attached to a *CFile*, *CArchive::Flush* writes the current contents of the buffer to the file.

*CString*s, *CRect*s, and other nonprimitive data types formed from MFC classes are serialized differently. MFC serializes a *CString*, for example, by outputting a character count followed by the characters themselves. The writing is done with *CArchive::Write*. Here's an excerpt from Arccore.cpp that shows how a *CString* containing less than 255 characters is serialized:

```
CArchive& AFXAPI operator<<(CArchive& ar, const CString& string)
{
         .
         .
         .
    if (string.GetData()->nDataLength < 255)
    {
        ar << (BYTE)string.GetData()->nDataLength;
    }
         .
         .
         .
    ar.Write(string.m_pchData,
        string.GetData()->nDataLength*sizeof(TCHAR));
    return ar;
}
```

CArchive::Write copies a specified chunk of data to the archive's internal buffer and flushes the buffer if necessary to prevent overflows. Incidentally, if a *CString* serialized into an archive with the << operator contains Unicode characters, MFC writes a special 3-byte signature into the archive before the character count. This enables MFC to identify a serialized string's character type so that, if necessary, those characters can be converted to the format that a client expects when the string is deserialized from the archive. In other words, it's perfectly acceptable for a Unicode application to serialize a string and for an ANSI application to deserialize it, and vice versa.

The more interesting case is what happens when a *CObject* pointer is serialized into an archive. Here's the relevant code from Afx.inl:

```
_AFX_INLINE CArchive& AFXAPI operator<<(CArchive& ar,
    const CObject* pOb)
    { ar.WriteObject(pOb); return ar; }
```

As you can see, the << operator calls *CArchive::WriteObject* and passes it the pointer that appears on the right side of the insertion operator—for example, the *pLine* in

```
ar << pLine;
```

WriteObject ultimately calls the object's *Serialize* function to serialize the object's data members, but before it does, it writes additional information to the archive that identifies the class from which the object was created.

For example, suppose the object being serialized is an instance of *CLine*. The very first time it serializes a *CLine* to the archive, *WriteObject* inserts a *new class tag*—a 16-bit integer whose value is –1, or 0xFFFF—into the archive, followed by the object's 16-bit schema number, a 16-bit value denoting the number of characters in the class name, and finally the class name itself. *WriteObject* then calls the *CLine*'s *Serialize* function to serialize the *CLine*'s data members.

If a second *CLine* is written to the archive, *WriteObject* behaves differently. When it writes a new class tag to the archive, *WriteObject* adds the class name to an in-memory database (actually, an instance of *CMapPtrToPtr*) and assigns the class a unique identifier that is in reality an index into the database. If no other classes have been written to the archive, the first *CLine* written to disk is assigned an index of 1. When asked to write a second *CLine* to the archive, *WriteObject* checks the database, sees that *CLine* is already recorded, and instead of writing redundant information to the archive, writes a 16-bit value that consists of the class index ORed with an *old class tag* (0x8000). It then calls the *CLine*'s *Serialize* function as before. Thus, the first instance of a class written to an archive is marked with a new class tag, a schema number, and a class name; subsequent instances are tagged with 16-bit values whose lower 15 bits identify a previously recorded schema number and class name.

Figure 6-2 shows a hex dump of an archive that contains two serialized version 1 *CLine*s. The *CLine*s were written to the archive with the following code fragment:

```
// Create two CLines and initialize an array of pointers.
CLine line1 (CPoint (0, 0), CPoint (50, 50));
CLine line2 (CPoint (50, 50), CPoint (100, 0));
CLine* pLines[2] = { &line1, &line2 };
int nCount = 2;

// Serialize the CLines and the CLine count.
ar << nCount;
for (int i=0; i<nCount; i++)
    ar << pLines[i];
```

The hex dump is broken down so that each line in the listing represents one component of the archive. I've numbered the lines for reference. Line 1 contains the object count (2) written to the archive when the statement

```
ar << nCount;
```

was executed. Line 2 contains information written by *WriteObject* defining the *CLine* class. The first 16-bit value is the new class tag; the second is the class's schema number (1); and the third holds the length of the class name (5). The final 5 bytes on line 2

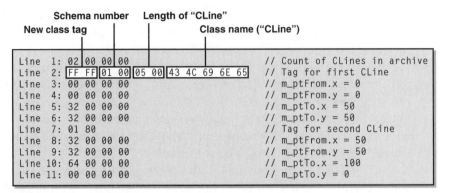

Figure 6-2. *Hex dump of an archive containing two CLines.*

hold the class name ("CLine"). Immediately following the class information, in lines 3 through 6, is the first serialized *CLine*: four 32-bit values that specify, in order, the *x* component of the *CLine*'s *m_ptFrom* data member, the *y* component of *m_ptFrom*, the *x* component of *m_ptTo*, and the *y* component of *m_ptTo*. Similar information for the second *CLine* appears on lines 8 through 11, but in between—on line 7—is a 16-bit tag that identifies the data that follows as a serialized *CLine*. *CLine*'s class index is 1 because it was the first class added to the archive. The 16-bit value 0x8001 is the class index ORed with an old class tag.

So far, so good. It's not difficult to understand what goes into the archive. Now let's see what happens when the *CLine*s are read out of the archive.

Assume that the *CLine*s are deserialized with the following code:

```
int nCount;
ar >> nCount;
CLine* pLines = new CLine[nCount];
for (int i=0; i<nCount; i++)
    ar >> pLines[i];
```

When the

```
ar >> nCount;
```

statement is executed, *CArchive* reaches into the archive, retrieves 4 bytes, and copies them to *nCount*. That sets the stage for the *for* loop that retrieves *CLine*s from the archive. Each time the

```
ar >> pLines[i];
```

statement is executed, the >> operator calls *CArchive::ReadObject* and passes in a NULL pointer. Here's the relevant code in Afx.inl:

```
_AFX_INLINE CArchive& AFXAPI operator>>(CArchive& ar, CObject*& pOb)
    { pOb = ar.ReadObject(NULL); return ar; }
_AFX_INLINE CArchive& AFXAPI operator>>(CArchive& ar,
    const CObject*& pOb)
    { pOb = ar.ReadObject(NULL); return ar; }
```

ReadObject calls another *CArchive* function named *ReadClass* to determine what kind of object it's about to deserialize. The first time through the loop, *ReadClass* reads one word from the archive, sees that it's a new class tag, and proceeds to read the schema number and class name from the archive. *ReadClass* then compares the schema number obtained from the archive to the schema number stored in the *CRuntimeClass* structure associated with the class whose name was just retrieved. (The DECLARE_SERIAL and IMPLEMENT_SERIAL macros create a static *CRuntimeClass* structure containing important information about a class, including its name and schema number. MFC maintains a linked list of *CRuntimeClass* structures that can be searched to locate run-time information for a particular class.) If the schemas are the same, *ReadClass* returns the *CRuntimeClass* pointer to *ReadObject*. *ReadObject*, in turn, calls *CreateObject* through the *CRuntimeClass* pointer to create a new instance of the class and then calls the object's *Serialize* function to load the data from the archive into the object's data members. The pointer to the new class instance returned by *ReadClass* is copied to the location specified by the caller—in this case, the address of *pLines[i]*.

As class information is read from the archive, *ReadObject* builds a class database in memory just as *WriteObject* does. When the second *CLine* is read from the archive, the 0x8001 tag preceding it tells *ReadClass* that it can get the *CRuntimeClass* pointer requested by *ReadObject* from the database.

That's basically what happens during the serialization process if all goes well. I've skipped many of the details, including the numerous error checks MFC performs and the special treatment given to NULL object pointers and multiple references to the same object.

What happens if the schema number read from the archive doesn't match the schema number stored in the corresponding *CRuntimeClass*? Enter versionable schemas. MFC first checks for a VERSIONABLE_SCHEMA flag in the schema number stored in the *CRuntimeClass*. If the flag is absent, MFC throws a *CArchiveException*. At that point, the serialization process is over; done; finis. There's very little you can do about it other than display an error message, which MFC will do for you if you don't catch the exception. If the VERSIONABLE_SCHEMA flag is present, however, MFC skips the call to *AfxThrowArchiveException* and stores the schema number where the application can retrieve it by calling *GetObjectSchema*. That's why VERSIONABLE_SCHEMA and *GetObjectSchema* are the keys that open the door to successful versioning of serializable classes.

Serializing *CObjects*

I'll close this chapter with a word of advice regarding the serialization of *CObjects*. MFC overloads *CArchive*'s insertion and extraction operators for *CObject* pointers, but not for *CObjects*. That means this will work:

```
CLine* pLine = new CLine (CPoint (0, 0), CPoint (100, 50));
ar << pLine;
```

But this won't:

```
CLine line (CPoint (0, 0), CPoint (100, 50));
ar << line;
```

In other words, *CObjects* can be serialized by pointer but not by value. This normally isn't a problem, but it can be troublesome if you write serializable classes that use other serializable classes as embedded data members and you want to serialize those data members.

One way to serialize *CObjects* by value instead of by pointer is to do your serialization and deserialization like this:

```
// Serialize.
CLine line (CPoint (0, 0), CPoint (100, 50));
ar << &line;

// Deserialize.
CLine* pLine;
ar >> pLine;
CLine line = *pLine; // Assumes CLine has a copy constructor.
delete pLine;
```

The more common approach, however, is to call the other class's *Serialize* function directly, as demonstrated here:

```
// Serialize.
CLine line (CPoint (0, 0), CPoint (100, 50));
line.Serialize (ar);

// Deserialize.
CLine line;
line.Serialize (ar);
```

Although calling *Serialize* directly is perfectly legal, you should be aware that it means doing without versionable schemas for the object that is being serialized. When you use the << operator to serialize an object pointer, MFC writes the object's schema number to the archive; when you call *Serialize* directly, it doesn't. If called to retrieve the schema number for an object whose schema is not recorded, *GetObjectSchema* will return −1 and the outcome of the deserialization process will depend on how gracefully *Serialize* handles unexpected schema numbers.

Chapter 7

Controls

One of the ingredients found in the recipe for nearly every successful Microsoft Windows application is the control. A *control* is a special kind of window designed to convey information to the user or to acquire input. Most controls appear in dialog boxes, but they work just fine in top-level windows and other nondialog windows, too. The push button is one example of a control; the edit control—a simple rectangle for entering and editing text—is another.

Controls reduce the tedium of Windows programming and promote a consistent user interface by providing canned implementations of common user interface elements. Controls are prepackaged objects that come complete with their own window procedures. An application that uses a push button control doesn't have to draw the push button on the screen and process mouse messages to know when the push button is clicked. Instead, it creates the push button with a simple function call and receives notifications whenever the push button is clicked. The control's WM_PAINT handler paints the push button on the screen, and other message handlers inside the control translate user input into notification messages.

Controls are sometimes referred to as *child window controls* because of the parent-child relationships that they share with other windows. Unlike top-level windows, which have no parents, controls are child windows that are parented to other windows. A child window moves when its parent moves, is automatically destroyed when its parent is destroyed, and is clipped to its parent's window rectangle. And when a control transmits a notification message signifying an input event, its parent is the recipient of that message.

Current versions of Windows come with more than 20 types of controls. Six, which we'll refer to as the *classic controls*, have been around since the first version of Windows and are implemented in User.exe. The others, which are collectively known as the *common controls,* are relatively new to Windows (most debuted in Windows 95) and are implemented in Comctl32.dll. This chapter introduces the classic controls and the MFC classes that encapsulate them. The common controls are covered in Chapter 16.

THE CLASSIC CONTROLS

Windows makes the classic controls available to the application programs that it hosts by registering six predefined WNDCLASSes. The control types, their WNDCLASSes, and the corresponding MFC classes are shown in the following table.

THE CLASSIC CONTROLS

Control Type	WNDCLASS	MFC Class
Buttons	"BUTTON"	*CButton*
List boxes	"LISTBOX"	*CListBox*
Edit controls	"EDIT"	*CEdit*
Combo boxes	"COMBOBOX"	*CComboBox*
Scroll bars	"SCROLLBAR"	*CScrollBar*
Static controls	"STATIC"	*CStatic*

A control is created by instantiating one of the MFC control classes and calling the resulting object's *Create* function. If *m_wndPushButton* is a *CButton* object, the statement

```
m_wndPushButton.Create (_T ("Start"), WS_CHILD | WS_VISIBLE |
    BS_PUSHBUTTON, rect, this, IDC_BUTTON);
```

creates a push button control labeled "Start." The first parameter is the text that appears on the button face. The second is the button style, which is a combination of conventional (WS_) window styles and button-specific (BS_) window styles. Together, WS_CHILD, WS_VISIBLE, and BS_PUSHBUTTON create a push button control that is a child of the window identified in the fourth parameter and that is visible on the screen. (If you omit WS_VISIBLE from the window style, the control won't become visible until you call *ShowWindow* on it.). *rect* is a RECT structure or a *CRect* object specifying the control's size and location, in pixels, relative to the upper left corner of its parent's client area. *this* identifies the parent window, and IDC_BUTTON is an integer value that identifies the control. This value is also known as the *child window ID* or *control ID*. It's important to assign a unique ID to each control you create within a given window so that you can map the control's notification messages to member functions in the parent window class.

List boxes and edit controls assume a "flat" look when they're created with *Create*. To endow them with the contemporary chiseled look that most users have grown accustomed to (Figure 7-1), you need to create list boxes and edit controls with *CreateEx* instead of *Create* and include a WS_EX_CLIENTEDGE flag in the extended style specified in the function's first parameter. If *m_wndListBox* is a *CListBox* object, the following statement creates a list box with chiseled edges and parents it to the window identified by the *this* pointer:

```
m_wndListBox.CreateEx (WS_EX_CLIENTEDGE, _T ("LISTBOX"), NULL,
    WS_CHILD | WS_VISIBLE | LBS_STANDARD, rect, this, IDC_LISTBOX);
```

As an alternative, you can derive your own class from *CListBox*, override *PreCreateWindow* in the derived class, and apply WS_EX_CLIENTEDGE to the window style in the *PreCreateWindow*, as demonstrated here:

```
BOOL CMyListBox::PreCreateWindow (CREATESTRUCT& cs)
{
    if (!CListBox::PreCreateWindow (cs))
        return FALSE;

    cs.dwExStyle |= WS_EX_CLIENTEDGE;
        :
        :
    return TRUE;
}
```

With *PreCreateWindow* implemented like this, a *CMyListBox* object will have chiseled borders regardless of how it's created.

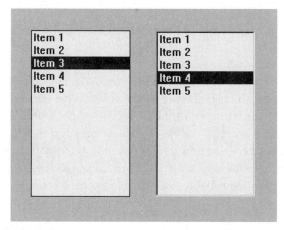

Figure 7-1. *A list box with flat edges (left) and chiseled edges (right).*

A control sends notifications to its parent in the form of WM_COMMAND messages. The kinds of notifications that are sent vary with the control type, but in each case, information encoded in the message's *wParam* and *lParam* parameters identifies the control that sent the message and the action that prompted the message. For example, the WM_COMMAND message sent when a push button is clicked contains the notification code BN_CLICKED in the upper 16 bits of *wParam*, the control ID in the lower 16 bits of *wParam*, and the control's window handle in *lParam*.

Rather than process raw WM_COMMAND messages, most MFC applications use message maps to link control notifications to class member functions. For example, the following message-map entry maps clicks of the push button whose control ID is IDC_BUTTON to the member function *OnButtonClicked*:

```
ON_BN_CLICKED (IDC_BUTTON, OnButtonClicked)
```

ON_BN_CLICKED is one of several control-related message-map macros that MFC provides. For example, there are ON_EN macros for edit controls and ON_LBN macros for list box controls. There's also the generic ON_CONTROL macro, which handles all notifications and all control types, and ON_CONTROL_RANGE, which maps identical notifications from two or more controls to a common notification handler.

Controls send messages to their parents, but it's no less common for parents to send messages to controls. For example, a check mark is placed in a check box control by sending the control a BM_SETCHECK message with *wParam* equal to BST-_CHECKED. MFC simplifies message-based control interfaces by building member functions into its control classes that wrap BM_SETCHECK and other control messages. For example, the statement

```
m_wndCheckBox.SetCheck (BST_CHECKED);
```

places a check mark inside a check box represented by a *CButton* object named *m_wndCheckBox*.

Because a control is a window, some of the member functions that the control classes inherit from *CWnd* are useful for control programming. For example, the same *SetWindowText* function that changes the text in a window's title bar inserts text into an edit control, too. Other useful *CWnd* functions include *GetWindowText*, which retrieves text from a control; *EnableWindow*, which enables and disables a control; and *SetFont*, which changes a control's font. If you want to do something to a control and can't find an appropriate member function in the control class, check *CWnd*'s list of member functions. You'll probably find the one you're looking for.

The *CButton* Class

CButton represents button controls based on the "BUTTON" WNDCLASS. Button controls come in four flavors: push buttons, check boxes, radio buttons, and group boxes. All four button types are shown in Figure 7-2.

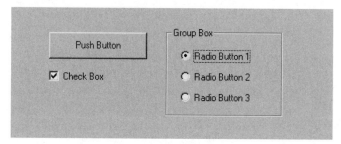

Figure 7-2. *The four types of button controls.*

When you create a button control, you specify which of the four button types you want to create by including one of the following flags in the button's window style:

Style	Description
BS_PUSHBUTTON	Creates a standard push button control
BS_DEFPUSHBUTTON	Creates a default push button; used in dialog boxes to identify the push button that's clicked if Enter is pressed
BS_CHECKBOX	Creates a check box control
BS_AUTOCHECKBOX	Creates a check box control that checks and unchecks itself when clicked
BS_3STATE	Creates a three-state check box control
BS_AUTO3STATE	Creates a three-state check box control that cycles through three states—checked, unchecked, and indeterminate—when clicked
BS_RADIOBUTTON	Creates a radio button control
BS_AUTORADIOBUTTON	Creates a radio button control that, when clicked, checks itself and unchecks other radio buttons in the group
BS_GROUPBOX	Creates a group box control

In addition, you can OR one or more of the following values into the window style to control the alignment of the text on the button face:

Style	Description
BS_LEFTTEXT	Moves the text accompanying a radio button or check box control from the button's right (the default) to its left
BS_RIGHTBUTTON	Same as BS_LEFTTEXT
BS_LEFT	Left justifies the button text in the control rectangle
BS_CENTER	Centers the button text in the control rectangle
BS_RIGHT	Right justifies the button text in the control rectangle
BS_TOP	Positions the button text at the top of the control rectangle
BS_VCENTER	Positions the button text in the center of the control rectangle vertically
BS_BOTTOM	Positions the button text at the bottom of the control rectangle
BS_MULTILINE	Allows text too long to fit on one line to be broken into two or more lines

There are other button styles, but most of them are rarely used. For example, BS_NOTIFY programs a button to send BN_DOUBLECLICKED, BN_KILLFOCUS, and BN_SETFOCUS notifications. BS_OWNERDRAW creates an *owner-draw* button—one whose appearance is maintained by the button's parent rather than the button itself. Owner-draw buttons have been largely superseded by bitmap buttons and icon buttons. You'll learn more about bitmap buttons and icon buttons later in this chapter.

Push Buttons

A push button is a button control created with the style BS_PUSHBUTTON. When clicked, a push button control sends its parent a BN_CLICKED notification encapsulated in a WM_COMMAND message. Absent the button style BS_NOTIFY, a push button sends no other types of notifications.

MFC's ON_BN_CLICKED macro links BN_CLICKED notifications to member functions in the parent window class. The message-map entry

```
ON_BN_CLICKED (IDC_BUTTON, OnButtonClicked)
```

connects *OnButtonClicked* to clicks of the push button whose control ID is IDC-_BUTTON. A trivial implementation of *OnButtonClicked* looks like this:

```
void CMainWindow::OnButtonClicked ()
{
    MessageBox (_T ("I've been clicked!"));
}
```

Like command handlers for menu items, BN_CLICKED handlers accept no parameters and return no values.

Check Boxes

Check boxes are buttons created with the style BS_CHECKBOX, BS_AUTOCHECKBOX, BS_3STATE, or BS_AUTO3STATE. BS_CHECKBOX and BS_AUTOCHECKBOX check boxes can assume two states: checked and unchecked. A check box is checked and unchecked with *CButton::SetCheck*:

```
m_wndCheckBox.SetCheck (BST_CHECKED);   // Check
m_wndCheckBox.SetCheck (BST_UNCHECKED); // Uncheck
```

To find out whether a check box is checked, use *CButton::GetCheck*. A return value equal to BST_CHECKED means the box is checked. BST_UNCHECKED means it's not.

Like push button controls, check boxes send BN_CLICKED notifications to their parents when clicked. The check mark in a BS_AUTOCHECKBOX check box toggles on and off automatically in response to button clicks. The check mark in a BS_CHECKBOX check box doesn't. Therefore, BS_CHECKBOX-style check boxes are of little use unless you write BN_CLICKED handlers to go with them. The following BN_CLICKED handler toggles *m_wndCheckBox*'s check mark on and off:

```
void CMainWindow::OnCheckBoxClicked ()
{
    m_wndCheckBox.SetCheck (m_wndCheckBox.GetCheck () ==
        BST_CHECKED ? BST_UNCHECKED : BST_CHECKED);
}
```

The BS_3STATE and BS_AUTO3STATE button styles create a check box that can assume a third state in addition to the checked and unchecked states. The third state is called the *indeterminate* state and is entered when the user clicks a BS_AUTO3STATE check box that is currently checked or when *SetCheck* is called with a BST_INDETERMINATE parameter:

```
m_wndCheckBox.SetCheck (BST_INDETERMINATE);
```

An indeterminate check box contains a grayed check mark. The indeterminate state is used to indicate that something is neither wholly on nor wholly off. For example, a word processing program might set a check box labeled "Bold" to the indeterminate state when the user selects a mix of normal and boldface text.

Radio Buttons

A radio button is a button control with the style BS_RADIOBUTTON or BS_AUTORADIOBUTTON. Radio buttons normally come in groups, with each button representing one in a list of mutually exclusive options. When clicked, a BS_AUTORADIOBUTTON radio button checks itself *and* unchecks the other radio buttons in the group. If you use the BS_RADIOBUTTON style instead, it's up to you to do the checking and unchecking using *CButton::SetCheck*.

Radio buttons send BN_CLICKED notifications to their parents, just as push buttons and check boxes do. The following BN_CLICKED handler checks the *m_wndRadioButton1* radio button and unchecks three other radio buttons in the same group:

```
void CMainWindow::OnRadioButton1Clicked ()
{
    m_wndRadioButton1.SetCheck (BST_CHECKED);
    m_wndRadioButton2.SetCheck (BST_UNCHECKED);
    m_wndRadioButton3.SetCheck (BST_UNCHECKED);
    m_wndRadioButton4.SetCheck (BST_UNCHECKED);
}
```

Unchecking the other radio buttons maintains the exclusivity of the selection. A BN_CLICKED handler isn't necessary for BS_AUTORADIOBUTTON radio buttons, though you can still provide one if you want to respond to changes in a radio button's state at the instant the button is clicked.

For BS_AUTORADIOBUTTON radio buttons to properly deselect the other buttons in the group, you must group the buttons so that Windows knows which buttons belong to the group. To create a group of BS_AUTORADIOBUTTON radio buttons, follow this procedure:

1. In your application's code, create the buttons in sequence, one after another; don't create any other controls in between.

2. To mark the beginning of the group, assign the style WS_GROUP to the first radio button you create.

3. If you create additional controls after the last radio button is created, assign the WS_GROUP style to the first additional control that you create. This implicitly marks the previous control (the last radio button) as the final one in the group. If there are no other controls after the radio buttons but there are other controls in the window, mark the first control with WS_GROUP to prevent the radio button group from wrapping around.

The following example demonstrates how to create four BS_AUTORADIO-BUTTON radio buttons belonging to one group and three belonging to another group, with a check box control in between:

```
m_wndRadioButton1.Create (_T ("COM1"), WS_CHILD | WS_VISIBLE |
    WS_GROUP | BS_AUTORADIOBUTTON, rect1, this, IDC_COM1);
m_wndRadioButton2.Create (_T ("COM2"), WS_CHILD | WS_VISIBLE |
    BS_AUTORADIOBUTTON, rect2, this, IDC_COM2);
m_wndRadioButton3.Create (_T ("COM3"), WS_CHILD | WS_VISIBLE |
    BS_AUTORADIOBUTTON, rect3, this, IDC_COM3);
```

```
m_wndRadioButton4.Create (_T ("COM4"), WS_CHILD ¦ WS_VISIBLE ¦
    BS_AUTORADIOBUTTON, rect4, this, IDC_COM4);
m_wndRadioButton1.SetCheck (BST_CHECKED);

m_wndCheckBox.Create (_T ("Save settings on exit"),
    WS_CHILD ¦ WS_VISIBLE ¦ WS_GROUP ¦ BS_AUTOCHECKBOX,
    rectCheckBox, this, IDC_SAVESETTINGS);

m_wndRadioButton5.Create (_T ("9600"), WS_CHILD ¦ WS_VISIBLE ¦
    WS_GROUP ¦ BS_AUTORADIOBUTTON, rect5, this, IDC_9600);
m_wndRadioButton6.Create (_T ("14400"), WS_CHILD ¦ WS_VISIBLE ¦
    BS_AUTORADIOBUTTON, rect6, this, IDC_14400);
m_wndRadioButton7.Create (_T ("28800"), WS_CHILD ¦ WS_VISIBLE ¦
    BS_AUTORADIOBUTTON, rect7, this, IDC_28800);
m_wndRadioButton5.SetCheck (BST_CHECKED);
```

Because of the BS_AUTORADIOBUTTON styles and the logical grouping provided by the WS_GROUP bits, checking any of the first four radio buttons automatically unchecks the other three in the group, and checking any radio button in the second group automatically unchecks the other two.

For good form, the code above calls *SetCheck* to check a button in each group. One of the buttons in a group of radio buttons should always be checked, even if the user has yet to provide any input. Radio buttons are never checked by default, so it's your responsibility to do the initializing.

Group Boxes

A group box is a button control created with the style BS_GROUPBOX. It is unlike other button controls in that it never receives the input focus and never sends notifications to its parent.

The sole function of the group box is to visually delineate control groups. Enclosing groups of controls in group boxes makes it apparent to the user which controls go together. Group boxes have nothing to do with the *logical* grouping of controls, so don't expect a series of radio buttons to function as a group simply because there's a group box around them.

The *CListBox* Class

MFC's *CListBox* class encapsulates list box controls, which display lists of text strings called *items*. A list box optionally sorts the items that are added to it, and scrolling is built in so that the number of items a list box can display isn't limited by the physical dimensions of the list box window.

List boxes are extremely useful for presenting lists of information and allowing users to select items from those lists. When an item is clicked or double-clicked, most list boxes (technically, those with LBS_NOTIFY in their window styles) notify their parents with WM_COMMAND messages. MFC simplifies the processing of these messages by providing ON_LBN message-map macros that you can use to route list box notifications to handling functions in the parent window class.

A standard list box displays text strings in a vertical column and allows only one item to be selected at a time. The currently selected item is highlighted with the system color COLOR_HIGHLIGHT. Windows supports a number of variations on the standard list box, including multiple-selection list boxes, multicolumn list boxes, and owner-draw list boxes that display images instead of text.

Creating a List Box

The following statement creates a standard list box from a *CListBox* object named *m_wndListBox*:

```
m_wndListBox.Create (WS_CHILD | WS_VISIBLE | LBS_STANDARD,
    rect, this, IDC_LISTBOX);
```

LBS_STANDARD combines the styles WS_BORDER, WS_VSCROLL, LBS_NOTIFY, and LBS_SORT to create a list box that has a border and a vertical scroll bar, that notifies its parent when the selection changes or an item is double-clicked, and that alphabetically sorts the strings that are added to it. By default, the scroll bar is visible only when the number of items in the list box exceeds the number that can be displayed. To make the scroll bar visible at all times, include the style LBS_DISABLENOSCROLL. A list box doesn't have a vertical scroll bar unless the style WS_VSCROLL or LBS-_STANDARD is included. Similarly, it doesn't have a border unless it is created with the style WS_BORDER or LBS_STANDARD. You might want to omit the border if you create a list box that encompasses the entire client area of its parent. These and other styles used to customize a list box's appearance and behavior are summarized in the table on the following page.

List boxes have keyboard interfaces built in. When a single-selection list box has the input focus, the up arrow, down arrow, Page Up, Page Down, Home, and End keys move the highlighted bar identifying the current selection. In addition, pressing a character key moves the selection to the next item beginning with that character. Keyboard input works in multiple-selection list boxes, too, but it's the position of a dotted focus rectangle, not the selection, that changes. Pressing the spacebar toggles the selection state of the item with the focus in a multiple-selection list box.

You can customize a list box's keyboard interface by including the LBS_WANT-KEYBOARDINPUT style and processing WM_VKEYTOITEM and WM_CHARTOITEM messages. An MFC application can map these messages to *OnVKeyToItem* and *OnChar-ToItem* handlers using the ON_WM_VKEYTOITEM and ON_WM_CHARTOITEM macros. A derived list box class can handle these messages itself by overriding the virtual *CListBox::VKeyToItem* and *CListBox::CharToItem* functions. One use for this capability is to create a self-contained list box class that responds to presses of Ctrl-D by deleting the item that is currently selected.

LIST BOX STYLES

Style	Description
LBS_STANDARD	Creates a "standard" list box that has a border and a vertical scroll bar, notifies its parent window when the selection changes or an item is double-clicked, and sorts items alphabetically.
LBS_SORT	Sorts items that are added to the list box.
LBS_NOSEL	Creates a list box whose items can be viewed but not selected.
LBS_NOTIFY	Creates a list box that notifies its parent when the selection changes or an item is double-clicked.
LBS_DISABLENOSC ROLL	Disables the list box's scroll bar when it isn't needed. Without this style, an unneeded scroll bar is hidden rather than disabled.
LBS_MULTIPLESEL	Creates a multiple-selection list box.
LBS_EXTENDEDSEL	Adds extended selection support to a multiple-selection list box.
LBS_MULTICOLUMN	Creates a multicolumn list box.
LBS_OWNERDRAWVARIABLE	Creates an owner-draw list box whose items can vary in height.
LBS_OWNERDRAWFIXED	Creates an owner-draw list box whose items are the same height.
LBS_USETABSTOPS	Configures the list box to expand tab characters in item text.
LBS_NOREDRAW	Creates a list box that doesn't automatically redraw itself when an item is added or removed.
LBS_HASSTRINGS	Creates a list box that "remembers" the strings added to it. Conventional list boxes have this style by default; owner-draw list boxes don't.
LBS_WANTKEYBOARDINPUT	Creates a list box that sends its parent a WM_VKEYTOITEM or WM_CHARTOITEM message when a key is pressed. This style is used to customize the list box's response to keyboard input.
LBS_NOINTEGRALHEIGHT	Allows a list box to assume any height. By default, Windows sets a list box's height to a multiple of the item height to prevent items from being partially clipped.

Because the default font that Windows uses for list boxes is proportionally spaced, it is virtually impossible to line up columns of information in a list box by separating them with space characters. One way to create a columnar list box display is to use *SetFont* to apply a fixed-pitch font to the list box. A better solution is to assign the list box the style LBS_USETABSTOPS and separate columns of information with tab characters. An LBS_USETABSTOPS list box treats tab characters the way a word processor does, automatically advancing to the next tab stop when a tab character is encountered. By default, tab stops are evenly spaced about eight character widths apart. You can change the default tab stop settings with the *CListBox::SetTabStops* function. *SetTabStops* measures distances in *dialog units*. One dialog unit is approximately equal to one-fourth the width of a character in the system font. The statement

```
m_wndListBox.SetTabStops (64);
```

sets the space between tab stops to 64 dialog units, and

```
int nTabStops[] = { 32, 48, 64, 128 };
m_wndListBox.SetTabStops (4, nTabStops);
```

places tab stops at 32, 48, 64, and 128 dialog units from the left margin.

By default, a list box repaints itself whenever an item is added or removed. Usually that's just what you want, but if you're adding hundreds or perhaps thousands of items in rapid-fire fashion, the repeated repaints produce an unsightly flashing effect and slow down the insertion process. You can use LBS_NOREDRAW to create a list box that doesn't automatically repaint itself. Such a list box will be repainted only when its client area is invalidated.

An alternative to using LBS_NOREDRAW is to disable redraws before beginning a lengthy insertion process and to reenable them after the last item is inserted. You can enable and disable redraws programmatically by sending a list box WM_SET-REDRAW messages, as shown here:

```
m_wndListBox.SendMessage (WM_SETREDRAW, FALSE, 0); // Disable redraws.
     ⋮
m_wndListBox.SendMessage (WM_SETREDRAW, TRUE, 0);  // Enable redraws.
```

A list box is automatically repainted when redraws are enabled with WM_SETREDRAW, so it's not necessary to follow up with a call to *Invalidate*.

Unless a list box is created with the style LBS_MULTIPLESEL, only one item can be selected at a time. In a single-selection list box, clicking an unselected item both selects that item and deselects the one that was formerly selected. In a multiple-selection list box, any number of items can be selected. Most multiple-selection list boxes are also created with the style LBS_EXTENDEDSEL, which enables extended selections. In an extended-selection list box, the user selects the first item by clicking it and selects subsequent items by clicking with the Ctrl key pressed. In addition, the user can select entire ranges of contiguous items by clicking the first item in the range and then clicking the last item in the range with the Shift key held down. The Ctrl and Shift keys can be combined to select multiple items and ranges, the net result being a handy interface for selecting arbitrary combinations of items.

The LBS_MULTICOLUMN style creates a multicolumn list box. Multicolumn list boxes are usually created with the WS_HSCROLL style so that their contents can be scrolled horizontally if not all the items can be displayed at once. (Multicolumn list boxes can't be scrolled vertically.) You can adjust the column width with the *CListBox::SetColumnWidth* function. Normally, the column width should be based on the average width of a character in the list box font. The default column width is enough to display about 16 characters in the default list box font, so if you'll be inserting strings longer than that, you should expand the column width to prevent columns from overlapping.

Adding and Removing Items

A list box is empty until items are added to it. Items are added with *CListBox::AddString* and *CListBox::InsertString*. The statement

```
m_wndListBox.AddString (string);
```

adds the *CString* object named *string* to the list box. If the list box style includes LBS_SORT, the string is positioned according to its lexical value; otherwise, it is added to the end of the list. *InsertString* adds an item to the list box at a location specified by a 0-based index. The statement

```
m_wndListBox.InsertString (3, string);
```

inserts *string* into the list box and makes it the fourth item. LBS_SORT has no effect on strings added with *InsertString*.

Both *AddString* and *InsertString* return a 0-based index specifying the string's position in the list box. If either function fails, it returns LB_ERRSPACE to indicate that the list box is full or LB_ERR to indicate that the insertion failed for other reasons. You shouldn't see the LB_ERRSPACE return value very often in 32-bit Windows because the capacity of a list box is limited only by available memory. *CListBox::GetCount* returns the number of items in a list box.

CListBox::DeleteString removes an item from a list box. It takes a single parameter: the index of the item to be removed. It returns the number of items remaining in the list box. To remove all items from a list box at once, use *CListBox::ResetContent*.

If desired, you can use *CListBox::SetItemDataPtr* or *CListBox::SetItemData* to associate a 32-bit pointer or a DWORD value with an item in a list box. A pointer or DWORD associated with an item can be retrieved with *CListBox::GetItemDataPtr* or *CListBox::GetItemData*. One use for this feature is to associate extra data with the items in a list box. For example, you could associate a data structure containing an address and a phone number with a list box item holding a person's name. Because *GetItemDataPtr* returns a pointer to a void data type, you'll need to cast the pointer that it returns.

Another technique programmers use to associate extra data—particularly text-based data—with list box items is to create an LBS_USETABSTOPS-style list box, set the first tab stop to a position beyond the list box's right border, and append a string consisting of a tab character followed by the extra data to the list box item. The text to the right of the tab character will be invisible, but *CListBox::GetText* will return the full text of the list box item—additional text included.

Finding and Retrieving Items

The *CListBox* class also includes member functions for getting and setting the current selection and for finding and retrieving items. *CListBox::GetCurSel* returns the 0-based index of the item that is currently selected. A return value equal to LB_ERR means that nothing is selected. *GetCurSel* is often called following a notification signifying that the selection changed or an item was double-clicked. A program can set the current selection with the *SetCurSel* function. Passing *SetCurSel* the value –1 deselects all items, causing the bar highlighting the current selection to disappear from the list box. To find out whether a particular item is selected, use *CListBox::GetSel*.

SetCurSel identifies an item by its index, but items can also be selected by content. *CListBox::SelectString* searches a single-selection list box for an item that begins with a specified text string and selects the item if a match is found. The statement

```
m_wndListBox.SelectString (-1, _T ("Times"));
```

starts the search with the first item in the list box and highlights the first item that begins with "Times"—for example, "Times New Roman" or "Times Roman." The search is not case-sensitive. The first parameter to *SelectString* specifies the index of the item before the one at which the search begins; –1 instructs the list box to start with item 0. If the search is begun anywhere else, the search will wrap around to the first item if necessary so that all list box items are searched.

To search a list box for a particular item without changing the selection, use *CListBox::FindString* or *CListBox::FindStringExact*. *FindString* performs a string search on a list box's contents and returns the index of the first item whose text matches or begins with a specified string. A return value equal to LB_ERR means that no match was found. *FindStringExact* does the same but reports a match only if the item text matches the search text exactly. Once you have an item's index in hand, you can retrieve the text of the item with *CListBox::GetText*. The following statements query the list box for the currently selected item and copy the text of that item to a *CString* named *string*:

```
CString string;
int nIndex = m_wndListBox.GetCurSel ();
if (nIndex != LB_ERR)
    m_wndListBox.GetText (nIndex, string);
```

An alternative form of *GetText* accepts a pointer to a character array rather than a *CString* reference. You can use *CListBox::GetTextLen* to determine how large the array should be before calling the array version of *GetText*.

Selections in multiple-selection list boxes are handled differently than selections in single-selection list boxes. In particular, the *GetCurSel*, *SetCurSel*, and *SelectString* functions don't work with multiple-selection list boxes. Instead, items are selected (and deselected) with the *SetSel* and *SelItemRange* functions. The following statements select items 0, 5, 6, 7, 8, and 9 and deselect item 3:

```
m_wndListBox.SetSel (0);
m_wndListBox.SelItemRange (TRUE, 5, 9);
m_wndListBox.SetSel (3, FALSE);
```

CListBox also provides the *GetSelCount* function for getting a count of selected items and the *GetSelItems* function for retrieving the indexes of all selected items. In a multiple-selection list box, the dotted rectangle representing the item with the focus can be moved without changing the current selection. The focus rectangle can be moved and queried with *SetCaretIndex* and *GetCaretIndex*. Most other list box functions, including *GetText*, *GetTextLen*, *FindString*, and *FindStringExact*, work the same for multiple-selection list boxes as they do for the single-selection variety.

List Box Notifications

A list box sends notifications to its parent window via WM_COMMAND messages. In an MFC application, list box notifications are mapped to class member functions with ON_LBN message-map entries. The table on the following page lists the six notification types and the corresponding ON_LBN macros. LBN_DBLCLK, LBN_SELCHANGE, and LBN_SELCANCEL notifications are sent only if the list box was created with the style LBS_NOTIFY or LBS_STANDARD. The others are sent regardless of list box style.

LIST BOX NOTIFICATIONS

Notification	Sent When	Message-Map Macro	LBS_NOTIFY Required?
LBN_SETFOCUS	The list box gains the input focus.	ON_LBN_SETFOCUS	No
LBN_KILLFOCUS	The list box loses the input focus.	ON_LBN_KILLFOCUS	No
LBN_ERRSPACE	An operation failed because of insufficient memory.	ON_LBN_ERRSPACE	No
LBN_DBLCLK	An item is double-clicked.	ON_LBN_DBLCLK	Yes
LBN_SELCHANGE	The selection changes.	ON_LBN_SELCHANGE	Yes
LBN_SELCANCEL	The selection is canceled.	ON_LBN_SELCANCEL	Yes

The two list box notifications that programmers rely on most are LBN_DBLCLK and LBN_SELCHANGE. LBN_DBLCLK is sent when a list box item is double-clicked. To determine the index of the item that was double-clicked in a single-selection list box, use *CListBox::GetCurSel*. The following code fragment displays the item in a message box:

```
// In CMainWindow's message map
ON_LBN_DBLCLK (IDC_LISTBOX, OnItemDoubleClicked)
        .
        .
        .
void CMainWindow::OnItemDoubleClicked ()
{
    CString string;
    int nIndex = m_wndListBox.GetCurSel ();
    m_wndListBox.GetText (nIndex, string);
    MessageBox (string);
}
```

For a multiple-selection list box, use *GetCaretIndex* instead of *GetCurSel* to determine which item was double-clicked.

A list box sends an LBN_SELCHANGE notification when the user changes the selection, but not when the selection is changed programmatically. A single-selection list box sends an LBN_SELCHANGE notification when the selection moves because of a mouse click or keystroke. A multiple-selection list box sends an LBN_SELCHANGE notification when an item is clicked, when an item's selection state is toggled with the spacebar, and when the focus rectangle is moved.

The *CStatic* Class

CStatic, which represents static controls created from the "STATIC" WNDCLASS, is the simplest of the MFC control classes. At least it *used* to be: Windows 95 added so many new features to static controls that *CStatic* now rivals *CButton* and some of the other control classes for complexity.

Static controls come in three flavors: text, rectangles, and images. Static text controls are often used to label other controls. The following statement creates a static text control that displays the string "Name":

```
m_wndStatic.Create (_T ("Name"), WS_CHILD | WS_VISIBLE | SS_LEFT,
    rect, this, IDC_STATIC);
```

SS_LEFT creates a static text control whose text is left-aligned. If the control text is too long to fit on one line, it wraps around to the next one. To prevent wrapping, use SS_LEFTNOWORDWRAP instead of SS_LEFT. Text can be centered horizontally or right-aligned in a static control by substituting SS_CENTER or SS_RIGHT for SS_LEFT or SS_LEFTNOWORDWRAP. Another alternative is the little-used SS_SIMPLE style, which is similar to SS_LEFT but creates a control whose text can't be altered with *CWnd::SetWindowText*.

By default, the text assigned to a static text control is aligned along the upper edge of the control rectangle. To center text vertically in the control rectangle, OR an SS_CENTERIMAGE flag into the control style. You can also draw a sunken border around a static control by including the style SS_SUNKEN.

A second use for static controls is to draw rectangles. The control style specifies the type of rectangle that is drawn. Here are the styles you can choose from:

Style	*Description*
SS_BLACKFRAME	Hollow rectangle painted in the system color COLOR-_WINDOWFRAME (default = black)
SS_BLACKRECT	Solid rectangle painted in the system color COLOR-_WINDOWFRAME (default = black)
SS_ETCHEDFRAME	Hollow rectangle with etched borders
SS_ETCHEDHORZ	Hollow rectangle with etched top and bottom borders
SS_ETCHEDVERT	Hollow rectangle with etched left and right borders
SS_GRAYFRAME	Hollow rectangle painted in the system color COLOR-_BACKGROUND (default = gray)
SS_GRAYRECT	Solid rectangle painted in the system color COLOR-_BACKGROUND (default = gray)
SS_WHITEFRAME	Hollow rectangle painted in the system color COLOR-_WINDOW (default = white)
SS_WHITERECT	Solid rectangle painted in the system color COLOR-_WINDOW (default = white)

The statement

```
m_wndStatic.Create (_T (""), WS_CHILD | WS_VISIBLE | SS_ETCHEDFRAME,
    rect, this, IDC_STATIC);
```

creates a static control that resembles a group box. For best results, you should draw etched rectangles on surfaces whose color is the same as the default dialog box color (the system color COLOR_3DFACE). A static rectangle control doesn't display text, even if you specify a nonnull text string in the call to *Create*.

A third use for static controls is to display images formed from bitmaps, icons, cursors, or GDI metafiles. A static image control uses one of the following styles:

Style	*Description*
SS_BITMAP	A static control that displays a bitmap
SS_ENHMETAFILE	A static control that displays a metafile
SS_ICON	A static control that displays an icon or a cursor

After creating an image control, you associate a bitmap, metafile, icon, or cursor with it by calling its *SetBitmap*, *SetEnhMetaFile*, *SetIcon*, or *SetCursor* function. The statements

```
m_wndStatic.Create (_T (""), WS_CHILD | WS_VISIBLE | SS_ICON,
    rect, this, IDC_STATIC);
m_wndStatic.SetIcon (hIcon);
```

create a static control that displays an icon and assign it the icon whose handle is *hIcon*. By default, the icon image is positioned in the upper left corner of the control, and if the image is larger than the control rectangle, the rectangle is automatically expanded so the image won't be clipped. To center the image in the control rectangle, OR SS_CENTERIMAGE into the control style. SS_CENTERIMAGE prevents the system from automatically sizing the control rectangle if it's too small to show the entire image, so if you use SS_CENTERIMAGE, be sure that the control rectangle is large enough to display the image. Sizing isn't an issue with SS_ENHMETAFILE-style controls because metafile images scale to match the control size. For a neat special effect, place a sunken border around an image control by ORing SS_SUNKEN into the control style.

By default, a static control sends no notifications to its parent. But a static control created with the SS_NOTIFY style sends the four types of notifications listed in the following table.

STATIC CONTROL NOTIFICATIONS

Notification	*Sent When*	*Message-Map Macro*
STN_CLICKED	The control is clicked.	ON_STN_CLICKED
STN_DBLCLK	The control is double-clicked.	ON_STN_DBLCLK
STN_DISABLE	The control is disabled.	ON_STN_DISABLE
STN_ENABLE	The control is enabled.	ON_STN_ENABLE

The STN_CLICKED and STN_DBLCLK notifications allow you to create static controls that respond to mouse clicks. The statements

```
// In CMainWindow's message map
ON_STN_CLICKED (IDC_STATIC, OnClicked)
     :
     :

// In CMainWindow::OnCreate
m_wndStatic.Create (_T ("Click me"), WS_CHILD | WS_VISIBLE |
    SS_CENTER | SS_CENTERIMAGE | SS_NOTIFY | SS_SUNKEN, rect,
    this, IDC_STATIC);
     :
     :

void CMainWindow::OnClicked ()
{
    m_wndStatic.PostMessage (WM_CLOSE, 0, 0);
}
```

create a static control that displays "Click me" in the center of a sunken rectangle and disappears from the screen when clicked. If a static control lacks the SS_NOTIFY style, mouse messages go through to the underlying window because the control's window procedure returns HTTRANSPARENT in response to WM_NCHITTEST messages.

The FontView Application

Let's put what we've learned so far about buttons, list boxes, and static controls to use in an application. The FontView program shown in Figure 7-3 lists the names of all the fonts installed on the host PC in a list box. When a font name is selected, a sample is drawn in the group box at the bottom of the window. The sample text is really a static control, so all FontView has to do to display a font sample is call the control's *SetFont* function. If the check box labeled Show TrueType Fonts Only is

Figure 7-3. *The FontView window.*

checked, non-TrueType fonts are excluded from the list. In addition to showing how push button, check box, list box, group box, and static controls are used, FontView also demonstrates a very important MFC programming technique—the use of C++ member functions as callback functions. The term *callback function* might not mean much to you at the moment, but you'll learn all about it shortly.

FontView's source code appears in Figure 7-4. The controls are created one by one in *CMainWindow::OnCreate*. All but one—the static control that displays the font sample—is assigned an 8-point MS Sans Serif font. Rather than use raw pixel counts to size and position the controls, FontView uses distances based on the width and height of 8-point MS Sans Serif characters to achieve independence from the physical resolution of the display device. The character height and width are measured by selecting the font into a device context and calling *CDC::GetTextMetrics* with a pointer to a TEXTMETRIC structure:

```
CFont* pOldFont = dc.SelectObject (&m_fontMain);
TEXTMETRIC tm;
dc.GetTextMetrics (&tm);
m_cxChar = tm.tmAveCharWidth;
m_cyChar = tm.tmHeight + tm.tmExternalLeading;
```

On return, the structure's *tmAveCharWidth* field holds the average character width. (Actual character width can vary from character to character in a proportionally spaced font.) Summing the *tmHeight* and *tmExternalLeading* fields yields the height of one line of text, including interline spacing.

FontView.h

```
class CMyApp : public CWinApp
{
public:
    virtual BOOL InitInstance ();
};

class CMainWindow : public CWnd
{
protected:
    int m_cxChar;
    int m_cyChar;

    CFont m_fontMain;
    CFont m_fontSample;

    CStatic m_wndLBTitle;
    CListBox m_wndListBox;
    CButton m_wndCheckBox;
    CButton m_wndGroupBox;
    CStatic m_wndSampleText;
    CButton m_wndPushButton;

    void FillListBox ();

public:
    CMainWindow ();

    static int CALLBACK EnumFontFamProc (ENUMLOGFONT* lpelf,
        NEWTEXTMETRIC* lpntm, int nFontType, LPARAM lParam);

protected:
    virtual void PostNcDestroy ();

    afx_msg int OnCreate (LPCREATESTRUCT lpcs);
    afx_msg void OnPushButtonClicked ();
    afx_msg void OnCheckBoxClicked ();
    afx_msg void OnSelChange ();

    DECLARE_MESSAGE_MAP ()
};
```

Figure 7-4. *The FontView application.*

(continued)

Figure 7-4. *continued*

FontView.cpp

```cpp
#include <afxwin.h>
#include "FontView.h"

#define IDC_PRINT      100
#define IDC_CHECKBOX   101
#define IDC_LISTBOX    102
#define IDC_SAMPLE     103


CMyApp myApp;

///////////////////////////////////////////////////////////////////////////
// CMyApp member functions

BOOL CMyApp::InitInstance ()
{
    m_pMainWnd = new CMainWindow;
    m_pMainWnd->ShowWindow (m_nCmdShow);
    m_pMainWnd->UpdateWindow ();
    return TRUE;
}


///////////////////////////////////////////////////////////////////////////
// CMainWindow message map and member functions

BEGIN_MESSAGE_MAP (CMainWindow, CWnd)
    ON_WM_CREATE ()
    ON_BN_CLICKED (IDC_PRINT, OnPushButtonClicked)
    ON_BN_CLICKED (IDC_CHECKBOX, OnCheckBoxClicked)
    ON_LBN_SELCHANGE (IDC_LISTBOX, OnSelChange)
END_MESSAGE_MAP ()

CMainWindow::CMainWindow ()
{
    CString strWndClass = AfxRegisterWndClass (
        0,
        myApp.LoadStandardCursor (IDC_ARROW),
        (HBRUSH) (COLOR_3DFACE + 1),
        myApp.LoadStandardIcon (IDI_WINLOGO)
    );
    CreateEx (0, strWndClass, _T ("FontView"),
        WS_OVERLAPPED | WS_SYSMENU | WS_CAPTION | WS_MINIMIZEBOX,
        CW_USEDEFAULT, CW_USEDEFAULT, CW_USEDEFAULT, CW_USEDEFAULT,
        NULL, NULL, NULL);
```

```
        CRect rect (0, 0, m_cxChar * 68, m_cyChar * 26);
        CalcWindowRect (&rect);

        SetWindowPos (NULL, 0, 0, rect.Width (), rect.Height (),
            SWP_NOZORDER | SWP_NOMOVE | SWP_NOREDRAW);
}

int CMainWindow::OnCreate (LPCREATESTRUCT lpcs)
{
        if (CWnd::OnCreate (lpcs) == -1)
            return -1;

        //
        // Create an 8-point MS Sans Serif font to use in the controls.
        //
        m_fontMain.CreatePointFont (80, _T ("MS Sans Serif"));

        //
        // Compute the average width and height of a character in the font.
        //
        CClientDC dc (this);
        CFont* pOldFont = dc.SelectObject (&m_fontMain);
        TEXTMETRIC tm;
        dc.GetTextMetrics (&tm);
        m_cxChar = tm.tmAveCharWidth;
        m_cyChar = tm.tmHeight + tm.tmExternalLeading;
        dc.SelectObject (pOldFont);

        //
        // Create the controls that will appear in the FontView window.
        //
        CRect rect (m_cxChar * 2, m_cyChar, m_cxChar * 48, m_cyChar * 2);
        m_wndLBTitle.Create (_T ("Typefaces"), WS_CHILD | WS_VISIBLE | SS_LEFT,
            rect, this);

        rect.SetRect (m_cxChar * 2, m_cyChar * 2, m_cxChar * 48,
            m_cyChar * 18);
        m_wndListBox.CreateEx (WS_EX_CLIENTEDGE, _T ("listbox"), NULL,
            WS_CHILD | WS_VISIBLE | LBS_STANDARD, rect, this, IDC_LISTBOX);

        rect.SetRect (m_cxChar * 2, m_cyChar * 19, m_cxChar * 48,
            m_cyChar * 20);
        m_wndCheckBox.Create (_T ("Show TrueType fonts only"), WS_CHILD |
            WS_VISIBLE | BS_AUTOCHECKBOX, rect, this, IDC_CHECKBOX);
```

(continued)

Figure 7-4. *continued*

```
    rect.SetRect (m_cxChar * 2, m_cyChar * 21, m_cxChar * 66,
        m_cyChar * 25);
    m_wndGroupBox.Create (_T ("Sample"),  WS_CHILD ¦ WS_VISIBLE ¦ BS_GROUPBOX,
        rect, this, (UINT) -1);

    rect.SetRect (m_cxChar * 4, m_cyChar * 22, m_cxChar * 64,
        (m_cyChar * 99) / 4);
    m_wndSampleText.Create (_T (""), WS_CHILD ¦ WS_VISIBLE ¦ SS_CENTER, rect,
        this, IDC_SAMPLE);

    rect.SetRect (m_cxChar * 50, m_cyChar * 2, m_cxChar * 66,
        m_cyChar * 4);
    m_wndPushButton.Create (_T ("Print Sample"), WS_CHILD ¦ WS_VISIBLE ¦
        WS_DISABLED ¦ BS_PUSHBUTTON, rect, this, IDC_PRINT);

    //
    // Set each control's font to 8-point MS Sans Serif.
    //
    m_wndLBTitle.SetFont (&m_fontMain, FALSE);
    m_wndListBox.SetFont (&m_fontMain, FALSE);
    m_wndCheckBox.SetFont (&m_fontMain, FALSE);
    m_wndGroupBox.SetFont (&m_fontMain, FALSE);
    m_wndPushButton.SetFont (&m_fontMain, FALSE);

    //
    // Fill the list box with typeface names and return.
    //
    FillListBox ();
    return 0;
}

void CMainWindow::PostNcDestroy ()
{
    delete this;
}

void CMainWindow::OnPushButtonClicked ()
{
    MessageBox (_T ("This feature is currently unimplemented. Sorry!"),
        _T ("Error"), MB_ICONINFORMATION ¦ MB_OK);
}

void CMainWindow::OnCheckBoxClicked ()
{
    FillListBox ();
    OnSelChange ();
}
```

```
void CMainWindow::OnSelChange ()
{
    int nIndex = m_wndListBox.GetCurSel ();

    if (nIndex == LB_ERR) {
        m_wndPushButton.EnableWindow (FALSE);
        m_wndSampleText.SetWindowText (_T (""));
    }
    else {
        m_wndPushButton.EnableWindow (TRUE);
        if ((HFONT) m_fontSample != NULL)
            m_fontSample.DeleteObject ();

        CString strFaceName;
        m_wndListBox.GetText (nIndex, strFaceName);

        m_fontSample.CreateFont (-m_cyChar * 2, 0, 0, 0, FW_NORMAL,
            0, 0, 0, DEFAULT_CHARSET, OUT_CHARACTER_PRECIS,
            CLIP_CHARACTER_PRECIS, DEFAULT_QUALITY, DEFAULT_PITCH |
            FF_DONTCARE, strFaceName);

        m_wndSampleText.SetFont (&m_fontSample);
        m_wndSampleText.SetWindowText (_T ("AaBbCcDdEeFfGg"));
    }
}

void CMainWindow::FillListBox ()
{
    m_wndListBox.ResetContent ();

    CClientDC dc (this);
    ::EnumFontFamilies ((HDC) dc, NULL, (FONTENUMPROC) EnumFontFamProc,
        (LPARAM) this);
}

int CALLBACK CMainWindow::EnumFontFamProc (ENUMLOGFONT* lpelf,
    NEWTEXTMETRIC* lpntm, int nFontType, LPARAM lParam)
{
    CMainWindow* pWnd = (CMainWindow*) lParam;

    if ((pWnd->m_wndCheckBox.GetCheck () == BST_UNCHECKED) ||
        (nFontType & TRUETYPE_FONTTYPE))
        pWnd->m_wndListBox.AddString (lpelf->elfLogFont.lfFaceName);
    return 1;
}
```

CMainWindow processes three types of control notifications: BN_CLICKED notifications from the push button, BN_CLICKED notifications from the check box, and LBN_SELCHANGE notifications from the list box. The corresponding message-map entries look like this:

```
ON_BN_CLICKED (IDC_PRINT, OnPushButtonClicked)
ON_BN_CLICKED (IDC_CHECKBOX, OnCheckBoxClicked)
ON_LBN_SELCHANGE (IDC_LISTBOX, OnSelChange)
```

OnPushButtonClicked is activated when the Print Sample button is clicked. Because printing is a complex undertaking in a Windows application, *OnPushButtonClicked* does nothing more than display a message box. *OnCheckBoxClicked* handles BN-_CLICKED notifications from the check box. Since the check box style includes a BS_AUTOCHECKBOX flag, the check mark toggles on and off automatically in response to button clicks. *OnCheckBoxClicked*'s job is to refresh the contents of the list box each time the check mark is toggled. To do that, it calls *CMainWindow::FillListBox* to reinitialize the list box and then calls *CMainWindow::OnSelChange* to update the sample text.

OnSelChange is also called whenever the list box selection changes. It calls *GetCurSel* to get the index of the currently selected item. If *GetCurSel* returns LB_ERR, indicating that nothing is selected, *OnSelChange* disables the push button and erases the sample text. Otherwise, it enables the button, retrieves the text of the selected item with *CListBox::GetText*, and creates a font whose typeface name equals the string returned by *GetText*. It then assigns the font to the static control and sets the control text to "AaBbCcDdEeFfGg."

Font Enumerations and Callback Functions

The job of filling the list box with font names falls to *CMainWindow::FillListBox*. *FillListBox* is called by *OnCreate* to initialize the list box when the program is started. It is also called by *OnCheckBoxClicked* to reinitialize the list box when the Show TrueType Fonts Only check box is clicked. *FillListBox* first clears the list box by calling *CListBox::ResetContent*. It then enumerates all the fonts installed in the system and adds the corresponding typeface names to the list box.

FillListBox begins the enumeration process by constructing a device context object named *dc*, using the *CDC* class's HDC operator to extract a device context handle, and passing that handle to the *::EnumFontFamilies* function:

```
CClientDC dc (this);
::EnumFontFamilies ((HDC) dc, NULL, (FONTENUMPROC) EnumFontFamProc,
    (LPARAM) this);
```

The NULL second parameter tells *::EnumFontFamilies* to enumerate all installed fonts. The next parameter is the address of a callback function. A *callback function* is a function in your application that Windows *calls back* with information you requested. For each font that *::EnumFontFamilies* enumerates, Windows calls your callback function one time. An *::EnumFontFamilies* callback function must be prototyped like this:

```
int CALLBACK EnumFontFamProc (ENUMLOGFONT* lpelf,
    NEWTEXTMETRIC* lpntm, int nFontType, LPARAM lParam)
```

lpelf is a pointer to an ENUMLOGFONT structure, which contains a wealth of information about the font, including its typeface name. *lpntm* is a pointer to a structure of type NEWTEXTMETRIC, which contains font metrics—height, average character width, and so on. *nFontType* specifies the font type. TrueType fonts are identified by logically ANDing *nFontType* with the value TRUETYPE_FONTTYPE. If the result is nonzero, the font is a TrueType font. The fourth and final parameter, *lParam*, is an optional 32-bit LPARAM value passed to *::EnumFontFamilies*. *FillListBox* passes the *this* pointer referring to *CMainWindow*, for reasons I'll explain in a moment.

FontView's callback function is a member of *CMainWindow*. It's actually the callback function, not *FillListBox*, that adds the typeface names to the list box. Each time *CMainWindow::EnumFontFamProc* is called, it casts the *lParam* value passed to it from *FillListBox* into a *CMainWindow* pointer:

```
CMainWindow* pWnd = (CMainWindow*) lParam;
```

It then uses the pointer to add the typeface name to the list box, but only if the Show TrueType Fonts Only check box is unchecked or the font is a TrueType font:

```
if ((pWnd->m_wndCheckBox.GetCheck () == BST_UNCHECKED) ||
    (nFontType & TRUETYPE_FONTTYPE))
    pWnd->m_wndListBox.AddString (lpelf->elfLogFont.lfFaceName);
return 1;
```

The nonzero return value tells Windows to continue the enumeration process. (The callback function can halt the process at any time by returning 0, a handy option to have if you've allocated a fixed amount of memory to store font information and the memory fills up.) After Windows has called *EnumFontFamProc* for the last time, the call that *FillListBox* placed to *::EnumFontFamilies* returns and the enumeration process is complete.

Why does *FillListBox* pass a *this* pointer to the callback function, and why does *EnumFontFamProc* cast the pointer to a *CMainWindow* pointer when it, too, is a member of *CMainWindow*? Look closely at the declaration for *CMainWindow* in FontView.h, and you'll see that *EnumFontFamProc* is a static member function. A static class member function doesn't receive a *this* pointer, so it can't access nonstatic members of its own class. To call *m_wndCheckBox*'s *GetCheck* function and *m_wnd-ListBox*'s *AddString*, *EnumFontFamProc* needs pointers to *m_wndCheckBox* and *m_wndListBox* or a pointer to the *CMainWindow* object to which those objects belong. By casting the *lParam* value passed to *FillListBox* to a *CMainWindow* pointer, *EnumFontFamProc* is able to access nonstatic members of the *CMainWindow* class just as if it were a nonstatic member function.

EnumFontFamProc is static because callbacks require special handling in C++ applications. Windows rigidly defines a callback function's interface—the parameters passed to it through its argument list. When a member function of a C++ class is declared, the compiler silently tacks on an extra argument to hold the *this* pointer. Unfortunately, the added parameter means that the callback function's argument list doesn't match the argument list Windows expects, and all sorts of bad things can happen as a result, including invalid memory access errors, the nemeses of all Windows programmers. There are several solutions to this problem, but declaring the callback to be a static member function is among the simplest and most direct. In C++, a static member function isn't passed a *this* pointer, so its argument list is unaltered.

Callback functions are common in Windows, so the technique demonstrated here is useful for more than just enumerating fonts. Many Windows API functions that rely on callbacks support an application-defined *lParam* value, which is perfect for passing *this* pointers to statically declared callback functions. Should you use an enumeration function that doesn't support an application-defined *lParam*, you'll have to resort to other means to make a pointer available. One alternative is to make the *this* pointer visible to the callback function by copying it to a global variable.

The *CEdit* Class

MFC's *CEdit* class encapsulates the functionality of edit controls. Edit controls are used for text entry and editing and come in two varieties: single-line and multiline. Single-line edit controls are perfect for soliciting one-line text strings such as names, passwords, and product IDs. (See Figure 7-5.) To see a multiline edit control in action, start the Notepad applet that comes with Windows. The client area of the Notepad window is a multiline edit control.

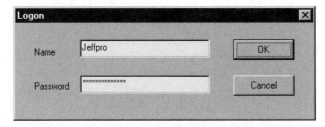

Figure 7-5. *A dialog box with two single-line edit controls.*

An edit control is limited to about 60 KB of text. That's not much of a restriction for single-line edit controls, but for a multiline edit control it can be constraining. If you need to handle large amounts of text, use the *rich edit control* instead—an enhanced version of the standard edit control that is part of the common controls library. Though designed to handle richly formatted text of the type seen in word processors, rich edit controls are quite capable of handling ordinary text, too. The Windows WordPad applet uses a rich edit control for text entry and editing. You'll use a rich edit control to build a WordPad-like application of your own in Chapter 12.

Creating an Edit Control

If *m_wndEdit* is a *CEdit* object, the statement

```
m_wndEdit.Create (WS_CHILD | WS_VISIBLE | WS_BORDER |
    ES_AUTOHSCROLL, rect, this, IDC_EDIT);
```

creates a single-line edit control that automatically scrolls horizontally when the caret moves beyond the control's border. Including ES_MULTILINE in the window style creates a multiline edit control instead:

```
m_wndEdit.Create (WS_CHILD | WS_VISIBLE | WS_BORDER |
    WS_HSCROLL | WS_VSCROLL | ES_MULTILINE, rect, this, IDC_EDIT);
```

WS_HSCROLL and WS_VSCROLL add horizontal and vertical scroll bars to the control. You can use *CEdit::SetRect* or *CEdit::SetRectNP* to define the control's editable area independent of the control's borders. One use for these functions is to define a page size that remains constant even if the control is resized. You can also use *CEdit::SetMargins* to specify left and right margin widths in pixels. The default margin widths are 0. The window styles listed in the table on the following page are specific to edit controls.

When it is first created, an edit control will accept only about 30,000 characters. You can raise or lower the limit with *CEdit::LimitText* or the Win32-specific *CEdit::Set-LimitText*. The following statement sets the maximum number of characters that an edit control will accept to 32:

```
m_wndEdit.SetLimitText (32);
```

When used with a multiline edit control, *SetLimitText* limits the total amount of text entered into the control, not the length of each line. There is no built-in way to limit the number of characters per line in a multiline edit control, but there are ways you can do it manually. One approach is to use *SetFont* to switch the edit control font to a fixed-pitch font and *CEdit::SetRect* to specify a formatting rectangle whose width is slightly greater than the width of a character times the desired number of characters per line.

EDIT CONTROL STYLES

Style	Description
ES_LEFT	Left-aligns text in the control.
ES_CENTER	Centers text in the control.
ES_RIGHT	Right-aligns text in the control.
ES_AUTOHSCROLL	Permits the edit control to scroll horizontally without a horizontal scroll bar. To add a horizontal scroll bar, include the style WS_HSCROLL.
ES_AUTOVSCROLL	Permits the edit control to scroll vertically without a vertical scroll bar. To add a vertical scroll bar, include the style WS_VSCROLL.
ES_MULTILINE	Creates a multiline edit control.
ES_LOWERCASE	Displays all characters in lowercase.
ES_UPPERCASE	Displays all characters in uppercase.
ES_PASSWORD	Displays asterisks instead of typed characters.
ES_READONLY	Creates an edit control whose text can't be edited.
ES_NOHIDESEL	Prevents the edit control from hiding the selection when the control loses the input focus.
ES_OEMCONVERT	Performs an ANSI-to-OEM-to-ANSI conversion on all characters typed into the control so that the application won't get unexpected results if it performs an ANSI-to-OEM conversion of its own. Obsolete.
ES_WANTRETURN	Programs the Enter key to insert line breaks instead of invoking the default push button for multiline edit controls used in dialog boxes.

Another function sometimes used to initialize an edit control is *CEdit::SetTabStops*, which sets the spacing between tab stops. Default tab stops are set about 8 character widths apart. You can space the tab stops however you like and can even vary the spacing between stops. Like *CListBox::SetTabStops*, *CEdit::SetTabStops* measures distances in dialog units.

Inserting and Retrieving Text

Text is inserted into an edit control with *SetWindowText* and retrieved with *GetWindowText*. *CEdit* inherits both functions from its base class, *CWnd*. The statement

```
m_wndEdit.SetWindowText (_T ("Hello, MFC"));
```

inserts the text string "Hello, MFC" into the edit control *m_wndEdit*, and

```
m_wndEdit.GetWindowText (string);
```

retrieves the text into a *CString* object named *string*. *GetWindowText* and *SetWindowText* work with both single-line and multiline edit controls. Text inserted with

SetWindowText replaces existing text, and *GetWindowText* returns all the text in the edit control, even if the text spans multiple lines. To erase all the text in an edit control, call *SetWindowText* with a null string:

```
m_wndEdit.SetWindowText (_T (""));
```

You can insert text into an edit control without erasing what's already there with *CEdit::ReplaceSel*. If one or more characters are selected when *ReplaceSel* is called, the inserted text replaces the selected text; otherwise, the new text is inserted at the current caret position.

A multiline edit control inserts line breaks automatically. If you'd like to know where the line breaks fall in text retrieved from a multiline edit control, use *CEdit::FmtLines* to enable soft line breaks before calling *GetWindowText*:

```
m_wndEdit.FmtLines (TRUE);
```

With soft line breaks enabled, each line is delimited with two carriage returns (13) followed by a line feed character (10). To disable soft line breaks, call *FmtLines* with a FALSE parameter:

```
m_wndEdit.FmtLines (FALSE);
```

Now line breaks won't be denoted in any special way. Hard returns—line breaks inserted manually when the user presses the Enter key—are signified by single carriage return/line feed pairs regardless of the *FmtLines* setting. *FmtLines* doesn't affect the appearance of the text in a multiline edit control. It affects only the way in which the control stores text internally and the format of text retrieved with *GetWindowText*.

To read just one line of text from a multiline edit control, use *CEdit::GetLine*. *GetLine* copies the contents of a line to a buffer whose address you provide. The line is identified with a 0-based index. The statement

```
m_wndEdit.GetLine (0, pBuffer, nBufferSize);
```

copies the first line of text in a multiline edit control to the buffer pointed to by *pBuffer*. The third parameter is the buffer size, in bytes (not characters). *GetLine* returns the number of bytes copied to the buffer. You can determine how much buffer space you need before retrieving a line with *CEdit::LineLength*. And you can find out how many lines of text a multiline edit control contains by calling *CEdit::GetLineCount*. Note that *GetLineCount* never returns 0; the return value is 1 even if no text has been entered.

Clear, Cut, Copy, Paste, and Undo

CEdit provides easy-to-use member functions that perform the programmatic equivalents of the Clear, Cut, Copy, Paste, and Undo items in the Edit menu. The statement

```
m_wndEdit.Clear ();
```

removes the selected text without affecting what's on the clipboard. The statement

```
m_wndEdit.Cut ();
```

removes the selected text and copies it to the clipboard. And the statement

```
m_wndEdit.Copy ();
```

copies the selected text to the clipboard without altering the contents of the edit control.

You can query an edit control for the current selection by calling *CEdit::GetSel*, which returns a DWORD value with two packed 16-bit integers specifying the indexes of the beginning and ending characters in the selection. An alternate form of *GetSel* copies the indexes to a pair of integers whose addresses are passed by reference. If the indexes are equal, no text is currently selected. The following *IsTextSelected* function, which you might add to an edit control class derived from *CEdit*, returns a nonzero value if a selection exists and 0 if one doesn't exist:

```
BOOL CMyEdit::IsTextSelected ()
{
    int nStart, nEnd;
    GetSel (nStart, nEnd);
    return (nStart != nEnd);
}
```

CEdit::Cut and *CEdit::Copy* do nothing if no text is selected.

Text can be selected programmatically with *CEdit::SetSel*. The statement

```
m_wndEdit.SetSel (100, 150);
```

selects 50 characters beginning with the 101st (the character whose 0-based index is 100) and scrolls the selection into view if it isn't visible already. To prevent scrolling, include a third parameter and set it equal to TRUE.

When programmatically selecting text in a multiline edit control, you often need to convert a line number and possibly an offset within that line into an index that can be passed to *SetSel*. *CEdit::LineIndex* accepts a 0-based line number and returns the index of the first character in that line. The next example uses *LineIndex* to determine the index of the first character in the eighth line of a multiline edit control, *LineLength* to retrieve the line's length, and *SetSel* to select everything on that line:

```
int nStart = m_wndEdit.LineIndex (7);
int nLength = m_wndEdit.LineLength (nStart);
m_wndEdit.SetSel (nStart, nStart + nLength);
```

CEdit also provides a function named *LineFromChar* for computing a line number from a character index.

CEdit::Paste pastes text into an edit control. The following statement pastes the text that currently resides in the Windows clipboard into an edit control named *m_wndEdit*:

```
m_wndEdit.Paste ();
```

If the clipboard contains no text, *CEdit::Paste* does nothing. If no text is selected when *Paste* is called, the clipboard text is inserted at the current caret position. If a selection exists, the text retrieved from the clipboard replaces the text selected in the control. You can determine ahead of time whether the clipboard contains text (and therefore whether the *Paste* function will actually do anything) by calling *::IsClipboardFormatAvailable*. The statement

```
BOOL bCanPaste = ::IsClipboardFormatAvailable (CF_TEXT);
```

sets *bCanPaste* to nonzero if text is available from the clipboard, and 0 if it isn't.

Edit controls also feature a built-in undo capability that "rolls back" the previous editing operation. The statement

```
m_wndEdit.Undo ();
```

undoes the last operation, provided that the operation can be undone. You can determine ahead of time whether calling *Undo* will accomplish anything with *CEdit::CanUndo*. A related function, *CEdit::EmptyUndoBuffer*, manually resets the undo flag so that subsequent calls to *Undo* will do nothing (and calls to *CanUndo* will return FALSE) until another editing operation is performed.

Edit Control Notifications

Edit controls send notifications to their parents to report various input events. In MFC applications, these notifications are mapped to handling functions with ON_EN message map macros. Edit control notifications and the corresponding message map macros are summarized in the table on the following page.

A common use for EN_CHANGE notifications is to dynamically update other controls as text is entered into an edit control. The following code updates a push button (*m_wndPushButton*) as text is entered into an edit control (*m_wndEdit*, ID=IDC_EDIT) so that the push button is enabled if the edit control contains at least one character and disabled if it doesn't:

```
// In CMainWindow's message map
ON_EN_CHANGE (IDC_EDIT, OnUpdatePushButton)
        :
        :
void CMainWindow::OnUpdatePushButton ()
{
    m_wndPushButton.EnableWindow (m_wndEdit.LineLength ());
}
```

EDIT CONTROL NOTIFICATIONS

Notification	Sent When	Message-Map Macro
EN_UPDATE	The control's text is about to change.	ON_EN_UPDATE
EN_CHANGE	The control's text has changed.	ON_EN_CHANGE
EN_KILLFOCUS	The edit control loses the input focus.	ON_EN_KILLFOCUS
EN_SETFOCUS	The edit control receives the input focus.	ON_EN_SETFOCUS
EN_HSCROLL	The edit control is scrolled horizontally using a scroll bar.	ON_EN_HSCROLL
EN_VSCROLL	The edit control is scrolled vertically using a scroll bar.	ON_EN_VSCROLL
EN_MAXTEXT	A character can't be entered because the edit control already contains the number of characters specified with *CEdit::LimitText* or *CEdit::SetLimitText*. This notification is also sent if a character can't be entered because the caret is at the right or the bottom edge of the control's formatting rectangle and the control doesn't support scrolling.	ON_EN_MAXTEXT
EN_ERRSPACE	An operation fails because of insufficient memory.	ON_EN_ERRSPACE

Providing interactive feedback of this nature is generally considered good user interface design. Most users would rather see a button remain disabled until all of the required information is entered than click a button and receive an error message.

Presto! Instant Notepad

The MyPad application, portions of whose source code are reproduced in Figure 7-6, uses a multiline edit control to create a near clone of the Windows Notepad applet. As you can see from the source code, the edit control does the bulk of the work. *CEdit* functions such as *Undo* and *Cut* allow you to implement commands in the Edit menu with just one line of code.

MyPad is a view-based application that I began by running the MFC AppWizard but unchecking the Document/View Architecture Support box in Step 1. To avoid unnecessary code, I unchecked the ActiveX Controls box in AppWizard's Step 3 dialog, too. After running AppWizard, I added a New command to the File menu and a Delete command to the Edit menu using the Visual C++ resource editor. I also used the resource editor to add an accelerator (Ctrl-N) for the New command. I then used ClassWizard to add command handlers, update handlers, and message handlers.

The view's WM_CREATE message handler creates the edit control by calling *Create* on the *CEdit* data member named *m_wndEdit*. *OnCreate* sets the control's width and height to 0, but *OnSize* resizes the control to fill the view's client area whenever the view receives a WM_SIZE message. The first WM_SIZE message arrives before the view becomes visible on the screen; subsequent WM_SIZE messages arrive anytime the MyPad window (and consequently, the view) is resized. A one-line WM_SET-FOCUS handler in the view class shifts the input focus to the edit control whenever the view receives the input focus.

MainFrm.h

```
// MainFrm.h : interface of the CMainFrame class
//
/////////////////////////////////////////////////////////////////////////

#if !defined(AFX_MAINFRM_H__0FA1D288_8471_11D2_8E53_006008A82731__INCLUDED_)
#define AFX_MAINFRM_H__0FA1D288_8471_11D2_8E53_006008A82731__INCLUDED_

#if _MSC_VER > 1000
#pragma once
#endif // _MSC_VER > 1000

#include "ChildView.h"

class CMainFrame : public CFrameWnd
{

public:
    CMainFrame();
protected:
    DECLARE_DYNAMIC(CMainFrame)

// Attributes
public:

// Operations
public:
```

Figure 7-6. *The MyPad application.*   *(continued)*

Figure 7-6. *continued*

```
// Overrides
    // ClassWizard generated virtual function overrides
    //{{AFX_VIRTUAL(CMainFrame)
    virtual BOOL PreCreateWindow(CREATESTRUCT& cs);
    virtual BOOL OnCmdMsg(UINT nID, int nCode, void* pExtra,
        AFX_CMDHANDLERINFO* pHandlerInfo);
    //}}AFX_VIRTUAL

// Implementation
public:
    virtual ~CMainFrame();
#ifdef _DEBUG
    virtual void AssertValid() const;
    virtual void Dump(CDumpContext& dc) const;
#endif
    CChildView     m_wndView;

// Generated message map functions
protected:
    //{{AFX_MSG(CMainFrame)
    afx_msg void OnSetFocus(CWnd *pOldWnd);
    afx_msg int OnCreate(LPCREATESTRUCT lpCreateStruct);
    //}}AFX_MSG
    DECLARE_MESSAGE_MAP()
};

/////////////////////////////////////////////////////////////////////////

//{{AFX_INSERT_LOCATION}}
// Microsoft Visual C++ will insert additional declarations
// immediately before the previous line.

#endif
// !defined(AFX_MAINFRM_H__0FA1D288_8471_11D2_8E53_006008A82731__INCLUDED_)
```

MainFrm.cpp

```
// MainFrm.cpp : implementation of the CMainFrame class
//

#include "stdafx.h"
#include "MyPad.h"

#include "MainFrm.h"
```

```
#ifdef _DEBUG
#define new DEBUG_NEW
#undef THIS_FILE
static char THIS_FILE[] = __FILE__;
#endif


/////////////////////////////////////////////////////////////////////////
// CMainFrame

IMPLEMENT_DYNAMIC(CMainFrame, CFrameWnd)

BEGIN_MESSAGE_MAP(CMainFrame, CFrameWnd)
    //{{AFX_MSG_MAP(CMainFrame)
    ON_WM_SETFOCUS()
    ON_WM_CREATE()
    //}}AFX_MSG_MAP
END_MESSAGE_MAP()


/////////////////////////////////////////////////////////////////////////
// CMainFrame construction/destruction

CMainFrame::CMainFrame()
{
}


CMainFrame::~CMainFrame()
{
}


BOOL CMainFrame::PreCreateWindow(CREATESTRUCT& cs)
{
    if( !CFrameWnd::PreCreateWindow(cs) )
        return FALSE;
    cs.dwExStyle &= ~WS_EX_CLIENTEDGE;
    cs.lpszClass = AfxRegisterWndClass(0);
    return TRUE;
}


/////////////////////////////////////////////////////////////////////////
// CMainFrame diagnostics

#ifdef _DEBUG
void CMainFrame::AssertValid() const
{
    CFrameWnd::AssertValid();
}
```

(continued)

Figure 7-6. *continued*

```
void CMainFrame::Dump(CDumpContext& dc) const
{
    CFrameWnd::Dump(dc);
}

#endif //_DEBUG

/////////////////////////////////////////////////////////////////////////////
// CMainFrame message handlers
void CMainFrame::OnSetFocus(CWnd* pOldWnd)
{
    // forward focus to the view window
    m_wndView.SetFocus();
}

BOOL CMainFrame::OnCmdMsg(UINT nID, int nCode, void* pExtra,
    AFX_CMDHANDLERINFO* pHandlerInfo)

{

    // let the view have first crack at the command
    if (m_wndView.OnCmdMsg(nID, nCode, pExtra, pHandlerInfo))
        return TRUE;

    // otherwise, do default handling
    return CFrameWnd::OnCmdMsg(nID, nCode, pExtra, pHandlerInfo);
}


int CMainFrame::OnCreate(LPCREATESTRUCT lpCreateStruct)
{
    if (CFrameWnd::OnCreate(lpCreateStruct) == -1)
        return -1;

    if (!m_wndView.Create(NULL, NULL, AFX_WS_DEFAULT_VIEW,
        CRect(0, 0, 0, 0), this, AFX_IDW_PANE_FIRST, NULL))
    {
        TRACE0("Failed to create view window\n");
        return -1;
    }
    return 0;
}
```

ChildView.h

```
// ChildView.h : interface of the CChildView class
//
/////////////////////////////////////////////////////////////////////////

#if !defined(AFX_CHILDVIEW_H__0FA1D28A_8471_11D2_8E53_006008A82731__INCLUDED_)
#define AFX_CHILDVIEW_H__0FA1D28A_8471_11D2_8E53_006008A82731__INCLUDED_

#if _MSC_VER > 1000
#pragma once
#endif // _MSC_VER > 1000


/////////////////////////////////////////////////////////////////////////
// CChildView window

class CChildView : public CWnd
{
// Construction
public:
    CChildView();

// Attributes
public:

// Operations
public:

// Overrides
    // ClassWizard generated virtual function overrides
    //{{AFX_VIRTUAL(CChildView)
    protected:
    virtual BOOL PreCreateWindow(CREATESTRUCT& cs);
    //}}AFX_VIRTUAL

// Implementation
public:
    virtual ~CChildView();

    // Generated message map functions
protected:
    BOOL IsTextSelected ();
    CEdit m_wndEdit;
    //{{AFX_MSG(CChildView)
```

(continued)

Figure 7-6. *continued*

```
    afx_msg void OnPaint();
    afx_msg void OnEditCut();
    afx_msg void OnEditCopy();
    afx_msg void OnEditPaste();
    afx_msg void OnEditDelete();
    afx_msg void OnEditUndo();
    afx_msg void OnUpdateEditCut(CCmdUI* pCmdUI);
    afx_msg void OnUpdateEditCopy(CCmdUI* pCmdUI);
    afx_msg void OnUpdateEditPaste(CCmdUI* pCmdUI);
    afx_msg void OnUpdateEditDelete(CCmdUI* pCmdUI);
    afx_msg void OnUpdateEditUndo(CCmdUI* pCmdUI);
    afx_msg int OnCreate(LPCREATESTRUCT lpCreateStruct);
    afx_msg void OnSize(UINT nType, int cx, int cy);
    afx_msg void OnFileNew();
    afx_msg void OnSetFocus(CWnd* pOldWnd);
    //}}AFX_MSG
    DECLARE_MESSAGE_MAP()
};


/////////////////////////////////////////////////////////////////////////////

//{{AFX_INSERT_LOCATION}}
// Microsoft Visual C++ will insert additional declarations
// immediately before the previous line.

#endif
// !defined(AFX_CHILDVIEW_H__0FA1D28A_8471_11D2_8E53_006008A82731__INCLUDED_)
```

ChildView.cpp

```
// ChildView.cpp : implementation of the CChildView class
//

#include "stdafx.h"
#include "MyPad.h"
#include "ChildView.h"

#ifdef _DEBUG
#define new DEBUG_NEW
#undef THIS_FILE
static char THIS_FILE[] = __FILE__;
#endif
```

```
////////////////////////////////////////////////////////////////////////
// CChildView

CChildView::CChildView()
{
}

CChildView::~CChildView()
{
}

BEGIN_MESSAGE_MAP(CChildView,CWnd )
    //{{AFX_MSG_MAP(CChildView)
    ON_WM_PAINT()
    ON_WM_CREATE()
    ON_WM_SIZE()
    ON_WM_SETFOCUS()
    ON_COMMAND(ID_EDIT_CUT, OnEditCut)
    ON_COMMAND(ID_EDIT_COPY, OnEditCopy)
    ON_COMMAND(ID_EDIT_PASTE, OnEditPaste)
    ON_COMMAND(ID_EDIT_DELETE, OnEditDelete)
    ON_COMMAND(ID_EDIT_UNDO, OnEditUndo)
    ON_UPDATE_COMMAND_UI(ID_EDIT_CUT, OnUpdateEditCut)
    ON_UPDATE_COMMAND_UI(ID_EDIT_COPY, OnUpdateEditCopy)
    ON_UPDATE_COMMAND_UI(ID_EDIT_PASTE, OnUpdateEditPaste)
    ON_UPDATE_COMMAND_UI(ID_EDIT_DELETE, OnUpdateEditDelete)
    ON_UPDATE_COMMAND_UI(ID_EDIT_UNDO, OnUpdateEditUndo)
    ON_COMMAND(ID_FILE_NEW, OnFileNew)
    //}}AFX_MSG_MAP
END_MESSAGE_MAP()


////////////////////////////////////////////////////////////////////////
// CChildView message handlers

BOOL CChildView::PreCreateWindow(CREATESTRUCT& cs)
{
    if (!CWnd::PreCreateWindow(cs))
        return FALSE;

    cs.dwExStyle |= WS_EX_CLIENTEDGE;
    cs.style &= ~WS_BORDER;
    cs.lpszClass = AfxRegisterWndClass(CS_HREDRAW|CS_VREDRAW|CS_DBLCLKS,
        ::LoadCursor(NULL, IDC_ARROW), HBRUSH(COLOR_WINDOW+1), NULL);

    return TRUE;
}
```

(continued)

Figure 7-6. *continued*

```
void CChildView::OnPaint()
{
    CPaintDC dc(this);
}


int CChildView::OnCreate(LPCREATESTRUCT lpCreateStruct)
{
    if (CWnd ::OnCreate(lpCreateStruct) == -1)
        return -1;

    m_wndEdit.Create (WS_CHILD | WS_VISIBLE | WS_VSCROLL | ES_MULTILINE |
        ES_AUTOVSCROLL, CRect (0, 0, 0, 0), this, IDC_EDIT);
    return 0;
}


void CChildView::OnSize(UINT nType, int cx, int cy)
{
    CWnd ::OnSize(nType, cx, cy);
    m_wndEdit.MoveWindow (0, 0, cx, cy);
}


void CChildView::OnSetFocus(CWnd* pOldWnd)
{
    m_wndEdit.SetFocus ();
}


void CChildView::OnEditCut()
{
    m_wndEdit.Cut ();
 }


void CChildView::OnEditCopy()
{
    m_wndEdit.Copy ();
}


void CChildView::OnEditPaste()
{
    m_wndEdit.Paste ();
}


void CChildView::OnEditDelete()
{
    m_wndEdit.Clear ();
}
```

```
void CChildView::OnEditUndo()
{
    m_wndEdit.Undo ();
}

void CChildView::OnUpdateEditCut(CCmdUI* pCmdUI)
{
    pCmdUI->Enable (IsTextSelected ());
}

void CChildView::OnUpdateEditCopy(CCmdUI* pCmdUI)
{
    pCmdUI->Enable (IsTextSelected ());
}

void CChildView::OnUpdateEditPaste(CCmdUI* pCmdUI)
{
    pCmdUI->Enable (::IsClipboardFormatAvailable (CF_TEXT));
}

void CChildView::OnUpdateEditDelete(CCmdUI* pCmdUI)
{
    pCmdUI->Enable (IsTextSelected ());
}

void CChildView::OnUpdateEditUndo(CCmdUI* pCmdUI)
{
    pCmdUI->Enable (m_wndEdit.CanUndo ());
}

void CChildView::OnFileNew()
{
    m_wndEdit.SetWindowText (_T (""));
}

BOOL CChildView::IsTextSelected()
{
    int nStart, nEnd;
    m_wndEdit.GetSel (nStart, nEnd);
    return (nStart != nEnd);
}
```

The *CComboBox* Class

The combo box combines a single-line edit control and a list box into one convenient package. Combo boxes come in three varieties: simple, drop-down, and drop-down list. Figure 7-7 shows a drop-down list combo box with its list displayed.

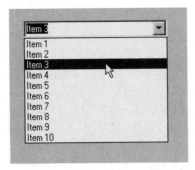

Figure 7-7. *A combo box with a drop-down list displayed.*

Simple combo boxes are the least used of the three combo box types. A simple combo box's list box is permanently displayed. When the user selects an item from the list, that item is automatically copied to the edit control. The user can also type text directly into the edit control. If the text the user enters matches an item in the list box, the item is automatically highlighted and scrolled into view.

A drop-down combo box differs from a simple combo box in that its list box is displayed only on demand. A drop-down list combo box works the same way but doesn't allow text to be typed into the edit control. This restriction effectively limits the user's selection to items appearing in the list box.

The style flags you pass to *Create* or *CreateEx* determine what type of combo box you create. CBS_SIMPLE creates a simple combo box, CBS_DROPDOWN creates a drop-down combo box, and CBS_DROPDOWNLIST creates a drop-down list combo box. Other styles control additional aspects of the combo box's appearance and behavior, as shown in the table on the following page. Many of these styles will look familiar because they're patterned after list box and edit control styles. CBS_AUTOHSCROLL, for example, does the same thing for the edit control portion of a combo box control that ES_AUTOHSCROLL does for a stand-alone edit control. When you create a combo box control, don't forget to include the style WS_VSCROLL if you want the list box to have a vertical scroll bar and WS_BORDER if you want the control's border to be visible. If *m_wndComboBox* is a *CComboBox* object, the statement

```
m_wndComboBox.Create (WS_CHILD | WS_VISIBLE | WS_BORDER |
    WS_VSCROLL | CBS_DROPDOWNLIST | CBS_SORT, rect, this,
    IDC_COMBOBOX);
```

creates a drop-down list combo box whose list box contains a vertical scroll bar when the number of items in the list box exceeds the number of items that can be displayed and that automatically sorts the items added to it. The control rectangle you specify in the call to *CComboBox::Create* should be large enough to encompass the list box part of the control as well as the edit box.

COMBO BOX STYLES

Style	*Description*
CBS_AUTOHSCROLL	Enables horizontal scrolling in the edit control portion of a combo box.
CBS_DISABLENOSCROLL	Disables the combo box list box's scroll bar when it isn't needed. Without this style, an unneeded scroll bar is hidden rather than disabled.
CBS_DROPDOWN	Creates a drop-down combo box.
CBS_DROPDOWNLIST	Creates a drop-down list combo box.
CBS_HASSTRINGS	Creates a combo box that "remembers" the strings added to it. Conventional combo boxes have this style by default; owner-draw combo boxes don't.
CBS_LOWERCASE	Forces all text in the combo box to lowercase.
CBS_NOINTEGRALHEIGHT	Prevents the combo box's list box height from having to be an exact multiple of the item height.
CBS_OEMCONVERT	A combo box whose edit control performs an ANSI-to-OEM-to-ANSI conversion on all characters so that the application won't get unexpected results if it performs an ANSI-to-OEM conversion of its own. Obsolete.
CBS_OWNERDRAWFIXED	Creates an owner-draw combo box whose items are all the same height.
CBS_OWNERDRAWVARIABLE	Creates an owner-draw combo box whose items can vary in height.
CBS_SIMPLE	Creates a simple combo box.
CBS_SORT	Automatically sorts items as they are added.
CBS_UPPERCASE	Forces all text in the combo box to uppercase.

Not surprisingly, the list of *CComboBox* member functions reads a lot like the list of member functions for *CEdit* and *CListBox*. Items are added to a combo box, for example, with *CComboBox::AddString* and *CComboBox::InsertString*, and the maximum character count for a combo box's edit control is set with *CComboBox::LimitText*. The *GetWindowText* and *SetWindowText* functions that *CComboBox* inherits from *CWnd* get and set the text in the edit control. Functions unique to combo boxes include *GetLBText*, which retrieves the text of an item identified by a 0-based index; *GetLBTextLen*, which returns the length of an item, in characters; *ShowDropDown*, which hides or displays the drop-down list box; and *GetDroppedState*, which returns a value indicating whether the drop-down list is currently displayed.

Combo Box Notifications

Combo boxes send notifications to their parents much as edit controls and list boxes do. The following table lists the notifications the parent can expect, the corresponding MFC message-map macros, and the types of combo boxes the notifications apply to.

COMBO BOX NOTIFICATIONS

Notification	Message-Macro Map	Simple	Drop-Down	Drop-Down List
CBN_DROPDOWN Sent when the drop-down list is displayed.	ON_CBN_DROPDOWN		✓	✓
CBN_CLOSEUP Sent when the drop-down list is closed.	ON_CBN_CLOSEUP		✓	✓
CBN_DBLCLK Sent when an item is double-clicked.	ON_CBN_DBLCLK	✓		
CBN_SELCHANGE Sent when the selection changes.	ON_CBN_SELCHANGE	✓	✓	✓
CBN_SELENDOK Sent when a selection is made.	ON_CBN_SELENDOK	✓	✓	✓
CBN_SELENDCANCEL Sent when a selection is canceled.	ON_CBN_SELENDCANCEL		✓	✓
CBN_EDITUPDATE Sent when the text in the edit control is about to change.	N_CBN_EDITUPDATE	✓	✓	
CBN_EDITCHANGE Sent when the text in the edit control has changed.	ON_CBN_EDITCHANGE	✓	✓	
CBN_KILLFOCUS Sent when the combo box loses the input focus.	ON_CBN_KILLFOCUS	✓	✓	✓
CBN_SETFOCUS Sent when the combo box receives the input focus.	ON_CBN_SETFOCUS	✓	✓	✓
CBN_ERRSPACE Sent when an operation fails because of insufficient memory.	ON_CBN_ERRSPACE	✓	✓	✓

Not all notifications apply to all combo box types. CBN_DROPDOWN and CBN_CLOSEUP notifications, for example, aren't sent to CBS_SIMPLE combo boxes because a simple combo box's list box doesn't open and close. By the same token, CBS_DROPDOWN and CBS_DROPDOWNLIST-style combo boxes don't receive CBN-_DBLCLK notifications because the items in their lists can't be double-clicked. (Why? Because the list box closes after the first click.) CBN_EDITUPDATE and CBN_EDIT-CHANGE notifications are equivalent to EN_UPDATE and EN_CHANGE notifications sent by edit controls, and CBN_SELCHANGE is to combo boxes as LBN_SELCHANGE is to list boxes.

One nuance you should be aware of when processing CBN_SELCHANGE notifications is that when a notification arrives, the edit control might not have been updated to match the list box selection. Therefore, you should use *GetLBText* to retrieve the newly selected text instead of *GetWindowText*. You can get the index of the selected item with *CComboBox::GetCurSel*.

The *CScrollBar* Class

MFC's *CScrollBar* class encapsulates scroll bar controls created from the "SCROLLBAR" WNDCLASS. Scroll bar controls are identical in most respects to the "window" scroll bars used in Chapter 2's Accel application. But whereas window scroll bars are created by adding WS_VSCROLL and WS_HSCROLL flags to the window style, scroll bar controls are created explicitly with *CScrollBar::Create*. And though a window scroll bar runs the full length of the window's client area and is inherently glued to the window border, scroll bar controls can be placed anywhere in the window and can be set to any height and width.

You create vertical scroll bars by specifying the style SBS_VERT and horizontal scroll bars by specifying SBS_HORZ. If *m_wndVScrollBar* and *m_wndHScrollBar* are *CScrollBar* objects, the statements

```
m_wndVScrollBar.Create (WS_CHILD ¦ WS_VISIBLE ¦ WS_BORDER ¦
    SBS_VERT, rectVert, this, IDC_VSCROLLBAR);
m_wndHScrollBar.Create (WS_CHILD ¦ WS_VISIBLE ¦ WS_BORDER ¦
    SBS_HORZ, rectHorz, this, IDC_HSCROLLBAR);
```

create two scroll bar controls, one vertical and the other horizontal.

You can query Windows for the standard width of a vertical scroll bar or the standard height of a horizontal scroll bar with the *::GetSystemMetrics* API function. The following code fragment sets *nWidth* and *nHeight* to the system's standard scroll bar width and height:

```
int nWidth = ::GetSystemMetrics (SM_CXVSCROLL);
int nHeight = ::GetSystemMetrics (SM_CYHSCROLL);
```

An alternative method for creating a scroll bar with a standard height or width is to specify the style SBS_TOPALIGN, SBS_BOTTOMALIGN, SBS_LEFTALIGN, or SBS-_RIGHTALIGN when creating it. SBS_LEFTALIGN and SBS_RIGHTALIGN align a vertical scroll bar control along the left or right border of the rectangle specified in the call to *Create* and assign it a standard width. SBS_TOPALIGN and SBS_BOTTOMALIGN align a horizontal scroll bar control along the top or bottom border of the rectangle and assign it a standard height.

Unlike the other classic controls, scroll bar controls don't send WM_COMMAND messages; they send WM_VSCROLL and WM_HSCROLL messages instead. MFC applications process these messages with *OnVScroll* and *OnHScroll* handlers, as described in Chapter 2. I didn't mention two scroll bar notification codes in Chapter 2 because they apply only to scroll bar controls. SB_TOP means that the user pressed the Home key while the scroll bar had the input focus, and SB_BOTTOM means the user pressed End.

MFC's *CScrollBar* class includes a handful of functions for manipulating scroll bars, most of which should seem familiar to you because they work just like the similarly named *CWnd* functions. *CScrollBar::GetScrollPos* and *CScrollBar::SetScrollPos* get and set the scroll bar's thumb position. *CScrollBar::GetScrollRange* and *CScrollBar::Set-ScrollRange* get and set the scroll bar range. You use *CScrollBar::SetScrollInfo* to set the range, position, and thumb size in one step. For details, refer to the discussion of *CWnd::SetScrollInfo* in Chapter 2.

ADVANCED CONTROL PROGRAMMING

One of the benefits of programming controls the MFC way is the ease with which you can modify a control's behavior by deriving classes of your own from the MFC control classes. It's easy, for example, to create an edit control that accepts only numbers or a list box that displays pictures instead of text. You can also build reusable, self-contained control classes that respond to their own notification messages.

The remainder of this chapter is about techniques you can use to shape the controls to make them work the way *you* want them to work by combining the best features of C++ and MFC.

Numeric Edit Controls

The MFC control classes are useful in their own right because they provide an object-oriented interface to the built-in control types. But their utility is enhanced by the fact that you can use them as base classes for control classes of your own. By adding new message handlers to a derived class or overriding message handlers acquired through inheritance, you can modify certain aspects of the control's behavior while leaving other aspects unchanged.

A perfect example of a derived control class is a numeric edit control. A normal edit control accepts a wide range of characters, including numbers, letters of the alphabet, and punctuation symbols. A numeric edit control accepts only numbers. It's perfect for entering phone numbers, serial numbers, IP addresses, and other numeric data.

Creating a numeric edit control is no big deal in an MFC application because the basic features of an edit control are defined in *CEdit*. Thanks to C++ inheritance and MFC message mapping, you can derive a control class from *CEdit* and supply custom message handlers to change the way the control responds to user input. The following *CNumEdit* class models an edit control that accepts numbers but rejects all other characters:

```
class CNumEdit : public CEdit
{
protected:
    afx_msg void OnChar (UINT nChar, UINT nRepCnt, UINT nFlags);
    DECLARE_MESSAGE_MAP ()
};

BEGIN_MESSAGE_MAP (CNumEdit, CEdit)
    ON_WM_CHAR ()
END_MESSAGE_MAP ()

void CNumEdit::OnChar (UINT nChar, UINT nRepCnt, UINT nFlags)
{
    if (((nChar >= _T ('0')) && (nChar <= _T ('9'))) ||
        (nChar == VK_BACK))
        CEdit::OnChar (nChar, nRepCnt, nFlags);
}
```

How does *CNumEdit* work? When an edit control has the input focus and a character key is pressed, the control receives a WM_CHAR message. By deriving a new class from *CEdit*, mapping WM_CHAR messages to the derived class's *OnChar* handler, and designing *OnChar* so that it passes WM_CHAR messages to the base class if and only if the character encoded in the message is a number, you create an edit control that rejects nonnumeric characters. VK_BACK is included in the list of acceptable character codes so that the Backspace key won't cease to function. It's not necessary to test for other editing keys such as Home and Del because they, unlike the Backspace key, don't generate WM_CHAR messages.

Owner-Draw List Boxes

By default, items in a list box consist of strings of text. Should you need a list box that displays graphical images instead of text, you can create an owner-draw list box—one whose contents are drawn by your application, not by Windows—by following two simple steps.

1. Derive a new list box class from *CListBox,* and override *CListBox::Measure-Item* and *CListBox::DrawItem.* Also override *PreCreateWindow,* and make sure that either LBS_OWNERDRAWFIXED or LBS_OWNERDRAWVARIABLE is included in the list box style.

2. Instantiate the derived class, and use *Create* or *CreateEx* to create the list box.

Functionally, owner-draw list boxes are similar to owner-draw menus. When an item in an owner-draw list box needs to be drawn (or redrawn), Windows sends the list box's parent a WM_DRAWITEM message with a pointer to a DRAWITEMSTRUCT structure containing a device context handle, a 0-based index identifying the item to be drawn, and other information. Before the first WM_DRAWITEM message arrives, the list box's parent receives one or more WM_MEASUREITEM messages requesting the height of the list box's items. If the list box style is LBS_OWNERDRAWFIXED, WM_MEASUREITEM is sent just once. For LBS_OWNERDRAWVARIABLE list boxes, a WM_MEASUREITEM message is sent for each item. MFC calls the list box object's virtual *DrawItem* function when the parent receives a WM_DRAWITEM message and *MeasureItem* when it receives a WM_MEASUREITEM message. Therefore, you don't have to modify the parent window class or worry about message maps and message handlers; just override *DrawItem* and *MeasureItem* in the list box class, and your list box can do its own drawing without any help from its parent.

CListBox supports two other owner-draw overridables in addition to *DrawItem* and *MeasureItem.* The first is *CompareItem.* If an owner-draw list box is created with the style LBS_SORT and items are added to it with *AddString, CListBox::CompareItem* must be overridden with a version that compares two arbitrary items packaged in COMPAREITEMSTRUCT structures. The overridden function must return −1 if item 1 comes before item 2, 0 if the items are lexically equal, or 1 if item 1 comes after item 2. Owner-draw list boxes are seldom created with the style LBS_SORT because nontextual data typically has no inherent order. (How would you sort a list of colors, for example?) And if you don't use LBS_SORT, you don't have to write a *CompareItem* function. If you don't implement *CompareItem* in a derived owner-draw list box class, it's prudent to override *PreCreateWindow* and make sure the list box style doesn't include LBS_SORT.

The final owner-draw list box overridable is *DeleteItem.* It's called when an item is deleted with *DeleteString,* when the list box's contents are erased with *ResetContent,* and when a list box containing one or more items is destroyed. *DeleteItem* is called once per item, and it receives a pointer to a DELETEITEMSTRUCT structure containing information about the item. If a list box uses per-item resources (for example, bitmaps) that need to be freed when an item is removed or the list box is destroyed, override *DeleteItem* and use it to free those resources.

The following *COwnerDrawListBox* class is a nearly complete C++ implementation of an LBS_OWNERDRAWFIXED-style owner-draw list box:

```cpp
class COwnerDrawListBox : public CListBox
{
public:
    virtual BOOL PreCreateWindow (CREATESTRUCT&);
    virtual void MeasureItem (LPMEASUREITEMSTRUCT);
    virtual void DrawItem (LPDRAWITEMSTRUCT);
};

BOOL COwnerDrawListBox::PreCreateWindow (CREATESTRUCT& cs)
{
    if (!CListBox::PreCreateWindow (cs))
        return FALSE;

    cs.style &= ~(LBS_OWNERDRAWVARIABLE | LBS_SORT);
    cs.style |= LBS_OWNERDRAWFIXED;
    return TRUE;
}

void COwnerDrawListBox::MeasureItem (LPMEASUREITEMSTRUCT lpmis)
{
    lpmis->itemHeight = 32;     // Item height in pixels
}

void COwnerDrawListBox::DrawItem (LPDRAWITEMSTRUCT lpdis)
{
    CDC dc;
    dc.Attach (lpdis->hDC);
    CRect rect = lpdis->rcItem;
    UINT nIndex = lpdis->itemID;

    CBrush* pBrush = new CBrush (::GetSysColor ((lpdis->itemState &
        ODS_SELECTED) ? COLOR_HIGHLIGHT : COLOR_WINDOW));
    dc.FillRect (rect, pBrush);
    delete pBrush;

    if (lpdis->itemState & ODS_FOCUS)
        dc.DrawFocusRect (rect);

    if (nIndex != (UINT) -1) {
        // Draw the item.
    }
    dc.Detach ();
}
```

Before you use *COwnerDrawListBox* in an application of your own, change the 32 in *COwnerDrawListBox::MeasureItem* to the desired item height in pixels and replace the comment "Draw the item" in *COwnerDrawListBox::DrawItem* with code that draws the item whose index is *nIndex*. Use the *dc* device context object to do the drawing and restrict your output to the rectangle specified by *rect*, and the list box should function superbly. (Be sure to preserve the state of the device context so that it's the same going out as it was coming in.) *COwnerDrawListBox*'s implementation of *DrawItem* paints the item's background with the system color COLOR_HIGHLIGHT if the item is selected (if the *lpdis->itemState*'s ODS_SELECTED bit is set) or COLOR_WINDOW if it isn't, and it draws a focus rectangle if the item has the input focus (if the *lpdis->itemState*'s ODS_FOCUS bit is set). All you have to do is draw the item itself. The *PreCreateWindow* override ensures that LBS_OWNERDRAWFIXED is set and that LBS_OWNERDRAWVARIABLE isn't. It also clears the LBS_SORT bit to prevent calls to *CompareItem*.

A final feature needed to transform *COwnerDrawListBox* into a complete class is an *AddItem* function that can be called to add a nontextual item to the list box. For a list box that displays bitmaps, for example, *AddItem* might look like this:

```
int COwnerDrawListBox::AddItem (HBITMAP hBitmap)
{
    int nIndex = AddString (_T (""));
    if ((nIndex != LB_ERR) && (nIndex != LB_ERRSPACE))
        SetItemData (nIndex, (DWORD) hBitmap);
    return nIndex;
}
```

In this example, *AddItem* uses *SetItemData* to associate a bitmap handle with a list box index. For a given item, the list box's *DrawItem* function can retrieve the bitmap handle with *GetItemData* and draw the bitmap. Bitmaps are resources that must be deleted when they're no longer needed. You can either leave it to the list box's parent to delete the bitmaps or override *CListBox::DeleteItem* and let the list box delete them itself. The choice is up to you.

The IconView application shown in Figure 7-8 uses an owner-draw list box class named *CIconListBox* to displays icons. *CIconListBox* overrides the *PreCreateWindow*, *MeasureItem*, and *DrawItem* functions it inherits from *CListBox* and adds two functions of its own. *AddIcon* adds an icon to the list box, and *ProjectImage* "projects" an icon onto a display surface, shrinking or expanding the image as needed to fit a specified rectangle. IconView's source code is shown in Figure 7-9 on page 368.

The only form of input that IconView accepts is drag-and-drop. To try it out, grab an EXE, DLL, or ICO file with the left mouse button, drag it to the IconView window, and release the mouse button. Any icons contained in the file will be displayed in the list box, and an enlarged image of the first icon will be displayed in the Detail window. To get a close-up view of any of the other icons in the file, just click the icon or cursor through the list with the up and down arrow keys.

Figure 7-8. *IconView showing the icons contained in Pifmgr.dll.*

IconView uses MFC's handy *CDC::DrawIcon* function to draw icons into the list box. The core code is found in *CIconListBox::DrawItem*:

```
if (nIndex != (UINT) -1)
    dc.DrawIcon (rect.left + 4, rect.top + 2,
        (HICON) GetItemData (nIndex));
```

Icon handles are stored with *SetItemData* and retrieved with *GetItemData*. The call to *DrawIcon* is skipped if *nIndex*—the index of the currently selected list box item— is −1. That's important, because *DrawItem* is called with a list box index of −1 when an empty list box receives the input focus. *DrawItem's* job in that case is to draw a focus rectangle around the nonexistent item 0. You shouldn't assume that *DrawItem* will always be called with a valid item index.

CMainWindow's OnPaint handler does nothing more than construct a paint device context and call the list box's *ProjectImage* function to draw a blown-up version of the currently selected icon in the window's client area. *ProjectImage* uses the *CDC* functions *BitBlt* and *StretchBlt* to project the image. This code probably won't make a lot of sense to you right now, but its meaning will be crystal clear once you've read about bitmaps in Chapter 15.

The drag-and-drop mechanism that IconView uses is a primitive form of drag- and-drop that was introduced in Windows 3.1. Briefly, the call to *DragAcceptFiles* in *CMainWindow::OnCreate* registers *CMainWindow* as a drop target. Once registered, the window receives a WM_DROPFILES message whenever a file is dragged from the shell and dropped on top of it. *CMainWindow::OnDropFiles* responds to WM_DROPFILES messages by using the *::DragQueryFile* API function to retrieve the name of the file that was dropped. It then uses *::ExtractIcon* to extract icons from the file and *CIconListBox::AddIcon* to add the icons to the list box.

In Chapter 19, you'll learn about a richer form of drag-and-drop called *OLE drag-and-drop.* "Old" drag-and-drop is still supported in 32-bit Windows, but it's not nearly as flexible as OLE drag-and-drop. That's why I haven't gone into more detail about it. Once you see OLE drag-and-drop in action, I think you'll agree that time spent understanding Windows 3.1-style drag-and-drop is time better spent elsewhere.

IconView.h

```
class CMyApp : public CWinApp
{
public:
    virtual BOOL InitInstance ();
};

class CIconListBox : public CListBox
{
public:
    virtual BOOL PreCreateWindow (CREATESTRUCT& cs);
    virtual void MeasureItem (LPMEASUREITEMSTRUCT lpmis);
    virtual void DrawItem (LPDRAWITEMSTRUCT lpdis);
    int AddIcon (HICON hIcon);
    void ProjectImage (CDC* pDC, LPRECT pRect, COLORREF clrBackColor);
};

class CMainWindow : public CWnd
{
protected:
    int m_cxChar;
    int m_cyChar;

    CFont m_font;
    CRect m_rcImage;

    CButton m_wndGroupBox;
    CIconListBox m_wndIconListBox;
    CStatic m_wndLabel;

public:
    CMainWindow ();

protected:
    virtual void PostNcDestroy ();

    afx_msg int OnCreate (LPCREATESTRUCT lpcs);
    afx_msg void OnPaint ();
```

Figure 7-9. *The IconView application.*

```
    afx_msg void OnSetFocus (CWnd* pWnd);
    afx_msg void OnDropFiles (HDROP hDropInfo);
    afx_msg void OnSelChange ();

    DECLARE_MESSAGE_MAP ()
};
```

IconView.cpp

```
#include <afxwin.h>
#include "IconView.h"

#define IDC_LISTBOX 100

CMyApp myApp;

/////////////////////////////////////////////////////////////////////////
// CMyApp member functions

BOOL CMyApp::InitInstance ()
{
    m_pMainWnd = new CMainWindow;
    m_pMainWnd->ShowWindow (m_nCmdShow);
    m_pMainWnd->UpdateWindow ();
    return TRUE;
}

/////////////////////////////////////////////////////////////////////////
// CMainWindow message map and member functions

BEGIN_MESSAGE_MAP (CMainWindow, CWnd)
    ON_WM_CREATE ()
    ON_WM_PAINT ()
    ON_WM_SETFOCUS ()
    ON_WM_DROPFILES ()
    ON_LBN_SELCHANGE (IDC_LISTBOX, OnSelChange)
END_MESSAGE_MAP ()

CMainWindow::CMainWindow ()
{
    CString strWndClass = AfxRegisterWndClass (
        0,
        myApp.LoadStandardCursor (IDC_ARROW),
        (HBRUSH) (COLOR_3DFACE + 1),
        myApp.LoadStandardIcon (IDI_WINLOGO)
    );
```

(continued)

Figure 7-9. *continued*

```
    CreateEx (0, strWndClass, _T ("IconView"),
        WS_OVERLAPPED | WS_SYSMENU | WS_CAPTION | WS_MINIMIZEBOX,
        CW_USEDEFAULT, CW_USEDEFAULT, CW_USEDEFAULT, CW_USEDEFAULT,
        NULL, NULL, NULL);

    CRect rect (0, 0, m_cxChar * 84, m_cyChar * 21);
    CalcWindowRect (&rect);

    SetWindowPos (NULL, 0, 0, rect.Width (), rect.Height (),
        SWP_NOZORDER | SWP_NOMOVE | SWP_NOREDRAW);
}

int CMainWindow::OnCreate (LPCREATESTRUCT lpcs)
{
    if (CWnd::OnCreate (lpcs) == -1)
        return -1;

    m_font.CreatePointFont (80, _T ("MS Sans Serif"));

    CClientDC dc (this);
    CFont* pOldFont = dc.SelectObject (&m_font);
    TEXTMETRIC tm;
    dc.GetTextMetrics (&tm);
    m_cxChar = tm.tmAveCharWidth;
    m_cyChar = tm.tmHeight + tm.tmExternalLeading;
    dc.SelectObject (pOldFont);

    m_rcImage.SetRect (m_cxChar * 4, m_cyChar * 3, m_cxChar * 46,
        m_cyChar * 19);

    m_wndGroupBox.Create (_T ("Detail"),  WS_CHILD | WS_VISIBLE | BS_GROUPBOX,
        CRect (m_cxChar * 2, m_cyChar, m_cxChar * 48, m_cyChar * 20),
        this, (UINT) -1);

    m_wndLabel.Create (_T ("Icons"), WS_CHILD | WS_VISIBLE | SS_LEFT,
        CRect (m_cxChar * 50, m_cyChar, m_cxChar * 82, m_cyChar * 2),
        this);

    m_wndIconListBox.Create (WS_CHILD | WS_VISIBLE | WS_VSCROLL |
        WS_BORDER | LBS_NOTIFY | LBS_NOINTEGRALHEIGHT,
        CRect (m_cxChar * 50, m_cyChar * 2, m_cxChar * 82, m_cyChar * 20),
        this, IDC_LISTBOX);

    m_wndGroupBox.SetFont (&m_font);
    m_wndLabel.SetFont (&m_font);
    DragAcceptFiles ();
    return 0;
}
```

```
void CMainWindow::PostNcDestroy ()
{
    delete this;
}

void CMainWindow::OnPaint ()
{
    CPaintDC dc (this);
    m_wndIconListBox.ProjectImage (&dc, m_rcImage,
        ::GetSysColor (COLOR_3DFACE));
}

void CMainWindow::OnSetFocus (CWnd* pWnd)
{
    m_wndIconListBox.SetFocus ();
}

void CMainWindow::OnDropFiles (HDROP hDropInfo)
{
    //
    // Find out how many files were dropped.
    //
    int nCount = ::DragQueryFile (hDropInfo, (UINT) -1, NULL, 0);

    if (nCount == 1) { // One file at a time, please
        m_wndIconListBox.ResetContent ();
        //
        // Extract the file's icons and add them to the list box.
        //
        char szFile[MAX_PATH];
        ::DragQueryFile (hDropInfo, 0, szFile, sizeof (szFile));
        int nIcons = (int) ::ExtractIcon (NULL, szFile, (UINT) -1);

        if (nIcons) {
            HICON hIcon;
            for (int i=0; i<nIcons; i++) {
                hIcon = ::ExtractIcon (AfxGetInstanceHandle (),
                    szFile, i);
                m_wndIconListBox.AddIcon (hIcon);
            }
        }

        //
        // Put the file name in the main window's title bar.
        //
        CString strWndTitle = szFile;
        strWndTitle += _T (" - IconView");
        SetWindowText (strWndTitle);
```

(continued)

371

Figure 7-9. *continued*

```
        //
        // Select item number 0.
        //
        CClientDC dc (this);
        m_wndIconListBox.SetCurSel (0);
        m_wndIconListBox.ProjectImage (&dc, m_rcImage,
            ::GetSysColor (COLOR_3DFACE));
    }
    ::DragFinish (hDropInfo);
}

void CMainWindow::OnSelChange ()
{
    CClientDC dc (this);
    m_wndIconListBox.ProjectImage (&dc, m_rcImage,
        ::GetSysColor (COLOR_3DFACE));
}


///////////////////////////////////////////////////////////////////////
// CIconListBox member functions

BOOL CIconListBox::PreCreateWindow (CREATESTRUCT& cs)
{
    if (!CListBox::PreCreateWindow (cs))
        return FALSE;

    cs.dwExStyle |= WS_EX_CLIENTEDGE;
    cs.style &= ~(LBS_OWNERDRAWVARIABLE | LBS_SORT);
    cs.style |= LBS_OWNERDRAWFIXED;
    return TRUE;
}

void CIconListBox::MeasureItem (LPMEASUREITEMSTRUCT lpmis)
{
    lpmis->itemHeight = 36;
}

void CIconListBox::DrawItem (LPDRAWITEMSTRUCT lpdis)
{
    CDC dc;
    dc.Attach (lpdis->hDC);
    CRect rect = lpdis->rcItem;
    int nIndex = lpdis->itemID;

    CBrush* pBrush = new CBrush;
```

```
        pBrush->CreateSolidBrush (::GetSysColor ((lpdis->itemState &
            ODS_SELECTED) ? COLOR_HIGHLIGHT : COLOR_WINDOW));
        dc.FillRect (rect, pBrush);
        delete pBrush;

        if (lpdis->itemState & ODS_FOCUS)
            dc.DrawFocusRect (rect);

        if (nIndex != (UINT) -1)
            dc.DrawIcon (rect.left + 4, rect.top + 2,
                (HICON) GetItemData (nIndex));

        dc.Detach ();
}

int CIconListBox::AddIcon (HICON hIcon)
{
    int nIndex = AddString (_T (""));
    if ((nIndex != LB_ERR) && (nIndex != LB_ERRSPACE))
        SetItemData (nIndex, (DWORD) hIcon);
    return nIndex;
}

void CIconListBox::ProjectImage (CDC* pDC, LPRECT pRect,
    COLORREF clrBackColor)
{
    CDC dcMem;
    dcMem.CreateCompatibleDC (pDC);

    CBitmap bitmap;
    bitmap.CreateCompatibleBitmap (pDC, 32, 32);
    CBitmap* pOldBitmap = dcMem.SelectObject (&bitmap);

    CBrush* pBrush = new CBrush (clrBackColor);
    dcMem.FillRect (CRect (0, 0, 32, 32), pBrush);
    delete pBrush;

    int nIndex = GetCurSel ();
    if (nIndex != LB_ERR)
        dcMem.DrawIcon (0, 0, (HICON) GetItemData (nIndex));

    pDC->StretchBlt (pRect->left, pRect->top, pRect->right - pRect->left,
        pRect->bottom - pRect->top, &dcMem, 0, 0, 32, 32, SRCCOPY);

    dcMem.SelectObject (pOldBitmap);
}
```

Graphical Push Buttons

MFC includes three derived control classes of its own: *CCheckListBox*, *CDragListBox*, and *CBitmapButton*. *CCheckListBox* turns a normal list box into a "check" list box—a list box with a check box by each item and added functions such as *GetCheck* and *SetCheck* for getting and setting check box states. *CDragListBox* creates a list box that supports its own primitive form of drag-and-drop. *CBitmapButton* encapsulates owner-draw push buttons that display pictures instead of text. It supplies its own *DrawItem* handler that draws a push button in response to WM_DRAWITEM messages. All you have to do is create the button and supply four bitmaps representing the button in various states.

CBitmapButton was a boon back in the days of 16-bit Windows because it simplified the task of creating graphical push buttons. Today, however, owner-draw push buttons are rarely used. Two button styles that were first introduced in Windows 95—BS_BITMAP and BS_ICON—make graphical push buttons a breeze by taking a single image and creating a push button from it. A BS_BITMAP-style push button (henceforth, a *bitmap push button*) displays a bitmap on the face of a push button. A BS_ICON-style push button (an *icon push button*) displays an icon. Most developers prefer icon push buttons because icons, unlike bitmaps, can have transparent pixels. Transparent pixels are great for displaying nonrectangular images on button faces because they decouple the image's background color from the button color.

Creating an icon push button is a two-step process:

1. Create a push button whose style includes a BS_ICON flag.

2. Call the button's *SetIcon* function, and pass in an icon handle.

The following example creates an icon push button from an icon whose resource ID is IDI_OK:

```
m_wndIconButton.Create (_T (""), WS_CHILD | WS_VISIBLE | BS_ICON,
    rect, this, IDC_BUTTON);
m_wndIconButton.SetIcon (AfxGetApp ()->LoadIcon (IDI_OK));
```

The icon is drawn in the center of the button unless you alter its alignment by applying one or more of the following button styles:

Button Style	Description
BS_LEFT	Aligns the icon image with the left edge of the button face
BS_RIGHT	Aligns the icon image with the right edge of the button face
BS_TOP	Aligns the icon image with the top edge of the button face
BS_BOTTOM	Aligns the icon image with the bottom edge of the button face
BS_CENTER	Centers the icon image horizontally
BS_VCENTER	Centers the icon image vertically

Chapter 8's Phone application uses icon push buttons to represent the OK and Cancel buttons in a dialog box.

The procedure for creating a bitmap button is almost the same as the one for creating an icon button. Just change BS_ICON to BS_BITMAP and *SetIcon* to *SetBitmap* and you're set. Of course, you'll have to replace the call to *LoadIcon* with code that loads a bitmap, too. You'll learn how that's done in Chapter 15.

One problem to watch out for when you're using icon push buttons is what happens when the button becomes disabled. Windows generates a disabled button image from the button's icon, but the results aren't always what you'd expect. In general, the simpler the image, the better. Unfilled figures render better when disabled than filled figures.

Customizing a Control's Colors

The most glaring deficiency in the Windows control architecture is that there's no obvious way to change a control's colors. You can change a control's font with *SetFont*, but there is no equivalent function for changing a control's colors.

MFC supports two mechanisms for changing a control's colors. Both rely on the fact that before a control paints itself, it sends its parent a message containing the handle of the device context used to do the painting. The parent can call *CDC::SetTextColor* and *CDC::SetBkColor* on that device context to alter the attributes of any text drawn by the control. It can also alter the control's background color by returning a brush handle (HBRUSH).

The message that a control sends to its parent prior to painting varies with the control type. For example, a list box sends a WM_CTLCOLORLISTBOX message; a static control sends a WM_CTLCOLORSTATIC message. In any event, the message's *wParam* holds the device context handle, and *lParam* holds the control's window handle. If a window processes a static control's WM_CTLCOLORSTATIC messages by setting the device context's text color to red and background color to white and returning a brush handle for a blue brush, the control text will be red, the gaps in and between characters will be white, and the control background—everything inside the control's borders not covered by text—will be blue.

MFC's ON_WM_CTLCOLOR message-map macro directs WM_CTLCOLOR messages of all types to a handler named *OnCtlColor*. *OnCtlColor* is prototyped as follows:

```
afx_msg HBRUSH OnCtlColor (CDC* pDC, CWnd* pWnd, UINT nCtlColor)
```

pDC is a pointer to the control's device context, *pWnd* is a *CWnd* pointer that identifies the control itself, and *nCtlColor* identifies the type of WM_CTLCOLOR message that prompted the call. Here are the possible values for *nCtlColor*.

nCtlColor	Control Type or Window Type
CTLCOLOR_BTN	Push button. Processing this message has no effect on a button's appearance.
CTLCOLOR_DLG	Dialog box.
CTLCOLOR_EDIT	Edit control and the edit control part of a combo box.
CTLCOLOR_LISTBOX	List box and the list box part of a combo box.
CTLCOLOR_MSGBOX	Message box.
CTLCOLOR_SCROLLBAR	Scroll bar.
CTLCOLOR_STATIC	Static control, check box, radio button, group box, read-only or disabled edit control, and the edit control in a disabled combo box.

Five *nCtlColor* values pertain to controls, and two—CTLCOLOR_DLG and CTL-COLOR_MSGBOX—apply to dialog boxes and message boxes. (That's right: You can control the color of dialog boxes and message boxes by processing WM_CTLCOLOR messages.) Static controls aren't the only controls that send WM_CTLCOLORSTATIC messages. You'd think that a radio button would send a WM_CTLCOLORBTN message, but in fact it sends a WM_CTLCOLORSTATIC message in 32-bit Windows.

One way, then, to change a control's colors is to implement *OnCtlColor* in the parent window class. The following *OnCtlColor* implementation changes the color of a static text control named *m_wndText* to white-on-red in a frame window:

```
HBRUSH CMainWindow::OnCtlColor (CDC* pDC, CWnd* pWnd,
    UINT nCtlColor)
{
    if (m_wndText.m_hWnd == pWnd->m_hWnd) {
        pDC->SetTextColor (RGB (255, 255, 255));
        pDC->SetBkColor (RGB (255, 0, 0));
        return (HBRUSH) m_brRedBrush;
    }
    CFrameWnd::OnCtlColor (pDC, pWnd, nCtlColor);
}
```

m_brRedBrush is a *CMainWindow* data member whose type is *CBrush*. It is initialized as follows:

```
m_brRedBrush.CreateSolidBrush (RGB (255, 0, 0));
```

Note that this implementation of *OnCtlColor* compares the window handle of the control whose color it wishes to change with the window handle of the control that generated the message. If the two are not equal, the message is forwarded to the base class. If this check were not performed, *OnCtlColor* would affect all the controls in *CMainWindow*, not just *m_wndText*.

That's one way to change a control's color. The problem with this technique is that it's up to the parent to do the changing. What happens if you want to derive a control class of your own and include in it a *SetColor* function for modifying the control's color?

A derived control class can set its own colors by using MFC's ON_WM_CTL-COLOR_REFLECT macro to pass WM_CTLCOLOR messages that aren't handled by the control's parent back to the control. Here's the code for a *CStatic*-like control that paints itself white-on-red:

```
class CColorStatic : public CStatic
{
public:
    CColorStatic ();

protected:
    CBrush m_brRedBrush;
    afx_msg HBRUSH CtlColor (CDC* pDC, UINT nCtlColor);
    DECLARE_MESSAGE_MAP ()
};

BEGIN_MESSAGE_MAP (CColorStatic, CStatic)
    ON_WM_CTLCOLOR_REFLECT ()
END_MESSAGE_MAP ()

CColorStatic::CColorStatic ()
{
    m_brRedBrush.CreateSolidBrush (RGB (255, 0, 0));
}

HBRUSH CColorStatic::CtlColor (CDC* pDC, UINT nCtlColor)
{
    pDC->SetTextColor (RGB (255, 255, 255));
    pDC->SetBkColor (RGB (255, 0, 0));
    return (HBRUSH) m_brRedBrush;
}
```

CtlColor is similar to *OnCtlColor*, but it doesn't receive the *pWnd* parameter that *OnCtlColor* does. It doesn't need to because the control to which the message applies is implicit in the call.

The ColorText application shown in Figure 7-10 uses a static text control whose colors are configurable. *CColorStatic* implements the control. This version of *CColorStatic* is more versatile than the one in the previous paragraph because rather than use hardcoded colors, it includes member functions named *SetTextColor* and *SetBkColor* that can be used to change its colors. When ColorText's Red, Green, or Blue radio button is clicked, the control's text color changes. The button click activates a handler that calls the control's *SetTextColor* function. (See Figure 7-11.) ColorText doesn't use the control's

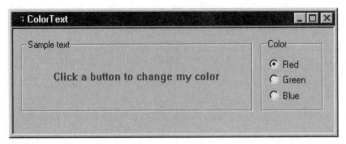

Figure 7-10. *The ColorText window.*

SetBkColor function, but I included the function anyway for completeness. *SetBkColor* controls the fill color drawn behind the text. *CColorStatic*'sdefault colors are black (foreground) and the system color COLOR_3DFACE (background), but a simple function call is sufficient to change either one.

ColorText.h

```
#define IDC_RED      100
#define IDC_GREEN    101
#define IDC_BLUE     102

class CColorStatic : public CStatic
{
protected:
    COLORREF m_clrText;
    COLORREF m_clrBack;
    CBrush m_brBkgnd;

public:
    CColorStatic ();
    void SetTextColor (COLORREF clrText);
    void SetBkColor (COLORREF clrBack);

protected:
    afx_msg HBRUSH CtlColor (CDC* pDC, UINT nCtlColor);
    DECLARE_MESSAGE_MAP ()
};

class CMyApp : public CWinApp
{
public:
    virtual BOOL InitInstance ();
};
```

Figure 7-11. *The ColorText application.*

```
class CMainWindow : public CFrameWnd
{
protected:
    int m_cxChar;
    int m_cyChar;
    CFont m_font;

    CColorStatic m_wndText;
    CButton m_wndRadioButtonRed;
    CButton m_wndRadioButtonGreen;
    CButton m_wndRadioButtonBlue;
    CButton m_wndGroupBox1;
    CButton m_wndGroupBox2;

public:
    CMainWindow ();

protected:
    afx_msg int OnCreate (LPCREATESTRUCT lpcs);
    afx_msg void OnRedButtonClicked ();
    afx_msg void OnGreenButtonClicked ();
    afx_msg void OnBlueButtonClicked ();

    DECLARE_MESSAGE_MAP ()
};
```

ColorText.cpp

```
#include <afxwin.h>
#include "ColorText.h"

CMyApp myApp;

//////////////////////////////////////////////////////////////////////
// CMyApp member functions

BOOL CMyApp::InitInstance ()
{
    m_pMainWnd = new CMainWindow;
    m_pMainWnd->ShowWindow (m_nCmdShow);
    m_pMainWnd->UpdateWindow ();
    return TRUE;
}

//////////////////////////////////////////////////////////////////////
// CMainWindow message map and member functions
```

(continued)

Figure 7-11. *continued*

```
BEGIN_MESSAGE_MAP (CMainWindow, CFrameWnd)
    ON_WM_CREATE ()
    ON_BN_CLICKED (IDC_RED, OnRedButtonClicked)
    ON_BN_CLICKED (IDC_GREEN, OnGreenButtonClicked)
    ON_BN_CLICKED (IDC_BLUE, OnBlueButtonClicked)
END_MESSAGE_MAP ()

CMainWindow::CMainWindow ()
{
    CString strWndClass = AfxRegisterWndClass (
        0,
        myApp.LoadStandardCursor (IDC_ARROW),
        (HBRUSH) (COLOR_3DFACE + 1),
        myApp.LoadStandardIcon (IDI_WINLOGO)
    );

    Create (strWndClass, _T ("ColorText"));
}

int CMainWindow::OnCreate (LPCREATESTRUCT lpcs)
{
    if (CFrameWnd::OnCreate (lpcs) == -1)
        return -1;

    m_font.CreatePointFont (80, _T ("MS Sans Serif"));

    CClientDC dc (this);
    CFont* pOldFont = dc.SelectObject (&m_font);
    TEXTMETRIC tm;
    dc.GetTextMetrics (&tm);
    m_cxChar = tm.tmAveCharWidth;
    m_cyChar = tm.tmHeight + tm.tmExternalLeading;
    dc.SelectObject (pOldFont);

    m_wndGroupBox1.Create (_T ("Sample text"), WS_CHILD | WS_VISIBLE |
        BS_GROUPBOX, CRect (m_cxChar * 2, m_cyChar, m_cxChar * 62,
        m_cyChar * 8), this, UINT (-1));

    m_wndText.Create (_T ("Click a button to change my color"),
        WS_CHILD | WS_VISIBLE | SS_CENTER, CRect (m_cxChar * 4,
        m_cyChar * 4, m_cxChar * 60, m_cyChar * 6), this);

    m_wndGroupBox2.Create (_T ("Color"), WS_CHILD | WS_VISIBLE |
        BS_GROUPBOX, CRect (m_cxChar * 64, m_cyChar, m_cxChar * 80,
        m_cyChar * 8), this, UINT (-1));
```

```
    m_wndRadioButtonRed.Create (_T ("Red"), WS_CHILD | WS_VISIBLE |
        WS_GROUP | BS_AUTORADIOBUTTON, CRect (m_cxChar * 66, m_cyChar * 3,
        m_cxChar * 78, m_cyChar * 4), this, IDC_RED);

    m_wndRadioButtonGreen.Create (_T ("Green"), WS_CHILD | WS_VISIBLE |
        BS_AUTORADIOBUTTON, CRect (m_cxChar * 66, (m_cyChar * 9) / 2,
        m_cxChar * 78, (m_cyChar * 11) / 2), this, IDC_GREEN);

    m_wndRadioButtonBlue.Create (_T ("Blue"), WS_CHILD | WS_VISIBLE |
        BS_AUTORADIOBUTTON, CRect (m_cxChar * 66, m_cyChar * 6,
        m_cxChar * 78, m_cyChar * 7), this, IDC_BLUE);

    m_wndRadioButtonRed.SetCheck (1);
    m_wndText.SetTextColor (RGB (255, 0, 0));

    m_wndGroupBox1.SetFont (&m_font, FALSE);
    m_wndGroupBox2.SetFont (&m_font, FALSE);
    m_wndRadioButtonRed.SetFont (&m_font, FALSE);
    m_wndRadioButtonGreen.SetFont (&m_font, FALSE);
    m_wndRadioButtonBlue.SetFont (&m_font, FALSE);
    return 0;
}

void CMainWindow::OnRedButtonClicked ()
{
    m_wndText.SetTextColor (RGB (255, 0, 0));
}

void CMainWindow::OnGreenButtonClicked ()
{
    m_wndText.SetTextColor (RGB (0, 255, 0));
}

void CMainWindow::OnBlueButtonClicked ()
{
    m_wndText.SetTextColor (RGB (0, 0, 255));
}

/////////////////////////////////////////////////////////////////////////
// CColorStatic message map and member functions

BEGIN_MESSAGE_MAP (CColorStatic, CStatic)
    ON_WM_CTLCOLOR_REFLECT ()
END_MESSAGE_MAP ()

CColorStatic::CColorStatic ()
```

(continued)

Figure 7-11. *continued*

```
{
    m_clrText = RGB (0, 0, 0);
    m_clrBack = ::GetSysColor (COLOR_3DFACE);
    m_brBkgnd.CreateSolidBrush (m_clrBack);
}

void CColorStatic::SetTextColor (COLORREF clrText)
{
    m_clrText = clrText;
    Invalidate ();
}

void CColorStatic::SetBkColor (COLORREF clrBack)
{
    m_clrBack = clrBack;
    m_brBkgnd.DeleteObject ();
    m_brBkgnd.CreateSolidBrush (clrBack);
    Invalidate ();
}

HBRUSH CColorStatic::CtlColor (CDC* pDC, UINT nCtlColor)
{
    pDC->SetTextColor (m_clrText);
    pDC->SetBkColor (m_clrBack);
    return (HBRUSH) m_brBkgnd;
}
```

Different controls respond to actions performed by *OnCtlColor* and *CtlColor* handlers in different ways. You've seen how static controls respond to *CDC::SetTextColor* and *CDC::SetBkColor*. For a scroll bar control, *SetTextColor* and *SetBkColor* do nothing, but the brush handle returned by a WM_CTLCOLORSCROLLBAR message handler sets the color of the scroll bar's shaft. For a list box, *SetTextColor* and *SetBkColor* affect unhighlighted list box items but have no effect on highlighted items, and the brush handle controls the color of the list box's background—anything on an empty or unhighlighted line that isn't painted over with text. For a push button, *OnCtlColor* and *CtlColor* have no effect whatsoever because Windows uses system colors to draw push button controls. If *nCtlType* contains the code CTLCOLOR_BTN, you might as well pass it on to the base class because nothing you do to the device context will affect how the control is drawn.

Message Reflection

ON_WM_CTLCOLOR_REFLECT is one of several message-map macros introduced in MFC 4.0 that permit notification messages to be reflected back to the controls that sent them. Message reflection is a powerful tool for building reusable control classes because it empowers derived control classes to implement their own behavior independent of their parents. Previous versions of MFC reflected certain messages back to the controls that sent them using a virtual *CWnd* function named *OnChildNotify*. Modern versions of MFC make the concept of message reflection generic so that a derived control class can map *any* message sent to its parent to a class member function. You saw an example of message reflection at work in the previous section when we derived a new class from *CStatic* and allowed it to handle its own WM_CTLCOLOR messages.

The following table contains a list of the message reflection macros MFC provides and short descriptions of what they do.

MFC MESSAGE REFLECTION MACROS

Macro	*Description*
ON_CONTROL_REFLECT	Reflects notifications relayed through WM_COMMAND messages
ON_NOTIFY_REFLECT	Reflects notifications relayed through WM_NOTIFY messages
ON_UPDATE_COMMAND_UI_REFLECT	Reflects update notifications to toolbars, status bars, and other user interface objects
ON_WM_CTLCOLOR_REFLECT	Reflects WM_CTLCOLOR messages
ON_WM_DRAWITEM_REFLECT	Reflects WM_DRAWITEM messages sent by owner-draw controls
ON_WM_MEASUREITEM_REFLECT	Reflects WM_MEASUREITEM messages sent by owner-draw controls
ON_WM_COMPAREITEM_REFLECT	Reflects WM_COMPAREITEM messages sent by owner-draw controls
ON_WM_DELETEITEM_REFLECT	Reflects WM_DELETEITEM messages sent by owner-draw controls
ON_WM_CHARTOITEM_REFLECT	Reflects WM_CHARTOITEM messages sent by list boxes
ON_WM_VKEYTOITEM_REFLECT	Reflects WM_VKEYTOITEM messages sent by list boxes
ON_WM_HSCROLL_REFLECT	Reflects WM_HSCROLL messages sent by scroll bars
ON_WM_VSCROLL_REFLECT	Reflects WM_VSCROLL messages sent by scroll bars
ON_WM_PARENTNOTIFY_REFLECT	Reflects WM_PARENTNOTIFY messages

Suppose you want to write a list box class that responds to its own LBN_DBLCLK notifications by displaying a message box containing the text of the item that was double-clicked. In an SDK-style application, the list box's parent would have to process the notification message and pop up the message box. In an MFC application, the list box can handle the notification and display the message box itself. Here's a derived list box class that does just that:

```
class CMyListBox : public CListBox
{
protected:
    afx_msg void OnDoubleClick ();
    DECLARE_MESSAGE_MAP ()
};

BEGIN_MESSAGE_MAP (CMyListBox, CListBox)
    ON_CONTROL_REFLECT (LBN_DBLCLK, OnDoubleClick)
END_MESSAGE_MAP ()

void CMyListBox::OnDoubleClick ()
{
    CString string;
    int nIndex = GetCurSel ();
    GetText (nIndex, string);
    MessageBox (string);
}
```

The ON_CONTROL_REFLECT entry in the derived class's message map tells MFC to call *CMyListBox::OnDoubleClick* anytime the list box sends an LBN_DBLCLK notification to its parent. It's worth noting that the notification is reflected only if the parent doesn't process the notification itself—that is, if the parent's message map doesn't include an ON_LBN_DBLCLK entry for this list box. The parent receives precedence, which is consistent with the fact that Windows expects the parent to process any notifications in which it is interested.

Chapter 8

Dialog Boxes and Property Sheets

In the real world, most controls appear not in top-level windows but in dialog boxes. A *dialog box,* also known as a *dialog*, is a window that pops up to solicit input from the user. The window that appears when you select Open from an application's File menu is one example of a dialog box; the window that pops up when you select File-Print is another. Dialog boxes are simpler to create than ordinary windows because a few statements in an RC file are sufficient to define a dialog box and all the controls it contains.

Dialog boxes come in two basic varieties: modal and modeless. A *modal* dialog box disables the window to which it is assigned—its *owner*—until the dialog box is dismissed. It's an application's way of saying, "I can't do anything else until you supply me with the input I need." A *modeless* dialog box behaves more like a conventional window. Its owner can be reactivated even while the dialog box is displayed.

MFC encapsulates the functionality of both modal and modeless dialog boxes in the class named *CDialog*. Dialog box programming is relatively easy when you use the Microsoft Windows SDK, but it's even easier with MFC. You can often build even complex dialog boxes with just a few lines of code, which speeds program development and reduces the likelihood of errors. MFC also provides convenient C++ implementations of the Windows *common dialogs*—Open dialogs, Print dialogs, and other dialog boxes commonly found in Windows applications.

A close cousin of the dialog box is the property sheet. A *property sheet* is essentially a dialog box with tabbed pages. Property sheets are great for lending a higher level of organization to the controls in a dialog. They're also space-efficient, allowing more controls to fit in a finite amount of space, and they're fast becoming commonplace in Windows applications. MFC makes property sheet handling simple with its *CPropertySheet* and *CPropertyPage* classes. Take it from someone who's been there: if you've programmed property sheets without a class library, you'll appreciate the work MFC does to make dealing with property sheets fundamentally no different from—and no more difficult than—dealing with ordinary dialog boxes.

MODAL DIALOG BOXES AND THE *CDIALOG* CLASS

Creating a modal dialog box is a three-step process:

1. Create a dialog box template describing the dialog and the controls that it contains.

2. Construct a *CDialog* object that encapsulates the dialog template.

3. Call *CDialog::DoModal* to display the dialog box.

For very simple dialogs, you can sometimes instantiate *CDialog* directly. More often, however, you'll need to derive a dialog class of your own so that you can customize its behavior. Let's begin by examining the ingredients that go into a modal dialog box. After that, we'll apply what we've learned to modeless dialogs and property sheets.

The Dialog Box Template

The first step in creating a dialog box is to create a dialog box template. A template defines the fundamental properties of a dialog box, from the controls it contains to its width and height. Although it's possible to create dialog box templates programmatically by assembling DLGTEMPLATE and DLGITEMTEMPLATE structures in memory, most dialog box templates are resources compiled from statements in an application's RC file. These statements can be hand-coded, but more often they are written to the RC file by a resource editor that supports the visual editing of dialog box templates.

The following RC statements define a dialog box template whose resource ID is IDD_MYDIALOG. The dialog box described by this template contains four controls: a single-line edit control for entering text, a static text control that serves as a label for the edit control, an OK button, and a Cancel button:

```
IDD_MYDIALOG DIALOG 0, 0, 160, 68
STYLE DS_MODALFRAME | WS_POPUP | WS_VISIBLE | WS_CAPTION | WS_SYSMENU
```

```
CAPTION "Enter Your Name"
FONT 8, "MS Sans Serif"
BEGIN
    LTEXT           "&Name", -1, 8, 14, 24, 8
    EDITTEXT        IDC_NAME, 34, 12, 118, 12, ES_AUTOHSCROLL
    DEFPUSHBUTTON   "OK", IDOK, 60, 34, 40, 14, WS_GROUP
    PUSHBUTTON      "Cancel", IDCANCEL, 112, 34, 40, 14, WS_GROUP
END
```

The numbers on the first line specify the template's resource ID (IDD_MYDIALOG), the dialog box's default position (0,0, which would place the dialog in the upper left corner of its owner's client area save for the fact that MFC automatically centers a modal dialog box whose position is 0,0), and the dialog box's dimensions (160,68). All measurements are expressed in dialog box units. Horizontally, one dialog box unit is equal to one-fourth the average width of a character in the dialog box font. Vertically, one dialog box unit equals one-eighth the character height. Because characters are generally about twice as tall as they are wide, the distance represented by one horizontal dialog box unit is roughly equal to that of one vertical dialog box unit. Measuring distances in dialog box units rather than pixels allows you to define a dialog box's relative proportions independent of the screen resolution.

The STYLE statement in the dialog box template specifies the dialog box's window style. You should always include WS_POPUP in a dialog box's window style. You should typically include WS_VISIBLE, too, so that you don't have to call *ShowWindow* to make the dialog box visible on the screen. WS_CAPTION gives the dialog box a title bar, and WS_SYSMENU adds a close button to the title bar. Styles prefixed with DS_ are specific to dialog boxes. By convention, modal dialog boxes are assigned the style DS_MODALFRAME. In early versions of Windows, this style placed a thick border around the dialog box. Today, DS_MODALFRAME has subtle effects on a dialog box's behavior but does nothing to its appearance. Other interesting dialog styles include DS_CENTER, which centers a dialog box on the screen, DS_ABSALIGN, which positions a dialog relative to the upper left corner of the screen instead of the upper left corner of its owner, and DS_CONTEXTHELP, which adds a question mark button to the dialog box's title bar so that the user can get context-sensitive help regarding the dialog box's controls.

You can create a *system-modal* dialog box by including DS_SYSMODAL in the STYLE statement. In 16-bit Windows, a system-modal dialog box disables all other windows in the system until it is dismissed and is typically used to report critical errors that must be attended to before further processing is performed. In 32-bit Windows, where processes are physically isolated from one another by the operating system, DS_SYSMODAL simply makes the dialog box a topmost window—that is, one that is always displayed on top of other windows. The dialog box overlays all other windows, but the user is free to switch to other applications while the dialog box is displayed.

The CAPTION statement specifies the text that appears in the dialog box's title bar. You can also set the title programmatically with the *SetWindowText* function a *CDialog* object inherits from *CWnd*.

FONT specifies the dialog box font, which is automatically assigned to all the controls in the dialog. The statement

```
FONT 8, "MS Sans Serif"
```

is somewhat redundant because 8-point MS Sans Serif is the default font in current versions of Windows. If your dialogs will be used in older (pre-Windows 95) versions of Windows, this statement ensures that the dialog will use 8-point MS Sans Serif. You can use *CWnd::SetFont* to change the fonts assigned to individual controls in a dialog box.

The statements between BEGIN and END define the dialog box's controls. Each statement defines one control, specifying its type (push button, check box, list box, and so on), its control ID, its position, its width and height, and its style. For static and button controls, you can specify the control text, too. In the example on the preceding page, the LTEXT statement creates a static text control whose ID is −1, whose text is left-aligned in the control rectangle, whose upper left corner lies 8 horizontal dialog box units to the right of and 14 vertical dialog box units below the dialog box's upper left corner, and whose width and height are 24 horizontal dialog box units and 8 vertical dialog box units, respectively. The ampersand in the control text makes Alt-N a shortcut for the edit control created on the following line.

LTEXT is one of several resource statements used to define controls in dialog box templates; a complete list appears in the table on the next page. In essence, these statements are shorthand ways of creating the same kinds of controls we created in Chapter 7 by instantiating a control class and calling the resulting object's *Create* or *CreateEx* function. Each keyword has certain default styles associated with it, and all build in the styles WS_CHILD and WS_VISIBLE. Buttons and edit controls also include the style WS_TABSTOP so that they can be tabbed to with the Tab key. If desired, you can remove an implicit style with the NOT operator. For example, the following resource statement creates an edit control minus the default WS_TABSTOP style:

```
EDITTEXT IDC_EDIT, 32, 16, 96, 12, NOT WS_TABSTOP
```

You can also define dialog box controls with the more generic CONTROL keyword. Sometimes you'll see a dialog box template defined this way:

```
IDD_MYDIALOG DIALOG 0, 0, 160, 68
STYLE DS_MODALFRAME ¦ WS_POPUP ¦ WS_VISIBLE ¦ WS_CAPTION ¦ WS_SYSMENU
CAPTION "Enter Your Name"
BEGIN
    CONTROL    "&Name", -1, "STATIC", SS_LEFT, 8, 14, 24, 8
    CONTROL    "", IDC_NAME, "EDIT", WS_BORDER ¦ ES_AUTOHSCROLL ¦
               ES_LEFT ¦ WS_TABSTOP, 34, 12, 118, 12
```

RESOURCE STATEMENTS FOR CREATING DIALOG BOX CONTROLS

Keyword	*Control Type*	*Default Styles*
LTEXT	Static control with left-aligned text	SS_LEFT | WS_GROUP
CTEXT	Static control with centered text	SS_CENTER | WS_GROUP
RTEXT	Static control with right-aligned text	SS_RIGHT | WS_GROUP
PUSHBUTTON	Push button	BS_PUSHBUTTON | WS_TABSTOP
DEFPUSHBUTTON	Default push button	BS_DEFPUSHBUTTON | WS_TABSTOP
EDITTEXT	Edit control	ES_LEFT | WS_BORDER | WS_TABSTOP
CHECKBOX	Check box	BS_CHECKBOX | WS_TABSTOP
AUTOCHECKBOX	Automatic check box	BS_AUTOCHECKBOX | WS_TABSTOP
STATE3	Three-state check box	BS_3STATE | WS_TABSTOP
AUTO3STATE	Automatic three-state check box	BS_AUTO3STATE | WS_TABSTOP
RADIOBUTTON	Radio button	BS_RADIOBUTTON | WS_TABSTOP
AUTORADIOBUTTON	Automatic radio button	BS_AUTORADIOBUTTON | WS_TABSTOP
GROUPBOX	Group box	BS_GROUPBOX
LISTBOX	List box	LBS_NOTIFY | WS_BORDER
COMBOBOX	Combo box	CBS_SIMPLE
SCROLLBAR	Scroll bar	SBS_HORZ
ICON	Static icon control	SS_ICON

```
    CONTROL    "OK", IDOK, "BUTTON", BS_DEFPUSHBUTTON |
               WS_TABSTOP | WS_GROUP, 60, 34, 40, 14
    CONTROL    "Cancel", IDCANCEL, "BUTTON", BS_PUSHBUTTON |
               WS_TABSTOP | WS_GROUP, 112, 34, 40, 14
END
```

This dialog template is equivalent to the one on pages 386–387. The styles WS_CHILD and WS_VISIBLE are implicit in a CONTROL statement, but all other styles must be specified explicitly. The third parameter in a CONTROL statement specifies the WND-CLASS the control is based on—"BUTTON" for push buttons, radio buttons, check boxes, and group boxes; "EDIT" for edit controls; and so on. Because the WNDCLASS is specified explicitly, you can use CONTROL to create custom controls whose WNDCLASSes are registered with *::RegisterClass*. It's with CONTROL statements, in fact, that you add progress bars, spin buttons, and other common controls to a dialog box. You'll learn more about the common controls in Chapter 16.

Today it's rare for programmers to create dialog box templates by hand. Using Visual C++'s Insert/Resource command, you can insert a dialog box resource into a project and edit it visually. Figure 8-1 shows the Visual C++ dialog editor at work. You add controls to a dialog box by picking them from the Controls toolbar and literally drawing them into the dialog window. (If the Controls toolbar isn't visible, you can make it visible by selecting Customize from the Tools menu, clicking the Toolbars tab, and placing a check mark next to Controls.) You modify a dialog box's properties—its STYLE, CAPTION, FONT, and so on—by making selections in the dialog box's property sheet, which you display by right-clicking the dialog box and selecting Properties from the context menu.

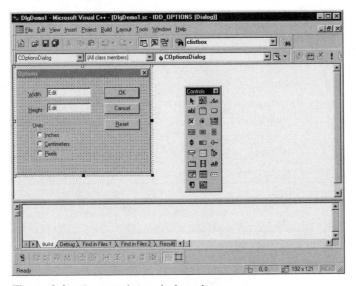

Figure 8-1. *The Visual C++ dialog editor.*

The Dialog Box Keyboard Interface

Windows supplies every dialog box with a keyboard interface that lets the user move the input focus among controls with the Tab key, cycle among the controls within a group using the arrow keys, and more. When you define a dialog box template in an RC file, you implicitly define the dialog box's keyboard interface, too. Here are the elements of the dialog box template that affect the keyboard interface:

- The order in which the controls are defined

- The use of ampersands in control text to designate shortcut keys

- The use of the WS_GROUP style to group controls

- The use of DEFPUSHBUTTON to designate the default push button

The order of the control-creation statements in the dialog template determines the *tab order*—the order in which the input focus is passed around when the user presses Tab or Shift-Tab. Most dialog editors, including the one that's built into Visual C++, let you specify the tab order visually. Under the hood, they simply reorder the resource statements to match the tab order. A control can't be tabbed to unless it includes the style WS_TABSTOP. That's why many of the resource statements discussed in the previous section include WS_TABSTOP by default.

Dialog boxes support shortcut keys for those users who prefer the keyboard over the mouse. You can create a shortcut key for a push button, a radio button, or a check box control by preceding the shortcut character in the control text with an ampersand, as in

```
PUSHBUTTON "&Reset", IDC_RESET, 112, 34, 40, 24, WS_GROUP
```

Now presses of Alt-R (or simply R if the input focus rests on another button control) will click the Reset button unless another control has been assigned the same mnemonic, in which case repeated presses of the shortcut key will cycle the input focus between the two controls. For list boxes, edit controls, and other controls that have no control text per se, you define a shortcut key by preceding the statement that creates the control with a statement that creates a static control and including an ampersand in the static control's text. For example, the statements

```
LTEXT      "&Name", -1, 8, 14, 24, 8
EDITTEXT   IDC_NAME, 34, 12, 118, 12, ES_AUTOHSCROLL
```

create a static control labeled "Name" and a single-line edit control to the right of it. Pressing Alt-N moves the input focus to the edit control.

Another element of the keyboard interface to consider when creating a dialog box template, especially if the dialog box includes radio buttons, is the grouping of the controls. Recall from Chapter 7 that BS_AUTORADIOBUTTON-style radio buttons must be grouped if Windows is to uncheck all the other buttons in the group when one of the buttons is clicked. Windows also uses radio button groupings to determine how to cycle the input focus among radio buttons when the arrow keys are pressed. To define a group of radio buttons, first make sure that the buttons occupy consecutive positions in the tab order—that is, if the first button in the group is control number 5 in the tab order, that the second button is number 6, that the third button is number 7, and so on. Then assign the style WS_GROUP to the first radio button in the group and to the first control that comes after the group in the tab order. Windows programmers often assign WS_GROUP to push buttons and check boxes, too, so that the arrow keys won't move the input focus when the input focus rests on a push button or a check box.

A final point to consider as you design a dialog box's keyboard interface is which push button should serve as the default. In most dialog boxes, you designate one push button (typically the OK button) as the default push button by creating it with a DEFPUSHBUTTON statement or assigning it the BS_DEFPUSHBUTTON style. When the Enter key is pressed, Windows simulates a click of the default push button in the dialog box. If the input focus is on a non-push-button control, the default push button is the one designated as the default in the dialog box template. As the input focus is cycled among push buttons, however, the "defaultness" moves with it. You can always tell which push button is the default by the thick border Windows draws around it.

All elements of a dialog box's keyboard interface can be specified visually in the Visual C++ dialog editor. You specify the tab order by selecting Tab Order from the Layout menu and clicking the controls in order. The dialog editor uses numbered boxes to show the tab order, as you can see in Figure 8-2. To apply the WS_GROUP style to a control, check the Group box in the control's property sheet. The property sheet is displayed by clicking the control with the right mouse button and selecting Properties. To make a push button the default push button, check the Default Button box in the button's property sheet.

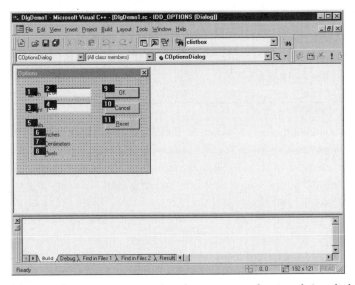

Figure 8-2. *A dialog box's tab order as seen in the Visual C++ dialog editor.*

The *CDialog* Class

For all but the most trivial dialog boxes, the next step in creating a modal dialog is to derive a class from *CDialog* and use it to define the dialog box's behavior. *CDialog* includes three key functions that you can override to initialize the dialog box and respond to clicks of the OK and Cancel buttons: *OnInitDialog*, *OnOK*, and *OnCancel*. Although each of these functions corresponds to a dialog box message, you don't need a message map to process them because *CDialog* does the message mapping for you and exposes the corresponding functions as ordinary virtual functions. *CDialog* also provides default implementations of all three, so you can frequently get away without overriding any of them if you take advantage of MFC's Dialog Data Exchange and Dialog Data Validation mechanisms, which we'll cover later in this chapter.

When a dialog box is created, it receives a WM_CREATE message just as any other window does. But when the WM_CREATE message arrives, the controls specified in the dialog box template have yet to be created and therefore can't be initialized. The dialog box is, in effect, empty. The internal window procedure that Windows uses to process dialog box messages responds to WM_CREATE messages by creating the dialog box's controls. After its controls are created, the dialog box receives a WM_INITDIALOG message affording it the opportunity to perform any necessary initializations, including those involving the controls. In a *CDialog*-derived class, the WM_INITDIALOG message activates the dialog box's *OnInitDialog* function, which is prototyped as follows:

```
virtual BOOL OnInitDialog ()
```

OnInitDialog is where you do anything you need to do to get the dialog box ready for action—for example, check a radio button or insert text into an edit control. At the moment *OnInitDialog* is called, the dialog box is extant in memory but not yet visible on the screen. The user won't see what you do in *OnInitDialog*, but he or she *will* see the results.

The value returned from *OnInitDialog* tells Windows what to do with the input focus. If *OnInitDialog* returns TRUE, Windows assigns the input focus to the first control in the tab order. To assign the input focus to a control other than the first one, call that control's *SetFocus* function in *OnInitDialog* and return FALSE from *OnInitDialog* to prevent Windows from setting the input focus itself. You can get a *CWnd* pointer through which to call *SetFocus* by passing the control ID to *GetDlgItem*, as demonstrated here:

```
GetDlgItem (IDC_EDIT)->SetFocus ();
```

If you override *OnInitDialog*, you should call the base class's *OnInitDialog* handler for reasons that we'll get into shortly.

When the user clicks the dialog box's OK button, the dialog box receives a WM_COMMAND message reporting the button click, and MFC in turn calls the dialog's virtual *OnOK* function. For this mechanism to work properly, you must assign the OK button the special ID value IDOK, as shown in the following resource statement:

```
DEFPUSHBUTTON "OK", IDOK, 60, 34, 40, 24, WS_GROUP
```

You can override *OnOK* to perform specialized processing before the dialog box is dismissed, which might include extracting data from the controls in the dialog box and possibly validating the data (for example, making sure that a numeric value retrieved from an edit control falls within an allowable range). If you do provide your own implementation of *OnOK*, be sure to close it out by calling *EndDialog* to dismiss the dialog box or by calling the base class's *OnOK* handler to dismiss it for you. Otherwise, the dialog box won't disappear when OK is clicked.

You must assign a Cancel button the predefined ID IDCANCEL for *OnCancel* to be called when the button is clicked. Be aware that even if your dialog box doesn't include a Cancel button, *OnCancel* will still be called if the Esc key is pressed or the close button in the dialog box's title bar is clicked. *OnCancel* isn't usually overridden because data typically doesn't need to be read from the dialog's controls if changes are canceled. *CDialog::OnCancel* calls *EndDialog* with an IDCANCEL parameter to dismiss the dialog box and inform the caller that changes in the dialog box controls should be ignored.

With the exception of the WM_INITDIALOG message, which is unique to dialog boxes, dialog boxes receive the same messages that conventional windows do. You can map any of these messages to the dialog class's member functions using a message map. For example, if your dialog box includes a Reset button whose ID is IDC_RESET and you want *OnReset* to be called when the button is clicked, you can use the following message-map entry to connect the two:

```
ON_BN_CLICKED (IDC_RESET, OnReset)
```

Dialog boxes can even handle WM_PAINT messages—somewhat unusual but doable nonetheless. Most dialog boxes don't need *OnPaint* handlers because controls repaint themselves when the area of the dialog box that they occupy is invalidated.

Getting Help from ClassWizard

Although deriving dialog classes from *CDialog* by hand is perfectly acceptable, most MFC programmers today prefer to let ClassWizard do it for them. It's easy: invoke ClassWizard, click its Add Class button, select New from the menu that appears under the button, and fill in a class name, base class name (*CDialog*), and resource ID, as shown in Figure 8-3. The resource ID that you specify must be that of a dialog resource. If you want to override *OnInitDialog*, *OnOK*, or *OnCancel* in the derived class, you can do so after ClassWizard has performed the derivation.

That's one way to get to ClassWizard's New Class dialog box, but it's not the only way. In the dialog editor, double-click the body of the dialog box. Visual C++ will prompt you with a message asking if you want to create a new class. If you answer OK, ClassWizard will pop up and the New Class dialog box will appear with the name of the base class and the resource ID already filled in.

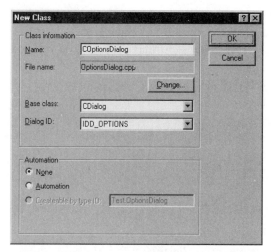

Figure 8-3. *Using ClassWizard to derive from CDialog.*

You can also use ClassWizard to write message handlers for a dialog's controls. Suppose you want to write a BN_CLICKED handler for a push button, and the push button's control ID is IDC_RESET. Here's how to go about it:

1. Right-click the dialog class in the ClassView window.

2. Select Add Windows Message Handler from the context menu.

3. Select the button ID (IDC_RESET) in the Class Or Object To Handle box.

4. Click BN_CLICKED in the New Windows Messages/Events box.

5. Click the Add Handler button, and enter a function name.

When you're done, the function whose name you entered will be present in the dialog class and will be wired to the push button via an ON_BN_CLICKED entry in the dialog's message map.

Creating a Modal Dialog Box

Once you've defined the dialog box template and declared the dialog class, creating a modal dialog box is a simple matter of constructing an object from your *CDialog*-derived class and calling that object's *DoModal* function. *DoModal* doesn't return until after the dialog box is dismissed. When *DoModal* does return, its return value is the value that was passed to *EndDialog*. Applications typically test the *DoModal* return value and take action only if the return value is IDOK, indicating that the dialog box was dismissed with the OK button. If the return value is anything else (most likely IDCANCEL), the information entered into the dialog box is ignored.

CDialog defines two constructors: one that accepts a string dialog template resource ID and a *CWnd* pointer identifying the dialog box's owner, and another that accepts an integer dialog template resource ID and a *CWnd* pointer identifying the dialog box's owner. The *CWnd* pointer can be omitted, in which case the application's main window becomes the dialog's owner. To make derived dialog classes more objectlike and more self-contained, MFC programmers often provide their own constructors that build in references to the dialog templates. You could write a simple inline constructor for *CMyDialog* like this:

```
CMyDialog::CMyDialog (CWnd* pParentWnd = NULL) :
    CDialog (IDD_MYDIALOG, pParentWnd) {}
```

This constructor simplifies the code that creates the dialog box and eliminates the possibility of inadvertently passing the constructor the wrong resource identifier:

```
CMyDialog dlg;
dlg.DoModal ();
```

When the user dismisses the dialog box by clicking OK or Cancel, *DoModal* returns and the function that called *DoModal* continues. If the action taken following the call to *DoModal* depends on whether the data entered in the dialog box was okayed or canceled (and it almost inevitably will), you can test the return value, like this:

```
CMyDialog dlg;
if (dlg.DoModal () == IDOK) {
    // The user clicked OK; do something!
}
```

By default, the only values *DoModal* will return are IDOK and IDCANCEL. However, you can write your dialog class to return other values by calling *EndDialog* with a value other than IDOK or IDCANCEL. You could, for example, include an End This Application button in a dialog box and wire it into the program as follows:

```
// In the dialog class
BEGIN_MESSAGE_MAP (CMyDialog, CDialog)
    ON_BN_CLICKED (IDC_ENDAPP, OnEndThisApplication)
END_MESSAGE_MAP ()
    .
    .
    .
void CMyDialog::OnEndThisApplication ()
{
    EndDialog (IDC_ENDAPP);
}
```

```
// Elsewhere in the application
CMyDialog dlg;
int nReturn = dlg.DoModal ();
if (nReturn == IDOK) {
    // The user clicked OK; do something!
}
else if (nReturn == IDC_ENDAPP)
    PostMessage (WM_CLOSE, 0, 0);
```

When the user clicks End This Application in the dialog box, the return value IDC_ENDAPP alerts the caller that the user wants to terminate the application. Consequently, a WM_CLOSE message is posted to the message queue to initiate a shutdown. IDC_ENDAPP and other user-defined values passed to *EndDialog* should be assigned ID values equal to 3 or higher to avoid conflicting with the predefined IDOK and IDCANCEL button IDs.

Dialog Data Exchange and Dialog Data Validation

A typical dialog box presents a list of options to the user, gathers input regarding those options, and makes that input available to the application that created the dialog box. A convenient way to expose the input is to map it to public member variables in the dialog class. The application that uses the dialog box can then access the data by reading or writing the dialog object's member variables.

Suppose your dialog box contains two single-line edit controls in which the user enters a name and a phone number. To expose the name and number input by the user to the application that creates the dialog, declare two *CString* member variables in your dialog class:

```
class CMyDialog : public CDialog
{
public:
    CMyDialog::CMyDialog (CWnd* pParentWnd = NULL) :
        CDialog (IDD_MYDIALOG, pParentWnd) {}
    CString m_strName;
    CString m_strPhone;
        :
        :
};
```

To solicit a name and phone number from the user, display the dialog and retrieve the values of *m_strName* and *m_strPhone* after the dialog is dismissed:

```
CMyDialog dlg;
if (dlg.DoModal () == IDOK) {
    CString strName = dlg.m_strName;
    CString strPhone = dlg.m_strPhone;
```

(continued)

```
        TRACE (_T ("Name=%s, Phone=%s"), strName, strPhone);
}
```

You could modify the code slightly to initialize the edit controls with a default name and phone number:

```
CMyDialog dlg;
dlg.m_strName = _T ("Jeff");
dlg.m_strPhone = _T ("555-1212");
if (dlg.DoModal () == IDOK) {
    CString strName = dlg.m_strName;
    CString strPhone = dlg.m_strPhone;
    TRACE (_T ("Name=%s, Phone=%s"), strName, strPhone);
}
```

These examples assume that *m_strName* and *m_strPhone* are intrinsically linked to the dialog's edit controls—that is, that the strings assigned to these variables are magically inserted into the edit controls and that strings read from these variables are the strings the user entered into the edit controls.

The coupling of a dialog's controls and data members doesn't happen by itself; you have to make it happen. One way to perform the coupling is to override *OnInitDialog* and *OnOK* in the derived dialog class and include code that transfers data between the controls and the data members. Assuming the edit controls' IDs are IDC_NAME and IDC_PHONE, here's a revised version of *CMyDialog* that demonstrates this technique:

```
class CMyDialog : public CDialog
{
public:
    CMyDialog::CMyDialog (CWnd* pParentWnd = NULL) :
        CDialog (IDD_MYDIALOG, pParentWnd) {}
    CString m_strName;
    CString m_strPhone;
protected:
    virtual BOOL OnInitDialog ();
    virtual void OnOK ();
};

BOOL CMyDialog::OnInitDialog ()
{
    CDialog::OnInitDialog ();
    SetDlgItemText (IDC_NAME, m_strName);
    SetDlgItemText (IDC_PHONE, m_strPhone);
    return TRUE;
}

void CMyDialog::OnOK ()
{
    GetDlgItemText (IDC_NAME, m_strName);
    GetDlgItemText (IDC_PHONE, m_strPhone);
```

```
    CDialog::OnOK ();
}
```

Structuring *CMyDialog* this way ensures that strings written to *m_strName* and *m_strPhone* before the dialog is created will appear in the edit controls and that strings entered in those edit controls will be copied to *m_strName* and *m_strPhone* when the dialog is dismissed with the OK button.

Imagine how trivial the implementation of *CMyDialog* would be if you didn't have to initialize the controls in *OnInitDialog* and read them back in *OnOK*—that is, if you could provide a "data map" of sorts correlating controls to member variables. Sound farfetched? It's not. In fact, that's exactly what MFC's Dialog Data Exchange (DDX) mechanism is for. It's simple to use, and in many cases, it completely obviates the need to supply custom *OnInitDialog* and *OnOK* functions, even if your dialog box contains dozens of controls.

You enact DDX by overriding a virtual function named *DoDataExchange* in each class you derive from *CDialog*. In the override, you use DDX functions provided by MFC to transfer data between the dialog's controls and data members. Here's a *DoDataExchange* implementation that links two *CString* data members (*m_strName* and *m_strPhone*) to a pair of edit controls (IDC_NAME and IDC_PHONE):

```
void CMyDialog::DoDataExchange (CDataExchange* pDX)
{
    DDX_Text (pDX, IDC_NAME, m_strName);
    DDX_Text (pDX, IDC_PHONE, m_strPhone);
}
```

MFC calls *DoDataExchange* once when the dialog is created (when the dialog box receives a WM_INITDIALOG message) and again when the OK button is clicked. The *pDX* parameter is a pointer to a *CDataExchange* object supplied by MFC. Among other things, the *CDataExchange* object tells *DDX_Text* in which direction the information is flowing—that is, whether data is being transferred from the data members to the controls or from the controls to the data members. Once it has determined the direction of data flow, *DDX_Text* performs the actual data transfer. Thus, one *DoDataExchange* function is sufficient to copy data from data members to controls when the dialog is created and from the controls to the data members when the dialog is dismissed.

DDX_Text is one of several DDX functions that MFC provides; a partial list is shown in the table on the next page. The relationship between a control and a data member depends on the DDX function connecting the two. For example, an int variable linked to a group of radio buttons with *DDX_Radio* holds a 0-based index identifying one member of the group. If the int's value is 2 when the dialog is created, *DDX_Radio* checks the third button in the group. When the OK button is clicked, *DDX_Radio* copies the index of the currently selected button to the member

DIALOG DATA EXCHANGE (DDX) FUNCTIONS

DDX Function	Description
DDX_Text	Associates a BYTE, an int, a short, a UINT, a long, a DWORD, a *CString*, a string, a float, a double, a *COleDateTime*, or a *COleCurrency* variable with an edit control
DDX_Check	Associates an int variable with a check box control
DDX_Radio	Associates an int variable with a group of radio buttons
DDX_LBIndex	Associates an int variable with a list box
DDX_LBString	Associates a *CString* variable with a list box
DDX_LBStringExact	Associates a *CString* variable with a list box
DDX_CBIndex	Associates an int variable with a combo box
DDX_CBString	Associates a *CString* variable with a combo box
DDX_CBStringExact	Associates a *CString* variable with a combo box
DDX_Scroll	Associates an int variable with a scroll bar

variable. An int connected to a scroll bar with *DDX_Scroll* specifies the position of the scroll bar thumb, and an int associated with a check box with *DDX_Check* specifies the check box's state—BST_CHECKED, BST_UNCHECKED, or, for three-state check boxes, BST_INDETERMINATE. If an int is linked to an edit control with *DDX_Text*, MFC automatically converts the integer into a text string when transferring the value to the edit control and the string to an integer when transferring data from the edit control.

A related mechanism called Dialog Data Validation (DDV) allows MFC to validate the values entered into a dialog's controls before the dialog is dismissed. DDV functions fall into two categories: those that validate numeric variables to ensure that they fall within specified limits and one that validates a *CString* variable to verify that its length doesn't exceed a certain value. Here's a *DoDataExchange* function that uses *DDX_Text* to connect an int member variable to an edit control and *DDV_MinMaxInt* to perform a range check on the value when the dialog's OK button is clicked:

```
void CMyDialog::DoDataExchange (CDataExchange* pDX)
{
    DDX_Text (pDX, IDC_COUNT, m_nCount);
    DDV_MinMaxInt (pDX, m_nCount, 0, 100);
}
```

If the value displayed in the edit control is less than 0 or greater than 100 when OK is clicked, *DDV_MinMaxInt* transfers the input focus to the control and displays an error message. For a given data member, the DDV function call should immediately follow the DDX function call to enable MFC to set the input focus to the proper control if the validation proves negative.

DDV_MinMaxInt is one of several DDV functions that MFC provides. The following table lists the DDV functions that pertain to the classic controls. The DDV range-validation routines are not overloaded to accept multiple data types, so if you write a *DoDataExchange* function by hand, you must be careful to match the function to the data type.

DIALOG DATA VALIDATION (DDV) FUNCTIONS

Function	*Description*
DDV_MinMaxByte	Verifies that a BYTE value falls within specified limits
DDV_MinMaxInt	Verifies that an int value falls within specified limits
DDV_MinMaxLong	Verifies that a long value falls within specified limits
DDV_MinMaxUInt	Verifies that a UINT value falls within specified limits
DDV_MinMaxDWord	Verifies that a DWORD value falls within specified limits
DDV_MinMaxFloat	Verifies that a float value falls within specified limits
DDV_MinMaxDouble	Verifies that a double value falls within specified limits
DDV_MaxChars	On entry, uses an EM_LIMITTEXT message to limit the number of characters that can be entered into an edit control; on exit, verifies that the control contains no more than the specified number of characters

The code that drives DDX and DDV is found in *CDialog*. When the dialog box is created, *CDialog::OnInitDialog* calls the *UpdateData* function a dialog object inherits from *CWnd* with a FALSE parameter. *UpdateData*, in turn, creates a *CDataExchange* object and calls the dialog's *DoDataExchange* function, passing it a pointer to the *CDataExchange* object. Each DDX function called by *DoDataExchange* initializes a control using the value of a member variable. Later, when the user clicks OK, *CDialog::OnOK* calls *UpdateData* with a TRUE parameter, causing the DDX functions to do just the opposite of what they did earlier. Any DDV functions present in *DoDataExchange* take this opportunity to validate the user's input. Earlier I mentioned the importance of calling the base class's *OnOK* and *OnInitDialog* functions if you override them in a derived class. Now you know why. If you fail to call the base class implementations of these functions, the framework won't get the opportunity to call *UpdateData* and DDX and DDV won't work.

What DDX and DDV amount to is a painless way to get data in and out of dialog box controls and perform simple validation procedures on the data. In practice, DDX and DDV prevent you from having to override *OnInitDialog* and *OnOK* simply to transfer data between a dialog's controls and data members.

More Help from ClassWizard

In an application crafted with the MFC wizards, you can add DDX and DDV functions to *DoDataExchange* by hand, or you can let ClassWizard add them for you. ClassWizard will even add member variables to a dialog class for you. Here's the procedure for adding a data member to a dialog class *and* associating it with a control via DDX or DDV:

1. Invoke ClassWizard, and go to the Member Variables page. (See Figure 8-4.)

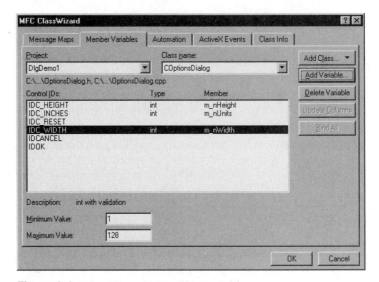

Figure 8-4. *ClassWizard's Member Variables page.*

2. Select the dialog class's name in the Class Name box.

3. Highlight the ID of the control that you want to associate with a member variable in the Control IDs box, and click the Add Variable button.

4. Type the member variable name into the Add Member Variable dialog box shown in Figure 8-5, and select the variable type from the Variable Type box. Then click OK.

If you examine the dialog class's source code after dismissing ClassWizard, you'll find that ClassWizard has added the member variable to the class declaration and also added a DDX statement to *DoDataExchange* connecting the member variable to a control. If the variable type is numeric, you can enter minimum and maximum values into the edit controls at the bottom of the Member Variables page and ClassWizard will add a *DDV_MinMax* statement, too. For string variables, you can enter a maximum character count and ClassWizard will add a *DDV_MaxChars* statement.

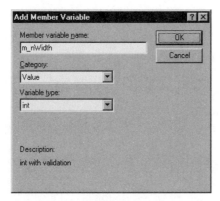

Figure 8-5. *ClassWizard's Add Member Variable dialog box.*

Interacting with the Controls in a Dialog

Does the presence of DDX and DDV mean that you'll never again have to write code to interact with the controls in a dialog box? Hardly. You might, for example, need to call *CListBox* functions on a list box control to add strings to the list box in *OnInitDialog*. To do that, you'll need a *CListBox* pointer to the list box. The question is, How do you get that pointer?

You can get a *CWnd* pointer to any control in a dialog with *CWnd::GetDlgItem*. The following code sample uses *GetDlgItem* and *CWnd::EnableWindow* to interactively enable the control whose ID is IDC_CHECK:

```
CWnd* pWnd = GetDlgItem (IDC_CHECK);
pWnd->EnableWindow (TRUE);
```

This code works fine because *GetDlgItem* returns a generic *CWnd* pointer and *EnableWindow* is a *CWnd* function. But consider the following code sample:

```
CListBox* pListBox = (CListBox*) GetDlgItem (IDC_LIST);
pListBox->AddString (_T ("One"));
pListBox->AddString (_T ("Two"));
pListBox->AddString (_T ("Three"));
```

This code works, but only because MFC is specifically architected to make it work. Because *GetDlgItem* returns a *CWnd* pointer, casting it to a *CListBox* pointer and calling a *CListBox* function through it is poor programming practice at best and dangerous at worst. In fact, in some situations, this technique simply won't work.

A better solution for calling non-*CWnd* functions on a control in a dialog box is MFC's *CWnd::Attach* function. With *Attach*, you can declare an instance of a control class (for example, *CListBox*) and dynamically attach it to a dialog box control. Here's how you'd use *Attach* to add strings to a list box.

```
CListBox wndListBox;
wndListBox.Attach (GetDlgItem (IDC_LIST)->m_hWnd);
wndListBox.AddString (_T ("One"));
wndListBox.AddString (_T ("Two"));
wndListBox.AddString (_T ("Three"));
wndListBox.Detach ();
```

When a *CListBox* object is declared on the stack as shown in this example, it's important to call *Detach* before the *CListBox* object goes out of scope. Otherwise, *CListBox*'s destructor will destroy the list box and the list box will suddenly disappear from the dialog box.

MFC's *DDX_Control* function offers a seamless mechanism for attaching an instance of an MFC control class to a control in a dialog box. Placing the following statement in a derived dialog class's *DoDataExchange* function transparently connects a *CListBox* data member named *m_wndListBox* to a list box control whose ID is IDC_LIST:

```
DDX_Control (pDX, IDC_LIST, m_wndListBox);
```

Now adding strings to the list box is a simple matter of calling *AddString* on *m_wndListBox*:

```
m_wndListBox.AddString (_T ("One"));
m_wndListBox.AddString (_T ("Two"));
m_wndListBox.AddString (_T ("Three"));
```

DDX_Control offers added value because rather than simply encapsulate a control's window handle as *Attach* does, *DDX_Control* dynamically subclasses the control so that messages sent to the control first pass through the object specified in *DDX_Control*'s third parameter. This is the easiest and most effective way to make a control in a dialog box behave like an object of a derived control class—for example, to make an edit control behave like a *CNumEdit* instead of an ordinary *CEdit*. You'll see an example demonstrating how to use a derived control class in a dialog box in the Phones application at the end of this chapter.

You can use ClassWizard to add *DDX_Control* statements to *DoDataExchange*. To do it, go to the Member Variables page and use the Add Variable button to add a member variable to the dialog class. But this time, select Control rather than Value in the Add Member Variable dialog box's Category box. Then pick a control class in the Variable Type box and click OK until you exit ClassWizard. Now, if you check the dialog class, you'll find that ClassWizard has added both the member variable and a *DDX_Control* statement connecting the variable to the control.

The DlgDemo1 Application

The DlgDemo1 application pictured in Figure 8-6 is a simple view-based program that draws a colored rectangle in the upper left corner of the view. The File menu features an Options command that displays a dialog box through which you can alter the rectangle's width, height, and units of measurement.

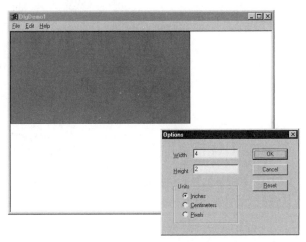

Figure 8-6. *The DlgDemo1 window and dialog box.*

I created DlgDemo1 with AppWizard and used ClassWizard to derive the dialog class, write message handlers, and so on. Portions of the source code are reproduced in Figure 8-7. The dialog box is an instance of *COptionsDialog*, which encapsulates the dialog resource IDD_OPTIONS. *COptionsDialog* has three public data members—*m_nWidth*, *m_nHeight*, and *m_nUnits*—which represent the rectangle's width, height, and units of measurement, respectively. Each data member is bound to a control (or group of controls) in the dialog box via DDX. An *m_nUnits* value equal to 0 represents inches, while 1 represents centimeters and 2 represents pixels. The view class *CChildView* contains identically named member variables that *CChildView::OnPaint* uses to paint the rectangle.

When the Options command is selected from the File menu, the command handler *CChildView::OnFileOptions* instantiates *COptionsDialog*; copies the current width, height, and units values to the dialog object's member variables; and displays the dialog with *DoModal*. If *DoModal* returns IDOK, *OnFileOptions* reads the width, height, and units values from the dialog's data members and copies them to the view's data members. Then it calls *Invalidate* to repaint the view, which refreshes the rectangle to conform to the new parameters.

MainFrm.h

```
// MainFrm.h : interface of the CMainFrame class
//
/////////////////////////////////////////////////////////////////////////////

#if !defined(AFX_MAINFRM_H__AC8095E8_902A_11D2_8E53_006008A82731__INCLUDED_)
#define AFX_MAINFRM_H__AC8095E8_902A_11D2_8E53_006008A82731__INCLUDED_

#if _MSC_VER > 1000
#pragma once
#endif // _MSC_VER > 1000

#include "ChildView.h"

class CMainFrame : public CFrameWnd
{

public:
    CMainFrame();
protected:
    DECLARE_DYNAMIC(CMainFrame)

// Attributes
public:

// Operations
public:

// Overrides
    // ClassWizard generated virtual function overrides
    //{{AFX_VIRTUAL(CMainFrame)
    virtual BOOL PreCreateWindow(CREATESTRUCT& cs);
    virtual BOOL OnCmdMsg(UINT nID, int nCode, void* pExtra,
        AFX_CMDHANDLERINFO* pHandlerInfo);
    //}}AFX_VIRTUAL
// Implementation
public:
    virtual ~CMainFrame();
#ifdef _DEBUG
    virtual void AssertValid() const;
    virtual void Dump(CDumpContext& dc) const;
#endif
    CChildView    m_wndView;

// Generated message map functions
protected:
```

Figure 8-7. *The DlgDemo1 application.*

```
    //{{AFX_MSG(CMainFrame)
    afx_msg void OnSetFocus(CWnd *pOldWnd);
    afx_msg int OnCreate(LPCREATESTRUCT lpCreateStruct);
    //}}AFX_MSG
    DECLARE_MESSAGE_MAP()
};


/////////////////////////////////////////////////////////////////////////


//{{AFX_INSERT_LOCATION}}
// Microsoft Visual C++ will insert additional declarations
// immediately before the previous line.

#endif
// !defined(AFX_MAINFRM_H__AC8095E8_902A_11D2_8E53_006008A82731__INCLUDED_)
```

MainFrm.cpp

```
// MainFrm.cpp : implementation of the CMainFrame class
//

#include "stdafx.h"
#include "DlgDemo1.h"

#include "MainFrm.h"

#ifdef _DEBUG
#define new DEBUG_NEW
#undef THIS_FILE
static char THIS_FILE[] = __FILE__;
#endif

/////////////////////////////////////////////////////////////////////////
// CMainFrame

IMPLEMENT_DYNAMIC(CMainFrame, CFrameWnd)

BEGIN_MESSAGE_MAP(CMainFrame, CFrameWnd)
    //{{AFX_MSG_MAP(CMainFrame)

    ON_WM_SETFOCUS()
    ON_WM_CREATE()
    //}}AFX_MSG_MAP
END_MESSAGE_MAP()


/////////////////////////////////////////////////////////////////////////
// CMainFrame construction/destruction
```

(continued)

Figure 8-7. *continued*

```
CMainFrame::CMainFrame()
{
}


CMainFrame::~CMainFrame()
{
}


BOOL CMainFrame::PreCreateWindow(CREATESTRUCT& cs)
{
    if( !CFrameWnd::PreCreateWindow(cs) )
        return FALSE;
    cs.dwExStyle &= ~WS_EX_CLIENTEDGE;
    cs.lpszClass = AfxRegisterWndClass(0);
    return TRUE;
}


/////////////////////////////////////////////////////////////////////////////
// CMainFrame diagnostics

#ifdef _DEBUG
void CMainFrame::AssertValid() const
{
    CFrameWnd::AssertValid();
}


void CMainFrame::Dump(CDumpContext& dc) const
{
    CFrameWnd::Dump(dc);
}


#endif //_DEBUG


/////////////////////////////////////////////////////////////////////////////
// CMainFrame message handlers
void CMainFrame::OnSetFocus(CWnd* pOldWnd)
{
    // forward focus to the view window
    m_wndView.SetFocus();
}


BOOL CMainFrame::OnCmdMsg(UINT nID, int nCode, void* pExtra,
    AFX_CMDHANDLERINFO* pHandlerInfo)
{
    // let the view have first crack at the command
    if (m_wndView.OnCmdMsg(nID, nCode, pExtra, pHandlerInfo))
        return TRUE;
```

```
    // otherwise, do default handling
    return CFrameWnd::OnCmdMsg(nID, nCode, pExtra, pHandlerInfo);
}

int CMainFrame::OnCreate(LPCREATESTRUCT lpCreateStruct)
{
    if (CFrameWnd::OnCreate(lpCreateStruct) == -1)
        return -1;

    if (!m_wndView.Create(NULL, NULL, AFX_WS_DEFAULT_VIEW,
        CRect(0, 0, 0, 0), this, AFX_IDW_PANE_FIRST, NULL))
        return -1;

    return 0;
}
```

ChildView.h

```
// ChildView.h : interface of the CChildView class
//
/////////////////////////////////////////////////////////////////////////

#if !defined(AFX_CHILDVIEW_H__AC8095EA_902A_11D2_8E53_006008A82731__INCLUDED_)

#define AFX_CHILDVIEW_H__AC8095EA_902A_11D2_8E53_006008A82731__INCLUDED_

#if _MSC_VER > 1000
#pragma once
#endif // _MSC_VER > 1000


/////////////////////////////////////////////////////////////////////////
// CChildView window

class CChildView : public CWnd
{
// Construction
public:
    CChildView();

// Attributes
public:

// Operations
public:
```

(continued)

Figure 8-7. *continued*

```
// Overrides
    // ClassWizard generated virtual function overrides
    //{{AFX_VIRTUAL(CChildView)
    protected:
    virtual BOOL PreCreateWindow(CREATESTRUCT& cs);
    //}}AFX_VIRTUAL

// Implementation
public:
    virtual ~CChildView();

    // Generated message map functions
protected:
    int m_nUnits;
    int m_nHeight;
    int m_nWidth;
    //{{AFX_MSG(CChildView)
    afx_msg void OnPaint();
    afx_msg void OnFileOptions();
    //}}AFX_MSG
    DECLARE_MESSAGE_MAP()
};


/////////////////////////////////////////////////////////////////////////////

//{{AFX_INSERT_LOCATION}}
// Microsoft Visual C++ will insert additional declarations immediately
// before the previous line.

#endif
//defined(AFX_CHILDVIEW_H__AC8095EA_902A_11D2_8E53_006008A82731__INCLUDED_)
```

ChildView.cpp

```
// ChildView.cpp : implementation of the CChildView class
//

#include "stdafx.h"
#include "DlgDemo1.h"
#include "OptionsDialog.h"
#include "ChildView.h"

#ifdef _DEBUG
#define new DEBUG_NEW
#undef THIS_FILE
```

```
static char THIS_FILE[] = __FILE__;
#endif

/////////////////////////////////////////////////////////////////////////
// CChildView

CChildView::CChildView()
{
    m_nWidth = 4;
    m_nHeight = 2;
    m_nUnits = 0;
}

CChildView::~CChildView()
{
}

BEGIN_MESSAGE_MAP(CChildView,CWnd )
    //{{AFX_MSG_MAP(CChildView)
    ON_WM_PAINT()
    ON_COMMAND(ID_FILE_OPTIONS, OnFileOptions)
    //}}AFX_MSG_MAP
END_MESSAGE_MAP()

/////////////////////////////////////////////////////////////////////////
// CChildView message handlers

BOOL CChildView::PreCreateWindow(CREATESTRUCT& cs)
{
    if (!CWnd::PreCreateWindow(cs))
        return FALSE;

    cs.dwExStyle |= WS_EX_CLIENTEDGE;
    cs.style &= ~WS_BORDER;
    cs.lpszClass = AfxRegisterWndClass(CS_HREDRAW|CS_VREDRAW|CS_DBLCLKS,
        ::LoadCursor(NULL, IDC_ARROW), HBRUSH(COLOR_WINDOW+1), NULL);

    return TRUE;
}

void CChildView::OnPaint()
{
    CPaintDC dc(this); // Device context for painting.

    CBrush brush (RGB (255, 0, 255));
    CBrush* pOldBrush = dc.SelectObject (&brush);
```

(continued)

Figure 8-7. *continued*

```
    switch (m_nUnits) {

    case 0: // Inches.
        dc.SetMapMode (MM_LOENGLISH);
        dc.Rectangle (0, 0, m_nWidth * 100, -m_nHeight * 100);
        break;

    case 1: // Centimeters.
        dc.SetMapMode (MM_LOMETRIC);
        dc.Rectangle (0, 0, m_nWidth * 100, -m_nHeight * 100);
        break;

    case 2: // Pixels.
        dc.SetMapMode (MM_TEXT);
        dc.Rectangle (0, 0, m_nWidth, m_nHeight);
        break;
    }
    dc.SelectObject (pOldBrush);
}

void CChildView::OnFileOptions()
{
    COptionsDialog dlg;

    dlg.m_nWidth = m_nWidth;
    dlg.m_nHeight = m_nHeight;
    dlg.m_nUnits = m_nUnits;

    if (dlg.DoModal () == IDOK) {
        m_nWidth = dlg.m_nWidth;
        m_nHeight = dlg.m_nHeight;
        m_nUnits = dlg.m_nUnits;
        Invalidate ();
    }
}
```

OptionsDialog.h

```
#if !defined(AFX_OPTIONSDIALOG_H__AC8095F0_902A_11D2_8E53_006008A82731__INCLUDED_)
#define AFX_OPTIONSDIALOG_H__AC8095F0_902A_11D2_8E53_006008A82731__INCLUDED_

#if _MSC_VER > 1000
#pragma once
#endif // _MSC_VER > 1000
// OptionsDialog.h : header file
//
```

Chapter 8 **Dialog Boxes and Property Sheets**

```
/////////////////////////////////////////////////////////////////////////
// COptionsDialog dialog

class COptionsDialog : public CDialog
{
// Construction
public:
    COptionsDialog(CWnd* pParent = NULL);   // standard constructor

// Dialog Data
    //{{AFX_DATA(COptionsDialog)
    enum { IDD = IDD_OPTIONS };
    int        m_nWidth;
    int        m_nHeight;
    int        m_nUnits;
    //}}AFX_DATA

// Overrides
    // ClassWizard generated virtual function overrides
    //{{AFX_VIRTUAL(COptionsDialog)
    protected:
    virtual void DoDataExchange(CDataExchange* pDX);    // DDX/DDV support
    //}}AFX_VIRTUAL

// Implementation
protected:

    // Generated message map functions
    //{{AFX_MSG(COptionsDialog)
    afx_msg void OnReset();
    //}}AFX_MSG
    DECLARE_MESSAGE_MAP()
};

//{{AFX_INSERT_LOCATION}}
// Microsoft Visual C++ will insert additional declarations immediately
// before the previous line.

#endif
//!defined(
//    AFX_OPTIONSDIALOG_H__AC8095F0_902A_11D2_8E53_006008A82731__INCLUDED_)
```

OptionsDialog.cpp

```
// OptionsDialog.cpp : implementation file
//
```

(continued)

Figure 8-7. *continued*

```
#include "stdafx.h"
#include "DlgDemo1.h"
#include "OptionsDialog.h"

#ifdef _DEBUG
#define new DEBUG_NEW
#undef THIS_FILE
static char THIS_FILE[] = __FILE__;
#endif

/////////////////////////////////////////////////////////////////////////////
// COptionsDialog dialog

COptionsDialog::COptionsDialog(CWnd* pParent /*=NULL*/)
    : CDialog(COptionsDialog::IDD, pParent)
{
    //{{AFX_DATA_INIT(COptionsDialog)
    m_nWidth = 0;
    m_nHeight = 0;
    m_nUnits = -1;
    //}}AFX_DATA_INIT
}

void COptionsDialog::DoDataExchange(CDataExchange* pDX)
{
    CDialog::DoDataExchange(pDX);
    //{{AFX_DATA_MAP(COptionsDialog)
    DDX_Text(pDX, IDC_WIDTH, m_nWidth);
    DDV_MinMaxInt(pDX, m_nWidth, 1, 128);
    DDX_Text(pDX, IDC_HEIGHT, m_nHeight);
    DDX_Radio(pDX, IDC_INCHES, m_nUnits);
    //}}AFX_DATA_MAP
}

BEGIN_MESSAGE_MAP(COptionsDialog, CDialog)
    //{{AFX_MSG_MAP(COptionsDialog)
    ON_BN_CLICKED(IDC_RESET, OnReset)
    //}}AFX_MSG_MAP
END_MESSAGE_MAP()

/////////////////////////////////////////////////////////////////////////////
// COptionsDialog message handlers

void COptionsDialog::OnReset()
{
    m_nWidth = 4;
    m_nHeight = 2;

    m_nUnits = 0;
    UpdateData (FALSE);
}
```

Here's a synopsis of the procedure I used to write DlgDemo1. You can create the application, too, by following these steps:

1. Use AppWizard to create a project named DlgDemo1. In AppWizard's Step 1 dialog box, choose Single Document as the application type and uncheck the Document/View Architecture Support box. Uncheck the following boxes in the Step 3 and Step 4 dialog boxes:

   - ❏ ActiveX Controls
   - ❏ 3D Controls
   - ❏ Docking Toolbar
   - ❏ Initial Status Bar

   Accept the AppWizard defaults everywhere else.

2. Add the following member variables to *CChildView*. Make the member variables protected, and initialize them in the view's constructor.

Variable Name	Type	Initial Value
m_nWidth	int	4
m_nHeight	int	2
m_nUnits	int	0

3. Implement the view's *OnPaint* function.

4. To compensate for a bug in Visual C++ 6.0, add a WM_CREATE message handler to the frame window class *CMainFrame* and add code to create the view.

5. Use the Insert-Resource command to add a new dialog resource to the project. Change the dialog's resource ID to IDD_OPTIONS by right-clicking IDD_DIALOG1 in ResourceView, selecting Properties from the context menu, and entering the new ID. While you're at it, change the dialog's caption to "Options."

6. Edit the dialog box so that it resembles the one in Figure 8-6. The table on the following page lists the controls in the dialog box and their IDs. Be sure to create the radio buttons one after another so that they will be assigned consecutive control IDs. The OK and Cancel buttons are provided for you, so you don't need to add them separately.

Control Type	Control Text	Control ID
Static	"&Width"	IDC_STATIC
Static	"&Height"	IDC_STATIC
Edit	None	IDC_WIDTH
Edit	None	IDC_HEIGHT
Group box	"Units"	IDC_STATIC
Radio button	"&Inches"	IDC_INCHES
Radio button	"&Centimeters"	IDC_CENTIMETERS
Radio button	"&Pixels"	IDC_PIXELS
Push button	"&Reset"	IDC_RESET
Push button	"OK"	IDOK
Push button	"Cancel"	IDCANCEL

7. Select Tab Order from the Layout menu, and set the tab order shown in Figure 8-2. You can test the tab order by selecting Tab Order again to exit tab order mode, selecting Test from the Layout menu and using the Tab key to tab among the dialog box's controls. Note that you must manually select one of the radio buttons before the Tab key will move the input focus to a radio button.

8. Let Windows know that the three radio buttons are a group by marking the first control in the group (the Inches radio button) and the first control in the tab order following the final control in the group (the OK button) with the style WS_GROUP. You can test the grouping by choosing Test from the Layout menu, clicking one of the radio buttons, and pressing the up or down arrow key a few times. If the radio buttons are properly grouped, the input focus will cycle among the radio buttons.

9. Double-click the dialog box in the dialog editor, and use ClassWizard to derive a dialog class named *COptionsDialog*. After you dismiss ClassWizard, *COptionsDialog* should appear in the ClassView window.

10. Use ClassWizard to add three int member variables to the dialog class: one (*m_nUnits*) that's linked to the radio button IDC_INCHES, another (*m_nWidth*) that's linked to the IDC_WIDTH edit control, and a third (*m_nHeight*) that's linked to the IDC_HEIGHT edit control. Set the minimum and maximum values for *m_nWidth* and *m_nHeight* to 1 and 128, respectively.

> **NOTE** Be sure that you create int member variables for the edit controls, not *CString* member variables, by selecting int in the Add Member Variable dialog box's Variable Type field. *CString* is the default. If you make a mistake, use the Delete Variable button to delete the member variable and try again.

11. Open the menu resource IDR_MAINFRAME, and add an Options command to the File menu. Enter "&Options..." for the text of the menu item and ID_FILE_OPTIONS for the command ID.

12. Add the following #include to the view's CPP file:

```
#include "OptionsDialog.h"
```

Then add a command handler named *OnFileOptions* to the view class that's called when the Options command is selected. Implement the function as shown in Figure 8-7.

13. Add a BN_CLICKED handler named *OnReset* to the dialog class that sets *m_nWidth* to 4, *m_nHeight* to 2, and *m_nUnits* to 0 when the Reset button is clicked. Implement the handler as shown in Figure 8-7.

14. Run the application, and use the File/Options command to display the Options dialog box. Test your handiwork by entering various widths and heights and selecting different units of measurement.

Notice how *COptionsDialog::OnReset* is implemented. It's perfectly legal to call *UpdateData* yourself to transfer data between a dialog's controls and data members. In this case, *UpdateData* is called with a FALSE paraméter to transfer data from the member variables to the controls. To read data out of the controls and into the member variables, pass *UpdateData* a TRUE parameter.

MODELESS DIALOG BOXES

Once you've mastered modal dialog boxes, you'll discover that modeless dialog boxes are just a variation on what you've already learned. Modal and modeless dialog boxes are more alike than they are different. The key differences between them include the following:

- Whereas a modal dialog box is displayed by calling *CDialog::DoModal*, modeless dialog boxes are displayed with *CDialog::Create*. Unlike *DoModal*, which doesn't return until the dialog box is dismissed, *Create* returns as soon as the dialog box is created. Therefore, the dialog box is still displayed when *Create* returns.

■   Modeless dialog boxes are dismissed by calling *DestroyWindow*, not *End-Dialog*. You mustn't allow *CDialog::OnOK* or *CDialog::OnCancel* to be called on a modeless dialog box, because both call *EndDialog*.

■   Modal dialog classes are usually instantiated on the stack so that destruction is automatic. Modeless dialog classes are instantiated with *new* so that the dialog object won't be destroyed prematurely. One way to ensure that the modeless dialog object is deleted when the dialog box is destroyed is to override *CDialog::PostNcDestroy* in the derived dialog class and execute a *delete this* statement.

There are other differences between modal and modeless dialog boxes that MFC handles for you. For example, the message loop of an SDK application that uses a modeless dialog box must be modified to call *::IsDialogMessage* to forward messages to the dialog box. An MFC application requires no such modification because *::IsDialogMessage* is called automatically.

In general, MFC makes dialog handling generic so that using modeless dialog boxes is little different than using modal dialog boxes. Let's prove it by converting DlgDemo1's dialog box into a modeless dialog box.

The DlgDemo2 Application

Figure 8-8's DlgDemo2 application is functionally identical to DlgDemo1 in all respects but one: the Options dialog box is modeless rather than modal. Following convention, the OK and Cancel buttons are now labeled Apply and Close. The Apply button applies the settings entered in the dialog box to the rectangle but doesn't dismiss the dialog box. The Close button removes the dialog box from the screen and discards any changes, just like the Cancel button in DlgDemo1. Despite the name changes, the button IDs are still IDOK and IDCANCEL. This means that we can still use *OnOK* and *OnCancel* to process button clicks and that Enter and Esc still serve as the buttons' keyboard equivalents.

MainFrm.h

```
// MainFrm.h : interface of the CMainFrame class
//
/////////////////////////////////////////////////////////////////////////////

#if
!defined(AFX_MAINFRM_H__7040DB88_9039_11D2_8E53_006008A82731__INCLUDED_)
#define  AFX_MAINFRM_H__7040DB88_9039_11D2_8E53_006008A82731__INCLUDED_
```

Figure 8-8. *The DlgDemo2 application.*

```
#if _MSC_VER > 1000
#pragma once
#endif // _MSC_VER > 1000

#include "ChildView.h"

class CMainFrame : public CFrameWnd
{

public:
    CMainFrame();
protected:
    DECLARE_DYNAMIC(CMainFrame)

// Attributes
public:

// Operations
public:

// Overrides
    // ClassWizard generated virtual function overrides
    //{{AFX_VIRTUAL(CMainFrame)
    virtual BOOL PreCreateWindow(CREATESTRUCT& cs);
    virtual BOOL OnCmdMsg(UINT nID, int nCode, void* pExtra,
        AFX_CMDHANDLERINFO* pHandlerInfo);
    //}}AFX_VIRTUAL

// Implementation
public:
    virtual ~CMainFrame();
#ifdef _DEBUG
    virtual void AssertValid() const;
    virtual void Dump(CDumpContext& dc) const;
#endif
    CChildView    m_wndView;

// Generated message map functions
protected:
    //{{AFX_MSG(CMainFrame)
    afx_msg void OnSetFocus(CWnd *pOldWnd);
    afx_msg int OnCreate(LPCREATESTRUCT lpCreateStruct);
    //}}AFX_MSG
    afx_msg LRESULT OnApply (WPARAM wParam, LPARAM lParam);
    afx_msg LRESULT OnDialogDestroyed (WPARAM wParam, LPARAM lParam);
    DECLARE_MESSAGE_MAP()
};
```

(continued)

Figure 8-8. *continued*

```
/////////////////////////////////////////////////////////////////////////

//{{AFX_INSERT_LOCATION}}
// Microsoft Visual C++ will insert additional declarations immediately
// before the previous line.

#endif
// !defined(AFX_MAINFRM_H__7040DB88_9039_11D2_8E53_006008A82731__INCLUDED_)
```

MainFrm.cpp

```
// MainFrm.cpp : implementation of the CMainFrame class
//

#include "stdafx.h"
#include "DlgDemo2.h"
#include "OptionsDialog.h"
#include "MainFrm.h"

#ifdef _DEBUG
#define new DEBUG_NEW
#undef THIS_FILE
static char THIS_FILE[] = __FILE__;
#endif

/////////////////////////////////////////////////////////////////////////
// CMainFrame

IMPLEMENT_DYNAMIC(CMainFrame, CFrameWnd)

BEGIN_MESSAGE_MAP(CMainFrame, CFrameWnd)
    //{{AFX_MSG_MAP(CMainFrame)
    ON_WM_SETFOCUS()
    ON_WM_CREATE()
    //}}AFX_MSG_MAP
    ON_MESSAGE (WM_USER_APPLY, OnApply)
    ON_MESSAGE (WM_USER_DIALOG_DESTROYED, OnDialogDestroyed)
END_MESSAGE_MAP()

/////////////////////////////////////////////////////////////////////////
// CMainFrame construction/destruction

CMainFrame::CMainFrame()
{
}
```

```
CMainFrame::~CMainFrame()
{
}


BOOL CMainFrame::PreCreateWindow(CREATESTRUCT& cs)
{
    if( !CFrameWnd::PreCreateWindow(cs) )
        return FALSE;
    cs.dwExStyle &= ~WS_EX_CLIENTEDGE;
    cs.lpszClass = AfxRegisterWndClass(0);
    return TRUE;
}


/////////////////////////////////////////////////////////////////////////
// CMainFrame diagnostics

#ifdef _DEBUG
void CMainFrame::AssertValid() const
{
    CFrameWnd::AssertValid();
}


void CMainFrame::Dump(CDumpContext& dc) const
{
    CFrameWnd::Dump(dc);
}


#endif //_DEBUG

/////////////////////////////////////////////////////////////////////////
// CMainFrame message handlers
void CMainFrame::OnSetFocus(CWnd* pOldWnd)
{
    // forward focus to the view window
    m_wndView.SetFocus();
}

BOOL CMainFrame::OnCmdMsg(UINT nID, int nCode, void* pExtra,
    AFX_CMDHANDLERINFO* pHandlerInfo)
{
    // let the view have first crack at the command
    if (m_wndView.OnCmdMsg(nID, nCode, pExtra, pHandlerInfo))
        return TRUE;

    // otherwise, do default handling
    return CFrameWnd::OnCmdMsg(nID, nCode, pExtra, pHandlerInfo);
}
```

(continued)

Figure 8-8. *continued*

```
int CMainFrame::OnCreate(LPCREATESTRUCT lpCreateStruct)
{
    if (CFrameWnd::OnCreate(lpCreateStruct) == -1)
        return -1;

    if (!m_wndView.Create(NULL, NULL, AFX_WS_DEFAULT_VIEW,
        CRect(0, 0, 0, 0), this, AFX_IDW_PANE_FIRST, NULL))
        return -1;

    return 0;
}

LRESULT CMainFrame::OnApply (WPARAM wParam, LPARAM lParam)
{
    m_wndView.SendMessage (WM_USER_APPLY, wParam, lParam);
    return 0;
}

LRESULT CMainFrame::OnDialogDestroyed (WPARAM wParam, LPARAM lParam)
{
    m_wndView.SendMessage (WM_USER_DIALOG_DESTROYED, wParam, lParam);
    return 0;
}
```

ChildView.h

```
// ChildView.h : interface of the CChildView class
//
//////////////////////////////////////////////////////////////////////

#if
!defined(AFX_CHILDVIEW_H__7040DB8A_9039_11D2_8E53_006008A82731__INCLUDED_)
#define AFX_CHILDVIEW_H__7040DB8A_9039_11D2_8E53_006008A82731__INCLUDED_

#if _MSC_VER > 1000
#pragma once
#endif // _MSC_VER > 1000

//////////////////////////////////////////////////////////////////////
// CChildView window

class CChildView : public CWnd
{
```

```
// Construction
public:
    CChildView();

// Attributes
public:

// Operations
public:

// Overrides
    // ClassWizard generated virtual function overrides
    //{{AFX_VIRTUAL(CChildView)
    protected:
    virtual BOOL PreCreateWindow(CREATESTRUCT& cs);
    //}}AFX_VIRTUAL

// Implementation
public:
    virtual ~CChildView();

    // Generated message map functions
protected:
    COptionsDialog* m_pDlg;
    int m_nUnits;
    int m_nHeight;
    int m_nWidth;
    //{{AFX_MSG(CChildView)
    afx_msg void OnPaint();
    afx_msg void OnFileOptions();
    //}}AFX_MSG
    afx_msg LRESULT OnApply (WPARAM wParam, LPARAM lParam);
    afx_msg LRESULT OnDialogDestroyed (WPARAM wParam, LPARAM lParam);
    DECLARE_MESSAGE_MAP()
};


/////////////////////////////////////////////////////////////////////////////

//{{AFX_INSERT_LOCATION}}
// Microsoft Visual C++ will insert additional declarations immediately
// before the previous line.

#endif
// !defined(
//    AFX_CHILDVIEW_H__7040DB8A_9039_11D2_8E53_006008A82731__INCLUDED_)
```

(continued)

Figure 8-8. *continued*

ChildView.cpp

```
// ChildView.cpp : implementation of the CChildView class
//

#include "stdafx.h"
#include "DlgDemo2.h"
#include "OptionsDialog.h"
#include "ChildView.h"

#ifdef _DEBUG
#define new DEBUG_NEW
#undef THIS_FILE
static char THIS_FILE[] = __FILE__;
#endif

/////////////////////////////////////////////////////////////////////////////
// CChildView

CChildView::CChildView()
{
    m_nWidth = 4;
    m_nHeight = 2;
    m_nUnits = 0;
    m_pDlg = NULL;
}

CChildView::~CChildView()
{
}

BEGIN_MESSAGE_MAP(CChildView,CWnd )
    //{{AFX_MSG_MAP(CChildView)
    ON_WM_PAINT()
    ON_COMMAND(ID_FILE_OPTIONS, OnFileOptions)
    //}}AFX_MSG_MAP
    ON_MESSAGE (WM_USER_APPLY, OnApply)
    ON_MESSAGE (WM_USER_DIALOG_DESTROYED, OnDialogDestroyed)
END_MESSAGE_MAP()

/////////////////////////////////////////////////////////////////////////////
// CChildView message handlers

BOOL CChildView::PreCreateWindow(CREATESTRUCT& cs)
{
    if (!CWnd::PreCreateWindow(cs))
        return FALSE;
```

```
        cs.dwExStyle |= WS_EX_CLIENTEDGE;
        cs.style &= ~WS_BORDER;
        cs.lpszClass = AfxRegisterWndClass(CS_HREDRAW|CS_VREDRAW|CS_DBLCLKS,
            ::LoadCursor(NULL, IDC_ARROW), HBRUSH(COLOR_WINDOW+1), NULL);

    return TRUE;
}

void CChildView::OnPaint()
{
    CPaintDC dc(this); // Device context for painting.

    CBrush brush (RGB (255, 0, 255));
    CBrush* pOldBrush = dc.SelectObject (&brush);

    switch (m_nUnits) {

    case 0: // Inches.
        dc.SetMapMode (MM_LOENGLISH);
        dc.Rectangle (0, 0, m_nWidth * 100, -m_nHeight * 100);
        break;

    case 1: // Centimeters.
        dc.SetMapMode (MM_LOMETRIC);
        dc.Rectangle (0, 0, m_nWidth * 100, -m_nHeight * 100);
        break;

    case 2: // Pixels.
        dc.SetMapMode (MM_TEXT);
        dc.Rectangle (0, 0, m_nWidth, m_nHeight);
        break;
    }
    dc.SelectObject (pOldBrush);
}

void CChildView::OnFileOptions()
{
    //
    // If the dialog box already exists, display it.
    //
    if (m_pDlg != NULL)
        m_pDlg->SetFocus ();

    //
    // If the dialog box doesn't already exist, create it.
    //
    else {
        m_pDlg = new COptionsDialog;
        m_pDlg->m_nWidth = m_nWidth;
```

(continued)

425

Figure 8-8. *continued*

```
        m_pDlg->m_nHeight = m_nHeight;
        m_pDlg->m_nUnits = m_nUnits;
        m_pDlg->Create (IDD_OPTIONS);
        m_pDlg->ShowWindow (SW_SHOW);
    }
}

LRESULT CChildView::OnApply (WPARAM wParam, LPARAM lParam)
{
    RECTPROP* prp = (RECTPROP*) lParam;
    m_nWidth = prp->nWidth;
    m_nHeight = prp->nHeight;
    m_nUnits = prp->nUnits;
    Invalidate ();
    return 0;
}

LRESULT CChildView::OnDialogDestroyed (WPARAM wParam, LPARAM lParam)
{
    m_pDlg = NULL;
    return 0;
}
```

OptionsDialog.h

```
#if
!defined(AFX_OPTIONSDIALOG_H__7040DB90_9039_11D2_8E53_006008A82731__INCLUDED_)
#define
AFX_OPTIONSDIALOG_H__7040DB90_9039_11D2_8E53_006008A82731__INCLUDED_

#if _MSC_VER > 1000
#pragma once
#endif // _MSC_VER > 1000
// OptionsDialog.h : header file
//

/////////////////////////////////////////////////////////////////////////////
// COptionsDialog dialog

class COptionsDialog : public CDialog
{
// Construction
public:
    COptionsDialog(CWnd* pParent = NULL);   // standard constructor
```

```
// Dialog Data
    //{{AFX_DATA(COptionsDialog)
    enum { IDD = IDD_OPTIONS };
    int        m_nWidth;
    int        m_nHeight;
    int        m_nUnits;
    //}}AFX_DATA

// Overrides
    // ClassWizard generated virtual function overrides
    //{{AFX_VIRTUAL(COptionsDialog)
    protected:
    virtual void DoDataExchange(CDataExchange* pDX);    // DDX/DDV support
    virtual void PostNcDestroy();
    //}}AFX_VIRTUAL
    virtual void OnOK ();
    virtual void OnCancel ();

// Implementation
protected:

    // Generated message map functions
    //{{AFX_MSG(COptionsDialog)
    afx_msg void OnReset();
    //}}AFX_MSG
    DECLARE_MESSAGE_MAP()
};

//{{AFX_INSERT_LOCATION}}
// Microsoft Visual C++ will insert additional declarations immediately
// before the previous line.

#endif
// !defined(
//     AFX_OPTIONSDIALOG_H__7040DB90_9039_11D2_8E53_006008A82731__INCLUDED_)
```

OptionsDialog.cpp

```
// OptionsDialog.cpp : implementation file
//

#include "stdafx.h"
#include "DlgDemo2.h"
#include "OptionsDialog.h"
```

(continued)

Figure 8-8. *continued*

```
#ifdef _DEBUG
#define new DEBUG_NEW
#undef THIS_FILE
static char THIS_FILE[] = __FILE__;
#endif


/////////////////////////////////////////////////////////////////////////////
// COptionsDialog dialog

COptionsDialog::COptionsDialog(CWnd* pParent /*=NULL*/)
    : CDialog(COptionsDialog::IDD, pParent)
{
    //{{AFX_DATA_INIT(COptionsDialog)
    m_nWidth = 0;
    m_nHeight = 0;
    m_nUnits = -1;
    //}}AFX_DATA_INIT
}

void COptionsDialog::DoDataExchange(CDataExchange* pDX)
{
    CDialog::DoDataExchange(pDX);
    //{{AFX_DATA_MAP(COptionsDialog)
    DDX_Text(pDX, IDC_WIDTH, m_nWidth);
    DDX_Text(pDX, IDC_HEIGHT, m_nHeight);
    DDX_Radio(pDX, IDC_INCHES, m_nUnits);
    //}}AFX_DATA_MAP
}

BEGIN_MESSAGE_MAP(COptionsDialog, CDialog)
    //{{AFX_MSG_MAP(COptionsDialog)
    ON_BN_CLICKED(IDC_RESET, OnReset)
    //}}AFX_MSG_MAP
END_MESSAGE_MAP()


/////////////////////////////////////////////////////////////////////////////
// COptionsDialog message handlers

void COptionsDialog::OnReset()
{
    m_nWidth = 4;
    m_nHeight = 2;
    m_nUnits = 0;
    UpdateData (FALSE);
}

void COptionsDialog::OnOK ()
```

```
{
    UpdateData (TRUE);

    RECTPROP rp;
    rp.nWidth = m_nWidth;
    rp.nHeight = m_nHeight;
    rp.nUnits = m_nUnits;

    AfxGetMainWnd ()->SendMessage (WM_USER_APPLY, 0, (LPARAM) &rp);
}

void COptionsDialog::OnCancel ()
{
    DestroyWindow ();
}

void COptionsDialog::PostNcDestroy ()
{
    CDialog::PostNcDestroy ();
    AfxGetMainWnd ()->SendMessage (WM_USER_DIALOG_DESTROYED, 0, 0);
    delete this;
}
```

As before, the Options dialog box is invoked by selecting Options from the File menu. Here's the code in *OnFileOptions* that constructs the dialog object, initializes the dialog's data members, and creates the dialog box:

```
m_pDlg = new COptionsDialog;
m_pDlg->m_nWidth = m_nWidth;
m_pDlg->m_nHeight = m_nHeight;
m_pDlg->m_nUnits = m_nUnits;
m_pDlg->Create (IDD_OPTIONS);
m_pDlg->ShowWindow (SW_SHOW);
```

To avoid automatic destruction, the dialog object is created on the heap rather than on the stack. The dialog pointer is saved in *CChildView::m_pDlg*, which is initialized to NULL by *CChildView*'s constructor and reset to NULL when the dialog box is destroyed. Any member function of *CChildView* can determine whether the dialog box is currently displayed by checking *m_pDlg* for a non-NULL value. This turns out to be quite useful because before creating the Options dialog box, *OnFileOptions* checks *m_pDlg* to see whether the dialog box is already displayed. If the answer is yes, *OnFileOptions* uses the *m_pDlg* pointer to set the focus to the existing dialog box rather than create a new one:

```
if (m_pDlg != NULL)
    m_pDlg->SetFocus ();
```

Without this precaution, every invocation of File-Options would create a new instance of the dialog, even if other instances already existed. There's normally no reason to have two or more copies of the same dialog box on the screen at the same time, so you shouldn't allow the user to open multiple instances of a modeless dialog box unless circumstances warrant it.

Processing the Apply and Close Buttons

One of the fundamental differences in implementing modal and modeless dialog boxes with MFC is how the dialog classes handle *OnOK* and *OnCancel*. A modal dialog class rarely overrides *OnCancel* because the default implementation in *CDialog* calls *EndDialog* to close the dialog box and return IDCANCEL. *OnOK* rarely needs to be overridden because the *CDialog* implementation of *OnOK* calls *UpdateData* to update the dialog's data members before dismissing the dialog box. If the dialog box's controls and data members are linked via DDX or DDV, the default action provided by *CDialog::OnOK* is usually sufficient.

A modeless dialog box, by contrast, almost always overrides *OnOK* and *On-Cancel*. As mentioned earlier, it's important to prevent *CDialog::OnOK* and *CDialog-::OnCancel* from being called in a modeless dialog box because modeless dialog boxes are dismissed with *DestroyWindow*, not *EndDialog*. You should override *OnOK* if any button in the dialog box has the ID IDOK. You should always override *OnCancel* because an IDCANCEL notification is sent when the user presses the Esc key or clicks the dialog box's close button, regardless of whether the dialog box contains a Cancel button.

Because clicking DlgDemo2's Apply and Close buttons generates calls to *On-OK* and *OnCancel*, both functions are overridden in *COptionsDialog*. *COptions-Dialog::OnOK* contains the following statements:

```
UpdateData (TRUE);

RECTPROP rp;
rp.nWidth = m_nWidth;
rp.nHeight = m_nHeight;
rp.nUnits = m_nUnits;

AfxGetMainWnd ()->SendMessage (WM_USER_APPLY, 0, (LPARAM) &rp);
```

The first statement updates the dialog's member variables to match the current state of the controls. A modeless dialog box that uses DDX or DDV must call *UpdateData* itself because calling *CDialog::OnOK* and letting it call *UpdateData* is out of the question. The next block of statements instantiates the RECTPROP structure declared in Stdafx.h and copies the new settings from the dialog's data members to the data structure. The final statement sends a message to the application's main window telling it to apply the settings contained in the RECTPROP structure to the dialog box.

WM_USER_APPLY is a user-defined message that's defined this way in Stdafx.h:

```
#define WM_USER_APPLY WM_USER+0x100
```

WM_USER, which is defined as 0x400 in the header file Winuser.h, specifies the low end of a range of message IDs an application can use without conflicting with the message IDs of standard Windows messages such as WM_CREATE and WM_PAINT. An application is free to use message IDs from WM_USER's 0x400 through 0x7FFF for its own purposes. Messages in this range are referred to as *user-defined messages*. Because dialog boxes use some message IDs in this range themselves, DlgDemo2 arbitrarily adds 0x100 to WM_USER to avoid conflicts.

A message transmitted with *SendMessage* includes two parameters the sender can use to pass data to the receiver: a 32-bit value of type WPARAM and another 32-bit value whose type is LPARAM. When *COptionsDialog::OnOK* sends a message to the main window, it sends along a pointer to a RECTPROP structure containing the settings retrieved from the dialog box. The main window processes the message with *CMainFrame::OnApply*, which is referenced in the message map with the following statement:

```
ON_MESSAGE (WM_USER_APPLY, OnApply);
```

When activated, *OnApply* forwards the message to the view:

```
LRESULT CMainFrame::OnApply (WPARAM wParam, LPARAM lParam)
{
    m_wndView.SendMessage (WM_USER_APPLY, wParam, lParam);
    return 0;
}
```

CChildView::OnApply, in turn, copies the values out of the data structure and into its own data members. It then invalidates the view to force a repaint incorporating the new settings:

```
LRESULT CChildView::OnApply (WPARAM wParam, LPARAM lParam)
{
    RECTPROP* prp = (RECTPROP*) lParam;
    m_nWidth = prp->nWidth;
    m_nHeight = prp->nHeight;
    m_nUnits = prp->nUnits;
    Invalidate ();
    return 0;
}
```

The value returned by a handler for a user-defined message is returned to the caller through *SendMessage*. DlgDemo2 attaches no meaning to the return value, so both *CMainFrame::OnApply* and *CChildView::OnApply* return 0.

COptionsDialog::OnCancel contains just one statement: a call to *DestroyWindow* to destroy the dialog box. Ultimately, this action activates *COptionsDialog::PostNcDestroy*, which is implemented as follows:

```
void COptionsDialog::PostNcDestroy ()
{
    CDialog::PostNcDestroy ();
    AfxGetMainWnd ()->SendMessage (WM_USER_DIALOG_DESTROYED, 0, 0);
    delete this;
}
```

This *SendMessage* sends a different user-defined message to the main window. The main window's WM_USER_DIALOG_DESTROYED handler, *CMainFrame::OnDialogDestroyed*, forwards the message to the view, whose WM_USER_DIALOG_DESTROYED handler responds by setting *m_pDlg* to NULL. Its work almost done, *PostNcDestroy* finishes up by executing a *delete this* statement to delete the dialog object created by *CChildView::OnFileOptions*.

USING A DIALOG BOX AS A MAIN WINDOW

If you write an application whose primary user interface is a dialog-like collection of controls, you should consider using a dialog box as a main window. Charles Petzold immortalizes this technique with the HEXCALC program featured in his book *Programming Windows*. Scores of developers have used similar techniques for creating small, utility-type application programs whose main windows are more easily defined in dialog templates than within the programmatic confines of *OnCreate* handlers.

Writing a dialog-based application is a snap thanks to AppWizard. One of the options in AppWizard's Step 1 dialog box is a radio button labeled Dialog Based. Checking this button prompts AppWizard to generate an application whose main window is a dialog box. AppWizard creates the dialog resource for you and derives a dialog class from *CDialog*. It also emits a special version of *InitInstance* that instantiates the dialog class and calls its *DoModal* function to display the dialog box on the screen when the application is started. All you have to do is add controls to the dialog in the resource editor and write message handlers to respond to control events. The AppWizard-generated code handles everything else.

The DlgCalc application shown in Figure 8-9 is an example of a dialog-based MFC application. DlgCalc is a calculator applet. It differs from the calculator applet supplied with Windows in one important respect: it uses postfix notation, which is also known as *reverse Polish notation*, or RPN. Postfix notation is the form of data entry used by Hewlett-Packard calculators. Once you've grown accustomed to postfix notation, you'll never want to use a conventional calculator again.

Figure 8-9. *The DlgCalc window.*

DlgCalc's source code appears in Figure 8-10. The main window is created in *CDlgCalcApp::InitInstance*, which constructs a *CDlgCalcDlg* object, copies the object's address to the application object's *m_pMainWnd* data member, and calls *DoModal* to display the window:

```
CDlgCalcDlg dlg;
m_pMainWnd = &dlg;
dlg.DoModal ();
```

CDlgCalcDlg is the dialog class that AppWizard derived from *CDialog*. The window created from it is a dialog box in every sense of the term, but it doubles as a main window since it has no parent and its address is tucked away in *m_pMainWnd*. I deleted some of the code that AppWizard placed in *InitInstance*—notably, the code that tests *DoModal*'s return value—because it served no purpose in this application. I also deleted the WM_QUERYDRAGICON handler that AppWizard included in the dialog class and the AppWizard-generated *OnPaint* code that paints the application icon when the window is minimized because neither is needed unless your application will be run on old versions of Windows—specifically, versions that use the Windows 3.*x*–style shell.

DlgCalc.h

```
// DlgCalc.h : main header file for the DLGCALC application
//

#if
!defined(AFX_DLGCALC_H__F42970C4_9047_11D2_8E53_006008A82731__INCLUDED_)
#define  AFX_DLGCALC_H__F42970C4_9047_11D2_8E53_006008A82731__INCLUDED_

#if _MSC_VER > 1000
#pragma once
#endif // _MSC_VER > 1000
```

Figure 8-10. *The DlgCalc application.* (continued)

Figure 8-10. *continued*

```
#ifndef __AFXWIN_H__
    #error include 'stdafx.h' before including this file for PCH
#endif

#include "resource.h"        // main symbols

/////////////////////////////////////////////////////////////////////////
// CDlgCalcApp:
// See DlgCalc.cpp for the implementation of this class
//

class CDlgCalcApp : public CWinApp
{
public:
    CDlgCalcApp();

// Overrides
    // ClassWizard generated virtual function overrides
    //{{AFX_VIRTUAL(CDlgCalcApp)
    public:
    virtual BOOL InitInstance();
    //}}AFX_VIRTUAL

// Implementation

    //{{AFX_MSG(CDlgCalcApp)
    //}}AFX_MSG
    DECLARE_MESSAGE_MAP()
};


/////////////////////////////////////////////////////////////////////////

//{{AFX_INSERT_LOCATION}}
// Microsoft Visual C++ will insert additional declarations immediately
// before the previous line.

#endif
// !defined(AFX_DLGCALC_H__F42970C4_9047_11D2_8E53_006008A82731__INCLUDED_)
```

DlgCalc.cpp

```
// DlgCalc.cpp : Defines the class behaviors for the application.
//

#include "stdafx.h"
#include "DlgCalc.h"
#include "DlgCalcDlg.h"
```

```
#ifdef _DEBUG
#define new DEBUG_NEW
#undef THIS_FILE
static char THIS_FILE[] = __FILE__;
#endif


/////////////////////////////////////////////////////////////////////////
// CDlgCalcApp

BEGIN_MESSAGE_MAP(CDlgCalcApp, CWinApp)
    //{{AFX_MSG_MAP(CDlgCalcApp)
    //}}AFX_MSG
    ON_COMMAND(ID_HELP, CWinApp::OnHelp)
END_MESSAGE_MAP()

/////////////////////////////////////////////////////////////////////////
// CDlgCalcApp construction

CDlgCalcApp::CDlgCalcApp()
{
}


/////////////////////////////////////////////////////////////////////////
// The one and only CDlgCalcApp object

CDlgCalcApp theApp;

/////////////////////////////////////////////////////////////////////////
// CDlgCalcApp initialization

BOOL CDlgCalcApp::InitInstance()
{
    CDlgCalcDlg dlg;
    m_pMainWnd = &dlg;
    dlg.DoModal ();
    return FALSE;
}
```

DlgCalcDlg.h

```
// DlgCalcDlg.h : header file
//

#if
!defined(AFX_DLGCALCDLG_H__F42970C6_9047_11D2_8E53_006008A82731__INCLUDED_)
#define  AFX_DLGCALCDLG_H__F42970C6_9047_11D2_8E53_006008A82731__INCLUDED_
```

(continued)

Figure 8-10. *continued*

```
#if _MSC_VER > 1000
#pragma once
#endif // _MSC_VER > 1000


/////////////////////////////////////////////////////////////////////////////
// CDlgCalcDlg dialog

class CDlgCalcDlg : public CDialog
{
// Construction
public:
    void UpdateDisplay (LPCTSTR pszDisplay);
    CDlgCalcDlg(CWnd* pParent = NULL);    // standard constructor

// Dialog Data
    //{{AFX_DATA(CDlgCalcDlg)
    enum { IDD = IDD_DLGCALC_DIALOG };
        // NOTE: the ClassWizard will add data members here
    //}}AFX_DATA

    // ClassWizard generated virtual function overrides
    //{{AFX_VIRTUAL(CDlgCalcDlg)
    public:
    virtual BOOL PreTranslateMessage(MSG* pMsg);
    protected:
    virtual void DoDataExchange(CDataExchange* pDX);    // DDX/DDV support
    virtual BOOL OnCommand(WPARAM wParam, LPARAM lParam);
    //}}AFX_VIRTUAL

// Implementation
protected:
    void DropStack();
    void LiftStack();
    void DisplayXRegister();

    double m_dblStack[4];
    double m_dblMemory;
    CString m_strDisplay;
    CString m_strFormat;
    CRect m_rect;
    int m_cxChar;
    int m_cyChar;

    BOOL m_bFixPending;
    BOOL m_bErrorFlag;
```

```
    BOOL m_bDecimalInString;
    BOOL m_bStackLiftEnabled;
    BOOL m_bNewX;

    HICON m_hIcon;
    HACCEL m_hAccel;

    // Generated message map functions
    //{{AFX_MSG(CDlgCalcDlg)
    virtual BOOL OnInitDialog();
    afx_msg void OnPaint();
    afx_msg void OnAdd();
    afx_msg void OnSubtract();
    afx_msg void OnMultiply();
    afx_msg void OnDivide();
    afx_msg void OnEnter();
    afx_msg void OnChangeSign();
    afx_msg void OnExponent();
    afx_msg void OnStore();
    afx_msg void OnRecall();
    afx_msg void OnFix();
    afx_msg void OnClear();
    afx_msg void OnDecimal();
    afx_msg void OnDelete();
    //}}AFX_MSG
    afx_msg void OnDigit(UINT nID);
    DECLARE_MESSAGE_MAP()
};

//{{AFX_INSERT_LOCATION}}
// Microsoft Visual C++ will insert additional declarations immediately
// before the previous line.

#endif
// !defined(
//    AFX_DLGCALCDLG_H__F42970C6_9047_11D2_8E53_006008A82731__INCLUDED_)
```

DlgCalcDlg.cpp

```
// DlgCalcDlg.cpp : implementation file
//

#include "stdafx.h"
#include "DlgCalc.h"
#include "DlgCalcDlg.h"
```

(continued)

Figure 8-10. *continued*

```
#ifdef _DEBUG
#define new DEBUG_NEW
#undef THIS_FILE
static char THIS_FILE[] = __FILE__;
#endif

/////////////////////////////////////////////////////////////////////////
// CDlgCalcDlg dialog

CDlgCalcDlg::CDlgCalcDlg(CWnd* pParent /*=NULL*/)
    : CDialog(CDlgCalcDlg::IDD, pParent)
{
    //{{AFX_DATA_INIT(CDlgCalcDlg)
        // NOTE: the ClassWizard will add member initialization here
    //}}AFX_DATA_INIT
    m_hIcon = AfxGetApp()->LoadIcon(IDR_MAINFRAME);
    m_hAccel = ::LoadAccelerators (AfxGetInstanceHandle (),
        MAKEINTRESOURCE (IDR_ACCEL));

    m_bFixPending = FALSE;
    m_bErrorFlag = FALSE;
    m_bDecimalInString = FALSE;
    m_bStackLiftEnabled = FALSE;
    m_bNewX = TRUE;

    for (int i=0; i<4; i++)
        m_dblStack[i] = 0.0;
    m_dblMemory = 0.0;
    m_strFormat = _T ("%0.2f");
}

void CDlgCalcDlg::DoDataExchange(CDataExchange* pDX)
{
    CDialog::DoDataExchange(pDX);
    //{{AFX_DATA_MAP(CDlgCalcDlg)
        // NOTE: the ClassWizard will add DDX and DDV calls here
    //}}AFX_DATA_MAP
}

BEGIN_MESSAGE_MAP(CDlgCalcDlg, CDialog)
    //{{AFX_MSG_MAP(CDlgCalcDlg)
    ON_WM_PAINT()
    ON_BN_CLICKED(IDC_ADD, OnAdd)
    ON_BN_CLICKED(IDC_SUBTRACT, OnSubtract)
    ON_BN_CLICKED(IDC_MULTIPLY, OnMultiply)
    ON_BN_CLICKED(IDC_DIVIDE, OnDivide)
```

```
    ON_BN_CLICKED(IDC_ENTER, OnEnter)
    ON_BN_CLICKED(IDC_CHGSIGN, OnChangeSign)
    ON_BN_CLICKED(IDC_EXP, OnExponent)
    ON_BN_CLICKED(IDC_STO, OnStore)
    ON_BN_CLICKED(IDC_RCL, OnRecall)
    ON_BN_CLICKED(IDC_FIX, OnFix)
    ON_BN_CLICKED(IDC_CLX, OnClear)
    ON_BN_CLICKED(IDC_DECIMAL, OnDecimal)
    ON_BN_CLICKED(IDC_DEL, OnDelete)
    //}}AFX_MSG_MAP
    ON_CONTROL_RANGE (BN_CLICKED, IDC_0, IDC_9, OnDigit)
END_MESSAGE_MAP()

/////////////////////////////////////////////////////////////////////////
// CDlgCalcDlg message handlers

BOOL CDlgCalcDlg::OnInitDialog()
{
    CDialog::OnInitDialog();

    //
    // Set the application's icon.
    //
    SetIcon(m_hIcon, TRUE);
    SetIcon(m_hIcon, FALSE);

    //
    // Remove the Size and Maximize commands from the system menu.
    //
    CMenu* pMenu = GetSystemMenu (FALSE);
    pMenu->DeleteMenu (SC_SIZE, MF_BYCOMMAND);
    pMenu->DeleteMenu (SC_MAXIMIZE, MF_BYCOMMAND);

    //
    // Initialize m_rect with the coordinates of the control representing
    // the calculator's output window. Then destroy the control.
    //
    CWnd* pWnd = GetDlgItem (IDC_DISPLAYRECT);
    pWnd->GetWindowRect (&m_rect);
    pWnd->DestroyWindow ();
    ScreenToClient (&m_rect);

    //
    // Initialize m_cxChar and m_cyChar with the average character width
    // and height.
    //
    TEXTMETRIC tm;
    CClientDC dc (this);
```

(continued)

Figure 8-10. *continued*

```
    dc.GetTextMetrics (&tm);
    m_cxChar = tm.tmAveCharWidth;
    m_cyChar = tm.tmHeight - tm.tmDescent;

    //
    // Initialize the calculator's output window and return.
    //
    DisplayXRegister ();
    return TRUE;
}

void CDlgCalcDlg::OnPaint()
{
    CPaintDC dc (this);
    dc.DrawEdge (m_rect, EDGE_SUNKEN, BF_RECT);
    UpdateDisplay (m_strDisplay);
}

BOOL CDlgCalcDlg::PreTranslateMessage(MSG* pMsg)
{
    if (m_hAccel != NULL)
        if (::TranslateAccelerator (m_hWnd, m_hAccel, pMsg))
            return TRUE;

    return CDialog::PreTranslateMessage (pMsg);
}

BOOL CDlgCalcDlg::OnCommand(WPARAM wParam, LPARAM lParam)
{
    int nID = (int) LOWORD (wParam);

    if (m_bErrorFlag && (nID != IDC_CLX)) {
        ::MessageBeep (MB_ICONASTERISK);
        return TRUE;
    }

    if (m_bFixPending &&
        ((nID < IDC_0) || (nID > IDC_9)) &&
        (nID != IDC_CLX)) {
        ::MessageBeep (MB_ICONASTERISK);
        return TRUE;
    }
    return CDialog::OnCommand (wParam, lParam);
}
```

```
void CDlgCalcDlg::OnDigit(UINT nID)
{
    TCHAR cDigit = (char) nID;

    if (m_bFixPending) {
        m_strFormat.SetAt (3, cDigit - IDC_0 + 0x30);
        DisplayXRegister ();
        m_bFixPending = FALSE;
        m_bStackLiftEnabled = TRUE;
        m_bNewX = TRUE;
        return;
    }

    if (m_bNewX) {
        m_bNewX = FALSE;
        if (m_bStackLiftEnabled) {
            m_bStackLiftEnabled = FALSE;
            LiftStack ();
        }
        m_bDecimalInString = FALSE;
        m_strDisplay.Empty ();
    }

    int nLength = m_strDisplay.GetLength ();
    if ((nLength == MAXCHARS) ||
        ((nLength == (MAXCHARS - 10)) && !m_bDecimalInString))
        ::MessageBeep (MB_ICONASTERISK);
    else {
        m_strDisplay += (cDigit - IDC_0 + 0x30);
        UpdateDisplay (m_strDisplay);
        m_dblStack[0] = _tcstod (m_strDisplay.GetBuffer (0), NULL);
    }
}

void CDlgCalcDlg::OnAdd()
{
    m_dblStack[0] += m_dblStack[1];
    DisplayXRegister ();
    DropStack ();
    m_bStackLiftEnabled = TRUE;
    m_bNewX = TRUE;
}

void CDlgCalcDlg::OnSubtract()
{
    m_dblStack[0] = m_dblStack[1] - m_dblStack[0];
    DisplayXRegister ();
```

(continued)

Figure 8-10. *continued*

```
    DropStack ();
    m_bStackLiftEnabled = TRUE;
    m_bNewX = TRUE;
}

void CDlgCalcDlg::OnMultiply()
{
    m_dblStack[0] *= m_dblStack[1];
    DisplayXRegister ();
    DropStack ();
    m_bStackLiftEnabled = TRUE;
    m_bNewX = TRUE;
}

void CDlgCalcDlg::OnDivide()
{
    if (m_dblStack[0] == 0.0) {
        m_bErrorFlag = TRUE;
        ::MessageBeep (MB_ICONASTERISK);
        UpdateDisplay (CString (_T ("Divide by zero")));
    }
    else {
        m_dblStack[0] = m_dblStack[1] / m_dblStack[0];
        DisplayXRegister ();
        DropStack ();
        m_bStackLiftEnabled = TRUE;
        m_bNewX = TRUE;
    }
}

void CDlgCalcDlg::OnEnter()
{
    LiftStack ();
    DisplayXRegister ();
    m_bStackLiftEnabled = FALSE;
    m_bNewX = TRUE;
}

void CDlgCalcDlg::OnChangeSign()
{
    if (m_dblStack[0] != 0.0) {
        m_dblStack[0] = -m_dblStack[0];
        if (m_strDisplay[0] == _T ('-')) {
            int nLength = m_strDisplay.GetLength ();
            m_strDisplay = m_strDisplay.Right (nLength - 1);
        }
```

```
            else
                m_strDisplay = _T ("-") + m_strDisplay;
            UpdateDisplay (m_strDisplay);
    }
}

void CDlgCalcDlg::OnExponent()
{
    if (((m_dblStack[1] == 0.0) && (m_dblStack[0] < 0.0)) ||
        ((m_dblStack[1] == 0.0) && (m_dblStack[0] == 0.0)) ||
        ((m_dblStack[1] < 0.0) &&
        (floor (m_dblStack[0]) != m_dblStack[0]))) {
        m_bErrorFlag = TRUE;
        ::MessageBeep (MB_ICONASTERISK);
        UpdateDisplay (CString (_T ("Invalid operation")));
    }
    else {
        m_dblStack[0] = pow (m_dblStack[1], m_dblStack[0]);
        DisplayXRegister ();
        DropStack ();
        m_bStackLiftEnabled = TRUE;
        m_bNewX = TRUE;
    }
}

void CDlgCalcDlg::OnStore()
{
    DisplayXRegister ();
    m_dblMemory = m_dblStack[0];
    m_bStackLiftEnabled = TRUE;
    m_bNewX = TRUE;
}

void CDlgCalcDlg::OnRecall()
{
    LiftStack ();
    m_dblStack[0] = m_dblMemory;
    DisplayXRegister ();
    m_bStackLiftEnabled = TRUE;
    m_bNewX = TRUE;
}

void CDlgCalcDlg::OnFix()
{
    m_bFixPending = TRUE;
}
```

(continued)

Figure 8-10. *continued*

```
void CDlgCalcDlg::OnClear()
{
    if (m_bFixPending) {
        m_bFixPending = FALSE;
        return;
    }

    m_bErrorFlag = FALSE;
    m_dblStack[0] = 0.0;
    DisplayXRegister ();
    m_bStackLiftEnabled = FALSE;
    m_bNewX = TRUE;
}

void CDlgCalcDlg::OnDecimal()
{
    if (m_bNewX) {
        m_bNewX = FALSE;
        if (m_bStackLiftEnabled) {
            m_bStackLiftEnabled = FALSE;
            LiftStack ();
        }
        m_bDecimalInString = FALSE;
        m_strDisplay.Empty ();
    }

    int nLength = m_strDisplay.GetLength ();
    if ((nLength == MAXCHARS) || (m_bDecimalInString))
        ::MessageBeep (MB_ICONASTERISK);
    else {
        m_bDecimalInString = TRUE;
        m_strDisplay += (char) 0x2E;
        UpdateDisplay (m_strDisplay);
        m_dblStack[0] = strtod (m_strDisplay.GetBuffer (0), NULL);
    }
}

void CDlgCalcDlg::OnDelete()
{
    int nLength = m_strDisplay.GetLength ();

    if (!m_bNewX && (nLength != 0)) {
        if (m_strDisplay[nLength - 1] == _T ('.'))
            m_bDecimalInString = FALSE;
        m_strDisplay = m_strDisplay.Left (nLength - 1);
```

```
        UpdateDisplay (m_strDisplay);
        m_dblStack[0] = strtod (m_strDisplay.GetBuffer (0), NULL);
    }
}

void CDlgCalcDlg::LiftStack()
{
    for (int i=3; i>0; i--)
        m_dblStack[i] = m_dblStack[i-1];
}

void CDlgCalcDlg::DropStack()
{
    for (int i=1; i<3; i++)
        m_dblStack[i] = m_dblStack[i+1];
}

void CDlgCalcDlg::DisplayXRegister()
{
    double dblVal = m_dblStack[0];

    if ((dblVal >= 1000000000000.0) || (dblVal <= -1000000000000.0)) {
        UpdateDisplay (CString (_T ("Overflow error")));
        m_bErrorFlag = TRUE;
        MessageBeep (MB_ICONASTERISK);
    }
    else {
        m_strDisplay.Format (m_strFormat, dblVal);
        UpdateDisplay (m_strDisplay);
    }
}

void CDlgCalcDlg::UpdateDisplay(LPCTSTR pszDisplay)
{
    CClientDC dc (this);
    CFont* pOldFont = dc.SelectObject (GetFont ());
    CSize size = dc.GetTextExtent (pszDisplay);

    CRect rect = m_rect;
    rect.InflateRect (-2, -2);
    int x = rect.right - size.cx - m_cxChar;
    int y = rect.top + ((rect.Height () - m_cyChar) / 2);

    dc.ExtTextOut (x, y, ETO_OPAQUE, rect, pszDisplay, NULL);
    dc.SelectObject (pOldFont);
}
```

By default, the main window in a dialog-based application created by AppWizard doesn't have a minimize button. I added one to the title bar by opening the dialog box in the dialog editor and checking Minimize Button in the dialog's property sheet.

The bulk of the code in DlgCalcDlg.cpp is there to process clicks of the calculator buttons. Thanks to this code, DlgCalc works very much like a genuine RPN calculator. To add 2 and 2, for example, you would type

2 <Enter> 2 +

To multiply 3.46 by 9, add 13, divide by 10, and raise the result to a power of 2.5, you would type

3.46 <Enter> 9 * 13 + 10 / 2.5 <Exp>

The Sto key copies the number in the calculator display to memory (stores it), and Rcl recalls it. Clx clears the calculator display (the "x" in "Clx" is a reference to the calculator's X register, whose contents are always shown in the calculator display), and the ± button changes the sign of the number that's currently displayed. Fix sets the number of digits displayed to the right of the decimal point. To change from two decimal places to four, click Fix and then the 4 button. The Del button deletes the rightmost character in the numeric display. For each button on the face of the calculator, there is an equivalent key on the keyboard, as shown in the following table. The P key assigned to the ± button is a crude mnemonic for "plus or minus." Most users find it slow going to click calculator buttons with the mouse, so the keyboard shortcuts are an important part of this application's user interface.

KEYBOARD EQUIVALENTS FOR DLGCALC'S CALCULATOR BUTTONS

Button(s)	Key(s)	Button(s)	Key(s)
±	P	0–9	0–9
Exp	E	-	-
Sto	S	+	+
Rcl	R	x	*
Enter	Enter	÷	/
Fix	F	.	.
Clx	C	Del	Del, Backspace

Processing Keyboard Messages

Because it's unusual for a dialog box to implement its own keyboard interface on top of the one that Windows provides, DlgCalc's keyboard processing logic deserves a closer look.

A fundamental problem with processing keystrokes in a dialog box is that WM_CHAR messages are processed by *::IsDialogMessage*, which is called from every MFC dialog's message loop. You can add an *OnChar* handler to a dialog class, but it will never get called if *::IsDialogMessage* sees keyboard messages before *::Translate-Message* does. Another problem is that once a control gets the input focus, subsequent keyboard messages go to the control instead of to the dialog window.

To circumvent these problems, I decided to use accelerators to process keyboard input. I first created an accelerator resource by selecting the Resource command from Visual C++'s Insert menu and double-clicking "Accelerator." Then I added accelerators for all the keys on the face of the calculator—"1" for the IDC_1 button, "2" for the IDC_2 button, and so on. Next I added an HACCEL member variable to *CDlgCalcDlg* and inserted the following statement into *CDlgCalcDlg*'s constructor to load the accelerators:

```
m_hAccel = ::LoadAccelerators (AfxGetInstanceHandle (),
    MAKEINTRESOURCE (IDR_ACCEL1));
```

Finally, I overrode *PreTranslateMessage* and replaced it with a version that calls *::TranslateAccelerator* on each message that the dialog receives:

```
BOOL CCalcDialog::PreTranslateMessage (MSG* pMsg)
{
    if (m_hAccel != NULL)
        if (::TranslateAccelerator (m_hWnd, m_hAccel, pMsg))
            return TRUE;

    return CDialog::PreTranslateMessage (pMsg);
}
```

This way, *::TranslateAccelerator* sees keyboard messages even before *::IsDialog-Message* does, and messages corresponding to accelerator keys are magically transformed into WM_COMMAND messages. Because the accelerator keys are assigned the same command IDs as the calculator's push buttons, the same ON_BN_CLICKED handlers process button clicks *and* keypresses.

Preprocessing WM_COMMAND Messages

Before a WM_COMMAND message emanating from a control is routed through a class's message map, MFC calls the class's virtual *OnCommand* function. The default implementation of *OnCommand* is the starting point for a command routing system put in place to ensure that all relevant objects associated with a running application program, including the document, view, and application objects used in document/view applications, see the message and get a crack at processing it. If desired, an application can preprocess WM_COMMAND messages by overriding *OnCommand*. When preprocessing is complete, the application can call the base class's *OnCommand* function to pass the message on for normal processing, or it can "eat" the message by returning without calling the base class. An *OnCommand* handler that doesn't call the base class should return TRUE to inform Windows that message processing is complete.

DlgCalc does something else unusual for an MFC application: it overrides *OnCommand* and filters out selected WM_COMMAND messages if either one of a pair of *CDlgCalcDlg* member variables—*m_bErrorFlag* or *m_bFixPending*—is nonzero. *CDlgCalcDialog::OnCommand* begins by obtaining the ID of the control that generated the message from the low word of the *wParam* value passed to it by MFC:

```
int nID = (int) LOWORD (wParam);
```

It then examines *m_bErrorFlag*, which, if nonzero, indicates that a divide-by-zero or other error has occurred. The user must click Clx to clear the display after an error occurs, so *OnCommand* rejects all buttons but Clx if *m_bErrorFlag* is nonzero:

```
if (m_bErrorFlag && (nID != IDC_CLX)) {
    ::MessageBeep (MB_ICONASTERISK);
    return TRUE;
}
```

Similarly, if the *m_bFixPending* flag is set, indicating that the calculator is awaiting a press of a numeric key following a press of the Fix key, all buttons other than 0 through 9 and the Clx key, which cancels a pending fix operation, are rejected:

```
if (m_bFixPending &&
    ((nID < IDC_0) || (nID > IDC_9)) &&
    (nID != IDC_CLX)) {
    ::MessageBeep (MB_ICONASTERISK);
    return TRUE;
}
```

In both cases, the *::MessageBeep* API function is called to produce an audible tone signifying an invalid button press. The base class's *OnCommand* handler is called only if *m_bErrorFlag* and *m_bFixPending* are both 0. Putting the code that tests these flags in the *OnCommand* handler prevents the code from having to be duplicated in every ON_BN_CLICKED handler.

Another item of interest related to WM_COMMAND messages is the fact that DlgCalc processes clicks of the 0 through 9 buttons with a common handler. An ON_CONTROL_RANGE statement hand-coded into the message map directs BN_CLICKED notifications from each of the 10 buttons to *CDlgCalcDlg::OnDigit*:

```
ON_CONTROL_RANGE (BN_CLICKED, IDC_0, IDC_9, OnDigit)
```

An ON_CONTROL_RANGE handler receives a UINT parameter identifying the control that sent the notification, and it returns void. In DlgCalc's case, the alternative to ON_CONTROL_RANGE would have been 10 separate ON_BN_CLICKED macros and a handler that called *CWnd::GetCurrentMessage* to retrieve the control ID from the message's *wParam*. One message-map entry is obviously more memory-efficient than ten, and the job of extracting control IDs from message parameters is best left to MFC when possible to ensure compatibility with future versions of Windows.

PROPERTY SHEETS

One feature of Windows that programmers of every stripe will appreciate is property sheets—tabbed dialog boxes containing pages of controls that the user can switch among with mouse clicks. Property sheets live in the common controls library provided with every copy of Windows. They're something of a chore to program using the Windows API, but they're relatively easy to implement in MFC thanks to the support provided by the framework. In fact, adding a property sheet to an MFC application isn't all that different from adding a dialog box. An MFC application that uses property sheets and runs on Windows 95 or later or Windows NT 3.51 or later uses the operating system's native property sheet implementation. On other platforms, MFC's private implementation is used instead.

The functionality of property sheets is neatly encapsulated in a pair of MFC classes named *CPropertySheet* and *CPropertyPage*. *CPropertySheet* represents the property sheet itself and is derived from *CWnd*. *CPropertyPage* represents a page in a property sheet and is derived from *CDialog*. Both are defined in the header file Afxdlgs.h. Like dialog boxes, property sheets can be modal or modeless. *CPropertySheet::DoModal* creates a modal property sheet, and *CPropertySheet::Create* creates a modeless property sheet.

The general procedure for creating a modal property sheet goes like this:

1. For each page in the property sheet, create a dialog template defining the page's contents and characteristics. Set the dialog title to the title you want to appear on the tab at the top of the property sheet page.

2. For each page in the property sheet, derive a dialog-like class from *CPropertyPage* that includes public data members linked to the page's controls via DDX or DDV.

3. Derive a property sheet class from *CPropertySheet*. Instantiate the property sheet class and the property sheet page classes you derived in step 2. Use *CPropertySheet::AddPage* to add the pages to the property sheet in the order in which you want them to appear.

4. Call the property sheet's *DoModal* function to display it on the screen.

To simplify property sheet creation, most MFC programmers declare instances of their property sheet page classes inside the derived property sheet class. They also write the property sheet class's constructor such that it calls *AddPage* to add the pages to the property sheet. The class declarations for a simple property sheet and its pages might look like this:

```
class CFirstPage : public CPropertyPage
{
public:
    CFirstPage () : CPropertyPage (IDD_FIRSTPAGE) {};
    // Declare CFirstPage's data members here.

protected:
    virtual void DoDataExchange (CDataExchange*);
};

class CSecondPage : public CPropertyPage
{
public:
    CSecondPage () : CPropertyPage (IDD_SECONDPAGE) {};
    // Declare CSecondPage's data members here.

protected:
    virtual void DoDataExchange (CDataExchange*);
};

class CMyPropertySheet : public CPropertySheet
{
public:
    CFirstPage m_firstPage;          // First page
    CSecondPage m_secondPage;        // Second page

    // Constructor adds the pages automatically.
    CMyPropertySheet (LPCTSTR pszCaption,
        CWnd* pParentWnd = NULL) :
        CPropertySheet (pszCaption, pParentWnd, 0)
    {
        AddPage (&m_firstPage);
        AddPage (&m_secondPage);
    }
};
```

In this example, *CFirstPage* represents the first page in the property sheet, and *CSecondPage* represents the second. The associated dialog resources, which are referenced in the pages' class constructors, are IDD_FIRSTPAGE and IDD_SECONDPAGE.

With this infrastructure in place, a modal property sheet featuring the caption "Properties" in its title bar can be constructed and displayed with two simple statements:

```
CMyPropertySheet ps (_T ("Properties"));
ps.DoModal ();
```

Like *CDialog::DoModal, CPropertySheet::DoModal* returns IDOK if the property sheet was dismissed with the OK button, or IDCANCEL otherwise.

The dialog templates for property sheet pages shouldn't include OK and Cancel buttons because the property sheet provides these buttons. A property sheet also includes an Apply button and an optional Help button. The Apply button is disabled when the property sheet first appears and is enabled when a property sheet page calls the *SetModified* function it inherits from *CPropertyPage* and passes in TRUE. *SetModified* should be called anytime the settings embodied in the property sheet are changed—for example, whenever the text of an edit control is modified or a radio button is clicked. To trap clicks of the Apply button, you must include an ON_BN_CLICKED handler in the derived property sheet class. The button's ID is ID_APPLY_NOW. The click handler should call *UpdateData* with a TRUE parameter to update the active page's member variables and transmit the current property values to the property sheet's owner. Afterward, the click handler should disable the Apply button by calling *SetModified* with a FALSE parameter—once for each of the property sheet pages.

Note that the Apply button's ON_BN_CLICKED handler calls *UpdateData* for only the *active property sheet page*—the one that's currently displayed. That's important, because property sheet pages aren't physically created until they are activated by the person using the property sheet. Calling *UpdateData* for a property sheet page whose tab hasn't been clicked results in an assertion error from MFC. The framework calls *UpdateData* for the active page when the user switches to another page, so when the user clicks the Apply button, the only page whose data members need to be updated is the page that's currently active. You can get a pointer to the active page with *CPropertySheet::GetActivePage*.

Using DDX and DDV to transfer data between controls and data members in property sheet pages and to validate data extracted from the controls is more than a matter of convenience; it allows MFC to do much of the dirty work involved in property sheet handling. The first time a property sheet page is displayed, for example, the page's *OnInitDialog* function is called. The default implementation of *OnInitDialog* calls *UpdateData* to initialize the page's controls. If the user then clicks a tab to activate another page, the current page's *OnKillActive* function is called and the framework calls *UpdateData* to retrieve and validate the controls' data. Shortly thereafter, the newly activated page receives an *OnSetActive* notification and possibly an

OnInitDialog notification, too. If the user then goes on to click the property sheet's OK button, the current page's *OnOK* handler is called and the framework calls *Update-Data* to retrieve and validate that page's data.

The point is that a property sheet works the way it does because the framework provides default implementations of key virtual functions that govern the property sheet's behavior. You can customize a property sheet's operation by overriding the pages' *OnInitDialog*, *OnSetActive*, *OnKillActive*, *OnOK*, and *OnCancel* functions and performing specialized processing of your own; but if you do, be sure to call the equivalent functions in the base class so that the framework can do its part. And if you don't use DDX and DDV, you need to override *all* of these functions for every page in the property sheet to ensure that each page's data is handled properly. DDX and DDV simplify property sheet usage by letting the framework do the bulk of the work.

The PropDemo Application

The PropDemo application shown in Figure 8-11 is similar to DlgDemo1 and Dlg-Demo2, but it uses a property sheet instead of a dialog box to expose configuration settings to the user. The property sheet's Size page contains controls for setting the size of the ellipse displayed in the view. The Color page contains controls for modifying the ellipse's color. The property sheet is modal, so the main window can't be reactivated while the property sheet is displayed.

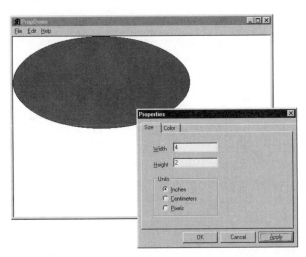

Figure 8-11. *The PropDemo window and property sheet.*

Selected portions of PropDemo's source code are reproduced in Figure 8-12. *CMyPropertySheet* represents the property sheet itself, and *CSizePage* and *CColorPage* represent the property sheet pages. All three classes were derived with ClassWizard. Instances of *CSizePage* and *CColorPage* named *m_sizePage* and *m_colorPage* are declared in *CMyPropertySheet* so that the page objects will be constructed automatically when the property sheet object is constructed. Furthermore, both *m_sizePage* and *m_colorPage* are declared public so that they can be accessed from outside of *CMyPropertySheet*.

The property sheet is created by *CChildView::OnFileProperties* when the user selects the Properties command from the File menu. After constructing a *CMyPropertySheet* object on the stack, *OnFileProperties* copies the current settings—width, height, units, and color—to the corresponding member variables in the property sheet page objects:

```
CMyPropertySheet ps (_T ("Properties"));
ps.m_sizePage.m_nWidth = m_nWidth;
ps.m_sizePage.m_nHeight = m_nHeight;
ps.m_sizePage.m_nUnits = m_nUnits;
ps.m_colorPage.m_nColor = m_nColor;
```

OnFileProperties then displays the property sheet by calling *DoModal*. If the property sheet is dismissed with the OK button, the new settings are copied from the property sheet pages and *Invalidate* is called to repaint the view and apply the changes:

```
if (ps.DoModal () == IDOK) {
    m_nWidth = ps.m_sizePage.m_nWidth;
    m_nHeight = ps.m_sizePage.m_nHeight;
    m_nUnits = ps.m_sizePage.m_nUnits;
    m_nColor = ps.m_colorPage.m_nColor;
    Invalidate ();
}
```

Both *CSizePage* and *CColorPage* map ON_BN_CLICKED notifications from radio buttons and EN_CHANGE notifications from edit controls to a class member function named *OnChange*. *OnChange* contains just one statement: a call to *SetModified* to enable the property sheet's Apply button. Consequently, any button click in a property sheet page, or any change to the text of an edit control, automatically enables the Apply button if it isn't already enabled.

When the Apply button is clicked, *CMyPropertySheet*'s *OnApply* function takes control. It first calls *UpdateData* on the active property sheet page to transfer the user's input from the page's controls to its data members. It then initializes an ELLPROP structure with the property settings obtained from each page's data members and sends a message to the main window containing the structure's address. The main window forwards the message to the view, which responds by copying the property values to its own data members and calling *Invalidate* to force a repaint. After *SendMessage* returns, *OnApply* disables the Apply button by calling each property sheet page's *SetModified* function.

MainFrm.h

```
// MainFrm.h : interface of the CMainFrame class
//
//////////////////////////////////////////////////////////////////////

#if
!defined(AFX_MAINFRM_H__9CE2B4A8_9067_11D2_8E53_006008A82731__INCLUDED_)
#define  AFX_MAINFRM_H__9CE2B4A8_9067_11D2_8E53_006008A82731__INCLUDED_

#if _MSC_VER > 1000
#pragma once
#endif // _MSC_VER > 1000

#include "ChildView.h"

class CMainFrame : public CFrameWnd
{

public:
    CMainFrame();
protected:
    DECLARE_DYNAMIC(CMainFrame)

// Attributes
public:

// Operations
public:

// Overrides
    // ClassWizard generated virtual function overrides
    //{{AFX_VIRTUAL(CMainFrame)
    virtual BOOL PreCreateWindow(CREATESTRUCT& cs);
    virtual BOOL OnCmdMsg(UINT nID, int nCode, void* pExtra,
        AFX_CMDHANDLERINFO* pHandlerInfo);
    //}}AFX_VIRTUAL

// Implementation
public:
    virtual ~CMainFrame();
#ifdef _DEBUG
    virtual void AssertValid() const;
    virtual void Dump(CDumpContext& dc) const;
#endif
    CChildView    m_wndView;
```

Figure 8-12. *The PropDemo application.*

```
// Generated message map functions
protected:
    //{{AFX_MSG(CMainFrame)
    afx_msg void OnSetFocus(CWnd *pOldWnd);
    afx_msg int OnCreate(LPCREATESTRUCT lpCreateStruct);
    //}}AFX_MSG
    afx_msg LRESULT OnApply (WPARAM wParam, LPARAM lParam);
    DECLARE_MESSAGE_MAP()
};

/////////////////////////////////////////////////////////////////////////

//{{AFX_INSERT_LOCATION}}
// Microsoft Visual C++ will insert additional declarations immediately
// before the previous line.

#endif
// !defined(AFX_MAINFRM_H__9CE2B4A8_9067_11D2_8E53_006008A82731__INCLUDED_)
```

MainFrm.cpp

```
// MainFrm.cpp : implementation of the CMainFrame class
//

#include "stdafx.h"
#include "PropDemo.h"

#include "MainFrm.h"

#ifdef _DEBUG
#define new DEBUG_NEW
#undef THIS_FILE
static char THIS_FILE[] = __FILE__;
#endif

/////////////////////////////////////////////////////////////////////////
// CMainFrame

IMPLEMENT_DYNAMIC(CMainFrame, CFrameWnd)

BEGIN_MESSAGE_MAP(CMainFrame, CFrameWnd)
    //{{AFX_MSG_MAP(CMainFrame)
    ON_WM_SETFOCUS()
    ON_WM_CREATE()
```

(continued)

Figure 8-12. *continued*

```
    //}}}AFX_MSG_MAP
    ON_MESSAGE (WM_USER_APPLY, OnApply)
END_MESSAGE_MAP()

/////////////////////////////////////////////////////////////////////////////
// CMainFrame construction/destruction

CMainFrame::CMainFrame()
{
}

CMainFrame::~CMainFrame()
{
}

BOOL CMainFrame::PreCreateWindow(CREATESTRUCT& cs)
{
    if( !CFrameWnd::PreCreateWindow(cs) )
        return FALSE;
    cs.dwExStyle &= ~WS_EX_CLIENTEDGE;
    cs.lpszClass = AfxRegisterWndClass(0);
    return TRUE;
}

/////////////////////////////////////////////////////////////////////////////
// CMainFrame diagnostics

#ifdef _DEBUG
void CMainFrame::AssertValid() const
{
    CFrameWnd::AssertValid();
}

void CMainFrame::Dump(CDumpContext& dc) const
{
    CFrameWnd::Dump(dc);
}

#endif //_DEBUG

/////////////////////////////////////////////////////////////////////////////
// CMainFrame message handlers
void CMainFrame::OnSetFocus(CWnd* pOldWnd)
{
    // forward focus to the view window
    m_wndView.SetFocus();
}
```

```
BOOL CMainFrame::OnCmdMsg(UINT nID, int nCode, void* pExtra,
    AFX_CMDHANDLERINFO* pHandlerInfo)
{
    // let the view have first crack at the command
    if (m_wndView.OnCmdMsg(nID, nCode, pExtra, pHandlerInfo))
        return TRUE;

    // otherwise, do default handling
    return CFrameWnd::OnCmdMsg(nID, nCode, pExtra, pHandlerInfo);
}


int CMainFrame::OnCreate(LPCREATESTRUCT lpCreateStruct)
{
    if (CFrameWnd::OnCreate(lpCreateStruct) == -1)
        return -1;

    if (!m_wndView.Create(NULL, NULL, AFX_WS_DEFAULT_VIEW,
        CRect(0, 0, 0, 0), this, AFX_IDW_PANE_FIRST, NULL))
        return -1;

    return 0;
}

LRESULT CMainFrame::OnApply (WPARAM wParam, LPARAM lParam)
{
    m_wndView.SendMessage (WM_USER_APPLY, wParam, lParam);
    return 0;
}
```

ChildView.h

```
// ChildView.h : interface of the CChildView class
//
/////////////////////////////////////////////////////////////////////////

#if
!defined(AFX_CHILDVIEW_H__9CE2B4AA_9067_11D2_8E53_006008A82731__INCLUDED_)
#define AFX_CHILDVIEW_H__9CE2B4AA_9067_11D2_8E53_006008A82731__INCLUDED_

#if _MSC_VER > 1000
#pragma once
#endif // _MSC_VER > 1000
```

(continued)

Figure 8-12. *continued*

```
//////////////////////////////////////////////////////////////////////////
// CChildView window

class CChildView : public CWnd
{
// Construction
public:
    CChildView();

// Attributes
public:

// Operations
public:

// Overrides
    // ClassWizard generated virtual function overrides
    //{{AFX_VIRTUAL(CChildView)
    protected:
    virtual BOOL PreCreateWindow(CREATESTRUCT& cs);
    //}}AFX_VIRTUAL

// Implementation
public:
    virtual ~CChildView();

    // Generated message map functions
protected:
    int m_nUnits;
    int m_nHeight;
    int m_nWidth;
    int m_nColor;
    //{{AFX_MSG(CChildView)
    afx_msg void OnPaint();
    afx_msg void OnFileProperties();
    //}}AFX_MSG
    afx_msg LRESULT OnApply (WPARAM wParam, LPARAM lParam);
    DECLARE_MESSAGE_MAP()
};

//////////////////////////////////////////////////////////////////////////

//{{AFX_INSERT_LOCATION}}
// Microsoft Visual C++ will insert additional declarations immediately
// before the previous line.

#endif
//!defined(AFX_CHILDVIEW_H__9CE2B4AA_9067_11D2_8E53_006008A82731__INCLUDED_)
```

ChildView.cpp

```cpp
// ChildView.cpp : implementation of the CChildView class
//

#include "stdafx.h"
#include "PropDemo.h"
#include "ChildView.h"
#include "MyPropertySheet.h"

#ifdef _DEBUG
#define new DEBUG_NEW
#undef THIS_FILE
static char THIS_FILE[] = __FILE__;
#endif

/////////////////////////////////////////////////////////////////////////////
// CChildView

CChildView::CChildView()
{
    m_nWidth = 4;
    m_nHeight = 2;
    m_nUnits = 0;
    m_nColor = 0;
}

CChildView::~CChildView()
{
}

BEGIN_MESSAGE_MAP(CChildView,CWnd )
    //{{AFX_MSG_MAP(CChildView)
    ON_WM_PAINT()
    ON_COMMAND(ID_FILE_PROPERTIES, OnFileProperties)
    //}}AFX_MSG_MAP
    ON_MESSAGE (WM_USER_APPLY, OnApply)
END_MESSAGE_MAP()

/////////////////////////////////////////////////////////////////////////////
// CChildView message handlers

BOOL CChildView::PreCreateWindow(CREATESTRUCT& cs)
{
    if (!CWnd::PreCreateWindow(cs))
        return FALSE;

    cs.dwExStyle |= WS_EX_CLIENTEDGE;
    cs.style &= ~WS_BORDER;
```

(continued)

Figure 8-12. *continued*

```
    cs.lpszClass = AfxRegisterWndClass(CS_HREDRAW|CS_VREDRAW|CS_DBLCLKS,
        ::LoadCursor(NULL, IDC_ARROW), HBRUSH(COLOR_WINDOW+1), NULL);

    return TRUE;
}

void CChildView::OnPaint()
{
    CPaintDC dc(this); // Device context for painting.

    CBrush brush (CColorPage::m_clrColors[m_nColor]);
    CBrush* pOldBrush = dc.SelectObject (&brush);

    switch (m_nUnits) {

    case 0: // Inches.
        dc.SetMapMode (MM_LOENGLISH);
        dc.Ellipse (0, 0, m_nWidth * 100, -m_nHeight * 100);
        break;

    case 1: // Centimeters.
        dc.SetMapMode (MM_LOMETRIC);
        dc.Ellipse (0, 0, m_nWidth * 100, -m_nHeight * 100);
        break;

    case 2: // Pixels.
        dc.SetMapMode (MM_TEXT);
        dc.Ellipse (0, 0, m_nWidth, m_nHeight);
        break;
    }
    dc.SelectObject (pOldBrush);
}

void CChildView::OnFileProperties()
{
    CMyPropertySheet ps (_T ("Properties"));
    ps.m_sizePage.m_nWidth = m_nWidth;
    ps.m_sizePage.m_nHeight = m_nHeight;
    ps.m_sizePage.m_nUnits = m_nUnits;
    ps.m_colorPage.m_nColor = m_nColor;

    if (ps.DoModal () == IDOK) {
        m_nWidth = ps.m_sizePage.m_nWidth;
        m_nHeight = ps.m_sizePage.m_nHeight;
        m_nUnits = ps.m_sizePage.m_nUnits;
        m_nColor = ps.m_colorPage.m_nColor;
        Invalidate ();
    }
}
```

```
LRESULT CChildView::OnApply (WPARAM wParam, LPARAM lParam)
{
    ELLPROP* pep = (ELLPROP*) lParam;
    m_nWidth = pep->nWidth;
    m_nHeight = pep->nHeight;
    m_nUnits = pep->nUnits;
    m_nColor = pep->nColor;
    Invalidate ();
    return 0;
}
```

MyPropertySheet.h

```
#if
!defined(AFX_MYPROPERTYSHEET_H__418271A3_90D4_11D2_8E53_006008A82731__INCLUDED_)
#define
AFX_MYPROPERTYSHEET_H__418271A3_90D4_11D2_8E53_006008A82731__INCLUDED_

#include "SizePage.h"    // Added by ClassView
#include "ColorPage.h"    // Added by ClassView
#if _MSC_VER > 1000
#pragma once
#endif // _MSC_VER > 1000
// MyPropertySheet.h : header file
//

/////////////////////////////////////////////////////////////////////////
// CMyPropertySheet

class CMyPropertySheet : public CPropertySheet
{
    DECLARE_DYNAMIC(CMyPropertySheet)

// Construction
public:
    CMyPropertySheet(UINT nIDCaption, CWnd* pParentWnd = NULL,
        UINT iSelectPage = 0);
    CMyPropertySheet(LPCTSTR pszCaption, CWnd* pParentWnd = NULL,
        UINT iSelectPage = 0);

// Attributes
public:
    CColorPage m_colorPage;
    CSizePage m_sizePage;

// Operations
public:
```

(continued)

Figure 8-12. *continued*

```
// Overrides
    // ClassWizard generated virtual function overrides
    //{{AFX_VIRTUAL(CMyPropertySheet)
    //}}AFX_VIRTUAL

// Implementation
public:
    virtual ~CMyPropertySheet();

    // Generated message map functions
protected:
    //{{AFX_MSG(CMyPropertySheet)
        // NOTE - the ClassWizard will add and remove
        // member functions here.
    //}}AFX_MSG
    afx_msg void OnApply ();
    DECLARE_MESSAGE_MAP()
};


/////////////////////////////////////////////////////////////////////////

//{{AFX_INSERT_LOCATION}}
// Microsoft Visual C++ will insert additional declarations immediately
// before the previous line.

#endif
// !defined(
//   AFX_MYPROPERTYSHEET_H__418271A3_90D4_11D2_8E53_006008A82731__INCLUDED_)
```

MyPropertySheet.cpp

```
// MyPropertySheet.cpp : implementation file
//

#include "stdafx.h"
#include "PropDemo.h"
#include "MyPropertySheet.h"

#ifdef _DEBUG
#define new DEBUG_NEW
#undef THIS_FILE
static char THIS_FILE[] = __FILE__;
#endif
```

```
///////////////////////////////////////////////////////////////////////////
// CMyPropertySheet

IMPLEMENT_DYNAMIC(CMyPropertySheet, CPropertySheet)

CMyPropertySheet::CMyPropertySheet(UINT nIDCaption, CWnd* pParentWnd,
    UINT iSelectPage) : CPropertySheet(nIDCaption, pParentWnd, iSelectPage)
{
    AddPage (&m_sizePage);
    AddPage (&m_colorPage);
}

CMyPropertySheet::CMyPropertySheet(LPCTSTR pszCaption, CWnd* pParentWnd,
    UINT iSelectPage) : CPropertySheet(pszCaption, pParentWnd, iSelectPage)
{
    AddPage (&m_sizePage);
    AddPage (&m_colorPage);
}

CMyPropertySheet::~CMyPropertySheet()
{
}

BEGIN_MESSAGE_MAP(CMyPropertySheet, CPropertySheet)
    //{{AFX_MSG_MAP(CMyPropertySheet)
        // NOTE - the ClassWizard will add and remove mapping macros here.
    //}}AFX_MSG_MAP
    ON_BN_CLICKED (ID_APPLY_NOW, OnApply)
END_MESSAGE_MAP()

///////////////////////////////////////////////////////////////////////////
// CMyPropertySheet message handlers

void CMyPropertySheet::OnApply ()
{
    GetActivePage ()->UpdateData (TRUE);

    ELLPROP ep;
    ep.nWidth = m_sizePage.m_nWidth;
    ep.nHeight = m_sizePage.m_nHeight;
    ep.nUnits = m_sizePage.m_nUnits;
    ep.nColor = m_colorPage.m_nColor;

    GetParent ()->SendMessage (WM_USER_APPLY, 0, (LPARAM) &ep);

    m_sizePage.SetModified (FALSE);
    m_colorPage.SetModified (FALSE);
}
```

(continued)

Figure 8-12. *continued*

SizePage.h

```
#if
!defined(AFX_SIZEPAGE_H__418271A1_90D4_11D2_8E53_006008A82731__INCLUDED_)
#define  AFX_SIZEPAGE_H__418271A1_90D4_11D2_8E53_006008A82731__INCLUDED_

#if _MSC_VER > 1000
#pragma once
#endif // _MSC_VER > 1000
// SizePage.h : header file
//


/////////////////////////////////////////////////////////////////////////////
// CSizePage dialog

class CSizePage : public CPropertyPage
{
    DECLARE_DYNCREATE(CSizePage)

// Construction
public:
    CSizePage();
    ~CSizePage();

// Dialog Data
    //{{AFX_DATA(CSizePage)
    enum { IDD = IDD_SIZE_PAGE };
    int        m_nWidth;
    int        m_nHeight;
    int        m_nUnits;
    //}}AFX_DATA


// Overrides
    // ClassWizard generate virtual function overrides
    //{{AFX_VIRTUAL(CSizePage)
    protected:
    virtual void DoDataExchange(CDataExchange* pDX);    // DDX/DDV support
    //}}AFX_VIRTUAL

// Implementation
protected:
    // Generated message map functions
    //{{AFX_MSG(CSizePage)
        // NOTE: the ClassWizard will add member functions here
```

```
    //}}AFX_MSG
    afx_msg void OnChange ();
    DECLARE_MESSAGE_MAP()

};

//{{AFX_INSERT_LOCATION}}
// Microsoft Visual C++ will insert additional declarations immediately
// before the previous line.

#endif
//!defined(AFX_SIZEPAGE_H__418271A1_90D4_11D2_8E53_006008A82731__INCLUDED_)
```

SizePage.cpp

```
// SizePage.cpp : implementation file
//

#include "stdafx.h"
#include "PropDemo.h"
#include "SizePage.h"

#ifdef _DEBUG
#define new DEBUG_NEW
#undef THIS_FILE
static char THIS_FILE[] = __FILE__;
#endif

/////////////////////////////////////////////////////////////////////////////
// CSizePage property page

IMPLEMENT_DYNCREATE(CSizePage, CPropertyPage)

CSizePage::CSizePage() : CPropertyPage(CSizePage::IDD)
{
    //{{AFX_DATA_INIT(CSizePage)
    m_nWidth = 0;
    m_nHeight = 0;
    m_nUnits = -1;
    //}}AFX_DATA_INIT
}

CSizePage::~CSizePage()
{
}
```

(continued)

Figure 8-12. *continued*

```
void CSizePage::DoDataExchange(CDataExchange* pDX)
{
    CPropertyPage::DoDataExchange(pDX);
    //{{AFX_DATA_MAP(CSizePage)
    DDX_Text(pDX, IDC_WIDTH, m_nWidth);
    DDV_MinMaxInt(pDX, m_nWidth, 1, 128);
    DDX_Text(pDX, IDC_HEIGHT, m_nHeight);
    DDV_MinMaxInt(pDX, m_nHeight, 1, 128);
    DDX_Radio(pDX, IDC_INCHES, m_nUnits);
    //}}AFX_DATA_MAP
}

BEGIN_MESSAGE_MAP(CSizePage, CPropertyPage)
    //{{AFX_MSG_MAP(CSizePage)
        // NOTE: the ClassWizard will add message map macros here
    //}}AFX_MSG_MAP
    ON_EN_CHANGE (IDC_WIDTH, OnChange)
    ON_EN_CHANGE (IDC_HEIGHT, OnChange)
    ON_BN_CLICKED (IDC_INCHES, OnChange)
    ON_BN_CLICKED (IDC_CENTIMETERS, OnChange)
    ON_BN_CLICKED (IDC_PIXELS, OnChange)
END_MESSAGE_MAP()

/////////////////////////////////////////////////////////////////////////
// CSizePage message handlers

void CSizePage::OnChange ()
{
    SetModified (TRUE);
}
```

ColorPage.h

```
#if
!defined(AFX_COLORPAGE_H__418271A2_90D4_11D2_8E53_006008A82731__INCLUDED_)
#define AFX_COLORPAGE_H__418271A2_90D4_11D2_8E53_006008A82731__INCLUDED_

#if _MSC_VER > 1000
#pragma once
#endif // _MSC_VER > 1000
// ColorPage.h : header file
//
```

```
///////////////////////////////////////////////////////////////////////////
// CColorPage dialog

class CColorPage : public CPropertyPage
{
    DECLARE_DYNCREATE(CColorPage)

// Construction
public:
    CColorPage();
    ~CColorPage();
    static const COLORREF m_clrColors[3];

// Dialog Data
    //{{AFX_DATA(CColorPage)
    enum { IDD = IDD_COLOR_PAGE };
    int         m_nColor;
    //}}AFX_DATA

// Overrides
    // ClassWizard generate virtual function overrides
    //{{AFX_VIRTUAL(CColorPage)
    protected:
    virtual void DoDataExchange(CDataExchange* pDX);    // DDX/DDV support
    //}}AFX_VIRTUAL

// Implementation
protected:
    // Generated message map functions
    //{{AFX_MSG(CColorPage)
        // NOTE: the ClassWizard will add member functions here
    //}}AFX_MSG
    afx_msg void OnChange ();
    DECLARE_MESSAGE_MAP()

};


//{{AFX_INSERT_LOCATION}}
// Microsoft Visual C++ will insert additional declarations immediately
// before the previous line.

#endif
//defined(AFX_COLORPAGE_H__418271A2_90D4_11D2_8E53_006008A82731__INCLUDED_)
```

(continued)

Figure 8-12. *continued*

ColorPage.cpp

```cpp
// ColorPage.cpp : implementation file
//

#include "stdafx.h"
#include "PropDemo.h"
#include "ColorPage.h"

#ifdef _DEBUG
#define new DEBUG_NEW
#undef THIS_FILE
static char THIS_FILE[] = __FILE__;
#endif

/////////////////////////////////////////////////////////////////////////////
// CColorPage property page

IMPLEMENT_DYNCREATE(CColorPage, CPropertyPage)

const COLORREF CColorPage::m_clrColors[3] = {
    RGB (255,   0,   0),    // Red
    RGB (  0, 255,   0),    // Green
    RGB (  0,   0, 255)     // Blue
};

CColorPage::CColorPage() : CPropertyPage(CColorPage::IDD)
{
    //{{AFX_DATA_INIT(CColorPage)
    m_nColor = -1;
    //}}AFX_DATA_INIT
}

CColorPage::~CColorPage()
{
}

void CColorPage::DoDataExchange(CDataExchange* pDX)
{
    CPropertyPage::DoDataExchange(pDX);
    //{{AFX_DATA_MAP(CColorPage)
    DDX_Radio(pDX, IDC_RED, m_nColor);
    //}}AFX_DATA_MAP
}

BEGIN_MESSAGE_MAP(CColorPage, CPropertyPage)
    //{{AFX_MSG_MAP(CColorPage)
        // NOTE: the ClassWizard will add message map macros here
```

```
    //}}AFX_MSG_MAP
    ON_BN_CLICKED (IDC_RED, OnChange)
    ON_BN_CLICKED (IDC_GREEN, OnChange)
    ON_BN_CLICKED (IDC_BLUE, OnChange)
END_MESSAGE_MAP()


/////////////////////////////////////////////////////////////////////////
// CColorPage message handlers

void CColorPage::OnChange ()
{
    SetModified (TRUE);
}
```

THE COMMON DIALOGS

Some dialog boxes appear so frequently in application programs that they have right-fully taken their places as part of the operating system. Before Windows 3.1, programmers had to write their own Open and Save As dialog boxes to get a file name from the user before opening or saving a file. Because both the design and the implementation of these dialog boxes were left up to the programmer, every Open and Save As dialog box was different, and some were far inferior to others. Windows 3.1 fixed this long-standing problem by providing standard implementations of these and other commonly used dialog boxes in a DLL known as the *common dialog library*. Windows 95 enhanced the library with improved versions of the Windows 3.1 common dialogs and a new Page Setup dialog box for entering page layouts. Windows 98 and Windows 2000 further refine the common dialogs to make them more functional than ever.

MFC provides C++ interfaces to the common dialogs with the classes shown in the following table.

THE COMMON DIALOG CLASSES

Class	*Dialog Type(s)*
CFileDialog	Open and Save As dialog boxes
CPrintDialog	Print and Print Setup dialog boxes
CPageSetupDialog	Page Setup dialog boxes
CFindReplaceDialog	Find and Replace dialog boxes
CColorDialog	Color dialog boxes
CFontDialog	Font dialog boxes

In an SDK-style application, a common dialog is invoked by filling in the fields of a data structure and calling an API function such as *::GetOpenFileName*. When the function returns, certain fields of the data structure contain values input by the user. MFC simplifies the interface by providing default input values for most fields and member functions for retrieving data entered into the dialog box. In an MFC application, getting a file name from the user before opening a file is normally no more complicated than this:

```
TCHAR szFilters[] =
    _T ("Text files (*.txt)¦*.txt¦All files (*.*)¦*.*¦¦");

CFileDialog dlg (TRUE, _T ("txt"), _T ("*.txt"),
    OFN_FILEMUSTEXIST ¦ OFN_HIDEREADONLY, szFilters);

if (dlg.DoModal () == IDOK) {
    filename = dlg.GetPathName ();
    // Open the file and read it.
        :
        :
}
```

The TRUE parameter passed to *CFileDialog*'s constructor tells MFC to display an Open dialog box rather than a Save As dialog box. The "txt" and "*.txt" parameters specify the default file name extension—the extension that is appended to the file name if the user doesn't enter an extension—and the text that initially appears in the dialog's File Name box. The OFN values are bit flags that specify the dialog's properties. OFN_FILEMUSTEXIST tells the dialog to test the file name the user enters and reject it if the file doesn't exist, and OFN_HIDEREADONLY hides the read-only check box that appears in the dialog box by default. *szFilters* points to a string specifying the file types the user can select from. When *DoModal* returns, the file name that the user entered, complete with path name, can be retrieved with *CFileDialog::GetPathName*. Other useful *CFileDialog* functions include *GetFileName*, which retrieves a file name without the path, and *GetFileTitle*, which retrieves a file name with neither path nor extension.

Generally, you'll find that MFC's common dialog classes are exceptionally easy to use, in part because you can often instantiate a common dialog class directly and avoid deriving classes of your own.

Modifying the Common Dialogs

You can modify the behavior of *CFileDialog* and other common dialog classes in a number of ways. One method involves nothing more than changing the parameters passed to the dialog's constructor. For example, *CFileDialog::CFileDialog*'s fourth parameter accepts about two dozen different bit flags affecting the dialog's appearance and behavior. One use for these flags is to create an Open dialog box that features a multiple-selection list box in which the user can select several files instead of just one. Rather than construct the dialog like this,

```
CFileDialog dlg (TRUE, _T ("txt"), _T ("*.txt"),
    OFN_FILEMUSTEXIST | OFN_HIDEREADONLY, szFilters);
```

you would do it like this:

```
CFileDialog dlg (TRUE, _T ("txt"), _T ("*.txt"),
    OFN_FILEMUSTEXIST | OFN_HIDEREADONLY | OFN_ALLOWMULTISELECT,
    szFilters);
```

After *DoModal* returns, a list of file names is stored in the buffer referenced by the dialog object's *m_ofn.lpstrFile* data member. The file names are easily retrieved from the buffer with *CFileDialog*'s *GetStartPosition* and *GetNextPathName* functions.

When you construct a dialog box from *CFileDialog*, the class constructor fills in the fields of an OPENFILENAME structure with values defining the title for the dialog window, the initial directory, and other parameters. The structure's address is subsequently passed to *::GetOpenFileName* or *::GetSaveFileName*. Some of the values used to initialize the structure are taken from *CFileDialog*'s constructor parameter list, but other parameters are filled with default values appropriate for the majority of applications. Another way to customize an Open or a Save As dialog box is to modify the fields of the OPENFILENAME structure after constructing the dialog object but before calling *DoModal*. The OPENFILENAME structure is accessible through the public data member *m_ofn*.

Suppose you'd like to change the title of a multiple-selection file dialog to "Select File(s)" instead of "Open." In addition, you'd like the file name filter that was selected when the dialog box was closed to be selected again the next time the dialog box is displayed. Here's how you could make these changes:

```
CFileDialog dlg (TRUE, _T ("txt"), NULL,
    OFN_FILEMUSTEXIST | OFN_ALLOWMULTISELECT,
    szFilters);

dlg.m_ofn.nFilterIndex = m_nFilterIndex;
static char szTitle[] = _T ("Select File(s)");
dlg.m_ofn.lpstrTitle = szTitle;

if (dlg.DoModal () == IDOK) {
    m_nFilterIndex = dlg.m_ofn.nFilterIndex;
        .
        .
        .
}
```

When the program is started, *m_nFilterIndex* should be set to 1. The first time the dialog box is created, the first file filter will be selected by default. When the user dismisses the dialog box with the OK button, the index of the currently selected filter is copied out of the OPENFILENAME structure and saved in *m_nFilterIndex*. The next time the dialog box is invoked, the same filter will be selected automatically. In other words, the dialog box will remember the user's filter selection. For a more thorough encapsulation, you could make *m_nFilterIndex* a part of the dialog box rather than a member of an external class by deriving your own dialog class from *CFileDialog*, declaring *m_nFilterIndex* to be a static member variable of that class, and initializing it to 1 before constructing a *CMyFileDialog* object for the first time.

You can implement more extensive changes by deriving your own dialog class from *CFileDialog* and overriding key virtual functions. In addition to *OnOK* and *OnCancel*, you can override the virtual functions *OnFileNameOK*, *OnLBSelChanged-Notify*, and *OnShareViolation* to customize the way the dialog box validates file names, responds to changes in file name selections, and handles sharing violations. You can override *OnInitDialog* to perform all sorts of stunts, such as increasing the size of the dialog box and adding or deleting controls. (If you override *CFileDialog::OnInitDialog*, be sure to call the base class version from your own implementation.) You could, for example, stretch the dialog box horizontally and create a preview area that displays a thumbnail sketch of the contents of the currently selected file. By overriding *OnLBSel-ChangedNotify*, you could update the preview window when the selection changes.

The Phones Application

This chapter's final application, Phones, brings together into one project many of the concepts discussed in this chapter and in Chapter 7. As you can see in Figure 8-13, Phones is a simple phone list program that stores names and phone numbers. Names and phone numbers are entered and edited in a modal dialog box that features a standard edit control for names, a numeric edit control for phone numbers, and icon push buttons. Data entered into the application can be saved to disk and read back using the File menu's Open, Save, and Save As commands. Phones uses *CFileDialog* to solicit file names from the user and *CStdioFile* to perform its file I/O. It also uses the derived list box class *CPhonesListBox* as the base class for *CChildView*, and it uses message reflection in that class to allow the list box to respond to its own double-click notifications. I hand-edited the AppWizard-generated *CChildView* class to change the base class from *CWnd* to *CPhonesListBox*. Pertinent portions of the application's source code are shown in Figure 8-14.

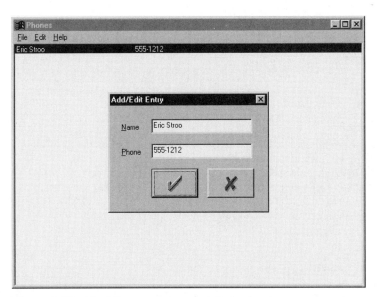

Figure 8-13. *The Phones window and dialog box.*

MainFrm.h

```
// MainFrm.h : interface of the CMainFrame class
//
/////////////////////////////////////////////////////////////////////

#if
!defined(AFX_MAINFRM_H__7BE4B248_90ED_11D2_8E53_006008A82731__INCLUDED_)
#define  AFX_MAINFRM_H__7BE4B248_90ED_11D2_8E53_006008A82731__INCLUDED_

#if _MSC_VER > 1000
#pragma once
#endif // _MSC_VER > 1000

#include "ChildView.h"

class CMainFrame : public CFrameWnd
{

public:
    CMainFrame();
protected:
    DECLARE_DYNAMIC(CMainFrame)
```

Figure 8-14. *The Phones application.*   *(continued)*

Figure 8-14. *continued*

```
// Attributes
public:

// Operations
public:

// Overrides
    // ClassWizard generated virtual function overrides
    //{{AFX_VIRTUAL(CMainFrame)
    virtual BOOL PreCreateWindow(CREATESTRUCT& cs);
    virtual BOOL OnCmdMsg(UINT nID, int nCode, void* pExtra,
        AFX_CMDHANDLERINFO* pHandlerInfo);
    //}}AFX_VIRTUAL

// Implementation
public:
    virtual ~CMainFrame();
#ifdef _DEBUG
    virtual void AssertValid() const;
    virtual void Dump(CDumpContext& dc) const;
#endif
    CChildView      m_wndView;

// Generated message map functions
protected:
    //{{AFX_MSG(CMainFrame)
    afx_msg void OnSetFocus(CWnd *pOldWnd);
    afx_msg int OnCreate(LPCREATESTRUCT lpCreateStruct);
    //}}AFX_MSG
    DECLARE_MESSAGE_MAP()
};

///////////////////////////////////////////////////////////////////////////

//{{AFX_INSERT_LOCATION}}
// Microsoft Visual C++ will insert additional declarations immediately
// before the previous line.

#endif
// !defined(AFX_MAINFRM_H__7BE4B248_90ED_11D2_8E53_006008A82731__INCLUDED_)
```

MainFrm.cpp

```
// MainFrm.cpp : implementation of the CMainFrame class
//
```

```
#include "stdafx.h"
#include "Phones.h"
#include "PhonesListBox.h"
#include "MainFrm.h"

#ifdef _DEBUG
#define new DEBUG_NEW
#undef THIS_FILE
static char THIS_FILE[] = __FILE__;
#endif

/////////////////////////////////////////////////////////////////////////////
// CMainFrame

IMPLEMENT_DYNAMIC(CMainFrame, CFrameWnd)

BEGIN_MESSAGE_MAP(CMainFrame, CFrameWnd)
    //{{AFX_MSG_MAP(CMainFrame)
    ON_WM_SETFOCUS()
    ON_WM_CREATE()
    //}}AFX_MSG_MAP
END_MESSAGE_MAP()

/////////////////////////////////////////////////////////////////////////////
// CMainFrame construction/destruction

CMainFrame::CMainFrame()
{
}

CMainFrame::~CMainFrame()
{
}

BOOL CMainFrame::PreCreateWindow(CREATESTRUCT& cs)
{
    if( !CFrameWnd::PreCreateWindow(cs) )
        return FALSE;
    cs.dwExStyle &= ~WS_EX_CLIENTEDGE;
    cs.lpszClass = AfxRegisterWndClass(0);
    return TRUE;
}

/////////////////////////////////////////////////////////////////////////////
// CMainFrame diagnostics
```

(continued)

Figure 8-14. *continued*

```
#ifdef _DEBUG
void CMainFrame::AssertValid() const
{
    CFrameWnd::AssertValid();
}

void CMainFrame::Dump(CDumpContext& dc) const
{
    CFrameWnd::Dump(dc);
}

#endif //_DEBUG

/////////////////////////////////////////////////////////////////////////////
// CMainFrame message handlers
void CMainFrame::OnSetFocus(CWnd* pOldWnd)
{
    // forward focus to the view window
    m_wndView.SetFocus();
}

BOOL CMainFrame::OnCmdMsg(UINT nID, int nCode, void* pExtra,
    AFX_CMDHANDLERINFO* pHandlerInfo)
{
    // let the view have first crack at the command
    if (m_wndView.OnCmdMsg(nID, nCode, pExtra, pHandlerInfo))
        return TRUE;

    // otherwise, do default handling
    return CFrameWnd::OnCmdMsg(nID, nCode, pExtra, pHandlerInfo);
}

int CMainFrame::OnCreate(LPCREATESTRUCT lpCreateStruct)
{
    if (CFrameWnd::OnCreate(lpCreateStruct) == -1)
        return -1;

    if (!m_wndView.Create(WS_CHILD | WS_VISIBLE | LBS_USETABSTOPS |
        LBS_SORT | LBS_NOTIFY | LBS_NOINTEGRALHEIGHT, CRect(0, 0, 0, 0),
        this, AFX_IDW_PANE_FIRST))
        return -1;

    return 0;
}
```

ChildView.h

```cpp
// ChildView.h : interface of the CChildView class
//
/////////////////////////////////////////////////////////////////////

#if
!defined(AFX_CHILDVIEW_H__7BE4B24A_90ED_11D2_8E53_006008A82731__INCLUDED_)
#define  AFX_CHILDVIEW_H__7BE4B24A_90ED_11D2_8E53_006008A82731__INCLUDED_

#if _MSC_VER > 1000
#pragma once
#endif // _MSC_VER > 1000


/////////////////////////////////////////////////////////////////////
// CChildView window

class CChildView : public CPhonesListBox
{
// Construction
public:
    CChildView();

// Attributes
public:

// Operations
public:

// Overrides
    // ClassWizard generated virtual function overrides
    //{{AFX_VIRTUAL(CChildView)
    protected:
    virtual BOOL PreCreateWindow(CREATESTRUCT& cs);
    //}}AFX_VIRTUAL

// Implementation
public:
    virtual ~CChildView();

    // Generated message map functions
protected:
    BOOL SaveFile (LPCTSTR pszFile);
    BOOL LoadFile (LPCTSTR pszFile);
    static const TCHAR m_szFilters[];
    CString m_strPathName;
```

(continued)

Figure 8-14. *continued*

```
    //{{AFX_MSG(CChildView)
    afx_msg void OnNewEntry();
    afx_msg void OnFileOpen();
    afx_msg void OnFileSave();
    afx_msg void OnFileSaveAs();
    //}}AFX_MSG
    DECLARE_MESSAGE_MAP()
};


//////////////////////////////////////////////////////////////////////

//{{AFX_INSERT_LOCATION}}
// Microsoft Visual C++ will insert additional declarations immediately
// before the previous line.

#endif
// !defined(
//    AFX_CHILDVIEW_H__7BE4B24A_90ED_11D2_8E53_006008A82731__INCLUDED_)
```

ChildView.cpp

```
// ChildView.cpp : implementation of the CChildView class
//

#include "stdafx.h"
#include "Phones.h"
#include "PhonesListBox.h"
#include "ChildView.h"

#ifdef _DEBUG
#define new DEBUG_NEW
#undef THIS_FILE
static char THIS_FILE[] = __FILE__;
#endif

//////////////////////////////////////////////////////////////////////
// CChildView

const TCHAR CChildView::m_szFilters[] =
    _T ("Phone Files (*.phn)¦*.phn¦All Files (*.*)¦*.*¦¦");

CChildView::CChildView()
{
}
```

```
CChildView::~CChildView()
{
}


BEGIN_MESSAGE_MAP(CChildView, CPhonesListBox)
    //{{AFX_MSG_MAP(CChildView)
    ON_COMMAND(ID_FILE_NEW, OnNewEntry)
    ON_COMMAND(ID_FILE_OPEN, OnFileOpen)
    ON_COMMAND(ID_FILE_SAVE, OnFileSave)
    ON_COMMAND(ID_FILE_SAVE_AS, OnFileSaveAs)
    //}}AFX_MSG_MAP
END_MESSAGE_MAP()


/////////////////////////////////////////////////////////////////////////////
// CChildView message handlers

BOOL CChildView::PreCreateWindow(CREATESTRUCT& cs)
{
    if (!CPhonesListBox::PreCreateWindow(cs))
        return FALSE;

    cs.dwExStyle |= WS_EX_CLIENTEDGE;
    cs.style &= ~WS_BORDER;
    return TRUE;
}


void CChildView::OnNewEntry()
{
    NewEntry ();
}


void CChildView::OnFileOpen()
{
    CFileDialog dlg (TRUE, _T ("phn"), _T ("*.phn"),
        OFN_FILEMUSTEXIST | OFN_HIDEREADONLY, m_szFilters);

    if (dlg.DoModal () == IDOK) {
        if (LoadFile (dlg.GetPathName ())) {
            m_strPathName = dlg.GetPathName ();
            SetCurSel (0);
        }
    }
}


void CChildView::OnFileSave()
{
    if (!m_strPathName.IsEmpty ())
```

(continued)

Figure 8-14. *continued*

```
            SaveFile (m_strPathName);
    else // Need a file name first.
        OnFileSaveAs ();
}

void CChildView::OnFileSaveAs()
{
    CFileDialog dlg (FALSE, _T ("phn"), m_strPathName,
        OFN_OVERWRITEPROMPT | OFN_PATHMUSTEXIST | OFN_HIDEREADONLY,
        m_szFilters);

    if (dlg.DoModal () == IDOK)
        if (SaveFile (dlg.GetPathName ()))
            m_strPathName = dlg.GetPathName ();
}

BOOL CChildView::LoadFile(LPCTSTR pszFile)
{
    BOOL bResult = FALSE;

    try {
        CStdioFile file (pszFile, CFile::modeRead);
        ResetContent ();
        DWORD dwCount;
        file.Read (&dwCount, sizeof (dwCount));
        if (dwCount) {
            for (int i=0; i<(int) dwCount; i++) {
                CString string;
                file.ReadString (string);
                AddString (string);
            }
        }
        bResult = TRUE;
    }
    catch (CFileException* e) {
        e->ReportError ();
        e->Delete ();
    }
    return bResult;
}

BOOL CChildView::SaveFile(LPCTSTR pszFile)
{
    BOOL bResult = FALSE;

    try {
        CStdioFile file (pszFile, CFile::modeWrite | CFile::modeCreate);
```

```
        DWORD dwCount = GetCount ();
        file.Write (&dwCount, sizeof (dwCount));
        if (dwCount) {
            for (int i=0; i<(int) dwCount; i++) {
                CString string;
                GetText (i, string);
                string += _T ("\n");
                file.WriteString (string);
            }
        }
        bResult = TRUE;
    }
    catch (CFileException* e) {
        e->ReportError ();
        e->Delete ();
    }
    return bResult;
}
```

PhonesListBox.h

```
#if
!defined(AFX_PHONESLISTBOX_H__7BE4B250_90ED_11D2_8E53_006008A82731__INCLUDED_)
#define
AFX_PHONESLISTBOX_H__7BE4B250_90ED_11D2_8E53_006008A82731__INCLUDED_

#if _MSC_VER > 1000
#pragma once
#endif // _MSC_VER > 1000
// PhonesListBox.h : header file
//

/////////////////////////////////////////////////////////////////////////
// CPhonesListBox window

class CPhonesListBox : public CListBox
{
// Construction
public:
    CPhonesListBox();

// Attributes
public:

// Operations
public:
```

(continued)

Figure 8-14. *continued*

```
// Overrides
    // ClassWizard generated virtual function overrides
    //{{AFX_VIRTUAL(CPhonesListBox)
    //}}AFX_VIRTUAL

// Implementation
public:
    void NewEntry();
    virtual ~CPhonesListBox();

    // Generated message map functions
protected:
    CFont m_font;
    //{{AFX_MSG(CPhonesListBox)
    afx_msg int OnCreate(LPCREATESTRUCT lpCreateStruct);
    afx_msg void OnEditItem();
    //}}AFX_MSG

    DECLARE_MESSAGE_MAP()
};


///////////////////////////////////////////////////////////////////////

//{{AFX_INSERT_LOCATION}}
// Microsoft Visual C++ will insert additional declarations immediately
// before the previous line.

#endif
// !defined(
//    AFX_PHONESLISTBOX_H__7BE4B250_90ED_11D2_8E53_006008A82731__INCLUDED_)
```

PhonesListBox.cpp

```
// PhonesListBox.cpp : implementation file
//

#include "stdafx.h"
#include "Phones.h"
#include "PhonesListBox.h"
#include "PhoneEdit.h"
#include "EditDialog.h"

#ifdef _DEBUG
#define new DEBUG_NEW
```

```
#undef THIS_FILE
static char THIS_FILE[] = __FILE__;
#endif

/////////////////////////////////////////////////////////////////////
// CPhonesListBox

CPhonesListBox::CPhonesListBox()
{
}

CPhonesListBox::~CPhonesListBox()
{
}

BEGIN_MESSAGE_MAP(CPhonesListBox, CListBox)
    //{{AFX_MSG_MAP(CPhonesListBox)
    ON_WM_CREATE()
    ON_CONTROL_REFLECT(LBN_DBLCLK, OnEditItem)
    //}}AFX_MSG_MAP
END_MESSAGE_MAP()

/////////////////////////////////////////////////////////////////////
// CPhonesListBox message handlers

int CPhonesListBox::OnCreate(LPCREATESTRUCT lpCreateStruct)
{
    if (CListBox::OnCreate(lpCreateStruct) == -1)
        return -1;

    m_font.CreatePointFont (80, _T ("MS Sans Serif"));
    SetFont (&m_font, FALSE);
    SetTabStops (128);
    return 0;
}

void CPhonesListBox::OnEditItem()
{
    CEditDialog dlg;

    CString strItem;
    int nIndex = GetCurSel ();
    GetText (nIndex, strItem);
    int nPos = strItem.Find (_T ('\t'));

    dlg.m_strName = strItem.Left (nPos);
    dlg.m_strPhone = strItem.Right (strItem.GetLength () - nPos - 1);
```

(continued)

Figure 8-14. *continued*

```
    if (dlg.DoModal () == IDOK) {
        strItem = dlg.m_strName + _T ("\t") + dlg.m_strPhone;
        DeleteString (nIndex);
        AddString (strItem);
    }
    SetFocus ();
}

void CPhonesListBox::NewEntry()
{
    CEditDialog dlg;
    if (dlg.DoModal () == IDOK) {
        CString strItem = dlg.m_strName + _T ("\t") + dlg.m_strPhone;
        AddString (strItem);
    }
    SetFocus ();
}
```

EditDialog.h

```
#if
!defined(AFX_EDITDIALOG_H__7BE4B252_90ED_11D2_8E53_006008A82731__INCLUDED_)
#define  AFX_EDITDIALOG_H__7BE4B252_90ED_11D2_8E53_006008A82731__INCLUDED_

#if _MSC_VER > 1000
#pragma once
#endif // _MSC_VER > 1000
// EditDialog.h : header file
//

/////////////////////////////////////////////////////////////////////////
// CEditDialog dialog

class CEditDialog : public CDialog
{
// Construction
public:
    CEditDialog(CWnd* pParent = NULL);   // standard constructor

// Dialog Data
    //{{AFX_DATA(CEditDialog)
    enum { IDD = IDD_EDITDLG };
    CButton     m_wndOK;
    CButton     m_wndCancel;
```

```
    CPhoneEdit      m_wndPhoneEdit;
    CString     m_strName;
    CString     m_strPhone;
    //}}AFX_DATA

// Overrides
    // ClassWizard generated virtual function overrides
    //{{AFX_VIRTUAL(CEditDialog)
    protected:
    virtual void DoDataExchange(CDataExchange* pDX);     // DDX/DDV support
    //}}AFX_VIRTUAL

// Implementation
protected:

    // Generated message map functions
    //{{AFX_MSG(CEditDialog)
    virtual BOOL OnInitDialog();
    //}}AFX_MSG
    DECLARE_MESSAGE_MAP()
};

//{{AFX_INSERT_LOCATION}}
// Microsoft Visual C++ will insert additional declarations immediately
// before the previous line.

#endif
// !defined(
//     AFX_EDITDIALOG_H__7BE4B252_90ED_11D2_8E53_006008A82731__INCLUDED_)
```

EditDialog.cpp

```
// EditDialog.cpp : implementation file
//

#include "stdafx.h"
#include "Phones.h"
#include "PhoneEdit.h"
#include "EditDialog.h"

#ifdef _DEBUG
#define new DEBUG_NEW
#undef THIS_FILE
static char THIS_FILE[] = __FILE__;
#endif
```

(continued)

Figure 8-14. *continued*

```
//////////////////////////////////////////////////////////////////////////
// CEditDialog dialog

CEditDialog::CEditDialog(CWnd* pParent /*=NULL*/)
    : CDialog(CEditDialog::IDD, pParent)
{
    //{{AFX_DATA_INIT(CEditDialog)
    m_strName = _T("");
    m_strPhone = _T("");
    //}}AFX_DATA_INIT
}

void CEditDialog::DoDataExchange(CDataExchange* pDX)
{
    CDialog::DoDataExchange(pDX);
    //{{AFX_DATA_MAP(CEditDialog)
    DDX_Control(pDX, IDOK, m_wndOK);
    DDX_Control(pDX, IDCANCEL, m_wndCancel);
    DDX_Control(pDX, IDC_PHONE, m_wndPhoneEdit);
    DDX_Text(pDX, IDC_NAME, m_strName);
    DDV_MaxChars(pDX, m_strName, 32);
    DDX_Text(pDX, IDC_PHONE, m_strPhone);
    //}}AFX_DATA_MAP
}

BEGIN_MESSAGE_MAP(CEditDialog, CDialog)
    //{{AFX_MSG_MAP(CEditDialog)
    //}}AFX_MSG_MAP
END_MESSAGE_MAP()


//////////////////////////////////////////////////////////////////////////
// CEditDialog message handlers

BOOL CEditDialog::OnInitDialog()
{
    CDialog::OnInitDialog();
    m_wndOK.SetIcon (AfxGetApp ()->LoadIcon (IDI_OK));
    m_wndCancel.SetIcon (AfxGetApp ()->LoadIcon (IDI_CANCEL));
    return TRUE;
}
```

PhoneEdit.h

```
#if !defined(AFX_PHONEEDIT_H__7BE4B251_90ED_11D2_8E53_006008A82731__INCLUDED_)
#define AFX_PHONEEDIT_H__7BE4B251_90ED_11D2_8E53_006008A82731__INCLUDED_
```

```
#if _MSC_VER > 1000
#pragma once
#endif // _MSC_VER > 1000
// PhoneEdit.h : header file
//

/////////////////////////////////////////////////////////////////////////////
// CPhoneEdit window

class CPhoneEdit : public CEdit
{
// Construction
public:
    CPhoneEdit();

// Attributes
public:

// Operations
public:

// Overrides
    // ClassWizard generated virtual function overrides
    //{{AFX_VIRTUAL(CPhoneEdit)
    //}}AFX_VIRTUAL

// Implementation
public:
    virtual ~CPhoneEdit();

    // Generated message map functions
protected:
    //{{AFX_MSG(CPhoneEdit)
    afx_msg void OnChar(UINT nChar, UINT nRepCnt, UINT nFlags);
    //}}AFX_MSG

    DECLARE_MESSAGE_MAP()
};

/////////////////////////////////////////////////////////////////////////////

//{{AFX_INSERT_LOCATION}}
// Microsoft Visual C++ will insert additional declarations immediately
// before the previous line.

#endif
//!defined(AFX_PHONEEDIT_H__7BE4B251_90ED_11D2_8E53_006008A82731__INCLUDED_)
```

(continued)

Figure 8-14. *continued*

PhoneEdit.cpp

```cpp
// PhoneEdit.cpp : implementation file
//

#include "stdafx.h"
#include "Phones.h"
#include "PhoneEdit.h"

#ifdef _DEBUG
#define new DEBUG_NEW
#undef THIS_FILE
static char THIS_FILE[] = __FILE__;
#endif

/////////////////////////////////////////////////////////////////////////////
// CPhoneEdit

CPhoneEdit::CPhoneEdit()
{
}

CPhoneEdit::~CPhoneEdit()
{
}

BEGIN_MESSAGE_MAP(CPhoneEdit, CEdit)
    //{{AFX_MSG_MAP(CPhoneEdit)
    ON_WM_CHAR()
    //}}AFX_MSG_MAP
END_MESSAGE_MAP()

/////////////////////////////////////////////////////////////////////////////
// CPhoneEdit message handlers

void CPhoneEdit::OnChar(UINT nChar, UINT nRepCnt, UINT nFlags)
{
    if (((nChar >= _T ('0')) && (nChar <= _T ('9'))) ||
        (nChar == VK_BACK) || (nChar == _T ('(')) || (nChar == _T (')')) ||
        (nChar == _T ('-')) || (nChar == _T (' ')))

        CEdit::OnChar(nChar, nRepCnt, nFlags);
}
```

One of the most subtle yet important elements of Phones' source code is the innocent-looking statement

```
DDX_Control (pDX, IDC_PHONE, m_wndPhoneEdit);
```

in EditDialog.cpp. *m_wndPhoneEdit* is an instance of the *CEdit*-derived class *CPhoneEdit*, which represents an edit control that filters out nonnumeric characters. But *m_wndPhoneEdit* is linked to IDC_PHONE, which is an ordinary edit control created from the dialog template. The only reason IDC_PHONE acts like a *CPhoneEdit* instead of a *CEdit* is that *DDX_Control* subclasses the control and routes messages destined for the control through *m-wndPhoneEdit*'s message map. The moral is both simple and profound. Whenever you want a control in a dialog box to behave as if it were an instance of a derived control class, map the control to a class instance with *DDX_Control*. Otherwise, any special behavior built into the derived class will go unused.

Phones does a reasonable job of demonstrating how MFC's *CFileDialog* class is used and how documents can be written to disk and read back. What it doesn't do very well is safeguard the user's data. If a list of names and phone numbers contains unsaved changes and another list is loaded or the application is shut down, Phones doesn't prompt you to save your changes. That's not how a real application should behave. Phones has other shortcomings, too, such as the fact that it doesn't register a file name extension with the operating system so that a saved file can be opened with a double-click. But don't despair: document handling is infinitely cleaner when performed in the context of the document/view architecture, and in the next chapter, we'll finally begin writing document/view applications. Once we do, MFC will handle many of the mundane chores expected of Windows applications, such as registering file name extensions and giving users the opportunity to save changes. If you've never written a document/view application before, you'll be pleasantly surprised at the level of support the framework provides.

Part II

The Document/View Architecture

Chapter 9

Documents, Views, and the Single Document Interface

In the early days of MFC, applications were architected in very much the same style as the sample programs in the first three chapters of this book. In MFC 1.0, an application had two principal components: an application object representing the application itself and a window object representing the application's window. The application object's primary duty was to create a window, and the window in turn processed messages. Other than the fact that it provided general-purpose classes such as *CString* and *CTime* to represent objects unrelated to Microsoft Windows, MFC was little more than a thin wrapper around the Windows API that grafted an object-oriented interface onto windows, dialog boxes, device contexts, and other objects already present in Windows in one form or another.

MFC 2.0 changed the way Windows applications are written by introducing the document/view architecture. In a document/view application, the application's data is represented by a document object and views of that data are represented by view objects. Documents and views work together to process the user's input and draw textual and graphical representations of the resulting data. MFC's *CDocument* class is the base class for document objects, and *CView* is the base class for view objects. The application's main window, whose behavior is modeled in MFC's *CFrameWnd* and *CMDIFrameWnd* classes, is no longer the focal point for message processing but serves primarily as a container for views, toolbars, status bars, and other user interface objects.

A programming model that separates documents from their views provides many benefits, not the least of which is that it more clearly defines the division of labor among software components and results in a higher degree of modularity. But the more compelling reason to take advantage of MFC's document/view architecture is that it simplifies the development process. Code to perform routine chores such as prompting the user to save unsaved data before a document is closed is provided for you by the framework. So is code to transform ordinary applications into Active Document servers, to save documents to disk and read them back, to simplify printing, and much more.

MFC supports two types of document/view applications. *Single document interface* (SDI) applications support just one open document at a time. *Multiple document interface* (MDI) applications permit two or more documents to be open concurrently and also support multiple views of a given document. The WordPad applet is an SDI application; Microsoft Word is an MDI application. The framework hides many of the differences between the two user interface models so that writing an MDI application is not much different than writing an SDI application, but today developers are discouraged from using the multiple document interface because the SDI model promotes a more document-centric user interface. If the user is to edit two documents simultaneously, Microsoft would prefer that each document be displayed in a separate instance of your application. This chapter therefore examines the document/view architecture with a decided emphasis on the single document interface. Everything that you learn here, however, applies to MDI applications as well, and for completeness we'll examine the multiple document interface as well as methods for supporting multiple views in SDI applications in Chapter 11.

DOCUMENT/VIEW FUNDAMENTALS

Let's begin our exploration of the document/view architecture with a conceptual look at the various objects involved and the relationships they share with one another. Figure 9-1 shows a schematic representation of an SDI document/view application. The frame window is the application's top-level window. It's normally a WS_OVERLAPPED-WINDOW-style window with a resizing border, a title bar, a system menu, and minimize, maximize, and close buttons. The view is a child window sized to fit the frame window so that it becomes, for all practical purposes, the frame window's client area.

The application's data is stored in the document object, a visible representation of which appears in the view. For an SDI application, the frame window class is derived from *CFrameWnd*, the document class is derived from *CDocument*, and the view class is derived from *CView* or a related class such as *CScrollView*.

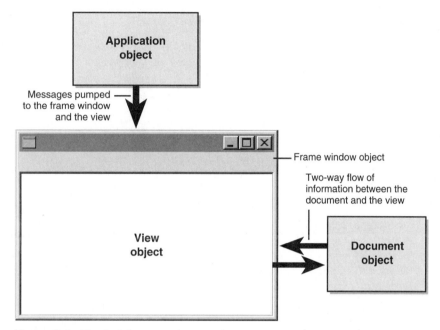

Figure 9-1. *The SDI document/view architecture.*

The arrows represent data flow. The application object provides the message loop that pumps messages to the frame window and the view. The view object translates mouse and keyboard input into commands that operate on the data stored in the document object, and the document object provides the data that the view needs to render its output. The individual objects interact in other ways, too, but you'll find the big picture easier to grasp after you've learned more about the role each object plays in a program's operation and have written a document/view application or two of your own.

The architecture depicted in Figure 9-1 has very real implications for the design and operation of an application program. In an MFC 1.0–style application, a program's data is often stored in member variables declared in the frame window class. The frame window draws "views" of that data by accessing its own member variables and using GDI functions encapsulated in the *CDC* class to draw into its client area. The document/view architecture enforces a modular program design by encapsulating data in a stand-alone document object and providing a view object for the program's screen output. A document/view application never grabs a client-area device context for its frame window and draws into it; instead, it draws into the view. It *looks* as if the drawing is being done in the frame window, but in reality all output goes to the view. You can draw into the frame window if you want to, but you won't see the output because the client area of an SDI frame window is completely obscured by the view.

The *InitInstance* Function Revisited

One of the most interesting aspects of an SDI document/view application is the way in which the frame window, document, and view objects are created. If you look at the *InitInstance* function for an SDI application generated by AppWizard, you'll see something like this:

```
CSingleDocTemplate* pDocTemplate;
pDocTemplate = new CSingleDocTemplate (
    IDR_MAINFRAME,
    RUNTIME_CLASS (CMyDoc),
    RUNTIME_CLASS (CMainFrame),
    RUNTIME_CLASS (CMyView)
);
AddDocTemplate (pDocTemplate);
        .
        .
        .

CCommandLineInfo cmdInfo;
ParseCommandLine (cmdInfo);

if (!ProcessShellCommand (cmdInfo))
    return FALSE;

m_pMainWnd->ShowWindow (SW_SHOW);
m_pMainWnd->UpdateWindow ();
```

This code is quite different from the startup code in the sample programs in Part I of this book. Let's look more closely at this *InitInstance* function to see what it takes to get a document/view application up and running.

To begin with, the statements

```
CSingleDocTemplate* pDocTemplate;
pDocTemplate = new CSingleDocTemplate (
    IDR_MAINFRAME,
    RUNTIME_CLASS (CMyDoc),
    RUNTIME_CLASS (CMainFrame),
    RUNTIME_CLASS (CMyView)
);
```

create an SDI document template from MFC's *CSingleDocTemplate* class. The SDI document template is a crucial element of an SDI document/view application. It identifies the document class used to manage the application's data, the frame window class that encloses views of that data, and the view class used to draw visual representations of the data. The document template also stores a resource ID that the framework uses to load menus, accelerators, and other resources that shape the application's user interface. AppWizard uses the resource ID IDR_MAINFRAME in the code that it generates. The RUNTIME_CLASS macro surrounding the class names returns a pointer to a *CRuntimeClass* structure for the specified class, which enables the framework to create objects of that class at run time. This dynamic creation mechanism is another important element of the document/view architecture. I'll describe how it works a little later in this chapter.

After the document template is created, the statement

```
AddDocTemplate (pDocTemplate);
```

adds it to the list of document templates maintained by the application object. Each template registered in this way defines one document type the application supports. SDI applications register just one document type, but MDI applications can—and sometimes do—register several types.

The statements

```
CCommandLineInfo cmdInfo;
ParseCommandLine (cmdInfo);
```

use *CWinApp::ParseCommandLine* to initialize a *CCommandLineInfo* object with values reflecting the parameters entered on the command line, which often include a document file name. The statements

```
if (!ProcessShellCommand (cmdInfo))
    return FALSE;
```

"process" the command line parameters. Among other things, *ProcessShellCommand* calls *CWinApp::OnFileNew* to start the application with an empty document if no file name was entered on the command line, or *CWinApp::OpenDocumentFile* to load a document if a document name was specified. It's during this phase of the program's execution that the framework creates the document, frame window, and view objects using the information stored in the document template. (In case you're wondering, the document object is created first, followed by the frame window and then the view.) *ProcessShellCommand* returns TRUE if the initialization succeeds and FALSE if it doesn't. If initialization is successful, the statements

```
m_pMainWnd->ShowWindow (SW_SHOW);
m_pMainWnd->UpdateWindow ();
```

display the application's frame window (and by extension, the view) on the screen.

After the application is started and the document, frame window, and view objects are created, the message loop kicks in and the application begins to retrieve and process messages. Unlike MFC 1.0–type applications, which typically map all messages to member functions of the frame window class, document/view applications divide message processing among the application, document, view, and frame window objects. The framework does a lot of work in the background to make this division of labor possible. In Windows, only windows can receive messages, so MFC implements a sophisticated command-routing mechanism that sends certain types of messages from one object to another in a predefined order until one of the objects processes the message or the message is passed to *::DefWindowProc* for default processing. When we discuss command routing later in this chapter, it will become abundantly clear why command routing is a powerful feature of MFC whose absence would severely inhibit the usefulness of the document/view architecture.

The Document Object

In a document/view application, data is stored in a document object. The document object is created when the framework instantiates a class derived from *CDocument*. The term *document* is somewhat misleading because it stirs up visions of word processors and spreadsheet programs and other types of applications that deal with what we traditionally think of as documents. In reality, the "document" part of document/view is much more general than that. A document can be almost anything, from a deck of cards in a poker simulation to an online connection to a remote data source; it is an abstract representation of a program's data that draws a clear boundary between how the data is stored and how it is presented to the user. Typically, the document object provides public member functions that other objects, primarily views, can use to access the document's data. All handling of the data is performed by the document object itself.

A document's data is often stored in member variables of the derived document class. The Scribble tutorial supplied with Microsoft Visual C++ exposes its data directly to other objects by declaring its data members public, but stricter encapsulation is achieved by making document data private and providing public member functions for accessing it. The document object in a text editing program, for example, might store characters in a *CByteArray* object and provide *AddChar* and *RemoveChar* functions so that the view can convert the mouse and keyboard messages it receives into commands to add and remove characters. Other functions, such as *AddLine* and *DeleteLine*, could further enrich the interface between the document object and the views connected to it.

CDocument Operations

In MFC literature, "operation" is the term used to describe nonvirtual class member functions. A derived document class inherits several important operations from *CDocument*, some of which are listed in the following table.

KEY *CDOCUMENT* OPERATIONS

Function	*Description*
GetFirstViewPosition	Returns a POSITION value that can be passed to *GetNextView* to begin enumerating the views associated with this document
GetNextView	Returns a *CView* pointer to the next view in the list of views associated with this document
GetPathName	Retrieves the document's file name and path—for example, "C:\Documents\Personal\MyFile.doc"; returns an empty string if the document hasn't been named
GetTitle	Retrieves the document's title—for example, "MyFile"; returns an empty string if the document hasn't been named
IsModified	Returns a nonzero value if the document contains unsaved data or 0 if it doesn't
SetModifiedFlag	Sets or clears the document's modified flag, which indicates whether the document contains unsaved data
UpdateAllViews	Updates all views associated with the document by calling each view's *OnUpdate* function

Of these functions, *SetModifiedFlag* and *UpdateAllViews* are the two that you'll use the most. You should call *SetModifiedFlag* whenever the document's data is modified. This function sets a flag inside the document object that tells MFC the document contains unsaved data, which allows MFC to prompt the user before closing a document that contains unsaved changes. You can determine for yourself whether a document is "dirty" with *IsModified*. *UpdateAllViews* commands all the views attached to a document to update themselves. Under the hood, *UpdateAllViews* calls each view's *OnUpdate* function, whose default action is to invalidate the view to force a repaint. In an application that supports multiple views of its documents, calling *UpdateAllViews* whenever the document's data changes keeps all the different views in sync. Even a single-view application can call *UpdateAllViews* to refresh the view based on the data currently contained in the document.

A document object can enumerate its views and communicate with each view individually by using *GetFirstViewPosition* and *GetNextView* to walk the list of views. The excerpt on the following page from the MFC source code file Doccore.ccp demonstrates how *UpdateAllViews* uses *GetFirstViewPosition* and *GetNextView* to call each view's *OnUpdate* function.

```
POSITION pos = GetFirstViewPosition();
while (pos != NULL)
{
    CView* pView = GetNextView(pos);
        .
        .
        .
    pView->OnUpdate(pSender, lHint, pHint);
}
```

Given that *OnUpdate* is a protected member function of *CView*, you might wonder how this code can even compile. The answer is that *CDocument* is declared a friend of *CView* in Afxwin.h. You can freely call *GetFirstViewPosition* and *GetNextView* from your own code, but you can call *OnUpdate* from your document class only if you, too, declare the document to be a friend of the view.

CDocument Overridables

CDocument also includes several virtual functions, or "overridables," that can be overridden to customize a document's behavior. Some of these functions are almost always overridden in a derived document class. The four most commonly used overridables are shown in the following table.

KEY *CDOCUMENT* OVERRIDABLES

Function	Description
OnNewDocument	Called by the framework when a new document is created. Override to apply specific initializations to the document object each time a new document is created.
OnOpenDocument	Called by the framework when a document is loaded from disk. Override to apply specific initializations to the document object each time a document is loaded.
DeleteContents	Called by the framework to delete the document's contents. Override to free memory and other resources allocated to the document before it is closed.
Serialize	Called by the framework to serialize the document to or from disk. Override to provide document-specific serialization code so that documents can be loaded and saved.

In an SDI application, MFC instantiates the document object once—when the application starts up—and reuses that object over and over as document files are opened and closed. Because the document object is created just one time, initializations performed by the document's class constructor are executed only once, too. But what if your derived document class contains member variables that you want to reinitialize whenever a new document is created or an existing document is loaded from disk?

That's where *OnNewDocument* and *OnOpenDocument* come in. MFC calls the document's *OnNewDocument* function whenever a new document is created. Typically, that occurs when the user chooses New from the File menu. MFC calls *OnOpenDocument* when a document is loaded from disk—that is, whenever the user selects Open from the File menu. You can perform one-time initializations in an SDI document class's constructor. But if you want to perform certain initializations anytime a document is created or opened, you must override *OnNewDocument* or *OnOpenDocument*.

MFC provides default implementations of *OnNewDocument* and *OnOpenDocument* that shoulder the burden of creating new documents and opening existing documents. If you override *OnNewDocument* and *OnOpenDocument*, you should call the equivalent functions in the base class, as shown here:

```
BOOL CMyDoc::OnNewDocument ()
{
    if (!CDocument::OnNewDocument ())
        return FALSE;
    // Insert application-specific initialization code here.
    return TRUE;
}

BOOL CMyDoc::OnOpenDocument (LPCTSTR lpszPathName)
{
    if (!CDocument::OnOpenDocument (lpszPathName))
        return FALSE;
    // Insert application-specific initialization code here.
    return TRUE;
}
```

Generally speaking, MFC applications more commonly override *OnNewDocument* than *OnOpenDocument*. Why? Because *OnOpenDocument* indirectly calls the document's *Serialize* function, which initializes a document's persistent data members with values retrieved from a document file. Only nonpersistent data members— those that aren't initialized by *Serialize*—need to be initialized in *OnOpenDocument*. *OnNewDocument*, by contrast, performs no default initialization of the document's data members. If you add data members to a document class and want those data members reinitialized whenever a new document is created, you need to override *OnNewDocument*.

Before a new document is created or opened, the framework calls the document object's virtual *DeleteContents* function to delete the document's existing data. Therefore, an SDI application can override *CDocument::DeleteContents* and take the opportunity to free any resources allocated to the document and perform other necessary cleanup chores in preparation for reusing the document object. MDI applications generally follow this model also, although MDI document objects differ from SDI document objects in that they are individually created and destroyed as the user opens and closes documents.

When a document is opened or saved, the framework calls the document object's *Serialize* function to serialize the document's data. You implement the *Serialize* function so that it streams the document's data in and out; the framework does everything else, including opening the file for reading or writing and providing a *CArchive* object to insulate you from the vagaries of physical disk I/O. A derived document class's *Serialize* function is typically structured like this:

```
void CMyDoc::Serialize (CArchive& ar)
{
    if (ar.IsStoring ()) {
        // Write the document's persistent data to the archive.
    }
    else { // Loading, not storing
        // Read the document's persistent data from the archive.
    }
}
```

In place of the comments, you include code that streams the document's persistent data to or from an archive using the serialization mechanism described in Chapter 6. For a simple document class whose data consists of two strings stored in *CString* member variables named *m_strName* and *m_strPhone*, you could write *Serialize* like this:

```
void CMyDoc::Serialize (CArchive& ar)
{
    if (ar.IsStoring ()) {
        ar << m_strName << m_strPhone;
    }
    else { // Loading, not storing.
        ar >> m_strName >> m_strPhone;
    }
}
```

If your document's data is composed of primitive data types and serializable classes like *CString*, writing a *Serialize* function is exceedingly easy because all input and output can be performed with the << and >> operators. For structures and other nonserializable data types, you can use the *CArchive* functions *Read* and *Write*. *CArchive* even includes *ReadString* and *WriteString* functions for serializing raw strings. If all else fails, you can call *CArchive::GetFile* to get a *CFile* pointer for interacting directly with the file attached to the archive. You'll see this technique used in Chapter 13's HexDump program.

Other *CDocument* overridables that aren't used as often but that can be useful include *OnCloseDocument*, which is called when a document is closed; *OnSaveDocument*, which is called when a document is saved; *SaveModified*, which is called before a document containing unsaved data is closed to ask the user whether changes should be saved; and *ReportSaveLoadException*, which is called when an error occurs during serialization. There are others, but for the most part they constitute advanced overridables that you'll rarely find occasion to use.

The View Object

Whereas the sole purpose of a document object is to manage an application's data, view objects exist for two purposes: to render visual representations of a document on the screen and to translate the user's input—particularly mouse and keyboard messages—into commands that operate on the document's data. Thus, documents and views are tightly interrelated, and information flows between them in both directions.

MFC's *CView* class defines the basic properties of a view. MFC also includes a family of view classes derived from *CView* that add functionality to views. *CScrollView*, for example, adds scrolling capabilities to *CView*. *CScrollView* and other *CView* derivatives are discussed in Chapter 10.

The *GetDocument* Function

A document object can have any number of views associated with it, but a view always belongs to just one document. The framework stores a pointer to the associated document object in a view's *m_pDocument* data member and exposes that pointer through the view's *GetDocument* member function. Just as a document object can identify its views using *GetFirstViewPosition* and *GetNextView*, a view can identify its document by calling *GetDocument*.

When AppWizard generates the source code for a view class, it overrides the base class's *GetDocument* function with one that casts *m_pDocument* to the appropriate document type and returns the result. This override allows type-safe access to the document object and eliminates the need for an explicit cast each time *GetDocument* is called.

CView Overridables

Like the *CDocument* class, *CView* includes several virtual member functions that you can override in a derived class to customize a view's behavior. The key overridables are shown in the following table. The most important is a pure virtual function named *OnDraw*, which is called each time the view receives a WM_PAINT message. In non-document/view applications, WM_PAINT messages are processed by *OnPaint* handlers that use *CPaintDC* objects to do their drawing. In document/view applications, the framework fields the WM_PAINT message, creates a *CPaintDC* object, and calls the view's *OnDraw* function with a pointer to the *CPaintDC* object. The following implementation of *OnDraw* retrieves a *CString* from the document object and displays it in the center of the view:

```
void CMyView::OnDraw (CDC* pDC)
{
    CMyDoc* pDoc = GetDocument ();
    CString string = pDoc->GetString ();
    CRect rect;
    GetClientRect (&rect);
    pDC->DrawText (string, rect,
        DT_SINGLELINE | DT_CENTER | DT_VCENTER);
}
```

Notice that *OnDraw* uses the supplied device context pointer rather than instantiate a device context of its own.

KEY *CVIEW* OVERRIDABLES

Function	Description
OnDraw	Called to draw the document's data. Override to paint views of a document.
OnInitialUpdate	Called when a view is first attached to a document. Override to initialize the view object each time a document is created or loaded.
OnUpdate	Called when the document's data has changed and the view needs to be updated. Override to implement "smart" update behavior that redraws only the part of the view that needs redrawing rather than the entire view.

The fact that the view doesn't have to construct its own device context object is a minor convenience. The real reason the framework uses *OnDraw* is so that the same code can be used for output to a window, for printing, and for print previewing. When a WM_PAINT message arrives, the framework passes the view a pointer to a screen device context so that output will go to the window. When a document is printed, the framework calls the same *OnDraw* function and passes it a pointer to a printer device context. Because the GDI is a device-independent graphics system, the same code can produce identical (or nearly identical) output on two different devices if it uses two different device contexts. MFC takes advantage of this fact to make printing—usually a chore in Windows—a less laborious undertaking. In fact, printing from a document/view application is typically *much* easier than printing from a conventional application. You'll learn all about MFC's print architecture in Chapter 13.

Two other *CView* functions you'll frequently override in derived view classes are *OnInitialUpdate* and *OnUpdate*. Views, like documents, are constructed once and then reused over and over in SDI applications. An SDI view's *OnInitialUpdate* function gets called whenever a document is opened or created. The default implementation of *OnInitialUpdate* calls *OnUpdate*, and the default implementation of *OnUpdate* in turn invalidates the view's client area to force a repaint. Use *OnInitialUpdate* to initialize data members of the view class, and perform other view-related initializations on a per-document basis. In a *CScrollView*-derived class, for example, it's common for *OnInitialUpdate* to call the view's *SetScrollSizes* function to initialize scrolling parameters. It's important to call the base class version of *OnInitialUpdate* from an overridden version, or the view won't be updated when a new document is opened or created.

OnUpdate is called when a document's data is modified and someone—usually either the document object or one of the views—calls *UpdateAllViews*. You never *have* to override *OnUpdate* because the default implementation calls *Invalidate*. But in practice, you'll often override *OnUpdate* to optimize performance by repainting just the part of the view that needs updating rather than repainting the entire view. These so-called intelligent updates are especially helpful in multiple-view applications because they eliminate unsightly flashing in secondary views. You'll see what I mean in the Chapter 11 sample program named Sketch.

At any given time in a multiple-view application, one view is the *active* view and other views are said to be *inactive*. Generally, the active view is the one with the input focus. A view can determine when it is activated and deactivated by overriding *CView::OnActivateView*. The first parameter to *OnActivateView* is nonzero if the view is being activated and 0 if it is being deactivated. The second and third parameters are *CView* pointers identifying the views that are being activated and deactivated, respectively. If the pointers are equal, the application's frame window was activated without causing a change in the active view. View objects sometimes use this feature of the *OnActivateView* function to realize a palette. A frame window can get and set the active view with the functions *CFrameWnd::GetActiveView* and *CFrameWnd::SetActiveView*.

The Frame Window Object

So far, we've looked at the roles that application objects, document objects, and view objects play in document/view applications. But we've yet to consider the frame window object, which defines the application's physical workspace on the screen and serves as a container for a view. An SDI application uses just one frame window—a *CFrameWnd* that serves as the application's top-level window and frames the view. As you'll discover in the next chapter, an MDI application uses two different types of frame windows—a *CMDIFrameWnd* that acts as a top-level window and *CMDIChild-Wnd* windows that float within the top-level frame window and frame views of the application's documents.

Frame windows play an important and often misunderstood role in the operation of document/view applications. Beginning MFC programmers often think of a frame window as simply a window. In fact, a frame window is an intelligent object that orchestrates much of what goes on behind the scenes in a document/view application. For example, MFC's *CFrameWnd* class provides *OnClose* and *OnQueryEndSession* handlers that make sure the user gets a chance to save a dirty document before the application terminates or Windows shuts down. *CFrameWnd* also handles the all-important task of resizing a view when the frame window is resized, and it knows how to work with toolbars, status bars, and other user interface objects. It also includes member functions for manipulating toolbars and status bars, identifying active documents and views, and more.

Perhaps the best way to understand the contribution the *CFrameWnd* class makes is to compare it to the more generic *CWnd* class. The *CWnd* class is basically a C++ wrapper around an ordinary window. *CFrameWnd* is derived from *CWnd* and adds all the bells and whistles a frame window needs to assume a proactive role in the execution of a document/view application.

Dynamic Object Creation

If the framework is to create document, view, and frame window objects during the course of a program's execution, the classes from which those objects are constructed must support a feature known as *dynamic creation*. MFC's DECLARE_DYNCREATE and IMPLEMENT_DYNCREATE macros make it easy to write dynamically creatable classes. Here's all you have to do:

1. Derive the class from *CObject*.

2. Call DECLARE_DYNCREATE in the class declaration. DECLARE_DYNCREATE accepts just one parameter—the name of the dynamically creatable class.

3. Call IMPLEMENT_DYNCREATE from outside the class declaration. IMPLEMENT_DYNCREATE accepts two parameters—the name of the dynamically creatable class and the name of its base class.

You can create an instance of a class that uses these macros at run time with a statement like this one:

```
RUNTIME_CLASS (CMyClass)->CreateObject ();
```

Using this statement is basically no different than using the *new* operator to create a *CMyClass* object, but it circumvents a shortcoming of the C++ language that prevents statements like these from working:

```
CString strClassName = _T ("CMyClass");
CMyClass* ptr = new strClassName;
```

The compiler, of course, will try to construct an object from a class named "strClassName" because it doesn't realize that *strClassName* is a variable name and not a literal class name. What MFC's dynamic object creation mechanism amounts to is a means for applications to register classes in such a way that the framework can create objects of those classes.

What happens under the hood when you write a class that's dynamically creatable? The DECLARE_DYNCREATE macro adds three members to the class declaration: a static *CRuntimeClass* data member, a virtual function named *GetRuntimeClass*, and a static function named *CreateObject*. When you write

```
DECLARE_DYNCREATE (CMyClass)
```

the C++ preprocessor outputs this:

```
public:
    static const AFX_DATA CRuntimeClass classCMyClass;
    virtual CRuntimeClass* GetRuntimeClass() const;
    static CObject* PASCAL CreateObject();
```

IMPLEMENT_DYNCREATE initializes the *CRuntimeClass* structure with information such as the class name and the size of each class instance. It also provides the *GetRuntimeClass* and *CreateObject* functions. If IMPLEMENT_DYNCREATE is called like this:

```
IMPLEMENT_DYNCREATE (CMyClass, CBaseClass)
```

CreateObject is implemented like this:

```
CObject* PASCAL CMyClass::CreateObject()
    { return new CMyClass; }
```

Early versions of MFC used a different implementation of *CreateObject* that allocated memory using the size information stored in the class's *CRuntimeClass* structure and manually initialized an object in that memory space. Today's implementation of *CreateObject* is truer to the C++ language because if a dynamically creatable class overloads the *new* operator, *CreateObject* will use the overloaded operator.

More on the SDI Document Template

Earlier in this chapter, you saw how an SDI document template object is created from the *CSingleDocTemplate* class. The template's constructor was passed four parameters: an integer value equal to IDR_MAINFRAME and three RUNTIME_CLASS pointers. The purpose of the three RUNTIME_CLASS macros should be clear by now, so let's look more closely at the integer passed in the first parameter, which is actually a multipurpose resource ID that identifies the following four resources:

- The application icon
- The application's menu
- The accelerator table that goes with the menu
- A *document string* that specifies, among other things, the default file name extension for documents created by this application and the default name for untitled documents

In an SDI document/view application, the framework creates the top-level window by creating a frame window object using run-time class information stored in the document template and then calling that object's *LoadFrame* function. One of the parameters *LoadFrame* accepts is a resource ID identifying the four resources listed above. Not surprisingly, the resource ID that the framework passes to *LoadFrame* is the same one supplied to the document template. *LoadFrame* creates a frame window and loads the associated menu, accelerators, and icon all in one step, but if the process is to work, you must assign all these resources the same ID. That's why the RC file that AppWizard generates for a document/view application uses the same ID for a variety of different resources.

The document string is a string resource formed from a combination of as many as seven substrings separated by "\n" characters. Each substring describes one characteristic of the frame window or document type. In left-to-right order, the substrings have the following meaning for an SDI application:

■ The title that appears in the frame window's title bar. This is usually the name of the application—for example, "Microsoft Draw."

■ The title assigned to new documents. If this substring is omitted, the default is "Untitled."

■ A descriptive name for the document type that appears along with other document types in a dialog box when the user selects New from the File menu in an MDI application that registers two or more document types. This substring isn't used in SDI applications.

■ A descriptive name for the document type combined with a wildcard file specification that includes the default file name extension—for example, "Drawing Files (*.drw)." This string is used in Open and Save As dialog boxes.

■ The default file name extension for documents of this type—for example, ".drw."

■ A name with no spaces that identifies the document type in the registry— for example, "Draw.Document." If the application calls *CWinApp::Register-ShellFileTypes* to register its document types, this substring becomes the default value for the HKEY_CLASSES_ROOT subkey named after the document's file name extension.

■ A descriptive name for the document type—for example, "Microsoft Draw Document." Unlike the substring preceding it in the document string, this substring can include spaces. If the application uses *CWinApp::Register-ShellFileTypes* to register its document types, this substring is the human-readable name the shell displays in property sheets.

You don't have to supply all seven substrings; you can omit individual substrings by following a "\n" separator character with another "\n," and you can omit trailing null substrings altogether. If you build an application with AppWizard, AppWizard creates the document string for you using information entered in the Advanced Options dialog box that's displayed when you click the Advanced button in AppWizard's Step 4 dialog box. The resource statements for a typical SDI document string look like this:

```
STRINGTABLE
BEGIN
    IDR_MAINFRAME "Microsoft Draw\n\n\nDraw Files(*.drw)\n.drw\n
        Draw.Document\nMicrosoft Draw Document"
END
```

STRINGTABLE creates a string table resource (a resource consisting of one or more text strings, each identifiable by a unique resource ID) just as DIALOG creates a dialog resource and MENU creates a menu resource. When this application is started with an empty document, its frame window will have the title "Untitled - Microsoft Draw." The default file name extension for documents saved by this application is ".drw," and "Draw Files (*.drw)" will be one of the file type choices listed in the Open and Save As dialog boxes.

Should the need ever arise, you can retrieve individual substrings from a document string with MFC's *CDocTemplate::GetDocString* function. For example, the statements

```
CString strDefExt;
pDocTemplate->GetDocString (strDefExt, CDocTemplate::filterExt);
```

copy the document's default file name extension to the *CString* variable named *strDefExt*.

Registering Document Types with the Operating System Shell

In Windows, you can double-click a document icon or right-click it and select Open from the context menu to open the document along with the application that created it. In addition, you can print a document by selecting Print from its context menu or dragging the document icon and dropping it over a printer icon.

For these operations to work, an application must register its document types with the operating system shell, which involves writing a series of entries to the HKEY_CLASSES_ROOT branch of the registry that identify each document type's file name extension and the commands used to open and print files of that type. Some applications perform this registration by supplying a REG file the user can merge into the registry or by writing the necessary entries into the registry programmatically with *::RegCreateKey*, *::RegSetValue*, and other Win32 registry functions. An MFC application, however, can make one simple function call and register every document type it supports. Calling *CWinApp::RegisterShellFileTypes* and passing in a TRUE parameter after calling *AddDocTemplate* forges critical links between the application, the documents it creates, and the operating system shell. When it creates a document/view application, AppWizard automatically includes a call to *RegisterShellFileTypes* in the application class's *InitInstance* function.

A related *CWinApp* function named *EnableShellOpen* adds a nifty feature to MDI document/view applications. If an MDI application registers its document type(s) with *RegisterShellFileTypes* and *EnableShellOpen* and the user double-clicks a document icon while the application is running, the shell doesn't automatically start a second instance of the application; first, it uses Dynamic Data Exchange (DDE) to send an "open" command to the existing instance and passes along the document's file name. A DDE handler built into MFC's *CDocManager* class responds by calling *OnOpen-*

Document to open the document. Thus, the document appears in a new window inside the top-level MDI frame, just as if it had been opened with the application's File-Open command. Similar DDE commands allow running application instances to fulfill print requests placed through the operating system shell.

Command Routing

One of the most remarkable features of the document/view architecture is that an application can handle command messages almost anywhere. *Command messages* is MFC's term for the WM_COMMAND messages that are generated when items are selected from menus, keyboard accelerators are pressed, and toolbar buttons are clicked. The frame window is the physical recipient of most command messages, but command messages can be handled in the view class, the document class, or even the application class by simply including entries for the messages you want to handle in the class's message map. Command routing lets you put command handlers where it makes the most sense to put them rather than relegate them all to the frame window class. Update commands for menu items, toolbar buttons, and other user interface objects are also subject to command routing, so you can put ON-_UPDATE_COMMAND_UI handlers in nonframe window classes as well.

The mechanism that makes command routing work lies deep within the bowels of MFC. When a frame window receives a WM_COMMAND message, it calls the virtual *OnCmdMsg* function featured in all *CCmdTarget*-derived classes to begin the routing process. The *CFrameWnd* implementation of *OnCmdMsg* looks like this:

```
BOOL CFrameWnd::OnCmdMsg(...)
{
    // Pump through current view FIRST.
    CView* pView = GetActiveView();
    if (pView != NULL && pView->OnCmdMsg(...))
        return TRUE;

    // Then pump through frame.
    if (CWnd::OnCmdMsg(...))
        return TRUE;

    // Last but not least, pump through application.
    CWinApp* pApp = AfxGetApp();
    if (pApp != NULL && pApp->OnCmdMsg(...))
        return TRUE;

    return FALSE;
}
```

CFrameWnd::OnCmdMsg first routes the message to the active view by calling the view's *OnCmdMsg* function. If *pView->OnCmdMsg* returns 0, indicating that the view didn't process the message (that is, that the view's message map doesn't contain an entry for this particular message), the frame window tries to handle the message itself by calling *CWnd::OnCmdMsg*. If that, too, fails, the frame window then tries the application object. Ultimately, if none of the objects processes the message, *CFrameWnd::OnCmdMsg* returns FALSE and the framework passes the message to *::DefWindowProc* for default processing.

This explains how a command message received by a frame window gets routed to the active view and the application object, but what about the document object? When *CFrameWnd::OnCmdMsg* calls the active view's *OnCmdMsg* function, the view first tries to handle the message itself. If it doesn't have a handler for the message, the view calls the document's *OnCmdMsg* function. If the document can't handle the message, it passes it up the ladder to the document template. Figure 9-2 shows the path that a command message travels when it's delivered to an SDI frame window. The active view gets first crack at the message, followed by the document associated with that view, the document template, the frame window, and finally the application object. The routing stops if any object along the way processes the message, but it continues all the way up to *::DefWindowProc* if none of the objects' message maps contains an entry for the message. Routing is much the same for command messages delivered to MDI frame windows, with the framework making sure that all the relevant objects, including the child window frame that surrounds the active MDI view, get the opportunity to weigh in.

The value of command routing becomes apparent when you look at how a typical document/view application handles commands from menus, accelerators, and toolbar buttons. By convention, the File-New, File-Open, and File-Exit commands are mapped to the application object, where *CWinApp* provides *OnFileNew*, *OnFileOpen*, and *OnAppExit* command handlers for them. File-Save and File-Save As are normally handled by the document object, which provides default command handlers named *CDocument::OnFileSave* and *CDocument::OnFileSaveAs*. Commands to show and hide toolbars and status bars are handled by the frame window using *CFrameWnd* member functions, and most other commands are handled by either the document or the view.

An important point to keep in mind as you consider where to put your message handlers is that only command messages and user interface updates are subject to routing. Standard Windows messages such as WM_CHAR, WM_LBUTTONDOWN, WM_CREATE, and WM_SIZE must be handled by the window that receives the message. Mouse and keyboard messages generally go to the view, and most other messages go to the frame window. Document objects and application objects never receive noncommand messages.

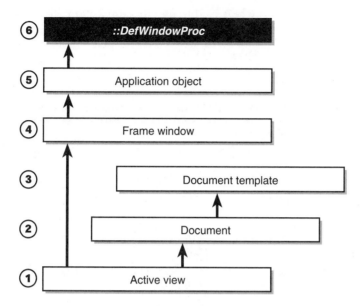

Figure 9-2. *Routing of command messages sent to an SDI frame window.*

Predefined Command IDs and Command Handlers

When you write a document/view application, you typically don't write the handlers for all the menu commands yourself. *CWinApp*, *CDocument*, *CFrameWnd*, and other MFC classes provide default handlers for common menu commands such as File-Open and File-Save. In addition, the framework provides an assortment of standard menu item command IDs, such as ID_FILE_OPEN and ID_FILE_SAVE, many of which are "prewired" into the message maps of classes that use them.

The table on the following page lists the most commonly used predefined command IDs and their associated command handlers. The "Prewired?" column indicates whether the handler is called automatically (Yes) or called only if a corresponding entry is added to the class's message map (No). You enable a prewired handler by assigning the corresponding ID to a menu item; a handler that isn't prewired is enabled only if you link the menu item ID to the function with a message-map entry. For example, you'll find default implementations of the File-New and File-Open commands in *CWinApp*'s *OnFileNew* and *OnFileOpen* functions, but neither function is connected to the application unless you provide an ON_COMMAND message-map entry for it. *CWinApp::OnAppExit*, on the other hand, works all by itself and requires no message-map entry. All you have to do is assign the File-Exit menu item the ID ID_APP_EXIT, and *OnAppExit* will magically be called to end the application when the user selects Exit from the File menu. Why? Because *CWinApp*'s message map contains an

```
ON_COMMAND (ID_APP_EXIT, OnAppExit)
```

entry, and message maps, like other class members, are passed on by inheritance.

PREDEFINED COMMAND IDs AND COMMAND HANDLERS

Command ID	Menu Item	Default Handler	Prewired?
File menu			
ID_FILE_NEW	New	*CWinApp::OnFileNew*	No
ID_FILE_OPEN	Open	*CWinApp::OnFileOpen*	No
ID_FILE_SAVE	Save	*CDocument::OnFileSave*	Yes
ID_FILE_SAVE_AS	Save As	*CDocument::OnFileSaveAs*	Yes
ID_FILE_PAGE_SETUP	Page Setup	None	N/A
ID_FILE_PRINT_SETUP	Print Setup	*CWinApp::OnFilePrintSetup*	No
ID_FILE_PRINT	Print	*CView::OnFilePrint*	No
ID_FILE_PRINT_PREVIEW	Print Preview	*CView::OnFilePrintPreview*	No
ID_FILE_SEND_MAIL	Send Mail	*CDocument::OnFileSendMail*	No
ID_FILE_MRU_FILE1–	N/A	*CWinApp::OnOpenRecentFile*	Yes
ID_FILE_MRU_FILE16			
ID_APP_EXIT	Exit	*CWinApp::OnAppExit*	Yes
Edit menu			
ID_EDIT_CLEAR	Clear	None	N/A
ID_EDIT_CLEAR_ALL	Clear All	None	N/A
ID_EDIT_CUT	Cut	None	N/A
ID_EDIT_COPY	Copy	None	N/A
ID_EDIT_PASTE	Paste	None	N/A
ID_EDIT_PASTE_LINK	Paste Link	None	N/A
ID_EDIT_PASTE_SPECIAL	Paste Special	None	N/A
ID_EDIT_FIND	Find	None	N/A
ID_EDIT_REPLACE	Replace	None	N/A
ID_EDIT_UNDO	Undo	None	N/A
ID_EDIT_REDO	Redo	None	N/A
ID_EDIT_REPEAT	Repeat	None	N/A
ID_EDIT_SELECT_ALL	Select All	None	N/A
View menu			
ID_VIEW_TOOLBAR	Toolbar	*CFrameWnd::OnBarCheck*	Yes
ID_VIEW_STATUS_BAR	Status Bar	*CFrameWnd::OnBarCheck*	Yes

Command ID	Menu Item	Default Handler	Prewired?
Window menu (MDI applications only)			
ID_WINDOW_NEW	New Window	*CMDIFrameWnd::OnWindowNew*	Yes
ID_WINDOW_ARRANGE	Arrange All	*CMDIFrameWnd::OnMDIWindowCmd*	Yes
ID_WINDOW_CASCADE	Cascade	*CMDIFrameWnd::OnMDIWindowCmd*	Yes
ID_WINDOW_TILE_HORZ	Tile Horizontal	*CMDIFrameWnd::OnMDIWindowCmd*	Yes
ID_WINDOW_TILE_VERT	Tile Vertical	*CMDIFrameWnd::OnMDIWindowCmd*	Yes
Help menu			
ID_APP_ABOUT	About AppName	None	N/A

MFC also provides update handlers for some commands, including these:

- *CFrameWnd::OnUpdateControlBarMenu* for the ID_VIEW_TOOLBAR and ID_VIEW_STATUS_BAR commands

- *CMDIFrameWnd::OnUpdateMDIWindowCmd* for the ID_WINDOW_-_ARRANGE, ID_WINDOW_CASCADE, ID_WINDOW_TILE_HORZ, ID-_WINDOW_TILE_VERT, and ID_WINDOW_NEW commands

- *CDocument::OnUpdateFileSendMail* for the ID_FILE_SEND_MAIL command

MFC's *CEditView* and *CRichEditView* classes include command handlers for some of the items in the Edit menu, but other views must provide their own.

You don't have to use the predefined command IDs or command handlers the framework provides. You can always strike out on your own and define custom command IDs, perhaps supplying message map entries to correlate your command IDs with default command handlers. You can even replace the default command handlers with handlers of your own. In short, you can use as much or as little of the framework's support as you want to. But the more you lean on the framework, the less code you'll have to write yourself.

YOUR FIRST DOCUMENT/VIEW APPLICATION

Now that you have an idea of what the document/view architecture is all about and a feel for some of the implementation details, let's write a document/view application. If some of the concepts covered in the first part of this chapter seem a little abstract, seeing the code for a working document/view application should help bring things into focus.

The SdiSquares Application

The program shown in Figure 9-3 is an SDI document/view application that displays a grid of squares four rows deep and four columns wide. Initially, each square is colored white. However, you can change a square's color by clicking it with the left mouse button. By default, clicking changes a square's color to red. You can select alternate colors from the Color menu and thereby create a multicolored grid containing squares of up to six different colors.

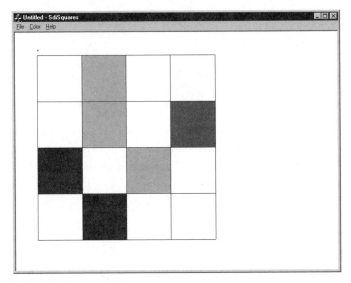

Figure 9-3. *The SdiSquares window.*

Though SdiSquares is but a rudimentary document/view application, it demonstrates all the basic tenets of the document/view architecture. Four fundamental classes play critical roles in the application's operation:

- The application class *CSquaresApp*, which is derived from *CWinApp*

- The frame window class *CMainFrame*, which is derived from *CFrameWnd*

- The document class *CSquaresDoc*, which is derived from *CDocument*

- The view class *CSquaresView*, which is derived from *CView*

The source code for these classes is reproduced in Figure 9-4 beginning on page 519.

In SdiSquares, a "document" consists of a two-dimensional array of COLORREF values defining the color of each square, plus an additional COLORREF value that defines the "current color"—the color assigned to a square when it is clicked.

The colors of the squares are stored in a protected *CSquaresDoc* member variable named *m_clrGrid*, which is a 4 by 4 array of COLORREF values. The current color is stored in a separate *CSquaresDoc* member variable named *m_clrCurrentColor*. In the document's *OnNewDocument* function, all 16 elements of *m_clrGrid* are initialized to white and *m_clrCurrentColor* is initialized to red. These variables are initialized in *OnNewDocument* instead of *CSquaresDoc*'s constructor to ensure that they are reset whenever a new document is created. If they were initialized in the document's constructor instead, they would be initialized only once—when the application starts up— and would retain their current values when a new document is created since an SDI application constructs a document object just one time and reuses it as documents are created and destroyed.

To expose the document's data to the view, *CSquaresDoc* implements three public member functions. *GetCurrentColor* returns the current color (the value of *m_clrCurrentColor*). *GetSquare* returns the color of the square at a given row and column address (*m_clrGrid[i][j]*). *SetSquare* assigns a color to the square at a specified row and column address. After assigning a color to a square, *SetSquare* calls the document's *SetModifiedFlag* to mark the document as dirty and *UpdateAllViews* to force the view to repaint to show the updated grid:

```
m_clrGrid[i][j] = color;
SetModifiedFlag (TRUE);
UpdateAllViews (NULL);
```

GetCurrentColor, *GetSquare*, and *SetSquare* serve as a bridge between the document and the view. The view can't access the document's data members directly since they are protected, but it can call the document's accessor functions because they are declared public.

The view's *OnDraw* function draws the grid on the screen. The colored squares are drawn by a nested *for* loop that iterates through the grid one row and one column at a time. Each iteration through the loop, the view retrieves the color of the corresponding square by calling the document's *GetSquare* function through the *pDoc* pointer that holds the value returned by *GetDocument*:

```
CSquaresDoc* pDoc = GetDocument();
ASSERT_VALID(pDoc);
        .
        .
        .
for (int i=0; i<4; i++) {
    for (int j=0; j<4; j++) {
        COLORREF color = pDoc->GetSquare (i, j);
        CBrush brush (color);
        int x1 = (j * 100) + 50;
```

(continued)

```
        int y1 = (i * -100) - 50;
        int x2 = x1 + 100;
        int y2 = y1 - 100;
        CRect rect (x1, y1, x2, y2);
        pDC->FillRect (rect, &brush);
    }
}
```

AppWizard inserted the calls to *GetDocument* and ASSERT_VALID; I added all the other statements in *OnDraw*. *OnDraw* uses negative *y* values in its computations because it does its drawing in the MM_LOENGLISH mapping mode, where client-area *y* coordinates are negative.

The view includes a WM_LBUTTONDOWN handler that converts the click co-ordinates from device coordinates to MM_LOENGLISH coordinates and then tests to see which, if any, of the squares was clicked. If the click occurred in a square, *CSquaresView::OnLButtonDown* calls the document's *GetCurrentColor* function to retrieve the current color:

```
CSquaresDoc* pDoc = GetDocument ();
COLORREF clrCurrentColor = pDoc->GetCurrentColor ();
```

It then calls the document's *SetSquare* function to assign that color to the square in which the click occurred:

```
pDoc->SetSquare (i, j, clrCurrentColor);
```

You can clearly see here how the public member functions added to *CSquaresDoc* are used to bridge the gulf between the document and the view, and why *GetDocument* is such an important function. And because the view has no notion of how the document's data is physically stored, you could alter the document's internal storage mechanism without affecting the view class one bit.

I placed the command and update handlers for the commands in the Color menu in the document class because *m_clrCurrentColor* is a member of the document class. The command handlers simply assign an RGB color value to *m_clrCurrentColor*. The update handlers use *CCmdUI::SetRadio* to bullet the current color. Rather than write six separate command handlers and six separate update handlers, I could have used MFC's ON_COMMAND_RANGE and ON_UPDATE_COMMAND_UI_RANGE macros to service all six menu items with one command handler and one update handler. Because ClassWizard provides no means for outputting RANGE macros, however, these macros, if used, would have to be added by hand.

When the user saves an SdiSquares document to disk or reads it back, MFC calls the document's *Serialize* function. *CSquaresDoc::Serialize* responds by serializing *m_clrGrid* and *m_clrCurrentColor* to the archive if the document is being saved or by serializing them *from* the archive if the document is being loaded. Here's the code that does the work:

```
void CSquaresDoc::Serialize(CArchive& ar)
{
    if (ar.IsStoring())
    {
        for (int i=0; i<4; i++)
            for (int j=0; j<4; j++)
                ar << m_clrGrid[i][j];
        ar << m_clrCurrentColor;
    }
    else
    {
        for (int i=0; i<4; i++)
            for (int j=0; j<4; j++)
                ar >> m_clrGrid[i][j];
        ar >> m_clrCurrentColor;
    }
}
```

Because a COLORREF is a DWORD and MFC overloads the << and >> operators for DWORDs, *m_clrGrid* and *m_clrCurrentColor* values can be serialized with syntactical ease. AppWizard generates a do-nothing *Serialize* function that includes the call to *IsStoring*. You supply the code that streams the document's persistent data in and out. Note that MFC handles the dirty work of displaying an Open or Save As dialog to the user, opening the file for reading or writing, and so on. That's why the process of saving and loading documents is typically much less work in document/view applications than it is in conventional applications.

As you can probably tell from Figure 9-4, I used AppWizard to generate Sdi-Squares' initial source code and ClassWizard to write message handlers, command handlers, and update handlers. I didn't touch the code that AppWizard generated for the application class and frame window class because I didn't need to. The bulk of my work involved the document and view classes, which is typical of the document/view application development process.

SdiSquares.h

```
// SdiSquares.h : main header file for the SDISQUARES application
//

#if !defined(
    AFX_SDISQUARES_H__00156CE5_BB17_11D2_A2FD_0000861BAE71__INCLUDED_)
#define  AFX_SDISQUARES_H__00156CE5_BB17_11D2_A2FD_0000861BAE71__INCLUDED_

#if _MSC_VER > 1000
#pragma once
#endif // _MSC_VER > 1000
```

Figure 9-4. *The SdiSquares application*   *(continued)*

Figure 9-4. *continued*

```
#ifndef __AFXWIN_H__
    #error include 'stdafx.h' before including this file for PCH
#endif

#include "resource.h"          // main symbols

/////////////////////////////////////////////////////////////////////////////
// CSquaresApp:
// See SdiSquares.cpp for the implementation of this class
//

class CSquaresApp : public CWinApp
{
public:
    CSquaresApp();

// Overrides
    // ClassWizard generated virtual function overrides
    //{{AFX_VIRTUAL(CSquaresApp)
    public:
    virtual BOOL InitInstance();
    //}}AFX_VIRTUAL

// Implementation
    //{{AFX_MSG(CSquaresApp)
    afx_msg void OnAppAbout();
        // NOTE - the ClassWizard will add and remove member functions here.
        //    DO NOT EDIT what you see in these blocks of generated code !
    //}}AFX_MSG
    DECLARE_MESSAGE_MAP()
};

/////////////////////////////////////////////////////////////////////////////

//{{AFX_INSERT_LOCATION}}
// Microsoft Visual C++ will insert additional declarations
// immediately before the previous line.

#endif
// !defined(
//     AFX_SDISQUARES_H__00156CE5_BB17_11D2_A2FD_0000861BAE71__INCLUDED_)
```

SdiSquares.cpp

```
// SdiSquares.cpp : Defines the class behaviors for the application.
//
```

```
#include "stdafx.h"
#include "SdiSquares.h"

#include "MainFrm.h"
#include "SquaresDoc.h"
#include "SquaresView.h"

#ifdef _DEBUG
#define new DEBUG_NEW
#undef THIS_FILE
static char THIS_FILE[] = __FILE__;
#endif

/////////////////////////////////////////////////////////////////////////////
// CSquaresApp

BEGIN_MESSAGE_MAP(CSquaresApp, CWinApp)
    //{{AFX_MSG_MAP(CSquaresApp)
    ON_COMMAND(ID_APP_ABOUT, OnAppAbout)
        // NOTE - the ClassWizard will add and remove mapping macros here.
        //     DO NOT EDIT what you see in these blocks of generated code!
    //}}AFX_MSG_MAP
    // Standard file based document commands
    ON_COMMAND(ID_FILE_NEW, CWinApp::OnFileNew)
    ON_COMMAND(ID_FILE_OPEN, CWinApp::OnFileOpen)
END_MESSAGE_MAP()

/////////////////////////////////////////////////////////////////////////////
// CSquaresApp construction

CSquaresApp::CSquaresApp()
{
    // TODO: add construction code here,
    // Place all significant initialization in InitInstance
}

/////////////////////////////////////////////////////////////////////////////
// The one and only CSquaresApp object

CSquaresApp theApp;

/////////////////////////////////////////////////////////////////////////////
// CSquaresApp initialization

BOOL CSquaresApp::InitInstance()
{
    // Standard initialization
    // If you are not using these features and wish to reduce the size
```

(continued)

Figure 9-4. *continued*

```
    //  of your final executable, you should remove from the following
    //  the specific initialization routines you do not need.

    // Change the registry key under which our settings are stored.
    // TODO: You should modify this string to be something appropriate
    // such as the name of your company or organization.
    SetRegistryKey(_T("Local AppWizard-Generated Applications"));

    LoadStdProfileSettings();  // Load standard INI file
                               // options (including MRU)

    // Register the application's document templates.  Document templates
    //  serve as the connection between documents, frame windows and views.

    CSingleDocTemplate* pDocTemplate;
    pDocTemplate = new CSingleDocTemplate(
        IDR_MAINFRAME,
        RUNTIME_CLASS(CSquaresDoc),
        RUNTIME_CLASS(CMainFrame),          // main SDI frame window
        RUNTIME_CLASS(CSquaresView));
    AddDocTemplate(pDocTemplate);

    // Enable DDE Execute open
    EnableShellOpen();
    RegisterShellFileTypes(TRUE);

    // Parse command line for standard shell commands, DDE, file open
    CCommandLineInfo cmdInfo;
    ParseCommandLine(cmdInfo);

    // Dispatch commands specified on the command line
    if (!ProcessShellCommand(cmdInfo))
        return FALSE;

    // The one and only window has been initialized, so show and update it.
    m_pMainWnd->ShowWindow(SW_SHOW);
    m_pMainWnd->UpdateWindow();

    // Enable drag/drop open
    m_pMainWnd->DragAcceptFiles();

    return TRUE;
}
```

```
///////////////////////////////////////////////////////////////////////////
// CAboutDlg dialog used for App About

class CAboutDlg : public CDialog
{
public:
    CAboutDlg();

// Dialog Data
    //{{AFX_DATA(CAboutDlg)
    enum { IDD = IDD_ABOUTBOX };
    //}}AFX_DATA

    // ClassWizard generated virtual function overrides
    //{{AFX_VIRTUAL(CAboutDlg)
    protected:
    virtual void DoDataExchange(CDataExchange* pDX);      // DDX/DDV support
    //}}AFX_VIRTUAL

// Implementation
protected:
    //{{AFX_MSG(CAboutDlg)
        // No message handlers
    //}}AFX_MSG
    DECLARE_MESSAGE_MAP()
};

CAboutDlg::CAboutDlg() : CDialog(CAboutDlg::IDD)
{
    //{{AFX_DATA_INIT(CAboutDlg)
    //}}AFX_DATA_INIT
}

void CAboutDlg::DoDataExchange(CDataExchange* pDX)
{
    CDialog::DoDataExchange(pDX);
    //{{AFX_DATA_MAP(CAboutDlg)
    //}}AFX_DATA_MAP
}

BEGIN_MESSAGE_MAP(CAboutDlg, CDialog)
    //{{AFX_MSG_MAP(CAboutDlg)
        // No message handlers
    //}}AFX_MSG_MAP
END_MESSAGE_MAP()
```

(continued)

Figure 9-4. *continued*

```
// App command to run the dialog
void CSquaresApp::OnAppAbout()
{
    CAboutDlg aboutDlg;
    aboutDlg.DoModal();
}


/////////////////////////////////////////////////////////////////////////////
// CSquaresApp message handlers
```

MainFrm.h

```
// MainFrm.h : interface of the CMainFrame class
//
/////////////////////////////////////////////////////////////////////////////

#if !defined(
    AFX_MAINFRM_H__00156CE9_BB17_11D2_A2FD_0000861BAE71__INCLUDED_)
#define AFX_MAINFRM_H__00156CE9_BB17_11D2_A2FD_0000861BAE71__INCLUDED_

#if _MSC_VER > 1000
#pragma once
#endif // _MSC_VER > 1000

class CMainFrame : public CFrameWnd
{

protected: // create from serialization only
    CMainFrame();
    DECLARE_DYNCREATE(CMainFrame)

// Attributes
public:

// Operations
public:

// Overrides
    // ClassWizard generated virtual function overrides
    //{{AFX_VIRTUAL(CMainFrame)
    virtual BOOL PreCreateWindow(CREATESTRUCT& cs);
    //}}AFX_VIRTUAL
```

```
// Implementation
public:
    virtual ~CMainFrame();
#ifdef _DEBUG
    virtual void AssertValid() const;
    virtual void Dump(CDumpContext& dc) const;
#endif

// Generated message map functions
protected:
    //{{AFX_MSG(CMainFrame)
        // NOTE - the ClassWizard will add and remove member functions here.
        //    DO NOT EDIT what you see in these blocks of generated code!
    //}}AFX_MSG
    DECLARE_MESSAGE_MAP()
};


/////////////////////////////////////////////////////////////////////////

//{{AFX_INSERT_LOCATION}}
// Microsoft Visual C++ will insert additional declarations
// immediately before the previous line.

#endif
// !defined(AFX_MAINFRM_H__00156CE9_BB17_11D2_A2FD_0000861BAE71__INCLUDED_)
```

MainFrm.cpp

```
// MainFrm.cpp : implementation of the CMainFrame class
//

#include "stdafx.h"
#include "SdiSquares.h"

#include "MainFrm.h"

#ifdef _DEBUG
#define new DEBUG_NEW
#undef THIS_FILE
static char THIS_FILE[] = __FILE__;
#endif


/////////////////////////////////////////////////////////////////////////
// CMainFrame
```

(continued)

Figure 9-4. *continued*

```
IMPLEMENT_DYNCREATE(CMainFrame, CFrameWnd)

BEGIN_MESSAGE_MAP(CMainFrame, CFrameWnd)
    //{{AFX_MSG_MAP(CMainFrame)
        // NOTE - the ClassWizard will add and remove mapping macros here.
        //      DO NOT EDIT what you see in these blocks of generated code !
    //}}AFX_MSG_MAP
END_MESSAGE_MAP()

/////////////////////////////////////////////////////////////////////////////
// CMainFrame construction/destruction

CMainFrame::CMainFrame()
{
    // TODO: add member initialization code here

}

CMainFrame::~CMainFrame()
{
}

BOOL CMainFrame::PreCreateWindow(CREATESTRUCT& cs)
{
    if( !CFrameWnd::PreCreateWindow(cs) )
        return FALSE;
    // TODO: Modify the Window class or styles here by modifying
    //   the CREATESTRUCT cs

    return TRUE;
}

/////////////////////////////////////////////////////////////////////////////
// CMainFrame diagnostics

#ifdef _DEBUG
void CMainFrame::AssertValid() const
{
    CFrameWnd::AssertValid();
}

void CMainFrame::Dump(CDumpContext& dc) const
{
    CFrameWnd::Dump(dc);
}

#endif //_DEBUG
```

```
/////////////////////////////////////////////////////////////////////////
// CMainFrame message handlers
```

SquaresDoc.h

```
// SquaresDoc.h : interface of the CSquaresDoc class
//
/////////////////////////////////////////////////////////////////////////

#if !defined(
    AFX_SQUARESDOC_H__00156CEB_BB17_11D2_A2FD_0000861BAE71__INCLUDED_)
#define AFX_SQUARESDOC_H__00156CEB_BB17_11D2_A2FD_0000861BAE71__INCLUDED_

#if _MSC_VER > 1000
#pragma once
#endif // _MSC_VER > 1000

class CSquaresDoc : public CDocument
{
protected: // create from serialization only
    CSquaresDoc();
    DECLARE_DYNCREATE(CSquaresDoc)

// Attributes
public:

// Operations
public:

// Overrides
    // ClassWizard generated virtual function overrides
    //{{AFX_VIRTUAL(CSquaresDoc)
    public:
    virtual BOOL OnNewDocument();
    virtual void Serialize(CArchive& ar);
    //}}AFX_VIRTUAL

// Implementation
public:
    void SetSquare (int i, int j, COLORREF color);
    COLORREF GetSquare (int i, int j);
    COLORREF GetCurrentColor();
    virtual ~CSquaresDoc();
```

(continued)

Figure 9-4. *continued*

```
#ifdef _DEBUG
    virtual void AssertValid() const;
    virtual void Dump(CDumpContext& dc) const;
#endif

protected:

// Generated message map functions
protected:
    COLORREF m_clrCurrentColor;
    COLORREF m_clrGrid[4][4];
    //{{AFX_MSG(CSquaresDoc)
    afx_msg void OnColorRed();
    afx_msg void OnColorYellow();
    afx_msg void OnColorGreen();
    afx_msg void OnColorCyan();
    afx_msg void OnColorBlue();
    afx_msg void OnColorWhite();
    afx_msg void OnUpdateColorRed(CCmdUI* pCmdUI);
    afx_msg void OnUpdateColorYellow(CCmdUI* pCmdUI);
    afx_msg void OnUpdateColorGreen(CCmdUI* pCmdUI);
    afx_msg void OnUpdateColorCyan(CCmdUI* pCmdUI);
    afx_msg void OnUpdateColorBlue(CCmdUI* pCmdUI);
    afx_msg void OnUpdateColorWhite(CCmdUI* pCmdUI);
    //}}AFX_MSG
    DECLARE_MESSAGE_MAP()
};

//////////////////////////////////////////////////////////////////////////

//{{AFX_INSERT_LOCATION}}
// Microsoft Visual C++ will insert additional declarations
// immediately before the previous line.

#endif
// !defined(
//      AFX_SQUARESDOC_H__00156CEB_BB17_11D2_A2FD_0000861BAE71__INCLUDED_)
```

SquaresDoc.cpp

```
// SquaresDoc.cpp : implementation of the CSquaresDoc class
//
```

```
#include "stdafx.h"
#include "SdiSquares.h"

#include "SquaresDoc.h"

#ifdef _DEBUG
#define new DEBUG_NEW
#undef THIS_FILE
static char THIS_FILE[] = __FILE__;
#endif

/////////////////////////////////////////////////////////////////////////////
// CSquaresDoc

IMPLEMENT_DYNCREATE(CSquaresDoc, CDocument)

BEGIN_MESSAGE_MAP(CSquaresDoc, CDocument)
    //{{AFX_MSG_MAP(CSquaresDoc)
    ON_COMMAND(ID_COLOR_RED, OnColorRed)
    ON_COMMAND(ID_COLOR_YELLOW, OnColorYellow)
    ON_COMMAND(ID_COLOR_GREEN, OnColorGreen)
    ON_COMMAND(ID_COLOR_CYAN, OnColorCyan)
    ON_COMMAND(ID_COLOR_BLUE, OnColorBlue)
    ON_COMMAND(ID_COLOR_WHITE, OnColorWhite)
    ON_UPDATE_COMMAND_UI(ID_COLOR_RED, OnUpdateColorRed)
    ON_UPDATE_COMMAND_UI(ID_COLOR_YELLOW, OnUpdateColorYellow)
    ON_UPDATE_COMMAND_UI(ID_COLOR_GREEN, OnUpdateColorGreen)
    ON_UPDATE_COMMAND_UI(ID_COLOR_CYAN, OnUpdateColorCyan)
    ON_UPDATE_COMMAND_UI(ID_COLOR_BLUE, OnUpdateColorBlue)
    ON_UPDATE_COMMAND_UI(ID_COLOR_WHITE, OnUpdateColorWhite)
    //}}AFX_MSG_MAP
END_MESSAGE_MAP()

/////////////////////////////////////////////////////////////////////////////
// CSquaresDoc construction/destruction

CSquaresDoc::CSquaresDoc()
{
    // TODO: add one-time construction code here

}

CSquaresDoc::~CSquaresDoc()
{
}
```

(continued)

Figure 9-4. *continued*

```
BOOL CSquaresDoc::OnNewDocument()
{
    if (!CDocument::OnNewDocument())
        return FALSE;

    for (int i=0; i<4; i++)
        for (int j=0; j<4; j++)
            m_clrGrid[i][j] = RGB (255, 255, 255);

    m_clrCurrentColor = RGB (255, 0, 0);
    return TRUE;
}



/////////////////////////////////////////////////////////////////////////////
// CSquaresDoc serialization

void CSquaresDoc::Serialize(CArchive& ar)
{
    if (ar.IsStoring())
    {
        for (int i=0; i<4; i++)
            for (int j=0; j<4; j++)
                ar << m_clrGrid[i][j];
        ar << m_clrCurrentColor;
    }
    else
    {
        for (int i=0; i<4; i++)
            for (int j=0; j<4; j++)
                ar >> m_clrGrid[i][j];
        ar >> m_clrCurrentColor;
    }
}


/////////////////////////////////////////////////////////////////////////////
// CSquaresDoc diagnostics

#ifdef _DEBUG
void CSquaresDoc::AssertValid() const
{
    CDocument::AssertValid();
}
```

```
void CSquaresDoc::Dump(CDumpContext& dc) const
{
    CDocument::Dump(dc);
}
#endif //_DEBUG

/////////////////////////////////////////////////////////////////////////////
// CSquaresDoc commands

COLORREF CSquaresDoc::GetCurrentColor()
{
    return m_clrCurrentColor;
}

COLORREF CSquaresDoc::GetSquare(int i, int j)
{
    ASSERT (i >= 0 && i <= 3 && j >= 0 && j <= 3);
    return m_clrGrid[i][j];
}

void CSquaresDoc::SetSquare(int i, int j, COLORREF color)
{
    ASSERT (i >= 0 && i <= 3 && j >= 0 && j <= 3);
    m_clrGrid[i][j] = color;
    SetModifiedFlag (TRUE);
    UpdateAllViews (NULL);
}

void CSquaresDoc::OnColorRed()
{
    m_clrCurrentColor = RGB (255, 0, 0);
}

void CSquaresDoc::OnColorYellow()
{
    m_clrCurrentColor = RGB (255, 255, 0);
}

void CSquaresDoc::OnColorGreen()
{
    m_clrCurrentColor = RGB (0, 255, 0);
}

void CSquaresDoc::OnColorCyan()
{
    m_clrCurrentColor = RGB (0, 255, 255);
}x
```

(continued)

Figure 9-4. *continued*

```
void CSquaresDoc::OnColorBlue()
{
    m_clrCurrentColor = RGB (0, 0, 255);
}

void CSquaresDoc::OnColorWhite()
{
    m_clrCurrentColor = RGB (255, 255, 255);
}

void CSquaresDoc::OnUpdateColorRed(CCmdUI* pCmdUI)
{
    pCmdUI->SetRadio (m_clrCurrentColor == RGB (255, 0, 0));
}

void CSquaresDoc::OnUpdateColorYellow(CCmdUI* pCmdUI)
{
    pCmdUI->SetRadio (m_clrCurrentColor == RGB (255, 255, 0));
}

void CSquaresDoc::OnUpdateColorGreen(CCmdUI* pCmdUI)
{
    pCmdUI->SetRadio (m_clrCurrentColor == RGB (0, 255, 0));
}

void CSquaresDoc::OnUpdateColorCyan(CCmdUI* pCmdUI)
{
    pCmdUI->SetRadio (m_clrCurrentColor == RGB (0, 255, 255));
}

void CSquaresDoc::OnUpdateColorBlue(CCmdUI* pCmdUI)
{
    pCmdUI->SetRadio (m_clrCurrentColor == RGB (0, 0, 255));
}

void CSquaresDoc::OnUpdateColorWhite(CCmdUI* pCmdUI)
{
    pCmdUI->SetRadio (m_clrCurrentColor == RGB (255, 255, 255));
}
```

SquaresView.h

```
// SquaresView.h : interface of the CSquaresView class
//
/////////////////////////////////////////////////////////////////////////

#if !defined(
    AFX_SQUARESVIEW_H__00156CED_BB17_11D2_A2FD_0000861BAE71__INCLUDED_)
#define  AFX_SQUARESVIEW_H__00156CED_BB17_11D2_A2FD_0000861BAE71__INCLUDED_

#if _MSC_VER > 1000
#pragma once
#endif // _MSC_VER > 1000


class CSquaresView : public CView
{
protected: // create from serialization only
    CSquaresView();
    DECLARE_DYNCREATE(CSquaresView)

// Attributes
public:
    CSquaresDoc* GetDocument();

// Operations
public:

// Overrides
    // ClassWizard generated virtual function overrides
    //{{AFX_VIRTUAL(CSquaresView)
    public:
    virtual void OnDraw(CDC* pDC);  // overridden to draw this view
    virtual BOOL PreCreateWindow(CREATESTRUCT& cs);
    protected:
    //}}AFX_VIRTUAL

// Implementation
public:
    virtual ~CSquaresView();
#ifdef _DEBUG
    virtual void AssertValid() const;
    virtual void Dump(CDumpContext& dc) const;
#endif

protected:
```

(continued)

Figure 9-4. *continued*

```
// Generated message map functions
protected:
    //{{AFX_MSG(CSquaresView)
    afx_msg void OnLButtonDown(UINT nFlags, CPoint point);
    //}}AFX_MSG
    DECLARE_MESSAGE_MAP()
};

#ifndef _DEBUG  // debug version in SquaresView.cpp
inline CSquaresDoc* CSquaresView::GetDocument()
    { return (CSquaresDoc*)m_pDocument; }
#endif

/////////////////////////////////////////////////////////////////////////////

//{{AFX_INSERT_LOCATION}}
// Microsoft Visual C++ will insert additional declarations
// immediately before the previous line.

#endif
// !defined(
//      AFX_SQUARESVIEW_H__00156CED_BB17_11D2_A2FD_0000861BAE71__INCLUDED_)
```

SquaresView.cpp

```
// SquaresView.cpp : implementation of the CSquaresView class
//

#include "stdafx.h"
#include "SdiSquares.h"

#include "SquaresDoc.h"
#include "SquaresView.h"

#ifdef _DEBUG
#define new DEBUG_NEW
#undef THIS_FILE
static char THIS_FILE[] = __FILE__;
#endif

/////////////////////////////////////////////////////////////////////////////
// CSquaresView
```

```
IMPLEMENT_DYNCREATE(CSquaresView, CView)

BEGIN_MESSAGE_MAP(CSquaresView, CView)
    //{{AFX_MSG_MAP(CSquaresView)
    ON_WM_LBUTTONDOWN()
    //}}AFX_MSG_MAP
END_MESSAGE_MAP()

/////////////////////////////////////////////////////////////////////////
// CSquaresView construction/destruction

CSquaresView::CSquaresView()
{
    // TODO: add construction code here

}

CSquaresView::~CSquaresView()
{
}

BOOL CSquaresView::PreCreateWindow(CREATESTRUCT& cs)
{
    // TODO: Modify the Window class or styles here by modifying
    //   the CREATESTRUCT cs

    return CView::PreCreateWindow(cs);
}

/////////////////////////////////////////////////////////////////////////
// CSquaresView drawing

void CSquaresView::OnDraw(CDC* pDC)
{
    CSquaresDoc* pDoc = GetDocument();
    ASSERT_VALID(pDoc);

    //
    // Set the mapping mode to MM_LOENGLISH.
    //
    pDC->SetMapMode (MM_LOENGLISH);

    //
    // Draw the 16 squares.
    //x
```

(continued)

Figure 9-4. *continued*

```
    for (int i=0; i<4; i++) {
        for (int j=0; j<4; j++) {
            COLORREF color = pDoc->GetSquare (i, j);
            CBrush brush (color);
            int x1 = (j * 100) + 50;
            int y1 = (i * -100) - 50;
            int x2 = x1 + 100;
            int y2 = y1 - 100;
            CRect rect (x1, y1, x2, y2);
            pDC->FillRect (rect, &brush);
        }
    }

    //
    // Then the draw the grid lines surrounding them.
    //
    for (int x=50; x<=450; x+=100) {
        pDC->MoveTo (x, -50);
        pDC->LineTo (x, -450);
    }

    for (int y=-50; y>=-450; y-=100) {
        pDC->MoveTo (50, y);
        pDC->LineTo (450, y);
    }
}

/////////////////////////////////////////////////////////////////////////
// CSquaresView diagnostics

#ifdef _DEBUG
void CSquaresView::AssertValid() const
{
    CView::AssertValid();
}

void CSquaresView::Dump(CDumpContext& dc) const
{
    CView::Dump(dc);
}

CSquaresDoc* CSquaresView::GetDocument() // non-debug version is inline
{
    ASSERT(m_pDocument->IsKindOf(RUNTIME_CLASS(CSquaresDoc)));
    return (CSquaresDoc*)m_pDocument;
}
#endif //_DEBUG
```

```
///////////////////////////////////////////////////////////////////////////
// CSquaresView message handlers

void CSquaresView::OnLButtonDown(UINT nFlags, CPoint point)
{
    CView::OnLButtonDown(nFlags, point);

    //
    // Convert to click coordinates to MM_LOENGLISH units.
    //
    CClientDC dc (this);
    dc.SetMapMode (MM_LOENGLISH);
    CPoint pos = point;
    dc.DPtoLP (&pos);

    //
    // If a square was clicked, set its color to the current color.
    //
    if (pos.x >= 50 && pos.x <= 450 && pos.y <= -50 && pos.y >= -450) {
        int i = (-pos.y - 50) / 100;
        int j = (pos.x - 50) / 100;
        CSquaresDoc* pDoc = GetDocument ();
        COLORREF clrCurrentColor = pDoc->GetCurrentColor ();
        pDoc->SetSquare (i, j, clrCurrentColor);
    }
}
```

SdiSquares Step by Step

It's important to understand how SdiSquares works, but it's also important to understand how it was created. When you use AppWizard and ClassWizard to craft MFC applications, the wizards write part of the code and you write the rest. Moreover, there's a process involved. Although I don't intend to document every single button click required to create SdiSquares, I would be remiss if I didn't provide at least an overview of the process. Here, then, is a step-by-step account of how SdiSquares came together and how you can create the application yourself.

1. Use AppWizard to create a new project named SdiSquares. In AppWizard's Step 1 dialog box, choose Single Document as the application type and check the Document/View Architecture Support box, as shown in Figure 9-5. In the Step 3 dialog box, uncheck the ActiveX Controls box. In Step 4, uncheck Docking Toolbar, Initial Status Bar, Printing And Print Preview, and 3D Controls. Also in the Step 4 dialog box, click the Advanced button and type the

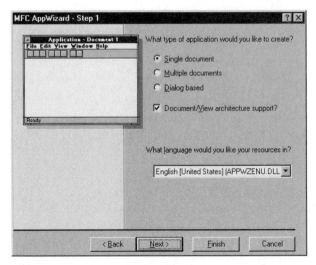

Figure 9-5. *Creating an SDI document/view application with AppWizard.*

letters *sqr* into the File Extension box (as shown in Figure 9-6) to define the default file name extension for SdiSquares documents. In the Step 6 dialog box, manually edit the class names to match the ones in Figure 9-4. Everywhere else, accept the AppWizard defaults.

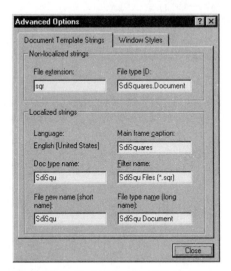

Figure 9-6. *Specifying the default file name extension for SdiSquares documents.*

2. Add the member variables *m_clrGrid* and *m_clrCurrentColor* to the document class, and add code to initialize them to *OnNewDocument*. AppWizard overrides *OnNewDocument,* so all you have to do is add the statements that initialize the data members.

3. Add the member functions *GetCurrentColor*, *GetSquare*, and *SetSquare* to the document class. Be sure to make them public member functions, since they must be accessible to the view.

4. Modify the *Serialize* function that AppWizard included in the document class to serialize *m_clrGrid* and *m_clrCurrentColor*.

5. Implement the view's *OnDraw* function. AppWizard generates a do-nothing *OnDraw* function; you write the code to perform application-specific duties.

6. Add the WM_LBUTTONDOWN handler (*OnLButtonDown*) to the view. You can add the message handler by hand or use ClassWizard to add it. I used ClassWizard.

7. Open the AppWizard-generated application menu for editing, delete the Edit menu, and add the Color menu. Then write command and update handlers for the new menu items. As with message handlers, you can add command and update handlers manually or you can add them with ClassWizard's help. Once again, I used ClassWizard.

You can add a nice finishing touch by editing the application's icons. AppWizard generated two icons when it created the project. IDR_MAINFRAME is the application icon—the one that appears in the frame window's title bar. IDR_SDISQUTYPE is the application's *document icon*, which is used to represent SdiSquares document files in the operating system shell. The document icon is registered with the system when *InitInstance* calls *RegisterShellFileTypes*.

DOC + VIEW = LESS WORK FOR YOU

As you play around with SdiSquares, notice how much of the application's functionality is provided by MFC. For example, documents can be opened and saved, despite the fact that we added a mere eight lines of code in support of such operations. If you change the color of a square and attempt to open another document or exit the application, a message box appears asking if you'd like to save your changes first. Double-clicking an SdiSquares document file in the operating system shell automatically starts SdiSquares and loads the document. MFC provides these features and more because we built the application using documents and views. You'll see other benefits of using the document/view architecture in chapters to come.

The first time I ever looked at a minimal MFC application generated by App-Wizard, I was dumbfounded by how relatively little code there was. What I didn't realize at the time was that the framework provided entire chunks of the application by way of innocent-looking message-map entries like this one:

```
ON_COMMAND (ID_FILE_OPEN, CWinApp::OnFileNew)
```

Still other parts of the program (notably the File menu's Save and Save As commands) were also implemented by the framework but weren't even visible as message-map entries because the message mapping was performed in the base class. All in all, it looked as if a lot of magic was going on, and it was clear to me that I was going to have to do some digging before I would fully understand the mechanics of doc/view.

As I soon found out, there's nothing magic about the document/view architecture—just some clever coding hidden in preprocessor macros and thousands of lines of code written to handle routine (and not-so-routine) chores such as resizing a view when a frame window is resized and carrying on DDE conversations with the shell. Many programmers fail to see the big picture because they don't take the time to look under the hood at the code AppWizard generates for them. SdiSquares is a document/view application in existential form, unobscured by nonessential extras. If you understand SdiSquares, you're well on your way to understanding the document/view architecture.

Chapter 10

Scroll Views, HTML Views, and Other View Types

MFC's *CView* class defines the basic functionality of views, but it is just one of several view classes that MFC places at your disposal. Related classes such as *CScrollView*, *CTreeView*, and *CHtmlView*—all of which are derived, either directly or indirectly, from *CView*—express added functionality that's yours for the asking when you use them as base classes for view classes of your own. The table on the following page lists the view classes that are available in MFC 6.0 and later.

CView was introduced in Chapter 9, where it was used as the base class for the view in SdiSquares. In this chapter, we'll look at some of the other view classes that MFC offers and examine practical sample code demonstrating their use. First up is *CScrollView*, which, next to *CView*, is probably the view class that MFC programmers use most often.

MFC VIEW CLASSES

Class Name	Description
CView	Root class for all view classes
CCtrlView	Base class for *CEditView, CRichEditView, CListView*, and *CTreeView*; can be used to create view classes based on other types of controls
CEditView	Wraps the multiline edit control and adds print, search, and search-and-replace capabilities
CRichEditView	Wraps the rich edit control
CListView	Wraps the list view control
CTreeView	Wraps the tree view control
CHtmlView	Creates views from HTML files and other media supported by the Microsoft Internet Explorer WebBrowser control
CScrollView	Adds scrolling capabilities to *CView*; base class for *CFormView*
CFormView	Implements scrollable "form" views created from dialog templates
CRecordView	*CFormView* derivative designed to display records obtained from an ODBC database
CDaoRecordView	DAO version of *CRecordView*
COleDBRecordView	OLE DB version of *CRecordView*

SCROLL VIEWS

CScrollView adds basic scrolling capabilities to *CView*. It includes handlers for WM_VSCROLL and WM_HSCROLL messages that allow MFC to do the bulk of the work involved in scrolling a window in response to scroll bar messages. It also includes member functions that you can call to perform fundamental tasks such as scrolling to a specified position and retrieving the current scroll position. Because *CScrollView* handles scrolling entirely on its own, you have to do very little to make it work other than implement *OnDraw*. You can usually implement *OnDraw* in a *CScrollView* exactly as you do in a *CView*. Unless you want to tweak it to optimize scrolling performance, *OnDraw* requires little or no special logic to support scrolling.

CScrollView Basics

Using *CScrollView* to create a scrolling view is simplicity itself. Here are the three basic steps. The term *physical view* refers to the view window and the space that it occupies on the screen, and *logical view* describes the virtual workspace that can be viewed by using the scroll bars:

1. Derive your application's view class from *CScrollView*. If you use App-Wizard to create the project, you can select *CScrollView* from the list of base classes presented in AppWizard's Step 6 dialog box, as shown in Figure 10-1.

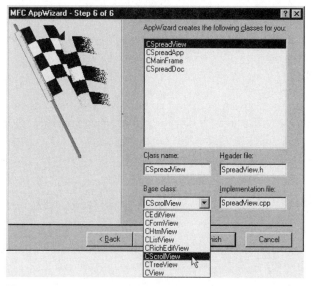

Figure 10-1. *Using AppWizard to create a CScrollView-based application.*

2. Override *OnInitialUpdate* in the view class, and call *SetScrollSizes* to specify the view's logical dimensions. This is your means of telling MFC how large an area the scrollable view should cover. If you use AppWizard to create the project and choose *CScrollView* in the Step 6 dialog box, AppWizard overrides *OnInitialUpdate* for you and inserts a call to *SetScrollSizes* that sets the view's logical width and height to 100 pixels.

3. Implement *OnDraw* as if the view were a conventional *CView*.

A scroll view created in this manner automatically scrolls in response to scroll bar events. It automatically factors the scroll position into the output from *OnDraw*. It also hides its scroll bars if the physical view size exceeds the logical view size and sizes the scroll bar thumbs to reflect the relative proportions of the physical and logical views when the scroll bars are visible.

CScrollView::SetScrollSizes accepts four parameters, two of which are optional. In order, here are those parameters:

- An integer specifying the mapping mode (required)

- A SIZE structure or *CSize* object specifying the view's logical dimensions (required)

- A SIZE structure or *CSize* object specifying the *page size*—the amount by which MFC scrolls the view when the scroll bar shaft is clicked (optional)

- A SIZE structure or *CSize* object specifying the line size—the amount by which MFC scrolls the view when the scroll bar arrows are clicked (optional)

If you omit either or both of the final two parameters, MFC uses sensible defaults for the page size and the line size. Here's an *OnInitialUpdate* function that sets the logical view size to 1,280 pixels wide and 1,024 pixels high:

```
void CMyView::OnInitialUpdate ()
{
    CScrollView::OnInitialUpdate ();
    SetScrollSizes (MM_TEXT, CSize (1280, 1024));
}
```

And here's one that sets the view's dimensions to those of an 8½-by-11-inch page:

```
void CMyView::OnInitialUpdate ()
{
    CScrollView::OnInitialUpdate ();
    SetScrollSizes (MM_LOENGLISH, CSize (850, 1100));
}
```

The next one does the same as the last one, but it also programs the view to scroll 2 inches in response to SB_PAGEUP/DOWN/LEFT/RIGHT events and ¼ inch in response to SB_LINEUP/DOWN/LEFT/RIGHT events:

```
void CMyView::OnInitialUpdate ()
{
    CScrollView::OnInitialUpdate ();
    SetScrollSizes (MM_LOENGLISH, CSize (850, 1100),
        CSize (200, 200), CSize (25, 25));
}
```

The mapping mode specified in *SetScrollSizes'* first parameter determines the units of measurement for the second, third, and fourth parameters. You can specify any mapping mode except MM_ISOTROPIC and MM_ANISOTROPIC. When *OnDraw* is called, the mapping mode has already been set to the one specified in the call to *SetScrollSizes*. Therefore, you needn't call *SetMapMode* yourself when you implement *OnDraw*.

Is that all there is to creating a scrolling view? Almost. You should remember two basic principles when using a *CScrollView*:

- If you draw in the view outside of *OnDraw*, call *CScrollView::OnPrepareDC* to allow MFC to factor the mapping mode and scroll position into the output.

- If you do any hit-testing in response to mouse messages, use *CDC ::DPtoLP* to convert the click coordinates from device coordinates to logical coordinates to factor the mapping mode and scroll position into the hit-test.

A bit of background on how a *CScrollView* works will clarify why these principles are important—and why an ordinary *OnDraw* function that knows nothing about scrolling magically adjusts its output to match the current scroll position when it's part of a *CScrollView*.

When a scroll event occurs, *CScrollView* captures the ensuing message with its *OnVScroll* or *OnHScroll* message handler and calls *::ScrollWindow* to scroll the view horizontally or vertically. Soon after, the view's *OnPaint* function is called to paint the portion of the window that was invalidated by *::ScrollWindow*. Here's the *OnPaint* handler that *CScrollView* inherits from *CView*:

```
CPaintDC dc(this);
OnPrepareDC(&dc);
OnDraw(&dc);
```

Before it calls *OnDraw*, *CView::OnPaint* calls the virtual *OnPrepareDC* function. *CScrollView* overrides *OnPrepareDC* and in it calls *CDC::SetMapMode* to set the mapping mode and *CDC::SetViewportOrg* to translate the viewport origin an amount that equals the horizontal and vertical scroll positions. Consequently, the scroll positions are automatically factored in when *OnDraw* repaints the view. Thanks to *CScroll View::OnPrepareDC*, a generic *OnDraw* function ported from a *CView* to a *CScrollView* automatically adapts to changes in the scroll position.

Now think about what happens if you instantiate a device context class on your own, outside the view's *OnDraw* function, and draw something in a *CScrollView*. Unless you first call *OnPrepareDC* to prepare the device context as *OnPaint* does, *SetViewportOrg* won't get called and drawing will be performed relative to the upper left corner of the physical view rather than to the upper left corner of the logical view. Views of a document get out of kilter pretty quickly if they're drawn using two different coordinate systems. Therefore, when you draw in a *CScrollView* window outside of *OnDraw* like this:

```
CClientDC dc (this);
// Draw something with dc.
```

Make it a habit to pass the device context to *OnPrepareDC* first, like this:

```
CClientDC dc (this);
OnPrepareDC (&dc);
// Draw something with dc.
```

By the same token, if you have the coordinates of a point in a *CScrollView* in device coordinates and want to find the corresponding position in the logical view, use *CDC::DPtoLP* to convert the device coordinates to logical coordinates. Call *OnPrepareDC* first to set the mapping mode and factor in the scroll position. Here's a WM_LBUTTONDOWN handler that performs a simple hit-test to determine whether the click point lies in the upper or lower half of the logical view:

```
void CMyView::OnLButtonDown (UINT nFlags, CPoint point)
{
    CPoint pos = point;
    CClientDC dc (this);
    OnPrepareDC (&dc);
    dc.DPtoLP (&pos);

    CSize size = GetTotalSize ();
    if (::abs (pos.y) < (size.cy / 2)) {
        // Upper half was clicked.
    }
    else {
        // Lower half was clicked.
    }
}
```

CPoint objects passed to *OnLButtonDown* and other mouse message handlers always contain device coordinates, so conversion is essential if you want to know the coordinates of the corresponding point in logical view space.

CScrollView Operations

CScrollView includes a handful of member functions that you can use to operate on a scroll view programmatically. For example, you can retrieve the current horizontal or vertical scroll position from a *CScrollView* by calling *GetScrollPosition*:

```
CPoint pos = GetScrollPosition ();
```

You can scroll to a given position programmatically with *ScrollToPosition*:

```
ScrollToPosition (CPoint (100, 100));
```

And you can measure the view's logical width and height with *GetTotalSize*:

```
CSize size = GetTotalSize ();
int nWidth = size.cx;
int nHeight = size.cy;
```

One of *CScrollView*'s more interesting member functions is *SetScaleToFit-Size*. Suppose you'd like to implement a Zoom To Fit command in your application that scales the entire logical view to fit the physical view. It's easy with *SetScale-ToFitSize*:

```
SetScaleToFitSize (GetTotalSize ());
```

To restore the view to its default scrollable form, simply call *SetScrollSizes* again. Incidentally, you can call *SetScrollSizes* multiple times throughout the life of an application to adjust scrolling parameters on the fly. For example, if the size of the logical view grows as data is added to the document, it's perfectly legal to use *Set-ScrollSizes* to increase the view's logical dimensions each time the document grows.

Optimizing Scrolling Performance

CScrollView is architected in such a way that the *OnDraw* code you write doesn't have to explicitly factor in the scroll position. Consequently, an *OnDraw* function borrowed from a *CView* generally works without modification in a *CScrollView*. But "works" and "performs acceptably" are two different things.

CScrollView stresses a view's *OnDraw* function far more than a *CView* does because scrolling precipitates more calls to *OnDraw*. Very often, a call to *OnDraw* induced by a scroll bar event requires only a few rows of pixels to be painted. If *OnDraw* attempts to paint the entire view, the GDI eliminates unnecessary output by clipping pixels outside the invalid rectangle. But clipping takes time, with the result that scrolling performance can range from fine to abysmal depending on how many CPU cycles *OnDraw* wastes trying to paint outside the invalid rectangle.

After you get a scroll view working, you should test its performance by dragging the scroll bar thumb. If the window scrolls acceptably, you're done. But if it doesn't (and in practice, it probably won't more often than it will), you should modify the view's *OnDraw* function so that it identifies the invalid rectangle and, to the extent possible, limits its painting to those pixels that fall inside the rectangle.

The key to optimizing *OnDraw* is a *CDC* function named *GetClipBox*. Called on the device context object passed to *OnDraw*, *GetClipBox* initializes a RECT structure or *CRect* object with the size and location, in logical coordinates, of the invalid rectangle, as shown here:

```
CRect rect;
pDC->GetClipBox (&rect);
```

A *CRect* initialized in this manner tells you what part of the view needs redrawing. How you use this information is highly application-specific. The sample program in the next section, which displays a spreadsheet in a scrollable view, translates the coordinates returned by *GetClipBox* into row and column numbers and uses the results to paint only those cells that fall within (either in whole or in part) the invalid rectangle. This is just one example of how *GetClipBox* can be used to optimize painting by eliminating unnecessary output. You'll see additional examples in subsequent chapters.

The ScrollDemo Application

The ScrollDemo application shown in Figure 10-2 demonstrates many of the principles discussed in the preceding sections. ScrollDemo displays a spreadsheet that measures 26 columns wide and 99 rows high. One cell in the spreadsheet—the "current cell"—is highlighted in light blue. Clicking a cell with the left mouse button makes that cell the current cell and moves the highlight. The spreadsheet is displayed in a scrollable view defined by the *CScrollView*-derived class named *CScrollDemoView*. *CScrollDemoView*'s source code appears in Figure 10-3.

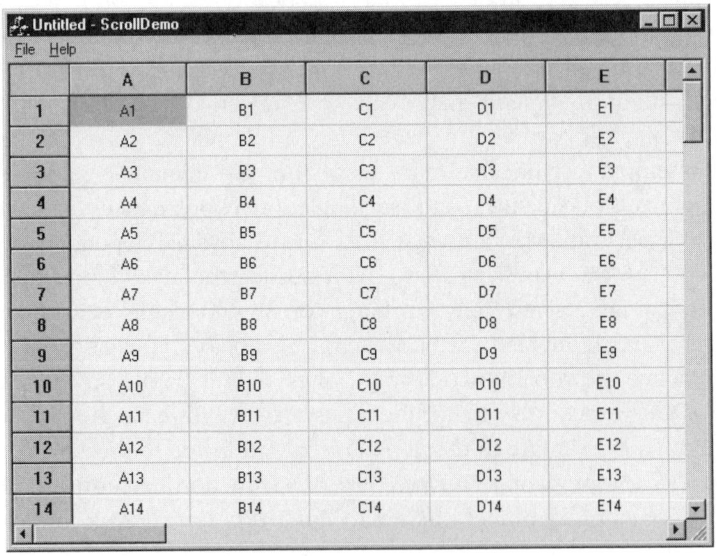

Figure 10-2. *The ScrollDemo window.*

ScrollDemoView.h

```
// ScrollDemoView.h : interface of the CScrollDemoView class
//
/////////////////////////////////////////////////////////////////////

#if
!defined(AFX_SCROLLDEMOVIEW_H__DCCF4E0D_9735_11D2_8E53_006008A82731__INCLUDED_)
#define
AFX_SCROLLDEMOVIEW_H__DCCF4E0D_9735_11D2_8E53_006008A82731__INCLUDED_

#if _MSC_VER > 1000
#pragma once
#endif // _MSC_VER > 1000


class CScrollDemoView : public CScrollView
{
protected: // create from serialization only
    CScrollDemoView();
    DECLARE_DYNCREATE(CScrollDemoView)

// Attributes
public:
    CScrollDemoDoc* GetDocument();

// Operations
public:

// Overrides
    // ClassWizard generated virtual function overrides
    //{{AFX_VIRTUAL(CScrollDemoView)
    public:
    virtual void OnDraw(CDC* pDC);  // overridden to draw this view
    virtual BOOL PreCreateWindow(CREATESTRUCT& cs);
    protected:
    virtual void OnInitialUpdate(); // called first time after construct
    //}}AFX_VIRTUAL

// Implementation
public:
    virtual ~CScrollDemoView();
#ifdef _DEBUG
    virtual void AssertValid() const;
    virtual void Dump(CDumpContext& dc) const;
#endif
```

Figure 10-3. *The ScrollDemo application* *(continued)*

Figure 10-3. *continued*

```
protected:

// Generated message map functions
protected:
    BOOL m_bSmooth;
    void GetCellRect (int row, int col, LPRECT pRect);
    void DrawAddress (CDC* pDC, int row, int col);
    void DrawPointer (CDC* pDC, int row, int col, BOOL bHighlight);
    CFont m_font;
    int m_nCurrentCol;
    int m_nCurrentRow;
    int m_nRibbonWidth;
    int m_nCellHeight;
    int m_nCellWidth;
    //{{AFX_MSG(CScrollDemoView)
    afx_msg void OnLButtonDown(UINT nFlags, CPoint point);
    //}}AFX_MSG
    DECLARE_MESSAGE_MAP()
};

#ifndef _DEBUG  // debug version in ScrollDemoView.cpp
inline CScrollDemoDoc* CScrollDemoView::GetDocument()
    { return (CScrollDemoDoc*)m_pDocument; }
#endif

//////////////////////////////////////////////////////////////////////////

//{{AFX_INSERT_LOCATION}}
// Microsoft Visual C++ will insert additional declarations immediately
// before the previous line.

#endif
// !defined(
//      AFX_SCROLLDEMOVIEW_H__DCCF4E0D_9735_11D2_8E53_006008A82731__INCLUDED_)
```

ScrollDemoView.cpp

```
// ScrollDemoView.cpp : implementation of the CScrollDemoView class
//

#include "stdafx.h"
#include "ScrollDemo.h"
#include "ScrollDemoDoc.h"
```

```
#include "ScrollDemoView.h"
#ifdef _DEBUG
#define new DEBUG_NEW
#undef THIS_FILE
static char THIS_FILE[] = __FILE__;
#endif

/////////////////////////////////////////////////////////////////////////
// CScrollDemoView

IMPLEMENT_DYNCREATE(CScrollDemoView, CScrollView)

BEGIN_MESSAGE_MAP(CScrollDemoView, CScrollView)
    //{{AFX_MSG_MAP(CScrollDemoView)
    ON_WM_LBUTTONDOWN()
    //}}AFX_MSG_MAP
END_MESSAGE_MAP()

/////////////////////////////////////////////////////////////////////////
// CScrollDemoView construction/destruction

CScrollDemoView::CScrollDemoView()
{
    m_font.CreatePointFont (80, _T ("MS Sans Serif"));
}

CScrollDemoView::~CScrollDemoView()
{
}

BOOL CScrollDemoView::PreCreateWindow(CREATESTRUCT& cs)
{
    return CScrollView::PreCreateWindow(cs);
}

/////////////////////////////////////////////////////////////////////////
// CScrollDemoView drawing

void CScrollDemoView::OnDraw(CDC* pDC)
{
    CScrollDemoDoc* pDoc = GetDocument();
    ASSERT_VALID(pDoc);

    //
    // Draw the grid lines.
```

(continued)

Figure 10-3. *continued*

```
//
CSize size = GetTotalSize ();

CPen pen (PS_SOLID, 0, RGB (192, 192, 192));
CPen* pOldPen = pDC->SelectObject (&pen);
for (int i=0; i<99; i++) {
    int y = (i * m_nCellHeight) + m_nCellHeight;
    pDC->MoveTo (0, y);
    pDC->LineTo (size.cx, y);
}

for (int j=0; j<26; j++) {
    int x = (j * m_nCellWidth) + m_nRibbonWidth;
    pDC->MoveTo (x, 0);
    pDC->LineTo (x, size.cy);
}

pDC->SelectObject (pOldPen);

//
// Draw the bodies of the rows and column headers.
//
CBrush brush;
brush.CreateStockObject (LTGRAY_BRUSH);

CRect rcTop (0, 0, size.cx, m_nCellHeight);
pDC->FillRect (rcTop, &brush);
CRect rcLeft (0, 0, m_nRibbonWidth, size.cy);
pDC->FillRect (rcLeft, &brush);

pDC->MoveTo (0, m_nCellHeight);
pDC->LineTo (size.cx, m_nCellHeight);
pDC->MoveTo (m_nRibbonWidth, 0);
pDC->LineTo (m_nRibbonWidth, size.cy);

pDC->SetBkMode (TRANSPARENT);

//
// Add numbers and button outlines to the row headers.
//
for (i=0; i<99; i++) {
    int y = (i * m_nCellHeight) + m_nCellHeight;
    pDC->MoveTo (0, y);
    pDC->LineTo (m_nRibbonWidth, y);

    CString string;
    string.Format (_T ("%d"), i + 1);
```

```
            CRect rect (0, y, m_nRibbonWidth, y + m_nCellHeight);
            pDC->DrawText (string, &rect, DT_SINGLELINE |
                DT_CENTER | DT_VCENTER);

            rect.top++;
            pDC->Draw3dRect (rect, RGB (255, 255, 255),
                RGB (128, 128, 128));
        }

        //
        // Add letters and button outlines to the column headers.
        //
        for (j=0; j<26; j++) {
            int x = (j * m_nCellWidth) + m_nRibbonWidth;
            pDC->MoveTo (x, 0);
            pDC->LineTo (x, m_nCellHeight);

            CString string;
            string.Format (_T ("%c"), j + 'A');

            CRect rect (x, 0, x + m_nCellWidth, m_nCellHeight);
            pDC->DrawText (string, &rect, DT_SINGLELINE |
                DT_CENTER | DT_VCENTER);

            rect.left++;
            pDC->Draw3dRect (rect, RGB (255, 255, 255),
                RGB (128, 128, 128));
        }

        //
        // Draw address labels into the individual cells.
        //
        CRect rect;
        pDC->GetClipBox (&rect);
        int nStartRow = max (0, (rect.top - m_nCellHeight) / m_nCellHeight);
        int nEndRow = min (98, (rect.bottom - 1) / m_nCellHeight);
        int nStartCol = max (0, (rect.left - m_nRibbonWidth) / m_nCellWidth);
        int nEndCol = min (25, ((rect.right + m_nCellWidth - 1) -
            m_nRibbonWidth) / m_nCellWidth);

        for (i=nStartRow; i<=nEndRow; i++)
            for (j=nStartCol; j<=nEndCol; j++)
                DrawAddress (pDC, i, j);

        //
        // Draw the cell pointer.
        //
        DrawPointer (pDC, m_nCurrentRow, m_nCurrentCol, TRUE);
}
```

(continued)

Figure 10-3. *continued*

```
void CScrollDemoView::OnInitialUpdate()
{
    CScrollView::OnInitialUpdate();

    m_nCurrentRow = 0;
    m_nCurrentCol = 0;
    m_bSmooth = FALSE;

    CClientDC dc (this);
    m_nCellWidth = dc.GetDeviceCaps (LOGPIXELSX);
    m_nCellHeight = dc.GetDeviceCaps (LOGPIXELSY) / 4;
    m_nRibbonWidth = m_nCellWidth / 2;

    int nWidth = (26 * m_nCellWidth) + m_nRibbonWidth;
    int nHeight = m_nCellHeight * 100;
    SetScrollSizes (MM_TEXT, CSize (nWidth, nHeight));
}

///////////////////////////////////////////////////////////////////////////
// CScrollDemoView diagnostics

#ifdef _DEBUG
void CScrollDemoView::AssertValid() const
{
    CScrollView::AssertValid();
}

void CScrollDemoView::Dump(CDumpContext& dc) const
{
    CScrollView::Dump(dc);
}

CScrollDemoDoc* CScrollDemoView::GetDocument() // non-debug version is
                                                            inline
{
    ASSERT(m_pDocument->IsKindOf(RUNTIME_CLASS(CScrollDemoDoc)));
    return (CScrollDemoDoc*)m_pDocument;
}
#endif //_DEBUG

///////////////////////////////////////////////////////////////////////////
// CScrollDemoView message handlers

void CScrollDemoView::OnLButtonDown(UINT nFlags, CPoint point)
{
    CScrollView::OnLButtonDown(nFlags, point);
```

```
    //
    // Convert the click point to logical coordinates.
    //
    CPoint pos = point;
    CClientDC dc (this);
    OnPrepareDC (&dc);
    dc.DPtoLP (&pos);

    //
    // If a cell was clicked, move the cell pointer.
    //
    CSize size = GetTotalSize ();
    if (pos.x > m_nRibbonWidth && pos.x < size.cx &&
        pos.y > m_nCellHeight && pos.y < size.cy) {

        int row = (pos.y - m_nCellHeight) / m_nCellHeight;
        int col = (pos.x - m_nRibbonWidth) / m_nCellWidth;
        ASSERT (row >= 0 && row <= 98 && col >= 0 && col <= 25);

        DrawPointer (&dc, m_nCurrentRow, m_nCurrentCol, FALSE);
        m_nCurrentRow = row;
        m_nCurrentCol = col;
        DrawPointer (&dc, m_nCurrentRow, m_nCurrentCol, TRUE);
    }
}

void CScrollDemoView::DrawPointer(CDC *pDC, int row, int col,
    BOOL bHighlight)
{
    CRect rect;
    GetCellRect (row, col, &rect);
    CBrush brush (bHighlight ? RGB (0, 255, 255) :
        ::GetSysColor (COLOR_WINDOW));
    pDC->FillRect (rect, &brush);
    DrawAddress (pDC, row, col);
}

void CScrollDemoView::DrawAddress(CDC *pDC, int row, int col)
{
    CRect rect;
    GetCellRect (row, col, &rect);

    CString string;
    string.Format (_T ("%c%d"), col + _T ('A'), row + 1);

    pDC->SetBkMode (TRANSPARENT);
    CFont* pOldFont = pDC->SelectObject (&m_font);
```

(continued)

Figure 10-3. *continued*

```
        pDC->DrawText (string, rect, DT_SINGLELINE | DT_CENTER | DT_VCENTER);
        pDC->SelectObject (pOldFont);
}


void CScrollDemoView::GetCellRect(int row, int col, LPRECT pRect)
{
    pRect->left = m_nRibbonWidth + (col * m_nCellWidth) + 1;
    pRect->top = m_nCellHeight + (row * m_nCellHeight) + 1;
    pRect->right = pRect->left + m_nCellWidth - 1;
    pRect->bottom = pRect->top + m_nCellHeight - 1;
}
```

Because *CScrollView* manages most aspects of scrolling, ScrollDemo includes remarkably little code to explicitly support scrolling operations. It does, however, use *GetClipBox* to optimize *OnDraw*'s performance. Rather than attempt to paint all 2,574 spreadsheet cells every time it's called, *OnDraw* translates the clip box into starting and ending row and column numbers and paints only those cells that fall within these ranges. The pertinent code is near the end of *OnDraw*:

```
CRect rect;
pDC->GetClipBox (&rect);
int nStartRow = max (0, (rect.top - m_nCellHeight) / m_nCellHeight);
int nEndRow = min (98, (rect.bottom - 1) / m_nCellHeight);
int nStartCol = max (0, (rect.left - m_nRibbonWidth) / m_nCellWidth);
int nEndCol = min (25, ((rect.right + m_nCellWidth - 1) -
    m_nRibbonWidth) / m_nCellWidth);

for (i=nStartRow; i<=nEndRow; i++)
    for (j=nStartCol; j<=nEndCol; j++)
        DrawAddress (pDC, i, j);
```

As an experiment, try modifying the *for* loop to paint every cell:

```
for (i=0; i<99; i++)
    for (j=0; j<26; j++)
        DrawAddress (pDC, i, j);
```

Then try scrolling the spreadsheet. You'll quickly see why optimizing *OnDraw* is a necessity rather than an option in many scroll views.

Another interesting experiment involves the view's *OnLButtonDown* function, which moves the cell highlight in response to mouse clicks. Before using the *CPoint* object passed to it to determine the row and column number in which the click occurred, *OnLButtonDown* converts the *CPoint*'s device coordinates to logical coordinates with the following statements:

```
CPoint pos = point;
CClientDC dc (this);
OnPrepareDC (&dc);
dc.DPtoLP (&pos);
```

To see what happens if *OnLButtonDown* fails to take the scroll position into account in a *CScrollView*, delete the call to *DPtoLP* and try clicking around in the spreadsheet after scrolling it a short distance horizontally or vertically.

Converting an Ordinary View into a Scroll View

What happens if you use AppWizard to generate a *CView*-based application and later decide you want a *CScrollView*? You can't use the MFC wizards to convert a *CView* into a *CScrollView* after the fact, but you *can* perform the conversion by hand. Here's how:

1. Search the view's header file and CPP file and change all occurrences of *CView* to *CScrollView*, except where *CView** occurs in a function's parameter list.

2. Override *OnInitialUpdate* if it isn't overridden already, and insert a call to *SetScrollSizes*.

If you perform step 1 but forget step 2, you'll know it as soon as you run the application because MFC will assert on you. MFC can't manage a scroll view if it doesn't know the view's logical dimensions.

HTML VIEWS

One of MFC's most powerful new classes is *CHtmlView*, which converts the Web-Browser control that's the heart and soul of Microsoft Internet Explorer into a full-fledged MFC view. *CHtmlView* displays HTML documents. You provide a URL, which can reference a document on the Internet, on an intranet, or even on a local hard disk, and *CHtmlView* displays the document the same way Internet Explorer displays it. From the underlying WebBrowser control, *CHtmlView* inherits a treasure trove of added functionality, from the ability to go backward or forward in a history list with a simple function call to the ability to host Dynamic HTML (DHTML) documents. *CHtmlView* is also an Active Document container, which means it can be used to display documents created by Microsoft Word, Microsoft Excel, and other Active Document servers. It can even display the contents of folders on a hard disk—just like Internet Explorer.

CHtmlView is a complex class because it includes dozens of member functions that provide a C++ interface to the WebBrowser control. Despite its complexity, however, it is an exceedingly easy class to use. With just a handful of member functions, you can build applications that rival Internet Explorer itself for richness and functionality. In fact, you can use CHtmlView and other MFC classes such as CToolBar to build an Internet Explorer knock-off in less than a day. Visual C++ comes with an MFC sample named MFCIE that demonstrates how. If you're willing to forego a few bells and whistles, you can build a basic browser in minutes. Do note that because CHtmlView derives most of its functionality from the WebBrowser control, and because the WebBrowser control is part of Internet Explorer, an application that uses CHtmlView can be run only on systems equipped with Internet Explorer 4.0 or later.

CHtmlView Operations

A good way to begin learning about CHtmlView is to get acquainted with its non-virtual member functions, or operations. The following table lists the operations that the majority of programmers will find the most useful. For information on the others (and there are many), refer to the MFC documentation.

KEY CHTMLVIEW OPERATIONS

Function	Description
GetBusy	Indicates whether a download is in progress
GetLocationName	If an HTML page is displayed, retrieves the page's title; if a file or folder is currently displayed, retrieves the file or folder name
GetLocationURL	Retrieves the URL of the resource that is currently displayed—for example, http://www.microsoft.com/ or file://C:/HTML Files/Clock.htm
GoBack	Goes to the previous item in the history list
GoForward	Goes to the next item in the history list
Navigate	Displays the resource at the specified URL
Refresh	Reloads the resource that is currently displayed
Stop	Stops loading a resource

The actions performed by these functions should be obvious to anyone familiar with Internet Explorer. For example, if you were writing a browser, you could wire up the Back, Forward, Refresh, and Stop buttons with these one-line command handlers:

```
// In CMyView's message map
ON_COMMAND (ID_BACK, OnBack)
```

```
ON_COMMAND (ID_FORWARD, OnForward)
ON_COMMAND (ID_REFRESH, OnRefresh)
ON_COMMAND (ID_STOP, OnStop)
    :
    :

void CMyView::OnBack ()
{
    GoBack ();
}

void CMyView::OnForward ()
{
    GoForward ();
}

void CMyView::OnRefresh ()
{
    Refresh ();
}

void CMyView::OnStop ()
{
    Stop ();
}
```

The WebBrowser control exposes huge chunks of its functionality through a COM interface named *IWebBrowser2*. Most nonvirtual *CHtmlView* member functions, including the ones shown here, are little more than C++ wrappers around calls to *IWebBrowser2* methods.

When the user clicks a hyperlink in an HTML document, *CHtmlView* automatically jumps to the associated URL. You can go to other URLs programmatically with the *Navigate* function. The statement

```
Navigate (_T ("http://www.microsoft.com"));
```

displays the main page of Microsoft's web site. *Navigate* also accepts file-based URLs. For example, the statement

```
Navigate (_T ("file://c:/my documents/budget.xls"));
```

displays an Excel spreadsheet in an HTML view. It works because Excel is an Active Document server, but it does require that Excel be installed on the host PC. Passing a path name identifying a folder rather than a file works, too:

```
Navigate (_T ("file://c:/my documents"));
```

A related *CHtmlView* function named *Navigate2* does everything *Navigate* does and more. Because it will accept pointers to ITEMIDLIST structures in lieu of path names, *Navigate2* can be used to access objects anywhere in the shell's namespace. *Navigate*, by contrast, is limited to file system objects only.

CHtmlView Overridables

CHtmlView includes several virtual functions that you can override in a derived class to obtain up-to-date information about the state of the WebBrowser control and the resources that it displays. A sampling of these functions appears in the following table.

KEY *CHTML VIEW* OVERRIDABLES

Function	Description
OnNavigateComplete2	Called after navigating to a new URL
OnBeforeNavigate2	Called before navigating to a new URL
OnProgressChange	Called to provide an update on the status of a download
OnDownloadBegin	Called to indicate that a download is about to begin
OnDownloadComplete	Called to indicate that a download is complete
OnTitleChange	Called when the document title changes
OnDocumentComplete	Called to indicate that a document was successfully downloaded

Unfortunately, the Visual C++ documentation provides only sketchy information about why or when these functions are called. That's why a transcript can be so revealing. Here's a log of the calls that took place when *CHtmlView::Navigate* was called to go to *home.microsoft.com*:

```
OnBeforeNavigate2 ("http://home.microsoft.com/")
OnDownloadBegin ()
OnProgressChange (100/10000)
OnProgressChange (150/10000)
OnProgressChange (150/10000)
OnProgressChange (200/10000)
OnProgressChange (250/10000)
OnProgressChange (300/10000)
OnProgressChange (350/10000)
OnProgressChange (400/10000)
OnProgressChange (450/10000)
OnProgressChange (500/10000)
OnProgressChange (550/10000)
OnDownloadComplete ()
OnDownloadBegin ()
```

```
OnProgressChange (600/10000)
OnProgressChange (650/10000)
OnProgressChange (700/10000)
OnProgressChange (750/10000)
OnProgressChange (800/10000)
OnProgressChange (850/10000)
OnProgressChange (900/10000)
OnProgressChange (950/10000)
OnProgressChange (1000/10000)
OnProgressChange (1050/10000)
OnProgressChange (1100/10000)
OnProgressChange (1150/10000)
OnProgressChange (1200/10000)
OnProgressChange (1250/10000)
OnProgressChange (131400/1000000)
OnTitleChange ("http://home.microsoft.com/")
OnNavigateComplete2 ("http://home.microsoft.com/")
OnTitleChange ("MSN.COM")
OnProgressChange (146500/1000000)
OnTitleChange ("MSN.COM")
OnProgressChange (158200/1000000)
OnProgressChange (286500/1000000)
OnProgressChange (452300/1000000)
OnTitleChange ("MSN.COM")
OnProgressChange (692800/1000000)
OnProgressChange (787000/1000000)
OnTitleChange ("MSN.COM")
         .
         .
         .

OnDownloadComplete ()
OnTitleChange ("MSN.COM")
OnDocumentComplete ("http://home.microsoft.com/")
OnProgressChange (0/0)
```

You can clearly see the call to *OnBeforeNavigate2* advertising the WebBrowser control's intent to jump to a new URL, the call to *OnNavigateComplete2* after a connection was established, and the call to *OnDocumentComplete* once the page was fully downloaded. In between, you see calls to *OnDownloadBegin* and *OnDownloadComplete* marking the downloading of individual page elements and calls to *OnProgressChange* noting the progress of those downloads. *OnProgressChange* receives two parameters: a long specifying the number of bytes downloaded thus far and a long specifying the number of bytes to be downloaded. Dividing the first by the second and multiplying by 100 yields a percentage-done figure that can be displayed in a progress bar or other control. A call to *OnProgressChange* with a first parameter equal to −1 or a pair of 0 parameters is another indication that a download is complete.

The MFCIE sample shipped with Visual C++ provides one example of how these functions can be used. It uses *OnTitleChange* to update the document title displayed in its title bar, *OnBeforeNavigate2* to begin playing an animation indicating a download is in progress, and *OnDocumentComplete* to stop the animation and update the URL displayed in its address bar. In essence, it uses *OnBeforeNavigate2* and *OnDocumentComplete* to mark the beginning and end of a document download and *OnTitleChange* to display the title parsed from the HTML.

Utilizing DHTML in *CHtmlView*-Based Applications

Writing specialized browsers for in-house use is a fine way to put *CHtmlView* to work, but *CHtmlView* has plenty of other uses, too. Some MFC developers find *CHtmlView* interesting because it can be used to write thin clients. A *thin client* is an application that derives all or part of its functionality from HTML code, DHTML code, or other web programming media. A full discourse on DHTML is beyond the scope of this book, but a sample will help to demonstrate how *CHtmlView* and DHTML together can be a potent mix.

Suppose you'd like to write a Windows application that simulates a digital clock. One way to do it is to fire up Visual C++ and write an MFC clock application. An alternate approach is to create a *CHtmlView*-based application that runs a DHTML script that in turn runs the clock. The chief advantage to the latter technique is that the application's look and feel is defined in an ordinary HTML file. Anyone with access to the HTML file can customize the application's user interface using tools as unsophisticated as Notepad. Modifying the user interface of a compiled executable, by contrast, requires more elaborate measures.

Because DHTML is language-independent, DHTML scripts can be written in any scripting language for which a scripting engine is available. Most DHTML scripts are written in JavaScript, which is a dialect of the Java programming language, or Microsoft Visual Basic, Scripting Edition (VBScript), which comes from Visual Basic. The following HTML file is based on a sample provided on MSDN. It uses DHTML and embedded JavaScript to display a ticking digital clock:

```
<HTML>
<HEAD><TITLE>DHTML Clock Demo</TITLE></HEAD>
<BODY BGCOLOR="#FF0000">
<H1 STYLE="font-family:comic sans ms" ALIGN=center>DHTML Clock</H1>
<DIV ID=Clock ALIGN=center
STYLE="font-family:arial; font-size:64; color:#FFFFFF">
 </DIV>

<SCRIPT LANGUAGE="JavaScript">
<!--
function tick() {
```

```
    var hours, minutes, seconds, ampm;
    var today = new Date();
    var h = today.getHours();
    var m = today.getMinutes();
    var s = today.getSeconds();

    if (h < 12) {
        hours = h + ":";
        ampm = "A.M.";
    }
    else if (h == 12) {
        hours = "12:";
        ampm = "P.M.";
    }
    else {
        h = h - 12;
        hours = h + ":";
        ampm = "P.M.";
    }

    if (m < 10)
        minutes = "0" + m + ":";
    else
        minutes = m + ":";

    if (s < 10)
        seconds = "0" + s + " ";
    else
        seconds = s + " ";

    Clock.innerHTML = hours + minutes + seconds + ampm;
    window.setTimeout("tick();", 100);
}
window.onload = tick;
-->
</SCRIPT>
</BODY>
</HTML>
```

Figure 10-4 on the following page shows a *CHtmlView*-based application named HtmlClock that uses this HTML script as the basis for a clock program. The HTML is stored in a file named Clock.htm. When HtmlClock is started, the view's *OnInitial-Update* function passes the path to Clock.htm to the *Navigate* function. (Because of the way the path name is formulated, Clock.htm must be located in the same directory as HtmlClock.exe.) Under the hood, *Navigate* passes the path name to the WebBrowser control, and the WebBrowser control loads the file, parses the HTML, and executes the script.

Figure 10-4. *The HtmlClock window.*

The source code for HtmlClock's view class appears in Figure 10-5. To create Html-Clock, I used AppWizard to create an SDI document/view program with a *CHtmlView*-based view. I modified the AppWizard-supplied *OnInitialUpdate* function to load Clock.htm, added an *OnTitleChange* function that displays the page title ("DHTML Clock Demo") in the frame window's title bar, and trimmed most of the AppWizard-generated entries from the application's menu.

HtmlClock merely scratches the surface of what you can do with HTML views. For example, you can run Java applets in HTML views, and you can write C++ code that interacts with DHTML objects. *CHtmlView* is also the perfect tool for building HTML-based help systems. If HTML remains the industry darling that it is today, *CHtmlView* can be the ticket that gets you into the ball.

HtmlClockView.h

```
// HtmlClockView.h : interface of the CHtmlClockView class
//
/////////////////////////////////////////////////////////////////////////////

#if !defined(
//      AFX_HTMLCLOCKVIEW_H__D39825ED_99C0_11D2_8E53_006008A82731__INCLUDED_)
#define AFX_HTMLCLOCKVIEW_H__D39825ED_99C0_11D2_8E53_006008A82731__INCLUDED_
#if _MSC_VER > 1000
```

Figure 10-5. *The HtmlClock application.*

```
#pragma once
#endif // _MSC_VER > 1000


class CHtmlClockView : public CHtmlView
{
protected: // create from serialization only
    CHtmlClockView();
    DECLARE_DYNCREATE(CHtmlClockView)

// Attributes
public:
    CHtmlClockDoc* GetDocument();

// Operations
public:

// Overrides
    // ClassWizard generated virtual function overrides
    //{{AFX_VIRTUAL(CHtmlClockView)
    public:
    virtual void OnDraw(CDC* pDC);  // overridden to draw this view
    virtual BOOL PreCreateWindow(CREATESTRUCT& cs);
    virtual void OnTitleChange(LPCTSTR lpszText);
    protected:
    virtual void OnInitialUpdate(); // called first time after construct
    //}}AFX_VIRTUAL

// Implementation
public:
    virtual ~CHtmlClockView();
#ifdef _DEBUG
    virtual void AssertValid() const;
    virtual void Dump(CDumpContext& dc) const;
#endif

protected:

// Generated message map functions
protected:
    //{{AFX_MSG(CHtmlClockView)
        // NOTE - the ClassWizard will add and remove member functions here.
        //    DO NOT EDIT what you see in these blocks of generated code !
    //}}AFX_MSG
    DECLARE_MESSAGE_MAP()
};
```

(continued)

Figure 10-5. *continued*

```
#ifndef _DEBUG  // debug version in HtmlClockView.cpp
inline CHtmlClockDoc* CHtmlClockView::GetDocument()
    { return (CHtmlClockDoc*)m_pDocument; }
#endif


/////////////////////////////////////////////////////////////////////////

//{{AFX_INSERT_LOCATION}}
// Microsoft Visual C++ will insert additional declarations immediately
// before the previous line.

#endif
// !defined(
//      AFX_HTMLCLOCKVIEW_H__D39825ED_99C0_11D2_8E53_006008A82731__INCLUDED_)
```

HtmlClockView.cpp

```
// HtmlClockView.cpp : implementation of the CHtmlClockView class
//

#include "stdafx.h"
#include "HtmlClock.h"

#include "HtmlClockDoc.h"
#include "HtmlClockView.h"

#ifdef _DEBUG
#define new DEBUG_NEW
#undef THIS_FILE
static char THIS_FILE[] = __FILE__;
#endif


/////////////////////////////////////////////////////////////////////////
// CHtmlClockView

IMPLEMENT_DYNCREATE(CHtmlClockView, CHtmlView)

BEGIN_MESSAGE_MAP(CHtmlClockView, CHtmlView)
    //{{AFX_MSG_MAP(CHtmlClockView)
        // NOTE - the ClassWizard will add and remove mapping macros here.
        //    DO NOT EDIT what you see in these blocks of generated code!
    //}}AFX_MSG_MAP
END_MESSAGE_MAP()
```

```
/////////////////////////////////////////////////////////////////////////
// CHtmlClockView construction/destruction

CHtmlClockView::CHtmlClockView()
{
}

CHtmlClockView::~CHtmlClockView()
{
}

BOOL CHtmlClockView::PreCreateWindow(CREATESTRUCT& cs)
{
    return CHtmlView::PreCreateWindow(cs);
}


/////////////////////////////////////////////////////////////////////////
// CHtmlClockView drawing

void CHtmlClockView::OnDraw(CDC* pDC)
{
    CHtmlClockDoc* pDoc = GetDocument();
    ASSERT_VALID(pDoc);
}

void CHtmlClockView::OnInitialUpdate()
{
    CHtmlView::OnInitialUpdate();

    TCHAR szPath[MAX_PATH];
    ::GetModuleFileName (NULL, szPath, sizeof (szPath) / sizeof (TCHAR));

    CString string = szPath;
    int nIndex = string.ReverseFind (_T ('\\'));
    ASSERT (nIndex != -1);
    string = string.Left (nIndex + 1) + _T ("Clock.htm");
    Navigate (string);
}


/////////////////////////////////////////////////////////////////////////
// CHtmlClockView diagnostics

#ifdef _DEBUG
void CHtmlClockView::AssertValid() const
{
    CHtmlView::AssertValid();
}
```

(continued)

Figure 10-5. *continued*

```
void CHtmlClockView::Dump(CDumpContext& dc) const
{
    CHtmlView::Dump(dc);
}

CHtmlClockDoc* CHtmlClockView::GetDocument() // non-debug version is inline
{
    ASSERT(m_pDocument->IsKindOf(RUNTIME_CLASS(CHtmlClockDoc)));
    return (CHtmlClockDoc*)m_pDocument;
}
#endif //_DEBUG

/////////////////////////////////////////////////////////////////////////////
// CHtmlClockView message handlers

void CHtmlClockView::OnTitleChange(LPCTSTR lpszText)
{
    CHtmlView::OnTitleChange(lpszText);
    AfxGetMainWnd ()->SetWindowText (lpszText);
}
```

TREE VIEWS

MFC's *CTreeView* class enables programmers to create views similar to the one featured in the left pane of Windows Explorer. Tree views display treelike structures containing items composed of text and images. Items can have subitems, and collections of subitems, or *subtrees,* can be expanded and collapsed to display and hide the information contained therein. Tree views are ideal for depicting data that's inherently hierarchical, such as the directory structure of a hard disk. If you do even a moderate amount of Windows programming, you'll probably find plenty of uses for tree views.

    CTreeView is a relatively simple class because it derives most of its functionality from the tree view control, which is one of the members of the common controls library Microsoft Windows 95 introduced to the world. In MFC, *CTreeCtrl* provides the programmatic interface to tree view controls. A tree view is programmed by calling *CTreeCtrl* functions on the underlying tree view control. The *CTreeView* function *GetTreeCtrl* returns a *CTreeCtrl* reference to that control. Thus, to determine how many items a tree view contains, you don't use a *CTreeView* function; instead, you call *CTreeCtrl::GetCount*, like this:

```
UINT nCount = GetTreeCtrl ().GetCount ();
```

This paradigm—call a member function of the view to acquire a reference to the corresponding control—is shared by all of MFC's *CCtrlView*-derived classes.

Initializing a Tree View

A tree view control supports several special window styles that influence its appearance and operation. Six of those styles are available on all systems running Windows 95 or later or Microsoft Windows NT 3.51 or later; additional styles are available on systems on which Internet Explorer 3.0 is installed, and even more styles are supported on systems equipped with Internet Explorer 4.0 or later. (For a discussion of the interdependencies between the common controls and Internet Explorer, see Chapter 16.) You can apply any of the supported styles to a tree view by ORing them into the *style* field of the CREATESTRUCT structure passed to *PreCreateWindow*. The six styles available to all tree views are listed in the following table.

TREE VIEW STYLES

Style	*Description*
TVS_HASLINES	Adds lines connecting subitems to their parents.
TVS_LINESATROOT	Adds lines connecting items at the top level, or root, of the hierarchy. This style is valid only if TVS_HASLINES is also specified.
TVS_HASBUTTONS	Adds buttons containing plus or minus signs to items that have subitems. Clicking a button expands or collapses the associated subtree.
TVS_EDITLABELS	Enables in-place label editing notifications.
TVS_DISABLEDRAGDROP	Disables drag-and-drop notifications.
TVS_SHOWSELALWAYS	Specifies that the item that's currently selected should always be highlighted. By default, the highlight is removed when the control loses the input focus.

Each item in a tree view control consists of a text string (also known as a *label*) and optionally an image from an image list. The image list is another of the control types introduced in Windows 95. In MFC, image lists are represented by instances of the class *CImageList*. Think of an image list as a collection of like-sized bitmaps in which each bitmap is identified by a 0-based index. The statements

```
CImageList il;
il.Create (IDB_IMAGES, 16, 1, RGB (255, 0, 255));
```

create an image list from a bitmap resource (ID=IDB_IMAGES) containing one or more images. Each image is 16 pixels wide, as indicated by *Create*'s second parameter. The COLORREF value in the final parameter specifies that magenta is the image lists's transparency color. When images from the image list are displayed in a tree view, only the nonmagenta pixels will be displayed.

If you want to include images as well as text in a tree view, you must create and initialize an image list and use *CTreeCtrl::SetImageList* to assign it to the tree view.

If *il* is a *CImageList* object, the statement

```
GetTreeCtrl ().SetImageList (&il, TVSIL_NORMAL);
```

associates the image list with the control. TVSIL_NORMAL tells the tree view that the images in the image list will be used to represent both selected and unselected items. You can assign a separate TVSIL_STATE image list to the tree view to represent items that assume application-defined states. Note that the image list must not be destroyed before the tree view is destroyed; if it is, the images will disappear from the control.

    CTreeCtrl::InsertItem adds an item to a tree view control. Items are identified by HTREEITEM handles, and one of the parameters input to *InsertItem* is the HTREE-ITEM handle of the item's parent. A subitem is created when an item is added to a tree view and parented to another item. Root items—items in the uppermost level of the tree—are created by specifying TVI_ROOT as the parent. The following code sample initializes a tree view with the names of two 1970s rock groups along with subtrees listing some of their albums:

```
// Root items first, with automatic sorting.
HTREEITEM hEagles = GetTreeCtrl ().InsertItem (_T ("Eagles"),
    TVI_ROOT, TVI_SORT);
HTREEITEM hDoobies = GetTreeCtrl ().InsertItem (_T ("Doobie Brothers"),
    TVI_ROOT, TVI_SORT);

// Eagles subitems second (no sorting).
GetTreeCtrl ().InsertItem (_T ("Eagles"), hEagles);
GetTreeCtrl ().InsertItem (_T ("On the Border"), hEagles);
GetTreeCtrl ().InsertItem (_T ("Hotel California"), hEagles);
GetTreeCtrl ().InsertItem (_T ("The Long Run"), hEagles);

// Doobie subitems third (no sorting).
GetTreeCtrl ().InsertItem (_T ("Toulouse Street"), hDoobies);
GetTreeCtrl ().InsertItem (_T ("The Captain and Me"), hDoobies);
GetTreeCtrl ().InsertItem (_T ("Stampede"), hDoobies);
```

Passing a TVI_SORT flag to *InsertItem* automatically sorts items added to the tree with respect to other items in the same subtree. The default is TVI_LAST, which simply adds the item to the end of the list. You can also specify TVI_FIRST to add an item to the head of the list.

    That's one way to add items to a tree view control. You also have several other options for adding items because *CTreeCtrl* provides four different versions of *Insert-Item*. Let's take the example in the previous paragraph a little further and assume that you'd like to include images as well as text in the tree view items. Suppose you've created an image list that contains two images. Image 0 depicts a guitar, and image 1 depicts an album cover. You'd like guitars to appear alongside the names of the rock groups and album images to appear next to album titles. Here's what the code to initialize the control looks like:

```
// Add the image list to the control.
GetTreeCtrl ().SetImageList (pImageList, TVSIL_NORMAL);

// Root items first, with automatic sorting
HTREEITEM hEagles = GetTreeCtrl ().InsertItem (_T ("Eagles"),
    0, 0, TVI_ROOT, TVI_SORT);
HTREEITEM hDoobies = GetTreeCtrl ().InsertItem (_T ("Doobie Brothers"),
    0, 0, TVI_ROOT, TVI_SORT);

// Eagles subitems second (no sorting)
GetTreeCtrl ().InsertItem (_T ("Eagles"), 1, 1, hEagles);
GetTreeCtrl ().InsertItem (_T ("On the Border"), 1, 1, hEagles);
GetTreeCtrl ().InsertItem (_T ("Hotel California"), 1, 1, hEagles);
GetTreeCtrl ().InsertItem (_T ("The Long Run"), 1, 1, hEagles);

// Doobie subitems third (no sorting)
GetTreeCtrl ().InsertItem (_T ("Toulouse Street"), 1, 1, hDoobies);
GetTreeCtrl ().InsertItem (_T ("The Captain and Me"), 1, 1, hDoobies);
GetTreeCtrl ().InsertItem (_T ("Stampede"), 1, 1, hDoobies);
```

The second and third parameters passed to this form of *InsertItem* are image indexes. The first specifies the image the tree view will display when the item isn't selected, and the second specifies the image it will display when the item *is* selected. Specifying the same index for both means that the same image will be used to represent the item in both states. The tree view control in the left pane of Windows Explorer uses an image depicting a closed folder for nonselected folder items and an open folder for selected folder items. Thus, if you move the highlight up and down with the arrow keys, a folder "opens" when you highlight it and closes when you highlight another item.

Tree View Member Functions and Notifications

CTreeCtrl provides a wide range of member functions for manipulating the underlying tree view control and acquiring information about its items. *DeleteItem*, for example, removes an item from the control, and *DeleteAllItems* removes all the items. *Expand* expands or collapses a subtree. *SetItemText* changes an item's label; *GetItemText* retrieves it. *SortChildren* sorts the items in a subtree. You name it, and there's probably a *CTreeCtrl* function for doing it.

The key to nearly every one of these functions is an HTREEITEM handle identifying the item that's the target of the operation. If you'd like, you can save the handles returned by *InsertItem* in an array or a linked list or some other structure so that you can reference them again later. You can retrieve the handle of the selected item with *CTreeCtrl::GetSelectedItem*. And if necessary, you can start with the first item in a tree view control and enumerate items one by one using *GetParentItem*, *GetChildItem*, *GetNextItem*, *GetNextSiblingItem*, and other *CTreeCtrl* functions.

Once items are added to it, a tree view is capable of processing most user input on its own. The user can browse the items in the tree by expanding and collapsing branches and can make selections by pointing and clicking. You can add even more capabilities to a tree view (or customize its default response to conventional input) by processing the notifications shown in the following table. Notifications come in the form of WM_NOTIFY messages, and in most cases, *lParam* points to an NM_TREE-VIEW structure containing additional information about the event that prompted the message. Here are just a few uses for tree view notifications:

- Enable in-place label editing so that the user can edit text in a tree view

- Update item text and images dynamically by passing LPSTR_TEXTCALL-BACK and I_IMAGECALLBACK parameters to *InsertItem* and processing TVN_GETDISPINFO notifications

- Customize the control's response to keyboard input by processing TVN-_KEYDOWN notifications

- Support drag-and-drop operations

There are more uses (of course!), but this short list should give you an idea of the wide-ranging flexibility of a tree view control.

TREE VIEW NOTIFICATIONS

Notification	Sent When
TVN_BEGINDRAG	A drag-and-drop operation is begun with the left mouse button. Not sent if the control has the style TVS_DISABLEDRAGDROP.
TVN_BEGINRDRAG	A drag-and-drop operation is begun with the right mouse button. Not sent if the control has the style TVS_DISABLEDRAGDROP.
TVN_BEGINLABELEDIT	A label editing operation is begun. Sent only if the control has the style TVS_EDITLABELS.
TVN_ENDLABELEDIT	A label editing operation is completed. Sent only if the control has the style TVS_EDITLABELS.
TVN_GETDISPINFO	The control needs additional information to display an item. Sent if the item text is LPSTR_TEXTCALLBACK or the image index is I_IMAGECALLBACK.
TVN_DELETEITEM	An item is deleted.
TVN_ITEMEXPANDED	A subtree has expanded or collapsed.
TVN_ITEMEXPANDING	A subtree is about to expand or collapse.
TVN_KEYDOWN	A key is pressed while the control has the input focus.
TVN_SELCHANGED	The selection has changed.
TVN_SELCHANGING	The selection is about to change.
TVN_SETDISPINFO	The information in a TV_DISPINFO structure needs to be updated.

The DriveTree Application

The DriveTree application shown in Figure 10-6 uses a *CTreeView*-derived class named *CDriveView* to provide an interactive view of the host PC's drive and directory structure. *CDriveView::OnInitialUpdate* uses *SetImageList* to import an image list containing bitmaps for different drive types and then calls a helper function named *AddDrives* to initialize the drive list. *AddDrives* uses the Win32 *::GetLogical-Drives* function to identify the logical drives in the system. For each drive, it calls *CDriveView::AddDriveItem* to add a "drive item"—a tree view item representing a drive—to the tree's uppermost level. *::GetLogicalDrives* returns a DWORD value with "on" bits identifying the valid logical drives, where bit 0 corresponds to drive A:, bit 1 to drive B:, and so on. *AddDrives* needs just a few lines of code to enumerate the drives in the system and create a drive item for each. (See Figure 10-7 beginning on page 575.)

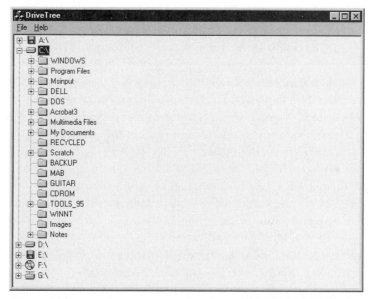

Figure 10-6. *The DriveTree window.*

AddDriveItem uses *CTreeCtrl::InsertItem* to add drive items to the tree. For each drive item that it adds, it also adds a "dummy" subitem so that a plus sign will appear next to the drive item. To determine a drive's type—floppy drive, hard disk, and so on—so that it can assign the drive an image from the image list, *AddDriveItem* uses the *::GetDriveType* API function. Given a string specifying the path to a drive's root directory, *::GetDriveType* returns a UINT value identifying the drive type. The possible return values are listed on the following page.

Return Value	Meaning
DRIVE_UNKNOWN	The drive type is unknown.
DRIVE_NO_ROOT_DIR	The drive lacks a root directory.
DRIVE_REMOVABLE	The drive is removable (returned for floppy drives and other removable-media drives such as Zip drives).
DRIVE_FIXED	The drive is fixed (returned for hard disks).
DRIVE_REMOTE	The drive is remote (returned for network drives).
DRIVE_CDROM	The drive is a CD-ROM drive.
DRIVE_RAMDISK	The drive is a RAM disk.

AddDriveItem uses a *switch-case* block to handle each of the possible return values. A series of ILI values defined near the top of DriveView.cpp correlates drive types and image indexes.

Much of the remaining code in DriveView.cpp is devoted to processing TVN-_ITEMEXPANDING notifications. For performance reasons, *CDriveView* doesn't initialize itself with items representing every directory on every drive. Instead, it adds directory items to a subtree just before the subtree is displayed and removes them when the subtree is collapsed. If a collapsed subtree contains at least one directory, a single child item is inserted so that a plus sign will appear next to the subtree. That child item is never seen because it's deleted before the subtree is expanded and replaced with items representing actual directories. An ON_NOTIFY_REFLECT entry in the message map reflects TVN_ITEMEXPANDING notifications so that *CDriveView* can handle them itself. The notification handler *OnItemExpanding* either adds items to the subtree or removes them, depending on whether the *action* field of the NM-_TREEVIEW structure indicates that the subtree is about to expand or collapse. *OnItemExpanding* uses the helper function *AddDirectories* to populate a branch of the tree with items. *AddDirectories*, in turn, uses the *::FindFirstFile* and *::FindNextFile* functions discussed in Chapter 6 to enumerate directories.

Removing the Document Name from the Title Bar

DriveTree doesn't use its document object at all. Its File menu doesn't include document-handling commands. And it doesn't display a document name in its title bar because it doesn't make sense to display a document name when the application doesn't support the loading and saving of documents. But because MFC automatically adds the document name to the title bar, you must take special steps to prevent MFC from inserting a document name.

You'll find the code responsible for removing the document name in the frame window class. *CMainFrame::PreCreateWindow* contains the statement

```
cs.style &= ~FWS_ADDTOTITLE;
```

FWS_ADDTOTITLE is a special window style specific to MFC that's included in frame windows by default. Windows that have this style have document names added to their window titles; windows that lack this style don't. By stripping the FWS_ADD-TOTITLE bit from the window style in *PreCreateWindow*, *CMainFrame* prevents the framework from modifying its window title. You can use this technique to remove the document name from the title bar of any document/view application.

MainFrm.h

```
// MainFrm.h : interface of the CMainFrame class
//
//////////////////////////////////////////////////////////////////////////////

#if
!defined(AFX_MAINFRM_H__090B3829_959D_11D2_8E53_006008A82731__INCLUDED_)
#define  AFX_MAINFRM_H__090B3829_959D_11D2_8E53_006008A82731__INCLUDED_

#if _MSC_VER > 1000
#pragma once
#endif // _MSC_VER > 1000

class CMainFrame : public CFrameWnd
{

protected: // create from serialization only
    CMainFrame();
    DECLARE_DYNCREATE(CMainFrame)

// Attributes
public:

// Operations
public:

// Overrides
    // ClassWizard generated virtual function overrides
    //{{AFX_VIRTUAL(CMainFrame)
    virtual BOOL PreCreateWindow(CREATESTRUCT& cs);
    //}}AFX_VIRTUAL
```

Figure 10-7. *The DriveTree application.*   *(continued)*

Figure 10-7. *continued*

```
// Implementation
public:
    virtual ~CMainFrame();
#ifdef _DEBUG
    virtual void AssertValid() const;
    virtual void Dump(CDumpContext& dc) const;
#endif

// Generated message map functions
protected:
    //{{AFX_MSG(CMainFrame)
        // NOTE - the ClassWizard will add and remove member functions here.
        //    DO NOT EDIT what you see in these blocks of generated code!
    //}}AFX_MSG
    DECLARE_MESSAGE_MAP()
};

/////////////////////////////////////////////////////////////////////////

//{{AFX_INSERT_LOCATION}}
// Microsoft Visual C++ will insert additional declarations immediately
// before the previous line.

#endif
// !defined(
//      AFX_MAINFRM_H__090B3829_959D_11D2_8E53_006008A82731__INCLUDED_)
```

MainFrm.cpp

```
// MainFrm.cpp : implementation of the CMainFrame class
//

#include "stdafx.h"
#include "DriveTree.h"

#include "MainFrm.h"

#ifdef _DEBUG
#define new DEBUG_NEW
#undef THIS_FILE
static char THIS_FILE[] = __FILE__;
#endif

/////////////////////////////////////////////////////////////////////////
// CMainFrame
```

```
IMPLEMENT_DYNCREATE(CMainFrame, CFrameWnd)

BEGIN_MESSAGE_MAP(CMainFrame, CFrameWnd)
    //{{AFX_MSG_MAP(CMainFrame)
        // NOTE - the ClassWizard will add and remove mapping macros here.
        //      DO NOT EDIT what you see in these blocks of generated code !
    //}}AFX_MSG_MAP
END_MESSAGE_MAP()

/////////////////////////////////////////////////////////////////////////
// CMainFrame construction/destruction

CMainFrame::CMainFrame()
{
}

CMainFrame::~CMainFrame()
{
}

BOOL CMainFrame::PreCreateWindow(CREATESTRUCT& cs)
{
    if( !CFrameWnd::PreCreateWindow(cs) )
        return FALSE;

    cs.style &= ~FWS_ADDTOTITLE;
    return TRUE;
}

/////////////////////////////////////////////////////////////////////////
// CMainFrame diagnostics

#ifdef _DEBUG
void CMainFrame::AssertValid() const
{
    CFrameWnd::AssertValid();
}

void CMainFrame::Dump(CDumpContext& dc) const
{
    CFrameWnd::Dump(dc);
}

#endif //_DEBUG

/////////////////////////////////////////////////////////////////////////
// CMainFrame message handlers
```

(continued)

Figure 10-7. *continued*

DriveView.h

```
// DriveTreeView.h : interface of the CDriveView class
//
///////////////////////////////////////////////////////////////////

#if
!defined(AFX_DRIVETREEVIEW_H__090B382D_959D_11D2_8E53_006008A82731__INCLUDED_)
#define
AFX_DRIVETREEVIEW_H__090B382D_959D_11D2_8E53_006008A82731__INCLUDED_

#if _MSC_VER > 1000
#pragma once
#endif // _MSC_VER > 1000


class CDriveView : public CTreeView
{
protected: // create from serialization only
    CDriveView();
    DECLARE_DYNCREATE(CDriveView)

// Attributes
public:
    CDriveTreeDoc* GetDocument();

// Operations
public:

// Overrides
    // ClassWizard generated virtual function overrides
    //{{AFX_VIRTUAL(CDriveView)
    public:
    virtual void OnDraw(CDC* pDC);  // overridden to draw this view
    virtual BOOL PreCreateWindow(CREATESTRUCT& cs);
    protected:
    virtual void OnInitialUpdate(); // called first time after construct
    //}}AFX_VIRTUAL

// Implementation
public:
    virtual ~CDriveView();
#ifdef _DEBUG
    virtual void AssertValid() const;
    virtual void Dump(CDumpContext& dc) const;
#endif
```

```
protected:

// Generated message map functions
protected:
    BOOL AddDriveItem (LPCTSTR pszDrive);
    int AddDirectories (HTREEITEM hItem, LPCTSTR pszPath);
    void DeleteAllChildren (HTREEITEM hItem);
    void DeleteFirstChild (HTREEITEM hItem);
    CString GetPathFromItem (HTREEITEM hItem);
    BOOL SetButtonState (HTREEITEM hItem, LPCTSTR pszPath);
    int AddDrives ();
    CImageList m_ilDrives;
    //{{AFX_MSG(CDriveView)
    afx_msg void OnItemExpanding(NMHDR* pNMHDR, LRESULT* pResult);
    //}}AFX_MSG
    DECLARE_MESSAGE_MAP()
};

#ifndef _DEBUG  // debug version in DriveTreeView.cpp
inline CDriveTreeDoc* CDriveView::GetDocument()
    { return (CDriveTreeDoc*)m_pDocument; }
#endif

/////////////////////////////////////////////////////////////////////////////

//{{AFX_INSERT_LOCATION}}
// Microsoft Visual C++ will insert additional declarations immediately
// before the previous line.

#endif
// !defined(
//     AFX_DRIVETREEVIEW_H__090B382D_959D_11D2_8E53_006008A82731__INCLUDED_)
```

DriveView.cpp

```
// DriveTreeView.cpp : implementation of the CDriveView class
//

#include "stdafx.h"
#include "DriveTree.h"

#include "DriveTreeDoc.h"
#include "DriveView.h"
#ifdef _DEBUG
```

(continued)

Figure 10-7. *continued*

```
#define new DEBUG_NEW
#undef THIS_FILE
static char THIS_FILE[] = __FILE__;
#endif

// Image indexes
#define ILI_HARD_DISK       0
#define ILI_FLOPPY          1
#define ILI_CD_ROM          2
#define ILI_NET_DRIVE       3
#define ILI_CLOSED_FOLDER   4
#define ILI_OPEN_FOLDER     5


/////////////////////////////////////////////////////////////////////////
// CDriveView

IMPLEMENT_DYNCREATE(CDriveView, CTreeView)

BEGIN_MESSAGE_MAP(CDriveView, CTreeView)
    //{{AFX_MSG_MAP(CDriveView)
    ON_NOTIFY_REFLECT(TVN_ITEMEXPANDING, OnItemExpanding)
    //}}AFX_MSG_MAP
END_MESSAGE_MAP()

/////////////////////////////////////////////////////////////////////////
// CDriveView construction/destruction

CDriveView::CDriveView()
{
}


CDriveView::~CDriveView()
{
}

BOOL CDriveView::PreCreateWindow(CREATESTRUCT& cs)
{
    if (!CTreeView::PreCreateWindow (cs))
        return FALSE;

    cs.style |= TVS_HASLINES | TVS_LINESATROOT | TVS_HASBUTTONS |
        TVS_SHOWSELALWAYS;
    return TRUE;
}


/////////////////////////////////////////////////////////////////////////
// CDriveView drawing
```

```
void CDriveView::OnDraw(CDC* pDC)
{
    CDriveTreeDoc* pDoc = GetDocument();
    ASSERT_VALID(pDoc);
    // TODO: add draw code for native data here
}

void CDriveView::OnInitialUpdate()
{
    CTreeView::OnInitialUpdate();

    //
    // Initialize the image list.
    //
    m_ilDrives.Create (IDB_DRIVEIMAGES, 16, 1, RGB (255, 0, 255));
    GetTreeCtrl ().SetImageList (&m_ilDrives, TVSIL_NORMAL);

    //
    // Populate the tree view with drive items.
    //
    AddDrives ();

    //
    // Show the folders on the current drive.
    //
    TCHAR szPath[MAX_PATH];
    ::GetCurrentDirectory (sizeof (szPath) / sizeof (TCHAR), szPath);
    CString strPath = szPath;
    strPath = strPath.Left (3);

    HTREEITEM hItem = GetTreeCtrl ().GetNextItem (NULL, TVGN_ROOT);
    while (hItem != NULL) {
        if (GetTreeCtrl ().GetItemText (hItem) == strPath)
            break;
        hItem = GetTreeCtrl ().GetNextSiblingItem (hItem);
    }

    if (hItem != NULL) {
        GetTreeCtrl ().Expand (hItem, TVE_EXPAND);
        GetTreeCtrl ().Select (hItem, TVGN_CARET);
    }
}

/////////////////////////////////////////////////////////////////////////
// CDriveView diagnostics
```

(continued)

Figure 10-7. *continued*

```
#ifdef _DEBUG
void CDriveView::AssertValid() const
{
    CTreeView::AssertValid();
}


void CDriveView::Dump(CDumpContext& dc) const
{
    CTreeView::Dump(dc);
}


CDriveTreeDoc* CDriveView::GetDocument() // non-debug version is inline
{
    ASSERT(m_pDocument->IsKindOf(RUNTIME_CLASS(CDriveTreeDoc)));
    return (CDriveTreeDoc*)m_pDocument;
}
#endif //_DEBUG


/////////////////////////////////////////////////////////////////////////
// CDriveView message handlers

int CDriveView::AddDrives()
{
    int nPos = 0;
    int nDrivesAdded = 0;
    CString string = _T ("?:\\");

    DWORD dwDriveList = ::GetLogicalDrives ();

    while (dwDriveList) {
        if (dwDriveList & 1) {
            string.SetAt (0, _T ('A') + nPos);
            if (AddDriveItem (string))
                nDrivesAdded++;
        }
        dwDriveList >>= 1;
        nPos++;
    }
    return nDrivesAdded;
}


BOOL CDriveView::AddDriveItem(LPCTSTR pszDrive)
{
    CString string;
    HTREEITEM hItem;

    UINT nType = ::GetDriveType (pszDrive);
```

```
    switch (nType) {

    case DRIVE_REMOVABLE:
        hItem = GetTreeCtrl ().InsertItem (pszDrive, ILI_FLOPPY,
            ILI_FLOPPY);
        GetTreeCtrl ().InsertItem (_T (""), ILI_CLOSED_FOLDER,
            ILI_CLOSED_FOLDER, hItem);
        break;

    case DRIVE_FIXED:
    case DRIVE_RAMDISK:
        hItem = GetTreeCtrl ().InsertItem (pszDrive, ILI_HARD_DISK,
            ILI_HARD_DISK);
        SetButtonState (hItem, pszDrive);
        break;

    case DRIVE_REMOTE:
        hItem = GetTreeCtrl ().InsertItem (pszDrive, ILI_NET_DRIVE,
            ILI_NET_DRIVE);
        SetButtonState (hItem, pszDrive);
        break;

    case DRIVE_CDROM:
        hItem = GetTreeCtrl ().InsertItem (pszDrive, ILI_CD_ROM,
            ILI_CD_ROM);
        GetTreeCtrl ().InsertItem (_T (""), ILI_CLOSED_FOLDER,
            ILI_CLOSED_FOLDER, hItem);
        break;

    default:
        return FALSE;
    }
    return TRUE;
}

BOOL CDriveView::SetButtonState(HTREEITEM hItem, LPCTSTR pszPath)
{
    HANDLE hFind;
    WIN32_FIND_DATA fd;
    BOOL bResult = FALSE;

    CString strPath = pszPath;
    if (strPath.Right (1) != _T ("\\"))
        strPath += _T ("\\");
    strPath += _T ("*.*");

    if ((hFind = ::FindFirstFile (strPath, &fd)) == INVALID_HANDLE_VALUE)
        return bResult;
```

(continued)

Figure 10-7. *continued*

```
    do {
        if (fd.dwFileAttributes & FILE_ATTRIBUTE_DIRECTORY) {
            CString strComp = (LPCTSTR) &fd.cFileName;
            if ((strComp != _T (".")) && (strComp != _T (".."))) {
                GetTreeCtrl ().InsertItem (_T (""), ILI_CLOSED_FOLDER,
                    ILI_CLOSED_FOLDER, hItem);
                bResult = TRUE;
                break;
            }
        }
    } while (::FindNextFile (hFind, &fd));

    ::FindClose (hFind);
    return bResult;
}

void CDriveView::OnItemExpanding(NMHDR* pNMHDR, LRESULT* pResult)
{
    NM_TREEVIEW* pNMTreeView = (NM_TREEVIEW*)pNMHDR;
    HTREEITEM hItem = pNMTreeView->itemNew.hItem;
    CString string = GetPathFromItem (hItem);

    *pResult = FALSE;

    if (pNMTreeView->action == TVE_EXPAND) {
        DeleteFirstChild (hItem);
        if (AddDirectories (hItem, string) == 0)
            *pResult = TRUE;
    }
    else { // pNMTreeView->action == TVE_COLLAPSE
        DeleteAllChildren (hItem);
        if (GetTreeCtrl ().GetParentItem (hItem) == NULL)
            GetTreeCtrl ().InsertItem (_T (""), ILI_CLOSED_FOLDER,
                ILI_CLOSED_FOLDER, hItem);
        else
            SetButtonState (hItem, string);
    }
}

CString CDriveView::GetPathFromItem(HTREEITEM hItem)
{
    CString strResult = GetTreeCtrl ().GetItemText (hItem);

    HTREEITEM hParent;
    while ((hParent = GetTreeCtrl ().GetParentItem (hItem)) != NULL) {
        CString string = GetTreeCtrl ().GetItemText (hParent);
        if (string.Right (1) != _T ("\\"))
            string += _T ("\\");
```

```
            strResult = string + strResult;
            hItem = hParent;
        }
        return strResult;
}

void CDriveView::DeleteFirstChild(HTREEITEM hItem)
{
    HTREEITEM hChildItem;
    if ((hChildItem = GetTreeCtrl ().GetChildItem (hItem)) != NULL)
        GetTreeCtrl ().DeleteItem (hChildItem);
}

void CDriveView::DeleteAllChildren(HTREEITEM hItem)
{
    HTREEITEM hChildItem;
    if ((hChildItem = GetTreeCtrl ().GetChildItem (hItem)) == NULL)
        return;

    do {
        HTREEITEM hNextItem =
            GetTreeCtrl ().GetNextSiblingItem (hChildItem);
        GetTreeCtrl ().DeleteItem (hChildItem);
        hChildItem = hNextItem;
    } while (hChildItem != NULL);
}

int CDriveView::AddDirectories(HTREEITEM hItem, LPCTSTR pszPath)
{
    HANDLE hFind;
    WIN32_FIND_DATA fd;
    HTREEITEM hNewItem;

    int nCount = 0;

    CString strPath = pszPath;
    if (strPath.Right (1) != _T ("\\"))
        strPath += _T ("\\");
    strPath += _T ("*.*");

    if ((hFind = ::FindFirstFile (strPath, &fd)) == INVALID_HANDLE_VALUE) {
        if (GetTreeCtrl ().GetParentItem (hItem) == NULL)
            GetTreeCtrl ().InsertItem (_T (""), ILI_CLOSED_FOLDER,
                ILI_CLOSED_FOLDER, hItem);
        return 0;
    }
```

(continued)

Figure 10-7. *continued*

```
   do {
       if (fd.dwFileAttributes & FILE_ATTRIBUTE_DIRECTORY) {
           CString strComp = (LPCTSTR) &fd.cFileName;
           if ((strComp != _T (".")) && (strComp != _T (".."))) {
               hNewItem =
                   GetTreeCtrl ().InsertItem ((LPCTSTR) &fd.cFileName,
                   ILI_CLOSED_FOLDER, ILI_OPEN_FOLDER, hItem);

               CString strNewPath = pszPath;
               if (strNewPath.Right (1) != _T ("\\"))
                   strNewPath += _T ("\\");

               strNewPath += (LPCTSTR) &fd.cFileName;
               SetButtonState (hNewItem, strNewPath);
               nCount++;
           }
       }
   } while (::FindNextFile (hFind, &fd));

   ::FindClose (hFind);
   return nCount;
}
```

LIST VIEWS

List views are similar to tree views in that they provide a powerful infrastructure for presenting complex collections of data to the user. But whereas tree views are ideal for depicting hierarchical relationships, list views are best suited for presenting "flat" collections of data, such as lists of file names.

Like items in a tree view, items in a list view can include both text and images. In addition, items can have text-only *subitems* containing additional information about the associated items. The subitems are visible when the control is in "report" mode, which is one of four presentation styles that a list view supports. The other presentation styles are large icon mode, small icon mode, and list mode. You can see examples of all four presentation styles by starting the Windows Explorer and using the View menu to change the view in the right pane. The Large Icons command in the View menu corresponds to large icon mode, Small Icons corresponds to small icon mode, List corresponds to list mode, and Details corresponds to report mode.

Initializing a List View

MFC's *CListView* class is the base class for list views. *CListView* derives most of its functionality from list view controls, which, like tree view controls, are part of the common controls library. MFC wraps list view controls in the class *CListCtrl*. To program a list view, you call *CListView::GetListCtrl* to acquire a *CListCtrl* reference to the control that appears inside the list view, and then you call *CListCtrl* functions using the returned reference.

When you derive from *CListView*, you'll almost always override *PreCreate-Window* in the derived class and apply one or more default styles to the view. The following table lists the styles that all list views support. Additional list view styles are available on systems running Internet Explorer 3.0 or later.

LIST VIEW STYLES

Style	*Description*
LVS_ICON	Selects large icon mode.
LVS_SMALLICON	Selects small icon mode.
LVS_LIST	Selects list mode.
LVS_REPORT	Selects report mode.
LVS_NOCOLUMNHEADER	Removes the header control that's normally displayed in report mode.
LVS_NOSORTHEADER	Disables the LVN_COLUMNCLICK notifications that are sent by default when a column header is clicked in report mode.
LVS_ALIGNLEFT	Aligns items along the left border in large and small icon mode.
LVS_ALIGNTOP	Aligns items along the top border in large and small icon mode.
LVS_AUTOARRANGE	Automatically arranges items in rows and columns in large and small icon mode.
LVS_EDITLABELS	Enables in-place label editing notifications.
LVS_NOLABELWRAP	Restricts labels to single lines in large icon mode.
LVS_NOSCROLL	Disables scrolling. Scrolling is enabled by default.
LVS_OWNERDRAWFIXED	Specifies that the control's owner will draw the items in response to WM_DRAWITEM messages.
LVS_SHAREIMAGELISTS	Prevents a list view from automatically deleting the image lists associated with it when the view itself is deleted.
LVS_SINGLESEL	Disables multiple-selection support.
LVS_SHOWSELALWAYS	Specifies that the selected items should always be highlighted. By default, the highlight is removed when the view loses the input focus.
LVS_SORTASCENDING	Specifies that items should be sorted in ascending order (for example, A through Z).
LVS_SORTDESCENDING	Specifies that items should be sorted in descending order (for example, Z through A).

Like a tree view control, a list view control is empty when it's first created. Initialization is a five-step process:

1. Create a pair of image lists containing images for the list view items. One image list contains "large" images used in large icon mode; the other contains "small" images used in small icon, list, and report modes.

2. Use *CListCtrl::SetImageList* to associate the image lists with the list view control. Pass *SetImageList* an LVSIL_NORMAL flag for the image list containing large images and an LVSIL_SMALL flag for the image list containing small images.

3. Add columns to the list view control with *CListCtrl::InsertColumn*. The leftmost column displays the items added to the control. The columns to the right display subitems and are visible only in report mode.

4. Add items to the control with *CListCtrl::InsertItem*.

5. Assign text strings to the item's subitems with *CListCtrl::SetItemText*.

This procedure isn't as difficult as it sounds. The following code fragment initializes a list view with items representing eight of the states in the United States. Each item consists of a label and an image. The label is the name of a state, and the image presumably shows a thumbnail rendition of the state's outline. Each item also contains a pair of subitems: a text string naming the state capital and a text string describing the state's land area. In report mode, the subitems appear in columns under headers labeled "Capital" and "Area (sq. miles)."

```
static CString text[8][3] = {
    _T ("Tennessee"),        _T ("Nashville"),     _T ("41,154"),
    _T ("Alabama"),          _T ("Montgomery"),    _T ("50,766"),
    _T ("Mississippi"),      _T ("Jackson"),       _T ("47,234"),
    _T ("Florida"),          _T ("Tallahassee"),   _T ("54,157"),
    _T ("Georgia"),          _T ("Atlanta"),       _T ("58,060"),
    _T ("Kentucky"),         _T ("Frankfort"),     _T ("39,674"),
    _T ("North Carolina"),   _T ("Raleigh"),       _T ("48,843"),
    _T ("South Carolina"),   _T ("Columbia"),      _T ("30,207")
};

// Assign image lists.
GetListCtrl ().SetImageList (&ilLarge, LVSIL_NORMAL);
GetListCtrl ().SetImageList (&ilSmall, LVSIL_SMALL);

// Add columns.
GetListCtrl ().InsertColumn (0, _T ("State"), LVCFMT_LEFT, 96);
GetListCtrl ().InsertColumn (1, _T ("Capital"), LVCFMT_LEFT, 96);
GetListCtrl ().InsertColumn (2, _T ("Area (sq. miles)"),
    LVCFMT_RIGHT, 96);
```

```
// Add items and subitems.
for (int i=0; i<8; i++) {
    GetListCtrl ().InsertItem (i, (LPCTSTR) text[i][0], i);
    GetListCtrl ().SetItemText (i, 1, (LPCTSTR) text[i][1]);
    GetListCtrl ().SetItemText (i, 2, (LPCTSTR) text[i][2]);
}
```

The parameters passed to *InsertColumn* specify, in order, the column's 0-based in-dex, the label that appears at the top of the column, the column's alignment (whether data displayed in the column is left justified, right justified, or centered), and the column width in pixels. You can base column widths on the widths of characters in the control font by using *CListCtrl::GetStringWidth* to convert text strings into pixel counts. The parameters passed to *InsertItem* specify the item's 0-based index, the item label, and the index of the corresponding images in the image lists. The parameters passed to *SetItemText* specify the item number, the subitem number, and the subitem text, in that order.

Changing the Presentation Style

When a list view is created, its presentation style—LVS_ICON, LVS_SMALLICON, LVS_LIST, or LVS_REPORT—determines whether it starts up in large icon mode, small icon mode, list mode, or report mode. The default presentation style is applied in *PreCreateWindow*. However, you can switch modes on the fly by changing the presentation style. The following statement switches a list view to small icon mode:

```
ModifyStyle (LVS_TYPEMASK, LVS_SMALLICON);
```

Similarly, this statement switches the view to report mode:

```
ModifyStyle (LVS_TYPEMASK, LVS_REPORT);
```

ModifyStyle is a *CWnd* function that's handed down through inheritance to *CListView*. The first parameter passed to *ModifyStyle* specifies the style bits to turn off, and the second parameter specifies the style bits to turn on. LVS_TYPEMASK is a mask for all four presentation styles.

LVS_ICON, LVS_SMALLICON, LVS_LIST, and LVS_REPORT aren't true bit flags, so LVS_TYPEMASK also comes in handy when you query a list view to determine its current presentation style. The following code won't work:

```
// Wrong!
DWORD dwStyle = GetStyle ();
if (dwStyle & LVS_ICON)
    // Large icon mode.
else if (dwStyle & LVS_SMALLICON)
    // Small icon mode.
else if (dwStyle & LVS_LIST)
    // List mode.
```

(continued)

```
else if (dwStyle & LVS_REPORT)
    // Report mode.
```

But this code will:

```
DWORD dwStyle = GetStyle () & LVS_TYPEMASK;
if (dwStyle == LVS_ICON)
    // Large icon mode.
else if (dwStyle == LVS_SMALLICON)
    // Small icon mode.
else if (dwStyle == LVS_LIST)
    // List mode.
else if (dwStyle == LVS_REPORT)
    // Report mode.
```

This is the proper technique for determining the view type before updating menu items or other user interface objects that depend on the list view's presentation style.

Sorting in a List View

When a list view that lacks the LVS_NOCOLUMNHEADER style switches to report mode, it automatically displays a header control with buttonlike "header items" captioning each column. The user can change the column widths by dragging the vertical dividers separating the header items. (For a nice touch, you can retrieve the column widths with *CListCtrl::GetColumnWidth* before destroying a list view and save the widths in the registry. Restore the column widths the next time the list view is created, and the user's column width preferences will be persistent.) Unless a list view has the style LVS_NOSORTHEADER, clicking a header item sends an LVN_COLUMN-CLICK notification to the list view's parent. The message's *lParam* points to an NM_LIST-VIEW structure, and the structure's *iSubItem* field contains a 0-based index identifying the column that was clicked.

An application's usual response to an LVN_COLUMNCLICK notification is to call *CListCtrl::SortItems* to sort the list view items. Great, you say. Now I can create a list view that sorts, and I won't have to write the code to do the sorting. You do have to provide a callback function that the control's built-in sorting routine can call to compare a pair of arbitrarily selected items, but writing a comparison function is substantially less work than writing a full-blown bubble sort or quick sort routine. And the fact that the comparison function is application-defined means that you enjoy complete control over how the items in a list view control are lexically ordered.

The bad news is that the comparison function receives just three parameters: the 32-bit *lParam* values of the two items being compared and an application-defined *lParam* value that equals the second parameter passed to *SortItems*. You can assign an item an *lParam* value in the call to *InsertItem* or in a separate call to *CListCtrl-::SetItemData*. Unless an application maintains a private copy of each item's data and stores a value in *lParam* that allows the item's data to be retrieved, the comparison function can't possibly do its job. It's not difficult for an application to allocate its own per-item memory and stuff pointers into the items' *lParam*s, but it does complicate matters a bit because the memory must be deallocated, too. And an application that stores its own item data uses memory inefficiently if it assigns text strings to the list view's items and subitems because then the data ends up being stored in memory twice. You can avoid such wastefulness by specifying LPSTR_TEXTCALLBACK for the item and subitem text and providing text to the list view control in response to LVN_GETDISPINFO notifications. But this, too, complicates the program logic and means that the infrastructure required to support *CListCtrl::SortItems* isn't as simple as it first appears. In just a moment, we'll develop an application that implements sortable columns in a list view so that you can see firsthand how it's done.

Hit-Testing in a List View

You can respond to mouse clicks in a list view by processing NM_CLICK, NM_DBLCLK, NM_RCLICK, and NM_RDBLCLK notifications. Very often, the way you respond to these events will depend on what, if anything, was under the cursor when the click (or double-click) occurred. You can use *CListCtrl::HitTest* to perform hit-testing on the items in a list view. Given the coordinates of a point, *HitTest* returns the index of the item at that point or at −1 if the point doesn't correspond to an item.

The following code demonstrates how to process double clicks in a list view. The ON_NOTIFY_REFLECT entry in the message map reflects NM_DBLCLK notifications back to the list view. The NM_DBLCLK handler echoes the name of the item that was double-clicked to the debug output window using MFC's TRACE macro:

```
// In CMyListView's message map
ON_NOTIFY_REFLECT (NM_DBLCLK, OnDoubleClick)
    :
    :
void CMyListView::OnDoubleClick (NMHDR* pnmh, LRESULT* pResult)
{
    DWORD dwPos = ::GetMessagePos ();
    CPoint point ((int) LOWORD (dwPos), (int) HIWORD (dwPos));
    GetListCtrl ().ScreenToClient (&point);

    int nIndex;
    if ((nIndex = GetListCtrl ().HitTest (point)) != -1) {
        CString string = GetListCtrl ().GetItemText (nIndex, 0);
        TRACE (_T ("%s was double-clicked\n"), string);
    }
    *pResult = 0;
}
```

NM_DBLCLK notifications don't include cursor coordinates, so the cursor position is retrieved with *::GetMessagePos*. The screen coordinates returned by *::GetMessagePos* are converted into client coordinates local to the list view and passed to *CListCtrl-::HitTest*. If *HitTest* returns an item index, the index is used to retrieve the item's text.

The WinDir Application

The WinDir application pictured in Figure 10-8 is so named because its output is reminiscent of the MS-DOS DIR command, albeit in a graphical format. It uses a *CListView-*derived class named *CFileView* to display a list of all the files in a specified directory. You pick the directory by selecting the New Directory command from the File menu and entering a path name. After retrieving the path name that you entered, WinDir passes the path name to *CFileView::Refresh* to display the directory's contents. You can see this for yourself in FileView.cpp, which, along with other parts of WinDir's source code, is reproduced in Figure 10-9.

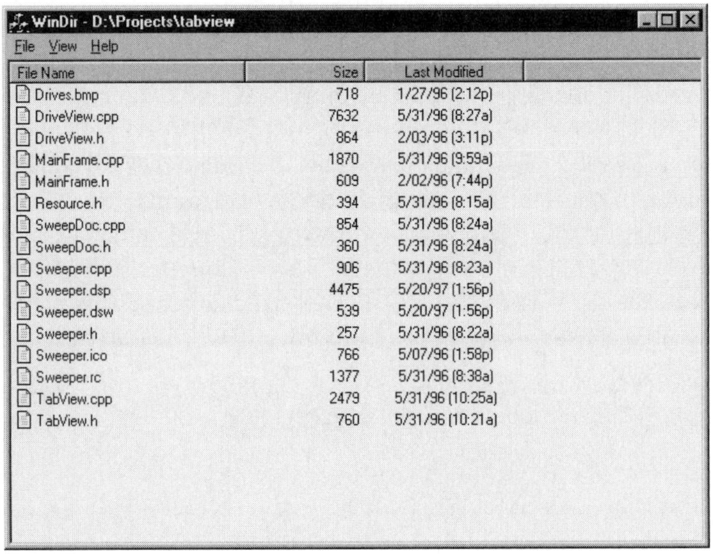

Figure 10-8. *The WinDir window.*

Here's a synopsis of how *CFileView* works. First, *CFileView::Refresh* builds a list of file names using *::FindFirstFile* and *::FindNextFile*. For each file that it identifies, *Refresh* adds an item to the list view by calling *CFileView::AddItem*. *AddItem*, in turn, allocates memory for an ITEMINFO data structure (defined in FileView.h); initializes the structure with the file's name, size, and date-and-time stamp; and adds an item to the list view whose *lParam* is the structure's address. Here's how it looks with error-checking code removed:

```
ITEMINFO* pItem;
pItem = new ITEMINFO;

pItem->strFileName = pfd->cFileName;
pItem->nFileSizeLow = pfd->nFileSizeLow;
pItem->ftLastWriteTime = pfd->ftLastWriteTime;

LV_ITEM lvi;
lvi.mask = LVIF_TEXT ¦ LVIF_IMAGE ¦ LVIF_PARAM;
lvi.iItem = nIndex;
lvi.iSubItem = 0;
lvi.iImage = 0;
lvi.pszText = LPSTR_TEXTCALLBACK;
lvi.lParam = (LPARAM) pItem;

GetListCtrl ().InsertItem (&lvi);
```

Notice the LPSTR_TEXTCALLBACK value specified in the LV_ITEM structure's *pszText* field. Rather than assign the item a text string, *AddItem* tells the list view, "Call me back when you need a label for the item." It's not necessary to initialize the subitems because LPSTR_TEXTCALLBACK is the default for subitems.

MainFrm.h

```
// MainFrm.h : interface of the CMainFrame class
//
/////////////////////////////////////////////////////////////////////////////

#if
!defined(AFX_MAINFRM_H__18BD7B7C_95C6_11D2_8E53_006008A82731__INCLUDED_)
#define  AFX_MAINFRM_H__18BD7B7C_95C6_11D2_8E53_006008A82731__INCLUDED_

#if _MSC_VER > 1000
#pragma once
#endif // _MSC_VER > 1000

class CMainFrame : public CFrameWnd
{

protected: // create from serialization only
    CMainFrame();
    DECLARE_DYNCREATE(CMainFrame)

// Attributes
public:
```

Figure 10-9. *The WinDir application.*   (*continued*)

Figure 10-9. *continued*

```
// Operations
public:

// Overrides
    // ClassWizard generated virtual function overrides
    //{{AFX_VIRTUAL(CMainFrame)
    virtual BOOL PreCreateWindow(CREATESTRUCT& cs);
    //}}AFX_VIRTUAL

// Implementation
public:
    virtual ~CMainFrame();
#ifdef _DEBUG
    virtual void AssertValid() const;
    virtual void Dump(CDumpContext& dc) const;
#endif

// Generated message map functions
protected:
    //{{AFX_MSG(CMainFrame)
        // NOTE - the ClassWizard will add and remove member functions here.
        //      DO NOT EDIT what you see in these blocks of generated code!
    //}}AFX_MSG
    DECLARE_MESSAGE_MAP()
};

///////////////////////////////////////////////////////////////////////////

//{{AFX_INSERT_LOCATION}}
// Microsoft Visual C++ will insert additional declarations immediately
// before the previous line.

#endif
// !defined(AFX_MAINFRM_H__18BD7B7C_95C6_11D2_8E53_006008A82731__INCLUDED_)
```

MainFrm.cpp

```
// MainFrm.cpp : implementation of the CMainFrame class
//

#include "stdafx.h"
#include "WinDir.h"
```

```
#include "MainFrm.h"

#ifdef _DEBUG
#define new DEBUG_NEW
#undef THIS_FILE
static char THIS_FILE[] = __FILE__;
#endif

/////////////////////////////////////////////////////////////////////////
// CMainFrame

IMPLEMENT_DYNCREATE(CMainFrame, CFrameWnd)

BEGIN_MESSAGE_MAP(CMainFrame, CFrameWnd)
    //{{AFX_MSG_MAP(CMainFrame)
        // NOTE - the ClassWizard will add and remove mapping macros here.
        //      DO NOT EDIT what you see in these blocks of generated code !
    //}}AFX_MSG_MAP
END_MESSAGE_MAP()

/////////////////////////////////////////////////////////////////////////
// CMainFrame construction/destruction

CMainFrame::CMainFrame()
{
}

CMainFrame::~CMainFrame()
{
}

BOOL CMainFrame::PreCreateWindow(CREATESTRUCT& cs)
{
    if( !CFrameWnd::PreCreateWindow(cs) )
        return FALSE;

    cs.style &= ~FWS_ADDTOTITLE;
    return TRUE;
}

/////////////////////////////////////////////////////////////////////////
// CMainFrame diagnostics

#ifdef _DEBUG
void CMainFrame::AssertValid() const
```

(continued)

Figure 10-9. *continued*

```
{
    CFrameWnd::AssertValid();
}

void CMainFrame::Dump(CDumpContext& dc) const
{
    CFrameWnd::Dump(dc);
}

#endif //_DEBUG


/////////////////////////////////////////////////////////////////////////
//
// CMainFrame message handlers
```

FileView.h

```
// FileView.h : interface of the CFileView class
//
/////////////////////////////////////////////////////////////////////////
//

#if
!defined(AFX_FILEVIEW_H__18BD7B80_95C6_11D2_8E53_006008A82731__INCLUDED_)
#define  AFX_FILEVIEW_H__18BD7B80_95C6_11D2_8E53_006008A82731__INCLUDED_

#if _MSC_VER > 1000
#pragma once
#endif // _MSC_VER > 1000

typedef struct tagITEMINFO {
    CString     strFileName;
    DWORD       nFileSizeLow;
    FILETIME    ftLastWriteTime;
} ITEMINFO;

class CFileView : public CListView
{
protected: // create from serialization only
    CFileView();
    DECLARE_DYNCREATE(CFileView)

// Attributes
public:
    CWinDirDoc* GetDocument();
```

```
// Operations
public:
    static int CALLBACK CompareFunc (LPARAM lParam1, LPARAM lParam2,
        LPARAM lParamSort);

// Overrides
    // ClassWizard generated virtual function overrides
    //{{AFX_VIRTUAL(CFileView)
    public:
    virtual void OnDraw(CDC* pDC);  // overridden to draw this view
    virtual BOOL PreCreateWindow(CREATESTRUCT& cs);
    protected:
    virtual void OnInitialUpdate(); // called first time after construct
    //}}AFX_VIRTUAL

// Implementation
public:
    int Refresh (LPCTSTR pszPath);
    virtual ~CFileView();
#ifdef _DEBUG
    virtual void AssertValid() const;
    virtual void Dump(CDumpContext& dc) const;
#endif

protected:

// Generated message map functions
protected:
    CString m_strPath;
    void FreeItemMemory ();
    BOOL AddItem (int nIndex, WIN32_FIND_DATA* pfd);
    CImageList m_ilSmall;
    CImageList m_ilLarge;
    //{{AFX_MSG(CFileView)
    afx_msg void OnDestroy();
    afx_msg void OnGetDispInfo(NMHDR* pNMHDR, LRESULT* pResult);
    afx_msg void OnColumnClick(NMHDR* pNMHDR, LRESULT* pResult);
    afx_msg void OnViewLargeIcons();
    afx_msg void OnViewSmallIcons();
    afx_msg void OnViewList();
    afx_msg void OnViewDetails();
    afx_msg void OnUpdateViewLargeIcons(CCmdUI* pCmdUI);
    afx_msg void OnUpdateViewSmallIcons(CCmdUI* pCmdUI);
    afx_msg void OnUpdateViewList(CCmdUI* pCmdUI);
    afx_msg void OnUpdateViewDetails(CCmdUI* pCmdUI);
    afx_msg void OnFileNewDirectory();
    //}}AFX_MSG
    DECLARE_MESSAGE_MAP()
};
```

(continued)

Figure 10-9. *continued*

```
#ifndef _DEBUG  // debug version in FileView.cpp
inline CWinDirDoc* CFileView::GetDocument()
    { return (CWinDirDoc*)m_pDocument; }
#endif


///////////////////////////////////////////////////////////////////////////

//{{AFX_INSERT_LOCATION}}
// Microsoft Visual C++ will insert additional declarations immediately
// before the previous line.

#endif
// !defined(
//      AFX_FILEVIEW_H__18BD7B80_95C6_11D2_8E53_006008A82731__INCLUDED_)
```

FileView.cpp

```
// FileView.cpp : implementation of the CFileView class
//

#include "stdafx.h"
#include "WinDir.h"
#include "PathDialog.h"
#include "WinDirDoc.h"
#include "FileView.h"

#ifdef _DEBUG
#define new DEBUG_NEW
#undef THIS_FILE
static char THIS_FILE[] = __FILE__;
#endif


///////////////////////////////////////////////////////////////////////////
// CFileView

IMPLEMENT_DYNCREATE(CFileView, CListView)

BEGIN_MESSAGE_MAP(CFileView, CListView)
    //{{AFX_MSG_MAP(CFileView)
    ON_WM_DESTROY()
    ON_NOTIFY_REFLECT(LVN_GETDISPINFO, OnGetDispInfo)
    ON_NOTIFY_REFLECT(LVN_COLUMNCLICK, OnColumnClick)
    ON_COMMAND(ID_VIEW_LARGE_ICONS, OnViewLargeIcons)
    ON_COMMAND(ID_VIEW_SMALL_ICONS, OnViewSmallIcons)
    ON_COMMAND(ID_VIEW_LIST, OnViewList)
```

```
    ON_COMMAND(ID_VIEW_DETAILS, OnViewDetails)
    ON_UPDATE_COMMAND_UI(ID_VIEW_LARGE_ICONS, OnUpdateViewLargeIcons)
    ON_UPDATE_COMMAND_UI(ID_VIEW_SMALL_ICONS, OnUpdateViewSmallIcons)
    ON_UPDATE_COMMAND_UI(ID_VIEW_LIST, OnUpdateViewList)
    ON_UPDATE_COMMAND_UI(ID_VIEW_DETAILS, OnUpdateViewDetails)
    ON_COMMAND(ID_FILE_NEW_DIR, OnFileNewDirectory)
    //}}AFX_MSG_MAP
END_MESSAGE_MAP()


/////////////////////////////////////////////////////////////////////////
// CFileView construction/destruction

CFileView::CFileView()
{
}


CFileView::~CFileView()
{
}


BOOL CFileView::PreCreateWindow(CREATESTRUCT& cs)
{
    if (!CListView::PreCreateWindow (cs))
        return FALSE;

    cs.style &= ~LVS_TYPEMASK;
    cs.style |= LVS_REPORT;
    return TRUE;
}


/////////////////////////////////////////////////////////////////////////
// CFileView drawing

void CFileView::OnDraw(CDC* pDC)
{
    CWinDirDoc* pDoc = GetDocument();
    ASSERT_VALID(pDoc);
    // TODO: add draw code for native data here
}


void CFileView::OnInitialUpdate()
{
    CListView::OnInitialUpdate();

    //
    // Initialize the image list.
    //
    m_ilLarge.Create (IDB_LARGEDOC, 32, 1, RGB (255, 0, 255));
```

(continued)

Figure 10-9. *continued*

```
    m_ilSmall.Create (IDB_SMALLDOC, 16, 1, RGB (255, 0, 255));

    GetListCtrl ().SetImageList (&m_ilLarge, LVSIL_NORMAL);
    GetListCtrl ().SetImageList (&m_ilSmall, LVSIL_SMALL);

    //
    // Add columns to the list view.
    //
    GetListCtrl ().InsertColumn (0, _T ("File Name"), LVCFMT_LEFT, 192);
    GetListCtrl ().InsertColumn (1, _T ("Size"), LVCFMT_RIGHT, 96);
    GetListCtrl ().InsertColumn (2, _T ("Last Modified"), LVCFMT_CENTER, 128);

    //
    // Populate the list view with items.
    //
    TCHAR szPath[MAX_PATH];
    ::GetCurrentDirectory (sizeof (szPath) / sizeof (TCHAR), szPath);
    Refresh (szPath);
}

/////////////////////////////////////////////////////////////////////////////
// CFileView diagnostics

#ifdef _DEBUG
void CFileView::AssertValid() const
{
    CListView::AssertValid();
}

void CFileView::Dump(CDumpContext& dc) const
{
    CListView::Dump(dc);
}

CWinDirDoc* CFileView::GetDocument() // non-debug version is inline
{
    ASSERT(m_pDocument->IsKindOf(RUNTIME_CLASS(CWinDirDoc)));
    return (CWinDirDoc*)m_pDocument;
}
#endif //_DEBUG

/////////////////////////////////////////////////////////////////////////////
// CFileView message handlers

int CFileView::Refresh(LPCTSTR pszPath)
{
    CString strPath = pszPath;
    if (strPath.Right (1) != _T ("\\"))
```

```
            strPath += _T ("\\");
        strPath += _T ("*.*");

        HANDLE hFind;
        WIN32_FIND_DATA fd;
        int nCount = 0;

        if ((hFind = ::FindFirstFile (strPath, &fd)) != INVALID_HANDLE_VALUE) {
            //
            // Delete existing items (if any).
            //
            GetListCtrl ().DeleteAllItems ();

            //
            // Show the path name in the frame window's title bar.
            //
            TCHAR szFullPath[MAX_PATH];
            ::GetFullPathName (pszPath, sizeof (szFullPath) / sizeof (TCHAR),
                szFullPath, NULL);
            m_strPath = szFullPath;

            CString strTitle = _T ("WinDir - ");
            strTitle += szFullPath;
            AfxGetMainWnd ()->SetWindowText (strTitle);

            //
            // Add items representing files to the list view.
            //
            if (!(fd.dwFileAttributes & FILE_ATTRIBUTE_DIRECTORY))
                AddItem (nCount++, &fd);

            while (::FindNextFile (hFind, &fd)) {
                if (!(fd.dwFileAttributes & FILE_ATTRIBUTE_DIRECTORY))
                    if (!AddItem (nCount++, &fd))
                        break;
            }
            ::FindClose (hFind);
        }
        return nCount;
    }

BOOL CFileView::AddItem(int nIndex, WIN32_FIND_DATA *pfd)
{
    //
    // Allocate a new ITEMINFO structure and initialize it with information
    // about the item.
```

(continued)

Figure 10-9. *continued*

```
    //
    ITEMINFO* pItem;
    try {
        pItem = new ITEMINFO;
    }
    catch (CMemoryException* e) {
        e->Delete ();
        return FALSE;
    }

    pItem->strFileName = pfd->cFileName;
    pItem->nFileSizeLow = pfd->nFileSizeLow;
    pItem->ftLastWriteTime = pfd->ftLastWriteTime;

    //
    // Add the item to the list view.
    //
    LV_ITEM lvi;
    lvi.mask = LVIF_TEXT | LVIF_IMAGE | LVIF_PARAM;
    lvi.iItem = nIndex;
    lvi.iSubItem = 0;
    lvi.iImage = 0;
    lvi.pszText = LPSTR_TEXTCALLBACK;
    lvi.lParam = (LPARAM) pItem;

    if (GetListCtrl ().InsertItem (&lvi) == -1)
        return FALSE;

    return TRUE;
}

void CFileView::FreeItemMemory()
{
    int nCount = GetListCtrl ().GetItemCount ();
    if (nCount) {
        for (int i=0; i<nCount; i++)
            delete (ITEMINFO*) GetListCtrl ().GetItemData (i);
    }
}

void CFileView::OnDestroy()
{
    FreeItemMemory ();
    CListView::OnDestroy ();
}

void CFileView::OnGetDispInfo(NMHDR* pNMHDR, LRESULT* pResult)
```

```
{
    CString string;
    LV_DISPINFO* pDispInfo = (LV_DISPINFO*) pNMHDR;

    if (pDispInfo->item.mask & LVIF_TEXT) {
        ITEMINFO* pItem = (ITEMINFO*) pDispInfo->item.lParam;

        switch (pDispInfo->item.iSubItem) {

        case 0: // File name.
            ::lstrcpy (pDispInfo->item.pszText, pItem->strFileName);
            break;

        case 1: // File size.
            string.Format (_T ("%u"), pItem->nFileSizeLow);
            ::lstrcpy (pDispInfo->item.pszText, string);
            break;

        case 2: // Date and time.
            CTime time (pItem->ftLastWriteTime);

            BOOL pm = FALSE;
            int nHour = time.GetHour ();
            if (nHour == 0)
                nHour = 12;
            else if (nHour == 12)
                pm = TRUE;
            else if (nHour > 12) {
                nHour -= 12;
                pm = TRUE;
            }

            string.Format (_T ("%d/%0.2d/%0.2d (%d:%0.2d%c)"),
                time.GetMonth (), time.GetDay (), time.GetYear () % 100,
                nHour, time.GetMinute (), pm ? _T ('p') : _T ('a'));
            ::lstrcpy (pDispInfo->item.pszText, string);
            break;
        }
    }
    *pResult = 0;
}

void CFileView::OnColumnClick(NMHDR* pNMHDR, LRESULT* pResult)
{
    NM_LISTVIEW* pNMListView = (NM_LISTVIEW*) pNMHDR;
    GetListCtrl ().SortItems (CompareFunc, pNMListView->iSubItem);
    *pResult = 0;
}
```

(continued)

Figure 10-9. *continued*

```
int CALLBACK CFileView::CompareFunc (LPARAM lParam1, LPARAM lParam2,
    LPARAM lParamSort)
{
    ITEMINFO* pItem1 = (ITEMINFO*) lParam1;
    ITEMINFO* pItem2 = (ITEMINFO*) lParam2;
    int nResult;

    switch (lParamSort) {

    case 0: // File name.
        nResult = pItem1->strFileName.CompareNoCase (pItem2->strFileName);
        break;

    case 1: // File size.
        nResult = pItem1->nFileSizeLow - pItem2->nFileSizeLow;
        break;

    case 2: // Date and time.
        nResult = ::CompareFileTime (&pItem1->ftLastWriteTime,
            &pItem2->ftLastWriteTime);
        break;
    }
    return nResult;
}

void CFileView::OnViewLargeIcons()
{
    ModifyStyle (LVS_TYPEMASK, LVS_ICON);
}

void CFileView::OnViewSmallIcons()
{
    ModifyStyle (LVS_TYPEMASK, LVS_SMALLICON);
}

void CFileView::OnViewList()
{
    ModifyStyle (LVS_TYPEMASK, LVS_LIST);
}

void CFileView::OnViewDetails()
{
    ModifyStyle (LVS_TYPEMASK, LVS_REPORT);
}
```

```
void CFileView::OnUpdateViewLargeIcons(CCmdUI* pCmdUI)
{
    DWORD dwCurrentStyle = GetStyle () & LVS_TYPEMASK;
    pCmdUI->SetRadio (dwCurrentStyle == LVS_ICON);
}


void CFileView::OnUpdateViewSmallIcons(CCmdUI* pCmdUI)
{
    DWORD dwCurrentStyle = GetStyle () & LVS_TYPEMASK;
    pCmdUI->SetRadio (dwCurrentStyle == LVS_SMALLICON);
}


void CFileView::OnUpdateViewList(CCmdUI* pCmdUI)
{
    DWORD dwCurrentStyle = GetStyle () & LVS_TYPEMASK;
    pCmdUI->SetRadio (dwCurrentStyle == LVS_LIST);
}


void CFileView::OnUpdateViewDetails(CCmdUI* pCmdUI)
{
    DWORD dwCurrentStyle = GetStyle () & LVS_TYPEMASK;
    pCmdUI->SetRadio (dwCurrentStyle == LVS_REPORT);
}


void CFileView::OnFileNewDirectory()
{
    CPathDialog dlg;
    dlg.m_strPath = m_strPath;
    if (dlg.DoModal () == IDOK)
        Refresh (dlg.m_strPath);
}
```

CFileView uses callbacks for item and subitem text so that it can maintain its own item data without forcing the control to maintain copies of the data, too. Callbacks come in the form of LVN_GETDISPINFO notifications, which *CFileView* reflects to its own *OnGetDispInfo* handler with an ON_NOTIFY_REFLECT message-map entry. When *OnGetDispInfo* is called, *pNMHDR* points to an LV_DISPINFO structure. The structure's *item.lParam* field contains the address of the ITEMINFO structure for the item in question, and the *item.iSubItem* field contains the index of the requested subitem. *CFileView::OnGetDispInfo* formulates a text string from the data stored in the ITEMINFO structure's *strFileName*, *nFileSizeLow*, or *ftLastWriteTime* field and copies the result to the address contained in the LV_DISPINFO structure's *item.pszText* field. The list view then displays the text on the screen.

CFileView maintains its own item data so that *CListCtrl::SortItems* can be called and *CFileView::CompareFunc* can retrieve any or all of an item's data by dereferencing the pointer stored in the item's *lParam*. If the user clicks a column header while the list view is in report mode, an ON_NOTIFY_REFLECT entry in the message map activates *CFileView::OnColumnClick*, and *OnColumnClick*, in turn, calls the list view's *SortItems* function, passing in the index of the column that was clicked:

```
GetListCtrl ().SortItems (CompareFunc, pNMListView->iSubItem);
```

CompareFunc is the application-defined sorting routine called to compare pairs of items. It's declared static because it's a callback function. *CompareFunc* uses the ITEMINFO pointers passed in *lParam1* and *lParam2* to retrieve the data for the items it's asked to compare and uses the column index in *lParamSort* to determine which of the items' subitems to use as the basis for the comparison. The entire function requires fewer than 20 lines of code:

```
int CALLBACK CFileView::CompareFunc (LPARAM lParam1, LPARAM lParam2,
    LPARAM lParamSort)
{
    ITEMINFO* pItem1 = (ITEMINFO*) lParam1;
    ITEMINFO* pItem2 = (ITEMINFO*) lParam2;
    int nResult;

    switch (lParamSort) {

    case 0: // File name.
        nResult =
            pItem1->strFileName.CompareNoCase (pItem2->strFileName);
        break;

    case 1: // File size.
        nResult = pItem1->nFileSizeLow - pItem2->nFileSizeLow;
        break;

    case 2: // Date and time.
        nResult = ::CompareFileTime (&pItem1->ftLastWriteTime,
            &pItem2->ftLastWriteTime);
        break;
    }
    return nResult;
}
```

A negative return value from *CompareFunc* indicates that item 1 is less than (should come before) item 2, 0 means that they're equal, and a positive return value means that item 1 is greater than item 2. The *::CompareFileTime* API function makes it easy to compare dates and times encapsulated in FILETIME values. You can also create *CTime* objects from FILETIME values and use <, >, and other operators to compare dates and times.

It might not be obvious to you yet, but you just saw why a list view with sortable columns must store its own data. The only information *CompareFunc* receives about the items it's asked to compare is the items' *lParam* values. Therefore, *lParam* has to provide full access to all of an item's data. One way to make sure that it does is to store item data in memory allocated by the application (in WinDir's case, in ITEMINFO structures allocated with *new*) and to store a pointer to the data in each item's own *lParam*. Storing item data yourself rather than converting it to text and handing it over to the list view provides greater flexibility in sorting because the data can be stored in binary form. How else could you sort the information that appears in *CFileView*'s Last Modified column? A string sort wouldn't work very well because "1/1/96" comes before "9/30/85" even though the former represents a later calendar date. But since *CFileView* stores dates and times in their native FILETIME format, sorting is a piece of cake.

A final note concerning *CFileView* has to do with the method used to delete the ITEMINFO structures allocated by *AddItem*. *CFileView::FreeItemMemory* deallocates the memory set aside for each item by iterating through the items in the list view and calling *delete* on the pointers stored in the items' *lParams*. *FreeItemMemory* is called by the view's WM_DESTROY handler to free the ITEMINFO structures before the application shuts down.

DO-IT-YOURSELF CONTROL VIEWS

CTreeView and *CListView* are examples of *control views*—views whose functionality comes from a Windows control. Both are derived from *CCtrlView*, which is also the base class for *CEditView* and *CRichEditView*. *CCtrlView* provides the basic functionality common to all control views. By using it as a base class, you can create control views of your own that wrap other types of Windows controls.

To demonstrate, the following *CCtrlView*-derived class defines a tabbed view, which is simply a view wrapped around a Win32 tab control. When displayed, it looks like a normal view except that it has property sheet–like tabs at the top:

```
class CTabView : public CCtrlView
{
    DECLARE_DYNCREATE (CTabView)
public:
    CTabView () :
        CCtrlView (_T ("SysTabControl32"), AFX_WS_DEFAULT_VIEW) {}
```

(continued)

```
    CTabCtrl& GetTabCtrl () const { return *(CTabCtrl*) this; }
    virtual BOOL PreCreateWindow (CREATESTRUCT& cs);
    virtual void OnInitialUpdate ();
};

IMPLEMENT_DYNCREATE (CTabView, CCtrlView)

BOOL CTabView::PreCreateWindow (CREATESTRUCT& cs)
{
    ::InitCommonControls ();
    if (!CCtrlView::PreCreateWindow (cs))
        return FALSE;
    cs.style |= TCS_FIXEDWIDTH; // Fixed-width tabs.
    return TRUE;
}

void CTabView::OnInitialUpdate ()
{
    static CString strLabel[] = {
        _T ("Tab No. 1"),
        _T ("Tab No. 2"),
        _T ("Tab No. 3")
    };

    // Set the tab width to 96 pixels.
    GetTabCtrl ().SetItemSize (CSize (96, 0));

    // Add three tabs.
    TC_ITEM item;
    item.mask = TCIF_TEXT;
    for (int i=0; i<3; i++) {
        item.pszText = (LPTSTR) (LPCTSTR) strLabel[i];
        item.cchTextMax = strLabel[i].GetLength ();
        GetTabCtrl ().InsertItem (i, &item);
    }
}
```

The key features of this class are the default constructor, which passes the base class's constructor the name of the tab control's WNDCLASS ("SysTabControl32"); the *GetTabCtrl* function, which returns a reference to the underlying tab control; and *OnInitialUpdate*, which adds three tabs to the control. *PreCreateWindow* also plays an important role by initializing the common controls library and applying default styles to the control.

Chapter 11

Multiple Documents and Multiple Views

Document/view applications aren't limited to just one document and one view of a document's data. Using splitter windows provided by MFC, a single document interface (SDI) application can present two or more views of the same document in resizeable "panes" that subdivide the frame window's client area. The document/view architecture also extends to multiple document interface (MDI) applications that support multiple views of a document, multiple open documents, and even multiple document types. Although Microsoft discourages the use of the multiple document interface, applications that rely on the MDI model are still prevalent and probably will be for some time to come, as evidenced by the continued success of Microsoft Word and other leading Microsoft Windows applications.

In Chapter 9, you saw what it takes to write an SDI document/view application. You'll find it a simple matter to extend that paradigm to encompass multiple documents and multiple views. In this chapter, we'll first examine MFC's support for MDI applications and see how easy it is to build an MDI application. Then we'll look at how splitter windows are used to provide multiple views of documents open in SDI applications.

MFC AND THE MULTIPLE DOCUMENT INTERFACE

From a user's point of view, five fundamental characteristics distinguish MDI applications from SDI applications:

- MDI applications permit the user to have two or more documents open for editing at once. SDI applications, by contrast, require the user to close the currently open document before opening another.

- MDI applications sometimes support multiple document types. For example, an all-in-one word processing, spreadsheet, and charting program might be implemented as an MDI application that supports three document types: word processing documents containing text, spreadsheet documents containing spreadsheets, and chart documents containing charts.

- MDI applications feature a Window menu with a New Window command for opening secondary views of a document and commands for arranging the windows in which the views appear. The Window menu also contains a list of open views. Selecting a view from this menu makes that view the active view and the document associated with that view the active document.

- SDI applications generally feature just one menu. MDI applications have at least two: one that's displayed when no documents are open and another that's displayed when at least one document is open. Some MDI applications have more than two menus. An MDI application that supports multiple document types generally implements one menu per document type.

- SDI applications use just one frame window—the top-level frame window that serves as the application's main window and frames views of open documents. MDI applications use two: a top-level frame window and *child frames* or *document frames* that float within the top-level frame window and frame views of open documents.

Without help from a framework such as MFC, MDI applications require more effort to create than SDI applications. For example, it's the developer's responsibility to update the menu that appears in the top-level frame window as documents are opened, closed, and switched between. It's the developer's responsibility to implement the Window menu. And it's the developer's responsibility to create and manage the document frames that float within the top-level frame window. Under the hood, these and other features of the MDI user interface model translate into dozens of annoying little implementation details that you (or someone) must account for.

That's the bad news. The good news is that MFC's document/view architecture abstracts the user interface model so that writing MDI applications is only slightly different than writing SDI applications. Like their SDI counterparts, MDI document/view applications store data in document objects based on *CDocument* and present views of that data in view objects based on *CView* or one of its derivatives. The chief structural differences between MDI and SDI applications built with MFC are as follows:

■ MDI applications derive their top-level frame window classes from *CMDIFrameWnd* rather than *CFrameWnd*.

■ MDI applications use classes based on *CMDIChildWnd* to represent the child frame windows that frame views of their documents.

■ MDI applications use *CMultiDocTemplate* rather than *CSingleDocTemplate* to create document templates. The frame window class referenced in *CMultiDocTemplate*'s constructor is the child frame window class rather than the top-level frame window class.

■ MDI applications have at least two menu resources, as opposed to SDI's one. One is displayed when no documents are open; the other is displayed when at least one document is open.

These are the differences that you see. On the inside, MFC devotes hundreds of lines of code to MDI-specific chores such as dynamically switching menus and creating new views of open documents. In short, the framework manages almost every aspect of an MDI application's user interface to spare you the chore of having to do it yourself. And to a large extent, details that aren't automatically handled for you by MFC are handled by AppWizard. If you choose Multiple Documents instead of Single Documents in AppWizard's Step 1 dialog box (shown in Figure 11-1), AppWizard emits an MDI application skeleton. From that point on, writing an MDI application is just like writing an SDI application. You just write a document/view application; MFC handles all the rest.

Well, MFC handles *almost* all the rest. You mustn't forget one important implementation detail. That "detail" is the subject of the next section.

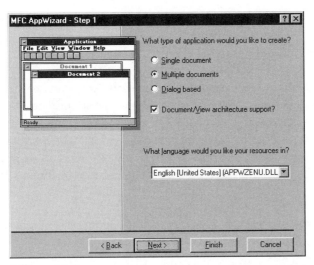

Figure 11-1. *Using AppWizard to create an MDI application.*

Synchronizing Multiple Views of a Document

When you elect to use the MDI user interface model, you implicitly afford your users the freedom to display multiple concurrent views of a document. A user editing a 100-page document might use this feature of your application to display pages 1 and 100 side by side for comparison.

When the New Window command is selected from the Window menu, an MFC-provided command handler pulls up the document template, extracts *CRuntimeClass* pointers identifying the view class and the frame window class, and instantiates a new view and a new frame window (a child frame, not a top-level frame) to go with it. Under the hood, the secondary view's address is added to the linked list of views maintained by the document object so that the document is aware that two independent views of it are visible on the screen. If either view is asked to repaint, it calls *GetDocument* to acquire a pointer to the document object, queries the document for the data it needs, and repaints. Because both views are connected to the same document object (that is, *GetDocument* returns the same pointer in either view), each enjoys access to the same set of document data. Moreover, the architecture is scalable: it works just as well for hundreds of open views as it does for two.

So far, so good. Now consider what happens if the user edits the document in one of the views. If the change is visible (or has consequences that are visible) in the other views, the other views should be updated to reflect the change. The catch is that the update doesn't happen automatically; it's up to you to make sure that when the document is edited in one view, other views—if they exist—are updated, too. The framework provides the mechanism to make this happen in the form of *CDocument-::UpdateAllViews* and *CView::OnUpdate*, which were briefly discussed in Chapter 9. It's now time to examine these functions more closely.

Suppose you write a program editor that uses the MDI architecture to allow the user to display multiple views of a source code file. If a change made to a file in one view is visible in the others, all views of that file should be updated to reflect the change. That's what *UpdateAllViews* is for. When a document's data is modified in a multiple-view application, someone—either the object that made the modification (usually a view object) or the document object—should call *UpdateAllViews* to update the views. *UpdateAllViews* iterates through the list of views associated with the document, calling each view's virtual *OnUpdate* function.

CView provides a trivial implementation of *OnUpdate* that invalidates the view and forces a call to *OnDraw*. If a full repaint is what you want, there's no need to override *OnUpdate*. If, however, you want to make updates as efficient as possible by repainting only the part of the view that changed, you can override *OnUpdate* in the view class and make use of hint information passed to *UpdateAllViews*. *Update-AllViews* is prototyped as follows:

```
void UpdateAllViews (CView* pSender, LPARAM lHint = 0L,
    CObject* pHint = NULL)
```

The function prototype for *OnUpdate* looks very similar:

```
virtual void OnUpdate (CView* pSender, LPARAM lHint,
    CObject* pHint)
```

lHint and *pHint* carry hint information from *UpdateAllViews* to *OnUpdate*. How you use these parameters is highly application-specific. A simple use for hint information is to pass the address of a RECT structure or a *CRect* object specifying what part of the view needs updating. *OnUpdate* can use that information in a call to *InvalidateRect*, as demonstrated here:

```
// In the document class
UpdateAllViews (NULL, 1, (CObject*) pRect);
    ⋮
    ⋮
// In the view class
void CMyView::OnUpdate (CView* pSender, LPARAM lHint, CObject* pHint)
{
```

(continued)

```
    if (lHint == 1) {
        CRect* pRect = (CRect*) pHint;
        InvalidateRect (pRect);
        return;
    }
    CView::OnUpdate (pSender, lHint, pHint);
}
```

If the document's data consists of an array of *CObjects* and *UpdateAllViews* is called because a new *CObject* was added to the document, *pHint* might be used to pass the new *CObject*'s address. The following example assumes that *pLine* holds a pointer to an instance of a *CObject*-derived class named *CLine* and that *CLine* includes a public member function named *Draw* that can be called to render the *CLine* on the screen:

```
// In the document class
UpdateAllViews (NULL, 1, pLine);

    .
    .
    .

// In the view class
void CMyView::OnUpdate (CView* pSender, LPARAM lHint, CObject* pHint)
{
    if (lHint == 1) {
        CLine* pLine = (CLine*) pHint;
        CClientDC dc (this);
        pLine->Draw (&dc);
        return;
    }
    CView::OnUpdate (pSender, lHint, pHint);
}
```

In both examples, *OnUpdate* forwards the call to the base class if *lHint* is anything other than the application-specific value passed to *UpdateAllViews*. That's important, because MFC sometimes calls *OnUpdate* itself with *lHint* equal to 0. You can use any nonzero value that you like for *lHint*. You can even define multiple "hint sets" that assign different meanings to *pHint* and use *lHint* to identify the hint type.

You can use *UpdateAllViews*' first parameter, *pSender*, to omit a view from the update cycle. If *pSender* is NULL, *UpdateAllViews* calls each view's *OnUpdate* function. If *pSender* is non-NULL, *UpdateAllViews* calls *OnUpdate* on every view *except* the one identified by *pSender*. When a function in the document class calls *UpdateAllViews*, it typically sets *pSender* to NULL so that all the views will be updated. If a view calls *UpdateAllViews*, however, it can set *pSender* to *this* to prevent its own *OnUpdate* function from being called. If the view has already updated itself in response to user input, its *OnUpdate* function doesn't need to be called. If, however, the view hasn't already updated itself because it performs all of its updating in *OnUpdate*, it should pass *UpdateAllViews* a NULL first parameter.

The sample program in the next section makes trivial use of *UpdateAllViews* by calling it without hint parameters. Secondary views are updated by the default implementation of *OnUpdate*. Later in this chapter, we'll develop a more ambitious multiple-view application that passes hint information to *UpdateAllViews* and makes use of that information in *OnUpdate*.

The MdiSquares Application

The MdiSquares application shown in Figure 11-2 is an MDI version of Chapter 9's SdiSquares. The document and view classes that it uses are identical to those used in SdiSquares, save for the fact that MdiSquares' view class draws the squares slightly smaller to conserve screen space.

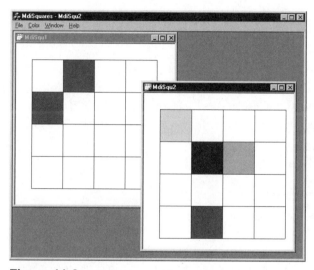

Figure 11-2. *MdiSquares with two documents open.*

When you run MdiSquares, the first document is opened automatically. You can open additional documents by selecting New from the File menu. To open another view of a document, select New Window from the Window menu. Observe that if you have two views of a document displayed and you click a square in one view, the square's color changes in both views. That's because the document's *SetSquare* function, which the view calls to add a color to a square, calls *UpdateAllViews* after recording the square's color in *m_clrGrid*. Here's the relevant statement in SquaresDoc.cpp:

```
UpdateAllViews (NULL);
```

Because no hint information is passed in the call, and because *CSquaresView* doesn't override *OnUpdate*, each view is repainted in its entirety when *SetSquare* is called. If you look closely, you can see the views flash each time you click a square. The flashing is a consequence of the fact that the entire view is being erased and repainted each time *UpdateAllViews* is called.

SquaresDoc.cpp and other MdiSquares source code files are shown in Figure 11-3. The main frame window class, *CMainFrame*, represents the application's top-level window. Views are displayed in instances of the child frame window class, *CChildFrame*. Notice that in *InitInstance*, *CChildFrame*, not *CMainFrame*, is identified as the frame window class when the document template is initialized:

```
CMultiDocTemplate* pDocTemplate;
pDocTemplate = new CMultiDocTemplate(
    IDR_MDISQUTYPE,
    RUNTIME_CLASS(CSquaresDoc),
    RUNTIME_CLASS(CChildFrame), // custom MDI child frame
    RUNTIME_CLASS(CSquaresView));
```

Consequently, calling *ProcessShellCommand* in an MDI application creates a new child frame but not a top-level frame window. As a result, an MDI application must create the top-level frame window itself before calling *ProcessShellCommand*. The code that creates MdiSquares' main window is found elsewhere in *InitInstance*:

```
CMainFrame* pMainFrame = new CMainFrame;
if (!pMainFrame->LoadFrame(IDR_MAINFRAME))
    return FALSE;
m_pMainWnd = pMainFrame;
```

This code and all the other code in *CMdiSquaresApp*, *CMainFrame*, and *CChildFrame* was generated by AppWizard. Unless you code an MDI application by hand, you'll perform the bulk of your work in the document and view classes.

If you open MdiSquares in Visual C++ and browse its list of resources, you'll see that it has two icons, two menus, and two document strings. Their resource IDs are IDR_MAINFRAME and IDR_MDISQUTYPE. Here's how these resources are used:

- The IDR_MAINFRAME icon is displayed in the title bar of the top-level window. The IDR_MDISQUTYPE icon is displayed in the title bars of the child frames. You can use the same icon for both if you like, but most MDI applications use a different icon for document windows.

- The IDR_MAINFRAME menu is displayed when no documents are open. The IDR_MDISQUTYPE menu is displayed when at least one document is open. The IDR_MAINFRAME menu is a minimal menu that features a File menu with New, Open, and Exit commands and a recently used file list, but little else. IDR_ MDISQUTYPE, on the other hand, is a full-blown menu with all the commands that pertain to MdiSquares documents.

■ The IDR_MAINFRAME document string contains nothing more than the title that appears in the main window's title bar. The IDR_ MDISQUTYPE document string contains all relevant information about the document type, including the default file name extension.

Except for the relatively minor differences discussed in this section, MdiSquares and SdiSquares are virtually identical. That's one of the benefits of using MFC's document/view architecture: once you know how to write SDI applications, you know how to write MDI applications, too.

MdiSquares.h

```
// MdiSquares.h : main header file for the MDISQUARES application
//

#if
!defined(AFX_MDISQUARES_H__36D513DB_9CA0_11D2_8E53_006008A82731__INCLUDED_)
#define  AFX_MDISQUARES_H__36D513DB_9CA0_11D2_8E53_006008A82731__INCLUDED_

#if _MSC_VER > 1000
#pragma once
#endif // _MSC_VER > 1000

#ifndef __AFXWIN_H__
    #error include 'stdafx.h' before including this file for PCH
#endif

#include "resource.h"        // main symbols


/////////////////////////////////////////////////////////////////////////////
// CMdiSquaresApp:
// See MdiSquares.cpp for the implementation of this class
//

class CMdiSquaresApp : public CWinApp
{
public:
    CMdiSquaresApp();

// Overrides
    // ClassWizard generated virtual function overrides
    //{{AFX_VIRTUAL(CMdiSquaresApp)
    public:
    virtual BOOL InitInstance();
    //}}AFX_VIRTUAL
```

Figure 11-3. *The MdiSquares application.* *(continued)*

Figure 11-3. *continued*

```
// Implementation
    //{{AFX_MSG(CMdiSquaresApp)
    afx_msg void OnAppAbout();
        // NOTE - the ClassWizard will add and remove member functions here.
        //     DO NOT EDIT what you see in these blocks of generated code !
    //}}AFX_MSG
    DECLARE_MESSAGE_MAP()
};


/////////////////////////////////////////////////////////////////////////////

//{{AFX_INSERT_LOCATION}}
// Microsoft Visual C++ will insert additional declarations immediately
// before the previous line.

#endif
// !defined(
//     AFX_MDISQUARES_H__36D513DB_9CA0_11D2_8E53_006008A82731__INCLUDED_)
```

MdiSquares.cpp

```
// MdiSquares.cpp : Defines the class behaviors for the application.
//

#include "stdafx.h"
#include "MdiSquares.h"

#include "MainFrm.h"
#include "ChildFrm.h"
#include "SquaresDoc.h"
#include "SquaresView.h"

#ifdef _DEBUG
#define new DEBUG_NEW
#undef THIS_FILE
static char THIS_FILE[] = __FILE__;
#endif


/////////////////////////////////////////////////////////////////////////////
// CMdiSquaresApp

BEGIN_MESSAGE_MAP(CMdiSquaresApp, CWinApp)
    //{{AFX_MSG_MAP(CMdiSquaresApp)
```

```
    ON_COMMAND(ID_APP_ABOUT, OnAppAbout)
        // NOTE - the ClassWizard will add and remove mapping macros here.
        //      DO NOT EDIT what you see in these blocks of generated code!
    //}}AFX_MSG_MAP
    // Standard file based document commands
    ON_COMMAND(ID_FILE_NEW, CWinApp::OnFileNew)
    ON_COMMAND(ID_FILE_OPEN, CWinApp::OnFileOpen)
END_MESSAGE_MAP()


/////////////////////////////////////////////////////////////////////////////
// CMdiSquaresApp construction

CMdiSquaresApp::CMdiSquaresApp()
{
}


/////////////////////////////////////////////////////////////////////////////
// The one and only CMdiSquaresApp object

CMdiSquaresApp theApp;

/////////////////////////////////////////////////////////////////////////////
// CMdiSquaresApp initialization

BOOL CMdiSquaresApp::InitInstance()
{
    SetRegistryKey(_T("Local AppWizard-Generated Applications"));

    LoadStdProfileSettings();  // Load standard INI file
                               // options (including MRU)

    CMultiDocTemplate* pDocTemplate;
    pDocTemplate = new CMultiDocTemplate(
        IDR_MDISQUTYPE,
        RUNTIME_CLASS(CSquaresDoc),
        RUNTIME_CLASS(CChildFrame), // custom MDI child frame
        RUNTIME_CLASS(CSquaresView));
    AddDocTemplate(pDocTemplate);

    // create main MDI Frame window
    CMainFrame* pMainFrame = new CMainFrame;
    if (!pMainFrame->LoadFrame(IDR_MAINFRAME))
        return FALSE;
    m_pMainWnd = pMainFrame;

    // Enable drag/drop open
    m_pMainWnd->DragAcceptFiles();
```

(continued)

Figure 11-3. *continued*

```
    // Enable DDE Execute open
    EnableShellOpen();
    RegisterShellFileTypes(TRUE);

    // Parse command line for standard shell commands, DDE, file open
    CCommandLineInfo cmdInfo;
    ParseCommandLine(cmdInfo);

    // Dispatch commands specified on the command line
    if (!ProcessShellCommand(cmdInfo))
        return FALSE;

    // The main window has been initialized, so show and update it.
    pMainFrame->ShowWindow(m_nCmdShow);
    pMainFrame->UpdateWindow();

    return TRUE;
}


/////////////////////////////////////////////////////////////////////////////
// CAboutDlg dialog used for App About

class CAboutDlg : public CDialog
{
public:
    CAboutDlg();

// Dialog Data
    //{{AFX_DATA(CAboutDlg)
    enum { IDD = IDD_ABOUTBOX };
    //}}AFX_DATA

    // ClassWizard generated virtual function overrides
    //{{AFX_VIRTUAL(CAboutDlg)
    protected:
    virtual void DoDataExchange(CDataExchange* pDX);    // DDX/DDV support
    //}}AFX_VIRTUAL

// Implementation
protected:
    //{{AFX_MSG(CAboutDlg)
        // No message handlers
    //}}AFX_MSG
    DECLARE_MESSAGE_MAP()
};
```

```
CAboutDlg::CAboutDlg() : CDialog(CAboutDlg::IDD)
{
    //{{AFX_DATA_INIT(CAboutDlg)
    //}}AFX_DATA_INIT
}

void CAboutDlg::DoDataExchange(CDataExchange* pDX)
{
    CDialog::DoDataExchange(pDX);
    //{{AFX_DATA_MAP(CAboutDlg)
    //}}AFX_DATA_MAP
}

BEGIN_MESSAGE_MAP(CAboutDlg, CDialog)
    //{{AFX_MSG_MAP(CAboutDlg)
        // No message handlers
    //}}AFX_MSG_MAP
END_MESSAGE_MAP()

// App command to run the dialog
void CMdiSquaresApp::OnAppAbout()
{
    CAboutDlg aboutDlg;
    aboutDlg.DoModal();
}

/////////////////////////////////////////////////////////////////////////
// CMdiSquaresApp message handlers
```

MainFrm.h

```
// MainFrm.h : interface of the CMainFrame class
//
/////////////////////////////////////////////////////////////////////////

#if
!defined(AFX_MAINFRM_H__36D513DF_9CA0_11D2_8E53_006008A82731__INCLUDED_)
#define AFX_MAINFRM_H__36D513DF_9CA0_11D2_8E53_006008A82731__INCLUDED_

#if _MSC_VER > 1000
#pragma once
#endif // _MSC_VER > 1000

class CMainFrame : public CMDIFrameWnd
```

(continued)

Figure 11-3. *continued*

```
{
    DECLARE_DYNAMIC(CMainFrame)
public:
    CMainFrame();

// Attributes
public:

// Operations
public:

// Overrides
    // ClassWizard generated virtual function overrides
    //{{AFX_VIRTUAL(CMainFrame)
    virtual BOOL PreCreateWindow(CREATESTRUCT& cs);
    //}}AFX_VIRTUAL

// Implementation
public:
    virtual ~CMainFrame();
#ifdef _DEBUG
    virtual void AssertValid() const;
    virtual void Dump(CDumpContext& dc) const;
#endif

// Generated message map functions
protected:
    //{{AFX_MSG(CMainFrame)
        // NOTE - the ClassWizard will add and remove member functions
here.
        //      DO NOT EDIT what you see in these blocks of generated code!
    //}}AFX_MSG
    DECLARE_MESSAGE_MAP()
};

/////////////////////////////////////////////////////////////////////////

//{{AFX_INSERT_LOCATION}}
// Microsoft Visual C++ will insert additional declarations immediately
// before the previous line.

#endif
// !defined(
// AFX_MAINFRM_H__36D513DF_9CA0_11D2_8E53_006008A82731__INCLUDED_)
```

MainFrm.cpp

```cpp
// MainFrm.cpp : implementation of the CMainFrame class
//

#include "stdafx.h"
#include "MdiSquares.h"

#include "MainFrm.h"

#ifdef _DEBUG
#define new DEBUG_NEW
#undef THIS_FILE
static char THIS_FILE[] = __FILE__;
#endif

/////////////////////////////////////////////////////////////////////////////
// CMainFrame

IMPLEMENT_DYNAMIC(CMainFrame, CMDIFrameWnd)

BEGIN_MESSAGE_MAP(CMainFrame, CMDIFrameWnd)
    //{{AFX_MSG_MAP(CMainFrame)
        // NOTE - the ClassWizard will add and remove mapping macros here.
        //    DO NOT EDIT what you see in these blocks of generated code !
    //}}AFX_MSG_MAP
END_MESSAGE_MAP()

/////////////////////////////////////////////////////////////////////////////
// CMainFrame construction/destruction

CMainFrame::CMainFrame()
{
}

CMainFrame::~CMainFrame()
{
}

BOOL CMainFrame::PreCreateWindow(CREATESTRUCT& cs)
{
    if( !CMDIFrameWnd::PreCreateWindow(cs) )
        return FALSE;
    return TRUE;
}
```

(continued)

Figure 11-3. *continued*

```
//////////////////////////////////////////////////////////////////
// CMainFrame diagnostics

#ifdef _DEBUG
void CMainFrame::AssertValid() const
{
    CMDIFrameWnd::AssertValid();
}

void CMainFrame::Dump(CDumpContext& dc) const
{
    CMDIFrameWnd::Dump(dc);
}

#endif //_DEBUG


//////////////////////////////////////////////////////////////////
// CMainFrame message handlers
```

ChildFrm.h

```
// ChildFrm.h : interface of the CChildFrame class
//
//////////////////////////////////////////////////////////////////

#if
!defined(AFX_CHILDFRM_H__36D513E1_9CA0_11D2_8E53_006008A82731__INCLUDED_)
#define  AFX_CHILDFRM_H__36D513E1_9CA0_11D2_8E53_006008A82731__INCLUDED_

#if _MSC_VER > 1000
#pragma once
#endif // _MSC_VER > 1000

class CChildFrame : public CMDIChildWnd
{
    DECLARE_DYNCREATE(CChildFrame)
public:
    CChildFrame();

// Attributes
public:

// Operations
public:
```

```
// Overrides
    // ClassWizard generated virtual function overrides
    //{{AFX_VIRTUAL(CChildFrame)
    virtual BOOL PreCreateWindow(CREATESTRUCT& cs);
    //}}AFX_VIRTUAL

// Implementation
public:
    virtual ~CChildFrame();
#ifdef _DEBUG
    virtual void AssertValid() const;
    virtual void Dump(CDumpContext& dc) const;
#endif

// Generated message map functions
protected:
    //{{AFX_MSG(CChildFrame)
        // NOTE - the ClassWizard will add and remove member functions here.
        //     DO NOT EDIT what you see in these blocks of generated code!
    //}}AFX_MSG
    DECLARE_MESSAGE_MAP()
};


/////////////////////////////////////////////////////////////////////////////

//{{AFX_INSERT_LOCATION}}
// Microsoft Visual C++ will insert additional declarations immediately
// before the previous line.

#endif
// !defined(
//   AFX_CHILDFRM_H__36D513E1_9CA0_11D2_8E53_006008A82731__INCLUDED_)
```

ChildFrm.cpp

```
// ChildFrm.cpp : implementation of the CChildFrame class
//

#include "stdafx.h"
#include "MdiSquares.h"

#include "ChildFrm.h"
```

(continued)

Figure 11-3. *continued*

```
#ifdef _DEBUG
#define new DEBUG_NEW
#undef THIS_FILE
static char THIS_FILE[] = __FILE__;
#endif

///////////////////////////////////////////////////////////////////////////
// CChildFrame

IMPLEMENT_DYNCREATE(CChildFrame, CMDIChildWnd)

BEGIN_MESSAGE_MAP(CChildFrame, CMDIChildWnd)
    //{{AFX_MSG_MAP(CChildFrame)
        // NOTE - the ClassWizard will add and remove mapping macros here.
        //    DO NOT EDIT what you see in these blocks of generated code !
    //}}AFX_MSG_MAP
END_MESSAGE_MAP()

///////////////////////////////////////////////////////////////////////////
//
// CChildFrame construction/destruction

CChildFrame::CChildFrame()
{
}

CChildFrame::~CChildFrame()
{
}

BOOL CChildFrame::PreCreateWindow(CREATESTRUCT& cs)
{
    if( !CMDIChildWnd::PreCreateWindow(cs) )
        return FALSE;
    return TRUE;
}

///////////////////////////////////////////////////////////////////////////
// CChildFrame diagnostics

#ifdef _DEBUG
void CChildFrame::AssertValid() const
{
    CMDIChildWnd::AssertValid();
}
```

```
void CChildFrame::Dump(CDumpContext& dc) const
{
    CMDIChildWnd::Dump(dc);
}

#endif //_DEBUG


/////////////////////////////////////////////////////////////////////////
// CChildFrame message handlers
```

SquaresDoc.h

```
// SquaresDoc.h : interface of the CSquaresDoc class
//
/////////////////////////////////////////////////////////////////////////
//

#if
!defined(AFX_SQUARESDOC_H__36D513E3_9CA0_11D2_8E53_006008A82731__INCLUDED_)
#define  AFX_SQUARESDOC_H__36D513E3_9CA0_11D2_8E53_006008A82731__INCLUDED_

#if _MSC_VER > 1000
#pragma once
#endif // _MSC_VER > 1000


class CSquaresDoc : public CDocument
{
protected: // create from serialization only
    CSquaresDoc();
    DECLARE_DYNCREATE(CSquaresDoc)

// Attributes
public:

// Operations
public:

// Overrides
    // ClassWizard generated virtual function overrides
    //{{AFX_VIRTUAL(CSquaresDoc)
    public:
    virtual BOOL OnNewDocument();
    virtual void Serialize(CArchive& ar);
    //}}AFX_VIRTUAL
```

(continued)

Figure 11-3. *continued*

```
// Implementation
public:
    void SetSquare (int i, int j, COLORREF color);
    COLORREF GetSquare (int i, int j);
    COLORREF GetCurrentColor();
    virtual ~CSquaresDoc();
#ifdef _DEBUG
    virtual void AssertValid() const;
    virtual void Dump(CDumpContext& dc) const;
#endif

protected:

// Generated message map functions
protected:
    COLORREF m_clrCurrentColor;
    COLORREF m_clrGrid[4][4];
    //{{AFX_MSG(CSquaresDoc)
    afx_msg void OnColorRed();
    afx_msg void OnColorYellow();
    afx_msg void OnColorGreen();
    afx_msg void OnColorCyan();
    afx_msg void OnColorBlue();
    afx_msg void OnColorWhite();
    afx_msg void OnUpdateColorRed(CCmdUI* pCmdUI);
    afx_msg void OnUpdateColorYellow(CCmdUI* pCmdUI);
    afx_msg void OnUpdateColorGreen(CCmdUI* pCmdUI);
    afx_msg void OnUpdateColorCyan(CCmdUI* pCmdUI);
    afx_msg void OnUpdateColorBlue(CCmdUI* pCmdUI);
    afx_msg void OnUpdateColorWhite(CCmdUI* pCmdUI);
    //}}AFX_MSG
    DECLARE_MESSAGE_MAP()
};

///////////////////////////////////////////////////////////////////////////

//{{AFX_INSERT_LOCATION}}
// Microsoft Visual C++ will insert additional declarations immediately
// before the previous line.

#endif
// !defined(
//      AFX_SQUARESDOC_H__36D513E3_9CA0_11D2_8E53_006008A82731__INCLUDED_)
```

SquaresDoc.cpp

```cpp
// SquaresDoc.cpp : implementation of the CSquaresDoc class
//

#include "stdafx.h"
#include "MdiSquares.h"

#include "SquaresDoc.h"

#ifdef _DEBUG
#define new DEBUG_NEW
#undef THIS_FILE
static char THIS_FILE[] = __FILE__;
#endif

/////////////////////////////////////////////////////////////////////////////
// CSquaresDoc

IMPLEMENT_DYNCREATE(CSquaresDoc, CDocument)

BEGIN_MESSAGE_MAP(CSquaresDoc, CDocument)
    //{{AFX_MSG_MAP(CSquaresDoc)
    ON_COMMAND(ID_COLOR_RED, OnColorRed)
    ON_COMMAND(ID_COLOR_YELLOW, OnColorYellow)
    ON_COMMAND(ID_COLOR_GREEN, OnColorGreen)
    ON_COMMAND(ID_COLOR_CYAN, OnColorCyan)
    ON_COMMAND(ID_COLOR_BLUE, OnColorBlue)
    ON_COMMAND(ID_COLOR_WHITE, OnColorWhite)
    ON_UPDATE_COMMAND_UI(ID_COLOR_RED, OnUpdateColorRed)
    ON_UPDATE_COMMAND_UI(ID_COLOR_YELLOW, OnUpdateColorYellow)
    ON_UPDATE_COMMAND_UI(ID_COLOR_GREEN, OnUpdateColorGreen)
    ON_UPDATE_COMMAND_UI(ID_COLOR_CYAN, OnUpdateColorCyan)
    ON_UPDATE_COMMAND_UI(ID_COLOR_BLUE, OnUpdateColorBlue)
    ON_UPDATE_COMMAND_UI(ID_COLOR_WHITE, OnUpdateColorWhite)
    //}}AFX_MSG_MAP
END_MESSAGE_MAP()

/////////////////////////////////////////////////////////////////////////////
// CSquaresDoc construction/destruction

CSquaresDoc::CSquaresDoc()
{
}
```

(continued)

Figure 11-3. *continued*

```
CSquaresDoc::~CSquaresDoc()
{
}

BOOL CSquaresDoc::OnNewDocument()
{
    if (!CDocument::OnNewDocument())
        return FALSE;

    for (int i=0; i<4; i++)
        for (int j=0; j<4; j++)
            m_clrGrid[i][j] = RGB (255, 255, 255);

    m_clrCurrentColor = RGB (255, 0, 0);
    return TRUE;
}

/////////////////////////////////////////////////////////////////////////////
// CSquaresDoc serialization

void CSquaresDoc::Serialize(CArchive& ar)
{
    if (ar.IsStoring())
    {
        for (int i=0; i<4; i++)
            for (int j=0; j<4; j++)
                ar << m_clrGrid[i][j];
        ar << m_clrCurrentColor;
    }
    else
    {
        for (int i=0; i<4; i++)
            for (int j=0; j<4; j++)
                ar >> m_clrGrid[i][j];
        ar >> m_clrCurrentColor;
    }
}

/////////////////////////////////////////////////////////////////////////////
// CSquaresDoc diagnostics

#ifdef _DEBUG
void CSquaresDoc::AssertValid() const
```

```
{
    CDocument::AssertValid();
}

void CSquaresDoc::Dump(CDumpContext& dc) const
{
    CDocument::Dump(dc);
}
#endif //_DEBUG

/////////////////////////////////////////////////////////////////////////////
// CSquaresDoc commands

COLORREF CSquaresDoc::GetCurrentColor()
{
    return m_clrCurrentColor;
}

COLORREF CSquaresDoc::GetSquare(int i, int j)
{
    ASSERT (i >= 0 && i <= 3 && j >= 0 && j <= 3);
    return m_clrGrid[i][j];
}

void CSquaresDoc::SetSquare(int i, int j, COLORREF color)
{
    ASSERT (i >= 0 && i <= 3 && j >= 0 && j <= 3);
    m_clrGrid[i][j] = color;
    SetModifiedFlag (TRUE);
    UpdateAllViews (NULL);
}

void CSquaresDoc::OnColorRed()
{
    m_clrCurrentColor = RGB (255, 0, 0);
}

void CSquaresDoc::OnColorYellow()
{
    m_clrCurrentColor = RGB (255, 255, 0);
}
```

(continued)

Figure 11-3. *continued*

```
void CSquaresDoc::OnColorGreen()
{
    m_clrCurrentColor = RGB (0, 255, 0);
}

void CSquaresDoc::OnColorCyan()
{
    m_clrCurrentColor = RGB (0, 255, 255);
}

void CSquaresDoc::OnColorBlue()
{
    m_clrCurrentColor = RGB (0, 0, 255);
}

void CSquaresDoc::OnColorWhite()
{
    m_clrCurrentColor = RGB (255, 255, 255);
}

void CSquaresDoc::OnUpdateColorRed(CCmdUI* pCmdUI)
{
    pCmdUI->SetRadio (m_clrCurrentColor == RGB (255, 0, 0));
}

void CSquaresDoc::OnUpdateColorYellow(CCmdUI* pCmdUI)
{
    pCmdUI->SetRadio (m_clrCurrentColor == RGB (255, 255, 0));
}

void CSquaresDoc::OnUpdateColorGreen(CCmdUI* pCmdUI)
{
    pCmdUI->SetRadio (m_clrCurrentColor == RGB (0, 255, 0));
}

void CSquaresDoc::OnUpdateColorCyan(CCmdUI* pCmdUI)
{
    pCmdUI->SetRadio (m_clrCurrentColor == RGB (0, 255, 255));
}

void CSquaresDoc::OnUpdateColorBlue(CCmdUI* pCmdUI)
{
    pCmdUI->SetRadio (m_clrCurrentColor == RGB (0, 0, 255));
}
```

```
void CSquaresDoc::OnUpdateColorWhite(CCmdUI* pCmdUI)
{
    pCmdUI->SetRadio (m_clrCurrentColor == RGB (255, 255, 255));
}
```

SquaresView.h

```
// SquaresView.h : interface of the CSquaresView class
//
/////////////////////////////////////////////////////////////////////////////
/

#if
!defined(AFX_SQUARESVIEW_H__36D513E5_9CA0_11D2_8E53_006008A82731__INCLUDED_)
#define  AFX_SQUARESVIEW_H__36D513E5_9CA0_11D2_8E53_006008A82731__INCLUDED_

#if _MSC_VER > 1000
#pragma once
#endif // _MSC_VER > 1000


class CSquaresView : public CView
{
protected: // create from serialization only
    CSquaresView();
    DECLARE_DYNCREATE(CSquaresView)

// Attributes
public:
    CSquaresDoc* GetDocument();

// Operations
public:

// Overrides
    // ClassWizard generated virtual function overrides
    //{{AFX_VIRTUAL(CSquaresView)
    public:
    virtual void OnDraw(CDC* pDC);  // overridden to draw this view
    virtual BOOL PreCreateWindow(CREATESTRUCT& cs);
    protected:
    //}}AFX_VIRTUAL
```

(continued)

Figure 11-3. *continued*

```
// Implementation
public:
    virtual ~CSquaresView();
#ifdef _DEBUG
    virtual void AssertValid() const;
    virtual void Dump(CDumpContext& dc) const;
#endif

protected:

// Generated message map functions
protected:
    //{{AFX_MSG(CSquaresView)
    afx_msg void OnLButtonDown(UINT nFlags, CPoint point);
    //}}AFX_MSG
    DECLARE_MESSAGE_MAP()
};

#ifndef _DEBUG  // debug version in SquaresView.cpp
inline CSquaresDoc* CSquaresView::GetDocument()
    { return (CSquaresDoc*)m_pDocument; }
#endif

/////////////////////////////////////////////////////////////////////////////

//{{AFX_INSERT_LOCATION}}
// Microsoft Visual C++ will insert additional declarations immediately
// before the previous line.

#endif
// !defined(
//      AFX_SQUARESVIEW_H__36D513E5_9CA0_11D2_8E53_006008A82731__INCLUDED_)
```

SquaresView.cpp

```
// SquaresView.cpp : implementation of the CSquaresView class
//

#include "stdafx.h"
#include "MdiSquares.h"

#include "SquaresDoc.h"
#include "SquaresView.h"
```

```
#ifdef _DEBUG
#define new DEBUG_NEW
#undef THIS_FILE
static char THIS_FILE[] = __FILE__;
#endif


/////////////////////////////////////////////////////////////////////////
// CSquaresView

IMPLEMENT_DYNCREATE(CSquaresView, CView)

BEGIN_MESSAGE_MAP(CSquaresView, CView)
    //{{AFX_MSG_MAP(CSquaresView)
    ON_WM_LBUTTONDOWN()
    //}}AFX_MSG_MAP
END_MESSAGE_MAP()


/////////////////////////////////////////////////////////////////////////
// CSquaresView construction/destruction

CSquaresView::CSquaresView()
{
}


CSquaresView::~CSquaresView()
{
}


BOOL CSquaresView::PreCreateWindow(CREATESTRUCT& cs)
{
    return CView::PreCreateWindow(cs);
}


/////////////////////////////////////////////////////////////////////////
// CSquaresView drawing

void CSquaresView::OnDraw(CDC* pDC)
{
    CSquaresDoc* pDoc = GetDocument();
    ASSERT_VALID(pDoc);

    //
    // Set the mapping mode to MM_LOENGLISH.
    //
    pDC->SetMapMode (MM_LOENGLISH);
```

(continued)

Figure 11-3. *continued*

```
    //
    // Draw the 16 squares.
    //
    for (int i=0; i<4; i++) {
        for (int j=0; j<4; j++) {
            COLORREF color = pDoc->GetSquare (i, j);
            CBrush brush (color);
            int x1 = (j * 70) + 35;
            int y1 = (i * -70) - 35;
            int x2 = x1 + 70;
            int y2 = y1 - 70;
            CRect rect (x1, y1, x2, y2);
            pDC->FillRect (rect, &brush);
        }
    }

    //
    // Then draw the grid lines surrounding them.
    //
    for (int x=35; x<=315; x+=70) {
        pDC->MoveTo (x, -35);
        pDC->LineTo (x, -315);
    }

    for (int y=-35; y>=-315; y-=70) {
        pDC->MoveTo (35, y);
        pDC->LineTo (315, y);
    }
}

/////////////////////////////////////////////////////////////////////////////
// CSquaresView diagnostics

#ifdef _DEBUG
void CSquaresView::AssertValid() const
{
    CView::AssertValid();
}

void CSquaresView::Dump(CDumpContext& dc) const
{
    CView::Dump(dc);
}

CSquaresDoc* CSquaresView::GetDocument() // non-debug version is inline
```

```
{
    ASSERT(m_pDocument->IsKindOf(RUNTIME_CLASS(CSquaresDoc)));
    return (CSquaresDoc*)m_pDocument;
}
#endif //_DEBUG


/////////////////////////////////////////////////////////////////////////////
// CSquaresView message handlers

void CSquaresView::OnLButtonDown(UINT nFlags, CPoint point)
{
    CView::OnLButtonDown(nFlags, point);

    //
    // Convert click coordinates to MM_LOENGLISH units.
    //
    CClientDC dc (this);
    dc.SetMapMode (MM_LOENGLISH);
    CPoint pos = point;
    dc.DPtoLP (&pos);

    //
    // If a square was clicked, set its color to the current color.
    //
    if (pos.x >= 35 && pos.x <= 315 && pos.y <= -35 && pos.y >= -315) {
        int i = (-pos.y - 35) / 70;
        int j = (pos.x - 35) / 70;
        CSquaresDoc* pDoc = GetDocument ();
        COLORREF clrCurrentColor = pDoc->GetCurrentColor ();
        pDoc->SetSquare (i, j, clrCurrentColor);
    }
}
```

Supporting Multiple Document Types

An MDI application written with MFC supports multiple document instances by default.
A new document instance is created each time the user executes a File/New command. MDI applications can also support multiple document *types,* each character-
ized by a unique document template.

Suppose you want to add a second document type—say, circles documents—
to MdiSquares so that when File/New is selected, the user is given a choice of whether
to create a squares document or a circles document. Here's how you'd do it.

1. Derive a new document class and a new view class to serve the new document type. For the sake of this example, assume the classes are named *CCirclesDoc* and *CCirclesView*. Make the classes dynamically creatable, just like the document and view classes AppWizard generates.

2. Add four new resources to the project for circles documents: an icon, a menu, an accelerator (optional), and a document string. Assign all four resources the same resource ID—for example, IDR_CIRCLETYPE.

3. Modify *InitInstance* to create a new document template containing the resource ID and *CRuntimeClass* pointers for the document, view, and frame window classes. Then call *AddDocTemplate* and pass in the address of the document template object.

Here's an excerpt from an *InitInstance* function modified to register two document templates:

```
// AppWizard-generated code
CMultiDocTemplate* pDocTemplate;
pDocTemplate = new CMultiDocTemplate(
    IDR_MDISQUTYPE,
    RUNTIME_CLASS(CSquaresDoc),
    RUNTIME_CLASS(CChildFrame), // custom MDI child frame
    RUNTIME_CLASS(CSquaresView));
AddDocTemplate(pDocTemplate);

// Your code
pDocTemplate = new CMultiDocTemplate(
    IDR_CIRCLETYPE,
    RUNTIME_CLASS(CCirclesDoc),
    RUNTIME_CLASS(CChildFrame),
    RUNTIME_CLASS(CCirclesView));
AddDocTemplate(pDocTemplate);
```

That's basically all there is to it. This example uses *CChildFrame* as the child frame class for both document types, but you can derive a separate child frame class if you'd prefer.

When multiple document types are registered in this manner, MFC's File-New command handler displays a dialog box presenting the user with a choice of document types. The string that identifies each document type in the dialog box comes from the document string—specifically, from the third of the document string's seven possible substrings. With this infrastructure in place, it's relatively simple to write multifunction MDI applications that permit users to create and edit different kinds of documents. You can write SDI applications that support two or more document types, too, but the multiple document type paradigm is rarely used in single document applications.

Alternatives to MDI

The multiple document interface isn't the only game in town if you want to give your users the ability to edit several documents at once in one instance of your application. *The Windows Interface Guidelines for Software Design* outlines three alternatives to the MDI programming model:

■ A workspace-based model that groups related documents in objects called *workspaces* and allows documents contained in a workspace to be viewed and edited in MDI-like document frames that are children of a top-level frame window. Visual C++ is one example of an application that uses the workspace containment model.

■ A workbook model in which individual views occupy the full client area of a top-level frame window but only one view at a time is visible. The appearance is similar to that of a maximized document frame in an MDI application. Each view is tabbed so that the user can switch from one view to another with a button click as if the views were pages in a property sheet.

■ A project model that groups related documents in projects but allows individual documents to be edited in SDI-like frame windows. The primary difference between the project model and the MDI and workspace models is that in the project model there is no top-level frame window providing containment for document frames.

MFC doesn't support any of these alternatives directly, but you can always code them yourself. Alternative user interface models are on the radar screen of the MFC team at Microsoft, so it's very possible that a future version of MFC will support user interface models other than SDI and MDI.

SPLITTER WINDOWS

MDI applications inherently support multiple views of a document; SDI applications do not. For SDI applications, the best way to present two or more concurrent views of a document is to use a splitter window based on MFC's *CSplitterWnd* class. A splitter window is a window that can be divided into two or more panes horizontally, vertically, or both horizontally and vertically using movable splitter bars. Each pane contains one view of a document's data. The views are children of the splitter window, and the splitter window itself is normally a child of a frame window. In an SDI application, the splitter window is a child of the top-level frame window. In an MDI application, the splitter window is a child of an MDI document frame. A view positioned inside a splitter window can use *CView::GetParentFrame* to obtain a pointer to its parent frame window.

MFC supports two types of splitter windows: static and dynamic. The numbers of rows and columns in a static splitter window are set when the splitter is created and can't be changed by the user. The user is, however, free to resize individual rows and columns. A static splitter window can contain a maximum of 16 rows and 16 columns. For an example of an application that uses a static splitter, look no further than the Windows Explorer. Explorer's main window is divided in half vertically by a static splitter window.

A dynamic splitter window is limited to at most two rows and two columns, but it can be split and unsplit interactively. The views displayed in a dynamic splitter window's panes aren't entirely independent of each other: when a dynamic splitter window is split horizontally, the two rows have independent vertical scroll bars but share a horizontal scroll bar. Similarly, the two columns of a dynamic splitter window split vertically contain horizontal scroll bars of their own but share a vertical scroll bar. The maximum number of rows and columns a dynamic splitter window can be divided into are specified when the splitter is created. Thus, it's a simple matter to create a dynamic splitter window that can be split horizontally or vertically but not both. Visual C++ uses a dynamic splitter window to permit two or more sections of a source code file to be edited at once. (See Figure 11-4.)

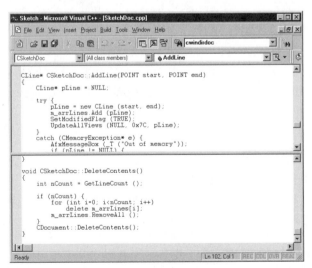

Figure 11-4. *A dynamic splitter showing two views of a document in Visual C++.*

One criterion for choosing between static and dynamic splitter windows is whether you want the user to be able to change the splitter's row and column configuration interactively. Use a dynamic splitter window if you do. Another factor in the decision is what kinds of views you plan to use in the splitter's panes. It's easy to use two or more different view classes in a static splitter window because you specify the type of view that goes in each pane. MFC manages the views in a dynamic splitter window, however, so a dynamic splitter uses the same view class for all of its views unless you derive a new class from *CSplitterWnd* and modify the splitter's default behavior.

Dynamic Splitter Windows

Dynamic splitter windows are created with MFC's *CSplitterWnd::Create* function. Creating and initializing a dynamic splitter window is a simple two-step procedure:

1. Add a *CSplitterWnd* data member to the frame window class.

2. Override the frame window's virtual *OnCreateClient* function, and call *CSplitterWnd::Create* to create a dynamic splitter window in the frame window's client area.

Assuming *m_wndSplitter* is a *CSplitterWnd* object that's a member of the frame window class *CMainFrame*, the following *OnCreateClient* override creates a dynamic splitter window inside the frame window:

```
BOOL CMainFrame::OnCreateClient (LPCREATESTRUCT lpcs,
    CCreateContext* pContext)
{
    return m_wndSplitter.Create (this, 2, 1, CSize (1, 1), pContext);
}
```

The first parameter to *CSplitterWnd::Create* identifies the splitter window's parent, which is the frame window. The second and third parameters specify the maximum number of rows and columns that the window can be split into. Because a dynamic splitter window supports a maximum of two rows and two columns, these parameter values will always be 1 or 2. The fourth parameter specifies each pane's minimum width and height in pixels. The framework uses these values to determine when panes should be created and destroyed as splitter bars are moved. *CSize* values equal to (1,1) specify that panes can be as little as 1 pixel wide and 1 pixel tall. The fifth parameter is a pointer to a *CCreateContext* structure provided by the framework. The structure's *m_pNewViewClass* member identifies the view class used to create views in the splitter's panes. The framework creates the initial view for you and puts it into the first pane. Other views of the same class are created automatically as additional panes are created.

CSplitterWnd::Create supports optional sixth and seventh parameters specifying the splitter window's style and its child window ID. In most instances, the defaults are fine. The default child window ID of AFX_IDW_PANE_FIRST is a magic number that enables a frame window to identify the splitter window associated with it. You need to modify the ID only if you create a second splitter window in a frame window that already contains a splitter.

Once a dynamic splitter window is created, the framework provides the logic to make it work. If the window is initially unsplit and the user drags a vertical splitter bar to the middle of the window, for example, MFC splits the window vertically and creates a view inside the new pane. Because the new view is created at run time, the view class must support dynamic creation. If the user later drags the vertical splitter bar to the left or right edge of the window (or close enough to the edge that either pane's width is less than the minimum width specified when the splitter window was created), MFC destroys the secondary pane and the view that appears inside it.

The *CSplitterWnd* class includes a number of useful member functions you can call on to query a splitter window for information. Among other things, you can ask for the number of rows or columns currently displayed, for the width or height of a row or a column, or for a *CView* pointer to the view in a particular row and column. If you'd like to add a Split command to your application's menu, include a menu item whose ID is ID_WINDOW_SPLIT. This ID is prewired to the command handler *CView::OnSplitCmd* and the update handler *CView::OnUpdateSplitCmd* in *CView*'s message map. Internally, *CView::OnSplitCmd* calls *CSplitterWnd::DoKeyboard-Split* to begin a tracking process that allows phantom splitter bars to be moved with the up and down arrow keys. Tracking ends when Enter is pressed to accept the new splitter position or Esc is pressed to cancel the operation.

The Sketch Application

The application shown in Figure 11-5 is a sketching application that you can use to create simple line drawings. To draw a line, press and hold the left mouse button and drag with the button held down. Releasing the left mouse button replaces the rubber-band line that follows the cursor with a real line. The Grid command in the View menu enables and disables snapping. When snapping is enabled, endpoints automatically snap to the nearest grid point.

Sketch's source code appears in Figure 11-6, beginning on page 645. In most respects, Sketch is a standard SDI document/view application. Lines drawn by the user are represented by instances of *CLine*, which includes *CPoint* member variables for storing a line's endpoints and a *Draw* function for drawing a line on the screen. The document object stores pointers to *CLine* objects in a dynamic array based on MFC's *CTypedPtrArray* class. Each time a line is drawn on the screen, the view, which uses mouse capturing to ensure that every WM_LBUTTONDOWN message is accompanied

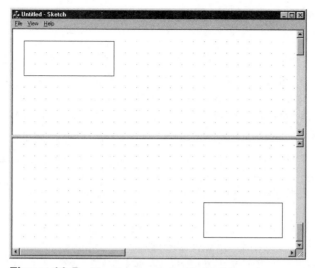

Figure 11-5. *The Sketch window halved by a dynamic splitter window.*

by a WM_LBUTTONUP message, calls the document's *AddLine* function and passes in the line's endpoints. *AddLine*, in turn, creates a new *CLine* object from those endpoints and records the *CLine*'s address in the array:

```
// In SketchDoc.h
typedef CTypedPtrArray<CObArray, CLine*> CLineArray;
    ⋮

CLineArray m_arrLines;

// In SketchDoc.cpp
CLine* CSketchDoc::AddLine(POINT from, POINT to)
{
    CLine* pLine = NULL;

    try {
        pLine = new CLine (from, to);
        m_arrLines.Add (pLine);
        SetModifiedFlag (TRUE);
        UpdateAllViews (NULL, 0x7C, pLine);
    }
    catch (CMemoryException* e) {
        AfxMessageBox (_T ("Out of memory"));
        if (pLine != NULL) {
            delete pLine;
            pLine = NULL;
        }
```

(continued)

```
        e->Delete ();
    }
    return pLine;
}
```

Because *CLine* is a serializable class, and because *CTypedPtrArray* is capable of serializing all of its serializable elements with a simple function call, one statement in *CSketchDoc::Serialize* saves or loads every line that the user has drawn:

```
m_arrLines.Serialize (ar);
```

CSketchDoc also overrides *DeleteContents* and uses it to delete all the *CLine* objects created by *AddLine* before the current document is discarded. Failure to dispose of the *CLine*s in this manner would result in memory leaks each time a document is closed.

What sets Sketch apart from a run-of-the-mill SDI document/view application is the fact that it uses a dynamic splitter window. The splitter window is created by the following statement in *CMainFrame::OnCreateClient*:

```
return m_wndSplitter.Create (this, 2, 1, CSize (8, 8), pContext);
```

Significantly, this is the only code anywhere in Sketch that's provided specifically for splitter windows; MFC handles all other aspects of the splitter's operation.

Concurrent views of a document displayed in a splitter window must be synchronized just like concurrent views in an MDI application. The call to *UpdateAllViews* in *CSketchDoc::AddLine* ensures that both views are updated if the window is split when a line is drawn. Rather than rely on the default implementation of *OnUpdate*, *CSketchView* overrides *OnUpdate* and performs a "smart update" by relying on hint information passed to *UpdateAllViews*. Specifically, each time a line is added to the document, *AddLine* calls *UpdateAllViews* and passes a *CLine* pointer referencing the new line in *pHint*:

```
UpdateAllViews (NULL, 0x7C, pLine);
```

The view's *OnUpdate* function casts *pHint* back to a *CLine* and asks the *CLine* to draw itself on the screen:

```
void CSketchView::OnUpdate(CView* pSender, LPARAM lHint, CObject* pHint)
{
    if (lHint == 0x7C) {
        CLine* pLine = (CLine*) pHint;
        ASSERT (pLine->IsKindOf (RUNTIME_CLASS (CLine)));
        CClientDC dc (this);
        OnPrepareDC (&dc);
        pLine->Draw (&dc);
        return;
    }
    CScrollView::OnUpdate (pSender, lHint, pHint);
}
```

This is much more efficient than redrawing the entire view with *OnDraw* because updating a view involves drawing just the one new line no matter how many lines are stored in the document. As a result, Sketch doesn't exhibit the flashing effect that afflicts MdiSquares.

Sketch.h

```
// Sketch.h : main header file for the SKETCH application
//

#if !defined(AFX_SKETCH_H__1260AFC5_9CAC_11D2_8E53_006008A82731__INCLUDED_)
#define AFX_SKETCH_H__1260AFC5_9CAC_11D2_8E53_006008A82731__INCLUDED_

#if _MSC_VER > 1000
#pragma once
#endif // _MSC_VER > 1000

#ifndef __AFXWIN_H__
    #error include 'stdafx.h' before including this file for PCH
#endif

#include "resource.h"        // main symbols

/////////////////////////////////////////////////////////////////////////////
// CSketchApp:
// See Sketch.cpp for the implementation of this class
//

class CSketchApp : public CWinApp
{
public:
    CSketchApp();

// Overrides
    // ClassWizard generated virtual function overrides
    //{{AFX_VIRTUAL(CSketchApp)
    public:
    virtual BOOL InitInstance();
    //}}AFX_VIRTUAL

// Implementation
    //{{AFX_MSG(CSketchApp)
    afx_msg void OnAppAbout();
```

Figure 11-6. *The Sketch application.*

(continued)

Figure 11-6. *continued*

```
        // NOTE - the ClassWizard will add and remove member functions here.
        //     DO NOT EDIT what you see in these blocks of generated code !
    //}}AFX_MSG
    DECLARE_MESSAGE_MAP()
};


//////////////////////////////////////////////////////////////////////////

//{{AFX_INSERT_LOCATION}}
// Microsoft Visual C++ will insert additional declarations immediately
// before the previous line.

#endif
// !defined(AFX_SKETCH_H__1260AFC5_9CAC_11D2_8E53_006008A82731__INCLUDED_)
```

Sketch.cpp

```
// Sketch.cpp : Defines the class behaviors for the application.
//

#include "stdafx.h"
#include "Line.h"
#include "Sketch.h"
#include "MainFrm.h"
#include "SketchDoc.h"
#include "SketchView.h"

#ifdef _DEBUG
#define new DEBUG_NEW
#undef THIS_FILE
static char THIS_FILE[] = __FILE__;
#endif


//////////////////////////////////////////////////////////////////////////
// CSketchApp

BEGIN_MESSAGE_MAP(CSketchApp, CWinApp)
    //{{AFX_MSG_MAP(CSketchApp)
    ON_COMMAND(ID_APP_ABOUT, OnAppAbout)
        // NOTE - the ClassWizard will add and remove mapping macros here.
        //     DO NOT EDIT what you see in these blocks of generated code!
```

```
    //}}AFX_MSG_MAP
    // Standard file based document commands
    ON_COMMAND(ID_FILE_NEW, CWinApp::OnFileNew)
    ON_COMMAND(ID_FILE_OPEN, CWinApp::OnFileOpen)
END_MESSAGE_MAP()

/////////////////////////////////////////////////////////////////////////////
// CSketchApp construction

CSketchApp::CSketchApp()
{
}

/////////////////////////////////////////////////////////////////////////////
// The one and only CSketchApp object

CSketchApp theApp;

/////////////////////////////////////////////////////////////////////////////
// CSketchApp initialization

BOOL CSketchApp::InitInstance()
{
    SetRegistryKey(_T("Local AppWizard-Generated Applications"));

    LoadStdProfileSettings();  // Load standard INI file
                               // options (including MRU)

    CSingleDocTemplate* pDocTemplate;
    pDocTemplate = new CSingleDocTemplate(
        IDR_MAINFRAME,
        RUNTIME_CLASS(CSketchDoc),
        RUNTIME_CLASS(CMainFrame),        // main SDI frame window
        RUNTIME_CLASS(CSketchView));
    AddDocTemplate(pDocTemplate);

    // Enable DDE Execute open
    EnableShellOpen();
    RegisterShellFileTypes(TRUE);

    // Parse command line for standard shell commands, DDE, file open
    CCommandLineInfo cmdInfo;
    ParseCommandLine(cmdInfo);
```

(continued)

Figure 11-6. *continued*

```
    // Dispatch commands specified on the command line
    if (!ProcessShellCommand(cmdInfo))
        return FALSE;

    // The one and only window has been initialized, so show and update it.
    m_pMainWnd->ShowWindow(SW_SHOW);
    m_pMainWnd->UpdateWindow();

    // Enable drag/drop open
    m_pMainWnd->DragAcceptFiles();

    return TRUE;
}

/////////////////////////////////////////////////////////////////////////////
// CAboutDlg dialog used for App About

class CAboutDlg : public CDialog
{
public:
    CAboutDlg();

// Dialog Data
    //{{AFX_DATA(CAboutDlg)
    enum { IDD = IDD_ABOUTBOX };
    //}}AFX_DATA

    // ClassWizard generated virtual function overrides
    //{{AFX_VIRTUAL(CAboutDlg)
    protected:
    virtual void DoDataExchange(CDataExchange* pDX);    // DDX/DDV support
    //}}AFX_VIRTUAL

// Implementation
protected:
    //{{AFX_MSG(CAboutDlg)
        // No message handlers
    //}}AFX_MSG
    DECLARE_MESSAGE_MAP()
};

CAboutDlg::CAboutDlg() : CDialog(CAboutDlg::IDD)
{
    //{{AFX_DATA_INIT(CAboutDlg)
    //}}AFX_DATA_INIT
}
```

```
void CAboutDlg::DoDataExchange(CDataExchange* pDX)
{
    CDialog::DoDataExchange(pDX);
    //{{AFX_DATA_MAP(CAboutDlg)
    //}}AFX_DATA_MAP
}


BEGIN_MESSAGE_MAP(CAboutDlg, CDialog)
    //{{AFX_MSG_MAP(CAboutDlg)
        // No message handlers
    //}}AFX_MSG_MAP
END_MESSAGE_MAP()


// App command to run the dialog
void CSketchApp::OnAppAbout()
{
    CAboutDlg aboutDlg;
    aboutDlg.DoModal();
}


/////////////////////////////////////////////////////////////////////
// CSketchApp message handlers
```

MainFrm.h

```
// MainFrm.h : interface of the CMainFrame class
//
/////////////////////////////////////////////////////////////////////
//

#if
!defined(AFX_MAINFRM_H__1260AFC9_9CAC_11D2_8E53_006008A82731__INCLUDED_)
#define  AFX_MAINFRM_H__1260AFC9_9CAC_11D2_8E53_006008A82731__INCLUDED_

#if _MSC_VER > 1000
#pragma once
#endif // _MSC_VER > 1000

class CMainFrame : public CFrameWnd
{

protected: // create from serialization only
    CMainFrame();
    DECLARE_DYNCREATE(CMainFrame)
```

(continued)

Figure 11-6. *continued*

```
// Attributes
public:

// Operations
public:

// Overrides
    // ClassWizard generated virtual function overrides
    //{{AFX_VIRTUAL(CMainFrame)
    public:
    virtual BOOL PreCreateWindow(CREATESTRUCT& cs);
    protected:
    virtual BOOL OnCreateClient(LPCREATESTRUCT lpcs,
        CCreateContext* pContext);
    //}}AFX_VIRTUAL

// Implementation
public:
    virtual ~CMainFrame();
#ifdef _DEBUG
    virtual void AssertValid() const;
    virtual void Dump(CDumpContext& dc) const;
#endif

// Generated message map functions
protected:
    CSplitterWnd m_wndSplitter;
    //{{AFX_MSG(CMainFrame)
        // NOTE - the ClassWizard will add and remove member functions here.
        //     DO NOT EDIT what you see in these blocks of generated code!
    //}}AFX_MSG
    DECLARE_MESSAGE_MAP()
};

/////////////////////////////////////////////////////////////////////////////

//{{AFX_INSERT_LOCATION}}
// Microsoft Visual C++ will insert additional declarations immediately
// before the previous line.

#endif
// !defined(AFX_MAINFRM_H__1260AFC9_9CAC_11D2_8E53_006008A82731__INCLUDED_)
```

MainFrm.cpp

```cpp
// MainFrm.cpp : implementation of the CMainFrame class
//

#include "stdafx.h"
#include "Sketch.h"

#include "MainFrm.h"

#ifdef _DEBUG
#define new DEBUG_NEW
#undef THIS_FILE
static char THIS_FILE[] = __FILE__;
#endif

/////////////////////////////////////////////////////////////////////////////
// CMainFrame

IMPLEMENT_DYNCREATE(CMainFrame, CFrameWnd)

BEGIN_MESSAGE_MAP(CMainFrame, CFrameWnd)
    //{{AFX_MSG_MAP(CMainFrame)
        // NOTE - the ClassWizard will add and remove mapping macros here.
        //     DO NOT EDIT what you see in these blocks of generated code !
    //}}AFX_MSG_MAP
END_MESSAGE_MAP()

/////////////////////////////////////////////////////////////////////////////
// CMainFrame construction/destruction

CMainFrame::CMainFrame()
{
}

CMainFrame::~CMainFrame()
{
}

BOOL CMainFrame::PreCreateWindow(CREATESTRUCT& cs)
{
    if( !CFrameWnd::PreCreateWindow(cs) )
        return FALSE;
    return TRUE;
}
```

(continued)

Figure 11-6. *continued*

```
//////////////////////////////////////////////////////////////////////
// CMainFrame diagnostics

#ifdef _DEBUG
void CMainFrame::AssertValid() const
{
    CFrameWnd::AssertValid();
}

void CMainFrame::Dump(CDumpContext& dc) const
{
    CFrameWnd::Dump(dc);
}

#endif //_DEBUG


//////////////////////////////////////////////////////////////////////
// CMainFrame message handlers


BOOL CMainFrame::OnCreateClient(LPCREATESTRUCT lpcs, CCreateContext*
pContext)
{
    return m_wndSplitter.Create (this, 2, 1, CSize (8, 8), pContext);
}
```

SketchDoc.h

```
// SketchDoc.h : interface of the CSketchDoc class
//
//////////////////////////////////////////////////////////////////////

#if
!defined(AFX_SKETCHDOC_H__1260AFCB_9CAC_11D2_8E53_006008A82731__INCLUDED_)
#define  AFX_SKETCHDOC_H__1260AFCB_9CAC_11D2_8E53_006008A82731__INCLUDED_

#if _MSC_VER > 1000
#pragma once
#endif // _MSC_VER > 1000

typedef CTypedPtrArray<CObArray, CLine*> CLineArray;
```

```
class CSketchDoc : public CDocument
{
protected: // create from serialization only
    CSketchDoc();
    DECLARE_DYNCREATE(CSketchDoc)

// Attributes
public:

// Operations
public:

// Overrides
    // ClassWizard generated virtual function overrides
    //{{AFX_VIRTUAL(CSketchDoc)
    public:
    virtual BOOL OnNewDocument();
    virtual void Serialize(CArchive& ar);
    virtual void DeleteContents();
    //}}AFX_VIRTUAL

// Implementation
public:
    CLine* GetLine (int nIndex);
    int GetLineCount ();
    CLine* AddLine (POINT from, POINT to);
    BOOL IsGridVisible ();
    virtual ~CSketchDoc();
#ifdef _DEBUG
    virtual void AssertValid() const;
    virtual void Dump(CDumpContext& dc) const;
#endif

protected:

// Generated message map functions
protected:
    CLineArray m_arrLines;
    BOOL m_bShowGrid;
    //{{AFX_MSG(CSketchDoc)
    afx_msg void OnViewGrid();
    afx_msg void OnUpdateViewGrid(CCmdUI* pCmdUI);
    //}}AFX_MSG
    DECLARE_MESSAGE_MAP()
};
```

(continued)

Figure 11-6. *continued*

```
///////////////////////////////////////////////////////////////////////
//{{AFX_INSERT_LOCATION}}
// Microsoft Visual C++ will insert additional declarations immediately
// before the previous line.

#endif
// !defined(
//      AFX_SKETCHDOC_H__1260AFCB_9CAC_11D2_8E53_006008A82731__INCLUDED_)
```

SketchDoc.cpp

```cpp
// SketchDoc.cpp : implementation of the CSketchDoc class
//

#include "stdafx.h"
#include "Line.h"
#include "Sketch.h"
#include "SketchDoc.h"

#ifdef _DEBUG
#define new DEBUG_NEW
#undef THIS_FILE
static char THIS_FILE[] = __FILE__;
#endif


///////////////////////////////////////////////////////////////////////
// CSketchDoc

IMPLEMENT_DYNCREATE(CSketchDoc, CDocument)

BEGIN_MESSAGE_MAP(CSketchDoc, CDocument)
    //{{AFX_MSG_MAP(CSketchDoc)
    ON_COMMAND(ID_VIEW_GRID, OnViewGrid)
    ON_UPDATE_COMMAND_UI(ID_VIEW_GRID, OnUpdateViewGrid)
    //}}AFX_MSG_MAP
END_MESSAGE_MAP()


///////////////////////////////////////////////////////////////////////
// CSketchDoc construction/destruction

CSketchDoc::CSketchDoc()
{
}
```

```
CSketchDoc::~CSketchDoc()
{
}


BOOL CSketchDoc::OnNewDocument()
{
    if (!CDocument::OnNewDocument())
        return FALSE;

    m_bShowGrid = TRUE;
    return TRUE;
}


/////////////////////////////////////////////////////////////////////////////
// CSketchDoc serialization

void CSketchDoc::Serialize(CArchive& ar)
{
    if (ar.IsStoring())
    {
        ar << m_bShowGrid;
    }
    else
    {
        ar >> m_bShowGrid;
    }
    m_arrLines.Serialize (ar);
}


/////////////////////////////////////////////////////////////////////////////
// CSketchDoc diagnostics

#ifdef _DEBUG
void CSketchDoc::AssertValid() const
{
    CDocument::AssertValid();
}

void CSketchDoc::Dump(CDumpContext& dc) const
{
    CDocument::Dump(dc);
}
#endif //_DEBUG
```

(continued)

Figure 11-6. *continued*

```
///////////////////////////////////////////////////////////////////////
// CSketchDoc commands

BOOL CSketchDoc::IsGridVisible()
{
    return m_bShowGrid;
}

void CSketchDoc::OnViewGrid()
{
    if (m_bShowGrid)
        m_bShowGrid = FALSE;
    else
        m_bShowGrid = TRUE;

    SetModifiedFlag (TRUE);
    UpdateAllViews (NULL);
}

void CSketchDoc::OnUpdateViewGrid(CCmdUI* pCmdUI)
{
    pCmdUI->SetCheck (m_bShowGrid);
}

CLine* CSketchDoc::AddLine(POINT from, POINT to)
{
    CLine* pLine = NULL;

    try {
        pLine = new CLine (from, to);
        m_arrLines.Add (pLine);
        SetModifiedFlag (TRUE);
        UpdateAllViews (NULL, 0x7C, pLine);
    }
    catch (CMemoryException* e) {
        AfxMessageBox (_T ("Out of memory"));
        if (pLine != NULL) {
            delete pLine;
            pLine = NULL;
        }
        e->Delete ();
    }
    return pLine;
}
```

```
int CSketchDoc::GetLineCount()
{
    return m_arrLines.GetSize ();
}

CLine* CSketchDoc::GetLine(int nIndex)
{
    ASSERT (nIndex < GetLineCount ());
    return m_arrLines[nIndex];
}

void CSketchDoc::DeleteContents()
{
    int nCount = GetLineCount ();

    if (nCount) {
        for (int i=0; i<nCount; i++)
            delete m_arrLines[i];
        m_arrLines.RemoveAll ();
    }
    CDocument::DeleteContents();
}
```

SketchView.h

```
// SketchView.h : interface of the CSketchView class
//
/////////////////////////////////////////////////////////////////////////////
//

#if
!defined(AFX_SKETCHVIEW_H__1260AFCD_9CAC_11D2_8E53_006008A82731__INCLUDED_)
#define  AFX_SKETCHVIEW_H__1260AFCD_9CAC_11D2_8E53_006008A82731__INCLUDED_

#if _MSC_VER > 1000
#pragma once
#endif // _MSC_VER > 1000


class CSketchView : public CScrollView
{
protected: // create from serialization only
    CSketchView();
    DECLARE_DYNCREATE(CSketchView)
```

(continued)

Figure 11-6. *continued*

```
// Attributes
public:
    CSketchDoc* GetDocument();

// Operations
public:

// Overrides
    // ClassWizard generated virtual function overrides
    //{{AFX_VIRTUAL(CSketchView)
    public:
    virtual void OnDraw(CDC* pDC);  // overridden to draw this view
    virtual BOOL PreCreateWindow(CREATESTRUCT& cs);
    protected:
    virtual void OnInitialUpdate(); // called first time after construct
    virtual void OnUpdate(CView* pSender, LPARAM lHint, CObject* pHint);
    //}}AFX_VIRTUAL

// Implementation
public:
    virtual ~CSketchView();
#ifdef _DEBUG
    virtual void AssertValid() const;
    virtual void Dump(CDumpContext& dc) const;
#endif

protected:

// Generated message map functions
protected:
    void InvertLine (CDC* pDC, POINT from, POINT to);
    CPoint m_ptFrom;
    CPoint m_ptTo;
    HCURSOR m_hCursor;
    //{{AFX_MSG(CSketchView)
    afx_msg BOOL OnSetCursor(CWnd* pWnd, UINT nHitTest, UINT message);
    afx_msg void OnLButtonDown(UINT nFlags, CPoint point);
    afx_msg void OnMouseMove(UINT nFlags, CPoint point);
    afx_msg void OnLButtonUp(UINT nFlags, CPoint point);
    //}}AFX_MSG
    DECLARE_MESSAGE_MAP()
};
```

```
#ifndef _DEBUG  // debug version in SketchView.cpp
inline CSketchDoc* CSketchView::GetDocument()
    { return (CSketchDoc*)m_pDocument; }
#endif


/////////////////////////////////////////////////////////////////////////

//{{AFX_INSERT_LOCATION}}
// Microsoft Visual C++ will insert additional declarations immediately
// before the previous line.

#endif
// !defined(
//      AFX_SKETCHVIEW_H__1260AFCD_9CAC_11D2_8E53_006008A82731__INCLUDED_)
```

SketchView.cpp

```
// SketchView.cpp : implementation of the CSketchView class
//

#include "stdafx.h"
#include "Line.h"
#include "Sketch.h"
#include "SketchDoc.h"
#include "SketchView.h"

#ifdef _DEBUG
#define new DEBUG_NEW
#undef THIS_FILE
static char THIS_FILE[] = __FILE__;
#endif


/////////////////////////////////////////////////////////////////////////
// CSketchView

IMPLEMENT_DYNCREATE(CSketchView, CScrollView)

BEGIN_MESSAGE_MAP(CSketchView, CScrollView)
    //{{AFX_MSG_MAP(CSketchView)
    ON_WM_SETCURSOR()
    ON_WM_LBUTTONDOWN()
```

(continued)

Figure 11-6. *continued*

```
    ON_WM_MOUSEMOVE()
    ON_WM_LBUTTONUP()
    //}}AFX_MSG_MAP
END_MESSAGE_MAP()


/////////////////////////////////////////////////////////////////////////
// CSketchView construction/destruction

CSketchView::CSketchView()
{
    m_hCursor = AfxGetApp ()->LoadStandardCursor (IDC_CROSS);
}


CSketchView::~CSketchView()
{
}


BOOL CSketchView::PreCreateWindow(CREATESTRUCT& cs)
{
    return CScrollView::PreCreateWindow(cs);
}


/////////////////////////////////////////////////////////////////////////
// CSketchView drawing

void CSketchView::OnDraw(CDC* pDC)
{
    CSketchDoc* pDoc = GetDocument();
    ASSERT_VALID(pDoc);

    //
    // Draw the snap grid.
    //
    if (pDoc->IsGridVisible ()) {
        for (int x=25; x<1600; x+=25)
            for (int y=-25; y>-1200; y-=25)
                pDC->SetPixel (x, y, RGB (128, 128, 128));
    }

    //
    // Draw the lines.
    //
    int nCount = pDoc->GetLineCount ();
    if (nCount) {
        for (int i=0; i<nCount; i++)
```

```
            pDoc->GetLine (i)->Draw (pDC);
    }
}

void CSketchView::OnInitialUpdate()
{
    CScrollView::OnInitialUpdate();
    SetScrollSizes(MM_LOENGLISH, CSize (1600, 1200));
}

/////////////////////////////////////////////////////////////////////////////
// CSketchView diagnostics

#ifdef _DEBUG
void CSketchView::AssertValid() const
{
    CScrollView::AssertValid();
}

void CSketchView::Dump(CDumpContext& dc) const
{
    CScrollView::Dump(dc);
}

CSketchDoc* CSketchView::GetDocument() // non-debug version is inline
{
    ASSERT(m_pDocument->IsKindOf(RUNTIME_CLASS(CSketchDoc)));
    return (CSketchDoc*)m_pDocument;
}
#endif //_DEBUG

/////////////////////////////////////////////////////////////////////////////
// CSketchView message handlers

BOOL CSketchView::OnSetCursor(CWnd* pWnd, UINT nHitTest, UINT message)
{
    ::SetCursor (m_hCursor);
    return TRUE;
}

void CSketchView::OnLButtonDown(UINT nFlags, CPoint point)
{
    CScrollView::OnLButtonDown(nFlags, point);

    CPoint pos = point;
```

(continued)

Figure 11-6. *continued*

```
    CClientDC dc (this);
    OnPrepareDC (&dc);
    dc.DPtoLP (&pos);

    if (GetDocument ()->IsGridVisible ()) {
        pos.x = ((pos.x + 12) / 25) * 25;
        pos.y = ((pos.y - 12) / 25) * 25;
    }

    m_ptFrom = pos;
    m_ptTo = pos;
    SetCapture ();
}

void CSketchView::OnMouseMove(UINT nFlags, CPoint point)
{
    CScrollView::OnMouseMove(nFlags, point);

    if (GetCapture () == this) {
        CPoint pos = point;
        CClientDC dc (this);
        OnPrepareDC (&dc);
        dc.DPtoLP (&pos);

        if (GetDocument ()->IsGridVisible ()) {
            pos.x = ((pos.x + 12) / 25) * 25;
            pos.y = ((pos.y - 12) / 25) * 25;
        }

        if (m_ptTo != pos) {
            InvertLine (&dc, m_ptFrom, m_ptTo);
            InvertLine (&dc, m_ptFrom, pos);
            m_ptTo = pos;
        }
    }
}

void CSketchView::OnLButtonUp(UINT nFlags, CPoint point)
{
    CScrollView::OnLButtonUp(nFlags, point);

    if (GetCapture () == this) {
        ::ReleaseCapture ();

        CPoint pos = point;
        CClientDC dc (this);
```

```
            OnPrepareDC (&dc);
            dc.DPtoLP (&pos);

            if (GetDocument ()->IsGridVisible ()) {
                pos.x = ((pos.x + 12) / 25) * 25;
                pos.y = ((pos.y - 12) / 25) * 25;
            }

            InvertLine (&dc, m_ptFrom, m_ptTo);

            CSketchDoc* pDoc = GetDocument ();
            CLine* pLine = pDoc->AddLine (m_ptFrom, m_ptTo);
        }
    }

void CSketchView::InvertLine(CDC *pDC, POINT from, POINT to)
{
    int nOldMode = pDC->SetROP2 (R2_NOT);
    pDC->MoveTo (from);
    pDC->LineTo (to);
    pDC->SetROP2 (nOldMode);
}

void CSketchView::OnUpdate(CView* pSender, LPARAM lHint, CObject* pHint)
{
    if (lHint == 0x7C) {
        CLine* pLine = (CLine*) pHint;
        ASSERT (pLine->IsKindOf (RUNTIME_CLASS (CLine)));
        CClientDC dc (this);
        OnPrepareDC (&dc);
        pLine->Draw (&dc);
        return;
    }
    CScrollView::OnUpdate (pSender, lHint, pHint);
}
```

Static Splitter Windows

Static splitter windows are handled much like dynamic splitter windows except that an extra step is required to create them. Static splitters are created with *CSplitterWnd::CreateStatic* rather than *CSplitterWnd::Create*, and because MFC doesn't automatically create the views displayed in a static splitter window, it's up to you to create the views after *CreateStatic* returns. *CSplitterWnd* provides a function named *CreateView* for this purpose. The procedure for adding a static splitter window to a frame window goes like this.

1. Add a *CSplitterWnd* data member to the frame window class.

2. Override the frame window's *OnCreateClient* function, and call *CSplitter-Wnd::CreateStatic* to create a static splitter window.

3. Use *CSplitterWnd::CreateView* to create a view in each of the splitter window's panes.

One of the chief advantages of using a static splitter window is that because you put the views in the panes, you control what kinds of views are placed there. The following example creates a static splitter window that contains two different kinds of views:

```
BOOL CMainFrame::OnCreateClient (LPCREATESTRUCT lpcs,
    CCreateContext* pContext)
{
    if (!m_wndSplitter.CreateStatic (this, 1, 2) ||
        !m_wndSplitter.CreateView (0, 0, RUNTIME_CLASS (CTextView),
            CSize (128, 0), pContext) ||
        !m_wndSplitter.CreateView (0, 1, RUNTIME_CLASS (CPictureView),
            CSize (0, 0), pContext))
        return FALSE;

    return TRUE;
}
```

The parameters passed to *CreateStatic* identify the splitter window's parent as well as the number of rows and columns that the splitter contains. *CreateView* is called once for each pane. Panes are identified by 0-based row and column numbers. In this example, the first call to *CreateView* inserts a view of type *CTextView* into the left pane (row 0, column 0), and the second inserts a view of type *CPictureView* into the right pane (row 0, column 1). The views aren't instantiated directly but are created by MFC. Therefore, you pass *CRuntimeClass* pointers to *CreateView* instead of pointers to existing *CView* objects. As with a dynamic splitter window, the views used in a static splitter window must be dynamically creatable or the framework can't use them.

The *CSize* objects passed to *CreateView* specify the panes' initial sizes. In this case, the *CTextView* pane will start out 128 pixels wide and the *CPictureView* pane will occupy the remaining width of the window. The width specified for the right pane and the heights specified for both the left and the right panes are 0 because the framework ignores these values. When a splitter window contains only one row, that row will occupy the full height of the parent's client area no matter what *CSize* values you specify. Similarly, if a splitter window contains *n* columns, the rightmost column will occupy all the space between the right edge of column *n*−1 and the edge of its parent.

The Wanderer Application

The Wanderer application shown in Figure 11-7 uses a static splitter window to mimic the look and feel of the Windows Explorer. The splitter window divides the frame window into two panes. The left pane contains a *CDriveView*, which is a *CTreeView* customized to display the directory structure of the host PC. The right pane contains a *CFileView*, which is a *CListView* that lists the files in the directory selected in the *CDriveView*.

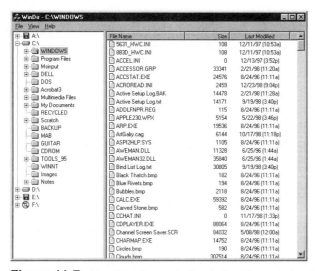

Figure 11-7. *The Wanderer window halved by a static splitter window.*

The *CDriveView* and *CFileView* classes that Wanderer uses are almost identical to the classes of the same name introduced in Chapter 10. I modified *CDriveView* slightly by adding a handler for reflected TVN_SELCHANGED notifications indicating that the tree view selection changed. That handler translates the selected item into a path name and uses *UpdateAllViews'* *pHint* parameter to transmit the path name to the *CFileView*:

```
void CDriveView::OnSelectionChanged(NMHDR* pNMHDR, LRESULT* pResult)
{
    NM_TREEVIEW* pNMTreeView = (NM_TREEVIEW*) pNMHDR;
    CString strPath = GetPathFromItem (pNMTreeView->itemNew.hItem);
    GetDocument ()->UpdateAllViews (this, 0x5A,
        (CObject*) (LPCTSTR) strPath);
    *pResult = 0;
}
```

I also modified *CFileView* to respond to calls to *OnUpdate* by displaying the contents of the directory identified by *pHint* if *lHint* equals 0x5A:

```
void CFileView::OnUpdate(CView* pSender, LPARAM lHint, CObject* pHint)
{
    if (lHint == 0x5A) {
        FreeItemMemory ();
        GetListCtrl ().DeleteAllItems ();
        Refresh ((LPCTSTR) pHint);
        return;
    }
    CListView::OnUpdate (pSender, lHint, pHint);
}
```

Together, these two modifications couple the left and right panes in such a way that the view on the right-hand side is updated whenever the directory selected on the left-hand side changes.

The static splitter window is created and initialized in *CMainFrame::OnCreate-Client*. After creating the splitter window, *OnCreateClient* uses *CreateView* to place a *CDriveView* in the left pane and a *CFileView* in the right pane. (See Figure 11-8.) The only thing that's unusual about Wanderer's implementation of *OnCreateClient* is that it creates the right-hand view first and the left-hand view second. The reason why is simple. The *CDriveView*'s *OnInitialUpdate* function calls *UpdateAllViews* to tell the *CFileView* which directory is selected; the *CFileView*'s *OnUpdate* function, in turn, displays the contents of that directory. But if the *CDriveView* is created first, the *CFileView* doesn't exist when *CDriveView::OnInitialUpdate* is called. Creating the *CFileView* first is one way to circumvent this problem.

Wanderer.h

```
// Wanderer.h : main header file for the WANDERER application
//

#if
!defined(AFX_WANDERER_H__AE0A6FFA_9B0F_11D2_8E53_006008A82731__INCLUDED_)
#define  AFX_WANDERER_H__AE0A6FFA_9B0F_11D2_8E53_006008A82731__INCLUDED_

#if _MSC_VER > 1000
#pragma once
#endif // _MSC_VER > 1000

#ifndef __AFXWIN_H__
    #error include 'stdafx.h' before including this file for PCH
#endif
```

Figure 11-8. *The Wanderer application.*

```
#include "resource.h"        // main symbols

/////////////////////////////////////////////////////////////////////////
// CWandererApp:
// See Wanderer.cpp for the implementation of this class
//

class CWandererApp : public CWinApp
{
public:
    CWandererApp();

// Overrides
    // ClassWizard generated virtual function overrides
    //{{AFX_VIRTUAL(CWandererApp)
    public:
    virtual BOOL InitInstance();
    //}}AFX_VIRTUAL

// Implementation
    //{{AFX_MSG(CWandererApp)
    afx_msg void OnAppAbout();
        // NOTE - the ClassWizard will add and remove member functions here.
        //     DO NOT EDIT what you see in these blocks of generated code !
    //}}AFX_MSG
    DECLARE_MESSAGE_MAP()
};


/////////////////////////////////////////////////////////////////////////

//{{AFX_INSERT_LOCATION}}
// Microsoft Visual C++ will insert additional declarations immediately
// before the previous line.

#endif
// !defined(
//     AFX_WANDERER_H__AE0A6FFA_9B0F_11D2_8E53_006008A82731__INCLUDED_)
```

Wanderer.cpp

```
// Wanderer.cpp : Defines the class behaviors for the application.
//
```

(continued)

Figure 11-8. *continued*

```
#include "stdafx.h"
#include "Wanderer.h"

#include "MainFrm.h"
#include "WandererDoc.h"
#include "DriveView.h"

#ifdef _DEBUG
#define new DEBUG_NEW
#undef THIS_FILE
static char THIS_FILE[] = __FILE__;
#endif


//////////////////////////////////////////////////////////////////////
// CWandererApp

BEGIN_MESSAGE_MAP(CWandererApp, CWinApp)
    //{{AFX_MSG_MAP(CWandererApp)
    ON_COMMAND(ID_APP_ABOUT, OnAppAbout)
        // NOTE - the ClassWizard will add and remove mapping macros here.
        //     DO NOT EDIT what you see in these blocks of generated code!
    //}}AFX_MSG_MAP
    // Standard file based document commands
    ON_COMMAND(ID_FILE_NEW, CWinApp::OnFileNew)
    ON_COMMAND(ID_FILE_OPEN, CWinApp::OnFileOpen)
END_MESSAGE_MAP()


//////////////////////////////////////////////////////////////////////
// CWandererApp construction

CWandererApp::CWandererApp()
{
    // TODO: add construction code here,
    // Place all significant initialization in InitInstance
}


//////////////////////////////////////////////////////////////////////
// The one and only CWandererApp object

CWandererApp theApp;


//////////////////////////////////////////////////////////////////////
// CWandererApp initialization

BOOL CWandererApp::InitInstance()
{
    // Standard initialization
```

```
    // If you are not using these features and wish to reduce the size
    //  of your final executable, you should remove from the following
    //  the specific initialization routines you do not need.

    // Change the registry key under which our settings are stored.
    // TODO: You should modify this string to be something appropriate
    //  such as the name of your company or organization.
    SetRegistryKey(_T("Local AppWizard-Generated Applications"));

    LoadStdProfileSettings();  // Load standard INI file
                               // options (including MRU)

    // Register the application's document templates.  Document templates
    //  serve as the connection between documents, frame windows and views.

    CSingleDocTemplate* pDocTemplate;
    pDocTemplate = new CSingleDocTemplate(
        IDR_MAINFRAME,
        RUNTIME_CLASS(CWandererDoc),
        RUNTIME_CLASS(CMainFrame),         // main SDI frame window
        RUNTIME_CLASS(CDriveView));
    AddDocTemplate(pDocTemplate);

    // Parse command line for standard shell commands, DDE, file open
    CCommandLineInfo cmdInfo;
    ParseCommandLine(cmdInfo);

    // Dispatch commands specified on the command line
    if (!ProcessShellCommand(cmdInfo))
        return FALSE;

    // The one and only window has been initialized, so show and update it.
    m_pMainWnd->ShowWindow(SW_SHOW);
    m_pMainWnd->UpdateWindow();

    return TRUE;
}


/////////////////////////////////////////////////////////////////////////////
// CAboutDlg dialog used for App About

class CAboutDlg : public CDialog
{
public:
    CAboutDlg();
```

(continued)

Figure 11-8. *continued*

```
// Dialog Data
    //{{AFX_DATA(CAboutDlg)
    enum { IDD = IDD_ABOUTBOX };
    //}}AFX_DATA

    // ClassWizard generated virtual function overrides
    //{{AFX_VIRTUAL(CAboutDlg)
    protected:
    virtual void DoDataExchange(CDataExchange* pDX);     // DDX/DDV support
    //}}AFX_VIRTUAL

// Implementation
protected:
    //{{AFX_MSG(CAboutDlg)
        // No message handlers
    //}}AFX_MSG
    DECLARE_MESSAGE_MAP()
};

CAboutDlg::CAboutDlg() : CDialog(CAboutDlg::IDD)
{
    //{{AFX_DATA_INIT(CAboutDlg)
    //}}AFX_DATA_INIT
}

void CAboutDlg::DoDataExchange(CDataExchange* pDX)
{
    CDialog::DoDataExchange(pDX);
    //{{AFX_DATA_MAP(CAboutDlg)
    //}}AFX_DATA_MAP
}

BEGIN_MESSAGE_MAP(CAboutDlg, CDialog)
    //{{AFX_MSG_MAP(CAboutDlg)
        // No message handlers
    //}}AFX_MSG_MAP
END_MESSAGE_MAP()

// App command to run the dialog
void CWandererApp::OnAppAbout()
{
    CAboutDlg aboutDlg;
    aboutDlg.DoModal();
}


/////////////////////////////////////////////////////////////////////////////
// CWandererApp message handlers
```

MainFrm.h

```
// MainFrm.h : interface of the CMainFrame class
//
///////////////////////////////////////////////////////////////////////
//

#if
!defined(AFX_MAINFRM_H__AE0A6FFE_9B0F_11D2_8E53_006008A82731__INCLUDED_)
#define  AFX_MAINFRM_H__AE0A6FFE_9B0F_11D2_8E53_006008A82731__INCLUDED_

#if _MSC_VER > 1000
#pragma once
#endif // _MSC_VER > 1000

class CMainFrame : public CFrameWnd
{

protected: // create from serialization only
    CMainFrame();
    DECLARE_DYNCREATE(CMainFrame)

// Attributes
public:

// Operations
public:

// Overrides
    // ClassWizard generated virtual function overrides
    //{{AFX_VIRTUAL(CMainFrame)
    public:
    virtual BOOL PreCreateWindow(CREATESTRUCT& cs);
    virtual BOOL OnCmdMsg(UINT nID, int nCode, void* pExtra,
        AFX_CMDHANDLERINFO* pHandlerInfo);
    protected:
    virtual BOOL OnCreateClient(LPCREATESTRUCT lpcs,
        CCreateContext* pContext);
    //}}AFX_VIRTUAL

// Implementation
public:
    virtual ~CMainFrame();
#ifdef _DEBUG
    virtual void AssertValid() const;
    virtual void Dump(CDumpContext& dc) const;
#endif
```

(continued)

Figure 11-8. *continued*

```
// Generated message map functions
protected:
    CSplitterWnd m_wndSplitter;
    //{{AFX_MSG(CMainFrame)
        // NOTE - the ClassWizard will add and remove member functions here.
        //     DO NOT EDIT what you see in these blocks of generated code!
    //}}AFX_MSG
    DECLARE_MESSAGE_MAP()
};


////////////////////////////////////////////////////////////////////////

//{{AFX_INSERT_LOCATION}}
// Microsoft Visual C++ will insert additional declarations immediately
// before the previous line.

#endif
//  !defined(AFX_MAINFRM_H__AE0A6FFE_9B0F_11D2_8E53_006008A82731__INCLUDED_)
```

MainFrm.cpp

```
// MainFrm.cpp : implementation of the CMainFrame class
//

#include "stdafx.h"
#include "Wanderer.h"
#include "WandererDoc.h"
#include "DriveView.h"
#include "FileView.h"
#include "MainFrm.h"

#ifdef _DEBUG
#define new DEBUG_NEW
#undef THIS_FILE
static char THIS_FILE[] = __FILE__;
#endif


////////////////////////////////////////////////////////////////////////
// CMainFrame

IMPLEMENT_DYNCREATE(CMainFrame, CFrameWnd)

BEGIN_MESSAGE_MAP(CMainFrame, CFrameWnd)
    //{{AFX_MSG_MAP(CMainFrame)
```

```
            // NOTE - the ClassWizard will add and remove mapping macros here.
            //      DO NOT EDIT what you see in these blocks of generated code !
        //}}AFX_MSG_MAP
    END_MESSAGE_MAP()


    /////////////////////////////////////////////////////////////////////////
    // CMainFrame construction/destruction

    CMainFrame::CMainFrame()
    {
    }


    CMainFrame::~CMainFrame()
    {
    }


    BOOL CMainFrame::PreCreateWindow(CREATESTRUCT& cs)
    {
        if( !CFrameWnd::PreCreateWindow(cs) )
            return FALSE;

        cs.style &= ~FWS_ADDTOTITLE;
        return TRUE;
    }


    /////////////////////////////////////////////////////////////////////////
    // CMainFrame diagnostics

    #ifdef _DEBUG
    void CMainFrame::AssertValid() const
    {
        CFrameWnd::AssertValid();
    }


    void CMainFrame::Dump(CDumpContext& dc) const
    {
        CFrameWnd::Dump(dc);
    }


    #endif //_DEBUG

    /////////////////////////////////////////////////////////////////////////
    // CMainFrame message handlers


    BOOL CMainFrame::OnCreateClient(LPCREATESTRUCT lpcs,
        CCreateContext* pContext)
```

(continued)

Figure 11-8. *continued*

```
{
    //
    // Note: Create the CFileView first so the CDriveView's OnInitialUpdate
    // function can call OnUpdate on the CFileView.
    //
    if (!m_wndSplitter.CreateStatic (this, 1, 2) ||
        !m_wndSplitter.CreateView (0, 1, RUNTIME_CLASS
            (CFileView), CSize (0, 0), pContext) ||
        !m_wndSplitter.CreateView (0, 0, RUNTIME_CLASS (CDriveView),
            CSize (192, 0), pContext))
        return FALSE;

    return TRUE;
}

BOOL CMainFrame::OnCmdMsg(UINT nID, int nCode, void* pExtra,
    AFX_CMDHANDLERINFO* pHandlerInfo)
{
    //
    // Route to standard command targets first.
    //
    if (CFrameWnd::OnCmdMsg (nID, nCode, pExtra, pHandlerInfo))
        return TRUE;

    //
    // Route to inactive views second.
    //
    CWandererDoc* pDoc = (CWandererDoc*) GetActiveDocument ();
    if (pDoc != NULL) { // Important!
        return pDoc->RouteCmdToAllViews (GetActiveView (),
            nID, nCode, pExtra, pHandlerInfo);
    }
    return FALSE;
}
```

WandererDoc.h

```
// WandererDoc.h : interface of the CWandererDoc class
//
//////////////////////////////////////////////////////////////////////////
//

#if
!defined(AFX_WANDERERDOC_H__AE0A7000_9B0F_11D2_8E53_006008A82731__INCLUDED_)
#define  AFX_WANDERERDOC_H__AE0A7000_9B0F_11D2_8E53_006008A82731__INCLUDED_
```

```
#if _MSC_VER > 1000
#pragma once
#endif // _MSC_VER > 1000


class CWandererDoc : public CDocument
{
protected: // create from serialization only
    CWandererDoc();
    DECLARE_DYNCREATE(CWandererDoc)

// Attributes
public:

// Operations
public:

// Overrides
    // ClassWizard generated virtual function overrides
    //{{AFX_VIRTUAL(CWandererDoc)
    public:
    virtual BOOL OnNewDocument();
    virtual void Serialize(CArchive& ar);
    //}}AFX_VIRTUAL

// Implementation
public:
    BOOL RouteCmdToAllViews (CView* pView, UINT nID, int nCode,
        void* pExtra, AFX_CMDHANDLERINFO* pHandlerInfo);
    virtual ~CWandererDoc();
#ifdef _DEBUG
    virtual void AssertValid() const;
    virtual void Dump(CDumpContext& dc) const;
#endif

protected:

// Generated message map functions
protected:
    //{{AFX_MSG(CWandererDoc)
        // NOTE - the ClassWizard will add and remove member functions here.
        //    DO NOT EDIT what you see in these blocks of generated code !
    //}}AFX_MSG
    DECLARE_MESSAGE_MAP()
};
```

(continued)

Figure 11-8. *continued*

```
//////////////////////////////////////////////////////////////////////

//{{AFX_INSERT_LOCATION}}
// Microsoft Visual C++ will insert additional declarations immediately
// before the previous line.

#endif
// !defined(
//      AFX_WANDERERDOC_H__AE0A7000_9B0F_11D2_8E53_006008A82731__INCLUDED_)
```

WandererDoc.cpp

```cpp
// WandererDoc.cpp : implementation of the CWandererDoc class
//

#include "stdafx.h"
#include "Wanderer.h"

#include "WandererDoc.h"

#ifdef _DEBUG
#define new DEBUG_NEW
#undef THIS_FILE
static char THIS_FILE[] = __FILE__;
#endif

//////////////////////////////////////////////////////////////////////
// CWandererDoc

IMPLEMENT_DYNCREATE(CWandererDoc, CDocument)

BEGIN_MESSAGE_MAP(CWandererDoc, CDocument)
    //{{AFX_MSG_MAP(CWandererDoc)
        // NOTE - the ClassWizard will add and remove mapping macros here.
        //     DO NOT EDIT what you see in these blocks of generated code!
    //}}AFX_MSG_MAP
END_MESSAGE_MAP()

//////////////////////////////////////////////////////////////////////
// CWandererDoc construction/destruction

CWandererDoc::CWandererDoc()
{
}
```

```
CWandererDoc::~CWandererDoc()
{
}


BOOL CWandererDoc::OnNewDocument()
{
    if (!CDocument::OnNewDocument())
        return FALSE;
    return TRUE;
}


/////////////////////////////////////////////////////////////////////////
// CWandererDoc serialization

void CWandererDoc::Serialize(CArchive& ar)
{
    if (ar.IsStoring())
    {
        // TODO: add storing code here
    }
    else
    {
        // TODO: add loading code here
    }
}


/////////////////////////////////////////////////////////////////////////
// CWandererDoc diagnostics

#ifdef _DEBUG
void CWandererDoc::AssertValid() const
{
    CDocument::AssertValid();
}


void CWandererDoc::Dump(CDumpContext& dc) const
{
    CDocument::Dump(dc);
}
#endif //_DEBUG


/////////////////////////////////////////////////////////////////////////
// CWandererDoc commands

BOOL CWandererDoc::RouteCmdToAllViews(CView *pView, UINT nID, int nCode,
    void *pExtra, AFX_CMDHANDLERINFO *pHandlerInfo)
```

(continued)

677

Figure 11-8. *continued*

```
{
    POSITION pos = GetFirstViewPosition ();

    while (pos != NULL) {
        CView* pNextView = GetNextView (pos);
        if (pNextView != pView) {
            if (pNextView->OnCmdMsg (nID, nCode, pExtra, pHandlerInfo))
                return TRUE;
        }
    }
    return FALSE;
}
```

DriveView.h

```
// DriveTreeView.h : interface of the CDriveView class
//
//////////////////////////////////////////////////////////////////////////////

#if
!defined(AFX_DRIVETREEVIEW_H__090B382D_959D_11D2_8E53_006008A82731__INCLUDED_)
#define  AFX_DRIVETREEVIEW_H__090B382D_959D_11D2_8E53_006008A82731__INCLUDED_

#if _MSC_VER > 1000
#pragma once
#endif // _MSC_VER > 1000


class CDriveView : public CTreeView
{
protected: // create from serialization only
    CDriveView();
    DECLARE_DYNCREATE(CDriveView)

// Attributes
public:
    CWandererDoc* GetDocument();

// Operations
public:
```

```
// Overrides
    // ClassWizard generated virtual function overrides
    //{{AFX_VIRTUAL(CDriveView)
    public:
    virtual void OnDraw(CDC* pDC);  // overridden to draw this view
    virtual BOOL PreCreateWindow(CREATESTRUCT& cs);
    protected:
    virtual void OnInitialUpdate(); // called first time after construct
    //}}AFX_VIRTUAL

// Implementation
public:
    virtual ~CDriveView();
#ifdef _DEBUG
    virtual void AssertValid() const;
    virtual void Dump(CDumpContext& dc) const;
#endif

protected:

// Generated message map functions
protected:
    BOOL AddDriveItem (LPCTSTR pszDrive);
    int AddDirectories (HTREEITEM hItem, LPCTSTR pszPath);
    void DeleteAllChildren (HTREEITEM hItem);
    void DeleteFirstChild (HTREEITEM hItem);
    CString GetPathFromItem (HTREEITEM hItem);
    BOOL SetButtonState (HTREEITEM hItem, LPCTSTR pszPath);
    int AddDrives ();
    CImageList m_ilDrives;
    //{{AFX_MSG(CDriveView)
    afx_msg void OnItemExpanding(NMHDR* pNMHDR, LRESULT* pResult);
    afx_msg void OnSelectionChanged(NMHDR* pNMHDR, LRESULT* pResult);
    //}}AFX_MSG
    DECLARE_MESSAGE_MAP()
};

#ifndef _DEBUG  // debug version in DriveTreeView.cpp
inline CWandererDoc* CDriveView::GetDocument()
    { return (CWandererDoc*)m_pDocument; }
#endif
```

(continued)

Figure 11-8. *continued*

```
//////////////////////////////////////////////////////////////////////

//{{AFX_INSERT_LOCATION}}
// Microsoft Visual C++ will insert additional declarations immediately
// before the previous line.

#endif
// !defined(
//
AFX_DRIVETREEVIEW_H__090B382D_959D_11D2_8E53_006008A82731__INCLUDED_)
```

DriveView.cpp

```cpp
// DriveTreeView.cpp : implementation of the CDriveView class
//

#include "stdafx.h"
#include "Wanderer.h"

#include "WandererDoc.h"
#include "DriveView.h"

#ifdef _DEBUG
#define new DEBUG_NEW
#undef THIS_FILE
static char THIS_FILE[] = __FILE__;
#endif

// Image indexes
#define ILI_HARD_DISK       0
#define ILI_FLOPPY          1
#define ILI_CD_ROM          2
#define ILI_NET_DRIVE       3
#define ILI_CLOSED_FOLDER   4
#define ILI_OPEN_FOLDER     5


//////////////////////////////////////////////////////////////////////
// CDriveView

IMPLEMENT_DYNCREATE(CDriveView, CTreeView)

BEGIN_MESSAGE_MAP(CDriveView, CTreeView)
    //{{AFX_MSG_MAP(CDriveView)
    ON_NOTIFY_REFLECT(TVN_ITEMEXPANDING, OnItemExpanding)
```

```
        ON_NOTIFY_REFLECT(TVN_SELCHANGED, OnSelectionChanged)
    //}}AFX_MSG_MAP
END_MESSAGE_MAP()


/////////////////////////////////////////////////////////////////////////////
// CDriveView construction/destruction

CDriveView::CDriveView()
{
}


CDriveView::~CDriveView()
{
}   .


BOOL CDriveView::PreCreateWindow(CREATESTRUCT& cs)
{
    if (!CTreeView::PreCreateWindow (cs))
        return FALSE;

    cs.style |= TVS_HASLINES | TVS_LINESATROOT | TVS_HASBUTTONS |
        TVS_SHOWSELALWAYS;
    return TRUE;
}


/////////////////////////////////////////////////////////////////////////////
// CDriveView drawing

void CDriveView::OnDraw(CDC* pDC)
{
    CWandererDoc* pDoc = GetDocument();
    ASSERT_VALID(pDoc);
}

void CDriveView::OnInitialUpdate()
{
    CTreeView::OnInitialUpdate();

    //
    // Initialize the image list.
    //
    m_ilDrives.Create (IDB_DRIVEIMAGES, 16, 1, RGB (255, 0, 255));
    GetTreeCtrl ().SetImageList (&m_ilDrives, TVSIL_NORMAL);

    //
    // Populate the tree view with drive items.
    //
```

(continued)

Figure 11-8. *continued*

```
    AddDrives ();

    //
    // Show the folders on the current drive.
    //
    TCHAR szPath[MAX_PATH];
    ::GetCurrentDirectory (sizeof (szPath) / sizeof (TCHAR), szPath);
    CString strPath = szPath;
    strPath = strPath.Left (3);

    HTREEITEM hItem = GetTreeCtrl ().GetNextItem (NULL, TVGN_ROOT);
    while (hItem != NULL) {
        if (GetTreeCtrl ().GetItemText (hItem) == strPath)
            break;
        hItem = GetTreeCtrl ().GetNextSiblingItem (hItem);
    }

    if (hItem != NULL) {
        GetTreeCtrl ().Expand (hItem, TVE_EXPAND);
        GetTreeCtrl ().Select (hItem, TVGN_CARET);
    }

    //
    // Initialize the list view.
    //
    strPath = GetPathFromItem (GetTreeCtrl ().GetSelectedItem ());
    GetDocument ()->UpdateAllViews (this, 0x5A,
        (CObject*) (LPCTSTR) strPath);
}

/////////////////////////////////////////////////////////////////////////
// CDriveView diagnostics

#ifdef _DEBUG
void CDriveView::AssertValid() const
{
    CTreeView::AssertValid();
}

void CDriveView::Dump(CDumpContext& dc) const
{
    CTreeView::Dump(dc);
}
```

```
CWandererDoc* CDriveView::GetDocument() // non-debug version is inline
{
    ASSERT(m_pDocument->IsKindOf(RUNTIME_CLASS(CWandererDoc)));
    return (CWandererDoc*)m_pDocument;
}
#endif //_DEBUG

/////////////////////////////////////////////////////////////////////////////
// CDriveView message handlers

int CDriveView::AddDrives()
{
    int nPos = 0;
    int nDrivesAdded = 0;
    CString string = _T ("?:\\");

    DWORD dwDriveList = ::GetLogicalDrives ();

    while (dwDriveList) {
        if (dwDriveList & 1) {
            string.SetAt (0, _T ('A') + nPos);
            if (AddDriveItem (string))
                nDrivesAdded++;
        }
        dwDriveList >>= 1;
        nPos++;
    }
    return nDrivesAdded;
}

BOOL CDriveView::AddDriveItem(LPCTSTR pszDrive)
{
    CString string;
    HTREEITEM hItem;

    UINT nType = ::GetDriveType (pszDrive);

    switch (nType) {

    case DRIVE_REMOVABLE:
        hItem = GetTreeCtrl ().InsertItem (pszDrive, ILI_FLOPPY,
            ILI_FLOPPY);
        GetTreeCtrl ().InsertItem (_T (""), ILI_CLOSED_FOLDER,
            ILI_CLOSED_FOLDER, hItem);
        break;
```

(continued)

Figure 11-8. *continued*

```
    case DRIVE_FIXED:
    case DRIVE_RAMDISK:
        hItem = GetTreeCtrl ().InsertItem (pszDrive, ILI_HARD_DISK,
            ILI_HARD_DISK);
        SetButtonState (hItem, pszDrive);
        break;

    case DRIVE_REMOTE:
        hItem = GetTreeCtrl ().InsertItem (pszDrive, ILI_NET_DRIVE,
            ILI_NET_DRIVE);
        SetButtonState (hItem, pszDrive);
        break;

    case DRIVE_CDROM:
        hItem = GetTreeCtrl ().InsertItem (pszDrive, ILI_CD_ROM,
            ILI_CD_ROM);
        GetTreeCtrl ().InsertItem (_T (""), ILI_CLOSED_FOLDER,
            ILI_CLOSED_FOLDER, hItem);
        break;

    default:
        return FALSE;
    }
    return TRUE;
}

BOOL CDriveView::SetButtonState(HTREEITEM hItem, LPCTSTR pszPath)
{
    HANDLE hFind;
    WIN32_FIND_DATA fd;
    BOOL bResult = FALSE;

    CString strPath = pszPath;
    if (strPath.Right (1) != _T ("\\"))
        strPath += _T ("\\");
    strPath += _T ("*.*");

    if ((hFind = ::FindFirstFile (strPath, &fd)) == INVALID_HANDLE_VALUE)
        return bResult;

    do {
        if (fd.dwFileAttributes & FILE_ATTRIBUTE_DIRECTORY) {
            CString strComp = (LPCTSTR) &fd.cFileName;
```

```
                if ((strComp != _T (".")) && (strComp != _T (".."))) {
                    GetTreeCtrl ().InsertItem (_T (""), ILI_CLOSED_FOLDER,
                        ILI_CLOSED_FOLDER, hItem);
                    bResult = TRUE;
                    break;
                }
            }
        } while (::FindNextFile (hFind, &fd));

    ::FindClose (hFind);
    return bResult;
}

void CDriveView::OnItemExpanding(NMHDR* pNMHDR, LRESULT* pResult)
{
    NM_TREEVIEW* pNMTreeView = (NM_TREEVIEW*)pNMHDR;
    HTREEITEM hItem = pNMTreeView->itemNew.hItem;
    CString string = GetPathFromItem (hItem);

    *pResult = FALSE;

    if (pNMTreeView->action == TVE_EXPAND) {
        DeleteFirstChild (hItem);
        if (AddDirectories (hItem, string) == 0)
            *pResult = TRUE;
    }
    else { // pNMTreeView->action == TVE_COLLAPSE
        DeleteAllChildren (hItem);
        if (GetTreeCtrl ().GetParentItem (hItem) == NULL)
            GetTreeCtrl ().InsertItem (_T (""), ILI_CLOSED_FOLDER,
                ILI_CLOSED_FOLDER, hItem);
        else
            SetButtonState (hItem, string);
    }
}

CString CDriveView::GetPathFromItem(HTREEITEM hItem)
{
    CString strResult = GetTreeCtrl ().GetItemText (hItem);

    HTREEITEM hParent;
    while ((hParent = GetTreeCtrl ().GetParentItem (hItem)) != NULL) {
        CString string = GetTreeCtrl ().GetItemText (hParent);
```

(continued)

Figure 11-8. *continued*

```
        if (string.Right (1) != _T ("\\"))
            string += _T ("\\");
        strResult = string + strResult;
        hItem = hParent;
    }
    return strResult;
}

void CDriveView::DeleteFirstChild(HTREEITEM hItem)
{
    HTREEITEM hChildItem;
    if ((hChildItem = GetTreeCtrl ().GetChildItem (hItem)) != NULL)
        GetTreeCtrl ().DeleteItem (hChildItem);
}

void CDriveView::DeleteAllChildren(HTREEITEM hItem)
{
    HTREEITEM hChildItem;
    if ((hChildItem = GetTreeCtrl ().GetChildItem (hItem)) == NULL)
        return;

    do {
        HTREEITEM hNextItem =
            GetTreeCtrl ().GetNextSiblingItem (hChildItem);
        GetTreeCtrl ().DeleteItem (hChildItem);
        hChildItem = hNextItem;
    } while (hChildItem != NULL);
}

int CDriveView::AddDirectories(HTREEITEM hItem, LPCTSTR pszPath)
{
    HANDLE hFind;
    WIN32_FIND_DATA fd;
    HTREEITEM hNewItem;

    int nCount = 0;

    CString strPath = pszPath;
    if (strPath.Right (1) != _T ("\\"))
        strPath += _T ("\\");
    strPath += _T ("*.*");

    if ((hFind = ::FindFirstFile (strPath, &fd)) == INVALID_HANDLE_VALUE) {
        if (GetTreeCtrl ().GetParentItem (hItem) == NULL)
            GetTreeCtrl ().InsertItem (_T (""), ILI_CLOSED_FOLDER,
                ILI_CLOSED_FOLDER, hItem);
        return 0;
    }
```

```
    do {
        if (fd.dwFileAttributes & FILE_ATTRIBUTE_DIRECTORY) {
            CString strComp = (LPCTSTR) &fd.cFileName;
            if ((strComp != _T (".")) && (strComp != _T (".."))) {
                hNewItem =
                    GetTreeCtrl ().InsertItem ((LPCTSTR) &fd.cFileName,
                    ILI_CLOSED_FOLDER, ILI_OPEN_FOLDER, hItem);

                CString strNewPath = pszPath;
                if (strNewPath.Right (1) != _T ("\\"))
                    strNewPath += _T ("\\");

                strNewPath += (LPCTSTR) &fd.cFileName;
                SetButtonState (hNewItem, strNewPath);
                nCount++;
            }
        }
    } while (::FindNextFile (hFind, &fd));

    ::FindClose (hFind);
    return nCount;
}

void CDriveView::OnSelectionChanged(NMHDR* pNMHDR, LRESULT* pResult)
{
    NM_TREEVIEW* pNMTreeView = (NM_TREEVIEW*) pNMHDR;
    CString strPath = GetPathFromItem (pNMTreeView->itemNew.hItem);
    GetDocument ()->UpdateAllViews (this, 0x5A,
        (CObject*) (LPCTSTR) strPath);
    *pResult = 0;
}
```

FileView.h

```
// FileView.h : interface of the CFileView class
//
//////////////////////////////////////////////////////////////////////
//

#if
!defined(AFX_FILEVIEW_H__18BD7B80_95C6_11D2_8E53_006008A82731__INCLUDED_)
#define AFX_FILEVIEW_H__18BD7B80_95C6_11D2_8E53_006008A82731__INCLUDED_

#if _MSC_VER > 1000
#pragma once
#endif // _MSC_VER > 1000
```

(continued)

Figure 11-8. *continued*

```
typedef struct tagITEMINFO {
    CString     strFileName;
    DWORD       nFileSizeLow;
    FILETIME    ftLastWriteTime;
} ITEMINFO;

class CFileView : public CListView
{
protected: // create from serialization only
    CFileView();
    DECLARE_DYNCREATE(CFileView)

// Attributes
public:
    CWandererDoc* GetDocument();

// Operations
public:
    static int CALLBACK CompareFunc (LPARAM lParam1, LPARAM lParam2,
        LPARAM lParamSort);

// Overrides
    // ClassWizard generated virtual function overrides
    //{{AFX_VIRTUAL(CFileView)
    public:
    virtual void OnDraw(CDC* pDC);  // overridden to draw this view
    virtual BOOL PreCreateWindow(CREATESTRUCT& cs);
    protected:
    virtual void OnInitialUpdate(); // called first time after construct
    virtual void OnUpdate(CView* pSender, LPARAM lHint, CObject* pHint);
    //}}AFX_VIRTUAL

// Implementation
public:
    int Refresh (LPCTSTR pszPath);
    virtual ~CFileView();
#ifdef _DEBUG
    virtual void AssertValid() const;
    virtual void Dump(CDumpContext& dc) const;
#endif

protected:

// Generated message map functions
protected:
    CString m_strPath;
    void FreeItemMemory ();
```

```
        BOOL AddItem (int nIndex, WIN32_FIND_DATA* pfd);
        CImageList m_ilSmall;
        CImageList m_ilLarge;
        //{{AFX_MSG(CFileView)
        afx_msg void OnDestroy();
        afx_msg void OnGetDispInfo(NMHDR* pNMHDR, LRESULT* pResult);
        afx_msg void OnColumnClick(NMHDR* pNMHDR, LRESULT* pResult);
        afx_msg void OnViewLargeIcons();
        afx_msg void OnViewSmallIcons();
        afx_msg void OnViewList();
        afx_msg void OnViewDetails();
        afx_msg void OnUpdateViewLargeIcons(CCmdUI* pCmdUI);
        afx_msg void OnUpdateViewSmallIcons(CCmdUI* pCmdUI);
        afx_msg void OnUpdateViewList(CCmdUI* pCmdUI);
        afx_msg void OnUpdateViewDetails(CCmdUI* pCmdUI);
        //}}AFX_MSG
        DECLARE_MESSAGE_MAP()
};

#ifndef _DEBUG  // debug version in FileView.cpp
inline CWandererDoc* CFileView::GetDocument()
    { return (CWandererDoc*)m_pDocument; }
#endif

////////////////////////////////////////////////////////////////////////////

//{{AFX_INSERT_LOCATION}}
// Microsoft Visual C++ will insert additional declarations immediately
// before the previous line.

#endif
//
!defined(AFX_FILEVIEW_H__18BD7B80_95C6_11D2_8E53_006008A82731__INCLUDED_)
```

FileView.cpp

```
// FileView.cpp : implementation of the CFileView class
//

#include "stdafx.h"
#include "Wanderer.h"
#include "WandererDoc.h"
#include "FileView.h"
```

(continued)

Figure 11-8. *continued*

```
#ifdef _DEBUG
#define new DEBUG_NEW
#undef THIS_FILE
static char THIS_FILE[] = __FILE__;
#endif


/////////////////////////////////////////////////////////////////////////////
// CFileView

IMPLEMENT_DYNCREATE(CFileView, CListView)

BEGIN_MESSAGE_MAP(CFileView, CListView)
    //{{AFX_MSG_MAP(CFileView)
    ON_WM_DESTROY()
    ON_NOTIFY_REFLECT(LVN_GETDISPINFO, OnGetDispInfo)
    ON_NOTIFY_REFLECT(LVN_COLUMNCLICK, OnColumnClick)
    ON_COMMAND(ID_VIEW_LARGE_ICONS, OnViewLargeIcons)
    ON_COMMAND(ID_VIEW_SMALL_ICONS, OnViewSmallIcons)
    ON_COMMAND(ID_VIEW_LIST, OnViewList)
    ON_COMMAND(ID_VIEW_DETAILS, OnViewDetails)
    ON_UPDATE_COMMAND_UI(ID_VIEW_LARGE_ICONS, OnUpdateViewLargeIcons)
    ON_UPDATE_COMMAND_UI(ID_VIEW_SMALL_ICONS, OnUpdateViewSmallIcons)
    ON_UPDATE_COMMAND_UI(ID_VIEW_LIST, OnUpdateViewList)
    ON_UPDATE_COMMAND_UI(ID_VIEW_DETAILS, OnUpdateViewDetails)
    //}}AFX_MSG_MAP
END_MESSAGE_MAP()


/////////////////////////////////////////////////////////////////////////////
// CFileView construction/destruction

CFileView::CFileView()
{
}


CFileView::~CFileView()
{
}


BOOL CFileView::PreCreateWindow(CREATESTRUCT& cs)
{
    if (!CListView::PreCreateWindow (cs))
        return FALSE;

    cs.style &= ~LVS_TYPEMASK;
    cs.style |= LVS_REPORT;
    return TRUE;
}
```

```
/////////////////////////////////////////////////////////////////////////
// CFileView drawing

void CFileView::OnDraw(CDC* pDC)
{
    CWandererDoc* pDoc = GetDocument();
    ASSERT_VALID(pDoc);
    // TODO: add draw code for native data here
}


void CFileView::OnInitialUpdate()
{
    CListView::OnInitialUpdate();

    //
    // Initialize the image list.
    //
    m_ilLarge.Create (IDB_LARGEDOC, 32, 1, RGB (255, 0, 255));
    m_ilSmall.Create (IDB_SMALLDOC, 16, 1, RGB (255, 0, 255));

    GetListCtrl ().SetImageList (&m_ilLarge, LVSIL_NORMAL);
    GetListCtrl ().SetImageList (&m_ilSmall, LVSIL_SMALL);

    //
    // Add columns to the list view.
    //
    GetListCtrl ().InsertColumn (0, _T ("File Name"), LVCFMT_LEFT, 192);
    GetListCtrl ().InsertColumn (1, _T ("Size"), LVCFMT_RIGHT, 96);
    GetListCtrl ().InsertColumn (2, _T ("Last Modified"), LVCFMT_CENTER,
        128);

    //
    // Populate the list view with items.
    //
    TCHAR szPath[MAX_PATH];
    ::GetCurrentDirectory (sizeof (szPath) / sizeof (TCHAR), szPath);
    Refresh (szPath);
}


/////////////////////////////////////////////////////////////////////////
// CFileView diagnostics

#ifdef _DEBUG
void CFileView::AssertValid() const
{
    CListView::AssertValid();
}
```

(continued)

Figure 11-8. *continued*

```
void CFileView::Dump(CDumpContext& dc) const
{
    CListView::Dump(dc);
}

CWandererDoc* CFileView::GetDocument() // non-debug version is inline
{
    ASSERT(m_pDocument->IsKindOf(RUNTIME_CLASS(CWandererDoc)));
    return (CWandererDoc*)m_pDocument;
}
#endif //_DEBUG

/////////////////////////////////////////////////////////////////////////////
// CFileView message handlers

int CFileView::Refresh(LPCTSTR pszPath)
{
    CString strPath = pszPath;
    if (strPath.Right (1) != _T ("\\"))
        strPath += _T ("\\");
    strPath += _T ("*.*");

    HANDLE hFind;
    WIN32_FIND_DATA fd;
    int nCount = 0;

    if ((hFind = ::FindFirstFile (strPath, &fd)) != INVALID_HANDLE_VALUE) {
        //
        // Delete existing items (if any).
        //
        GetListCtrl ().DeleteAllItems ();

        //
        // Show the path name in the frame window's title bar.
        //
        TCHAR szFullPath[MAX_PATH];
        ::GetFullPathName (pszPath, sizeof (szFullPath) / sizeof (TCHAR),
            szFullPath, NULL);
        m_strPath = szFullPath;

        CString strTitle = _T ("WinDir - ");
        strTitle += szFullPath;
        AfxGetMainWnd ()->SetWindowText (strTitle);

        //
        // Add items representing files to the list view.
        //
```

```
            if (!(fd.dwFileAttributes & FILE_ATTRIBUTE_DIRECTORY))
                AddItem (nCount++, &fd);

            while (::FindNextFile (hFind, &fd)) {
                if (!(fd.dwFileAttributes & FILE_ATTRIBUTE_DIRECTORY))
                    if (!AddItem (nCount++, &fd))
                        break;
            }
            ::FindClose (hFind);
        }
        return nCount;
}

BOOL CFileView::AddItem(int nIndex, WIN32_FIND_DATA *pfd)
{
    //
    // Allocate a new ITEMINFO structure and initialize it with information
    // about the item.
    //
    ITEMINFO* pItem;
    try {
        pItem = new ITEMINFO;
    }
    catch (CMemoryException* e) {
        e->Delete ();
        return FALSE;
    }

    pItem->strFileName = pfd->cFileName;
    pItem->nFileSizeLow = pfd->nFileSizeLow;
    pItem->ftLastWriteTime = pfd->ftLastWriteTime;

    //
    // Add the item to the list view.
    //
    LV_ITEM lvi;
    lvi.mask = LVIF_TEXT | LVIF_IMAGE | LVIF_PARAM;
    lvi.iItem = nIndex;
    lvi.iSubItem = 0;
    lvi.iImage = 0;
    lvi.pszText = LPSTR_TEXTCALLBACK;
    lvi.lParam = (LPARAM) pItem;

    if (GetListCtrl ().InsertItem (&lvi) == -1)
        return FALSE;

    return TRUE;
}
```

(continued)

Figure 11-8. *continued*

```
void CFileView::FreeItemMemory()
{
    int nCount = GetListCtrl ().GetItemCount ();
    if (nCount) {
        for (int i=0; i<nCount; i++)
            delete (ITEMINFO*) GetListCtrl ().GetItemData (i);
    }
}

void CFileView::OnDestroy()
{
    FreeItemMemory ();
    CListView::OnDestroy ();
}

void CFileView::OnGetDispInfo(NMHDR* pNMHDR, LRESULT* pResult)
{
    CString string;
    LV_DISPINFO* pDispInfo = (LV_DISPINFO*) pNMHDR;

    if (pDispInfo->item.mask & LVIF_TEXT) {
        ITEMINFO* pItem = (ITEMINFO*) pDispInfo->item.lParam;

        switch (pDispInfo->item.iSubItem) {

        case 0: // File name
            ::lstrcpy (pDispInfo->item.pszText, pItem->strFileName);
            break;

        case 1: // File size
            string.Format (_T ("%u"), pItem->nFileSizeLow);
            ::lstrcpy (pDispInfo->item.pszText, string);
            break;

        case 2: // Date and time
            CTime time (pItem->ftLastWriteTime);

            BOOL pm = FALSE;
            int nHour = time.GetHour ();
            if (nHour == 0)
                nHour = 12;
            else if (nHour == 12)
                pm = TRUE;
            else if (nHour > 12) {
                nHour -= 12;
                pm = TRUE;
            }
```

```
            string.Format (_T ("%d/%0.2d/%0.2d (%d:%0.2d%c)"),
                time.GetMonth (), time.GetDay (), time.GetYear () % 100,
                nHour, time.GetMinute (), pm ? _T ('p') : _T ('a'));
            ::lstrcpy (pDispInfo->item.pszText, string);
            break;
        }
    }
    *pResult = 0;
}

void CFileView::OnColumnClick(NMHDR* pNMHDR, LRESULT* pResult)
{
    NM_LISTVIEW* pNMListView = (NM_LISTVIEW*) pNMHDR;
    GetListCtrl ().SortItems (CompareFunc, pNMListView->iSubItem);
    *pResult = 0;
}

int CALLBACK CFileView::CompareFunc (LPARAM lParam1, LPARAM lParam2,
    LPARAM lParamSort)
{
    ITEMINFO* pItem1 = (ITEMINFO*) lParam1;
    ITEMINFO* pItem2 = (ITEMINFO*) lParam2;
    int nResult;

    switch (lParamSort) {

    case 0: // File name
        nResult = pItem1->strFileName.CompareNoCase (pItem2->strFileName);
        break;

    case 1: // File size
        nResult = pItem1->nFileSizeLow - pItem2->nFileSizeLow;
        break;

    case 2: // Date and time
        nResult = ::CompareFileTime (&pItem1->ftLastWriteTime,
            &pItem2->ftLastWriteTime);
        break;
    }
    return nResult;
}

void CFileView::OnViewLargeIcons()
{
    ModifyStyle (LVS_TYPEMASK, LVS_ICON);
}
```

(continued)

Figure 11-8. *continued*

```
void CFileView::OnViewSmallIcons()
{
    ModifyStyle (LVS_TYPEMASK, LVS_SMALLICON);
}

void CFileView::OnViewList()
{
    ModifyStyle (LVS_TYPEMASK, LVS_LIST);
}

void CFileView::OnViewDetails()
{
    ModifyStyle (LVS_TYPEMASK, LVS_REPORT);
}

void CFileView::OnUpdateViewLargeIcons(CCmdUI* pCmdUI)
{
    DWORD dwCurrentStyle = GetStyle () & LVS_TYPEMASK;
    pCmdUI->SetRadio (dwCurrentStyle == LVS_ICON);
}

void CFileView::OnUpdateViewSmallIcons(CCmdUI* pCmdUI)
{
    DWORD dwCurrentStyle = GetStyle () & LVS_TYPEMASK;
    pCmdUI->SetRadio (dwCurrentStyle == LVS_SMALLICON);
}

void CFileView::OnUpdateViewList(CCmdUI* pCmdUI)
{
    DWORD dwCurrentStyle = GetStyle () & LVS_TYPEMASK;
    pCmdUI->SetRadio (dwCurrentStyle == LVS_LIST);
}

void CFileView::OnUpdateViewDetails(CCmdUI* pCmdUI)
{
    DWORD dwCurrentStyle = GetStyle () & LVS_TYPEMASK;
    pCmdUI->SetRadio (dwCurrentStyle == LVS_REPORT);
}

void CFileView::OnUpdate(CView* pSender, LPARAM lHint, CObject* pHint)
{
    if (lHint == 0x5A) {
        FreeItemMemory ();
        GetListCtrl ().DeleteAllItems ();
        Refresh ((LPCTSTR) pHint);
        return;
    }
    CListView::OnUpdate (pSender, lHint, pHint);
}
```

I created Wanderer by using AppWizard to generate the source code for a standard SDI document/view application, plugging in Chapter 10's *CDriveView* and *CFileView* classes and modifying them as described above, adding a *CSplitterWnd* member variable to *CMainFrame*, overriding *OnCreateClient*, and inserting calls *CreateStatic* and *CreateView*. However, there is another way to create Explorer-like applications. If you select Windows Explorer instead of MFC Standard in AppWizard's Step 5 dialog box (shown in Figure 11-9), AppWizard adds code to create a static splitter window. It also derives a pair of view classes—one from *CTreeView*, the other from *CListView* or the view class of your choice—and places them in the splitter window's panes. Unfortunately, the AppWizard-generated view classes add little to the base classes from which they derive, so while AppWizard will get you started, you still have to write a fair amount of code to create an Explorer-type application.

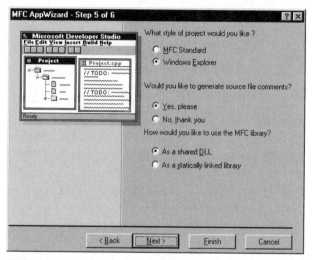

Figure 11-9. *Using AppWizard to create an Explorer-style application.*

Despite the outward similarities between Wanderer and the Windows Explorer, there is a fundamental difference between these applications that goes well beyond their feature lists. Wanderer is a *file browser* that displays drive, directory, and file names. Explorer is a *namespace browser* that serves as a virtual window into the shell's namespace. You can see how the shell's namespace is structured and what kinds of objects it includes by studying the left pane of an Explorer window. The desktop object sits at the uppermost level of the hierarchy, followed by My Computer, Network Neighborhood, and Recycle Bin at the next level, drives at the level beneath that, and so on. Drives, directories, and files are merely a subset of the shell's namespace. The namespace also includes printers, printer folders, and other objects for which there are no direct analogues in the file system. The operating system shell supports a set of API functions all its own that applications can use to access its namespace. Some are conventional API functions with names such as *::SHGetDesktopFolder*; others are COM functions accessed through *IShellFolder* interfaces. For more information, search MSDN for articles on the shell's namespace.

Custom Command Routing

As you already know, MFC's *CFrameWnd* class routes the command messages and user interface (UI) update messages it receives to other objects so that the frame window doesn't have to process commands from menu items and other UI objects. Thanks to command routing, events involving menu items and toolbar buttons can be handled just as easily in the application class, the document class, or the view class as they can in the frame window class. Chapter 9 described the command routing mechanism, and Figure 9-2 documented the path a command or a UI update message follows after an SDI frame window receives it. The active view sees the message first, followed by the document, the document template, the frame window, and finally the application object. For most document/view applications, the command routing sequence depicted in Figure 9-2 is adequate because it gives each object that's likely to want to see a command or an update message a crack at processing it.

Every now and then you'll run into an application for which default command routing isn't sufficient. Wanderer is one of them, and here's why. Commands and UI updates for the view items in Wanderer's View menu are processed in the *CFileView* class. When *CFileView* is the active view, its command and update handlers work just fine because the active view is included in the framework's routing list. But when *CDriveView* is the active view, *CFileView* isn't notified of events involving View commands because it's not the active view. Consequently, the commands in the Options menu are grayed out and can't be selected when the *CDriveView* in the left pane has the input focus.

To circumvent this problem, Wanderer modifies the command routing sequence so that command and update messages that aren't handled by any of the standard command targets are routed to inactive views. The work is done in *CMainFrame::OnCmdMsg*, which first forwards command and update messages to the standard command targets by calling *CFrameWnd::OnCmdMsg*:

```
if (CFrameWnd::OnCmdMsg (nID, nCode, pExtra, pHandlerInfo))
    return TRUE;
```

If *CFrameWnd::OnCmdMsg* returns 0, indicating that none of the standard command targets handled the message, *CMainFrame::OnCmdMsg* calls a function in the document class to route the message to all the inactive views:

```
CWandererDoc* pDoc = (CWandererDoc*) GetActiveDocument ();
if (pDoc != NULL) { // Important!
    return pDoc->RouteCmdToAllViews (GetActiveView (),
        nID, nCode, pExtra, pHandlerInfo);
}
```

CWandererDoc::RouteCmdToAllViews iterates through the views associated with the document and calls each view's *OnCmdMsg* function:

```
BOOL CWandererDoc::RouteCmdToAllViews(CView *pView, UINT nID, int nCode,
    void *pExtra, AFX_CMDHANDLERINFO *pHandlerInfo)
{
    POSITION pos = GetFirstViewPosition ();

    while (pos != NULL) {
        CView* pNextView = GetNextView (pos);
        if (pNextView != pView) {
            if (pNextView->OnCmdMsg (nID, nCode, pExtra, pHandlerInfo))
                return TRUE;
        }
    }
    return FALSE;
}
```

CMainFrame::OnCmdMsg passes *RouteCmdToAllViews* a pointer to the active view so that *RouteCmdToAllViews* can avoid calling the active view's *OnCmdMsg* function. The active view has already been called as part of the standard command routing sequence, so calling it again is wasteful. The frame window provides the pointer to the active view because the document class has no concept of active and inactive views. By the same token, a frame window knows which view is active but doesn't how many views there are. That's why *CMainFrame* calls a function in the document class to iterate through all the views rather than enumerate the views itself.

Note that the *CView* pointer returned by *GetNextView* must be cast upward to *CCmdTarget* pointers in some versions of MFC because those versions erroneously declare *OnCmdMsg* as protected in *CView*. Thankfully, this bug is fixed in MFC 6.

Custom routing is a powerful tool for routing commands and UI update messages to nonstandard command targets. You can tap into the command routing sequence just about anywhere you want to by overriding the right *OnCmdMsg* function. In general, you should call the base class version of *OnCmdMsg* from an override to keep default command routing intact. And be careful about whose *OnCmdMsg* functions you call because it's possible to fall into a recursive loop in which object A calls object B and object B calls object A. You wouldn't, for example, want to call a view's *OnCmdMsg* function from a document's *OnCmdMsg* function because the view calls the document as part of the standard command routing sequence.

Three-Way Splitter Windows

You can create a three-way splitter window similar to the one featured in Microsoft Outlook Express by nesting static splitter windows. The following *OnCreateClient* function creates a three-way static splitter that's divided into two columns. The right column is further subdivided into two rows. The user can adjust the relative sizes of the panes by dragging the splitter bars, but the basic layout of the splitter can't be changed because the splitters are static rather than dynamic:

```
BOOL CMainFrame::OnCreateClient (LPCREATESTRUCT lpCreateStruct,
    CCreateContext* pContext)
{
    if (!m_wndSplitter1.CreateStatic (this, 1, 2) ||
        !m_wndSplitter1.CreateView (0, 0, RUNTIME_CLASS (CTextView),
            CSize (128, 0), pContext) ||
        !m_wndSplitter2.CreateStatic (&m_wndSplitter1, 2, 1, WS_CHILD |
            WS_VISIBLE, m_wndSplitter1.IdFromRowCol (0, 1)) ||
        !m_wndSplitter2.CreateView (0, 0, RUNTIME_CLASS (CPictureView),
            CSize (0, 128), pContext) ||
        !m_wndSplitter2.CreateView (1, 0, RUNTIME_CLASS (CPictureView),
            CSize (0, 0), pContext))
        return FALSE;
    return TRUE;
}
```

Here's a synopsis of what happens in the *if* statement that creates and initializes the three-way splitter:

1. The first splitter window is created by calling *CreateStatic* on the *CSplitterWnd* data member *m_wndSplitter1*. This splitter window contains one row and two columns.

2. A *CTextView* is added to *m_wndSplitter1*'s first (left) pane with *CreateView*.

3. A second splitter window is created in the right pane of the first splitter window by calling *m_wndSplitter2*'s *CreateStatic* function. *m_wndSplitter2* is parented to *m_wndSplitter1* rather than to the frame window and assigned a child window ID that identifies it as the pane in row 0, column 1. The proper ID for *m_wndSplitter2* is obtained by calling *CSplitterWnd::IdFromRowCol*, which uses simple math to convert a row and column number into a numeric offset that's added to AFX_IDW_PANE_FIRST.

4. *CreateView* is called twice to add a *CPictureView* to each *m_wndSplitter2* pane.

Using a dynamic splitter window for *m_wndSplitter2* would require a little more work because of some of the assumptions that MFC makes when it creates new views to fill dynamically created splitter panes. If you try to nest a dynamic splitter window inside a static splitter window like this:

```
BOOL CMainFrame::OnCreateClient (LPCREATESTRUCT lpCreateStruct,
    CCreateContext* pContext)
```

```
{
    if (!m_wndSplitter1.CreateStatic (this, 1, 2) ||
        !m_wndSplitter1.CreateView (0, 0, RUNTIME_CLASS (CTextView),
            CSize (128, 0), pContext) ||
        !m_wndSplitter2.Create (&m_wndSplitter1, 2, 1, CSize (1, 1),
            pContext, WS_CHILD | WS_VISIBLE | WS_HSCROLL |
            WS_VSCROLL | SPLS_DYNAMIC_SPLIT,
            m_wndSplitter1.IdFromRowCol (0, 1)))
        return FALSE;
    return TRUE;
}
```

you'll sometimes generate access violations when splitting the dynamic splitter window. The reason why is rooted deep in the framework. When a dynamic splitter window splits, *CSplitterWnd* calls *CreateView* with a NULL *pContext* pointer to create a view for the new pane. Seeing that *pContext* is NULL, *CreateView* queries the frame window for a pointer to the active view and uses that view as a model for the new view. If the *CTextView* window happens to be the active view when a split occurs, the framework will see that the view isn't a child of the dynamic splitter and will create an "empty" view that isn't attached to a document object. The first time that view tries to access its document, an access violation will occur.

The secret to successfully nesting a dynamic splitter window inside a static splitter window involves two steps:

1. Derive a class from *CSplitterWnd,* and replace *CSplitterWnd::SplitRow* in the derived class with the following implementation:

    ```
    BOOL CNestedSplitterWnd::SplitRow (int cyBefore)
    {
        GetParentFrame ()->
            SetActiveView ((CView*) GetPane (0, 0));
        return CSplitterWnd::SplitRow (cyBefore);
    }
    ```

2. Make the nested dynamic splitter an instance of the derived class rather than an instance of *CSplitterWnd*.

SplitRow is a virtual *CSplitterWnd* function that's called when a horizontal splitter bar is dragged to create a new pane. The version of *SplitRow* shown above makes the view in the dynamic splitter window's uppermost pane the active view before the split occurs, which neatly circumvents the dynamic view creation problems that result when the active view is a child of the static splitter window. The override uses *GetParentFrame* instead of *GetParent* because the dynamic splitter window's parent is actually the static splitter window, not the frame window, and a frame window function (not a splitter window function) sets the active view.

Dynamic Splitter Windows with Multiple View Types

The previous section demonstrates one way in which a splitter window can be customized by deriving from *CSplitterWnd* and overriding *CSplitterWnd::SplitRow*. The *CSplitterWnd* class includes other virtual functions you can override to customize a splitter window's behavior. One of those functions is *CreateView*, which MFC calls to create a new view when a dynamic splitter window is split. You can create a dynamic splitter window that displays different types of views in different panes by deriving a class from *CSplitterWnd*, overriding *CreateView*, and calling *CSplitterWnd::CreateView* with a *CRuntimeClass* pointer to the view of your choice.

The following *CreateView* override forces a *CTextView* into the pane at row 1, column 0, regardless of the type of view contained in row 0, column 0:

```
BOOL CDynaSplitterWnd::CreateView (int row, int col,
    CRuntimeClass* pViewClass, SIZE sizeInit,
    CCreateContext* pContext)
{
    if ((row == 1) && (col == 0))
        return CSplitterWnd::CreateView (row, col,
            RUNTIME_CLASS (CTextView), sizeInit, pContext);

    return CSplitterWnd::CreateView (row, col, pViewClass,
        sizeInit, pContext);
}
```

You'll probably have to modify this code for every different splitter window you use because the view class is hardwired to the row and column number. However, you could build a generic (and reusable) dynamic splitter class that supports multiple view types by adding a *RegisterView* function that correlates view types identified by *CRuntimeClass* pointers to row and column numbers. Before *CSplitterWnd::Create* is called, the splitter window could be initialized with information about the type of view that goes in each pane, and *CreateView* could then use that information to generate the appropriate views.

Chapter 12

Toolbars, Status Bars, and Rebars

In this chapter, we'll continue our look at MFC by examining two new classes that you can use to enhance your applications' user interfaces: *CToolBar* and *CStatusBar*. *CToolBar* implements toolbars—ribbonlike windows containing push buttons (and sometimes other types of controls) that provide swift access to commonly used commands. *CStatusBar* is MFC's status bar class. A status bar is a window that displays context-sensitive help for menu items and toolbar buttons as well as other helpful information. Adding toolbars and status bars to MFC applications is easy because *CToolBar* and *CStatusBar* provide thorough encapsulations of these ubiquitous user interface (UI) elements.

Another feature of MFC that you'll learn about in this chapter is the new *CReBar* class, which wraps the rebar controls that were introduced with Microsoft Internet Explorer. Rebars convert ordinary toolbars into the stylized toolbars (also known as "coolbars") featured in Internet Explorer, Microsoft Visual C++, and other Microsoft applications. They are also the basis for "command bars"—menu bars with items that highlight like push buttons when the cursor passes over them—similar to the one that serves as the main menu in Visual C++. Thanks to *CReBar*, an MFC programmer can transform a *CToolBar* into a coolbar with just one or two lines of code. You'll see how in just a few moments.

TOOLBARS

A toolbar's purpose is to provide one-click access to commonly used commands. Toolbar buttons typically serve as shortcuts for menu commands, but they can also implement commands that don't appear in a menu. MFC's *CToolBar* class takes a bitmap resource containing images for the faces of the toolbar buttons and an array of button IDs and creates a toolbar object that docks to the side of a frame window or floats in its own mini frame window. Toolbar buttons are assigned command IDs just as menu items are. Clicking a toolbar button produces a WM_COMMAND message just as if a menu item had been selected. If a menu item and a toolbar button are assigned the same command ID, one command handler can serve them both. With a little work, you can add combo boxes, check boxes, and other non-push-button controls to a toolbar. You can also convert ordinary push buttons into "check push buttons" that stay up or down when clicked or "radio push buttons" that work like radio buttons. MFC provides functions for hiding and displaying toolbars, saving and restoring toolbar states, and much more.

In early versions of MFC, *CToolBar* was a stand-alone class whose functionality came entirely from MFC. Today, *CToolBar* derives much of its functionality from the toolbar control in Comctl32.dll. A separate and more primitive MFC class named *CToolBarCtrl* provides an MFC interface to toolbar controls. That's useful to know, because if you want to do something with a *CToolBar* and can't find a suitable member function, *CToolBarCtrl* might have the member function you're looking for. You can call *CToolBarCtrl* functions on a *CToolBar* if you first call *CToolBar::GetToolBarCtrl* to acquire a *CToolBarCtrl* reference to the underlying control. Most of the time, however, *CToolBar* will do everything you need and then some. With that in mind, let's see what it takes to get a *CToolBar* up and running.

Creating and Initializing a Toolbar

You create a toolbar by constructing a *CToolBar* object and calling *CToolBar::Create*. Because a toolbar is a child of the application's main frame window and is normally created when the frame window is created, the usual practice is to add a *CToolBar* member to the frame window class and call *Create* from the frame window's *OnCreate* handler. If *m_wndToolBar* is a *CToolBar* data member, the statement

```
m_wndToolBar.Create (this);
```

creates a toolbar that is a child of *this*. Two parameters are implicit in the call: the toolbar's style and its child-window ID. The default style is WS_CHILD | WS_VISIBLE | CBRS_TOP. You can change the toolbar style by adding a second parameter to *Create* or by calling the *SetBarStyle* function that a toolbar inherits from its base class, *CControlBar*, after the toolbar is created. For example, to replace CBRS_TOP with

CBRS_BOTTOM so that the toolbar aligns itself along the bottom of its parent, you could create it like this:

```
m_wndToolBar.Create (this, WS_CHILD | WS_VISIBLE | CBRS_BOTTOM);
```

Or you could create it like this:

```
m_wndToolBar.Create (this);
m_wndToolBar.SetBarStyle ((m_wndToolBar.GetBarStyle () &
    ~CBRS_TOP) | CBRS_BOTTOM);
```

CToolBar::Create also accepts an optional third parameter specifying the toolbar ID. The default is AFX_IDW_TOOLBAR. There's no need to change the toolbar ID unless you write an application that contains two or more toolbars. In a multitoolbar application, you should assign each toolbar a unique ID.

A freshly created toolbar is empty, so the next step is to add buttons to it. One way to add buttons is to call *CToolBar::LoadBitmap* to load a bitmap resource containing images for the button faces and *CToolBar::SetButtons* to tell the toolbar how many buttons it will have and what the buttons' command IDs are. The following statements create a toolbar and initialize it with the images stored in the bitmap resource IDR_TOOLBAR and the IDs in the array *nButtonIDs*. The special ID-_SEPARATOR value places a small gap a few pixels wide between buttons.

```
// In the RC file
IDR_TOOLBAR BITMAP Toolbar.bmp

// In the CPP file
static UINT nButtonIDs[] = {
    ID_FILE_NEW,
    ID_FILE_OPEN,
    ID_FILE_SAVE,
    ID_SEPARATOR,
    ID_EDIT_CUT,
    ID_EDIT_COPY,
    ID_EDIT_PASTE,
    ID_EDIT_UNDO,
    ID_SEPARATOR,
    ID_FILE_PRINT
};

m_wndToolBar.Create (this);
m_wndToolBar.LoadBitmap (IDR_TOOLBAR);
m_wndToolBar.SetButtons (nButtonIDs, 10);
```

The bitmap resource contains all of the toolbar button images, positioned end to end like frames in a filmstrip, as shown in Figure 12-1 on the following page. By default, each image is 16 pixels wide and 15 pixels high. The button itself measures 24 pixels

Toolbar bitmap

The resulting toolbar

Figure 12-1. *Toolbar images and a toolbar created from them.*

by 22 pixels. You can change both the image size and the button size with *CTool-Bar::SetSizes*. Drawing professional-looking toolbar buttons requires a little artistic flair, but for standard items such as New, Open, Save, Cut, Copy, Paste, and Print, you can borrow images from the Toolbar.bmp bitmap supplied with Visual C++.

A second method for creating the toolbar buttons is to add a TOOLBAR resource describing the button IDs and image sizes to the application's RC file and call *CToolBar::LoadToolBar* with the resource ID. The following statements create and initialize a toolbar that is identical to the one in the previous paragraph:

```
// In the RC file
IDR_TOOLBAR BITMAP Toolbar.bmp

IDR_TOOLBAR TOOLBAR 16, 15
BEGIN
    BUTTON ID_FILE_NEW
    BUTTON ID_FILE_OPEN
    BUTTON ID_FILE_SAVE
    SEPARATOR
    BUTTON ID_EDIT_CUT
    BUTTON ID_EDIT_COPY
    BUTTON ID_EDIT_PASTE
    BUTTON ID_EDIT_UNDO
    SEPARATOR
    BUTTON ID_FILE_PRINT
END

// In the CPP file
m_wndToolBar.Create (this);
m_wndToolBar.LoadToolBar (IDR_TOOLBAR);
```

When you use a TOOLBAR resource, you can change the image size simply by changing the numbers in the resource statement. *LoadToolBar* loads the toolbar images, sets the button IDs, and sets the button sizes all in one step. When you ask AppWizard to include a toolbar in an application, it uses this method to define the toolbar.

Fortunately, you don't have to create and edit TOOLBAR resources by hand. When AppWizard adds a toolbar to an application, it creates a TOOLBAR resource and a bitmap to go with it. You can also add TOOLBAR resources to a project with Visual C++'s Insert-Resource command. Once it's added, a TOOLBAR resource and its button bitmaps can be edited visually in Visual C++'s resource editor.

By default, toolbar buttons contain images but not text. You can add text strings to the faces of the buttons with *CToolBar::SetButtonText*. After you've specified the text of each button, use *CToolBar::SetSizes* to adjust the button sizes to accommodate the text strings. The following statements create a toolbar from IDR_TOOLBAR and add descriptive text to each button face:

```
// In the RC file
IDR_TOOLBAR BITMAP Toolbar.bmp

IDR_TOOLBAR TOOLBAR 40, 19
    ⋮

// In the CPP file
m_wndToolBar.Create (this);
m_wndToolBar.LoadToolBar (IDR_TOOLBAR);

m_wndToolBar.SetButtonText (0, _T ("New"));
m_wndToolBar.SetButtonText (1, _T ("Open"));
m_wndToolBar.SetButtonText (2, _T ("Save"));
m_wndToolBar.SetButtonText (4, _T ("Cut"));
m_wndToolBar.SetButtonText (5, _T ("Copy"));
m_wndToolBar.SetButtonText (6, _T ("Paste"));
m_wndToolBar.SetButtonText (7, _T ("Undo"));
m_wndToolBar.SetButtonText (9, _T ("Print"));

m_wndToolBar.SetSizes (CSize (48, 42), CSize (40, 19));
```

The resulting toolbar is shown in Figure 12-2. The first parameter passed to *SetButtonText* specifies the button's index, with 0 representing the leftmost button on the toolbar, 1 representing the button to its right, and so on. *SetSizes* must be called *after* the button text is added, not before, or the button sizes won't stick. Also, the width of the button bitmaps must be expanded to make room for the button text. In this example, the button bitmaps in Toolbar.bmp were expanded to a width of 40 pixels each, and the height was changed to 19 pixels to make the resulting buttons roughly square.

Figure 12-2. *Toolbar buttons with text.*

Unless you take steps to have them do otherwise, toolbar buttons behave like standard push buttons: they go down when clicked and pop back up when released.

You can use MFC's *CToolBar::SetButtonStyle* function to create check push buttons that stay down until they're clicked again and radio push buttons that stay down until another toolbar button is clicked. The following statements create a text formatting toolbar that contains check push buttons for selecting bold, italic, and underlined text and radio push buttons for selecting left aligned, centered, or right aligned text.

```
// In the RC file
IDR_TOOLBAR BITMAP Toolbar.bmp

IDR_TOOLBAR TOOLBAR 16, 15
BEGIN
    BUTTON ID_CHAR_BOLD
    BUTTON ID_CHAR_ITALIC
    BUTTON ID_CHAR_UNDERLINE
    SEPARATOR
    BUTTON ID_PARA_LEFT
    BUTTON ID_PARA_CENTER
    BUTTON ID_PARA_RIGHT
END

// In the CPP file
m_wndToolBar.Create (this);
m_wndToolBar.LoadToolBar (IDR_TOOLBAR);

m_wndToolBar.SetButtonStyle (0, TBBS_CHECKBOX);
m_wndToolBar.SetButtonStyle (1, TBBS_CHECKBOX);
m_wndToolBar.SetButtonStyle (2, TBBS_CHECKBOX);
m_wndToolBar.SetButtonStyle (4, TBBS_CHECKGROUP);
m_wndToolBar.SetButtonStyle (5, TBBS_CHECKGROUP);
m_wndToolBar.SetButtonStyle (6, TBBS_CHECKGROUP);
```

The TBBS_CHECKBOX style creates a check push button. TBBS_CHECKGROUP, which is equivalent to TBBS_CHECKBOX | TBBS_GROUP, creates a radio push button. Because buttons 4, 5, and 6 share the TBBS_CHECKGROUP style, clicking any one of them "checks" that button and unchecks the others. Buttons 0, 1, and 2, however, operate independently of each other and toggle up and down only when clicked. Other toolbar button styles that you can specify through *SetButtonStyle* include TBBS_BUTTON, which creates a standard push button, and TBBS_SEPARATOR, which creates a button separator. The complementary *CToolBar::GetButtonStyle* function retrieves button styles.

When you add radio push buttons to a toolbar, you should also check one member of each group to identify the default selection. The following code expands on the example in the previous paragraph by checking the ID_PARA_LEFT button:

```
int nState =
    m_wndToolBar.GetToolBarCtrl ().GetState (ID_PARA_LEFT);
m_wndToolBar.GetToolBarCtrl ().SetState (ID_PARA_LEFT, nState ¦
    TBSTATE_CHECKED);
```

As described earlier in the chapter, *CToolBar::GetToolBarCtrl* returns a reference to the *CToolBarCtrl* that provides the basic functionality for a *CToolBar*. *CToolBar-Ctrl::GetState* returns the state of a toolbar button, and *CToolBarCtrl::SetState* changes the button state. Setting the TBSTATE_CHECKED flag in the parameter passed to *SetState* checks the button.

In practice, you might never need *SetButtonStyle* because in an MFC program you can convert standard push buttons into check push buttons and radio push buttons by providing update handlers that use *CCmdUI::SetCheck* to do the checking and unchecking. I'll have more to say about this aspect of toolbar buttons in just a moment.

Docking and Floating

One feature that *CToolBar* provides for free is the ability for the user to grab a toolbar with the mouse, detach it from its frame window, and either dock it to another side of the window or allow it to float free in a mini frame window of its own. You can control which (if any) sides of the frame window a toolbar can be docked to and other docking and floating characteristics. You can also create highly configurable toolbars that can be docked, floated, and resized at the user's behest and static tool palettes that permanently float and retain rigid row and column configurations.

When a toolbar is first created, it's affixed to the side of its frame window and can't be detached. Floating and docking are enabled by calling the toolbar's *Enable-Docking* function (*CControlBar::EnableDocking*) with bit flags specifying which sides of the frame window the toolbar will allow itself to be docked to and by calling the frame window's *EnableDocking* function (*CFrameWnd::EnableDocking*) with bit flags specifying which sides of the window are valid docking targets. The following values can be ORed together and passed to either *EnableDocking* function:

Bit Flag	*Description*
CBRS_ALIGN_LEFT	Permit docking to the left side of the frame window
CBRS_ALIGN_RIGHT	Permit docking to the right side of the frame window
CBRS_ALIGN_TOP	Permit docking to the top of the frame window
CBRS_ALIGN_BOTTOM	Permit docking to the bottom of the frame window
CBRS_ALIGN_ANY	Permit docking to any side of the frame window

Called from a member function of a frame window class, the statements

```
m_wndToolBar.EnableDocking (CBRS_ALIGN_ANY);
EnableDocking (CBRS_ALIGN_ANY);
```

enable the toolbar represented by *m_wndToolBar* to be docked to any side of its parent. The statements

```
m_wndToolBar.EnableDocking (CBRS_ALIGN_TOP | CBRS_ALIGN_BOTTOM);
EnableDocking (CBRS_ALIGN_ANY);
```

restrict docking to the top and bottom of the frame window. It might seem redundant for both the toolbar and the frame window to specify docking targets, but the freedom to configure the toolbar's docking parameters and the frame window's docking parameters independently comes in handy when a frame window contains more than one toolbar and each has different docking requirements. For example, if *m_wndToolBar1* and *m_wndToolBar2* belong to the same frame window, the statements

```
m_wndToolBar1.EnableDocking (CBRS_ALIGN_TOP | CBRS_ALIGN_BOTTOM);
m_wndToolBar2.EnableDocking (CBRS_ALIGN_LEFT | CBRS_ALIGN_RIGHT);
EnableDocking (CBRS_ALIGN_ANY);
```

enable *m_wndToolBar1* to be docked top and bottom and *m_wndToolBar2* to be docked left and right.

Toolbars are docked and undocked programmatically with the *CFrameWnd* member functions *DockControlBar* and *FloatControlBar*. *DockControlBar* docks a toolbar to its parent frame. The statement

```
DockControlBar (&m_wndToolBar);
```

docks *m_wndToolBar* in its default location—the inside top of the frame window. The statement

```
DockControlBar (&m_wndToolBar, AFX_IDW_DOCKBAR_RIGHT);
```

docks the toolbar to the right edge of the frame window. To exercise even finer control over a toolbar's placement, you can pass *DockControlBar* a *CRect* object or a pointer to a RECT structure containing a docking position. Until *DockControlBar* is called, a toolbar can't be detached from its parent, even if docking has been enabled with *CControlBar::EnableDocking* and *CFrameWnd::EnableDocking*.

FloatControlBar is the opposite of *DockControlBar*. It's called to detach a toolbar from its frame window and tell it to begin floating. The framework calls this function when the user drags a docked toolbar and releases it in an undocked position, but you can float a toolbar yourself by calling *FloatControlBar* and passing in a *CPoint* parameter specifying the position of the toolbar's upper left corner in screen coordinates:

```
FloatControlBar (&m_wndToolBar, CPoint (x, y));
```

You can also pass *FloatControlBar* a third parameter equal to CBRS_ALIGN_TOP to orient the toolbar horizontally or CBRS_ALIGN_LEFT to orient it vertically. Call *FloatControlBar* instead of *DockControlBar* to create a toolbar that's initially floating instead of docked. If you call *EnableDocking* with a 0 and then call *FloatControlBar*, you get a floating toolbar that can't be docked to the side of a frame window. MFC programmers sometimes use this technique to create stand-alone tool palette windows. You can determine whether a toolbar is docked or floating at any given moment by calling *CControlBar::IsFloating*. You can also add a title to the mini frame window that surrounds a floating toolbar by calling the toolbar's *SetWindowText* function.

By default, a floating toolbar aligns itself horizontally when docked to the top or bottom of a frame window and vertically when it's docked on the left or right, but it can't be realigned while it's floating. You can give the user the ability to resize a floating toolbar by adding a CBRS_SIZE_DYNAMIC flag to the toolbar style. Conversely, you can make sure that a toolbar's size and shape remain fixed (even when the toolbar is docked) by using CBRS_SIZE_FIXED. One use for CBRS_SIZE_FIXED is to create floating tool palette windows with permanent row and column configurations. You can create static tool palettes containing multiple rows of buttons by using the TBBS_WRAPPED style to tell *CToolBar* where the line breaks are. A toolbar button with the style TBBS_WRAPPED is analogous to a carriage return/line feed pair in a text file: what comes after it begins on a new line. Assuming IDR_TOOLBAR represents a toolbar containing nine buttons, the following sample code creates a fixed tool palette window containing three rows of three buttons each:

```
m_wndToolBar.Create (this);
m_wndToolBar.LoadToolBar (IDR_TOOLBAR);
m_wndToolBar.SetBarStyle (m_wndToolBar.GetBarStyle () |
    CBRS_SIZE_FIXED);

m_wndToolBar.SetButtonStyle (2,
    m_wndToolBar.GetButtonStyle (0) | TBBS_WRAPPED);
m_wndToolBar.SetButtonStyle (5,
    m_wndToolBar.GetButtonStyle (0) | TBBS_WRAPPED);

EnableDocking (CBRS_ALIGN_ANY);
m_wndToolBar.EnableDocking (0);
FloatControlBar (&m_wndToolBar, CPoint (x, y));
```

Adding TBBS_WRAPPED bits to the buttons whose indexes are 2 and 5 creates a line break every third button. And because the tool palette's *EnableDocking* function is called with a 0, the tool palette floats indefinitely and can't be docked to a frame window.

If an application uses two or more toolbars, you can include a CBRS_FLOAT_MULTI flag in the toolbars' *EnableDocking* functions and allow the user to dock floating toolbars together to form composite toolbars that share a common mini frame window. Unfortunately, the CBRS_FLOAT_MULTI and CBRS_SIZE_DYNAMIC styles are incompatible with each other, so you can't use both in the same toolbar.

Controlling a Toolbar's Visibility

Most applications that incorporate toolbars feature commands for hiding and displaying them. An MFC application can use the *CFrameWnd* member function *OnBarCheck* to toggle a toolbar on or off. Called with a toolbar ID, *OnBarCheck* hides the toolbar if it's visible or displays it if it's hidden. A related member function named *OnUpdateControlBarMenu* updates the menu containing the command that toggles a toolbar on or off by checking or unchecking the menu item whose ID matches the toolbar ID. *OnBarCheck* and *OnUpdateControlBarMenu* work with status bars, too; all you have to do is pass a status bar ID instead of a toolbar ID.

If your application has only one toolbar and that toolbar is assigned the default ID AFX_IDW_TOOLBAR, you can create a menu item that toggles the toolbar on and off by assigning the menu item the special ID value ID_VIEW_TOOLBAR. For a status bar, use ID_VIEW_STATUS_BAR instead. No message mapping is necessary because *CFrameWnd*'s message map contains entries mapping these "magic" menu item IDs to the appropriate *CFrameWnd* member functions:

```
ON_UPDATE_COMMAND_UI (ID_VIEW_STATUS_BAR, OnUpdateControlBarMenu)
ON_COMMAND_EX (ID_VIEW_STATUS_BAR, OnBarCheck)
ON_UPDATE_COMMAND_UI (ID_VIEW_TOOLBAR, OnUpdateControlBarMenu)
ON_COMMAND_EX (ID_VIEW_TOOLBAR, OnBarCheck)
```

ON_COMMAND_EX is similar to ON_COMMAND, but an ON_COMMAND_EX handler, unlike an ON_COMMAND handler, receives a UINT parameter containing the ID of the UI object that generated the message. *OnBarCheck* assumes that the toolbar ID and the menu item ID are the same and uses that ID to hide or display the toolbar.

If your application uses a toolbar whose ID isn't AFX_IDW_TOOLBAR, you can connect the toolbar to command and update handlers that control its visibility in two ways. The simplest method is to assign the toolbar and the corresponding menu item the same ID and to map that ID to *OnBarCheck* and *OnUpdateControlBarMenu* in the main frame window's message map. If the menu item ID is ID_VIEW_TOOLBAR2, here's what the message-map entries will look like:

```
ON_UPDATE_COMMAND_UI (ID_VIEW_TOOLBAR2, OnUpdateControlBarMenu)
ON_COMMAND_EX (ID_VIEW_TOOLBAR2, OnBarCheck)
```

Don't forget that for this method to work, the toolbar *must* be assigned the same ID as the menu item.

The second approach is to provide your own command and update handlers and use *CFrameWnd::ShowControlBar* to hide and display the toolbar. You can determine whether a toolbar is currently visible or invisible by checking the WS_VISIBLE bit of the value returned by *GetStyle*:

```
// In CMainFrame's message map
ON_COMMAND (ID_VIEW_TOOLBAR2, OnViewToolbar2)
ON_UPDATE_COMMAND_UI (ID_VIEW_TOOLBAR2, OnUpdateViewToolbar2UI)
    :
    :
void CMainFrame::OnViewToolbar2 ()
{
    ShowControlBar (&m_wndToolBar2, (m_wndToolBar2.GetStyle() &
        WS_VISIBLE) == 0, FALSE);
}

void CMainFrame::OnUpdateViewToolbar2UI (CCmdUI* pCmdUI)
{
    pCmdUI->SetCheck ((m_wndToolBar2.GetStyle () &
        WS_VISIBLE) ? 1 : 0);
}
```

Don't try to toggle a toolbar's visibility by turning the WS_VISIBLE flag on or off, because there's more to hiding and displaying a toolbar than flipping a style bit. When a toolbar is toggled on or off (or docked or undocked), for example, MFC resizes the view to compensate for the change in the visible area of the frame window's client area. *ShowControlBar* takes these and other factors into account when it hides or displays a toolbar. For details, see the code for *CFrameWnd::ShowControlBar* in the MFC source code file Winfrm.cpp.

Keeping Toolbar Buttons in Sync with Your Application

Toolbar buttons are connected to command handlers in your source code the same way menu items are connected: through message maps. You can assign toolbar buttons update handlers just as you can menu items. That's one reason MFC passes an update handler a pointer to a *CCmdUI* object instead of a pointer to a *CMenu* or a *CButton*: the same *CCmdUI* functions that update menu items are equally capable of updating toolbar buttons. Calling *CCmdUI::SetCheck* during a menu update checks or unchecks the menu item. Calling the same function during a toolbar update checks or unchecks a toolbar button by pushing it down or popping it back up. Because *CCmdUI* abstracts the physical nature of UI objects, one update handler can do the updating for a toolbar button and a menu item as long as both objects share the same ID.

Suppose your application has an Edit menu with a Paste command that's enabled when there's text on the clipboard and disabled when there isn't. Furthermore, suppose that the application has a Paste toolbar button that performs the same action as Edit-Paste. Both the menu item and the toolbar button are assigned the predefined command ID ID_EDIT_PASTE, and ID_EDIT_PASTE is mapped to a handler named *OnEditPaste* with the following message-map entry.

```
ON_COMMAND (ID_EDIT_PASTE, OnEditPaste)
```

To update the Paste menu item each time the Edit menu is displayed, you also map ID_EDIT_PASTE to an update handler named *OnUpdateEditPasteUI*:

```
ON_UPDATE_COMMAND_UI (ID_EDIT_PASTE, OnUpdateEditPasteUI)
```

OnUpdateEditPasteUI uses *CCmdUI::Enable* to enable or disable the Paste command based on the value returned by *::IsClipboardFormatAvailable*:

```
void CMyClass::OnUpdateEditPasteUI (CCmdUI* pCmdUI)
{
    pCmdUI->Enable (::IsClipboardFormatAvailable (CF_TEXT));
}
```

With this infrastructure in place, a paste operation can be performed by selecting Paste from the Edit menu or by clicking the Paste button in the toolbar. In addition, the handler that keeps the menu item in sync with the clipboard state also updates the toolbar button. The only difference between menu item updates and toolbar updates is the timing of calls to the update handler. For a menu item, the framework calls the update handler in response to WM_INITMENUPOPUP messages. For a toolbar button, the framework calls the update handler during idle periods in which there are no messages for the application to process. Thus, although menu updates are deferred until just before a menu is displayed, toolbar buttons are updated almost immediately when a state change occurs. It's a good thing, too, because toolbar buttons, unlike menu items, are visible at all times. The physical calling mechanism is transparent to the application, which simply provides an update handler and then trusts the framework to call it as needed.

Earlier I mentioned that you can use update handlers to create check push buttons and radio push buttons without changing the button styles. It's easy: just provide an update handler for each button and use *CCmdUI::SetCheck* or *CCmdUI::SetRadio* to do the checking and unchecking. If a button's command handler toggles a Boolean variable between TRUE and FALSE, and if its update handler checks or unchecks the button based on the value of the variable, the button acts like a check push button. If the command handler sets the variable value to TRUE and sets the values of other buttons in the group to FALSE, the button acts like a radio push button. The following message-map entries, command handlers, and update handlers make a group of three toolbar buttons behave like radio push buttons:

```
// In CMyClass's message map
ON_COMMAND (ID_BUTTON1, OnButton1)
ON_COMMAND (ID_BUTTON2, OnButton2)
ON_COMMAND (ID_BUTTON3, OnButton3)
ON_UPDATE_COMMAND_UI (ID_BUTTON1, OnUpdateButton1)
ON_UPDATE_COMMAND_UI (ID_BUTTON2, OnUpdateButton2)
ON_UPDATE_COMMAND_UI (ID_BUTTON3, OnUpdateButton3)
```

```
    ⋮

void CMyClass::OnButton1 ()
{
    m_bButton1Down = TRUE;
    m_bButton2Down = FALSE;
    m_bButton3Down = FALSE;
}

void CMyClass::OnButton2 ()
{
    m_bButton1Down = FALSE;
    m_bButton2Down = TRUE;
    m_bButton3Down = FALSE;
}

void CMyClass::OnButton3 ()
{
    m_bButton1Down = FALSE;
    m_bButton2Down = FALSE;
    m_bButton3Down = TRUE;
}

void CMyClass::OnUpdateButton1 (CCmdUI* pCmdUI)
{
    pCmdUI->SetCheck (m_bButton1Down);
}

void CMyClass::OnUpdateButton2 (CCmdUI* pCmdUI)
{
    pCmdUI->SetCheck (m_bButton2Down);
}

void CMyClass::OnUpdateButton3 (CCmdUI* pCmdUI)
{
    pCmdUI->SetCheck (m_bButton3Down);
}
```

With these command and update handlers in place, it's irrelevant whether the toolbar buttons are TBBS_CHECKGROUP buttons or ordinary TBBS_BUTTON buttons. Clicking any one of the buttons sets the other button-state variables to FALSE, and the update handlers respond by drawing the buttons in their new states.

Adding ToolTips and Flyby Text

When toolbars first began appearing in Microsoft Windows applications, they were sometimes more hindrance than help because the meanings of the buttons weren't always clear from the pictures on the buttons' faces. Some UI designers sought to alleviate this problem by adding text to the buttons. Others went one step further and invented *ToolTips*—small windows with descriptive text such as "Open" and "Paste" that appear on the screen when the cursor pauses over a toolbar button for a half second or so. (See Figure 12-3.) Today, ToolTips are commonplace in Windows applications, and they offer a unique solution to the problem of button ambiguity because they make context-sensitive help for toolbar buttons readily available without requiring a commensurate increase in button size.

Figure 12-3. *A floating toolbar with a ToolTip displayed.*

Adding ToolTips to an MFC toolbar is easy. Simply add CBRS_TOOLTIPS to the toolbar style and create a string table resource containing ToolTip text. The string IDs match the ToolTips to the toolbar buttons. If you use standard MFC command IDs such as ID_FILE_OPEN and ID_EDIT_PASTE and include Afxres.h in your application's RC file, the framework provides the ToolTip text for you. For other command IDs, you provide the ToolTip text by supplying string resources with IDs that match the toolbar button IDs. The following code sample creates a toolbar with buttons for performing common text-formatting operations and ToolTips to go with the buttons:

```
// In the RC file
IDR_TOOLBAR BITMAP Toolbar.bmp

IDR_TOOLBAR TOOLBAR 16, 15
BEGIN
    BUTTON ID_CHAR_BOLD
    BUTTON ID_CHAR_ITALIC
    BUTTON ID_CHAR_UNDERLINE
    SEPARATOR
    BUTTON ID_PARA_LEFT
    BUTTON ID_PARA_CENTER
    BUTTON ID_PARA_RIGHT
END

STRINGTABLE
BEGIN
    ID_CHAR_BOLD        "\nBold"
    ID_CHAR_ITALIC      "\nItalic"
    ID_CHAR_UNDERLINE   "\nUnderline"
    ID_PARA_LEFT        "\nAlign Left"
    ID_PARA_CENTER      "\nAlign Center"
    ID_PARA_RIGHT       "\nAlign Right"
END
```

```
// In the CPP file
m_wndToolBar.Create (this, WS_CHILD | WS_VISIBLE |
    CBRS_TOP | CBRS_TOOLTIPS);
m_wndToolBar.LoadToolBar (IDR_TOOLBAR);
```

When the cursor pauses over a toolbar button and there's a string resource whose ID matches the button ID, the framework displays the text following the newline character in a ToolTip window. The ToolTip disappears when the cursor moves. In the old days, you had to set timers, monitor mouse movements, and subclass windows to make ToolTips work. Nowadays, that functionality is provided for you.

If your application features a status bar as well as a toolbar, you can configure the toolbar to display "flyby" text in addition to (or in lieu of) ToolTips by setting the CBRS_FLYBY bit in the toolbar style. Flyby text is descriptive text displayed in the status bar when the cursor pauses over a toolbar button. ToolTip text should be short and to the point, but flyby text can be lengthier. Did you wonder why the string resources in the previous paragraph began with "\n" characters? That's because the same string resource identifies flyby text and ToolTip text. Flyby text comes before the newline character, and ToolTip text comes after. Here's what the previous code sample would look like if it were modified to include flyby text as well as ToolTips:

```
// In the RC file
IDR_TOOLBAR BITMAP Toolbar.bmp

IDR_TOOLBAR TOOLBAR 16, 15
BEGIN
    BUTTON ID_CHAR_BOLD
    BUTTON ID_CHAR_ITALIC
    BUTTON ID_CHAR_UNDERLINE
    SEPARATOR
    BUTTON ID_PARA_LEFT
    BUTTON ID_PARA_CENTER
    BUTTON ID_PARA_RIGHT
END

STRINGTABLE
BEGIN
    ID_CHAR_BOLD        "Toggle boldface on or off\nBold"
    ID_CHAR_ITALIC      "Toggle italic on or off\nItalic"
    ID_CHAR_UNDERLINE   "Toggle underline on or off\nUnderline"
    ID_PARA_LEFT        "Align text flush left\nAlign Left"
    ID_PARA_CENTER      "Center text between margins\nAlign Center"
    ID_PARA_RIGHT       "Align text flush right\nAlign Right"
END
```

(continued)

```
// In the CPP file
m_wndToolBar.Create (this, WS_CHILD | WS_VISIBLE |
    CBRS_TOP | CBRS_TOOLTIPS | CBRS_FLYBY);
m_wndToolBar.LoadToolBar (IDR_TOOLBAR);
```

If menu items share the same IDs as the toolbar buttons, the text preceding the newline character in the corresponding string resource is also displayed when a menu item is highlighted. We'll discuss this and other features of status bars shortly.

You can assign ToolTips and flyby text to toolbar buttons visually using the resource editor in Visual C++. With a toolbar resource open for editing, double-clicking a toolbar button displays the button's property sheet. You can then type a string into the Prompt box to assign flyby text, ToolTip text, or both to the button, as shown in Figure 12-4.

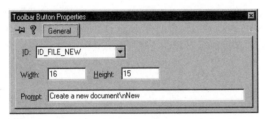

Figure 12-4. *Assigning ToolTip text and flyby text to a toolbar button.*

Adding Non-Push-Button Controls to a Toolbar

Push buttons far outnumber the other types of controls found on toolbars, but *CTool-Bar*s can also include non-push-button controls such as combo boxes and check boxes. Suppose you'd like to add a combo box to a toolbar so that the user can select a type-face or a font size or something else from a drop-down list. Here's how to do it.

The first step is to include either a button separator or a dummy push button—a push button with an arbitrary command ID and button image—in the TOOLBAR resource where you want the combo box to appear. The following TOOLBAR resource definition uses a separator as a placeholder for a combo box that appears to the right of the final push button:

```
IDR_TOOLBAR TOOLBAR 16, 15
BEGIN
    BUTTON      ID_CHAR_BOLD
    BUTTON      ID_CHAR_ITALIC
    BUTTON      ID_CHAR_UNDERLINE
    SEPARATOR
    BUTTON      ID_PARA_LEFT
    BUTTON      ID_PARA_CENTER
    BUTTON      ID_PARA_RIGHT
    SEPARATOR       // Space between button and combo box
    SEPARATOR       // Placeholder for combo box
END
```

The second step is to use *CToolBar::SetButtonInfo* to increase the width of the placeholder to make room for the combo box and then to create a combo box in that space. Assuming that the toolbar is represented by a toolbar class derived from *CToolBar*, that *m_wndComboBox* is a *CComboBox* data member in the derived class, that IDC_COMBOBOX is the combo box's control ID, and that *nWidth* and *nHeight* hold the desired combo box dimensions, here's an excerpt from the derived class's *OnCreate* handler demonstrating how to create the combo box:

```
SetButtonInfo (8, IDC_COMBOBOX, TBBS_SEPARATOR, nWidth);
CRect rect;
GetItemRect (8, &rect);
rect.bottom = rect.top + nHeight;
m_wndComboBox.Create (WS_CHILD | WS_VISIBLE | WS_VSCROLL |
    CBS_SORT | CBS_DROPDOWNLIST, rect, this, IDC_COMBOBOX);
```

The call to *CToolBar::SetButtonInfo* assigns the placeholder the same ID as the combo box and expands the placeholder horizontally so that its width equals the desired width of the combo box. Before *CComboBox::Create* is called to create the combo box, *CToolBar::GetItemRect* is called to retrieve the placeholder's control rectangle. That rectangle is then heightened to make room for the list box part of the combo box, and the combo box is created over the top of the placeholder. The combo box is parented to the toolbar so that it will move when the toolbar moves. The toolbar also receives the combo box's WM_COMMAND messages, but thanks to command routing, the notifications that the combo box sends to its parent can be processed by the frame window, the view, and other standard command targets.

What about ToolTips and flyby text for non-push-button controls? As far as the framework is concerned, the combo box is just another control on the toolbar and can include ToolTips and flyby text just as push button controls can. All you have to do to add ToolTip and flyby text to the combo box is define a string resource whose ID is IDC_COMBOBOX. A ToolTip window will automatically appear when the cursor pauses over the combo box, and the flyby text will appear in the status bar.

Updating Non-Push-Button Controls

It wouldn't make sense to assign an update handler to a combo box in a toolbar because *CCmdUI* isn't designed to handle combo boxes. But MFC provides an alternative update mechanism that's ideal for non-push-button controls. *CControlBar::OnUpdateCmdUI* is a virtual function the framework calls as part of its idle-processing regimen. A derived toolbar class can override *OnUpdateCmdUI* and take the opportunity to update controls that don't have UI update handlers. *OnUpdateCmdUI* is the perfect solution for keeping custom toolbar controls in sync with other parts of the application, and doing it in a passive way that closely mimics the update mechanism used for toolbar buttons and menu items.

Let's say you've derived a toolbar class named *CStyleBar* from *CToolBar* that includes a combo box with a list of all the fonts installed in the system. As the user moves the caret through a document, you want to update the combo box so that the item selected in it is the name of the typeface at the current caret position. Rather than respond to each change in the caret position by updating the combo box selection directly, you can override *OnUpdateCmdUI* as shown here:

```
void CStyleBar::OnUpdateCmdUI (CFrameWnd* pTarget,
    BOOL bDisableIfNoHndler)
{
    CToolBar::OnUpdateCmdUI (pTarget, bDisableIfNoHndler);
    CString string = GetTypefaceAtCaret ();
    if (m_wndComboBox.SelectString (-1, string) == CB_ERR)
        m_wndComboBox.SetCurSel (-1);
}
```

GetTypefaceAtCaret is a *CStyleBar* helper function that retrieves font information from the document or from the view and returns a *CString* with the typeface name. After *GetTypefaceAtCaret* returns, *CComboBox::SelectString* is called to select the corresponding combo box item, and *CComboBox::SetCurSel* is called with a −1 to blank the visible portion of the combo box if *SelectString* fails. With this simple update handler in place, the combo box selection will stay in sync with the caret as the user cursors through the document. The MyWord application presented later in this chapter uses a similar *OnUpdateCmdUI* handler to keep a pair of combo boxes—one for typefaces and one for font sizes—in sync with the caret position.

Generally speaking, you can ignore the *pTarget* and *bDisableIfNoHndler* parameters passed to *OnUpdateCmdUI*. But be sure to call *CToolBar::OnUpdateCmdUI* from the derived class's *OnUpdateCmdUI* function to avoid short-circuiting the update handlers for conventional toolbar buttons.

Making Toolbar Settings Persistent

MFC provides two convenient functions that you can use to preserve toolbar settings across sessions: *CFrameWnd::SaveBarState* and *CFrameWnd::LoadBarState*. *SaveBarState* writes information about each toolbar's docked or floating state, position, orientation, and visibility to the registry or a private INI file. (In Windows 95 and Windows 98 and in all versions of Windows NT, you should call *CWinApp::SetRegistryKey* from the application class's *InitInstance* function so that *SaveBarState* will use the registry.) If your application includes a status bar, *SaveBarState* records information about the status bar, too. Calling *LoadBarState* when the application restarts reads the settings back from the registry and restores each toolbar and status bar to its previous state. Normally, *LoadBarState* is called from the main frame window's *OnCreate* handler after the toolbars and status bars are created, and *SaveBarState* is called from the frame window's *OnClose* handler. If you'd also like to save control bar settings if Windows is shut down while your application is running, call *SaveBarState* from an *OnEndSession* handler, too.

You shouldn't call *SaveBarState* from the frame window's *OnDestroy* handler if you want to preserve the states of floating toolbars as well as docked toolbars. A docked toolbar is a child of the frame window it's docked to, but a floating toolbar is a child of the mini frame window that surrounds it. The mini frame window is a popup window owned by the frame window, but it's not a child of the frame window. (A popup window is a window with the style WS_POPUP; a child window has the WS_CHILD style instead.) The distinction is important because popup windows owned by a frame window are destroyed before the frame window is destroyed. Child windows, on the other hand, are destroyed *after* their parents are destroyed. A floating toolbar no longer exists when the frame window's *OnDestroy* function is called. Consequently, if it's called from *OnDestroy*, *SaveBarState* will fail to save state information for toolbars that aren't docked to the frame window.

Toolbar Support in AppWizard

You can use AppWizard to add a basic toolbar to an application. Checking the Docking Toolbar box in AppWizard's Step 4 dialog box (shown in Figure 12-5) adds a simple toolbar containing push buttons for File-Open, File-Save, and other commonly used commands. Besides creating the TOOLBAR resource and button bitmap, AppWizard adds a *CToolBar* data member named *m_wndToolBar* to the main frame window class and includes in the frame window's *OnCreate* handler code to create the toolbar and to enable docking.

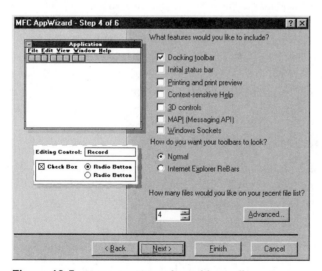

Figure 12-5. *Using AppWizard to add a toolbar.*

AppWizard's toolbar-creation code uses *CToolBar::CreateEx* rather than *CTool-Bar::Create* to create a toolbar, and it passes CBRS_GRIPPER and TBSTYLE_FLAT flags to *CreateEx*. CBRS_GRIPPER draws a thin vertical bar, or "gripper," down the left edge of the toolbar. TBSTYLE_FLAT creates a "flat" toolbar—one with flat buttons whose edges are visible only when the cursor is over them—like the ones in Visual C++. Flat toolbars are only supported on systems that have Internet Explorer installed. Fortunately, they degrade gracefully on older systems by assuming the visage of ordinary toolbars.

STATUS BARS

It has become common, even expected, for Windows applications to include status bars that display context-sensitive help for toolbar buttons and menu items. SDK-style Windows applications customarily display descriptive help text for menu items by trapping WM_MENUSELECT messages and updating the status bar. MFC provides an easier way. When a *CStatusBar* is connected to a frame window, it automatically displays a string of help text when a menu item is highlighted. If the application includes a toolbar, and if the toolbar style includes a CBRS_FLYBY flag, the status bar also displays flyby text for toolbar buttons. The best part is that all you're responsible for besides creating and initializing the status bar (something that requires just a few lines of code) is providing the help text in the form of string resources in your application's RC file. The framework does the rest.

Status bars can do much more than just display help text, of course. A status bar can be divided into one or more areas that are variously referred to as panes, panels, or indicators. The text of each pane can be set individually, so one pane can display the current line number or page number in a document while another displays menu and toolbar help and still others display the current Caps Lock and Num Lock states. Some status bars even contain progress controls that report percentage-complete figures for potentially lengthy operations such as document saving and loading.

Creating and Initializing a Status Bar

In MFC, a status bar is an instance of *CStatusBar*. An application that uses a status bar typically declares a *CStatusBar* object as a member of the frame window class. Then the frame window's *OnCreate* handler creates the status bar with a statement like this one:

```
m_wndStatusBar.Create (this);
```

The lone argument passed to *Create* identifies the status bar's parent window. Passing a *this* pointer referring to a frame window makes the status bar a child of the frame window. A status bar created in this way doesn't need to be destroyed before the application terminates because it's destroyed automatically when its parent is destroyed. *CStatusBar::Create* also accepts parameters specifying the status bar's style and child window ID, but the default values MFC provides for these parameters do quite nicely for most applications.

After it's created, a status bar is initialized by calling *CStatusBar::SetIndicators*. *SetIndicators* specifies the number of panes the status bar will contain and optionally assigns string resources to individual panes. The statements

```
UINT nIndicator = ID_SEPARATOR;
m_wndStatusBar.Create (this);
m_wndStatusBar.SetIndicators (&nIndicator, 1);
```

create a simple status bar containing just one pane. ID_SEPARATOR is a generic ID that says no string resource is associated with this pane. You can create a simple "binary" pane that indicates whether a particular feature of your application is on or off by specifying a string resource ID instead of ID_SEPARATOR and connecting the pane to an update handler that uses *CCmdUI::Enable* to enable and disable the pane. An enabled pane displays the string resource assigned to it, but a disabled pane is blank. The status bar created by the following code sample includes a pane that displays the text string "INS" when the application is in insert mode and nothing when it's in overstrike mode. This example assumes that insert mode is on when *m_bInsert* is nonzero and off when *m_bInsert* is 0:

```
// In the RC file
STRINGTABLE
BEGIN
    ID_INDICATOR_INS "INS"
END

// In CMainFrame's message map
ON_UPDATE_COMMAND_UI (ID_INDICATOR_INS, OnUpdateIndicator)

// In CMainFrame::OnCreate
static UINT nIndicators[] = {
    ID_SEPARATOR,
    ID_INDICATOR_INS
};

m_wndStatusBar.Create (this);
m_wndStatusBar.SetIndicators (nIndicators, 2);

// Elsewhere in CMainFrame
void CMainFrame::OnUpdateIndicator (CCmdUI* pCmdUI)
{
    pCmdUI->Enable (m_bInsert);
}
```

In this example, the frame window handles the UI update commands. In a real application, it might be more appropriate to make *OnUpdateIndicator* a member of the document or the view class. ID_INDICATOR_INS is a symbolic constant defined elsewhere in the application; MFC doesn't define it for you.

MFC defines four special indicator IDs for status bar panes that display keyboard states and maps them to a common update handler in the *CFrameWnd* class:

- ID_INDICATOR_CAPS, which corresponds to the Caps Lock key

- ID_INDICATOR_NUM, which corresponds to the Num Lock key

- ID_INDICATOR_SCRL, which corresponds to the Scroll Lock key

- ID_INDICATOR_KANA, which corresponds to the Kana key on Japanese keyboards

A status bar pane assigned the ID value ID_INDICATOR_CAPS displays the word "CAP" when Caps Lock is on. Similarly, an ID_INDICATOR_NUM pane displays "NUM" when Num Lock is on, an ID_INDICATOR_SCRL pane displays "SCRL" when Scroll Lock is on, and an ID_INDICATOR_KANA pane displays "KANA" when Kana mode is enabled on Japanese keyboards. The framework (in reality, *CFrameWnd::OnUpdate-KeyIndicator*) keeps these indicators in sync with the keyboard. Consequently, you can create a status bar with Caps Lock, Num Lock, and Scroll Lock indicators simply by adding the magic ID values to the array passed to *SetIndicators*:

```
static UINT nIndicators[] = {
    ID_SEPARATOR,
    ID_INDICATOR_CAPS,
    ID_INDICATOR_NUM,
    ID_INDICATOR_SCRL
};

m_wndStatusBar.Create (this);
m_wndStatusBar.SetIndicators (nIndicators, 4);
```

The resulting status bar is shown in Figure 12-6. The blank pane indicates that Scroll Lock is inactive. *CStatusBar* automatically positions all panes after the first at the far right end of the status bar and stretches the leftmost pane to fill the remaining space. It sizes the other panes so that they're just wide enough to display the text strings assigned to them. Panes other than the first are also drawn "indented" so that they're visible even when they're blank.

Figure 12-6. *Status bar with Caps Lock, Num Lock, and Scroll Lock indicators.*

Providing Context-Sensitive Help for Menu Items

When you assign the first (leftmost) pane in a status bar the value ID_SEPARATOR, you enable a special feature of MFC that is elegant in both design and simplicity. When the user highlights a menu item, the framework checks to see whether the application's EXE file contains a string resource whose ID equals the menu item ID. If the search turns up a match, the string resource is loaded and displayed in the status bar pane. As a result, you can provide context-sensitive help for your application's menus by providing string resources whose IDs match the menu item IDs. If a menu item and a toolbar button share the same ID, the same string resource doubles as help text for the menu item and as flyby text for the toolbar.

As it does for toolbar buttons, the framework provides default help strings for ID_FILE_NEW, ID_FILE_OPEN, and other common command IDs. It also provides default help strings for commands found in the system menu. (For a complete list of predefined IDs and the help text and ToolTip text associated with them, look in the MFC source code file Prompts.rc.) Simply include the header file Afxres.h in your application's RC file, and the framework's predefined string resources will be included, too. If you use AppWizard to create the application, Afxres.h is included for you. Rather than add string resources for other menu items by hand, you can double-click a menu item in the menu editor and enter a string in the Menu Item Properties window's Prompt box.

You can override the help text for predefined menu item IDs by defining your own string resources with identical ID values. For a nice touch, include an

```
AFX_IDS_IDLEMESSAGE "Ready"
```

statement in your application's string table, and the framework will display the word "Ready" in the status bar when no menu is pulled down or no item is selected. As usual, this is done for you if you use AppWizard to add a status bar to your application.

Creating Custom Status Bar Panes

Now you know how to display help text in a status bar, add Caps Lock, Num Lock, and Scroll Lock indicators, and create simple on/off indicators by combining string resources and update handlers. But what about more complex status bars like the ones featured in Microsoft Word, Microsoft Excel, Microsoft PowerPoint, and other Windows applications? How, for example, would you create a status bar pane that displays the time of day or the current page number?

For starters, you can add panes to a status bar and size them any way you want using *CStatusBar*'s *SetPaneInfo* function. *SetPaneInfo* accepts four parameters: the 0-based index of the pane whose attributes you want to modify and the pane's ID, style, and width, in that order. The pane style specifies whether the pane will be drawn indented, protruding, or flush with the face of the status bar. It also determines whether the pane is currently enabled or disabled and identifies variable-width panes that expand and contract with the status bar. The style is a combination of one or more of the following values:

Style	Description
SBPS_NOBORDERS	Draws the pane flush with the surface of the status bar.
SBPS_POPOUT	Draws the pane so that it protrudes from the status bar.
SBPS_NORMAL	Draws the pane so that it is indented into the status bar.
SBPS_DISABLED	Disables the pane. Disabled panes don't display text.
SBPS_STRETCH	Stretches the pane to fill unused space when the status bar is resized. Only one pane per status bar can have this style.
SBPS_OWNERDRAW	Creates an owner-draw pane.

The following code creates a status bar with three custom panes. The first pane is 64 pixels wide and is drawn flush with the surface of the status bar. The second is also 64 pixels wide, but it protrudes from the status bar. The third is a variable-width pane whose right edge follows the right edge of the status bar. It's drawn with an indented border.

```
static UINT nIndicators[] = {
    ID_SEPARATOR,
    ID_SEPARATOR,
    ID_SEPARATOR
};

m_wndStatusBar.Create (this);
m_wndStatusBar.SetIndicators (nIndicators, 3);

m_wndStatusBar.SetPaneInfo (0, ID_SEPARATOR, SBPS_NOBORDERS, 64);
m_wndStatusBar.SetPaneInfo (1, ID_SEPARATOR, SBPS_POPOUT, 64);
m_wndStatusBar.SetPaneInfo (2, ID_SEPARATOR, SBPS_NORMAL |
    SBPS_STRETCH, 0);
```

In a real application, you'll probably want to avoid hard pixel counts and, instead, base pane widths on a scalable screen metric such as the average width of a character in the status bar font. You can get a *CFont* pointer for the default status bar font by calling the *GetFont* function a *CStatusBar* inherits from *CWnd*.

Once a custom pane is created, it's your job to tell the status bar what to display inside the pane. You can add text to a pane in two ways. You can call *CStatusBar::SetPaneText* to set the text directly, or you can assign the pane an update handler and let the update handler set the text with *CCmdUI::SetText*. Which method you use depends on how you want the pane to be updated. The following code fragment

sets a timer to fire every 200 milliseconds and uses *SetPaneText* to update an hours-
:minutes:seconds display in pane 2. (Windows timers are discussed in Chapter 14.)
In this case, the ID assigned to the pane in the call to *SetIndicators* or *SetPaneInfo* is
irrelevant because *SetPaneText* identifies panes by index.

```
// In CMainFrame::OnCreate
SetTimer (ID_TIMER, 200, NULL);
        .
        .
        .
void CMainFrame::OnTimer (UINT nTimerID)
{
    CTime time = CTime::GetCurrentTime ();
    int nSecond = time.GetSecond ();
    int nMinute = time.GetMinute ();
    int nHour = time.GetHour () % 12;

    CString string;
    string.Format (_T ("%0.2d:%0.2d:%0.2d"), nHour, nMinute, nSecond);
    m_wndStatusBar.SetPaneText (2, string);
}
```

An alternative approach is to assign the pane a unique ID such as ID_INDICATOR-
_TIME and connect it to an update handler with a message-map entry. Now the time-
of-day display in the status bar will be continually updated by the framework.

```
// In the message map
ON_UPDATE_COMMAND_UI (ID_INDICATOR_TIME, OnUpdateTime)
        .
        .
        .
void CMainFrame::OnUpdateTime (CCmdUI* pCmdUI)
{
    CTime time = CTime::GetCurrentTime ();
    int nSecond = time.GetSecond ();
    int nMinute = time.GetMinute ();
    int nHour = time.GetHour () % 12;

    CString string;
    string.Format (_T ("%0.2d:%0.2d:%0.2d"), nHour, nMinute, nSecond);
    pCmdUI->SetText (string);
}
```

The best way to define ID_INDICATOR_TIME is to add a string resource with that ID
to your application. Assign the string a dummy value such as "MMMMM," and MFC
will use the width of the string to size the status bar pane. Incidentally, you can include a leading tab character ("\t") in text written to a status bar to center the text in
the pane or two leading tab characters ("\t\t") to right-align the text.

Status Bar Support in AppWizard

You can use AppWizard to add a status bar to an MFC application by checking the Initial Status Bar box in AppWizard's Step 4 dialog box, as shown in Figure 12-7. AppWizard responds by adding a *CStatusBar* member variable to the main frame window class and hooking it up with an *OnCreate* handler that creates a four-pane status bar: an ID_SEPARATOR pane in which help text appears and indicator panes for the Caps Lock, Num Lock, and Scroll Lock keys.

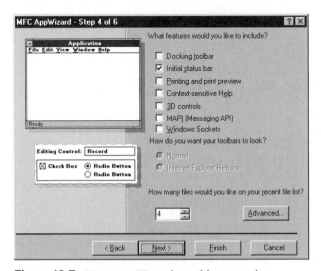

Figure 12-7. *Using AppWizard to add a status bar.*

One of the first questions new MFC programmers ask about AppWizard-generated status bars is, "How do I get rid of the keyboard indicator panes?" The answer is simple. Begin by finding the following statements in the CPP file for the AppWizard-generated main frame window class:

```
static UINT indicators[] =
{
    ID_SEPARATOR,           // status line indicator
    ID_INDICATOR_CAPS,
    ID_INDICATOR_NUM,
    ID_INDICATOR_SCRL,
};
```

Then remove the final three entries so that the array looks like this:

```
static UINT indicators[] =
{
    ID_SEPARATOR            // status line indicator
};
```

That's all there is to it. Rebuild the application and the indicator panes will be no more.

PUTTING IT ALL TOGETHER: THE MYWORD APPLICATION

The sample program shown in Figure 12-8 demonstrates many of the principles discussed in the preceding sections. MyWord is a miniature word processor built around a *CRichEditView*. MFC's *CRichEditView* class is like a *CEditView* on steroids; based on the rich text edit control supplied in the common controls library, it features superior text formatting capabilities and the ability to read and write rich text format (RTF) files with a simple function call. MyWord doesn't use all the features of a *CRichEditView*; in fact, it barely scratches the surface. (For a more in-depth look at *CRichEditView*, see the Wordpad sample program provided with MFC. The Wordpad files are the actual source code for the Wordpad applet that ships with Windows.) But MyWord packs a lot of punch for a program that's only a few hundred lines long, and it's a good starting point for writing *CRichEditView*-based applications of your own.

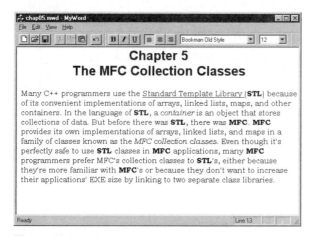

Figure 12-8. *The MyWord window.*

MyWord uses two toolbars and one status bar. The main toolbar includes buttons that serve as shortcuts for the New, Open, and Save items in the File menu and the Cut, Copy, Paste, and Undo items in the Edit menu. The other toolbar, which I'll refer to as the *style bar,* includes check push buttons for setting the character format (bold, italic, and underline), radio push buttons for setting the paragraph alignment (left aligned, centered, and right aligned), and combo boxes for selecting typefaces and font sizes. Both toolbars can be detached from the frame window, floated, and docked at other locations; and both can be resized while they're floating. Try it: Drag the main toolbar to the right side of the window, and dock it in a vertical position. Grab the style bar and release it in the center of the window so that it becomes a floating palette. Use the View menu to hide and display the toolbars and the status bar. You can also hide a toolbar by clicking the close button in the mini frame window it floats in when it's detached from the main frame window. To redisplay the toolbar, simply select the Toolbar or Style Bar command in the View menu.

The status bar at the bottom of MyWord's frame window displays help text for menu items and toolbar controls. It also includes Caps Lock and Num Lock indicators and a line number display that's continually updated as the caret moves through the document. The Caps Lock and Num Lock indicators were added using MFC's predefined ID_INDICATOR_CAPS and ID_INDICATOR_NUM IDs. The line number indicator is updated by an ON_UPDATE_COMMAND_UI handler that, when called, retrieves the current line number from the *CRichEditView*, formulates a text string containing the line number, and updates the status bar display with *CCmdUI::SetText*. The line number pane is sized to fit the dummy string "Line 00000," whose resource ID, ID_INDICATOR_LINE, is identical to the status bar pane's ID. The dummy string is never seen because the pane is updated with a real line number before the status bar appears on the screen.

I used AppWizard to begin MyWord. I checked the Docking Toolbar and Initial Status Bar options in AppWizard's Step 4 dialog box, and in Step 6, I selected *CRichEditView* as the base class for the view. I next derived a class named *CStyleBar* to represent the style bar, added a *CStyleBar* data member to the frame window class, and modified the frame window's *OnCreate* function to create the style bar. (I used ClassWizard to perform the class derivation, but because ClassWizard doesn't support *CToolBar* as a base class, I derived *CStyleBar* from *CCmdTarget* and then manually patched up the code to change the base class to *CToolBar*.) I used Visual C++'s Insert-Resource command to create the toolbar resource from which the style bar is created, and I added buttons in the toolbar editor. Finishing MyWord was a matter of writing the command handlers, update handlers, and ordinary class member functions that form the core of the application.

The source code for MyWord's frame window, document, view, and style bar classes is listed in Figure 12-9. Take a moment to look it over to see how the toolbars and status bar are handled. Then flip forward a few pages to read about pertinent parts of the source code in greater detail.

MainFrm.h

```
// MainFrm.h : interface of the CMainFrame class
//
/////////////////////////////////////////////////////////////////////////////

#if !defined(
    AFX_MAINFRM_H__C85C9089_A154_11D2_8E53_006008A82731__INCLUDED_)
#define AFX_MAINFRM_H__C85C9089_A154_11D2_8E53_006008A82731__INCLUDED_
```

Figure 12-9. *The MyWord application.*

```
#include "StyleBar.h"    // Added by ClassView
#if _MSC_VER > 1000
#pragma once
#endif // _MSC_VER > 1000


class CMainFrame : public CFrameWnd
{

protected: // create from serialization only
    CMainFrame();
    DECLARE_DYNCREATE(CMainFrame)

// Attributes
public:

// Operations
public:

// Overrides
    // ClassWizard generated virtual function overrides
    //{{AFX_VIRTUAL(CMainFrame)
    virtual BOOL PreCreateWindow(CREATESTRUCT& cs);
    //}}AFX_VIRTUAL

// Implementation
public:
    virtual ~CMainFrame();
#ifdef _DEBUG
    virtual void AssertValid() const;
    virtual void Dump(CDumpContext& dc) const;
#endif

protected:  // control bar embedded members
    CStyleBar    m_wndStyleBar;
    CStatusBar   m_wndStatusBar;
    CToolBar     m_wndToolBar;
// Generated message map functions
protected:
    BOOL CreateToolBar ();
    BOOL CreateStyleBar ();
    BOOL CreateStatusBar ();
    //{{AFX_MSG(CMainFrame)
    afx_msg int OnCreate(LPCREATESTRUCT lpCreateStruct);
    afx_msg void OnClose();
    //}}AFX_MSG
    DECLARE_MESSAGE_MAP()
};
```

(continued)

Figure 12-9. *continued*

```
///////////////////////////////////////////////////////////////////////////

//{{AFX_INSERT_LOCATION}}
// Microsoft Visual C++ will insert additional declarations
// immediately before the previous line.

#endif
// !defined(AFX_MAINFRM_H__C85C9089_A154_11D2_8E53_006008A82731__INCLUDED_)
```

MainFrm.cpp

```
// MainFrm.cpp : implementation of the CMainFrame class
//

#include "stdafx.h"
#include "MyWord.h"

#include "MainFrm.h"

#ifdef _DEBUG
#define new DEBUG_NEW
#undef THIS_FILE
static char THIS_FILE[] = __FILE__;
#endif

///////////////////////////////////////////////////////////////////////////
// CMainFrame

IMPLEMENT_DYNCREATE(CMainFrame, CFrameWnd)

BEGIN_MESSAGE_MAP(CMainFrame, CFrameWnd)
    //{{AFX_MSG_MAP(CMainFrame)
    ON_WM_CREATE()
    ON_WM_CLOSE()
    //}}AFX_MSG_MAP

ON_COMMAND_EX (IDW_STYLE_BAR, OnBarCheck)
    ON_UPDATE_COMMAND_UI (IDW_STYLE_BAR, OnUpdateControlBarMenu)
END_MESSAGE_MAP()

///////////////////////////////////////////////////////////////////////////
// CMainFrame construction/destruction

CMainFrame::CMainFrame()
{
}
```

```
CMainFrame::~CMainFrame()
{
}

int CMainFrame::OnCreate(LPCREATESTRUCT lpCreateStruct)
{
    if (CFrameWnd::OnCreate(lpCreateStruct) == -1)
        return -1;

    //
    // Tell the frame window to permit docking.
    //
    EnableDocking (CBRS_ALIGN_ANY);

    //
    // Create the toolbar, style bar, and status bar.
    //
    if (!CreateToolBar () ||
        !CreateStyleBar () ||
        !CreateStatusBar ())
        return -1;

    //
    // Load the saved bar state (if any).
    //
    LoadBarState (_T ("MainBarState"));
    return 0;
}

BOOL CMainFrame::PreCreateWindow(CREATESTRUCT& cs)
{
    if( !CFrameWnd::PreCreateWindow(cs) )
        return FALSE;
    return TRUE;
}
/////////////////////////////////////////////////////////////////////////////
// CMainFrame diagnostics

#ifdef _DEBUG
void CMainFrame::AssertValid() const
{
    CFrameWnd::AssertValid();
}

void CMainFrame::Dump(CDumpContext& dc) const
{
```

(continued)

Figure 12-9. *continued*

```
    CFrameWnd::Dump(dc);
}

#endif //_DEBUG

//////////////////////////////////////////////////////////////////////////
// CMainFrame message handlers

void CMainFrame::OnClose()
{
    SaveBarState (_T ("MainBarState"));
    CFrameWnd::OnClose();
}

BOOL CMainFrame::CreateToolBar()
{
    if (!m_wndToolBar.Create (this) ||
        !m_wndToolBar.LoadToolBar (IDR_MAINFRAME))
        return FALSE;

    m_wndToolBar.SetBarStyle (m_wndToolBar.GetBarStyle () |
        CBRS_TOOLTIPS | CBRS_FLYBY | CBRS_SIZE_DYNAMIC);

    m_wndToolBar.SetWindowText (_T ("Main"));
    m_wndToolBar.EnableDocking (CBRS_ALIGN_ANY);
    DockControlBar (&m_wndToolBar);
    return TRUE;
}

BOOL CMainFrame::CreateStyleBar()
{
    if (!m_wndStyleBar.Create (this, WS_CHILD | WS_VISIBLE | CBRS_TOP |
        CBRS_TOOLTIPS | CBRS_FLYBY | CBRS_SIZE_DYNAMIC, IDW_STYLE_BAR))
        return FALSE;

    m_wndStyleBar.SetWindowText (_T ("Styles"));
    m_wndStyleBar.EnableDocking (CBRS_ALIGN_TOP | CBRS_ALIGN_BOTTOM);
    DockControlBar (&m_wndStyleBar);
    return TRUE;
}

BOOL CMainFrame::CreateStatusBar()
{
    static UINT nIndicators[] = {
```

```
        ID_SEPARATOR,
        ID_INDICATOR_LINE,
        ID_INDICATOR_CAPS,
        ID_INDICATOR_NUM
    };

    if (!m_wndStatusBar.Create (this))
        return FALSE;

    m_wndStatusBar.SetIndicators (nIndicators, 4);
    return TRUE;
}
```

MyWordDoc.h

```cpp
// MyWordDoc.h : interface of the CMyWordDoc class
//
//////////////////////////////////////////////////////////////////////

#if !defined(
    AFX_MYWORDDOC_H__C85C908B_A154_11D2_8E53_006008A82731__INCLUDED_)
#define AFX_MYWORDDOC_H__C85C908B_A154_11D2_8E53_006008A82731__INCLUDED_

#if _MSC_VER > 1000
#pragma once
#endif // _MSC_VER > 1000


class CMyWordDoc : public CRichEditDoc
{
protected: // create from serialization only
    CMyWordDoc();
    DECLARE_DYNCREATE(CMyWordDoc)

// Attributes
public:

// Operations
public:

// Overrides
    // ClassWizard generated virtual function overrides
    //{{AFX_VIRTUAL(CMyWordDoc)
    public:
```

(continued)

Figure 12-9. *continued*

```
    virtual BOOL OnNewDocument();
    virtual void Serialize(CArchive& ar);
    //}}AFX_VIRTUAL
    virtual CRichEditCntrItem* CreateClientItem(REOBJECT* preo) const;


// Implementation
public:
    virtual ~CMyWordDoc();
#ifdef _DEBUG
    virtual void AssertValid() const;
    virtual void Dump(CDumpContext& dc) const;
#endif

protected:

// Generated message map functions
protected:
    //{{AFX_MSG(CMyWordDoc)
        // NOTE - the ClassWizard will add and remove member functions here.
        //    DO NOT EDIT what you see in these blocks of generated code !
    //}}AFX_MSG
    DECLARE_MESSAGE_MAP()
};


/////////////////////////////////////////////////////////////////////////////

//{{AFX_INSERT_LOCATION}}
// Microsoft Visual C++ will insert additional declarations
// immediately before the previous line.

#endif
// !defined(
//     AFX_MYWORDDOC_H__C85C908B_A154_11D2_8E53_006008A82731__INCLUDED_)
```

MyWordDoc.cpp

```
// MyWordDoc.cpp : implementation of the CMyWordDoc class
//

#include "stdafx.h"
#include "MyWord.h"

#include "MyWordDoc.h"
#include "CntrItem.h"
```

```
#ifdef _DEBUG
#define new DEBUG_NEW
#undef THIS_FILE
static char THIS_FILE[] = __FILE__;
#endif


/////////////////////////////////////////////////////////////////////////
// CMyWordDoc

IMPLEMENT_DYNCREATE(CMyWordDoc, CRichEditDoc)

BEGIN_MESSAGE_MAP(CMyWordDoc, CRichEditDoc)
    //{{AFX_MSG_MAP(CMyWordDoc)
        // NOTE - the ClassWizard will add and remove mapping macros here.
        //    DO NOT EDIT what you see in these blocks of generated code!
    //}}AFX_MSG_MAP
    // Enable default OLE container implementation
    ON_UPDATE_COMMAND_UI(ID_OLE_EDIT_LINKS,
        CRichEditDoc::OnUpdateEditLinksMenu)
    ON_COMMAND(ID_OLE_EDIT_LINKS, CRichEditDoc::OnEditLinks)
    ON_UPDATE_COMMAND_UI_RANGE(ID_OLE_VERB_FIRST,
        ID_OLE_VERB_LAST, CRichEditDoc::OnUpdateObjectVerbMenu)
END_MESSAGE_MAP()

/////////////////////////////////////////////////////////////////////////
// CMyWordDoc construction/destruction

CMyWordDoc::CMyWordDoc()
{
}


CMyWordDoc::~CMyWordDoc()
{
}


BOOL CMyWordDoc::OnNewDocument()
{
    if (!CRichEditDoc::OnNewDocument())
        return FALSE;
    return TRUE;
}
CRichEditCntrItem* CMyWordDoc::CreateClientItem(REOBJECT* preo) const
{
    return new CMyWordCntrItem(preo, (CMyWordDoc*) this);
}
```

(continued)

Figure 12-9. *continued*

```
///////////////////////////////////////////////////////////////////////
// CMyWordDoc serialization

void CMyWordDoc::Serialize(CArchive& ar)
{
    CRichEditDoc::Serialize(ar);
}


///////////////////////////////////////////////////////////////////////
// CMyWordDoc diagnostics

#ifdef _DEBUG
void CMyWordDoc::AssertValid() const
{
    CRichEditDoc::AssertValid();
}

void CMyWordDoc::Dump(CDumpContext& dc) const
{
    CRichEditDoc::Dump(dc);
}
#endif //_DEBUG


///////////////////////////////////////////////////////////////////////
// CMyWordDoc commands
```

MyWordView.h

```
// MyWordView.h : interface of the CMyWordView class
//
///////////////////////////////////////////////////////////////////////

#if !defined(
    AFX_MYWORDVIEW_H__C85C908D_A154_11D2_8E53_006008A82731__INCLUDED_)
#define AFX_MYWORDVIEW_H__C85C908D_A154_11D2_8E53_006008A82731__INCLUDED_

#if _MSC_VER > 1000
#pragma once
#endif // _MSC_VER > 1000

class CMyWordCntrItem;

class CMyWordView : public CRichEditView
{
```

```
protected: // create from serialization only
    CMyWordView();
    DECLARE_DYNCREATE(CMyWordView)

// Attributes
public:
    CMyWordDoc* GetDocument();

// Operations
public:
    void GetFontInfo (LPTSTR pszFaceName, int& nSize);
    void ChangeFont (LPCTSTR pszFaceName);
    void ChangeFontSize (int nSize);

// Overrides
    // ClassWizard generated virtual function overrides
    //{{AFX_VIRTUAL(CMyWordView)
    public:
    virtual BOOL PreCreateWindow(CREATESTRUCT& cs);
    protected:
    virtual void OnInitialUpdate(); // called first time after construct
    //}}AFX_VIRTUAL

// Implementation
public:
    virtual ~CMyWordView();
#ifdef _DEBUG
    virtual void AssertValid() const;
    virtual void Dump(CDumpContext& dc) const;
#endif

protected:

// Generated message map functions
protected:
    //{{AFX_MSG(CMyWordView)
    afx_msg void OnDestroy();
    afx_msg void OnCharBold();
    afx_msg void OnCharItalic();
    afx_msg void OnCharUnderline();
    afx_msg void OnParaLeft();
    afx_msg void OnParaCenter();
    afx_msg void OnParaRight();
    afx_msg void OnUpdateCharBold(CCmdUI* pCmdUI);
    afx_msg void OnUpdateCharItalic(CCmdUI* pCmdUI);
    afx_msg void OnUpdateCharUnderline(CCmdUI* pCmdUI);
```

(continued)

Figure 12-9. *continued*

```
    afx_msg void OnUpdateParaLeft(CCmdUI* pCmdUI);
    afx_msg void OnUpdateParaCenter(CCmdUI* pCmdUI);
    afx_msg void OnUpdateParaRight(CCmdUI* pCmdUI);
    //}}AFX_MSG
    afx_msg void OnUpdateLineNumber (CCmdUI* pCmdUI);
    DECLARE_MESSAGE_MAP()
};

#ifndef _DEBUG  // debug version in MyWordView.cpp
inline CMyWordDoc* CMyWordView::GetDocument()
    { return (CMyWordDoc*)m_pDocument; }
#endif


/////////////////////////////////////////////////////////////////////////

//{{AFX_INSERT_LOCATION}}
// Microsoft Visual C++ will insert additional declarations
// immediately before the previous line.

#endif
// !defined(
//     AFX_MYWORDVIEW_H__C85C908D_A154_11D2_8E53_006008A82731__INCLUDED_)
```

MyWordView.cpp

```
// MyWordView.cpp : implementation of the CMyWordView class
//

#include "stdafx.h"
#include "MyWord.h"

#include "MyWordDoc.h"
#include "CntrItem.h"
#include "MyWordView.h"

#ifdef _DEBUG
#define new DEBUG_NEW
#undef THIS_FILE
static char THIS_FILE[] = __FILE__;
#endif


/////////////////////////////////////////////////////////////////////////
// CMyWordView

IMPLEMENT_DYNCREATE(CMyWordView, CRichEditView)
```

```
BEGIN_MESSAGE_MAP(CMyWordView, CRichEditView)
    //{{AFX_MSG_MAP(CMyWordView)
    ON_WM_DESTROY()
    ON_COMMAND(ID_CHAR_BOLD, OnCharBold)
    ON_COMMAND(ID_CHAR_ITALIC, OnCharItalic)
    ON_COMMAND(ID_CHAR_UNDERLINE, OnCharUnderline)
    ON_COMMAND(ID_PARA_LEFT, OnParaLeft)
    ON_COMMAND(ID_PARA_CENTER, OnParaCenter)
    ON_COMMAND(ID_PARA_RIGHT, OnParaRight)
    ON_UPDATE_COMMAND_UI(ID_CHAR_BOLD, OnUpdateCharBold)
    ON_UPDATE_COMMAND_UI(ID_CHAR_ITALIC, OnUpdateCharItalic)
    ON_UPDATE_COMMAND_UI(ID_CHAR_UNDERLINE, OnUpdateCharUnderline)
    ON_UPDATE_COMMAND_UI(ID_PARA_LEFT, OnUpdateParaLeft)
    ON_UPDATE_COMMAND_UI(ID_PARA_CENTER, OnUpdateParaCenter)
    ON_UPDATE_COMMAND_UI(ID_PARA_RIGHT, OnUpdateParaRight)
    //}}AFX_MSG_MAP
    ON_UPDATE_COMMAND_UI(ID_INDICATOR_LINE, OnUpdateLineNumber)
END_MESSAGE_MAP()


/////////////////////////////////////////////////////////////////////////////
// CMyWordView construction/destruction

CMyWordView::CMyWordView()
{
}


CMyWordView::~CMyWordView()
{
}


BOOL CMyWordView::PreCreateWindow(CREATESTRUCT& cs)
{
    return CRichEditView::PreCreateWindow(cs);
}


void CMyWordView::OnInitialUpdate()
{
    CRichEditView::OnInitialUpdate();

    CHARFORMAT cf;
    cf.cbSize = sizeof (CHARFORMAT);
    cf.dwMask = CFM_BOLD | CFM_ITALIC | CFM_UNDERLINE |
        CFM_PROTECTED | CFM_STRIKEOUT | CFM_FACE | CFM_SIZE;
    cf.dwEffects = 0;
    cf.yHeight = 240; // 240 twips == 12 points
```

(continued)

Figure 12-9. *continued*

```
    ::lstrcpy (cf.szFaceName, _T ("Times New Roman"));
    SetCharFormat (cf);
}


void CMyWordView::OnDestroy()
{
    // Deactivate the item on destruction; this is important
    // when a splitter view is being used.
    CRichEditView::OnDestroy();
    COleClientItem* pActiveItem = GetDocument()->GetInPlaceActiveItem(this);
    if (pActiveItem != NULL && pActiveItem->GetActiveView() == this)
    {
        pActiveItem->Deactivate();
        ASSERT(GetDocument()->GetInPlaceActiveItem(this) == NULL);
    }
}


/////////////////////////////////////////////////////////////////////////////
// CMyWordView diagnostics

#ifdef _DEBUG
void CMyWordView::AssertValid() const
{
    CRichEditView::AssertValid();
}


void CMyWordView::Dump(CDumpContext& dc) const
{
    CRichEditView::Dump(dc);
}


CMyWordDoc* CMyWordView::GetDocument() // non-debug version is inline
{
    ASSERT(m_pDocument->IsKindOf(RUNTIME_CLASS(CMyWordDoc)));
    return (CMyWordDoc*)m_pDocument;
}
#endif //_DEBUG


/////////////////////////////////////////////////////////////////////////////
// CMyWordView message handlers

void CMyWordView::OnCharBold()
{
    CHARFORMAT cf;
    cf = GetCharFormatSelection ();
```

```
    if (!(cf.dwMask & CFM_BOLD) !! !(cf.dwEffects & CFE_BOLD))
        cf.dwEffects = CFE_BOLD;
    else
        cf.dwEffects = 0;

    cf.dwMask = CFM_BOLD;
    SetCharFormat (cf);
}

void CMyWordView::OnCharItalic()
{
    CHARFORMAT cf;
    cf = GetCharFormatSelection ();

    if (!(cf.dwMask & CFM_ITALIC) !! !(cf.dwEffects & CFE_ITALIC))
        cf.dwEffects = CFE_ITALIC;
    else
        cf.dwEffects = 0;

    cf.dwMask = CFM_ITALIC;
    SetCharFormat (cf);
}

void CMyWordView::OnCharUnderline()
{
    CHARFORMAT cf;
    cf = GetCharFormatSelection ();

    if (!(cf.dwMask & CFM_UNDERLINE) !! !(cf.dwEffects & CFE_UNDERLINE))
        cf.dwEffects = CFE_UNDERLINE;
    else
        cf.dwEffects = 0;

    cf.dwMask = CFM_UNDERLINE;
    SetCharFormat (cf);
}

void CMyWordView::OnParaLeft()
{
    OnParaAlign (PFA_LEFT);
}

void CMyWordView::OnParaCenter()
{
    OnParaAlign (PFA_CENTER);
}
```

(continued)

Figure 12-9. *continued*

```
void CMyWordView::OnParaRight()
{
    OnParaAlign (PFA_RIGHT);
}

void CMyWordView::OnUpdateCharBold(CCmdUI* pCmdUI)
{
    OnUpdateCharEffect (pCmdUI, CFM_BOLD, CFE_BOLD);
}

void CMyWordView::OnUpdateCharItalic(CCmdUI* pCmdUI)
{
    OnUpdateCharEffect (pCmdUI, CFM_ITALIC, CFE_ITALIC);
}

void CMyWordView::OnUpdateCharUnderline(CCmdUI* pCmdUI)
{
    OnUpdateCharEffect (pCmdUI, CFM_UNDERLINE, CFE_UNDERLINE);
}

void CMyWordView::OnUpdateParaLeft(CCmdUI* pCmdUI)
{
    OnUpdateParaAlign (pCmdUI, PFA_LEFT);
}

void CMyWordView::OnUpdateParaCenter(CCmdUI* pCmdUI)
{
    OnUpdateParaAlign (pCmdUI, PFA_CENTER);
}

void CMyWordView::OnUpdateParaRight(CCmdUI* pCmdUI)
{
    OnUpdateParaAlign (pCmdUI, PFA_RIGHT);
}

void CMyWordView::OnUpdateLineNumber(CCmdUI* pCmdUI)
{
    int nLine = GetRichEditCtrl ().LineFromChar (-1) + 1;

    CString string;
    string.Format (_T ("Line %d"), nLine);
    pCmdUI->Enable (TRUE);
    pCmdUI->SetText (string);
}

void CMyWordView::ChangeFont(LPCTSTR pszFaceName)
```

```
{
    CHARFORMAT cf;
    cf.cbSize = sizeof (CHARFORMAT);
    cf.dwMask = CFM_FACE;
    ::lstrcpy (cf.szFaceName, pszFaceName);
    SetCharFormat (cf);
}

void CMyWordView::ChangeFontSize(int nSize)
{
    CHARFORMAT cf;
    cf.cbSize = sizeof (CHARFORMAT);
    cf.dwMask = CFM_SIZE;
    cf.yHeight = nSize;
    SetCharFormat (cf);
}

void CMyWordView::GetFontInfo(LPTSTR pszFaceName, int& nSize)
{
    CHARFORMAT cf = GetCharFormatSelection ();
    ::lstrcpy (pszFaceName,
        cf.dwMask & CFM_FACE ? cf.szFaceName : _T (""));
    nSize = cf.dwMask & CFM_SIZE ? cf.yHeight : -1;
}
```

StyleBar.h

```
#if !defined(
    AFX_STYLEBAR_H__C85C9099_A154_11D2_8E53_006008A82731__INCLUDED_)
#define AFX_STYLEBAR_H__C85C9099_A154_11D2_8E53_006008A82731__INCLUDED_

#if _MSC_VER > 1000
#pragma once
#endif // _MSC_VER > 1000
// StyleBar.h : header file
//


/////////////////////////////////////////////////////////////////////////////
// CStyleBar command target

class CStyleBar : public CToolBar
{
// Attributes
public:
```

(continued)

Figure 12-9. *continued*

```
// Operations
public:
    static int CALLBACK EnumFontNameProc (ENUMLOGFONT* lpelf,
    NEWTEXTMETRIC* lpntm, int nFontType, LPARAM lParam);

// Overrides
    // ClassWizard generated virtual function overrides
    //{{AFX_VIRTUAL(CStyleBar)
    //}}AFX_VIRTUAL
    virtual void OnUpdateCmdUI (CFrameWnd* pTarget,
        BOOL bDisableIfNoHndler);

// Implementation
protected:
    void InitTypefaceList (CDC* pDC);
    CFont m_font;
    CComboBox m_wndFontNames;
    CComboBox m_wndFontSizes;
    // Generated message map functions
    //{{AFX_MSG(CStyleBar)
    afx_msg int OnCreate(LPCREATESTRUCT lpCreateStruct);
    //}}AFX_MSG
    afx_msg void OnSelectFont ();
    afx_msg void OnSelectSize ();
    afx_msg void OnCloseUp ();
    DECLARE_MESSAGE_MAP()
};

////////////////////////////////////////////////////////////////////////////

//{{AFX_INSERT_LOCATION}}
// Microsoft Visual C++ will insert additional declarations
// immediately before the previous line.

#endif
// !defined(
//      AFX_STYLEBAR_H__C85C9099_A154_11D2_8E53_006008A82731__INCLUDED_)
```

StyleBar.cpp

```
// StyleBar.cpp : implementation file
//

#include "stdafx.h"
```

```
#include "MyWord.h"
#include "MyWordDoc.h"
#include "MyWordView.h"
#include "StyleBar.h"

#ifdef _DEBUG
#define new DEBUG_NEW
#undef THIS_FILE
static char THIS_FILE[] = __FILE__;
#endif

/////////////////////////////////////////////////////////////////////////
// CStyleBar

BEGIN_MESSAGE_MAP(CStyleBar, CToolBar)
    //{{AFX_MSG_MAP(CStyleBar)
    ON_WM_CREATE()
    //}}AFX_MSG_MAP
    ON_CBN_SELENDOK (IDC_FONTNAMES, OnSelectFont)
    ON_CBN_SELENDOK (IDC_FONTSIZES, OnSelectSize)
    ON_CBN_CLOSEUP (IDC_FONTNAMES, OnCloseUp)
    ON_CBN_CLOSEUP (IDC_FONTSIZES, OnCloseUp)
END_MESSAGE_MAP()

/////////////////////////////////////////////////////////////////////////
// CStyleBar message handlers

int CStyleBar::OnCreate(LPCREATESTRUCT lpCreateStruct)
{
    static int nFontSizes[] = {
        8, 9, 10, 11, 12, 14, 16, 18, 20, 22, 24, 26, 28, 32, 36, 48, 72
    };

    if (CToolBar::OnCreate(lpCreateStruct) == -1)
        return -1;

    //
    // Load the toolbar.
    //
    if (!LoadToolBar (IDR_STYLE_BAR))
        return -1;

    //
    // Create an 8-point MS Sans Serif font for the combo boxes.
    //
```

(continued)

Figure 12-9. *continued*

```
CClientDC dc (this);
m_font.CreatePointFont (80, _T ("MS Sans Serif"));
CFont* pOldFont = dc.SelectObject (&m_font);

TEXTMETRIC tm;
dc.GetTextMetrics (&tm);
int cxChar = tm.tmAveCharWidth;
int cyChar = tm.tmHeight + tm.tmExternalLeading;

dc.SelectObject (pOldFont);

//
// Add the font name combo box to the toolbar.
//
SetButtonInfo (8, IDC_FONTNAMES, TBBS_SEPARATOR, cxChar * 32);

CRect rect;
GetItemRect (8, &rect);
rect.bottom = rect.top + (cyChar * 16);

if (!m_wndFontNames.Create (WS_CHILD | WS_VISIBLE | WS_VSCROLL |
    CBS_DROPDOWNLIST | CBS_SORT, rect, this, IDC_FONTNAMES))
    return -1;

m_wndFontNames.SetFont (&m_font);
InitTypefaceList (&dc);

//
// Add the font size combo box to the toolbar.
//
SetButtonInfo (10, IDC_FONTSIZES, TBBS_SEPARATOR, cxChar * 12);

GetItemRect (10, &rect);
rect.bottom = rect.top + (cyChar * 14);

if (!m_wndFontSizes.Create (WS_CHILD | WS_VISIBLE | WS_VSCROLL |
    CBS_DROPDOWNLIST, rect, this, IDC_FONTSIZES))
    return -1;

m_wndFontSizes.SetFont (&m_font);

CString string;
int nCount = sizeof (nFontSizes) / sizeof (int);
for (int i=0; i<nCount; i++) {
    string.Format (_T ("%d"), nFontSizes[i]);
    m_wndFontSizes.AddString (string);
```

```
    }
    return 0;
}

void CStyleBar::OnSelectFont ()
{
    TCHAR szFaceName[LF_FACESIZE];
    int nIndex = m_wndFontNames.GetCurSel ();
    m_wndFontNames.GetLBText (nIndex, szFaceName);

    CMyWordView* pView =
        (CMyWordView*) ((CFrameWnd*) AfxGetMainWnd ())->GetActiveView ();
    pView->ChangeFont (szFaceName);
}

void CStyleBar::OnSelectSize ()
{
    TCHAR szSize[8];
    int nIndex = m_wndFontSizes.GetCurSel ();
    m_wndFontSizes.GetLBText (nIndex, szSize);

    int nSize = atoi (szSize) * 20; // Need twips

    CMyWordView* pView =
        (CMyWordView*) ((CFrameWnd*) AfxGetMainWnd ())->GetActiveView ();
    pView->ChangeFontSize (nSize);
}

void CStyleBar::OnCloseUp ()
{
    ((CFrameWnd*) AfxGetMainWnd ())->GetActiveView ()->SetFocus ();
}

void CStyleBar::InitTypefaceList (CDC* pDC)
{
    ::EnumFontFamilies (pDC->m_hDC, NULL,
        (FONTENUMPROC) EnumFontNameProc, (LPARAM) this);
}

int CALLBACK CStyleBar::EnumFontNameProc (ENUMLOGFONT* lpelf,
    NEWTEXTMETRIC* lpntm, int nFontType, LPARAM lParam)
{
    CStyleBar* pWnd = (CStyleBar*) lParam;
    if (nFontType & TRUETYPE_FONTTYPE)
        pWnd->m_wndFontNames.AddString (lpelf->elfLogFont.lfFaceName);
    return 1;
}
```

(continued)

Figure 12-9. *continued*

```
void CStyleBar::OnUpdateCmdUI (CFrameWnd* pTarget, BOOL bDisableIfNoHndler)
{
    CToolBar::OnUpdateCmdUI (pTarget, bDisableIfNoHndler);

    CWnd* pWnd = GetFocus ();
    if ((pWnd == &m_wndFontNames) || (pWnd == &m_wndFontSizes))
        return;

    //
    // Get the font name and size.
    //
    int nTwips;
    TCHAR szFaceName[LF_FACESIZE];

    CMyWordView* pView =
        (CMyWordView*) ((CFrameWnd*) AfxGetMainWnd ())->GetActiveView ();
    pView->GetFontInfo (szFaceName, nTwips);

    //
    // Update the font name combo box.
    //
    TCHAR szSelection[LF_FACESIZE];
    m_wndFontNames.GetWindowText (szSelection,
        sizeof (szSelection) / sizeof (TCHAR));

    if (::lstrcmp (szFaceName, szSelection) != 0) {
        if (szFaceName[0] == 0)
            m_wndFontNames.SetCurSel (-1);
        else {
            if (m_wndFontNames.SelectString (-1, szFaceName) == CB_ERR)
                m_wndFontNames.SetCurSel (-1);
        }
    }

    //
    // Update the font size combo box.
    //
    TCHAR szSize[4];
    m_wndFontSizes.GetWindowText (szSize,
        sizeof (szSize) / sizeof (TCHAR));
    int nSizeFromComboBox = atoi (szSize);
    int nSizeFromView = nTwips / 20;
```

```
if (nSizeFromComboBox != nSizeFromView) {
    if (nTwips == -1)
        m_wndFontSizes.SetCurSel (-1);
    else {
        CString string;
        string.Format (_T ("%d"), nSizeFromView);
        if (m_wndFontSizes.SelectString (-1, string) == CB_ERR)
            m_wndFontSizes.SetCurSel (-1);
    }
}
}
```

The Main Toolbar

MyWord's main toolbar is a standard *CToolBar* that's created along with the style bar and status bar in *CMainFrame::OnCreate*. After the main toolbar is created, the styles CBRS_TOOLTIPS, CBRS_FLYBY, and CBRS_SIZE_DYNAMIC are added and *CToolBar::EnableDocking* is called with a CBRS_ALIGN_ANY parameter so that the toolbar can be docked to any side of the frame window. *DockControlBar* is called to dock the toolbar in its default location at the top of the window so that it can be detached and floated. The call to *LoadBarState* in *CMainFrame::OnCreate* restores the toolbar to its previous location if the application has been run before.

Handlers for all the buttons on the main toolbar—and for all the items in MyWord's menus, for that matter—are provided by the framework. As usual, *CWinApp* provides handlers for the New, Open, and Exit commands in the File menu, and *CDocument* handles the Save and Save As commands. *CRichEditView* provides handlers for the items in the Edit menu (all prewired into the message map, of course), and *CFrameWnd* handles the commands in the View menu. *CRichEditView* also provides update handlers for Edit commands, which explains why the Cut, Copy, Paste, and Undo buttons in the toolbar are automatically enabled and disabled in response to actions performed by the user. To see what I mean, type a line or two of text and highlight a few characters to form a selection. The Cut and Copy buttons will light up when the first character is selected and blink out again when the selection is canceled. Updates are automatic because of the following entries in *CRichEditView*'s message map:

```
ON_UPDATE_COMMAND_UI (ID_EDIT_CUT, OnUpdateNeedSel)
ON_UPDATE_COMMAND_UI (ID_EDIT_COPY, OnUpdateNeedSel)
```

Scan the *CRichEditView* message map in the MFC source code file Viewrich.cpp to see the full range of commands for which *CRichEditView* provides default command and update handlers.

The Style Bar

MyWord's style bar is an instance of the *CToolBar*-derived class *CStyleBar*. The style bar is constructed when the frame window is constructed and created in *CMainFrame::OnCreate*, but it also contains its own *OnCreate* handler that creates and initializes the font name and font size combo boxes. Other *CStyleBar* member functions include *OnSelectFont*, which applies typefaces selected from the font name combo box; *OnSelectSize*, which applies sizes selected from the font size combo box; *OnCloseUp*, which restores the input focus to the view when either combo box's drop-down list box is closed; *InitTypefaceList* and *EnumFontNameProc*, which work together to enumerate fonts and add their names to the font name combo box; and *OnUpdateCmdUI*, which updates the combo boxes so that the font name and the font size shown in the style bar are consistent with the character at the caret or the characters in a selection.

MyWord's view class provides command and update handlers for the buttons in the style bar. Clicking the Bold button, for example, activates *CMyWordView::OnCharBold*, which is implemented as follows:

```
void CMyWordView::OnCharBold ()
{
    CHARFORMAT cf;
    cf = GetCharFormatSelection ();

    if (!(cf.dwMask & CFM_BOLD) ¦¦ !(cf.dwEffects & CFE_BOLD))
        cf.dwEffects = CFE_BOLD;
    else
        cf.dwEffects = 0;

    cf.dwMask = CFM_BOLD;
    SetCharFormat (cf);
}
```

GetCharFormatSelection is a *CRichEditView* function that returns a CHARFORMAT structure containing information about the text that is currently selected in the view or, if there is no selection, about the default character format. *SetCharFormat* is another *CRichEditView* function that applies the text attributes described in a CHARFORMAT structure to the selected text. If no text is currently selected, *SetCharFormat* sets the view's default character format.

Boldface text is toggled on or off by setting the CFM_BOLD bit in the *dwMask* field of the CHARFORMAT structure passed to *SetCharFormat* and either setting or clearing the CFE_BOLD bit in the structure's *dwEffects* field. To determine the proper setting for the CFE_BOLD flag, *OnCharBold* inspects both the CFM_BOLD and CFE_BOLD flags in the CHARFORMAT structure returned by *GetCharFormatSelection*. The CFM_BOLD flag is clear if the current selection includes a mix of bold and nonbold text. If CFM_BOLD is set, either the selection consists entirely of bold or nonbold text or no text is currently selected. In either case, the CFE_BOLD flag indicates whether the selected (or default) text is bold or nonbold. *OnCharBold* can be called in five possible scenarios. The following table describes each set of circumstances and documents the result. The view's *OnCharItalic* and *OnCharUnderline* handlers use similar logic to toggle italic and underline on and off.

Circumstances Under Which **OnCharBold** *Is Called*	**dwMask & CFM_BOLD**	**dwEffects & CFE_BOLD**	*Action Taken* **by OnCharBold**
One or more characters are selected; the selection contains a mix of bold and nonbold text.	0	Undefined	Makes all characters in the selection bold.
One or more characters are selected; the selection consists entirely of bold text.	Nonzero	Nonzero	Makes all characters in the selection nonbold.
One or more characters are selected; the selection consists entirely of nonbold text.	Nonzero	0	Makes all characters in the selection bold.
No text is selected; the default character format is bold.	Nonzero	Nonzero	Sets the default character format to nonbold.
No text is selected; the default character format is nonbold.	Nonzero	0	Sets the default character format to bold.

The handlers for the paragraph alignment buttons are simpler because their actions don't depend on the current paragraph alignment. *CRichEditView* provides a convenient *OnParaAlign* function for setting the paragraph alignment to left, right, or centered. (Unfortunately, neither a *CRichEditView* nor the rich edit control that is the foundation for a *CRichEditView* supports fully justified text that extends the width between both margins.) The statement

```
OnParaAlign (PFA_LEFT);
```

in *OnParaLeft* selects left-aligned text. If no text is selected in the view, *OnParaAlign* reformats the paragraph that contains the caret. If text is selected, all paragraphs touched by the selection are transformed so that the text in them is left aligned.

Each button in the style bar is mapped to an update handler that calls either *CRichEditView::OnUpdateCharEffect* or *CRichEditView::OnUpdateParaAlign*. In addition to checking and unchecking the buttons as appropriate, these *CRichEditView* functions also set a button to the indeterminate state when a selection includes a mix of character formats or paragraph alignments. For a simple demonstration, try this test. First enter some text if you haven't already. Then highlight some characters, click the Italic button to italicize the selection, and select a range of characters that includes both italicized and nonitalicized text. Because *OnUpdateCharItalic* calls *OnUpdate-CharEffect*, the Italic button will become half-grayed, indicating that the selection contains a mix of character formats. And because each style bar button is assigned an update handler, the buttons behave like check push buttons and radio push buttons even though none is assigned the TBBS_CHECKBOX or TBBS_CHECKGROUP style.

When a font name or a font size is selected from the combo boxes, the style bar retrieves the font name or font size and calls a public member function of the view class to implement the change. Selecting a font name activates *CStyleBar::OnSelectFont*, which passes the new typeface name to the view through *CMyWordView::ChangeFont*. *ChangeFont*, in turn, changes the font in the view by setting the CFM_FACE flag in a CHARFORMAT structure's *dwMask* field, copying the typeface name to the structure's *szFaceName* field and calling *SetCharFormat*:

```
void CMyWordView::ChangeFont (LPCTSTR pszFaceName)
{
    CHARFORMAT cf;
    cf.cbSize = sizeof (CHARFORMAT);
    cf.dwMask = CFM_FACE;
    ::lstrcpy (cf.szFaceName, pszFaceName);
    SetCharFormat (cf);
}
```

CStyleBar::OnSelectSize uses a similar procedure to change the font size through the view's *ChangeFontSize* member function. Font sizes passed to *CRichEditView*s are expressed in twips, where 1 twip equals $1/20$ of a point. Therefore, *OnSelectSize* multiplies the point size retrieved from the combo box by 20 to convert points to twips before calling *ChangeFontSize*.

Which brings up a question: Because the command message generated when an item is selected from a combo box is subject to command routing, why doesn't MyWord let the view handle combo box notifications directly? Actually, that *would* be ideal. But it would also pose a problem. Because the combo boxes are protected members of the style bar class, the view would have no way of retrieving the selected item from the combo box. We could fix that by making the combo boxes public data members and the style bar a public data member of the frame window class, but protected data members provide stricter encapsulation. Letting the style bar handle combo box notifications and pass the information to the view through public member functions allows the style bar to hide its data yet still communicate style changes to the view.

So that the items selected in the combo boxes will match the character format in the view as the caret is moved through the document and selections are made, *CStyleBar* overrides the *OnUpdateCmdUI* function it inherits from *CToolBar* and updates the combo boxes based on information obtained from the view. After verifying that neither of the combo boxes has the input focus so that the combo boxes won't flicker if *OnUpdateCmdUI* is called while a drop-down list box is displayed, *OnUpdate-CmdUI* calls *CMyWordView::GetFontInfo* to get the current font name and size. If the font name obtained from the view doesn't match the font name selected in the font name combo box, *OnUpdateCmdUI* changes the combo box selection. Similarly, the selection is updated in the font size combo box if the size shown in the combo box doesn't match the size reported by *GetFontInfo*. Leaving the current selection intact if it hasn't changed prevents the combo boxes from flickering as a result of repeated (and unnecessary) updates. The update handler is also smart enough to blank the combo box selection if the font name or font size obtained from *GetFontInfo* doesn't match any of the items in the combo box or if the text selected in the view contains a mixture of typefaces or font sizes.

One thing *CStyleBar* doesn't do is update the list of typefaces in the font name combo box if the pool of installed fonts changes while MyWord is running. When fonts are added or deleted, Windows sends all top-level windows a WM_FONTCHANGE message notifying them of the change. To respond to changes in font availability while an application is running, include an ON_WM_FONTCHANGE entry in the frame window's message map and an *OnFontChange* handler to go with it. The message-map entry and handler must be members of the frame window class because WM-_FONTCHANGE messages are not routed, whereas command messages are.

To simplify the logic for updating the selection in the font size combo box, MyWord's style bar lists TrueType fonts only. If the font name combo box included raster fonts as well, the font size combo box would need to be reinitialized each time the selection changed in the font name combo box because raster fonts come in a limited number of sizes. Limiting the user's choice of fonts to TrueType only makes the point sizes listed in the font size combo box independent of the typeface selected in the font name combo box because TrueType fonts can be accurately rendered in any point size from 1 through 999.

More About *CRichEditView*

Most of MyWord's functionality comes from *CRichEditView*, which is built around the powerful rich text edit control provided in the common controls library. MFC's *CRichEditView* class doesn't act alone in encapsulating the features of a rich text edit control; help comes from *CRichEditDoc* and *CRichEditCntrItem*. *CRichEditDoc* represents the data stored in a *CRichEditView*, which can include linked and embedded OLE objects, and *CRichEditCntrItem* represents OLE objects contained in a *CRichEditView*.

When you derive a view class from *CRichEditView*, you must also derive a document class from *CRichEditDoc* and override *CRichEditDoc::CreateClientItem*, which is pure virtual. MyWord's *CMyWordDoc* document class implements *CreateClientItem* by creating a *CRichEditCntrItem* object and returning a pointer:

```
CRichEditCntrItem* CMyWordDoc::CreateClientItem (REOBJECT* preo) const
{
    return new CMyWordCntrItem (preo, (CMyWordDoc*) this);
}
```

This simple override enables the Paste and Paste Special commands in the Edit menu to paste OLE items into the document. For a demonstration, copy a picture created with the Windows Paint applet to the clipboard and paste it into a MyWord document. Then double-click the embedded image in MyWord, and Paint will merge its menus and toolbars with MyWord's menus and toolbars so that you can edit the picture in place. If the document is saved, the embedded Paint object is saved, too, so that it will come back up just as you left it when you reload the document.

In case you hadn't noticed, MyWord is fully capable of saving the documents you create and loading them back in. It can even read RTF files created by other word processors and serialize OLE objects. Yet *CMyWordDoc::Serialize* contains just one statement:

```
CRichEditDoc::Serialize(ar);
```

You won't find any other serialization code in *CMyWordDoc* because *CRichEditDoc* can handle serialization on its own. *CRichEditDoc::Serialize* streams data to and from a *CRichEditView* by calling the view's *Serialize* function, which in turn relies on the streaming capabilities built into a rich text edit control. (For more information, see the documentation for the EM_STREAMIN and EM_STREAMOUT messages that can be sent to a rich text edit control and the equivalent *StreamIn* and *StreamOut* function members of MFC's *CRichEditCtrl* class.) It's relatively easy to write an SDK application that saves and loads documents in a rich text edit control, but it's downright simple to do it in MFC because *CRichEditDoc* and *CRichEditView* work together with other components of the framework to handle all phases of the serialization process for you.

By default, *CRichEditDoc* serializes documents in rich text format. You can instruct a *CRichEditDoc* to write text files that lack formatting information and OLE objects by setting the *CRichEditDoc* data member *m_bRTF* equal to FALSE before storing a document. By the same token, you can read files in plain text format by setting *m_bRTF* to FALSE before dearchiving a document. It wouldn't be hard to give MyWord the ability to read and write text files as well as rich text format files, but you'd have to add some logic to the front end of the deserialization process to identify the type of file that's about to be read. *CRichEditDoc* won't load a text file if *m_bRTF* is TRUE, and if it reads a rich text format document with *m_bRTF* equal to FALSE, it converts

RTF formatting commands to ordinary text. A full treatment of *CRichEditDoc* serialization options is beyond the scope of this book, but if you're interested in learning more, a good place to start is the Wordpad source code provided with MFC.

REBARS

Internet Explorer 3.0 introduced a new control type to Windows: the rebar control. A rebar is a container for other controls. You populate a rebar control by adding *bands* to it; each band can include a child window such as a toolbar, push button, or combo box. You can add as many bands as you like, and once the rebar is displayed, the user can move and resize the bands to configure the rebar control to his or her liking. Each band in a rebar can optionally have an image from an image list, a label (text string), and a bitmap associated with it. The image and label, if used, are displayed on the face of the band. The bitmap, if used, is tiled horizontally and vertically to form a stylized background for whatever else happens to be displayed in the band. Remember the toolbar with the textured background in Internet Explorer 3.0? That toolbar was actually a rebar control wrapped around an otherwise rather ordinary toolbar control. A bitmap provided the textured background.

MFC 6.0 introduced two new classes to simplify the programming of rebar controls: *CReBar* and *CReBarCtrl*. *CReBarCtrl* is a low-level class that provides a very thin wrapper around a raw rebar control. *CReBar* is a high-level class that makes it almost as easy to add rebars to an MFC application as it is to add toolbars and status bars. *CReBar* publishes just three member functions:

- *Create*, which creates a rebar from a *CReBar* object
- *GetReBarCtrl*, which returns a *CReBarCtrl* reference to the underlying rebar control
- *AddBar*, which adds a band to the rebar

With *CReBar* and its member functions to help out, creating rebar-type toolbars like the ones used in Visual C++ could hardly be easier. The following example converts an MFC toolbar into a rebar by first creating a *CToolBar* and then making it a band in a *CReBar*:

```
m_wndToolBar.CreateEx (this);
m_wndToolBar.LoadToolBar (IDR_TOOLBAR);
m_wndReBar.Create (this);
m_wndReBar.AddBar (&m_wndToolBar);
```

You can use *AddBar*'s optional second and third parameters to specify a label and a background bitmap. For example, if *m_bitmap* is a *CBitmap* object, the statements

```
m_bitmap.LoadBitmap (IDB_BKGND);
m_wndToolBar.CreateEx (this, TBSTYLE_FLAT ¦ TBSTYLE_TRANSPARENT);
m_wndToolBar.LoadToolBar (IDR_TOOLBAR);
m_wndReBar.Create (this);
m_wndReBar.AddBar (&m_wndToolBar, _T ("Main"), &m_bitmap);
```

assign the toolbar the label "Main" and use the bitmap resource whose ID is IDB_BKGND as the toolbar's background. When you use a background bitmap in this manner, it's important to create the toolbar with the styles TBSTYLE_FLAT and TBSTYLE-_TRANSPARENT and to use light gray as the toolbar buttons' background color. Otherwise, the button backgrounds are drawn over the top of the background bitmap, and you won't get the effect you were hoping for.

If you check the Internet Explorer ReBars box in AppWizard's Step 4 dialog box (shown in Figure 12-10), AppWizard wraps a rebar around the toolbar that it generates. If you want to do more with the rebar, such as add a label or a bitmap, or if your application features multiple toolbars and you want to wrap each of them in a rebar, you must add the code yourself.

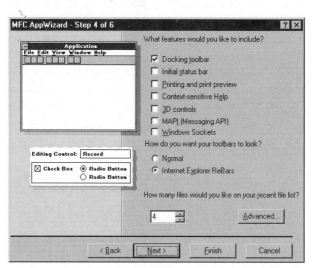

Figure 12-10. *Using AppWizard to wrap a rebar around a toolbar.*

Chapter 13

Printing and Print Previewing

For beginning programmers, learning to print is one of the single most daunting aspects of Microsoft Windows programming. Printing has never been easy in Windows because the same GDI that provides a device-independent interface to every kind of printer imaginable makes you jump through hoops to print a simple document. The GDI also gives you such precise control over the output that users expect a lot from Windows applications that produce printed documents. The good news is that the same GDI functions you use to draw on the screen can be used to draw on a sheet of paper. The bad news is that printing entails lots of extra details, from paginating the output to giving the user the means to terminate an unfinished print job. And if you really want your product to be competitive, you should probably support print previewing so that the user can see exactly what the printed output will look like before he or she sends the first page to the printer.

In Chapters 9 through 12, you saw how the document/view architecture simplifies the development of single document interface (SDI) and multiple document interface (MDI) applications by letting MFC take over key aspects of a program's operation. In this chapter, you'll learn how the same document/view architecture simplifies printing and print previewing. Even MFC-style printing isn't something to be taken lightly, but thanks to the support the framework offers, the tedium of writing and testing code that renders documents on printers and other hardcopy devices is sharply reduced. And once you've given an application the ability to print, print previewing comes almost for free.

PRINTING WITH DOCUMENTS AND VIEWS

MFC's print architecture is built around a kernel formed by GDI printing functions and virtual *CView* member functions. To understand what's on the outside, it helps to first understand what's on the inside. Here's the approach we'll take in this chapter as we study the code that enables an MFC application to support printing and print previewing:

- Look at the Windows printing model, and examine the steps an SDK-style application goes through to print a document.

- Understand the relationship between the Windows print architecture and the MFC print architecture and the mechanics of printing from MFC applications.

- Develop a bare-bones printing program that demonstrates how the same code can be used to send output to either the screen or the printer.

- Develop a more ambitious printing program whose printing and previewing capabilities are on a par with those of commercial applications.

As you'll discover, printing from an MFC application isn't altogether different than rendering to the screen except for the fact that printed output must be paginated. Because MFC handles almost everything else, much of the effort you expend writing printing code will be devoted to figuring out where the page breaks go and how to position your output on the printed page.

The Windows Print Architecture

Printing a document from a Windows application without the benefit of MFC involves a number of steps. You begin by obtaining a device context (DC) for the printer that output will go to. Just as an application needs a screen DC to send output to the screen, it needs a printer DC to send output to a printer. If you know the device name of the printer you want to print to, you can create a device context yourself with the Win32 *::CreateDC* function or MFC's *CDC::CreateDC*:

```
CDC dc;
dc.CreateDC (NULL, _T ("HP LaserJet IIP"), NULL, NULL);
```

If you don't know the device name but would like the application to print to the default printer, you can use MFC's handy *CPrintDialog::GetDefaults* and *CPrintDialog::GetPrinterDC* functions to create the device context:

```
CDC dc;
CPrintDialog dlg (FALSE);
dlg.GetDefaults ();
dc.Attach (dlg.GetPrinterDC ());
```

If you'd like to let the user select a printer, you can use *CPrintDialog::DoModal* to display a Print dialog (one of the common dialogs supplied by the operating system) and call *CPrintDialog::GetPrinterDC* to get a DC after the dialog is dismissed:

```
CDC dc;
CPrintDialog dlg (FALSE);
if (dlg.DoModal () == IDOK)
    dc.Attach (dlg.GetPrinterDC ());
```

To prevent resource leakage, you should delete a printer DC obtained by any of these methods when it's no longer needed. If the *CDC* object to which you attach the DC is created on the stack, deletion is automatic.

Once you have a printer DC in hand, you're ready to begin printing. The next step is to call *::StartDoc* or its MFC equivalent, *CDC::StartDoc*, to mark the beginning of the print job. *CDC::StartDoc* accepts just one parameter: a pointer to a DOCINFO structure containing a descriptive name for the document that's about to be printed, the name of the file the output will go to if you're printing to a file rather than a printer, and other information about the print job. The statements

```
DOCINFO di;
::ZeroMemory (&di, sizeof (DOCINFO));
di.cbSize = sizeof (DOCINFO);
di.lpszDocName = _T ("Budget Figures for the Current Fiscal Year");
dc.StartDoc (&di);
```

start a print job on the printer associated with the *CDC* object *dc*. If you open a printer window while the document is printing, the string "Budget Figures for the Current Fiscal Year" will identify the print job. If *StartDoc* fails, it returns a 0 or a less-than-0 value. If it succeeds, it returns a positive integer that equals the print job ID. You can use the print job ID in conjunction with Win32 print control functions such as *::GetJob* and *::SetJob*.

Next comes output to the page. Text and graphics are rendered on a printer with GDI functions. If *dc* refers to a screen device context, the statement

```
dc.Ellipse (0, 0, 100, 100);
```

draws an ellipse 100 logical units wide and 100 logical units high on the screen. If *dc* refers to a printer device context, the circle is drawn to the printer instead. Pages of output are framed between calls to *CDC::StartPage* and *CDC::EndPage,* which mark the beginning and end of each page. A document that contains *nPageCount* pages of output could be printed as follows:

```
for (int i=1; i<=nPageCount; i++) {
    dc.StartPage ();
    // Print page i
    dc.EndPage ();
}
```

In a simplified sense, calling *EndPage* is analogous to outputting a form feed character to the printer. In between *StartPage* and *EndPage*, you print the page by calling *CDC* member functions. Your application should call *StartPage* and *EndPage* even if the document contains only one page.

A common mistake that programmers make the first time they write printing code is failing to initialize the printer DC for each page. In Windows 95 and Windows 98, the device context's default attributes are restored each time *StartPage* is called. You can't just select a font or set the mapping mode right after the DC is created and expect those attributes to remain in effect indefinitely as you can for a screen DC. Instead, you must reinitialize the printer DC for each page. (In Microsoft Windows NT 3.5 and later, a printer DC retains its settings across calls to *StartPage* and *EndPage*, but even a Windows NT application should reinitialize the device context at the beginning of each page if it's to work under Windows 95 and Windows 98, too.) If you print using the MM_LOENGLISH mapping mode, for example, you should call *CDC-::SetMapMode* at the beginning of each page, like this:

```
for (int i=1; i<=nPageCount; i++) {
    dc.StartPage ();
    dc.SetMapMode (MM_LOENGLISH);
    // Print page i.
    dc.EndPage ();
}
```

If you do it this way instead:

```
dc.SetMapMode (MM_LOENGLISH);
for (int i=1; i<=nPageCount; i++) {
    dc.StartPage ();
    // Print page i.
    dc.EndPage ();
}
```

printing will be performed in the default MM_TEXT mapping mode.

After it prints the final page, an application terminates a print job by calling *CDC::EndDoc*. Printing is made slightly more complicated by the fact that *EndDoc* shouldn't be called if a previous call to *EndPage* returned a code indicating that the print job had already been terminated by the GDI. *EndPage* returns a signed integer value greater than 0 if the page was successfully output to the printer. A 0 or negative return value indicates either that an error occurred or that the user canceled the print job while the page was being printed. In either of those two events, the return code will equal one of the following values.

Return Code	Description
SP_ERROR	The print job was aborted for an unspecified reason.
SP_APPABORT	The print job was aborted because the user clicked the Cancel button in the dialog box that displays the status of the print job.
SP_USERABORT	The print job was aborted because the user canceled it through the operating system shell.
SP_OUTOFDISK	The system is out of disk space, so no further printer data can be spooled.
SP_OUTOFMEMORY	The system is out of memory, so no further printer data can be spooled.

The following loop prints each page of a document and calls *EndDoc* at the end of the print job if and only if each page was successfully printed:

```
if (dc.StartDoc (&di) > 0) {
    BOOL bContinue = TRUE;

    for (int i=1; i<=nPageCount && bContinue; i++) {
        dc.StartPage ();
        // Initialize the device context.
        // Print page i.
        if (dc.EndPage () <= 0)
            bContinue = FALSE;
    }

    if (bContinue)
        dc.EndDoc ();
    else
        dc.AbortDoc ();
}
```

CDC::AbortDoc signals the end of an uncompleted print job just as *EndDoc* signals the end of a successful print job. *AbortDoc* can also be called between calls to *StartPage* and *EndPage* to terminate a print job before the final page is printed.

The Abort Procedure and the Abort Dialog

If that's all there was to sending output to a printer under Windows, printing wouldn't be such a formidable task after all. But there's more. Because a large print job can take minutes or even hours to complete, the user should be able to terminate a print job before it's finished. Windows applications traditionally give the user the means to cancel a print job by displaying a print status dialog containing a Cancel button. Clicking the Cancel button cancels printing by forcing *EndPage* to return SP_APPABORT. The mechanism that links the Cancel button to the printing code in your application is a function that Windows calls an *abort procedure*.

An abort procedure is an exported callback function that Windows calls repeatedly as it processes printed output. It's prototyped as follows:

```
BOOL CALLBACK AbortProc (HDC hDC, int nCode)
```

hDC holds the handle of the printer device context. *nCode* is 0 if printing is proceeding smoothly or SP_OUTOFDISK if the print spooler is temporarily out of disk space. *nCode* is usually ignored because the print spooler responds to an SP_OUTOFDISK condition by waiting around for more disk space to come free. The abort procedure's job is twofold:

■ To check the message queue with *::PeekMessage* and retrieve and dispatch any waiting messages

■ To tell Windows whether printing should continue by returning TRUE (to continue printing) or FALSE (to abort)

You pass Windows the address of your abort procedure by calling *::SetAbortProc* or *CDC::SetAbortProc*. A very simple abort procedure looks like this:

```
BOOL CALLBACK AbortProc (HDC hDC, int nCode)
{
    MSG msg;
    while (::PeekMessage (&msg, NULL, 0, 0, PM_NOREMOVE))
        AfxGetThread ()->PumpMessage ();
    return TRUE;
}
```

The message loop inside *AbortProc* allows the WM_COMMAND message generated when the print status dialog's Cancel button is clicked to make it through to the window procedure even though the application is busy printing. In 16-bit Windows, the message loop plays an important role in multitasking by yielding so that the print spooler and other processes running in the system can get CPU time. In Windows 95 and Windows 98, yielding in the abort procedure enhances multitasking performance when 32-bit applications print to 16-bit printer drivers by reducing contention for the Win16Mutex—an internal flag that locks 32-bit applications out of the 16-bit kernel while a 16-bit application executes code there.

Before it begins printing (before calling *StartDoc*), the application calls *SetAbortProc* to set the abort procedure, disables its own window by calling *CWnd::EnableWindow* with a FALSE parameter, and displays the print status or "abort" dialog—a modeless dialog box containing a Cancel button and usually one or more static controls listing the document's file name and the number of the page that's currently being printed. Disabling the main window ensures that no other input will interrupt the printing process. The window is reenabled when printing is finished and the dialog box is destroyed. The dialog, meanwhile, sets a flag—call it *bUserAbort*—from FALSE to TRUE if the Cancel button is clicked. And the abort procedure is modified so that it returns FALSE to shut down printing if *bUserAbort* is TRUE.

```
BOOL CALLBACK AbortProc (HDC hDC, int nCode)
{
    MSG msg;
    while (!bUserAbort &&
        ::PeekMessage (&msg, NULL, 0, 0, PM_NOREMOVE))
        AfxGetThread ()->PumpMessage ();
    return !bUserAbort;
}
```

Thus, printing proceeds unimpeded if the Cancel button isn't clicked because *Abort-Proc* always returns a nonzero value. But if Cancel is clicked, *bUserAbort* changes from FALSE to TRUE, the next call to *AbortProc* returns 0, and Windows terminates the printing process. *EndPage* returns SP_APPABORT, and the call to *EndDoc* is subsequently bypassed.

Print Spooling

Everything I've described up to this point constitutes the "front end" of the printing process—the part the application is responsible for. Windows handles the back end, which is a joint effort on the part of the GDI, the print spooler, the printer driver, and other components of the 32-bit print subsystem. Windows supports two kinds of print spooling: EMF (enhanced metafile) print spooling and "raw" print spooling. If EMF print spooling is enabled, GDI calls executed through the printer DC are written to an enhanced metafile on the hard disk and stored there until the print spooler, which runs in a separate thread, unspools the commands and "plays" them into the printer driver. If raw print spooling (the only option available on PostScript printers) is selected instead, output is processed through the printer driver and spooled to disk in raw form. Spooling can also be disabled. In that case, GDI commands are transmitted directly to the printer driver each time *EndPage* is called. Print spooling speeds the return-to-application time by preventing a program from having to wait for the printer to physically print each page of output. Spooling metafile commands instead of raw printer data further improves the return-to-application time by decoupling the performance of the application from the performance of the printer driver.

Fortunately, applications can safely ignore what happens at the back end of the printing process and concentrate on the front end. Still, many details must be attended to before an application can get down to the real business of printing—paginating the output and executing GDI calls between *StartPage* and *EndPage* to render each page on the printer, for example. With this background in mind, let's see what MFC can do to help.

The MFC Print Architecture

MFC's simplified print architecture is just one more reason that Windows programmers are migrating away from the SDK and toward object-oriented development environments. When you add print capabilities to a document/view application, you can forget about most of the code samples in the previous section. The framework creates a printer DC for you and deletes the DC when printing is finished. The framework also calls *StartDoc* and *EndDoc* to begin and end the print job and *StartPage* and *EndPage* to bracket GDI calls for individual pages. The framework even supplies the dialog box that displays the status of the print job and the abort procedure that shuts down the print operation if the user clicks the Cancel button. And in some cases, the same *OnDraw* function that renders a document on the screen can render it on the printer and in a print preview window, too.

The key to printing from a document/view application is a set of virtual *CView* functions the framework calls at various stages during the printing process. These functions are listed in the following table. Which of them you override and what you do in the overrides depend on the content of your printed output. At the very least, you'll always override *OnPreparePrinting* and call *DoPreparePrinting* so that the framework will display a Print dialog and create a printer DC for you. A minimal *OnPreparePrinting* override looks like this:

```
BOOL CMyView::OnPreparePrinting (CPrintInfo* pInfo)
{
    return DoPreparePrinting (pInfo);
}
```

A nonzero return from *OnPreparePrinting* begins the printing process, and a 0 return cancels the print job before it begins. *DoPreparePrinting* returns 0 if the user cancels the print job by clicking the Cancel button in the Print dialog, if no printers are installed, or if the framework is unable to create a printer DC.

KEY *CVIEW* PRINT OVERRIDABLES

Function	*Description*
OnPreparePrinting	Called at the onset of a print job. Override to call *DoPreparePrinting* and to provide the framework with the page count (if known) and other information about the print job.
OnBeginPrinting	Called just before printing begins. Override to allocate fonts and other resources required for printing.
OnPrepareDC	Called before each page is printed. Override to position the viewport origin and set a clipping region before *OnDraw* prints the next page.
OnPrint	Called before each page is printed. Override to print headers, footers, and other page elements that aren't drawn by *OnDraw* or to print without relying on *OnDraw*.
OnEndPrinting	Called when printing is finished. Override to deallocate resources allocated in *OnBeginPrinting*.

Before proceeding, let me take a moment to explain the two basic approaches to printing from an MFC application. The first is to let *OnDraw* handle both screen output and printed output. The second is to let *OnDraw* handle screen output and *OnPrint* handle printed output. Most experienced MFC developers would agree that the let-*OnDraw*-do-it-all method is highly overrated. It almost inevitably requires you to add print-specific logic to *OnDraw*, and you usually end up overriding *OnPrint* anyway to print page numbers, headers, footers, and other page elements that appear only on the printed page. So while it's true that a view's *OnDraw* function can write to both the screen and the printer, it's usually more practical to put printer output logic in *OnPrint* and screen output logic in *OnDraw*. I'll discuss both approaches in this chapter, but I'll emphasize the latter.

More on the *OnPreparePrinting* Function

The *CPrintInfo* object passed to *OnPreparePrinting* contains information describing the parameters of the print job, including the minimum and maximum page numbers. The minimum and maximum page numbers default to 1 and 0xFFFF, respectively, with 0xFFFF signaling the framework that the maximum page number is unknown. If your application knows how many pages the document contains when *OnPreparePrinting* is called, it should inform MFC by calling *CPrintInfo::SetMaxPage* before calling *DoPreparePrinting*:

```
BOOL CMyView::OnPreparePrinting (CPrintInfo* pInfo)
{
    pInfo->SetMaxPage (10);
    return DoPreparePrinting (pInfo);
}
```

MFC, in turn, displays the maximum page number—in this case, 10—in the To box of the Print dialog.

SetMinPage and *SetMaxPage* are two of several *CPrintInfo* member functions you can call to specify print parameters or to query the framework about print options entered by the user. *GetFromPage* and *GetToPage* return the starting and ending page numbers the user entered in the Print dialog. Be sure to call them after *DoPreparePrinting*, because it's *DoPreparePrinting* that displays the dialog. *CPrintInfo* also includes several public data members, including an *m_pPD* variable that points to the initialized *CPrintDialog* object through which *DoPreparePrinting* displays the Print dialog. You can use this pointer to customize the Print dialog before it appears on the screen and to extract information from the dialog by calling *CPrintDialog* functions or accessing *CPrintDialog* data members directly. Later in the chapter, you'll see an example demonstrating how and why this is done.

The *OnBeginPrinting* and *OnEndPrinting* Functions

Often the maximum page number depends on the size of the printable area of each page output from the printer. Unfortunately, until the user has selected a printer and the framework has created a printer DC, you can only guess what that printable area will be. If you don't set the maximum page number in *OnPreparePrinting*, you should set it in *OnBeginPrinting* if possible. *OnBeginPrinting* receives a pointer to an initialized *CPrintInfo* structure and a pointer to a *CDC* object representing the printer DC the framework created when you called *DoPreparePrinting*. You can determine the dimensions of the printable page area in *OnBeginPrinting* by calling *CDC::GetDeviceCaps* twice—once with a HORZRES parameter and once with a VERTRES parameter. The following *OnBeginPrinting* override uses *GetDeviceCaps* to determine the height of the printable page area in pixels and uses that information to inform the framework how many pages the document contains:

```
void CMyView::OnBeginPrinting (CDC* pDC, CPrintInfo* pInfo)
{
    int nPageHeight = pDC->GetDeviceCaps (VERTRES);
    int nDocLength = GetDocument ()->GetDocLength ();
    int nMaxPage = max (1, (nDocLength + (nPageHeight - 1)) /
        nPageHeight);
    pInfo->SetMaxPage (nMaxPage);
}
```

In this example, *GetDocLength* is a document function that returns the length of the document in pixels. *CPrintInfo* contains a data member named *m_rectDraw* that describes the printable page area in logical coordinates, but don't try to use *m_rectDraw* in *OnBeginPrinting* because it isn't initialized until after *OnBeginPrinting* returns.

Calling *SetMaxPage* in either *OnPreparePrinting* or *OnBeginPrinting* lets the framework know how many times it should call *OnPrint* to print a page. If it's impossible (or simply inconvenient) to determine the document length before printing begins, you can perform *print-time pagination* by overriding *OnPrepareDC* and setting *CPrintInfo::m_bContinuePrinting* to TRUE or FALSE each time *OnPrepareDC* is called. An *m_bContinuePrinting* value equal to FALSE terminates the print job. If you don't call *SetMaxPage*, the framework assumes the document is only one page long. Therefore, you must override *OnPrepareDC* and set *m_bContinuePrinting* to print documents that are more than one page long if you don't set the maximum page number with *SetMaxPage*.

OnBeginPrinting is also the best place to create fonts and other GDI resources used in the printing process. Suppose that *OnDraw* uses a GDI font to output text to the screen and that the font height is based on the current screen metrics. To print a WYSIWYG version of that font on the printer, you must create a separate font that's scaled to printer metrics rather than to screen metrics. By creating the font in *OnBegin-Printing* and deleting it in *OnEndPrinting*, you ensure that the font exists only for the period of time that it is needed and also avoid the overhead of re-creating it each time a page is printed.

OnEndPrinting is the counterpart of *OnBeginPrinting*. It's a great place to free fonts and other resources allocated in *OnBeginPrinting*. If there are no resources to free, or if you didn't override *OnBeginPrinting* to begin with, you probably don't need to override *OnEndPrinting*, either.

The *OnPrepareDC* Function

OnPrepareDC is called once for each page of the printed document. One reason to override *OnPrepareDC* is to perform print-time pagination as described in the previous section. Another reason to override *OnPrepareDC* is to calculate a new viewport origin from the current page number so that *OnDraw* can output the current page to the printer. Like *OnBeginPrinting*, *OnPrepareDC* receives a pointer to a device context and a pointer to a *CPrintInfo* object. Unlike *OnBeginPrinting*, *OnPrepareDC* is called before screen repaints as well as in preparation for outputting a page to the printer. If the call to *OnPrepareDC* precedes a screen repaint, the *CDC* pointer refers to a screen DC and the *CPrintInfo* pointer is NULL. If *OnPrepareDC* is called as part of the printing process, the *CDC* pointer references a printer DC and the *CPrintInfo* pointer is non-NULL. In the latter case, you can obtain the page number of the page that's about to be printed from the *CPrintInfo* object's public *m_nCurPage* data member. You can determine whether *OnPrepareDC* was called for the screen or the printer by calling *CDC::IsPrinting* through the *CDC* pointer passed in the parameter list.

The following implementation of *OnPrepareDC* moves the viewport origin in the *y* direction so that the device point (0,0)—the pixel in the upper left corner of the printed page—corresponds to the logical point in the upper left corner of the document's current page. *m_nPageHeight* is a *CMyView* data member that holds the printable page height:

```
void CMyView::OnPrepareDC (CDC* pDC, CPrintInfo* pInfo)
{
    CView::OnPrepareDC (pDC, pInfo);
    if (pDC->IsPrinting ()) { // If printing...
        int y = (pInfo->m_nCurPage - 1) * m_nPageHeight;
        pDC->SetViewportOrg (0, -y);
    }
}
```

Setting the viewport origin this way ensures that an *OnDraw* function that tries to draw the entire document will actually draw only the part that corresponds to the current page. This example assumes that you want to use the entire printable area of the page. Often it's also necessary to set a clipping region to restrict the part of the document that's printed to something less than the page's full printable area. Rectangular regions are created with *CRgn::CreateRectRgn* and selected into DCs to serve as clipping regions with *CDC::SelectClipRgn*.

As a rule, you need to override *OnPrepareDC* only if you use *OnDraw* to draw to both the screen and the printed page. If you do all your printing from *OnPrint*, there's no need to override *OnPrepareDC*. When you do override it, you should call the base class before doing anything else so that the default implementation will get a chance to do its thing. Calling the base class's *OnPrepareDC* is especially important when your view class is derived from *CScrollView* because *CScrollView::OnPrepareDC* sets the viewport origin for screen DCs to match the current scroll position. When a call to *CScrollView::OnPrepareDC* returns, the DC's mapping mode is set to the mapping mode specified in the call to *SetScrollSizes*. If your view class isn't derived from *CScrollView*, *OnPrepareDC* is a good place to call *SetMapMode* to set the device context's mapping mode.

The *OnPrint* Function

After calling *OnPrepareDC* for a given page, the framework calls *CView::OnPrint*. Like many other *CView* printing functions, *OnPrint* receives a pointer to the printer DC and a pointer to a *CPrintInfo* object. The default implementation in Viewcore.cpp verifies the validity of *pDC* and calls *OnDraw*:

```
void CView::OnPrint(CDC* pDC, CPrintInfo*)
{
    ASSERT_VALID(pDC);

    // Override and set printing variables based on page number
    OnDraw(pDC);                        // Call Draw
}
```

What you do when you override *OnPrint* (and whether you override it at all) depends on how the application does its printing. If *OnDraw* handles both screen output and printed output, override *OnPrint* to print page elements that don't appear on the screen. The following *OnPrint* function calls a local member function named *PrintHeader* to print a header at the top of the page, another local member function named *PrintPageNumber* to print a page number at the bottom of the page, and *OnDraw* to print the body of the page:

```
void CMyView::OnPrint (CDC* pDC, CPrintInfo* pInfo)
{
    PrintHeader (pDC);
    PrintPageNumber (pDC, pInfo->m_nCurPage);
```

```
    // Set the viewport origin and/or clipping region before
    // calling OnDraw...
    OnDraw (pDC);
}
```

Any adjustments made to the printer DC with *SetViewportOrg* or *SelectClipRgn* so that *OnDraw* will draw just the part of the document that corresponds to the current page should now be made in *OnPrint* rather than *OnPrepareDC* to prevent headers and page numbers from being affected.

 If instead you elect to do all your printing from *OnPrint*, you override *OnPrint* and include in it code to output one printed page. To determine which page *OnPrint* has been called to print, check *CPrintInfo::m_nCurPage*.

CView::OnFilePrint and Other Command Handlers

Printing usually begins when the user selects the Print command from the File menu, so MFC provides a *CView::OnFilePrint* function you can connect to the ID_FILE_PRINT menu item through the view's message map. Figure 13-1 shows what happens when *OnFilePrint* is called and when in the printing process each virtual *CView* printing function is called. It also shows how the MFC print architecture meshes with the Windows print architecture: if you take away the dark rectangles representing the virtual *CView* functions that the framework calls, you're left with a pretty good schematic of the Windows printing model. Notice that *OnPrepareDC* is called twice per page when your code executes under Windows 95 or Windows 98. The first call to *OnPrepareDC* is made to preserve compatibility with 16-bit versions of MFC, which called *OnPrepareDC* before *StartPage* and got away with it because in 16-bit Windows *EndPage*, not *StartPage*, resets the device context. The second call to *OnPrepareDC* is made because in Windows 95 and Windows 98, changes made to the device context in the first call to *OnPrepareDC* are nullified when *StartDoc* is called.

 MFC also provides predefined command IDs and default command handlers for the File menu's Print Preview and Print Setup commands. The File-Print Preview command (ID=ID_FILE_PRINT_PREVIEW) is handled by *CView::OnFilePrintPreview*, and File-Print Setup (ID=ID_FILE_PRINT_SETUP) is handled by *CWinApp::OnFilePrintSetup*. Like *OnFilePrint*, these command handlers are not prewired into the message maps of the classes to which they belong. To enable these handlers, you must do the message mapping yourself. If you use AppWizard to generate the skeleton of an application that prints, the message mapping is done for you. AppWizard also maps ID_FILE_PRINT_DIRECT to *CView::OnFilePrint* to enable "direct" printing—printing performed not by the user's selecting Print from the File menu but by the user's selecting Print from a document's context menu or dropping a document icon onto a printer.

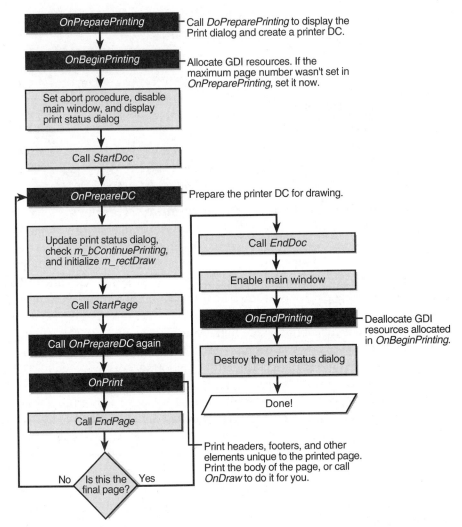

Figure 13-1. *Overview of the MFC print architecture.*

Print Previewing

Once a document/view application is endowed with the ability to print, adding print previewing is as simple as adding a Print Preview command to the File menu (ID=ID_FILE_PRINT_PREVIEW) and adding an entry to the message map to connect this command ID to *CView::OnFilePrintPreview*. A lot of code backs up *OnFile-PrintPreview* (see the MFC source code file Viewprev.cpp for details), but what happens in *OnFilePrintPreview* is pretty simple. *OnFilePrintPreview* takes over the frame window and fills it with a view created from a special *CScrollView*-derived class named

CPreviewView. It also adds a toolbar with buttons for going to the next or the previous page, switching between one-page and two-page views, zooming in and out, and so on. *CPreviewView::OnDraw* draws a white rectangle representing a printed page (or two rectangles if two-page view is selected), sets some scaling parameters so that the printable area of the white rectangle matches the printable area of a real page, and calls *OnPrint* to draw in the rectangle. As far as your application is concerned, output is being sent to the printer; the same virtual functions that get called during printing also get called during print preview. But in reality, output goes to the print preview window instead.

Part of the magic that makes print previewing work is the fact that the device context referenced in the *pDC* parameter passed to *CView* printing functions is actually two device contexts in one. Every *CDC* object contains two device context handles: one for an "output DC" (*m_hDC*) and another for an "attribute DC" (*m_hAttribDC*). MFC uses the output DC for calls that produce physical output and the attribute DC for calls that request information about the device context—the current text color or current background mode, for example. Most of the time, *m_hDC* and *m_hAttribDC* hold the same device context handle. But during print previewing, *m_hDC* references the screen DC where pages are previewed and *m_hAttribDC* references the printer DC. The result? If your application uses *GetDeviceCaps* or other *CDC* functions to query the GDI about the printer's capabilities or the properties of the printed page, the information it gets back is genuine because it comes from the printer DC. But all physical output goes to the screen DC.

When the user closes the print preview window, the framework calls a virtual *CView* function named *OnEndPrintPreview* to notify the application that print preview is about to end. The default implementation of *OnEndPrintPreview* calls *OnEndPrinting*, reactivates the original view, and destroys the print preview window. Programmers sometimes override *OnEndPrintPreview* in order to scroll the view of the document to the last page displayed in print preview mode. (By default, the scroll position in the original view is preserved so that scrolling in print preview mode doesn't affect the original view.) The following *OnEndPrintPreview* override demonstrates how you can link the scroll position in the original view to the scroll position in the print preview window for a *CScrollView*:

```
void CMyView::OnEndPrintPreview (CDC* pDC, CPrintInfo* pInfo,
    POINT point, CPreviewView* pView)
{
    UINT nPage = pInfo->m_nCurPage;
    POINT pt;
    // Convert nPage into a scroll position in pt.
    ScrollToPosition (pt);
    CScrollView::OnEndPrintPreview (pDC, pInfo, point, pView);
}
```

You'll have to supply the code that converts the current page number into a scroll position yourself. Don't rely on the *point* parameter passed to *OnEndPrintPreview* to tell you anything; in current versions of MFC, *point* always equals (0,0). You should call the base class's *OnEndPrintPreview* function from the overridden version so that the framework can exit print preview mode and restore the frame window to its original state.

If your printing code needs to discriminate between real printing and printing performed in print preview mode, it can check the *m_bPreview* data member of the *CPrintInfo* object referenced in calls to *OnBeginPrinting*, *OnPrint*, and other print overridables. *m_bPreview* is nonzero if the document is being previewed and 0 if it isn't. In addition, *CPrintInfo::m_nNumPreviewPages* can be inspected to determine whether one or two pages are displayed.

A BARE-BONES PRINTING APPLICATION

The EZPrint application shown in Figure 13-2 demonstrates the minimum amount of work a document/view application must do to support printing and print previewing.

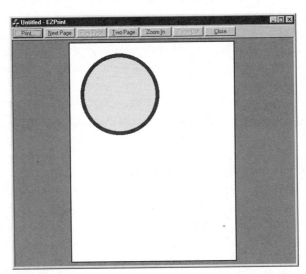

Figure 13-2. *The EZPrint application displaying a print preview.*

An EZPrint "document" contains a blue circle 10 centimeters (1,000 units in the MM_LOMETRIC mapping mode) in diameter with a yellow interior. The application's File menu contains just four items: Print, Print Preview, Print Setup, and Exit. The Print and Print Preview commands are mapped to *CView::OnFilePrint* and *CView::On-FilePrintPreview* in *CEZPrintView*'s message map, and the Print Setup command is mapped to *CWinApp::OnFilePrintSetup* in *CEZPrintApp*'s message map. AppWizard performed all the message mapping. The Print command displays a Print dialog box in which the user can specify printing options such as the desired printer, the print range, and the number of copies. Print Preview puts the application in print preview mode. Print Setup displays a Print Setup dialog box. You can use the Print Setup dialog box to choose a printer, select a paper size, and specify the page orientation—portrait or landscape.

I used AppWizard to create the EZPrint project. In the Step 4 dialog box (shown in Figure 13-3), I checked the Printing And Print Preview box to add printing support. Checking this box prompts AppWizard to make three modifications to the code that it generates:

- Add Print, Print Preview, and Print Setup commands to the File menu.

- Modify the message map to connect the Print, Print Preview, and Print Setup commands to MFC-provided command handlers.

- Override *OnPreparePrinting*, *OnBeginPrinting*, and *OnEndPrinting* in the view class.

AppWizard's *OnPreparePrinting* function includes a call to *DoPreparePrinting*. Its *OnBeginPrinting* and *OnEndPrinting* functions do nothing, so you can delete them if you don't use them. I left them in, but EZPrint would work just as well without them. All of EZPrint's printing code is found in the view class, whose source code is reproduced in Figure 13-4.

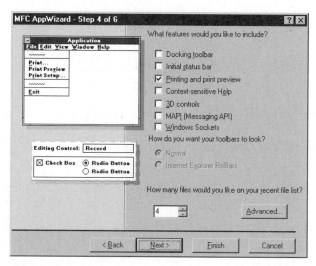

Figure 13-3. *Using AppWizard to add printing and print previewing support.*

There's not a lot to say about EZPrint's printing and print previewing capabilities other than that MFC does the bulk of the work. *CEZPrintView::OnDraw* renders all the output, regardless of whether that output is destined for the screen, a printer, or a print preview window. So that the circle will have the same proportions regardless of where it is drawn, *OnDraw* does all of its drawing using the MM_LOMETRIC mapping mode. That's important, because pixel-per-inch values for screens and printers are rarely the same. If you drew to the screen and the printer in the MM_TEXT mapping mode, the circle would be a lot smaller on a 600 dpi printer than it would be on the screen. To get WYSIWYG results, you'd have to scale the circle's height and width manually during printing and print previewing using ratios derived from pixel-per-inch counts for the screen and printer. Using a mapping mode in which logical units scale to physical distances rather than pixel counts allows the GDI to do the scaling and ensures that *OnDraw* can produce consistent results no matter where the output is rendered.

EZPrintView.h

```
// EZPrintView.h : interface of the CEZPrintView class
//
/////////////////////////////////////////////////////////////////////////////

#if !defined(
    AFX_EZPRINTVIEW_H__3A83FDED_A3E6_11D2_8E53_006008A82731__INCLUDED_)
#define AFX_EZPRINTVIEW_H__3A83FDED_A3E6_11D2_8E53_006008A82731__INCLUDED_

#if _MSC_VER > 1000
#pragma once
#endif // _MSC_VER > 1000


class CEZPrintView : public CView
{
protected: // create from serialization only
    CEZPrintView();
    DECLARE_DYNCREATE(CEZPrintView)

// Attributes
public:
    CEZPrintDoc* GetDocument();

// Operations
public:

// Overrides
    // ClassWizard generated virtual function overrides
    //{{AFX_VIRTUAL(CEZPrintView)
    public:
    virtual void OnDraw(CDC* pDC);  // overridden to draw this view
```

Figure 13-4. *The EZPrint application.*

```
    virtual BOOL PreCreateWindow(CREATESTRUCT& cs);
    protected:
    virtual BOOL OnPreparePrinting(CPrintInfo* pInfo);
    virtual void OnBeginPrinting(CDC* pDC, CPrintInfo* pInfo);
    virtual void OnEndPrinting(CDC* pDC, CPrintInfo* pInfo);
    //}}AFX_VIRTUAL

// Implementation
public:
    virtual ~CEZPrintView();
#ifdef _DEBUG
    virtual void AssertValid() const;
    virtual void Dump(CDumpContext& dc) const;
#endif

protected:

// Generated message map functions
protected:
    //{{AFX_MSG(CEZPrintView)
        // NOTE - the ClassWizard will add and remove member functions here.
        //     DO NOT EDIT what you see in these blocks of generated code !
    //}}AFX_MSG
    DECLARE_MESSAGE_MAP()
};

#ifndef _DEBUG  // debug version in EZPrintView.cpp
inline CEZPrintDoc* CEZPrintView::GetDocument()
    { return (CEZPrintDoc*)m_pDocument; }
#endif

/////////////////////////////////////////////////////////////////////////

//{{AFX_INSERT_LOCATION}}
// Microsoft Visual C++ will insert additional declarations
// immediately before the previous line.

#endif
// !defined(
//     AFX_EZPRINTVIEW_H__3A83FDED_A3E6_11D2_8E53_006008A82731__INCLUDED_)
```

EZPrintView.cpp

```
// EZPrintView.cpp : implementation of the CEZPrintView class
//
```

(continued)

Figure 13-4 *continued*

```
#include "stdafx.h"
#include "EZPrint.h"

#include "EZPrintDoc.h"
#include "EZPrintView.h"

#ifdef _DEBUG
#define new DEBUG_NEW
#undef THIS_FILE
static char THIS_FILE[] = __FILE__;
#endif

/////////////////////////////////////////////////////////////////////////
// CEZPrintView

IMPLEMENT_DYNCREATE(CEZPrintView, CView)

BEGIN_MESSAGE_MAP(CEZPrintView, CView)
    //{{AFX_MSG_MAP(CEZPrintView)
        // NOTE - the ClassWizard will add and remove mapping macros here.
        //    DO NOT EDIT what you see in these blocks of generated code!
    //}}AFX_MSG_MAP
    // Standard printing commands
    ON_COMMAND(ID_FILE_PRINT, CView::OnFilePrint)
    ON_COMMAND(ID_FILE_PRINT_DIRECT, CView::OnFilePrint)
    ON_COMMAND(ID_FILE_PRINT_PREVIEW, CView::OnFilePrintPreview)
END_MESSAGE_MAP()

/////////////////////////////////////////////////////////////////////////
// CEZPrintView construction/destruction

CEZPrintView::CEZPrintView()
{
}

CEZPrintView::~CEZPrintView()
{
}

BOOL CEZPrintView::PreCreateWindow(CREATESTRUCT& cs)
{
    return CView::PreCreateWindow(cs);
}

/////////////////////////////////////////////////////////////////////////
// CEZPrintView drawing
```

```
void CEZPrintView::OnDraw(CDC* pDC)
{
    CPen pen (PS_SOLID, 50, RGB (0, 0, 255));
    CBrush brush (RGB (255, 255, 0));

    pDC->SetMapMode (MM_LOMETRIC);
    CPen* pOldPen = pDC->SelectObject (&pen);
    CBrush* pOldBrush = pDC->SelectObject (&brush);

    pDC->Ellipse (100, -100, 1100, -1100);

    pDC->SelectObject (pOldBrush);
    pDC->SelectObject (pOldPen);
}


/////////////////////////////////////////////////////////////////////////////
// CEZPrintView printing

BOOL CEZPrintView::OnPreparePrinting(CPrintInfo* pInfo)
{
    return DoPreparePrinting(pInfo);
}

void CEZPrintView::OnBeginPrinting(CDC* /*pDC*/, CPrintInfo* /*pInfo*/)
{
    // TODO: add extra initialization before printing
}

void CEZPrintView::OnEndPrinting(CDC* /*pDC*/, CPrintInfo* /*pInfo*/)
{
    // TODO: add cleanup after printing
}


/////////////////////////////////////////////////////////////////////////////
// CEZPrintView diagnostics

#ifdef _DEBUG
void CEZPrintView::AssertValid() const
{
    CView::AssertValid();
}

void CEZPrintView::Dump(CDumpContext& dc) const
{
    CView::Dump(dc);
}
```

(continued)

Figure 13-4 *continued*

```
CEZPrintDoc* CEZPrintView::GetDocument() // non-debug version is inline
{
    ASSERT(m_pDocument->IsKindOf(RUNTIME_CLASS(CEZPrintDoc)));
    return (CEZPrintDoc*)m_pDocument;
}
#endif //_DEBUG

///////////////////////////////////////////////////////////////////////////
// CEZPrintView message handlers
```

Black-and-White Print Previews

MFC's print preview support isn't perfect. EZPrint's preview page shows the circle in full-blown color even if the only printer attached to your PC is a black-and-white model. (Naturally, the circle *will* be printed in color if you print it on a color printer.) You can add a nice touch to your print preview code by doing your rendering in shades of gray if both the following conditions are true when *OnPrint* or *OnDraw* is called:

- *pInfo->m_bPreview* is nonzero *(OnPrint)* or
  pDC->m_hDC is not equal to *pDC->m_hAttribDC (OnDraw)*.

- *pDC->GetDeviceCaps (NUMCOLORS)* returns 2, indicating that the printer is a monochrome device.

You can convert RGB color values into shades of gray with this formula:

```
r/g/b = (red * 0.30) + (green * 0.59) + (blue * 0.11)
```

The following statement creates a gray brush that simulates on the screen how yellow (RGB (255, 255, 0)) will look on a monochrome output device:

```
CBrush brush (RGB (227, 227, 227));
```

I got the value 227 by plugging the color components 255, 255, and 0 into the color conversion formula.

To see a simple demonstration of black-and-white print previewing, replace the lines

```
CPen pen (PS_SOLID, 50, RGB (0, 0, 255));
CBrush brush (RGB (255, 255, 0));
```

in EZPrint's *CPrintView::OnDraw* function with these:

```
BOOL bMono = (pDC->GetDeviceCaps (NUMCOLORS) == 2) &&
    (pDC->m_hDC != pDC->m_hAttribDC); // True only for preview mode.
CPen pen (PS_SOLID, 50, bMono ? RGB (28, 28, 28) : RGB (0, 0, 255));
CBrush brush (bMono ? RGB (227, 227, 227) : RGB (255, 255, 0));
```

Print previews will now be rendered in shades of gray when the default printer is a black-and-white model. Comparing *m_hDC* to *m_hAttribDC* is a sneaky way to detect print preview mode when *CPrintInfo* information isn't available.

A MORE COMPLEX PRINTING APPLICATION

EZPrint is okay for a start, but it's hardly representative of the kinds of applications found in the real world. It doesn't have to deal with pagination because its documents contain one page each. It creates the GDI resources it needs each time *OnDraw* is called, so it doesn't use *OnBeginPrinting* and *OnEndPrinting* to allocate printer-specific resources. It doesn't override *OnPrepareDC* and *OnPrint* at all, because nothing in EZPrint distinguishes a printed view from an onscreen view.

The HexDump application shown in Figure 13-5 better represents the kinds of applications that you're likely to have to write. HexDump is a hexadecimal viewing program that displays the contents of any file in binary form. Printed pages have a header at the top that includes the file name (prefaced with a path name if there's room) and the page number. The header is underscored with a thin horizontal line. The line is drawn with *CDC::MoveTo* and *CDC::LineTo*; all other output is performed with *CDC::TextOut*. Figure 13-6 shows one page of a document in print preview mode. When printing a document, HexDump queries the printer for the dimensions of the printable page and adjusts its output accordingly. The page height is used to compute the number of lines printed per page, and the page width is used to center the output horizontally no matter what the page size or orientation.

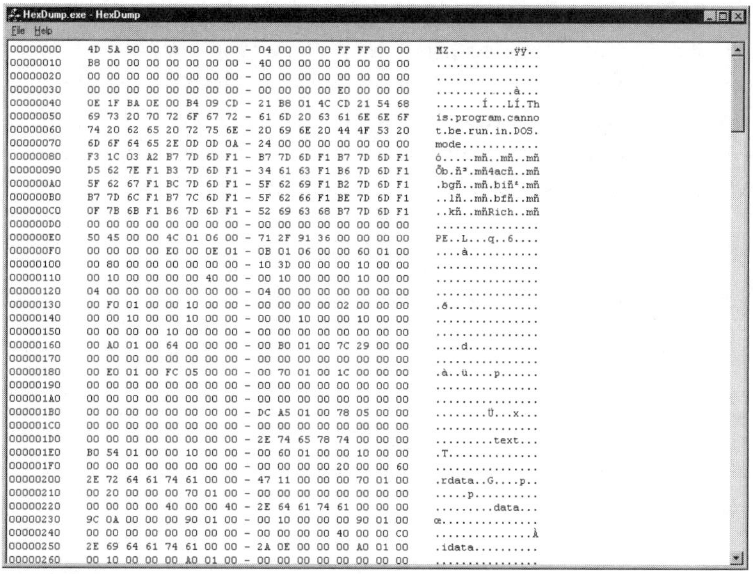

Figure 13-5. *HexDump showing a binary view of a file.*

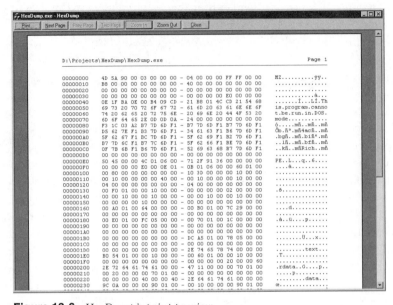

Figure 13-6. *HexDump's print preview.*

CHexView::OnDraw produces all of HexDump's screen output. To repaint the view, *OnDraw* calls *CDC::GetClipBox* to identify the rectangle that needs repainting, converts the *y* coordinates of the rectangle's top and bottom into starting and ending line numbers, and draws just those lines that need repainting. The font used in the output is a 10-point Courier New screen font initialized in *CHexView::OnCreate*. The current scroll position is factored into the output automatically because *CHexView* is derived from *CScrollView*. Because *OnDraw* does the minimum amount of painting necessary, scrolling performance is acceptable even if the document is very large. To see how sluggish a *CScrollView* can become when a large document is loaded and *OnDraw* isn't optimized, try rewriting *OnDraw* so that it attempts to draw the entire document each time it's called. All you have to do is replace these two lines:

```
UINT nStart = rect.top / m_cyScreen;
UINT nEnd = min (m_nLinesTotal - 1,
    (rect.bottom + m_cyScreen - 1) / m_cyScreen);
```

with these:

```
UINT nStart = 0;
UINT nEnd = m_nLinesTotal - 1;
```

Then load a file whose size is 10 KB or 20 KB and do some scrolling up and down. It will quickly become apparent why *OnDraw* goes to the trouble of converting the clip box into a range of line numbers.

HexDump does all its printing in *OnPrint*. *CHexView::OnPrint* calls *CHexView-
::PrintPageHeader* to print the header at the top of the page and *CHexView::Print-
Page* to print the body of the page. *OnBeginPrinting* sets the stage by initializing
m_fontPrinter with a 10-point Courier New font sized for the printer (notice the printer
device context pointer passed in *CreatePointFont*'s third parameter), *m_cyPrinter* with
the interline spacing, *m_nLinesPerPage* with the number of lines per page based on
the page height, *m_cxOffset* with the *x* indent required to center printed lines on the
page, and *m_cxWidth* with the width of each line of text. *PrintPage* calculates starting and ending line numbers from the current page number and the number of lines
per page. The *for* loop that does the drawing is similar to the *for* loop in *OnDraw*,
differing only in how it aligns the text on the page and in the fact that it uses
m_fontPrinter for its output instead of *m_fontScreen*. When printing (or print previewing) is complete, *OnEndPrinting* cleans up by deleting the printer font created
by *OnBeginPrinting*.

Could *OnDraw* have been written to handle both screen and printer output? Sure.
But HexDump's code (Figure 13-7) is arguably simpler and more straightforward the
way it's written now. MFC programmers sometimes make the mistake of feeling that
they *have* to do their printing as well as their screen updating in *OnDraw*. HexDump
not only demonstrates that it doesn't have to be that way but also provides a working
example of an application that does its printing and screen updating separately.

HexDoc.h

```
// HexDoc.h : interface of the CHexDoc class
//
/////////////////////////////////////////////////////////////////////////////

#if !defined(AFX_HEXDOC_H__3A83FDFE_A3E6_11D2_8E53_006008A82731__INCLUDED_)
#define AFX_HEXDOC_H__3A83FDFE_A3E6_11D2_8E53_006008A82731__INCLUDED_

#if _MSC_VER > 1000
#pragma once
#endif // _MSC_VER > 1000


class CHexDoc : public CDocument
{
protected: // create from serialization only
    CHexDoc();
    DECLARE_DYNCREATE(CHexDoc)

// Attributes
public:
```

Figure 13-7. *The HexDump program.*   *(continued)*

Figure 13-7 *continued*

```
// Operations
public:
    UINT GetBytes(UINT nIndex, UINT nCount, PVOID pBuffer);
    UINT GetDocumentLength();

// Overrides
    // ClassWizard generated virtual function overrides
    //{{AFX_VIRTUAL(CHexDoc)
    public:
    virtual BOOL OnNewDocument();
    virtual void Serialize(CArchive& ar);
    virtual void DeleteContents();
    //}}AFX_VIRTUAL

// Implementation
public:
    virtual ~CHexDoc();
#ifdef _DEBUG
    virtual void AssertValid() const;
    virtual void Dump(CDumpContext& dc) const;
#endif

protected:

// Generated message map functions
protected:
    BYTE* m_pFileData;
    UINT m_nDocLength;
    //{{AFX_MSG(CHexDoc)
        // NOTE - the ClassWizard will add and remove member functions here.
        //    DO NOT EDIT what you see in these blocks of generated code !
    //}}AFX_MSG
    DECLARE_MESSAGE_MAP()
};

///////////////////////////////////////////////////////////////////////////

//{{AFX_INSERT_LOCATION}}
// Microsoft Visual C++ will insert additional declarations
// immediately before the previous line.

#endif
// !defined(AFX_HEXDOC_H__3A83FDFE_A3E6_11D2_8E53_006008A82731__INCLUDED_)
```

HexDoc.cpp

```cpp
// HexDoc.cpp : implementation of the CHexDoc class
//

#include "stdafx.h"
#include "HexDump.h"

#include "HexDoc.h"

#ifdef _DEBUG
#define new DEBUG_NEW
#undef THIS_FILE
static char THIS_FILE[] = __FILE__;
#endif

/////////////////////////////////////////////////////////////////////////////
// CHexDoc

IMPLEMENT_DYNCREATE(CHexDoc, CDocument)

BEGIN_MESSAGE_MAP(CHexDoc, CDocument)
    //{{AFX_MSG_MAP(CHexDoc)
        // NOTE - the ClassWizard will add and remove mapping macros here.
        //    DO NOT EDIT what you see in these blocks of generated code!
    //}}AFX_MSG_MAP
END_MESSAGE_MAP()

/////////////////////////////////////////////////////////////////////////////
// CHexDoc construction/destruction

CHexDoc::CHexDoc()
{
    m_nDocLength = 0;
    m_pFileData = NULL;
}

CHexDoc::~CHexDoc()
{
}

BOOL CHexDoc::OnNewDocument()
{
    if (!CDocument::OnNewDocument())
        return FALSE;
    return TRUE;
}
```

(continued)

Figure 13-7 *continued*

```
//////////////////////////////////////////////////////////////////////////
// CHexDoc serialization

void CHexDoc::Serialize(CArchive& ar)
{
    if (ar.IsLoading ()) {
        CFile* pFile = ar.GetFile ();
        m_nDocLength = (UINT) pFile->GetLength ();

        //
        // Allocate a buffer for the file data.
        //
        try {
            m_pFileData = new BYTE[m_nDocLength];
        }
        catch (CMemoryException* e) {
            m_nDocLength = 0;
            throw e;
        }

        //
        // Read the file data into the buffer.
        //
        try {
            pFile->Read (m_pFileData, m_nDocLength);
        }
        catch (CFileException* e) {
            delete[] m_pFileData;
            m_pFileData = NULL;
            m_nDocLength = 0;
            throw e;
        }
    }
}

//////////////////////////////////////////////////////////////////////////
// CHexDoc diagnostics

#ifdef _DEBUG
void CHexDoc::AssertValid() const
{
    CDocument::AssertValid();
}

void CHexDoc::Dump(CDumpContext& dc) const
{
    CDocument::Dump(dc);
}
#endif //_DEBUG
```

```
/////////////////////////////////////////////////////////////////////////
// CHexDoc commands

void CHexDoc::DeleteContents()
{
    CDocument::DeleteContents();

    if (m_pFileData != NULL) {
        delete[] m_pFileData;
        m_pFileData = NULL;
        m_nDocLength = 0;
    }
}

UINT CHexDoc::GetBytes(UINT nIndex, UINT nCount, PVOID pBuffer)
{
    if (nIndex >= m_nDocLength)
        return 0;

    UINT nLength = nCount;
    if ((nIndex + nCount) > m_nDocLength)
        nLength = m_nDocLength - nIndex;

    ::CopyMemory (pBuffer, m_pFileData + nIndex, nLength);
    return nLength;
}

UINT CHexDoc::GetDocumentLength()
{
    return m_nDocLength;
}
```

HexView.h

```
// HexView.h : interface of the CHexView class
//
/////////////////////////////////////////////////////////////////////////

#if !defined(
    AFX_HEXVIEW_H__3A83FE00_A3E6_11D2_8E53_006008A82731__INCLUDED_)
#define AFX_HEXVIEW_H__3A83FE00_A3E6_11D2_8E53_006008A82731__INCLUDED_

#if _MSC_VER > 1000
#pragma once
#endif // _MSC_VER > 1000
```

(continued)

Figure 13-7 *continued*

```
class CHexView : public CScrollView
{
protected: // create from serialization only
    CHexView();
    DECLARE_DYNCREATE(CHexView)

// Attributes
public:
    CHexDoc* GetDocument();

// Operations
public:

// Overrides
    // ClassWizard generated virtual function overrides
    //{{AFX_VIRTUAL(CHexView)
    public:
    virtual void OnDraw(CDC* pDC);  // overridden to draw this view
    virtual BOOL PreCreateWindow(CREATESTRUCT& cs);
    protected:
    virtual void OnInitialUpdate(); // called first time after construct
    virtual BOOL OnPreparePrinting(CPrintInfo* pInfo);
    virtual void OnBeginPrinting(CDC* pDC, CPrintInfo* pInfo);
    virtual void OnEndPrinting(CDC* pDC, CPrintInfo* pInfo);
    virtual void OnPrint(CDC* pDC, CPrintInfo* pInfo);
    //}}AFX_VIRTUAL

// Implementation
public:
    virtual ~CHexView();
#ifdef _DEBUG
    virtual void AssertValid() const;
    virtual void Dump(CDumpContext& dc) const;
#endif

protected:

// Generated message map functions
protected:
    void FormatLine(CHexDoc* pDoc, UINT nLine, CString& string);
    void PrintPageHeader(CHexDoc* pDoc, CDC* pDC, UINT nPageNumber);
    void PrintPage(CHexDoc* pDoc, CDC* pDC, UINT nPageNumber);
    UINT m_cxWidth;
    UINT m_cxOffset;
    UINT m_nLinesPerPage;
    UINT m_nLinesTotal;
```

```
    UINT m_cyPrinter;
    UINT m_cyScreen;
    CFont m_fontPrinter;
    CFont m_fontScreen;
    //{{AFX_MSG(CHexView)
    afx_msg int OnCreate(LPCREATESTRUCT lpCreateStruct);
    //}}AFX_MSG
    DECLARE_MESSAGE_MAP()
};

#ifndef _DEBUG  // debug version in HexView.cpp
inline CHexDoc* CHexView::GetDocument()
    { return (CHexDoc*)m_pDocument; }
#endif

/////////////////////////////////////////////////////////////////////////

//{{AFX_INSERT_LOCATION}}
// Microsoft Visual C++ will insert additional declarations
// immediately before the previous line.

#endif
// !defined(AFX_HEXVIEW_H__3A83FE00_A3E6_11D2_8E53_006008A82731__INCLUDED_)
```

HexView.cpp

```
// HexView.cpp : implementation of the CHexView class
//

#include "stdafx.h"
#include "HexDump.h"

#include "HexDoc.h"
#include "HexView.h"

#ifdef _DEBUG
#define new DEBUG_NEW
#undef THIS_FILE
static char THIS_FILE[] = __FILE__;
#endif

#define PRINTMARGIN 2

/////////////////////////////////////////////////////////////////////////
// CHexView
```

(continued)

Figure 13-7 *continued*

```
IMPLEMENT_DYNCREATE(CHexView, CScrollView)

BEGIN_MESSAGE_MAP(CHexView, CScrollView)
    //{{AFX_MSG_MAP(CHexView)
    ON_WM_CREATE()
    //}}AFX_MSG_MAP
    // Standard printing commands
    ON_COMMAND(ID_FILE_PRINT, CScrollView::OnFilePrint)
    ON_COMMAND(ID_FILE_PRINT_DIRECT, CScrollView::OnFilePrint)
    ON_COMMAND(ID_FILE_PRINT_PREVIEW, CScrollView::OnFilePrintPreview)
END_MESSAGE_MAP()

/////////////////////////////////////////////////////////////////////////////
// CHexView construction/destruction

CHexView::CHexView()
{
}

CHexView::~CHexView()
{
}

BOOL CHexView::PreCreateWindow(CREATESTRUCT& cs)
{
    return CScrollView::PreCreateWindow(cs);
}

/////////////////////////////////////////////////////////////////////////////
// CHexView drawing

void CHexView::OnDraw(CDC* pDC)
{
    CHexDoc* pDoc = GetDocument();
    ASSERT_VALID(pDoc);

    if (m_nLinesTotal != 0) {
        CRect rect;
        pDC->GetClipBox (&rect);

        UINT nStart = rect.top / m_cyScreen;
        UINT nEnd = min (m_nLinesTotal - 1,
            (rect.bottom + m_cyScreen - 1) / m_cyScreen);

        CFont* pOldFont = pDC->SelectObject (&m_fontScreen);
        for (UINT i=nStart; i<=nEnd; i++) {
```

```
                CString string;
                FormatLine (pDoc, i, string);
                pDC->TextOut (2, (i * m_cyScreen) + 2, string);
            }
        pDC->SelectObject (pOldFont);
    }
}

void CHexView::OnInitialUpdate()
{
    CScrollView::OnInitialUpdate();

    UINT nDocLength = GetDocument ()->GetDocumentLength ();
    m_nLinesTotal = (nDocLength + 15) / 16;

    SetScrollSizes (MM_TEXT, CSize (0, m_nLinesTotal * m_cyScreen),
        CSize (0, m_cyScreen * 10), CSize (0, m_cyScreen));
    ScrollToPosition (CPoint (0, 0));
}

/////////////////////////////////////////////////////////////////////////////
// CHexView printing

BOOL CHexView::OnPreparePrinting(CPrintInfo* pInfo)
{
    // default preparation
    return DoPreparePrinting(pInfo);
}

void CHexView::OnBeginPrinting(CDC* pDC, CPrintInfo* pInfo)
{
    //
    // Create a printer font.
    //
    m_fontPrinter.CreatePointFont (100, _T ("Courier New"), pDC);

    //
    // Compute the width and height of a line in the printer font.
    //
    TEXTMETRIC tm;
    CFont* pOldFont = pDC->SelectObject (&m_fontPrinter);
    pDC->GetTextMetrics (&tm);
    m_cyPrinter = tm.tmHeight + tm.tmExternalLeading;
    CSize size = pDC->GetTextExtent (_T ("--------1--------2--------" \
        "3--------4--------5--------6--------7--------8-"), 81);
    pDC->SelectObject (pOldFont);
    m_cxWidth = size.cx;
```

(continued)

791

Figure 13-7 *continued*

```
    //
    // Compute the page count.
    //
    m_nLinesPerPage = (pDC->GetDeviceCaps (VERTRES) -
        (m_cyPrinter * (3 + (2 * PRINTMARGIN)))) / m_cyPrinter;
    UINT nMaxPage = max (1, (m_nLinesTotal + (m_nLinesPerPage - 1)) /
        m_nLinesPerPage);
    pInfo->SetMaxPage (nMaxPage);

    //
    // Compute the horizontal offset required to center
    // each line of output.
    //
    m_cxOffset = (pDC->GetDeviceCaps (HORZRES) - size.cx) / 2;
}

void CHexView::OnPrint(CDC* pDC, CPrintInfo* pInfo)
{
    CHexDoc* pDoc = GetDocument ();
    PrintPageHeader (pDoc, pDC, pInfo->m_nCurPage);
    PrintPage (pDoc, pDC, pInfo->m_nCurPage);
}

void CHexView::OnEndPrinting(CDC* pDC, CPrintInfo* pInfo)
{
    m_fontPrinter.DeleteObject ();
}


//////////////////////////////////////////////////////////////////////////
// CHexView diagnostics

#ifdef _DEBUG
void CHexView::AssertValid() const
{
    CScrollView::AssertValid();
}

void CHexView::Dump(CDumpContext& dc) const
{
    CScrollView::Dump(dc);
}

CHexDoc* CHexView::GetDocument() // non-debug version is inline
{
    ASSERT(m_pDocument->IsKindOf(RUNTIME_CLASS(CHexDoc)));
    return (CHexDoc*)m_pDocument;
}
#endif //_DEBUG
```

```
/////////////////////////////////////////////////////////////////////////////
// CHexView message handlers

int CHexView::OnCreate(LPCREATESTRUCT lpCreateStruct)
{
    if (CScrollView::OnCreate(lpCreateStruct) == -1)
        return -1;

    //
    // Create a screen font.
    //
    m_fontScreen.CreatePointFont (100, _T ("Courier New"));

    //
    // Compute the height of one line in the screen font.
    //
    CClientDC dc (this);
    TEXTMETRIC tm;
    CFont* pOldFont = dc.SelectObject (&m_fontScreen);
    dc.GetTextMetrics (&tm);
    m_cyScreen = tm.tmHeight + tm.tmExternalLeading;
    dc.SelectObject (pOldFont);
    return 0;
}

void CHexView::FormatLine(CHexDoc* pDoc, UINT nLine, CString& string)
{
    //
    // Get 16 bytes and format them for output.
    //
    BYTE b[17];
    ::FillMemory (b, 16, 32);
    UINT nCount = pDoc->GetBytes (nLine * 16, 16, b);

    string.Format (_T ("%0.8X    %0.2X %0.2X %0.2X %0.2X %0.2X %0.2X " \
        "%0.2X %0.2X - %0.2X %0.2X %0.2X %0.2X %0.2X %0.2X %0.2X " \
        "%0.2X    "), nLine * 16,
        b[0], b[1], b[2], b[3], b[4], b[5], b[6], b[7],
        b[8], b[9], b[10], b[11], b[12], b[13], b[14], b[15]);

    //
    // Replace non-printable characters with periods.
    //
    for (UINT i=0; i<nCount; i++) {
        if (!::IsCharAlphaNumeric (b[i]))
            b[i] = 0x2E;
    }
```

(continued)

Figure 13-7 *continued*

```
    //
    // If less than 16 bytes were retrieved, erase to the end of the line.
    //
    b[nCount] = 0;
    string += b;

    if (nCount < 16) {
        UINT pos1 = 59;
        UINT pos2 = 60;
        UINT j = 16 - nCount;

        for (i=0; i<j; i++) {
            string.SetAt (pos1, _T (' '));
            string.SetAt (pos2, _T (' '));
            pos1 -= 3;
            pos2 -= 3;
            if (pos1 == 35) {
                string.SetAt (35, _T (' '));
                string.SetAt (36, _T (' '));
                pos1 = 33;
                pos2 = 34;
            }
        }
    }
}

void CHexView::PrintPageHeader(CHexDoc* pDoc, CDC* pDC, UINT nPageNumber)
{
    //
    // Formulate the text that appears at the top of page.
    //
    CString strHeader = pDoc->GetPathName ();
    if (strHeader.GetLength () > 68)
        strHeader = pDoc->GetTitle ();

    CString strPageNumber;
    strPageNumber.Format (_T ("Page %d"), nPageNumber);

    UINT nSpaces =
        81 - strPageNumber.GetLength () - strHeader.GetLength ();
    for (UINT i=0; i<nSpaces; i++)
        strHeader += _T (' ');
    strHeader += strPageNumber;

    //
    // Output the text.
    //
```

```
    UINT y = m_cyPrinter * PRINTMARGIN;
    CFont* pOldFont = pDC->SelectObject (&m_fontPrinter);
    pDC->TextOut (m_cxOffset, y, strHeader);

    //
    // Draw a horizontal line underneath the line of text.
    //
    y += (m_cyPrinter * 3) / 2;
    pDC->MoveTo (m_cxOffset, y);
    pDC->LineTo (m_cxOffset + m_cxWidth, y);

    pDC->SelectObject (pOldFont);
}

void CHexView::PrintPage(CHexDoc* pDoc, CDC* pDC, UINT nPageNumber)
{
    if (m_nLinesTotal != 0) {
        UINT nStart = (nPageNumber - 1) * m_nLinesPerPage;
        UINT nEnd = min (m_nLinesTotal - 1, nStart + m_nLinesPerPage - 1);

        CFont* pOldFont = pDC->SelectObject (&m_fontPrinter);
        for (UINT i=nStart; i<=nEnd; i++) {
            CString string;
            FormatLine (pDoc, i, string);
            UINT y = ((i - nStart) + PRINTMARGIN + 3) * m_cyPrinter;
            pDC->TextOut (m_cxOffset, y, string);
        }
        pDC->SelectObject (pOldFont);
    }
}
```

A Unique Approach to Serialization

One aspect of HexDump that deserves special mention is the unusual way in which it serializes documents. When *CHexDoc::Serialize* is called to read a document from disk, it doesn't read from an archive. Instead, it allocates a buffer whose size equals the file size and reads the file into the buffer with *CFile::Read*. With exception handling statements removed, here's how it looks in code:

```
if (ar.IsLoading ()) {
    CFile* pFile = ar.GetFile ();
    m_nDocLength = (UINT) pFile->GetLength ();
    m_pFileDate = new BYTE[m_nDocLength];
    pFile->Read (m_pFileDate, m_nDocLength);
}
```

CArchive::GetFile returns a *CFile* pointer for the file associated with the archive so that an application can call *CFile* functions on it directly. This is one way an MFC application can read and write binary documents stored by someone else. When the document's *DeleteContents* function is called, HexDump frees the buffer containing the raw file data:

```
delete[] m_pFileData;
```

HexDump doesn't serialize the contents of a file back to disk because it's a hex viewer and not a hex editor, but if it did allow documents to be edited and saved, it would use *CFile::Write* to write modified documents back to disk the same way it uses *CFile::Read* to read them into memory.

Allocating a buffer whose size equals the file size isn't the most efficient approach to serializing and viewing large documents because it means that an entire document has to fit into memory at once. There are workarounds (memory-mapped files being one solution that comes to mind), but in HexDump's case it turns out to be a moot point because the limitations imposed by the *CScrollView* are typically more constraining than the limitations imposed by available memory. To see what I mean, find a file that's a few hundred kilobytes in length and load it into HexDump. If it's running on Windows 95 or Windows 98, HexDump won't display more than about a thousand lines of the file. How come?

The problem arises from the 16-bit heritage of Windows 95 and Windows 98. In both these operating systems, scroll bar ranges are 16-bit values. Before *CHexView::OnInitialUpdate* calls *SetScrollSizes*, it computes the view's virtual height by multiplying the number of lines in the document by the number of pixels per line. If the height of a line is 16 pixels and the document contains 1,000 lines, the resulting height is 16,000. For small documents, that's fine; but a *CScrollView* can't handle heights greater than 32,767—the largest positive value that can be represented with a signed 16-bit integer—because that's the upper limit of a scroll bar's range. The result? If you load a document that contains too many lines, the *CScrollView* shows only part of the document even though printing and previewing work adequately. To modify HexDump to handle large documents, your best bet is to create a *CView* with a scroll bar and process scroll bar messages yourself. For more information about processing scroll bar messages in MFC applications, refer to Chapter 2.

Printing Tips and Tricks

Here are a few tips, tricks, and answers to frequently asked questions to help you write better printing code and resolve problems that aren't addressed in this chapter's sample programs.

Using the Print Dialog's Selection Button

The Print dialog that MFC displays before printing begins includes a Selection radio button that the user can click to print the current selection rather than the entire document or a range of pages. By default, the button is disabled. You can enable it by adding the following statement to *OnPreparePrinting* just before the call to *DoPreparePrinting*:

```
pInfo->m_pPD->m_pd.Flags &= ~PD_NOSELECTION;
```

To select the radio button after it's enabled, add this statement as well:

```
pInfo->m_pPD->m_pd.Flags |= PD_SELECTION;
```

The *m_pPD* data member of the *CPrintInfo* structure passed to *OnPreparePrinting* points to the *CPrintDialog* object that *DoPreparePrinting* uses to display the Print dialog box. *CPrintDialog::m_pd* holds a reference to the PRINTDLG structure the dialog is based on, and PRINTDLG's *Flags* field holds bit flags that define the dialog box's properties. Removing the PD_NOSELECTION flag added by *CPrintInfo*'s constructor enables the Selection button, and adding a PD_SELECTION flag selects the button. If *DoPreparePrinting* returns a nonzero value, indicating that the dialog was dismissed with the OK button, you can find out whether the Selection button was selected by calling *CPrintDialog::PrintSelection*. A nonzero return value means the button was selected; 0 means it wasn't:

```
if (pInfo->m_pPD->PrintSelection ()) {
    // Print the current selection.
}
```

You can call *PrintSelection* and other *CPrintDialog* functions that return information about settings entered in a Print or Print Setup dialog through the *pInfo* parameter passed to *OnPreparePrinting* after *DoPreparePrinting* returns. You can also call them through the *pInfo* parameter passed to *OnBeginPrinting* and other *CView* print overridables.

You can use *CPrintInfo::m_pPD* in other ways to modify the appearance and behavior of the Print dialog that *DoPreparePrinting* displays. Refer to the documentation that accompanies Visual C++ for more information about PRINTDLG and its data members.

Assume Nothing—And Test Thoroughly!

When you send output to the printed page, it's generally a mistake to assume anything about the printable area of the pages you'll be printing. Even if you know you're printing to, say, an 8½-by-11-inch page, the printable page area will differ for different printers. The printable page area can even differ for the same printer and the same paper size depending on which printer driver is being used, and the horizontal and vertical dimensions of the printable page area will be switched if the user opts to print in landscape rather than portrait mode. Rather than assume you have a given amount of space to work with, do as HexDump does and call *GetDeviceCaps* through the *CDC* pointer provided to *CView* print functions to determine the printable page area each time you print, or use *CPrintInfo::m_rectDraw* in your *OnPrint* function. This simple precaution will enable your printing code to work with any printer Windows can throw at it and will greatly reduce the number of problem reports you receive from users.

As you've already learned, calling *GetDeviceCaps* with HORZRES and VERTRES parameters returns the horizontal and vertical dimensions of the printable page area. You can pass the following values to *GetDeviceCaps* to get more information about a printer or other hardcopy device:

Value	*Description*
HORZRES	Returns the width of the printable page area in pixels.
VERTRES	Returns the height of the printable page area in pixels.
HORSIZE	Returns the width of the printable page area in millimeters.
VERTSIZE	Returns the height of the printable page area in millimeters.
LOGPIXELSX	Returns the number of pixels per inch in the horizontal direction (300 for a 300-dpi printer).
LOGPIXELSY	Returns the number of pixels per inch in the vertical direction (300 for a 300-dpi printer).
PHYSICALWIDTH	Returns the page width in pixels (2,550 for an 8½-by-11-inch page on a 300-dpi printer).
PHYSICALHEIGHT	Returns the page height in pixels (3,300 for an 8½-by-11-inch page on a 300-dpi printer).
PHYSICALOFFSETX	Returns the distance in pixels from the left side of the page to the beginning of the page's printable area.
PHYSICALOFFSETY	Returns the distance in pixels from the top of the page to the beginning of the page's printable area.
TECHNOLOGY	Returns a value that identifies the type of output device the DC pertains to. The most common return values are DT_RASDISPLAY for screens, DT_RASPRINTER for printers, and DT_PLOTTER for plotters.
RASTERCAPS	Returns a series of bit flags identifying the level of GDI support provided by the printer driver. For example, an RC_BITBLT flag indicates that the printer supports *BitBlt*s, and RC_STRETCHBLT indicates that the printer supports *StretchBlt*s.
NUMCOLORS	Returns the number of colors the printer supports. The return value is 2 for black-and-white printers.

You've already seen one use for the *GetDeviceCaps* NUMCOLORS parameter: to detect when a black-and-white printer is being used so that you draw print previews in shades of gray. The PHYSICALOFFSETX and PHYSICALOFFSETY parameters are useful for setting margin widths based on information the user enters in a Page Setup dialog. (MFC's *CWinApp::OnFilePrintSetup* function displays a Print Setup dialog instead of a Page Setup dialog, but you can display a Page Setup dialog yourself using MFC's *CPageSetupDialog* class.) If the user wants 1-inch margins on the left side of the page, for example, you can subtract the PHYSICALOFFSETX value returned by *GetDeviceCaps* from the number of pixels printed per inch (LOGPIXELSX) to compute the *x* offset from the left of the printable page area where printing should begin. If the printer driver returns accurate information, the resulting margin will fall within a few pixels of being exactly 1 inch. You can use the HORZRES, VERTRES, LOGPIXELSX, LOGPIXELSY, PHYSICALWIDTH, PHYSICALHEIGHT, PHYSICAL-OFFSETX, and PHYSICALOFFSETY values to characterize the printable area of a page and pinpoint exactly where on the page the printable area lies.

If you're concerned about the occasional hardcopy device that won't draw bitmaps, you can find out whether *CDC::BitBlt* and *CDC::StretchBlt* are supported by calling *GetDeviceCaps* with a RASTERCAPS parameter and checking the return flags. For the most part, only vector devices such as plotters don't support the GDI's *Blt* functions. If the driver for a raster device doesn't support blitting directly, the GDI will compensate by doing the blitting itself. You can determine outright whether printed output is destined for a plotter by calling *GetDeviceCaps* with a TECHNOLOGY parameter and checking to see if the return value equals DT_PLOTTER.

When you use a number of different printers to test an application that prints, you'll find that printer drivers are maddeningly inconsistent in the information they report and the output they produce. For example, some printer drivers return the same values for PHYSICALWIDTH and PHYSICALHEIGHT as they return for HORZRES and VERTRES. And sometimes an ordinary GDI function such as *CDC::TextOut* will work fine on hundreds of printers but will fail on one particular model because of a driver bug. Other times, a GDI function won't fail outright but will behave differently on different printers. I once ran across a printer driver that defaulted to the TRANSPARENT background mode even though other drivers for the same family of printers correctly set the device context's default background mode to OPAQUE. Printer drivers are notoriously flaky, so you need to anticipate problems and test as thoroughly as you can on as many printers as possible. The more ambitious your program's printing needs, the more likely that driver quirks will require you to write workarounds for problems that crop up only on certain printers.

Adding Default Pagination Support

HexDump calls *CPrintInfo::SetMaxPage* from *OnBeginPrinting* rather than from *OnPreparePrinting* because the pagination process relies on the printable page area and *OnBeginPrinting* is the first virtual *CView* function that's called with a pointer to a printer DC. Because the maximum page number isn't set until after *OnPrepare-Printing* returns, the From box in the Print dialog is filled in (with a 1) but the To box isn't. Some users might think it incongruous that an application can correctly paginate a document for print preview but can't fill in the maximum page number in a dialog box. In addition to displaying the maximum page number correctly, many commercial applications display page breaks outside print preview and "Page *mm* of *nn*" strings in status bars. How do these applications know how the document will be paginated when they don't know what printer the document will be printed on or what the page orientation will be?

The answer is that they don't know for sure, so they make their best guess based on the properties of the default printer. The following code snippet initializes a *CSize* object with the pixel dimensions of the printable page area on the default printer or the last printer that the user selected in Print Setup. You can call it from *OnPrepare-Printing* or elsewhere to compute a page count or to get the information you need to provide other forms of default pagination support:

```
CSize size;
CPrintInfo pi;
if (AfxGetApp ()->GetPrinterDeviceDefaults (&pi.m_pPD->m_pd)) {
    HDC hDC = pi.m_pPD->m_pd.hDC;
    if (hDC == NULL)
        hDC = pi.m_pPD->CreatePrinterDC ();
    if (hDC != NULL) {
        CDC dc;
        dc.Attach (hDC);
        size.cx = dc.GetDeviceCaps (VERTRES);
        size.cy = dc.GetDeviceCaps (HORZRES);
        ::DeleteDC (dc.Detach ());
    }
}
```

CWinApp::GetPrinterDeviceDefaults initializes a PRINTDLG structure with values describing the default printing configuration. A 0 return means that the function failed, which usually indicates that no printers are installed or that a default printer hasn't been designated. *CPrintInfo::CreatePrinterDC* creates a device context handle from the information in the PRINTDLG structure encapsulated in a *CPrintInfo* object. With the device context in hand, it's a simple matter to wrap it in a *CDC* object and use *CDC::GetDeviceCaps* to measure the printable page area.

Enumerating Printers

Sometimes it's useful to be able to build a list of all the printers available so that the user can select a printer outside a Print or Print Setup dialog box. The following routine uses the Win32 *::EnumPrinters* function to enumerate the printers currently installed and adds an entry for each to the combo box pointed to by *pComboBox*.

```
#include <winspool.h>
    :
    :
DWORD dwSize, dwPrinters;
::EnumPrinters (PRINTER_ENUM_LOCAL, NULL, 5,
    NULL, 0, &dwSize, &dwPrinters);

BYTE* pBuffer = new BYTE[dwSize];

::EnumPrinters (PRINTER_ENUM_LOCAL, NULL, 5,
    pBuffer, dwSize, &dwSize, &dwPrinters);

if (dwPrinters != 0) {
    PRINTER_INFO_5* pPrnInfo = (PRINTER_INFO_5*) pBuffer;
    for (UINT i=0; i<dwPrinters; i++) {
        pComboBox->AddString (pPrnInfo->pPrinterName);
        pPrnInfo++;
    }
}

delete[] pBuffer;
```

The first call to *::EnumPrinters* retrieves the amount of buffer space needed to hold an array of PRINTER_INFO_5 structures describing individual printers. The second call to *::EnumPrinters* initializes the buffer pointed to by *pBuffer* with an array of PRINTER_INFO_5 structures. On return, *dwPrinters* holds a count of the printers enumerated (which equals the count of PRINTER_INFO_5 structures copied to the buffer), and each structure's *pPrinterName* field holds a pointer to a zero-delimited string containing the device name of the associated printer. Enumerating printers with PRINTER_INFO_5 structures is fast because no remote calls are required; all information needed to fill the buffer is obtained from the registry. For fast printer enumerations in Windows NT or Windows 2000, use PRINTER_INFO_4 structures instead.

If a printer is selected from the combo box and you want to create a device context for it, you can pass the device name copied from the PRINTER_INFO_5 structure to *CDC::CreateDC* as follows:

```
CString strPrinterName;
int nIndex = pComboBox->GetCurSel ();
pComboBox->GetLBText (nIndex, strPrinterName);

CDC dc;
dc.CreateDC (NULL, strPrinterName, NULL, NULL);
```

You can use the resulting *CDC* object just like the *CDC* objects whose addresses are passed to *OnBeginPrinting* and other *CView* print functions.

Part III

Beyond the Basics

Chapter 14

Timers and Idle Processing

Not all actions that Microsoft Windows applications undertake are performed in response to user input. Some processing is inherently time-based, such as autosave operations that save documents at 10-minute intervals and updates that involve a clock displayed in a status bar. Windows helps out by providing *timers* that you can program to send notifications at regular intervals. Another form of temporal processing is *idle processing*—work performed during "idle" periods when no messages are waiting in the message queue. MFC supplies a framework for idle-time processing in the form of a virtual function named *OnIdle* that is called whenever the message pump in *CWinThread* goes to the message queue and finds it empty.

In the first half of this chapter, we'll examine timers, which can be programmed for intervals as low as 55 milliseconds. Here are just a few of the ways in which you can put timers to use:

- In applications that display wall-clock time. Most such applications set a timer to fire at intervals ranging from a half second to as many as 60 seconds. When a timer notification arrives, these applications update the display to reflect the current time.

- In unattended backup programs, disk defragmenters, and other applications that lie dormant until a specified time.

- In resource monitors, free-memory gauges, and other applications that monitor the state of the system.

In the second half of the chapter, we'll look at idle processing—what it is, how it works, and how you can use it to perform background processing tasks in MFC applications.

TIMERS

You only need to know about two functions to use timers. *CWnd::SetTimer* programs a timer to fire at specified intervals, and *CWnd::KillTimer* stops a running timer. Depending on the parameters passed to *SetTimer*, a timer notifies an application that a time interval has elapsed in one of two ways:

- By sending a specified window a WM_TIMER message

- By calling an application-defined callback function

The WM_TIMER method is the simpler of the two, but the callback method is sometimes preferable, particularly when multiple timers are used. Both types of timer notifications receive low priority when they are sent to an application. They are processed only when the message queue is devoid of other messages.

Timer notifications are never allowed to stack up in the message queue. If you set a timer to fire every 100 milliseconds and a full second goes by while your application is busy processing other messages, it won't suddenly receive ten rapid-fire timer notifications when the message queue empties. Instead, it will receive just one. You needn't worry that if you take too much time to process a timer notification, another will arrive before you're finished with the previous one and start a race condition. Still, a Windows application should never spend an excessive amount of time processing a message unless processing has been delegated to a background thread because responsiveness will suffer if the primary thread goes too long without checking the message queue.

Setting a Timer: Method 1

The easiest way to set a timer is to call *SetTimer* with a timer ID and a timer interval and then map WM_TIMER messages to an *OnTimer* function. A timer ID is a nonzero value that uniquely identifies the timer. When *OnTimer* is activated in response to a WM_TIMER message, the timer ID is passed as an argument. If you use only one timer, the ID value probably won't interest you because all WM_TIMER messages will originate from the same timer. An application that employs two or more timers can use the timer ID to identify the timer that generated a particular message.

The timer interval passed to *SetTimer* specifies the desired length of time between consecutive WM_TIMER messages in thousandths of a second. Valid values range from 1 through the highest number a 32-bit integer will hold: $2^{32} - 1$ milliseconds, which equals slightly more than 49½ days. The statement

```
SetTimer (1, 500, NULL);
```

allocates a timer, assigns it an ID of 1, and programs it to send the window whose *SetTimer* function was called a WM_TIMER message every 500 milliseconds. The NULL third parameter configures the timer to send WM_TIMER messages rather than call a callback function. Although the programmed interval is 500 milliseconds, the window will actually receive a WM_TIMER message about once every 550 milliseconds because the hardware timer on which Windows timers are based ticks once every 54.9 milliseconds, give or take a few microseconds, on most systems (particularly Intel-based systems). In effect, Windows rounds the value you pass to *SetTimer* up to the next multiple of 55 milliseconds. Thus, the statement

```
SetTimer (1, 1, NULL);
```

programs a timer to send a WM_TIMER message roughly every 55 milliseconds, as does the statement

```
SetTimer (1, 50, NULL);
```

But change the timer interval to 60, as in

```
SetTimer (1, 60, NULL);
```

and WM_TIMER messages will arrive, on average, every 110 milliseconds.

How regular is the spacing between WM_TIMER messages once a timer is set? The following list of elapsed times between timer messages was taken from a 32-bit Windows application that programmed a timer to fire at 500-millisecond intervals:

Notification No.	Interval	Notification No.	Interval
1	0.542 second	11	0.604 second
2	0.557 second	12	0.550 second
3	0.541 second	13	0.549 second
4	0.503 second	14	0.549 second
5	0.549 second	15	0.550 second
6	0.549 second	16	0.508 second
7	1.936 seconds	17	0.550 second
8	0.261 second	18	0.549 second
9	0.550 second	19	0.549 second
10	0.549 second	20	0.550 second

As you can see, the average elapsed time is very close to 550 milliseconds, and most of the individual elapsed times are close to 550 milliseconds, too. The only significant perturbation, the elapsed time of 1.936 seconds between the sixth and seventh WM_TIMER messages, occurred as the window was being dragged across the screen. It's obvious from this list that Windows doesn't allow timer messages to accumulate in the message queue. If it did, the window would have received three or four timer messages in quick succession following the 1.936-second delay.

The lesson to be learned from this is that you can't rely on timers for stopwatch-like accuracy. If you write a clock application that programs a timer for 1,000-millisecond intervals and updates the display each time a WM_TIMER message arrives, you shouldn't assume that 60 WM_TIMER messages means that 1 minute has passed. Instead, you should check the current time whenever a message arrives and update the clock accordingly. Then if the flow of timer messages is interrupted, the clock's accuracy will be maintained.

If you write an application that demands precision timing, you can use Windows multimedia timers in lieu of conventional timers and program them for intervals of 1 millisecond or less. Multimedia timers offer superior precision and are ideal for specialized applications such as MIDI sequencers, but they also incur more overhead and can adversely impact other processes running in the system.

The value returned by *SetTimer* is the timer ID if the function succeeded or 0 if it failed. In 16-bit versions of Windows, timers were a shared global resource and only a limited number were available. In 32-bit Windows, the number of timers the system can dole out is virtually unlimited. Failures are rare, but it's still prudent to check the return value just in case the system is critically low on resources. (Don't forget, too, that a little discretion goes a long way. An application that sets too many timers can drag down the performance of the entire system.) The timer ID returned by *SetTimer* equals the timer ID specified in the function's first parameter unless you specify 0, in which case *SetTimer* will return a timer ID of 1. *SetTimer* won't fail if you assign two or more timers the same ID. Rather, it will assign duplicate IDs as requested.

You can also use *SetTimer* to change a previously assigned time-out value. If timer 1 already exists, the statement

```
SetTimer (1, 1000, NULL);
```

reprograms it for intervals of 1,000 milliseconds. Reprogramming a timer also resets its internal clock so that the next notification won't arrive until the specified time period has elapsed.

Responding to WM_TIMER Messages

MFC's ON_WM_TIMER message-map macro directs WM_TIMER messages to a class member function named *OnTimer*. *OnTimer* is prototyped as follows:

```
afx_msg void OnTimer (UINT nTimerID)
```

nTimerID is the ID of the timer that generated the message. You can do anything in *OnTimer* that you can do in other message processing functions, including grabbing a device context and painting in a window. The following code sample uses an

OnTimer handler to draw ellipses of random sizes and colors in a frame window's client area. The timer is programmed for 100-millisecond intervals in the window's *OnCreate* handler:

```
BEGIN_MESSAGE_MAP (CMainWindow, CFrameWnd)
    ON_WM_CREATE ()
    ON_WM_TIMER ()
END_MESSAGE_MAP ()

int CMainWindow::OnCreate (LPCREATESTRUCT lpcs)
{
    if (CFrameWnd::OnCreate (lpcs) == -1)
        return -1;

    if (!SetTimer (ID_TIMER_ELLIPSE, 100, NULL)) {
        MessageBox (_T ("Error: SetTimer failed"));
        return -1;
    }
    return 0;
}

void CMainWindow::OnTimer (UINT nTimerID)
{
    CRect rect;
    GetClientRect (&rect);

    int x1 = rand () % rect.right;
    int x2 = rand () % rect.right;
    int y1 = rand () % rect.bottom;
    int y2 = rand () % rect.bottom;

    CClientDC dc (this);
    CBrush brush (RGB (rand () % 255, rand () % 255,
        rand () % 255));
    CBrush* pOldBrush = dc.SelectObject (&brush);
    dc.Ellipse (min (x1, x2), min (y1, y2), max (x1, x2),
        max (y1, y2));
    dc.SelectObject (pOldBrush);
}
```

Here's how the same code fragment would look if the application were modified to use two timers—one for drawing ellipses and another for drawing rectangles:

```
BEGIN_MESSAGE_MAP (CMainWindow, CFrameWnd)
    ON_WM_CREATE ()
    ON_WM_TIMER ()
END_MESSAGE_MAP ()
```

(continued)

```
int CMainWindow::OnCreate (LPCREATESTRUCT lpcs)
{
    if (CFrameWnd::OnCreate (lpcs) == -1)
        return -1;

    if (!SetTimer (ID_TIMER_ELLIPSE, 100, NULL) ||
        !SetTimer (ID_TIMER_RECTANGLE, 100, NULL)) {
        MessageBox (_T ("Error: SetTimer failed"));
        return -1;
    }
    return 0;
}

void CMainWindow::OnTimer (UINT nTimerID)
{
    CRect rect;
    GetClientRect (&rect);

    int x1 = rand () % rect.right;
    int x2 = rand () % rect.right;
    int y1 = rand () % rect.bottom;
    int y2 = rand () % rect.bottom;

    CClientDC dc (this);
    CBrush brush (RGB (rand () % 255, rand () % 255, rand () % 255));
    CBrush* pOldBrush = dc.SelectObject (&brush);
    if (nTimerID == ID_TIMER_ELLIPSE)
        dc.Ellipse (min (x1, x2), min (y1, y2), max (x1, x2),
            max (y1, y2));
    else // nTimerID == ID_TIMER_RECTANGLE
        dc.Rectangle (min (x1, x2), min (y1, y2), max (x1, x2),
            max (y1, y2));
    dc.SelectObject (pOldBrush);
}
```

As you can see, this version of *OnTimer* inspects the *nTimerID* value passed to it to decide whether to draw an ellipse or a rectangle.

You might not write too many applications that draw ellipses and rectangles endlessly, but using timer messages to execute a certain task or a sequence of tasks repeatedly provides an easy solution to a common problem encountered in Windows programming. Suppose you write an application with two push button controls labeled "Start" and "Stop" and that clicking the Start button starts a drawing loop that looks like this:

```
m_bContinue = TRUE;
while (m_bContinue)
    DrawRandomEllipse ();
```

The loop draws ellipses over and over until the Stop button is clicked, which sets *m_bContinue* to FALSE so that the *while* loop will fall through. It looks reasonable, but try it and you'll find that it doesn't work. Once Start is clicked, the *while* loop runs until the Windows session is terminated or the application is aborted with Task Manager. Why? Because the statement that sets *m_bContinue* to FALSE gets executed only if the WM_COMMAND message generated by the Stop button is retrieved, dispatched, and routed through the message map to the corresponding ON_COMMAND handler. But as long as the *while* loop is spinning in a continuous cycle without checking for messages, the WM_COMMAND message sits idly in the message queue, waiting to be retrieved. *m_bContinue* never changes from TRUE to FALSE, and the program gets stuck in an infinite loop.

You can solve this problem in several ways. One solution is to do the drawing in a secondary thread so that the primary thread can continue to pump messages. Another is to add a message pump to the *while* loop to periodically check the message queue as ellipses are drawn. A third solution is to draw ellipses in response to WM_TIMER messages. In between WM_TIMER messages, other messages will continue to be processed as normal. The only drawback to this solution is that drawing ellipses at a rate of more than about 18 per second requires multiple timers, whereas a thread that starts drawing the next ellipse as soon as the previous one is finished might draw hundreds of ellipses per second, depending on the speed of the video hardware and the sizes of the ellipses.

An important point to take home here is that WM_TIMER messages are not processed asynchronously with respect to other messages. That is, one WM_TIMER message will never interrupt another WM_TIMER message in the same thread, nor will it interrupt a nontimer message, for that matter. WM_TIMER messages wait their turn in the message queue just as other messages do and aren't processed until they are retrieved and dispatched by the message loop. If a regular message handling function and an *OnTimer* function use a common member variable, you can safely assume that accesses to the variable won't overlap as long as the two message handlers belong to the same window or to windows running on the same thread.

Setting a Timer: Method 2

Timers don't have to generate WM_TIMER messages. If you prefer, you can configure a timer to call a callback function inside your application rather than send it a WM_TIMER message. This method is often used in applications that use multiple timers so that each timer can be assigned a unique handling function.

A common misconception among Windows programmers is that timer callbacks are processed more expediently than timer messages because callbacks are called directly by the operating system whereas WM_TIMER messages are placed in the message queue. In reality, timer callbacks and timer messages are handled identically up to the point at which *::DispatchMessage* is called. When a timer fires, Windows sets a flag in the message queue to indicate that a timer message or callback is waiting to be processed. (The on/off nature of the flag explains why timer notifications don't stack up in the message queue. The flag isn't incremented when a timer interval elapses but is merely set to "on.") If *::GetMessage* finds that the message queue is empty and that no windows need repainting, it checks the timer flag. If the flag is set, *::GetMessage* builds a WM_TIMER message that is subsequently dispatched by *::DispatchMessage*. If the timer that generated the message is of the WM_TIMER variety, the message is dispatched to the window procedure. But if a callback function is registered instead, *::DispatchMessage* calls the callback function. Therefore, callback timers enjoy virtually no performance advantage over message timers. Callbacks are subject to slightly less overhead than messages because neither a message map nor a window procedure is involved, but the difference is all but immeasurable. In practice, you'll find that WM_TIMER-type timers and callback timers work with the same regularity (or irregularity, depending on how you look at it).

To set a timer that uses a callback, specify the name of the callback function in the third parameter to *SetTimer*, like this:

```
SetTimer (ID_TIMER, 100, TimerProc);
```

The callback procedure, which is named *TimerProc* in this example, is prototyped as follows:

```
void CALLBACK TimerProc (HWND hWnd, UINT nMsg,
    UINT nTimerID, DWORD dwTime)
```

The *hWnd* parameter to *TimerProc* contains the window handle, *nMsg* contains the message ID WM_TIMER, *nTimerID* holds the timer ID, and *dwTime* specifies the number of milliseconds that have elapsed since Windows was started. (Some documentation says that *dwTime* "specifies the system time in Coordinated Universal Time format." Don't believe it; it's a bug in the documentation.) The callback function should be a static member function or a global function to prevent a *this* pointer from being passed to it. For more information on callback functions and the problems that nonstatic member functions pose for C++ applications, refer to Chapter 7.

One obstacle you'll encounter when using a static member function as a timer callback is that the timer procedure doesn't receive a user-defined *lParam* value as some Windows callback functions do. When we used a static member function to field callbacks from *::EnumFontFamilies* in Chapter 7, we passed a *CMainWindow* pointer in *lParam* to permit the callback function to access nonstatic class members. In a timer procedure, you have to obtain that pointer by other means if you want to access nonstatic function and data members. Fortunately, you can get a pointer to your application's main window with MFC's *AfxGetMainWnd* function:

```
CMainWindow* pMainWnd = (CMainWindow*) AfxGetMainWnd ();
```

Casting the return value to a *CMainWindow* pointer is necessary if you want to access *CMainWindow* function and data members because the pointer returned by *AfxGetMainWnd* is a generic *CWnd* pointer. Once *pMainWnd* is initialized in this way, a *TimerProc* function that is also a member of *CMainWindow* can access nonstatic *CMainWindow* function and data members as if it, too, were a nonstatic member function.

Stopping a Timer

The counterpart to *CWnd::SetTimer* is *CWnd::KillTimer*, which stops a timer and stops the flow of WM_TIMER messages or timer callbacks. The following statement releases the timer whose ID is 1:

```
KillTimer (1);
```

A good place to kill a timer created in *OnCreate* is in the window's *OnClose* or *OnDestroy* handler. If an application fails to free a timer before it terminates, 32-bit versions of Windows will clean up after it when the process ends. Still, good form dictates that every call to *SetTimer* should be paired with a call to *KillTimer* to ensure that timer resources are properly deallocated.

THE CLOCK APPLICATION

The Clock application shown in Figure 14-1 uses a timer set to fire at 1-second intervals to periodically redraw a set of clock hands simulating an analog clock. Clock isn't a document/view application; it uses the MFC 1.0–style application architecture described in the first few chapters of this book. All of its source code, including the RC file, was generated by hand. (See Figure 14-2.) Besides demonstrating how to use a timer in a Windows application, Clock introduces a new MFC class named *CTime* and a new message, WM_MINMAXINFO. It also has several other interesting features that have nothing to do with timers, including these:

■ A command in the system menu for removing the window's title bar

■ A command in the system menu for making Clock's window a topmost window—one that's drawn on top of other windows even when it's running in the background

■ A persistent frame window that remembers its size and position

■ A frame window that can be dragged by its client area

We'll go over these and other unique aspects of the application in the sections that follow.

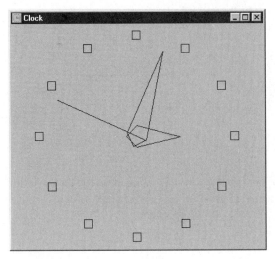

Figure 14-1. *The Clock window.*

Resource.h

```
#define IDM_SYSMENU_FULL_WINDOW      16
#define IDM_SYSMENU_STAY_ON_TOP      32
#define IDI_APPICON                 100
```

Clock.rc

```
#include <afxres.h>
#include "Resource.h"

IDI_APPICON ICON Clock.ico
```

Clock.h

```
class CMyApp : public CWinApp
{
public:
    virtual BOOL InitInstance ();
};

class CMainWindow : public CFrameWnd
{
```

Figure 14-2. *The Clock application.*

```
protected:
    BOOL m_bFullWindow;
    BOOL m_bStayOnTop;

    int m_nPrevSecond;
    int m_nPrevMinute;
    int m_nPrevHour;

    void DrawClockFace (CDC* pDC);
    void DrawSecondHand (CDC* pDC, int nLength, int nScale, int nDegrees,
        COLORREF clrColor);
    void DrawHand (CDC* pDC, int nLength, int nScale, int nDegrees,
        COLORREF clrColor);

    void SetTitleBarState ();
    void SetTopMostState ();
    void SaveWindowState ();
    void UpdateSystemMenu (CMenu* pMenu);

public:
    CMainWindow ();
    virtual BOOL PreCreateWindow (CREATESTRUCT& cs);
    BOOL RestoreWindowState ();

protected:
    afx_msg int OnCreate (LPCREATESTRUCT lpcs);
    afx_msg void OnGetMinMaxInfo (MINMAXINFO* pMMI);
    afx_msg void OnTimer (UINT nTimerID);
    afx_msg void OnPaint ();
    afx_msg UINT OnNcHitTest (CPoint point);
    afx_msg void OnSysCommand (UINT nID, LPARAM lParam);
    afx_msg void OnContextMenu (CWnd* pWnd, CPoint point);
    afx_msg void OnEndSession (BOOL bEnding);
    afx_msg void OnClose ();

    DECLARE_MESSAGE_MAP ()
};
```

Clock.cpp

```
#include <afxwin.h>
#include <math.h>
#include "Clock.h"
#include "Resource.h"
```

(continued)

Figure 14-2 *continued*

```
#define SQUARESIZE 20
#define ID_TIMER_CLOCK 1

CMyApp myApp;

/////////////////////////////////////////////////////////////////////////
// CMyApp member functions

BOOL CMyApp::InitInstance ()
{
    SetRegistryKey (_T ("Programming Windows with MFC"));
    m_pMainWnd = new CMainWindow;
    if (!((CMainWindow*) m_pMainWnd)->RestoreWindowState ())
        m_pMainWnd->ShowWindow (m_nCmdShow);
    m_pMainWnd->UpdateWindow ();
    return TRUE;
}

/////////////////////////////////////////////////////////////////////////
// CMainWindow message map and member functions

BEGIN_MESSAGE_MAP (CMainWindow, CFrameWnd)
    ON_WM_CREATE ()
    ON_WM_PAINT ()
    ON_WM_TIMER ()
    ON_WM_GETMINMAXINFO ()
    ON_WM_NCHITTEST ()
    ON_WM_SYSCOMMAND ()
    ON_WM_CONTEXTMENU ()
    ON_WM_ENDSESSION ()
    ON_WM_CLOSE ()
END_MESSAGE_MAP ()

CMainWindow::CMainWindow ()
{
    m_bAutoMenuEnable = FALSE;

    CTime time = CTime::GetCurrentTime ();
    m_nPrevSecond = time.GetSecond ();
    m_nPrevMinute = time.GetMinute ();
    m_nPrevHour = time.GetHour () % 12;

    CString strWndClass = AfxRegisterWndClass (
        CS_HREDRAW | CS_VREDRAW,
        myApp.LoadStandardCursor (IDC_ARROW),
```

```
            (HBRUSH) (COLOR_3DFACE + 1),
            myApp.LoadIcon (IDI_APPICON)     );

    Create (strWndClass, _T ("Clock"));
}

BOOL CMainWindow::PreCreateWindow (CREATESTRUCT& cs)
{
    if (!CFrameWnd::PreCreateWindow (cs))
        return FALSE;

    cs.dwExStyle &= ~WS_EX_CLIENTEDGE;
    return TRUE;
}

int CMainWindow::OnCreate (LPCREATESTRUCT lpcs)
{
    if (CFrameWnd::OnCreate (lpcs) == -1)
        return -1;

    //
    // Set a timer to fire at 1-second intervals.
    //
    if (!SetTimer (ID_TIMER_CLOCK, 1000, NULL)) {
        MessageBox (_T ("SetTimer failed"), _T ("Error"),
            MB_ICONSTOP | MB_OK);
        return -1;
    }

    //
    // Customize the system menu.
    //
    CMenu* pMenu = GetSystemMenu (FALSE);
    pMenu->AppendMenu (MF_SEPARATOR);
    pMenu->AppendMenu (MF_STRING, IDM_SYSMENU_FULL_WINDOW,
        _T ("Remove &Title"));
    pMenu->AppendMenu (MF_STRING, IDM_SYSMENU_STAY_ON_TOP,
        _T ("Stay on To&p"));
    return 0;
}

void CMainWindow::OnClose ()
{
    SaveWindowState ();
    KillTimer (ID_TIMER_CLOCK);
    CFrameWnd::OnClose ();
}
```

(continued)

Figure 14-2 *continued*

```
void CMainWindow::OnEndSession (BOOL bEnding)
{
    if (bEnding)
        SaveWindowState ();
    CFrameWnd::OnEndSession (bEnding);
}

void CMainWindow::OnGetMinMaxInfo (MINMAXINFO* pMMI)
{
    pMMI->ptMinTrackSize.x = 120;
    pMMI->ptMinTrackSize.y = 120;
}

UINT CMainWindow::OnNcHitTest (CPoint point)
{
    UINT nHitTest = CFrameWnd::OnNcHitTest (point);
    if ((nHitTest == HTCLIENT) && (::GetAsyncKeyState (MK_LBUTTON) < 0))
        nHitTest = HTCAPTION;
    return nHitTest;
}

void CMainWindow::OnSysCommand (UINT nID, LPARAM lParam)
{
    UINT nMaskedID = nID & 0xFFF0;

    if (nMaskedID == IDM_SYSMENU_FULL_WINDOW) {
        m_bFullWindow = m_bFullWindow ? 0 : 1;
        SetTitleBarState ();
        return;
    }
    else if (nMaskedID == IDM_SYSMENU_STAY_ON_TOP) {
        m_bStayOnTop = m_bStayOnTop ? 0 : 1;
        SetTopMostState ();
        return;
    }
    CFrameWnd::OnSysCommand (nID, lParam);
}

void CMainWindow::OnContextMenu (CWnd* pWnd, CPoint point)
{
    CRect rect;
    GetClientRect (&rect);
    ClientToScreen (&rect);
```

```
    if (rect.PtInRect (point)) {
        CMenu* pMenu = GetSystemMenu (FALSE);
        UpdateSystemMenu (pMenu);

        int nID = (int) pMenu->TrackPopupMenu (TPM_LEFTALIGN |
            TPM_LEFTBUTTON | TPM_RIGHTBUTTON | TPM_RETURNCMD, point.x,
            point.y, this);

        if (nID > 0)
            SendMessage (WM_SYSCOMMAND, nID, 0);

        return;
    }
    CFrameWnd::OnContextMenu (pWnd, point);
}

void CMainWindow::OnTimer (UINT nTimerID)
{
    //
    // Do nothing if the window is minimized.
    //
    if (IsIconic ())
        return;

    //
    // Get the current time and do nothing if it hasn't changed.
    //
    CTime time = CTime::GetCurrentTime ();
    int nSecond = time.GetSecond ();
    int nMinute = time.GetMinute ();
    int nHour = time.GetHour () % 12;

    if ((nSecond == m_nPrevSecond) &&
        (nMinute == m_nPrevMinute) &&
        (nHour == m_nPrevHour))
        return;

    //
    // Center the origin and switch to the MM_ISOTROPIC mapping mode.
    //
    CRect rect;
    GetClientRect (&rect);

    CClientDC dc (this);
    dc.SetMapMode (MM_ISOTROPIC);
    dc.SetWindowExt (1000, 1000);
    dc.SetViewportExt (rect.Width (), -rect.Height ());
```

(continued)

Figure 14-2 *continued*

```
    dc.SetViewportOrg (rect.Width () / 2, rect.Height () / 2);

    //
    // If minutes have changed, erase the hour and minute hands.
    //
    COLORREF clrColor = ::GetSysColor (COLOR_3DFACE);

    if (nMinute != m_nPrevMinute) {
        DrawHand (&dc, 200, 4, (m_nPrevHour * 30) + (m_nPrevMinute / 2),
            clrColor);
        DrawHand (&dc, 400, 8, m_nPrevMinute * 6, clrColor);
        m_nPrevMinute = nMinute;
        m_nPrevHour = nHour;
    }

    //
    // If seconds have changed, erase the second hand and redraw all hands.
    //
    if (nSecond != m_nPrevSecond) {
        DrawSecondHand (&dc, 400, 8, m_nPrevSecond * 6, clrColor);
        DrawSecondHand (&dc, 400, 8, nSecond * 6, RGB (0, 0, 0));
        DrawHand (&dc, 200, 4, (nHour * 30) + (nMinute / 2),
            RGB (0, 0, 0));
        DrawHand (&dc, 400, 8, nMinute * 6, RGB (0, 0, 0));
        m_nPrevSecond = nSecond;
    }
}

void CMainWindow::OnPaint ()
{
    CRect rect;
    GetClientRect (&rect);

    CPaintDC dc (this);
    dc.SetMapMode (MM_ISOTROPIC);
    dc.SetWindowExt (1000, 1000);
    dc.SetViewportExt (rect.Width (), -rect.Height ());
    dc.SetViewportOrg (rect.Width () / 2, rect.Height () / 2);

    DrawClockFace (&dc);
    DrawHand (&dc, 200, 4, (m_nPrevHour * 30) +
        (m_nPrevMinute / 2), RGB (0, 0, 0));
    DrawHand (&dc, 400, 8, m_nPrevMinute * 6, RGB (0, 0, 0));
    DrawSecondHand (&dc, 400, 8, m_nPrevSecond * 6, RGB (0, 0, 0));
}
```

```
void CMainWindow::DrawClockFace (CDC* pDC)
{
    static CPoint point[12] = {
        CPoint (   0,  450),    // 12 o'clock
        CPoint ( 225,  390),    // 1 o'clock
        CPoint ( 390,  225),    // 2 o'clock
        CPoint ( 450,    0),    // 3 o'clock
        CPoint ( 390, -225),    // 4 o'clock
        CPoint ( 225, -390),    // 5 o'clock
        CPoint (   0, -450),    // 6 o'clock
        CPoint (-225, -390),    // 7 o'clock
        CPoint (-390, -225),    // 8 o'clock
        CPoint (-450,    0),    // 9 o'clock
        CPoint (-390,  225),    // 10 o'clock
        CPoint (-225,  390),    // 11 o'clock
    };

    pDC->SelectStockObject (NULL_BRUSH);

    for (int i=0; i<12; i++)
        pDC->Rectangle (point[i].x - SQUARESIZE,
            point[i].y + SQUARESIZE, point[i].x + SQUARESIZE,
            point[i].y - SQUARESIZE);
}

void CMainWindow::DrawHand (CDC* pDC, int nLength, int nScale,
    int nDegrees, COLORREF clrColor)
{
    CPoint point[4];
    double nRadians = (double) nDegrees * 0.017453292;

    point[0].x = (int) (nLength * sin (nRadians));
    point[0].y = (int) (nLength * cos (nRadians));

    point[2].x = -point[0].x / nScale;
    point[2].y = -point[0].y / nScale;

    point[1].x = -point[2].y;
    point[1].y = point[2].x;

    point[3].x = -point[1].x;
    point[3].y = -point[1].y;

    CPen pen (PS_SOLID, 0, clrColor);
    CPen* pOldPen = pDC->SelectObject (&pen);
```

(continued)

Figure 14-2 *continued*

```
    pDC->MoveTo (point[0]);
    pDC->LineTo (point[1]);
    pDC->LineTo (point[2]);
    pDC->LineTo (point[3]);
    pDC->LineTo (point[0]);

    pDC->SelectObject (pOldPen);
}

void CMainWindow::DrawSecondHand (CDC* pDC, int nLength, int nScale,
    int nDegrees, COLORREF clrColor)
{
    CPoint point[2];
    double nRadians = (double) nDegrees * 0.017453292;

    point[0].x = (int) (nLength * sin (nRadians));
    point[0].y = (int) (nLength * cos (nRadians));

    point[1].x = -point[0].x / nScale;
    point[1].y = -point[0].y / nScale;

    CPen pen (PS_SOLID, 0, clrColor);
    CPen* pOldPen = pDC->SelectObject (&pen);

    pDC->MoveTo (point[0]);
    pDC->LineTo (point[1]);

    pDC->SelectObject (pOldPen);
}

void CMainWindow::SetTitleBarState ()
{
    CMenu* pMenu = GetSystemMenu (FALSE);

    if (m_bFullWindow ) {
        ModifyStyle (WS_CAPTION, 0);
        pMenu->ModifyMenu (IDM_SYSMENU_FULL_WINDOW, MF_STRING,
            IDM_SYSMENU_FULL_WINDOW, _T ("Restore &Title"));
    }
    else {
        ModifyStyle (0, WS_CAPTION);
        pMenu->ModifyMenu (IDM_SYSMENU_FULL_WINDOW, MF_STRING,
            IDM_SYSMENU_FULL_WINDOW, _T ("Remove &Title"));
    }
    SetWindowPos (NULL, 0, 0, 0, 0, SWP_NOMOVE | SWP_NOSIZE |
        SWP_NOZORDER | SWP_DRAWFRAME);
```

```
}

void CMainWindow::SetTopMostState ()
{
    CMenu* pMenu = GetSystemMenu (FALSE);

    if (m_bStayOnTop) {
        SetWindowPos (&wndTopMost, 0, 0, 0, 0, SWP_NOMOVE | SWP_NOSIZE);
        pMenu->CheckMenuItem (IDM_SYSMENU_STAY_ON_TOP, MF_CHECKED);
    }
    else {
        SetWindowPos (&wndNoTopMost, 0, 0, 0, 0, SWP_NOMOVE | SWP_NOSIZE);
        pMenu->CheckMenuItem (IDM_SYSMENU_STAY_ON_TOP, MF_UNCHECKED);
    }
}

BOOL CMainWindow::RestoreWindowState ()
{
    CString version = _T ("Version 1.0");
    m_bFullWindow = myApp.GetProfileInt (version, _T ("FullWindow"), 0);
    SetTitleBarState ();
    m_bStayOnTop = myApp.GetProfileInt (version, _T ("StayOnTop"), 0);
    SetTopMostState ();

    WINDOWPLACEMENT wp;
    wp.length = sizeof (WINDOWPLACEMENT);
    GetWindowPlacement (&wp);

    if (((wp.flags =
            myApp.GetProfileInt (version, _T ("flags"), -1)) != -1) &&
        ((wp.showCmd =
            myApp.GetProfileInt (version, _T ("showCmd"), -1)) != -1) &&
        ((wp.rcNormalPosition.left =
            myApp.GetProfileInt (version, _T ("x1"), -1)) != -1) &&
        ((wp.rcNormalPosition.top =
            myApp.GetProfileInt (version, _T ("y1"), -1)) != -1) &&
        ((wp.rcNormalPosition.right =
            myApp.GetProfileInt (version, _T ("x2"), -1)) != -1) &&
        ((wp.rcNormalPosition.bottom =
            myApp.GetProfileInt (version, _T ("y2"), -1)) != -1)) {

        wp.rcNormalPosition.left = min (wp.rcNormalPosition.left,
            ::GetSystemMetrics (SM_CXSCREEN) -
            ::GetSystemMetrics (SM_CXICON));
        wp.rcNormalPosition.top = min (wp.rcNormalPosition.top,
            ::GetSystemMetrics (SM_CYSCREEN) -
            ::GetSystemMetrics (SM_CYICON));
```

(continued)

Figure 14-2 *continued*

```
        SetWindowPlacement (&wp);
        return TRUE;
    }
    return FALSE;
}


void CMainWindow::SaveWindowState ()
{
    CString version = _T ("Version 1.0");
    myApp.WriteProfileInt (version, _T ("FullWindow"), m_bFullWindow);
    myApp.WriteProfileInt (version, _T ("StayOnTop"), m_bStayOnTop);

    WINDOWPLACEMENT wp;
    wp.length = sizeof (WINDOWPLACEMENT);
    GetWindowPlacement (&wp);

    myApp.WriteProfileInt (version, _T ("flags"), wp.flags);
    myApp.WriteProfileInt (version, _T ("showCmd"), wp.showCmd);
    myApp.WriteProfileInt (version, _T ("x1"), wp.rcNormalPosition.left);
    myApp.WriteProfileInt (version, _T ("y1"), wp.rcNormalPosition.top);
    myApp.WriteProfileInt (version, _T ("x2"), wp.rcNormalPosition.right);
    myApp.WriteProfileInt (version, _T ("y2"), wp.rcNormalPosition.bottom);
}


void CMainWindow::UpdateSystemMenu (CMenu* pMenu)
{
    static UINT nState[2][5] = {
        { MFS_GRAYED,  MFS_ENABLED, MFS_ENABLED,
          MFS_ENABLED, MFS_DEFAULT },
        { MFS_DEFAULT, MFS_GRAYED,  MFS_GRAYED,
          MFS_ENABLED, MFS_GRAYED  }
    };

    if (IsIconic ()) // Shouldn't happen, but let's be safe
        return;

    int i = 0;
    if (IsZoomed ())
        i = 1;

    CString strMenuText;
    pMenu->GetMenuString (SC_RESTORE, strMenuText, MF_BYCOMMAND);
    pMenu->ModifyMenu (SC_RESTORE, MF_STRING | nState[i][0], SC_RESTORE,
        strMenuText);

    pMenu->GetMenuString (SC_MOVE, strMenuText, MF_BYCOMMAND);
    pMenu->ModifyMenu (SC_MOVE, MF_STRING | nState[i][1], SC_MOVE,
```

```
            strMenuText);

    pMenu->GetMenuString (SC_SIZE, strMenuText, MF_BYCOMMAND);
    pMenu->ModifyMenu (SC_SIZE, MF_STRING | nState[i][2], SC_SIZE,
        strMenuText);

    pMenu->GetMenuString (SC_MINIMIZE, strMenuText, MF_BYCOMMAND);
    pMenu->ModifyMenu (SC_MINIMIZE, MF_STRING | nState[i][3], SC_MINIMIZE,
        strMenuText);

    pMenu->GetMenuString (SC_MAXIMIZE, strMenuText, MF_BYCOMMAND);
    pMenu->ModifyMenu (SC_MAXIMIZE, MF_STRING | nState[i][4], SC_MAXIMIZE,
        strMenuText);

    SetMenuDefaultItem (pMenu->m_hMenu, i ? SC_RESTORE :
        SC_MAXIMIZE, FALSE);
}
```

Processing Timer Messages

Clock uses *SetTimer* to program a timer in *OnCreate*. The timer is destroyed in *OnClose* with *KillTimer*. When a WM_TIMER message arrives, *CMainWindow::OnTimer* gets the current time and compares the hour, minute, and second to the hour, minute, and second previously recorded in the member variables *m_nPrevHour*, *m_nPrevMinute*, and *m_nPrevSecond*. If the current hour, minute, and second equal the hour, minute, and second recorded earlier, *OnTimer* does nothing. Otherwise, it records the new time and moves the clock hands. *CMainWindow::DrawHand* draws the hour and minute hands, and *CMainWindow::DrawSecondHand* draws the second hand. A hand is moved by calling the corresponding drawing function twice: once to erase the hand by drawing over it with the window background color (COLOR_3DFACE) and once to draw the hand—in black—in its new position.

With this *OnTimer* mechanism in place, the clock's second hand is moved roughly once per second and the hour and minute hands are moved whenever the current number of minutes past the hour no longer equals the previously recorded minutes-past-the-hour. Because the hands are drawn to reflect the current time and not some assumed time based on the number of WM_TIMER messages received, it doesn't matter if WM_TIMER messages are skipped as the window is dragged or resized. If you watch closely, you'll see that the second hand occasionally advances by two seconds rather than one. That's because every now and then a WM_TIMER message arrives just before a new second ticks off and the next WM_TIMER message arrives a split second after the next new second. You could prevent this from happening by lowering the timer interval to, say, 0.5 second. The cost would be more overhead to the system, but the added overhead would be minimal because *OnTimer* is structured so that it redraws the clock hands (by far the most labor-intensive part of the process) only if the time has changed since the last timer message.

Before doing anything else, *OnTimer* calls the main window's *IsIconic* function to determine whether the window is currently minimized. *IsIconic* returns nonzero for a minimized window and 0 for an unminimized window. (A complementary function, *CWnd::IsZoomed*, returns a nonzero value if a window is maximized and 0 if it isn't.) If *IsIconic* returns nonzero, *OnTimer* exits immediately to prevent the clock display from being updated when the window isn't displayed. When a minimized window calls *GetClientRect* in Windows 95 or higher or Windows NT 4.0 or higher, the returned rectangle is a NULL rectangle—one whose coordinates equal 0. The application can try to paint in this rectangle, but the GDI will clip the output. Checking for a minimized window upon each timer tick reduces the load on the CPU by eliminating unnecessary drawing.

If you'd rather that Clock not sit idle while its window is minimized, try rewriting the beginning of the *OnTimer* function so that it looks like this:

```
CTime time = CTime::GetCurrentTime ();
int nSecond = time.GetSecond ();
int nMinute = time.GetMinute ();
int nHour = time.GetHour () % 12;

if (IsIconic ()) {
    CString time;
    time.Format (_T ("%0.2d:%0.2d:%0.2d"), nHour, nMinute, nSecond);
    SetWindowText (time);
    return;
}

else {
    SetWindowText (_T ("Clock"));
        .
        .
        .
}
```

An application can change the text displayed next to its icon in the taskbar by changing the window title with *CWnd::SetWindowText*. If modified as shown above, Clock will tick off the seconds in the taskbar while it is minimized.

Getting the Current Time: The *CTime* Class

To query the system for the current time, Clock uses a *CTime* object. *CTime* is an MFC class that represents times and dates. It includes convenient member functions for getting the date, time, day of the week (Sunday, Monday, Tuesday, and so on), and other information. Overloaded operators such as +, −, and > allow you to manipulate times and dates with the ease of simple integers.

The *CTime* member functions that interest us are *GetCurrentTime*, which is a static function that returns a *CTime* object initialized to the current date and time; *GetHour*, which returns the hour (0 through 23); *GetMinute*, which returns the number of minutes past the hour (0 through 59); and *GetSecond*, which returns the number of seconds (0 through 59). *OnTimer* uses the following statements to retrieve the current hour, minute, and second so that it can determine whether the clock display needs to be updated:

```
CTime time = CTime::GetCurrentTime ();
int nSecond = time.GetSecond ();
int nMinute = time.GetMinute ();
int nHour = time.GetHour () % 12;
```

The modulo-12 operation applied to *GetHour*'s return value converts the hour to an integer from 0 through 11. *CMainWindow*'s constructor uses similar code to initialize *m_nPrevHour*, *m_nPrevMinute*, and *m_nPrevSecond*.

Using the MM_ISOTROPIC Mapping Mode

Up to now, most of the applications that we've developed have used the default MM_TEXT mapping mode. The mapping mode governs how Windows converts the logical units passed to *CDC* drawing functions into device units (pixels) on the display. In the MM_TEXT mapping mode, logical units and device units are one and the same, so if an application draws a line from (0,0) to (50,100), the line extends from the pixel in the upper left corner of the display surface to the pixel that lies 50 pixels to the right of and 100 pixels below the upper left corner. This assumes, of course, that the drawing origin hasn't been moved from its default location in the upper left corner of the display surface.

MM_TEXT is fine for most applications, but you can use other GDI mapping modes to lessen an application's dependency on the physical characteristics of the display. (For a review of GDI mapping modes, refer to Chapter 2.) In the MM_LO-ENGLISH mapping mode, for example, one logical unit is equal to 1/100 of an inch, so if you want to draw a line exactly 1 inch long, you can use a length of 100 units and Windows will factor in the number of pixels per inch when it scan-converts the line into pixels. The conversion might not be perfect for screen DCs because Windows uses assumed pixel-per-inch values for screens that aren't based on the physical screen size. Windows can obtain precise pixel-per-inch values for printers and other hardcopy devices, however, so by using MM_LOENGLISH for printer output, you really can draw a line 1 inch long.

Clock uses the MM_ISOTROPIC mapping mode, in which logical units measured along the *x* axis have the same physical dimensions as logical units measured along the *y* axis. Before drawing the clock's face and hands in response to a WM_TIMER or WM_PAINT message, Clock measures the window's client area with *GetClientRect* and creates a device context. Then it sets the mapping mode to MM_ISOTROPIC, moves the origin of the coordinate system so that the logical point (0,0) lies at the center of the window's client area, and sets the window extents so that the window's client area measures 1,000 logical units in each direction. Here's how it looks in code:

```
CRect rect;
GetClientRect (&rect);

CClientDC dc (this); // In OnPaint, use CPaintDC instead.
dc.SetMapMode (MM_ISOTROPIC);
dc.SetWindowExt (1000, 1000);
dc.SetViewportExt (rect.Width (), -rect.Height ());
dc.SetViewportOrg (rect.Width () / 2, rect.Height () / 2);
```

The negative value passed to *SetViewportExt* specifying the viewport's physical height orients the coordinate system such that values of *y* increase in the upward direction. If the negative sign were omitted, increasing values of *y* would move down the screen rather than up because Windows numbers pixels at the bottom of the screen higher than it does pixels at the top. Figure 14-3 shows what the coordinate system looks like after it is transformed. The coordinate system is centered in the window's client area, and values of *x* and *y* increase as you move to the right and up. The result is a four-quadrant Cartesian coordinate system that happens to be a very convenient model for drawing an analog clock face.

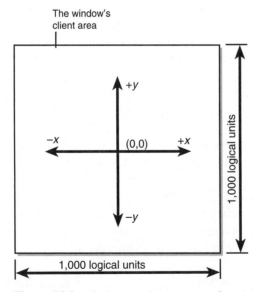

Figure 14-3. *Clock's coordinate system for screen output.*

Once you've configured the coordinate system this way, you can write the routines that draw the clock's face and hands without regard for the physical dimensions of the window. When *DrawHand* is called to draw a clock hand, the length value passed in the second parameter is either 200 for an hour hand or 400 for a minute hand. *DrawSecondHand*, too, is passed a length of 400. Because the distance from the origin of the coordinate system to any edge of the window is 500 logical units, the minute and second hands extend outward 80 percent of the distance to the nearest window edge and the hour hand spans 40 percent of the distance. If you used the MM_TEXT mapping mode instead, you'd have to scale every coordinate and every distance manually before passing it to the GDI.

Hiding and Displaying the Title Bar

Clock's system menu contains two extra commands: Remove Title and Stay On Top. Remove Title removes the window's title bar so that the clock face fills the entire window. You can restore the title bar by displaying the system menu again and selecting Restore Title, which appears where Remove Title used to be. The magic underlying this transformation is simple, yet adding or removing a title bar on the fly is enough to make even seasoned Windows programmers scratch their heads in bewilderment the first time they try it.

The secret lies in *CMainWindow::SetTitleBarState*. The attribute that determines whether a window has a title bar is the WS_CAPTION style bit, which is included in the WS_OVERLAPPEDWINDOW style used by most frame windows. Creating a window without a title bar is as simple as omitting WS_CAPTION from the window style. It follows that you can remove a title bar from a window that already exists by stripping the WS_CAPTION bit. MFC's *CWnd::ModifyStyle* function changes a window's style with one simple function call. When Remove/Restore Title is selected from Clock's system menu, *CMainWindow::OnSysCommand* toggles the value stored in *CMainWindow::m_bFullWindow* from 0 to 1 or 1 to 0 and then calls *CMainWindow::SetTitleBarState*, which adds or removes the WS_CAPTION style based on the current value of *m_bFullWindow*:

```
if (m_bFullWindow ) {
    ModifyStyle (WS_CAPTION, 0);
    pMenu->ModifyMenu (IDM_SYSMENU_FULL_WINDOW, MF_STRING,
        IDM_SYSMENU_FULL_WINDOW, _T ("Restore &Title"));
}
else {
    ModifyStyle (0, WS_CAPTION);
    pMenu->ModifyMenu (IDM_SYSMENU_FULL_WINDOW, MF_STRING,
        IDM_SYSMENU_FULL_WINDOW, _T ("Remove &Title"));
}
```

The first parameter passed to *ModifyStyle* specifies the style or styles to remove, and the second parameter specifies the style or styles to add. *SetTitleBarState* also sets the menu item text to match the state of the style bit: "Remove Title" if the title bar is displayed and "Restore Title" if it isn't.

Toggling WS_CAPTION on and off is only half the battle, however. The trick is getting the window's nonclient area to repaint once the window style is changed. Calling *CWnd::Invalidate* won't do it, but calling *SetWindowPos* with a SWP_DRAW-FRAME parameter will:

```
SetWindowPos (NULL, 0, 0, 0, 0, SWP_NOMOVE | SWP_NOSIZE |
    SWP_NOZORDER | SWP_DRAWFRAME);
```

The combination of *SetWindowPos* and SWP_DRAWFRAME causes the entire window, including the title bar, to redraw. The other SWP flags passed to *SetWindowPos* preserve the window's position, size, and position in the z-order—the front-to-back ordering of windows that determines which windows are painted on top of others.

Implementing Client-Area Drag

One problem with a window without a title bar is that it can't be repositioned with the mouse. Windows are dragged by their title bars, and when there's no title bar, the user has nothing to grab onto. Clock solves this little dilemma by playing a trick with the window's WM_NCHITTEST handler so that the window can be dragged by its client area, a feature Windows programmers call *client-area drag*.

In Windows, every mouse message is preceded by a WM_NCHITTEST message containing screen coordinates identifying the cursor location. The message is normally handled by *::DefWindowProc*, which returns a code that tells Windows what part of the window the cursor is over. Windows uses the return value to decide what type of mouse message to send. For example, if the left mouse button is clicked over the window's title bar, *::DefWindowProc*'s WM_NCHITTEST handler returns HTCAP-TION and Windows sends the window a WM_NCLBUTTONDOWN message. If *::DefWindowProc* returns HTCLIENT instead, Windows converts the cursor coordinates from screen coordinates to client coordinates and passes them to the window in a WM_LBUTTONDOWN message.

The fact that an application sees mouse messages in raw form makes for some interesting possibilities. The following *OnNcHitTest* handler implements client-area drag by fooling Windows into thinking that the mouse is over the title bar when in fact it's over the window's client area:

```
UINT CMainWindow::OnNcHitTest (CPoint point)
{
    UINT nHitTest = CFrameWnd::OnNcHitTest (point);
    if (nHitTest == HTCLIENT)
        nHitTest = HTCAPTION;
    return nHitTest;
}
```

With this *OnNcHitTest* handler in place, a window is as easily dragged by its client area as by its title bar. And it works even if the window doesn't *have* a title bar. Try it:

click the left mouse button in Clock's client area, and move the mouse with the button held down. The window should go wherever the mouse goes.

Clock uses an *OnNcHitTest* handler similar to the one shown above. The only difference is that Clock verifies that the left mouse button is down before replacing an HTCLIENT return code with HTCAPTION so that other mouse messages—particularly right-button mouse messages that precede WM_CONTEXTMENU messages—will get through unscathed:

```
UINT CMainWindow::OnNcHitTest (CPoint point)
{
    UINT nHitTest = CFrameWnd::OnNcHitTest (point);
    if ((nHitTest == HTCLIENT) &&
        (::GetAsyncKeyState (MK_LBUTTON) < 0))
        nHitTest = HTCAPTION;
    return nHitTest;
}
```

The call to *::GetAsyncKeyState* checks the left mouse button and returns a negative value if the button is currently down.

Using the System Menu as a Context Menu

Removing a window's title bar has other implications, too. Without a title bar, the user has nothing to click on to display the system menu so that the title bar can be restored. Clock's solution is an *OnContextMenu* handler that displays the system menu as a context menu when the right mouse button is clicked in the window's client area. Popping up a system menu at an arbitrary location is easier said than done because there's no convenient API function for displaying a system menu programmatically. Clock demonstrates one technique that you can use to do it yourself.

When Clock's client area is clicked with the right mouse button, *CMainWindow's* *OnContextMenu* handler retrieves a *CMenu* pointer to the system menu with *GetSystemMenu* and displays the menu with *CMenu::TrackPopupMenu*:

```
CMenu* pMenu = GetSystemMenu (FALSE);
    :
int nID = (int) pMenu->TrackPopupMenu (TPM_LEFTALIGN |
    TPM_LEFTBUTTON | TPM_RIGHTBUTTON | TPM_RETURNCMD, point.x,
    point.y, this);
```

One problem with this solution is that commands selected from the menu produce WM_COMMAND messages instead of WM_SYSCOMMAND messages. To compensate, Clock passes *TrackPopupMenu* a TPM_RETURNCMD flag instructing it to return the ID of the selected menu item. If *TrackPopupMenu* returns a positive, nonzero value, indicating that an item was selected, Clock sends itself a WM_SYSCOMMAND message with *wParam* equal to the menu item ID as shown on the next page.

```
if (nID > 0)
    SendMessage (WM_SYSCOMMAND, nID, 0);
```

Consequently, *OnSysCommand* gets called to process selections from the pseudo–system menu just as it does for selections from the real system menu. To prevent the framework from disabling the items added to the system menu because of the lack of ON_COMMAND handlers, *CMainWindow*'s constructor sets *m_bAutoMenuEnable* to FALSE. Normally, the framework's automatic enabling and disabling of menu items doesn't affect items added to the system menu, but Clock's system menu is an exception because it's treated as a conventional menu when it's displayed with *TrackPopupMenu*.

So far, so good. There's just one problem remaining. Windows interactively enables and disables certain commands in the system menu so that the selection of commands available is consistent with the window state. For example, the Move, Size, and Maximize commands are grayed in a maximized window's system menu but the Restore and Minimize commands are not. If the same window is restored to its unmaximized size, Restore is grayed out but all other commands are enabled. Unfortunately, when you get a menu pointer with *GetSystemMenu*, the menu items haven't been updated yet. Therefore, *OnContextMenu* calls a *CMainWindow* function named *UpdateSystemMenu* to manually update the menu item states based on the current state of the window. After *UpdateSystemMenu* updates the system menu by placing a series of calls to *CMenu::GetMenuString* and *CMenu::ModifyMenu*, it uses the *::SetMenuDefaultItem* API function to set the default menu item (the one displayed in boldface type) to either Restore or Maximize, depending on the window state. *UpdateSystemMenu* is hardly an ideal solution, but it works, and to date I haven't found a better way to keep the items in a programmatically displayed system menu in sync with the window the menu belongs to.

Topmost Windows

One of the innovations Windows 3.1 introduced was the notion of a *topmost window*—a window whose position in the z-order is implicitly higher than those of conventional, or nontopmost, windows. Normally, the window at the top of the z-order is painted on top of other windows, the window that's second in the z-order is painted on top of windows other than the first, and so on. A topmost window, however, receives priority over other windows so that it's not obscured even if it's at the bottom of the z-order. It's always visible, even while it's running in the background.

The Windows taskbar is the perfect example of a topmost window. By default, the taskbar is designated a topmost window so that it will be drawn on top of other windows. If two (or more) topmost windows are displayed at the same time, the normal rules of z-ordering determine the visibility of each one relative to the other. You should use topmost windows sparingly because if all windows were topmost windows, a topmost window would no longer be accorded priority over other windows.

The difference between a topmost window and a nontopmost window is an extended window style bit. WS_EX_TOPMOST makes a window a topmost window. You can create a topmost frame window by including a WS_EX_TOPMOST flag in the call to *Create*, like this:

```
Create (NULL, _T ("MyWindow"), WS_OVERLAPPEDWINDOW, rectDefault,
    NULL, NULL, WS_EX_TOPMOST);
```

The alternative is to add the style bit after the window is created by calling *Set-WindowPos* with a *&wndTopMost* parameter, as shown here:

```
SetWindowPos (&wndTopMost, 0, 0, 0, 0, SWP_NOMOVE | SWP_NOSIZE);
```

You can convert a topmost window into a nontopmost window by calling *SetWindowPos* with the first parameter equal to *&wndNoTopMost* rather than *&wndTopMost*.

Clock uses *SetWindowPos* to make its window a topmost window when Stay On Top is checked in the system menu and a nontopmost window when Stay On Top is unchecked. The work is done by *CMainWindow::SetTopMostState*, which is called by *OnSysCommand*. When Stay On Top is checked, Clock is visible on the screen at all times, even if it's running in the background and it overlaps the application running in the foreground.

Making Configuration Settings Persistent

Clock is the first program presented thus far that makes program settings persistent by recording them on disk. The word *persistent* comes up a lot in discussions of Windows programming. Saying that a piece of information is persistent means that it's preserved across sessions. If you want Clock to run in a tiny window in the lower right corner of your screen, you can size it and position it once and it will automatically come back up in the same size and position the next time it's started. For users who like to arrange their desktops a certain way, little touches like this one make the difference between a good application and a great one. Other Clock configuration settings are preserved, too, including the title bar and stay-on-top states.

The key to preserving configuration information across sessions is to store it on the hard disk so that it can be read back again the next time the application is started. In 16-bit Windows, applications commonly use *::WriteProfileString*, *::GetProfileString*, and other API functions to store configuration settings in Win.ini or private INI files. In 32-bit Windows, INI files are still supported for backward compatibility, but programmers are discouraged from using them. 32-bit applications should store configuration settings in the registry instead.

The registry is a binary database that serves as a central data repository for the operating system and the applications it hosts. Information stored in the registry is organized hierarchically using a system of keys and subkeys, which are analogous to directories and subdirectories on a hard disk. Keys can contain data entries just as directories can contain files. Data entries have names and can be assigned text or binary values. The uppermost level in the registry's hierarchy is a set of six root keys named HKEY_CLASSES_ROOT, HKEY_USERS, HKEY_CURRENT_USER, HKEY_LOCAL-_MACHINE, HKEY_CURRENT_CONFIG, and HKEY_DYN_DATA. Per Microsoft's recommendations, Windows applications should store private configuration settings under the key

```
HKEY_CURRENT_USER\Software\CompanyName\ProductName\Version
```

where *CompanyName* is the company name, *ProductName* is the product name, and *Version* is the product's version number. A registry entry that records the user-selectable window background color for version 2.0 of a product named WidgetMaster from WinWidgets, Inc., might look like this:

```
HKEY_CURRENT_USER\Software\WinWidgets, Inc.\WidgetMaster\Version 2.0\BkgndColor=4
```

Because the information is stored under HKEY_CURRENT_USER, it is maintained on a per-user basis. That is, if another user logs in and runs the same application but selects a different background color, a separate *BkgndColor* value will be recorded for that user.

The Win32 API includes an assortment of functions for reading and writing to the registry, but MFC provides a layer on top of the API that makes reading and writing application-specific registry values no different from using ordinary INI files. A call to *CWinApp::SetRegistryKey* with the name of a registry key directs the framework to use the registry instead of an INI file. The key name passed to *SetRegistryKey* corresponds to the company name—for example, "WinWidgets, Inc." in the example above. String and numeric values are written to the registry with *CWinApp*'s *WriteProfileString* and *WriteProfileInt* functions and read back with *GetProfileString* and *GetProfileInt*. In an application named MyWord.exe, the statements

```
SetRegistryKey (_T ("WordSmith"));
WriteProfileInt (_T ("Version 1.0"), _T ("MRULength"), 8);
```

create the following numeric registry entry:

```
HKEY_CURRENT_USER\Software\WordSmith\MYWORD\Version 1.0\MRULength=8
```

The statement

```
m_nMRULength = GetProfileInt (_T ("Version 1.0"), _T ("MRULength"), 4);
```

reads it back and returns 4 if the entry doesn't exist. Note that MFC generates the product name for you by stripping the .exe extension from the executable file name.

Before it terminates, Clock records the following configuration settings in the registry:

■ The value of *CMainWindow::m_bFullWindow*, which indicates whether the title bar is displayed

■ The value of *CMainWindow::m_bStayOnTop*, which indicates whether Stay On Top is selected

■ The size and position of the frame window

The next time it starts up, Clock reads the settings back. The full complement of entries that Clock stores in the registry is shown in Figure 14-4. The *CMainWindow* functions *SaveWindowState* and *RestoreWindowState* do the reading and writing. *SaveWindowState* is called from the window's *OnClose* and *OnEndSession* handlers, which are called just before the application closes and just before Windows shuts down, respectively. If Windows is shut down, a running application doesn't receive a WM_CLOSE message, but it does receive a WM_ENDSESSION message. If you want to know whether Windows is preparing to shut down, simply add an ON_WM__ENDSESSION entry to the main window's message map and write an *OnEndSession* handler to go with it. The *bEnding* parameter passed to *OnEndSession* indicates whether Windows is in fact shutting down. A nonzero value means it is; 0 means Windows was about to shut down but another application vetoed the operation. A WM_ENDSESSION message is preceded by a WM_QUERYENDSESSION message, in which each application is given a chance to say yes or no to an impending shutdown.

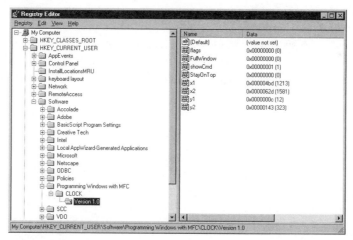

Figure 14-4. *Clock's registry entries as seen in Registry Editor (RegEdit.exe).*

Clock's title bar and stay-on-top settings are saved to the HKEY_CURRENT-_USER\Software\Programming Windows with MFC\CLOCK\Version 1.0 branch of the registry with the following statements in *SaveWindowState*.

```
CString version = _T ("Version 1.0");
myApp.WriteProfileInt (version, _T ("FullWindow"), m_bFullWindow);
myApp.WriteProfileInt (version, _T ("StayOnTop"), m_bStayOnTop);
```

The settings are read back and applied to the window in *RestoreWindowState*:

```
CString version = _T ("Version 1.0");
m_bFullWindow = myApp.GetProfileInt (version, _T ("FullWindow"), 0);
SetTitleBarState ();
m_bStayOnTop = myApp.GetProfileInt (version, _T ("StayOnTop"), 0);
SetTopMostState ();
```

RestoreWindowState is called by *CMyApp::InitInstance* right after the window is created but before it's displayed on the screen.

Saving and restoring the window's size and position is a little trickier. If you've never written an application with a window that remembers its size and position, you might think it would be a simple matter of saving the coordinates returned by *CWnd::GetWindowRect* so that they can be passed to *Create* or *CreateEx*. But there's more to it than that. If you fail to take into account the window's current state (minimized, maximized, or neither minimized nor maximized), all kinds of bad things can happen. For example, if you pass the coordinates of a maximized window to *Create* or *CreateEx*, the resultant window will occupy the full extent of the screen but its title bar will have a maximize box instead of a restore box. A persistent window that's closed while it's minimized or maximized should come back up in the minimized or maximized state, and it should also remember its normal size so that restoring it will restore its former size.

The key to preserving a window's size and position and taking relevant state information into account lies in a pair of *CWnd* functions named *GetWindowPlacement* and *SetWindowPlacement*. Each accepts the address of a WINDOWPLACEMENT structure, which is defined as follows:

```
typedef struct tagWINDOWPLACEMENT {
    UINT   length;
    UINT   flags;
    UINT   showCmd;
    POINT  ptMinPosition;
    POINT  ptMaxPosition;
    RECT   rcNormalPosition;
} WINDOWPLACEMENT;
```

WINDOWPLACEMENT brings together in one place everything Windows needs to know to characterize a window's screen state. *length* specifies the size of the WINDOWPLACEMENT structure. Both *CWnd::GetWindowPlacement* and *CWnd::SetWindowPlacement* fill in this field for you. *flags* contains zero or more bit flags specifying information about minimized windows. The WPF_RESTORETOMAXIMIZED flag, if present, indicates that a minimized window will be maximized when it is restored.

showCmd specifies the window's current display state. It is set to SW_SHOW-MINIMIZED if the window is minimized, SW_SHOWMAXIMIZED if the window is maximized, or SW_SHOWNORMAL if the window is neither minimized nor maximized. *ptMinPosition* and *ptMaxPosition* hold the screen coordinates of the window's upper left corner when it is minimized and maximized, respectively. (Don't rely on *ptMinPosition* to tell you anything; in current versions of Windows, *ptMinPosition* is set to (3000,3000) when a window is minimized.) *rcNormalPosition* contains the screen coordinates of the window's "normal," or unminimized and unmaximized, screen position. When a window is minimized or maximized, *rcNormalPosition* specifies the position and size the window will be restored to—provided, of course, that the WPF_RESTORETOMAXIMIZED flag isn't set to force a restored window to full screen.

You can preserve a window's screen state across sessions by saving the *flags*, *showCmd*, and *rcNormalPosition* values in the window's WINDOWPLACEMENT structure and restoring these values when the window is re-created. You don't need to save *ptMinPosition* and *ptMaxPosition* because Windows fills in their values when the window is minimized or maximized. Clock's *SaveWindowState* function uses *GetWindowPlacement* to initialize a WINDOWPLACEMENT structure and then writes the pertinent members of that structure to the registry. The window state is restored when *CMyApp::InitInstance* calls *CMainWindow::RestoreWindowState*, which in turn calls *GetWindowPlacement* to fill in a WINDOWPLACEMENT structure; reads the *flags*, *showCmd*, and *rcNormalPosition* values from the registry; copies them to the structure; and calls *SetWindowPlacement*. The SW_SHOWMINIMIZED, SW_SHOWMAXIMIZED, or SW_SHOWNORMAL parameter passed to *SetWindowPlacement* in *showCmd* makes the window visible, so there's no need to call *ShowWindow* if *RestoreWindowState* returns TRUE, indicating that the window state was successfully restored. In fact, you should skip the usual call placed to *ShowWindow* from *InitInstance* if *RestoreWindowState* returns TRUE because the application object's *m_nCmdShow* parameter might alter the window's state. Clock's *InitInstance* function looks like this:

```
BOOL CMyApp::InitInstance ()
{
    SetRegistryKey (_T ("Programming Windows with MFC"));
    m_pMainWnd = new CMainWindow;
    if (!((CMainWindow*) m_pMainWnd)->RestoreWindowState ())
        m_pMainWnd->ShowWindow (m_nCmdShow);
    m_pMainWnd->UpdateWindow ();
    return TRUE;
}
```

The first time Clock is executed, *ShowWindow* is called in the normal way because *RestoreWindowState* returns FALSE. In subsequent invocations, the window's size, position, and visibility state are set by *RestoreWindowState,* and *ShowWindow* is skipped.

Before calling *SetWindowPlacement* to apply the state values retrieved from the registry, *RestoreWindowState* ensures that a window positioned near the edge of a 1,024-by-768 screen won't disappear if Windows is restarted in 640-by-480 or 800-by-600 mode by comparing the window's normal position with the screen extents:

```
wp.rcNormalPosition.left = min (wp.rcNormalPosition.left,
    ::GetSystemMetrics (SM_CXSCREEN) -
    ::GetSystemMetrics (SM_CXICON));
wp.rcNormalPosition.top = min (wp.rcNormalPosition.top,
    ::GetSystemMetrics (SM_CYSCREEN) -
    ::GetSystemMetrics (SM_CYICON));
```

Called with SM_CXSCREEN and SM_CYSCREEN parameters, *::GetSystemMetrics* returns the screen's width and height, respectively, in pixels. If the window coordinates retrieved from the registry are 700 and 600 and Windows is running at a resolution of 640 by 480, this simple procedure transforms the 700 and 600 into 640 and 480 minus the width and height of an icon. Rather than appear out of sight off the screen and probably leave the user wondering why the application didn't start, the window will appear just inside the lower right corner of the screen.

A good way to test a program that preserves a window's position and size is to resize the window to some arbitrary size, maximize it, minimize it, and then close the application with the window minimized. When the program is restarted, the window should come up minimized, and clicking the minimized window's icon in the taskbar should remaximize it. Clicking the restore button should restore the window's original size and position. Try this procedure with Clock, and you should find that it passes the test with flying colors.

Controlling the Window Size: The WM_GETMINMAXINFO Message

A final aspect of Clock that deserves scrutiny is its *OnGetMinMaxInfo* handler. As a window is being resized, it receives a series of WM_GETMINMAXINFO messages with *lParam* pointing to a MINMAXINFO structure containing information about the window's minimum and maximum "tracking" sizes. You can limit a window's minimum and maximum sizes programmatically by processing WM_GETMINMAXINFO messages and copying the minimum width and height to the x and y members of the structure's *ptMinTrackSize* field and the maximum width and height to the x and y members of the *ptMaxTrackSize* field. Clock prevents its window from being reduced to less than 120 pixels horizontally and vertically with the following *OnGetMinMaxInfo* handler:

```
void CMainWindow::OnGetMinMaxInfo (MINMAXINFO* pMMI)
{
    pMMI->ptMinTrackSize.x = 120;
```

```
        pMMI->ptMinTrackSize.y = 120;
}
```

The tracking dimensions copied to MINMAXINFO are measured in device units, or pixels. In this example, the window's maximum size is unconstrained because *pMMI->ptMaxTrackSize* is left unchanged. You could limit the maximum window size to one-half the screen size by adding the statements

```
pMMI->ptMaxTrackSize.x = ::GetSystemMetrics (SM_CXSCREEN) / 2;
pMMI->ptMaxTrackSize.y = ::GetSystemMetrics (SM_CYSCREEN) / 2;
```

to the message handler.

IDLE PROCESSING

Because MFC's application class, *CWinApp*, provides the message loop that retrieves and dispatches messages, it's a simple matter for *CWinApp* to call a function in your application when no messages are waiting to be processed. If you look at the source code for the *CWinThread::Run* function that gets called by *WinMain* to start the message loop, you'll see something that looks like this:

```
BOOL bIdle = TRUE;
LONG lIdleCount = 0;

for (;;)
{
    while (bIdle &&
        !::PeekMessage(&m_msgCur, NULL, NULL, NULL, PM_NOREMOVE))
    {
        if (!OnIdle(lIdleCount++))
            bIdle = FALSE;
    }

    do
    {
        if (!PumpMessage())
            return ExitInstance();

        if (IsIdleMessage(&m_msgCur))
        {
            bIdle = TRUE;
            lIdleCount = 0;
        }

    } while (::PeekMessage(&m_msgCur, NULL, NULL, NULL, PM_NOREMOVE));
}
```

Before it calls *PumpMessage* to retrieve and dispatch a message, *Run* calls *::PeekMessage* with a PM_NOREMOVE flag to check the message queue. If a message is waiting, *::PeekMessage* copies it to an MSG structure and returns a nonzero value but doesn't remove the message from the queue. If no messages are waiting, *::PeekMessage* returns 0. Unlike *::GetMessage*, *::PeekMessage* doesn't wait for a message to appear in the message queue before returning; it returns immediately. If *::PeekMessage* returns nonzero, indicating that messages are waiting to be processed, *CWinThread::Run* enters a *do-while* loop that calls *CWinThread::PumpMessage* repeatedly to retrieve and dispatch the messages. But if *::PeekMessage* returns 0 and the *bIdle* flag is set, *CWinThread::Run* calls a member function named *OnIdle* to give the application an opportunity to perform idle processing. Because *OnIdle* is a virtual function and because *CWinApp* is derived from *CWinThread*, a derived application class can hook into the idle loop by replacing *CWinApp::OnIdle* with an *OnIdle* function of its own.

Back in the days of Windows 3.*x,* when applications were inherently single-threaded, *OnIdle* was the perfect place to perform background processing tasks such as print spooling and garbage collecting. In 32-bit Windows, *CWinApp::OnIdle*'s usefulness is greatly diminished because low-priority tasks can be performed more efficiently in background threads of execution. *OnIdle* still has legitimate uses, however. MFC uses it to update toolbar buttons and other always-visible user interface objects by calling update handlers registered in the message map. It also takes advantage of times when the application isn't busy processing messages by deleting temporary objects created by functions such as *CWnd::FromHandle* and *CWnd::GetMenu.*

When you call *FromHandle* to convert a window handle into a *CWnd* pointer, MFC consults an internal table called a *handle map* that correlates *CWnd* objects and window handles. If it finds the handle it's looking for, MFC returns a pointer to the corresponding *CWnd* object. If the window handle doesn't appear in the handle map because a corresponding *CWnd* doesn't exist, however, *FromHandle* creates a temporary *CWnd* object and returns its address to the caller. The next time *OnIdle* is called (which doesn't occur until after the message handler that called *FromHandle* returns), MFC cleans up by deleting the temporary *CWnd* object. That's why the documentation for some MFC functions warns that returned pointers might be temporary and "should not be stored for later use." What that really means is that an object referenced by one of these temporary pointers isn't guaranteed to exist outside the scope of the current message handler because, once that handler returns, *OnIdle* is liable to be called—and the object deleted—at any moment.

Using *OnIdle*

An MFC application can enact its own idle-processing regimen by overriding the virtual *OnIdle* function that it inherits from *CWinApp*. *OnIdle* is prototyped as follows:

```
virtual BOOL OnIdle (LONG lCount)
```

lCount is a 32-bit value that specifies the number of times *OnIdle* has been called since the last message was processed. The count continually increases until the message loop in *CWinThread::Run* calls *PumpMessage* to retrieve and dispatch another message. The count is then reset to 0 and starts again. WM_PAINT messages, WM_SYSTIMER messages, and certain mouse messages don't cause *lCount* to be reset. (WM_SYSTIMER is an undocumented message Windows uses internally.) *lCount* can be used as a rough measure of the time elapsed since the last message or of the length of time the application has been idle. If you have two background tasks you'd like to perform during idle time, one that's high priority and another that's low, you can use *lCount* to determine when to execute each task. For example, you might perform the high-priority task each time *lCount* reaches 10 and the low-priority task when *lCount* hits 100 or even 1,000.

If you could log the calls to an application's *OnIdle* function without slowing it down, you'd find that 1,000 is not all that high a number. Typically, *OnIdle* is called 100 or more times per second when the message queue is empty, so a low-priority background task that kicks off when *lCount* reaches 1,000 is typically executed when the mouse and keyboard are idle for a few seconds. A high-priority task that begins when *lCount* reaches 10 is executed much more often because the count frequently reaches or exceeds 10, even when the message loop is relatively busy. Idle processing should be carried out as quickly as possible because message traffic is blocked until *OnIdle* returns.

The value that *OnIdle* returns determines whether *OnIdle* will be called again. If *OnIdle* returns a nonzero value, it's called again if the message queue is still empty. If *OnIdle* returns 0, however, further calls are suspended until another message finds its way into the message queue and the idle state is reentered after the message is dispatched. The mechanism that makes this work is the *bIdle* flag in *CWinThread::Run*, which is initially set to TRUE but is set to FALSE if *OnIdle* returns FALSE. The *while* loop that calls *OnIdle* tests the value of *bIdle* at the beginning of each iteration and falls through if *bIdle* is FALSE. *bIdle* is set to TRUE again when a message shows up in the message queue and *PumpMessage* is called. As a practical matter, you can save a few CPU cycles by returning FALSE from *OnIdle* if your background processing is complete for the moment and you don't want *OnIdle* to be called again until the flow of messages resumes. Be careful, however, not to return FALSE before the framework has finished its most recent spate of idle-processing chores and thus deprive it of the idle time it needs.

The cardinal rule to follow when using *OnIdle* is to call the base class version of *OnIdle* from the overridden version. The following *OnIdle* override demonstrates the proper technique. The base class's *OnIdle* function is called first, and after the call returns, the application performs its own idle processing:

```
BOOL CMyApp::OnIdle (LONG lCount)
```

(continued)

```
{
    CWinApp::OnIdle (lCount);
    DoIdleWork (); // Do custom idle processing.
    return TRUE;
}
```

It turns out that the framework does its processing when *lCount* is 0 and 1. There-fore, an even better approach is to accord higher priority to the framework's *OnIdle* handler by delaying the start of your own idle processing until *lCount* reaches a value of 2 or higher:

```
BOOL CMyApp::OnIdle (LONG lCount)
{
    CWinApp::OnIdle (lCount);
    if (lCount == 2)
        DoIdleWork (); // Do custom idle processing.
    return TRUE;
}
```

You can see for yourself what MFC does during idle time by examining the source code for *CWinThread::OnIdle* in Thrdcore.cpp and *CWinApp::OnIdle* in Appcore.cpp.

Because the *OnIdle* implementations in the previous paragraph always returns TRUE, calls to *OnIdle* will continue unabated even if both you and the framework are finished with *OnIdle* for the time being. The following *OnIdle* override reduces overhead by returning FALSE when both MFC's idle processing and the application's idle processing are complete:

```
BOOL CMyApp::OnIdle (LONG lCount)
{
    BOOL bContinue = CWinApp::OnIdle (lCount);
    if (lCount == 2)
        DoIdleWork (); // Do custom idle processing.
    return (bContinue || lCount < 2);
}
```

The fact that application-specific idle processing isn't started until *lCount* equals 2 means that the framework won't be deprived of the idle time it needs if the application's *OnIdle* function returns FALSE.

It's important to perform idle processing as quickly as possible to avoid adversely impacting the application's responsiveness. If necessary, break up large *OnIdle* tasks into smaller, more manageable pieces and process one piece at a time in successive calls to *OnIdle*. The following *OnIdle* function begins its work when *lCount* reaches 2 and continues responding to *OnIdle* calls until *DoIdleWork* returns 0:

```
BOOL CMyApp::OnIdle (LONG lCount)
{
    BOOL bMFCContinue = CWinApp::OnIdle (lCount);
```

```
    BOOL bAppContinue = TRUE;
    if (lCount >= 2)
        bAppContinue = DoIdleWork (); // Do custom idle processing.
    return (bMFCContinue || bAppContinue);
}
```

Because *DoIdleWork*'s return value is also used as *OnIdle*'s return value, *OnIdle* will cease to be called once *DoIdleWork* has completed its appointed task.

Idle Processing vs. Multithreading

In Chapter 17, you'll learn about another way to perform background tasks that involves multiple threads of execution. Multithreading is a powerful programming paradigm that's ideal for performing two or more tasks in parallel. It's also scalable: on a multiprocessor system containing *n* CPUs, Windows NT and Windows 2000 will execute up to *n* threads concurrently by scheduling each to run on a different processor. (Windows 95 and Windows 98, by contrast, force all threads to share a single CPU, even on multiprocessor systems.)

Given the robust multithreading support in 32-bit Windows, it's reasonable to ask when, if at all, you should use idle processing in lieu of multithreading. Here are two answers:

- When you have background tasks to perform that must execute in the application's primary thread. User interface–related tasks tend to be very thread-sensitive. That's one reason why MFC performs user interface updates in the primary thread.

- When you have background tasks to perform and the application that you're writing must work in 16-bit Windows as well as in 32-bit Windows. Multithreading is not supported in 16-bit Windows.

In these situations, performing background tasks in *OnIdle* makes a lot of sense. Under any other circumstances, multithreading is in all likelihood the proper solution.

Chapter 15

Bitmaps, Palettes, and Regions

Getting a firm grasp of the Microsoft Windows GDI is an important milestone on the road to becoming a Windows programmer because all graphical output to screens, printers, and other devices is performed through the GDI. So far in this book, we've used three of the six MFC classes that represent GDI objects: *CPen*, *CBrush*, and *CFont*. In this chapter, we'll examine the remaining three: *CPalette*, *CBitmap*, and *CRgn*.

CPalette represents palettes—tables of color that allow Windows to balance the sometimes conflicting needs of applications that demand more colors than the video adapter can provide. If every video adapter displayed 24-bits-per-pixel color (8 bits each for red, green, and blue), palettes would be unnecessary. But 256-color video adapters are a fact of life and probably will be for some time to come. By default, a Windows application that executes in a 256-color environment has access to only 20 colors. If you're careful about how you pick your colors and make those colors part of a palette, you can expand the selection to 256 colors and write Windows applications whose color output is almost as good on 256-color screens as it is on screens that display millions of colors. In this chapter, you'll see how to use palettes in your applications to generate color output as rich as the hardware will allow.

MFC's *CBitmap* class represents GDI bitmaps. *CBitmap* is a primitive class that does very little on its own. Combined with MFC's *CDC* class, however, *CBitmap* makes it relatively easy to draw on virtual display surfaces in memory, load bitmap resources, and display simple bitmap images on the screen. You can also use *CBitmap* to build more capable bitmap classes that exploit the capabilities of the Windows device-independent bitmap (DIB) engine. One technique you'll see demonstrated in this chapter is a method for creating DIB sections from BMP files and attaching them to ordinary *CBitmap* objects—all in just three lines of code.

CRgn is one of MFC's more obscure classes, but one that you can use for some exotic graphics effects. Rather than spoil the fun, I'll leave the details for the end of the chapter.

PALETTES

Have you ever written a Windows application that makes generous use of color only to find that the output looks crummy on 16-color and 256-color video adapters? There's not a whole lot you can do about it when the adapter itself supports only 16 colors, but you can do plenty to improve output on 256-color devices. The key to better color output is MFC's *CPalette* class. Before we get into the specifics of *CPalette*, let's briefly review how color information is encoded in Windows and what Windows does with the color information that you provide.

How Windows Uses Color

One of the benefits of a device-independent output model is that you can specify the colors an application uses without regard for the physical characteristics of the output device. When you pass a color to the Windows GDI, you pass a COLORREF value containing 8 bits each for red, green, and blue. The RGB macro combines individual red, green, and blue values into a single COLORREF. The statement

```
COLORREF clr = RGB (255, 0, 255);
```

creates a COLORREF value named *clr* that represents magenta—the color you get when you mix equal parts red and blue. Conversely, you can extract 8-bit red, green, and blue values from a COLORREF value with the *GetRValue*, *GetGValue*, and *GetBValue* macros. A number of GDI functions, including those that create pens and brushes, accept COLORREF values.

What the GDI does with the COLORREF values you pass it depends on several factors, including the color resolution of the video hardware and the context in which the colors are used. In the simplest and most desirable scenario, the video adapter is a 24-bits-per-pixel device and COLORREF values translate directly into colors on the screen. Video adapters that support 24-bit color, or *true color,* are becoming increasingly common, but Windows still runs on millions of PCs whose video adapters are limited to 4 or 8 bits per pixel. Typically, these devices are *palletized devices,* meaning that they support a wide range of colors but can display only a limited number of colors at one time. A standard VGA, for example, can display 262,144 different colors—6 bits each for red, green, and blue. However, a VGA running at a resolution of

640 by 480 pixels can display only 16 different colors at once because each pixel is limited to 4 bits of color information in the video buffer. The more common case is a video adapter that can display more than 16.7 million colors but can display only 256 colors at once. The 256 colors that can be displayed are determined from RGB values that are programmed into the adapter's hardware palette.

Windows handles palletized devices by preprogramming a standard selection of colors into the adapter's hardware palette. A 256-color adapter is preprogrammed with the 20 so-called *static colors* shown in the following table. The four colors marked with asterisks are subject to change at the operating system's behest, so you shouldn't write code that depends on their presence.

STATIC PALETTE COLORS

Color	R	G	B	Color	R	G	B
Black	0	0	0	Cream*	255	251	240
Dark red	128	0	0	Intermediate gray*	160	160	164
Dark green	0	128	0	Medium gray	128	128	128
Dark yellow	128	128	0	Red	255	0	0
Dark blue	0	0	128	Green	0	255	0
Dark magenta	128	0	128	Yellow	255	255	0
Dark cyan	0	128	128	Blue	0	0	255
Light gray	192	192	192	Magenta	255	0	255
Money green*	192	220	192	Cyan	0	255	255
Sky blue*	166	202	240	White	255	255	255

* Denotes default colors that are subject to change.

When you draw on a palletized device, the GDI maps each COLORREF value to the nearest static color using a simple color-matching algorithm. If you pass a COLORREF value to a function that creates a pen, Windows assigns the pen the nearest static color. If you pass a COLOREF value to a function that creates a brush and there isn't a matching static color, Windows dithers the brush color using static colors. Because the static colors include a diverse (if limited) assortment of hues, Windows can do a reasonable job of simulating any COLORREF value you throw at it. A picture painted with 100 different shades of red won't come out very well because Windows will simulate all 100 shades with just two reds. But you're guaranteed that red won't undergo a wholesale transformation to blue, green, or some other color, because the static colors are always there and are always available.

For many applications, the primitive form of color mapping that Windows performs using static colors is good enough. But for others, accurate color output is a foremost concern and 20 colors just won't get the job done. In a single-tasking environment such as MS-DOS, a program running on a 256-color adapter can program the hardware palette itself and use any 256 colors it wants. In Windows, applications can't be allowed to program the hardware palette directly because the video adapter is a shared resource. So how do you take advantage of the 236 colors left unused in a 256-color adapter after Windows adds the 20 static colors? The answer lies in a GDI object known as a logical palette.

Logical Palettes and the *CPalette* Class

A *logical palette* is a table of RGB color values that tells Windows what colors an application would like to display. A related term, *system palette*, refers to the adapter's hardware color palette. At an application's request, the palette manager built into Windows will transfer the colors in a logical palette to unused entries in the system palette—a process known as *realizing a palette*—so that the application can take full advantage of the video adapter's color capabilities. With the help of a logical palette, an application running on a 256-color video adapter can use the 20 static colors plus an additional 236 colors of its choosing. And because all requests to realize a palette go through the GDI, the palette manager can serve as an arbitrator between programs with conflicting color needs and thus ensure that the system palette is used cooperatively.

What happens if two or more applications realize logical palettes and the sum total of the colors they request is more than the 236 additional colors a 256-color video adapter can handle? The palette manager assigns color priorities based on each window's position in the z-order. The window at the top of the z-order receives top priority, the window that's second gets the next highest priority, and so on. If the foreground window realizes a palette of 200 colors, all 200 get mapped to the system palette. If a background window then realizes a palette of, say, 100 colors, 36 get programmed into the unused slots remaining in the system palette and 64 get mapped to the nearest matching colors. That's the worst case. Unless directed to do otherwise, the palette manager avoids duplicating entries in the system palette. Therefore, if 4 of the foreground window's colors and 10 of the background window's colors match static colors, and if another 10 of the background window's colors match nonstatic colors in the foreground window, the background window ends up getting 60 exact matches in the system palette.

You can see the palette manager at work by switching Windows to 256-color mode, launching two instances of the Windows Paint applet, loading a different 256-color bitmap in each, and clicking back and forth between the two. The bitmap in the foreground will always look the best because it gets first crack at the system palette. The bitmap in the background gets what's left over. If both bitmaps use similar colors, the background image won't look too bad. But if the colors are vastly different—

for example, if bitmap A contains lots of bright, vibrant colors whereas bitmap B uses primarily earth tones—the image in the background window might be so color-corrupted that it's hardly recognizable. The palette manager's role in the process is to try to satisfy the needs of both programs. When those needs conflict, the foreground window receives priority over all others so that the application the user is working with looks the best.

Creating a Logical Palette

Writing an application that uses a logical palette isn't difficult. In MFC, logical palettes are represented by the *CPalette* class and are created and initialized with *CPalette* member functions. Once a logical palette is created, it can be selected into a device context and realized with *CDC* member functions.

CPalette provides two member functions for palette creation. *CreatePalette* creates a custom palette from RGB values you specify; *CreateHalftonePalette* creates a "halftone" palette containing a generic and fairly uniform distribution of colors. Custom palettes give better results when an image contains few distinctly different colors but many subtle variations in tone. Halftone palettes work well for images containing a wide range of colors. The statements

```
CPalette palette;
palette.CreateHalftonePalette (pDC);
```

create a halftone palette tailored to the device context pointed to by *pDC*. If the device context corresponds to a 256-color device, the halftone palette will also contain 256 colors. Twenty of the colors will match the static colors; the other 236 will expand the selection of colors available by adding subtler shades of red, green, and blue and mixtures of these primary colors. Specifically, a 256-color halftone palette includes all the colors in a 6-by-6-by-6-color cube (colors composed of six shades each of red, green, and blue), plus an array of grays for gray-scale imaging and other colors handpicked by the GDI. Passing a NULL DC handle to *CreateHalftonePalette* creates a 256-color halftone palette independent of the characteristics of the output device. However, because *CPalette::CreateHalftonePalette* mistakenly asserts in debug builds if passed a NULL DC handle, you must drop down to the Windows API to take advantage of this feature:

```
CPalette palette;
palette.Attach (::CreateHalftonePalette (NULL));
```

::CreateHalftonePalette is the API equivalent of *CPalette::CreateHalftonePalette*.

Creating a custom palette is a little more work because before you call *CreatePalette*, you must initialize a LOGPALETTE structure with entries describing the palette's colors. LOGPALETTE is defined as follows.

```
typedef struct tagLOGPALETTE {
    WORD            palVersion;
    WORD            palNumEntries;
    PALETTEENTRY    palPalEntry[1];
} LOGPALETTE;
```

palVersion specifies the LOGPALETTE version number; in all current releases of Windows, it should be set to 0x300. *palNumEntries* specifies the number of colors in the palette. *palPalEntry* is an array of PALETTEENTRY structures defining the colors. The number of elements in the array should equal the value of *palNumEntries*. PALETTEENTRY is defined like this:

```
typedef struct tagPALETTEENTRY {
    BYTE peRed;
    BYTE peGreen;
    BYTE peBlue;
    BYTE peFlags;
} PALETTEENTRY;
```

peRed, *peGreen*, and *peBlue* specify a color's 8-bit RGB components. *peFlags* contains zero or more bit flags describing the *type* of palette entry. It can be set to any of the values shown here, or to 0 to create a "normal" palette entry:

Flag	*Description*
PC_EXPLICIT	Creates a palette entry that specifies an index into the system palette rather than an RGB color. Used by programs that display the contents of the system palette.
PC_NOCOLLAPSE	Creates a palette entry that's mapped to an unused entry in the system palette even if there's already an entry for that color. Used to ensure the uniqueness of palette colors.
PC_RESERVED	Creates a palette entry that's private to this application. When a PC_RESERVED entry is added to the system palette, it isn't mapped to colors in other logical palettes even if the colors match. Used by programs that perform palette animation.

Most of the time, *peFlags* is simply set to 0. We'll discuss one use for the PC_RESERVED flag later in this chapter, in the section on palette animation.

The PALETTEENTRY array in the LOGPALETTE structure is declared with just one array element because Windows has no way of anticipating how many colors a logical palette will contain. As a result, you can't just declare an instance of LOGPALETTE on the stack and fill it in; instead, you have to allocate memory for it based on the number of PALETTEENTRY structures it contains. The following code allocates a "full" LOGPALETTE structure on the stack and then creates a logical palette containing 32 shades of red:

```
struct {
    LOGPALETTE lp;
    PALETTEENTRY ape[31];
} pal;

LOGPALETTE* pLP = (LOGPALETTE*) &pal;
pLP->palVersion = 0x300;
pLP->palNumEntries = 32;

for (int i=0; i<32; i++) {
    pLP->palPalEntry[i].peRed = i * 8;
    pLP->palPalEntry[i].peGreen = 0;
    pLP->palPalEntry[i].peBlue = 0;
    pLP->palPalEntry[i].peFlags = 0;
}

CPalette palette;
palette.CreatePalette (pLP);
```

Like other GDI objects, logical palettes should be deleted when they're no longer needed. A logical palette represented by a *CPalette* object is automatically deleted when the corresponding *CPalette* object is deleted or goes out of scope.

How many entries can a logical palette contain? As many as you want it to. Of course, the number of colors that can be mapped directly to the system palette is limited by the capabilities of the video adapter. If you realize a palette containing 1,024 colors on a 256-color output device, only the first 236 will be mapped directly; the remaining colors will be matched as closely as possible to colors already in the system palette. When you use logical palettes (especially large ones), it's helpful to arrange the colors in order of importance, where *palPalEntry*[0] defines the most important color, *palPalEntry*[1] defines the next most important color, and so on. The palette manager maps palette colors in array order, so by putting important colors first, you increase the chances that those colors will be displayed in their native form. In general, you shouldn't make a logical palette any larger than it has to be. Large palettes take longer to realize, and the more palette colors a foreground window uses, the fewer colors the palette manager can make available to palette-aware windows lower in the z-order.

After a palette is created, you can retrieve individual palette entries with *CPalette::GetPaletteEntries* or change them with *CPalette::SetPaletteEntries*. You can also resize a palette with *CPalette::ResizePalette*. If the palette is enlarged, the new palette entries initially contain all 0s.

Realizing a Logical Palette

For a logical palette to be effective, it must be selected into a device context and realized before any drawing takes place. The current logical palette is a device context attribute, just as the current pen and brush are device context attributes. (In case you're wondering, a device context's default logical palette is a trivial one whose entries correspond to the static colors.) The following *OnPaint* handler selects the logical palette *m_palette* into a paint device context and realizes the palette before repainting the screen:

```
void CMainWindow::OnPaint ()
{
    CPaintDC dc (this);
    CPalette* pOldPalette = dc.SelectPalette (&m_palette, FALSE);
    dc.RealizePalette ();
    // Do some drawing.
    dc.SelectPalette (pOldPalette, FALSE);
}
```

In this example, the pointer to the default palette is saved and used later to select *m_palette* out of the device context. Note that palettes are selected with *CDC::SelectPalette* instead of *CDC::SelectObject*. The second parameter is a BOOL value that, if TRUE, forces the palette to behave as if it were in the background even when the window that selected it is in the foreground. Background palettes can be handy in applications that use multiple palettes, but normally you'll specify FALSE in calls to *SelectPalette*. *CDC::RealizePalette* realizes the palette that's currently selected into the device context by asking the palette manager to map colors from the logical palette to the system palette.

Drawing with Palette Colors

Once you create a palette, select it into a device context, and realize it, you're ready to start drawing. If you use *CDC::BitBlt* to display a bitmap, the realized colors are used automatically. But if you're drawing images with brushes or pens or using functions such as *CDC::FloodFill* that use neither a brush nor a pen directly but do accept COLORREF values, there's something else you must consider.

The RGB macro is one of three macros that create COLORREF values. The others are PALETTEINDEX and PALETTERGB. Which of the three macros you use determines how the GDI treats the resultant COLORREF. When you draw with a COLORREF value created with the RGB macro, the GDI ignores the colors that were added to the system palette when the logical palette was realized and uses only the static colors. If you want the GDI to use *all* the palette colors, use the PALETTERGB macro. PALETTERGB creates a *palette-relative* color. The PALETTEINDEX macro creates a COLORREF value that specifies an index into a logical palette rather than an RGB color value. This value is called a *palette-index* color value. It's the fastest kind of color to draw with because it prevents the GDI from having to match RGB color values to colors in the logical palette.

The following code sample demonstrates how all three macros are used:

```
void CMainWindow::OnPaint ()
{
    CPaintDC dc (this);

    // Select and realize a logical palette.
    CPalette* pOldPalette = dc.SelectPalette (&m_palette, FALSE);
    dc.RealizePalette ();

    // Create three pens.
    CPen pen1 (PS_SOLID, 16, RGB (242, 36, 204));
    CPen pen2 (PS_SOLID, 16, PALETTERGB (242, 36, 204));
    CPen pen3 (PS_SOLID, 16, PALETTEINDEX (3));

    // Do some drawing.
    dc.MoveTo (0, 0);
    CPen* pOldPen = dc.SelectObject (&pen1);
    dc.LineTo (300, 0);           // Nearest static color
    dc.SelectObject (&pen2);
    dc.LineTo (150, 200);         // Nearest static or palette color
    dc.SelectObject (&pen3);
    dc.LineTo (0, 0);             // Exact palette color
    dc.SelectObject (pOldPen);

    // Select the palette out of the device context.
    dc.SelectPalette (pOldPalette, FALSE);
}
```

Because pens use solid, undithered colors and because its COLORREF value is specified with an RGB macro, *pen1* draws with the static color that most closely approximates the RGB value (242, 36, 204). *pen2*, on the other hand, is assigned the nearest matching color from the static colors or *m_palette*. *pen3* uses the color in the system palette that corresponds to the fourth color (index=3) in the logical palette, regardless of what that color might be.

The WM_QUERYNEWPALETTE and WM_PALETTECHANGED Messages

When you write an application that uses a logical palette, you should include handlers for a pair of messages named WM_QUERYNEWPALETTE and WM_PALETTECHANGED. WM_QUERYNEWPALETTE is sent to a top-level window when it or one of its children receives the input focus. WM_PALETTECHANGED is sent to all top-level windows in the system when a palette realization results in a change to the system palette. An application's normal response to either message is to realize its palette and repaint itself. Realizing a palette and repainting in response to a WM_QUERYNEWPALETTE message enables a window that was just brought to the foreground to put on its best face by taking advantage of the fact that it now has top priority in realizing its palette. Realizing a palette and repainting in response to a WM_PALETTECHANGED message enable background windows to adapt to changes in the system palette and take advantage of any unused entries that remain after windows higher in the z-order have realized their palettes.

The following message handler demonstrates a typical response to a WM_QUERY-NEWPALETTE message:

```
// In the message map
ON_WM_QUERYNEWPALETTE ()
    :
    :

BOOL CMainWindow::OnQueryNewPalette ()
{
    CClientDC dc (this);
    CPalette* pOldPalette = dc.SelectPalette (&m_palette, FALSE);

    UINT nCount;
    if (nCount = dc.RealizePalette ())
        Invalidate ();

    dc.SelectPalette (pOldPalette, FALSE);
    return nCount;
}
```

The general strategy is to realize a palette and force a repaint by invalidating the window's client area. The value returned by *RealizePalette* is the number of palette entries that were mapped to entries in the system palette. A 0 return value means that realizing the palette had no effect, which should be extremely rare for a foreground window. If *RealizePalette* returns 0, you should skip the call to *Invalidate*. *OnQueryNewPalette* should return a nonzero value if a logical palette was realized and 0 if it wasn't. It should also return 0 if it tried to realize a palette but *RealizePalette* returned 0. The return value isn't used in current versions of Windows.

WM_PALETTECHANGED messages are handled in a similar way. Here's what a typical *OnPaletteChanged* handler looks like:

```
// In the message map
ON_WM_PALETTECHANGED ()
    :
    :

void CMainWindow::OnPaletteChanged (CWnd* pFocusWnd)
```

```
{
    if (pFocusWnd != this) {
        CClientDC dc (this);
        CPalette* pOldPalette = dc.SelectPalette (&m_palette,
            FALSE);
        if (dc.RealizePalette ())
            Invalidate ();
        dc.SelectPalette (pOldPalette, FALSE);
    }
}
```

The *CWnd* pointer passed to *OnPaletteChanged* identifies the window that prompted the WM_PALETTECHANGED message by realizing a palette. To avoid unnecessary recursion and possible infinite loops, *OnPaletteChanged* should do nothing if *pFocusWnd* points to its own window. That's the reason for the *if* statement that compares *pFocusWnd* to *this*.

Rather than perform full repaints in response to WM_PALETTECHANGED messages, applications can optionally call *CDC::UpdateColors* instead. *UpdateColors* updates a window by matching the color of each pixel to the colors in the system palette. It's usually faster than a full repaint, but the results typically aren't as good because the color matching is done based on the contents of the system palette *before* it changed. If you use *UpdateColors*, maintain a variable that counts the number of times *UpdateColors* has been called. Then every third or fourth time, do a full repaint and reset the counter to 0. This will prevent the colors in a background window from becoming too out of sync with the colors in the system palette.

Handling Palette Messages in Document/View Applications

The *OnQueryNewPalette* and *OnPaletteChanged* handlers in the previous section assume that the window to be updated is the application's main window. In a document/view application, that's not the case; the views need updating, not the top-level window. The ideal solution would be to put the *OnQueryNewPalette* and *OnPaletteChanged* handlers in the view class, but that won't work because views don't receive palette messages—only top-level windows do.

What most document/view applications do instead is have their main windows update the views in response to palette messages. The following *OnQueryNewPalette* and *OnPaletteChanged* handlers work well for most SDI applications:

```
BOOL CMainFrame::OnQueryNewPalette ()
{
    CDocument* pDoc = GetActiveDocument ();
    if (pDoc != NULL)
        GetActiveDocument ()->UpdateAllViews (NULL);
    return TRUE;
}
```

(continued)

```
void CMainFrame::OnPaletteChanged (CWnd* pFocusWnd)
{
    if (pFocusWnd != this) {
        CDocument* pDoc = GetActiveDocument ();
        if (pDoc != NULL)
            GetActiveDocument ()->UpdateAllViews (NULL);
    }
}
```

Palettes are a little trickier in MDI applications. If each open document has a unique palette associated with it (as is often the case), the active view should be redrawn using a foreground palette and inactive views should be redrawn using background palettes. Another issue with MDI applications that use multiple palettes is the need to update the views' colors as the user clicks among views. The best solution is to override *CView::OnActivateView* so that a view knows when it's activated or deactivated and can realize its palette accordingly. For a good example of palette handling in MDI applications, see the DIBLOOK sample program provided with Visual C++.

Determining Whether a Logical Palette Is Needed

Now that you understand the mechanics of palette usage, ask yourself this question: How do I know if I need a logical palette in the first place? If color accuracy is of paramount concern, you'll probably want to use a logical palette when your application runs on a palletized 256-color video adapter. But the same application doesn't need a logical palette when the hardware color depth is 24 bits because in that environment perfect color output comes for free. And if the application runs on a standard 16-color VGA, palettes are extraneous because the system palette contains 16 static colors that leave no room for colors in logical palettes.

You can determine at run time whether a logical palette will improve color output by calling *CDC::GetDeviceCaps* with a RASTERCAPS parameter and checking the RC_PALETTE bit in the return value, as demonstrated here:

```
CClientDC dc (this);
BOOL bUsePalette = FALSE;
if (dc.GetDeviceCaps (RASTERCAPS) & RC_PALETTE)
    bUsePalette = TRUE;
```

RC_PALETTE is set in palettized color modes and clear in nonpalettized modes. Generally speaking, the RC_PALETTE bit is set in 8-bit color modes and clear in 4-bit and 24-bit color modes. The RC_PALETTE bit is also clear if the adapter is running in 16-bit color ("high color") mode, which for most applications produces color output every bit as good as true color. Don't make the mistake some programmers have made and rely on bit counts to tell you whether to use a palette. As sure as you do, you'll run across an oddball video adapter that defies the normal conventions and fools your application into using a palette when a palette isn't needed or not using a palette when a palette would help.

What happens if you ignore the RC_PALETTE setting and use a logical palette regardless of color depth? The application will still work because the palette manager works even on nonpalettized devices. If RC_PALETTE is 0, palettes can still be created and selected into device contexts, but calls to *RealizePalette* do nothing. PALETTEINDEX values are dereferenced and converted into RGB colors in the logical palette, and PALETTERGB values are simply treated as if they were standard RGB color values. *OnQueryNewPalette* and *OnPaletteChanged* aren't called because no WM_QUERYNEWPALETTE and WM_PALETTECHANGED messages are sent. As explained in an excellent article, "The Palette Manager: How and Why," available on the Microsoft Developer Network (MSDN), "The goal is to allow applications to use palettes in a device-independent fashion and to not worry about the actual palette capabilities of the device driver."

Still, you can avoid wasted CPU cycles by checking the RC_PALETTE flag and skipping palette-related function calls if the flag is clear. And if your application *relies* on the presence of hardware palette support and won't work without it—for example, if it uses palette animation, a subject we'll get to in a moment—you can use RC_PALETTE to determine whether your application is even capable of running on the current hardware.

An equally important question to ask yourself when considering whether to use logical palettes is, "How accurate does my program's color output need to be?" Applications that draw using colors that match the static colors don't need palettes at all. On the other hand, a bitmap file viewer almost certainly needs palette support because without it all but the simplest bitmaps would look terrible on 256-color video adapters. Assess your program's color needs, and do as little work as you have to. You'll write better applications as a result.

The PaletteDemo Application

The application shown in Figure 15-1 demonstrates basic palette-handling technique in a non-document/view application. PaletteDemo uses a series of blue brushes to paint a background that fades smoothly from blue to black. Moreover, it produces a beautiful gradient fill even on 256-color video adapters. The key to the high quality of its output on 256-color screens is PaletteDemo's use of a logical palette containing 64 shades of blue, ranging from almost pure black (R=0, G=0, B=3) to high-intensity blue (R=0, G=0, B=255). Brush colors are specified using palette-relative COLORREF values so that the GDI will match the brush colors to colors in the system palette after the logical palette is realized. You can judge the results for yourself by running PaletteDemo in both 8-bit and 24-bit color modes and seeing that the output is identical. Only when it is run in 16-color mode does PaletteDemo fail to produce a smooth gradient fill. But even then the results aren't bad because the GDI dithers the brush colors.

Figure 15-1. *The PaletteDemo window.*

Here are a few points of interest in PaletteDemo's source code, which appears in Figure 15-2. For starters, PaletteDemo's main window paints the gradient-filled background in response to WM_ERASEBKGND messages. WM_ERASEBKGND messages are sent to erase a window's background before a WM_PAINT handler paints the foreground. A WM_ERASEBKGND handler that paints a custom window background as PaletteDemo does should return a nonzero value to notify Windows that the background has been "erased." (For a cool effect, see what happens when a WM_ERASEBKGND handler paints nothing but returns TRUE anyway. What do you get? A see-through window!) Otherwise, Windows erases the background itself by filling the window's client area with the WNDCLASS's background brush.

PaletteDemo creates the logical palette that it uses to paint the window background in *CMainWindow::OnCreate*. The palette itself is a *CPalette* data member named *m_palette*. Before creating the palette, *OnCreate* checks *CDC::GetDeviceCaps*'s return value for an RC_PALETTE bit. If the bit isn't set, *OnCreate* leaves *m_palette* uninitialized. Before selecting and realizing the palette, *CMainWindow::OnEraseBkgnd* checks *m_palette* to determine whether a palette exists:

```
if ((HPALETTE) m_palette != NULL) {
    pOldPalette = pDC->SelectPalette (&m_palette, FALSE);
    pDC->RealizePalette ();
}
```

CPalette's HPALETTE operator returns the handle of the palette attached to a *CPalette* object. A NULL handle means *m_palette* is uninitialized. *OnEraseBkgnd* adapts itself to the environment it's run in by selecting and realizing a logical palette if and only if the video hardware is palettized. The *DoGradientFill* function that draws the window background works with or without a palette because brush colors are specified with PALETTERGB macros.

One consideration that PaletteDemo doesn't address is what happens if the color depth changes while the application is running. You can account for such occurrences by processing WM_DISPLAYCHANGE messages, which are sent when the user changes the screen's resolution or color depth, and reinitializing the palette based on the new settings. There is no ON_WM_DISPLAYCHANGE macro, so you have to do the message mapping manually with ON_MESSAGE. The *wParam* parameter encapsulated in a WM_DISPLAYCHANGE message contains the new color depth expressed as the number of bits per pixel, and the low and high words of *lParam* contain the latest horizontal and vertical screen resolution in pixels.

WM_DISPLAYCHANGE isn't only for applications that use palettes. You should also use it if, for example, you initialize variables with the average width and height of a character in the system font when the application starts and later use those variables to size and position your output. If the variables aren't reinitialized when the screen resolution changes, subsequent output might be distorted.

PaletteDemo.h

```
class CMyApp : public CWinApp
{
public:
    virtual BOOL InitInstance ();
};

class CMainWindow : public CFrameWnd
{
protected:
    CPalette m_palette;
    void DoGradientFill (CDC* pDC, LPRECT pRect);
    void DoDrawText (CDC* pDC, LPRECT pRect);

public:
    CMainWindow ();

protected:
    afx_msg int OnCreate (LPCREATESTRUCT lpcs);
    afx_msg BOOL OnEraseBkgnd (CDC* pDC);
    afx_msg void OnPaint ();
    afx_msg BOOL OnQueryNewPalette ();
    afx_msg void OnPaletteChanged (CWnd* pFocusWnd);
    DECLARE_MESSAGE_MAP ()
};
```

Figure 15-2. *The PaletteDemo application.* *(continued)*

Figure 15-2 *continued*

PaletteDemo.cpp

```
#include <afxwin.h>
#include "PaletteDemo.h"

CMyApp myApp;

/////////////////////////////////////////////////////////////////////////
// CMyApp member functions

BOOL CMyApp::InitInstance ()
{
    m_pMainWnd = new CMainWindow;
    m_pMainWnd->ShowWindow (m_nCmdShow);
    m_pMainWnd->UpdateWindow ();
    return TRUE;
}


/////////////////////////////////////////////////////////////////////////
// CMainWindow message map and member functions

BEGIN_MESSAGE_MAP (CMainWindow, CFrameWnd)
    ON_WM_CREATE ()
    ON_WM_ERASEBKGND ()
    ON_WM_PAINT ()
    ON_WM_QUERYNEWPALETTE ()
    ON_WM_PALETTECHANGED ()
END_MESSAGE_MAP ()

CMainWindow::CMainWindow ()
{
    Create (NULL, _T ("Palette Demo"));
}

int CMainWindow::OnCreate (LPCREATESTRUCT lpcs)
{
    if (CFrameWnd::OnCreate (lpcs) == -1)
        return -1;

    //
    // Create a logical palette if running on a palettized adapter.
    //
    CClientDC dc (this);
    if (dc.GetDeviceCaps (RASTERCAPS) & RC_PALETTE) {
        struct {
```

```
            LOGPALETTE lp;
            PALETTEENTRY ape[63];
        } pal;

        LOGPALETTE* pLP = (LOGPALETTE*) &pal;
        pLP->palVersion = 0x300;
        pLP->palNumEntries = 64;

        for (int i=0; i<64; i++) {
            pLP->palPalEntry[i].peRed = 0;
            pLP->palPalEntry[i].peGreen = 0;
            pLP->palPalEntry[i].peBlue = 255 - (i * 4);
            pLP->palPalEntry[i].peFlags = 0;
        }
        m_palette.CreatePalette (pLP);
    }
    return 0;
}

BOOL CMainWindow::OnEraseBkgnd (CDC* pDC)
{
    CRect rect;
    GetClientRect (&rect);

    CPalette* pOldPalette;
    if ((HPALETTE) m_palette != NULL) {
        pOldPalette = pDC->SelectPalette (&m_palette, FALSE);
        pDC->RealizePalette ();
    }

    DoGradientFill (pDC, &rect);

    if ((HPALETTE) m_palette != NULL)
        pDC->SelectPalette (pOldPalette, FALSE);
    return TRUE;
}

void CMainWindow::OnPaint ()
{
    CRect rect;
    GetClientRect (&rect);
    CPaintDC dc (this);
    DoDrawText (&dc, &rect);
}

BOOL CMainWindow::OnQueryNewPalette ()
```

(continued)

Figure 15-2 *continued*

```
{
    if ((HPALETTE) m_palette == NULL)     // Shouldn't happen, but
        return 0;                         // let's be sure.

    CClientDC dc (this);
    CPalette* pOldPalette = dc.SelectPalette (&m_palette, FALSE);

    UINT nCount;
    if (nCount = dc.RealizePalette ())
        Invalidate ();

    dc.SelectPalette (pOldPalette, FALSE);
    return nCount;
}

void CMainWindow::OnPaletteChanged (CWnd* pFocusWnd)
{
    if ((HPALETTE) m_palette == NULL)     // Shouldn't happen, but
        return;                           // let's be sure.

    if (pFocusWnd != this) {
        CClientDC dc (this);
        CPalette* pOldPalette = dc.SelectPalette (&m_palette, FALSE);
        if (dc.RealizePalette ())
            Invalidate ();
        dc.SelectPalette (pOldPalette, FALSE);
    }
}

void CMainWindow::DoGradientFill (CDC* pDC, LPRECT pRect)
{
    CBrush* pBrush[64];
    for (int i=0; i<64; i++)
        pBrush[i] = new CBrush (PALETTERGB (0, 0, 255 - (i * 4)));

    int nWidth = pRect->right - pRect->left;
    int nHeight = pRect->bottom - pRect->top;
    CRect rect;

    for (i=0; i<nHeight; i++) {
        rect.SetRect (0, i, nWidth, i + 1);
        pDC->FillRect (&rect, pBrush[(i * 63) / nHeight]);
    }

    for (i=0; i<64; i++)
```

```
        delete pBrush[i];
}

void CMainWindow::DoDrawText (CDC* pDC, LPRECT pRect)
{
    CFont font;
    font.CreatePointFont (720, _T ("Comic Sans MS"));

    pDC->SetBkMode (TRANSPARENT);
    pDC->SetTextColor (RGB (255, 255, 255));

    CFont* pOldFont = pDC->SelectObject (&font);
    pDC->DrawText (_T ("Hello, MFC"), -1, pRect, DT_SINGLELINE |
        DT_CENTER | DT_VCENTER);
    pDC->SelectObject (pOldFont);
}
```

Palette Animation

One of the more novel uses for a logical palette is for performing palette animation. Conventional computer animation is performed by repeatedly drawing, erasing, and redrawing images on the screen. Palette animation involves no drawing and erasing, but it can make images move just the same. A classic example of palette animation is a simulated lava flow that cycles shades of red, orange, and yellow to produce an image that resembles lava flowing down a hill. What's interesting is that the image is drawn only once. The illusion of motion is created by repeatedly reprogramming the system palette so that red becomes orange, orange becomes yellow, yellow becomes red, and so on. Palette animation is fast because it doesn't involve moving any pixels. A simple value written to a palette register on a video adapter can change the color of an entire screen full of pixels in the blink of an eye—to be precise, in the $^{1}/_{60}$ of a second or so it takes for a monitor's electron guns to complete one screen refresh cycle.

What does it take to do palette animation in Windows? Just these three steps:

1. Call *GetDeviceCaps,* and check RC_PALETTE to verify that palettes are supported. Palette animation won't work if the RC_PALETTE bit isn't set.

2. Create a logical palette containing the colors you want to animate, and mark each palette entry with a PC_RESERVED flag. Only palette entries marked PC_RESERVED can be used for palette animation.

3. Draw an image using colors in the logical palette, and then call *CPalette-::AnimatePalette* repeatedly to change the palette colors. Each time you change the palette with *AnimatePalette*, the colors in the image will change accordingly.

Figure 15-3. *The LivePalette window.*

The LivePalette application in Figure 15-3 and Figure 15-4 demonstrates how palette animation works. The window background is painted with bands of color (eight different colors in all) from PC_RESERVED entries in a logical palette. Brush colors are specified with PALETTEINDEX values. PALETTERGB values would work, too, but ordinary RGB values wouldn't because pixels whose colors will be animated must be painted with colors marked PC_RESERVED in the logical palette, not static colors. LivePalette sets a timer to fire every 500 milliseconds, and *OnTimer* animates the palette as follows:

```
PALETTEENTRY pe[8];
m_palette.GetPaletteEntries (7, 1, pe);
m_palette.GetPaletteEntries (0, 7, &pe[1]);
m_palette.AnimatePalette (0, 8, pe);
```

The calls to *CPalette::GetPaletteEntries* initialize an array of PALETTEENTRY structures with values from the logical palette and simultaneously rotate every color up one position so that color 7 becomes color 0, color 0 becomes color 1, and so on. *AnimatePalette* then updates the colors on the screen by copying the values from the array directly to the corresponding entries in the system palette. It isn't necessary to call *RealizePalette* because the equivalent of a palette realization has already been performed.

The remainder of the program is very similar to the previous section's PaletteDemo program, with one notable exception: If RC_PALETTE is NULL, *InitInstance* displays a message box informing the user that palette animation isn't supported in the present environment and shuts down the application by returning FALSE. You'll see this message if you run LivePalette in anything other than a 256-color video mode.

LivePalette.h

```
class CMyApp : public CWinApp
{
public:
    virtual BOOL InitInstance ();
};

class CMainWindow : public CFrameWnd
{
protected:
    CPalette m_palette;
    void DoBkgndFill (CDC* pDC, LPRECT pRect);
    void DoDrawText (CDC* pDC, LPRECT pRect);

public:
    CMainWindow ();

protected:
    afx_msg int OnCreate (LPCREATESTRUCT lpcs);
    afx_msg BOOL OnEraseBkgnd (CDC* pDC);
    afx_msg void OnPaint ();
    afx_msg void OnTimer (UINT nTimerID);
    afx_msg BOOL OnQueryNewPalette ();
    afx_msg void OnPaletteChanged (CWnd* pFocusWnd);
    afx_msg void OnDestroy ();
    DECLARE_MESSAGE_MAP ()
};
```

LivePalette.cpp

```
#include <afxwin.h>
#include "LivePalette.h"

CMyApp myApp;

//////////////////////////////////////////////////////////////////////////
// CMyApp member functions

BOOL CMyApp::InitInstance ()
{
    //
    // Verify that the host system is running in a palettized video mode.
    //
    CClientDC dc (NULL);
```

Figure 15-4. *The LivePalette application.*

(continued)

Figure 15-4 *continued*

```
    if ((dc.GetDeviceCaps (RASTERCAPS) & RC_PALETTE) == 0) {
        AfxMessageBox (_T ("Palette animation is not supported on this " \
            "device. Set the color depth to 256 colors and try again."),
            MB_ICONSTOP | MB_OK);
        return FALSE;
    }

    //
    // Initialize the application as normal.
    //
    m_pMainWnd = new CMainWindow;
    m_pMainWnd->ShowWindow (m_nCmdShow);
    m_pMainWnd->UpdateWindow ();
    return TRUE;
}

///////////////////////////////////////////////////////////////////////
// CMainWindow message map and member functions

BEGIN_MESSAGE_MAP (CMainWindow, CFrameWnd)
    ON_WM_CREATE ()
    ON_WM_ERASEBKGND ()
    ON_WM_PAINT ()
    ON_WM_TIMER ()
    ON_WM_QUERYNEWPALETTE ()
    ON_WM_PALETTECHANGED ()
    ON_WM_DESTROY ()
END_MESSAGE_MAP ()

CMainWindow::CMainWindow ()
{
    Create (NULL, _T ("Palette Animation Demo"));
}

int CMainWindow::OnCreate (LPCREATESTRUCT lpcs)
{
    static BYTE bColorVals[8][3] = {
        128, 128, 128,  // Dark Gray
        0,    0, 255,  // Blue
        0,  255,   0,  // Green
        0,  255, 255,  // Cyan
        255,   0,   0,  // Red
        255,   0, 255,  // Magenta
        255, 255,   0,  // Yellow
        192, 192, 192   // Light gray
    };
```

```
    if (CFrameWnd::OnCreate (lpcs) == -1)
        return -1;

    //
    // Create a palette to support palette animation.
    //
    struct {
        LOGPALETTE lp;
        PALETTEENTRY ape[7];
    } pal;

    LOGPALETTE* pLP = (LOGPALETTE*) &pal;
    pLP->palVersion = 0x300;
    pLP->palNumEntries = 8;

    for (int i=0; i<8; i++) {
        pLP->palPalEntry[i].peRed = bColorVals[i][0];
        pLP->palPalEntry[i].peGreen = bColorVals[i][1];
        pLP->palPalEntry[i].peBlue = bColorVals[i][2];
        pLP->palPalEntry[i].peFlags = PC_RESERVED;
    }

    m_palette.CreatePalette (pLP);

    //
    // Program a timer to fire every half-second.
    //
    SetTimer (1, 500, NULL);
    return 0;
}

void CMainWindow::OnTimer (UINT nTimerID)
{
    PALETTEENTRY pe[8];
    m_palette.GetPaletteEntries (7, 1, pe);
    m_palette.GetPaletteEntries (0, 7, &pe[1]);
    m_palette.AnimatePalette (0, 8, pe);
}

BOOL CMainWindow::OnEraseBkgnd (CDC* pDC)
{
    CRect rect;
    GetClientRect (&rect);

    CPalette* pOldPalette;
    pOldPalette = pDC->SelectPalette (&m_palette, FALSE);
    pDC->RealizePalette ();
```

(continued)

Figure 15-4 *continued*

```
    DoBkgndFill (pDC, &rect);

    pDC->SelectPalette (pOldPalette, FALSE);
    return TRUE;
}

void CMainWindow::OnPaint ()
{
    CRect rect;
    GetClientRect (&rect);
    CPaintDC dc (this);
    DoDrawText (&dc, &rect);
}

BOOL CMainWindow::OnQueryNewPalette ()
{
    CClientDC dc (this);
    dc.SelectPalette (&m_palette, FALSE);

    UINT nCount;
    if (nCount = dc.RealizePalette ())
        Invalidate ();

    return nCount;
}

void CMainWindow::OnPaletteChanged (CWnd* pFocusWnd)
{
    if (pFocusWnd != this) {
        CClientDC dc (this);
        dc.SelectPalette (&m_palette, FALSE);
        if (dc.RealizePalette ())
            Invalidate ();
    }
}

void CMainWindow::OnDestroy ()
{
    KillTimer (1);
}

void CMainWindow::DoBkgndFill (CDC* pDC, LPRECT pRect)
{
    CBrush* pBrush[8];
    for (int i=0; i<8; i++)
        pBrush[i] = new CBrush (PALETTEINDEX (i));
```

```
    int nWidth = pRect->right - pRect->left;
    int nHeight = (pRect->bottom - pRect->top) / 8;

    CRect rect;
    int y1, y2;

    for (i=0; i<8; i++) {
        y1 = i * nHeight;
        y2 = (i == 7) ? pRect->bottom - pRect->top : y1 + nHeight;
        rect.SetRect (0, y1, nWidth, y2);
        pDC->FillRect (&rect, pBrush[i]);
    }

    for (i=0; i<8; i++)
        delete pBrush[i];
}

void CMainWindow::DoDrawText (CDC* pDC, LPRECT pRect)
{
    CFont font;
    font.CreatePointFont (720, _T ("Comic Sans MS"));

    pDC->SetBkMode (TRANSPARENT);
    pDC->SetTextColor (RGB (255, 255, 255));

    CFont* pOldFont = pDC->SelectObject (&font);
    pDC->DrawText (_T ("Hello, MFC"), -1, pRect, DT_SINGLELINE |
        DT_CENTER | DT_VCENTER);
    pDC->SelectObject (pOldFont);
}
```

The *::SetSystemPaletteUse* Function

A final word on palette usage: if your application absolutely, unequivocally has to have access to the entire system palette and not just the unused color entries that remain after the static colors are added, it can call *::SetSystemPaletteUse* with a device context handle and a SYSPAL_NOSTATIC parameter to reduce the number of static colors from 20 to 2—black and white. On a 256-color video adapter, this means that 254 instead of just 236 colors can be copied from a logical palette to the system palette. The Win32 API documentation makes it pretty clear how *::SetSystemPaletteUse* and its companion function *::GetSystemPaletteUse* are used, so I'll say no more about them here. However, realize that replacing the static colors with colors of your own is an extremely unfriendly thing to do because it could corrupt the colors of title bars, push buttons, and other window elements throughout the entire system. Don't do it unless you have to.

BITMAPS

The bitmapped image, or simply *bitmap,* is a staple of modern computer graphics because it allows computers to store complex images in the form of 1s and 0s. In Windows, bitmaps are GDI objects that are handled at a fairly high level just like fonts, brushes, pens, and other GDI objects. You can create bitmaps with a paint program, embed them as resources in an application's EXE file, and load them with a simple function call; or you can create bitmaps on the fly by using GDI functions to draw to virtual display surfaces in memory. Once created, a bitmap can be displayed on the screen or reproduced on the printer with a few simple function calls.

Two types of bitmaps are supported in 32-bit Windows: *device-dependent bitmaps* (DDBs) and *device-independent bitmaps* (DIBs). Also supported in 32-bit Windows is a variation on the device-independent bitmap that was first introduced in Windows NT—something programmers refer to as a *DIB section.* DDBs are the simplest of the lot as well as the most limiting. They also happen to be the only type of bitmap that MFC thoroughly encapsulates. We'll get the fundamentals out of the way first by covering *CBitmap*s and DDBs, and later we'll move on to the more powerful DIBs and DIB sections. As you read, be aware that I'll often use the term *bitmap* interchangeably with the more specific terms *DDB, DIB,* and *DIB section.* Which type of bitmap I'm referring to (or whether I'm using the term generically) should be clear from the context of the discussion.

DDBs and the *CBitmap* Class

It goes without saying that before you can do anything with a bitmap, you must first create it. One way to create a bitmap is to construct a *CBitmap* object and call *CBitmap::CreateCompatibleBitmap*:

```
CBitmap bitmap;
bitmap.CreateCompatibleBitmap (&dc, nWidth, nHeight);
```

In this example, *dc* represents a screen device context and *nWidth* and *nHeight* are the bitmap's dimensions in pixels. The reason *CreateCompatibleBitmap* requires a device context pointer is that the format of the resulting DDB is closely tied to the architecture of the output device. Providing a pointer to a device context enables Windows to structure the DDB so that it's compatible with the device on which you intend to display it. The alternative is to call *CBitmap::CreateBitmap* or *CBitmap::CreateBitmapIndirect* and specify the number of color planes and number of bits per pixel per color plane, both of which are device-dependent values. These days, about the only practical use for *CreateBitmap* and *CreateBitmapIndirect* is for creating monochrome bitmaps. Monochrome bitmaps are sometimes useful even in color environments, as one of this chapter's sample programs will demonstrate.

A DDB created with *CreateCompatibleBitmap* initially contains random data. If you want to do something with the DDB—say, display it in a window—you'll probably want to draw something into the bitmap first. You can use GDI functions to draw into a bitmap by first creating a special type of device context known as a *memory device context* (DC) and then selecting the bitmap into the memory DC. In essence, a bitmap selected into a memory DC becomes the device context's display surface, just as the display surface that corresponds to a screen DC is the screen itself. The following code creates an uninitialized DDB that measures 100 pixels square. It then creates a memory DC, selects the bitmap into it, and initializes all the pixels in the bitmap to blue:

```
CClientDC dcScreen (this);
CBitmap bitmap;
bitmap.CreateCompatibleBitmap (&dcScreen, 100, 100);

CDC dcMem;
dcMem.CreateCompatibleDC (&dcScreen);

CBrush brush (RGB (0, 0, 255));
CBitmap* pOldBitmap = dcMem.SelectObject (&bitmap);
dcMem.FillRect (CRect (0, 0, 100, 100), &brush);
dcMem.SelectObject (pOldBitmap);
```

CDC::CreateCompatibleDC creates a memory DC that's compatible with the specified device context. The device context whose address you pass in is usually a screen DC, but it could just as easily be a printer DC if the image you're preparing is destined for a printer rather than the screen. Once a bitmap is selected into a memory DC, you can draw to the memory DC (and hence into the bitmap) using the same *CDC* member functions you use to draw to a screen or printer DC.

The big difference between drawing to a memory DC and drawing to a screen DC is that pixels drawn to a memory DC aren't displayed. To display them, you have to copy them from the memory DC to a screen DC. Drawing to a memory DC first and then transferring pixels to a screen DC can be useful for replicating the same image on the screen several times. Rather than draw the image anew each time, you can draw it once in a memory DC and then transfer the image to a screen DC as many times as you want. (Be aware, however, that many display adapters will perform better if you copy the image from the memory DC to the screen DC one time and then replicate the image already present in the screen DC as needed.) Bitmaps play an important role in the process because when a memory DC is first created it contains just one pixel you can draw to, and that pixel is a monochrome pixel. Selecting a bitmap into a memory DC gives you a larger display surface to draw on and also more colors to work with as long as the bitmap isn't monochrome.

Blitting Bitmaps to Screens and Other Devices

How do you draw a bitmap on the screen? Bitmaps can't be selected into nonmemory DCs; if you try, *SelectObject* will return NULL. But you can use *CDC::BitBlt* or *CDC::StretchBlt* to "blit" pixels from a memory DC to a screen DC. *BitBlt* transfers a block of pixels from one DC to another and preserves the block's dimensions; *StretchBlt* transfers a block of pixels between DCs and scales the block to the dimensions you specify. If *dcMem* is a memory DC that contains a 100-pixel by 100-pixel bitmap image and *dcScreen* is a screen DC, the statement

```
dcScreen.BitBlt (0, 0, 100, 100, &dcMem, 0, 0, SRCCOPY);
```

copies the image to the screen DC and consequently displays it on the screen. The first two parameters passed to *BitBlt* specify the coordinates of the image's upper left corner in the destination (screen) DC, the next two specify the width and height of the block to be transferred, the fifth is a pointer to the source (memory) DC, the sixth and seventh specify the coordinates of the upper left corner of the block of pixels in the source DC, and the eighth and final parameter specifies the type of raster operation to be used in the transfer. SRCCOPY copies the pixels unchanged from the memory DC to the screen DC.

You can shrink or expand a bitmap as it's blitted by using *StretchBlt* instead of *BitBlt*. *StretchBlt*'s argument list looks a lot like *BitBlt*'s, but it includes an additional pair of parameters specifying the width and height of the resized image. The following statement blits a 100-by-100 image from a memory DC to a screen DC and stretches the image to fit a 50-by-200 rectangle:

```
dcScreen.StretchBlt (0, 0, 50, 200, &dcMem, 0, 0, 100, 100, SRCCOPY);
```

By default, rows and columns of pixels are simply removed from the resultant image when the width or height in the destination DC is less than the width or height in the source DC. You can call *CDC::SetStretchBltMode* before calling *StretchBlt* to specify other stretching modes that use various methods to preserve discarded color information. Refer to the documentation on *SetStretchBltMode* for further details, but be advised that the most potentially useful alternative stretching mode—HALFTONE, which uses dithering to simulate colors that can't be displayed directly—works in Windows NT and Windows 2000 but not in Windows 95 and Windows 98.

You can get information about a bitmap by passing a pointer to a BITMAP structure to *CBitmap::GetBitmap*. BITMAP is defined as follows:

```
typedef struct tagBITMAP {
    LONG    bmType;
    LONG    bmWidth;
    LONG    bmHeight;
    LONG    bmWidthBytes;
    WORD    bmPlanes;
```

```
    WORD    bmBitsPixel;
    LPVOID  bmBits;
} BITMAP;
```

The *bmType* field always contains 0. *bmWidth* and *bmHeight* specify the bitmap's dimensions in pixels. *bmWidthBytes* specifies the length (in bytes) of each line in the bitmap and is always a multiple of 2 because rows of bits are padded to 16-bit boundaries. *bmPlanes* and *bmBitsPixel* specify the number of color planes and the number of pixels per bit in each color plane. If *bm* is an initialized BITMAP, you can determine the maximum number of colors the bitmap can contain by using the following statement:

```
int nColors = 1 << (bm.bmPlanes * bm.bmBitsPixel);
```

Finally, *bmBits* contains a NULL pointer following a call to *GetBitmap* if the bitmap is a DDB. If *bitmap* represents a *CBitmap* object, the statements

```
BITMAP bm;
bitmap.GetBitmap (&bm);
```

initialize *bm* with information about the bitmap.

The bitmap dimensions returned by *GetBitmap* are expressed in device units (pixels), but both *BitBlt* and *StretchBlt* use logical units. If you want to write a generic *DrawBitmap* function that blits a bitmap to a DC, you must anticipate the possibility that the DC might be set to a mapping mode other than MM_TEXT. The following *DrawBitmap* function, which is designed to be a member function of a class derived from *CBitmap*, works in all mapping modes. *pDC* points to the device context the bitmap is being blitted to; *x* and *y* specify the location of the image's upper left corner at the destination:

```
void CMyBitmap::DrawBitmap (CDC* pDC, int x, int y)
{
    BITMAP bm;
    GetBitmap (&bm);
    CPoint size (bm.bmWidth, bm.bmHeight);
    pDC->DPtoLP (&size);

    CPoint org (0, 0);
    pDC->DPtoLP (&org);

    CDC dcMem;
    dcMem.CreateCompatibleDC (pDC);
    CBitmap* pOldBitmap = dcMem.SelectObject (this);
    dcMem.SetMapMode (pDC->GetMapMode ());
    pDC->BitBlt (x, y, size.x, size.y, &dcMem, org.x, org.y, SRCCOPY);
    dcMem.SelectObject (pOldBitmap);
}
```

Because of some inadvertent skullduggery that MFC's *CDC::DPtoLP* function performs on *CSize* objects, the *size* variable that holds the bitmap's dimensions is a *CPoint* object, not a *CSize* object. When you pass *CDC::DPtoLP* the address of a *CPoint* object, the call goes straight through to the *::DPtoLP* API function and the conversion is performed properly, even if one or more of the coordinates comes back negative. But when you pass *CDC::DPtoLP* the address of a *CSize* object, MFC performs the conversion itself and converts any negatives to positives. It might make intuitive sense that sizes shouldn't be negative, but that's exactly what *BitBlt* expects in mapping modes in which the *y* axis points upward.

Bitmap Resources

If all you want to do is display a predefined bitmap image—one created with the Visual C++ resource editor or any paint program or image editor that generates BMP files— you can add a bitmap resource to your application's RC file like this:

```
IDB_MYLOGO BITMAP Logo.bmp
```

Then you can load it like this:

```
CBitmap bitmap;
bitmap.LoadBitmap (IDB_MYLOGO);
```

In this example, IDB_MYLOGO is the bitmap's integer resource ID and Logo.bmp is the name of the file that contains the bitmap image. You can also assign a bitmap resource a string ID and load it this way:

```
bitmap.LoadBitmap (_T ("MyLogo"));
```

LoadBitmap accepts resource IDs of either type. After loading a bitmap resource, you display it the way you display any other bitmap—by selecting it into a memory DC and blitting it to a screen DC. Splash screens like the one you see when Visual C++ starts up are typically stored as bitmap resources and loaded with *LoadBitmap* (or its API equivalent, *::LoadBitmap*) just before they're displayed.

CBitmap includes a related member function named *LoadMappedBitmap* that loads a bitmap resource and transforms one or more colors in the bitmap to the colors you specify. *LoadMappedBitmap* is a wrapper around *::CreateMappedBitmap*, which was added to the API so that colors in bitmaps used to paint owner-draw buttons, toolbar buttons, and other controls could be transformed into system colors upon loading. The statement

```
bitmap.LoadMappedBitmap (IDB_BITMAP);
```

loads a bitmap resource and automatically transforms black pixels to the system color COLOR_BTNTEXT, dark gray (R=128, G=128, B=128) pixels to COLOR_BTNSHADOW, light gray (R=192, G=192, B=192) pixels to COLOR _BTNFACE, white pixels to COLOR-_BTNHIGHLIGHT, dark blue (R=0, G=0, B=128) pixels to COLOR_HIGHLIGHT, and magenta (R=255, G=0, B=255) pixels to COLOR_WINDOW. The idea behind mapping magenta to COLOR_WINDOW is that you can add "transparent" pixels to a bitmap by coloring them magenta. If *LoadMappedBitmap* transforms magenta pixels into COLOR_WINDOW pixels and the bitmap is displayed against a COLOR_WINDOW background, the remapped pixels will be invisible against the window background.

You can perform custom color conversions by passing *LoadMappedBitmap* a pointer to an array of COLORMAP structures specifying the colors you want changed and the colors you want to change them to. One use for custom color mapping is for simulating transparent pixels by transforming an arbitrary background color to the background color of your choice. Later in this chapter, we'll examine a technique for drawing bitmaps with transparent pixels that works with any kind of background (even those that aren't solid) and requires no color mapping.

DIBs and DIB Sections

The problem with device-dependent bitmaps is—well, that they're device-dependent. You can manipulate the bits in a DDB directly using *CBitmap::GetBitmapBits* and *CBitmap::SetBitmapBits*, but because pixel color data is stored in a device-dependent format, it's difficult to know what to do with the data returned by *GetBitmapBits* (or what to pass to *SetBitmapBits*) unless the bitmap is monochrome. Worse, the color information encoded in a DDB is meaningful only to the device driver that displays it. If you write a DDB to disk on one PC and read it back on another, there's a very good chance that the colors won't come out the same. DDBs are fine for loading and displaying bitmap resources (although you'll get poor results if a bitmap resource contains more colors than your hardware is capable of displaying) and for drawing images in memory DCs before rendering them on an output device. But their lack of portability makes them unsuitable for just about anything else.

That's why Windows 3.0 introduced the device-independent bitmap, or DIB. The term *DIB* describes a device-independent format for storing bitmap data, a format that's meaningful outside the context of a display driver and even outside the framework of Windows itself. When you call *::CreateBitmap* (the API equivalent of *CBitmap::CreateBitmap*) to create a bitmap, you get back an HBITMAP handle. When you call *::CreateDIBitmap* to create a bitmap, you also get back an HBITMAP. The difference is what's inside. Pixel data passed to *::CreateBitmap* is stored in device driver format, but pixel data passed to *::CreateDIBitmap* is stored in DIB format. Moreover, the DIB format includes color information that enables different device drivers to interpret colors consistently. The API includes a pair of functions named *::GetDIBits* and *::SetDIBits* for reading and writing DIB-formatted bits. It also includes functions for rendering raw DIB data stored in a buffer owned by the application to an output device. Windows BMP files store bitmaps in DIB format, so it's relatively easy to write a function that uses *::CreateDIBitmap* to convert the contents of a BMP file into a GDI bitmap object.

DIB sections are similar to DIBs and were created to solve a performance problem involving the *::StretchDIBits* function in Windows NT. Some graphics programs allocate a buffer to hold DIB bits and then render those bits directly to the screen with *::StretchDIBits*. By not passing the bits to *::CreateDIBitmap* and creating an HBITMAP, the programs enjoy direct access to the bitmap data but can still display the bitmap on the screen. Unfortunately, the client/server architecture of Windows NT and Windows 2000 dictates that bits blitted from a buffer on the client side be copied to a buffer on the server side before they're transferred to the frame buffer, and the extra overhead causes *::StretchDIBits* to perform sluggishly.

Rather than compromise the system architecture, the Windows NT team came up with DIB sections. A DIB section is the Windows NT and Windows 2000 equivalent of having your cake and eating it, too: you can select a DIB section into a DC and blit it to the screen (thus avoiding the undesirable memory-to-memory moves), but you can also access the bitmap bits directly. Speed isn't as much of an issue with the *::StretchDIBits* function in Windows 95 and Windows 98 because these operating systems are architected differently than Windows NT and Windows 2000, but Windows 95 and Windows 98 support DIB sections just as Windows NT and Windows 2000 do and also offer some handy API functions for dealing with them. Win32 programmers are encouraged to use DIB sections in lieu of ordinary DIBs and DDBs whenever possible to give the operating system the greatest amount of flexibility in handling bitmap data.

The bad news about DIBs and DIB sections is that current versions of MFC don't encapsulate them. To use DIBs and DIB sections in your MFC applications, you have to either resort to the API or write your own classes to encapsulate the relevant API functions. Writing a basic *CDib* class or extending *CBitmap* to include functions for DIBs and DIB sections isn't difficult, but I'm not going to do either here because it's very likely that some future version of MFC will include a comprehensive set of classes representing DIBs and DIB sections. What I'll do instead is show you how to get the most out of MFC's *CBitmap* class and how to combine *CBitmap* with API functions to get some very DIB-like behavior out of ordinary *CBitmap*s.

Blits, Raster Operations, and Color Mapping

The most common use for *CDC::BitBlt* is to blit bitmap images to the screen. But *BitBlt* does more than just transfer raw bits. In reality, it's a complex function that computes the color of each pixel it outputs by using Boolean operations to combine pixels from the source DC, the destination DC, and the brush currently selected in the destination DC. The SRCCOPY raster-op code is simple; it merely copies pixels from the source to the destination. Other raster-op codes aren't so simple. MERGEPAINT, for example, inverts the colors of the source pixels with a Boolean NOT operation and ORs the result with the pixel colors at the destination. *BitBlt* supports 256 raster-op codes in all. The 15 shown in the following table are given names with *#define* statements in Wingdi.h.

BitBlt Raster-Op Codes

Name	Binary Equivalent	Operation(s) Performed
SRCCOPY	0xCC0020	dest = source
SRCPAINT	0xEE0086	dest = source OR dest
SRCAND	0x8800C6	dest = source AND dest
SRCINVERT	0x660046	dest = source XOR dest
SRCERASE	0x440328	dest = source AND (NOT dest)
NOTSRCCOPY	0x330008	dest = (NOT source)
NOTSRCERASE	0x1100A6	dest = (NOT src) AND (NOT dest)
MERGECOPY	0xC000CA	dest = (source AND pattern)
MERGEPAINT	0xBB0226	dest = (NOT source) OR dest
PATCOPY	0xF00021	dest = pattern
PATPAINT	0xFB0A09	dest = pattern OR (NOT src) OR dest
PATINVERT	0x5A0049	dest = pattern XOR dest
DSTINVERT	0x550009	dest = (NOT dest)
BLACKNESS	0x000042	dest = BLACK
WHITENESS	0xFF0062	dest = WHITE

You can derive custom raster-op codes by applying the logical operations you want to the bit values in the following list and using the result to look up a DWORD-sized raster-op code in the "Ternary Raster Operations" section of Microsoft's Platform SDK.

Pat	1 1 1 1 0 0 0 0
Src	1 1 0 0 1 1 0 0
Dest	1 0 1 0 1 0 1 0

Pat (for "pattern") represents the color of the brush selected into the destination DC; *Src* represents the pixel color in the source DC; and *Dest* represents the pixel color in the destination DC. Let's say you want to find a raster-op code that inverts a source bitmap, ANDs it with the pixels at the destination, and ORs the result with the brush color. First apply these same operations to each column of bits in the list. The result is shown here:

Pat	1 1 1 1 0 0 0 0	
Src	1 1 0 0 1 1 0 0	
Dest	1 0 1 0 1 0 1 0	
	1 1 1 1 0 0 1 0	= 0xF2

Look up 0xF2 in the ternary raster operations table, and you'll find that the full raster-op code is 0xF20B05. Consequently, you can pass *BitBlt* the hex value 0xF20B05 instead of SRCCOPY or some other raster-op code and it will perform the raster operation described above.

So what can you *do* with all those raster-op codes? The truth is that in color environments you probably won't use many of them. After SRCCOPY, the next most useful raster operations are SRCAND, SRCINVERT, and SRCPAINT. But as the sample program in the next section demonstrates, using an unnamed raster-op code can sometimes reduce the number of steps required to achieve a desired result.

BitBlt is part of a larger family of *CDC* blitting functions that includes *StretchBlt* (which we've already discussed), *PatBlt*, *MaskBlt*, and *PlgBlt*. *PatBlt* combines pixels in a rectangle in the destination DC with the brush selected into the device context, basically duplicating the subset of *BitBlt* raster operations that don't use a source DC. *MaskBlt* combines pixels in source and destination DCs and uses a monochrome bitmap as a mask. One raster operation (the "foreground" raster operation) is performed on pixels that correspond to 1s in the mask, and another raster operation (the "background" raster operation) is performed on pixels that correspond to 0s in the mask. *PlgBlt* blits a rectangular block of pixels in a source DC to a parallelogram in the destination DC and optionally uses a monochrome bitmap as a mask during the transfer. Pixels that correspond to 1s in the mask are blitted to the parallelogram; pixels that correspond to 0s in the mask are not. Unfortunately, *MaskBlt* and *PlgBlt* are supported in Windows NT 3.1 and higher and in Windows 2000 but not in Windows 95 and Windows 98. If you call either of them in Windows 95 or Windows 98, you'll get a 0 return, indicating that the function failed.

Some output devices (notably plotters) don't support *BitBlt* and other blitting functions. To determine whether *BitBlt*s are supported on a given device, get a device context and call *GetDeviceCaps* with a RASTERCAPS parameter. If the RC_BITBLT bit is set in the return value, the device supports *BitBlt*s; if the RC_STRETCHBLT bit is set, the device also supports *StretchBlt*s. There are no specific RASTERCAPS bits for other blit functions, but if you're writing for Windows NT and *BitBlt* isn't supported, you should assume that *PatBlt*, *MaskBlt*, and *PlgBlt* aren't supported, either. Generally, plotters and other vector-type devices that don't support blits will set the RC_NONE bit in the value returned by *GetDeviceCaps* to indicate that they don't support raster operations of any type.

BitBlt and other blitting functions produce the best results (and also perform the best) when the color characteristics of the source and destination DCs match. If you blit a 256-color bitmap to a 16-color destination DC, Windows must map the colors in the source DC to the colors in the destination DC. On some occasions, however, you can use color mapping to your advantage. When *BitBlt* blits a monochrome bitmap to a color DC, it converts 0 bits to the destination DC's current foreground color (*CDC::SetTextColor*) and 1 bits to the destination DC's current background color (*CDC::SetBkColor*). Conversely, when it blits a color bitmap to a monochrome DC, *BitBlt* converts pixels that match the destination DC's background color to 1 and all other pixels to 0. You can use the latter form of color mapping to create a monochrome mask from a color bitmap and use that mask in a routine that blits all pixels except those of a certain color from a bitmap to a screen DC, in effect creating transparent pixels in the bitmap.

Sound interesting? Icons implement transparent pixels by storing two bitmaps for every icon image: a monochrome AND mask and a color XOR mask. You can draw bitmaps with transparent pixels by writing an output routine that uses *BitBlt*s and raster operations to build the AND and XOR masks on the fly. The BitmapDemo sample program in the next section shows how.

The BitmapDemo Application

BitmapDemo is a non-document/view application created with AppWizard that demonstrates how to load a bitmap resource and *BitBlt* it to the screen. It also shows how to make clever use of *BitBlt*s and raster-op codes to blit irregularly shaped images by designating one color in the bitmap as the transparency color. The program's output consists of a rectangular array of bitmap images drawn against a background that fades from blue to black. When Draw Opaque is checked in the Options menu, bitmaps are blitted to the screen unchanged, producing the result shown in Figure 15-5. If Draw Transparent is checked instead, red pixels are removed from the bitmaps when they're blitted to the screen. The result is pictured in Figure 15-6.

Figure 15-5. *The BitmapDemo window with transparency disabled.*

Figure 15-6. *The BitmapDemo window with transparency enabled.*

BitmapDemo uses a *CBitmap*-derived class named *CMaskedBitmap* to represent bitmaps. *CMaskedBitmap* contains two member functions that *CBitmap* doesn't: a *Draw* function for blitting a bitmap to a DC and a *DrawTransparent* function for blitting a bitmap to a DC and simultaneously filtering out all pixels of a specified color. With *CMaskedBitmap* to lend a hand, the statements

```
CMaskedBitmap bitmap;
bitmap.LoadBitmap (IDB_BITMAP);
bitmap.Draw (pDC, x, y);
```

are all you need to create a bitmap object, load a bitmap resource into it, and draw that bitmap on the device represented by *pDC*. The *x* and *y* parameters specify the placement of the bitmap's upper left corner. The statements

```
CMaskedBitmap bitmap;
bitmap.LoadBitmap (IDB_BITMAP);
bitmap.DrawTransparent (pDC, x, y, RGB (255, 0, 255));
```

do the same but don't blit any pixels in the bitmap whose color is bright magenta— RGB (255, 0, 255). With *CMaskedBitmap* to help out, drawing bitmaps with "holes" or nonrectangular profiles is easy: just assign all the transparent pixels in the bitmap a common color and pass that color to *DrawTransparent*. *DrawTransparent* will see to it that the transparent pixels don't get blitted along with the others.

The source code for *CMaskedBitmap::Draw* should look familiar to you: it's identical to the *DrawBitmap* function discussed earlier. *CMaskedBitmap::Draw-Transparent* is a little more complicated. The comments in the source code should help you understand what's going on. If the comments don't make things clear enough, here's a summary of the steps involved in blitting a bitmap to the screen but omitting pixels of a certain color:

1. Create a memory DC, and select the bitmap into it.

2. Create a second memory DC, and select in a monochrome bitmap whose size is identical to that of the original bitmap. Create an AND mask by setting the background color of the memory DC created in step 1 to the transparency color and blitting the bitmap to the DC. The resultant AND mask has 1s everywhere the original bitmap has pixels whose color equals the transparency color and 0s everywhere else.

3. Create a third memory DC, and select in a bitmap whose size and color characteristics match those of the original bitmap. Create an XOR mask in this DC by first blitting the image from the memory DC created in step 1 to this DC with a SRCCOPY raster-op code and then blitting the AND mask to this DC with the raster-op code 0x220326.

4. Create a fourth memory DC, and select in a bitmap whose size and color characteristics match those of the original bitmap. Blit the pixels from the rectangle in which the bitmap will go in the output DC to the newly created memory DC.

5. Create the final image in the memory DC created in step 4 by first blitting in the AND mask with a SRCAND raster-op code and then blitting in the XOR mask with a SRCINVERT raster-op code.

6. Copy the image from the memory DC to the output DC.

Notice how *BitBlt* is used to generate the AND mask in step 2. Because the destination DC is monochrome, the GDI translates pixels whose color equals the background color to 1s and all other pixels to 0s at the destination. It's important to set the source DC's background color equal to the bitmap's transparency color first so that the transformation will be performed properly. If you look at the code in *CMaskedBitmap::DrawTransparent* that corresponds to step 2, you'll see that the destination DC's size and color characteristics are set by using *CBitmap::CreateBitmap* to create a monochrome bitmap whose dimensions equal the dimensions of the original bitmap and then selecting the monochrome bitmap into the DC. You control the size of a memory DC's display surface and the number of colors that it supports by selecting a bitmap into it. That's why you see so many calls to *CreateBitmap* and *CreateCompatibleBitmap* in *DrawTransparent*.

One other point of interest in *DrawTransparent* is the raster-op code 0x220326 used in step 3, which performs the following raster operation involving pixels at the source and destination.

```
dest = (NOT src) AND dest
```

You can accomplish the same thing using "standard" raster-op codes by calling *BitBlt* twice: once with the raster-op code NOTSRCCOPY to invert the image in the source DC and again with SRCAND to AND the inverted image with the pixels in the destination DC. One *BitBlt* is obviously more efficient than two, but don't be surprised if the 0x220326 code doesn't perform any faster than the NOTSRCCOPY/SRCAND combination on some PCs. Most display drivers are optimized to perform certain raster operations faster than others, and it's always possible that a NOTSRCCOPY or a SRCAND will execute very quickly but a 0x220326 won't.

As you experiment with BitmapDemo (whose source code appears in Figure 15-7), notice that the window takes longer to repaint when BitmapDemo draws transparent pixels. That's because *DrawTransparent* has to do a lot more work than *Draw* to get a single image to the screen. The worst performance hit occurs when *DrawTransparent* generates the same AND and XOR masks over and over again. If you want the functionality of *DrawTransparent* in an application in which output performance is critical (for example, if you use transparent bitmaps to create spritelike objects that move about the screen), you should modify the *CMaskedBitmap* class so that the masks are generated just once and then reused as needed. Performance can also be improved by applying the AND and XOR masks directly to the destination DC rather than to a memory DC containing a copy of the pixels at the destination, but the small amount of flickering produced by the short delay between the application of the masks might be too much if you're using the bitmap for animation.

MainFrm.h

```
// MainFrm.h : interface of the CMainFrame class
//
/////////////////////////////////////////////////////////////////////////////

#if !defined(
    AFX_MAINFRM_H__D71EF549_A6FE_11D2_8E53_006008A82731__INCLUDED_)
#define AFX_MAINFRM_H__D71EF549_A6FE_11D2_8E53_006008A82731__INCLUDED_

#if _MSC_VER > 1000
#pragma once
#endif // _MSC_VER > 1000

#include "ChildView.h"

class CMainFrame : public CFrameWnd
{
```

Figure 15-7. *The BitmapDemo application.*

```
public:
    CMainFrame();
protected:
    DECLARE_DYNAMIC(CMainFrame)

// Attributes
public:

// Operations
public:

// Overrides
    // ClassWizard generated virtual function overrides
    //{{AFX_VIRTUAL(CMainFrame)
    virtual BOOL PreCreateWindow(CREATESTRUCT& cs);
    virtual BOOL OnCmdMsg(UINT nID, int nCode, void* pExtra,
        AFX_CMDHANDLERINFO* pHandlerInfo);
    //}}AFX_VIRTUAL

// Implementation
public:
    virtual ~CMainFrame();
#ifdef _DEBUG
    virtual void AssertValid() const;
    virtual void Dump(CDumpContext& dc) const;
#endif

protected:  // control bar embedded members
    CStatusBar  m_wndStatusBar;
    CChildView      m_wndView;

// Generated message map functions
protected:
    //{{AFX_MSG(CMainFrame)
    afx_msg int OnCreate(LPCREATESTRUCT lpCreateStruct);
    afx_msg void OnSetFocus(CWnd *pOldWnd);
    afx_msg BOOL OnQueryNewPalette();
    afx_msg void OnPaletteChanged(CWnd* pFocusWnd);
    //}}AFX_MSG
    DECLARE_MESSAGE_MAP()
};

////////////////////////////////////////////////////////////////////////////

//{{AFX_INSERT_LOCATION}}
```

(continued)

Figure 15-7 *continued*

```
// Microsoft Visual C++ will insert additional declarations
// immediately before the previous line.

#endif
// !defined(
//     AFX_MAINFRM_H__D71EF549_A6FE_11D2_8E53_006008A82731__INCLUDED_)
```

MainFrm.cpp

```
// MainFrm.cpp : implementation of the CMainFrame class
//

#include "stdafx.h"
#include "BitmapDemo.h"
#include "MaskedBitmap.h"
#include "MainFrm.h"

#ifdef _DEBUG
#define new DEBUG_NEW
#undef THIS_FILE
static char THIS_FILE[] = __FILE__;
#endif


/////////////////////////////////////////////////////////////////////////
// CMainFrame

IMPLEMENT_DYNAMIC(CMainFrame, CFrameWnd)

BEGIN_MESSAGE_MAP(CMainFrame, CFrameWnd)
    //{{AFX_MSG_MAP(CMainFrame)
    ON_WM_CREATE()
    ON_WM_SETFOCUS()
    ON_WM_QUERYNEWPALETTE()
    ON_WM_PALETTECHANGED()
    //}}AFX_MSG_MAP
END_MESSAGE_MAP()

static UINT indicators[] =
{
    ID_SEPARATOR
};


/////////////////////////////////////////////////////////////////////////
// CMainFrame construction/destruction
```

```
CMainFrame::CMainFrame()
{
}

CMainFrame::~CMainFrame()
{
}

int CMainFrame::OnCreate(LPCREATESTRUCT lpCreateStruct)
{
    if (CFrameWnd::OnCreate(lpCreateStruct) == -1)
        return -1;
    // create a view to occupy the client area of the frame
    if (!m_wndView.Create(NULL, NULL, AFX_WS_DEFAULT_VIEW,
        CRect(0, 0, 0, 0), this, AFX_IDW_PANE_FIRST, NULL))
    {
        TRACE0("Failed to create view window\n");
        return -1;
    }

    if (!m_wndStatusBar.Create(this) ||
        !m_wndStatusBar.SetIndicators(indicators,
          sizeof(indicators)/sizeof(UINT)))
    {
        TRACE0("Failed to create status bar\n");
        return -1;      // fail to create
    }

    return 0;
}

BOOL CMainFrame::PreCreateWindow(CREATESTRUCT& cs)
{
    if( !CFrameWnd::PreCreateWindow(cs) )
        return FALSE;
    // TODO: Modify the Window class or styles here by modifying
    //  the CREATESTRUCT cs

    cs.dwExStyle &= ~WS_EX_CLIENTEDGE;
    cs.lpszClass = AfxRegisterWndClass(0);
    return TRUE;
}

/////////////////////////////////////////////////////////////////////
// CMainFrame diagnostics
```

(continued)

Figure 15-7 *continued*

```
#ifdef _DEBUG
void CMainFrame::AssertValid() const
{
    CFrameWnd::AssertValid();
}

void CMainFrame::Dump(CDumpContext& dc) const
{
    CFrameWnd::Dump(dc);
}

#endif //_DEBUG

//////////////////////////////////////////////////////////////////////////
// CMainFrame message handlers
void CMainFrame::OnSetFocus(CWnd* pOldWnd)
{
    // forward focus to the view window
    m_wndView.SetFocus();
}

BOOL CMainFrame::OnCmdMsg(UINT nID, int nCode, void* pExtra,
    AFX_CMDHANDLERINFO* pHandlerInfo)
{
    // let the view have first crack at the command
    if (m_wndView.OnCmdMsg(nID, nCode, pExtra, pHandlerInfo))
        return TRUE;

    // otherwise, do default handling
    return CFrameWnd::OnCmdMsg(nID, nCode, pExtra, pHandlerInfo);
}

BOOL CMainFrame::OnQueryNewPalette()
{
    m_wndView.Invalidate ();
    return TRUE;
}

void CMainFrame::OnPaletteChanged(CWnd* pFocusWnd)
{
    m_wndView.Invalidate ();
}
```

ChildView.h

```
// ChildView.h : interface of the CChildView class
//
/////////////////////////////////////////////////////////////////////////////

#if !defined(
    AFX_CHILDVIEW_H__D71EF54B_A6FE_11D2_8E53_006008A82731__INCLUDED_)
#define AFX_CHILDVIEW_H__D71EF54B_A6FE_11D2_8E53_006008A82731__INCLUDED_

#if _MSC_VER > 1000
#pragma once
#endif // _MSC_VER > 1000


/////////////////////////////////////////////////////////////////////////////
// CChildView window

class CChildView : public CWnd
{
// Construction
public:
    CChildView();

// Attributes
public:

// Operations
public:

// Overrides
    // ClassWizard generated virtual function overrides
    //{{AFX_VIRTUAL(CChildView)
    protected:
    virtual BOOL PreCreateWindow(CREATESTRUCT& cs);
    //}}AFX_VIRTUAL

// Implementation
public:
    virtual ~CChildView();

    // Generated message map functions
protected:
    void DoGradientFill (CDC* pDC, LPRECT pRect);
    CPalette m_palette;
    CMaskedBitmap m_bitmap;
    BOOL m_bDrawOpaque;
    //{{AFX_MSG(CChildView)
```

(continued)

Figure 15-7 *continued*

```
    afx_msg void OnPaint();
    afx_msg int OnCreate(LPCREATESTRUCT lpCreateStruct);
    afx_msg BOOL OnEraseBkgnd(CDC* pDC);
    afx_msg void OnOptionsDrawOpaque();
    afx_msg void OnOptionsDrawTransparent();
    afx_msg void OnUpdateOptionsDrawOpaque(CCmdUI* pCmdUI);
    afx_msg void OnUpdateOptionsDrawTransparent(CCmdUI* pCmdUI);
    //}}AFX_MSG
    DECLARE_MESSAGE_MAP()
};


/////////////////////////////////////////////////////////////////////////


//{{AFX_INSERT_LOCATION}}
// Microsoft Visual C++ will insert additional declarations
// immediately before the previous line.

#endif
// !defined(
//      AFX_CHILDVIEW_H__D71EF54B_A6FE_11D2_8E53_006008A82731__INCLUDED_)
```

ChildView.cpp

```
// ChildView.cpp : implementation of the CChildView class
//

#include "stdafx.h"
#include "BitmapDemo.h"
#include "MaskedBitmap.h"
#include "ChildView.h"

#ifdef _DEBUG
#define new DEBUG_NEW
#undef THIS_FILE
static char THIS_FILE[] = __FILE__;
#endif


/////////////////////////////////////////////////////////////////////////
// CChildView

CChildView::CChildView()
{
    m_bDrawOpaque = TRUE;
}
```

```
CChildView::~CChildView()
{
}

BEGIN_MESSAGE_MAP(CChildView,CWnd )
    //{{AFX_MSG_MAP(CChildView)
    ON_WM_PAINT()
    ON_WM_CREATE()
    ON_WM_ERASEBKGND()
    ON_COMMAND(ID_OPTIONS_DRAW_OPAQUE, OnOptionsDrawOpaque)
    ON_COMMAND(ID_OPTIONS_DRAW_TRANSPARENT, OnOptionsDrawTransparent)
    ON_UPDATE_COMMAND_UI(ID_OPTIONS_DRAW_OPAQUE, OnUpdateOptionsDrawOpaque)
    ON_UPDATE_COMMAND_UI(ID_OPTIONS_DRAW_TRANSPARENT,
        OnUpdateOptionsDrawTransparent)
    //}}AFX_MSG_MAP
END_MESSAGE_MAP()

/////////////////////////////////////////////////////////////////////////////
// CChildView message handlers

BOOL CChildView::PreCreateWindow(CREATESTRUCT& cs)
{
    if (!CWnd::PreCreateWindow(cs))
        return FALSE;

    cs.dwExStyle != WS_EX_CLIENTEDGE;
    cs.style &= ~WS_BORDER;
    cs.lpszClass = AfxRegisterWndClass(CS_HREDRAW|CS_VREDRAW|CS_DBLCLKS,
        ::LoadCursor(NULL, IDC_ARROW), HBRUSH(COLOR_WINDOW+1), NULL);

    return TRUE;
}

void CChildView::OnPaint()
{
    CRect rect;
    GetClientRect (&rect);
    CPaintDC dc (this);

    BITMAP bm;
    m_bitmap.GetBitmap (&bm);
    int cx = (rect.Width () / (bm.bmWidth + 8)) + 1;
    int cy = (rect.Height () / (bm.bmHeight + 8)) + 1;

    int i, j, x, y;
    for (i=0; i<cx; i++) {
```

(continued)

Figure 15-7 *continued*

```
        for (j=0; j<cy; j++) {
            x = 8 + (i * (bm.bmWidth + 8));
            y = 8 + (j * (bm.bmHeight + 8));
            if (m_bDrawOpaque)
                m_bitmap.Draw (&dc, x, y);
            else
                m_bitmap.DrawTransparent (&dc, x, y, RGB (255, 0, 0));
        }
    }
}

int CChildView::OnCreate(LPCREATESTRUCT lpCreateStruct)
{
    if (CWnd ::OnCreate(lpCreateStruct) == -1)
        return -1;

    //
    // Load the bitmap.
    //
    m_bitmap.LoadBitmap (IDB_BITMAP);

    //
    // Create a palette for a gradient fill if this is a palettized device.
    //
    CClientDC dc (this);
    if (dc.GetDeviceCaps (RASTERCAPS) & RC_PALETTE) {
        struct {
            LOGPALETTE lp;
            PALETTEENTRY ape[63];
        } pal;

        LOGPALETTE* pLP = (LOGPALETTE*) &pal;
        pLP->palVersion = 0x300;
        pLP->palNumEntries = 64;

        for (int i=0; i<64; i++) {
            pLP->palPalEntry[i].peRed = 0;
            pLP->palPalEntry[i].peGreen = 0;
            pLP->palPalEntry[i].peBlue = 255 - (i * 4);
            pLP->palPalEntry[i].peFlags = 0;
        }
        m_palette.CreatePalette (pLP);
    }
    return 0;
}
```

```
BOOL CChildView::OnEraseBkgnd(CDC* pDC)
{
    CRect rect;
    GetClientRect (&rect);

    CPalette* pOldPalette;
    if ((HPALETTE) m_palette != NULL) {
        pOldPalette = pDC->SelectPalette (&m_palette, FALSE);
        pDC->RealizePalette ();
    }

    DoGradientFill (pDC, &rect);

    if ((HPALETTE) m_palette != NULL)
        pDC->SelectPalette (pOldPalette, FALSE);
    return TRUE;
}

void CChildView::DoGradientFill(CDC *pDC, LPRECT pRect)
{
    CBrush* pBrush[64];
    for (int i=0; i<64; i++)
        pBrush[i] = new CBrush (PALETTERGB (0, 0, 255 - (i * 4)));

    int nWidth = pRect->right - pRect->left;
    int nHeight = pRect->bottom - pRect->top;
    CRect rect;

    for (i=0; i<nHeight; i++) {
        rect.SetRect (0, i, nWidth, i + 1);
        pDC->FillRect (&rect, pBrush[(i * 63) / nHeight]);
    }

    for (i=0; i<64; i++)
        delete pBrush[i];
}

void CChildView::OnOptionsDrawOpaque()
{
    m_bDrawOpaque = TRUE;
    Invalidate ();
}

void CChildView::OnOptionsDrawTransparent()
{
    m_bDrawOpaque = FALSE;
```

(continued)

Figure 15-7 *continued*

```
    Invalidate ();
}

void CChildView::OnUpdateOptionsDrawOpaque(CCmdUI* pCmdUI)
{
    pCmdUI->SetCheck (m_bDrawOpaque ? 1 : 0);
}

void CChildView::OnUpdateOptionsDrawTransparent(CCmdUI* pCmdUI)
{
    pCmdUI->SetCheck (m_bDrawOpaque ? 0 : 1);
}
```

MaskedBitmap.h

```
// MaskedBitmap.h: interface for the CMaskedBitmap class.
//
/////////////////////////////////////////////////////////////////////////

#if !defined(
    AFX_MASKEDBITMAP_H__D71EF554_A6FE_11D2_8E53_006008A82731__INCLUDED_)
#define AFX_MASKEDBITMAP_H__D71EF554_A6FE_11D2_8E53_006008A82731__INCLUDED_

#if _MSC_VER > 1000
#pragma once
#endif // _MSC_VER > 1000

class CMaskedBitmap : public CBitmap
{
public:
    void DrawTransparent (CDC* pDC, int x, int y,
        COLORREF clrTransparency);
    void Draw (CDC* pDC, int x, int y);
};

#endif
// !defined(
//      AFX_MASKEDBITMAP_H__D71EF554_A6FE_11D2_8E53_006008A82731__INCLUDED_)
```

MaskedBitmap.cpp

```
// MaskedBitmap.cpp: implementation of the CMaskedBitmap class.
//
```

```
/////////////////////////////////////////////////////////////////////

#include "stdafx.h"
#include "BitmapDemo.h"
#include "MaskedBitmap.h"

#ifdef _DEBUG
#undef THIS_FILE
static char THIS_FILE[]=__FILE__;
#define new DEBUG_NEW
#endif

void CMaskedBitmap::Draw(CDC *pDC, int x, int y)
{
    BITMAP bm;
    GetBitmap (&bm);
    CPoint size (bm.bmWidth, bm.bmHeight);
    pDC->DPtoLP (&size);

    CPoint org (0, 0);
    pDC->DPtoLP (&org);

    CDC dcMem;
    dcMem.CreateCompatibleDC (pDC);
    CBitmap* pOldBitmap = dcMem.SelectObject (this);
    dcMem.SetMapMode (pDC->GetMapMode ());

    pDC->BitBlt (x, y, size.x, size.y, &dcMem, org.x, org.y, SRCCOPY);

    dcMem.SelectObject (pOldBitmap);
}

void CMaskedBitmap::DrawTransparent(CDC *pDC, int x, int y,
    COLORREF clrTransparency)
{
    BITMAP bm;
    GetBitmap (&bm);
    CPoint size (bm.bmWidth, bm.bmHeight);
    pDC->DPtoLP (&size);

    CPoint org (0, 0);
    pDC->DPtoLP (&org);

    //
    // Create a memory DC (dcImage) and select the bitmap into it.
    //
    CDC dcImage;
```

(continued)

Figure 15-7 *continued*

```
    dcImage.CreateCompatibleDC (pDC);
    CBitmap* pOldBitmapImage = dcImage.SelectObject (this);
    dcImage.SetMapMode (pDC->GetMapMode ());


    //
    // Create a second memory DC (dcAnd) and in it create an AND mask.
    //
    CDC dcAnd;
    dcAnd.CreateCompatibleDC (pDC);
    dcAnd.SetMapMode (pDC->GetMapMode ());

    CBitmap bitmapAnd;
    bitmapAnd.CreateBitmap (bm.bmWidth, bm.bmHeight, 1, 1, NULL);
    CBitmap* pOldBitmapAnd = dcAnd.SelectObject (&bitmapAnd);

    dcImage.SetBkColor (clrTransparency);
    dcAnd.BitBlt (org.x, org.y, size.x, size.y, &dcImage, org.x, org.y,
        SRCCOPY);


    //
    // Create a third memory DC (dcXor) and in it create an XOR mask.
    //
    CDC dcXor;
    dcXor.CreateCompatibleDC (pDC);
    dcXor.SetMapMode (pDC->GetMapMode ());

    CBitmap bitmapXor;
    bitmapXor.CreateCompatibleBitmap (&dcImage, bm.bmWidth, bm.bmHeight);
    CBitmap* pOldBitmapXor = dcXor.SelectObject (&bitmapXor);

    dcXor.BitBlt (org.x, org.y, size.x, size.y, &dcImage, org.x, org.y,
        SRCCOPY);

    dcXor.BitBlt (org.x, org.y, size.x, size.y, &dcAnd, org.x, org.y,
        0x220326);


    //
    // Copy the pixels in the destination rectangle to a temporary
    // memory DC (dcTemp).
    //
    CDC dcTemp;
    dcTemp.CreateCompatibleDC (pDC);
    dcTemp.SetMapMode (pDC->GetMapMode ());

    CBitmap bitmapTemp;
    bitmapTemp.CreateCompatibleBitmap (&dcImage, bm.bmWidth, bm.bmHeight);
```

```
    CBitmap* pOldBitmapTemp = dcTemp.SelectObject (&bitmapTemp);

    dcTemp.BitBlt (org.x, org.y, size.x, size.y, pDC, x, y, SRCCOPY);

    //
    // Generate the final image by applying the AND and XOR masks to
    // the image in the temporary memory DC.
    //
    dcTemp.BitBlt (org.x, org.y, size.x, size.y, &dcAnd, org.x, org.y,
        SRCAND);

    dcTemp.BitBlt (org.x, org.y, size.x, size.y, &dcXor, org.x, org.y,
        SRCINVERT);

    //
    // Blit the resulting image to the screen.
    //
    pDC->BitBlt (x, y, size.x, size.y, &dcTemp, org.x, org.y, SRCCOPY);

    //
    // Restore the default bitmaps.
    //
    dcTemp.SelectObject (pOldBitmapTemp);
    dcXor.SelectObject (pOldBitmapXor);
    dcAnd.SelectObject (pOldBitmapAnd);
    dcImage.SelectObject (pOldBitmapImage);
}
```

Both Windows 98 and Windows 2000 support a new API function named *::TransparentBlt* that performs the equivalent of a *StretchBlt* and also accepts a transparency color. Like BitmapDemo's *DrawTransparent* function, *::TransparentBlt* skips pixels whose color equals the transparency color. I didn't use *::TransparentBlt* because I wanted BitmapDemo to work as well on down-level systems as it works on Windows 98 and Windows 2000 systems. Which of these transparency functions you should use depends on the platforms you're targeting.

Writing a BMP File Viewer

The disk-and-drive image drawn by BitmapDemo looks pretty good because it's a simple 16-color bitmap whose colors match the static colors in the system palette. As long as you draw the bitmaps yourself and stick to the colors in the default palette, bitmaps will display just fine without custom *CPalette*s. But if you write an application that reads arbitrary BMP files created by other programs and you rely on the default palette for color mapping, bitmaps containing 256 or more colors will be posterized—some rather severely. You can dramatically improve the quality of the output by creating a *CPalette* whose colors match the colors in the bitmap. The sample program in this section demonstrates how. It also shows one way that MFC programmers can combine *CBitmap*s with DIB sections to create more functional bitmaps.

The sample program, which I'll call Vista, is shown in Figure 15-8. Vista is a document/view BMP file viewer that will read virtually any BMP file containing any number of colors and draw a reasonable representation of it on a screen that's capable of displaying 256 or more colors. (Vista works with 16-color screens, too, but don't expect a lot from the output if the bitmap contains more than 16 colors.) The source code, selected portions of which appear in Figure 15-9 (beginning on page 899), is surprisingly simple. Other than the code that creates a logical palette after a BMP file is read from disk, the application includes very little other than the standard stuff that forms the core of every document/view application.

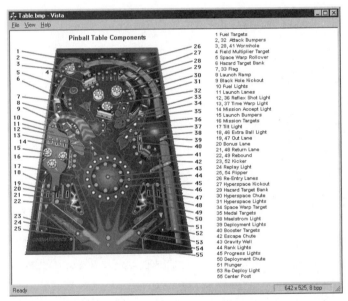

Figure 15-8. *The Vista window with a bitmap displayed.*

The view's *OnDraw* function displays bitmaps on the screen by selecting the logical palette associated with the bitmap into the device context (provided such a palette exists) and *BitBlt*ing the bitmap to a *CScrollView*. *OnDraw* retrieves the logical palette by calling the document's *GetPalette* function, and it retrieves the bitmap by calling the document's *GetBitmap* function. *GetPalette* returns a *CPalette* pointer to the palette that the document object creates when the bitmap is loaded. A NULL return means that no palette is associated with the bitmap, which in turn means that Vista is running on a nonpalettized video adapter. *GetBitmap* returns a pointer to the bitmap that constitutes the document itself. Vista's document class *CVistaDoc* stores the bitmap in a *CBitmap* data member named *m_bitmap* and the palette (if any) that goes with the bitmap in a *CPalette* member named *m_palette*. The bitmap and palette objects are initialized when the document's *OnOpenDocument* function is called (when the user selects Open from the File menu) and destroyed when the document's *DeleteContents* function is called.

One simple statement in *OnOpenDocument* reads the BMP file named in the function's parameter list:

```
HBITMAP hBitmap = (HBITMAP) ::LoadImage (NULL, lpszPathName,
    IMAGE_BITMAP, 0, 0, LR_LOADFROMFILE | LR_CREATEDIBSECTION);
```

The value returned by *::LoadImage* is a valid HBITMAP if the DIB section was successfully created and NULL if it wasn't. If *::LoadImage* fails, it's highly likely that the file doesn't contain a DIB. *OnOpenDocument* indicates as much in the error message it displays when *::LoadImage* returns NULL. If the HBITMAP isn't NULL, *OnOpenDocument* attaches it to *m_bitmap*. The document (bitmap) is now loaded and ready to be displayed—almost.

If Vista is running on a palettized display device, the bitmap probably won't look very good unless there's a logical palette to go with it. After *::LoadImage* returns, *OnOpenDocument* grabs a device context and calls *GetDeviceCaps* to determine whether palettes are supported. If the return value doesn't contain an RC_PALETTE flag, *OnOpenDocument* returns immediately and leaves *m_palette* uninitialized. Otherwise, *OnOpenDocument* initializes *m_palette* with a logical palette.

To determine how best to create the palette, *OnOpenDocument* first finds out how many colors the bitmap contains by calling *GetObject* with a pointer to a DIBSECTION structure. One of the members of a DIBSECTION structure is a BITMAP-INFOHEADER structure, and the BITMAPINFOHEADER structure's *biClrUsed* and *biBitCount* fields reveal the number of colors in the bitmap. If *biClrUsed* is nonzero, it specifies the color count. If *biClrUsed* is 0, the number of colors equals

```
1 << biBitCount
```

The following code in *OnOpenDocument* sets *nColors* equal to the number of colors in the bitmap:

```
DIBSECTION ds;
m_bitmap.GetObject (sizeof (DIBSECTION), &ds);

int nColors;
if (ds.dsBmih.biClrUsed != 0)
    nColors = ds.dsBmih.biClrUsed;
else
    nColors = 1 << ds.dsBmih.biBitCount;
```

What *OnOpenDocument* does next depends on the value of *nColors*. If *nColors* is greater than 256, indicating that the bitmap has a color depth of 16, 24, or 32 bits (images stored in BMP files always use 1-bit, 4-bit, 8-bit, 16-bit, 24-bit, or 32-bit color), *OnOpenDocument* creates a halftone palette by calling *CPalette::CreateHalftonePalette* with a pointer to the screen DC it obtained earlier:

```
if (nColors > 256)
    m_palette.CreateHalftonePalette (&dc);
```

In return, the system creates a generic palette with a rainbow of colors that's suited to the device context. In most cases, a logical palette created by *CreateHalftonePalette* will contain 256 colors. That's not enough to allow a bitmap containing thousands or perhaps millions of colors to be displayed with 100 percent accuracy, but it will produce much better results than you'd get if you used the device context's default palette.

If *nColors* is less than or equal to 256, *OnOpenDocument* initializes *m_palette* with a logical palette whose colors match the colors in the bitmap. The key to matching the bitmap's colors is the API function *::GetDIBColorTable*, which copies the color table associated with a 1-bit, 4-bit, or 8-bit DIB section to an array of RGBQUAD structures. That array, in turn, is used to initialize an array of PALETTEENTRY structures and create a logical palette:

```
RGBQUAD* pRGB = new RGBQUAD[nColors];

CDC memDC;
memDC.CreateCompatibleDC (&dc);
CBitmap* pOldBitmap = memDC.SelectObject (&m_bitmap);
::GetDIBColorTable ((HDC) memDC, 0, nColors, pRGB);
memDC.SelectObject (pOldBitmap);

UINT nSize = sizeof (LOGPALETTE) +
    (sizeof (PALETTEENTRY) * (nColors - 1));
LOGPALETTE* pLP = (LOGPALETTE*) new BYTE[nSize];

pLP->palVersion = 0x300;
pLP->palNumEntries = nColors;

for (int i=0; i<nColors; i++) {
    pLP->palPalEntry[i].peRed = pRGB[i].rgbRed;
    pLP->palPalEntry[i].peGreen = pRGB[i].rgbGreen;
    pLP->palPalEntry[i].peBlue = pRGB[i].rgbBlue;
    pLP->palPalEntry[i].peFlags = 0;
}

m_palette.CreatePalette (pLP);
```

::GetDIBColorTable works only if the DIB section is selected into a device context, so *OnOpenDocument* creates a memory DC and selects *m_bitmap* into it before making the call. The rest is just detail: allocating memory for a LOGPALETTE structure, transferring the RGBQUAD values from the color table to the corresponding PALETTE-

ENTRY entries, and calling *CreatePalette*. Once it has a palette to work with, Vista will display most 256-color bitmaps with stunning accuracy on 256-color screens.

For a nice touch, Vista includes a readout in its status bar that identifies the bitmap's dimensions and color depth (bits per pixel). The status bar is updated when *OnOpenDocument* sends Vista's main window a WM_USER_UPDATE_STATS message containing a pointer to the string that it wants to appear in the status bar pane. A message handler in the frame window class fields the message and updates the status bar accordingly.

MainFrm.h

```
// MainFrm.h : interface of the CMainFrame class
//
/////////////////////////////////////////////////////////////////////////////

#if !defined(
    AFX_MAINFRM_H__3597FEA9_A70E_11D2_8E53_006008A82731__INCLUDED_)
#define AFX_MAINFRM_H__3597FEA9_A70E_11D2_8E53_006008A82731__INCLUDED_

#if _MSC_VER > 1000
#pragma once
#endif // _MSC_VER > 1000

class CMainFrame : public CFrameWnd
{

protected: // create from serialization only
    CMainFrame();
    DECLARE_DYNCREATE(CMainFrame)

// Attributes
public:

// Operations
public:

// Overrides
    // ClassWizard generated virtual function overrides
    //{{AFX_VIRTUAL(CMainFrame)
    virtual BOOL PreCreateWindow(CREATESTRUCT& cs);
    //}}AFX_VIRTUAL

// Implementation
public:
    virtual ~CMainFrame();
```

Figure 15-9. *The Vista application.*

(continued)

Figure 15-9 *continued*

```
#ifdef _DEBUG
    virtual void AssertValid() const;
    virtual void Dump(CDumpContext& dc) const;
#endif

protected:  // control bar embedded members
    CStatusBar   m_wndStatusBar;

// Generated message map functions
protected:
    //{{AFX_MSG(CMainFrame)
    afx_msg int OnCreate(LPCREATESTRUCT lpCreateStruct);
    afx_msg BOOL OnQueryNewPalette();
    afx_msg void OnPaletteChanged(CWnd* pFocusWnd);
    //}}AFX_MSG
    afx_msg LRESULT OnUpdateImageStats (WPARAM wParam, LPARAM lParam);
    DECLARE_MESSAGE_MAP()
};


///////////////////////////////////////////////////////////////////////////

//{{AFX_INSERT_LOCATION}}
// Microsoft Visual C++ will insert additional declarations
// immediately before the previous line.

#endif
// !defined(AFX_MAINFRM_H__3597FEA9_A70E_11D2_8E53_006008A82731__INCLUDED_)
```

MainFrm.cpp

```
// MainFrm.cpp : implementation of the CMainFrame class
//

#include "stdafx.h"
#include "Vista.h"

#include "MainFrm.h"

#ifdef _DEBUG
#define new DEBUG_NEW
#undef THIS_FILE
static char THIS_FILE[] = __FILE__;
#endif
```

```
/////////////////////////////////////////////////////////////////////////
// CMainFrame

IMPLEMENT_DYNCREATE(CMainFrame, CFrameWnd)

BEGIN_MESSAGE_MAP(CMainFrame, CFrameWnd)
    //{{AFX_MSG_MAP(CMainFrame)
    ON_WM_CREATE()
    ON_WM_QUERYNEWPALETTE()
    ON_WM_PALETTECHANGED()
    //}}AFX_MSG_MAP
    ON_MESSAGE (WM_USER_UPDATE_STATS, OnUpdateImageStats)
END_MESSAGE_MAP()

static UINT indicators[] =
{
    ID_SEPARATOR,
    ID_SEPARATOR
};

/////////////////////////////////////////////////////////////////////////
// CMainFrame construction/destruction

CMainFrame::CMainFrame()
{
}

CMainFrame::~CMainFrame()
{
}

int CMainFrame::OnCreate(LPCREATESTRUCT lpCreateStruct)
{
    if (CFrameWnd::OnCreate(lpCreateStruct) == -1)
        return -1;

    //
    // Create the status bar.
    //
    if (!m_wndStatusBar.Create(this) ||
        !m_wndStatusBar.SetIndicators(indicators,
            sizeof(indicators)/sizeof(UINT)))
    {
        TRACE0("Failed to create status bar\n");
        return -1;       // fail to create
    }
```

(continued)

Figure 15-9 *continued*

```
    //
    // Size the status bar's rightmost pane to hold a text string.
    //
    TEXTMETRIC tm;
    CClientDC dc (this);
    CFont* pFont = m_wndStatusBar.GetFont ();
    CFont* pOldFont = dc.SelectObject (pFont);
    dc.GetTextMetrics (&tm);
    dc.SelectObject (pOldFont);

    int cxWidth;
    UINT nID, nStyle;
    m_wndStatusBar.GetPaneInfo (1, nID, nStyle, cxWidth);
    cxWidth = tm.tmAveCharWidth * 24;
    m_wndStatusBar.SetPaneInfo (1, nID, nStyle, cxWidth);
    return 0;
}

BOOL CMainFrame::PreCreateWindow(CREATESTRUCT& cs)
{
    if( !CFrameWnd::PreCreateWindow(cs) )
        return FALSE;
    return TRUE;
}

/////////////////////////////////////////////////////////////////////////
// CMainFrame diagnostics

#ifdef _DEBUG
void CMainFrame::AssertValid() const
{
    CFrameWnd::AssertValid();
}

void CMainFrame::Dump(CDumpContext& dc) const
{
    CFrameWnd::Dump(dc);
}

#endif //_DEBUG

/////////////////////////////////////////////////////////////////////////
// CMainFrame message handlers

BOOL CMainFrame::OnQueryNewPalette()
```

```
{
    CDocument* pDoc = GetActiveDocument ();
    if (pDoc != NULL)
        GetActiveDocument ()->UpdateAllViews (NULL);
    return TRUE;
}


void CMainFrame::OnPaletteChanged(CWnd* pFocusWnd)
{
    if (pFocusWnd != this) {
        CDocument* pDoc = GetActiveDocument ();
        if (pDoc != NULL)
            GetActiveDocument ()->UpdateAllViews (NULL);
    }
}


LRESULT CMainFrame::OnUpdateImageStats (WPARAM wParam, LPARAM lParam)
{
    m_wndStatusBar.SetPaneText (1, (LPCTSTR) lParam, TRUE);
    return 0;
}
```

VistaDoc.h

```
// VistaDoc.h : interface of the CVistaDoc class
//
/////////////////////////////////////////////////////////////////////

#if !defined(
    AFX_VISTADOC_H__3597FEAB_A70E_11D2_8E53_006008A82731__INCLUDED_)
#define AFX_VISTADOC_H__3597FEAB_A70E_11D2_8E53_006008A82731__INCLUDED_

#if _MSC_VER > 1000
#pragma once
#endif // _MSC_VER > 1000


class CVistaDoc : public CDocument
{
protected: // create from serialization only
    CVistaDoc();
    DECLARE_DYNCREATE(CVistaDoc)

// Attributes
public:
```

(continued)

Figure 15-9 *continued*

```
// Operations
public:

// Overrides
    // ClassWizard generated virtual function overrides
    //{{AFX_VIRTUAL(CVistaDoc)
    public:
    virtual BOOL OnNewDocument();
    virtual void Serialize(CArchive& ar);
    virtual BOOL OnOpenDocument(LPCTSTR lpszPathName);
    virtual void DeleteContents();
    //}}AFX_VIRTUAL

// Implementation
public:
    CPalette* GetPalette();
    CBitmap* GetBitmap();
    virtual ~CVistaDoc();
#ifdef _DEBUG
    virtual void AssertValid() const;
    virtual void Dump(CDumpContext& dc) const;
#endif

protected:

// Generated message map functions
protected:
    CPalette m_palette;
    CBitmap m_bitmap;
    //{{AFX_MSG(CVistaDoc)
        // NOTE - the ClassWizard will add and remove member functions here.
        //    DO NOT EDIT what you see in these blocks of generated code !
    //}}AFX_MSG
    DECLARE_MESSAGE_MAP()
};

//////////////////////////////////////////////////////////////////////

//{{AFX_INSERT_LOCATION}}
// Microsoft Visual C++ will insert additional declarations
// immediately before the previous line.

#endif
// !defined(
//    AFX_VISTADOC_H__3597FEAB_A70E_11D2_8E53_006008A82731__INCLUDED_)
```

VistaDoc.cpp

```cpp
// VistaDoc.cpp : implementation of the CVistaDoc class
//

#include "stdafx.h"
#include "Vista.h"

#include "VistaDoc.h"

#ifdef _DEBUG
#define new DEBUG_NEW
#undef THIS_FILE
static char THIS_FILE[] = __FILE__;
#endif

/////////////////////////////////////////////////////////////////////////
// CVistaDoc

IMPLEMENT_DYNCREATE(CVistaDoc, CDocument)

BEGIN_MESSAGE_MAP(CVistaDoc, CDocument)
    //{{AFX_MSG_MAP(CVistaDoc)
        // NOTE - the ClassWizard will add and remove mapping macros here.
        //    DO NOT EDIT what you see in these blocks of generated code!
    //}}AFX_MSG_MAP
END_MESSAGE_MAP()

/////////////////////////////////////////////////////////////////////////
// CVistaDoc construction/destruction

CVistaDoc::CVistaDoc()
{
}

CVistaDoc::~CVistaDoc()
{
}

BOOL CVistaDoc::OnNewDocument()
{
    if (!CDocument::OnNewDocument())
        return FALSE;
    return TRUE;
}
```

(continued)

Figure 15-9 *continued*

```
/////////////////////////////////////////////////////////////////////////
// CVistaDoc serialization

void CVistaDoc::Serialize(CArchive& ar)
{
    if (ar.IsStoring())
    {
        // TODO: add storing code here
    }
    else
    {
        // TODO: add loading code here
    }
}

/////////////////////////////////////////////////////////////////////////
// CVistaDoc diagnostics

#ifdef _DEBUG
void CVistaDoc::AssertValid() const
{
    CDocument::AssertValid();
}

void CVistaDoc::Dump(CDumpContext& dc) const
{
    CDocument::Dump(dc);
}
#endif //_DEBUG

/////////////////////////////////////////////////////////////////////////
// CVistaDoc commands

BOOL CVistaDoc::OnOpenDocument(LPCTSTR lpszPathName)
{
    if (!CDocument::OnOpenDocument (lpszPathName))
        return FALSE;

    //
    // Open the file and create a DIB section from its contents.
    //
    HBITMAP hBitmap = (HBITMAP) ::LoadImage (NULL, lpszPathName,
        IMAGE_BITMAP, 0, 0, LR_LOADFROMFILE | LR_CREATEDIBSECTION);

    if (hBitmap == NULL) {
        CString string;
```

```
        string.Format (_T ("%s does not contain a DIB"), lpszPathName);
        AfxMessageBox (string);
        return FALSE;
    }

    m_bitmap.Attach (hBitmap);

    //
    // Return now if this device doesn't support palettes.
    //
    CClientDC dc (NULL);
    if ((dc.GetDeviceCaps (RASTERCAPS) & RC_PALETTE) == 0)
        return TRUE;

    //
    // Create a palette to go with the DIB section.
    //
    if ((HBITMAP) m_bitmap != NULL) {
        DIBSECTION ds;
        m_bitmap.GetObject (sizeof (DIBSECTION), &ds);

        int nColors;
        if (ds.dsBmih.biClrUsed != 0)
            nColors = ds.dsBmih.biClrUsed;
        else
            nColors = 1 << ds.dsBmih.biBitCount;

        //
        // Create a halftone palette if the DIB section contains more
        // than 256 colors.
        //
        if (nColors > 256)
            m_palette.CreateHalftonePalette (&dc);

        //
        // Create a custom palette from the DIB section's color table
        // if the number of colors is 256 or less.
        //
        else {
            RGBQUAD* pRGB = new RGBQUAD[nColors];

            CDC memDC;
            memDC.CreateCompatibleDC (&dc);
            CBitmap* pOldBitmap = memDC.SelectObject (&m_bitmap);
            ::GetDIBColorTable ((HDC) memDC, 0, nColors, pRGB);
            memDC.SelectObject (pOldBitmap);
```

(continued)

Figure 15-9 *continued*

```
            UINT nSize = sizeof (LOGPALETTE) +
                (sizeof (PALETTEENTRY) * (nColors - 1));
            LOGPALETTE* pLP = (LOGPALETTE*) new BYTE[nSize];

            pLP->palVersion = 0x300;
            pLP->palNumEntries = nColors;

            for (int i=0; i<nColors; i++) {
                pLP->palPalEntry[i].peRed = pRGB[i].rgbRed;
                pLP->palPalEntry[i].peGreen = pRGB[i].rgbGreen;
                pLP->palPalEntry[i].peBlue = pRGB[i].rgbBlue;
                pLP->palPalEntry[i].peFlags = 0;
            }

            m_palette.CreatePalette (pLP);
            delete[] pLP;
            delete[] pRGB;
        }
    }
    return TRUE;
}

void CVistaDoc::DeleteContents()
{
    if ((HBITMAP) m_bitmap != NULL)
        m_bitmap.DeleteObject ();

    if ((HPALETTE) m_palette != NULL)
        m_palette.DeleteObject ();

    CDocument::DeleteContents();
}

CBitmap* CVistaDoc::GetBitmap()
{
    return ((HBITMAP) m_bitmap == NULL) ? NULL : &m_bitmap;
}

CPalette* CVistaDoc::GetPalette()
{
    return ((HPALETTE) m_palette == NULL) ? NULL : &m_palette;
}
```

VistaView.h

```
// VistaView.h : interface of the CVistaView class
//
/////////////////////////////////////////////////////////////////////////

#if !defined(
    AFX_VISTAVIEW_H__3597FEAD_A70E_11D2_8E53_006008A82731__INCLUDED_)
#define AFX_VISTAVIEW_H__3597FEAD_A70E_11D2_8E53_006008A82731__INCLUDED_

#if _MSC_VER > 1000
#pragma once
#endif // _MSC_VER > 1000


class CVistaView : public CScrollView
{
protected: // create from serialization only
    CVistaView();
    DECLARE_DYNCREATE(CVistaView)

// Attributes
public:
    CVistaDoc* GetDocument();

// Operations
public:

// Overrides
    // ClassWizard generated virtual function overrides
    //{{AFX_VIRTUAL(CVistaView)
    public:
    virtual void OnDraw(CDC* pDC);  // overridden to draw this view
    virtual BOOL PreCreateWindow(CREATESTRUCT& cs);
    protected:
    virtual void OnInitialUpdate(); // called first time after construct
    //}}AFX_VIRTUAL

// Implementation
public:
    virtual ~CVistaView();
#ifdef _DEBUG
    virtual void AssertValid() const;
    virtual void Dump(CDumpContext& dc) const;
#endif
```

(continued)

Figure 15-9 *continued*

```
protected:

// Generated message map functions
protected:
    //{{AFX_MSG(CVistaView)
        // NOTE - the ClassWizard will add and remove member functions here.
        //    DO NOT EDIT what you see in these blocks of generated code !
    //}}AFX_MSG
    DECLARE_MESSAGE_MAP()
};

#ifndef _DEBUG  // debug version in VistaView.cpp
inline CVistaDoc* CVistaView::GetDocument()
    { return (CVistaDoc*)m_pDocument; }
#endif


/////////////////////////////////////////////////////////////////////////////

//{{AFX_INSERT_LOCATION}}
// Microsoft Visual C++ will insert additional declarations
// immediately before the previous line.

#endif
// !defined(
//     AFX_VISTAVIEW_H__3597FEAD_A70E_11D2_8E53_006008A82731__INCLUDED_)
```

VistaView.cpp

```
// VistaView.cpp : implementation of the CVistaView class
//

#include "stdafx.h"
#include "Vista.h"

#include "VistaDoc.h"
#include "VistaView.h"

#ifdef _DEBUG
#define new DEBUG_NEW
#undef THIS_FILE
static char THIS_FILE[] = __FILE__;
#endif
```

```
/////////////////////////////////////////////////////////////////////
// CVistaView

IMPLEMENT_DYNCREATE(CVistaView, CScrollView)

BEGIN_MESSAGE_MAP(CVistaView, CScrollView)
    //{{AFX_MSG_MAP(CVistaView)
        // NOTE - the ClassWizard will add and remove mapping macros here.
        //     DO NOT EDIT what you see in these blocks of generated code!
    //}}AFX_MSG_MAP
END_MESSAGE_MAP()

/////////////////////////////////////////////////////////////////////
// CVistaView construction/destruction

CVistaView::CVistaView()
{
}

CVistaView::~CVistaView()
{
}

BOOL CVistaView::PreCreateWindow(CREATESTRUCT& cs)
{
    return CScrollView::PreCreateWindow(cs);
}

/////////////////////////////////////////////////////////////////////
// CVistaView drawing

void CVistaView::OnDraw(CDC* pDC)
{
    CVistaDoc* pDoc = GetDocument();
    ASSERT_VALID(pDoc);

    CBitmap* pBitmap = pDoc->GetBitmap ();

    if (pBitmap != NULL) {
        CPalette* pOldPalette;
        CPalette* pPalette = pDoc->GetPalette ();

        if (pPalette != NULL) {
            pOldPalette = pDC->SelectPalette (pPalette, FALSE);
            pDC->RealizePalette ();
        }
```

(continued)

Figure 15-9 *continued*

```
        DIBSECTION ds;
        pBitmap->GetObject (sizeof (DIBSECTION), &ds);

        CDC memDC;
        memDC.CreateCompatibleDC (pDC);
        CBitmap* pOldBitmap = memDC.SelectObject (pBitmap);

        pDC->BitBlt (0, 0, ds.dsBm.bmWidth, ds.dsBm.bmHeight, &memDC,
            0, 0, SRCCOPY);

        memDC.SelectObject (pOldBitmap);

        if (pPalette != NULL)
            pDC->SelectPalette (pOldPalette, FALSE);
    }
}

void CVistaView::OnInitialUpdate()
{
    CScrollView::OnInitialUpdate ();

    CString string;
    CSize sizeTotal;
    CBitmap* pBitmap = GetDocument ()->GetBitmap ();

    //
    // If a bitmap is loaded, set the view size equal to the bitmap size.
    // Otherwise, set the view's width and height to 0.
    //
    if (pBitmap != NULL) {
        DIBSECTION ds;
        pBitmap->GetObject (sizeof (DIBSECTION), &ds);
        sizeTotal.cx = ds.dsBm.bmWidth;
        sizeTotal.cy = ds.dsBm.bmHeight;
        string.Format (_T ("\t%d x %d, %d bpp"), ds.dsBm.bmWidth,
            ds.dsBm.bmHeight, ds.dsBmih.biBitCount);
    }
    else {
        sizeTotal.cx = sizeTotal.cy = 0;
        string.Empty ();
    }

    AfxGetMainWnd ()->SendMessage (WM_USER_UPDATE_STATS, 0,
        (LPARAM) (LPCTSTR) string);
    SetScrollSizes (MM_TEXT, sizeTotal);
}
```

```
/////////////////////////////////////////////////////////////////////////
// CVistaView diagnostics

#ifdef _DEBUG
void CVistaView::AssertValid() const
{
    CScrollView::AssertValid();
}

void CVistaView::Dump(CDumpContext& dc) const
{
    CScrollView::Dump(dc);
}

CVistaDoc* CVistaView::GetDocument() // non-debug version is inline
{
    ASSERT(m_pDocument->IsKindOf(RUNTIME_CLASS(CVistaDoc)));
    return (CVistaDoc*)m_pDocument;
}
#endif //_DEBUG


/////////////////////////////////////////////////////////////////////////
// CVistaView message handlers
```

More on the *::LoadImage* Function

One reason Vista can do so much with so little code is that the *::LoadImage* function
allows a DIB section to be built from a BMP file with just one statement. Here's that
statement again:

```
HBITMAP hBitmap = (HBITMAP) ::LoadImage (NULL, lpszPathName,
    IMAGE_BITMAP, 0, 0, LR_LOADFROMFILE | LR_CREATEDIBSECTION);
```

::LoadImage is to DIB sections what *::LoadBitmap* and *CDC::LoadBitmap* are to DDBs.
But it's also much more. I won't rehash all the input values it accepts because you
can get that from the documentation, but here's a short summary of some of the things
you can do with *::LoadImage*:

- Load bitmap resources, and create DDBs and DIB sections from them.

- Load bitmaps stored in BMP files, and create DDBs and DIB sections from
  them.

- Automatically convert three shades of gray (RGB (128, 128, 128), RGB
  (192, 192, 192), and RGB (223, 223, 223)) to the system colors
  COLOR_3DSHADOW, COLOR_3DFACE, and COLOR_3DLIGHT as an
  image is loaded.

■ Automatically convert the color of the pixel in the upper left corner of the bitmap to the system color COLOR_WINDOW or COLOR_3DFACE so that the pixel and others like it will be invisible against a COLOR_WINDOW or COLOR_3DFACE background.

■ Convert a color image to monochrome.

Keep in mind that *::LoadImage*'s color-mapping capabilities work only with images that contain 256 or fewer colors. DIBs with 256 or fewer colors contain built-in color tables that make color mapping fast and efficient. Rather than examine every pixel in the image to perform a color conversion, *::LoadImage* simply modifies the color table.

Vista demonstrates how *::LoadImage* can be used to create a DIB section from a BMP file and attach it to a *CBitmap* object. One advantage of loading a bitmap as a DIB section instead of as an ordinary DDB is that you can call functions such as *::GetDIBColorTable* on it. Had the LR_CREATEDIBSECTION flag been omitted from the call to *::LoadImage*, we would have been unable to access the bitmap's color table and create a logical palette from it. In general, your applications will port more easily to future versions of Windows (and probably perform better, too) if you now start using DIB sections instead of DDBs whenever possible.

REGIONS

MFC's *CRect* class represents rectangles—simple regions of space enclosed by four boundaries aligned at right angles. More complex regions of space can be represented with the *CRgn* class, which encapsulates GDI objects called, appropriately enough, *regions*. The most common use for regions is to create complex patterns that serve as clipping boundaries for GDI drawing functions. But you can use *CRgn* in other ways, too. Here's a brief look at regions and some of the interesting things that you can do with them.

Regions and the *CRgn* Class

CRgn provides functions for creating geometrically shaped regions, combining existing regions to create more complex regions, and performing certain operations such as hit-testing a region or retrieving a region's bounding rectangle. The *CDC* class provides tools for drawing with a region once it's created—for example, filling a region with a brush color or using it to clip other drawing operations. Let's see first how regions are created. Then we'll look at the *CDC* functions that act on regions and finish up by building a sample program that uses regions to generate some rather unusual output.

Creating Regions

After a *CRgn* object is constructed, a region is created and attached to it by calling one of several member functions the *CRgn* class provides for region creation. The pertinent *CRgn* functions are summarized in the following table.

CRGN REGION-CREATION FUNCTIONS

Function	Description
CreateRectRgn	Creates a rectangular region from a set of coordinates
CreateRectRgnIndirect	Creates a rectangular region from a RECT structure or a *CRect* object
CreateEllipticRgn	Creates an elliptical region from a set of coordinates
CreateEllipticRgnIndirect	Creates an elliptical region from a RECT structure or a *CRect* object
CreateRoundRectRgn	Creates a rectangular region with rounded corners
CreatePolygonRgn	Creates a polygonal region from a set of points
CreatePolyPolygonRgn	Creates a region composed of multiple polygons from a set of points
CreateFromPath	Creates a region from a path
CreateFromData	Creates a region by applying two-dimensional coordinate transformations to an existing region
CopyRgn	Creates a region that is a copy of an existing region

The use of most of these functions is straightforward. For example, to create an elliptical region from a *CRect* object named *rect* that defines a bounding box, you can write

```
CRgn rgn;
rgn.CreateEllipticRgnIndirect(&rect);
```

To create a rectangular region with rounded corners, you'd do it this way instead:

```
CRgn rgn;
rgn.CreateRoundRectRgn (rect.left, rect.top, rect.right,
    rect.bottom, nCornerWidth, nCornerHeight);
```

nCornerWidth and *nCornerHeight* represent the horizontal and vertical dimensions, respectively, of the ellipses used to round the corners. All coordinates passed to functions that create regions are logical coordinates. Like other GDI objects, a region must be deleted when it's no longer needed. Creating a *CRgn* on the stack makes destruction automatic because when a *CRgn* goes out of scope it destroys the GDI region it's attached to.

One of the most powerful region-creation functions is *CRgn::CreateFromPath*, which converts the device context's current path into a region. A *path* is an outline generated by bracketing calls to other GDI drawing functions between calls to *CDC-::BeginPath* and *CDC::EndPath*. The following statements generate a simple elliptical path and convert it into a region:

```
dc.BeginPath ();                    // Define a path.
dc.Ellipse (0, 0, 400, 200);
dc.EndPath ();

CRgn rgn;                           // Convert the path into a region.
rgn.CreateFromPath (&dc);
```

There's nothing remarkable about this code because you could do the same thing by simply calling *CRgn::CreateEllipticRgn*. But what's cool about *CreateFromPath* is that you can create paths from more complex objects such as Bézier curves and text outlines. The following statements create a region from the characters in the text string "Hello, MFC":

```
dc.BeginPath ();
dc.TextOut (0, 0, CString (_T ("Hello, MFC")));
dc.EndPath ();
```

Once created, the path can be converted into a region with *CRgn::CreateFromPath*. *Ellipse* and *TextOut* are but two of several *CDC* drawing functions that work with *BeginPath* and *EndPath*; for a complete list, refer to the MFC documentation for the API function *::BeginPath*. (The subset of GDI drawing functions that can be used to generate paths varies slightly between Windows 95 and Windows 98 and Windows NT and Windows 2000, so watch out.) You can also use paths in ways unrelated to regions. To learn about the drawing operations you can perform with paths, see the MFC documentation for the *CDC* functions *FillPath*, *StrokePath*, *StrokeAndFillPath*, and *WidenPath*.

Another way to create complex regions is to combine existing regions with *CRgn::CombineRgn*. *CombineRgn* accepts three parameters: *CRgn* pointers to the two regions to be combined (region 1 and region 2) and an integer value specifying the combine mode. The combine mode can be any one of the five values listed here:

Mode	*Description*
RGN_COPY	Sets the region equal to region 1
RGN_AND	Sets the region equal to the intersection of regions 1 and 2
RGN_OR	Sets the region equal to the union of regions 1 and 2
RGN_DIFF	Sets the region equal to the area bounded by region 1 minus the area bounded by region 2
RGN_XOR	Sets the region equal to the nonoverlapping areas of regions 1 and 2

The combine mode tells the GDI what Boolean operations to use to combine the regions. The statements

```
CRgn rgn1, rgn2, rgn3;
rgn1.CreateEllipticRgn (0, 0, 100, 100);
rgn2.CreateEllipticRgn (40, 40, 60, 60);
rgn3.CreateRectRgn (0, 0, 1, 1);
rgn3.CombineRgn (&rgn1, &rgn2, RGN_DIFF);
```

create a donut-shaped region consisting of a circle with a hole in the middle. Note that *CombineRgn* can't be called until the region it's called for is created by some other means (that is, until there's an HRGN to go with the *CRgn*). That's why this example calls *CreateRectRgn* to create a trivial rectangular region for *rgn3* before calling *CombineRgn*.

Using Regions

Just what can you do with a region after it's created? To start with, the following *CDC* drawing functions use regions:

- *CDC::FillRgn* fills a region using a specified brush.

- *CDC::PaintRgn* fills a region using the current brush.

- *CDC::InvertRgn* inverts the colors in a region.

- *CDC::FrameRgn* borders a region with a specified brush.

You can also invalidate a region with *CWnd::InvalidateRgn*. Internally, Windows uses regions rather than rectangles to track the invalid areas of a window. When you call *CDC::GetClipBox*, what you get back is a rectangle that bounds the window's invalid region. That region could be a simple rectangle, or it could be something much more complex.

You can perform hit-testing in regions with *CRgn::PtInRegion*. Let's say you create an elliptical region that's centered in a window's client area. You used *PaintRgn* or *FillRgn* to paint the region a different color from the window background color, and now you want to know when the user clicks the left mouse button inside the ellipse. If *m_rgn* is the *CRgn* object, here's what the *OnLButtonDown* handler might look like:

```
void CMyWindow::OnLButtonDown (UINT nFlags, CPoint point)
{
    CClientDC dc (this);
    dc.DPtoLP (&point); // Convert to logical coordinates.
    if (m_rgn.PtInRegion (point)) {
        // The point falls within the region.
    }
}
```

MFC's *CRect* class provides an analogous function for rectangles: *PtInRect*. In fact, there are many parallels in the API (and in MFC member functions) between regions and rectangles: *InvalidateRect* and *InvalidateRgn*, *FillRect* and *FillRgn*, and so on. Rectangle functions are faster, so when possible you should avoid using region functions to operate on simple rectangles and use the equivalent rectangle functions instead.

Regions really pay off when you use them as clipping boundaries for complex graphic images. A region can be selected into a device context with *CDC::SelectObject* or *CDC::SelectClipRgn*. Once selected, the region serves as a clipping boundary for all subsequent output to the device context. The RegionDemo application in the next section uses a clipping region to create an image that would be murderously difficult to draw by other means. But with a region acting as a virtual stencil for graphics output, the image is relatively easy to render. The drawback to complex clipping regions is that they're slow. But sometimes using a clipping region is the only practical way to get the output you're looking for. If you want to use a path as a clipping region, you don't have to convert it into a region and then select it into a device context. You can select the path directly into the device context with *CDC::SelectClipPath*.

One of the more imaginative uses for a region is to pass it to the *CWnd::SetWindowRgn* function so that it becomes a window region. A *window region* is a clipping region for an entire window. Windows doesn't allow anything outside the window region to be painted, including title bars and other nonclient-area window elements. Create an elliptical region and pass its handle to *SetWindowRgn*, and you'll get an elliptical window. If the window is a top-level window and its title bar is hidden from view, use an *OnNcHitTest* handler to convert HTCLIENT hit-test codes into HTCAPTION codes so that the window can be dragged by its client area. A more practical use for nonrectangular window regions is to create stylized text bubbles that are actually windows and that receive messages just as other windows do. With *SetWindowRgn* to assist you, it's not terribly difficult to create a popup window class that displays help text in a window shaped like a thought balloon and that automatically destroys itself when it's clicked.

The RegionDemo Application

Figure 15-10 shows the output from an application named RegionDemo, which uses a clipping region to draw a radial array of lines forming the words "Hello, MFC." The clipping region is generated from a path, and the path, in turn, is generated by calling *CDC::TextOut* between calls to *CDC::BeginPath* and *CDC::EndPath*. All the work is done in *OnPaint*. Look over the source code in Figure 15-11; it should be pretty apparent what's going on in each phase of the output, with the possible exception of the code that uses two different *CRgn* objects and various calls to *CRgn* member functions to generate the final clipping region (*rgn1*) that is selected into the device context with *CDC::SelectClipRgn*.

Figure 15-10. *The RegionDemo window.*

RegionDemo.h

```
class CMyApp : public CWinApp
{
public:
    virtual BOOL InitInstance ();
};

class CMainWindow : public CFrameWnd
{
public:
    CMainWindow ();

protected:
    afx_msg void OnPaint ();
    DECLARE_MESSAGE_MAP ()
};
```

RegionDemo.cpp

```
#include <afxwin.h>
#include <math.h>
#include "RegionDemo.h"
```

Figure 15-11. *The RegionDemo application.* *(continued)*

Figure 15-11 *continued*

```
CMyApp myApp;

/////////////////////////////////////////////////////////////////////////
// CMyApp member functions

BOOL CMyApp::InitInstance ()
{
    m_pMainWnd = new CMainWindow;
    m_pMainWnd->ShowWindow (m_nCmdShow);
    m_pMainWnd->UpdateWindow ();
    return TRUE;
}


/////////////////////////////////////////////////////////////////////////
// CMainWindow message map and member functions

BEGIN_MESSAGE_MAP (CMainWindow, CFrameWnd)
    ON_WM_PAINT ()
END_MESSAGE_MAP ()

CMainWindow::CMainWindow ()
{
    Create (NULL, _T ("Region Demo"));
}

void CMainWindow::OnPaint ()
{
    CPaintDC dc (this);

    //
    // Create a 72-point Times New Roman font.
    //
    CFont font;
    font.CreatePointFont (720, _T ("Times New Roman"));

    //
    // Create a clipping region from the text string "Hello, MFC."
    //
    CRect rect;
    GetClientRect (&rect);
    CString string ("Hello, MFC");

    CFont* pOldFont = dc.SelectObject (&font);
    CSize size = dc.GetTextExtent (string);
    int x = (rect.Width () - size.cx) / 2;
```

```
TEXTMETRIC tm;
dc.GetTextMetrics (&tm);
int y = (rect.Height () - tm.tmHeight) / 2;

dc.BeginPath ();
dc.TextOut (x, y, string);
dc.EndPath ();
dc.SelectObject (pOldFont);

CRect rcText;
CRgn rgn1, rgn2;
rgn1.CreateFromPath (&dc);
rgn1.GetRgnBox (&rcText);
rgn2.CreateRectRgnIndirect (&rcText);
rgn1.CombineRgn (&rgn2, &rgn1, RGN_DIFF);

dc.SelectClipRgn (&rgn1);

//
// Draw a radial array of lines.
//
dc.SetViewportOrg (rect.Width () / 2, rect.Height () / 2);
double fRadius = hypot (rect.Width () / 2, rect.Height () / 2);

for (double fAngle = 0.0; fAngle < 6.283; fAngle += 0.01745) {
    dc.MoveTo (0, 0);
    dc.LineTo ((int) ((fRadius * cos (fAngle)) + 0.5),
        (int) ((fRadius * sin (fAngle)) + 0.5));
}
}
```

Here's a blow-by-blow analysis of the code that creates the clipping region after the path outlining the characters in the text string is created. The statement

```
rgn1.CreateFromPath (&dc);
```

initializes *rgn1* with a region that matches the path. Figure 15-12 shows what this first region looks like. The interior of the region is a rectangle with the outline of the letters "Hello, MFC" stamped out in the middle. (Some graphics systems—notably PostScript—handle paths generated from character outlines differently by making the interiors of the regions the interiors of the characters themselves. The GDI does essentially the opposite, creating a region from the characters' bounding box and then subtracting the areas enclosed by the character outlines.) Next, the statements

```
rgn1.GetRgnBox (&rcText);
rgn2.CreateRectRgnIndirect (&rcText);
```

copy *rgn1*'s bounding box to a *CRect* object named *rcText* and create a region (*rgn2*)

Hello, MFC

Figure 15-12. *The path generated from the text string "Hello, MFC."*

from it. The final statement effectively inverts *rgn1* by subtracting *rgn1* from *rgn2*:

```
rgn1.CombineRgn (&rgn2, &rgn1, RGN_DIFF);
```

The resulting region is one whose interior exactly matches the insides of the characters drawn by *TextOut*. After the region is selected into the device context, a radial array of lines is drawn outward at 1-degree increments from the center of the window's client area. Because the lines are clipped to the boundaries of the region, nothing is drawn outside the character outlines.

You could make RegionDemo slightly more efficient by moving the code that generates the region out of *OnPaint* and into *OnCreate*. The region would no longer have to be generated anew each time the window is repainted, but it would need to be repositioned with *CRgn::OffsetRgn* to keep it centered. Eliminating redundant calls to *CRgn* functions improves the speed of the output somewhat, but the biggest performance hit still comes when the lines drawn on the screen are clipped to the region's boundaries. That complex clipping regions exact a price in performance is a fact of life in computer graphics, so it's wise to avoid using nonrectangular clipping regions except in cases in which there's no reasonable alternative.

Chapter 16

The Common Controls

Since version 1.0, Microsoft Windows has provided a core set of controls that includes push buttons, radio buttons, list boxes, and other common user interface (UI) objects. Windows 95 and Windows NT 3.51 expanded the selection of controls available by including 15 new control types in a DLL named Comctl32.dll. Collectively known as the *common controls,* these controls run the gamut from simple progress controls, which provide graphical feedback regarding the progress of ongoing operations, to richer and more complex tree view controls, which present hierarchical views of data in treelike structures whose branches expand and collapse in response to mouse clicks. Microsoft Internet Explorer adds even more controls to Comctl32.dll, bringing the total number of common controls supported on today's platforms to 20. The suite of controls provided by Internet Explorer includes controls for selecting dates and times, entering Internet Protocol (IP) addresses, and more.

Common controls are used throughout Windows and are an important part of the operating system's look and feel. Figure 16-1 shows how Windows uses some of the common controls. The header control in the Explorer window is a part of the list view control, but header controls can also be created apart from list views. The magnifying glass that moves in a circle while Find performs a search is an animation control. So are the pieces of paper that fly across the screen when files are moved, copied, or deleted. As you'll see later, animation controls make it easy to display simple animations by playing back sequences recorded in Windows Audio Video Interleaved (AVI) format.

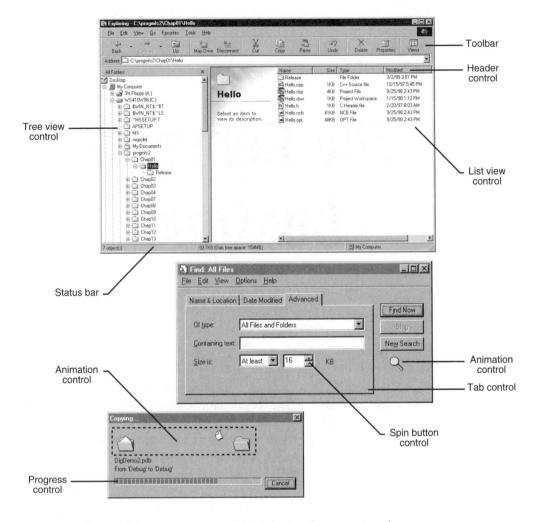

Figure 16-1. *Common controls and the Windows user interface.*

In this chapter, I'll introduce the common controls and their MFC interfaces. I'll begin with an overview of the common controls and then explain how they're created and the unique way in which they send notifications to their parents. After that, we'll examine several of the common controls in detail and go over sample code demonstrating their use.

COMMON CONTROL FUNDAMENTALS

MFC provides classes to wrap the common controls just as it provides classes to wrap the core control types implemented in User.exe. The following table shows the 20 types of common controls, the WNDCLASSes on which they're based, and the

THE COMMON CONTROLS

Control Type	*WNDCLASS*	*WNDCLASS Alias*	*MFC Class*
Animation	"SysAnimate32"	ANIMATE_CLASS	*CAnimateCtrl*
ComboBoxEx*	"ComboBoxEx32"	WC_COMBOBOXEX	*CComboBoxEx*
Date-Time*	"SysDateTimePick32"	DATETIMEPICK_CLASS	*CDateTimeCtrl*
Header	"SysHeader32"	WC_HEADER	*CHeaderCtrl*
Hotkey	"msctls_hotkey32"	HOTKEY_CLASS	*CHotKeyCtrl*
Image list	N/A	N/A	*CImageList*
IP address**	"SysIPAddress32"	WC_IPADDRESS	*CIPAddressCtrl*
List view	"SysListView32"	WC_LISTVIEW	*CListCtrl*
Month calendar*	"SysMonthCal32"	MONTHCAL_CLASS	*CMonthCalCtrl*
Progress	"msctls_progress32"	PROGRESS_CLASS	*CProgressCtrl*
Property sheet	N/A	N/A	*CPropertySheet*
Rebar*	"ReBarWindow32"	REBARCLASSNAME	*CReBarCtrl*
Rich edit	"RichEdit20A" (ANSI) or "RichEdit20W" (Unicode)	RICHEDIT_CLASS	*CRichEditCtrl*
Slider	"msctls_trackbar32"	TRACKBAR_CLASS	*CSliderCtrl*
Spin button	"msctls_updown32"	UPDOWN_CLASS	*CSpinButtonCtrl*
Status bar	"msctls_statusbar32"	STATUSCLASSNAME	*CStatusBarCtrl*
Tab	"SysTabControl32"	WC_TABCONTROL	*CTabCtrl*
Toolbar	"ToolbarWindow32"	TOOLBARCLASSNAME	*CToolBarCtrl*
ToolTip	"tooltips_class32"	TOOLTIPS_CLASS	*CToolTipCtrl*
Tree view	"SysTreeView32"	WC_TREEVIEW	*CTreeCtrl*

* Requires Internet Explorer 3.0 or later

** Requires Internet Explorer 4.0 or later

corresponding MFC classes. It also shows aliases for those WNDCLASSes defined in the header file Commctrl.h. Image lists and property sheets don't have WNDCLASSes because they're not controls in the strict sense of the word, but they're nearly always counted among the common controls because their code resides in Comctl32.dll. You'll sometimes see drag list boxes shown with the common controls. I didn't include them here because drag list boxes aren't stand-alone controls; they're conventional list boxes that are converted into "drag" list boxes by a function in Comctl32.dll. MFC provides a convenient implementation of drag list boxes in *CDragListBox*, so for more information, see the documentation for *CDragListBox*.

As you can see from the table, some of the common controls are only supported on systems that have a particular version of Internet Explorer installed. That's because when you install Internet Explorer, the setup program silently upgrades Comctl32.dll, too. Many times in this chapter I'll say something like "This style is only supported on systems equipped with Internet Explorer 3.0 or later" or "This feature requires Internet Explorer 4.0." In truth, it's not Internet Explorer that's required but the version of Comctl32.dll that comes with that version of Internet Explorer. Because installing a more recent version of Internet Explorer is presently the only legal way to get the latest version of Comctl32.dll, Internet Explorer is a reasonable basis for documenting version dependencies.

Given the common controls' myriad dependencies on the version of Comctl32.dll that's installed and the fact that some systems don't have Internet Explorer installed at all, you might wonder how to determine at run time whether a given feature is supported provided that you know what version of Comctl32.dll it requires. Here's a simple routine that returns Comctl32.dll's major and minor version numbers. It returns 4.0 if the Comctl32.dll installed on the host system is one that predates Internet Explorer 3.0, and 0.0 if Comctl32.dll isn't installed at all:

```
void GetComctlVersion(DWORD &dwMajor, DWORD &dwMinor)
{
    dwMajor = dwMinor = 0;
    HINSTANCE hLib = ::LoadLibrary (_T ("Comctl32.dll"));
    if (hLib != NULL) {
        DLLGETVERSIONPROC pDllGetVersion =
            (DLLGETVERSIONPROC) ::GetProcAddress (hLib, _T ("DllGetVersion"));
        if (pDllGetVersion) { // IE 3.0 or higher
            DLLVERSIONINFO dvi;
            ::ZeroMemory (&dvi, sizeof (dvi));
            dvi.cbSize = sizeof (dvi);
            HRESULT hr = (*pDllGetVersion) (&dvi);
            if (SUCCEEDED (hr)) {
                dwMajor = dvi.dwMajorVersion;
                dwMinor = dvi.dwMinorVersion;
            }
        }
        else { // Pre-IE 3.0
            dwMajor = 4;
            dwMinor = 0;
        }
        ::FreeLibrary (hLib);
    }
}
```

You also need a way to translate Internet Explorer version numbers into Comctl32.dll version numbers. Here's a table that will help:

Internet Explorer Version	Comctl32.dll Version
3.0	4.70
4.0	4.71
4.01	4.72

Now if I say that a certain feature requires Internet Explorer 3.0 or later and you want to determine at run time whether that feature is supported, you can do this:

```
DWORD dwMajor, dwMinor;
GetComctlVersion (dwMajor, dwMinor);
if ((dwMajor == 4 && dwMinor >= 70) !! dwMajor > 4) {
    // The feature is supported.
}
else {
    // The feature is not supported.
}
```

Yes, it's ugly. But it's the only option currently available.

Creating a Common Control

There are two ways to create a common control without resorting to API functions. The first method is to instantiate the corresponding MFC control class and call the resulting object's *Create* function, as demonstrated here:

```
#include <afxcmn.h>
    .
    .
    .

CProgressCtrl wndProgress;
wndProgress.Create (WS_CHILD ! WS_VISIBLE ! WS_BORDER,
    CRect (x1, y1, x2, y2), this, IDC_PROGRESS);
```

The header file Afxcmn.h contains the declarations for *CProgressCtrl* and other common control classes. The second method is to add a CONTROL statement to a dialog template. When the dialog box is created, the control is created, too. The following CONTROL statement creates a progress control in a dialog box:

```
CONTROL "", IDC_PROGRESS, PROGRESS_CLASS, WS_BORDER, 32, 32, 80, 16
```

When you create a common control this way, you can specify either the literal WNDCLASS name or its alias, whichever you prefer. The Visual C++ dialog editor writes CONTROL statements for you when you use it to add common controls to a dialog box.

Most of the common controls support their own window styles, which you can combine with WS_CHILD, WS_VISIBLE, and other standard window styles. The table on the following page shows the "generic" common control styles that, at least in theory, aren't specific to any particular control type. As an MFC programmer, you'll rarely have occasion to manipulate these styles directly because many of them apply only to toolbars and status bars, and if you use *CToolBar* and *CStatusBar* instead of the more primitive *CToolBarCtrl* and *CStatusBarCtrl* classes to implement toolbars and status bars, the appropriate CCS styles are built in. These are by no means all the styles you can use with common controls. I'll point out control-specific styles when we examine individual control types.

COMMON CONTROL STYLES

Style	Description
CCS_TOP	Positions the control at the top of its parent's client area and matches the control's width to the width of its parent. Toolbars have this style by default.
CCS_BOTTOM	Positions the control at the bottom of its parent's client area and matches the control's width to the width of its parent. Status bars have this style by default.
CCS_LEFT*	Positions the control at the left end of its parent's client area.
CCS_RIGHT*	Positions the control at the right end of its parent's client area.
CCS_VERT*	Orients the control vertically rather than horizontally.
CCS_NOMOVEX*	Causes the control to resize and move itself vertically but not horizontally when its parent is resized.
CCS_NOMOVEY	Causes the control to resize and move itself horizontally but not vertically when its parent is resized. Header controls have this style by default.
CCS_NORESIZE	Prevents the control from resizing itself when the size of its parent changes. If this style is specified, the control assumes the width and height specified in the control rectangle.
CCS_NOPARENTALIGN	Prevents the control from sticking to the top or bottom of its parent's client area. A control with this style retains its position relative to the upper left corner of its parent's client area. If this style is combined with CCS_TOP or CCS_BOTTOM, the control assumes a default height but its width and position don't change when its parent is resized.
CCS_NODIVIDER	Eliminates the divider drawn at the top of a toolbar control.
CCS_ADJUSTABLE	Enables a toolbar control's built-in customization features. Double-clicking a toolbar of this type displays a Customize Toolbar dialog box.

* Requires Internet Explorer 3.0 or later

Once you've created a common control, you manipulate it using member functions of the corresponding control class. For controls created from dialog templates, you can use any of the techniques described in Chapter 8 to manufacture type-specific references for accessing a control's function and data members. For example, the following statement links a *CProgressCtrl* member variable named *m_wndProgress* to the progress control whose ID is IDC_PROGRESS:

```
DDX_Control (pDX, IDC_PROGRESS, m_wndProgress);
```

This statement must appear in a dialog class's *DoDataExchange* function. Rather than add the statement manually, you can use ClassWizard if you'd like. See Chapter 8 for a description of how to use ClassWizard to bind a member variable in a dialog class to a control in the dialog box.

When you use the common controls in an SDK-style application, you must call either *::InitCommonControls* or the newer *::InitCommonControlsEx* to load Comctl32.dll and register the controls' WNDCLASSes before creating the first control. In an MFC application, MFC calls these functions for you. It first tries to call *::InitCommonControlsEx*. If the attempt fails because Internet Explorer 3.0 or later isn't installed (Internet Explorer adds *::InitCommonControlsEx* to the Win32 API), MFC falls back and calls *::InitCommonControls*, which is supported on any system running Windows 95 or higher or Windows NT 3.51 or higher.

MFC calls *::InitCommonControls(Ex)* whenever a dialog box is created or a common control class's *Create* function is called. If for some reason you decide to create a common control or a dialog box that contains a common control using the Windows API instead of MFC, or if you create a common control with *CreateEx* instead of *Create*, you should call *::InitCommonControls* or *::InitCommonControlsEx* yourself. A good place to do that is in the main window's *OnCreate* handler or *InitInstance*, although you can defer the call until just before the control or dialog box is created if you'd prefer. It's not harmful to call *::InitCommonControls(Ex)* multiple times during an application's lifetime.

Processing Notifications: The WM_NOTIFY Message

Unlike the classic controls, which send notifications to their parents using WM_COMMAND messages, most common controls package their notifications in WM_NOTIFY messages. A WM_NOTIFY message's *wParam* holds the child window ID of the control that sent the message, and *lParam* holds a pointer to either an NMHDR structure or a structure that's a superset of NMHDR. NMHDR is defined as follows:

```
typedef struct tagNMHDR {
    HWND hwndFrom;
    UINT idFrom;
    UINT code;
} NMHDR;
```

hwndFrom holds the control's window handle, *idFrom* holds the control ID (the same value that's passed in *wParam*), and *code* specifies the notification code. The following notifications are transmitted by virtually all of the common controls.

Notification	*Sent When*
NM_CLICK	The control is clicked with the left mouse button.
NM_DBLCLK	The control is double-clicked with the left mouse button.
NM_RCLICK	The control is clicked with the right mouse button.
NM_RDBLCLK	The control is double-clicked with the right mouse button.
NM_RETURN	The Enter key is pressed while the control has the input focus.
NM_KILLFOCUS	The control loses the input focus.
NM_SETFOCUS	The control gains the input focus.
NM_OUTOFMEMORY	An operation on the control has failed because of insufficient memory.

Systems on which Internet Explorer 3.0 or later is installed support a richer assortment of NM notifications. For example, certain control types, including some of the original common controls that aren't unique to Internet Explorer but that are enhanced when Internet Explorer is installed, send NM_CUSTOMDRAW notifications so that their owners can customize their appearance. Others send NM_SETCURSOR notifications that their owners can use to apply custom cursors. The documentation for individual controls notes the "special" NM notifications, if any, that the controls send.

Most common controls define additional notification codes to signify control-specific events. For example, a tree view control notifies its parent when a subtree is expanded by sending it a WM_NOTIFY message with *code* equal to TVN_ITEM-EXPANDED. *lParam* points to an NM_TREEVIEW structure, which contains the following data members:

```
typedef struct _NM_TREEVIEW {
    NMHDR    hdr;
    UINT     action;
    TV_ITEM  itemOld;
    TV_ITEM  itemNew;
    POINT    ptDrag;
} NM_TREEVIEW;
```

Notice that the structure's first member is an NMHDR structure, making NM_TREEVIEW a functional superset of NMHDR. The type of structure *lParam* points to depends on the type of control the notification came from. It sometimes even depends on the notification code. For instance, the *lParam* accompanying a TVN_GETDISPINFO notification from a tree view control points to a TV_DISPINFO structure, which is defined differently than NM_TREEVIEW is:

```
typedef struct _TV_DISPINFO {
    NMHDR   hdr;
    TV_ITEM item;
} TV_DISPINFO;
```

How do you know what kind of pointer to cast *lParam* to? You start by casting to an NMHDR pointer and examining the notification code. Then, if necessary, you can recast to a more specific pointer type, as demonstrated here:

```
NMHDR* pnmh = (NMHDR*) lParam;
switch (pnmh->code) {

case TVN_ITEMEXPANDED:
    NM_TREEVIEW* pnmtv = (NM_TREEVIEW*) pnmh;
    // Process the notification.
    break;

case TVN_GETDISPINFO:
    NM_DISPINFO* pnmdi = (NM_DISPINFO*) pnmh;
    // Process the notification.
    break;
}
```

If the window that processes these notifications contains two or more tree view controls, it can examine the *hwndFrom* or *idFrom* field of the NMHDR structure to determine which control sent the notification.

switch statements like the one above are usually unnecessary in MFC applications, because notifications encapsulated in WM_NOTIFY messages are mapped to class member functions with ON_NOTIFY and ON_NOTIFY_RANGE macros. In addition, WM_NOTIFY notifications can be reflected to derived control classes using ON_NOTIFY_REFLECT. (MFC also supports extended forms of these macros named ON_NOTIFY_EX, ON_NOTIFY_EX_RANGE, and ON_NOTIFY_REFLECT_EX.) The following message-map entries map TVN_ITEMEXPANDED and TVN_GETDISPINFO notifications from a tree view control whose ID is IDC_TREEVIEW to handling functions named *OnItemExpanded* and *OnGetDispInfo*:

```
ON_NOTIFY (TVN_ITEMEXPANDED, IDC_TREEVIEW, OnItemExpanded)
ON_NOTIFY (TVN_GETDISPINFO, IDC_TREEVIEW, OnGetDispInfo)
```

Casting to specific pointer types is performed inside the notification handlers:

```
void CMyWindow::OnItemExpanded (NMHDR* pnmh, LRESULT* pResult)
{
    NM_TREEVIEW* pnmtv = (NM_TREEVIEW*) pnmh;
    // Process the notification.
}
```

(continued)

```
void CMyWindow::OnGetDispInfo (NMHDR* pnmh, LRESULT* pResult)
{
    NM_DISPINFO* pnmdi = (NM_DISPINFO*) pnmh;
    // Process the notification.
}
```

The *pnmh* parameter passed to an ON_NOTIFY handler is identical to the WM-_NOTIFY message's *lParam*. The *pResult* parameter points to a 32-bit LRESULT variable that receives the handler's return value. Many notifications attach no meaning to the return value, in which case the handler can safely ignore *pResult*. But sometimes what happens after the handler returns depends on the value of *pResult*. For example, you can prevent branches of a tree view control from being expanded by processing TVN_ITEMEXPANDING notifications and setting *pResult* to a nonzero value. A 0 return value, on the other hand, allows the expansion to occur:

```
// In the message map
ON_NOTIFY (TVN_ITEMEXPANDING, IDC_TREEVIEW, OnItemExpanding)
        :
        :
void OnItemExpanding (NMHDR* pnmh, LRESULT* pResult)
{
    NM_TREEVIEW* pnmtv = (NM_TREEVIEW*) pnmh;
    if (...) {
        *pResult = TRUE; // Under certain conditions, prevent
        return;          // the expansion from taking place.
    }
    *pResult = 0;        // Allow the expansion to proceed.
}
```

A TVN_ITEMEXPANDING notification differs from a TVN_ITEMEXPANDED notification in that it is sent *before* an item in a tree view control is expanded, not after. As with the standard control types, you can ignore notifications you're not interested in and process only those that are meaningful to your application. Windows provides appropriate default responses for unhandled notifications.

SLIDER, SPIN BUTTON, AND TOOLTIP CONTROLS

Now that you're familiar with the general characteristics of the common controls, let's look at specifics for a few of the control types. We'll start with sliders, spin buttons, and ToolTip controls, which are all relatively simple to program and which are also generic enough that they can be put to use in a variety of applications. After we've looked at these controls and the corresponding MFC control classes, we'll write a sample program that uses a slider control and a pair of spin buttons in a dialog box and also uses a ToolTip control to provide context-sensitive help. Rather than use a raw *CToolTipCtrl* to implement the ToolTip control, we'll use *CToolTipCtrl* as a base class for a class of our own and add a pair of handy member functions that correct a rather severe deficiency in MFC's ToolTip implementation.

Slider Controls

Slider controls, also known as *trackbar controls,* are similar to the sliding volume controls found on many radios and stereo systems. A slider has a thumb that moves like the thumb in a scroll bar. After you create a slider, you set the minimum and maximum values representing the extremes of the thumb's travel and optionally set the initial thumb position. The user can then reposition the thumb by dragging it with the left mouse button or clicking the channel in which the thumb slides. When a slider has the input focus, its thumb can also be moved with the arrow keys, the Page Up and Page Down keys, and the Home and End keys. A simple function call returns an integer representing the thumb position. If desired, you can respond to positional changes as the thumb is moved by processing control notifications. Figure 16-2 shows what a simple slider control looks like. Tick marks denote the positions the thumb can assume.

Figure 16-2. *A horizontal slider with tick marks denoting thumb stops.*

The table on the following page shows slider-specific control styles. A slider can be oriented horizontally or vertically. The default orientation if neither TBS_HORZ nor TBS_VERT is specified is horizontal. The TBS_AUTOTICKS style marks thumb stops with tick marks. If the slider's range is 0 through 8, TBS_AUTOTICKS creates nine tick marks—one at each end of the slider and seven in between. TBS_NOTICKS removes the tick marks altogether, and TBS_NOTHUMB creates a slider that has no thumb. If you specify neither TBS_AUTOTICKS nor TBS_NOTICKS, the slider has a tick mark at each end but none in between. By default, tick marks are drawn below a horizontal slider and to the right of a vertical slider. You can move the tick marks to the top or the left by specifying TBS_TOP or TBS_LEFT, or you can use TBS_BOTH to create a slider that has tick marks both above and below or to its right and left.

SLIDER CONTROL STYLES

Style	Description
TBS_HORZ	Orients the slider horizontally.
TBS_VERT	Orients the slider vertically.
TBS_LEFT	Draws tick marks to the left of a vertical slider.
TBS_RIGHT	Draws tick marks to the right of a vertical slider.
TBS_TOP	Draws tick marks above a horizontal slider.
TBS_BOTTOM	Draws tick marks below a horizontal slider.
TBS_BOTH	Draws tick marks both above and below a horizontal slider or to the left and right of a vertical slider.
TBS_NOTICKS	Removes tick marks from the slider.
TBS_AUTOTICKS	Positions a tick mark at each stop in the slider's range.
TBS_FIXEDLENGTH	Allows the thumb size to be modified by sending the control a TBM_SETTHUMBLENGTH message.
TBS_NOTHUMB	Removes the thumb from the slider.
TBS_ENABLESELRANGE	Widens the slider's channel so that a selection range can be displayed.
TBS_TOOLTIPS*	Adds a dynamic ToolTip control that moves with the thumb and displays the thumb position. Use *CSlider-Ctrl::SetToolTips* to replace the default ToolTip control with one of your own.

*   Requires Internet Explorer 3.0 or later

MFC represents sliders with the *CSliderCtrl* class. A slider's range and thumb position are set with *CSliderCtrl::SetRange* and *CSliderCtrl::SetPos*. The related *CSlider-Ctrl::GetRange* and *CSliderCtrl::GetPos* functions retrieve range and position information. If *m_wndSlider* is a *CSliderCtrl*, the statements

```
m_wndSlider.SetRange (0, 8);
m_wndSlider.SetPos (2);
```

set the slider's range to 0 through 8 and its thumb position to 2.

A slider control assigned the style TBS_AUTOTICKS draws tick marks at each incremental thumb position. You can adjust the distance between tick marks with *CSliderCtrl::SetTicFreq*. The following statement configures a slider control to draw tick marks at every other thumb stop:

```
m_wndSlider.SetTicFreq (2);
```

To create a slider with tick marks at irregular intervals, omit the TBS_AUTOTICKS style and use *CSliderCtrl::SetTic* to put tick marks where you want them. The statements

```
m_wndSlider.SetRange (0, 8);
m_wndSlider.SetTic (2);
m_wndSlider.SetTic (3);
m_wndSlider.SetTic (6);
m_wndSlider.SetPos (2);
```

place tick marks at 2, 3, and 6 in addition to the ones drawn at 0 and 8.

The TBS_ENABLESELRANGE style creates a slider with a wide channel suitable for displaying a selection range. The selection range is set with *CSliderCtrl::SetSelection* and is represented by a bar drawn in the system color COLOR_HIGHLIGHT. The statements

```
m_wndSlider.SetRange (0, 8);
m_wndSlider.SetSelection (3, 7);
```

set the range to 0 through 8 and the selection to 3 through 7, producing the slider seen in Figure 16-3. Setting a selection doesn't limit the thumb's travel; the thumb can still be positioned anywhere in the slider range. If you want to limit the thumb's travel to the selection range or allow the user to alter the selection, you must implement a custom slider control UI. The most practical approach to customizing the UI is to derive a class from *CSliderCtrl* and add message handlers that change the way the control responds to presses of the Home, End, Page Up, Page Down, and arrow keys and clicks of the left mouse button. To perform default processing on selected messages, simply pass those messages to the base class.

Figure 16-3. *A slider with a selection range.*

As its thumb is moved, a slider sends its parent WM_HSCROLL or WM_VSCROLL messages as a scroll bar does. An *OnHScroll* or *OnVScroll* handler for a slider control receives three parameters: a notification code, an integer specifying the latest thumb position, and a *CScrollBar* pointer that can be cast to a *CSliderCtrl* pointer. The table on the following page shows the nine possible notification codes and the actions that generate them. The thumb position passed to *OnHScroll* or *OnVScroll* is valid only when the notification code is TB_THUMBPOSITION or TB_THUMBTRACK. Use *CSlider-Ctrl::GetPos* to retrieve the thumb position in response to other types of notifications.

SLIDER NOTIFICATIONS

Notification	Sent When
TB_TOP	The Home key is pressed while the slider has the input focus.
TB_BOTTOM	The End key is pressed while the slider has the input focus.
TB_LINEDOWN	The down or right arrow key is pressed while the slider has the input focus.
TB_LINEUP	The up or left arrow key is pressed while the slider has the input focus.
TB_PAGEDOWN	The Page Down key is pressed while the slider has the input focus, or the channel is clicked right of the thumb in a horizontal slider or below the thumb in a vertical slider.
TB_PAGEUP	The Page Up key is pressed while the slider has the input focus, or the channel is clicked left of the thumb in a horizontal slider or above the thumb in a vertical slider.
TB_THUMBTRACK	The thumb is dragged to a new position with the mouse.
TB_THUMBPOSITION	The left mouse button is released after the thumb is dragged.
TB_ENDTRACK	The key or mouse button used to move the thumb to a new position is released.

One use for slider notifications is for dynamically updating an image on the screen in response to positional changes. The Settings page of the system's Display Properties property sheet, which you can display by right-clicking the desktop and selecting Properties from the context menu, processes TB_THUMBTRACK notifications from the slider in the Screen Area box and redraws an image of the computer screen each time the thumb moves to preview the effect the new setting will have on the desktop.

CSliderCtrl provides more than two dozen functions you can use to operate on slider controls. Other useful member functions include *SetPageSize*, which sets the number of units the thumb moves when the channel is clicked with the mouse or when Page Up or Page Down is pressed; *GetTic*, *GetTicPos*, *GetTicArray*, and *GetNumTicks*, which return information about tick marks; and *ClearSel*, which removes a selection range. See the MFC documentation for more information regarding these and other *CSliderCtrl* function members.

Spin Button Controls

Spin button controls, which are also known as *up-down controls,* are small windows containing arrows that point up and down or left and right. Like scroll bars and sliders, spin buttons maintain their own ranges and positions. Clicking the up or right arrow increments the current position, and clicking the down or left arrow decrements it. Spin button controls send their parents notification messages before and after each positional change, but often those notifications are ignored because spin buttons are capable of doing some extraordinarily useful things on their own.

You can choose from the styles shown in the following table when you create a spin button control. UDS_SETBUDDYINT creates a spin button control that automatically updates an integer value displayed in a "buddy" control, which is typically an edit control or a static text control. When a UDS_SETBUDDYINT-style spin button control undergoes a positional change, it converts the integer describing the new position into a text string (think *_itoa*) and uses *::SetWindowText* to display the string in its buddy. UDS_SETBUDDYINT makes it trivial to add a set of arrows to an edit control so that the user can enter a number by either typing it at the keyboard or dialing it in with the mouse.

SPIN BUTTON CONTROL STYLES

Style	*Description*
UDS_HORZ	Orients the arrows horizontally rather than vertically.
UDS_WRAP	Causes the position to wrap around if it's decremented or incremented beyond the minimum or maximum.
UDS_ARROWKEYS	Adds a keyboard interface. If a spin button control with this style has the input focus, the up and down arrow keys increment and decrement its position.
UDS_NOTHOUSANDS	Removes thousands separators so that 1,234,567 is displayed as 1234567.
UDS_SETBUDDYINT	Creates a spin button control that updates the text of a designated buddy control when the position is incremented or decremented.
UDS_AUTOBUDDY	Selects the previous control in the *z*-order as the spin button's buddy.
UDS_ALIGNRIGHT	Attaches the spin button control to the right inside border of its buddy.
UDS_ALIGNLEFT	Attaches the spin button control to the left inside border of its buddy.

You can connect a spin button control to its buddy in two ways. You can explicitly link the two by calling *CSpinButtonCtrl::SetBuddy* with a *CWnd* pointer identifying the buddy control, or you can specify UDS_AUTOBUDDY when creating the spin button control, which automatically selects the previous control in the *z*-order as the spin button's buddy. In a dialog template, the statements

```
EDITTEXT    IDC_EDIT, 60, 80, 40, 14, ES_AUTOHSCROLL
CONTROL     "", IDC_SPIN, "msctls_updown32", UDS_SETBUDDYINT |
            UDS_AUTOBUDDY | UDS_ALIGNRIGHT, 0, 0, 0, 0
```

create a single-line edit control and attach a spin button control to its right inside border, as shown in Figure 16-4. The edit control is shrunk by the width of the spin button control, and the spin button's height is adjusted to match the height of its buddy. Consequently, the edit control and the spin button control together occupy the same amount of space as the original edit control. Information regarding a spin button control's size and position is ignored when UDS_ALIGNLEFT or UDS_ALIGNRIGHT is specified.

Figure 16-4. *A spin button control attached to an edit control.*

By default, a UDS_SETBUDDYINT spin button control displays numbers in decimal format and inserts a thousands separator every third digit. You can configure the control to display hexadecimal numbers instead with *CSpinButtonCtrl::SetBase*:

```
m_wndSpinButton.SetBase (16);
```

Hex numbers are preceded by 0x characters so that it's obvious they are hexadecimal. Calling *SetBase* with a 10 switches output back to decimal format. You can remove separators from decimal numbers by specifying UDS_NOTHOUSANDS when you create the control; thousands separators are omitted from hex numbers by default.

You set a spin button control's range and position with *CSpinButtonCtrl::SetRange* and *CSpinButtonCtrl::SetPos*. Valid minimums and maximums range from −32,767 through 32,767, but the difference between the low and high ends of the range can't exceed 32,767. It's legal to specify a maximum that's less than the minimum. When you do, the actions of the arrows are reversed. On systems with Internet Explorer 4.0 or later installed, spin button controls support 32-bit ranges whose minimums and maximums can be set and retrieved with the aptly named *CSliderCtrl* functions *SetRange32* and *GetRange32*.

Each discrete click of an arrow in a spin button control (or press of an arrow key if the control's style includes UDS_ARROWKEYS) increments or decrements the position by 1. If you press and hold a button, the increments change to ±5 after 2 seconds and ±20 after 5 seconds. You can alter the number of seconds that elapse before the incremental value changes and also control the magnitude of the changes with *CSpinButtonCtrl::SetAccel*. *SetAccel* accepts two parameters: a pointer to an array of UDACCEL structures and the number of structures in the array. The following statements configure a spin button control to increment or decrement the position by 1 for the first 2 seconds, 2 for the next 2 seconds, 10 for the next 2 seconds, and 100 for the remainder of the time a button is held down:

```
UDACCEL uda[4];
uda[0].nSec = 0;
uda[0].nInc = 1;
uda[1].nSec = 2;
uda[1].nInc = 2;
uda[2].nSec = 4;
uda[2].nInc = 10;
uda[3].nSec = 8;
uda[3].nInc = 100;
pSpinButton->SetAccel (4, uda);
```

Another use for *SetAccel* is to specify incremental values other than 1. If you'd like each button click to increment or decrement the position by 5, call *SetAccel* like this:

```
UDACCEL uda;
uda.nSec = 0;
uda.nInc = 5;
pSpinButton->SetAccel (1, &uda);
```

You can retrieve accelerator values by passing the address of an array of UDACCEL structures to *CSpinButton::GetAccel*. But there's a trick: How do you know how many structures to allocate space for? This fact wasn't documented prior to Visual C++ 6, but calling *GetAccel* as shown here returns the number of UDACCEL structures in the accelerator array:

```
UINT nCount = pSpinButton->GetAccel (0, NULL);
```

Once the count is known, you can allocate a buffer for the array and retrieve it like this:

```
UDACCEL* puda = new UDACCEL[nCount];
pSpinButton->GetAccel (nCount, puda);
// Do something with the array.
delete[] puda;
```

See? Nothing to it when you know the secret.

Before its position is incremented or decremented, a spin button control sends its parent a WM_NOTIFY message with a notification code equal to UDN_DELTAPOS and an *lParam* pointing to an NM_UPDOWN structure. Inside the structure are integers specifying the current position (*iPos*) and the amount by which the position is about to change (*iDelta*). A UDN_DELTAPOS handler must set **pResult* to FALSE to allow the change to occur. To purposely prevent an increment or decrement operation being carried out, have the handler set **pResult* to TRUE, and then return TRUE from *OnNotify*. UDN_DELTAPOS notifications are followed by WM_HSCROLL or WM_VSCROLL messages (depending on whether the spin button is oriented horizontally or vertically) reporting the new position. Clicking the down arrow when the control's current position is 8 produces the following sequence of messages.

Message	Notification Code	Parameters
WM_NOTIFY	UDN_DELTAPOS	$iPos$=8, $iDelta$=−1
WM_VSCROLL	SB_THUMBPOSITION	$nPos$=7
WM_VSCROLL	SB_ENDSCROLL	$nPos$=7

If the button is held down for more than a half second or so, several UDN_DELTAPOS and SB_THUMBPOSITION notifications are sent in sequence.

ToolTip Controls

A ToolTip is a miniature help-text window that appears when the cursor pauses over a "tool" such as a button on a toolbar or a control in a dialog box. A ToolTip control is a control that monitors mouse movements and automatically displays a ToolTip when the cursor remains motionless over a tool for a predetermined period of time. MFC provides a convenient C++ interface to ToolTip controls through the *CToolTipCtrl* class. With *CToolTipCtrl* to help out, it's relatively easy to add ToolTips to controls in dialog boxes and implement other forms of interactive help. You simply create a ToolTip control and register the tools for which you'd like ToolTips displayed and the text of the ToolTips. For the most part, the control does the rest.

CToolTipCtrl::Create creates a ToolTip control. (ToolTip controls can also be created from dialog templates, but the more common approach is to add a *CToolTipCtrl* data member to the dialog class and call *Create* from *OnInitDialog* instead.) If *m_ctlTT* is a *CToolTipCtrl* data member of a window class, the statement

```
m_ctlTT.Create (this);
```

creates a ToolTip control. *CToolTipCtrl::Create* accepts an optional second parameter specifying the control's style. The only two styles supported are TTS_ALWAYSTIP and TTS_NOPREFIX. By default, ToolTips appear over active windows only. A TTS_ALWAYSTIP-style ToolTip control displays ToolTips over both active and inactive windows. TTS_NOPREFIX tells the control not to strip ampersands from ToolTip text. The default behavior is to ignore ampersands so that you can use the same text strings for menus and ToolTips.

After you create a ToolTip control, the next step is to add tools to it. A tool is either another window—usually a child window control that belongs to the ToolTip control's parent—or a rectangular area of a window. *CToolTipCtrl::AddTool* registers a tool and the ToolTip text that goes with it. One ToolTip control can have any number of tools associated with it. The statement

```
m_ctlTT.AddTool (pWnd, _T ("This is a window"), NULL, 0);
```

assigns the ToolTip text "This is a window" to the window identified by *pWnd*. The second parameter passed to *AddTool* can be a pointer to a text string or the ID of a string resource, whichever you prefer. Similarly, the statement

```
m_ctlTT.AddTool (pWnd, _T ("This is a rectangle"),
    CRect (32, 32, 64, 64), IDT_RECTANGLE);
```

creates a tool from the specified rectangle in *pWnd*'s client area. IDT_RECTANGLE is a nonzero integer that identifies the rectangle and is analogous to a child window ID identifying a control.

So far, so good. There's just one problem. A ToolTip control has to be able to see the mouse messages a tool receives so that it can monitor mouse events and know when to display a ToolTip, but Windows sends mouse messages to the window underneath the cursor. In the examples above, it's up to you to forward mouse messages going to *pWnd* to the ToolTip control. If *pWnd* corresponds to a top-level window or a dialog box, forwarding mouse messages is no big deal because you can map the relevant mouse messages to handlers in the window class or dialog class and relay them to the ToolTip control with *CToolTipCtrl::RelayEvent*. But if *pWnd* points to a child window control or any window other than your own, you have to resort to window subclassing or other devices in order to see mouse messages going to the window and relay them to the ToolTip control. Late in the beta cycle of Windows 95, the operating system architects recognized this problem and gave ToolTip controls the ability to do their own subclassing. Unfortunately, this feature has yet to be folded into *CToolTipCtrl*. So to make ToolTips truly easy to use, you must customize the *CToolTipCtrl* class by adding some smarts of your own.

Whenever I use a ToolTip control in an MFC application, I first derive a class from *CToolTipCtrl* named *CMyToolTipCtrl* and add a pair of member functions that take advantage of the fact that a ToolTip control can do its own subclassing. Here's what the derived class looks like:

```
class CMyToolTipCtrl : public CToolTipCtrl
{
public:
    BOOL AddWindowTool (CWnd* pWnd, LPCTSTR pszText);
    BOOL AddRectTool (CWnd* pWnd, LPCTSTR pszText,
        LPCRECT pRect, UINT nIDTool);
};

BOOL CMyToolTipCtrl::AddWindowTool (CWnd* pWnd, LPCTSTR pszText)
{
    TOOLINFO ti;
    ti.cbSize = sizeof (TOOLINFO);
    ti.uFlags = TTF_IDISHWND | TTF_SUBCLASS;
    ti.hwnd = pWnd->GetParent ()->GetSafeHwnd ();
    ti.uId = (UINT) pWnd->GetSafeHwnd ();
```

(continued)

```
        ti.hinst = AfxGetInstanceHandle ();
        ti.lpszText = (LPTSTR) pszText;

        return (BOOL) SendMessage (TTM_ADDTOOL, 0, (LPARAM) &ti);
}

BOOL CMyToolTipCtrl::AddRectTool (CWnd* pWnd, LPCTSTR pszText,
    LPCRECT lpRect, UINT nIDTool)
{
    TOOLINFO ti;
    ti.cbSize = sizeof (TOOLINFO);
    ti.uFlags = TTF_SUBCLASS;
    ti.hwnd = pWnd->GetSafeHwnd ();
    ti.uId = nIDTool;
    ti.hinst = AfxGetInstanceHandle ();
    ti.lpszText = (LPTSTR) pszText;
    ::CopyRect (&ti.rect, lpRect);

        return (BOOL) SendMessage (TTM_ADDTOOL, 0, (LPARAM) &ti);
}
```

With this infrastructure in place, creating a tool from a child window control—subclassing and all—requires just one simple statement:

```
m_ctlTT.AddWindowTool (pWnd, _T ("This is a window"));
```

Creating a tool from a rectangle in a window is equally simple:

```
m_ctlTT.AddRectTool (pWnd, _T ("This is a rectangle"),
    CRect (32, 32, 64, 64), IDT_RECTANGLE);
```

The *pWnd* parameter passed to *AddWindowTool* identifies the window the ToolTip will be applied to. The *pWnd* parameter passed to *AddRectTool* references the window whose client area contains the rectangle referenced in the third parameter. Because of the TTF_SUBCLASS flag passed in the *uFlags* field of the TOOLINFO structure, the ToolTip control will do its own window subclassing and mouse messages don't have to be relayed manually.

Dynamic ToolTips

If you specify LPSTR_TEXTCALLBACK for the ToolTip text when you call *AddTool*, *AddWindowTool*, or *AddRectTool*, the ToolTip control will send a notification to its parent requesting a text string before displaying a ToolTip. You can use LPSTR_TEXTCALLBACK to create dynamic ToolTips whose text varies from one invocation to the next. Text callbacks come in the form of WM_NOTIFY messages with a notification code equal to TTN_NEEDTEXT and *lParam* pointing to a structure of type TOOLTIPTEXT. TOOLTIPTEXT is defined as follows:

```
typedef struct {
    NMHDR      hdr;
    LPTSTR     lpszText;
    char       szText[80];
    HINSTANCE  hinst;
    UINT       uFlags;
} TOOLTIPTEXT;
```

A ToolTip control's parent responds to TTN_NEEDTEXT notifications in one of three ways: by copying the address of a text string to the TOOLTIPTEXT structure's *lpszText* field; by copying the text (as many as 80 characters, including the zero terminator) directly to the structure's *szText* field; or by copying a string resource ID to *lpszText* and copying the application's instance handle, which an MFC application can obtain with *AfxGetInstanceHandle*, to *hinst*. The *idFrom* field of the NMHDR structure that's nested inside the TOOLTIPTEXT structure contains either a window handle or an application-defined tool ID identifying the tool for which text is needed.

The following example demonstrates how to create a dynamic ToolTip for a rectangular region of a dialog box. The rectangle's application-defined tool ID is IDT_RECTANGLE, and the text displayed in the ToolTip window is the current time:

```
// In the message map
ON_NOTIFY (TTN_NEEDTEXT, NULL, OnNeedText)

        :
        :

BOOL CMyDialog::OnInitDialog ()
{
    m_ctlTT.Create (this);
    m_ctlTT.AddRectTool (this, LPSTR_TEXTCALLBACK,
        CRect (0, 0, 32, 32), IDT_RECTANGLE);
    return TRUE;
}


void CMyDialog::OnNeedText (NMHDR* pnmh, LRESULT* pResult)
{
    TOOLTIPTEXT* pttt = (TOOLTIPTEXT*) pnmh;
    if (pttt->hdr.idFrom == IDT_RECTANGLE) {
        CString string;
        CTime time = CTime::GetCurrentTime ();
        string.Format (_T ("%0.2d:%0.2d:%0.2d"), time.GetHour () % 12,
            time.GetMinute (), time.GetSecond ());
        ::lstrcpy (pttt->szText, (LPCTSTR) string);
    }
}
```

Notice the NULL child window ID specified in the second parameter to the ON_NOTIFY macro in *CMyDialog*'s message map. This parameter must be NULL because *CToolTipCtrl::Create* registers a NULL child window ID for ToolTip controls.

MFC's *CToolTipCtrl* class includes an assortment of member functions you can use to operate on ToolTip controls. For example, you can use *GetText* to retrieve the text assigned to a tool, *UpdateTipText* to change ToolTip text, *Activate* to activate and deactivate a ToolTip control, and *SetDelayTime* to change the delay time—the number of milliseconds the cursor must remain motionless before a ToolTip is displayed. The default delay time is 500 milliseconds.

The GridDemo Application

The GridDemo application, whose source code appears in Figure 16-6, provides a practical demonstration of slider controls, spin button controls, and ToolTip controls. GridDemo divides a frame window's client area into a grid by drawing intersecting horizontal and vertical lines. By default, the grid contains 8 rows and 8 columns and grid lines are drawn in a medium shade of gray. You can vary the number of rows and columns as well as the darkness of the grid lines by choosing Grid Settings from the Options menu and entering the new settings in the dialog box shown in Figure 16-5. The slider control selects the line weight, and the values entered into the edit controls control the numbers of rows and columns. Valid values range from 2 through 64; you can type in the numbers or use the arrow buttons. When the cursor pauses over the slider or either of the edit controls, a ToolTip window appears with a short description of the tool underneath.

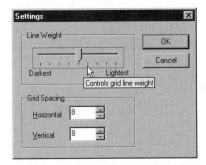

Figure 16-5. *GridDemo's Settings dialog box with a ToolTip displayed.*

ChildView.h

```
// ChildView.h : interface of the CChildView class
//
/////////////////////////////////////////////////////////////////////////////

#if !defined(
    AFX_CHILDVIEW_H__A4559BAA_ABE5_11D2_8E53_006008A82731__INCLUDED_)
```

Figure 16-6. *The GridDemo application.*

```
#define AFX_CHILDVIEW_H__A4559BAA_ABE5_11D2_8E53_006008A82731__INCLUDED_

#if _MSC_VER > 1000
#pragma once
#endif // _MSC_VER > 1000


/////////////////////////////////////////////////////////////////////////////
// CChildView window

class CChildView : public CWnd
{
// Construction
public:
    CChildView();

// Attributes
public:

// Operations
public:

// Overrides
    // ClassWizard generated virtual function overrides
    //{{AFX_VIRTUAL(CChildView)
    protected:
    virtual BOOL PreCreateWindow(CREATESTRUCT& cs);
    //}}AFX_VIRTUAL

// Implementation
public:
    virtual ~CChildView();

    // Generated message map functions
protected:
    int m_nWeight;
    int m_cy;
    int m_cx;
    //{{AFX_MSG(CChildView)
    afx_msg void OnPaint();
    afx_msg void OnOptionsGridSettings();
    //}}AFX_MSG
    DECLARE_MESSAGE_MAP()
};


/////////////////////////////////////////////////////////////////////////////

//{{AFX_INSERT_LOCATION}}
```

(continued)

Figure 16-6 *continued*

```
// Microsoft Visual C++ will insert additional declarations
// immediately before the previous line.

#endif
// !defined(
//     AFX_CHILDVIEW_H__A4559BAA_ABE5_11D2_8E53_006008A82731__INCLUDED_)
```

ChildView.cpp

```cpp
// ChildView.cpp : implementation of the CChildView class
//

#include "stdafx.h"
#include "GridDemo.h"
#include "ChildView.h"
#include "SettingsDialog.h"

#ifdef _DEBUG
#define new DEBUG_NEW
#undef THIS_FILE
static char THIS_FILE[] = __FILE__;
#endif


/////////////////////////////////////////////////////////////////////////
// CChildView

CChildView::CChildView()
{
    m_cx = 8;
    m_cy = 8;
    m_nWeight = 4;
}

CChildView::~CChildView()
{
}

BEGIN_MESSAGE_MAP(CChildView,CWnd )
    //{{AFX_MSG_MAP(CChildView)
    ON_WM_PAINT()
    ON_COMMAND(ID_OPTIONS_GRID_SETTINGS, OnOptionsGridSettings)
    //}}AFX_MSG_MAP
END_MESSAGE_MAP()
```

```
/////////////////////////////////////////////////////////////////////////
// CChildView message handlers

BOOL CChildView::PreCreateWindow(CREATESTRUCT& cs)
{
    if (!CWnd::PreCreateWindow(cs))
        return FALSE;

    cs.dwExStyle |= WS_EX_CLIENTEDGE;
    cs.style &= ~WS_BORDER;
    cs.lpszClass = AfxRegisterWndClass(CS_HREDRAW|CS_VREDRAW|CS_DBLCLKS,
        ::LoadCursor(NULL, IDC_ARROW), HBRUSH(COLOR_WINDOW+1), NULL);

    return TRUE;
}

void CChildView::OnPaint()
{
    CRect rect;
    GetClientRect (&rect);

    int nShade = m_nWeight * 32;
    if (nShade != 0)
        nShade--;

    CPaintDC dc (this);
    CPen pen (PS_SOLID, 1, RGB (nShade, nShade, nShade));
    CPen* pOldPen = dc.SelectObject (&pen);

    int x;
    for (int i=1; i<m_cx; i++) {
        x = (rect.Width () * i) / m_cx;
        dc.MoveTo (x, 0);
        dc.LineTo (x, rect.Height ());
    }

    int y;
    for (i=1; i<m_cy; i++) {
        y = (rect.Height () * i) / m_cy;
        dc.MoveTo (0, y);
        dc.LineTo (rect.Width (), y);
    }

    dc.SelectObject (pOldPen);
}
```

(continued)

Figure 16-6 *continued*

```
void CChildView::OnOptionsGridSettings()
{
    CSettingsDialog dlg;

    dlg.m_cx = m_cx;
    dlg.m_cy = m_cy;
    dlg.m_nWeight = m_nWeight;

    if (dlg.DoModal () == IDOK) {
        m_cx = dlg.m_cx;
        m_cy = dlg.m_cy;
        m_nWeight = dlg.m_nWeight;
        Invalidate ();
    }
}
```

SettingsDialog.h

```
#if !defined(
    AFX_SETTINGSDIALOG_H__A4559BB0_ABE5_11D2_8E53_006008A82731__INCLUDED_)
#define
    AFX_SETTINGSDIALOG_H__A4559BB0_ABE5_11D2_8E53_006008A82731__INCLUDED_

#include "MyToolTipCtrl.h"      // Added by ClassView
#if _MSC_VER > 1000
#pragma once
#endif // _MSC_VER > 1000
// SettingsDialog.h : header file
//


/////////////////////////////////////////////////////////////////////////
// CSettingsDialog dialog

class CSettingsDialog : public CDialog
{
// Construction
public:
    int m_nWeight;
    CSettingsDialog(CWnd* pParent = NULL);   // standard constructor

// Dialog Data
    //{{AFX_DATA(CSettingsDialog)
    enum { IDD = IDD_SETTINGDLG };
```

```
    CSpinButtonCtrl    m_wndSpinVert;
    CSpinButtonCtrl    m_wndSpinHorz;
    CSliderCtrl    m_wndSlider;
    int        m_cx;
    int        m_cy;
    //}}AFX_DATA

// Overrides
    // ClassWizard generated virtual function overrides
    //{{AFX_VIRTUAL(CSettingsDialog)
    protected:
    virtual void DoDataExchange(CDataExchange* pDX);    // DDX/DDV support
    //}}AFX_VIRTUAL

// Implementation
protected:
    CMyToolTipCtrl m_ctlTT;
    // Generated message map functions
    //{{AFX_MSG(CSettingsDialog)
    virtual BOOL OnInitDialog();
    virtual void OnOK();
    //}}AFX_MSG
    DECLARE_MESSAGE_MAP()
};

//{{AFX_INSERT_LOCATION}}
// Microsoft Visual C++ will insert additional declarations
// immediately before the previous line.

#endif
// !defined(
//    AFX_SETTINGSDIALOG_H__A4559BB0_ABE5_11D2_8E53_006008A82731__INCLUDED_)
```

SettingsDialog.cpp

```
// SettingsDialog.cpp : implementation file
//

#include "stdafx.h"
#include "GridDemo.h"
#include "MyToolTipCtrl.h"
#include "SettingsDialog.h"
```

(continued)

Figure 16-6 *continued*

```
#ifdef _DEBUG
#define new DEBUG_NEW
#undef THIS_FILE
static char THIS_FILE[] = __FILE__;
#endif


//////////////////////////////////////////////////////////////////////
// CSettingsDialog dialog

CSettingsDialog::CSettingsDialog(CWnd* pParent /*=NULL*/)
    : CDialog(CSettingsDialog::IDD, pParent)
{
    //{{AFX_DATA_INIT(CSettingsDialog)
    m_cx = 0;
    m_cy = 0;
    //}}AFX_DATA_INIT
}


void CSettingsDialog::DoDataExchange(CDataExchange* pDX)
{
    CDialog::DoDataExchange(pDX);
    //{{AFX_DATA_MAP(CSettingsDialog)
    DDX_Control(pDX, IDC_SPINVERT, m_wndSpinVert);
    DDX_Control(pDX, IDC_SPINHORZ, m_wndSpinHorz);
    DDX_Control(pDX, IDC_SLIDER, m_wndSlider);
    DDX_Text(pDX, IDC_EDITHORZ, m_cx);
    DDX_Text(pDX, IDC_EDITVERT, m_cy);
    //}}AFX_DATA_MAP
}


BEGIN_MESSAGE_MAP(CSettingsDialog, CDialog)
    //{{AFX_MSG_MAP(CSettingsDialog)
    //}}AFX_MSG_MAP
END_MESSAGE_MAP()


//////////////////////////////////////////////////////////////////////
// CSettingsDialog message handlers

BOOL CSettingsDialog::OnInitDialog()
{
    CDialog::OnInitDialog();

    //
    // Initialize the slider control.
    //
```

```
    m_wndSlider.SetRange (0, 8);
    m_wndSlider.SetPos (m_nWeight);

    //
    // Initialize the spin button controls.
    //
    m_wndSpinHorz.SetRange (2, 64);
    m_wndSpinVert.SetRange (2, 64);

    //
    // Create and initialize a tooltip control.
    //
    m_ctlTT.Create (this);
    m_ctlTT.AddWindowTool (GetDlgItem (IDC_SLIDER),
        MAKEINTRESOURCE (IDS_SLIDER));
    m_ctlTT.AddWindowTool (GetDlgItem (IDC_EDITHORZ),
        MAKEINTRESOURCE (IDS_EDITHORZ));
    m_ctlTT.AddWindowTool (GetDlgItem (IDC_EDITVERT),
        MAKEINTRESOURCE (IDS_EDITVERT));
    return TRUE;
}

void CSettingsDialog::OnOK()
{
    //
    // Read the slider control's thumb position
    // before dismissing the dialog.
    //
    m_nWeight = m_wndSlider.GetPos ();
    CDialog::OnOK();
}
```

MyToolTipCtrl.h

```
#if !defined(
    AFX_MYTOOLTIPCTRL_H__A4559BB1_ABE5_11D2_8E53_006008A82731__INCLUDED_)
#define
    AFX_MYTOOLTIPCTRL_H__A4559BB1_ABE5_11D2_8E53_006008A82731__INCLUDED_

#if _MSC_VER > 1000
#pragma once
#endif // _MSC_VER > 1000
// MyToolTipCtrl.h : header file
//
```

(continued)

Figure 16-6 *continued*

```
/////////////////////////////////////////////////////////////////////////
// CMyToolTipCtrl window

class CMyToolTipCtrl : public CToolTipCtrl
{
// Construction
public:
    CMyToolTipCtrl();

// Attributes
public:

// Operations
public:

// Overrides
    // ClassWizard generated virtual function overrides
    //{{AFX_VIRTUAL(CMyToolTipCtrl)
    //}}AFX_VIRTUAL

// Implementation
public:
    BOOL AddRectTool (CWnd* pWnd, LPCTSTR pszText, LPCRECT pRect,
        UINT nIDTool);
    BOOL AddWindowTool (CWnd* pWnd, LPCTSTR pszText);
    virtual ~CMyToolTipCtrl();

    // Generated message map functions
protected:
    //{{AFX_MSG(CMyToolTipCtrl)
        // NOTE - the ClassWizard will add and remove member functions here.
    //}}AFX_MSG

    DECLARE_MESSAGE_MAP()
};


/////////////////////////////////////////////////////////////////////////

//{{AFX_INSERT_LOCATION}}
// Microsoft Visual C++ will insert additional declarations
// immediately before the previous line.

#endif
// !defined(
//     AFX_MYTOOLTIPCTRL_H__A4559BB1_ABE5_11D2_8E53_006008A82731__INCLUDED_)
```

MyToolTipCtrl.cpp

```cpp
// MyToolTipCtrl.cpp : implementation file
//

#include "stdafx.h"
#include "GridDemo.h"
#include "MyToolTipCtrl.h"

#ifdef _DEBUG
#define new DEBUG_NEW
#undef THIS_FILE
static char THIS_FILE[] = __FILE__;
#endif

/////////////////////////////////////////////////////////////////////////////
// CMyToolTipCtrl

CMyToolTipCtrl::CMyToolTipCtrl()
{
}

CMyToolTipCtrl::~CMyToolTipCtrl()
{
}


BEGIN_MESSAGE_MAP(CMyToolTipCtrl, CToolTipCtrl)
    //{{AFX_MSG_MAP(CMyToolTipCtrl)
        // NOTE - the ClassWizard will add and remove mapping macros here.
    //}}AFX_MSG_MAP
END_MESSAGE_MAP()

/////////////////////////////////////////////////////////////////////////////
// CMyToolTipCtrl message handlers

BOOL CMyToolTipCtrl::AddWindowTool(CWnd *pWnd, LPCTSTR pszText)
{
    TOOLINFO ti;
    ti.cbSize = sizeof (TOOLINFO);
    ti.uFlags = TTF_IDISHWND | TTF_SUBCLASS;
    ti.hwnd = pWnd->GetParent ()->GetSafeHwnd ();
    ti.uId = (UINT) pWnd->GetSafeHwnd ();
    ti.hinst = AfxGetInstanceHandle ();
    ti.lpszText = (LPTSTR) pszText;
```

(continued)

Figure 16-6 *continued*

```
    return (BOOL) SendMessage (TTM_ADDTOOL, 0, (LPARAM) &ti);
}


BOOL CMyToolTipCtrl::AddRectTool(CWnd *pWnd, LPCTSTR pszText,
    LPCRECT pRect, UINT nIDTool)
{
    TOOLINFO ti;
    ti.cbSize = sizeof (TOOLINFO);
    ti.uFlags = TTF_SUBCLASS;
    ti.hwnd = pWnd->GetSafeHwnd ();
    ti.uId = nIDTool;
    ti.hinst = AfxGetInstanceHandle ();
    ti.lpszText = (LPTSTR) pszText;
    ::CopyRect (&ti.rect, pRect);

    return (BOOL) SendMessage (TTM_ADDTOOL, 0, (LPARAM) &ti);
}
```

The ToolTip control is an instance of *CMyToolTipCtrl*. Rather than hardcode the ToolTip text into the calls to *AddWindowTool*, I elected to put the text in the application's string table. String resources are identified by their resource IDs. In the calls to *AddWindowTool*, IDS_SLIDER, IDS_EDITHORZ, and IDS_EDITVERT are the resource IDs:

```
m_ctlTT.AddWindowTool (GetDlgItem (IDC_SLIDER),
    MAKEINTRESOURCE (IDS_SLIDER));
m_ctlTT.AddWindowTool (GetDlgItem (IDC_EDITHORZ),
    MAKEINTRESOURCE (IDS_EDITHORZ));
m_ctlTT.AddWindowTool (GetDlgItem (IDC_EDITVERT),
    MAKEINTRESOURCE (IDS_EDITVERT));
```

You can see the text associated with these resource IDs by opening the project, switching to ResourceView, and viewing the string table.

The slider and spin button controls are part of the dialog template and are programmed using *CSliderCtrl* and *CSpinButtonCtrl* member functions. The slider's range and initial position are set in *OnInitDialog*, and the final thumb position is retrieved in *OnOK*. The spin buttons' ranges are also initialized in *OnInitDialog*, but their positions don't have to be explicitly set or retrieved because the edit controls that the spin buttons are buddied to are served by Dialog Data Exchange (DDX) and Dialog Data Validation (DDV) routines.

Speaking of DDX and DDV: With few exceptions, MFC doesn't provide DDX routines to move data between common controls and dialog data members or DDV routines to validate input to common controls. When you use only classic controls in a dialog, you frequently don't have to override *OnInitDialog* and *OnOK* because you (or ClassWizard) can populate *DoDataExchange* with statements that transfer data between the dialog's member variables and its controls. When you use common controls, however, it's up to you to initialize the controls and perform data exchanges. That's why *CSettingsDialog::OnInitDialog* contains these statements:

```
m_wndSlider.SetRange (0, 8);
m_wndSlider.SetPos (m_nWeight);
    :
    :
m_wndSpinHorz.SetRange (2, 64);
m_wndSpinVert.SetRange (2, 64);
```

And *CSettingsDialog::OnOK* contains this one:

```
m_nWeight = m_wndSlider.GetPos ();
```

These statements do what DDX would have done had it been supported. (Interestingly enough, MFC 6 includes a *DDX_Slider* function that performs DDX on slider controls, but it's fatally flawed because it initializes a slider with a position but not a range. Try it and you'll see what I mean.) *m_wndSlider* is a *CSliderCtrl* member variable that I added to the dialog class with ClassWizard. *m_wndSpinHorz* and *m_wnd-SpinVert* are *CSpinButtonCtrl* member variables; I added them with ClassWizard as well. All three are linked to controls in the dialog via *DDX_Control* statements in *DoDataExchange*.

Because GridDemo doesn't create a logical palette with shades of gray representing the different line weight settings, the full range of line weights isn't visible on 16-color and 256-color video adapters. As an exercise, you might try adding palette support by adding a *CPalette* data member to the frame window and using PALETTERGB or PALETTEINDEX colors to draw the grid lines. Refer to Chapter 15 for more information on GDI palettes and MFC's *CPalette* class.

IMAGE LISTS AND COMBOBOXEX CONTROLS

Chapter 10's DriveTree and WinDir programs used image lists to provide iconlike images to a tree view and a list view. At the time, I didn't say much about image lists other than that they hold collections of bitmapped images and that MFC wraps them with the class *CImageList*. As it turns out, image lists are extraordinarily useful not only for supplying images to other controls, but also for blitting bitmaps with special effects such as transparency and blending. We'll examine these and other features of image lists in the next section.

When Internet Explorer 3.0 or later is installed, it replaces Comctl32.dll with a newer version that includes enhanced versions of the existing controls as well as several new common control types. One of those new control types is the extended combo box control, better known as the ComboBoxEx control. A ComboBoxEx control differs from a standard combo box control in several important respects, most notably in the fact that it can display images next to each item. Not surprisingly, the images come from an image list. You can combine image lists and ComboBoxEx controls to create drop-down lists containing both graphics and text.

In the sections that follow, I'll use a broad brush to paint a picture of image lists and ComboBoxEx controls and introduce the fundamental principles involved in programming them. Then you'll see just how powerful image lists and ComboBoxEx controls can be by developing a combo box that depicts path names visually.

Image Lists

An image list is a collection of identically sized bitmap images joined together to form one logical unit. MFC's *CImageList* class provides functions for creating image lists, adding and deleting images, drawing images on the screen, writing image lists to an archive and reading them back, and more. Image lists are useful in and of themselves because many of the functions that operate on them have no direct counterparts elsewhere in Windows. But image lists were added to the operating system in the first place so that bitmaps could be grouped and passed as a unit to other common controls. When you supply images to a tree view control, for example, you don't pass it an array of *CBitmap*s; you pass it a handle to an image list (an HIMAGELIST) or a pointer to a *CImageList* object. Individual images are then referenced with 0-based indexes.

The best way to picture an image list is to think of a filmstrip with images laid horizontally from end to end. The leftmost image is image number 0, the one to its right is image number 1, and so on. The images can be any height and width, but they must all be the same height and width.

MFC provides three ways to create an image list. You can create an empty image list and add images to it with *CImageList::Add*; you can create an initialized image list from an existing bitmap containing an array of images; or you can create an initialized image list by merging images from existing image lists. *CImageList::Create* is overloaded to support all three creation methods. The second (and probably the most common) of these methods is illustrated in the following example. Suppose IDB_BITMAP is the resource ID of a bitmap that contains five images, each measuring 18 pixels wide and 16 pixels high. The bitmap itself is 90 pixels wide (5 times 18) and 16 pixels high. These statements create an image list from the bitmap:

```
CImageList il;
il.Create (IDB_BITMAP, 18, 1, CLR_NONE);
```

The first parameter passed to *Create* is the bitmap's resource ID. You can also pass a string resource ID for this parameter. The second parameter is the width, in pixels, of the individual images. Windows determines how many images to add to the list by dividing the bitmap width by the image width. The third parameter is the *grow size*. Image lists are sized dynamically just as arrays created from MFC collection classes are, and the grow size tells the image list how many additional images to make room for when more memory must be allocated to accommodate new images. The final parameter—CLR_NONE—creates an *unmasked* image list. Unmasked images are ordinary bitmaps that are blitted directly to the destination when they're drawn on the screen.

Passing *CImageList::Create* a COLORREF value instead of CLR_NONE creates a *masked* image list. In addition to storing color information for a masked image, Windows also stores a monochrome bit mask that allows it to distinguish between foreground and background pixels. The COLORREF value passed to *CImageList::Create* specifies the background color, and any pixel set to that color is assumed to be a background pixel. What's cool about masked images is the fact that you can call *CImageList::SetBkColor* before drawing from an image list and set the background color to any color you like. The background color in the original bitmap might be magenta, but if you set the background color to red and draw the image, all the magenta pixels will come out red. What's *really* cool is that you can pass *CImageList::SetBkColor* a CLR_NONE parameter and background pixels won't be drawn at all. Consequently, image lists provide a simple means of drawing bitmaps with transparent pixels. Remember the *DrawTransparent* function we developed in Chapter 15 for drawing nonrectangular bitmaps? An image list lets you do the same thing with less code. The image list method is faster, too, because the masks don't have to be generated anew each time the image is blitted to the screen.

CImageList::Draw draws images on the screen. The following statement draws the third image in the list (image number 2) to the screen DC referenced by the *CDC* pointer *pDC*:

```
il.Draw (pDC, 2, point, ILD_NORMAL);
```

point is a POINT structure containing the *x* and *y* coordinates of the point in the destination DC where the upper left corner of the image will be drawn. ILD_NORMAL is a flag that tells the *Draw* function to draw a masked image using the current background color. (This flag has no effect on unmasked images.) If you'd like background pixels to be transparent regardless of what the current background color happens to be, you can use an ILD_TRANSPARENT flag instead:

```
il.Draw (pDC, 2, point, ILD_TRANSPARENT);
```

For some truly interesting effects, try drawing a masked image with an ILD_BLEND25 or ILD_BLEND50 flag to blend in the system highlight color (COLOR_HIGHLIGHT). *CImageList::Draw* also accepts ILD_SELECTED and ILD_FOCUS flags, but they're nothing more than ILD_BLEND50 and ILD_BLEND25 in disguise. To see blending at work, select an icon on the Windows desktop. To show the icon in a selected state, the system dithers the icon with the system highlight color by drawing it with an ILD_BLEND50 flag.

An aside: Drawing with an ILD_TRANSPARENT flag or with the background color set to CLR_NONE is always a little slower than drawing an unmasked image. If an image contains transparent pixels but is being blitted to a solid background, use *CImageList::SetBkColor* to set the image list's background color to the color of the solid background and then call *CImageList::Draw* with an ILD_NORMAL flag. You'll improve performance and still get those transparent pixels you wanted.

ComboBoxEx Controls

ComboBoxEx controls exist to simplify the task of including images as well as text in combo boxes. Assuming that *m_wndCBEx* is a *ComboBoxEx* data member of a dialog class, that *m_wndCBEx* is mapped to a ComboBoxEx control in the dialog, and that *m_il* is an instance of *CImageList*, the following statements initialize the control with items labeled "Item 1" through "Item 5." Next to each item appears a folder image extracted from the image list. The image list, in turn, acquires the image from the bitmap resource IDB_IMAGE:

```
m_il.Create (IDB_IMAGE, 16, 1, RGB (255, 0, 255));
m_wndCBEx.SetImageList (&m_il);

for (int i=0; i<5; i++) {
    CString string;
    string.Format (_T ("Item %d"), i);

    COMBOBOXEXITEM cbei;
    cbei.mask = CBEIF_IMAGE | CBEIF_SELECTEDIMAGE | CBEIF_TEXT;
    cbei.iItem = i;
    cbei.pszText = (LPTSTR) (LPCTSTR) string;
    cbei.iImage = 0;
    cbei.iSelectedImage = 0;

    m_wndCBEx.InsertItem (&cbei);
}
```

The key functions used in this sample include *CComboBoxEx::SetImageList*, which associates an image list with a ComboBoxEx control, and *CComboBoxEx::InsertItem*, which adds an item to the control. *InsertItem* accepts a pointer to a COMBO-BOXEXITEM structure containing pertinent information about the item, including the item's text and the 0-based indexes of the images (if any) associated with the item. *iImage* identifies the image displayed next to the item when the item isn't selected, and *iSelectedImage* identifies the image that's displayed when the item is selected. Figure 16-7 shows the resulting control with its drop-down list displayed.

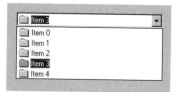

Figure 16-7. *A ComboBoxEx control containing both text and images.*

You can indent an item in a ComboBoxEx control by specifying a nonzero number of "spaces" in COMBOBOXEXITEM's *iIndent* field. Each space equals 10 pixels. The following example initializes a ComboBoxEx control that's identical to the one in the preceding example except for the fact that each successive item is indented one space more than the previous item:

```
m_il.Create (IDB_IMAGE, 16, 1, RGB (255, 0, 255));
m_wndCBEx.SetImageList (&m_il);

for (int i=0; i<5; i++) {
    CString string;
    string.Format (_T ("Item %d"), i);

    COMBOBOXEXITEM cbei;
    cbei.mask = CBEIF_IMAGE | CBEIF_SELECTEDIMAGE | CBEIF_TEXT |
        CBEIF_INDENT;
    cbei.iItem = i;
    cbei.pszText = (LPTSTR) (LPCTSTR) string;
    cbei.iImage = 0;
    cbei.iSelectedImage = 0;
    cbei.iIndent = i;

    m_wndCBEx.InsertItem (&cbei);
}
```

The result is shown in Figure 16-8. The ability to indent items an arbitrary number of spaces comes in handy when you use a ComboBoxEx control to display items that share a hierarchical relationship, such as the names of the individual directories comprising a path name.

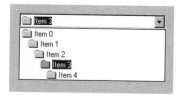

Figure 16-8. *A ComboBoxEx control containing indented items.*

InsertItem is one of four *CComboBoxEx* member functions that you can use to manipulate items in a ComboBoxEx control. The others are *DeleteItem*, which removes an item; *GetItem*, which copies the information about an item to a COMBOBOXEXITEM structure; and *SetItem*, which modifies an item using information supplied in a COMBOBOXEXITEM structure.

CComboBoxEx has just a handful of member functions of its own. Common operations such as selecting an item or retrieving the index of the selected item are performed with *CComboBox* member functions. Because *CComboBoxEx* derives from *CComboBox*, you can call *CComboBox* functions on a *CComboBoxEx*. For example, the statement

```
m_wndCBEx.SetCurSel (nIndex);
```

selects the item whose 0-based index is *nIndex*, and the statement

```
int nIndex = m_wndCBEx.GetCurSel ();
```

sets *nIndex* equal to the index of the currently selected item.

Like conventional combo boxes, ComboBoxEx controls come in three varieties: simple, drop-down, and drop-down list. You pick the type by choosing one of the three primary combo box styles: CBS_SIMPLE, CBS_DROPDOWN, or CBS_DROP-DOWNLIST. Other CBS styles, such as CBS_SORT, don't apply to ComboBoxEx controls and are ignored if you use them. ComboBoxEx controls do support a few styles of their own, however. These styles are known as *extended styles* and can't be applied in a dialog template or a *Create* statement; instead, you must apply them programmatically with *CComboBoxEx::SetExtendedStyle* after the control is created. The following table lists the extended styles that are supported on all platforms. To configure the control to treat text as case-sensitive, for example, you would write:

```
m_wndCBEx.SetExtendedStyle (CBES_EX_CASESENSITIVE,
    CBES_EX_CASESENSITIVE);
```

The second parameter you pass to *SetExtendedStyle* specifies the style or styles that you want to apply. The first parameter is a style mask that you can use to prevent other styles from being affected, too. Passing zero in parameter 1 effectively eliminates the mask.

COMBOBOXEX CONTROL EXTENDED STYLES

Style	*Description*
CBES_EX_CASESENSITIVE	Makes string searches case-sensitive
CBES_EX_NOEDITIMAGE	Suppresses item images
CBES_EX_NOEDITIMAGEINDENT	Suppresses item images and left-indents each item to remove the space normally reserved for the item image
CBES_EX_NOSIZELIMIT	Allows the ComboBoxEx control's height to be less than the height of the combo box contained inside the control

A ComboBoxEx control sends the same CBN notifications to its parent that a conventional combo box sends. It also supports the notifications of its own that are listed in the following table.

COMBOBOXEX NOTIFICATIONS

Notification	Sent When
CBEN_BEGINEDIT	The user displays the control's drop-down list or clicks the edit control to begin editing.
CBEN_ENDEDIT	The user selects an item from the control's list box or edits the control's text directly.
CBEN_DRAGBEGIN	The user drags an item in the control to begin a drag-and-drop operation.
CBEN_INSERTITEM	An item is added to the control.
CBEN_DELETEITEM	An item is removed from the control.
CBEN_GETDISPINFO	The control needs additional information—a text string, an image, an indentation level, or some combination thereof —about an item before displaying that item.
NM_SETCURSOR	The control is about to set the cursor in response to a WM-_SETCURSOR message.

MFC applications use ON_NOTIFY macros to map CBEN notifications to handling functions in the parent's window class. CBEN_GETDISPINFO notifications are sent only if the *pszText* field of a COMBOBOXEXITEM structure passed to *Insert-Item* contains LPSTR_TEXTCALLBACK, the *iImage* or *iSelectedImage* field contains I_IMAGECALLBACK, or the *iIndent* field contains I_INDENTCALLBACK. You can use these special values to create dynamic ComboBoxEx controls that supply text, images, and indentation levels on the fly rather than at the time the items are inserted.

The PathList Application

PathList, shown in Figure 16-9, is a dialog-based MFC application that uses a Combo-BoxEx control to depict path names. The control is an instance of *CPathComboBox*, which I derived from *CComboBoxEx*. *CPathComboBox* has two public member functions: *SetPath* and *GetPath*. When passed a fully qualified path name, *SetPath* parses the path name and adds indented items representing the individual directories that make up the path. (*SetPath* checks the drive letter but doesn't validate the remainder of the path name.) *GetPath* returns a fully qualified path name that corresponds to the drive or directory that is currently selected in the control.

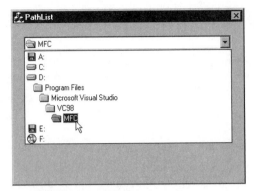

Figure 16-9. *The PathList window.*

The source code for PathList's dialog and ComboBoxEx classes is shown in Figure 16-10. PathList's dialog window does very little with the ComboBoxEx control other than host it. It calls *SetPath* with the path to the current directory when it starts up, and it displays the path name returned by *GetPath* when an item is selected. The control class *CPathComboBox* contains most of the interesting stuff, including the code that parses path names passed to *SetPath*, adds items to the control, removes the old items when the path name changes, and so on. Take the time to understand how it works and you'll be well on your way to understanding ComboBoxEx controls, too.

PathListDlg.h

```
// PathListDlg.h : header file
//

#if !defined(
    AFX_PATHLISTDLG_H__710413E6_AC66_11D2_8E53_006008A82731__INCLUDED_)
#define AFX_PATHLISTDLG_H__710413E6_AC66_11D2_8E53_006008A82731__INCLUDED_

#if _MSC_VER > 1000
#pragma once
#endif // _MSC_VER > 1000


/////////////////////////////////////////////////////////////////////////////
// CPathListDlg dialog

class CPathListDlg : public CDialog
{
// Construction
public:
    CPathListDlg(CWnd* pParent = NULL);     // standard constructor
```

Figure 16-10. *The PathList application.*

```
// Dialog Data
    //{{AFX_DATA(CPathListDlg)
    enum { IDD = IDD_PATHLIST_DIALOG };
    CPathComboBox    m_wndCBEx;
    //}}AFX_DATA

    // ClassWizard generated virtual function overrides
    //{{AFX_VIRTUAL(CPathListDlg)
    protected:
    virtual void DoDataExchange(CDataExchange* pDX);    // DDX/DDV support
    //}}AFX_VIRTUAL

// Implementation
protected:
    HICON m_hIcon;

    // Generated message map functions
    //{{AFX_MSG(CPathListDlg)
    virtual BOOL OnInitDialog();
    afx_msg void OnPaint();
    afx_msg HCURSOR OnQueryDragIcon();
    afx_msg void OnSelEndOK();
    //}}AFX_MSG
    DECLARE_MESSAGE_MAP()
};

//{{AFX_INSERT_LOCATION}}
// Microsoft Visual C++ will insert additional declarations
// immediately before the previous line.

#endif
// !defined(
//     AFX_PATHLISTDLG_H__710413E6_AC66_11D2_8E53_006008A82731__INCLUDED_)
```

PathListDlg.cpp

```
// PathListDlg.cpp : implementation file
//

#include "stdafx.h"
#include "PathList.h"
#include "PathComboBox.h"
#include "PathListDlg.h"
```

(continued)

Figure 16-10 *continued*

```
#ifdef _DEBUG
#define new DEBUG_NEW
#undef THIS_FILE
static char THIS_FILE[] = __FILE__;
#endif


/////////////////////////////////////////////////////////////////////////////
// CPathListDlg dialog

CPathListDlg::CPathListDlg(CWnd* pParent /*=NULL*/)
    : CDialog(CPathListDlg::IDD, pParent)
{
    //{{AFX_DATA_INIT(CPathListDlg)
    //}}AFX_DATA_INIT
    m_hIcon = AfxGetApp()->LoadIcon(IDR_MAINFRAME);
}

void CPathListDlg::DoDataExchange(CDataExchange* pDX)
{
    CDialog::DoDataExchange(pDX);
    //{{AFX_DATA_MAP(CPathListDlg)
    DDX_Control(pDX, IDC_CBEX, m_wndCBEx);
    //}}AFX_DATA_MAP
}

BEGIN_MESSAGE_MAP(CPathListDlg, CDialog)
    //{{AFX_MSG_MAP(CPathListDlg)
    ON_WM_PAINT()
    ON_WM_QUERYDRAGICON()
    ON_CBN_SELENDOK(IDC_CBEX, OnSelEndOK)
    //}}AFX_MSG_MAP
END_MESSAGE_MAP()


/////////////////////////////////////////////////////////////////////////////
// CPathListDlg message handlers

BOOL CPathListDlg::OnInitDialog()
{
    CDialog::OnInitDialog();

    SetIcon(m_hIcon, TRUE);
    SetIcon(m_hIcon, FALSE);

    //
    // Initialize the ComboBoxEx control.
    //
```

```
        TCHAR szPath[MAX_PATH];
        ::GetCurrentDirectory (sizeof (szPath) / sizeof (TCHAR), szPath);
        m_wndCBEx.SetPath (szPath);
        return TRUE;
}

void CPathListDlg::OnPaint()
{
        if (IsIconic())
        {
                CPaintDC dc(this); // device context for painting

                SendMessage(WM_ICONERASEBKGND, (WPARAM) dc.GetSafeHdc(), 0);

                // Center icon in client rectangle
                int cxIcon = GetSystemMetrics(SM_CXICON);
                int cyIcon = GetSystemMetrics(SM_CYICON);
                CRect rect;
                GetClientRect(&rect);
                int x = (rect.Width() - cxIcon + 1) / 2;
                int y = (rect.Height() - cyIcon + 1) / 2;

                // Draw the icon
                dc.DrawIcon(x, y, m_hIcon);
        }
        else
        {
                CDialog::OnPaint();
        }
}

HCURSOR CPathListDlg::OnQueryDragIcon()
{
        return (HCURSOR) m_hIcon;
}

void CPathListDlg::OnSelEndOK()
{
        //
        // Display the path just selected from the ComboBoxEx control.
        //
        MessageBox (m_wndCBEx.GetPath ());
}
```

(continued)

Figure 16-10 *continued*

PathComboBox.h

```
#if !defined(
    AFX_PATHCOMBOBOX_H__710413F1_AC66_11D2_8E53_006008A82731__INCLUDED_)
#define AFX_PATHCOMBOBOX_H__710413F1_AC66_11D2_8E53_006008A82731__INCLUDED_

#if _MSC_VER > 1000
#pragma once
#endif // _MSC_VER > 1000
// PathComboBox.h : header file
//

/////////////////////////////////////////////////////////////////////////////
// CPathComboBox window

class CPathComboBox : public CComboBoxEx
{
// Construction
public:
    CPathComboBox();

// Attributes
public:

// Operations
public:

// Overrides
    // ClassWizard generated virtual function overrides
    //{{AFX_VIRTUAL(CPathComboBox)
    //}}AFX_VIRTUAL

// Implementation
public:
    CString GetPath();
    BOOL SetPath (LPCTSTR pszPath);
    virtual ~CPathComboBox();

    // Generated message map functions
protected:
    void GetSubstring (int& nStart, CString& string, CString& result);
    int m_nIndexEnd;
    int m_nIndexStart;
    BOOL m_bFirstCall;
    CImageList m_il;
    //{{AFX_MSG(CPathComboBox)
```

```
        //}}AFX_MSG

    DECLARE_MESSAGE_MAP()
};

//////////////////////////////////////////////////////////////////////////

//{{AFX_INSERT_LOCATION}}
// Microsoft Visual C++ will insert additional declarations
// immediately before the previous line.

#endif
// !defined(
//      AFX_PATHCOMBOBOX_H__710413F1_AC66_11D2_8E53_006008A82731__INCLUDED_)
```

PathComboBox.cpp

```cpp
// PathComboBox.cpp : implementation file
//

#include "stdafx.h"
#include "PathList.h"
#include "PathComboBox.h"

#ifdef _DEBUG
#define new DEBUG_NEW
#undef THIS_FILE
static char THIS_FILE[] = __FILE__;
#endif

//////////////////////////////////////////////////////////////////////////
// CPathComboBox

CPathComboBox::CPathComboBox()
{
    m_bFirstCall = TRUE;
    m_nIndexStart = -1;
    m_nIndexEnd = -1;
}

CPathComboBox::~CPathComboBox()
{
}
```

(continued)

Figure 16-10 *continued*

```
BEGIN_MESSAGE_MAP(CPathComboBox, CComboBoxEx)
    //{{AFX_MSG_MAP(CPathComboBox)
    //}}AFX_MSG_MAP
END_MESSAGE_MAP()

/////////////////////////////////////////////////////////////////////////
// CPathComboBox message handlers

BOOL CPathComboBox::SetPath(LPCTSTR pszPath)
{
    if (m_bFirstCall) {
        m_bFirstCall = FALSE;

        //
        // Add an image list containing drive and folder images.
        //
        m_il.Create (IDB_IMAGES, 16, 1, RGB (255, 0, 255));
        SetImageList (&m_il);

        //
        // Add icons representing the drives on the host system.
        //
        int nPos = 0;
        int nCount = 0;
        CString string = _T ("?:\\");

        DWORD dwDriveList = ::GetLogicalDrives ();

        while (dwDriveList) {
            if (dwDriveList & 1) {
                string.SetAt (0, _T ('A') + nPos);
                CString strDrive = string.Left (2);
                UINT nType = ::GetDriveType (string);

                int nImage = 0;
                switch (nType) {

                case DRIVE_FIXED:
                    nImage = 0;
                    break;

                case DRIVE_REMOVABLE:
                    nImage = 1;
                    break;
```

```
                    case DRIVE_CDROM:
                        nImage = 2;
                        break;

                    case DRIVE_REMOTE:
                        nImage = 3;
                        break;
                }

                COMBOBOXEXITEM cbei;
                cbei.mask = CBEIF_TEXT | CBEIF_IMAGE | CBEIF_SELECTEDIMAGE;
                cbei.iItem = nCount++;
                cbei.pszText = (LPTSTR) (LPCTSTR) strDrive;
                cbei.iImage = nImage;
                cbei.iSelectedImage = nImage;
                InsertItem (&cbei);
            }
            dwDriveList >>= 1;
            nPos++;
        }
    }

    //
    // Find the item that corresponds to the drive specifier in pszPath.
    //
    CString strPath = pszPath;
    CString strDrive = strPath.Left (2);

    int nDriveIndex = FindStringExact (-1, strDrive);
    if (nDriveIndex == CB_ERR)
        return FALSE;

    //
    // Delete previously added folder items (if any).
    //
    if (m_nIndexStart != -1 && m_nIndexEnd != -1) {
        ASSERT (m_nIndexEnd >= m_nIndexStart);
        int nCount = m_nIndexEnd - m_nIndexStart + 1;
        for (int i=0; i<nCount; i++)
            DeleteItem (m_nIndexStart);
        if (m_nIndexStart < nDriveIndex)
            nDriveIndex -= nCount;
        m_nIndexStart = -1;
        m_nIndexEnd = -1;
    }
```

(continued)

Figure 16-10 *continued*

```
    //
    // Add items representing the directories in pszPath.
    //
    int nCount = 0;
    int nStringIndex = strPath.Find (_T ('\\'), 0);

    if (nStringIndex++ != -1) {
        CString strItem;
        GetSubstring (nStringIndex, strPath, strItem);

        while (!strItem.IsEmpty ()) {
            COMBOBOXEXITEM cbei;
            cbei.mask = CBEIF_TEXT | CBEIF_IMAGE | CBEIF_SELECTEDIMAGE |
                CBEIF_INDENT;
            cbei.iItem = nDriveIndex + ++nCount;
            cbei.pszText = (LPTSTR) (LPCTSTR) strItem;
            cbei.iImage = 4;
            cbei.iSelectedImage = 5;
            cbei.iIndent = nCount;
            InsertItem (&cbei);

            GetSubstring (nStringIndex, strPath, strItem);
        }
    }

    //
    // Record the indexes of the items that were added, too.
    //
    if (nCount) {
        m_nIndexStart = nDriveIndex + 1;
        m_nIndexEnd = nDriveIndex + nCount;
    }

    //
    // Finish up by selecting the final item.
    //
    int nResult = SetCurSel (nDriveIndex + nCount);
    return TRUE;
}

void CPathComboBox::GetSubstring(int& nStart, CString &string,
    CString &result)
{
    result = _T ("");
    int nLen = string.GetLength ();
```

```
        if (nStart >= nLen)
            return;

        int nEnd = string.Find (_T ('\\'), nStart);
        if (nEnd == -1) {
            result = string.Right (nLen - nStart);
            nStart = nLen;
        }
        else {
            result = string.Mid (nStart, nEnd - nStart);
            nStart = nEnd + 1;
        }
}

CString CPathComboBox::GetPath()
{
        //
        // Get the index of the selected item.
        //
        CString strResult;
        int nEnd = GetCurSel ();
        int nStart = nEnd + 1;

        //
        // Find the index of the "root" item.
        //
        COMBOBOXEXITEM cbei;
        do {
            cbei.mask = CBEIF_INDENT;
            cbei.iItem = --nStart;
            GetItem (&cbei);
        } while (cbei.iIndent != 0);

        //
        // Build a path name by combining all the items from the root item to
        // the selected item.
        //
        for (int i=nStart; i<=nEnd; i++) {
            TCHAR szItem[MAX_PATH];
            COMBOBOXEXITEM cbei;
            cbei.mask = CBEIF_TEXT;
            cbei.iItem = i;
            cbei.pszText = szItem;
            cbei.cchTextMax = sizeof (szItem) / sizeof (TCHAR);
            GetItem (&cbei);
```

(continued)

Figure 16-10 *continued*

```
      strResult += szItem;
      strResult += _T ("\\");
   }

   //
   // Strip the trailing backslash.
   //
   int nLen = strResult.GetLength ();
   strResult = strResult.Left (nLen - 1);
   return strResult;
}
```

PROGRESS CONTROLS AND ANIMATION CONTROLS

Comctl32.dll includes two convenient tools for providing visual feedback to users concerning the status of ongoing operations. The first is the progress control. A *progress control* is a vertical or horizontal rectangle containing a colored bar that grows as an operation approaches completion. The second is the *animation control*, which reduces the complex task of playing an AVI file to two simple function calls. Although animation controls enjoy a variety of uses, very often they are used simply to let the user know that a lengthy operation is underway.

Progress Controls

MFC represents progress controls with instances of the class *CProgressCtrl*. By default, a progress control is oriented horizontally and its bar is drawn as a series of line segments. You can orient a progress control vertically by assigning it the style PBS_VERTICAL, and you can change the bar from broken to solid with PBS_SMOOTH. (See Figure 16-11.) Unfortunately, neither style is supported in the absence of Internet Explorer 3.0 or later.

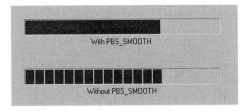

Figure 16-11. *Progress controls with and without the style PBS_SMOOTH.*

Like slider controls, progress controls have ranges and positions. If a progress control's range is 0 to 100 and its position is 20, the bar fills 20 percent of the control.

If the range is 100 to 400 and the position is 300, the bar extends two-thirds of the control's length. The default range is 0 to 100, but you can change it to anything you like with *CProgressCtrl::SetRange*. If *m_wndProgress* is a *CProgressCtrl* object, the statement

```
m_wndProgress.SetRange (100, 400);
```

sets the control's range to 100 to 400. *SetRange* limits its minimums and maximums to 16-bit values, but if Internet Explorer 3.0 or later is installed, you can specify 32-bit ranges using the newer *CProgressCtrl::SetRange32* function. To retrieve the current range, use *GetRange*. *GetRange* handles both 16-bit and 32-bit ranges.

Once you've created a progress control and set its range, you can set its position with *CProgressCtrl::SetPos*. The following example steps a progress control from 0 to 100 in about 2½ seconds by calling *SetPos* repeatedly from a loop that uses the *::Sleep* API function to ensure that each iteration requires at least 25 milliseconds:

```
m_wndProgress.SetRange (0, 100);
m_wndProgress.SetPos (0);
for (int i=0; i<100; i++) {
    m_wndProgress.SetPos (i);
    ::Sleep (25);
}
m_wndProgress.SetPos (0);
```

That's one way to step a progress control. You can also use the *OffsetPos* function to specify a new position that's relative to the current one. Here's the previous code sample rewritten to use *OffsetPos*:

```
m_wndProgress.SetRange (0, 100);
m_wndProgress.SetPos (0);
for (int i=0; i<100; i++) {
    m_wndProgress.OffsetPos (1);
    ::Sleep (25);
}
m_wndProgress.SetPos (0);
```

A third way to step a progress control is to assign the control a step size with *SetStep* and then to increment the position by the current step size with *StepIt*:

```
m_wndProgress.SetRange (0, 100);
m_wndProgress.SetPos (0);
m_wndProgress.SetStep (1);
for (int i=0; i<100; i++) {
    m_wndProgress.StepIt ();
    ::Sleep (25);
}
m_wndProgress.SetPos (0);
```

You can call the complementary *CProgressCtrl::GetPos* function at any time to retrieve the control's current position.

By default, the color of the bar in a progress control is the system color COLOR-_HIGHLIGHT, and the control's background color is COLOR_3DFACE. On systems equipped with Internet Explorer 4.0 or higher, you can change the bar color with a PBM_SETBARCOLOR message, and you can change the control's background color with a PBM_SETBKCOLOR message. Because *CProgressCtrl* lacks wrapper functions for these messages, you must send the messages yourself. For example, the statement

```
m_wndProgress.SendMessage (PBM_SETBARCOLOR, 0, (LPARAM) RGB (255, 0, 0));
```

changes *m_wndProgress*'s bar color to red.

One of the sample programs in the next chapter—ImageEdit—uses a progress control to provide visual feedback regarding an image processing operation. The progress control is attached to a status bar and in fact appears to be an ordinary status bar pane until the operation begins and the bar begins stepping across the face of the control. If you'd like to see a progress control in action, feel free to skip ahead and take a look at ImageEdit.

Animation Controls

Animation controls simplify the task of playing video clips in a dialog box or a window. The video clips must be in Windows AVI format, and they can have at most two streams inside them. If one of the streams is an audio stream, it is ignored. Visual Studio comes with a number of sample AVI files that work well in animation controls. One of those sample files, Findfile.avi, contains the circling magnifying glass featured in the system's Find utility. Another, Filecopy.avi, contains the "flying paper" clip you see when you drag-copy a large file or group of files from one folder to another.

CAnimateCtrl wraps the functionality of animation controls in an easy-to-use C++ class. Using *CAnimateCtrl* is simplicity itself. *CAnimateCtrl::Open* loads an AVI clip from a resource or an external file. *CAnimateCtrl::Play* begins playing the clip, *CAnimateCtrl::Stop* stops it, and *CAnimateCtrl::Close* unloads the clip. Assuming that *m_wndAnimate* is an instance of *CAnimateCtrl* and that it is associated with an animation control, the following code sample loads an AVI file named Findfile.avi and begins playing it:

```
m_wndAnimate.Open (_T ("Findfile.avi"));
m_wndAnimate.Play (0, -1, -1);
```

Open will accept a resource ID in lieu of a file name, enabling you to embed AVI clips as resources in EXE files:

```
// In the RC file
IDR_FINDFILE AVI "Findfile.avi"
    ⋮
    ⋮
// In the CPP file
m_wndAnimate.Open (IDR_FINDFILE);
m_wndAnimate.Play (0, -1, -1);
```

Play starts the animation and returns immediately; it doesn't wait around for the animation to stop. That's good, because it means the thread that called *Play* can continue working while the animation plays in the background.

Play accepts three parameters: the starting and ending frame numbers and the number of times the animation should be played. Specifying 0, −1, and −1 for these parameters tells the control to play all the frames and to repeat them indefinitely until *Stop* is called, like this:

```
m_wndAnimate.Stop ();
```

After you call *Stop*, you should call *Close* to remove the clip from memory if you don't intend to play it anymore:

```
m_wndAnimate.Close ();
```

Every call to *Open* should be accompanied by a call to *Close* to prevent resource leaks.

Animation controls support four styles that affect their appearance and operation. ACS_AUTOPLAY configures the control to begin playing an animation as soon as it is opened rather than waiting for *Play* to be called. ACS_CENTER centers the output in the control rectangle. Without this style, the clip plays in the upper left corner of the control rectangle and the control is resized to fit the frames contained in the animation. ACS_TRANSPARENT plays the animation using a transparent background instead of the background color designated inside the AVI file. Finally, ACS_TIMER prevents the control from launching a background thread to do its drawing. Rather than start another thread (threads consume resources, and too many threads can bog down the system), an ACS_TIMER-style animation control sets a timer in the caller's thread and uses timer callbacks to draw successive frames. ACS_TIMER is supported only on systems equipped with Internet Explorer 3.0 or later.

IP ADDRESS CONTROLS AND OTHER DATA-ENTRY CONTROLS

IP address controls, hotkey controls, month calendar controls, and date-time picker controls all have one characteristic in common: they exist to make it easy to solicit specially formatted input from the user. Some of them, such as the IP address control, are exceedingly simple; others, such as the date-time picker control, offer an intimidating array of options. All are relatively easy to program, however, especially when you use the wrapper classes provided by MFC. The sections that follow provide an overview of all four control types and present code samples demonstrating their use.

IP Address Controls

IP address controls facilitate the effortless entry of 32-bit IP addresses consisting of four 8-bit integer values separated by periods, as in 10.255.10.1. The control accepts numeric input only and is divided into four 3-digit fields, as shown in Figure 16-12. When the user types three digits into a field, the input focus automatically moves to the next field. IP address controls exist only on systems that have Internet Explorer 4.0 or later installed.

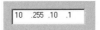

Figure 16-12. *The IP address control.*

MFC codifies the interface to IP address controls with *CIPAddressCtrl*. *CIPAddressCtrl* functions named *SetAddress* and *GetAddress* get IP addresses in and out. If *m_wndIPAddress* is a *CIPAddressCtrl* data member in a dialog class, the following *OnInitDialog* and *OnOK* functions initialize the control with the IP address stored in *m_nField1* through *m_nField4* when the dialog box is created and retrieve the IP address from the control when the dialog box is dismissed:

```
// In CMyDialog's class declaration
BYTE m_nField1, m_nField2, m_nField3, m_nField4;
    :
    :

BOOL CMyDialog::OnInitDialog ()
{
    CDialog::OnInitDialog ();
    m_wndIPAddress.SetAddress (m_nField1, m_nField2,
        m_nField3, m_nField4);
    return TRUE;
}

void CMyDialog::OnOK ()
{
    m_wndIPAddress.GetAddress (m_nField1, m_nField2,
        m_nField3, m_nField4);
    CDialog::OnOK ();
}
```

You can also empty an IP address control with *CIPAddressCtrl::ClearAddress* or find out whether it is currently empty with *CIPAddressCtrl::IsBlank*. Another *CIPAddressCtrl* member function, *SetFieldFocus*, programmatically moves the input focus to a specified field.

By default, each field in an IP address control accepts a value from 0 to 255. You can change the range of values that a given field will accept with *CIPAddress-Ctrl::SetFieldRange*. The following statement configures the control to restrict values entered into the control's first field to 10 through 100 and values entered in the final field to 100 through 155, inclusive:

```
m_wndIPAddress.SetFieldRange (0, 10, 100); // Field 1
m_wndIPAddress.SetFieldRange (3, 100, 155); // Field 4
```

The control prevents invalid values from being entered into a field by automatically converting values that fall outside the allowable range to the upper or lower limit of that range, whichever is appropriate.

IP address controls send four types of notifications to their owners. EN_SET-FOCUS and EN_KILLFOCUS notifications signify that the control gained or lost the input focus. EN_CHANGE notifications indicate that the data in the control has changed. All three notifications are encapsulated in WM_COMMAND messages. IP address controls also send IPN_FIELDCHANGED notifications when a field's value changes or the input focus moves from one field to another. IPN_FIELDCHANGED is unique among IP address control notifications in that it is transmitted in WM-_NOTIFY messages.

Hotkey Controls

Hotkey controls are similar in concept to IP address controls. The chief difference is that hotkey controls accept key combinations instead of IP addresses. A hotkey control is essentially a glorified edit control that automatically converts key combinations such as Ctrl-Alt-P into text strings suitable for displaying on the screen. Hotkey controls are so-called because the key combinations entered in them are sometimes converted into hotkeys with WM_SETHOTKEY messages. Data entered into a hotkey control doesn't have to be used for hotkeys, however; it can be used any way that you, the developer, see fit.

MFC represents hotkey controls with instances of *CHotKeyCtrl*. Member functions named *SetHotKey* and *GetHotKey* convert key combinations into text strings displayed by the control, and vice versa. The following statement initializes a hotkey control represented by the *CHotKeyCtrl* object *m_wndHotkey* with the key combination Ctrl-Alt-P. The control responds by displaying the text string "Ctrl + Alt + P":

```
m_wndHotkey.SetHotKey (_T ('P'), HOTKEYF_CONTROL ¦ HOTKEYF_ALT);
```

The next two statements read data from the hotkey control into variables named *wKeyCode*, which holds a virtual key code, and *wModifiers*, which holds bit flags specifying which, if any, modifier keys—Ctrl, Alt, and Shift—are included in the key combination:

```
WORD wKeyCode, wModifiers;
m_wndHotkey.GetHotKey (wKeyCode, wModifiers);
```

You can include similar calls to *SetHotKey* and *GetHotKey* in a dialog class's *OnInit-Dialog* and *OnOK* functions to transfer data between a hotkey control and data members of the dialog class.

By default, a hotkey control accepts key combinations that include any combination of the Ctrl, Shift, and Alt keys. You can restrict the combinations that the control will accept by calling *CHotKeyCtrl::SetRules*. *SetRules* accepts two parameters: an array of bit flags identifying invalid combinations of Ctrl, Shift, and Alt, and an array of bit flags specifying the combination of Ctrl, Shift, and Alt that should replace an invalid combination of modifier keys. For example, the statement

```
m_wndHotkey.SetRules (HKCOMB_A | HKCOMB_CA | HKCOMB_SA | HKCOMB_SCA, 0);
```

disallows any key combination that includes the Alt key, and the statement

```
m_wndHotkey.SetRules (HKCOMB_A | HKCOMB_CA | HKCOMB_SA | HKCOMB_SCA,
    HOTKEYF_CONTROL);
```

does the same but also directs the control to replace the modifiers in any key combination that includes the Alt key with the Ctrl key. See the *SetRules* documentation for a list of other supported HKCOMB flags.

Month Calendar Controls

The month calendar control, which I'll refer to simply as the *calendar control*, lets users input dates by picking them from a calendar rather than typing them into an edit control. (See Figure 16-13.) A calendar control can support single selections or multiple selections. Clicking a date in a single-selection calendar control makes that date the "current date." In a multiple-selection calendar control, the user can select a single date or a contiguous range of dates. You can set and retrieve the current selection, be it a single date or a range of dates, programmatically by sending messages to the control. MFC wraps these and other calendar control messages in member functions belonging to the *CMonthCalCtrl* class.

Figure 16-13. *The month calendar control.*

In a single-selection calendar control, *CMonthCalCtrl::SetCurSel* sets the current date and *CMonthCalCtrl::GetCurSel* retrieves it. The statement

```
m_wndCal.SetCurSel (CTime (1999, 9, 30, 0, 0, 0));
```

sets the current date to September 30, 1999, in the calendar control represented by *m_wndCal*. Ostensibly, the statements

```
CTime date;
m_wndCal.GetCurSel (date);
```

retrieve the date from the control by initializing *date* with the currently selected date. But watch out. Contrary to what the documentation says, a calendar control sometimes returns random data in the hours, minutes, seconds, and milliseconds fields of the SYSTEMTIME structure it uses to divulge dates in response to MCM_GETCURSEL messages. Because *CTime* factors the time into the dates it obtains from SYSTEMTIME structures, incrementing the day by 1, for example, if hours equals 25, *CTime* objects initialized by *CMonthCalCtrl::GetCurSel* can't be trusted. The solution is to retrieve the current date by sending the control an MCM_GETCURSEL message and zeroing the time fields of the SYSTEMTIME structure before converting it into a *CTime*, as demonstrated here:

```
SYSTEMTIME st;
m_wndCal.SendMessage (MCM_GETCURSEL, 0, (LPARAM) &st);
st.wHour = st.wMinute = st.wSecond = st.wMilliseconds = 0;
CTime date (st);
```

If you prefer, you can also use *CMonthCalCtrl*'s *SetRange* function to place upper and lower bounds on the dates that the control will allow the user to select.

The alternative to *SetCurSel* and *GetCurSel* is to use DDX to get dates in and out of a calendar control. MFC includes a DDX function named *DDX_MonthCalCtrl* that you can put in a dialog's *DoDataExchange* function to automatically transfer data between a calendar control and a *CTime* or *COleDateTime* data member. It even includes DDV functions for date validation. But guess what? *DDX_MonthCalCtrl* doesn't work because it uses *GetCurSel* to read the current date. Until this bug is fixed, your best recourse is to forego DDX and use the techniques described above to get and set the current date.

You can create a calendar control that allows the user to select a range of contiguous dates by including an MCS_MULTISELECT bit in the control's style. By default, a selection can't span more than 7 days. You can change that with *CMonthCalCtrl::SetMaxSelCount*. The statement

```
m_wndCal.SetMaxSelCount (14);
```

sets the upper limit on selection ranges to 14 days. The complementary *GetMaxSelCount* function returns the current maximum selection count.

To programmatically select a date or a range of dates in a multiple-selection calendar control, you must use *CMonthCalCtrl::SetSelRange* instead of *CMonthCalCtrl::SetCurSel*. (The latter fails if it's called on a multiple-selection calendar control.) The statements

```
m_wndCal.SetSelRange (CTime (1999, 9, 30, 0, 0, 0),
    CTime (1999, 9, 30, 0, 0, 0));
```

select September 30, 1999, in an MCS_MULTISELECT-style calendar control, and the statements

```
m_wndCal.SetSelRange (CTime (1999, 9, 16, 0, 0, 0),
    CTime (1999, 9, 30, 0, 0, 0));
```

select September 16 through September 30. This call will fail unless you first call *SetMaxSelCount* to set the maximum selection range size to 15 days or higher. To read the current selection, use *CMonthCalCtrl::GetSelRange* as demonstrated here:

```
CTime dateStart, dateEnd;
m_wndCal.GetSelRange (dateStart, dateEnd);
```

This example sets *dateStart* equal to the selection's start date and *dateEnd* to the end date. If just one day is selected, *dateStart* will equal *dateEnd*. Fortunately, *GetSelRange* doesn't suffer from the randomness problems that *GetCurSel* does.

Three calendar control styles allow you to alter a calendar control's appearance. MCS_NOTODAY removes the line that displays today's date at the bottom of the calendar; MCS_NOTODAYCIRCLE removes the circle that appears around today's date in the body of the calendar; and MCS_WEEKNUMBERS displays week numbers (1 through 52). You can further modify a calendar's appearance with *CMonthCalCtrl* functions. For example, you can change today's date (as displayed by the control) with *SetToday*, the day of the week that appears in the calendar's leftmost column with *SetFirstDayOfWeek*, and the control's colors with *SetColor*. You can even command the control to display certain dates in boldface type by calling its *SetDayState* function or processing MCN_GETDAYSTATE notifications. Be aware that *SetDayState* works (and MCN_GETDAYSTATE notifications are sent) only if MCS_DAYSTATE is included in the control style

If you'd like to know when the current date (or date range) changes in a calendar control, you can process either of two notifications. MCN_SELECT notifications are sent when the user selects a new date or range of dates. MCN_SELCHANGE notifications are sent when the user explicitly makes a selection *and* when the selection changes because the user scrolled the calendar backward or forward a month. In an MFC application, you can map these notifications to member functions in the parent window class with ON_NOTIFY or reflect them to functions in a derived control class with ON_NOTIFY_REFLECT.

Date-Time Picker Controls

Date-time picker controls, or *DTP controls*, provide developers with a simple, convenient, and easy-to-use means for soliciting dates and times from a user. A DTP control resembles an edit control, but rather than display ordinary text strings, it displays dates and times. Dates can be displayed in short format, as in 9/30/99, or long format, as in Thursday, September 30, 1999. Times are displayed in standard HH:MM:SS format followed by AM or PM. Custom date and time formats are also supported. Times and dates can be edited visually—for example, by clicking the control's up and down arrows or picking from a drop-down calendar control—or manually. MFC simplifies the interface to DTP controls with the wrapper class named *CDateTimeCtrl*.

Using a DTP control to solicit a time requires just one or two lines of code. First you assign the control the style DTS_TIMEFORMAT to configure it to display times rather than dates. Then you call *CDateTimeCtrl::SetTime* to set the time displayed in the control and *CDateTimeCtrl::GetTime* when you're ready to retrieve it. Assuming *m_wndDTP* is a *CDateTimeCtrl* data member in a dialog class and that *m_wndDTP* is mapped to a DTP control in the dialog, the following *OnInitDialog* and *OnOK* functions transfer data between the control and a *CTime* member variable in the dialog class:

```
// In CMyDialog's class declaration
CTime m_time;
       .
       .
       .

BOOL CMyDialog::OnInitDialog ()
{
    CDialog::OnInitDialog ();
    m_wndDTP.SetTime (&m_time);
    return TRUE;
}

void CMyDialog::OnOK ()
{
    m_wndDTP.GetTime (m_time);
    CDialog::OnOK ();
}
```

Rather than call *SetTime* and *GetTime* explicitly, you can use a *DDX_DateTimeCtrl* statement in the dialog's *DoDataExchange* function instead:

```
DDX_DateTimeCtrl (pDX, IDC_DTP, m_time);
```

If you use *DDX_DateTimeCtrl* to connect a DTP control to a dialog data member, you might also want to use MFC's *DDV_MinMaxDateTime* function to validate times retrieved from the control.

To display dates rather than times in a DTP control, replace DTS_TIMEFORMAT with either DTS_SHORTDATEFORMAT for short dates or DTS_LONGDATEFORMAT for long dates. You set and retrieve dates the same way you do times: with *SetTime* and *GetTime* or *DDX_DateTimeCtrl*. You can use *CDateTimeCtrl::SetRange* to limit the dates and times that a DTP control will accept.

A DTP control whose style includes DTS_UPDOWN has up and down arrows that the user can use to edit times and dates. If DTS_UPDOWN is omitted from the control style, a downward-pointing arrow similar to the arrow in a combo box replaces the up and down arrows. Clicking the downward-pointing arrow displays a drop-down calendar control, as illustrated in Figure 16-14. Thus, combining either of the date styles (DTS_SHORTDATEFORMAT or DTS_LONGDATEFORMAT) with DTS-_UPDOWN produces a DTP control in which dates are entered using up and down arrows; using either of the date styles without DTS_UPDOWN creates a control in which dates are picked from a calendar. By default, a calendar dropped down from a DTP control is left-aligned with the control. You can alter the alignment by including DTS_RIGHTALIGN in the control style. You can also use the DTS_APPCANPARSE style to allow the user to manually edit the text displayed in a DTP control. Even without this style, the keyboard's arrow keys can be used to edit time and date entries.

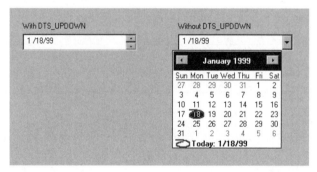

Figure 16-14. *Date-time picker controls with and without the style DTS_UPDOWN.*

CDateTimeCtrl's SetFormat function assigns custom formatting strings to a DTP control. For example, a formatting string of the form "H': 'mm': 'ss" programs a DTP control to display the time in 24-hour military format. Here's how *SetFormat* would be used to apply this formatting string:

```
m_wndDTP.SetFormat (_T ("H\':\'mm\':\'ss"));
```

In a formatting string, *H* represents a one-digit or two-digit hour in 24-hour format, *mm* represents a two-digit minute, and *ss* represents a two-digit second. The following table shows all the special characters that you can use in formatting strings. You can include literals, such as the colons in the example above, by enclosing them in single quotation marks. If you really want to get fancy, you can use Xs to define *call-*

back fields. A DTP control uses DTN_FORMAT and DTN_FORMATQUERY notifications to determine what to display in a callback field, enabling an application that processes these notifications to provide text to a DTP control at run time.

DTP FORMATTING CHARACTERS

Character(s)	Description
d	One-digit or two-digit day
dd	Two-digit day
ddd	Three-character day of the week abbreviation (for example, Mon or Tue)
dddd	Full day of the week name (for example, Monday or Tuesday)
b	One-digit or two-digit hour in 12-hour format
bb	Two-digit hour in 12-hour format
H	One-digit or two-digit hour in 24-hour format
HH	Two-digit hour in 24-hour format
m	One-digit or two-digit minute
mm	Two-digit minute
M	One-digit or two-digit month
MM	Two-digit month
MMM	Three-character month abbreviation (for example, Jan or Feb)
MMMM	Full month name (for example, January or February)
s	One-digit or two-digit second
ss	Two-digit second
t	Displays A for a.m. or P for p.m.
tt	Displays AM for a.m. or PM for p.m.
X	Callback field
y	One-digit year
yy	Two-digit year
yyyy	Four-digit year

DTP controls send a variety of other notifications to their parents. If you want to know when a drop-down calendar control is displayed, listen for DTN_DROPDOWN notifications. When a DTN_DROPDOWN notification arrives, you can call *CDateTimeCtrl::GetMonthCalCtrl* to acquire a *CMonthCalCtrl* pointer that you can use to modify the calendar control. If you simply want to know when the time or the date in a DTP control changes, process DTN_DATETIMECHANGE notifications. Consult the Platform SDK documentation on DTP controls for details concerning these and other DTP control notifications.

Chapter 17

Threads and Thread Synchronization

In the Microsoft Win32 environment, every running application constitutes a *process* and every process contains one or more threads of execution. A *thread* is a path of execution through a program's code, plus a set of resources (stack, register state, and so on) assigned by the operating system.

A fundamental difference between 16-bit and 32-bit versions of Microsoft Windows is that 32-bit Windows doesn't limit its applications to just one thread each. A process in a 32-bit Windows application begins its life as a single thread, but that thread can spawn additional threads. A preemptive scheduler in the operating system kernel divides CPU time among active threads so that they appear to run simultaneously. Threads are ideal for performing tasks in the background while processing user input in the foreground. They can also play more visible roles by creating windows and processing messages to those windows, just as the primary thread processes messages sent to an application's main window.

Multithreading isn't for everyone. Multithreaded applications are difficult to write and debug because the parallelism of concurrently running threads adds an extra layer of complexity to a program's code. Used properly, however, multiple threads can dramatically improve an application's responsiveness. A word processor that does its spell checking in a dedicated thread, for example, can continue to process messages in the primary thread and allow the user to continue to work while the spelling checker runs its course. What makes writing a threaded spelling checker difficult is that the spell checking thread will invariably have to synchronize its actions with other threads in the application. Most programmers have been conditioned to think about their code in synchronous terms—function A calls function B, function B performs some task and returns to A, and so on. But threads are asynchronous by nature. In a multithreaded application, you have to think about what happens if, say, two threads call function B at the same time or one thread reads a variable while another writes it. If function A launches function B in a separate thread, you also must anticipate the problems that could occur if function A continues to run while function B executes. For example, it's common to pass the address of a variable created on the stack in function A to function B for processing. But if function B is in another thread, the variable might no longer exist when function B gets around to accessing it. Even the most innocent-looking code can be fatally flawed when it involves two different threads.

MFC encapsulates threads of execution in the *CWinThread* class. It also encapsulates events, mutexes, and other Win32 thread synchronization objects in easy-to-use C++ classes. Does MFC make multithreading easier? Not exactly. Developers who have written multithreaded Windows applications in C are often surprised to learn that MFC adds complexities all its own. The key to writing multithreaded programs in MFC is having a keen understanding of what you're doing and knowing where the trouble spots are. This chapter will help you do both.

THREADS

As far as Windows is concerned, all threads are alike. MFC, however, distinguishes between two types of threads: *user interface* (UI) *threads* and *worker threads*. The difference between the two is that UI threads have message loops and worker threads don't. UI threads can create windows and process messages sent to those windows. Worker threads perform background tasks that receive no direct input from the user and therefore don't need windows and message loops.

The system itself provides two very good examples of how UI threads and worker threads can be used. When you open a folder in the operating system shell, the shell launches a UI thread that creates a window showing the folder's contents. If you drag-copy a group of files to the newly opened folder, that folder's thread performs the file transfers. (Sometimes the UI thread creates yet another thread—this time a worker thread—to copy the files.) The benefit of this multithreaded architecture is that, once the copy has begun, you can switch to windows opened onto other folders and continue working while the files are being copied in the background. Launching a UI thread that creates a window is conceptually similar to launching an application within an application. The most common use for UI threads is to create multiple windows serviced by separate threads of execution.

Worker threads are ideal for performing isolated tasks that can be broken off from the rest of the application and performed in the background. A classic example of a worker thread is the thread that an animation control uses to play AVI clips. That thread does little more than draw a frame, put itself to sleep for a fraction of a second, and wake up and repeat the process. It adds little to the processor's workload because it spends most of its life suspended between frames, and yet it also provides a valuable service. This is a great example of multithreaded design because the background thread is given a specific task to do and then allowed to perform that task over and over until the primary thread signals that it's time to end.

Creating a Worker Thread

The best way to launch a thread in an MFC application is to call *AfxBeginThread*. MFC defines two different versions of *AfxBeginThread*: one that starts a UI thread and another that starts a worker thread. The source code for both is found in Thrdcore.cpp. Don't use the Win32 *::CreateThread* function to create a thread in an MFC program unless the thread doesn't use MFC. *AfxBeginThread* isn't merely a wrapper around the Win32 *::CreateThread* function; in addition to launching a thread, it initializes internal state information used by the framework, performs sanity checks at various points during the thread creation process, and takes steps to ensure that functions in the C run-time library are accessed in a thread-safe manner.

AfxBeginThread makes it simple—almost trivial, in fact—to create a worker thread. When called, *AfxBeginThread* creates a new *CWinThread* object, launches a thread and attaches it to the *CWinThread* object, and returns a *CWinThread* pointer. The statement

```
CWinThread* pThread = AfxBeginThread (ThreadFunc, &threadInfo);
```

starts a worker thread and passes it the address of an application-defined data structure (&*threadInfo*) that contains input to the thread. *ThreadFunc* is the *thread function*—the function that gets executed when the thread itself begins to execute. A very simple thread function that spins in a loop eating CPU cycles and then terminates looks like this:

```
UINT ThreadFunc (LPVOID pParam)
{
    UINT nIterations = (UINT) pParam;
    for (UINT i=0; i<nIterations; i++);
    return 0;
}
```

In this example, the value passed in *pParam* isn't a pointer at all, but an ordinary UINT. Thread functions are described in more detail in the next section.

The worker thread form of *AfxBeginThread* accepts as many as four additional parameters that specify the thread's priority, stack size, creation flags, and security attributes. The complete function prototype is as follows:

```
CWinThread* AfxBeginThread (AFX_THREADPROC pfnThreadProc,
    LPVOID pParam, int nPriority = THREAD_PRIORITY_NORMAL,
    UINT nStackSize = 0, DWORD dwCreateFlags = 0,
    LPSECURITY_ATTRIBUTES lpSecurityAttrs = NULL)
```

nPriority specifies the thread's execution priority. High-priority threads are scheduled for CPU time before low-priority threads, but in practice, even threads with extremely low priorities usually get all the processor time they need. *nPriority* doesn't specify an absolute priority level. It specifies a priority level relative to the priority level of the process to which the thread belongs. The default is THREAD_PRIORITY_NORMAL, which assigns the thread the same priority as the process that owns it. You can change a thread's priority level at any time with *CWinThread::SetThreadPriority*.

The *nStackSize* parameter passed to *AfxBeginThread* specifies the thread's maximum stack size. In the Win32 environment, each thread receives its own stack. The 0 default *nStackSize* value allows the stack to grow as large as 1 MB. This doesn't mean that every thread requires a minimum of 1 MB of memory; it means that each thread is assigned 1 MB of address space in the larger 4-GB address space in which 32-bit Windows applications execute. Memory isn't committed (assigned) to the stack's address space until it's needed, so most thread stacks never use more than a few kilobytes of physical memory. Placing a limit on the stack size allows the operating system to trap runaway functions that recur endlessly and eventually consume the stack. The default limit of 1 MB is fine for almost all applications.

dwCreateFlags can be one of two values. The default value 0 tells the system to start executing the thread immediately. If CREATE_SUSPENDED is specified instead, the thread starts out in a suspended state and doesn't begin running until another thread (usually the thread that created it) calls *CWinThread::ResumeThread* on the suspended thread, as demonstrated here:

```
CWinThread* pThread = AfxBeginThread (ThreadFunc, &threadInfo,
    THREAD_PRIORITY_NORMAL, 0, CREATE_SUSPENDED);
    :
    :
pThread->ResumeThread (); // Start the thread
```

Sometimes it's useful to create a thread but defer its execution until later. The CREATE_SUSPENDED flag is your mechanism for enacting delayed execution.

The final parameter in *AfxBeginThread*'s argument list, *lpSecurityAttrs*, is a pointer to a SECURITY_ATTRIBUTES structure that specifies the new thread's security attributes and also tells the system whether child processes should inherit the thread handle. The NULL default value assigns the new thread the same properties the thread that created it has.

The Thread Function

A thread function is a callback function, so it must be either a static class member function or a global function declared outside a class. It is prototyped this way:

```
UINT ThreadFunc (LPVOID pParam)
```

pParam is a 32-bit value whose value equals the *pParam* passed to *AfxBeginThread*. Very often, *pParam* is the address of an application-defined data structure containing information passed to the worker thread by the thread that created it. It can also be a scalar value, a handle, or even a pointer to an object. Using the same thread function for two or more threads is perfectly legal, but you should be sensitive to reentrancy problems caused by global and static variables. As long as the variables (and objects) a thread uses are created on the stack, no reentrancy problems occur because each thread gets its own stack.

Creating a UI Thread

Creating a UI thread is an altogether different process than creating a worker thread. A worker thread is defined by its thread function, but a UI thread's behavior is governed by a dynamically creatable class derived from *CWinThread* that resembles an application class derived from *CWinApp*. The UI thread class shown below creates a top-level frame window that closes itself when clicked with the left mouse button. Closing the window terminates the thread, too, because *CWnd::OnNcDestroy* posts a WM_QUIT message to the thread's message queue. Posting a WM_QUIT message to a secondary thread ends the thread. Posting a WM_QUIT message to a primary thread ends the thread and ends the application, too.

```
// The CUIThread class
class CUIThread : public CWinThread
{
    DECLARE_DYNCREATE (CUIThread)

public:
    virtual BOOL InitInstance ();
};

IMPLEMENT_DYNCREATE (CUIThread, CWinThread)

BOOL CUIThread::InitInstance ()
{
    m_pMainWnd = new CMainWindow;
```

(continued)

```
    m_pMainWnd->ShowWindow (SW_SHOW);
    m_pMainWnd->UpdateWindow ();
    return TRUE;
}

// The CMainWindow class
class CMainWindow : public CFrameWnd
{
public:
    CMainWindow ();

protected:
    afx_msg void OnLButtonDown (UINT, CPoint);
    DECLARE_MESSAGE_MAP ()
};

BEGIN_MESSAGE_MAP (CMainWindow, CFrameWnd)
    ON_WM_LBUTTONDOWN ()
END_MESSAGE_MAP ()

CMainWindow::CMainWindow ()
{
    Create (NULL, _T ("UI Thread Window"));
}

void CMainWindow::OnLButtonDown (UINT nFlags, CPoint point)
{
    PostMessage (WM_CLOSE, 0, 0);
}
```

Notice the SW_SHOW parameter passed to *ShowWindow* in place of the normal *m_nCmdShow* parameter. *m_nCmdShow* is a *CWinApp* data member, so when you create a top-level window from a UI thread, it's up to you to specify the window's initial state.

You launch a *CUIThread* by calling the form of *AfxBeginThread* that accepts a *CRuntimeClass* pointer to the thread class:

```
CWinThread* pThread = AfxBeginThread (RUNTIME_CLASS (CUIThread));
```

The UI-thread version of *AfxBeginThread* accepts the same four optional parameters as the worker-thread version, but it doesn't accept a *pParam* value. Once started, a UI thread runs asynchronously with respect to the thread that created it.

Suspending and Resuming Threads

A running thread can be suspended with *CWinThread::SuspendThread* and started again with *CWinThread::ResumeThread*. A thread can call *SuspendThread* on itself, or another thread can call *SuspendThread* for it. However, a suspended thread can't call *ResumeThread* to wake itself up; someone else must call *ResumeThread* on its behalf. A suspended thread consumes next to no processor time and imposes essentially zero overhead on the system.

For each thread, Windows maintains a *suspend count* that's incremented by *SuspendThread* and decremented by *ResumeThread*. A thread is scheduled for processor time only when its suspend count is 0. If *SuspendThread* is called twice in succession, *ResumeThread* must be called twice also. A thread created without a CREATE_SUSPENDED flag has an initial suspend count of 0. A thread created with a CREATE_SUSPENDED flag begins with a suspend count of 1. Both *SuspendThread* and *ResumeThread* return the thread's previous suspend count, so you can make sure a thread gets resumed no matter how high its suspend count is by calling *ResumeThread* repeatedly until it returns 1. *ResumeThread* returns 0 if the thread it's called on isn't currently suspended.

Putting Threads to Sleep

A thread can put itself to sleep for a specified period of time by calling the API function *::Sleep*. A sleeping thread uses no processor time. The statement

```
::Sleep (10000);
```

suspends the current thread for 10 seconds.

One use for *::Sleep* is to implement threads whose actions are inherently time-based, such as the background thread in an animation control or a thread that moves the hands of a clock. *::Sleep* can also be used to relinquish the remainder of a thread's timeslice. The statement

```
::Sleep (0);
```

suspends the current thread and allows the scheduler to run other threads of equal or higher priority. If no other equal or higher priority threads are awaiting execution time, the function call returns immediately and the current thread resumes execution. In Microsoft Windows NT 4.0 and higher, you can yield to another thread by calling *::SwitchToThread*. Use *::Sleep (0)* if the code you're writing must work on all Win32 platforms.

If you write an application that uses multiple threads to draw to the screen, a few strategically placed *::Sleep (0)* statements can do wonders for the quality of the output. Suppose you're animating the motion of four objects and you assign each object its own thread. Each thread is responsible for moving one object across the screen. If you simply run each thread in a loop and allow it to grab for all the processor time it can get, the motion of the objects is likely to be grainy and irregular. But if you have each thread move its assigned object a few pixels and then call *::Sleep (0)*, the animation can be performed more smoothly.

The value you pass to *::Sleep* doesn't guarantee that the thread will be awakened at the precise moment that the time-out interval elapses. Passing *::Sleep* a value of 10,000 guarantees that the thread will awaken *sometime after* 10 seconds have elapsed. The thread might sleep for 10 seconds, or it might sleep for 20—it's all up to the operating system. In practice, the thread will usually begin running again a fraction of a second after the time-out interval elapses, but there are no guarantees. Presently, no method exists in any version of Windows to suspend a thread for a precise amount of time.

Terminating a Thread

Once a thread begins, it can terminate in two ways. A worker thread ends when the thread function executes a *return* statement or when any function anywhere in the thread calls *AfxEndThread*. A UI thread terminates when a WM_QUIT message is posted to its message queue or when the thread itself calls *AfxEndThread*. A thread can post a WM_QUIT message to itself with the API function *::PostQuitMessage*. *AfxEndThread*, *::PostQuitMessage*, and *return* all accept a 32-bit exit code that can be retrieved with *::GetExitCodeThread* after the thread has terminated. The following statement copies the exit code of the thread referenced by *pThread* to *dwExitCode*:

```
DWORD dwExitCode;
::GetExitCodeThread (pThread->m_hThread, &dwExitCode);
```

If called for a thread that's still executing, *::GetExitCodeThread* sets *dwExitCode* equal to STILL_ACTIVE (0x103). In this example, the thread handle passed to *::GetExitCodeThread* is retrieved from the *m_hThread* data member of the *CWinThread* object encapsulating the thread. Anytime you have a *CWinThread* and you want to call an API function that requires a thread handle, you can get that handle from *m_hThread*.

Autodeleting *CWinThread*s

The two-line code sample in the previous section looks innocent enough, but it's an accident waiting to happen unless you're aware of a peculiar characteristic of *CWinThread* and take steps to account for it.

You already know that *AfxBeginThread* creates a *CWinThread* object and returns its address to the caller. But how does that *CWinThread* get deleted? So that you don't have to call *delete* on a *CWinThread* pointer returned by *AfxBeginThread*, MFC calls *delete* on that pointer itself after the thread has terminated. Furthermore, *CWinThread*'s destructor uses the *::CloseHandle* API function to close the thread handle. Thread handles must be closed explicitly because they remain open even after the threads associated with them have terminated. They have to remain open; otherwise, functions such as *::GetExitCodeThread* couldn't possibly work.

On the surface, the fact that MFC automatically deletes *CWinThread* objects and closes the corresponding thread handles seems convenient. If MFC didn't handle these routine housekeeping chores for you, you'd have to handle them yourself. But there's a problem—at least a potential one. Look again at this statement:

```
::GetExitCodeThread (pThread->m_hThread, &dwExitCode);
```

There's nothing wrong with this code if the thread hasn't terminated, because *pThread* is still a valid pointer. But if the thread has terminated, it's highly likely that MFC has deleted the *CWinThread* object and that *pThread* is now an invalid pointer. (I say "highly likely" because a short window of time separates a thread's termination from the associated *CWinThread* object's deletion.) An obvious solution is to copy the thread handle from the *CWinThread* object to a local variable before the thread terminates and to use that handle in the call to *::GetExitCodeThread*, like this:

```
// While the thread is running
HANDLE hThread = pThread->m_hThread;
      .
      .
      .
// Sometime later
::GetExitCodeThread (hThread, &dwExitCode);
```

But this code, too, is buggy. Why? Because if the *CWinThread* object no longer exists, the thread handle no longer exists, either; it has long since been closed. Failure to take into account the autodeleting nature of *CWinThread*s and the *::CloseHandle* call executed by *CWinThread*'s destructor can lead to egregious programming errors if you use functions such as *::GetExitCodeThread* that assume a thread's handle is still valid even if the thread is no longer running.

Fortunately, this problem has a solution—two of them, in fact. The first solution is to prevent MFC from deleting a *CWinThread* object by setting the object's *m_bAutoDelete* data member equal to FALSE. The default is TRUE, which enables autodeletion. If you choose this route, you must remember to call *delete* on the *CWinThread* pointer returned by *AfxBeginThread*, or your application will suffer memory leaks. The following code fragment illustrates this point:

```
CWinThread* pThread = AfxBeginThread (ThreadFunc, NULL,
    THREAD_PRIORITY_NORMAL, 0, CREATE_SUSPENDED);
pThread->m_bAutoDelete = FALSE;
pThread->ResumeThread ();
      .
      .
      .
// Sometime later
DWORD dwExitCode;
```

(continued)

```
::GetExitCodeThread (pThread->m_hThread, &dwExitCode);
if (dwExitCode == STILL_ACTIVE) {
    // The thread is still running.
}
else {
    // The thread has terminated. Delete the CWinThread object.
    delete pThread;
}
```

Just as important as deleting the *CWinThread* object is creating the thread in a suspended state. If you don't, a small but very real chance exists that the new thread will run out its lifetime before the thread that created it executes the statement that sets *m_bAutoDelete* to FALSE. Remember: Once a thread is started, Windows gives you no guarantees about how much or how little CPU time that thread will be accorded.

The second solution is to allow the *CWinThread* to autodelete but to use the Win32 *::DuplicateHandle* function to create a copy of the thread handle. Thread handles are reference-counted, and using *::DuplicateHandle* to duplicate a newly opened thread handle bumps that handle's reference count up from 1 to 2. Consequently, when *CWinThread*'s destructor calls *::CloseHandle*, the handle isn't really closed; it simply has its reference count decremented. The downside is that you mustn't forget to call *::CloseHandle* yourself to close the handle. Here's an example:

```
CWinThread* pThread = AfxBeginThread (ThreadFunc, NULL,
    THREAD_PRIORITY_NORMAL, 0, CREATE_SUSPENDED);

HANDLE hThread;
::DuplicateHandle (GetCurrentProcess (), pThread->m_hThread,
    GetCurrentProcess (), &hThread, 0, FALSE, DUPLICATE_SAME_ACCESS);

pThread->ResumeThread ();
    .
    .
    .
// Sometime later
DWORD dwExitCode;
::GetExitCodeThread (hThread, &dwExitCode);
if (dwExitCode == STILL_ACTIVE) {
    // The thread is still running.
}
else {
    // The thread has terminated. Close the thread handle.
    ::CloseHandle (hThread);
}
```

Once again, the new thread is created in a suspended state so that the creating thread can be absolutely sure to execute code before the new thread ends.

Terminating Another Thread

Generally speaking, threads can terminate only themselves. If you want thread A to terminate thread B, you must set up a signaling mechanism that allows thread A to tell thread B to terminate itself. A simple variable can serve as a termination request flag, as demonstrated here:

```
// Thread A
nContinue = 1;
CWinThread* pThread = AfxBeginThread (ThreadFunc, &nContinue);
    :
    :
nContinue = 0; // Tell thread B to terminate.

// Thread B
UINT ThreadFunc (LPVOID pParam)
{
    int* pContinue = (int*) pParam;
    while (*pContinue) {
        // Work work work work
    }
    return 0;
}
```

In this example, thread B checks *nContinue* from time to time and terminates if *nContinue* changes from nonzero to 0. Normally it's not a terrific idea for two threads to access the same variable without synchronizing their actions, but in this case, it's acceptable because thread B is checking only to find out whether *nContinue* is 0. Of course, to prevent access violations, you need to ensure that *nContinue* doesn't go out of scope while thread B is running. You can do that by making *nContinue* a static or global variable.

Now suppose that you want to modify this example so that once thread A sets *nContinue* to 0, it pauses until thread B is no longer running. Here's the proper way to do it:

```
// Thread A
nContinue = 1;
CWinThread* pThread = AfxBeginThread (ThreadFunc, &nContinue);
    :
    :
HANDLE hThread = pThread->m_hThread; // Save the thread handle.
nContinue = 0; // Tell thread B to terminate.
::WaitForSingleObject (hThread, INFINITE);

// Thread B
UINT ThreadFunc (LPVOID pParam)
```

(continued)

```
{
    int* pContinue = (int*) pParam;
    while (*pContinue) {
        // Work work work work
    }
    return 0;
}
```

::WaitForSingleObject blocks the calling thread until the specified object—in this case, another thread—enters a "signaled" state. A thread becomes signaled when it terminates. When a thread blocks in *::WaitForSingleObject*, it waits very efficiently because it's effectively suspended until the function call returns. This example assumes that thread B won't end until thread A tells it to. If that's not the case—if thread B could end before thread A commands it to—thread A should create thread B in a suspended state and make a copy of the thread handle with *::DuplicateHandle*. Otherwise, thread A could get caught in the trap of passing an invalid thread handle to *::WaitForSingleObject*.

::WaitForSingleObject is an indispensable function that you'll use time and time again when writing multithreaded code. The first parameter passed to it is the handle of the object you want to wait on. (It can also be a process handle, the handle of a synchronization object, or a file change notification handle, among other things.) In the example above, thread A retrieves thread B's handle before setting *nContinue* to 0 because the *CWinThread* object representing thread B might no longer exist when the call to *::WaitForSingleObject* executes. The second parameter to *::WaitForSingle-Object* is the length of time you're willing to wait. INFINITE means wait as long as it takes. When you specify INFINITE, you take the chance that the calling thread could lock up if the object it's waiting on never becomes signaled. If you specify a number of milliseconds instead, as in

```
::WaitForSingleObject (hThread, 5000);
```

::WaitForSingleObject will return after the specified time—here 5 seconds—has elapsed even if the object hasn't become signaled. You can check the return value to determine why the function returned. WAIT_OBJECT_0 means that the object became signaled, and WAIT_TIMEOUT means that it didn't.

Given a thread handle or a valid *CWinThread* object wrapping a thread handle, you can quickly determine whether the thread is still running by calling *::WaitFor-SingleObject* and specifying 0 for the time-out period, as shown here:

```
if (::WaitForSingleObject (hThread, 0) == WAIT_OBJECT_0) {
    // The thread no longer exists.
}
else {
    // The thread is still running.
}
```

Called this way, *::WaitForSingleObject* doesn't wait; it returns immediately. A return value equal to WAIT_OBJECT_0 means that the thread is signaled (no longer exists), and a return value equal to WAIT_TIMEOUT means that the thread is nonsignaled (still exists). As usual, it's up to you to ensure that the handle you pass to *::WaitForSingleObject* is a valid one, either by duplicating the original thread handle or by preventing the *CWinThread* object from being autodeleted.

There is one way a thread can kill another thread directly, but you should use it only as a last resort. The statement

```
::TerminateThread (hThread, 0);
```

terminates the thread whose handle is *hThread* and assigns it an exit code of 0. The Win32 API reference documents some of the many problems *::TerminateThread* can cause, which range from orphaned thread synchronization objects to DLLs that don't get a chance to execute normal thread-shutdown code.

Threads, Processes, and Priorities

The scheduler is the component of the operating system that decides which threads run when and for how long. Thread scheduling is a complex task whose goal is to divide CPU time among multiple threads of execution as efficiently as possible to create the illusion that all of them are running at once. On machines with multiple CPUs, Windows NT and Windows 2000 really do run two or more threads at the same time by assigning different threads to different processors using a scheme called *symmetric multiprocessing,* or SMP. Windows 95 and Windows 98 are not SMP operating systems, so they schedule all of their threads on the same CPU even on multiprocessor PCs.

The scheduler uses a variety of techniques to improve multitasking performance and to try to ensure that each thread in the system gets an ample amount of CPU time. (For an inside look at the Windows NT scheduler, its strategies, and its algorithms, I highly recommend the book *Inside Windows NT*, second edition, by David Solomon.) Ultimately, however, the decision about which thread to execute next boils down to the thread with the highest priority. At any given moment, each thread is assigned a priority level from 0 through 31, with higher numbers indicating higher priorities. If a priority-11 thread is waiting to execute and all other threads vying for CPU time have priority levels of 10 or less, the priority-11 thread runs next. If two priority-11 threads are waiting to execute, the scheduler executes the one that has executed the least recently. When that thread's timeslice, or *quantum*, is up, the other priority-11 thread gets executed if all the other threads still have lower priorities. As a rule, the scheduler *always* gives the next timeslice to the waiting thread with the highest priority.

Does this mean that low-priority threads never get executed? Not at all. First, remember that Windows is a message-based operating system. If a thread calls *::GetMessage* and its message queue is empty, the thread blocks until a message becomes available. This gives lower priority threads a chance to execute. Most UI threads spend the vast majority of their time blocked on the message queue, so as long as a high-priority worker thread doesn't monopolize the CPU, even very low priority threads typically get all the CPU time they need. (A worker thread never blocks on the message queue because it doesn't process messages.)

The scheduler also plays a lot of tricks with priority levels to enhance the overall responsiveness of the system and to reduce the chance that any thread will be starved for CPU time. If a thread with a priority level of 7 goes for too long without receiving a timeslice, the scheduler may temporarily boost the thread's priority level to 8 or 9 or even higher to give it a chance to execute. Windows NT 3.*x* boosts the priorities of threads that belong to the foreground process to improve the responsiveness of the application in which the user is working, and Windows NT 4.0 Workstation boosts the threads' quantums. Windows also uses a technique called *priority inheritance* to prevent high-priority threads from blocking for too long on synchronization objects owned by low-priority threads. For example, if a priority-11 thread tries to claim a mutex owned by a priority-5 thread, the scheduler may boost the priority of the priority-5 thread so that the mutex will come free sooner.

How do thread priorities get assigned in the first place? When you call *AfxBeginThread* or *CWinThread::SetThreadPriority*, you specify a *relative thread priority*. The operating system combines the relative priority level with the priority class of the process that owns the thread (more about that in a moment) to compute a *base priority level* for the thread. The thread's actual priority level—a number from 0 through 31—can vary from moment to moment because of priority boosting and deboosting. You can't control boosting (and you wouldn't want to even if you could), but you can control the base priority level by setting the process priority class and the relative thread priority level.

Process Priority Classes

Most processes begin life with the priority class NORMAL_PRIORITY_CLASS. Once started, however, a process can change its priority by calling *::SetPriorityClass*, which accepts a process handle (obtainable with *::GetCurrentProcess*) and one of the specifiers shown in the following table.

PROCESS PRIORITY CLASSES

Priority Class	Description
IDLE_PRIORITY_CLASS	The process runs only when the system is idle—for example, when no other thread is waiting for a given CPU.
NORMAL_PRIORITY_CLASS	The default process priority class. The process has no special scheduling needs.
HIGH_PRIORITY_CLASS	The process receives priority over IDLE-_PRIORITY_CLASS and NORMAL_PRIORITY-_CLASS processes.
REALTIME_PRIORITY_CLASS	The process must have the highest possible priority, and its threads should preempt even threads belonging to HIGH_PRIORITY_CLASS processes.

Most applications don't need to change their priority classes. HIGH_PRIORITY-_CLASS and REALTIME_PRIORITY_CLASS processes can severely inhibit the responsiveness of the system and can even delay critical system activities such as flushing of the disk cache. One legitimate use of HIGH_PRIORITY_CLASS is for system applications that remain hidden most of the time but pop up a window when a certain input event occurs. These applications impose very little overhead on the system while they're blocked waiting for input, but once the input appears, they receive priority over normal applications. REALTIME_PRIORITY_CLASS is provided primarily for the benefit of real-time data acquisition programs that must have the lion's share of the CPU time in order to work properly. IDLE_PRIORITY_CLASS is ideal for screen savers, system monitors, and other low-priority applications that are designed to operate unobtrusively in the background.

Relative Thread Priorities

The table on the following page shows the relative thread priority values you can pass to *AfxBeginThread* and *CWinThread::SetThreadPriority*. The default is THREAD-_PRIORITY_NORMAL, which *AfxBeginThread* automatically assigns to a thread unless you specify otherwise. Normally, a THREAD_PRIORITY_NORMAL thread that belongs to a NORMAL_PRIORITY_CLASS process has a base priority level of 8. At various times, the thread's priority may be boosted for reasons mentioned earlier, but it will eventually return to 8. A THREAD_PRIORITY_LOWEST thread running in a HIGH_PRIORITY_CLASS background or foreground process has a base priority of 11. The actual numbers aren't as important as realizing that you can fine-tune the relative priorities of the threads within a process to achieve the best responsiveness and performance—and if necessary, you can adjust the priority of the process itself.

RELATIVE THREAD PRIORITIES

Priority Value	Description
THREAD_PRIORITY_IDLE	The thread's base priority level is 1 if the process's priority class is HIGH-_PRIORITY_CLASS or lower, or 16 if the process's priority class is REALTIME-_PRIORITY_CLASS.
THREAD_PRIORITY_LOWEST	The thread's base priority level is equal to the process's priority class minus 2.
THREAD_PRIORITY_BELOW_NORMAL	The thread's base priority level is equal to the process's priority class minus 1.
THREAD_PRIORITY_NORMAL	The default thread priority value. The thread's base priority level is equal to the process's priority class.
THREAD_PRIORITY_ABOVE_NORMAL	The thread's base priority level is equal to the process's priority class plus 1.
THREAD_PRIORITY_HIGHEST	The thread's base priority level is equal to the process's priority class plus 2.
THREAD_PRIORITY_TIME_CRITICAL	The thread's base priority level is 15 if the process's priority class is HIGH-_PRIORITY_CLASS or lower, or 31 if the process's priority class is REALTIME-_PRIORITY_CLASS.

Now that you understand where thread priorities come from and how they affect the scheduling process, let's talk about how you know when to adjust thread priorities and what values you should assign to them. As a rule, if a high priority is required, it's usually obvious. If it's not obvious that a thread requires a high priority, a normal thread priority will probably do. For most threads, the default THREAD-_PRIORITY_NORMAL is just fine. But if you're writing a communications program that uses a dedicated thread to read and buffer data from a serial port, you might miss bytes here and there unless the thread that does the reading and buffering has a relative priority value of THREAD_PRIORITY_HIGHEST or THREAD_PRIORITY-_TIME_CRITICAL.

One thing's for sure: if an application is a CPU hog and it's not designed to fulfill a specific purpose, such as performing real-time data acquisition on a PC dedicated to that task, the market will look upon it unfavorably. CPU time is a computer's most precious resource. Use it judiciously, and don't get caught in the trap of bumping up priority levels to make your own application execute 5 percent faster when doing so might subtract 50 percent from the speed and responsiveness of other applications.

Using C Run-Time Functions in Multithreaded Applications

Certain functions in the standard C run-time library pose problems for multithreaded applications. *strtok, asctime*, and several other C run-time functions use global variables to store intermediate data. If thread A calls one of these functions and thread B preempts thread A and calls the same function, global data stored by thread B could overwrite global data stored by thread A, or vice versa. One solution to this problem is to use thread synchronization objects to serialize access to C run-time functions. But even simple synchronization objects can be expensive in terms of processor time. Therefore, most modern C and C++ compilers come with two versions of the C run-time library: one that's thread-safe (can safely be called by two or more threads) and one that isn't. The thread-safe versions of the run-time library typically don't rely on thread synchronization objects. Instead, they store intermediate values in per-thread data structures.

Visual C++ comes with six versions of the C run-time library. Which one you should choose depends on whether you're compiling a debug build or a release build, whether you want to link with the C run-time library statically or dynamically, and, obviously, whether your application is single-threaded or multithreaded. The following table shows the library names and the corresponding compiler switches.

VISUAL C++ VERSIONS OF THE C RUN-TIME LIBRARY

Library Name	*Application Type*	*Switch*
Libc.lib	Single-threaded; static linking; release builds	/ML
Libcd.lib	Single-threaded; static linking; debug builds	/MLd
Libcmt.lib	Multithreaded; static linking; release builds	/MT
Libcmtd.lib	Multithreaded; static linking; debug builds	/MTd
Msvcrt.lib	Single-threaded or multithreaded; dynamic linking; release builds	/MD
Msvcrtd.lib	Single-threaded or multithreaded; dynamic linking; debug builds	/MDd

Libc.lib, Libcd.lib, Libcmt.lib, and Libcmtd.lib are static link libraries containing C run-time code; Msvcrt.lib and Msvcrtd.lib are import libraries that enable an application to dynamically link to functions in the Visual C++ C run-time DLL. Of course, you don't have to fuss with compiler switches unless you build your own make files. If you're using Visual C++, just select the appropriate entry in the Use Run-time Library field of the Project Settings dialog box and the IDE will add the switches for you. Even if you write a multithreaded application that doesn't use C run-time functions, you should link with one of the multithreaded libraries anyway because MFC calls certain C run-time functions itself.

In an MFC application, that's all you have to do to make calls to C run-time functions thread-safe. Simply set the compiler switches, and trust the class library to do the rest. In an SDK application, you must also replace calls to *::CreateThread* with calls to *_beginthreadex*. MFC programmers don't need to worry about *_beginthreadex* because *AfxBeginThread* calls it automatically.

Calling MFC Member Functions Across Thread Boundaries

Now for the bad news about writing multithreaded MFC applications. As long as threads don't call member functions belonging to objects created by other threads, there are few restrictions on what they can do. However, if thread A passes a *CWnd* pointer to thread B and thread B calls a member function of that *CWnd* object, MFC is likely to assert in a debug build. A release build might work fine—but then again, it might not. There's also the possibility that a debug build won't assert but that it won't work properly, either. It all depends on what happens inside the framework when that particular *CWnd* member function is called. You can avoid a potential minefield of problems by compartmentalizing your threads and having each thread use only those objects that it creates rather than rely on objects created by other threads. But for cases in which that's simply not practical, here are a few rules to go by.

First, many MFC member functions *can* be safely called on objects in other threads. Most of the inline functions defined in the INL files in MFC's Include directory can be called across thread boundaries because they are little more than wrappers around API functions. But calling a noninline member function is asking for trouble. For example, the following code, which passes a *CWnd* pointer named *pWnd* from thread A to thread B and has B call *CWnd::GetParent* through the pointer, works without any problems:

```
CWinThread* pThread = AfxBeginThread (ThreadFunc, pWnd);
    :
    :
UINT ThreadFunc (LPVOID pParam)
{
    CWnd* pWnd = (CWnd*) pParam;
    CWnd* pParent = pWnd->GetParent ();
    return 0;
}
```

Simply changing *GetParent* to *GetParentFrame*, however, causes an assertion:

```
CWinThread* pThread = AfxBeginThread (ThreadFunc, pWnd);
    :
    :
UINT ThreadFunc (LPVOID pParam)
```

```
{
    CWnd* pWnd = (CWnd*) pParam;
    // Get ready for an assertion!
    CWnd* pParent = pWnd->GetParentFrame ();
    return 0;
}
```

Why does *GetParent* work when *GetParentFrame* doesn't? Because *GetParent* calls through almost directly to the *::GetParent* function in the API. Here's how *CWnd-::GetParent* is defined in Afxwin2.inl, with a little reformatting thrown in to enhance readability:

```
_AFXWIN_INLINE CWnd* CWnd::GetParent () const
{
    ASSERT (::IsWindow (m_hWnd));
    return CWnd::FromHandle (::GetParent (m_hWnd));
}
```

No problem there; *m_hWnd* is valid because it's part of the *CWnd* object that *pWnd* points to, and *FromHandle* converts the HWND returned by *::GetParent* into a *CWnd* pointer.

But now consider what happens when you call *GetParentFrame*, whose source code is found in Wincore.cpp. The line that causes the assertion error is

```
ASSERT_VALID (this);
```

ASSERT_VALID calls *CWnd::AssertValid*, which performs a sanity check by making sure that the HWND associated with *this* appears in the permanent or temporary handle map the framework uses to convert HWNDs into *CWnd*s. Going from a *CWnd* to an HWND is easy because the HWND is a data member of the *CWnd*, but going from an HWND to a *CWnd* can be done only through the handle maps. And here's the problem: Handle maps are local to each thread and aren't visible to other threads. If thread A created the *CWnd* whose address is passed to ASSERT_VALID, the corresponding HWND won't appear in thread B's permanent or temporary handle map and MFC will assert. Many of MFC's noninline member functions call ASSERT_VALID, but inline functions don't—at least not in current releases.

Frequently, MFC's assertions protect you from calling functions that wouldn't work anyway. In a release build, *GetParentFrame* returns NULL when called from a thread other than the one in which the parent frame was created. But in cases in which assertion errors are spurious—that is, in cases in which the function would work okay despite the per-thread handle tables—you can avoid assertions by passing real handles instead of object pointers. For example, it's safe to call *CWnd::GetTopLevelParent* in a secondary thread if you call *FromHandle* first to create an entry in the thread's temporary handle map, as shown on the following page.

```
CWinThread* pThread = AfxBeginThread (ThreadFunc, pWnd->m_hWnd);
    :
    :
UINT ThreadFunc (LPVOID pParam)
{
    CWnd* pWnd = CWnd::FromHandle ((HWND) pParam);
    CWnd* pParent = pWnd->GetTopLevelParent ();
    return 0;
}
```

That's why the MFC documentation warns that windows, GDI objects, and other objects should be passed between threads using handles instead of pointers. In general, you'll have fewer problems if you pass handles and use *FromHandle* to re-create objects in the destination threads. But don't take that to mean that just any function will work. It won't.

What about calling member functions belonging to objects created from "pure" MFC classes such as *CDocument* and *CRect*—classes that don't wrap HWNDs, HDCs, or other handle types and therefore don't rely on handle maps? Just what you wanted to hear: some work and some don't. There's no problem with this code:

```
CWinThread* pThread = AfxBeginThread (ThreadFunc, pRect);
    :
    :
UINT ThreadFunc (LPVOID pParam)
{
    CRect* pRect = (CRect*) pParam;
    int nArea = pRect->Width () * pRect->Height ();
    return 0;
}
```

But this code will assert on you:

```
CWinThread* pThread = AfxBeginThread (ThreadFunc, pDoc);
    :
    :
UINT ThreadFunc (LPVOID pParam)
{
    CDocument* pDoc = pParam;
    pDoc->UpdateAllViews (NULL);
    return 0;
}
```

Even some seemingly innocuous functions such as *AfxGetMainWnd* don't work when they're called from anywhere but the application's primary thread.

The bottom line is that before you go calling member functions on MFC objects created in other threads, *you must understand the implications*. And the only way to understand the implications is to study the MFC source code to see how a particular member function behaves. Also keep in mind that MFC isn't thread-safe, a subject we'll discuss further later in this chapter. So even if a member function appears to be safe, ask yourself what might happen if thread B accessed an object created by thread A and thread A preempted thread B in the middle of the access.

This stuff is incredibly difficult to sort out and only adds to the complexity of writing multithreaded applications. That's why in the real world, multithreaded MFC applications tend to do the bulk of their user interface work in the main thread. If a background thread wants to update the user interface, it sends or posts a message to the main thread so that the main thread can do the updating. You'll see examples of this kind of messaging in this chapter's sample programs.

Your First Multithreaded Application

The application shown in Figure 17-1 demonstrates some of the basic principles involved in designing and implementing a multithreaded application. Sieve is a dialog-based application that uses the famous Sieve of Eratosthenes algorithm to compute the number of prime numbers between 2 and a number that you specify. The computation begins when you click the Start button and ends when a count appears in the box in the center of the window. Because counting primes is resource-intensive, Sieve does all its counting in a background thread. (To see just how resource-intensive counting primes can be, ask Sieve to count primes between 2 and 100,000,000. Unless your system has gobs of memory, you'll wait a while for the answer.) If the primary thread were to perform the counting, Sieve would be frozen to input for the duration. But because it delegates the task of counting primes to a worker thread, Sieve remains responsive to user input no matter how much time the computation requires.

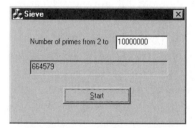

Figure 17-1. *The Sieve window.*

The thread that does the counting is launched by the Start button's ON_BN-_CLICKED handler, *OnStart*. You can see the source code yourself in Figure 17-2 (beginning on page 1007). Here's the code that launches the thread:

```
THREADPARMS* ptp = new THREADPARMS;
ptp->nMax = nMax;
ptp->hWnd = m_hWnd;
AfxBeginThread (ThreadFunc, ptp);
```

OnStart passes data to the worker thread in an application-defined data structure named THREADPARMS. One of the items included in the structure is the upper limit that the user typed into the dialog (*nMax*). The other is the dialog's window handle. The upper limit is passed to the *Sieve* function that does the actual counting. The dialog's window handle is used to post a message to the application's main window once the worker thread has arrived at a result:

```
int nCount = Sieve (nMax);
::PostMessage (hWnd, WM_USER_THREAD_FINISHED, (WPARAM) nCount, 0);
```

WM_USER_THREAD_FINISHED is a user-defined message ID defined in SieveDlg.h. The main window's WM_USER_THREAD_FINISHED handler retrieves the result from the message's *wParam* and displays it in the window.

Notice that storage for the THREADPARMS structure passed by address to the thread function is allocated in the primary thread and deallocated in the worker thread, as shown here:

```
// In the primary thread
THREADPARAMS* ptp = new THREADPARMS;
     ⋮
     ⋮
AfxBeginThread (ThreadFunc, ptp);

// In the worker thread
THREADPARMS* ptp = (THREADPARMS*) pParam;
     ⋮
     ⋮
delete ptp;
```

Why create the structure in one thread and delete it in another? Because if you create the structure on the stack in the primary thread, it might go out of scope before the other thread gets a chance to access it. This is one of those annoying little details that can cause seemingly random errors if you don't handle it properly. Allocating the structure with *new* ensures that scoping problems won't occur, and allocating memory in one thread and deleting it in another isn't harmful. Making the structure a class data member or declaring it globally is an equally effective method of ensuring that it doesn't go away too soon.

When an application's primary thread terminates, the process terminates and any other threads that belong to the process terminate, too. Multithreaded SDK applications typically don't bother to kill background threads before terminating, but MFC applications that end without terminating running background threads suffer memory leaks because the threads' *CWinThread* objects don't get autodeleted. Such leaks aren't a big deal because the operating system cleans them up almost immediately. However, if you'd rather leave nothing to chance, you can avoid leaking *CWinThread*s by deleting extant *CWinThread* objects just before your application shuts down. It's not harmful to delete a running *CWinThread*, but keep in mind that you can't call *CWinThread* functions on a deleted *CWinThread*, either.

Sieve.h

```
// Sieve.h : main header file for the SIEVE application
//

#if !defined(AFX_SIEVE_H__6DF40C9B_7EA1_11D1_8E53_E4D9F9C00000__INCLUDED_)
#define AFX_SIEVE_H__6DF40C9B_7EA1_11D1_8E53_E4D9F9C00000__INCLUDED_

#if _MSC_VER >= 1000
#pragma once
#endif // _MSC_VER >= 1000

#ifndef __AFXWIN_H__
    #error include 'stdafx.h' before including this file for PCH
#endif

#include "resource.h"        // main symbols

/////////////////////////////////////////////////////////////////////////////
// CSieveApp:
// See Sieve.cpp for the implementation of this class
//

class CSieveApp : public CWinApp
{
public:
    CSieveApp();

// Overrides
    // ClassWizard generated virtual function overrides
    //{{AFX_VIRTUAL(CSieveApp)
    public:
    virtual BOOL InitInstance();
    //}}AFX_VIRTUAL

// Implementation

    //{{AFX_MSG(CSieveApp)
        // NOTE - the ClassWizard will add and remove member functions here.
        //    DO NOT EDIT what you see in these blocks of generated code !
    //}}AFX_MSG
    DECLARE_MESSAGE_MAP()
};
```

Figure 17-2. *The Sieve application.*

(continued)

Figure 17-2 *continued*

```
//////////////////////////////////////////////////////////////////////////

//{{AFX_INSERT_LOCATION}}
// Microsoft Developer Studio will insert additional declarations
// immediately before the previous line.

#endif
// !defined(AFX_SIEVE_H__6DF40C9B_7EA1_11D1_8E53_E4D9F9C00000__INCLUDED_)
```

Sieve.cpp

```cpp
// Sieve.cpp : Defines the class behaviors for the application.
//

#include "stdafx.h"
#include "Sieve.h"
#include "SieveDlg.h"

#ifdef _DEBUG
#define new DEBUG_NEW
#undef THIS_FILE
static char THIS_FILE[] = __FILE__;
#endif

//////////////////////////////////////////////////////////////////////////
// CSieveApp

BEGIN_MESSAGE_MAP(CSieveApp, CWinApp)
    //{{AFX_MSG_MAP(CSieveApp)
        // NOTE - the ClassWizard will add and remove mapping macros here.
        //    DO NOT EDIT what you see in these blocks of generated code!
    //}}AFX_MSG
    ON_COMMAND(ID_HELP, CWinApp::OnHelp)
END_MESSAGE_MAP()

//////////////////////////////////////////////////////////////////////////
// CSieveApp construction

CSieveApp::CSieveApp()
{
    // TODO: add construction code here,
    // Place all significant initialization in InitInstance
}
```

```
/////////////////////////////////////////////////////////////////////////
// The one and only CSieveApp object

CSieveApp theApp;

/////////////////////////////////////////////////////////////////////////
// CSieveApp initialization

BOOL CSieveApp::InitInstance()
{
    // Standard initialization
    // If you are not using these features and wish to reduce the size
    //  of your final executable, you should remove from the following
    //  the specific initialization routines you do not need.

    CSieveDlg dlg;
    m_pMainWnd = &dlg;
    int nResponse = dlg.DoModal();
    if (nResponse == IDOK)
    {
        // TODO: Place code here to handle when the dialog is
        //  dismissed with OK
    }
    else if (nResponse == IDCANCEL)
    {
        // TODO: Place code here to handle when the dialog is
        //  dismissed with Cancel
    }

    // Since the dialog has been closed, return FALSE so that we exit the
    //  application, rather than start the application's message pump.
    return FALSE;
}
```

SieveDlg.h

```
// SieveDlg.h : header file
//

#if !defined(
    AFX_SIEVEDLG_H__6DF40C9D_7EA1_11D1_8E53_E4D9F9C00000__INCLUDED_)
#define AFX_SIEVEDLG_H__6DF40C9D_7EA1_11D1_8E53_E4D9F9C00000__INCLUDED_
```

(continued)

Figure 17-2 *continued*

```
#if _MSC_VER >= 1000
#pragma once
#endif // _MSC_VER >= 1000


#define WM_USER_THREAD_FINISHED WM_USER+0x100

UINT ThreadFunc (LPVOID pParam);
int Sieve (int nMax);

typedef struct tagTHREADPARMS {
    int nMax;
    HWND hWnd;
} THREADPARMS;

/////////////////////////////////////////////////////////////////////////////
// CSieveDlg dialog

class CSieveDlg : public CDialog
{
// Construction
public:
    CSieveDlg(CWnd* pParent = NULL);    // standard constructor

// Dialog Data
    //{{AFX_DATA(CSieveDlg)
    enum { IDD = IDD_SIEVE_DIALOG };
        // NOTE: the ClassWizard will add data members here
    //}}AFX_DATA

    // ClassWizard generated virtual function overrides
    //{{AFX_VIRTUAL(CSieveDlg)
    protected:
    virtual void DoDataExchange(CDataExchange* pDX);    // DDX/DDV support
    //}}AFX_VIRTUAL

// Implementation
protected:
    HICON m_hIcon;

    // Generated message map functions
    //{{AFX_MSG(CSieveDlg)
    virtual BOOL OnInitDialog();
    afx_msg void OnPaint();
    afx_msg HCURSOR OnQueryDragIcon();
    afx_msg void OnStart();
```

```
    //}}AFX_MSG
    afx_msg LONG OnThreadFinished (WPARAM wParam, LPARAM lParam);
    DECLARE_MESSAGE_MAP()
};


//{{AFX_INSERT_LOCATION}}
// Microsoft Developer Studio will insert additional declarations
// immediately before the previous line.


#endif
// !defined(
//      AFX_SIEVEDLG_H__6DF40C9D_7EA1_11D1_8E53_E4D9F9C00000__INCLUDED_)
```

SieveDlg.cpp

```cpp
// SieveDlg.cpp : implementation file
//

#include "stdafx.h"
#include "Sieve.h"
#include "SieveDlg.h"


#ifdef _DEBUG
#define new DEBUG_NEW
#undef THIS_FILE
static char THIS_FILE[] = __FILE__;
#endif


/////////////////////////////////////////////////////////////////////////
// CSieveDlg dialog

CSieveDlg::CSieveDlg(CWnd* pParent /*=NULL*/)
    : CDialog(CSieveDlg::IDD, pParent)
{
    //{{AFX_DATA_INIT(CSieveDlg)
        // NOTE: the ClassWizard will add member initialization here
    //}}AFX_DATA_INIT
    // Note that LoadIcon does not require a subsequent
    // DestroyIcon in Win32
    m_hIcon = AfxGetApp()->LoadIcon(IDR_MAINFRAME);
}


void CSieveDlg::DoDataExchange(CDataExchange* pDX)
```

(continued)

Figure 17-2 *continued*

```
{
    CDialog::DoDataExchange(pDX);
    //{{AFX_DATA_MAP(CSieveDlg)
        // NOTE: the ClassWizard will add DDX and DDV calls here
    //}}AFX_DATA_MAP
}

BEGIN_MESSAGE_MAP(CSieveDlg, CDialog)
    //{{AFX_MSG_MAP(CSieveDlg)
    ON_BN_CLICKED(IDC_START, OnStart)
    //}}AFX_MSG_MAP
    ON_MESSAGE (WM_USER_THREAD_FINISHED, OnThreadFinished)
END_MESSAGE_MAP()

/////////////////////////////////////////////////////////////////////////////
// CSieveDlg message handlers

BOOL CSieveDlg::OnInitDialog()
{
    CDialog::OnInitDialog();
    SetIcon(m_hIcon, TRUE);
    SetIcon(m_hIcon, FALSE);
    return TRUE;
}

void CSieveDlg::OnStart()
{
    int nMax = GetDlgItemInt (IDC_MAX);
    if (nMax < 10) {
        MessageBox (_T ("The number you enter must be 10 or higher"));
        GetDlgItem (IDC_MAX)->SetFocus ();
        return;
    }

    SetDlgItemText (IDC_RESULT, _T (""));
    GetDlgItem (IDC_START)->EnableWindow (FALSE);

    THREADPARMS* ptp = new THREADPARMS;
    ptp->nMax = nMax;
    ptp->hWnd = m_hWnd;
    AfxBeginThread (ThreadFunc, ptp);
}

LONG CSieveDlg::OnThreadFinished (WPARAM wParam, LPARAM lParam)
```

```
{
    SetDlgItemInt (IDC_RESULT, (int) wParam);
    GetDlgItem (IDC_START)->EnableWindow (TRUE);
    return 0;
}


/////////////////////////////////////////////////////////////////////////////
// Global functions

UINT ThreadFunc (LPVOID pParam)
{
    THREADPARMS* ptp = (THREADPARMS*) pParam;
    int nMax = ptp->nMax;
    HWND hWnd = ptp->hWnd;
    delete ptp;

    int nCount = Sieve (nMax);
    ::PostMessage (hWnd, WM_USER_THREAD_FINISHED, (WPARAM) nCount, 0);
    return 0;
}

int Sieve(int nMax)
{
    PBYTE pBuffer = new BYTE[nMax + 1];
    ::FillMemory (pBuffer, nMax + 1, 1);

    int nLimit = 2;
    while (nLimit * nLimit < nMax)
        nLimit++;

    for (int i=2; i<=nLimit; i++) {
        if (pBuffer[i]) {
            for (int k=i + i; k<=nMax; k+=i)
                pBuffer[k] = 0;
        }
    }

    int nCount = 0;
    for (i=2; i<=nMax; i++)
        if (pBuffer[i])
            nCount++;

    delete[] pBuffer;
    return nCount;
}
```

THREAD SYNCHRONIZATION

In the real world, you don't usually have the luxury of starting a thread and just letting it run. More often than not, that thread must coordinate its actions with other threads in the application. If two threads share a linked list, for example, accesses to the linked list must be serialized so that both threads don't try to modify it at the same time. Simply letting a thread go off and do its own thing can lead to all sorts of synchronization problems that show up only randomly in testing and that can often be fatal to the application.

Windows supports four types of synchronization objects that can be used to synchronize the actions performed by concurrently running threads:

- Critical sections
- Mutexes
- Events
- Semaphores

MFC encapsulates these objects in classes named *CCriticalSection*, *CMutex*, *CEvent*, and *CSemaphore*. It also includes a pair of classes named *CSingleLock* and *CMultiLock* that further abstract the interfaces to thread synchronization objects. In the sections that follow, I'll describe how to use these classes to synchronize the actions of concurrently executing threads.

Critical Sections

The simplest type of thread synchronization object is the critical section. Critical sections are used to serialize accesses performed on linked lists, simple variables, structures, and other resources that are shared by two or more threads. The threads must belong to the same process, because critical sections don't work across process boundaries.

The idea behind critical sections is that each thread that requires exclusive access to a resource can lock a critical section before accessing that resource and unlock it when the access is complete. If thread B attempts to lock a critical section that is currently locked by thread A, thread B blocks until the critical section comes free. While blocked, thread B waits in an extremely efficient wait state that consumes no processor time.

CCriticalSection::Lock locks a critical section, and *CCriticalSection::Unlock* unlocks it. Let's say that a document class includes a linked-list data member created from MFC's *CList* class and that two separate threads use the linked list. One writes to the list, and the other reads from it. To prevent the two threads from accessing the list at exactly the same time, you can protect the list with a critical section. The following example uses a globally declared *CCriticalSection* object to demonstrate how. (I've used global synchronization objects in the examples to ensure that the objects are equally visible to all the threads in a process, but no, synchronization objects don't have to have global scope.)

```
// Global data
CCriticalSection g_cs;
       .
       .
       .
// Thread A
g_cs.Lock ();
// Write to the linked list.
g_cs.Unlock ();
       .
       .
       .
// Thread B
g_cs.Lock ();
// Read from the linked list.
g_cs.Unlock ();
```

Now it's impossible for threads A and B to access the linked list at the same time because both guard the list with the same critical section. The diagram in Figure 17-3 illustrates how the critical section prevents overlapping read and write accesses by serializing the threads' actions.

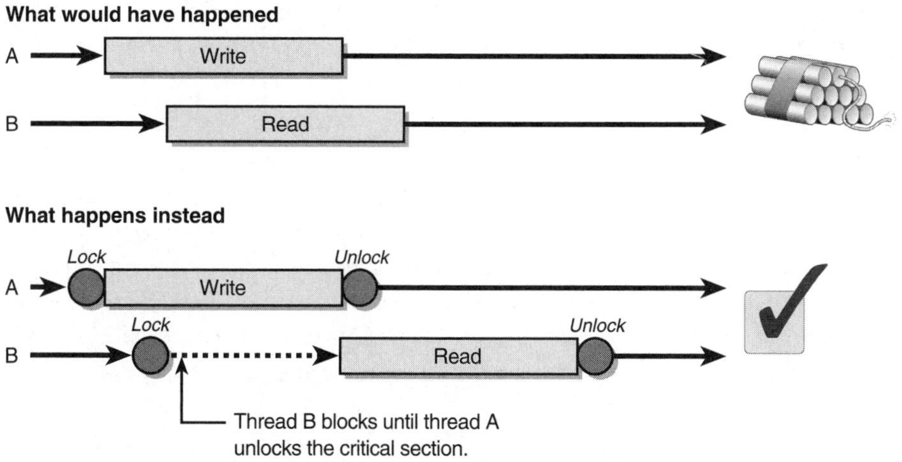

Figure 17-3. *Protecting a shared resource with a critical section.*

An alternate form of *CCriticalSection::Lock* accepts a time-out value, and some MFC documentation states that if you pass *Lock* a time-out value, it will return if the time-out period expires before the critical section comes free. The documentation is wrong. You can specify a time-out value if you want to, but *Lock* won't return until the critical section is unlocked.

It's obvious why a linked list should be protected from concurrent thread accesses, but what about simple variables? For example, suppose thread A increments a variable with the statement

```
nVar++;
```

and thread B does something else with the variable. Should *nVar* be protected with a critical section? In general, yes. What looks to be an atomic operation in a C++ program—even the application of a simple ++ operator—might compile into a sequence of several machine instructions. And one thread can preempt another between any two machine instructions. As a rule, it's a good idea to protect any data subject to simultaneous write accesses or simultaneous read and write accesses. A critical section is the perfect tool for the job.

The Win32 API includes a family of functions named *::InterlockedIncrement*, *::InterlockedDecrement*, *::InterlockedExchange*, *::InterlockedCompareExchange*, and *::InterlockedExchangeAdd* that you can use to safely operate on 32-bit values without explicitly using synchronization objects. For example, if *nVar* is a UINT, DWORD, or other 32-bit data type, you can increment it with the statement

```
::InterlockedIncrement (&nVar);
```

and the system will ensure that other accesses to *nVar* performed using *Interlocked* functions don't overlap. *nVar* should be aligned on a 32-bit boundary, or the *Interlocked* functions might fail on multiprocessor Windows NT systems. Also, *::InterlockedCompareExchange* and *::InterlockedExchangeAdd* are supported only in Windows NT 4.0 and higher and Windows 98.

Mutexes

Mutex is a contraction of the words *mutually* and *exclusive*. Like critical sections, mutexes are used to gain exclusive access to a resource shared by two or more threads. Unlike critical sections, mutexes can be used to synchronize threads running in the same process *or* in different processes. Critical sections are generally preferred to mutexes for intraprocess thread synchronization needs because critical sections are faster, but if you want to synchronize threads running in two or more different processes, mutexes are the answer.

Suppose two applications use a block of shared memory to exchange data. Inside that shared memory is a linked list that must be protected against concurrent thread accesses. A critical section won't work because it can't reach across process boundaries, but a mutex will do the job nicely. Here's what you do in each process before reading or writing the linked list:

```
// Global data
CMutex g_mutex (FALSE, _T ("MyMutex"));
   .
   .
   .
g_mutex.Lock ();
// Read or write the linked list.
g_mutex.Unlock ();
```

The first parameter passed to the *CMutex* constructor specifies whether the mutex is initially locked (TRUE) or unlocked (FALSE). The second parameter specifies the mutex's name, which is required if the mutex is used to synchronize threads in two different processes. You pick the name, but both processes must specify the same name so that the two *CMutex* objects will reference the same mutex object in the Windows kernel. Naturally, *Lock* blocks on a mutex locked by another thread, and *Unlock* frees the mutex so that others can lock it.

By default, *Lock* will wait forever for a mutex to become unlocked. You can build in a fail-safe mechanism by specifying a maximum wait time in milliseconds. In the following example, the thread waits for up to 1 minute before accessing the resource guarded by the mutex.

```
g_mutex.Lock (60000);
// Read or write the linked list.
g_mutex.Unlock ();
```

Lock's return value tells you why the function call returned. A nonzero return means that the mutex came free, and 0 indicates that the time-out period expired first. If *Lock* returns 0, it's normally prudent not to access the shared resource because doing so could result in an overlapping access. Thus, code that uses *Lock*'s time-out feature is normally structured like this:

```
if (g_mutex.Lock (60000)) {
    // Read or write the linked list.
    g_mutex.Unlock ();
}
```

There is one other difference between mutexes and critical sections. If a thread locks a critical section and terminates without unlocking it, other threads waiting for the critical section to come free will block indefinitely. However, if a thread that locks a mutex fails to unlock it before terminating, the system deems the mutex to be "abandoned" and automatically frees the mutex so that waiting threads can resume.

Events

MFC's *CEvent* class encapsulates Win32 event objects. An event is little more than a flag in the operating system kernel. At any given time, it can be in either of two states: raised (set) or lowered (reset). A set event is said to be in a signaled state, and a reset event is said to be nonsignaled. *CEvent::SetEvent* sets an event, and *CEvent::Reset-Event* resets it. A related function, *CEvent::PulseEvent*, sets and clears an event in one operation.

Events are sometimes described as "thread triggers." One thread calls *CEvent::Lock* to block on an event and wait for it to become set. Another thread sets the event and thereby releases the waiting thread. Setting the event is like pulling a trigger: it unblocks the waiting thread and allows it to resume executing. An event can have one thread or several threads blocking on it, and if your code is properly written, all waiting threads will be released when the event becomes set.

Windows supports two different types of events: autoreset events and manual-reset events. The difference between them is very simple, but the implications are far-reaching. An autoreset event is automatically reset to the nonsignaled state when a thread blocking on it is released. A manual-reset event doesn't reset automatically; it must be reset programmatically. The rules for choosing between autoreset and manual-reset events—and for using them once you've made your selection—are as follows:

■   If just one thread will be triggered by the event, use an autoreset event and release the waiting thread with *SetEvent*. There's no need to call *ResetEvent* because the event is reset automatically the moment the thread is released.

■   If two or more threads will be triggered by the event, use a manual-reset event and release all waiting threads with *PulseEvent*. Once more, you don't need to call *ResetEvent* because *PulseEvent* resets the event for you after releasing the threads.

It's vital to use a manual-reset event to trigger multiple threads. Why? Because an autoreset event would be reset the moment one of the threads was released and would therefore trigger just one thread. It's equally important to use *PulseEvent* to pull the trigger on a manual-reset event. If you use *SetEvent* and *ResetEvent*, you have no guarantee that all waiting threads will be released. *PulseEvent* not only sets and resets the event, but it also ensures that all threads waiting on the event are released before resetting the event.

An event is created by constructing a *CEvent* object. *CEvent::CEvent* accepts four parameters, all of them optional. It's prototyped as follows:

```
CEvent (BOOL bInitiallyOwn = FALSE,
    BOOL bManualReset = FALSE, LPCTSTR lpszName = NULL,
    LPSECURITY_ATTRIBUTES lpsaAttribute = NULL)
```

The first parameter, *bInitiallyOwn*, specifies whether the event object is initially signaled (TRUE) or nonsignaled (FALSE). The default is fine in most cases. *bManualReset* specifies whether the event is a manual-reset event (TRUE) or an autoreset event

(FALSE). The third parameter, *lpszName*, assigns a name to the event object. Like mutexes, events can be used to coordinate threads running in different processes, and for an event to span process boundaries, it must be assigned a name. If the threads that use the event belong to the same process, *lpszName* should be NULL. The final parameter, *lpsaAttribute*, is a pointer to a SECURITY_ATTRIBUTES structure describing the object's security attributes. NULL accepts the default security attributes, which are appropriate for most applications.

So how do you use events to synchronize threads? Here's an example involving one thread (thread A) that fills a buffer with data and another thread (thread B) that does something with that data. Assume that thread B must wait for a signal from thread A saying that the buffer is initialized and ready to go. An autoreset event is the perfect tool for the job:

```
// Global data
CEvent g_event; // Autoreset, initially nonsignaled
    ⋮
// Thread A
InitBuffer (&buffer); // Initialize the buffer.
g_event.SetEvent ();  // Release thread B.
    ⋮
// Thread B
g_event.Lock ();      // Wait for the signal.
```

Thread B calls *Lock* to block on the event object. Thread A calls *SetEvent* when it's ready to release thread B. Figure 17-4 shows what happens as a result.

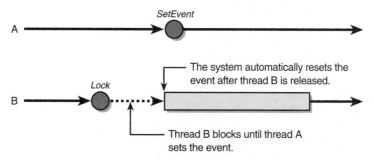

Figure 17-4. *Triggering a thread with an autoreset event.*

The lone parameter passed to *Lock* specifies how long the caller is willing to wait, in milliseconds. The default is INFINITE, which means wait as long as necessary. A nonzero return value means that *Lock* returned because the object became signaled; 0 means that the time-out period expired or an error occurred. MFC isn't doing anything fancy here. It's simply recasting the kernel's thread synchronization objects and the API functions that operate on them in a more object-oriented mold.

Autoreset events are fine for triggering single threads, but what if a thread C running in parallel with thread B does something entirely different with the buffered data? You need a manual-reset event to release B and C together because an autoreset event would release one or the other but not both. Here's the code to trigger two or more threads with a manual-reset event:

```
// Global data
CEvent g_event (FALSE, TRUE); // Nonsignaled, manual-reset
      .
      .
      .
// Thread A
InitBuffer (&buffer);  // Initialize the buffer.
g_event.PulseEvent (); // Release threads B and C.
      .
      .
      .
// Thread B
g_event.Lock ();        // Wait for the signal.
      .
      .
      .
// Thread C
g_event.Lock ();        // Wait for the signal.
```

Notice that thread A uses *PulseEvent* to pull the trigger, in accordance with the second of the two rules prescribed above. Figure 17-5 illustrates the effect of using a manual-reset event to trigger two threads.

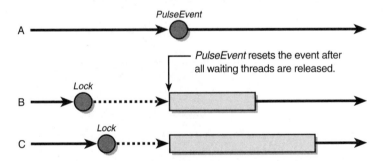

Figure 17-5. *Triggering two threads with a manual-reset event.*

To reiterate, use autoreset events and *CEvent::SetEvent* to release single threads blocking on an event, and use manual-reset events and *CEvent::PulseEvent* to release multiple threads. Abide by these simple rules and events will serve you capably and reliably.

Sometimes events aren't used as triggers but as primitive signaling mechanisms. For example, maybe thread B wants to know whether thread A has completed some task, but it doesn't want to block if the answer is no. Thread B can check the state of an event without blocking by passing *::WaitForSingleObject* the event handle and a time-out value of 0. The event handle can be retrieved from a *CEvent*'s *m_hObject* data member:

```
if (::WaitForSingleObject (g_event.m_hObject, 0) == WAIT_OBJECT_0) {
    // The event is signaled.
}
else {
    // The event is not signaled.
}
```

One caveat to be aware of when using an event in this manner is that if thread B will be checking the event repeatedly until it becomes set, make sure that the event is a manual-reset event and not an autoreset event. Otherwise, the very act of checking the event will reset it.

Semaphores

The fourth and final type of synchronization object is the semaphore. Events, critical sections, and mutexes are "all or nothing" objects in the sense that *Lock* blocks on them if any other thread has them locked. Semaphores are different. Semaphores maintain resource counts representing the number of resources available. Locking a semaphore decrements its resource count, and unlocking a semaphore increments the resource count. A thread blocks only if it tries to lock a semaphore whose resource count is 0. In that case, the thread blocks until another thread unlocks the semaphore and thereby raises the resource count or until a specified time-out period has elapsed. Semaphores can be used to synchronize threads within a process or threads that belong to different processes.

MFC represents semaphores with instances of the class *CSemaphore*. The statement

```
CSemaphore g_semaphore (3, 3);
```

constructs a semaphore object that has an initial resource count of 3 (parameter 1) and a maximum resource count of 3 (parameter 2). If the semaphore will be used to synchronize threads in different processes, you should include a third parameter assigning the semaphore a name. An optional fourth parameter points to a SECURITY-_ATTRIBUTES structure (default=NULL). Each thread that accesses a resource controlled by a semaphore can do so like this:

```
g_semaphore.Lock ();
// Access the shared resource.
g_semaphore.Unlock ();
```

As long as no more than three threads try to access the resource at the same time, *Lock* won't suspend the thread. But if the semaphore is locked by three threads and a fourth thread calls *Lock*, that thread will block until one of the other threads calls

Unlock. (See Figure 17-6.) To limit the time that *Lock* will wait for the semaphore's resource count to become nonzero, you can pass a maximum wait time (in milliseconds, as always) to the *Lock* function.

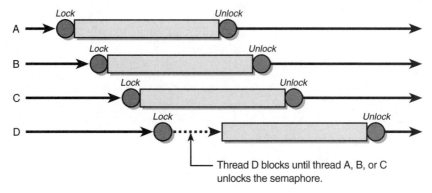

Figure 17-6. *Using a semaphore to guard a shared resource.*

CSemaphore::Unlock can be used to increment the resource count by more than 1 and also to find out what the resource count was before *Unlock* was called. For example, suppose the same thread calls *Lock* twice in succession to lay claim to two resources guarded by a semaphore. Rather than call *Unlock* twice, the thread can do its unlocking like this:

```
LONG lPrevCount;
g_semaphore.Unlock (2, &lPrevCount);
```

There are no functions in either MFC or the API that return a semaphore's resource count other than *CSemaphore::Unlock* and its API equivalent, *::ReleaseSemaphore.*

A classic use for semaphores is to allow a group of *m* threads to share *n* resources, where *m* is greater than *n*. For example, suppose you launch 10 worker threads and charge each with the task of gathering data. Whenever a thread fills a buffer with data, it transmits the data through an open socket, clears the buffer, and starts gathering data again. Now suppose that only three sockets are available at any given time. If you guard the socket pool with a semaphore whose resource count is 3 and code each thread so that it locks the semaphore before claiming a socket, threads will consume no CPU time while they wait for a socket to come free.

The *CSingleLock* and *CMultiLock* Classes

MFC includes a pair of classes named *CSingleLock* and *CMultiLock* that have *Lock* and *Unlock* functions of their own. You can wrap a critical section, mutex, event, or semaphore in a *CSingleLock* object and use *CSingleLock::Lock* to apply a lock, as demonstrated here:

```
CCriticalSection g_cs;
    :
    :

CSingleLock lock (&g_cs); // Wrap it in a CSingleLock.
lock.Lock ();             // Lock the critical section.
```

Is there any advantage to locking a critical section this way instead of calling the *CCriticalSection* object's *Lock* function directly? Sometimes, yes. Consider what happens if the following code throws an exception between the calls to *Lock* and *Unlock*:

```
g_cs.Lock ();
    :
    :

g_cs.Unlock ();
```

If an exception occurs, the critical section will remain locked forever because the call to *Unlock* will be bypassed. But look what happens if you architect your code this way:

```
CSingleLock lock (&g_cs);
lock.Lock ();
    :
    :

lock.Unlock ();
```

The critical section won't be left permanently locked. Why? Because the *CSingleLock* object is created on the stack, its destructor is called if an exception is thrown. *CSingleLock*'s destructor calls *Unlock* on the contained synchronization object. In other words, *CSingleLock* is a handy tool for making sure that a locked synchronization object gets unlocked even in the face of inopportune exceptions.

CMultiLock is an altogether different animal. By using a *CMultiLock*, a thread can block on up to 64 synchronization objects at once. And depending on how it calls *CMultiLock::Lock*, the thread can block until one of the synchronization objects comes free or until *all* of them come free. The following example demonstrates how a thread can block on two events and one mutex simultaneously. Be aware of the fact that events, mutexes, and semaphores can be wrapped in *CMultiLock* objects, but critical sections can't.

```
CMutex g_mutex;
CEvent g_event[2];
CSyncObject* g_pObjects[3] = { &g_mutex, &g_event[0], &g_event[1] };
    :
    :

// Block until all three objects become signaled.
CMultiLock multiLock (g_pObjects, 3);
multiLock.Lock ();
    :
    :
```

(continued)

1023

```
// Block until one of the three objects becomes signaled.
CMultiLock multiLock (g_pObjects, 3);
multiLock.Lock (INFINITE, FALSE);
```

CMultiLock::Lock accepts three parameters, all of which are optional. The first specifies a time-out value (default=INFINITE). The second specifies whether the thread should be awakened when one of the synchronization objects becomes unlocked (FALSE) or when all of them come unlocked (TRUE, the default). The third is a *wakeup mask* that specifies other conditions that will wake up the thread—for example, WM_PAINT messages or mouse-button messages. The default wakeup mask value of 0 prevents the thread from being awakened for any reason other than that the synchronization object (or objects) came free or the time-out period expired.

If a thread comes unblocked after calling *CMultiLock::Lock* to block until just one synchronization object becomes signaled, it's very often the case that the thread will need to know which synchronization object became signaled. The answer can be ascertained from *Lock*'s return value:

```
CMutex g_mutex;
CEvent g_event[2];
CSyncObject* g_pObjects[3] = { &g_mutex, &g_event[0], &g_event[1] };
            :
            :
CMultiLock multiLock (g_pObjects, 3);
DWORD dwResult = multiLock.Lock (INFINITE, FALSE);
DWORD nIndex = dwResult - WAIT_OBJECT_0;
if (nIndex == 0) {
    // The mutex became signaled.
}
else if (nIndex == 1) {
    // The first event became signaled.
}
else if (nIndex == 2) {
    // The second event became signaled.
}
```

Be aware that if you pass *Lock* a time-out value other than INFINITE, you should compare the return value to WAIT_TIMEOUT before subtracting WAIT_OBJECT_0 in case *Lock* returned because the time-out period expired. Also, if *Lock* returns because an abandoned mutex became signaled, you must subtract WAIT_ABANDONED_0 from the return value instead of WAIT_OBJECT_0. For further details, consult the documentation for *CMultiLock::Lock*.

Here's one example of a situation in which *CMultiLock* can be useful. Suppose three separate threads—threads A, B, and C—are working together to prepare data in a buffer. Once the data is ready, thread D transmits the data through a socket or writes it to a file. However, thread D can't be called until threads A, B, and C have completed their work. The solution? Create separate event objects to represent threads

A, B, and C, and let thread D use a *CMultiLock* object to block until all three events become signaled. As each thread completes its work, it sets the corresponding event object to the signaled state. Thread D therefore blocks until the last of the three threads signals that it's done.

Writing Thread-Safe Classes

MFC classes are thread-safe at the class level but not at the object level. Translated, this means that it's safe for two threads to access two separate instances of the same class but that problems could result if two threads are allowed to access the same instance at the same time. MFC's designers chose not to make it thread-safe at the object level for performance reasons. The simple act of locking an unlocked critical section can consume hundreds of clock cycles on a Pentium processor. If every access to an object of an MFC class locked a critical section, the performance of single-threaded applications would suffer needlessly.

To illustrate what it means for a class to be thread-safe, think about what might happen if two threads using the same *CString* object made no attempt to synchronize their actions. Let's say that thread A decides to set the string, whose name is *g_strFileName*, equal to the text string referenced by *pszFile*:

```
g_strFileName = pszFile;
```

At about the same time, thread B decides to display *g_strFileName* on the screen by passing it to *CDC::TextOut*:

```
pDC->TextOut (x, y, g_strFileName);
```

What gets displayed on the screen? The old value of *g_strFileName* or the new value? Maybe neither. Copying text to a *CString* object is a multistep operation that involves allocating buffer space to hold the text, performing a *memcpy* to copy the characters, setting the *CString* data member that stores the string length equal to the number of characters that were copied, adding a terminating 0 to the end, and so on. If thread B interrupts this process at the wrong moment, there's no telling what state the *CString* might be in when it's passed to *TextOut*. The output might be improperly truncated. Or *TextOut* might display garbage on the screen or cause an access violation.

One way to synchronize access to *g_strFileName* is to protect it with a critical section, as shown here:

```
// Global data
CCriticalSection g_cs;
     :
     :
// Thread A
g_cs.Lock ();
g_strFileName = pszFile;
```

(continued)

```
g_cs.Unlock ();
      ⋮
      ⋮
// Thread B
g_cs.Lock ();
pDC->TextOut (x, y, g_strFileName);
g_cs.Unlock ();
```

An alternative approach is to derive a class from *CString* and make the derived class thread-safe by building in a critical section that's automatically locked anytime an access occurs. Then the object itself ensures that accesses are performed in a thread-safe way, and it's no longer incumbent upon the application that *uses* the object to synchronize the actions of its threads.

Deriving a class and making it thread-safe is basically a matter of overriding every member function that reads or writes an object's data and wrapping calls to member functions in the base class with calls to lock and unlock a synchronization object that's a member of the derived class. Ditto for thread-safe classes that aren't derived from other classes but are designed from the ground up: add a *CCriticalSection* or *CMutex* data member to the class, and lock and unlock the synchronization object before and after every access.

It's not always possible to make a class entirely thread-safe. If a thread uses *GetBuffer* or an LPCTSTR operator to get a pointer to the text of a *CString*, for example, the *CString* itself has no control over what the caller does with that pointer. In that case, it's still the responsibility of the thread that uses the *CString* object to coordinate its accesses with those of other threads.

The point to take home from all of this is that objects are not thread-safe by default. You can use synchronization objects to access other objects in a thread-safe way, and you can develop classes that are inherently thread-safe by controlling access to objects created from those classes. But allowing one thread to read data from an object while another thread modifies the object's data—or vice versa—is a recipe for disaster. To make matters worse, errors of this nature often show up randomly in testing. You might run the application 1,000 times and never experience the debilitating effects of an overlapping access. But as sure as the possibility exists, someone using your application will experience a dual access that occurs at the worst possible moment and brings the entire application (and possibly the operating system, too) crashing to the ground.

The ImageEdit Application

The ImageEdit application shown in Figure 17-7 is an enhanced version of Chapter 15's Vista application, one that uses a separate thread to perform a complex image processing task in the background. When you select Convert To Gray Scale from the Effects menu, ImageEdit scans the current bitmap pixel by pixel, converts each pixel

Figure 17-7. *The ImageEdit window.*

to a shade of gray, and adjusts the color palette to display an accurate gray-scale rendition of the original color image. The conversion function is an ideal candidate for a worker thread because it can take anywhere from a few seconds to several minutes to run, depending on the size of the bitmap, the speed of the CPU, and other factors. The code that performs the conversion is far from optimal; in fact, its speed could be improved by a factor of 10 or more if it were rewritten to operate directly on the bitmap's bits rather than to call *CDC::GetPixel* and *CDC::SetPixel* on every pixel. But for demonstration purposes, it's fine. And using *CDC* pixel functions to get and set pixel colors allows us to do in about 20 lines of code what could easily require several hundred if we rewrote ImageEdit to process raw bitmap data.

The bulk of ImageEdit's source code is reproduced in Figure 17-8. I wanted to show a multithreaded document/view application in this chapter because there are certain issues unique to writing multithreaded document/view programs that don't come up in multithreaded SDK applications or in multithreaded MFC applications that don't use documents and views. For example, it's not unusual for a document object to launch a worker thread to process the document's data. But how can a background thread let the document object know that processing is complete? It can't post a message to the document because a document isn't a window. It's a bad idea for the document to block on an event waiting for the thread to complete its mission, because doing so would block the application's primary thread and effectively suspend the message loop. Yet the document usually needs to know when the thread is finished so that it can update its views. The question is, How?

(Text continues on page 1051.)

MainFrm.h

```
// MainFrm.h : interface of the CMainFrame class
//
/////////////////////////////////////////////////////////////////////////////

#if !defined(
    AFX_MAINFRM_H__9D77AEE8_AA14_11D2_8E53_006008A82731__INCLUDED_)
#define AFX_MAINFRM_H__9D77AEE8_AA14_11D2_8E53_006008A82731__INCLUDED_

#if _MSC_VER > 1000
#pragma once
#endif // _MSC_VER > 1000

class CMainFrame : public CFrameWnd
{

protected: // create from serialization only
    CMainFrame();
    DECLARE_DYNCREATE(CMainFrame)

// Attributes
public:

// Operations
public:

// Overrides
    // ClassWizard generated virtual function overrides
    //{{AFX_VIRTUAL(CMainFrame)
    virtual BOOL PreCreateWindow(CREATESTRUCT& cs);
    //}}AFX_VIRTUAL

// Implementation
public:
    virtual ~CMainFrame();
#ifdef _DEBUG
    virtual void AssertValid() const;
    virtual void Dump(CDumpContext& dc) const;
#endif

protected:  // control bar embedded members
    CSpecialStatusBar m_wndStatusBar;

// Generated message map functions
protected:
    int m_nPercentDone;
```

Figure 17-8. *The ImageEdit application.*

```
    //{{AFX_MSG(CMainFrame)
    afx_msg int OnCreate(LPCREATESTRUCT lpCreateStruct);
    afx_msg BOOL OnQueryNewPalette();
    afx_msg void OnPaletteChanged(CWnd* pFocusWnd);
    //}}AFX_MSG
    afx_msg LRESULT OnUpdateImageStats (WPARAM wParam, LPARAM lParam);
    afx_msg LRESULT OnThreadUpdate (WPARAM wParam, LPARAM lParam);
    afx_msg LRESULT OnThreadFinished (WPARAM wParam, LPARAM lParam);
    afx_msg LRESULT OnThreadAborted (WPARAM wParam, LPARAM lParam);
    DECLARE_MESSAGE_MAP()
};


///////////////////////////////////////////////////////////////////////////

//{{AFX_INSERT_LOCATION}}
// Microsoft Visual C++ will insert additional declarations
// immediately before the previous line.

#endif
// !defined(AFX_MAINFRM_H__9D77AEE8_AA14_11D2_8E53_006008A82731__INCLUDED_)
```

MainFrm.cpp

```
// MainFrm.cpp : implementation of the CMainFrame class
//

#include "stdafx.h"
#include "ImageEdit.h"
#include "ImageEditDoc.h"
#include "SpecialStatusBar.h"
#include "MainFrm.h"

#ifdef _DEBUG
#define new DEBUG_NEW
#undef THIS_FILE
static char THIS_FILE[] = __FILE__;
#endif


///////////////////////////////////////////////////////////////////////////
// CMainFrame

IMPLEMENT_DYNCREATE(CMainFrame, CFrameWnd)

BEGIN_MESSAGE_MAP(CMainFrame, CFrameWnd)
    //{{AFX_MSG_MAP(CMainFrame)
```

(continued)

Figure 17-8 *continued*

```
    ON_WM_CREATE()
    ON_WM_QUERYNEWPALETTE()
    ON_WM_PALETTECHANGED()
    //}}AFX_MSG_MAP
    ON_MESSAGE (WM_USER_UPDATE_STATS, OnUpdateImageStats)
    ON_MESSAGE (WM_USER_THREAD_UPDATE, OnThreadUpdate)
    ON_MESSAGE (WM_USER_THREAD_FINISHED, OnThreadFinished)
    ON_MESSAGE (WM_USER_THREAD_ABORTED, OnThreadAborted)
END_MESSAGE_MAP()

static UINT indicators[] =
{
    ID_SEPARATOR,
    ID_SEPARATOR,
    ID_SEPARATOR
};

/////////////////////////////////////////////////////////////////////////////
// CMainFrame construction/destruction

CMainFrame::CMainFrame()
{
    m_nPercentDone = -1;
}


CMainFrame::~CMainFrame()
{
}


int CMainFrame::OnCreate(LPCREATESTRUCT lpCreateStruct)
{
    if (CFrameWnd::OnCreate(lpCreateStruct) == -1)
        return -1;

    if (!m_wndStatusBar.Create(this))
    {
        TRACE0("Failed to create status bar\n");
        return -1;      // fail to create
    }
    return 0;
}


BOOL CMainFrame::PreCreateWindow(CREATESTRUCT& cs)
```

```
{
    if( !CFrameWnd::PreCreateWindow(cs) )
        return FALSE;
    return TRUE;
}


/////////////////////////////////////////////////////////////////////////////
// CMainFrame diagnostics

#ifdef _DEBUG
void CMainFrame::AssertValid() const
{
    CFrameWnd::AssertValid();
}


void CMainFrame::Dump(CDumpContext& dc) const
{
    CFrameWnd::Dump(dc);
}


#endif //_DEBUG


/////////////////////////////////////////////////////////////////////////////
// CMainFrame message handlers

BOOL CMainFrame::OnQueryNewPalette()
{
    CDocument* pDoc = GetActiveDocument ();
    if (pDoc != NULL)
        GetActiveDocument ()->UpdateAllViews (NULL);
    return TRUE;
}


void CMainFrame::OnPaletteChanged(CWnd* pFocusWnd)
{
    if (pFocusWnd != this) {
        CDocument* pDoc = GetActiveDocument ();
        if (pDoc != NULL)
            GetActiveDocument ()->UpdateAllViews (NULL);
    }
}


LRESULT CMainFrame::OnUpdateImageStats (WPARAM wParam, LPARAM lParam)
{
    m_wndStatusBar.SetImageStats ((LPCTSTR) lParam);
    return 0;
}
```

(continued)

Figure 17-8 *continued*

```
LRESULT CMainFrame::OnThreadUpdate (WPARAM wParam, LPARAM lParam)
{
    int nPercentDone = ((int) wParam * 100) / (int) lParam;
    if (nPercentDone != m_nPercentDone) {
        m_wndStatusBar.SetProgress (nPercentDone);
        m_nPercentDone = nPercentDone;
    }
    return 0;
}

LRESULT CMainFrame::OnThreadFinished (WPARAM wParam, LPARAM lParam)
{
    CImageEditDoc* pDoc = (CImageEditDoc*) GetActiveDocument ();
    if (pDoc != NULL) {
        pDoc->ThreadFinished ();
        m_wndStatusBar.SetProgress (0);
        m_nPercentDone = -1;
    }
    return 0;
}

LRESULT CMainFrame::OnThreadAborted (WPARAM wParam, LPARAM lParam)
{
    CImageEditDoc* pDoc = (CImageEditDoc*) GetActiveDocument ();
    if (pDoc != NULL) {
        pDoc->ThreadAborted ();
        m_wndStatusBar.SetProgress (0);
        m_nPercentDone = -1;
    }
    return 0;
}
```

ImageEditDoc.h

```
// ImageEditDoc.h : interface of the CImageEditDoc class
//
/////////////////////////////////////////////////////////////////////

#if !defined(
    AFX_IMAGEEDITDOC_H__9D77AEEA_AA14_11D2_8E53_006008A82731__INCLUDED_)
#define AFX_IMAGEEDITDOC_H__9D77AEEA_AA14_11D2_8E53_006008A82731__INCLUDED_

#if _MSC_VER > 1000
#pragma once
#endif // _MSC_VER > 1000
```

```
UINT ThreadFunc (LPVOID pParam);
LOGPALETTE* CreateGrayScale ();

class CImageEditDoc : public CDocument
{
protected: // create from serialization only
    CImageEditDoc();
    DECLARE_DYNCREATE(CImageEditDoc)

// Attributes
public:

// Operations
public:

// Overrides
    // ClassWizard generated virtual function overrides
    //{{AFX_VIRTUAL(CImageEditDoc)
    public:
    virtual BOOL OnNewDocument();
    virtual BOOL OnOpenDocument(LPCTSTR lpszPathName);
    virtual void DeleteContents();
    //}}AFX_VIRTUAL

// Implementation
public:
    void ThreadAborted();
    void ThreadFinished();
    CPalette* GetPalette();
    CBitmap* GetBitmap();
    virtual ~CImageEditDoc();
#ifdef _DEBUG
    virtual void AssertValid() const;
    virtual void Dump(CDumpContext& dc) const;
#endif

protected:

// Generated message map functions
protected:
    CCriticalSection m_cs;
    CEvent m_event;
    HANDLE m_hThread;
    BOOL m_bWorking;
    CPalette m_palette;
    CBitmap m_bitmap;
    //{{AFX_MSG(CImageEditDoc)
    afx_msg void OnGrayScale();
```

(continued)

Figure 17-8 *continued*

```
    afx_msg void OnUpdateGrayScale(CCmdUI* pCmdUI);
    //}}AFX_MSG
    DECLARE_MESSAGE_MAP()
};


/////////////////////////////////////////////////////////////////////////////

//{{AFX_INSERT_LOCATION}}
// Microsoft Visual C++ will insert additional declarations
// immediately before the previous line.

#endif
// !defined(
//      AFX_IMAGEEDITDOC_H__9D77AEEA_AA14_11D2_8E53_006008A82731__INCLUDED_)
```

ImageEditDoc.cpp

```
// ImageEditDoc.cpp : implementation of the CImageEditDoc class
//

#include "stdafx.h"
#include "ImageEdit.h"

#include "ImageEditDoc.h"

#ifdef _DEBUG
#define new DEBUG_NEW
#undef THIS_FILE
static char THIS_FILE[] = __FILE__;
#endif

/////////////////////////////////////////////////////////////////////////////
// CImageEditDoc

IMPLEMENT_DYNCREATE(CImageEditDoc, CDocument)

BEGIN_MESSAGE_MAP(CImageEditDoc, CDocument)
    //{{AFX_MSG_MAP(CImageEditDoc)
    ON_COMMAND(ID_EFFECTS_GRAY_SCALE, OnGrayScale)
    ON_UPDATE_COMMAND_UI(ID_EFFECTS_GRAY_SCALE, OnUpdateGrayScale)
    //}}AFX_MSG_MAP
END_MESSAGE_MAP()
```

```
/////////////////////////////////////////////////////////////////////////////
// CImageEditDoc construction/destruction

CImageEditDoc::CImageEditDoc() :
    m_event (FALSE, TRUE) // Manual-reset event, initially unowned
{
    m_hThread = NULL;
    m_bWorking = FALSE;
}


CImageEditDoc::~CImageEditDoc()
{
}


BOOL CImageEditDoc::OnNewDocument()
{
    if (!CDocument::OnNewDocument())
        return FALSE;
    return TRUE;
}


/////////////////////////////////////////////////////////////////////////////
// CImageEditDoc diagnostics

#ifdef _DEBUG
void CImageEditDoc::AssertValid() const
{
    CDocument::AssertValid();
}


void CImageEditDoc::Dump(CDumpContext& dc) const
{
    CDocument::Dump(dc);
}
#endif //_DEBUG


/////////////////////////////////////////////////////////////////////////////
// CImageEditDoc commands

BOOL CImageEditDoc::OnOpenDocument(LPCTSTR lpszPathName)
{
    //
    // Return now if an image is being processed.
    //
```

(continued)

Figure 17-8 *continued*

```
    if (m_bWorking) {
        AfxMessageBox (_T ("You can't open an image while another is " \
            "being converted"));
        return FALSE;
    }

    //
    // Let the base class do its thing.
    //
    if (!CDocument::OnOpenDocument (lpszPathName))
        return FALSE;

    //
    // Open the file and create a DIB section from its contents.
    //
    HBITMAP hBitmap = (HBITMAP) ::LoadImage (NULL, lpszPathName,
        IMAGE_BITMAP, 0, 0, LR_LOADFROMFILE | LR_CREATEDIBSECTION);

    if (hBitmap == NULL) {
        CString string;
        string.Format (_T ("%s does not contain a DIB"), lpszPathName);
        AfxMessageBox (string);
        return FALSE;
    }

    m_bitmap.Attach (hBitmap);

    //
    // Return now if this device doesn't support palettes.
    //
    CClientDC dc (NULL);
    if ((dc.GetDeviceCaps (RASTERCAPS) & RC_PALETTE) == 0)
        return TRUE;

    //
    // Create a palette to go with the DIB section.
    //
    if ((HBITMAP) m_bitmap != NULL) {
        DIBSECTION ds;
        m_bitmap.GetObject (sizeof (DIBSECTION), &ds);

        int nColors;
        if (ds.dsBmih.biClrUsed != 0)
            nColors = ds.dsBmih.biClrUsed;
```

```
        else
            nColors = 1 << ds.dsBmih.biBitCount;

        //
        // Create a halftone palette if the DIB section contains more
        // than 256 colors.
        //
        if (nColors > 256)
            m_palette.CreateHalftonePalette (&dc);

        //
        // Create a custom palette from the DIB section's color table
        // if the number of colors is 256 or less.
        //
        else {
            RGBQUAD* pRGB = new RGBQUAD[nColors];

            CDC memDC;
            memDC.CreateCompatibleDC (&dc);
            CBitmap* pOldBitmap = memDC.SelectObject (&m_bitmap);
            ::GetDIBColorTable ((HDC) memDC, 0, nColors, pRGB);
            memDC.SelectObject (pOldBitmap);

            UINT nSize = sizeof (LOGPALETTE) +
                (sizeof (PALETTEENTRY) * (nColors - 1));
            LOGPALETTE* pLP = (LOGPALETTE*) new BYTE[nSize];

            pLP->palVersion = 0x300;
            pLP->palNumEntries = nColors;

            for (int i=0; i<nColors; i++) {
                pLP->palPalEntry[i].peRed = pRGB[i].rgbRed;
                pLP->palPalEntry[i].peGreen = pRGB[i].rgbGreen;
                pLP->palPalEntry[i].peBlue = pRGB[i].rgbBlue;
                pLP->palPalEntry[i].peFlags = 0;
            }

            m_palette.CreatePalette (pLP);
            delete[] pLP;
            delete[] pRGB;
        }
    }
    return TRUE;
}
```

(continued)

Figure 17-8 *continued*

```
void CImageEditDoc::DeleteContents()
{
    if ((HBITMAP) m_bitmap != NULL)
        m_bitmap.DeleteObject ();

    if ((HPALETTE) m_palette != NULL)
        m_palette.DeleteObject ();

    CDocument::DeleteContents();
}

CBitmap* CImageEditDoc::GetBitmap()
{
    return ((HBITMAP) m_bitmap == NULL) ? NULL : &m_bitmap;
}

CPalette* CImageEditDoc::GetPalette()
{
    return ((HPALETTE) m_palette == NULL) ? NULL : &m_palette;
}

void CImageEditDoc::ThreadFinished()
{
    ASSERT (m_hThread != NULL);
    ::WaitForSingleObject (m_hThread, INFINITE);
    ::CloseHandle (m_hThread);
    m_hThread = NULL;
    m_bWorking = FALSE;

    //
    // Replace the current palette with a gray scale palette.
    //
    if ((HPALETTE) m_palette != NULL) {
        m_palette.DeleteObject ();
        LOGPALETTE* pLP = CreateGrayScale ();
        m_palette.CreatePalette (pLP);
        delete[] pLP;
    }

    //
    // Tell the view to repaint.
    //
    UpdateAllViews (NULL);
}
```

```
void CImageEditDoc::ThreadAborted()
{
    ASSERT (m_hThread != NULL);
    ::WaitForSingleObject (m_hThread, INFINITE);
    ::CloseHandle (m_hThread);
    m_hThread = NULL;
    m_bWorking = FALSE;
}

void CImageEditDoc::OnGrayScale()
{
    if (!m_bWorking) {
        m_bWorking = TRUE;
        m_event.ResetEvent ();

        //
        // Package data to pass to the image processing thread.
        //
        THREADPARMS* ptp = new THREADPARMS;
        ptp->pWnd = AfxGetMainWnd ();
        ptp->pBitmap = &m_bitmap;
        ptp->pPalette = &m_palette;
        ptp->pCriticalSection = &m_cs;
        ptp->pEvent = &m_event;

        //
        // Start the image processing thread and duplicate its handle.
        //
        CWinThread* pThread = AfxBeginThread (ThreadFunc, ptp,
            THREAD_PRIORITY_NORMAL, 0, CREATE_SUSPENDED);

        ::DuplicateHandle (GetCurrentProcess (),
            pThread->m_hThread, GetCurrentProcess (), &m_hThread,
            0, FALSE, DUPLICATE_SAME_ACCESS);

        pThread->ResumeThread ();
    }
    else
        //
        // Kill the image processing thread.
        //
        m_event.SetEvent ();
}
```

(continued)

Figure 17-8 *continued*

```
void CImageEditDoc::OnUpdateGrayScale(CCmdUI* pCmdUI)
{
    if (m_bWorking) {
        pCmdUI->SetText (_T ("Stop &Gray Scale Conversion"));
        pCmdUI->Enable ();
    }
    else {
        pCmdUI->SetText (_T ("Convert to &Gray Scale"));
        pCmdUI->Enable ((HBITMAP) m_bitmap != NULL);
    }
}


///////////////////////////////////////////////////////////////////////////
// Thread function and other globals

UINT ThreadFunc (LPVOID pParam)
{
    THREADPARMS* ptp = (THREADPARMS*) pParam;
    CWnd* pWnd = ptp->pWnd;
    CBitmap* pBitmap = ptp->pBitmap;
    CPalette* pPalette = ptp->pPalette;
    CCriticalSection* pCriticalSection = ptp->pCriticalSection;
    CEvent* pKillEvent = ptp->pEvent;
    delete ptp;

    DIBSECTION ds;
    pBitmap->GetObject (sizeof (DIBSECTION), &ds);
    int nWidth = ds.dsBm.bmWidth;
    int nHeight = ds.dsBm.bmHeight;

    //
    // Initialize one memory DC (memDC2) to hold a color copy of the
    // image and another memory DC (memDC1) to hold a gray scale copy.
    //
    CClientDC dc (pWnd);
    CBitmap bitmap1, bitmap2;
    bitmap1.CreateCompatibleBitmap (&dc, nWidth, nHeight);
    bitmap2.CreateCompatibleBitmap (&dc, nWidth, nHeight);

    CDC memDC1, memDC2;
    memDC1.CreateCompatibleDC (&dc);
    memDC2.CreateCompatibleDC (&dc);
    CBitmap* pOldBitmap1 = memDC1.SelectObject (&bitmap1);
    CBitmap* pOldBitmap2 = memDC2.SelectObject (&bitmap2);
```

```
CPalette* pOldPalette1 = NULL;
CPalette* pOldPalette2 = NULL;
CPalette grayPalette;

if (pPalette->m_hObject != NULL) {
    LOGPALETTE* pLP = CreateGrayScale ();
    grayPalette.CreatePalette (pLP);
    delete[] pLP;

    pOldPalette1 = memDC1.SelectPalette (&grayPalette, FALSE);
    pOldPalette2 = memDC2.SelectPalette (pPalette, FALSE);
    memDC1.RealizePalette ();
    memDC2.RealizePalette ();
}

//
// Copy the bitmap to memDC2.
//
CDC memDC3;
memDC3.CreateCompatibleDC (&dc);
pCriticalSection->Lock ();
CBitmap* pOldBitmap3 = memDC3.SelectObject (pBitmap);
memDC2.BitBlt (0, 0, nWidth, nHeight, &memDC3, 0, 0, SRCCOPY);
memDC3.SelectObject (pOldBitmap3);
pCriticalSection->Unlock ();

//
// Convert the colors in memDC2 to shades of gray in memDC1.
//
int x, y;
COLORREF crColor;
BYTE grayLevel;

for (y=0; y<nHeight; y++) {
    for (x=0; x<nWidth; x++) {
        crColor = memDC2.GetPixel (x, y);
        grayLevel = (BYTE)
            (((((UINT) GetRValue (crColor)) * 30) +
            (((UINT) GetGValue (crColor)) * 59) +
            (((UINT) GetBValue (crColor)) * 11)) / 100);
        memDC1.SetPixel (x, y,
            PALETTERGB (grayLevel, grayLevel, grayLevel));
    }
```

(continued)

Figure 17-8 *continued*

```
    //
    // Kill the thread if the pKillEvent event is signaled.
    //
    if (::WaitForSingleObject (pKillEvent->m_hObject, 0) ==
        WAIT_OBJECT_0) {

        memDC1.SelectObject (pOldBitmap1);
        memDC2.SelectObject (pOldBitmap2);

        if (pPalette->m_hObject != NULL) {
            memDC1.SelectPalette (pOldPalette1, FALSE);
            memDC2.SelectPalette (pOldPalette2, FALSE);
        }
        pWnd->PostMessage (WM_USER_THREAD_ABORTED, y + 1, 0);
        return (UINT) -1;
    }
    pWnd->SendMessage (WM_USER_THREAD_UPDATE, y + 1, nHeight);
}

//
// Copy the gray scale image over the original bitmap.
//
CPalette* pOldPalette3 = NULL;
if (pPalette->m_hObject != NULL) {
    pOldPalette3 = memDC3.SelectPalette (&grayPalette, FALSE);
    memDC3.RealizePalette ();
}
pCriticalSection->Lock ();
pOldBitmap3 = memDC3.SelectObject (pBitmap);
memDC3.BitBlt (0, 0, nWidth, nHeight, &memDC1, 0, 0, SRCCOPY);
memDC3.SelectObject (pOldBitmap3);
pCriticalSection->Unlock ();

//
// Clean up the memory DCs.
//
memDC1.SelectObject (pOldBitmap1);
memDC2.SelectObject (pOldBitmap2);

if (pPalette->m_hObject != NULL) {
    memDC1.SelectPalette (pOldPalette1, FALSE);
    memDC2.SelectPalette (pOldPalette2, FALSE);
    memDC3.SelectPalette (pOldPalette3, FALSE);
}
```

```
    //
    // Tell the frame window we're done.
    //
    pWnd->PostMessage (WM_USER_THREAD_FINISHED, 0, 0);
    return 0;
}

LOGPALETTE* CreateGrayScale ()
{
    UINT nSize = sizeof (LOGPALETTE) + (sizeof (PALETTEENTRY) * 63);
    LOGPALETTE* pLP = (LOGPALETTE*) new BYTE[nSize];

    pLP->palVersion = 0x300;
    pLP->palNumEntries = 64;

    for (int i=0; i<64; i++) {
        pLP->palPalEntry[i].peRed = i * 4;
        pLP->palPalEntry[i].peGreen = i * 4;
        pLP->palPalEntry[i].peBlue = i * 4;
        pLP->palPalEntry[i].peFlags = 0;
    }
    return pLP;
}
```

ImageEditView.h

```
// ImageEditView.h : interface of the CImageEditView class
//
/////////////////////////////////////////////////////////////////////////////

#if !defined(
    AFX_IMAGEEDITVIEW_H__9D77AEEC_AA14_11D2_8E53_006008A82731__INCLUDED_)
#define
    AFX_IMAGEEDITVIEW_H__9D77AEEC_AA14_11D2_8E53_006008A82731__INCLUDED_

#if _MSC_VER > 1000
#pragma once
#endif // _MSC_VER > 1000


class CImageEditView : public CScrollView
{
protected: // create from serialization only
    CImageEditView();
    DECLARE_DYNCREATE(CImageEditView)
```

(continued)

Figure 17-8 *continued*

```
// Attributes
public:
    CImageEditDoc* GetDocument();

// Operations
public:

// Overrides
    // ClassWizard generated virtual function overrides
    //{{AFX_VIRTUAL(CImageEditView)
    public:
    virtual void OnDraw(CDC* pDC);  // overridden to draw this view
    virtual BOOL PreCreateWindow(CREATESTRUCT& cs);
    protected:
    virtual void OnInitialUpdate(); // called first time after construct
    //}}AFX_VIRTUAL

// Implementation
public:
    virtual ~CImageEditView();
#ifdef _DEBUG
    virtual void AssertValid() const;
    virtual void Dump(CDumpContext& dc) const;
#endif

protected:

// Generated message map functions
protected:
    //{{AFX_MSG(CImageEditView)
    //}}AFX_MSG
    DECLARE_MESSAGE_MAP()
};

#ifndef _DEBUG  // debug version in ImageEditView.cpp
inline CImageEditDoc* CImageEditView::GetDocument()
    { return (CImageEditDoc*)m_pDocument; }
#endif


///////////////////////////////////////////////////////////////////////

//{{AFX_INSERT_LOCATION}}
// Microsoft Visual C++ will insert additional declarations
// immediately before the previous line.
```

```
#endif
// !defined(
//    AFX_IMAGEEDITVIEW_H__9D77AEEC_AA14_11D2_8E53_006008A82731__INCLUDED_)
```

ImageEditView.cpp

```
// ImageEditView.cpp : implementation of the CImageEditView class
//

#include "stdafx.h"
#include "ImageEdit.h"

#include "ImageEditDoc.h"
#include "ImageEditView.h"

#ifdef _DEBUG
#define new DEBUG_NEW
#undef THIS_FILE
static char THIS_FILE[] = __FILE__;
#endif

/////////////////////////////////////////////////////////////////////////
// CImageEditView

IMPLEMENT_DYNCREATE(CImageEditView, CScrollView)

BEGIN_MESSAGE_MAP(CImageEditView, CScrollView)
    //{{AFX_MSG_MAP(CImageEditView)
    //}}AFX_MSG_MAP
END_MESSAGE_MAP()

/////////////////////////////////////////////////////////////////////////
// CImageEditView construction/destruction

CImageEditView::CImageEditView()
{
}

CImageEditView::~CImageEditView()
{
}

BOOL CImageEditView::PreCreateWindow(CREATESTRUCT& cs)
{
    return CScrollView::PreCreateWindow(cs);
}
```

(continued)

Figure 17-8 *continued*

```
///////////////////////////////////////////////////////////////////////////
// CImageEditView drawing

void CImageEditView::OnDraw(CDC* pDC)
{
    CImageEditDoc* pDoc = GetDocument();
    ASSERT_VALID(pDoc);

    CBitmap* pBitmap = pDoc->GetBitmap ();

    if (pBitmap != NULL) {
        CPalette* pOldPalette;
        CPalette* pPalette = pDoc->GetPalette ();

        if (pPalette != NULL) {
            pOldPalette = pDC->SelectPalette (pPalette, FALSE);
            pDC->RealizePalette ();
        }

        DIBSECTION ds;
        pBitmap->GetObject (sizeof (DIBSECTION), &ds);

        CDC memDC;
        memDC.CreateCompatibleDC (pDC);
        CBitmap* pOldBitmap = memDC.SelectObject (pBitmap);

        pDC->BitBlt (0, 0, ds.dsBm.bmWidth, ds.dsBm.bmHeight, &memDC,
            0, 0, SRCCOPY);

        memDC.SelectObject (pOldBitmap);

        if (pPalette != NULL)
            pDC->SelectPalette (pOldPalette, FALSE);
    }
}

void CImageEditView::OnInitialUpdate()
{
    CScrollView::OnInitialUpdate ();

    CString string;
    CSize sizeTotal;
    CBitmap* pBitmap = GetDocument ()->GetBitmap ();
```

```
    //
    // If a bitmap is loaded, set the view size equal to the bitmap size.
    // Otherwise, set the view's width and height to 0.
    //
    if (pBitmap != NULL) {
        DIBSECTION ds;
        pBitmap->GetObject (sizeof (DIBSECTION), &ds);
        sizeTotal.cx = ds.dsBm.bmWidth;
        sizeTotal.cy = ds.dsBm.bmHeight;
        string.Format (_T ("\t%d x %d, %d bpp"), ds.dsBm.bmWidth,
            ds.dsBm.bmHeight, ds.dsBmih.biBitCount);
    }
    else {
        sizeTotal.cx = sizeTotal.cy = 0;
        string.Empty ();
    }

    AfxGetMainWnd ()->SendMessage (WM_USER_UPDATE_STATS, 0,
        (LPARAM) (LPCTSTR) string);
    SetScrollSizes (MM_TEXT, sizeTotal);
}


/////////////////////////////////////////////////////////////////////////////
// CImageEditView diagnostics

#ifdef _DEBUG
void CImageEditView::AssertValid() const
{
    CScrollView::AssertValid();
}

void CImageEditView::Dump(CDumpContext& dc) const
{
    CScrollView::Dump(dc);
}

CImageEditDoc* CImageEditView::GetDocument() // non-debug version is inline
{
    ASSERT(m_pDocument->IsKindOf(RUNTIME_CLASS(CImageEditDoc)));
    return (CImageEditDoc*)m_pDocument;
}
#endif //_DEBUG


/////////////////////////////////////////////////////////////////////////////
// CImageEditView message handlers
```

(continued)

Figure 17-8 *continued*

SpecialStatusBar.h

```
// SpecialStatusBar.h: interface for the CSpecialStatusBar class.
//
//////////////////////////////////////////////////////////////////////

#if !defined(
    AFX_SPECIALSTATUSBAR_H__4BA7D301_AA24_11D2_8E53_006008A82731__INCLUDED_)
#define
    AFX_SPECIALSTATUSBAR_H__4BA7D301_AA24_11D2_8E53_006008A82731__INCLUDED_

#if _MSC_VER > 1000
#pragma once
#endif // _MSC_VER > 1000

class CSpecialStatusBar : public CStatusBar
{
public:
    void SetProgress (int nPercent);
    void SetImageStats(LPCTSTR pszStats);
    CSpecialStatusBar();
    virtual ~CSpecialStatusBar();

protected:
    CProgressCtrl m_wndProgress;
    afx_msg int OnCreate (LPCREATESTRUCT lpcs);
    afx_msg void OnSize (UINT nType, int cx, int cy);
    DECLARE_MESSAGE_MAP ()
};

#endif
// !defined(
// AFX_SPECIALSTATUSBAR_H__4BA7D301_AA24_11D2_8E53_006008A82731__INCLUDED_)
```

SpecialStatusBar.cpp

```
// SpecialStatusBar.cpp: implementation of the CSpecialStatusBar class.
//
//////////////////////////////////////////////////////////////////////

#include "stdafx.h"
#include "ImageEdit.h"
#include "SpecialStatusBar.h"
```

```
#ifdef _DEBUG
#undef THIS_FILE
static char THIS_FILE[]=__FILE__;
#define new DEBUG_NEW
#endif

///////////////////////////////////////////////////////////////////////
// Construction/Destruction
///////////////////////////////////////////////////////////////////////

BEGIN_MESSAGE_MAP(CSpecialStatusBar, CStatusBar)
    ON_WM_CREATE ()
    ON_WM_SIZE ()
END_MESSAGE_MAP()

CSpecialStatusBar::CSpecialStatusBar()
{
}

CSpecialStatusBar::~CSpecialStatusBar()
{
}

int CSpecialStatusBar::OnCreate (LPCREATESTRUCT lpcs)
{
    static UINT nIndicators[] =
    {
        ID_SEPARATOR,
        ID_SEPARATOR,
        ID_SEPARATOR
    };

    if (CStatusBar::OnCreate (lpcs) == -1)
        return -1;

    //
    // Add panes to the status bar.
    //
    SetIndicators (nIndicators, sizeof (nIndicators) / sizeof (UINT));

    //
    // Size the status bar panes.
    //
    TEXTMETRIC tm;
    CClientDC dc (this);
    CFont* pFont = GetFont ();
```

(continued)

Figure 17-8 *continued*

```
        CFont* pOldFont = dc.SelectObject (pFont);
        dc.GetTextMetrics (&tm);
        dc.SelectObject (pOldFont);

        int cxWidth;
        UINT nID, nStyle;
        GetPaneInfo (1, nID, nStyle, cxWidth);
        SetPaneInfo (1, nID, nStyle, tm.tmAveCharWidth * 24);
        GetPaneInfo (2, nID, nStyle, cxWidth);
        SetPaneInfo (2, nID, SBPS_NOBORDERS, tm.tmAveCharWidth * 24);

        //
        // Place a progress control in the rightmost pane.
        //
        CRect rect;
        GetItemRect (2, &rect);
        m_wndProgress.Create (WS_CHILD | WS_VISIBLE | PBS_SMOOTH,
            rect, this, -1);
        m_wndProgress.SetRange (0, 100);
        m_wndProgress.SetPos (0);
        return 0;
}

void CSpecialStatusBar::OnSize (UINT nType, int cx, int cy)
{
        CStatusBar::OnSize (nType, cx, cy);

        //
        // Resize the rightmost pane to fit the resized status bar.
        //
        CRect rect;
        GetItemRect (2, &rect);
        m_wndProgress.SetWindowPos (NULL, rect.left, rect.top,
            rect.Width (), rect.Height (), SWP_NOZORDER);
}

void CSpecialStatusBar::SetImageStats(LPCTSTR pszStats)
{
        SetPaneText (1, pszStats, TRUE);
}

void CSpecialStatusBar::SetProgress(int nPercent)
{
        ASSERT (nPercent >= 0 && nPercent <= 100);
        m_wndProgress.SetPos (nPercent);
}
```

ImageEdit demonstrates a practical solution to the problem of how a worker thread can let a document object know when it's finished. When Convert To Gray Scale is selected from the Effects menu, the document's *OnGrayScale* function launches a background thread that executes the *ThreadFunc* function. *ThreadFunc* processes the bitmap and posts a WM_USER_THREAD_FINISHED message to the application's frame window just before it terminates. The frame window, in turn, calls the document's *ThreadFinished* function to notify the document that the image has been converted, and *ThreadFinished* calls *UpdateAllViews*.

Posting a message to the frame window and having it call down to the document object is *not* the same as having the thread function call a function in the document object directly because the *PostMessage* call performs a virtual transfer of control to the primary thread. If *ThreadFunc* called the document object itself, *UpdateAllViews* would be called in the context of the background thread and would fail.

For good measure, *ThreadFunc* sends a WM_USER_THREAD_UPDATE message to the main window each time it finishes converting another line in the bitmap. The frame window responds by updating a progress control embedded in the status bar, so the user is never left wondering when the gray-scale image will appear. WM_USER-_THREAD_UPDATE messages are sent rather than posted to make sure that the progress control is updated in real time. If WM_USER_THREAD_UPDATE messages were posted rather than sent, the background thread might post messages faster than the main window could process them on fast CPUs.

ImageEdit uses two thread synchronization objects: a *CEvent* object named *m_event* and a *CCriticalSection* object named *m_cs*. Both are members of the document class, and both are passed by address to the thread function in a THREADPARMS structure. The event object is used to terminate the worker thread if the user stops a gray-scale conversion midstream by selecting the Stop Gray Scale Conversion command from the Effects menu. To kill the thread, the primary thread sets the event to the signaled state:

```
m_event.SetEvent ();
```

Upon completion of each scan line, the conversion routine inside *ThreadFunc* checks the event object and terminates the thread if the event is signaled:

```
if (::WaitForSingleObject (pKillEvent->m_hObject, 0) ==
    WAIT_OBJECT_0) {
    :
    :
    pWnd->PostMessage (WM_USER_THREAD_ABORTED, y + 1, 0);
    return (UINT) -1;
}
```

The WM_USER_THREAD_ABORTED message alerts the frame window that the thread has been aborted. The frame window notifies the document by calling

CImageEditDoc::ThreadAborted, and *ThreadAborted* blocks on the thread handle just in case the thread hasn't quite terminated. Then it resets an internal flag indicating that the thread is no longer running.

The critical section prevents the application's two threads from trying to select the bitmap into a device context at the same time. The primary thread selects the bitmap into a device context when the view needs updating; the background thread selects the bitmap into a memory device context once when a gray-scale conversion begins and again when it ends. A bitmap can be selected into only one device context at a time, so if either thread tries to select the bitmap into a device context while the other has it selected into a device context, one of the threads will fail. (Palettes, on the other hand, can be selected into several device contexts concurrently, and *ThreadFunc* takes advantage of that fact when it performs a gray-scale conversion on a palettized device.) The odds that the two threads will try to select the bitmap at the same time are small, but the use of a critical section ensures that the code executed between calls to *SelectObject* won't be interrupted by a call to *SelectObject* from another thread. The bitmap doesn't stay selected into a device context for any appreciable length of time, so neither thread should have to wait long if the critical section is locked.

ImageEdit also demonstrates how to place a progress control in a status bar. ImageEdit's status bar is an instance of *CSpecialStatusBar*, which I derived from *CStatusBar*. *CSpecialStatusBar::OnCreate* adds three panes to the status bar. Then it creates a progress control and positions the control to exactly fit the rightmost pane. Because the sizes and positions of a status bar's panes can change when the status bar is resized, *CSpecialStatusBar* also includes an *OnSize* handler that adjusts the progress control to the rightmost pane. The result is a progress control that looks like an ordinary status bar pane until you begin stepping it with *CProgressCtrl::SetPos*.

ODDS AND ENDS

Here are a few odds and ends related to multitasking and multithreading that might be useful to you.

Message Pumps

A common misconception programmers have about multithreading is that it makes applications run faster. On a single-processor machine, it doesn't; however, it does make applications more *responsive*. One way to demonstrate the difference in responsiveness multithreading can make is to write an application that draws a few thousand ellipses in response to a menu command. If the drawing is done by the primary thread and the thread doesn't occasionally take time out to check its message queue and dispatch any waiting messages, input will be frozen until the drawing loop has run its course. If the same application is written so that drawing is done in a separate thread, it will continue to respond to user input while the drawing loop executes.

In a scenario as simple as this, however, multithreading might be overkill. An alternative solution is to use a *message pump* to keep the messages flowing while the primary thread draws ellipses. Suppose the message handler that does the drawing looks like this:

```
void CMainWindow::OnStartDrawing ()
{
    for (int i=0; i<NUMELLIPSES; i++)
        DrawRandomEllipse ();
}
```

If NUMELLIPSES is a large number, the program could be stuck for a long time once the *for* loop is started. You could try adding another menu command that sets a flag and interrupts the *for* loop, as shown here:

```
void CMainWindow::OnStartDrawing ()
{
    m_bQuit = FALSE;
    for (int i=0; i<NUMELLIPSES && !m_bQuit; i++)
        DrawRandomEllipse ();
}

void CMainWindow::OnStopDrawing ()
{
    m_bQuit = TRUE;
}
```

But that wouldn't work. Why not? Because the WM_COMMAND message that activates *OnStopDrawing* can't get through as long as the *for* loop in *OnStartDrawing* executes without pumping messages. In fact, a menu can't even be pulled down while the *for* loop is running.

This problem is easily solved with a message pump. Here's the proper way to execute a lengthy procedure in a single-threaded MFC program:

```
void CMainWindow::OnStartDrawing ()
{
    m_bQuit = FALSE;
    for (int i=0; i<NUMELLIPSES && !m_bQuit; i++) {
        DrawRandomEllipse ();
        if (!PeekAndPump ())
            break;
    }
}
```

(continued)

1053

```
void CMainWindow::OnStopDrawing ()
{
    m_bQuit = TRUE;
}

BOOL CMainWindow::PeekAndPump ()
{
    MSG msg;
    while (::PeekMessage (&msg, NULL, 0, 0, PM_NOREMOVE)) {
        if (!AfxGetApp ()->PumpMessage ()) {
            ::PostQuitMessage (0);
            return FALSE;
        }
    }
    LONG lIdle = 0;
    while (AfxGetApp ()->OnIdle (lIdle++));
    return TRUE;
}
```

PeekAndPump enacts a message loop within a message loop. Called at the conclusion of each iteration through *OnStartDrawing*'s *for* loop, *PeekAndPump* first calls *CWinThread::PumpMessage* to retrieve and dispatch messages if *::PeekMessage* indicates that messages are waiting in the queue. A 0 return from *PumpMessage* indicates that the last message retrieved and dispatched was a WM_QUIT message, which calls for special handling because the application won't terminate unless the WM_QUIT message is retrieved by the *main* message loop. That's why *PeekAndPump* posts another WM_QUIT message to the queue if *PumpMessage* returns 0, and why the *for* loop in *OnStartDrawing* falls through if *PeekAndPump* returns 0. If a WM_QUIT message doesn't prompt an early exit, *PeekAndPump* simulates the framework's idle mechanism by calling the application object's *OnIdle* function before returning.

With *PeekAndPump* inserted into the drawing loop, the WM_COMMAND message that activates *OnStopDrawing* is retrieved and dispatched normally. Because *OnStopDrawing* sets *m_bQuit* to TRUE, the drawing loop will fall through before the next ellipse is drawn.

Launching Other Processes

Win32 processes can launch other processes with the same ease with which they launch threads. The following statements launch Notepad.exe from the Windows directory of drive C:

```
STARTUPINFO si;
::ZeroMemory (&si, sizeof (STARTUPINFO));
si.cb = sizeof (STARTUPINFO);
PROCESS_INFORMATION pi;
```

```
if (::CreateProcess (NULL, _T ("C:\\Windows\\Notepad"), NULL,
    NULL, FALSE, NORMAL_PRIORITY_CLASS, NULL, NULL, &si, &pi)) {
    ::CloseHandle (pi.hThread);
    ::CloseHandle (pi.hProcess);
}
```

::CreateProcess is a versatile function that takes the name of (and optionally the path to) an executable file and then loads and executes it. If the drive and directory name are omitted from the executable file name, the system automatically searches for the file in the Windows directory, the Windows system directory, all directories in the current path, and in selected other locations. The file name can also include command line parameters, as in

```
"C:\\Windows\\Notepad C:\\Windows\\Desktop\\Ideas.txt"
```

::CreateProcess fills a PROCESS_INFORMATION structure with pertinent information about the process, including the process handle (*hProcess*) and the handle of the process's primary thread (*hThread*). You should close these handles with *::CloseHandle* after the process is started. If you have no further use for the handles, you can close them as soon as *::CreateProcess* returns.

A nonzero return from *::CreateProcess* means that the process was successfully launched. Win32 processes are launched and executed asynchronously, so *::CreateProcess* does *not* wait until the process has ended to return. If you'd like to launch another process and suspend the current process until the process that it launched terminates, call *::WaitForSingleObject* on the process handle, as shown here:

```
STARTUPINFO si;
::ZeroMemory (&si, sizeof (STARTUPINFO));
si.cb = sizeof (STARTUPINFO);
PROCESS_INFORMATION pi;

if (::CreateProcess (NULL, _T ("C:\\Windows\\Notepad"), NULL,
    NULL, FALSE, NORMAL_PRIORITY_CLASS, NULL, NULL, &si, &pi)) {
    ::CloseHandle (pi.hThread);
    ::WaitForSingleObject (pi.hProcess, INFINITE);
    ::CloseHandle (pi.hProcess);
}
```

Processes have exit codes just as threads do. If *::WaitForSingleObject* returns anything but WAIT_FAILED, you can call *::GetExitCodeProcess* to retrieve the process's exit code.

Sometimes the need arises to launch a process and delay just long enough to make sure the process is started and responding to user input. If process A launches process B and process B creates a window, for example, and process A wants to send that window a message, process A might have to wait for a moment after *::CreateProcess* returns to give process B time to create a window and begin processing messages. This problem is easily solved with the Win32 *::WaitForInputIdle* function:

```
STARTUPINFO si;
::ZeroMemory (&si, sizeof (STARTUPINFO));
si.cb = sizeof (STARTUPINFO);
PROCESS_INFORMATION pi;

if (::CreateProcess (NULL, _T ("C:\\Windows\\Notepad"), NULL,
    NULL, FALSE, NORMAL_PRIORITY_CLASS, NULL, NULL, &si, &pi)) {
    ::CloseHandle (pi.hThread);
    ::WaitForInputIdle (pi.hProcess, INFINITE);
    // Get B's window handle and send or post a message.
    ::CloseHandle (pi.hProcess);
}
```

::WaitForInputIdle suspends the current process until the specified process begins processing messages and empties its message queue. I didn't show the code to find the window handle because there isn't a simple MFC or API function you can call to convert a process handle into a window handle. Instead, you must use *::Enum-Windows*, *::FindWindow*, or a related function to search for the window based on some known characteristic of the owning process.

File Change Notifications

Earlier in this chapter, I mentioned that the HANDLE parameter passed to *::Wait-ForSingleObject* can be a "file change notification handle." The Win32 API includes a function named *::FindFirstChangeNotification* that returns a handle you can use to wake a blocked thread whenever a change occurs in a specified directory or its subdirectories—for example, when a file is renamed or deleted or a new directory is created.

Let's say you want to enhance Chapter 11's Wanderer application so that changes to the file system are instantly reflected in the left or right pane. The most efficient way to do it is to start a background thread and have it block on one or more file change notification handles. Here's what the thread function for a thread that monitors drive C: might look like:

```
UINT ThreadFunc (LPVOID pParam)
{
    HWND hwnd = (HWND) pParam; // Window to notify
    HANDLE hChange = ::FindFirstChangeNotification (_T ("C:\\"),
        TRUE, FILE_NOTIFY_CHANGE_FILE_NAME | FILE_NOTIFY_CHANGE_DIR_NAME);

    if (hChange == INVALID_HANDLE_VALUE) {
        TRACE (_T ("Error: FindFirstChangeNotification failed\n"));
        return (UINT) -1;
    }
```

```
while (...) {
    ::WaitForSingleObject (hChange, INFINITE);
    ::PostMessage (hwnd, WM_USER_CHANGE_NOTIFY, 0, 2);
    ::FindNextChangeNotification (hChange); // Reset
}
::FindCloseChangeNotification (hChange);
return 0;
}
```

The first parameter passed to *::FindFirstChangeNotification* identifies the directory you want to monitor, the second specifies whether you want to monitor just that directory (FALSE) or that directory and all its subdirectories (TRUE), and the third specifies the kinds of changes that the thread should be notified of. In this example, the thread will be awakened when a file is created, renamed, or deleted anywhere on the C: drive (FILE_NOTIFY_CHANGE_FILE_NAME) or when a directory is created, renamed, or deleted (FILE_NOTIFY_CHANGE_DIR_NAME). When the thread is awakened, it posts a user-defined message to the window whose handle was passed in *pParam*. The message's *lParam* holds a drive number (2 for drive C:). The window that receives the message—presumably the application's top-level frame window—can respond to the message by updating its views. Keep in mind that a thread awakened by a file change notification doesn't receive any information about the nature of the change or about where in the directory tree the change occurred, so it must scan the file system if it wants to determine what caused the file change notification.

It's also possible to structure the thread so that it monitors not just one drive, but several. All you would have to do is call *::FindFirstChangeNotification* once per drive to acquire a separate file change notification handle for each drive and use *::WaitForMultipleObjects* to block on all the file change notifications simultaneously. *::WaitForMultipleObjects* is the Win32 API equivalent of *CMultiLock::Lock*. Passing FALSE in the third parameter to a call to *::WaitForMultipleObjects* tells the system to wake the thread when any one of the objects that the thread is blocking on becomes signaled.

Part IV

COM, OLE, and ActiveX

Chapter 18

MFC and the Component Object Model

In the beginning, when MFC was still in its infancy, C++ programmers who began migrating from the Microsoft Windows API in favor of MFC did so because they wanted a class library to aid them in developing Windows applications. The conventional wisdom at the time said that MFC made Windows programming easier, but the truth of the matter was that Windows programming was still Windows programming. MFC simplified certain aspects of the development process, and for those few programmers prescient enough to adopt it early on, it eased the pain of porting 16-bit Windows applications to 32 bits. But even MFC could hardly claim to put a dent in the legendary Windows learning curve. That was true then, and it's still true today.

Today there is another, more compelling reason to use MFC. If the applications you develop have anything whatsoever to do with COM, OLE, or ActiveX, MFC can dramatically simplify the development process. By that, I mean MFC can cut the time required to develop an application (or a software component) by an order of magnitude. In this day and time, there is simply no good reason to develop certain types of software from scratch given that such good class libraries are available. COM, OLE, and ActiveX have been criticized for being overly complex and hopelessly arcane, but for better or worse, they're here to stay, and there's a very real chance that in the future you'll have to be a COM programmer if you want to program Windows.

So what are COM, OLE, and ActiveX, and what does MFC do to make them so much easier to program? I'm glad you asked, because the rest of this book is about MFC's support for all things COM. In this chapter, I'll begin by defining COM, OLE, and ActiveX, and then I'll introduce some of the unique and interesting ways in which MFC wraps its arms around them. In subsequent chapters, we'll tackle specific COM-based technologies such as Automation and ActiveX controls and you'll see how to use MFC to make them come to life.

THE COMPONENT OBJECT MODEL

COM is an acronym for Component Object Model. Simply put, COM is a way of building objects that is independent of any programming language. If you want the gory details, you can download the COM specification from Microsoft's Web site. But don't be too quick to pull out your browser: if this is your first exposure to COM, the specification might be a bit overwhelming. A better approach is to start slowly and allow yourself time to understand the big picture rather than risk getting mired in details that for the moment are unimportant.

C++ programmers are accustomed to writing classes that other C++ programmers can use. The problem with these classes is that *only* other C++ programmers can use them. COM tells us how to build objects in any programming language that can also be used in any programming language. In other words, COM transcends language-specific ways of building reusable objects and gives us a true binary standard for object architectures.

C++ classes have member functions; COM objects have *methods*. Methods are grouped into *interfaces* and are called through *interface pointers*. Interfaces exist to semantically bind together groups of related methods. For example, suppose you're writing a COM class that has methods named *Add*, *Subtract*, and *CheckSpelling*. Rather than make all three methods members of the same interface, you might assign *Add* and *Subtract* to an interface named *IMath* and *CheckSpelling* to an interface named *ISpelling*. (Prefacing interface names with a capital *I* for *Interface* is an almost universal COM programming convention.) Microsoft has predefined more than 100 interfaces that any COM object can support. These interfaces are called *standard interfaces*. User-defined interfaces such as *IMath* and *ISpelling* are *custom interfaces*. COM objects can use standard interfaces, custom interfaces, or a combination of the two.

Every COM object implements an interface named *IUnknown*. *IUnknown* contains just three methods:

Method Name	Description
QueryInterface	Returns a pointer to another interface
AddRef	Increments the object's reference count
Release	Decrements the object's reference count

One of the rules of COM says that given a pointer to an interface, a client can call any *IUnknown* method through that pointer as well as any methods that are specific to the interface. In other words, all interfaces must support the three *IUnknown* methods in addition to their own methods. This means that if you define an *IMath* interface with methods named *Add* and *Subtract*, the interface actually contains five methods: *QueryInterface, AddRef, Release, Add*, and *Subtract*. Most objects don't implement *IUnknown* as a separate interface. Because all interfaces include the *IUnknown* methods, most objects, if asked for an *IUnknown* pointer, simply return a pointer to one of their other interfaces.

Figure 18-1 shows a schematic of a simple COM object. The sticks, or "lollipops" as they're sometimes called, represent the object's interfaces. The *IUnknown* lollipop is often omitted because it's understood that every COM object implements *IUnknown*.

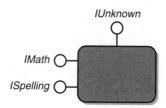

Figure 18-1. *A simple COM object.*

I've been using human-readable names such as *IMath* to refer to interfaces, but in truth, interfaces are identified by number, not by name. Every interface is uniquely identified by a 128-bit value called an *interface identifier*, or IID. So many different 128-bit numbers are possible that the chances of you and I ever picking the same IID at random are virtually nil. Therefore, it doesn't matter if two people on different sides of the planet happen to define incompatible versions of a custom interface named *IMath*. What counts is that the two *IMath* interfaces have different IIDs.

Microsoft Visual C++ comes with two tools for generating IIDs. One is a command line utility named Uuidgen. The other is a GUI application named Guidgen. Both utilities do their best to maximize the randomness of the 128-bit numbers they generate, even factoring in variables such as your network card's Ethernet ID and the time of day. You can generate IIDs programmatically with the COM API function *CoCreateGuid*. The *Guid* in *CoCreateGuid* stands for *globally unique identifier,* a generic term that describes any 128-bit identifier. An IID is simply a special GUID.

Instantiating a COM Object

COM classes, like interfaces, are identified by 128-bit values. GUIDs that identify classes are called *class IDs*, or CLSIDs. All a client needs to know in order to instantiate an object is the object's CLSID. COM has an API of its own that includes *activation functions* for creating object instances. The most commonly used activation function is *CoCreateInstance*, which accepts a CLSID and returns an interface pointer to an object. The following statements instantiate the COM class whose CLSID is *CLSID_Object* and cache a pointer to the object's *IMath* interface in *pMath*:

```
IMath* pMath;
CoCreateInstance (CLSID_Object, NULL,
    CLSCTX_SERVER, IID_IMath, (void**) &pMath);
```

IID_IMath is simply a variable that holds *IMath*'s 128-bit interface ID.

Once it has an interface pointer, a C++ client can call methods on that interface using the -> operator. The following statements call *IMath::Add* to add a pair of numbers:

```
int sum;
pMath->Add (2, 2, &sum);
```

Add doesn't return the sum of the two inputs directly; instead, it copies the result to an address specified by the caller—in this case, to the variable named *sum*. That's because COM methods return special 32-bit values called HRESULTs. An HRESULT tells the caller whether a call succeeded or failed. It can also provide detailed information about the nature of the failure if the call doesn't succeed. You might think that a method as simple as *Add* can never fail, but it *could* fail if the object that implements the method is running on a remote network server and the client is unable to contact the server because a cable has been disconnected. If that happens, the system steps in and returns an HRESULT informing the caller that the call didn't go through.

One aspect of COM that newcomers frequently find confusing is the fact that every externally creatable COM class (that is, every COM class that can be instantiated by passing a CLSID to *CoCreateInstance*) is accompanied by a *class object*. A class object is also a COM object. Its sole purpose in life is to create other COM objects. Passing a CLSID to *CoCreateInstance* appears to instantiate an object directly, but internally, *CoCreateInstance* first instantiates the object's class object and then asks the class object to create the object. Most class objects implement a special COM interface known as *IClassFactory* (or *IClassFactory2*, a newer version of the interface that is a functional superset of *IClassFactory*). A class object that implements *IClassFactory* is called a *class factory*. Given an *IClassFactory* interface pointer, a client creates an object instance by calling *IClassFactory::CreateInstance*. This method—*CreateInstance*—has been described as the COM equivalent of the *new* operator in C++.

Not all COM classes are externally creatable. Some are intended only for private use and can't be instantiated with *CoCreateInstance* because they have no CLSIDs and no class factories. C++ programmers instantiate these objects by calling *new* on the C++ classes that implement the objects. Typically, these objects play a part in implementing a COM-based protocol such as drag-and-drop data transfers. Some of MFC's COM classes fit this profile. You'll learn more about them when we discuss the various COM and ActiveX technologies that MFC supports.

Object Lifetimes

C++ programmers are used to creating heap-based objects using the C++ *new* operator. They're also accustomed to calling *delete* to delete the objects that they create with *new*. COM differs from C++ in this respect, because clients create object instances but they don't delete them. Instead, COM objects delete themselves. Here's why.

Suppose two or more clients are using the same instance of an object. Client A creates the object, and Client B attaches to the object by somehow acquiring an interface pointer. If Client A, unaware that Client B exists, deletes the object, Client B is left with an interface pointer that no longer points to anything. Because a COM client typically doesn't know (and doesn't care) whether it's the sole user of an object or one of many users, COM leaves it up to the object to delete itself. Deletion occurs when an internal reference count maintained by the object drops to 0. The reference count is a running count of the number of clients holding pointers to the object's interfaces.

For COM classes implemented in C++, the reference count is typically stored in a member variable. The count is incremented when *AddRef* is called and decremented when *Release* is called. (Remember that because *AddRef* and *Release* are *IUnknown* methods, they can be called through any interface pointer.) Implementations of *AddRef* and *Release* are normally no more complicated than this:

```
ULONG __stdcall CComClass::AddRef ()
{
    return ++m_lRef;
}

ULONG __stdcall CComClass::Release ()
{
    if (--m_lRef == 0) {
        delete this;
        return 0;
    }
    return m_lRef;
}
```

In this example, *CComClass* is a C++ class that represents a COM class. *m_lRef* is the member variable that holds the object's reference count. If every client calls *Release* when it's finished using an interface, the object conveniently deletes itself when the last client calls *Release*.

A bit of protocol is involved in using *AddRef* and *Release*. It's the responsibility of the object—not the client—to call *AddRef* whenever it hands out an interface pointer. However, it's the client's responsibility to call *Release*. Clients sometimes call *AddRef* themselves to indicate that they're making a copy of the interface pointer. In such cases, it's still up to the client (or whomever the client hands the copied interface pointer to) to call *Release* when the interface pointer is no longer needed.

Acquiring Interface Pointers

The *CoCreateInstance* example we examined earlier created an object and asked for an *IMath* interface pointer. Now suppose that the object also implements *ISpelling*. How would a client that holds an *IMath* pointer ask the object for an *ISpelling* pointer?

That's what the third of the three *IUnknown* methods is for. Given an interface pointer, a client can call *QueryInterface* through that pointer to get a pointer to any other interface that the object supports. Here's how it looks in code:

```
IMath* pMath;
HRESULT hr = CoCreateInstance (CLSID_Object, NULL,
    CLSCTX_SERVER, IID_IMath, (void**) &pMath);

if (SUCCEEDED (hr)) { // CoCreateInstance worked.

    :

    ISpelling* pSpelling;
    hr = pMath->QueryInterface (IID_ISpelling, (void**) &pSpelling);
    if (SUCCEEDED (hr)) {
        // Got the interface pointer!

        :

        pSpelling->Release ();
    }
    pMath->Release ();
}
```

Notice that this time, the client checks the HRESULT returned by *CoCreateInstance* to make sure that the activation request succeeded. Sometime after the object is created, the client uses *QueryInterface* to request an *ISpelling* pointer, once more checking the HRESULT rather than simply assuming that the pointer is valid. (The SUCCEEDED macro tells a client whether an HRESULT code signifies success or failure. A related macro named FAILED can be used to test for failure.) Both interfaces are released when they're no longer needed. When *Release* is called through the *IMath* pointer, the object deletes itself if no other clients are holding interface pointers.

> **NOTE** There is no COM function that you can call to enumerate all of an object's interfaces. The assumption is that the client knows what interfaces an object supports, so it can call *QueryInterface* to obtain pointers to any and all interfaces. An object can publish a list of the interfaces that it supports using a mechanism known as *type information*. Some COM objects make type information available to their clients, and some don't. Certain types of COM objects, ActiveX controls included, are *required* to publish type information. You'll see why when we examine the ActiveX control architecture in Chapter 21.

COM Servers

If COM is to create objects in response to activation requests, it must know where to find each object's executable file. An executable that implements a COM object is called a *COM server*. The HKEY_CLASSES_ROOT\CLSID section of the registry contains information that correlates CLSIDs and executable files. For example, if a server named MathSvr.exe implements Math objects and a client calls *CoCreateInstance* with Math's CLSID, COM looks up the CLSID in the registry, extracts the path to MathSvr.exe, and launches the EXE. The EXE, in turn, hands COM a class factory, and COM calls the class factory's *CreateInstance* method to create an instance of the Math object.

COM servers come in two basic varieties: in-process and out-of-process. In-process servers (often referred to as *in-proc* servers) are DLLs. They're called in-procs because in the Win32 environment, a DLL loads and runs in the same address space as its client. EXEs, in contrast, run in separate address spaces that are physically isolated from one another. In most cases, calls to in-proc objects are very fast because they're little more than calls to other addresses in memory. Calling a method on an in-proc object is much like calling a subroutine in your own application.

Out-of-process servers (also known as *out-of-proc* servers) come in EXEs. One advantage to packaging COM objects in EXEs is that clients and objects running in two different processes are protected from one another if one crashes. The disadvantage is speed. Calls to objects in other processes are roughly 1,000 times slower than calls to in-proc objects because of the overhead incurred when a method call crosses process boundaries.

Microsoft Windows NT 4.0 introduced Distributed COM (DCOM), which gives out-of-proc servers the freedom to run on remote network servers. It's simple to take an out-of-proc server that has been written, tested, and debugged locally and deploy it on a network. (As of Windows NT 4.0 Service Pack 2, in-proc servers can also run remotely using a mechanism that relies on surrogate EXEs to host the DLLs.) *CoCreateInstance* and other COM activation functions are fully capable of creating objects that reside elsewhere on the network. Even legacy COM servers written before DCOM came into existence can be remoted with a few minor registry changes.

To differentiate out-of-proc servers that serve up objects on the same machine from out-of-proc servers that run on remote machines, COM programmers use the terms *local server* and *remote server*. A local server is an EXE that runs on the same machine as its client; a remote server, in contrast, runs elsewhere on the network. Although there are important structural differences between in-proc and out-of-proc servers, there are no differences between local and remote servers. Objects designed with DCOM in mind are often tweaked to leverage the operating system's underlying security model or to improve performance. But optimizations aside, the fact remains that local servers and remote servers share the exact same server and object architectures.

Location Transparency

One of COM's most powerful features is location transparency. Simply put, location transparency means that a client neither knows nor cares where an object lives. The exact same sequence of instructions that calls a method on an object running in the same address space as the client also calls a method on an object running in another process or even on another machine. A lot of magic goes on behind the scenes to make location transparency work, but COM handles the bulk of it.

When a method call goes out to an object in another process or on another machine, COM *remotes* the call. As part of the remoting process, COM *marshals* the method's parameters and return values. Marshaling comes in many forms, but the most common type of marshaling essentially reproduces the caller's stack frame in the call recipient's address space. *Proxies* and *stubs* carry out most marshaling and remoting. When a client is handed an interface pointer to an object running in a process other than its own, COM creates an interface proxy in the client process and an interface stub in the server process. Interface pointers held by the client are really interface pointers to the proxy, which implements the same interfaces and methods as the real object. When a client calls a method on the object, the call goes to the proxy, which uses some type of interprocess communication (IPC) to forward the call to the stub. The stub unpackages the method parameters, calls the object, and marshals any return values back to the proxy. Figure 18-2 illustrates the relationship between clients, objects, proxies, and stubs.

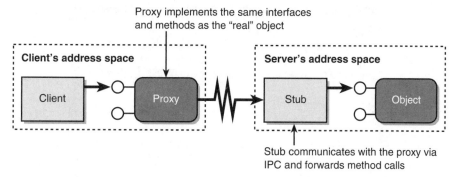

Figure 18-2. *Proxies and stubs.*

Where do proxies and stubs come from? If an object uses only standard interfaces, COM supplies the proxies and stubs. If an object uses custom interfaces, it's up to the object implementor to provide the proxies and stubs in the form of a proxy/stub DLL. The good news is that you rarely need to write a proxy/stub DLL by hand. Visual C++ comes with a tool called the MIDL (Microsoft Interface Definition Language) compiler that "compiles" IDL (Interface Definition Language) files, producing the source code for proxy/stub DLLs. The bad news is that now you have to learn another language—IDL. IDL has been called the lingua franca of COM. The better you know your IDL, the better equipped you are to optimize the performance of local and remote servers. You can avoid IDL and MIDL altogether by using an alternative marshaling strategy known as *custom marshaling,* but custom marshaling is so difficult to implement correctly that proxies and stubs are the way to go unless you have clear and compelling reasons to do otherwise. You can opt for other ways to avoid writing proxies and stubs if you're willing to make a few trade-offs in flexibility and performance. One of those other ways is Automation, which we'll discuss in Chapter 20.

The key to location transparency is the fact that when clients communicate with objects in other processes, they don't know that they're really communicating through proxies and stubs. All a client knows is that it has an interface pointer and that method calls through that interface pointer work. Now you know why.

Object Linking and Embedding

Before there was COM, there was object linking and embedding, better known by the acronym OLE. OLE allows you to place *content objects* created by one application in documents created by another application. One use for OLE is to place Excel spreadsheets inside Word documents. (See Figure 18-3.) In such a scenario, Excel acts as an OLE server by serving up an embedded or linked spreadsheet object (a "content object") and Word acts as an OLE container by hosting the object.

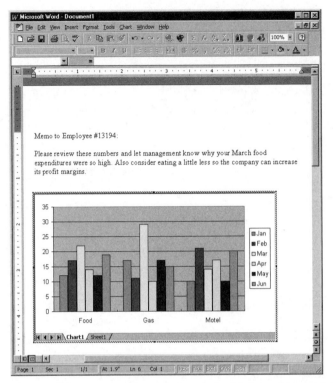

Figure 18-3. *A Microsoft Excel chart embedded in a Microsoft Word document.*

OLE is a complex software protocol that describes how OLE servers talk to OLE containers and vice versa. Microsoft built OLE 1.0 on top of Dynamic Data Exchange (DDE). DDE proved to be a less than ideal IPC mechanism, so Microsoft invented COM to serve as the underlying IPC mechanism for OLE 2.0. For a long time, Microsoft affixed the OLE label to all new COM technologies: Automation became OLE Automation, ActiveX controls were named OLE controls, and so on. Microsoft even went so far as to say that OLE was no longer an acronym; it was a *word*. It wasn't until the term *ActiveX* was coined in 1995 that Microsoft reversed itself and said, in effect, "We've changed our minds; OLE once again stands for object linking and embedding." Despite this reversal, many programmers still (erroneously) use the terms *COM* and *OLE* interchangeably. They are not synonymous. COM is the object model that forms the foundation for all OLE and ActiveX technologies. OLE is the technology that allows you to place Excel spreadsheets inside Word documents. Get used to this new world order, and you'll avoid the confusion that has stricken so many programmers.

Just how does OLE use COM? When an OLE server such as Excel serves up a spreadsheet object to a container such as Word, it creates one or more COM objects that implement certain standard interfaces such as *IOleObject* and *IViewObject*. Word, too, creates COM objects that conform to published specifications. The architecture is generic in that it isn't limited only to Word and Excel; any application can be an OLE container or server, or both. The container and the server communicate by calling methods through interface pointers. Thanks to location transparency, it doesn't matter that the container and the server are running in different processes, although some of OLE's COM interfaces must be implemented in proc to work around certain limitations of Windows. Because device context handles aren't portable between processes (for example, when a container asks a server to draw an object in the container's window), that part of the server must be implemented in proc.

Figure 18-4 shows a schematic of a simple embedding container. For each content object embedded in the container's document, the container implements a *site object*. At a minimum, a site object must implement the COM interfaces *IOleClientSite* and *IAdviseSink*. To talk to the container, the server calls methods through pointers to these interfaces. The simplicity of this diagram belies the inward complexity of real-life linking and embedding servers, but it nonetheless illustrates the role that COM plays as an enabling technology.

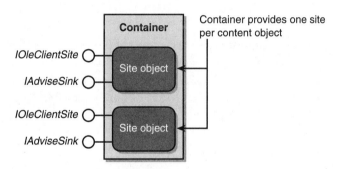

Figure 18-4. *A simple embedding container.*

For the record, linked objects and embedded objects are fundamentally different. Embedded objects are stored in the container's document file alongside the container's native document data. Linked objects, on the other hand, are stored in external files. The container's document stores only a *link* to the object, which is a fancy way of saying that the container stores the name of and path to the file that holds the object's data. Links can be more sophisticated than that. If you create a link to a range of cells in an Excel spreadsheet, for example, the link includes information identifying the range as well as the path to the file.

Active Documents

In my opinion, OLE is the least interesting of all the COM technologies that Microsoft has defined, so I won't cover it further in this book. (If you want to learn more about it, start with the OLE lessons in the Scribble tutorial that comes with Visual C++.)

However, one COM-based technology that has grown out of OLE at least deserves mention because it is potentially very useful. That technology is *Active Documents*.

The Active Documents protocol is a superset of object linking and embedding. It permits Active Document containers such as Microsoft Internet Explorer to open document files created by Active Document servers such as Word and Excel. Ever notice how you can open a Word DOC file or an Excel XLS file inside Internet Explorer? Internet Explorer appears to understand the Word and Excel file formats. It doesn't. What's really happening is that Internet Explorer talks to Word or Excel through—you guessed it—COM interfaces. Word or Excel runs in the background (you can prove that by viewing the task list while a DOC or XLS file is open in Internet Explorer) and essentially takes over the interior of Internet Explorer's window. You're really using Word or Excel, although it certainly doesn't look that way.

Active Documents really pay off when you post a Word or an Excel document on a Web site. If the machine on which Internet Explorer is running has Word and Excel installed, you can view DOC and XLS files as effortlessly as you do HTML pages. That's Active Documents at work.

ActiveX

First there was OLE. Next there was COM. And then along came ActiveX. When Microsoft turned its attention to the Internet in 1995, the software giant coined the term *ActiveX* to refer to a suite of COM-based technologies designed to make the Internet—and the World Wide Web in particular—more interactive. ActiveX controls are probably the best-known ActiveX technology, but there are others. If "Active" is in the name, it's an ActiveX technology: ActiveX controls, ActiveX Data Objects (ADO), Active Server Pages (ASP), and Active Documents, to name but a few. The roster is growing every day.

The one thing all ActiveX technologies have in common is that they're all COM-based. ActiveX controls, for example, are COM objects that conform to the rules of behavior set forth in Microsoft's OLE control (OCX) specifications. Applications that host ActiveX controls also implement COM interfaces; officially, they're known as ActiveX control containers.

Writing a full-blown ActiveX control—that is, one that can be plugged into a Web page or displayed in a window or a dialog box—is not a trivial undertaking. The ActiveX control architecture is complex. A typical ActiveX control implements more than a dozen COM interfaces, some of which contain more than 20 methods. Even something as seemingly simple as plugging an ActiveX control into a dialog box is far more complex than most people realize. To host an ActiveX control, a dialog box has to be an ActiveX control container, and containers must implement a number of COM interfaces of their own.

Fortunately, MFC does an excellent job of wrapping ActiveX controls and control containers. Check a box in AppWizard, and any dialog box instantly becomes a control container. You don't have to write a single line of code because MFC provides all the necessary infrastructure. MFC also simplifies ActiveX control development. Writing an ActiveX control from scratch can easily require two months of development time, but do it with MFC and you can write a fully functional control in a matter of hours. Why? Because MFC provides stock implementations of COM's ActiveX control interfaces. All you have to do is override a virtual function here and there and add the elements that make your control different from the rest.

MFC AND COM

The primary reason why MFC makes COM, OLE, and ActiveX programming simpler is that it provides canned implementations of common COM interfaces in classes such as *COleControl* and *COleControlSite*. COM has been described as an "empty API," which means that Microsoft defines the interfaces and the methods and tells you what the methods are supposed to do but leaves it up to *you*, the object implementor, to write the code. The good news is that as long as you're writing ActiveX controls, Automation servers, or other types of components that MFC explicitly supports, MFC implements the necessary COM interfaces for you.

In the next three chapters, you'll get acquainted with many of the MFC classes that implement COM interfaces. Right now, I want you to understand *how* MFC classes implement COM interfaces. To do that, you must understand the two techniques that COM programmers use to write C++ classes representing COM objects. The first is *multiple inheritance*. The second is *nested classes*. MFC uses only nested classes, but let's look at both techniques so that we can compare the relative merits of each.

Multiple Inheritance

C++ programmers define COM interfaces using the following syntax:

```
interface IUnknown
{
    virtual HRESULT __stdcall QueryInterface (REFIID riid, void** ppv) = 0;
    virtual ULONG __stdcall AddRef () = 0;
    virtual ULONG __stdcall Release () = 0;
};
```

The keyword *interface* is an alias for *struct*. Therefore, to the C++ programmer, an interface definition is a set of pure virtual functions logically bound together as members of a common structure. And because structures and classes are treated almost identically in C++, it's perfectly legal to derive one interface from another, like this:

```
interface IMath : public IUnknown
{
    virtual HRESULT __stdcall Add (int a, int b, int* pResult) = 0;
    virtual HRESULT __stdcall Subtract (int a, int b, int* pResult) = 0;
};
```

You can take advantage of the fact that interface definitions are merely sets of pure virtual functions when you develop C++ classes that represent COM objects. For example, you can declare a class that implements *IMath* like this:

```
class CComClass : public IMath
{
protected:
    long m_lRef;    // Reference count
public:
    CComClass ();
    virtual ~CComClass ();
    // IUnknown methods
    virtual HRESULT __stdcall QueryInterface (REFIID riid, void** ppv);
    virtual ULONG __stdcall AddRef ();
    virtual ULONG __stdcall Release ();
    // IMath methods
    virtual HRESULT __stdcall Add (int a, int b, int* pResult);
    virtual HRESULT __stdcall Subtract (int a, int b, int* pResult);
};
```

With this setup, you can implement *QueryInterface*, *AddRef*, *Release*, *Add*, and *Subtract* as member functions of class *CComClass*.

Now, suppose you want *CComClass* to implement not just one COM interface, but two. How do you do it? One approach is to derive *CComClass* from both *IMath* and another interface by using multiple inheritance, like so:

```
class CComClass : public IMath, public ISpelling
{
protected:
    long m_lRef;    // Reference count
public:
    CComClass ();
    virtual ~CComClass ();
    // IUnknown methods
    virtual HRESULT __stdcall QueryInterface (REFIID riid, void** ppv);
    virtual ULONG __stdcall AddRef ();
    virtual ULONG __stdcall Release ();
    // IMath methods
    virtual HRESULT __stdcall Add (int a, int b, int* pResult);
    virtual HRESULT __stdcall Subtract (int a, int b, int* pResult);
    // ISpelling methods
    virtual HRESULT __stdcall CheckSpelling (wchar_t* pString);
};
```

This approach has a couple of advantages. First, it's simple. To declare a class that implements *n* interfaces, you simply include all *n* interfaces in the class's list of base classes. Second, you have to implement *IUnknown* only once. If each interface were truly implemented separately, you'd have to implement *QueryInterface*, *AddRef*, and *Release* for each one. But with multiple inheritance, all methods supported by all interfaces are essentially merged into one implementation.

One of the more interesting aspects of using multiple inheritance to write COM classes is what happens when a client calls *QueryInterface* asking for an interface pointer. Let's say that the client asks for an *IMath* pointer. The proper way to return the interface pointer is to cast the *this* pointer to an *IMath**:

```
*ppv = (IMath*) this;
```

If the client asks for an *ISpelling* pointer instead, you cast to *ISpelling**:

```
*ppv = (ISpelling*) this;
```

If you omit the casts, the code will compile just fine but will probably blow up when one of the two interfaces is used. Why? Because a class formed with multiple inheritance contains multiple vtables and multiple vtable pointers, and without the cast, you don't know which vtable the *this* pointer references. In other words, the two casts shown here return different numeric values, even though *this* never varies. If a client asks for an *ISpelling* pointer and you return a plain (uncasted) *this* pointer, and if *this* happens to reference *IMath*'s vtable, the client calls *ISpelling* methods through an *IMath* vtable. That's a formula for disaster and is why COM classes that use multiple inheritance *always* cast to retrieve the proper vtable pointer.

Nested Classes

What's wrong with using multiple inheritance to implement COM classes? Nothing—provided that no two interfaces have methods with the same names and signatures. If *IMath* and *ISpelling* both contained methods named *Init* that had identical parameter lists but required separate implementations, you wouldn't be able to use multiple inheritance to define a class that implements both of them. Why? Because with multiple inheritance, the class would have just one member function named *Init*. It would therefore be impossible to implement *Init* separately for *IMath* and *ISpelling*.

This limitation is the reason MFC uses the nested class approach to implementing COM interfaces. Nested classes are a little more work and slightly less intuitive than multiple inheritance, but they're also suitably generic. You can use the nested class approach to implement *any* combination of COM interfaces in a single C++ class, regardless of the interfaces' characteristics. Here's how it works.

Suppose that *CComClass* implements *IMath* and *ISpelling* and that both interfaces have a method named *Init* that accepts no parameters.

```
virtual HRESULT __stdcall Init () = 0;
```

You can't use multiple inheritance in this case because of C++'s inability to support two semantically identical functions in one class. So instead, you define two subclasses, each of which implements one interface:

```
class CMath : public IMath
{
protected:
    CComClass* m_pParent;     // Back pointer to parent
public:
    CMath ();
    virtual ~CMath ();
    // IUnknown methods
    virtual HRESULT __stdcall QueryInterface (REFIID riid, void** ppv);
    virtual ULONG __stdcall AddRef ();
    virtual ULONG __stdcall Release ();
    // IMath methods
    virtual HRESULT __stdcall Add (int a, int b, int* pResult);
    virtual HRESULT __stdcall Subtract (int a, int b, int* pResult);
    virtual HRESULT __stdcall Init () = 0;
};

class CSpelling : public ISpelling
{
protected:
    CComClass* m_pParent;     // Back pointer to parent
public:
    CSpelling ();
    virtual ~CSpelling ();
    // IUnknown methods
    virtual HRESULT __stdcall QueryInterface (REFIID riid, void** ppv);
    virtual ULONG __stdcall AddRef ();
    virtual ULONG __stdcall Release ();
    // ISpelling methods
    virtual HRESULT __stdcall CheckSpelling (wchar_t* pString);
    virtual HRESULT __stdcall Init () = 0;
};
```

To make *CMath* and *CSpelling* nested classes, you declare them inside *CComClass*. Then you include in *CComClass* a pair of data members that are instances of *CMath* and *CSpelling*:

```
class CComClass : public IUnknown
{
protected:
    long m_lRef;          // Reference count
    class CMath : public IMath
```

```
    {
        [...]
    };
    CMath m_objMath;          // CMath object
    class CSpelling : public ISpelling
    {
        [...]
    };
    CSpelling m_objSpell;     // CSpelling object
public:
    CComClass ();
    virtual ~CComClass ();
    // IUnknown methods
    virtual HRESULT __stdcall QueryInterface (REFIID riid, void** ppv);
    virtual ULONG __stdcall AddRef ();
    virtual ULONG __stdcall Release ();
};
```

Notice that *CComClass* now derives only from *IUnknown*. It doesn't derive from *IMath* or *ISpelling* because the nested classes provide implementations of both interfaces. If a client calls *QueryInterface* asking for an *IMath* pointer, *CComClass* simply passes out a pointer to the *CMath* object:

```
*ppv = (IMath*) &m_objMath;
```

Similarly, if asked for an *ISpelling* pointer, *CComClass* returns a pointer to *m_objSpell*:

```
*ppv = (ISpelling*) &m_objSpell;
```

A key point to understand about the nested class approach is that the subobjects must delegate all calls to their *IUnknown* methods to the equivalent methods in the parent class. Notice that in place of a member variable that stores a reference count, each nested class stores a *CComClass* pointer. That pointer is a "back pointer" to the subobject's parent. Delegation is performed by calling *CComClass*'s *IUnknown* methods through the back pointer. Typically, the parent's constructor initializes the back pointers:

```
CComClass::CComClass ()
{
    [...]          // Normal initialization stuff goes here.
    m_objMath.m_pParent = this;
    m_objSpell.m_pParent = this;
}
```

The nested classes' implementations of *IUnknown* look like this:

```
HRESULT __stdcall CComClass::CMath::QueryInterface (REFIID riid, void** ppv)
{
    return m_pParent->QueryInterface (riid, ppv);
}
```

(continued)

```
ULONG __stdcall CComClass::CMath::AddRef ()
{
    return m_pParent->AddRef ();
}

ULONG __stdcall CComClass::CMath::Release ()
{
    return m_pParent->Release ();
}
```

Delegation of this sort is necessary for two reasons. First, if a client calls *AddRef* or *Release* on an interface implemented by a subobject, the parent's reference count should be adjusted, not the subobject's. Second, if a client calls *QueryInterface* on one of the subobjects, the parent must field the call because only the parent knows which nested classes are present and therefore which interfaces it implements.

MFC and Nested Classes

If you browse through the source code for MFC classes such as *COleControl*, you won't see anything that resembles the code in the previous section. That's because MFC hides its nested classes behind macros.

MFC's *COleDropTarget* class is a case in point. It's one of the simpler MFC COM classes, and it implements just one COM interface—a standard interface named *IDropTarget*. If you look inside Afxole.h, you'll see these statements near the end of *COleDropTarget*'s class declaration:

```
BEGIN_INTERFACE_PART(DropTarget, IDropTarget)
    [...]
    STDMETHOD(DragEnter)(LPDATAOBJECT, DWORD, POINTL, LPDWORD);
    STDMETHOD(DragOver)(DWORD, POINTL, LPDWORD);
    STDMETHOD(DragLeave)();
    STDMETHOD(Drop)(LPDATAOBJECT, DWORD, POINTL pt, LPDWORD);
END_INTERFACE_PART(DropTarget)
```

MFC's BEGIN_INTERFACE_PART macro defines a nested class that implements one COM interface. The class is named by prepending a capital *X* to the first parameter in the macro's parameter list. In this example, the nested class's name is *XDropTarget*. The END_INTERFACE_PART macro declares a member variable that's an instance of the nested class. Here's the code generated by the preprocessor:

```
class XDropTarget : public IDropTarget
{
public:
    STDMETHOD_(ULONG, AddRef)();
    STDMETHOD_(ULONG, Release)();
    STDMETHOD(QueryInterface)(REFIID iid, LPVOID* ppvObj);
    STDMETHOD(DragEnter)(LPDATAOBJECT, DWORD, POINTL, LPDWORD);
    STDMETHOD(DragOver)(DWORD, POINTL, LPDWORD);
```

```
    STDMETHOD(DragLeave)();
    STDMETHOD(Drop)(LPDATAOBJECT, DWORD, POINTL pt, LPDWORD);
} m_xDropTarget;
friend class XDropTarget;
```

Do you see the resemblance between the preprocessor output and the nested class example we looked at earlier? Notice that the name of the nested class instance is *m_x* plus the first parameter in the macro's parameter list—in this case, *m_xDropTarget*.

The nested class implements the three *IUnknown* methods plus the methods listed between BEGIN_INTERFACE_PART and END_INTERFACE_PART. *IDropTarget* has four methods—*DragEnter*, *DragOver*, *DragLeave*, and *Drop*—hence the methods named in the preceding code listing. Here's an excerpt from the MFC source code file Oledrop2.cpp showing how *IDropTarget*'s methods are implemented in the nested *XDropTarget* class:

```
STDMETHODIMP_(ULONG) COleDropTarget::XDropTarget::AddRef()
{
    [...]
}


STDMETHODIMP_(ULONG) COleDropTarget::XDropTarget::Release()
{
    [...]
}


STDMETHODIMP COleDropTarget::XDropTarget::QueryInterface(...)
{
    [...]
}


STDMETHODIMP COleDropTarget::XDropTarget::DragEnter(...)
{
    [...]
}


STDMETHODIMP COleDropTarget::XDropTarget::DragOver(...)
{
    [...]
}


STDMETHODIMP COleDropTarget::XDropTarget::DragLeave(...)
{
    [...]
}


STDMETHODIMP COleDropTarget::XDropTarget::Drop(...)
{
    [...]
}
```

The code inside the method implementations is unimportant for now. The key here is that a few innocent-looking macros in an MFC source code listing turn into a nested class that implements a full-blown COM interface. You can create a class that implements several COM interfaces by including one BEGIN_INTERFACE_PART/END-_INTERFACE_PART block for each interface. Moreover, you needn't worry about conflicts if two or more interfaces contain identical methods because the nested class technique permits each interface (and its methods) to be implemented independently.

How MFC Implements *IUnknown*

Let's go back and look more closely at *COleDropTarget*'s implementation of *Query-Interface*, *AddRef*, and *Release*. Here's the complete, unabridged version:

```
STDMETHODIMP_(ULONG) COleDropTarget::XDropTarget::AddRef()
{
    METHOD_PROLOGUE_EX_(COleDropTarget, DropTarget)
    return pThis->ExternalAddRef();
}

STDMETHODIMP_(ULONG) COleDropTarget::XDropTarget::Release()
{
    METHOD_PROLOGUE_EX_(COleDropTarget, DropTarget)
    return pThis->ExternalRelease();
}

STDMETHODIMP COleDropTarget::XDropTarget::QueryInterface(
    REFIID iid, LPVOID* ppvObj)
{
    METHOD_PROLOGUE_EX_(COleDropTarget, DropTarget)
    return pThis->ExternalQueryInterface(&iid, ppvObj);
}
```

Once more, what MFC is doing is hidden behind a macro. In this case, the macro is METHOD_PROLOGUE_EX_, which creates a stack variable named *pThis* that points to *XDropTarget*'s parent—that is, the *COleDropTarget* object of which the *XDropTarget* object is a member. Knowing this, you can see that *XDropTarget*'s *IUnknown* methods delegate to *COleDropTarget*. Which begs a question or two: What do *COleDrop-Target*'s *ExternalAddRef*, *ExternalRelease*, and *ExternalQueryInterface* functions do, and where do they come from?

The second question is easy to answer. All three functions are members of *CCmdTarget*, and *COleDropTarget* is derived from *CCmdTarget*. To answer the first question, we need to look at the function implementations inside *CCmdTarget*. Here's an excerpt from the MFC source code file Oleunk.cpp:

```
DWORD CCmdTarget::ExternalAddRef()
{
    [...]
    return InternalAddRef();
}

DWORD CCmdTarget::ExternalRelease()
{
    [...]
    return InternalRelease();
}

DWORD CCmdTarget::ExternalQueryInterface(const void* iid,
    LPVOID* ppvObj)
{
    [...]
    return InternalQueryInterface(iid, ppvObj);
}
```

ExternalAddRef, *ExternalRelease*, and *ExternalQueryInterface* call another set of *CCmd-Target* functions named *InternalAddRef*, *InternalRelease*, and *InternalQueryInterface*. The *Internal* functions are a little more complicated, but if you look at them, you'll find that they do just what *AddRef*, *Release*, and *QueryInterface* are supposed to do, albeit in an MFC way. So now we know that the nested class's *IUnknown* methods delegate to the parent class and that the parent class inherits implementations of these methods from *CCmdTarget*. Let's keep going.

Interface Maps

The most interesting *Internal* function is *InternalQueryInterface*. If you peek at it in Oleunk.cpp, you'll see that it calls a little-known function named *GetInterface*, which belongs to a little-known class named *CUnknown*. *GetInterface* does a table lookup to determine whether this class supports the specified interface. It then retrieves a pointer to the nested class that implements the interface and returns it to *Internal-QueryInterface*. So MFC uses a table-driven mechanism to implement *QueryInterface*. But where do the tables come from?

Once more, we can look to *COleDropTarget* for an example. At the very end of *COleDropTarget*'s class declaration is the statement

```
DECLARE_INTERFACE_MAP()
```

And in *COleDropTarget*'s implementation is this set of related statements:

```
BEGIN_INTERFACE_MAP(COleDropTarget, CCmdTarget)
    INTERFACE_PART(COleDropTarget, IID_IDropTarget, DropTarget)
END_INTERFACE_MAP()
```

DECLARE_INTERFACE_MAP is an MFC macro that declares an interface map—a table containing one entry for each interface that a class (in reality, a nested class) implements. BEGIN_INTERFACE_MAP and END_INTERFACE_MAP are also macros. They define the contents of the interface map. Just as message maps tell MFC which messages a class provides handlers for, interface maps tell MFC which COM interfaces a class supports and which nested classes provide the interface implementations. Each INTERFACE_PART macro that appears between BEGIN_INTERFACE_MAP and END_INTERFACE_MAP constitutes one entry in the table. In this example, the INTERFACE_PART statement tells MFC that the interface map is a member of *COleDropTarget*, that *COleDropTarget* implements the *IDropTarget* interface, and that the nested class containing the actual *IDropTarget* implementation is *XDropTarget*. INTERFACE_PART prepends an *X* to the class name in the same manner as BEGIN_INTERFACE_PART.

Because an interface map can contain any number of INTERFACE_PART macros, MFC classes aren't limited to one COM interface each; they can implement several. For each INTERFACE_PART entry that appears in a class's interface map, there is one BEGIN_INTERFACE_PART/END_INTERFACE_PART block in the class declaration. Take a look at *COleControl*'s interface map in Ctlcore.cpp and the numerous BEGIN_INTERFACE_PART/END_INTERFACE_PART blocks in AfxCtl.h and you'll see what I mean.

MFC and Aggregation

Does it seem curious that *CCmdTarget* has two sets of functions with *QueryInterface*, *AddRef*, and *Release* in their names? When I showed you the source code for the *External* functions, I omitted (for clarity) the part that explains why. Here it is again, but this time in unabbreviated form:

```
DWORD CCmdTarget::ExternalAddRef()
{
    // delegate to controlling unknown if aggregated
    if (m_pOuterUnknown != NULL)
        return m_pOuterUnknown->AddRef();

    return InternalAddRef();
}

DWORD CCmdTarget::ExternalRelease()
{
    // delegate to controlling unknown if aggregated
    if (m_pOuterUnknown != NULL)
        return m_pOuterUnknown->Release();

    return InternalRelease();
}
```

```
DWORD CCmdTarget::ExternalQueryInterface(const void* iid,
    LPVOID* ppvObj)
{
    // delegate to controlling unknown if aggregated
    if (m_pOuterUnknown != NULL)
        return m_pOuterUnknown->QueryInterface(*(IID*)iid, ppvObj);

    return InternalQueryInterface(iid, ppvObj);
}
```

Observe that the *External* functions call the *Internal* functions only if *m_pOuterUnknown* holds a NULL value. *m_pOuterUnknown* is a *CCmdTarget* member variable that holds an object's *controlling unknown*. If *m_pOuterUnknown* is not NULL, the *External* functions delegate through the pointer held in *m_pOuterUnknown*. If you're familiar with COM aggregation, you can probably guess what's going on here. But if aggregation is new to you, the preceding code requires further explanation.

COM has never supported inheritance in the way that C++ does. In other words, you can't derive one COM object from another in the way that you can derive one C++ class from another. However, COM does support two mechanisms—*containment* and *aggregation*—for object reuse.

Containment is the simpler of the two. To illustrate how it works, let's say you've written an object that contains a pair of methods named *Add* and *Subtract*. Now suppose someone else has written a COM object with *Multiply* and *Divide* methods that you'd like to incorporate into your object. One way to "borrow" the other object's methods is to have your object create the other object with *CoCreateInstance* and call its methods as needed. Your object is the outer object, the other object is the inner object, and if *m_pInnerObject* holds a pointer to the interface on the inner object that implements *Multiply* and *Divide*, you might also include *Multiply* and *Divide* methods in your object and implement them like this:

```
HRESULT __stdcall CComClass::Multiply (int a, int b, int* pResult)
{
    return m_pInnerObject->Multiply (a, b, pResult);
}

HRESULT __stdcall CComClass::Divide (int a, int b, int* pResult)
{
    return m_pInnerObject->Divide (a, b, pResult);
}
```

That's containment in a nutshell. Figure 18-5 shows the relationship between the inner and outer objects. Notice that the inner object's interface is exposed only to the outer object, not to the clients of the outer object.

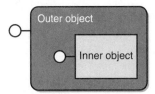

Figure 18-5. *Containment.*

Aggregation is altogether different. When one object aggregates another, the aggregate object exposes the interfaces of both the inner and the outer objects. (See Figure 18-6.) The client has no idea that the object is actually an aggregate of two or more objects.

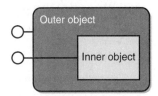

Figure 18-6. *Aggregation.*

Aggregation is similar to containment in that the outer object creates the inner object. But the similarities end there. For aggregation to work, the inner object and the outer object must work together to create the illusion that they're really one object. Both objects must adhere to a strict set of rules governing their behavior. One of those rules says that the outer object must pass its own *IUnknown* pointer to the inner object. This pointer becomes the inner object's controlling unknown. If a client calls an *IUnknown* method on the inner object, the inner object must delegate to the outer object by calling *QueryInterface*, *AddRef*, or *Release* through the controlling unknown. That's what happens when *CCmdTarget*'s *External* functions call *Query-Interface*, *AddRef*, or *Release* through *m_pOuterUnknown*. If the object is aggregated, *m_pOuterUnknown* is non-NULL and the *External* functions delegate to the outer object. Otherwise, the object isn't aggregated and the *Internal* functions are called instead.

A key difference between containment and aggregation is that any object can be contained by another object, but only objects that specifically support aggregation can be aggregated. MFC makes aggregation easy because it builds in aggregation support for free.

MFC and Class Factories

Any class library that places a friendly wrapper around COM should include support for class factories. COM class factories typically contain a lot of boilerplate code that varies little from one application to the next, so they're perfect candidates to be hidden away inside a C++ class.

MFC provides a canned implementation of COM class factories in *COleObject-Factory*. MFC's *COleObjectFactory* class implements two COM interfaces: *IClassFactory* and *IClassFactory2*. *IClassFactory2* is a superset of *IClassFactory*; it supports all of *IClassFactory*'s methods and adds licensing methods that are used primarily by ActiveX controls.

When you create a *COleObjectFactory*, you feed its constructor four critical pieces of information. The first is the CLSID of the object that the class factory creates. The second is a RUNTIME_CLASS pointer identifying the C++ class that implements objects of that type. The third is a BOOL that tells COM whether this server, if it's an EXE, is capable of creating multiple object instances. If this parameter is TRUE and 10 clients call *CoCreateInstance* on the COM class that this server implements, 10 different instances of the EXE are launched. If the parameter is FALSE, one instance of the EXE serves all 10 clients. The fourth and final parameter to *COleObjectFactory*'s constructor is the ProgID of the object that the class factory creates. ProgID is short for Program ID; it's a human-readable name (for example, "Math.Object") that can be used in lieu of a CLSID to identify a COM class. The following code fragment creates a *COleObjectFactory* that instantiates *CComClass* when CLSID_Math is passed to a COM activation function:

```
COleObjectFactory cf (
    CLSID_Math,                    // The object's CLSID
    RUNTIME_CLASS (CComClass),     // Class representing the object
    FALSE,                         // Many clients, one EXE
    _T ("Math.Object")             // The object's ProgID
);
```

Most MFC applications don't explicitly declare an instance of *COleObjectFactory*; instead, they use MFC's DECLARE_OLECREATE and IMPLEMENT_OLECREATE macros. When the preprocessor encounters

```
// In the class declaration
DECLARE_OLECREATE (CComClass)

// In the class implementation
IMPLEMENT_OLECREATE (CComClass, "Math.Object", 0x708813ac,
    0x88d6, 0x11d1, 0x8e, 0x53, 0x00, 0x60, 0x08, 0xa8, 0x27, 0x31)
```

it outputs this:

```
// In the class declaration
public:
    static COleObjectFactory factory;
    static const GUID guid;

// In the class implementation
COleObjectFactory CComClass::factory(CComClass::guid,
    RUNTIME_CLASS(CComClass), FALSE, _T("Math.Object"));
```

(continued)

```
const GUID CComClass::guid =
    { 0x708813ac, 0x88d6, 0x11d1, { 0x8e, 0x53, 0x00,
      0x60, 0x08, 0xa8, 0x27, 0x31} };
```

The one drawback to the OLECREATE macros is that they contain hardcoded references to *COleObjectFactory*. If you derive a class from *COleObjectFactory* and want to use it in an application, you must either discard the macros and hand-code the references to the derived class or write your own OLECREATE macros. Programmers occasionally do find it useful to derive their own classes from *COleObjectFactory* to modify the class factory's behavior. By overriding the virtual *OnCreateObject* function, for example, you can create a "singleton" class factory—a class factory that creates an object the first time *IClassFactory::CreateInstance* is called and hands out pointers to the existing object in response to subsequent activation requests.

Internally, MFC maintains a linked list of all the *COleObjectFactory* objects that an application creates. (Look inside *COleObjectFactory*'s constructor and you'll see the code that adds each newly instantiated object to the list.) *COleObjectFactory* includes handy member functions for registering all an application's class factories with the operating system and for registering the objects that the class factories create in the system registry. The statement

```
COleObjectFactory::UpdateRegistryAll ();
```

adds to the registry all the information required to create any object that is served up by this application's class factories. That's powerful, because the alternative is to write low-level code that relies on Win32 registry functions to update the registry yourself.

Putting It All in Perspective

Has this chapter covered everything there is to know about the relationship between MFC and COM? Hardly. There's plenty more, as you'll discover in the next three chapters. But this chapter has set the stage for the ones that follow. Now when you see a diagram like the one in Figure 18-1 (on page 1063), you'll understand what you're looking at and have a pretty good idea of how MFC implements it. Plus, when you look over a wizard-generated source code listing or dig down into the MFC source code, you'll know what statements like INTERFACE_PART and IMPLEMENT_OLE-CREATE mean.

If COM is new to you, you're probably feeling a little overwhelmed right now. Don't despair. Learning COM is a lot like learning to program Windows: You endure the obligatory six months of mental fog before it all begins to make sense. The good news is that you don't have to be an expert on COM to build COM-based applications with MFC. In fact, you don't have to know much about COM at all. But if you believe (as I do) that the best programmers are the ones who understand what goes on under the hood, the information presented in this chapter will serve you well in the long run.

Chapter 19

The Clipboard and OLE Drag-and-Drop

Since version 1.0, Microsoft Windows has supported the transfer of data through the clipboard. The clipboard is a centralized location where data can be stored en route from one application to another or on its way to another part of the same application. Even novices quickly grasp the clipboard's simple cut/copy/paste paradigm: select the data, cut it or copy it to the clipboard, and paste it somewhere else. Many applications feature Cut, Copy, and Paste commands in their Edit menus, and millions of Windows users know Ctrl-X, Ctrl-C, and Ctrl-V as the keyboard equivalents of these basic clipboard commands.

The original clipboard (which I'll refer to as the *legacy clipboard* or simply as *the clipboard*) is still present in Windows 98 and Windows 2000, but programmers are encouraged to forego using it in favor of a newer, more capable clipboard known as the *OLE clipboard*. The OLE clipboard is backward-compatible with the legacy clipboard, meaning that one application can copy data to the OLE clipboard and another application can retrieve that data from the legacy clipboard, and vice versa. More important, the OLE clipboard lets programmers do a few things that the legacy clipboard doesn't. To transfer a large bitmap using the legacy clipboard, for example, you must allocate enough memory to store the entire bitmap. Transfer the same bitmap through the OLE clipboard, however, and you can store the bitmap in a more sensible storage medium, such as in a file on a hard disk.

Closely related to the OLE clipboard is a visual method of transferring data called *OLE drag-and-drop*. OLE drag-and-drop simplifies cut/copy/paste by eliminating the middleman. Rather than requiring one command to move the data to the clipboard and another to paste it into a document, OLE drag-and-drop lets you grab a piece of data with the mouse and drag it to the desired location. Under the hood, a mechanism much like the OLE clipboard is used to facilitate the data transfer. But to the user, the transfer appears seamless—and very intuitive.

MFC doesn't provide explicit support for operations involving the legacy clipboard, but it does support the OLE clipboard and OLE drag-and-drop. Writing code to use either of these data transfer mechanisms is no picnic if you're doing it from scratch, but MFC makes it surprisingly simple.

The best way to understand the mechanics of the OLE clipboard and OLE drag-and-drop is to first understand how the legacy clipboard works. To that end, I'll begin this chapter with an overview of the legacy clipboard and a review of the Windows API functions used to access it. I'll then introduce the OLE clipboard and OLE drag-and-drop and demonstrate how to use MFC to develop applications that support both of them in no time flat.

THE LEGACY CLIPBOARD

Data is transferred to and from the legacy clipboard using a small subset of Windows API functions. The following table briefly summarizes those functions.

CLIPBOARD API FUNCTIONS

Function	*Description*
OpenClipboard	Opens the clipboard
CloseClipboard	Closes the clipboard
EmptyClipboard	Deletes the current contents of the clipboard
GetClipboardData	Retrieves data from the clipboard
SetClipboardData	Transfers data to the clipboard

Placing data on the clipboard is a four-step process:

1. Open the clipboard with *::OpenClipboard*.

2. Discard any data presently stored in the clipboard with *::EmptyClipboard*.

3. Use *::SetClipboardData* to transfer ownership of a global memory block or other object (for example, a bitmap handle) containing clipboard data to the clipboard.

4. Close the clipboard with *::CloseClipboard*.

A *global memory block* is a block of memory allocated with the *::GlobalAlloc* API function. *::GlobalAlloc* returns a handle of type HGLOBAL, which can be treated as a generic HANDLE in a Win32 application. A related function named *::GlobalLock* takes an HGLOBAL and returns a pointer to the memory block. Windows programmers don't use *::GlobalAlloc* much anymore because *::HeapAlloc* superseded it in the Win32 API. But *::GlobalAlloc* is still useful for clipboard programming because the clipboard requires a memory handle, not a pointer.

The following code places a text string on the clipboard by copying the text string to a global memory block and handing the memory block over to the clipboard:

```
char szText[]= "Hello, world"; // ANSI characters
if (::OpenClipboard (m_hWnd)) {
    ::EmptyClipboard ();

    HANDLE hData = ::GlobalAlloc (GMEM_MOVEABLE, ::lstrlen (szText) + 1);
    LPSTR pData = (LPSTR) ::GlobalLock (hData);
    ::lstrcpy (pData, szText);
    ::GlobalUnlock (hData);

    ::SetClipboardData (CF_TEXT, hData);
    ::CloseClipboard ();
}
```

Once a global memory block is handed over to the clipboard, the application that allocated the block should neither use it nor delete it. The clipboard now owns the memory and will release it at the appropriate time—specifically, the next time an application calls *::EmptyClipboard*.

The sole parameter passed to *::OpenClipboard* is the handle of the window that "owns" the clipboard while the clipboard is open. In an MFC application, of course, you can retrieve a *CWnd*'s window handle from its *m_hWnd* data member. *::Open-Clipboard* will fail if another application has the clipboard open. Forcing every application to open the clipboard before using it is the way that Windows synchronizes access to this shared resource and ensures that the clipboard's contents don't change while an application is using it.

Retrieving data from the clipboard is equally simple. Here are the steps:

1. Open the clipboard with *::OpenClipboard*.

2. Use *::GetClipboardData* to retrieve the handle of the global memory block or other object containing clipboard data.

3. Make a local copy of the data by copying it from the global memory block.

4. Close the clipboard with *::CloseClipboard*.

Here's how you can retrieve the text string placed on the clipboard in the previous example:

```
char szText[BUFLEN];
if (::OpenClipboard (m_hWnd)) {
    HANDLE hData = ::GetClipboardData (CF_TEXT);
    if (hData != NULL) {
        LPCSTR pData = (LPCSTR) ::GlobalLock (hData);
        if (::lstrlen (pData) < BUFLEN)
            ::lstrcpy (szText, pData);
        ::GlobalUnlock (hData);
    }
    ::CloseClipboard ();
}
```

If a text string is available from the clipboard, *szText* will hold a copy of it when this routine finishes.

Clipboard Formats

Both *::SetClipboardData* and *::GetClipboardData* accept an integer value specifying a clipboard format, which identifies the type of data involved in the transfer. The examples in the previous section used CF_TEXT, which identifies the data as ANSI text. Windows uses a separate clipboard format ID for Unicode text. (That's why both examples used the *char* data type instead of TCHAR.) CF_TEXT is one of several predefined clipboard formats that Windows supports. A partial list of clipboard formats is shown in the following table.

COMMONLY USED CLIPBOARD FORMATS

Format	Data Type
CF_BITMAP	Windows bitmap
CF_DIB	Device-independent bitmap
CF_ENHMETAFILE	GDI enhanced metafile
CF_METAFILEPICT	Old-style (nonenhanced) GDI metafile with sizing and mapping-mode information attached
CF_HDROP	List of file names in HDROP format
CF_PALETTE	GDI palette
CF_TEXT	Text composed of 8-bit ANSI characters
CF_TIFF	Bitmap in TIFF format
CF_UNICODETEXT	Text composed of 16-bit Unicode characters
CF_WAVE	Audio data in WAV format

You can use the predefined clipboard formats to transfer bitmaps, palettes, enhanced metafiles, and other objects as easily as you can transfer text. For example, if *m_bitmap* is a *CBitmap* data member that holds a bitmap, here's one way to make a copy of the bitmap and place it on the clipboard:

```
if (::OpenClipboard (m_hWnd)) {
    // Make a copy of the bitmap.
    BITMAP bm;
    CBitmap bitmap;
    m_bitmap.GetObject (sizeof (bm), &bm);
    bitmap.CreateBitmapIndirect (&bm);

    CDC dcMemSrc, dcMemDest;
    dcMemSrc.CreateCompatibleDC (NULL);
    CBitmap* pOldBitmapSrc = dcMemSrc.SelectObject (&m_bitmap);
    dcMemDest.CreateCompatibleDC (NULL);
    CBitmap* pOldBitmapDest = dcMemDest.SelectObject (&bitmap);

    dcMemDest.BitBlt (0, 0, bm.bmWidth, bm.bmHeight, &dcMemSrc,
        0, 0, SRCCOPY);
    HBITMAP hBitmap = (HBITMAP) bitmap.Detach ();

    dcMemDest.SelectObject (pOldBitmapDest);
    dcMemSrc.SelectObject (pOldBitmapSrc);

    // Place the copy on the clipboard.
    ::EmptyClipboard ();
    ::SetClipboardData (CF_BITMAP, hBitmap);
    ::CloseClipboard ();
}
```

To retrieve a bitmap from the clipboard, call *::GetClipboardData* and pass it a CF-_BITMAP parameter:

```
if (::OpenClipboard (m_hWnd)) {
    HBITMAP hBitmap = (HBITMAP) ::GetClipboardData (CF_BITMAP);
    if (hBitmap != NULL) {
        // Make a local copy of the bitmap.
    }
    ::CloseClipboard ();
}
```

Notice the pattern here. The application that places data on the clipboard tells Windows the data type. The application that retrieves the data asks for a particular data type. If data isn't available in that format, *::GetClipboardData* returns NULL. In the example above, *::GetClipboardData* returns NULL if the clipboard contains no CF_BITMAP-type data and the code that copies the bitmap is bypassed.

The system silently converts some clipboard formats to related data types when *::GetClipboardData* is called. For example, if application A copies a string of ANSI text to the clipboard (CF_TEXT) and application B calls *::GetClipboardData* requesting Unicode text (CF_UNICODETEXT), Windows 2000 converts the text to Unicode and *::GetClipboardData* returns a valid memory handle. Bitmaps benefit from implicit data conversions, too. Both Windows 98 and Windows 2000 convert a CF_BITMAP bitmap into a CF_DIB, and vice versa. This adds a welcome measure of portability to clipboard formats that represent different forms of the same basic data types.

The CF_HDROP Clipboard Format

One of the more interesting—and least documented—clipboard formats is CF_HDROP. When you retrieve CF_HDROP-formatted data from the clipboard, you get back an HDROP, which is actually a handle to a global memory block. Inside the memory block is a list of file names. Rather than read the file names by parsing the contents of the memory block, you can use the *::DragQueryFile* function. The following code retrieves an HDROP from the clipboard and stuffs all the file names into the list box referenced by the *CListBox* pointer *pListBox*:

```
if (::OpenClipboard (m_hWnd)) {
    HDROP hDrop = (HDROP) ::GetClipboardData (CF_HDROP);
    if (hDrop != NULL) {
        // Find out how many file names the HDROP contains.
        int nCount = ::DragQueryFile (hDrop, (UINT) -1, NULL, 0);
        // Enumerate the file names.
        if (nCount) {
            TCHAR szFile[MAX_PATH];
            for (int i=0; i<nCount; i++) {
                ::DragQueryFile (hDrop, i, szFile,
                    sizeof (szFile) / sizeof (TCHAR));
                pListBox->AddString (szFile);
            }
        }
    }
    ::CloseClipboard ();
}
```

Extracting file names from an HDROP is easy; inserting them is a bit more work. The memory block that an HDROP references contains a DROPFILES structure followed by a list of file names terminated by two consecutive NULL characters. DROPFILES is defined as follows in Shlobj.h:

```
typedef struct _DROPFILES {
    DWORD pFiles;               // Offset of file list
    POINT pt;                   // Drop coordinates
    BOOL fNC;                   // Client or nonclient area
    BOOL fWide;                 // ANSI or Unicode text
} DROPFILES, FAR * LPDROPFILES;
```

To create your own HDROP, you allocate a global memory block, initialize a DROPFILES structure inside it, and append a list of file names. The only DROPFILES fields you need to initialize are *pFiles*, which holds the offset relative to the beginning of the memory block of the first character in the list of file names, and *fWide*, which indicates whether the file names are composed of ANSI (*fWide*=FALSE) or Unicode (*fWide*=TRUE) characters. To illustrate, the following statements create an HDROP containing two file names and place the HDROP on the clipboard:

```
TCHAR szFiles[3][32] = {
    _T ("C:\\My Documents\\Book\\Chap20.doc"),
    _T ("C:\\My Documents\\Book\\Chap21.doc"),
    _T ("")
};

if (::OpenClipboard (m_hWnd)) {
    ::EmptyClipboard ();
    int nSize = sizeof (DROPFILES) + sizeof (szFiles);
    HANDLE hData = ::GlobalAlloc (GHND, nSize);
    LPDROPFILES pDropFiles = (LPDROPFILES) ::GlobalLock (hData);
    pDropFiles->pFiles = sizeof (DROPFILES);

#ifdef UNICODE
    pDropFiles->fWide = TRUE;
#else
    pDropFiles->fWide = FALSE;
#endif

    LPBYTE pData = (LPBYTE) pDropFiles + sizeof (DROPFILES);
    ::CopyMemory (pData, szFiles, sizeof (szFiles));
    ::GlobalUnlock (hData);
    ::SetClipboardData (CF_HDROP, hData);
    ::CloseClipboard ();
}
```

The GHND parameter passed to *::GlobalAlloc* in this example combines the GMEM-_MOVEABLE and GMEM_ZEROINIT flags. GMEM_ZEROINIT tells *::GlobalAlloc* to initialize all the bytes in the block to 0, which ensures that the uninitialized members of the DROPFILES structures are set to 0. As an aside, the GMEM_MOVEABLE flag is no longer necessary when you allocate global memory blocks to hand over to the clipboard in the Win32 environment, despite what the documentation might say. Its presence here is a tip of the hat to 16-bit Windows, which required us to allocate clipboard memory with both the GMEM_MOVEABLE and GMEM_DDESHARE flags.

HDROPs might seem like a curious way to pass around lists of file names. However, the Windows 98 and Windows 2000 shells use this format to cut, copy, and paste files. Here's a simple experiment you can perform to see for yourself how the shell uses HDROPs. Copy the sample code into an application, and change the file names to reference real files on your hard disk. Execute the code to transfer the HDROP to the clipboard. Then open a window onto a hard disk folder and select Paste from the window's Edit menu. The shell will respond by moving the files whose names appear in the HDROP into the folder.

Private Clipboard Formats

CF_TEXT, CF_BITMAP, and other predefined clipboard formats cover a wide range of data types, but they can't possibly include every type of data that an application might want to transfer through the clipboard. For this reason, Windows allows you to register your own private clipboard formats and use them in lieu of or in conjunction with standard clipboard formats.

Let's say you're writing a Widget application that creates widgets. You'd like your users to be able to cut or copy widgets to the clipboard and paste them elsewhere in the document (or perhaps into an entirely different document). To support such functionality, call the Win32 API function *::RegisterClipboardFormat* to register a private clipboard format for widgets:

```
UINT nID = ::RegisterClipboardFormat (_T ("Widget"));
```

The UINT you get back is the ID of your private clipboard format. To copy a widget to the clipboard, copy all the data needed to define the widget into a global memory block, and then call *::SetClipboardData* with the private clipboard format ID and the memory handle:

```
::SetClipboardData (nID, hData);
```

To retrieve the widget from the clipboard, pass the widget's clipboard format ID to *::GetClipboardData*:

```
HANDLE hData = ::GetClipboardData (nID);
```

Then lock the block to get a pointer and reconstruct the widget from the data in the memory block. The key here is that if 10 different applications (or 10 different instances of the same application) call *::RegisterClipboardFormat* with the same format name, all 10 will receive the same clipboard format ID. Thus, if application A copies a widget to the clipboard and application B retrieves it, the process will work just fine as long as both applications specify the same format name when they call *::Register-ClipboardFormat*.

Providing Data in Multiple Formats

Placing multiple items on the clipboard is perfectly legal as long as each item represents a different format. Applications do it all the time. It's an effective way to make data available to a wide range of applications—even those that don't understand your private clipboard formats.

Microsoft Excel is a good example of an application that uses multiple clipboard formats. When you select a range of spreadsheet cells in Excel and copy the selection to the clipboard, Excel places up to 30 items on the clipboard. One of those items uses a private clipboard format that represents native Excel spreadsheet data. Another is a CF_BITMAP rendition of the cells. The Paint utility that comes with Windows doesn't understand Excel's private clipboard format, but it can paste Excel spreadsheet cells into a bitmap. At least it *appears* that Paint can paste spreadsheet cells. In truth, it pastes a bitmapped image of those cells, not real spreadsheet cells. You can even paste Excel data into Notepad because one of the formats that Excel places on the clipboard is—you guessed it—CF_TEXT. By making spreadsheet data available in a wide range of formats, Excel increases the portability of its clipboard data.

How do you place two or more items on the clipboard? It's easy: Just call *::SetClipboardData* once for each format:

```
::SetClipboardData (nID, hPrivateData);
::SetClipboardData (CF_BITMAP, hBitmap);
::SetClipboardData (CF_TEXT, hTextData);
```

Now if an application calls *::GetClipboardData* asking for data in CF_TEXT format, CF_BITMAP format, or the private format specified by *nID*, the call will succeed and the caller will receive a non-NULL data handle in return.

Querying for Available Data Formats

One way to find out whether clipboard data is available in a particular format is to call *::GetClipboardData* and check for a NULL return value. Sometimes, however, you'll want to know in advance whether *::GetClipboardData* will succeed or to see all the formats that are currently available enumerated so that you can pick the one that best fits your needs. The following Win32 API functions let you do all this and more:

Function	Description
CountClipboardFormats	Returns the number of formats currently available
EnumClipboardFormats	Enumerates all available clipboard formats
IsClipboardFormatAvailable	Indicates whether data is available in a particular format
GetPriorityClipboardFormat	Given a prioritized list of formats, indicates which one is the first available

::IsClipboardFormatAvailable is the simplest of the four functions. To find out whether data is available in CF_TEXT format, call *::IsClipboardFormatAvailable* like this.

```
if (::IsClipboardFormatAvailable (CF_TEXT)) {
    // Yes, it's available.
}
else {
    // No, it's not available.
}
```

This function is often used to implement update handlers for the Edit menu's Paste command. Refer to page 357 in Chapter 7 for an example of this usage.

::IsClipboardFormatAvailable works even if the clipboard isn't open. But don't forget that clipboard data is subject to change when the clipboard isn't open. Don't make the mistake of writing code like this:

```
if (::IsClipboardFormatAvailable (CF_TEXT)) {
    if (::OpenClipboard (m_hWnd)) {
        HANDLE hData = ::GetClipboardData (CF_TEXT);
        LPCSTR pData = (LPCSTR) ::GlobalLock (hData);
            .
            .
            .
        ::CloseClipboard ();
    }
}
```

This code is buggy because in a multitasking environment, there's a small but very real chance that the data on the clipboard will be replaced after *::IsClipboardFormat-Available* executes but before *::GetClipboardData* is called. You can avoid this risk by opening the clipboard prior to calling *::IsClipboardFormatAvailable*:

```
if (::OpenClipboard (m_hWnd)) {
    if (::IsClipboardFormatAvailable (CF_TEXT)) {
        HANDLE hData = ::GetClipboardData (CF_TEXT);
        LPCSTR pData = (LPCSTR) ::GlobalLock (hData);
            .
            .
            .
    }
    ::CloseClipboard ();
}
```

This code will work just fine because only the application that has the clipboard open can change the clipboard's contents.

You can use *::EnumClipboardFormats* to iterate through a list of all available clipboard formats. Here's an example:

```
if (::OpenClipboard (m_hWnd)) {
    UINT nFormat = 0; // Must be 0 to start the iteration.
    while (nFormat = ::EnumClipboardFormats (nFormat)) {
        // Next clipboard format is in nFormat.
    }
    ::CloseClipboard ();
}
```

Because *::EnumClipboardFormats* returns 0 when it reaches the end of the list, the loop falls through after retrieving the last available format. If you simply want to know how many data formats are available on the clipboard, call *::CountClipboardFormats*.

The final clipboard data availability function, *::GetPriorityClipboardFormat*, simplifies the process of checking for not just one clipboard format, but several. Suppose your application is capable of pasting data in a private format stored in *nID*, in CF_TEXT format, or in CF_BITMAP format. You would prefer the private format, but if that's not available, you'll take CF_TEXT instead, or if all else fails, CF_BITMAP. Rather than write

```
if (::OpenClipboard (m_hWnd)) {
    if (::IsClipboardFormatAvailable (nID)) {
        // Perfect!
    }
    else if (::IsClipboardFormatAvailable (CF_TEXT)) {
        // Not the best, but I'll take it.
    }
    else if (::IsClipboardFormatAvailable (CF_BITMAP)) {
        // Better than nothing.
    }
    ::CloseClipboard ();
}
```

you can write

```
UINT nFormats[3] = {
    nID,          // First choice
    CF_TEXT,      // Second choice
    CF_BITMAP     // Third choice
};

if (::OpenClipboard (m_hWnd)) {
    UINT nFormat = ::GetPriorityClipboardFormat (nFormats, 3);
    if (nFormat > 0) {
        // nFormat holds nID, CF_TEXT, or CF_BITMAP.
    }
    ::CloseClipboard ();
}
```

::GetPriorityClipboardFormat's return value is the ID of the first format in the list that matches a format that is currently available. *::GetPriorityClipboardFormat* returns −1 if none of the formats is available or 0 if the clipboard is empty.

Delayed Rendering

One of the limitations of the legacy clipboard is that all data placed on it is stored in memory. For text strings and other simple data types, memory-based data transfers are both fast and efficient. But suppose someone copies a 10-MB bitmap to the clipboard. Until the clipboard is emptied, the bitmap will occupy 10 MB of RAM. And if no one pastes the bitmap, the memory allocated to hold it will have been used for naught.

To avoid such wastefulness, Windows supports *delayed rendering*. Delayed rendering allows an application to say, "I have data that I'll make available through the clipboard, but I'm not going to copy it to the clipboard until someone asks for it." How does delayed rendering work? First you call *::SetClipboardData* with a valid clipboard format ID but a NULL data handle. Then you respond to WM_RENDERFORMAT messages by physically placing the data on the clipboard with *::SetClipboardData*. The WM_RENDERFORMAT message is sent if and when an application calls *::GetClipboardData* asking for data in that particular format. If no one asks for the data, the message is never sent, and you'll never have to allocate that 10 MB of memory. Keep in mind that a WM_RENDERFORMAT message handler should *not* call *::OpenClipboard* and *::CloseClipboard* because the window that receives the message implicitly owns the clipboard at the time the message is received.

An application that processes WM_RENDERFORMAT messages must process WM_RENDERALLFORMATS messages, too. The WM_RENDERALLFORMATS message is sent if an application terminates while the clipboard holds NULL data handles that the application put there. The message handler's job is to open the clipboard, transfer to it the data that the application promised to provide through delayed rendering, and close the clipboard. Putting the data on the clipboard ensures that the data will be available to other applications after an application that uses delayed rendering is long gone.

A third clipboard message, WM_DESTROYCLIPBOARD, also plays a role in delayed rendering. This message informs an application that it's no longer responsible for providing delay-rendered data. It's sent when another application calls *::EmptyClipboard*. It's also sent after a WM_RENDERALLFORMATS message. If you're holding on to any resources in order to respond to WM_RENDERFORMAT and WM_RENDERALLFORMATS messages, you can safely free those resources when a WM_DESTROYCLIPBOARD message arrives.

Here's how an MFC application might use delayed rendering to place a bitmap on the clipboard:

```
// In CMyWindow's message map
ON_COMMAND (ID_EDIT_COPY, OnEditCopy)
ON_WM_RENDERFORMAT ()
ON_WM_RENDERALLFORMATS ()
    :
    :
// Elsewhere in CMyWindow
void CMyWindow::OnEditCopy ()
```

```
{
    ::SetClipboardData (CF_BITMAP, NULL);
}

void CMyWindow::OnRenderFormat (UINT nFormat)
{
    if (nFormat == CF_BITMAP) {
        // Make a copy of the bitmap, and store the handle in hBitmap.
            .
            .
            .
        ::SetClipboardData (CF_BITMAP, hBitmap);
    }
}

void CMyWindow::OnRenderAllFormats ()
{
    ::OpenClipboard (m_hWnd);
    OnRenderFormat (CF_BITMAP);
    ::CloseClipboard ();
}
```

This example isn't entirely realistic because if there's a possibility that the bitmap could change between the time it's copied to the clipboard and the time it's retrieved (a distinct possibility if the application is a bitmap editor and the bitmap is open for editing), *OnEditCopy* is obliged to make a copy of the bitmap in its current state. But think about it. If *OnEditCopy* makes a copy of the bitmap, the whole purpose of using delayed rendering is defeated. Delayed rendering is a tool for conserving memory, but if an application is obliged to make a copy of each item that is "copied" to the clipboard for delayed rendering, shouldn't it just copy the item to the clipboard outright?

Not necessarily. The snapshot can be stored on disk. Here's a revised version of the code that demonstrates how delayed rendering can conserve memory even if the data is subject to change:

```
// In CMyWindow's message map
ON_COMMAND (ID_EDIT_COPY, OnEditCopy)
ON_WM_RENDERFORMAT ()
ON_WM_RENDERALLFORMATS ()
ON_WM_DESTROYCLIPBOARD ()
    .
    .
    .
// Elsewhere in CMyWindow
void CMyWindow::OnEditCopy ()
{
    // Save the bitmap to a temporary disk file.
        .
        .
        .
```

(continued)

```
        ::SetClipboardData (CF_BITMAP, NULL);
}

void CMyWindow::OnRenderFormat (UINT nFormat)
{
    if (nFormat == CF_BITMAP) {
        // Re-create the bitmap from the data in the temporary file.
            .
            .
            .
        ::SetClipboardData (CF_BITMAP, hBitmap);
    }
}

void CMyWindow::OnRenderAllFormats ()
{
    ::OpenClipboard (m_hWnd);
    OnRenderFormat (CF_BITMAP);
    ::CloseClipboard ();
}

void CMyWindow::OnDestroyClipboard ()
{
    // Delete the temporary file.
}
```

The idea is to save a copy of the bitmap to a file in *OnEditCopy* and re-create the bitmap from the file in *OnRenderFormat*. Disk space is orders of magnitude cheaper than RAM, so this trade-off is acceptable in most situations.

Building a Reusable Clipboard Class

Given the nature of the clipboard, you might be surprised to discover that MFC doesn't provide a *CClipboard* class that encapsulates the clipboard API. You could write your own clipboard class without much difficulty, but there's really no good reason to bother. Why? Because the OLE clipboard does everything that the legacy clipboard does and then some, and because MFC does a thorough job of wrapping the OLE clipboard. Operations involving the OLE clipboard are considerably more complex than operations involving the legacy clipboard, but MFC levels the playing field. In fact, with MFC to lend a hand, using the OLE clipboard is no more difficult than using the legacy clipboard. The next several sections explain why.

THE OLE CLIPBOARD

The OLE clipboard is a modern-day version of the legacy clipboard. It is also backward-compatible. Thanks to some magic built into the OLE libraries, you can put a text string, a bitmap, or some other item on the OLE clipboard and an application that knows nothing about OLE can paste that item just as if it had come from the legacy clipboard. Conversely, an application can use the OLE clipboard to retrieve data from the legacy clipboard.

What's different about the OLE clipboard, and why is it superior to the old clipboard? There are two major differences between the two. First, the OLE clipboard is completely COM-based; all data is transferred by calling methods through pointers to COM interfaces. Second, the OLE clipboard supports storage media other than global memory. The legacy clipboard, in contrast, uses memory for *all* data transfers, which effectively limits the size of items transferred through the clipboard to the amount of memory available. Because of the legacy clipboard's inability to use media other than memory for data transfers, the compatibility between the legacy clipboard and the OLE clipboard is subject to the limitation that only items transferred through memory can be copied to one and retrieved from the other.

The first reason alone isn't enough to justify forsaking the legacy clipboard. COM is trendy and objects are cool, but without MFC, code that interacts with the OLE clipboard is much more complex than legacy clipboard code. But the second reason— the freedom to use alternative storage media—is just cause to use the OLE clipboard. Transferring a 4-GB bitmap through the legacy clipboard is impossible because current versions of Windows don't support memory objects that large. With the OLE clipboard, however, you can transfer anything that will fit on your hard disk. In fact, with a little ingenuity, you can transfer anything at all—even items too large to fit on a hard disk. Given the huge volumes of information that many modern applications are forced to deal with, the OLE clipboard can be a very handy tool indeed.

OLE Clipboard Basics

The first and most fundamental notion to understand about the OLE clipboard is that when you place an item of data on it, you don't actually place the data itself. Instead, you place a COM data object that encapsulates the data. A *data object* is a COM object that implements the *IDataObject* interface. *IDataObject* has two methods that play key roles in the operation of the OLE clipboard: *SetData* and *GetData*. Assuming that the data object is a generic data repository (as opposed to an object that is custom-fit to handle a particular set of data), a data provider stuffs data into the data object with *IDataObject::SetData*. It then places the object on the OLE clipboard with *::OleSetClipboard*. A data consumer calls *::OleGetClipboard* to get the clipboard data object's *IDataObject* pointer, and then it calls *IDataObject::GetData* to retrieve the data.

Figure 19-1 provides a conceptual look at OLE clipboard operations. This is a simplified view in that the *IDataObject* pointer returned by *::OleGetClipboard* isn't really the *IDataObject* pointer that was passed to *::OleSetClipboard*. Rather, it's a pointer to the *IDataObject* interface implemented by a system-provided clipboard data object that wraps the data object provided to *::OleSetClipboard* and also allows consumers

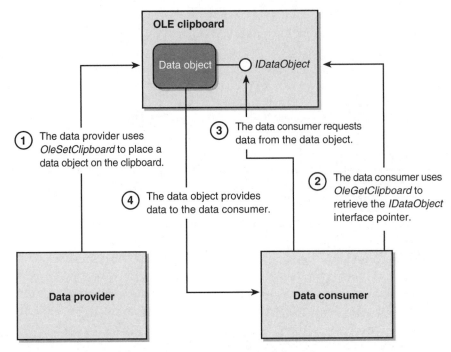

OLE clipboard

Data object ——○ *IDataObject*

① The data provider uses *OleSetClipboard* to place a data object on the clipboard.

③ The data consumer requests data from the data object.

④ The data object provides data to the data consumer.

② The data consumer uses *OleGetClipboard* to retrieve the *IDataObject* interface pointer.

Data provider

Data consumer

Figure 19-1. *Transferring data through the OLE clipboard.*

to access data on the legacy clipboard. Fortunately, this bit of indirection doesn't affect the code you write one iota. You simply use the *IDataObject* interface to interact with the data object. The system does the rest.

Using the OLE clipboard sounds reasonably simple, but nothing is simple when COM and OLE are involved. The hard part is writing the code for a data object and implementing not only *IDataObject::GetData* and *IDataObject::SetData* but also the other *IDataObject* methods. But first things first. Assuming that you've already implemented a data object and that *pdo* holds a pointer to the object's *IDataObject* interface, here's one way to place a text string on the OLE clipboard:

```
// Copy the text string to a global memory block.
char szText[] = "Hello, world";
HANDLE hData = ::GlobalAlloc (GMEM_MOVEABLE, ::lstrlen (szText) + 1);
LPSTR pData = (LPSTR) ::GlobalLock (hData);
::lstrcpy (pData, szText);
::GlobalUnlock (hData);

// Initialize a FORMATETC structure and a STGMEDIUM structure that
// describe the data and the location at which it's stored.
FORMATETC fe;
fe.cfFormat = CF_TEXT;                // Clipboard format=CF_TEXT
```

```
fe.ptd = NULL;                  // Target device=Screen
fe.dwAspect = DVASPECT_CONTENT; // Level of detail=Full content
fe.lindex = -1;                 // Index=Not applicable
fe.tymed = TYMED_HGLOBAL;       // Storage medium=Memory

STGMEDIUM stgm;
stgm.tymed = TYMED_HGLOBAL;     // Storage medium=Memory
stgm.hGlobal = hData;           // Handle to memory block
stgm.pUnkForRelease = NULL;     // Use ReleaseStgMedium

// Place the data object on the OLE clipboard.
pdo->SetData (&fe, &stgm, FALSE);
::OleSetClipboard (pdo);
pdo->Release ();
```

The *Release* call in the final statement assumes that the application that created the data object has no more use for it after handing it off to the OLE clipboard. Calling *Release* on the data object won't cause the object to self-delete because *::OleSet-Clipboard* performs an *AddRef* on the *IDataObject* pointer passed to it.

Retrieving the text string is a little less work because we don't have to create a data object. But the process still isn't quite as straightforward as the one for retrieving a string from the legacy clipboard:

```
char szText[BUFLEN];
IDataObject* pdo;
STGMEDIUM stgm;

FORMATETC fe = {
    CF_TEXT, NULL, DVASPECT_CONTENT, -1, TYMED_HGLOBAL
};

if (SUCCEEDED (::OleGetClipboard (&pdo))) {
    if (SUCCEEDED (pdo->GetData (&fe, &stgm) && stgm.hGlobal != NULL)) {
        LPCSTR pData = (LPCSTR) ::GlobalLock (stgm.hGlobal);
        if (::lstrlen (pData) < BUFLEN)
            ::lstrcpy (szText, pData);
        ::GlobalUnlock (stgm.hGlobal);
        ::ReleaseStgMedium (&stgm);
    }
    pdo->Release ();
}
```

If the data object can't provide the requested data, it returns an HRESULT signifying failure. The SUCCEEDED macro used in this example is the same one that we used to test HRESULTs in Chapter 18.

Two structures play key roles in the operation of *SetData* and *GetData*: FORMATETC and STGMEDIUM. FORMATETC describes the format of the data and identifies the type of *storage medium* (for example, global memory block or file) that holds the data. Here's how FORMATETC is defined in Objidl.h:

```
typedef struct tagFORMATETC {
    CLIPFORMAT cfFormat; // Clipboard format
    DVTARGETDEVICE *ptd; // Target device
    DWORD dwAspect;      // Level of detail
    LONG lindex;         // Page number or other index
    DWORD tymed;         // Type of storage medium
} FORMATETC;
```

The two most important fields are *cfFormat* and *tymed*. *cfFormat* holds a clipboard format ID. The ID can be a standard clipboard format ID such as CF_TEXT or CF_BITMAP, or it can be a private clipboard format ID. *tymed* identifies the type of storage medium and can be any one of the values listed in the following table. Most OLE clipboard data transfers still use old-fashioned global memory blocks, but as you can plainly see, FORMATETC supports other media types as well.

IDataObject STORAGE MEDIA TYPES

tymed *Flag*	*Storage Medium Type*
TYMED_HGLOBAL	Global memory block
TYMED_FILE	File
TYMED_ISTREAM	Stream object (implements interface *IStream*)
TYMED_ISTORAGE	Storage object (implements interface *IStorage*)
TYMED_GDI	GDI bitmap
TYMED_MFPICT	Metafile picture
TYMED_ENHMF	GDI enhanced metafile

FORMATETC identifies the storage medium type, but the STGMEDIUM structure identifies the storage medium itself. For example, if data is stored in a global memory block, the STGMEDIUM structure holds an HGLOBAL. If the data lives in a file instead, the STGMEDIUM holds a pointer to a character string that specifies the file name. STGMEDIUM holds other information as well. Here's how the structure is defined:

```
typedef struct tagSTGMEDIUM {
    DWORD tymed;
    union {
        HBITMAP hBitmap;              // TYMED_GDI
        HMETAFILEPICT hMetaFilePict;  // TYMED_MFPICT
```

```
        HENHMETAFILE hEnhMetaFile;      // TYMED_ENHMF
        HGLOBAL hGlobal;                // TYMED_HGLOBAL
        LPOLESTR lpszFileName;          // TYMED_FILE
        IStream *pstm;                  // TYMED_STREAM
        IStorage *pstg;                 // TYMED_STORAGE
    };
    IUnknown *pUnkForRelease;
} STGMEDIUM;
```

Here *tymed* holds a TYMED value that identifies the storage medium type, just as FORMATETC's *tymed* field does. *hBitmap*, *hMetaFilePict*, and other members of the embedded union identify the actual storage. Finally, *pUnkForRelease* holds a pointer to the COM interface whose *Release* method releases the storage medium. When an application retrieves an item from the OLE clipboard with *IDataObject::GetData*, that application is responsible for releasing the storage medium when it's no longer needed. For a memory block, "release" means to free the block; for a file, it means to delete the file. COM provides an API function named *::ReleaseStgMedium* that an application can call to release a storage medium. If you simply set *pUnkForRelease* to NULL when you initialize a STGMEDIUM, *::ReleaseStgMedium* will free the storage medium using logic that is appropriate for the storage medium type.

There's much more that could be written about these data structures, but the description offered here should be enough to enable you to understand the examples in the previous section. The first example initialized a FORMATETC structure to describe an ANSI text string (*cfFormat*=CF_TEXT) stored in a global memory block (*tymed*=TYMED_HGLOBAL). It also wrapped the memory block with a STGMEDIUM (*hGlobal*=*hData* and *tymed*=TYMED_HGLOBAL). Both structures were passed by address to *IDataObject::SetData*.

In the second example, a FORMATETC structure was initialized with the same parameters and the STGMEDIUM structure was left uninitialized. Both were passed to *IDataObject::GetData* to retrieve the text string. In this case, the parameters in the FORMATETC structure told the data object what kind of data and what type of storage medium the caller wanted. On return from *IDataObject::GetData*, the STGMEDIUM structure held the HGLOBAL through which the data could be accessed.

By now, you're probably beginning to understand why programming the OLE clipboard is more involved than programming the legacy clipboard. You haven't seen the half of it yet, however, because I haven't shown the code for the data object. Remember, a data object is a COM object that implements the *IDataObject* interface. *IDataObject* is part of a COM-based data transfer protocol that Microsoft has christened Uniform Data Transfer, or UDT. I mentioned earlier that *GetData* and *SetData* are just two of the *IDataObject* methods you must wrestle with. The table on the following page contains a complete list.

IDATAOBJECT **METHODS**

Method	Description
GetData	Retrieves data from the data object (object provides the storage medium)
GetDataHere	Retrieves data from the data object (caller provides the storage medium)
QueryGetData	Determines whether data is available in a particular format
GetCanonicalFormatEtc	Creates a different but logically equivalent FORMATETC
SetData	Provides data to the data object
EnumFormatEtc	Used to enumerate available data formats
DAdvise	Establishes an advisory connection to the data object
DUnadvise	Terminates an advisory connection
EnumDAdvise	Enumerates existing advisory connections

You don't have to implement all these methods to perform a simple clipboard data transfer (some methods can simply return the special COM error code E_NOTIMPL), but implementing *IDataObject* is still a nontrivial task. Copying a simple text string to the legacy clipboard requires just a few lines of code. Copying the same text string to the OLE clipboard can require several hundred lines, primarily because of the added overhead of implementing a full-blown COM data object.

If having to write hundreds of lines of code to copy a string to the clipboard seems silly, take heart. MFC greatly simplifies matters by providing the data object for you and by wrapping it in friendly C++ classes that hide the FORMATETC structures and the STGMEDIUM structures and other low-level nuts and bolts of the *IDataObject* interface. Generally speaking, using the OLE clipboard in an MFC application is no more difficult than using the legacy clipboard, particularly when you use global memory as the storage medium. And you retain the option of using files and other storage media as alternatives to global memory. All things considered, MFC's abstraction of the OLE clipboard is a big win for programmers. Let's see if you agree.

MFC, Global Memory, and the OLE Clipboard

MFC's OLE clipboard support is concentrated in two classes. The first, *COleDataSource*, models the provider side of clipboard operations. The second, *COleDataObject*, models the consumer side. In other words, you use *COleDataSource* to place data on the OLE clipboard and *COleDataObject* to retrieve it. Not surprisingly, *COleDataSource* contains a generic implementation of COM's *IDataObject* interface. You can see this implementation for yourself in the MFC source code file Oledobj2.cpp. If you're not familiar with the manner in which MFC classes implement COM interfaces, you might want to review Chapter 18 before reading the source code.

Placing an item that's stored in global memory on the OLE clipboard is easy when you let *COleDataSource* do the dirty work. Here are the steps:

1. Create a *COleDataSource* object on the heap (not on the stack).

2. Call *COleDataSource::CacheGlobalData* to hand the HGLOBAL to the *COleDataSource* object.

3. Place the object on the OLE clipboard by calling *COleDataSource::Set-Clipboard*.

The following example uses *COleDataSource* to make an ANSI text string available through the OLE clipboard:

```
char szText[] = "Hello, world"; // ANSI characters
HANDLE hData = ::GlobalAlloc (GMEM_MOVEABLE, ::lstrlen (szText) + 1);
LPSTR pData = (LPSTR) ::GlobalLock (hData);
::lstrcpy (pData, szText);
::GlobalUnlock (hData);

COleDataSource* pods = new COleDataSource;
pods->CacheGlobalData (CF_TEXT, hData);
pods->SetClipboard ();
```

Notice that the *COleDataSource* object is created on the heap, not on the stack. That fact is important because the object must remain in memory until a call to *IUnknown-::Release* drops the data object's reference count to 0, at which time the object self-deletes. If you were to create the *COleDataSource* on the stack, the object would be deleted the moment it went out of scope.

MFC's *COleDataObject* provides a handy mechanism for retrieving items from the OLE clipboard. Here's the procedure for retrieving an item stored in global memory:

1. Create a *COleDataObject* object.

2. Call *COleDataObject::AttachClipboard* to connect the *COleDataObject* to the OLE clipboard.

3. Use *COleDataObject::GetGlobalData* to retrieve the item.

4. Free the global memory block returned by *GetGlobalData*.

And here's how the text string placed on the OLE clipboard in the previous example is retrieved using *COleDataObject*:

```
char szText[BUFLEN];
COleDataObject odo;
```

(continued)

```
odo.AttachClipboard ();
HANDLE hData = odo.GetGlobalData (CF_TEXT);

if (hData != NULL) {
    LPCSTR pData = (LPCSTR) ::GlobalLock (hData);
    if (::lstrlen (pData) < BUFLEN)
        ::lstrcpy (szText, pData);
    ::GlobalUnlock (hData);
    ::GlobalFree (hData);
}
```

The *AttachClipboard* function creates a logical connection between a *COleDataObject* and the OLE clipboard. Once the connection is made, MFC transforms calls to *Get-GlobalData* and other *COleDataObject* data retrieval functions into *GetData* calls through the *IDataObject* pointer returned by *::OleGetClipboard*. Don't forget that it's your responsibility to free the global memory block returned by *GetGlobalData*. That requirement explains the call to *::GlobalFree* in the preceding example.

Using Alternative Storage Media

All the examples presented so far in this chapter have used global memory as the transfer medium. But remember that the OLE clipboard supports other media types, too. *COleDataSource::CacheGlobalData* and *COleDataObject::GetGlobalData* are hardwired to use global memory blocks. You can use the more generic *COleData-Source::CacheData* and *COleDataObject::GetData* functions to transfer data in other types of storage media.

The next example demonstrates how to transfer a text string through the OLE clipboard using a file as the transfer medium. The string is first copied into a temporary file. Then FORMATETC and STGMEDIUM structures are initialized with information describing the file and the data that it contains. Finally, the information is passed to *COleDataSource::CacheData*, and the data object is placed on the OLE clipboard with *COleDataSource::SetClipboard*:

```
char szText[] = "Hello, world";
TCHAR szPath[MAX_PATH], szFileName[MAX_PATH];
::GetTempPath (sizeof (szPath) / sizeof (TCHAR), szPath);
::GetTempFileName (szPath, _T ("tmp"), 0, szFileName);

CFile file;
if (file.Open (szFileName, CFile::modeCreate | CFile::modeWrite)) {
    file.Write (szText, ::lstrlen (szText) + 1);
    file.Close ();

    LPWSTR pwszFileName =
        (LPWSTR) ::CoTaskMemAlloc (MAX_PATH * sizeof (WCHAR));
```

```
#ifdef UNICODE
    ::lstrcpy (pwszFileName, szFileName);
#else
    ::MultiByteToWideChar (CP_ACP, MB_PRECOMPOSED, szFileName, -1,
        pwszFileName, MAX_PATH);
#endif

    FORMATETC fe = {
        CF_TEXT, NULL, DVASPECT_CONTENT, -1, TYMED_FILE
    };

    STGMEDIUM stgm;
    stgm.tymed = TYMED_FILE;
    stgm.lpszFileName = pwszFileName;
    stgm.pUnkForRelease = NULL;

    COleDataSource* pods = new COleDataSource;
    pods->CacheData (CF_TEXT, &stgm, &fe);
    pods->SetClipboard ();
}
```

The file name whose address is copied to the STGMEDIUM structure prior to calling *CacheData* must be composed of Unicode characters. This is always true, even in Windows 98. You must also allocate the file name buffer using the COM function *::CoTaskMemAlloc*. Among other things, this ensures that the buffer is properly freed when *::ReleaseStgMedium* calls *::CoTaskMemFree* on the buffer pointer.

On the consumer side, you can use *COleDataObject::GetData* to retrieve the string from the clipboard:

```
char szText[BUFLEN];
STGMEDIUM stgm;

FORMATETC fe = {
    CF_TEXT, NULL, DVASPECT_CONTENT, -1, TYMED_FILE
};

COleDataObject odo;
odo.AttachClipboard ();

if (odo.GetData (CF_TEXT, &stgm, &fe) && stgm.tymed == TYMED_FILE) {
    TCHAR szFileName[MAX_PATH];

#ifdef UNICODE
    ::lstrcpy (szFileName, stgm.lpszFileName);
#else
```

(continued)

```
    ::WideCharToMultiByte (CP_ACP, 0, stgm.lpszFileName,
        -1, szFileName, sizeof (szFileName) / sizeof (TCHAR), NULL, NULL);
#endif

    CFile file;
    if (file.Open (szFileName, CFile::modeRead)) {
        DWORD dwSize = file.GetLength ();
        if (dwSize < BUFLEN)
            file.Read (szText, (UINT) dwSize);
        file.Close ();
    }
    ::ReleaseStgMedium (&stgm);
}
```

When you retrieve data with *COleDataObject::GetData*, you are responsible for freeing the storage medium, which is why *::ReleaseStgMedium* is called in the final statement of this example.

Of course, transferring small text strings through files rather than global memory blocks doesn't make much sense. If the item being transferred is a large bitmap, however, such a transfer might make a lot of sense—especially if the bitmap is already stored on disk somewhere. I used text strings in this section's examples to make the code as simple and uncluttered as possible, but the principle represented here applies to data of all types.

Treating the OLE Clipboard as a *CFile*

MFC's *COleDataObject::GetFileData* function provides a handy abstraction of the OLE clipboard that enables data stored in any of the following storage media to be retrieved as if the clipboard were an ordinary *CFile*:

- TYMED_HGLOBAL
- TYMED_FILE
- TYMED_MFPICT
- TYMED_ISTREAM

If successful, *GetFileData* returns a pointer to a *CFile* object that wraps the item retrieved from the clipboard. You can call *CFile::Read* through that pointer to read the data out.

The following example demonstrates how to use *GetFileData* to retrieve a string from the OLE clipboard:

```
char szText[BUFLEN];
COleDataObject odo;
odo.AttachClipboard ();
```

```
CFile* pFile = odo.GetFileData (CF_TEXT);

if (pFile != NULL) {
    DWORD dwSize = pFile->GetLength ();
    if (dwSize < BUFLEN)
        pFile->Read (szText, (UINT) dwSize);
    delete pFile; // Don't forget this!
}
```

Again, notice that you are responsible for deleting the *CFile* object whose address is returned by *GetFileData*. If you forget to delete it, you'll suffer memory leaks.

The code above is the functional equivalent of the *GetData* example presented in the previous section, but with two added benefits. One, it's simpler. Two, it works whether data is stored in a global memory block, a file, or a stream. In other words, one size fits all. To get the same results with *GetData*, you'd have to do something like this:

```
char szText[BUFLEN];
STGMEDIUM stgm;

COleDataObject odo;
odo.AttachClipboard ();

FORMATETC fe = {
    CF_TEXT, NULL, DVASPECT_CONTENT, -1,
    TYMED_FILE | TYMED_HGLOBAL | TYMED_ISTREAM
};

if (odo.GetData (CF_TEXT, &stgm, &fe)) {
    switch (stgm.tymed) {

    case TYMED_FILE:
        // Read the string from a file.
            .
            .
            .
        break;

    case TYMED_HGLOBAL:
        // Read the string from a global memory block.
            .
            .
            .
        break;

    case TYMED_ISTREAM:
        // Read the string from a stream object.
            .
            .
            .
```

(continued)

```
        break;
    }
    ::ReleaseStgMedium (&stgm);
}
```

Notice the use of multiple TYMED flags in the FORMATETC structure passed to *GetData*. TYMED flags can be OR'd together in this manner to inform a data object that the caller will accept data in a variety of different storage media.

Multiple Formats and Multiple Storage Media

A data provider can call *CacheData* or *CacheGlobalData* as many times as necessary to make data available to data consumers in a variety of formats. The following code offers an item in two formats: a private format registered with *::RegisterClipboard-Format* (*nFormat*) and a CF_TEXT format:

```
COleDataSource* pods = new COleDataSource;
pods->CacheGlobalData (nFormat, hPrivateData);
pods->CacheGlobalData (CF_TEXT, hTextData);
pods->SetClipboard ();
```

You can also make multiple data items available in the same format but in different storage media. Suppose you want to make CF_TEXT data available in either a global memory block or a file. Assuming that *pwszFileName* has already been initialized to point to a file name (expressed in Unicode characters), here's how you go about it:

```
FORMATETC fe = {
    CF_TEXT, NULL, DVASPECT_CONTENT, -1, TYMED_FILE
};

STGMEDIUM stgm;
stgm.tymed = TYMED_FILE;
stgm.lpszFileName = pwszFileName;
stgm.pUnkForRelease = NULL;

COleDataSource* pods = new COleDataSource;
pods->CacheGlobalData (CF_TEXT, hTextData);    // TYMED_HGLOBAL
pods->CacheData (CF_TEXT, &stgm, &fe);         // TYMED_FILE
pods->SetClipboard ();
```

Calling *CacheData* and *CacheGlobalData* more than once and then placing the data object on the clipboard is analogous to calling *::SetClipboardData* multiple times to place two or more formats on the legacy clipboard. However, the legacy clipboard won't accept two items that are of the same format. The OLE clipboard will—as long as each FORMATETC structure has a unique *tymed* value, which is another way of saying that the items are stored in different types of storage media.

Checking Data Availability

The API function *::IsClipboardFormatAvailable* allows users of the legacy clipboard to find out whether data is available in a certain format. *COleDataObject::IsData-Available* lets OLE clipboard users do the same. The following code fragment checks to see whether CF_TEXT data is available in an HGLOBAL:

```
COleDataObject odo;
odo.AttachClipboard ();
if (odo.IsDataAvailable (CF_TEXT)) {
    // CF_TEXT is available in an HGLOBAL.
}
else {
    // CF_TEXT is not available in an HGLOBAL.
}
```

To check for storage media types other than global memory, you simply initialize a FORMATETC structure and pass its address to *IsDataAvailable*, as shown here:

```
COleDataObject odo;
odo.AttachClipboard ();

FORMATETC fe = {
    CF_TEXT, NULL, DVASPECT_CONTENT, -1, TYMED_ISTREAM
};

if (odo.IsDataAvailable (CF_TEXT, &fe)) {
    // CF_TEXT is available in a stream object.
}
else {
    // CF_TEXT is not available in a stream object.
}
```

If you want to, you can OR several TYMED flags into the *tymed* field of the FORMATETC structure passed to *IsDataAvailable*. The return value will be nonzero if data is available in any of the requested storage media.

> **NOTE** As a result of a bug in MFC 6.0, *COleDataObject::IsDataAvailable* sometimes returns a nonzero value if the requested data is available in *any* storage medium. In effect, the media type information passed to *IsDataAvailable* in a FORMATETC structure is ignored. Significantly, the bug manifests itself only if *IsDataAvailable* is called on a *COleDataObject* that's attached to the OLE clipboard, and it affects some data types (notably CF_TEXT data) more than others. *IsDataAvailable* works as advertised when *COleDataObject* is used to implement an OLE drop target.

Data consumers can use the *COleDataObject* functions *BeginEnumFormats* and *GetNextFormat* to enumerate the various formats available. The following code fragment enumerates all the formats available on the OLE clipboard:

```
COleDataObject odo;
odo.AttachClipboard ();

FORMATETC fe;
odo.BeginEnumFormats ();
while (odo.GetNextFormat (&fe)) {
    // FORMATETC structure describes the next available format.
}
```

If a particular data format is available in two or more types of storage media, *GetNextFormat* is supposed to either initialize the FORMATETC structure's *tymed* field with bit flags identifying each storage medium type or return a unique FORMATETC structure for each *tymed*. However, an interesting (and potentially aggravating) anomaly can occur. If the OLE clipboard contains two data items with identical *cfFormat*s but different *tymed*s, *GetNextFormat* will return information for only one of them. This appears to be a bug in the system-supplied clipboard data object whose *IDataObject* pointer is returned by *::OleGetClipboard*. If you need to know what media types a given clipboard format is available in, use *IsDataAvailable* to query for individual combinations of clipboard formats and storage media.

Delayed Rendering with *COleDataSource*

Does the OLE clipboard support delayed rendering? The short answer is yes, although in truth, MFC's implementation of *COleDataSource*, not the OLE clipboard, makes delayed rendering work. A glimpse under the hood of *COleDataSource* explains why.

A *COleDataSource* object is first and foremost a data cache. Internally, it maintains an array of FORMATETC and STGMEDIUM structures that describe the data that is currently available. When an application calls *CacheData* or *CacheGlobalData*, a STGMEDIUM structure with a *tymed* value that describes the storage medium type is added to the array. If an application calls *DelayRenderData* instead, a STGMEDIUM structure that contains a NULL *tymed* value is added to the array. When asked to retrieve that data, the *COleDataSource* sees the NULL *tymed* value and knows that the data was promised via delayed rendering. *COleDataSource* responds by calling a virtual function named *OnRenderData*. Your job is to override this function in a derived class so that you can provide the data on request.

Here's an example that demonstrates how to place a bitmap on the OLE clipboard using delayed rendering. The first step is to make a copy of the bitmap and store it in a file. (You could store it in memory, but that might defeat the purpose of using delayed rendering in the first place.) The second step is to call *DelayRenderData*:

```
FORMATETC fe = {
    CF_BITMAP, NULL, DVASPECT_CONTENT, -1, TYMED_GDI
};

CMyDataSource* pmds = new CMyDataSource;
pmds->DelayRenderData (CF_BITMAP, &fe);
pmds->SetClipboard ();
```

CMyDataSource is a *COleDataSource* derivative. Here's the *OnRenderData* function that renders the bitmap to a TYMED_GDI storage medium when the data source is asked to hand over the bitmap:

```
BOOL CMyDataSource::OnRenderData (LPFORMATETC lpFormatEtc,
    LPSTGMEDIUM lpStgMedium)
{
    if (COleDataSource::OnRenderData (lpFormatEtc, lpStgMedium))
        return TRUE;

    if (lpFormatEtc->cfFormat == CF_BITMAP &&
        lpFormatEtc->tymed & TYMED_GDI) {

        // Re-create the bitmap from the file, and store the
        // handle in hBitmap.
            :
            :

        lpFormatEtc->cfFormat = CF_BITMAP;
        lpFormatEtc->ptd = NULL;
        lpFormatEtc->dwAspect = DVASPECT_CONTENT;
        lpFormatEtc->lindex = -1;
        lpFormatEtc->tymed = TYMED_GDI;

        lpStgMedium->tymed = TYMED_GDI;
        lpStgMedium->hBitmap = hBitmap;
        lpStgMedium->pUnkForRelease = NULL;

        CacheData (CF_BITMAP, lpStgMedium, lpFormatEtc);
        return TRUE;
    }
    return FALSE;
}
```

Other than the fact that you have to derive a class and override *OnRenderData*, delayed rendering with a *COleDataSource* isn't much different from immediate rendering.

Other *COleDataSource* functions can sometimes simplify the delayed rendering code that you write. For example, if you intend to render data only to HGLOBAL storage media, you can override *OnRenderGlobalData* instead of *OnRenderData*. You can use a separate set of *COleDataSource* functions named *DelayRenderFileData* and *OnRenderFileData* functions to delay-render data using *CFile* output functions.

One detail to be aware of when you use *COleDataSource* delayed rendering is that if the storage type is TYMED_HGLOBAL, TYMED_FILE, TYMED_ISTREAM, or TYMED_ISTORAGE, the storage medium might be allocated before *OnRenderData* is called. If the storage medium is preallocated, *OnRenderData* must render the data into the existing storage medium rather than create a new storage medium itself. The *tymed* value in the STGMEDIUM structure whose address is passed to *OnRenderData* tells the tale. If *lpStgMedium->tymed* is TYMED_NULL, *OnRenderData* is responsible for allocating the storage medium. If *lpStgMedium->tymed* holds any other value, the caller has supplied the storage medium and *lpStgMedium->tymed* identifies the storage type. The following code sample demonstrates proper handling of *OnRenderData* for media types that are subject to preallocation:

```
BOOL CMyDataSource::OnRenderData (LPFORMATETC lpFormatEtc,
    LPSTGMEDIUM lpStgMedium)
{
    if (COleDataSource::OnRenderData (lpFormatEtc, lpStgMedium))
        return TRUE;

    if (lpStgMedium->tymed == TYMED_NULL) { // Medium is not preallocated.
        if (lpFormatEtc->tymed & TYMED_HGLOBAL) {
            // Allocate a global memory block, render the data
            // into it, and then copy the handle to lpStgMedium->hGlobal.
        }
    }
    else { // Medium is preallocated.
        if (lpStgMedium->tymed == TYMED_HGLOBAL) {
            // Render the data into the global memory block whose
            // handle is stored in lpStgMedium->hGlobal.
        }
    }
}
```

This example addresses only the case in which the storage medium is an HGLOBAL, but the principle should be clear nonetheless.

The most common reason for using *COleDataSource*'s brand of delayed rendering is to provide data in a variety of storage media without having to allocate each and every storage medium up front. If you're willing to provide, say, CF_TEXT data in several different media, you can call *DelayRenderData* and pass in a FORMATETC structure whose *tymed* field contains bit flags representing each of the media types that you support. Then you can render the data in any medium that the data consumer requests by inspecting the *tymed* field of the FORMATETC structure passed to *OnRenderData*. If the consumer asks for the data in a medium that you don't support, you can simply fail the call to *OnRenderData* by returning FALSE.

COleDataSource and *COleDataObject* in Review

You now know how to use MFC's *COleDataSource* and *COleDataObject* classes to interact with the OLE clipboard. Just to put things in perspective (and to reinforce what you've already learned), the following tables provide a brief summary of the most useful *COleDataSource* and *COleDataObject* member functions. These classes have other functions as well, but those listed here are the ones that you're most likely to need.

KEY *COLEDATASOURCE* MEMBER FUNCTIONS

Function	Description
SetClipboard	Places the *COleDataSource* on the OLE clipboard
CacheData	Provides data to the *COleDataSource*
CacheGlobalData	Provides data stored in global memory to the *COleDataSource*
DelayRenderData	Offers data for delayed rendering
DelayRenderFileData	Offers data for delayed rendering using *CFile* output functions
OnRenderData	Called to render data to an arbitrary storage medium
OnRenderFileData	Called to render data to a *CFile*
OnRenderGlobalData	Called to render data to an HGLOBAL

KEY *COLEDATAOBJECT* MEMBER FUNCTIONS

Function	Description
AttachClipboard	Attaches the *COleDataObject* to the OLE clipboard
GetData	Retrieves data from the data object to which the *COleDataObject* is attached
GetFileData	Retrieves data using *CFile* functions
GetGlobalData	Retrieves data in an HGLOBAL
IsDataAvailable	Determines whether data is available in a particular format and storage medium
BeginEnumFormats	Begins the process of enumerating available data formats
GetNextFormat	Fills a FORMATETC structure with information describing the next available data format

Earlier, I said that the primary reason to use the OLE clipboard is to gain the ability to use storage media other than global memory. That's true, but there's another reason, too. Thanks to the abstractions offered by *COleDataSource* and *COleData-Object*, once you write MFC code to utilize the OLE clipboard, you only have to do a little more work to add support for an even more convenient form of data transfer: OLE drag-and-drop. OLE drag-and-drop lets the user transfer data by grabbing it with the mouse and dragging it. Writing OLE drag-and-drop code without a class library to help out isn't any fun, but MFC makes the process as hassle-free as possible.

OLE DRAG-AND-DROP

If you've never seen OLE drag-and-drop in action, you can perform a simple demonstration using the source code editor in Visual C++. Begin by opening a source code file and highlighting a line of text. Grab the highlighted text with the left mouse button, and with the button held down, drag it down a few lines. Then release the mouse button. The text will disappear from its original location and appear where you dropped it, just as if you had performed a cut-and-paste operation. Repeat the operation with the Ctrl key held down, and the text will be copied rather than moved. That's OLE drag-and-drop. You used it to transfer text from one part of a document to another, but it works just as well if the destination is a different document or even a different application. And just as with the OLE clipboard, you can use OLE drag-and-drop to transfer any kind of data—not just text.

Programmatically, OLE drag-and-drop is very similar to the OLE clipboard. The data provider, or *drop source,* creates a data object that encapsulates the data and makes an *IDataObject* pointer available. The data consumer, or *drop target,* retrieves the *IDataObject* pointer and uses it to extract data from the data object.

One difference between OLE drag-and-drop and the OLE clipboard is how the *IDataObject* pointer changes hands. The OLE clipboard uses *::OleSetClipboard* and *::OleGetClipboard* to transfer the pointer from sender to receiver. In OLE drag-and-drop, the drop source initiates a drag-and-drop operation by passing an *IDataObject* pointer to *::DoDragDrop*. On the other end, any window interested in being a drop target registers itself with the system by calling the API function *::RegisterDragDrop*. If a drop occurs over a window that's registered in this way, the drop target is handed the *IDataObject* pointer passed to *::DoDragDrop*.

If that's all there was to it, OLE drag-and-drop wouldn't be difficult at all. What complicates matters is that OLE drag-and-drop requires three COM objects instead of just one:

- A data object that implements *IDataObject*
- A drop source object that implements *IDropSource*
- A drop target object that implements *IDropTarget*

The data object is identical to the one used for OLE clipboard transfers. The drop source and drop target objects are new. Figure 19-2 shows a schematic representation

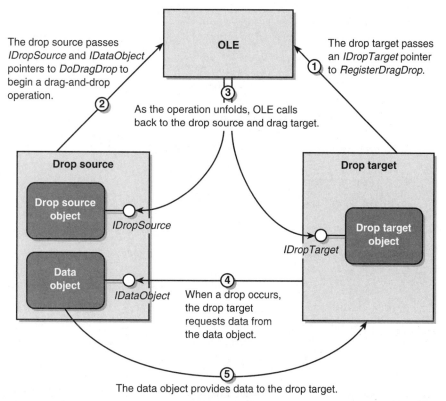

Figure 19-2. *Participants in an OLE drag-and-drop operation.*

of the participants in a drag-and-drop data transfer. On the sending end of the transaction is an application that implements two COM objects: a data object and a drop source object. (There's nothing to prevent one object from supporting both interfaces, but in practice, the objects are usually implemented separately.) On the receiving end is an application that implements a drop target object. Neither the drop source nor the drop target receives an *IDropSource* or *IDropTarget* pointer that references the other. Instead, the system acts as an intermediary and calls methods on both interfaces at the appropriate times.

Anatomy of a Drop Source

An OLE drag-and-drop operation begins when an application calls *::DoDragDrop* and passes in four key pieces of information:

- An *IDataObject* pointer
- An *IDropSource* pointer

- An input value containing one or more DROPEFFECT codes specifying what types of operations are allowed on the data (for example, move, copy, or both move and copy)

- A pointer to a DWORD that receives a DROPEFFECT code specifying what happened on the other end (for example, did a drop occur, and if it did, was the data moved or copied?)

::DoDragDrop returns when either of two conditions is met:

- A drop occurs.
- The operation is canceled.

The action that cancels a drag-and-drop operation varies from application to application and is ultimately determined by the drop source. In most cases, the stimulus is a press of the Esc key. If the operation is canceled or the drop target rejects the drop, *::DoDragDrop* copies the value DROPEFFECT_NONE to the address in the fourth parameter. If the drop is successful, *::DoDragDrop* copies one of the DROPEFFECT codes passed in the third parameter to the address in the fourth parameter so that the drop source will know precisely what occurred.

Assume that *pdo* and *pds* hold *IDataObject* and *IDropSource* pointers, respectively. The following statements initiate a drag-and-drop operation in which the data encapsulated in the data object can be either moved or copied:

```
DWORD dwEffect;
HRESULT hr = ::DoDragDrop (pdo, pds,
    DROPEFFECT_MOVE | DROPEFFECT_COPY, &dwEffect);
```

When *::DoDragDrop* returns, *dwEffect* tells the drop source what transpired on the other end. If *dwEffect* equals DROPEFFECT_NONE or DROPEFFECT_COPY, the drop source doesn't need to do anything more. If *dwEffect* equals DROPEFFECT_MOVE, however, the drop source must delete the data from the source document:

```
if (SUCCEEDED (hr) && dwEffect == DROPEFFECT_MOVE) {
    // Delete the original data from the document.
}
```

The code that deletes the data isn't shown because, obviously, it's application-specific.

Calls to *::DoDragDrop* are synchronous; that is, *::DoDragDrop* doesn't return until the operation has been completed or canceled. However, as a drag-and-drop operation is being performed, the system communicates with the drop source through the *IDropSource* pointer provided to *::DoDragDrop*. *IDropSource* is a simple interface that contains just two methods besides the *IUnknown* methods common to all COM interfaces:

IDROPSOURCE METHODS

Method	*Description*
GiveFeedback	Called each time the cursor moves or a key state changes to allow the drop source to update the cursor
QueryContinueDrag	Called when a key state or mouse button state changes to allow the drop source to specify whether to continue the operation, cancel it, or execute a drop

Whenever a change occurs in the state of a key or mouse button that might be of interest to the drop source, the drop source object's *QueryContinueDrag* method is called. *QueryContinueDrag* receives two parameters: a BOOL indicating whether the Esc key has been pressed and a DWORD containing flags that reflect the current state of the mouse buttons as well as the Ctrl, Alt, and Shift keys. Using this information, *QueryContinueDrag* must return one of three values telling the system what to do next:

Return Value	*Description*
S_OK	Continue the drag-and-drop operation
DRAGDROP_S_DROP	End the operation by executing a drop
DRAGDROP_S_CANCEL	Cancel the drag-and-drop operation

Typical responses are to cancel the operation if the Esc key has been pressed, to execute a drop if the left mouse button has been released, or to allow the operation to continue if neither of the first two conditions is true. The following *QueryContinueDrag* implementation embodies this logic:

```
HRESULT __stdcall CDropSource::QueryContinueDrag (BOOL fEscape,
    DWORD grfKeyState)
{
    if (fEscape)
        return DRAGDROP_S_CANCEL;     // Esc key was pressed.
    if (!(grfKeyState & MK_LBUTTON))
        return DRAGDROP_S_DROP;       // Left mouse button was released.
    return S_OK;                      // Let the operation continue.
}
```

This code assumes that the drag-and-drop operation began when the left mouse button was depressed. If you're implementing right-button drag instead, check the right mouse button (MK_RBUTTON) to determine whether to execute the drop. If you prefer to use a key other than Esc to cancel the operation, you can call *::GetAsyncKeyState* to read the key's state and use that value rather than *fEscape* to decide whether to return DRAGDROP_S_CANCEL.

As a drag-and-drop operation unfolds, the drop source receives a flurry of calls to its *IDropSource::GiveFeedback* method. *GiveFeedback* receives one function parameter: a DROPEFFECT code that tells the drop source what would happen if a drop were to occur right now. (As you'll see in the next section, this information comes from the drop target because ultimately it's the drop target that controls what happens on the other end.) *GiveFeedback*'s job is to inspect this parameter and update the cursor to provide visual feedback to the user. When you see the cursor change shape as it moves from window to window during a drag-and-drop data transfer or when you see a little plus sign appear next to the cursor when the Ctrl key is pressed, what you're actually seeing is the drop source's response to *IDropSource::GiveFeedback*.

If you want to, you can create your own cursors and display them each time *GiveFeedback* is called; however, the system provides several predefined cursors for just this purpose. To use them, simply return DRAGDROP_S_USEDEFAULTCURSORS from your *GiveFeedback* implementation. Rather than do this:

```
HRESULT __stdcall CDropSource::GiveFeedback (DWORD dwEffect)
{
    HCURSOR hCursor;
    switch (dwEffect) {
        // Inspect dwEffect, and load a cursor handle in hCursor.
    }
    ::SetCursor (hCursor);
    return S_OK;
}
```

you can do this:

```
HRESULT __stdcall CDropSource::GiveFeedback (DWORD dwEffect)
{
    return DRAGDROP_S_USEDEFAULTCURSORS;
}
```

That's all there is to most implementations of *IDropSource::GiveFeedback*. You can do more if you'd like, but you might as well use the default cursors unless you have compelling reasons to do otherwise.

Anatomy of a Drop Target

A window becomes an OLE drop target when an application calls *::RegisterDragDrop* and passes in the window's handle and a pointer to an *IDropTarget* interface:

```
::RegisterDragDrop (hWnd, pdt);
```

You unregister a drop target by calling *::RevokeDragDrop*. Although the system will clean up after you if you fail to call this function before a drop target window is destroyed, calling it yourself is good form.

When the cursor enters, leaves, or moves over a drop target window during a drag-and-drop operation, the system apprises the drop target of that fact by calling *IDropTarget* methods through the *IDropTarget* pointer provided to *::RegisterDragDrop*. *IDropTarget* has just the four methods listed in the following table.

IDropTarget METHODS

Method	*Description*
DragEnter	Called when the cursor enters the drop target window
DragOver	Called as the cursor moves over the drop target window
DragLeave	Called when the cursor leaves the drop target window or if the operation is canceled while the cursor is over the window
Drop	Called when a drop occurs

Both *DragEnter* and *DragOver* receive a pointer to a DWORD (among other things) in their parameter lists. When either of these methods is called, the drop target must let the drop source know what would happen if a drop were to occur by copying a DROPEFFECT value to the DWORD. The value copied to the DWORD is the value passed to the drop source's *GiveFeedback* method. *DragEnter* and *DragOver* also receive a set of cursor coordinates (in case the outcome of a drop depends on the current cursor position) and flags that specify the status of the Ctrl, Alt, and Shift keys and each of the mouse buttons. In addition, *DragEnter* receives an *IDataObject* pointer that it can use to query the data object. The following implementations of *DragEnter* and *DragOver* return DROPEFFECT_NONE, DROPEFFECT_MOVE, or DROPEFFECT_COPY to the data source depending on whether text is available from the data object and whether the Ctrl key is up (move) or down (copy):

```
HRESULT __stdcall CDropTarget::DragEnter (IDataObject* pDataObject,
    DWORD grfKeyState, POINTL pt, DWORD* pdwEffect)
{
    FORMATETC fe = {
        CF_TEXT, NULL, DVASPECT_CONTENT, -1, TYMED_HGLOBAL
    };

    if (pDataObject->QueryGetData (&fe) == S_OK) {
        m_bCanAcceptData = TRUE;
        *pdwEffect = (grfKeyState & MK_CONTROL) ?
            DROPEFFECT_COPY : DROPEFFECT_MOVE;
    }
    else {
        m_bCanAcceptData = FALSE;
        *pdwEffect = DROPEFFECT_NONE;
    }
    return S_OK;
}
```

(continued)

```
HRESULT __stdcall CDropTarget::DragOver (DWORD grfKeyState,
    POINTL pt, DWORD* pdwEffect)
{
    if (m_bCanAcceptData)
        *pdwEffect = (grfKeyState & MK_CONTROL) ?
            DROPEFFECT_COPY : DROPEFFECT_MOVE;
    else
        *pdwEffect = DROPEFFECT_NONE;
    return S_OK;
}
```

m_bCanAcceptData is a BOOL member variable that keeps a record of whether the data offered by the drop source is in a format that the drop target will accept. When *DragOver* is called, the drop target uses this value to determine whether to indicate that it's willing to accept a drop.

The drop target's *DragLeave* method is called if the cursor leaves the drop target window without executing a drop or if the drag-and-drop operation is canceled while the cursor is over the drop target window. The call to *DragLeave* gives the drop target the opportunity to clean up after itself by freeing any resources allocated in *DragEnter* or *DragOver* if the anticipated drop doesn't occur.

The final *IDropTarget* method, *Drop*, is called if (and only if) a drop occurs. Through its parameter list, *Drop* receives all the information it needs to process the drop, including an *IDataObject* pointer; a DWORD that specifies the state of the Ctrl, Alt, and Shift keys and the mouse buttons; and cursor coordinates. It also receives a DWORD pointer to which it must copy a DROPEFFECT value that informs the data source what happened as a result of the drop. The following *Drop* implementation retrieves a text string from the data object, provided that a text string is available:

```
HRESULT __stdcall CDropTarget::Drop (IDataObject* pDataObject,
    DWORD grfKeyState, POINTL pt, DWORD* pdwEffect)
{
    if (m_bCanAcceptData) {
        FORMATETC fe = {
            CF_TEXT, NULL, DVASPECT_CONTENT, -1, TYMED_HGLOBAL
        };

        STGMEDIUM stgm;

        if (SUCCEEDED (pDataObject->GetData (&fe, &stgm)) &&
            stgm.hGlobal != NULL) {
            // Copy the string from the global memory block.
                :
                :
            ::ReleaseStgMedium (&stgm);
            *pdwEffect = (grfKeyState & MK_CONTROL) ?
                DROPEFFECT_COPY : DROPEFFECT_MOVE;
```

```
            return S_OK;
        }
    }
    // If we make it to here, the drop did not succeed.
    *pdwEffect = DROPEFFECT_NONE;
    return S_OK;
}
```

A call to *Drop* isn't followed by a call to *DragLeave*, so if there's any cleaning up to do after the drop is completed, the *Drop* method should do it.

MFC Support for OLE Drag-and-Drop

Most of the work in writing OLE drag-and-drop code lies in implementing the COM objects. Fortunately, MFC will implement them for you. The same *COleDataSource* class that provides data objects for OLE clipboard operations works with OLE drag-and-drop, too. *COleDropSource* provides a handy implementation of the drop source object, and *COleDropTarget* provides the drop target object. Very often, you don't even have to instantiate *COleDropSource* yourself because *COleDataSource* does it for you. You will have to instantiate *COleDropTarget*, but you usually do that simply by adding a *COleDropTarget* member variable to the application's view class.

Suppose you'd like to transfer a text string using OLE drag-and-drop in an MFC application. Here's how to do it using a global memory block as the storage medium:

```
char szText[] = "Hello, world";
HANDLE hData = ::GlobalAlloc (GMEM_MOVEABLE, ::lstrlen (szText) + 1)
LPSTR pData = (LPSTR) ::GlobalLock (hData);
::lstrcpy (pData, szText);
::GlobalUnlock (hData);

COleDataSource ods;
ods.CacheGlobalData (CF_TEXT, hData);

DROPEFFECT de =
    ods.DoDragDrop (DROPEFFECT_MOVE | DROPEFFECT_COPY)

if (de == DROPEFFECT_MOVE) {
    // Delete the string from the document.
}
```

This code is strikingly similar to the code presented earlier in this chapter that used *COleDataSource* to place a text string on the OLE clipboard. Other than the fact that the *COleDataSource* object is created on the stack rather than on the heap (which is correct because, in this case, the object doesn't need to outlive the function that created it), the only real difference is that *COleDataSource::DoDragDrop* is called instead of *COleDataSource::SetClipboard*. *COleDataSource::DoDragDrop* is a wrapper around the API function of the same name. In addition to calling *::DoDragDrop* for you, it also creates the *COleDropSource* object whose *IDropSource* interface pointer is passed to *::DoDragDrop*.

If you'd rather create your own *COleDropSource* object, you can do so and pass it by address to *COleDataSource::DoDragDrop* in that function's optional third parameter. The only reason to create this object yourself is if you want to derive a class from *COleDropSource* and use it instead of *COleDropSource*. Programmers occasionally derive from *COleDropSource* and override its *GiveFeedback* and *Query-ContinueDrag* member functions to provide custom responses to the *IDropSource* methods of the same names.

MFC makes acting as a target for OLE drag-and-drop data transfers relatively easy, too. The first thing you do is add a *COleDropTarget* data member to the application's view class:

```
// In CMyView's class declaration
COleDropTarget m_oleDropTarget;
```

Then, in the view's *OnCreate* function, you call *COleDropTarget::Register* and pass in a pointer to the view object:

```
m_oleDropTarget.Register (this);
```

Finally, you override the view's *OnDragEnter*, *OnDragOver*, *OnDragLeave*, and *On-Drop* functions or some combination of them. These *CView* functions are coupled to the similarly named *IDropTarget* methods. For example, when the drop target object's *IDropTarget::Drop* method is called, *COleDropTarget::OnDrop* calls your view's *OnDrop* function. To respond to calls to *IDropTarget::Drop*, you simply override *CView::OnDrop*.

Here's an example that demonstrates how to override *OnDragEnter*, *OnDrag-Over*, and *OnDrop* in a *CScrollView*-derived class to make the view a drop target for text. *OnDragLeave* isn't overridden in this example because nothing special needs to be done when it's called. Notice that a preallocated *COleDataObject* is provided in each function's parameter list. This *COleDataObject* wraps the *IDataObject* pointer passed to the drop target's *IDropTarget* methods:

```
DROPEFFECT CMyView::OnDragEnter (COleDataObject* pDataObject,
    DWORD dwKeyState, CPoint point)
{
    CScrollView::OnDragEnter (pDataObject, dwKeyState, point);
    if (!pDataObject->IsDataAvailable (CF_TEXT))
        return DROPEFFECT_NONE;
    return (dwKeyState & MK_CONTROL) ?
        DROPEFFECT_COPY : DROPEFFECT_MOVE;
}
```

```
DROPEFFECT CMyView::OnDragOver (COleDataObject* pDataObject,
    DWORD dwKeyState, CPoint point)
{
    CScrollView::OnDragOver (pDataObject, dwKeyState, point);
    if (!pDataObject->IsDataAvailable (CF_TEXT))
        return DROPEFFECT_NONE;
    return (dwKeyState & MK_CONTROL) ?
        DROPEFFECT_COPY : DROPEFFECT_MOVE;
}

BOOL CMyView::OnDrop (COleDataObject* pDataObject, DROPEFFECT dropEffect,
    CPoint point)
{
    CScrollView::OnDrop (pDataObject, dropEffect, point);
    HANDLE hData = pDataObject->GetGlobalData (CF_TEXT);
    if (hData != NULL) {
        // Copy the string from the global memory block.
            :
            :
        ::GlobalFree (hData);
        return TRUE;     // Drop succeeded.
    }
    return FALSE;        // Drop failed.
}
```

This code looks a lot like the non-MFC version presented in the previous section. *OnDragEnter* and *OnDragOver* call *COleDataObject::IsDataAvailable* through the pointer provided in their parameter lists to determine whether text is available. If the answer is no, both functions return DROPEFFECT_NONE to indicate that they won't accept the drop. The drop source, in turn, will probably display a "no-drop" cursor. If text is available, *OnDragEnter* and *OnDragOver* return either DROPEFFECT_MOVE or DROPEFFECT_COPY, depending on whether the Ctrl key is down. *OnDrop* uses *COleDataObject::GetGlobalData* to retrieve the data when a drop occurs.

Drop Target Scrolling

The examples in the previous section assume that the drop target is a view-based application. You can use *COleDropTarget* to implement drop targeting in applications that don't have views by deriving your own class from *COleDropTarget* and overriding *OnDragEnter*, *OnDragOver*, *OnDragLeave*, and *OnDrop*. However, using a view as a drop target offers one very attractive benefit if the drop target has scroll bars: you get drop target scrolling for free, courtesy of MFC.

What is drop target scrolling? Suppose a drag-and-drop operation has begun and the user wants to drop the data at a location in a *CScrollView* that is currently scrolled out of sight. If the cursor pauses within a few pixels of the view's border, a *CScrollView* will automatically scroll itself for as long as the cursor remains in that vicinity. Thus, the user can move the cursor to the edge of the window and wait until the drop point scrolls into view. This is just one more detail you'd have to handle yourself if MFC didn't do if for you.

PUTTING IT ALL TOGETHER: THE WIDGET APPLICATION

The application shown in Figure 19-3 demonstrates one way to apply the concepts, principles, and code fragments presented in this chapter to the real world. Widget creates triangular "widgets" of various colors in response to commands on the Insert menu. You can transfer widgets to and from the OLE clipboard using the commands on the Edit menu. Before you can use the Cut and Copy commands, you must select a widget by clicking it. The widget will turn green to indicate that it is in a selected state. You can also move and copy widgets using OLE drag-and-drop. If you hold down the Ctrl key when a drop is performed, the widget is copied; otherwise, it's moved. For a graphical demonstration of OLE drag-and-drop in action, run two instances of Widget side by side and drag widgets back and forth between them.

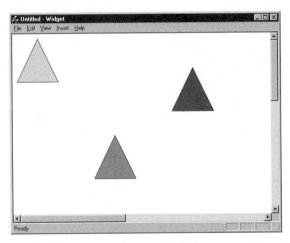

Figure 19-3. *The Widget window.*

Figure 19-4 shows the pertinent parts of Widget's source code. WidgetView.cpp contains most of the good stuff, including the handlers for the Cut, Copy, and Paste commands. It also contains the overridden versions of *OnDragEnter*, *OnDragOver*, *OnDragLeave*, and *OnDrop* as well as the code that initiates a drag-and-drop data transfer when the left mouse button is clicked. (See *OnLButtonDown*.) Widgets are transferred through global memory. Widget registers a private clipboard format for widgets and uses it in calls to *COleDataSource::CacheGlobalData* and *COleData-Object::GetGlobalData*. The ID is stored in the application object and retrieved using *CWidgetApp::GetClipboardFormat*.

Widget.h

```
// Widget.h : main header file for the WIDGET application
//

#if !defined(AFX_WIDGET_H__02909A45_3F5C_11D2_AC89_006008A8274D__INCLUDED_)
#define AFX_WIDGET_H__02909A45_3F5C_11D2_AC89_006008A8274D__INCLUDED_

#if _MSC_VER > 1000
#pragma once
#endif // _MSC_VER > 1000

#ifndef __AFXWIN_H__
    #error include 'stdafx.h' before including this file for PCH
#endif

#include "resource.h"        // main symbols

/////////////////////////////////////////////////////////////////////////////
// CWidgetApp:
// See Widget.cpp for the implementation of this class
//

class CWidgetApp : public CWinApp
{
public:
    UINT GetClipboardFormat ();
    CWidgetApp();

// Overrides
    // ClassWizard generated virtual function overrides
    //{{AFX_VIRTUAL(CWidgetApp)
    public:
    virtual BOOL InitInstance();
    //}}AFX_VIRTUAL

// Implementation
    //{{AFX_MSG(CWidgetApp)
    afx_msg void OnAppAbout();
        // NOTE - the ClassWizard will add and remove member functions here.
        //    DO NOT EDIT what you see in these blocks of generated code !
```

Figure 19-4. *The Widget application.*

(continued)

Figure 19-4. *continued*

```
    //}}AFX_MSG
    DECLARE_MESSAGE_MAP()
protected:
    UINT m_nFormat;
};


/////////////////////////////////////////////////////////////////////////////

//{{AFX_INSERT_LOCATION}}
// Microsoft Visual C++ will insert additional declarations
// immediately before the previous line.

#endif
// !defined(AFX_WIDGET_H__02909A45_3F5C_11D2_AC89_006008A8274D__INCLUDED_)
```

Widget.cpp

```
// Widget.cpp : Defines the class behaviors for the application.
//

#include "stdafx.h"
#include "Widget.h"

#include "MainFrm.h"
#include "WidgetDoc.h"
#include "WidgetView.h"

#ifdef _DEBUG
#define new DEBUG_NEW
#undef THIS_FILE
static char THIS_FILE[] = __FILE__;
#endif


/////////////////////////////////////////////////////////////////////////////
// CWidgetApp

BEGIN_MESSAGE_MAP(CWidgetApp, CWinApp)
    //{{AFX_MSG_MAP(CWidgetApp)
    ON_COMMAND(ID_APP_ABOUT, OnAppAbout)
        // NOTE - the ClassWizard will add and remove mapping macros here.
        //    DO NOT EDIT what you see in these blocks of generated code!
    //}}AFX_MSG_MAP
    // Standard file based document commands
```

```
    ON_COMMAND(ID_FILE_NEW, CWinApp::OnFileNew)
    ON_COMMAND(ID_FILE_OPEN, CWinApp::OnFileOpen)
END_MESSAGE_MAP()

/////////////////////////////////////////////////////////////////////////
// CWidgetApp construction

CWidgetApp::CWidgetApp()
{
    // TODO: add construction code here,
    // Place all significant initialization in InitInstance
}

/////////////////////////////////////////////////////////////////////////
// The one and only CWidgetApp object

CWidgetApp theApp;

/////////////////////////////////////////////////////////////////////////
// CWidgetApp initialization

BOOL CWidgetApp::InitInstance()
{
    if (!AfxOleInit ()) {
        AfxMessageBox (_T ("AfxOleInit failed"));
        return FALSE;
    }

    SetRegistryKey(_T("Local AppWizard-Generated Applications"));
    LoadStdProfileSettings();  // Load standard INI file
                               // options (including MRU)

    // Register the application's document templates.  Document templates
    // serve as the connection between documents, frame windows and views.

    CSingleDocTemplate* pDocTemplate;
    pDocTemplate = new CSingleDocTemplate(
        IDR_MAINFRAME,
        RUNTIME_CLASS(CWidgetDoc),
        RUNTIME_CLASS(CMainFrame),          // main SDI frame window
        RUNTIME_CLASS(CWidgetView));
    AddDocTemplate(pDocTemplate);

    // Enable DDE Execute open
    EnableShellOpen();
    RegisterShellFileTypes(TRUE);
```

(continued)

Figure 19-4. *continued*

```
    // Parse command line for standard shell commands, DDE, file open
    CCommandLineInfo cmdInfo;
    ParseCommandLine(cmdInfo);

    // Dispatch commands specified on the command line
    if (!ProcessShellCommand(cmdInfo))
        return FALSE;

    // The one and only window has been initialized, so show and update it.
    m_pMainWnd->ShowWindow(SW_SHOW);
    m_pMainWnd->UpdateWindow();

    // Enable drag/drop open
    m_pMainWnd->DragAcceptFiles();

    //
    // Register a private clipboard format for widgets.
    //
    m_nFormat = ::RegisterClipboardFormat (_T ("Widget"));
    return TRUE;
}


/////////////////////////////////////////////////////////////////////////
// CAboutDlg dialog used for App About

class CAboutDlg : public CDialog
{
public:
    CAboutDlg();

// Dialog Data
    //{{AFX_DATA(CAboutDlg)
    enum { IDD = IDD_ABOUTBOX };
    //}}AFX_DATA

    // ClassWizard generated virtual function overrides
    //{{AFX_VIRTUAL(CAboutDlg)
    protected:
    virtual void DoDataExchange(CDataExchange* pDX);    // DDX/DDV support
    //}}AFX_VIRTUAL

// Implementation
protected:
    //{{AFX_MSG(CAboutDlg)
        // No message handlers
    //}}AFX_MSG
    DECLARE_MESSAGE_MAP()
};
```

```
CAboutDlg::CAboutDlg() : CDialog(CAboutDlg::IDD)
{
    //{{AFX_DATA_INIT(CAboutDlg)
    //}}AFX_DATA_INIT
}

void CAboutDlg::DoDataExchange(CDataExchange* pDX)
{
    CDialog::DoDataExchange(pDX);
    //{{AFX_DATA_MAP(CAboutDlg)
    //}}AFX_DATA_MAP
}

BEGIN_MESSAGE_MAP(CAboutDlg, CDialog)
    //{{AFX_MSG_MAP(CAboutDlg)
        // No message handlers
    //}}AFX_MSG_MAP
END_MESSAGE_MAP()

// App command to run the dialog
void CWidgetApp::OnAppAbout()
{
    CAboutDlg aboutDlg;
    aboutDlg.DoModal();
}


/////////////////////////////////////////////////////////////////////////////
// CWidgetApp message handlers

UINT CWidgetApp::GetClipboardFormat()
{
    return m_nFormat;
}
```

WidgetDoc.h

```
// WidgetDoc.h : interface of the CWidgetDoc class
//
/////////////////////////////////////////////////////////////////////////////

#if !defined(
    AFX_WIDGETDOC_H__02909A4B_3F5C_11D2_AC89_006008A8274D__INCLUDED_)
#define AFX_WIDGETDOC_H__02909A4B_3F5C_11D2_AC89_006008A8274D__INCLUDED_

#if _MSC_VER > 1000
#pragma once
#endif // _MSC_VER > 1000
```

(continued)

Figure 19-4. *continued*

```cpp
#include "WidgetObj.h"
typedef CTypedPtrArray<CObArray, CWidget*> CWidgetArray;

class CWidgetDoc : public CDocument
{
protected: // create from serialization only
    CWidgetDoc();
    DECLARE_DYNCREATE(CWidgetDoc)

// Attributes
public:

// Operations
public:

// Overrides
    // ClassWizard generated virtual function overrides
    //{{AFX_VIRTUAL(CWidgetDoc)
    public:
    virtual BOOL OnNewDocument();
    virtual void Serialize(CArchive& ar);
    virtual void DeleteContents();
    //}}AFX_VIRTUAL

// Implementation
public:
    BOOL RemoveWidget (int nIndex);
    int AddWidget (int x, int y, COLORREF color);
    CWidget* GetWidget (int nIndex);
    int GetWidgetCount ();
    virtual ~CWidgetDoc();
#ifdef _DEBUG
    virtual void AssertValid() const;
    virtual void Dump(CDumpContext& dc) const;
#endif

protected:
    CWidgetArray m_arrWidgets;

// Generated message map functions
protected:
    //{{AFX_MSG(CWidgetDoc)
    afx_msg void OnInsertRedWidget();
    afx_msg void OnInsertBlueWidget();
    afx_msg void OnInsertYellowWidget();
    //}}AFX_MSG
    DECLARE_MESSAGE_MAP()
};
```

```
//////////////////////////////////////////////////////////////////////////

//{{AFX_INSERT_LOCATION}}
// Microsoft Visual C++ will insert additional declarations
// immediately before the previous line.

#endif
// !defined(
//      AFX_WIDGETDOC_H__02909A4B_3F5C_11D2_AC89_006008A8274D__INCLUDED_)
```

WidgetDoc.cpp

```
CWidgetDoc::~CWidgetDoc()
{
}

BOOL CWidgetDoc::OnNewDocument()
{
    if (!CDocument::OnNewDocument())
        return FALSE;

    return TRUE;
}


//////////////////////////////////////////////////////////////////////////
// CWidgetDoc serialization

void CWidgetDoc::Serialize(CArchive& ar)
{
    m_arrWidgets.Serialize (ar);
}

//////////////////////////////////////////////////////////////////////////
// CWidgetDoc diagnostics

#ifdef _DEBUG
void CWidgetDoc::AssertValid() const
{
    CDocument::AssertValid();
}

void CWidgetDoc::Dump(CDumpContext& dc) const
{
    CDocument::Dump(dc);
}
```

(continued)

Figure 19-4. *continued*

```
#endif //_DEBUG

///////////////////////////////////////////////////////////////////////////
// CWidgetDoc commands

void CWidgetDoc::DeleteContents()
{
    int i = m_arrWidgets.GetSize ();
    while (i)
        delete m_arrWidgets[--i];
    m_arrWidgets.RemoveAll ();
    CDocument::DeleteContents();
}

int CWidgetDoc::GetWidgetCount()
{
    return m_arrWidgets.GetSize ();
}

CWidget* CWidgetDoc::GetWidget(int nIndex)
{
    if (nIndex >= m_arrWidgets.GetSize ())
        return NULL;
    return (CWidget*) m_arrWidgets[nIndex];
}

int CWidgetDoc::AddWidget(int x, int y, COLORREF color)
{
    int nIndex = -1;
    CWidget* pWidget = NULL;

    try {
        pWidget = new CWidget (x, y, color);
        nIndex = m_arrWidgets.Add (pWidget);
        SetModifiedFlag ();
    }
    catch (CMemoryException* e) {
        AfxMessageBox (_T ("Out of memory"));
        if (pWidget != NULL)
            delete pWidget;
        e->Delete ();
        return -1;
    }
    return nIndex;
}
```

```
BOOL CWidgetDoc::RemoveWidget(int nIndex)
{
    if (nIndex >= m_arrWidgets.GetSize ())
        return FALSE;

    delete m_arrWidgets[nIndex];
    m_arrWidgets.RemoveAt (nIndex);
    return TRUE;
}

void CWidgetDoc::OnInsertBlueWidget()
{
    AddWidget (10, 10, RGB (0, 0, 255));
    UpdateAllViews (NULL);
}

void CWidgetDoc::OnInsertRedWidget()
{
    AddWidget (10, 10, RGB (255, 0, 0));
    UpdateAllViews (NULL);
}

void CWidgetDoc::OnInsertYellowWidget()
{
    AddWidget (10, 10, RGB (255, 255, 0));
    UpdateAllViews (NULL);
}
```

WidgetView.h

```
// WidgetView.h : interface of the CWidgetView class
//
/////////////////////////////////////////////////////////////////////

#if !defined(
    AFX_WIDGETVIEW_H__02909A4D_3F5C_11D2_AC89_006008A8274D__INCLUDED_)
#define AFX_WIDGETVIEW_H__02909A4D_3F5C_11D2_AC89_006008A8274D__INCLUDED_

#if _MSC_VER > 1000
#pragma once
#endif // _MSC_VER > 1000

typedef struct tagWIDGETINFO {
    int x;                  // x coordinate of widget's upper left corner
    int y;                  // y coordinate of widget's upper left corner
```

(continued)

Figure 19-4. *continued*

```
    int cx;                   // Horizontal drag offset
    int cy;                   // Vertical drag offset
    COLORREF color;           // The widget's color
} WIDGETINFO;

class CWidgetView : public CScrollView
{
protected: // create from serialization only
    CWidgetView();
    DECLARE_DYNCREATE(CWidgetView)

// Attributes
public:
    CWidgetDoc* GetDocument();

// Operations
public:

// Overrides
    // ClassWizard generated virtual function overrides
    //{{AFX_VIRTUAL(CWidgetView)
    public:
    virtual void OnDraw(CDC* pDC);  // overridden to draw this view
    virtual BOOL PreCreateWindow(CREATESTRUCT& cs);
    virtual DROPEFFECT OnDragEnter(COleDataObject* pDataObject,
        DWORD dwKeyState, CPoint point);
    virtual DROPEFFECT OnDragOver(COleDataObject* pDataObject,
        DWORD dwKeyState, CPoint point);
    virtual void OnDragLeave();
    virtual BOOL OnDrop(COleDataObject* pDataObject,
        DROPEFFECT dropEffect, CPoint point);
    protected:
    virtual void OnInitialUpdate(); // called first time after construct
    //}}AFX_VIRTUAL

// Implementation
public:
    virtual ~CWidgetView();
#ifdef _DEBUG
    virtual void AssertValid() const;
    virtual void Dump(CDumpContext& dc) const;
#endif

protected:
    CWidget* m_pTempWidget;
    CSize m_offset;
```

```
        CPoint m_pointLastImage;
        CPoint m_pointLastMsg;
        int m_nSel;
        COleDropTarget m_oleDropTarget;

// Generated message map functions
protected:
    //{{AFX_MSG(CWidgetView)
    afx_msg int OnCreate(LPCREATESTRUCT lpCreateStruct);
    afx_msg void OnLButtonDown(UINT nFlags, CPoint point);
    afx_msg void OnEditCut();
    afx_msg void OnEditCopy();
    afx_msg void OnEditPaste();
    afx_msg void OnEditDelete();
    afx_msg void OnUpdateEditCut(CCmdUI* pCmdUI);
    afx_msg void OnUpdateEditCopy(CCmdUI* pCmdUI);
    afx_msg void OnUpdateEditPaste(CCmdUI* pCmdUI);
    afx_msg void OnUpdateEditDelete(CCmdUI* pCmdUI);
    afx_msg void OnSetFocus(CWnd* pOldWnd);
    afx_msg void OnKillFocus(CWnd* pNewWnd);
    //}}AFX_MSG
    DECLARE_MESSAGE_MAP()
};

#ifndef _DEBUG  // debug version in WidgetView.cpp
inline CWidgetDoc* CWidgetView::GetDocument()
    { return (CWidgetDoc*)m_pDocument; }
#endif

/////////////////////////////////////////////////////////////////////////

//{{AFX_INSERT_LOCATION}}
// Microsoft Visual C++ will insert additional declarations
// immediately before the previous line.

#endif
// !defined(
//      AFX_WIDGETVIEW_H__02909A4D_3F5C_11D2_AC89_006008A8274D__INCLUDED_)
```

WidgetView.cpp

```
// WidgetView.cpp : implementation of the CWidgetView class
//

#include "stdafx.h"
#include "Widget.h"
```

(continued)

Figure 19-4. *continued*

```
#include "WidgetDoc.h"
#include "WidgetView.h"

#ifdef _DEBUG
#define new DEBUG_NEW
#undef THIS_FILE
static char THIS_FILE[] = __FILE__;
#endif

/////////////////////////////////////////////////////////////////////////
// CWidgetView

IMPLEMENT_DYNCREATE(CWidgetView, CScrollView)

BEGIN_MESSAGE_MAP(CWidgetView, CScrollView)
    //{{AFX_MSG_MAP(CWidgetView)
    ON_WM_CREATE()
    ON_WM_LBUTTONDOWN()
    ON_COMMAND(ID_EDIT_CUT, OnEditCut)
    ON_COMMAND(ID_EDIT_COPY, OnEditCopy)
    ON_COMMAND(ID_EDIT_PASTE, OnEditPaste)
    ON_COMMAND(ID_EDIT_DELETE, OnEditDelete)
    ON_UPDATE_COMMAND_UI(ID_EDIT_CUT, OnUpdateEditCut)
    ON_UPDATE_COMMAND_UI(ID_EDIT_COPY, OnUpdateEditCopy)
    ON_UPDATE_COMMAND_UI(ID_EDIT_PASTE, OnUpdateEditPaste)
    ON_UPDATE_COMMAND_UI(ID_EDIT_DELETE, OnUpdateEditDelete)
    ON_WM_SETFOCUS()
    ON_WM_KILLFOCUS()
    //}}AFX_MSG_MAP
END_MESSAGE_MAP()

/////////////////////////////////////////////////////////////////////////
// CWidgetView construction/destruction

CWidgetView::CWidgetView()
{
}

CWidgetView::~CWidgetView()
{
}

BOOL CWidgetView::PreCreateWindow(CREATESTRUCT& cs)
{
    return CScrollView::PreCreateWindow(cs);
}
```

```
/////////////////////////////////////////////////////////////////////////
// CWidgetView drawing

void CWidgetView::OnDraw(CDC* pDC)
{
    CWidgetDoc* pDoc = GetDocument();
    ASSERT_VALID(pDoc);

    int nCount = pDoc->GetWidgetCount ();
    if (nCount) {
        //
        // Draw all widgets.
        //
        for (int i=0; i<nCount; i++)
            pDoc->GetWidget (i)->Draw (pDC);

        //
        // Draw the selected widget if this view has the input focus.
        //
        if (m_nSel != -1 && CWnd::GetFocus () == this)
            pDoc->GetWidget (m_nSel)->DrawSelected (pDC);
    }
}

void CWidgetView::OnInitialUpdate()
{
    CScrollView::OnInitialUpdate();
    SetScrollSizes(MM_TEXT, CSize (1280, 1024));
    m_pTempWidget = NULL;
    m_nSel = -1;
}

/////////////////////////////////////////////////////////////////////////
// CWidgetView diagnostics

#ifdef _DEBUG
void CWidgetView::AssertValid() const
{
    CScrollView::AssertValid();
}

void CWidgetView::Dump(CDumpContext& dc) const
{
    CScrollView::Dump(dc);
}
```

(continued)

Figure 19-4. *continued*

```
CWidgetDoc* CWidgetView::GetDocument() // non-debug version is inline
{
    ASSERT(m_pDocument->IsKindOf(RUNTIME_CLASS(CWidgetDoc)));
    return (CWidgetDoc*)m_pDocument;
}
#endif //_DEBUG

/////////////////////////////////////////////////////////////////////////////
// CWidgetView message handlers

DROPEFFECT CWidgetView::OnDragEnter(COleDataObject* pDataObject,
    DWORD dwKeyState, CPoint point)
{
    CScrollView::OnDragEnter(pDataObject, dwKeyState, point);

    //
    // If a widget is available from the drop source, create a temporary
    // widget for drag imaging.
    //
    UINT nFormat = ((CWidgetApp*) AfxGetApp ())->GetClipboardFormat ();
    HGLOBAL hData = pDataObject->GetGlobalData (nFormat);

    if (hData != NULL) {
        WIDGETINFO* pWidgetInfo = (WIDGETINFO*) ::GlobalLock (hData);
        int x = point.x - pWidgetInfo->cx;
        int y = point.y - pWidgetInfo->cy;
        m_offset.cx = pWidgetInfo->cx;
        m_offset.cy = pWidgetInfo->cy;
        COLORREF color = pWidgetInfo->color;
        ::GlobalUnlock (hData);
        ::GlobalFree (hData);

        m_pTempWidget = new CWidget (x, y, color);
        m_pointLastImage.x = m_pointLastImage.y = -32000;
        m_pointLastMsg = point;

        //
        // Return DROPEFFECT_COPY if the Ctrl key is down, or
        // DROPEFFECT_MOVE if it is not.
        //
        return (dwKeyState & MK_CONTROL) ?
            DROPEFFECT_COPY : DROPEFFECT_MOVE;
    }
    //
    // The cursor isn't carrying a widget. Indicate that the drop target
    // will not accept a drop.
```

```
        //
        m_pTempWidget = NULL;
        return DROPEFFECT_NONE;
}

DROPEFFECT CWidgetView::OnDragOver(COleDataObject* pDataObject,
        DWORD dwKeyState, CPoint point)
{
        CScrollView::OnDragOver(pDataObject, dwKeyState, point);

        //
        // Return now if the object being dragged is not a widget.
        //
        if (m_pTempWidget == NULL)
                return DROPEFFECT_NONE;

        //
        // Convert the drag point to logical coordinates.
        //
        CClientDC dc (this);
        OnPrepareDC (&dc);
        dc.DPtoLP (&point);

        //
        // If the cursor has moved, erase the old drag image and
        // draw a new one.
        //
        if (point != m_pointLastMsg) {
                CPoint pt (point.x - m_offset.cx, point.y - m_offset.cy);
                m_pTempWidget->DrawDragImage (&dc, m_pointLastImage);
                m_pTempWidget->DrawDragImage (&dc, pt);
                m_pointLastImage = pt;
                m_pointLastMsg = point;
        }

        //
        // Return DROPEFFECT_COPY if the Ctrl key is down, or DROPEFFECT_MOVE
        // if it is not.
        //
        return (dwKeyState & MK_CONTROL) ?
                DROPEFFECT_COPY : DROPEFFECT_MOVE;
}

void CWidgetView::OnDragLeave()
{
        CScrollView::OnDragLeave();

        //
        // Erase the last drag image and delete the temporary widget.
```

(continued)

Figure 19-4. *continued*

```
    //
    if (m_pTempWidget != NULL) {
        CClientDC dc (this);
        OnPrepareDC (&dc);
        m_pTempWidget->DrawDragImage (&dc, m_pointLastImage);
        delete m_pTempWidget;
        m_pTempWidget = NULL;
    }
}

BOOL CWidgetView::OnDrop(COleDataObject* pDataObject,
    DROPEFFECT dropEffect, CPoint point)
{
    CScrollView::OnDrop(pDataObject, dropEffect, point);

    //
    // Convert the drop point to logical coordinates.
    //
    CClientDC dc (this);
    OnPrepareDC (&dc);
    dc.DPtoLP (&point);

    //
    // Erase the last drag image and delete the temporary widget.
    //
    if (m_pTempWidget != NULL) {
        m_pTempWidget->DrawDragImage (&dc, m_pointLastImage);
        delete m_pTempWidget;
        m_pTempWidget = NULL;
    }

    //
    // Retrieve the HGLOBAL from the data object and create a widget.
    //
    UINT nFormat = ((CWidgetApp*) AfxGetApp ())->GetClipboardFormat ();
    HGLOBAL hData = pDataObject->GetGlobalData (nFormat);

    if (hData != NULL) {
        WIDGETINFO* pWidgetInfo = (WIDGETINFO*) ::GlobalLock (hData);
        int x = point.x - pWidgetInfo->cx;
        int y = point.y - pWidgetInfo->cy;
        COLORREF color = pWidgetInfo->color;
        ::GlobalUnlock (hData);
        ::GlobalFree (hData);

        CWidgetDoc* pDoc = GetDocument ();
        m_nSel = pDoc->AddWidget (x, y, color);
```

```
            pDoc->UpdateAllViews (NULL);
            return TRUE;
        }
    return FALSE;
}

int CWidgetView::OnCreate(LPCREATESTRUCT lpCreateStruct)
{
    if (CScrollView::OnCreate(lpCreateStruct) == -1)
        return -1;

    m_oleDropTarget.Register (this);
    return 0;
}

void CWidgetView::OnLButtonDown(UINT nFlags, CPoint point)
{
    CScrollView::OnLButtonDown(nFlags, point);

    CWidgetDoc* pDoc = GetDocument ();
    int nCount = pDoc->GetWidgetCount ();

    if (nCount) {
        //
        // Convert the click point to logical coordinates.
        //
        CClientDC dc (this);
        OnPrepareDC (&dc);
        dc.DPtoLP (&point);

        //
        // Find out whether a widget was clicked.
        //
        int i;
        BOOL bHit = FALSE;
        for (i=nCount - 1; i>=0 && !bHit; i--) {
            CWidget* pWidget = pDoc->GetWidget (i);
            if (pWidget->PtInWidget (point)) {
                bHit = TRUE;
            }
        }

        //
        // If no widget was clicked, change the selection to NULL and exit.
        //
        if (!bHit) {
            m_nSel = -1;
            InvalidateRect (NULL, FALSE);
            return;
        }
```

(continued)

Figure 19-4. *continued*

```
        //
        // Select the widget that was clicked.
        //
        int nWidgetIndex = i + 1;

        if (m_nSel != nWidgetIndex) {
            m_nSel = nWidgetIndex;
            InvalidateRect (NULL, FALSE);
            UpdateWindow ();
        }

        //
        // Begin a drag-and-drop operation involving the selected widget.
        //
        HANDLE hData = ::GlobalAlloc (GMEM_MOVEABLE, sizeof (WIDGETINFO));

        WIDGETINFO* pWidgetInfo = (WIDGETINFO*) ::GlobalLock (hData);
        CWidget* pWidget = pDoc->GetWidget (nWidgetIndex);
        ASSERT (pWidget != NULL);
        CRect rect = pWidget->GetRect ();
        pWidgetInfo->cx = point.x - rect.left;
        pWidgetInfo->cy = point.y - rect.top;
        pWidgetInfo->color = pWidget->GetColor ();
        ::GlobalUnlock (hData);

        COleDataSource ods;
        UINT nFormat = ((CWidgetApp*) AfxGetApp ())->GetClipboardFormat ();
        ods.CacheGlobalData (nFormat, hData);

        int nOldSel = m_nSel;
        DROPEFFECT de = ods.DoDragDrop (DROPEFFECT_COPY | DROPEFFECT_MOVE);

        if (de == DROPEFFECT_MOVE) {
            pDoc->RemoveWidget (nWidgetIndex);
            int nCount = pDoc->GetWidgetCount ();
            if (nOldSel == m_nSel || nCount == 0)
                m_nSel = -1;
            else if (m_nSel >= nCount)
                m_nSel = nCount - 1;
            pDoc->UpdateAllViews (NULL);
        }
    }
}

void CWidgetView::OnEditCut()
{
    if (m_nSel != -1) {
        OnEditCopy ();
```

```
            OnEditDelete ();
    }
}

void CWidgetView::OnEditCopy()
{
    if (m_nSel != -1) {
        //
        // Copy data describing the currently selected widget to a
        // global memory block.
        //
        HANDLE hData = ::GlobalAlloc (GMEM_MOVEABLE, sizeof (WIDGETINFO));

        WIDGETINFO* pWidgetInfo = (WIDGETINFO*) ::GlobalLock (hData);
        CWidgetDoc* pDoc = GetDocument ();
        CWidget* pWidget = pDoc->GetWidget (m_nSel);
        ASSERT (pWidget != NULL);
        CRect rect = pWidget->GetRect ();
        pWidgetInfo->x = rect.left;
        pWidgetInfo->y = rect.top;
        pWidgetInfo->color = pWidget->GetColor ();
        ::GlobalUnlock (hData);

        //
        // Place the widget on the clipboard.
        //
        COleDataSource* pods = new COleDataSource;
        UINT nFormat = ((CWidgetApp*) AfxGetApp ())->GetClipboardFormat ();
        pods->CacheGlobalData (nFormat, hData);
        pods->SetClipboard ();
    }
}

void CWidgetView::OnEditPaste()
{
    //
    // Create a COleDataObject and attach it to the clipboard.
    //
    COleDataObject odo;
    odo.AttachClipboard ();

    //
    // Retrieve the HGLOBAL from the clipboard and create a widget.
    //
    UINT nFormat = ((CWidgetApp*) AfxGetApp ())->GetClipboardFormat ();
    HGLOBAL hData = odo.GetGlobalData (nFormat);
```

(continued)

Figure 19-4. *continued*

```
if (hData != NULL) {
        WIDGETINFO* pWidgetInfo = (WIDGETINFO*) ::GlobalLock (hData);
        int x = pWidgetInfo->x;
        int y = pWidgetInfo->y;
        COLORREF color = pWidgetInfo->color;
        ::GlobalUnlock (hData);
        ::GlobalFree (hData);

        CWidgetDoc* pDoc = GetDocument ();
        m_nSel = pDoc->AddWidget (x, y, color);
        pDoc->UpdateAllViews (NULL);
    }
}

void CWidgetView::OnEditDelete()
{
    if (m_nSel != -1) {
        CWidgetDoc* pDoc = GetDocument ();
        pDoc->RemoveWidget (m_nSel);
        m_nSel = -1;
        pDoc->UpdateAllViews (NULL);
    }
}

void CWidgetView::OnUpdateEditCut(CCmdUI* pCmdUI)
{
    pCmdUI->Enable (m_nSel != -1);
}

void CWidgetView::OnUpdateEditCopy(CCmdUI* pCmdUI)
{
    pCmdUI->Enable (m_nSel != -1);
}

void CWidgetView::OnUpdateEditPaste(CCmdUI* pCmdUI)
{
    UINT nFormat = ((CWidgetApp*) AfxGetApp ())->GetClipboardFormat ();
    pCmdUI->Enable (::IsClipboardFormatAvailable (nFormat));
}

void CWidgetView::OnUpdateEditDelete(CCmdUI* pCmdUI)
{
    pCmdUI->Enable (m_nSel != -1);
}

void CWidgetView::OnKillFocus(CWnd* pNewWnd)
{
```

```
        CScrollView::OnKillFocus(pNewWnd);
        InvalidateRect (NULL, FALSE);
}

void CWidgetView::OnSetFocus(CWnd* pOldWnd)
{
        CScrollView::OnSetFocus(pOldWnd);
        InvalidateRect (NULL, FALSE);
}
```

WidgetObj.h

```
#if !defined(
    AFX_WIDGETOBJ_H__02909A57_3F5C_11D2_AC89_006008A8274D__INCLUDED_)
#define AFX_WIDGETOBJ_H__02909A57_3F5C_11D2_AC89_006008A8274D__INCLUDED_

#if _MSC_VER > 1000
#pragma once
#endif // _MSC_VER > 1000
// WidgetObj.h : header file
//

/////////////////////////////////////////////////////////////////////////
// CWidget command target

class CWidget : public CObject
{
    DECLARE_SERIAL(CWidget)

// Attributes
public:

// Operations
public:
    CWidget();
    CWidget (int x, int y, COLORREF color);
    virtual ~CWidget();
    void DrawSelected (CDC* pDC);
    BOOL PtInWidget (POINT point);
    virtual void DrawDragImage (CDC* pDC, POINT point);
    virtual void Draw (CDC* pDC);
    COLORREF GetColor ();
    CRect GetRect ();

// Overrides
    // ClassWizard generated virtual function overrides
    //{{AFX_VIRTUAL(CWidget)
```

(continued)

Figure 19-4. *continued*

```
    //}}}AFX_VIRTUAL
    virtual void Serialize (CArchive& ar);

// Implementation
protected:
    COLORREF m_color;
    CRect m_rect;
};


/////////////////////////////////////////////////////////////////////////////

//{{AFX_INSERT_LOCATION}}
// Microsoft Visual C++ will insert additional declarations
// immediately before the previous line.

#endif
// !defined(
//     AFX_WIDGETOBJ_H__02909A57_3F5C_11D2_AC89_006008A8274D__INCLUDED_)
```

WidgetObj.cpp

```
// WidgetObj.cpp : implementation file
//

#include "stdafx.h"
#include "Widget.h"
#include "WidgetObj.h"

#ifdef _DEBUG
#define new DEBUG_NEW
#undef THIS_FILE
static char THIS_FILE[] = __FILE__;
#endif

/////////////////////////////////////////////////////////////////////////////
// CWidget

IMPLEMENT_SERIAL(CWidget, CObject, 1)

CWidget::CWidget()
{
    m_rect = CRect (0, 0, 90, 90);
    m_color = RGB (255, 0, 0);
}
CWidget::CWidget (int x, int y, COLORREF color)
{
```

```
    m_rect = CRect (x, y, x + 90, y + 90);
    m_color = color;
}


CWidget::~CWidget()
{
}


/////////////////////////////////////////////////////////////////////////
// CWidget message handlers

CRect CWidget::GetRect()
{
    return m_rect;
}


COLORREF CWidget::GetColor()
{
    return m_color;
}


void CWidget::Serialize (CArchive& ar)
{
    CObject::Serialize (ar);

    if (ar.IsStoring ())
        ar << m_rect << m_color;
    else
        ar >> m_rect >> m_color;
}


void CWidget::Draw(CDC *pDC)
{
    CBrush brush (m_color);
    CBrush* pOldBrush = pDC->SelectObject (&brush);

    CPoint points[3];
    points[0].x = m_rect.left;
    points[0].y = m_rect.bottom;
    points[1].x = m_rect.left + (m_rect.Width () / 2);
    points[1].y = m_rect.top;
    points[2].x = m_rect.right;
    points[2].y = m_rect.bottom;
    pDC->Polygon (points, 3);

    pDC->SelectObject (pOldBrush);
}
```

(continued)

Figure 19-4. *continued*

```
void CWidget::DrawSelected(CDC *pDC)
{
    CBrush brush (RGB (0, 255, 0));
    CBrush* pOldBrush = pDC->SelectObject (&brush);

    CPoint points[3];
    points[0].x = m_rect.left;
    points[0].y = m_rect.bottom;
    points[1].x = m_rect.left + (m_rect.Width () / 2);
    points[1].y = m_rect.top;
    points[2].x = m_rect.right;
    points[2].y = m_rect.bottom;
    pDC->Polygon (points, 3);

    pDC->SelectObject (pOldBrush);
}

void CWidget::DrawDragImage(CDC *pDC, POINT point)
{
    int nOldMode = pDC->SetROP2 (R2_NOT);
    CBrush* pOldBrush = (CBrush*) pDC->SelectStockObject (NULL_BRUSH);

    CPoint points[3];
    points[0].x = point.x;
    points[0].y = point.y + m_rect.Height ();
    points[1].x = point.x + (m_rect.Width () / 2);
    points[1].y = point.y;
    points[2].x = point.x + m_rect.Width ();
    points[2].y = point.y + m_rect.Height ();
    pDC->Polygon (points, 3);

    pDC->SelectObject (pOldBrush);
    pDC->SetROP2 (nOldMode);
}

BOOL CWidget::PtInWidget(POINT point)
{
    if (!m_rect.PtInRect (point))
        return FALSE;

    int cx = min (point.x - m_rect.left, m_rect.right - point.x);
    return ((m_rect.bottom - point.y) <= (2 * cx));
}
```

Widgets are represented by objects of the *CWidget* class, whose source code is found in WidgetObj.h and WidgetObj.cpp. To derive *CWidget*, I used ClassWizard to derive from *CCmdTarget* and then manually edited the source code to change the base class to *CObject*. I also changed the DYNCREATE macros inserted by ClassWizard into SERIAL macros and overrode *CObject::Serialize* to make *CWidget* a serializable class. These tweaks reduced the document's *Serialize* function to one simple statement:

```
m_arrWidgets.Serialize (ar);
```

m_arrWidgets is the *CWidgetDoc* member variable that stores *CWidget* pointers. A *CWidget* object is created when a command is selected from the Insert menu, when a widget is pasted from the clipboard, and when a widget is dropped over the Widget window.

The *CWidget* class has a pair of member functions named *Draw* and *DrawSelected* that draw a widget to an output device. *Draw* draws the widget in the unselected state; *DrawSelected* draws it in the selected state. The view's *OnDraw* code is a simple loop that retrieves *CWidget* pointers from the document one by one and asks each widget to draw itself. If the view has the input focus and a widget is currently selected (that is, if *CWidgetView::m_nSel* != −1), the selected widget is drawn again after all the other widgets are drawn:

```
for (int i=0; i<nCount; i++)
    pDoc->GetWidget (i)->Draw (pDC);
if (m_nSel != -1 && CWnd::GetFocus () == this)
    pDoc->GetWidget (m_nSel)->DrawSelected (pDC);
```

Drawing the selected widget last ensures that it is always visible on top of the others.

Another *CWidget* drawing function, *DrawDragImage*, is used for drag imaging. As you drag a widget across the screen, notice the triangular outline that follows the cursor. That's drag imaging. The operating system shell uses drag images for a similar effect when file system objects are dragged. Because the drop source is responsible for displaying the cursor during a drag-and-drop operation, programmers often assume that the drop source draws drag images by making them part of the cursor. That's generally not true. What really happens is that the drop target (not the drop source) draws the drag image in *OnDragOver*. For this to work, the drop target has to know what kind of payload the cursor is carrying so that it can draw an outline on the screen.

Widget handles drag imaging by creating a temporary widget object in *OnDragEnter*, caching the pointer in *CWidgetView::m_pTempWidget*, and calling the object's *DrawDragImage* function each time *OnDragOver* is called. Actually, *OnDragOver* calls *DrawDragImage* twice: once to erase the old drag image and once to draw a new one. *DrawDragImage* does its drawing in the R2_NOT drawing mode, so drawing a drag image on top of an old one effectively erases the old drag image. The position of the previous drag image is stored in *CWidgetView*'s *m_pointLastImage* data member. The temporary widget is deleted when *OnDragLeave* or *OnDrop* is called. This example demonstrates why overriding *OnDragLeave* is sometimes useful. In this case, *OnDragEnter* allocates a resource that must be freed even if a drop doesn't occur.

You can see drop target scrolling in action by dragging a widget and pausing within a few pixels of the view's lower or right border. After a brief delay, the view will begin scrolling and will continue scrolling until a drop occurs or the cursor moves away from the border. Drop target scrolling enables you to drop a widget in any part of the view without taking your finger off the mouse button to click a scroll bar. Again, drop target scrolling comes absolutely for free when the drop target is a *CScrollView*.

The *AfxOleInit* Function

When I used AppWizard to create the Widget project, I selected none of the OLE options in Step 3. When AppWizard is run this way, the generated source code doesn't include a call to the all-important *AfxOleInit* function, which initializes the OLE libraries. This function *must* be called before an MFC application touches COM or OLE in any way. Therefore, I added a call to *AfxOleInit* to the beginning of the application class's *InitInstance* function. This meant that I also had to add the statement

```
#include <afxole.h>
```

to Stdafx.h. Otherwise, the call to *AfxOleInit* wouldn't have compiled.

I mention this because if you write an application that uses COM or OLE but you don't select one of the OLE options in AppWizard, you must add the *AfxOleInit* call and the statement that #includes Afxole.h manually. If you don't, your application will compile just fine, but calls to functions such as *COleDataSource::DoDragDrop* will fail. I once lost half a day of work wondering why my clipboard code wasn't working when, by all appearances, I had done everything right. Then I realized that I had forgotten to include these crucial statements in my source code. If you write an application and find that calls to *DoDragDrop* or other OLE functions mysteriously fail, make sure that *AfxOleInit* is called when the application starts up. You'll save yourself a lot of grief.

Chapter 20

Automation

Imagine a world in which you could program any Microsoft Windows application using a sophisticated yet easy-to-use scripting language. Imagine further that all scripting languages were the same so that once you learned to write scripts for one application, you could write scripts for others, too. While you're at it, consider how useful it would be if programs written in Microsoft Visual C++, Microsoft Visual Basic, and other programming languages could also access the features exposed to this hypothetical language.

Sound too good to be true? It's not. Thanks to the COM-based technology known as Automation, any MFC application can be turned into a scriptable application. Automation is a standardized means for exposing an application's features to clients written in Visual Basic; Visual Basic for Applications (VBA); Visual Basic, Scripting Edition (VBScript); and other languages. It solves the problem posed by these languages' inability to talk to COM objects using conventional COM interfaces, but it isn't restricted to dialects of Visual Basic; clients written in C++ and other languages can also use Automation.

Microsoft is actively encouraging application developers to build Automation support into their programs and has led the way by building Automation capabilities into many of its flagship applications. Microsoft Excel, for example, is a powerful Automation server. So are Microsoft Word, Microsoft PowerPoint, and other Microsoft Office applications. By exposing an application's feature set through Automation, you make that application a powerful tool in the hands of users who are willing to learn a scripting language. You also give developers the means to use your application as a platform for building their own applications.

Automation is a versatile tool with talents that extend beyond mere scripting. It's also used to build software components for Active Server Pages, and it's one of the key technologies employed by ActiveX controls. In this chapter, you'll learn what Automation is, how it works, and how you can use MFC to write Automation-enabled applications. A Visual C++ programmer can have a simple Automation server up and running in no time flat. With a little know-how, you can build Automation servers that expose complex, hierarchically structured object models. Visual C++ and MFC also simplify the creation of Automation clients—programs that use the services provided by Automation servers.

AUTOMATION BASICS

Unlike a typical COM object, which exposes interfaces and methods, an Automation object exposes methods and properties. A *method* is a function that can be called by the object's clients. A *property* is an attribute of the object, such as a color or a file name.

Automation-aware languages such as Visual Basic shield the programmer from reference counting, interface pointers, and other idioms of COM. They also permit you to access Automation methods and properties as easily as you access local subroutines and variables. The following Visual Basic statements instantiate an Automation object and invoke a method named *Add* to add 2 and 2:

```
Dim Math as Object
Set Math = CreateObject ("Math.Object")
Sum = Math.Add (2, 2)
Set Math = Nothing
```

In this example, *Math* is a variable of type *Object*. "Math.Object" is the Automation object's ProgID. (Recall from Chapter 18 that a ProgID is the string analogue of a COM CLSID.) The final statement frees the object by performing the Visual Basic equivalent of calling *Release* through an interface pointer.

In Visual Basic, accessing an Automation property is syntactically similar to calling an Automation method. The next example creates a bank account object and sets the balance in the account by assigning a value to a property named *Balance*:

```
Dim Account as Object
Set Account = CreateObject ("BankAccount.Object")
Account.Balance = 100
```

Checking the balance in the account is as simple as reading the property value:

```
Amount = Account.Balance
```

Reading or writing an Automation property is analogous to accessing a public member variable in a C++ class. In truth, COM objects can't expose member variables any more than C++ objects can expose private data members. The illusion that an Automation object can expose values as well as methods is part of the magic of Automation.

Automation clients written in VBScript look very much like Automation clients written in Visual Basic. The following script uses VBScript's built-in *FileSystemObject* object, which is in reality an Automation object, to create a text file containing the string "Hello, world":

```
Set fso = CreateObject ("Scripting.FileSystemObject")
Set TextFile = fso.CreateTextFile ("C:\Hello.txt", True)
TextFile.WriteLine ("Hello, world")
TextFile.Close
```

To try this script for yourself, use Notepad or a program editor to enter these statements in a text file and save the file with the extension .vbs. Then double-click the file in the operating system shell or type START *filename*.vbs in a command prompt window. On Windows 98 and Windows 2000 systems, this will invoke the built-in Windows Scripting Host, which will open the file and execute the statements found inside it.

You can also write Automation clients in C++. The next section shows you how, but be warned that it isn't pretty because a C++ client doesn't have the Visual Basic run-time or a scripting engine to serve as a mediator between it and the Automation server. The good news is that Visual C++ aids in the creation of Automation clients by generating easy-to-use wrapper classes based on MFC's *COleDispatchDriver* class. You'll see what I mean later in this chapter.

IDispatch: The Root of All Automation

Automation looks fairly simple from the outside, and for a Visual Basic programmer, Automation *is* simple. But the fact that COM is involved should be a clue that what goes on under the hood is a far different story.

The key to understanding how Automation works lies in understanding the COM interface known as *IDispatch*. An Automation object is a COM object that implements *IDispatch*. *IDispatch* contains four methods (which are listed in the table on the following page), not counting the three *IUnknown* methods common to all COM interfaces. Of the four, *Invoke* and *GetIDsOfNames* are the most important. A client calls *Invoke* to call an Automation method or to read or write an Automation property. *Invoke* doesn't accept a method or a property name such as "Add" or "Balance." Instead, it accepts an integer *dispatch ID*, or *dispid*, that identifies the property or method. *GetIDsOfNames* converts a property name or a method name into a dispatch ID that can be passed to *Invoke*. Collectively, the methods and properties exposed through an *IDispatch* interface form a *dispinterface*.

THE *IDISPATCH* INTERFACE

Method	Description
Invoke	Calls an Automation method or accesses an Automation property
GetIDsOfNames	Returns the dispatch ID of a property or a method
GetTypeInfo	Retrieves an *ITypeInfo* pointer (if available) for accessing the Automation object's type information
GetTypeInfoCount	Returns 0 if the Automation object doesn't offer type information; returns 1 if it does

When Visual Basic encounters a statement like

```
Sum = Math.Add (2, 2)
```

it calls *GetIDsOfNames* to convert "Add" into a dispatch ID. It then calls *Invoke*, passing in the dispatch ID retrieved from *GetIDsOfNames*. Before calling *Invoke*, Visual Basic initializes an array of structures with the values of the method parameters—in this case, 2 and 2. It passes the array's address to *Invoke* along with the address of an empty structure that receives the method's return value (the sum of the two input parameters). The Automation object examines the dispatch ID, sees that it corresponds to the *Add* method, unpacks the input values, adds them together, and copies the sum to the structure provided by the caller.

A good way to picture this process is to see how a C++ programmer would call an Automation method. The following code is the C++ equivalent of the first example in the previous section:

```
// Convert the ProgID into a CLSID.
CLSID clsid;
::CLSIDFromProgID (OLESTR ("Math.Object"), &clsid);

// Create the object, and get a pointer to its IDispatch interface.
IDispatch* pDispatch;
::CoCreateInstance (clsid, NULL, CLSCTX_SERVER, IID_IDispatch,
    (void**) &pDispatch);

// Get the Add method's dispatch ID.
DISPID dispid;
OLECHAR* szName = OLESTR ("Add");
pDispatch->GetIDsOfNames (IID_NULL, &szName, 1,
    ::GetUserDefaultLCID (), &dispid);
```

```
// Prepare an argument list for the Add method.
VARIANTARG args[2];
DISPPARAMS params = { args, NULL, 2, 0 };
for (int i=0; i<2; i++) {
    ::VariantInit (&args[i]);    // Initialize the VARIANT.
    args[i].vt = VT_I4;          // Data type = 32-bit long
    V_I4 (&args[i]) = 2;         // Value = 2
}

// Call Add to add 2 and 2.
VARIANT result;
::VariantInit (&result);
pDispatch->Invoke (dispid, IID_NULL, ::GetUserDefaultLCID (),
    DISPATCH_METHOD, &params, &result, NULL, NULL);

// Extract the result.
long lResult = V_I4 (&result);

// Clear the VARIANTs.
::VariantClear (&args[0]);
::VariantClear (&args[1]);
::VariantClear (&result);

// Release the Automation object.
pDispatch->Release ();
```

You can plainly see the calls to *IDispatch::GetIDsOfNames* and *IDispatch::Invoke*, as well as the *::CoCreateInstance* statement that creates the Automation object. You can also see that input and output parameters are packaged in structures called VARIANT-ARGs, a subject that's covered in the next section.

You also use *IDispatch::Invoke* to access Automation properties. You can set the fourth parameter, which was equal to DISPATCH_METHOD in the preceding example, to DISPATCH_PROPERTYPUT or DISPATCH_PROPERTYGET to indicate that the value of the property named by the dispatch ID in parameter 1 is being set or retrieved. In addition, *IDispatch::Invoke* can return error information in an EXCEPINFO structure provided by the caller. The structure's address is passed in *Invoke*'s seventh parameter; a NULL pointer means the caller isn't interested in such information. *Invoke* also supports Automation methods and properties with optional and named arguments, which matters little to C++ clients but can simplify client code written in Visual Basic.

It should be evident from these examples that Automation leaves something to be desired for C++ programmers. It's faster and more efficient for C++ clients to call conventional COM methods than it is for them to call Automation methods.

Automation looks easy in Visual Basic for the simple reason that Visual Basic goes to great lengths to *make* it look easy. Peel away the façade, however, and Automation looks very different indeed.

Automation Data Types

One of the more interesting aspects of *IDispatch::Invoke* is how it handles input and output parameters. In Automation, all parameters are passed in data structures called VARIANTs. (Technically, input parameters are passed in VARIANTARGs and output parameters in VARIANTs, but because these structures are identical, developers often use the term VARIANT to describe both.) A VARIANT is, in essence, a self-describing data type. Inside a VARIANT is a union of data types for holding the VARIANT's data and a separate field for defining the data type. Here's how the structure is defined in Oaidl.idl:

```
struct tagVARIANT {
    union {
        struct __tagVARIANT {
            VARTYPE vt;
            WORD    wReserved1;
            WORD    wReserved2;
            WORD    wReserved3;
            union {
                LONG          lVal;        /* VT_I4             */
                BYTE          bVal;        /* VT_UI1            */
                SHORT         iVal;        /* VT_I2             */
                FLOAT         fltVal;      /* VT_R4             */
                DOUBLE        dblVal;      /* VT_R8             */
                VARIANT_BOOL  boolVal;     /* VT_BOOL           */
                _VARIANT_BOOL bool;        /* (obsolete)        */
                SCODE         scode;       /* VT_ERROR          */
                CY            cyVal;       /* VT_CY             */
                DATE          date;        /* VT_DATE           */
                BSTR          bstrVal;     /* VT_BSTR           */
                IUnknown *    punkVal;     /* VT_UNKNOWN        */
                IDispatch *   pdispVal;    /* VT_DISPATCH       */
                SAFEARRAY *   parray;      /* VT_ARRAY          */
                BYTE *        pbVal;       /* VT_BYREF!VT_UI1   */
                SHORT *       piVal;       /* VT_BYREF!VT_I2    */
                LONG *        plVal;       /* VT_BYREF!VT_I4    */
                FLOAT *       pfltVal;     /* VT_BYREF!VT_R4    */
```

```
        DOUBLE *         pdblVal;      /* VT_BYREF|VT_R8        */
        VARIANT_BOOL *pboolVal;        /* VT_BYREF|VT_BOOL      */
        _VARIANT_BOOL *pbool;          /* (obsolete)            */
        SCODE *          pscode;       /* VT_BYREF|VT_ERROR     */
        CY *             pcyVal;       /* VT_BYREF|VT_CY        */
        DATE *           pdate;        /* VT_BYREF|VT_DATE      */
        BSTR *           pbstrVal;     /* VT_BYREF|VT_BSTR      */
        IUnknown **      ppunkVal;     /* VT_BYREF|VT_UNKNOWN   */
        IDispatch **     ppdispVal;    /* VT_BYREF|VT_DISPATCH  */
        SAFEARRAY **     pparray;      /* VT_BYREF|VT_ARRAY     */
        VARIANT *        pvarVal;      /* VT_BYREF|VT_VARIANT   */
        PVOID            byref;        /* Generic ByRef         */
        CHAR             cVal;         /* VT_I1                 */
        USHORT           uiVal;        /* VT_UI2                */
        ULONG            ulVal;        /* VT_UI4                */
        INT              intVal;       /* VT_INT                */
        UINT             uintVal;      /* VT_UINT               */
        DECIMAL *        pdecVal;      /* VT_BYREF|VT_DECIMAL   */
        CHAR *           pcVal;        /* VT_BYREF|VT_I1        */
        USHORT *         puiVal;       /* VT_BYREF|VT_UI2       */
        ULONG *          pulVal;       /* VT_BYREF|VT_UI4       */
        INT *            pintVal;      /* VT_BYREF|VT_INT       */
        UINT *           puintVal;     /* VT_BYREF|VT_UINT      */
        struct __tagBRECORD {
            PVOID            pvRecord;
            IRecordInfo * pRecInfo;
        } __VARIANT_NAME_4;            /* VT_RECORD             */
      } __VARIANT_NAME_3;
    } __VARIANT_NAME_2;

    DECIMAL decVal;
  } __VARIANT_NAME_1;
};
```

The *vt* field holds one or more VT_ flags identifying the data type. Another field holds the actual value. For example, a VARIANT that represents a 32-bit long equal to 128 has a *vt* equal to VT_I4 and an *lVal* equal to 128. The header file Oleauto.h defines macros for reading and writing data encapsulated in VARIANTs. In addition, the system file Oleaut32.dll includes API functions, such as *::VariantInit* and *::VariantClear,* for managing and manipulating VARIANTs, and MFC's *COleVariant* class places a friendly wrapper around VARIANT data structures and the operations that can be performed on them.

When you write Automation objects, you must use Automation-compatible data types—that is, data types that can be represented with VARIANTs—for all the objects' properties and methods. The table on the following page summarizes the available data types.

VARIANT-COMPATIBLE DATA TYPES

Data Type	Description
BSTR	Automation string
BSTR*	Pointer to Automation string
BYTE	8-bit byte
BYTE*	Pointer to 8-bit byte
CHAR	8-bit character
CHAR*	Pointer to 8-bit character
CY	64-bit currency value
CY*	Pointer to 64-bit currency value
DATE	64-bit date and time value
DATE*	Pointer to 64-bit date and time value
DECIMAL*	Pointer to DECIMAL data structure
DOUBLE	Double-precision floating point value
DOUBLE*	Pointer to double-precision floating point value
FLOAT	Single-precision floating point value
FLOAT*	Pointer to single-precision floating point value
*IDispatch**	*IDispatch* interface pointer
*IDispatch***	Pointer to *IDispatch* interface pointer
INT	Signed integer (32 bits on Win32 platforms)
INT*	Pointer to signed integer
*IUnknown**	COM interface pointer
*IUnknown***	Pointer to COM interface pointer
LONG	32-bit signed integer
LONG*	Pointer to 32-bit signed integer
PVOID	Untyped pointer
SAFEARRAY*	SAFEARRAY pointer
SAFEARRAY**	Pointer to SAFEARRAY pointer
SCODE	COM HRESULT
SCODE*	Pointer to COM HRESULT
SHORT	16-bit signed integer
SHORT*	Pointer to 16-bit signed integer
UINT	Unsigned integer
UINT*	Pointer to unsigned integer
ULONG	32-bit unsigned integer
ULONG*	Pointer to 32-bit unsigned integer
USHORT	16-bit unsigned integer
USHORT*	Pointer to 16-bit unsigned integer
VARIANT*	Pointer to VARIANT data structure
VARIANT_BOOL	Automation Boolean
VARIANT_BOOL*	Pointer to Automation Boolean

Generally speaking, Automation's dependence on VARIANT-compatible data types is a limitation that can frustrate developers who are accustomed to building "pure" COM objects—objects that use conventional COM interfaces rather than dispinterfaces and are therefore less restricted in the types of data that they can use. However, using only Automation-compatible data types offers one advantage: COM knows how to marshal VARIANTs, so Automation objects don't require custom proxy/stub DLLs. The trade-off is that you can't use structures (or pointers to structures) in methods' parameter lists, and arrays require special handling because they must be encapsulated in structures called SAFEARRAYs.

The BSTR Data Type

Most of the data types presented in the preceding section are self-explanatory. Two, however, merit further explanation. BSTR (pronounced "Bee'-ster") is Automation's string data type. Unlike a C++ string, which is an array of characters followed by a zero delimiter, a BSTR is a counted string. The first four bytes hold the number of bytes (not characters) in the string; subsequent bytes hold the characters themselves. All characters in a BSTR are 16-bit Unicode characters. A BSTR value is actually a pointer to the first character in the string. (See Figure 20-1.) The string is, in fact, zero-delimited, which means that you can convert a BSTR into a C++ string pointer by casting it to an LPCWSTR.

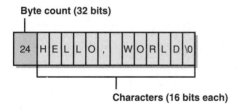

Figure 20-1. *The BSTR data type.*

In MFC, dealing with BSTRs frequently means converting *CStrings* to BSTRs and BSTRs to *CStrings*. *CString::AllocSysString* creates a BSTR from a *CString*:

```
CString string = _T ("Hello, world");
BSTR bstr = string.AllocSysString ();
```

AllocSysString will automatically convert ANSI characters to Unicode characters if the preprocessor symbol _UNICODE is not defined, indicating that this is an ANSI program build. *CString* also includes a member function named *SetSysString* that can be used to modify an existing BSTR.

Converting a BSTR into a *CString* is equally easy. *CString*'s LPCWSTR operator initializes a *CString* from a BSTR and conveniently converts the characters to 8-bit ANSI characters if the *CString* is of the ANSI variety:

```
CString string = (LPCWSTR) bstr;
```

Be aware that if a BSTR contains embedded zeros (a very real possibility since BSTRs are counted strings), turning it into a *CString* in this way will effectively truncate the string.

The SAFEARRAY Data Type

SAFEARRAY is Automation's array data type. It's called a "safe" array because in addition to holding the data comprising the array elements, it houses information regarding the number of dimensions in the array, the bounds of each dimension, and more.

A SAFEARRAY is actually a structure. It is defined this way in Oaidl.h:

```
typedef struct  tagSAFEARRAY
    {
    USHORT cDims;
    USHORT fFeatures;
    ULONG cbElements;
    ULONG cLocks;
    PVOID pvData;
    SAFEARRAYBOUND rgsabound[ 1 ];
    } SAFEARRAY;
```

SAFEARRAYBOUND is also a structure. It is defined like this:

```
typedef struct  tagSAFEARRAYBOUND
    {
    ULONG cElements;
    LONG lLbound;
    } SAFEARRAYBOUND;
```

The *cDims* field holds the number of dimensions in the SAFEARRAY. *rgsabound* is an embedded array that contains one element for each dimension. Each element defines the bounds (number of storage elements) of one dimension as well as the index of that dimension's lower bound. Unlike C++ arrays, which number their elements from 0 to *n*, a SAFEARRAY's elements can be numbered using any contiguous range of integers—for example, −5 to *n*−5. *fFeatures* holds flags specifying what kind of data the SAFEARRAY stores and how the SAFEARRAY is allocated. *cbElements* holds the size, in bytes, of each element. Finally, *pvData* points to the elements themselves.

The Windows API includes numerous functions for creating and using SAFE-ARRAYs; all begin with the name *SafeArray*. MFC has its own way of dealing with SAFEARRAYs in the form of a class named *COleSafeArray*. The following code creates a *COleSafeArray* object that represents a one-dimensional SAFEARRAY containing the integers 1 through 10:

```
COleSafeArray sa;
LONG lValues[] = { 1, 2, 3, 4, 5, 6, 7, 8, 9, 10 };
sa.CreateOneDim (VT_I4, 10, lValues);
```

The address of the VARIANT data structure in which the SAFEARRAY is stored can be retrieved with *COleSafeArray*'s LPVARIANT or LPCVARIANT operator:

```
VARIANT* pVariant = (LPVARIANT) sa;
```

One-dimensional arrays are relatively easy to create with *COleSafeArray*, but multi-dimensional arrays require more effort. Suffice it to say that even *COleSafeArray* can't make SAFEARRAYs as palatable to C++ programmers as ordinary arrays.

Late Binding vs. Early Binding

A C++ programmer seeing Automation for the first time might wonder why dispinterfaces should even exist: the reason for them is far from obvious. Given that Automation objects are inherently more complex and less efficient than their conventional COM counterparts, why not use custom COM interfaces instead of *IDispatch* interfaces and save developers a lot of time and trouble?

Dispinterfaces were created to allow Visual Basic programmers to use COM objects at a time when Visual Basic flatly didn't support conventional COM interfaces. In its early incarnations, Visual Basic couldn't call COM methods through ordinary interface pointers. Current versions of Visual Basic have partially eliminated this limitation, but to this day, many scripting languages, including VBScript, can talk to COM objects only through *IDispatch* interfaces.

What's so special about *IDispatch*? In a nutshell, it prevents a compiler (or an interpreter, as the case may be) from having to understand vtables. A COM interface pointer is really a pointer to a location inside the object that holds the address of a table of function pointers—in C++ parlance, a virtual function table, or vtable. If *pMath* holds an *IMath* interface pointer, when a C++ compiler encounters a statement like

```
pMath->Add (2, 2, &sum);
```

it resolves the call by emitting code that extracts the address of the *Add* method from the interface's vtable. It knows the vtable's layout because the interface definition was #included in a header file. And therein lies the problem. Scripting languages don't understand C++ interface definitions. These languages can't resolve a statement like the following one unless they can somehow pass the method name to the object and ask the object itself to resolve the call:

```
Sum = Math.Add (2, 2)
```

Scripting languages may not understand vtables, but they know *IDispatch* very well. Given a pointer to an *IDispatch* interface, they know where they can go in the vtable to find the addresses of *GetIDsOfNames* and *Invoke*. It's therefore a simple matter for them to call *IDispatch::Invoke* and "bind" to a method at run time.

That's the crux of *IDispatch*: shifting the responsibility for resolving method calls from the client to the object. Programmers call this *late binding* because the actual binding is done at run time. By contrast, we say that C++ clients use *early binding* because the bulk of the work required to resolve a method call is performed at compile time.

Dual Interfaces

The drawback to late binding is that it requires a run-time lookup that's not necessary in early binding. That impacts performance. And because of *IDispatch*'s reliance on dispatch IDs, each property or method access nominally requires two round-trips to the server: a call to *GetIDsOfNames* followed by a call to *Invoke*. A smart Automation client can minimize round-trips by caching dispatch IDs, but the fact remains that late binding is inherently less efficient than early binding.

The choice between an *IDispatch* interface and a conventional COM interface is a choice between flexibility and speed. An object that exposes its features through an *IDispatch* interface serves a wider variety of clients, but an object that uses ordinary COM interfaces serves late binding clients (particularly C++ clients) more efficiently.

Dual interfaces are the COM equivalent of having your cake and eating it, too. A dual interface is an interface that derives from *IDispatch*. Its vtable includes entries for *IDispatch* methods (*GetIDsOfNames*, *Invoke*, and so on) as well as custom methods. Figure 20-2 shows the layout of the vtable for a dual interface that permits methods named *Add* and *Subtract* to be accessed indirectly through *IDispatch::Invoke* or directly through the vtable. Clients that rely exclusively on *IDispatch* can call *Add* and *Subtract* through *IDispatch::Invoke*; they won't even realize that the custom portion of the vtable exists. C++ clients, on the other hand, will effectively ignore the *IDispatch* section of the vtable and use early binding to call *Add* and *Subtract*. Thus, the same object can support early and late binding. Notice that methods defined in the custom half of the vtable must use Automation-compatible data types, just as methods exposed through *IDispatch::Invoke* must.

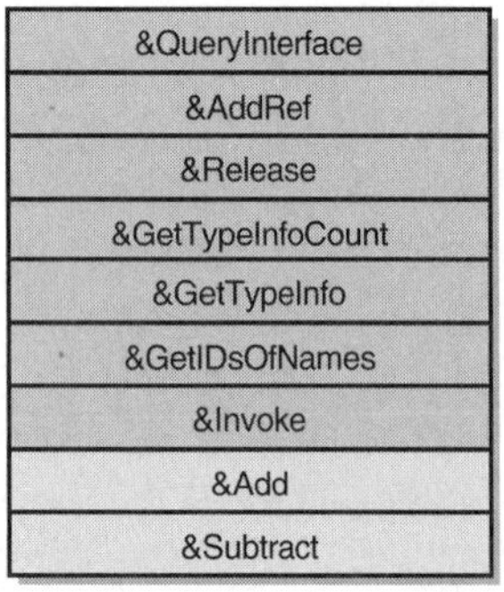

| &QueryInterface |
| &AddRef |
| &Release |
| &GetTypeInfoCount |
| &GetTypeInfo |
| &GetIDsOfNames |
| &Invoke |
| &Add |
| &Subtract |

Figure 20-2. *Virtual function table for a dual interface.*

For MFC programmers, the greatest impediment to dual interfaces is the amount of effort required to implement them. MFC Technical Note 65 describes how to add dual interfaces to an MFC Automation server, but the procedure isn't for the faint of heart. The best way to do dual interfaces today is to forego MFC and instead use the Active Template Library (ATL), which makes creating dual interfaces truly effortless.

Type Libraries

Most Automation servers are accompanied by type libraries. In his book *Inside COM* (1997, Microsoft Press), Dale Rogerson describes a type library as "a bag of information about interfaces and components." Given a type library, a client can find out all sorts of interesting things about a COM object, including which interfaces it implements, what methods are present in those interfaces, and what each method's parameter list looks like. A type library can be provided in a separate file (usually with the extension .tlb, although .olb is sometimes used instead) or as a resource embedded in the object's executable file. Regardless of how they're packaged, type libraries are registered in the registry so that clients can easily locate them.

Type libraries can be used in a variety of ways. ActiveX controls, for example, use type information (the kind of data found in type libraries) to tell control containers what kinds of events they're capable of firing. Type libraries can also be used to implement *IDispatch* interfaces and to provide information to object browsers. But the big reason type libraries are important to Automation programmers is that they permit Visual Basic clients to access a server's Automation methods and properties using the custom portion of a dual interface. Given type information, today's Visual Basic programs can even use conventional COM objects—ones that expose their functionality through custom COM interfaces instead of *IDispatch* interfaces. Type libraries aren't only for Visual Basic users, however; C++ programmers can use them, too. Shortly, you'll see how you can use ClassWizard to generate wrapper classes that simplify the writing of MFC Automation clients. Significantly, ClassWizard can work its magic only if a type library is available.

How do type libraries get created? You can create them programmatically using COM API functions and methods, but most are created from IDL files. MIDL will read an IDL file and produce a type library from the statements inside it. You can also create type libraries by defining objects and their interfaces in ODL files and compiling them with a special tool called MkTypeLib. IDL files are the preferred method, but Visual C++ still uses ODL files for MFC Automation servers. The following ODL statements define a type library that contains descriptions of an Automation component named Math and a dispinterface named *IAutoMath*:

```
[uuid (B617CC83-3C57-11D2-8E53-006008A82731), version (1.0)]
library AutoMath
{
    importlib ("stdole32.tlb");

    [uuid (B617CC84-3C57-11D2-8E53-006008A82731)]
```

(continued)

```
dispinterface IAutoMath
{
    properties:
        [id(1)] double Pi;
    methods:
        [id(2)] long Add (long a, long b);
        [id(3)] long Subtract (long a, long b);
};

[uuid (B617CC82-3C57-11D2-8E53-006008A82731)]
coclass Math
{
    [default] dispinterface IAutoMath;
};
};
```

The *importlib* statement in ODL is analogous to *#include* in C++. *uuid* assigns a GUID to an object or interface, and *dispinterface* defines a dispinterface. Statements inside a *dispinterface* block declare Automation methods and properties as well as their dispatch IDs. The object in this example features a property named *Pi* and methods named *Add* and *Subtract*. Their dispatch IDs are 1, 2, and 3, respectively.

When you write an MFC Automation server, AppWizard creates an ODL file and adds it to the project. Each time a method or property is added, ClassWizard modifies the ODL file so that the next build will produce an up-to-date type library. As long as you use the MFC wizards to craft MFC Automation servers, type libraries are a natural consequence of the build process and require no extra effort to generate.

MFC AUTOMATION SERVERS

You can use MFC to write stand-alone Automation components, but more often, you'll use its Automation support to expose an application's features to Automation clients. Exposing features this way has the very desirable effect of making the application scriptable.

You don't have to be an expert on *IDispatch* interfaces and VARIANTs to write MFC Automation servers because MFC disguises methods and properties as ordinary class member functions. In fact, it's so easy to write an MFC Automation server that Visual C++ programmers often use Automation components in situations where ordinary COM objects might make more sense.

Writing MFC Automation servers is easy because of the wizards. AppWizard adds the infrastructure needed to transform an application into an Automation server. ClassWizard reduces the chore of adding methods and properties to a few button clicks. The code generated by these wizards relies extensively on the Automation support already present in MFC. Before we go over the steps required to build an Automation server, let's look inside MFC and see what it does to make Automation possible.

MFC, *IDispatch*, and Dispatch Maps

The cornerstone of MFC's support for Automation servers is a built-in implementation of *IDispatch*. That implementation comes from a class named *COleDispatchImpl*, which is instantiated and folded into a *CCmdTarget* object by the *CCmdTarget-::EnableAutomation* function. This correctly implies that an MFC class that supports Automation must be derived, either directly or indirectly, from *CCmdTarget. EnableAutomation* is typically called in the class constructor.

When MFC's implementation of *IDispatch::Invoke* is called, MFC must somehow translate the method call or property access into a call to a class member function. Similarly, when *IDispatch::GetIDsOfNames* is called, MFC must translate the accompanying property or method name into a dispatch ID. It accomplishes both tasks using a *dispatch map*.

A dispatch map is a table that begins with BEGIN_DISPATCH_MAP and ends with END_DISPATCH_MAP. Statements in between define the object's methods and properties. Through the dispatch map, MFC's implementation of *IDispatch::Invoke* translates calls to Automation methods into calls to member functions in the class that houses the dispatch map. Automation properties are accessed through the dispatch map, too. The following dispatch map defines a method named *DebitAccount* and a property named *Balance* in a *CCmdTarget*-derived class named *CAutoClass*:

```
BEGIN_DISPATCH_MAP (CAutoClass, CCmdTarget)
    DISP_FUNCTION (CAutoClass, "DebitAccount", Debit, VT_I4, VTS_I4)
    DISP_PROPERTY_EX (CAutoClass, "Balance", GetBalance, SetBalance,
        VT_I4)
END_DISPATCH_MAP()
```

The DISP_FUNCTION macro names an Automation method and the member function that's called when the method is called. The VT_ and VTS_ values passed in the macro's argument list identify the method's return type and the types of arguments it accepts. DISP_PROPERTY_EX defines an Automation property and the get and set functions used to read and write the property's value. The fifth parameter to DISP-_PROPERTY_EX defines the property's type. In this example, *CAutoClass::Debit* will be called when the Automation object's *DebitAccount* method is called. *CAutoClass-::GetBalance* will be called to read *Balance*, and *CAutoClass::SetBalance* will be called to assign a value to it. DISP_FUNCTION and DISP_PROPERTY_EX are just two of several dispatch map macros defined in Afxdisp.h.

You might have noticed that neither of the dispatch map macros shown in the previous paragraph accepts a dispatch ID. MFC has a curious way of assigning dispatch IDs to methods and properties based on their position in the dispatch map and the derivation depth. MFC Technical Note 39 has the gory details. The positional dependency of the items in a dispatch map has one very serious implication for Automation programmers: The order of those items must agree with the dispatch IDs in the ODL file. This means that if you hand-edit a wizard-generated dispatch map and change the order of the items in any way, you must edit the ODL file, too. You can get away with editing the dispatch map and leaving the ODL file unchanged for clients that use late binding, but early binding clients will get terribly confused if the type library says one thing and *IDispatch* says another. For this reason, MFC provides alternative dispatch map macros that accept dispatch IDs; they, too, are documented in Technical Note 39. You still have to make sure that the dispatch IDs in the dispatch map and the ODL file agree, but the order of the statements in a dispatch map built with these macros is inconsequential. ClassWizard doesn't use the dispatch ID macros, so if you want to take advantage of them, you'll have to code them yourself.

Writing an Automation Server

You can write dispatch maps by hand if you want to, but it's more convenient to let ClassWizard write them for you. Here are the three basic steps involved in writing an MFC Automation server:

1. Run AppWizard and check the Automation box in the Step 3 dialog box (Step 2 if you choose Dialog Based in Step 1), as shown in Figure 20-3. In the Step 4 dialog box, click the Advanced button and type the server's ProgID into the File Type ID box. (See Figure 20-4.)

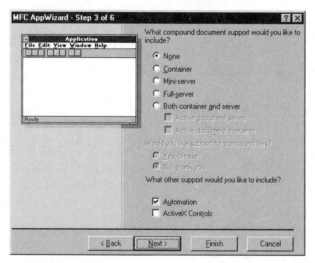

Figure 20-3. *Creating an MFC Automation server.*

2. Use the Add Method button on ClassWizard's Automation page to add Automation methods. (See Figure 20-5.)

3. Use the Add Property button on ClassWizard's Automation page to add Automation properties.

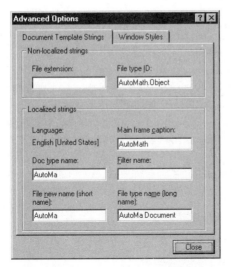

Figure 20-4. *Specifying an Automation server's ProgID.*

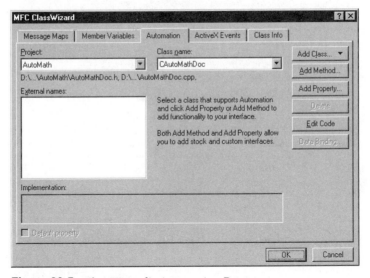

Figure 20-5. *ClassWizard's Automation Page.*

By default, only one of the classes present in an application created by AppWizard can have Automation properties and methods added to it. For a doc/view application, that class is the document class. For a dialog-based application, the "Automatable" class is a proxy class that's derived from *CCmdTarget* and attached to the dialog class. Why are these the only classes that will support Automation methods and properties? Because these are the only classes that AppWizard endows with the infrastructure necessary to act as Automation objects. Later in this chapter, you'll learn how to add other Automatable classes to an MFC Automation server so that it can host as many Automation objects as you like.

Adding Automation Methods

Adding an Automation method to an MFC Automation server is as simple as clicking ClassWizard's Add Method button and filling in the Add Method dialog box. (See Figure 20-6.) In the dialog box, External Name is the Automation method's name, and Internal Name is the name of the corresponding member function. The two names don't have to be the same, although they usually are. Return Type is the method's return type; it can be any Automation-compatible data type. Method parameters are defined in the Parameter List box. MFC handles the chore of unpackaging the VARIANTARGs containing the method parameters and packaging the method's return value in the VARIANT passed to *IDispatch::Invoke*.

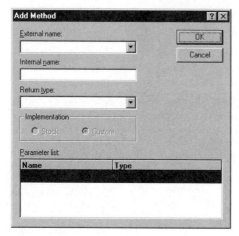

Figure 20-6. *ClassWizard's Add Method dialog box.*

When it adds an Automation method, ClassWizard makes four modifications to the project's source code files:

■ The function that implements the method is declared in the class's header file.

■ An empty function implementation is added to the class's CPP file.

■ A DISP_FUNCTION statement is added to the class's dispatch map.

■ The method and its dispatch ID are added to the project's ODL file.

After ClassWizard is finished, it's your job to implement the method by filling in the empty function body.

Adding Automation Properties

You can also use ClassWizard to add Automation properties. MFC distinguishes between two types of Automation properties:

■   Member variable properties

■   Get/set properties

A member variable property exposes a member variable as an Automation property. A get/set property is a property that's implemented by get and set functions in your source code. A member variable property makes sense if the property value lends itself to being stored in a class member variable and if the Automation server doesn't need control over values assigned to the property. You should use a get/set property instead if any of the following conditions is true:

■   The property value can't be stored in a simple member variable. For example, a *Visible* property controlling the visibility of an Automation server's window is usually implemented as a get/set property so that the get function can call *CWnd::IsWindowVisible* and the set function can call *CWnd::ShowWindow*.

■   The server wants to control the values assigned to a property. For example, if legitimate values range from 1 to 10, the set function could constrain property values to numbers in this range.

■   The property is a read-only property. In this case, the set function should call the *SetNotSupported* function an Automatable class inherits from *CCmdTarget* to generate a run-time error if a client attempts to alter the property value.

■   The property is a write-only property—for example, a password. A write-only property's get function should call *GetNotSupported* to generate a run-time error if a client attempts to read the property value.

To add a member variable property, click ClassWizard's Add Property button and select Member Variable. Then fill in the other fields of the Add Property dialog box pictured in Figure 20-7. External Name specifies the property name. Type is the property's Automation-compatible data type. Variable Name identifies the member variable that stores the property value. ClassWizard will add this member variable for you and wire it into the dispatch map. Notification Function specifies the name of the member function that's called when a client assigns a value to the property. You can enter any name you want into this box, and ClassWizard will add the function for you. If you don't care when the property value changes, leave this box blank, and no notification function will be added. Notification functions are useful when you want to respond immediately to changes in property values—for example, to repaint a window whose background color is exposed as a member variable property.

Under the hood, ClassWizard adds a DISP_PROPERTY statement to the class's dispatch map when a member variable property without a notification function is

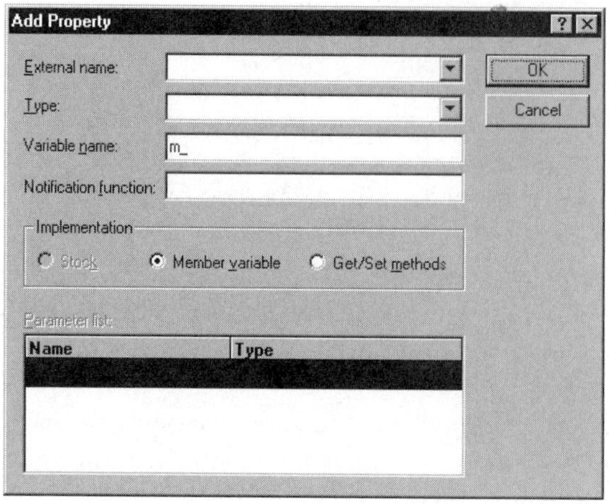

Figure 20-7. *Adding a member variable Automation property.*

added and a DISP_PROPERTY_NOTIFY macro when a member variable property *with* a notification function is added. It also declares the property in the project's ODL file.

If the Add Property dialog box's Get/Set Methods option is checked, ClassWizard adds a get/set property to the Automation server. (See Figure 20-8.) Besides adding member functions named Get*PropertyName* and Set*PropertyName* to the Automation class and declaring the property in the ODL file, ClassWizard adds either a DISP-_PROPERTY_EX or a DISP_PROPERTY_PARAM statement to the class's dispatch map. DISP_PROPERTY_PARAM defines a property with parameters; DISP_PROPERTY_EX defines a property without parameters. If you define parameters in the Parameter List box, a client must supply those input parameters when reading or writing the property. Automation servers sometimes use get/set properties with parameters to implement *indexed properties*, which are described later in this chapter in the section "A More Complex Automation Server."

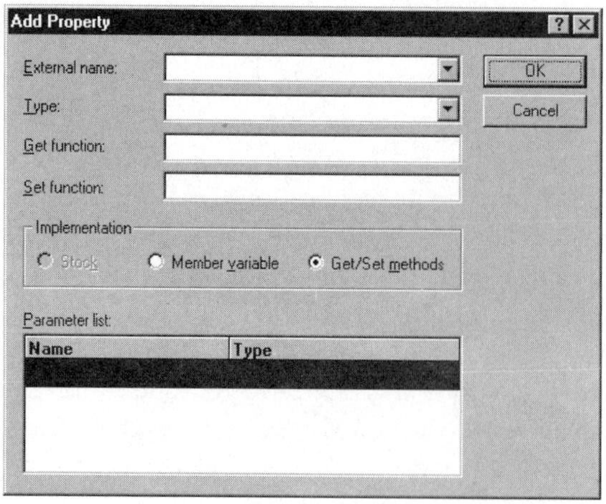

Figure 20-8. *Adding a get/set Automation property.*

A Simple Automation Server

To get your feet wet writing a living, breathing MFC Automation server, try this simple exercise:

1. Use AppWizard to start a new project named AutoMath. Choose Single Document in AppWizard's Step 1 dialog box to make the server a single document interface (SDI) application. Check the Automation box in Step 3 to make the application an Automation server, and in Step 4, click the Advanced button and type *AutoMath.Object* into the File Type ID box. This is the Automation object's ProgID.

2. On ClassWizard's Automation page, select *CAutoMathDoc* from the Class Name drop-down list, click Add Method, and fill in the Add Method dialog box as shown in Figure 20-9. Click OK followed by Edit Code to go to the method's empty function body, and implement it as follows:

```
long CAutoMathDoc::Add (long a, long b)
{
    return a + b;
}
```

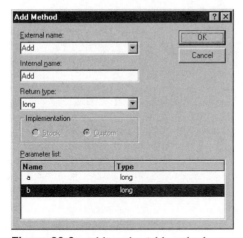

Figure 20-9. *Adding the Add method.*

3. Repeat step 2 to add an Automation method named *Subtract*. Implement the method as follows:

```
long CAutoMathDoc::Subtract (long a, long b)
{
    return a - b;
}
```

4. On ClassWizard's Automation page, click Add Property and add a get/set property named *Pi*. (See Figure 20-10.) Implement the property's get and set functions like this:

```
double CAutoMathDoc::GetPi ()
{
    return 3.1415926;
}

void CAutoMathDoc::SetPi (double newValue)
{
    SetNotSupported ();
}
```

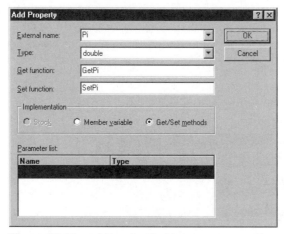

Figure 20-10. *Adding the Pi property.*

5. Build the application and run it once to register it on your system. (An MFC Automation server registers itself each time it's run. Registration involves writing the server's ProgID and other information to the host system's registry.)

Now you're ready to test the AutoMath server that you just created. To perform the test, enter the following VBScript statements into a text file named Test.vbs:

```
Set Math = CreateObject ("AutoMath.Object")
Sum = Math.Add (2, 2)
MsgBox ("2 + 2 = " + CStr (Sum))
MsgBox ("pi = " + CStr (Math.Pi))
```

Then execute the script by double-clicking the Test.vbs file icon. This will run the script under the auspices of the Windows Scripting Host. Two message boxes should appear on the screen. The first displays the sum of 2 and 2. The second displays the value of pi.

See? Automation is easy when you use MFC!

Automation Hierarchies

You can build Automation servers of arbitrary complexity by adding methods and properties ad infinitum. But Automation servers can grow unwieldy if they're weighted down with hundreds of methods and properties. That's why Automation programmers often "objectify" their servers' feature sets by implementing Automation hierarchies.

An Automation hierarchy is a set of Automation objects joined together to form a tree-structured object model. Figure 20-11 shows the top four levels of Microsoft Excel's Automation hierarchy. Rather than hang all its methods and properties off a single object, Excel divides them among a top-level *Application* object and numerous subobjects. The following Visual Basic code starts Excel and turns on the Caps Lock Correct feature, which gives Excel permission to fIX wORDS lIKE tHESE:

```
Dim Excel as Object
Set Excel = CreateObject ("Excel.Application")
Excel.AutoCorrect.CorrectCapsLock = 1
```

Caps Lock Correct is exposed to Automation clients as a property of the *AutoCorrect* object. *AutoCorrect*, in turn, is a subobject of the *Application* object. A hierarchical object model such as this one lends organization to the server's dispinterfaces and makes the programming model easier to learn.

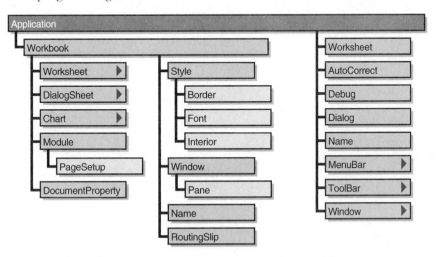

▶ Indicates that this object contains one or more subobjects that are not shown.

Figure 20-11. *The Excel object model.*

How difficult is it to implement Automation hierarchies in MFC Automation servers? Not difficult at all—once you know how. The secret is twofold. First, you add one Automatable class to the application for each subobject you want to implement. To each Automatable class, you add Automation methods and properties. Second, you wire up the hierarchy by connecting child objects to their parents. An object is made a child of another by adding a get/set property of type LPDISPATCH to the parent object and implementing the get function by returning the child's *IDispatch* interface pointer. You can retrieve the child object's *IDispatch* pointer by calling the *GetIDispatch* function the child object inherits from *CCmdTarget*.

Adding Automatable classes is easy, too. Simply click ClassWizard's Add Class button, select New, enter a class name, select *CCmdTarget* as the base class, and check the Automation option near the bottom of the dialog box. (See Figure 20-12.) To make the class externally createable (that is, to give it its own ProgID so that it, too, can be created by Automation clients), check Createable By Type ID instead and enter a ProgID in the box to its right.

Figure 20-12. *Adding an Automatable class.*

A More Complex Automation Server

The AutoPie application in Figure 20-13 is an MFC Automation server that implements the two-level object model shown in Figure 20-14. AutoPie draws pie charts depicting quarterly revenue values. The revenue values are exposed through an indexed property named *Revenue*, which belongs to the *Chart* object. The property is said to be *indexed* because accesses to it must be accompanied by a number from 1 to 4 specifying a quarter (first quarter, second quarter, and so on). Internally, *Revenue* is implemented as a get/set Automation property with one parameter in its parameter list.

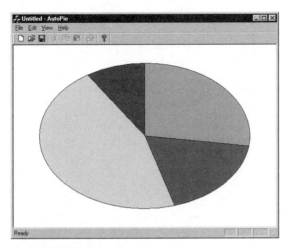

Figure 20-13. *The AutoPie window.*

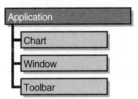

Figure 20-14. *AutoPie's object model.*

Revenue is just one of several properties that AutoPie exposes. The following list identifies all the Automation methods and properties that AutoPie supports as well as the objects to which those methods and properties belong:

Object	Properties	Methods
Application	N/A	Quit ( )
Chart	Revenue (*quarter*)	Save (*pathname*)
Window	Visible	Refresh ( )
Toolbar	Visible	N/A

The top-level *Application* object represents the application itself. Its lone method, *Quit*, terminates the application. The *Chart* object represents the pie chart. *Save* saves the quarterly revenue values to disk. *Window* represents the application's window. Its *Visible* property can be used to hide or display the window, and *Refresh* forces the window (and the chart displayed inside it) to repaint. Finally, the *Toolbar* object represents the window's toolbar, which can be toggled on and off by setting *Visible* to a 0 (off) or a nonzero (on) value.

You can test AutoPie using the following VBScript applet:

```
Set Pie = CreateObject ("AutoPie.Application")
Pie.Chart.Revenue (1) = 420
Pie.Chart.Revenue (2) = 234
Pie.Chart.Revenue (3) = 380
Pie.Chart.Revenue (4) = 640
Pie.Window.Visible = 1
MsgBox ("Click OK to double third-quarter revenues")
Pie.Chart.Revenue (3) = Pie.Chart.Revenue (3) * 2
Pie.Window.Refresh
Pie.Chart.Save ("C:\Chart.pie")
MsgBox ("Test completed")
```

When executed, the script starts the Automation server by passing AutoPie's ProgID to *CreateObject*. It then assigns revenue values and makes the AutoPie window visible. (By default, MFC Automation servers that aren't dialog-based don't show their windows when they're started by Automation clients.) Next the script displays a message box. When the message box is dismissed, the third-quarter revenue is read, multiplied by 2, and written back to the Automation server. Afterward, *Refresh* is called to update the pie chart. Finally, the *Chart* object's *Save* method is called to save the pie chart to a file, and a message box is displayed announcing that the test is complete.

Pertinent portions of AutoPie's source code are reproduced in Figure 20-15. The top-level *Application* object is represented by the application's document class. When I used AppWizard to generate the project, I entered "AutoPie.Application" for the ProgID. Because AppWizard automated the document class, *CAutoPieDoc* became a proxy of sorts for the *Application* object at the top of the hierarchy. The subobjects are represented by *CAutoChart*, *CAutoWindow*, and *CAutoToolbar*, which I derived from *CCmdTarget* using ClassWizard. Each is an Automatable class. (Refer to Figure 20-12.) After generating these classes, I used ClassWizard to add Automation methods and properties.

AutoPie.h

```
// AutoPie.h : main header file for the AUTOPIE application
//

#if !defined(
    AFX_AUTOPIE_H__3B5BA30B_3B72_11D2_AC82_006008A8274D__INCLUDED_)
#define AFX_AUTOPIE_H__3B5BA30B_3B72_11D2_AC82_006008A8274D__INCLUDED_

#if _MSC_VER > 1000
#pragma once
#endif // _MSC_VER > 1000
```

Figure 20-15. *The AutoPie program.*

```
#ifndef __AFX)WIN_H__
    #error include 'stdafx.h' before including this file for PCH
#endif

#include "resource.h"        // main symbols

/////////////////////////////////////////////////////////////////////////////
// CAutoPieApp:
// See AutoPie.cpp for the implementation of this class
//

class CAutoPieApp : public CWinApp
{
public:
    CAutoPieApp();

// Overrides
    // ClassWizard generated virtual function overrides
    //{{AFX_VIRTUAL(CAutoPieApp)
    public:
    virtual BOOL InitInstance();
    //}}AFX_VIRTUAL

// Implementation
    COleTemplateServer m_server;
        // Server object for document creation
    //{{AFX_MSG(CAutoPieApp)
    afx_msg void OnAppAbout();
        // NOTE - the ClassWizard will add and remove member functions here.
        //    DO NOT EDIT what you see in these blocks of generated code !
    //}}AFX_MSG
    DECLARE_MESSAGE_MAP()
};


/////////////////////////////////////////////////////////////////////////////


//{{AFX_INSERT_LOCATION}}
// Microsoft Visual C++ will insert additional declarations
// immediately before the previous line.

#endif
// !defined(AFX_AUTOPIE_H__3B5BA30B_3B72_11D2_AC82_006008A8274D__INCLUDED_)
```

(continued)

Figure 20-15 *continued*

AutoPie.cpp

```cpp
// AutoPie.cpp : Defines the class behaviors for the application.
//

#include "stdafx.h"
#include "AutoPie.h"

#include "MainFrm.h"
#include "AutoPieDoc.h"
#include "AutoPieView.h"

#ifdef _DEBUG
#define new DEBUG_NEW
#undef THIS_FILE
static char THIS_FILE[] = __FILE__;
#endif


/////////////////////////////////////////////////////////////////////////////
// CAutoPieApp

BEGIN_MESSAGE_MAP(CAutoPieApp, CWinApp)
    //{{AFX_MSG_MAP(CAutoPieApp)
    ON_COMMAND(ID_APP_ABOUT, OnAppAbout)
        // NOTE - the ClassWizard will add and remove mapping macros here.
        //    DO NOT EDIT what you see in these blocks of generated code!
    //}}AFX_MSG_MAP
    // Standard file based document commands
    ON_COMMAND(ID_FILE_NEW, CWinApp::OnFileNew)
    ON_COMMAND(ID_FILE_OPEN, CWinApp::OnFileOpen)
END_MESSAGE_MAP()


/////////////////////////////////////////////////////////////////////////////
// CAutoPieApp construction

CAutoPieApp::CAutoPieApp()
{
    // TODO: add construction code here,
    // Place all significant initialization in InitInstance
}


/////////////////////////////////////////////////////////////////////////////
// The one and only CAutoPieApp object

CAutoPieApp theApp;
```

```
// This identifier was generated to be statistically unique for your app.
// You may change it if you prefer to choose a specific identifier.

// {3B5BA306-3B72-11D2-AC82-006008A8274D}
static const CLSID clsid =
{ 0x3b5ba306, 0x3b72, 0x11d2,
    { 0xac, 0x82, 0x0, 0x60, 0x8, 0xa8, 0x27, 0x4d } };


/////////////////////////////////////////////////////////////////////////
// CAutoPieApp initialization

BOOL CAutoPieApp::InitInstance()
{
    // Initialize OLE libraries
    if (!AfxOleInit())
    {
        AfxMessageBox(IDP_OLE_INIT_FAILED);
        return FALSE;
    }

    // Standard initialization
    // If you are not using these features and wish to reduce the size
    //  of your final executable, you should remove from the following
    //  the specific initialization routines you do not need.

    // Change the registry key under which our settings are stored.
    // TODO: You should modify this string to be something appropriate
    // such as the name of your company or organization.
    SetRegistryKey(_T("Local AppWizard-Generated Applications"));

    LoadStdProfileSettings();  // Load standard INI file options
                               // (including MRU)

    // Register the application's document templates.  Document templates
    //  serve as the connection between documents, frame windows and views.

    CSingleDocTemplate* pDocTemplate;
    pDocTemplate = new CSingleDocTemplate(
        IDR_MAINFRAME,
        RUNTIME_CLASS(CAutoPieDoc),
        RUNTIME_CLASS(CMainFrame),        // main SDI frame window
        RUNTIME_CLASS(CAutoPieView));
    AddDocTemplate(pDocTemplate);

    // Connect the COleTemplateServer to the document template.
    //  The COleTemplateServer creates new documents on behalf
    //  of requesting OLE containers by using information
    //  specified in the document template.
```

(continued)

Figure 20-15 *continued*

```
    m_server.ConnectTemplate(clsid, pDocTemplate, TRUE);
        // Note: SDI applications register server objects only if /Embedding
        //   or /Automation is present on the command line.

    // Enable DDE Execute open
    EnableShellOpen();
    RegisterShellFileTypes(TRUE);

    // Parse command line for standard shell commands, DDE, file open
    CCommandLineInfo cmdInfo;
    ParseCommandLine(cmdInfo);

    // Check to see if launched as OLE server
    if (cmdInfo.m_bRunEmbedded || cmdInfo.m_bRunAutomated)
    {
        // Register all OLE server (factories) as running.  This enables
        //  the OLE libraries to create objects from other applications.
        COleTemplateServer::RegisterAll();

        // Application was run with /Embedding or /Automation.
        //  Don't show themain window in this case.
        return TRUE;
    }

    // When a server application is launched stand-alone, it is a good idea
    //  to update the system registry in case it has been damaged.
    m_server.UpdateRegistry(OAT_DISPATCH_OBJECT);
    COleObjectFactory::UpdateRegistryAll();

    // Dispatch commands specified on the command line
    if (!ProcessShellCommand(cmdInfo))
        return FALSE;

    // The one and only window has been initialized, so show and update it.
    m_pMainWnd->ShowWindow(SW_SHOW);
    m_pMainWnd->UpdateWindow();

    // Enable drag/drop open
    m_pMainWnd->DragAcceptFiles();

    return TRUE;
}

////////////////////////////////////////////////////////////////////////////
// CAboutDlg dialog used for App About

class CAboutDlg : public CDialog
```

```
{
public:
    CAboutDlg();

// Dialog Data
    //{{AFX_DATA(CAboutDlg)
    enum { IDD = IDD_ABOUTBOX };
    //}}AFX_DATA

    // ClassWizard generated virtual function overrides
    //{{AFX_VIRTUAL(CAboutDlg)
    protected:
    virtual void DoDataExchange(CDataExchange* pDX);    // DDX/DDV support
    //}}AFX_VIRTUAL

// Implementation
protected:
    //{{AFX_MSG(CAboutDlg)
        // No message handlers
    //}}AFX_MSG
    DECLARE_MESSAGE_MAP()
};

CAboutDlg::CAboutDlg() : CDialog(CAboutDlg::IDD)
{
    //{{AFX_DATA_INIT(CAboutDlg)
    //}}AFX_DATA_INIT
}

void CAboutDlg::DoDataExchange(CDataExchange* pDX)
{
    CDialog::DoDataExchange(pDX);
    //{{AFX_DATA_MAP(CAboutDlg)
    //}}AFX_DATA_MAP
}

BEGIN_MESSAGE_MAP(CAboutDlg, CDialog)
    //{{AFX_MSG_MAP(CAboutDlg)
        // No message handlers
    //}}AFX_MSG_MAP
END_MESSAGE_MAP()

// App command to run the dialog
void CAutoPieApp::OnAppAbout()
{
    CAboutDlg aboutDlg;
    aboutDlg.DoModal();
}
```

(continued)

Figure 20-15 *continued*

```
/////////////////////////////////////////////////////////////////////////////
// CAutoPieApp message handlers
```

AutoPieDoc.h

```
// AutoPieDoc.h : interface of the CAutoPieDoc class
//
/////////////////////////////////////////////////////////////////////////////

#if !defined(
    AFX_AUTOPIEDOC_H__3B5BA312_3B72_11D2_AC82_006008A8274D__INCLUDED_)
#define AFX_AUTOPIEDOC_H__3B5BA312_3B72_11D2_AC82_006008A8274D__INCLUDED_

#include "AutoChart.h"      // Added by ClassView
#include "AutoWindow.h"     // Added by ClassView
#include "AutoToolbar.h"    // Added by ClassView
#if _MSC_VER > 1000
#pragma once
#endif // _MSC_VER > 1000


class CAutoPieDoc : public CDocument
{
protected: // create from serialization only
    CAutoPieDoc();
    DECLARE_DYNCREATE(CAutoPieDoc)

// Attributes
public:

// Operations
public:

// Overrides
    // ClassWizard generated virtual function overrides
    //{{AFX_VIRTUAL(CAutoPieDoc)
    public:
    virtual BOOL OnNewDocument();
    virtual void Serialize(CArchive& ar);
    //}}AFX_VIRTUAL

// Implementation
public:
    void SetRevenue (int nQuarter, int nNewValue);
```

```
    int GetRevenue (int nQuarter);
    virtual ~CAutoPieDoc();
#ifdef _DEBUG
    virtual void AssertValid() const;
    virtual void Dump(CDumpContext& dc) const;
#endif

protected:

// Generated message map functions
protected:
    CAutoToolbar m_autoToolbar;
    CAutoWindow m_autoWindow;
    CAutoChart m_autoChart;
    int m_nRevenues[4];
    //{{AFX_MSG(CAutoPieDoc)
        // NOTE - the ClassWizard will add and remove member functions here.
        //    DO NOT EDIT what you see in these blocks of generated code !
    //}}AFX_MSG
    DECLARE_MESSAGE_MAP()

    // Generated OLE dispatch map functions
    //{{AFX_DISPATCH(CAutoPieDoc)
    afx_msg LPDISPATCH GetChart();
    afx_msg void SetChart(LPDISPATCH newValue);
    afx_msg LPDISPATCH GetWindow();
    afx_msg void SetWindow(LPDISPATCH newValue);
    afx_msg LPDISPATCH GetToolbar();
    afx_msg void SetToolbar(LPDISPATCH newValue);
    afx_msg void Quit();
    //}}AFX_DISPATCH
    DECLARE_DISPATCH_MAP()
    DECLARE_INTERFACE_MAP()
};

/////////////////////////////////////////////////////////////////////////////

//{{AFX_INSERT_LOCATION}}
// Microsoft Visual C++ will insert additional declarations
// immediately before the previous line.

#endif
// !defined(
//    AFX_AUTOPIEDOC_H__3B5BA312_3B72_11D2_AC82_006008A8274D__INCLUDED_)
```

(continued)

Figure 20-15 *continued*

AutoPieDoc.cpp

```cpp
// AutoPieDoc.cpp : implementation of the CAutoPieDoc class
//

#include "stdafx.h"
#include "AutoPie.h"

#include "AutoPieDoc.h"

#ifdef _DEBUG
#define new DEBUG_NEW
#undef THIS_FILE
static char THIS_FILE[] = __FILE__;
#endif

/////////////////////////////////////////////////////////////////////////////
// CAutoPieDoc

IMPLEMENT_DYNCREATE(CAutoPieDoc, CDocument)

BEGIN_MESSAGE_MAP(CAutoPieDoc, CDocument)
    //{{AFX_MSG_MAP(CAutoPieDoc)
        // NOTE - the ClassWizard will add and remove mapping macros here.
        //    DO NOT EDIT what you see in these blocks of generated code!
    //}}AFX_MSG_MAP
END_MESSAGE_MAP()

BEGIN_DISPATCH_MAP(CAutoPieDoc, CDocument)
    //{{AFX_DISPATCH_MAP(CAutoPieDoc)
    DISP_PROPERTY_EX(CAutoPieDoc, "Chart", GetChart, SetChart, VT_DISPATCH)
    DISP_PROPERTY_EX(CAutoPieDoc, "Window", GetWindow,
        SetWindow, VT_DISPATCH)
    DISP_PROPERTY_EX(CAutoPieDoc, "Toolbar", GetToolbar,
        SetToolbar, VT_DISPATCH)
    DISP_FUNCTION(CAutoPieDoc, "Quit", Quit, VT_EMPTY, VTS_NONE)
    //}}AFX_DISPATCH_MAP
END_DISPATCH_MAP()

// Note: we add support for IID_IAutoPie to support typesafe binding
// from VBA.  This IID must match the GUID that is attached to the
// dispinterface in the .ODL file.

// {3B5BA308-3B72-11D2-AC82-006008A8274D}
static const IID IID_IAutoPie =
```

```
{ 0x3b5ba308, 0x3b72, 0x11d2,

    { 0xac, 0x82, 0x0, 0x60, 0x8, 0xa8, 0x27, 0x4d } };

BEGIN_INTERFACE_MAP(CAutoPieDoc, CDocument)
    INTERFACE_PART(CAutoPieDoc, IID_IAutoPie, Dispatch)
END_INTERFACE_MAP()

/////////////////////////////////////////////////////////////////////////
// CAutoPieDoc construction/destruction

CAutoPieDoc::CAutoPieDoc()
{
    EnableAutomation();

    AfxOleLockApp();
}

CAutoPieDoc::~CAutoPieDoc()
{
    AfxOleUnlockApp();
}

BOOL CAutoPieDoc::OnNewDocument()
{
    if (!CDocument::OnNewDocument())
        return FALSE;

    m_nRevenues[0] = 1;
    m_nRevenues[1] = 1;
    m_nRevenues[2] = 1;
    m_nRevenues[3] = 1;
    return TRUE;
}

/////////////////////////////////////////////////////////////////////////
// CAutoPieDoc serialization

void CAutoPieDoc::Serialize(CArchive& ar)
{
    if (ar.IsStoring())
    {
        for (int i=0; i<4; i++)
            ar << m_nRevenues[i];
    }
    else
    {
        for (int i=0; i<4; i++)
            ar >> m_nRevenues[i];
```

(continued)

Figure 20-15 *continued*

```
    }
}

/////////////////////////////////////////////////////////////////////////
// CAutoPieDoc diagnostics

#ifdef _DEBUG
void CAutoPieDoc::AssertValid() const
{
    CDocument::AssertValid();
}

void CAutoPieDoc::Dump(CDumpContext& dc) const
{
    CDocument::Dump(dc);
}
#endif //_DEBUG

/////////////////////////////////////////////////////////////////////////
// CAutoPieDoc commands

int CAutoPieDoc::GetRevenue(int nQuarter)
{
    ASSERT (nQuarter >= 0 && nQuarter <= 3);
    return m_nRevenues[nQuarter];
}

void CAutoPieDoc::SetRevenue(int nQuarter, int nNewValue)
{
    ASSERT (nQuarter >= 0 && nQuarter <= 3);
    m_nRevenues[nQuarter] = nNewValue;
}

void CAutoPieDoc::Quit()
{
    AfxGetMainWnd ()->PostMessage (WM_CLOSE, 0, 0);
}

LPDISPATCH CAutoPieDoc::GetChart()
{
    return m_autoChart.GetIDispatch (TRUE);
}

void CAutoPieDoc::SetChart(LPDISPATCH newValue)
{
    SetNotSupported ();
}
```

```
LPDISPATCH CAutoPieDoc::GetWindow()
{
    return m_autoWindow.GetIDispatch (TRUE);
}

void CAutoPieDoc::SetWindow(LPDISPATCH newValue)
{
    SetNotSupported ();
}

LPDISPATCH CAutoPieDoc::GetToolbar()
{
    return m_autoToolbar.GetIDispatch (TRUE);
}

void CAutoPieDoc::SetToolbar(LPDISPATCH newValue)
{
    SetNotSupported ();
}
```

AutoChart.h

```
#if !defined(
    AFX_AUTOCHART_H__3B5BA31E_3B72_11D2_AC82_006008A8274D__INCLUDED_)
#define AFX_AUTOCHART_H__3B5BA31E_3B72_11D2_AC82_006008A8274D__INCLUDED_

#if _MSC_VER > 1000
#pragma once
#endif // _MSC_VER > 1000
// AutoChart.h : header file
//

#define ID_ERROR_OUTOFRANGE 100

/////////////////////////////////////////////////////////////////////////////
// CAutoChart command target

class CAutoChart : public CCmdTarget
{
    DECLARE_DYNCREATE(CAutoChart)

    CAutoChart();           // protected constructor used by dynamic creation

// Attributes
public:
    virtual ~CAutoChart();
```

(continued)

Figure 20-15 *continued*

```
// Operations
public:

// Overrides
    // ClassWizard generated virtual function overrides
    //{{AFX_VIRTUAL(CAutoChart)
    public:
    virtual void OnFinalRelease();
    //}}AFX_VIRTUAL

// Implementation
protected:
    // Generated message map functions
    //{{AFX_MSG(CAutoChart)
        // NOTE - the ClassWizard will add and remove member functions here.
    //}}AFX_MSG

    DECLARE_MESSAGE_MAP()
    // Generated OLE dispatch map functions
    //{{AFX_DISPATCH(CAutoChart)
    afx_msg BOOL Save(LPCTSTR pszPath);
    afx_msg long GetRevenue(short nQuarter);
    afx_msg void SetRevenue(short nQuarter, long nNewValue);
    //}}AFX_DISPATCH
    DECLARE_DISPATCH_MAP()
    DECLARE_INTERFACE_MAP()
};


/////////////////////////////////////////////////////////////////////////

//{{AFX_INSERT_LOCATION}}
// Microsoft Visual C++ will insert additional declarations
// immediately before the previous line.

#endif
// !defined(
//      AFX_AUTOCHART_H__3B5BA31E_3B72_11D2_AC82_006008A8274D__INCLUDED_)
```

AutoChart.cpp

```
// AutoChart.cpp : implementation file
//

#include "stdafx.h"
#include "AutoPie.h"
```

```
#include "AutoChart.h"
#include "AutoPieDoc.h"

#ifdef _DEBUG
#define new DEBUG_NEW
#undef THIS_FILE
static char THIS_FILE[] = __FILE__;
#endif

/////////////////////////////////////////////////////////////////////////////
// CAutoChart

IMPLEMENT_DYNCREATE(CAutoChart, CCmdTarget)

CAutoChart::CAutoChart()
{
    EnableAutomation();
}

CAutoChart::~CAutoChart()
{
}

void CAutoChart::OnFinalRelease()
{
    // When the last reference for an automation object is released
    // OnFinalRelease is called.  The base class will automatically
    // deletes the object.  Add additional cleanup required for your
    // object before calling the base class.

    CCmdTarget::OnFinalRelease();
}

BEGIN_MESSAGE_MAP(CAutoChart, CCmdTarget)
    //{{AFX_MSG_MAP(CAutoChart)
        // NOTE - the ClassWizard will add and remove mapping macros here.
    //}}AFX_MSG_MAP
END_MESSAGE_MAP()

BEGIN_DISPATCH_MAP(CAutoChart, CCmdTarget)
    //{{AFX_DISPATCH_MAP(CAutoChart)
    DISP_FUNCTION(CAutoChart, "Save", Save, VT_BOOL, VTS_BSTR)
    DISP_PROPERTY_PARAM(CAutoChart, "Revenue", GetRevenue,
        SetRevenue, VT_I4, VTS_I2)
    //}}AFX_DISPATCH_MAP
END_DISPATCH_MAP()
```

(continued)

Figure 20-15 *continued*

```
// Note: we add support for IID_IAutoChart to support typesafe binding
//  from VBA.  This IID must match the GUID that is attached to the
//  dispinterface in the .ODL file.

// {3B5BA31D-3B72-11D2-AC82-006008A8274D}
static const IID IID_IAutoChart =
{ 0x3b5ba31d, 0x3b72, 0x11d2,
    { 0xac, 0x82, 0x0, 0x60, 0x8, 0xa8, 0x27, 0x4d } };

BEGIN_INTERFACE_MAP(CAutoChart, CCmdTarget)
    INTERFACE_PART(CAutoChart, IID_IAutoChart, Dispatch)
END_INTERFACE_MAP()

/////////////////////////////////////////////////////////////////////////
// CAutoChart message handlers

BOOL CAutoChart::Save(LPCTSTR pszPath)
{
    CFrameWnd* pFrame = (CFrameWnd*) AfxGetMainWnd ();
    CAutoPieDoc* pDoc = (CAutoPieDoc*) pFrame->GetActiveDocument ();
    return pDoc->OnSaveDocument (pszPath);
}

long CAutoChart::GetRevenue(short nQuarter)
{
    long lResult = -1;

    if (nQuarter >= 1 && nQuarter <= 4) {
        CFrameWnd* pFrame = (CFrameWnd*) AfxGetMainWnd ();
        CAutoPieDoc* pDoc = (CAutoPieDoc*) pFrame->GetActiveDocument ();
        lResult = (long) pDoc->GetRevenue (nQuarter - 1);
    }
    else {
        //
        // If the quarter number is out of range, fail the call
        // and let the caller know precisely why it failed.
        //
        AfxThrowOleDispatchException (ID_ERROR_OUTOFRANGE,
            _T ("Invalid parameter specified when reading Revenue"));
    }
    return lResult;
}

void CAutoChart::SetRevenue(short nQuarter, long nNewValue)
{
    if (nQuarter >= 1 && nQuarter <= 4) {
        CFrameWnd* pFrame = (CFrameWnd*) AfxGetMainWnd ();
```

```
            CAutoPieDoc* pDoc = (CAutoPieDoc*) pFrame->GetActiveDocument ();
            pDoc->SetRevenue (nQuarter - 1, nNewValue);
    }
    else {
        //
        // If the quarter number is out of range, fail the call
        // and let the caller know precisely why it failed.
        //
        AfxThrowOleDispatchException (ID_ERROR_OUTOFRANGE,
            _T ("Invalid parameter specified when setting Revenue"));
    }
}
```

AutoWindow.h

```
#if !defined(
    AFX_AUTOWINDOW_H__3B5BA321_3B72_11D2_AC82_006008A8274D__INCLUDED_)
#define AFX_AUTOWINDOW_H__3B5BA321_3B72_11D2_AC82_006008A8274D__INCLUDED_

#if _MSC_VER > 1000
#pragma once
#endif // _MSC_VER > 1000
// AutoWindow.h : header file
//

/////////////////////////////////////////////////////////////////////////////
// CAutoWindow command target

class CAutoWindow : public CCmdTarget
{
    DECLARE_DYNCREATE(CAutoWindow)

    CAutoWindow();          // protected constructor used by dynamic creation

// Attributes
public:
    virtual ~CAutoWindow();

// Operations
public:

// Overrides
    // ClassWizard generated virtual function overrides
    //{{AFX_VIRTUAL(CAutoWindow)
    public:
```

(continued)

Figure 20-15 *continued*

```
virtual void OnFinalRelease();
    //}}AFX_VIRTUAL

// Implementation
protected:
    // Generated message map functions
    //{{AFX_MSG(CAutoWindow)
        // NOTE - the ClassWizard will add and remove member functions here.
    //}}AFX_MSG

    DECLARE_MESSAGE_MAP()
    // Generated OLE dispatch map functions
    //{{AFX_DISPATCH(CAutoWindow)
    afx_msg BOOL GetVisible();
    afx_msg void SetVisible(BOOL bNewValue);
    afx_msg void Refresh();
    //}}AFX_DISPATCH
    DECLARE_DISPATCH_MAP()
    DECLARE_INTERFACE_MAP()
};


//////////////////////////////////////////////////////////////////////

//{{AFX_INSERT_LOCATION}}
// Microsoft Visual C++ will insert additional declarations
// immediately before the previous line.

#endif
// !defined(
//      AFX_AUTOWINDOW_H__3B5BA321_3B72_11D2_AC82_006008A8274D__INCLUDED_)
```

AutoWindow.cpp

```
// AutoWindow.cpp : implementation file
//

#include "stdafx.h"
#include "AutoPie.h"
#include "AutoWindow.h"
#include "AutoPieDoc.h"

#ifdef _DEBUG
#define new DEBUG_NEW
#undef THIS_FILE
static char THIS_FILE[] = __FILE__;
#endif
```

```
/////////////////////////////////////////////////////////////////////////
// CAutoWindow

IMPLEMENT_DYNCREATE(CAutoWindow, CCmdTarget)

CAutoWindow::CAutoWindow()
{
    EnableAutomation();
}

CAutoWindow::~CAutoWindow()
{
}

void CAutoWindow::OnFinalRelease()
{
    // When the last reference for an automation object is released
    // OnFinalRelease is called.  The base class will automatically
    // deletes the object.  Add additional cleanup required for your
    // object before calling the base class.

    CCmdTarget::OnFinalRelease();
}

BEGIN_MESSAGE_MAP(CAutoWindow, CCmdTarget)
    //{{AFX_MSG_MAP(CAutoWindow)
        // NOTE - the ClassWizard will add and remove mapping macros here.
    //}}AFX_MSG_MAP
END_MESSAGE_MAP()

BEGIN_DISPATCH_MAP(CAutoWindow, CCmdTarget)
    //{{AFX_DISPATCH_MAP(CAutoWindow)
    DISP_PROPERTY_EX(CAutoWindow, "Visible", GetVisible,
        SetVisible, VT_BOOL)
    DISP_FUNCTION(CAutoWindow, "Refresh", Refresh, VT_EMPTY, VTS_NONE)
    //}}AFX_DISPATCH_MAP
END_DISPATCH_MAP()

// Note: we add support for IID_IAutoWindow to support typesafe binding
// from VBA.  This IID must match the GUID that is attached to the
// dispinterface in the .ODL file.

// {3B5BA320-3B72-11D2-AC82-006008A8274D}
static const IID IID_IAutoWindow =
{ 0x3b5ba320, 0x3b72, 0x11d2,
    { 0xac, 0x82, 0x0, 0x60, 0x8, 0xa8, 0x27, 0x4d } };
BEGIN_INTERFACE_MAP(CAutoWindow, CCmdTarget)
    INTERFACE_PART(CAutoWindow, IID_IAutoWindow, Dispatch)
END_INTERFACE_MAP()
```

(continued)

Figure 20-15 *continued*

```
///////////////////////////////////////////////////////////////////////////
// CAutoWindow message handlers

void CAutoWindow::Refresh()
{
    CFrameWnd* pFrame = (CFrameWnd*) AfxGetMainWnd ();
    CAutoPieDoc* pDoc = (CAutoPieDoc*) pFrame->GetActiveDocument ();
    pDoc->UpdateAllViews (NULL);
}

BOOL CAutoWindow::GetVisible()
{
    return AfxGetMainWnd ()->IsWindowVisible ();
}

void CAutoWindow::SetVisible(BOOL bNewValue)
{
    AfxGetMainWnd ()->ShowWindow (bNewValue ? SW_SHOW : SW_HIDE);
}
```

AutoToolbar.h

```
#if !defined(
    AFX_AUTOTOOLBAR_H__3B5BA324_3B72_11D2_AC82_006008A8274D__INCLUDED_)
#define AFX_AUTOTOOLBAR_H__3B5BA324_3B72_11D2_AC82_006008A8274D__INCLUDED_

#if _MSC_VER > 1000
#pragma once
#endif // _MSC_VER > 1000
// AutoToolbar.h : header file
//

///////////////////////////////////////////////////////////////////////////
// CAutoToolbar command target

class CAutoToolbar : public CCmdTarget
{
    DECLARE_DYNCREATE(CAutoToolbar)

    CAutoToolbar();          // protected constructor used by dynamic creation

// Attributes
public:
    virtual ~CAutoToolbar();

// Operations
public:

//Overrides
// ClassWizard generated virtual function overrides
```

```
    //{{AFX_VIRTUAL(CAutoToolbar)
    public:
    virtual void OnFinalRelease();
    //}}AFX_VIRTUAL

// Implementation
protected:
    // Generated message map functions
    //{{AFX_MSG(CAutoToolbar)
        // NOTE - the ClassWizard will add and remove member functions here.
    //}}AFX_MSG

    DECLARE_MESSAGE_MAP()
    // Generated OLE dispatch map functions
    //{{AFX_DISPATCH(CAutoToolbar)
    afx_msg BOOL GetVisible();
    afx_msg void SetVisible(BOOL bNewValue);
    //}}AFX_DISPATCH
    DECLARE_DISPATCH_MAP()
    DECLARE_INTERFACE_MAP()
};


////////////////////////////////////////////////////////////////////////////

//{{AFX_INSERT_LOCATION}}
// Microsoft Visual C++ will insert additional declarations
// immediately before the previous line.

#endif
// !defined(
//     AFX_AUTOTOOLBAR_H__3B5BA324_3B72_11D2_AC82_006008A8274D__INCLUDED_)
```

AutoToolbar.cpp

```
// AutoToolbar.cpp : implementation file
//

#include "stdafx.h"
#include "AutoPie.h"
#include "AutoToolbar.h"
#include "MainFrm.h"

#ifdef _DEBUG
#define new DEBUG_NEW
#undef THIS_FILE
static char THIS_FILE[] = __FILE__;
#endif
```

(continued)

Figure 20-15 *continued*

```
/////////////////////////////////////////////////////////////////////////
// CAutoToolbar

IMPLEMENT_DYNCREATE(CAutoToolbar, CCmdTarget)

CAutoToolbar::CAutoToolbar()
{
    EnableAutomation();
}

CAutoToolbar::~CAutoToolbar()
{
}

void CAutoToolbar::OnFinalRelease()
{
    // When the last reference for an automation object is released
    // OnFinalRelease is called.  The base class will automatically
    // deletes the object.  Add additional cleanup required for your
    // object before calling the base class.

    CCmdTarget::OnFinalRelease();
}

BEGIN_MESSAGE_MAP(CAutoToolbar, CCmdTarget)
    //{{AFX_MSG_MAP(CAutoToolbar)
        // NOTE - the ClassWizard will add and remove mapping macros here.
    //}}AFX_MSG_MAP
END_MESSAGE_MAP()

BEGIN_DISPATCH_MAP(CAutoToolbar, CCmdTarget)
    //{{AFX_DISPATCH_MAP(CAutoToolbar)
    DISP_PROPERTY_EX(CAutoToolbar, "Visible", GetVisible,
        SetVisible, VT_BOOL)
    //}}AFX_DISPATCH_MAP
END_DISPATCH_MAP()

// Note: we add support for IID_IAutoToolbar to support typesafe binding
//  from VBA.  This IID must match the GUID that is attached to the
//  dispinterface in the .ODL file.

// {3B5BA323-3B72-11D2-AC82-006008A8274D}
static const IID IID_IAutoToolbar =
{ 0x3b5ba323, 0x3b72, 0x11d2,
    { 0xac, 0x82, 0x0, 0x60, 0x8, 0xa8, 0x27, 0x4d } };

BEGIN_INTERFACE_MAP(CAutoToolbar, CCmdTarget)
    INTERFACE_PART(CAutoToolbar, IID_IAutoToolbar, Dispatch)
END_INTERFACE_MAP()
```

```
///////////////////////////////////////////////////////////////////////
// CAutoToolbar message handlers

BOOL CAutoToolbar::GetVisible()
{
    CMainFrame* pFrame = (CMainFrame*) AfxGetMainWnd ();
    return (pFrame->m_wndToolBar.GetStyle () & WS_VISIBLE) ?
        TRUE : FALSE;
}

void CAutoToolbar::SetVisible(BOOL bNewValue)
{
    CMainFrame* pFrame = (CMainFrame*) AfxGetMainWnd ();
    pFrame->ShowControlBar (&pFrame->m_wndToolBar, bNewValue, FALSE);
}
```

AutoPieView.h

```
// AutoPieView.h : interface of the CAutoPieView class
//
///////////////////////////////////////////////////////////////////////

#if !defined(
    AFX_AUTOPIEVIEW_H__3B5BA314_3B72_11D2_AC82_006008A8274D__INCLUDED_)
#define  AFX_AUTOPIEVIEW_H__3B5BA314_3B72_11D2_AC82_006008A8274D__INCLUDED_

#if _MSC_VER > 1000
#pragma once
#endif // _MSC_VER > 1000

#define PI 3.1415926

class CAutoPieView : public CView
{
protected: // create from serialization only
    CAutoPieView();
    DECLARE_DYNCREATE(CAutoPieView)

// Attributes
public:
    CAutoPieDoc* GetDocument();

// Operations
public:

// Overrides
    // ClassWizard generated virtual function overrides
    //{{AFX_VIRTUAL(CAutoPieView)
```

(continued)

Figure 20-15 *continued*

```
    public:
    virtual void OnDraw(CDC* pDC);  // overridden to draw this view
    virtual BOOL PreCreateWindow(CREATESTRUCT& cs);
    protected:
    //}}AFX_VIRTUAL

// Implementation
public:
    virtual ~CAutoPieView();
#ifdef _DEBUG
    virtual void AssertValid() const;
    virtual void Dump(CDumpContext& dc) const;
#endif

protected:

// Generated message map functions
protected:
    //{{AFX_MSG(CAutoPieView)
        // NOTE - the ClassWizard will add and remove member functions here.
        //    DO NOT EDIT what you see in these blocks of generated code !
    //}}AFX_MSG
    DECLARE_MESSAGE_MAP()
};

#ifndef _DEBUG  // debug version in AutoPieView.cpp
inline CAutoPieDoc* CAutoPieView::GetDocument()
    { return (CAutoPieDoc*)m_pDocument; }
#endif

/////////////////////////////////////////////////////////////////////////////
//{{AFX_INSERT_LOCATION}}
// Microsoft Visual C++ will insert additional declarations
// immediately before the previous line.

#endif
// !defined(
//    AFX_AUTOPIEVIEW_H__3B5BA314_3B72_11D2_AC82_006008A8274D__INCLUDED_)
```

AutoPieView.cpp

```
// AUTOPIEVIEW.CPP : IMPLEMENTATION OF THE CAUTOPIEVIEW CLASS
//

#include "stdafx.h"
#include "AutoPie.h"
#include "AutoPieDoc.h"
#include "AutoPieView.h"

#ifdef _DEBUG
```

```
#define new DEBUG_NEW
#undef THIS_FILE
static char THIS_FILE[] = __FILE__;
#endif

/////////////////////////////////////////////////////////////////////////
// CAutoPieView

IMPLEMENT_DYNCREATE(CAutoPieView, CView)

BEGIN_MESSAGE_MAP(CAutoPieView, CView)
    //{{AFX_MSG_MAP(CAutoPieView)
        // NOTE - the ClassWizard will add and remove mapping macros here.
        //      DO NOT EDIT what you see in these blocks of generated code!
    //}}AFX_MSG_MAP
END_MESSAGE_MAP()

/////////////////////////////////////////////////////////////////////////
// CAutoPieView construction/destruction

CAutoPieView::CAutoPieView()
{
    // TODO: add construction code here

}


CAutoPieView::~CAutoPieView()
{
}


BOOL CAutoPieView::PreCreateWindow(CREATESTRUCT& cs)
{
    // TODO: Modify the Window class or styles here by modifying
    //   the CREATESTRUCT cs

    return CView::PreCreateWindow(cs);
}

/////////////////////////////////////////////////////////////////////////
// CAutoPieView drawing

void CAutoPieView::OnDraw(CDC* pDC)
{
    CAutoPieDoc* pDoc = GetDocument();
    ASSERT_VALID(pDoc);

    CRect rect;
    GetClientRect (&rect);
    //
    // Initialize the mapping mode.
    //
```

(continued)

Figure 20-15 *continued*

```
    pDC->SetMapMode (MM_ANISOTROPIC);
    pDC->SetWindowExt (500, 500);
    pDC->SetWindowOrg (-250, -250);
    pDC->SetViewportExt (rect.Width (), rect.Height ());

    //
    // Create a set of brushes.
    //
    CBrush brFillColor[4];
    brFillColor[0].CreateSolidBrush (RGB (255,   0,   0));   // Red
    brFillColor[1].CreateSolidBrush (RGB (255, 255,   0));   // Yellow
    brFillColor[2].CreateSolidBrush (RGB (255,   0, 255));   // Magenta
    brFillColor[3].CreateSolidBrush (RGB (  0, 255, 255));   // Cyan

    //
    // Draw the pie chart.
    //
    int nTotal = 0;
    for (int i=0; i<4; i++)
        nTotal += pDoc->GetRevenue (i);

    int x1 = 0;
    int y1 = -1000;
    int nSum = 0;

    for (i=0; i<4; i++) {
        int nRevenue = pDoc->GetRevenue (i);
        if (nRevenue != 0) {
            nSum += nRevenue;
            int x2 = (int) (sin (((((double) nSum * 2 * PI) /
                (double) nTotal) + PI) * 1000);
            int y2 = (int) (cos (((((double) nSum * 2 * PI) /
                (double) nTotal) + PI) * 1000);
            pDC->SelectObject (&brFillColor[i]);
            pDC->Pie (-200, -200, 200, 200, x1, y1, x2, y2);
            x1 = x2;
            y1 = y2;
        }
    }
    pDC->SelectStockObject (WHITE_BRUSH);
}

/////////////////////////////////////////////////////////////////////////////
// CAutoPieView diagnostics

#ifdef _DEBUG
void CAutoPieView::AssertValid() const
{
    CView::AssertValid();
}
```

```
void CAutoPieView::Dump(CDumpContext& dc) const
{
    CView::Dump(dc);
}

CAutoPieDoc* CAutoPieView::GetDocument() // non-debug version is inline
{
    ASSERT(m_pDocument->IsKindOf(RUNTIME_CLASS(CAutoPieDoc)));
    return (CAutoPieDoc*)m_pDocument;
}
#endif //_DEBUG

/////////////////////////////////////////////////////////////////////////////
// CAutoPieView message handlers
```

To expose *CAutoWindow*, *CAutoChart*, and *CAutoToolbar* as subobjects of the *Application* object, I added *CAutoWindow*, *CAutoChart*, and *CAutoToolbar* data members named *m_autoWindow*, *m_autoChart*, and *m_autoToolbar* to the document class. I then added LPDISPATCH get/set properties named *Window*, *Chart*, and *Toolbar* to the document class and implemented the get functions by calling *GetIDispatch* on the embedded objects. If a client tries to write to these properties, the *SetNotSupported* calls in the set functions will serve notice that the properties are read-only:

```
LPDISPATCH CAutoPieDoc::GetChart()
{
    return m_autoChart.GetIDispatch (TRUE);
}

void CAutoPieDoc::SetChart(LPDISPATCH newValue)
{
    SetNotSupported ();
}

LPDISPATCH CAutoPieDoc::GetWindow()
{
    return m_autoWindow.GetIDispatch (TRUE);
}

void CAutoPieDoc::SetWindow(LPDISPATCH newValue)
{
    SetNotSupported ();
}

LPDISPATCH CAutoPieDoc::GetToolbar()
{
    return m_autoToolbar.GetIDispatch (TRUE);
}
```

(continued)

```
void CAutoPieDoc::SetToolbar(LPDISPATCH newValue)
{
    SetNotSupported ();
}
```

Passing TRUE to *GetIDispatch* ensures that *AddRef* is called on the *IDispatch* pointers retrieved from the subobjects. This protects the subobjects from premature deletion. It's up to the client to release the *IDispatch* pointers. Fortunately, VBScript clients do this automatically.

The *AfxThrowOleDispatchException* Function

SetNotSupported uses MFC's *AfxThrowOleDispatchException* function to fail attempts to write to read-only Automation properties. Sometimes it's useful to call *AfxThrowOleDispatchException* yourself. AutoPie does just that if a client specifies an invalid quarter number (a value outside the range 1 through 4) when reading or writing the *Chart* object's *Revenue* property. Here's an excerpt from AutoChart.cpp:

```
AfxThrowOleDispatchException (ID_ERROR_OUTOFRANGE,
    _T ("Invalid parameter specified when reading Revenue"));
```

AfxThrowOleDispatchException fails the call and provides a descriptive error message to the client. Most clients, particularly VBScript clients, display this error message to their users.

MFC AUTOMATION CLIENTS

MFC vastly simplifies the writing of Automation servers, but what about Automation clients? Good news: with a little help from ClassWizard, it's almost as easy to write an Automation client with MFC as it is to write it with Visual Basic.

The key is a class named *COleDispatchDriver*, which puts a friendly face on *IDispatch* pointers exported by running Automation servers. The *COleDispatchDriver* helper functions *InvokeHelper*, *SetProperty*, and *GetProperty* simplify method and property accesses, but interacting with an Automation object using these functions is only slightly better than calling *IDispatch::Invoke* directly. The real value of *COleDispatchDriver* lies in creating type-safe classes whose member functions provide easy access to Automation methods and properties. After all, it's easier for a C++ programmer to call a class member function than to call *IDispatch::Invoke*.

To derive a class from *COleDispatchDriver* that's tailored to a specific Automation server, click ClassWizard's Add Class button, select From A Type Library, and point ClassWizard to the server's type library. ClassWizard will read the type library and generate the new class. Inside that class you'll find member functions for calling the server's methods and get and set functions for accessing its properties. For example, if the server supports a method named *Add* and a property named *Pi*, the ClassWizard-generated class will include a member function named *Add* and accessor functions named *GetPi* and *SetPi*. If the wrapper class were named *CAutoMath* and the object's ProgID were "Math.Object," the object could be instantiated and programmed using statements like these:

```
CAutoMath math;
math.CreateDispatch (_T ("Math.Object"));
int sum = math.Add (2, 2);
double pi = math.GetPi ();
```

CreateDispatch uses *::CoCreateInstance* to create the Automation object. It caches the object's *IDispatch* pointer in a member variable named *m_lpDispatch*. Method calls and property accesses performed via *CAutoMath* member functions are translated into *IDispatch* calls to the object by *InvokeHelper* and other *COleDispatchDriver* functions.

The PieClient Application

Let's close out this chapter with an MFC Automation client. PieClient, a picture of which appears in Figure 20-16 and whose source code appears in Figure 20-17, is a dialog-based application whose main window features edit controls for entering and editing quarterly revenue values. Values entered in the controls are charted by AutoPie. PieClient drives AutoPie via Automation.

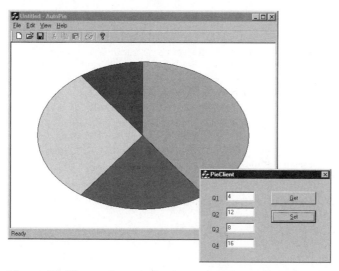

Figure 20-16. *PieClient acting as an Automation client to AutoPie.*

When started, PieClient calls *CreateDispatch* on a *CAutoPie* object named *m_autoPie* to start the Automation server:

```
BOOL bSuccess = m_autoPie.CreateDispatch (_T ("AutoPie.Application"));
```

When its Set button is clicked, PieClient gathers the revenue values from the edit controls and transmits them to the server by writing them to the *Chart* object's *Revenue* property:

```
m_autoChart.SetRevenue (1, GetDlgItemInt (IDC_Q1));
m_autoChart.SetRevenue (2, GetDlgItemInt (IDC_Q2));
m_autoChart.SetRevenue (3, GetDlgItemInt (IDC_Q3));
m_autoChart.SetRevenue (4, GetDlgItemInt (IDC_Q4));
```

It then repaints the pie chart by calling the *Window* object's *Refresh* method:

```
m_autoWindow.Refresh ();
```

Conversely, if the Get button is clicked, PieClient reads the property values from the Automation object and displays them in the edit controls.

m_autoChart and *m_autoWindow* are instances of *CAutoChart* and *CAutoWindow*. These classes and others—namely, *CAutoPie* and *CAutoToolbar*—are *COleDispatchDriver* derivatives that ClassWizard created from AutoPie's type library. *CAutoPie* represents the server's top-level *Application* object. The remaining classes represent the *Chart*, *Window*, and *Toolbar* subobjects. *m_autoPie* is initialized by *CreateDispatch*, but *m_autoChart* and *m_autoWindow* must be initialized separately because the corresponding subobjects are automatically created when the server is started. These initializations are performed by passing the *IDispatch* pointers returned by *CAutoPie*'s *GetChart* and *GetWindow* functions to *AttachDispatch*:

```
m_autoChart.AttachDispatch (m_autoPie.GetChart ());
m_autoWindow.AttachDispatch (m_autoPie.GetWindow ());
```

Because *m_autoPie*, *m_autoChart*, and *m_autoWindow* are embedded data members, they're automatically destroyed when the dialog object is destroyed. And when a *COleDispatchDriver*-object is destroyed, the *IDispatch* pointer that it wraps is released by the class destructor. That's why AutoPie closes when PieClient is closed. When the last pointer to an MFC Automation server's dispinterface is released, the server obediently shuts itself down.

PieClient.h

```
// PieClient.h : main header file for the PIECLIENT application
//

#if !defined(
    AFX_PIECLIENT_H__3B5BA32A_3B72_11D2_AC82_006008A8274D__INCLUDED_)
#define AFX_PIECLIENT_H__3B5BA32A_3B72_11D2_AC82_006008A8274D__INCLUDED_
```

Figure 20-17. *The PieClient program.*

```
#if _MSC_VER > 1000
#pragma once
#endif // _MSC_VER > 1000
#ifndef __AFXWIN_H__
    #error include 'stdafx.h' before including this file for PCH
#endif

#include "resource.h"        // main symbols

/////////////////////////////////////////////////////////////////////////////
// CPieClientApp:
// See PieClient.cpp for the implementation of this class
//

class CPieClientApp : public CWinApp
{
public:
    CPieClientApp();

// Overrides
    // ClassWizard generated virtual function overrides
    //{{AFX_VIRTUAL(CPieClientApp)
    public:
    virtual BOOL InitInstance();
    //}}AFX_VIRTUAL

// Implementation

    //{{AFX_MSG(CPieClientApp)
        // NOTE - the ClassWizard will add and remove member functions here.
        //    DO NOT EDIT what you see in these blocks of generated code !
    //}}AFX_MSG
    DECLARE_MESSAGE_MAP()
};


/////////////////////////////////////////////////////////////////////////////

//{{AFX_INSERT_LOCATION}}
// Microsoft Visual C++ will insert additional declarations
// immediately before the previous line.

#endif
// !defined(
//     AFX_PIECLIENT_H__3B5BA32A_3B72_11D2_AC82_006008A8274D__INCLUDED_)
```

(continued)

1209

Figure 20-17 *continued*

PieClient.cpp

```
// PieClient.cpp : Defines the class behaviors for the application.
//

#include "stdafx.h"
#include "PieClient.h"
#include "PieClientDlg.h"

#ifdef _DEBUG
#define new DEBUG_NEW
#undef THIS_FILE
static char THIS_FILE[] = __FILE__;
#endif


/////////////////////////////////////////////////////////////////////////////
// CPieClientApp

BEGIN_MESSAGE_MAP(CPieClientApp, CWinApp)
    //{{AFX_MSG_MAP(CPieClientApp)
        // NOTE - the ClassWizard will add and remove mapping macros here.
        //    DO NOT EDIT what you see in these blocks of generated code!
    //}}AFX_MSG
    ON_COMMAND(ID_HELP, CWinApp::OnHelp)
END_MESSAGE_MAP()

/////////////////////////////////////////////////////////////////////////////
// CPieClientApp construction

CPieClientApp::CPieClientApp()
{
    // TODO: add construction code here,
    // Place all significant initialization in InitInstance
}

/////////////////////////////////////////////////////////////////////////////
// The one and only CPieClientApp object

CPieClientApp theApp;

/////////////////////////////////////////////////////////////////////////////
// CPieClientApp initialization

BOOL CPieClientApp::InitInstance()
{
    if (!AfxOleInit ()) {
        AfxMessageBox (_T ("AfxOleInit failed"));
        return FALSE;
```

```
        }
        // Standard initialization
        // If you are not using these features and wish to reduce the size
        //  of your final executable, you should remove from the following
        //  the specific initialization routines you do not need.

        CPieClientDlg dlg;
        m_pMainWnd = &dlg;
        int nResponse = dlg.DoModal();
        if (nResponse == IDOK)
        {
            // TODO: Place code here to handle when the dialog is
            //  dismissed with OK
        }
        else if (nResponse == IDCANCEL)
        {
            // TODO: Place code here to handle when the dialog is
            //  dismissed with Cancel
        }

        // Since the dialog has been closed, return FALSE so that we exit the
        //  application, rather than start the application's message pump.
        return FALSE;
}
```

PieClientDlg.h

```
// PieClientDlg.h : header file
//

#if !defined(
    AFX_PIECLIENTDLG_H__3B5BA32C_3B72_11D2_AC82_006008A8274D__INCLUDED_)
#define AFX_PIECLIENTDLG_H__3B5BA32C_3B72_11D2_AC82_006008A8274D__INCLUDED_

#include "autopie.h"    // Added by ClassView
#if _MSC_VER > 1000
#pragma once
#endif // _MSC_VER > 1000


/////////////////////////////////////////////////////////////////////////////
// CPieClientDlg dialog

class CPieClientDlg : public CDialog
{
// Construction
public:
    CPieClientDlg(CWnd* pParent = NULL);    // standard constructor
```

(continued)

1211

Figure 20-17 *continued*

```
// Dialog Data
    //{{AFX_DATA(CPieClientDlg)
    enum { IDD = IDD_PIECLIENT_DIALOG };
    CButton    m_wndSet;
    CButton    m_wndGet;
    //}}AFX_DATA

    // ClassWizard generated virtual function overrides
    //{{AFX_VIRTUAL(CPieClientDlg)
    protected:
    virtual void DoDataExchange(CDataExchange* pDX);    // DDX/DDV support
    //}}AFX_VIRTUAL

// Implementation
protected:
    CAutoWindow m_autoWindow;
    CAutoChart m_autoChart;
    CAutoPie m_autoPie;
    HICON m_hIcon;

    // Generated message map functions
    //{{AFX_MSG(CPieClientDlg)
    virtual BOOL OnInitDialog();
    afx_msg void OnPaint();
    afx_msg HCURSOR OnQueryDragIcon();
    afx_msg void OnGet();
    afx_msg void OnSet();
    //}}AFX_MSG
    DECLARE_MESSAGE_MAP()
};

//{{AFX_INSERT_LOCATION}}
// Microsoft Visual C++ will insert additional declarations
// immediately before the previous line.

#endif
// !defined(
//    AFX_PIECLIENTDLG_H__3B5BA32C_3B72_11D2_AC82_006008A8274D__INCLUDED_)
```

PieClientDlg.cpp

```
// PieClientDlg.cpp : implementation file
//
```

```
#include "stdafx.h"
#include "PieClient.h"
#include "PieClientDlg.h"

#ifdef _DEBUG
#define new DEBUG_NEW
#undef THIS_FILE
static char THIS_FILE[] = __FILE__;
#endif

/////////////////////////////////////////////////////////////////////////
// CPieClientDlg dialog

CPieClientDlg::CPieClientDlg(CWnd* pParent /*=NULL*/)
    : CDialog(CPieClientDlg::IDD, pParent)
{
    //{{AFX_DATA_INIT(CPieClientDlg)
    //}}AFX_DATA_INIT
    // Note that LoadIcon does not require a subsequent
    // DestroyIcon in Win32
    m_hIcon = AfxGetApp()->LoadIcon(IDR_MAINFRAME);
}

void CPieClientDlg::DoDataExchange(CDataExchange* pDX)
{
    CDialog::DoDataExchange(pDX);
    //{{AFX_DATA_MAP(CPieClientDlg)
    DDX_Control(pDX, IDC_SET, m_wndSet);
    DDX_Control(pDX, IDC_GET, m_wndGet);
    //}}AFX_DATA_MAP
}

BEGIN_MESSAGE_MAP(CPieClientDlg, CDialog)
    //{{AFX_MSG_MAP(CPieClientDlg)
    ON_WM_PAINT()
    ON_WM_QUERYDRAGICON()
    ON_BN_CLICKED(IDC_GET, OnGet)
    ON_BN_CLICKED(IDC_SET, OnSet)
    //}}AFX_MSG_MAP
END_MESSAGE_MAP()

/////////////////////////////////////////////////////////////////////////
// CPieClientDlg message handlers

BOOL CPieClientDlg::OnInitDialog()
{
    CDialog::OnInitDialog();
```

(continued)

Figure 20-17 *continued*

```
    SetIcon(m_hIcon, TRUE);          // Set big icon
    SetIcon(m_hIcon, FALSE);         // Set small icon

    //
    // Start the Automation server.
    //
    BOOL bSuccess = m_autoPie.CreateDispatch (_T ("AutoPie.Application"));

    //
    // If CreateDispatch succeeded, initialize the m_autoChart and
    // m_autoWindow data members to represent the Chart and Window
    // subobjects, respectively. Then initialize the controls in
    // the dialog and make the server window visible.
    //
    if (bSuccess) {
        m_autoChart.AttachDispatch (m_autoPie.GetChart ());
        ASSERT (m_autoChart.m_lpDispatch != NULL);
        m_autoWindow.AttachDispatch (m_autoPie.GetWindow ());
        ASSERT (m_autoWindow.m_lpDispatch != NULL);
        OnGet ();
        m_autoWindow.SetVisible (TRUE);
    }

    //
    // If CreateDispatch failed, let the user know about it.
    //
    else {
        MessageBox (_T ("Error launching AutoPie. Run it once to " \
        "register it on this system and then try again."), _T ("Error"));
        m_wndGet.EnableWindow (FALSE);
        m_wndSet.EnableWindow (FALSE);
    }
    return TRUE;  // return TRUE unless you set the focus to a control
}

void CPieClientDlg::OnPaint()
{
    if (IsIconic())
    {
        CPaintDC dc(this); // device context for painting

        SendMessage(WM_ICONERASEBKGND, (WPARAM) dc.GetSafeHdc(), 0);

        // Center icon in client rectangle.
        int cxIcon = GetSystemMetrics(SM_CXICON);
```

```
        int cyIcon = GetSystemMetrics(SM_CYICON);
        CRect rect;
        GetClientRect(&rect);
        int x = (rect.Width() - cxIcon + 1) / 2;
        int y = (rect.Height() - cyIcon + 1) / 2;

        // Draw the icon.
        dc.DrawIcon(x, y, m_hIcon);
    }
    else
    {
        CDialog::OnPaint();
    }
}


HCURSOR CPieClientDlg::OnQueryDragIcon()
{
    return (HCURSOR) m_hIcon;
}


void CPieClientDlg::OnGet()
{
    //
    // Retrieve revenue values from the Automation server and display them.
    //
    SetDlgItemInt (IDC_Q1, m_autoChart.GetRevenue (1));
    SetDlgItemInt (IDC_Q2, m_autoChart.GetRevenue (2));
    SetDlgItemInt (IDC_Q3, m_autoChart.GetRevenue (3));
    SetDlgItemInt (IDC_Q4, m_autoChart.GetRevenue (4));
}


void CPieClientDlg::OnSet()
{
    //
    // Retrieve the revenue values displayed in the edit controls
    // and provide them to the Automation server.
    //
    m_autoChart.SetRevenue (1, GetDlgItemInt (IDC_Q1));
    m_autoChart.SetRevenue (2, GetDlgItemInt (IDC_Q2));
    m_autoChart.SetRevenue (3, GetDlgItemInt (IDC_Q3));
    m_autoChart.SetRevenue (4, GetDlgItemInt (IDC_Q4));

    //
    // Repaint the pie chart.
    //
    m_autoWindow.Refresh ();
}
```

(continued)

Figure 20-17 *continued*

AutoPie.h

```
// Machine generated IDispatch wrapper class(es) created with ClassWizard
///////////////////////////////////////////////////////////////////////////
// CAutoPie wrapper class

class CAutoPie : public COleDispatchDriver
{
public:
    CAutoPie() {}          // Calls COleDispatchDriver default constructor
    CAutoPie(LPDISPATCH pDispatch) : COleDispatchDriver(pDispatch) {}
    CAutoPie(const CAutoPie& dispatchSrc) :
        COleDispatchDriver(dispatchSrc) {}

// Attributes
public:
    LPDISPATCH GetChart();
    void SetChart(LPDISPATCH);
    LPDISPATCH GetWindow();
    void SetWindow(LPDISPATCH);
    LPDISPATCH GetToolbar();
    void SetToolbar(LPDISPATCH);

// Operations
public:
    void Quit();
};
///////////////////////////////////////////////////////////////////////////
// CAutoChart wrapper class

class CAutoChart : public COleDispatchDriver
{
public:
    CAutoChart() {}          // Calls COleDispatchDriver default constructor
    CAutoChart(LPDISPATCH pDispatch) : COleDispatchDriver(pDispatch) {}
    CAutoChart(const CAutoChart& dispatchSrc) :
        COleDispatchDriver(dispatchSrc) {}

// Attributes
public:

// Operations
public:
    BOOL Save(LPCTSTR pszPath);
    long GetRevenue(short nQuarter);
    void SetRevenue(short nQuarter, long nNewValue);
};
```

```
/////////////////////////////////////////////////////////////////////////
// CAutoWindow wrapper class

class CAutoWindow : public COleDispatchDriver
{
public:
    CAutoWindow() {}          // Calls COleDispatchDriver default constructor
    CAutoWindow(LPDISPATCH pDispatch) : COleDispatchDriver(pDispatch) {}
    CAutoWindow(const CAutoWindow& dispatchSrc) :
        COleDispatchDriver(dispatchSrc) {}

// Attributes
public:
    BOOL GetVisible();
    void SetVisible(BOOL);

// Operations
public:
    void Refresh();
};
/////////////////////////////////////////////////////////////////////////
// CAutoToolbar wrapper class

class CAutoToolbar : public COleDispatchDriver
{
public:
    CAutoToolbar() {}          // Calls COleDispatchDriver default constructor
    CAutoToolbar(LPDISPATCH pDispatch) : COleDispatchDriver(pDispatch) {}
    CAutoToolbar(const CAutoToolbar& dispatchSrc) :
        COleDispatchDriver(dispatchSrc) {}

// Attributes
public:
    BOOL GetVisible();
    void SetVisible(BOOL);

// Operations
public:
};
```

AutoPie.cpp

```
// Machine generated IDispatch wrapper class(es) created with ClassWizard

#include "stdafx.h"
#include "autopie.h"
```

(continued)

Figure 20-17 *continued*

```
#ifdef _DEBUG
#define new DEBUG_NEW
#undef THIS_FILE
static char THIS_FILE[] = __FILE__;
#endif

/////////////////////////////////////////////////////////////////////////////
// CAutoPie properties

LPDISPATCH CAutoPie::GetChart()
{
    LPDISPATCH result;
    GetProperty(0x1, VT_DISPATCH, (void*)&result);
    return result;
}

void CAutoPie::SetChart(LPDISPATCH propVal)
{
    SetProperty(0x1, VT_DISPATCH, propVal);
}

LPDISPATCH CAutoPie::GetWindow()
{
    LPDISPATCH result;
    GetProperty(0x2, VT_DISPATCH, (void*)&result);
    return result;
}

void CAutoPie::SetWindow(LPDISPATCH propVal)
{
    SetProperty(0x2, VT_DISPATCH, propVal);
}

LPDISPATCH CAutoPie::GetToolbar()
{
    LPDISPATCH result;
    GetProperty(0x3, VT_DISPATCH, (void*)&result);
    return result;
}

void CAutoPie::SetToolbar(LPDISPATCH propVal)
{
    SetProperty(0x3, VT_DISPATCH, propVal);
}
```

```
///////////////////////////////////////////////////////////////////////////
// CAutoPie operations

void CAutoPie::Quit()
{
    InvokeHelper(0x4, DISPATCH_METHOD, VT_EMPTY, NULL, NULL);
}


///////////////////////////////////////////////////////////////////////////
// CAutoChart properties

///////////////////////////////////////////////////////////////////////////
// CAutoChart operations

BOOL CAutoChart::Save(LPCTSTR pszPath)
{
    BOOL result;
    static BYTE parms[] =
        VTS_BSTR;
    InvokeHelper(0x1, DISPATCH_METHOD, VT_BOOL, (void*)&result, parms,
        pszPath);
    return result;
}

long CAutoChart::GetRevenue(short nQuarter)
{
    long result;
    static BYTE parms[] =
        VTS_I2;
    InvokeHelper(0x2, DISPATCH_PROPERTYGET, VT_I4, (void*)&result, parms,
        nQuarter);
    return result;
}

void CAutoChart::SetRevenue(short nQuarter, long nNewValue)
{
    static BYTE parms[] =
        VTS_I2 VTS_I4;
    InvokeHelper(0x2, DISPATCH_PROPERTYPUT, VT_EMPTY, NULL, parms,
        nQuarter, nNewValue);
}


///////////////////////////////////////////////////////////////////////////
// CAutoWindow properties
```

(continued)

Figure 20-17 *continued*

```
BOOL CAutoWindow::GetVisible()
{
    BOOL result;
    GetProperty(0x1, VT_BOOL, (void*)&result);
    return result;
}

void CAutoWindow::SetVisible(BOOL propVal)
{
    SetProperty(0x1, VT_BOOL, propVal);
}

/////////////////////////////////////////////////////////////////////////////
// CAutoWindow operations

void CAutoWindow::Refresh()
{
    InvokeHelper(0x2, DISPATCH_METHOD, VT_EMPTY, NULL, NULL);
}

/////////////////////////////////////////////////////////////////////////////
// CAutoToolbar properties

BOOL CAutoToolbar::GetVisible()
{
    BOOL result;
    GetProperty(0x1, VT_BOOL, (void*)&result);
    return result;
}

void CAutoToolbar::SetVisible(BOOL propVal)
{
    SetProperty(0x1, VT_BOOL, propVal);
}

/////////////////////////////////////////////////////////////////////////////
// CAutoToolbar operations
```

Stdafx.h

```
// stdafx.h : include file for standard system include files,
//  or project specific include files that are used frequently, but
//      are changed infrequently
//
```

```
#if !defined(AFX_STDAFX_H__3B5BA32E_3B72_11D2_AC82_006008A8274D__INCLUDED_)
#define AFX_STDAFX_H__3B5BA32E_3B72_11D2_AC82_006008A8274D__INCLUDED_

#if _MSC_VER > 1000
#pragma once
#endif // _MSC_VER > 1000

#define VC_EXTRALEAN        // Exclude rarely-used stuff from Windows headers

#include <afxwin.h>         // MFC core and standard components
#include <afxext.h>         // MFC extensions
#include <afxdtctl.h>       // MFC support for Internet Explorer 4
                            // Common Controls
#ifndef _AFX_NO_AFXCMN_SUPPORT
#include <afxcmn.h>                 // MFC support for Windows Common Controls
#endif // _AFX_NO_AFXCMN_SUPPORT
#include <afxdisp.h>

//{{AFX_INSERT_LOCATION}}
// Microsoft Visual C++ will insert additional declarations
// immediately before the previous line.

#endif
// !defined(AFX_STDAFX_H__3B5BA32E_3B72_11D2_AC82_006008A8274D__INCLUDED_)
```

Keep in mind that checking the Automation box in AppWizard makes an application an Automation server, not an Automation client. With the Automation option unchecked, however, AppWizard will not add an *AfxOleInit* call to *InitInstance*, nor will it #include Afxdisp.h in Stdafx.h. Both are necessary for Automation clients, so I added them by hand to PieClient. Without these additions, the code will compile just fine, but *CreateDispatch* will fail every time.

Connecting to a Running Automation Server

Thanks to ClassWizard-generated wrapper classes and their member functions, accessing an Automation server's methods and properties from a C++ program is almost as easy as accessing them from Visual Basic. But what if you want to connect two or more instances of PieClient to one instance of AutoPie? As it stands now, that's not possible because each instance of PieClient calls *CreateDispatch*, which creates a brand new instance of the Automation object.

You can modify PieClient and AutoPie to support multiple simultaneous connections by adding a few lines of code to each. On the server side, AutoPie needs to call the API function *::RegisterActiveObject* to register itself as an active object. Here's a modified version of *CAutoPieDoc*'s constructor that demonstrates how.

```
CAutoPieDoc::CAutoPieDoc ()
{
    // Wizard-generated code
    EnableAutomation ();
    AfxOleLockApp ();

    // Additional code that registers the running object
    IUnknown* pUnknown;
    GetIDispatch (FALSE)->
        QueryInterface (IID_IUnknown, (void**) &pUnknown);
    GetIDispatch (FALSE)->Release (); // Undo the AddRef
                                      // performed by QueryInterface.
    ::RegisterActiveObject (pUnknown, clsid, ACTIVEOBJECT_WEAK, &m_ulID);
}
```

In this example, *m_ulID* is an unsigned long member variable added to *CAutoPieDoc*. It receives a 32-bit value identifying the entry that *::RegisterActiveObject* added to COM's running object table. *clsid* is the object's CLSID; it's declared in AutoPie.cpp and made visible in AutoPieDoc.cpp by adding the statement

```
extern CLSID clsid;
```

to AutoPieDoc.cpp. For this *extern* statement to compile and link, you must remove the keywords *static* and *const* from the variable declaration in AutoPie.cpp.

So that clients won't attempt to connect to an Automation server that is no longer running, a version of AutoPie that registers itself in the running object table must unregister itself before it shuts down. The best way to do this is to override *OnFinalRelease* in *CAutoPieDoc* and call *::RevokeActiveObject*, as shown here:

```
void CAutoPieDoc::OnFinalRelease()
{
    ::RevokeActiveObject (m_ulID, NULL);
    CDocument::OnFinalRelease();
}
```

::RevokeActiveObject does the opposite of *::RegisterActiveObject*: Given a registration ID, it removes an object from the running object table. *OnFinalRelease* is a *CCmdTarget* function that's called just before an MFC COM object self-deletes.

The final modification needed to support multiple connections applies to the client, not the server. Before calling *CreateDispatch* to create the Automation object, PieClient should call *::GetActiveObject* to find out whether the object is already running. The following code connects to an existing object instance if such an instance exists or creates a new instance if it doesn't:

```
BOOL bSuccess = FALSE;

CLSID clsid;
if (SUCCEEDED (CLSIDFromProgID (OLESTR ("AutoPie.Application"), &clsid))) {
```

```
        IUnknown* pUnknown;
        if (SUCCEEDED (::GetActiveObject (clsid, NULL, &pUnknown))) {
            IDispatch* pDispatch;
            if (SUCCEEDED (pUnknown->QueryInterface (IID_IDispatch,
                (void**) &pDispatch))) {
                pDispatch->Release (); // Undo the AddRef performed
                                       // by QueryInterface.
                m_autoPie.AttachDispatch (pDispatch);
                bSuccess = TRUE;
            }
        }
    }

    if (!bSuccess)
        bSuccess = m_autoPie.CreateDispatch (_T ("AutoPie.Application"));

    if (!bSuccess) {
        // Error: Unable to connect to an existing object instance or
        // launch a new one.
    }
```

If you apply these modifications to AutoPie and PieClient, you'll find that no matter how many instances of PieClient you start, each will connect to the same Automation object. One drawback to the *::RegisterActiveObject/::GetActiveObject* method is that it's powerless over a network, even though Automation itself works just fine between machines. Attaching multiple clients to an Automation server on another machine requires an altogether different approach to the problem. That, however, is a topic for another day.

Chapter 21

ActiveX Controls

In the minds of most people, the term *ActiveX* conjures up visions of ActiveX controls displaying fancy animations and video streams in Web pages. In truth, ActiveX controls are just one piece of the puzzle called ActiveX. But as the penultimate COM technology and the most visible member of the ActiveX family, ActiveX controls enjoy a special distinction that sets them apart from run-of-the-mill COM objects.

ActiveX controls began their life in 1994 as "OLE controls." The first version of the OLE control specification, which is now referred to as OCX 94, outlined the structure of what would one day be known as ActiveX controls and was intended to provide developers with a generic, COM-based architecture for building reusable Microsoft Windows controls. The OLE control of 1994 was a replacement for custom control DLLs and Visual Basic controls (VBXs). The specification was revised in 1996 (OCX 96), and later that same year, OLE controls were officially renamed ActiveX controls and Microsoft Internet Explorer gained the ability to host ActiveX controls in Web pages. To this day, ActiveX controls serve a dual purpose. (See Figure 21-1.) Application developers can use them to enhance their programs, and Web developers can use them to create interactive Web content—"interactive" because unlike Active Server Pages and Common Gateway Interface (CGI) scripts, ActiveX controls execute on the client side of an HTTP connection.

Microsoft provides a number of tools for writing ActiveX controls, but none offer the balance of power and ease of use that Visual C++ and MFC do. Writing an ActiveX control from scratch can require weeks or even months of development time. You can write the same control with MFC in a matter of hours. In fact, you can write a simple control that works equally well in an application or a Web page in minutes with the tools that Visual C++ provides. One of those tools is the MFC ActiveX ControlWizard, which generates the initial source code for a control project. But make no mistake: it's MFC that's the belle of the ball, and without MFC or a similar class

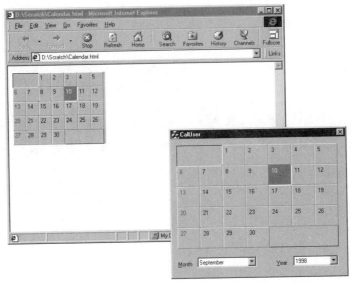

Figure 21-1. *Two instances of an ActiveX calendar control displayed side by side—in Internet Explorer and in an application program.*

library to help out, writing an ActiveX control would be right up there on a list of fun things to do with having your fingernails pulled out.

In this chapter, I'll begin with an overview of ActiveX controls and an explanation of how they work. I'll conclude with a few topics that aren't treated at length elsewhere in the chapter. In between, you'll learn how MFC supports ActiveX controls. Then you'll write your own control and an application that uses the control. You'll even test the control in a Web page. When you're done, I think you'll agree that even a subject as complex as ActiveX controls can be downright enjoyable when MFC is there to do the bulk of the work.

ACTIVEX CONTROL BASICS

So just what is an ActiveX control? Simply put, an ActiveX control is a COM object. But it's not just any COM object; it's a COM object that implements a certain set of interfaces that enable it to look and act like a control. There's some confusion over exactly what that set of interfaces is because, technically, the only interface that's required is *IUnknown*. When I use the term *ActiveX control* in this chapter, I'm talking about a *full-blown* control: an ActiveX control that works equally well in an MFC dialog, a Visual Basic form, or a Web page.

ActiveX controls leverage many of the technologies found elsewhere in COM. For example, most ActiveX controls expose methods and properties just as Automation servers do. They do it by implementing *IDispatch*. Most are also capable of being in-place activated, as OLE embedding servers are. They do that by implementing *IOleObject*, *IOleInPlaceActiveObject*, and other interfaces. ActiveX controls that expose properties generally provide a means for those properties to be stored persistently. They do that by implementing persistence interfaces such as *IPersistStreamInit* and *IPersistPropertyBag*. In short, ActiveX controls are complex objects that implement not just one COM interface, but many. In a moment, we'll examine those interfaces and the roles that they play in a control's operation.

Methods, Properties, and Events

Controls implement properties so that people using them can customize them to fit the needs of a particular application or Web page. For example, the calendar control that we'll build in this chapter exposes its background color as a property so that users can change its color. When you design an ActiveX control, try to anticipate all the things a user might want to change about its appearance or behavior and then make those characteristics of the control programmable by exposing them as properties.

Controls implement methods so that they can be called to do useful work. A calculator control might support methods for computing square roots and medians. A clock control wouldn't be complete without a method for setting the time. Control methods are nothing more than Automation methods, and they're added to a control the same way methods are added to an Automation server. You already know how to add methods to an Automation server (refer to Chapter 20 if you need a refresher), so you know how to add methods to an ActiveX control, too.

One feature that sets ActiveX controls apart from Automation servers is their ability to fire events. An *event* is a notification sent from a control to its container. A *container* is a window that hosts an ActiveX control. Windows controls send notifications to their owners by sending messages; ActiveX controls send notifications to their containers by firing events. Events are fired by calling Automation methods through interfaces—normally *IDispatch* interfaces—provided by control containers. A portion of the ActiveX control specification is devoted to the issue of how a control obtains a pointer to a container's *IDispatch* interface.

When you design an ActiveX control, you should think about what kinds of things could happen inside the control that a container might be interested in and code them as ActiveX events. For instance, an ActiveX push button control should fire an event when it's clicked. Remember that it's better to fire too many events than too few because a container can ignore those in which it has no interest.

Custom vs. Stock

Another feature that differentiates ActiveX controls from Automation servers is the fact that a control's methods, properties, and events come in two varieties: custom and stock. Custom methods, properties, and events are ordinary Automation methods, properties, and events: ones for which you pick the names and dispatch IDs. Stock methods, properties, and events are "standard" methods, properties, and events that use names and dispatch IDs prescribed in the ActiveX control specification. The idea behind stock attributes is that if a control exposes, say, its background color as a property, using a standard name (*BackColor*) and dispatch ID (–501) will promote uniformity among otherwise unrelated controls. If a Visual Basic user sees that your control has a property named *BackColor*, he or she will know exactly what that property does. If you call it something else, the meaning might be less obvious.

The control specification contains a rather lengthy list of stock methods, properties, and events, complete with names and dispatch IDs. MFC contains built-in implementations of most of them, and ClassWizard makes adding stock methods, properties, and events to a control a piece of cake.

Of course, you can forget about stock methods, properties, and events if you want to and make everything custom. But a savvy control designer will use them wherever applicable.

Ambient Properties

Another unique and interesting aspect of the ActiveX control architecture is that containers, too, can expose properties. Many times, a control needs to know something about the environment in which it's running before it can decide how to look or act. For example, if you want a control to blend in with its container, you might want to know the container's background color so that the control can paint its own background the same color. You can obtain these and other items of information by reading the container's ambient properties. An *ambient property* is an Automation property that's exposed through—you guessed it—*IDispatch*. The difference is that the container—not the control—implements the interface.

Like stock control properties, ambient properties have well-known names and dispatch IDs. (You'll see a list of the ambient properties that a container can support in a subsequent section of this chapter.) The ambient property named *BackColor*, for example, exposes the container's background color. A control can read the ambient property named *UserMode* to find out whether it's running in a design-time environment (for example, in the Visual Basic forms editor or the Visual C++ dialog editor) or a "user" environment (for example, in a Web page or a running application). All it needs is an *IDispatch* interface pointer and a dispatch ID. The *IDispatch* interface pointer comes from the container; the dispatch ID comes from the control specification.

Control States

At any given time, a control can be in either of two states: active or inactive. These terms have roots in object linking and embedding, but they can be defined accurately enough for our purposes without resorting to the usual OLE technojargon.

An active control is one that's alive and running in a container. The control's DLL is loaded (ActiveX controls are in-proc COM servers, so they live in DLLs), the control has a window of its own, and the control is able to paint to that window and respond to user input. I should say the control *might* have a window of its own, because one of the enhancements introduced in OCX 96 was the option to write windowless controls—controls that borrow real estate from their container and literally paint themselves into the container's window. A windowless control doesn't have a window even when it's active, but conceptually it's accurate to think of that control as having a window because both it and the container work very hard to foster that illusion.

An inactive control, by contrast, doesn't have a window of its own. It therefore consumes fewer system resources and is dead to user input. When a container deactivates a control, it asks the control for a metafile image that it can use to represent the control in the container's window. Then it destroys the control's window and draws the metafile to make it appear that the control is still there. The control will typically remain inactive until it's clicked. OCX 96 defines a new COM interface named *IPointerInactive* that an inactive control can use to sense mouse movements or change the shape of the cursor, or to request that the container activate it as soon as the mouse enters the control rectangle. The net result is the illusion that the control is active and accepting input all the while; the user is usually none the wiser.

Does it matter whether a control is active or inactive? It might, depending on what type of control you write. If your ActiveX control creates child window controls, for example, those child windows might render poorly into a metafile. Therefore, you might decide to do whatever you can to prevent the control from being deactivated. One of the options you have as a control designer is to tell the container you'd like the control to be active whenever it's visible. The container isn't absolutely required to honor that request, but most containers will.

Another reason to be aware of activation states is that controls repaint when they transition from one state to the other. If the control looks the same whether it's active or inactive (most do), this repainting can produce an annoying flicker. The solution to this problem is yet another OCX 96 enhancement called *flicker-free drawing*. I'll have more to say about these and other ActiveX control options when we examine the MFC ActiveX ControlWizard.

The ActiveX Control Architecture

Because an ActiveX control is a COM object, it can be defined in terms of the interfaces that it supports. However, because no one set of interfaces makes an ActiveX control an ActiveX control, the best we can hope to do is to diagram a *typical* ActiveX control and use it to paint a broad picture of the ActiveX control architecture. Figure 21-2 contains one such diagram.

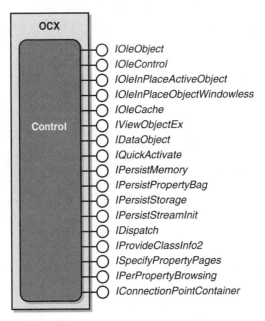

Figure 21-2. *A typical ActiveX control.*

The control depicted in Figure 21-2 is precisely what you get when you write an ActiveX control with MFC. The control object is housed in a Win32 DLL that's commonly referred to as an OCX. The "OC" in OCX stands for OLE Control. An OCX can house one control or several controls. It usually has a .ocx file name extension, but that's left to the discretion of the control creator. Some OCXs have the extension .dll instead.

Figure 21-2 is the perfect illustration of a full-blown ActiveX control, which can be more fully defined now as one that draws a visible manifestation of itself in a window; that supports methods, properties, and events; and that is equally at home in an application or on a Web page. Though technically none of these COM interfaces is required of an ActiveX control, as a practical matter, many of them *are* required if the control is to support the kinds of features normally associated with ActiveX controls. For example, a control must implement *IConnectionPointContainer* if it's to fire events. And it can't expose methods and properties without an *IDispatch* interface. In that sense, then, Figure 21-2 is a reasonable depiction of the objects that most people think of as ActiveX controls.

So just what do all those interfaces do? One could easily write a book about each interface and the role that it plays in the operation of an ActiveX control, but that level of detail isn't necessary here. The following table briefly describes each interface.

ACTIVEX CONTROL INTERFACES

Interface	Comments
IConnectionPointContainer	Exposes connection points for event interfaces
IDataObject	Makes presentation data available to the control container
IDispatch	Exposes the control's methods and properties
IOleCache	Controls the presentation data cache
IOleControl	Base interface for ActiveX controls
IOleInPlaceActiveObject	Base interface for embedded objects that support in-place activation
IOleInPlaceObjectWindowless	Allows the container to manage the activation and deactivation of both windowed and windowless controls
IOleObject	Base interface for embedded objects
IQuickActivate	Speeds control creation in containers that recognize this interface
IPerPropertyBrowsing	Allows containers to acquire information about control properties, such as each property's name
IPersistMemory	Allows the control to write property values to memory and read them back
IPersistPropertyBag	Allows the control to save property values in "property bag" objects provided by the container
IPersistStorage	Allows the control to save property values in storage objects
IPersistStreamInit	Allows the control to save property values in stream objects
IProvideClassInfo2	Makes type information available to the control container
ISpecifyPropertyPages	Allows the control to add pages to property sheets displayed by the container
IViewObjectEx	Allows the container to acquire images of inactive controls and paint windowless controls

IConnectionPointContainer indirectly enables containers to provide *IDispatch* interface pointers to controls for event firing. You already know that to fire an event, a control calls an Automation method on its container's *IDispatch* interface. To find out what kinds of events the control is capable of firing (and by extension, what methods the container must implement in order to respond to control events), most containers read the control's type information. Type information is accessed by calling the control's *IProvideClassInfo2::GetClassInfo* method and calling *ITypeInfo* methods through the returned *ITypeInfo* pointer.

If you were writing an ActiveX control from scratch (that is, without the aid of a class library), you'd have to understand the semantics of all these interfaces and others to the *n*th degree. But write a control with MFC and MFC will implement the interfaces for you. You don't even have to know that the interfaces are there; they just work.

ActiveX Control Containers

ActiveX control containers are complex COM objects in their own right. That's right: to host an ActiveX control, a container must implement COM interfaces, too. The exact set of interfaces required depends somewhat on the nature of the control that's being hosted, but control containers tend to be more uniform in the interfaces that they implement than controls are.

Figure 21-3 shows a typical ActiveX control container. For each control that it hosts, the container implements a *control site* object. Apart from the individual site objects, it also implements COM's *IOleContainer* and *IOleInPlaceFrame* interfaces. As the diagram shows, most containers provide two separate implementations of *IDispatch*. One exposes the container's ambient properties, and the other is provided to the control for event firing. The following table provides brief descriptions of commonly used ActiveX control container interfaces.

ACTIVEX CONTROL CONTAINER INTERFACES

Interface	Comments
IOleContainer	Base interface for embedding containers
IOleInPlaceFrame	Base interface for OLE containers that support in-place activation
IOleClientSite	Base interface for OLE containers
IOleInPlaceSite	Base interface for OLE containers that support in-place activation
IOleControlSite	Base interface for ActiveX control sites
IDispatch	Exposes the container's ambient properties
IDispatch	Traps events fired by a control
IPropertyNotifySink	Allows the control to notify the container about property changes and to ask permission before changing them

Writing a control container involves more than just implementing the required COM interfaces; you have to wrestle with a protocol, too. For example, when a control is created, a conversation ensues between it and its container. Among other things, the two exchange interface pointers, the container plugs *IDispatch* and *IPropertyNotifySink* (and perhaps other) interface pointers into connection points implemented by the control, and the container usually activates the control by calling its *IOleObject::DoVerb* method. In some cases, the container reads type information from the control so that it will know what to do when events are fired through its *IDispatch* interface.

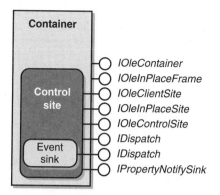

Figure 21-3. *A typical ActiveX control container.*

The conversations don't stop after the control is initialized; the control and its container are constantly responding to calls from each other by placing calls of their own. In other words, hosting an ActiveX control is a big job. That's all the more reason to build ActiveX control containers with MFC, which does an excellent job of hiding all these complexities under the hood and making it very easy to host ActiveX controls in any *CWnd*-derived object.

MFC Support for ActiveX Controls

MFC simplifies the writing of ActiveX controls and control containers by providing built-in implementations of the required COM interfaces and encapsulating the protocol that links ActiveX controls and control containers. For those COM methods that can't be implemented in a generic fashion, MFC provides virtual functions that you can override in a derived class to implement control-specific behavior. To a large extent, writing an ActiveX control with MFC is a matter of deriving from MFC base classes and overriding virtual functions here and there to add the logic that makes your control unique.

Though by no means exhaustive, the following sections highlight the MFC classes that provide the foundation for MFC's ActiveX control support.

COleControl

Much of MFC's ActiveX control support is found in *COleControl*. The base class for all MFC ActiveX controls, *COleControl* is a large and complex class that implements most of the COM interfaces shown in Figure 21-2. It also includes handlers for dozens of Windows messages and provides built-in implementations of stock methods, properties, and events.

When you derive a class from *COleControl* to represent an ActiveX control, you'll override some of its virtual functions, too. *COleControl* includes about sixty virtual functions, each of which is important in its own right. The two functions listed in the table at the top of the next page, however, stand out for their utter importance in the operation of a control.

KEY VIRTUAL *COLECONTROL* FUNCTIONS

Function	Description
OnDraw	Called to paint the control. Override to add control-specific painting logic.
DoPropExchange	Called to save or load a control's persistent properties. Override to support persistent control properties.

Both functions are overridden for you if you use the MFC ActiveX ControlWizard to create the control project. Issues that you should be aware of when implementing these functions in a derived class are covered later in this chapter.

COleControl also includes a diverse assortment of nonvirtual functions that a control programmer should be aware of. One of those functions is *InvalidateControl*. It should be used in lieu of *CWnd::Invalidate* to repaint a control because unlike *Invalidate*, it works with both windowed and windowless controls. The following table lists some of the nonvirtual functions that are useful when you're writing ActiveX controls with MFC.

KEY NONVIRTUAL *COLECONTROL* FUNCTIONS

Function	Description
Ambientxxx	Retrieves an ambient property value from the container (for example, *AmbientBackColor*)
Firexxx	Fires a stock event (for example, *FireClick*)
GetAmbientProperty	Retrieves the values of an ambient property for which no *Ambientxxx* function is defined
Getxxx	Retrieves the value of a stock property (for example, *GetBackColor*)
InitializeIIDs	Makes the IDs of the control's event interface and *IDispatch* interface known to MFC; normally called from the class constructor
InvalidateControl	Repaints the control
SerializeStockProps	Serializes the control's stock properties
SetModifiedFlag	Marks the control as dirty or not dirty (A "dirty" control is one that contains unsaved property changes.)
SetNotSupported	Generates an error when a client attempts to write to a read-only property
ThrowError	Signals that an error occurred; used in method implementations and property accessor functions
TranslateColor	Translates an OLE_COLOR value into a COLORREF value

You'll see some of these functions used in this chapter's sample control. Two of them—*InitializeIIDs* and *SerializeStockProps*—are automatically added to *COleControl*-derived classes by ControlWizard.

COleControlModule

Every MFC application includes a global instance of a *CWinApp*-derived class that represents the application itself. *COleControlModule* is to MFC ActiveX controls what *CWinApp* is to conventional MFC applications: It represents the server module (that is, the DLL) in which the control is housed.

    COleControlModule is a thin class that adds little to the functionality it inherits from its base class, *CWinApp*. Its primary contribution is an *InitInstance* function that calls *AfxOleInitModule* to enable COM support in an MFC DLL. It follows that if you override *InitInstance* in a *COleControlModule*-derived class, you should call the base class's *InitInstance* function before executing any code of your own. When Control-Wizard creates an ActiveX control project, it adds the call for you.

COlePropertyPage

Most ActiveX controls expose their properties to developers by implementing property sheet pages that are displayed by the control container. In ActiveX land, property pages are COM objects, complete with CLSIDs. A property page object—sometimes referred to as an *OLE property page*—is one that implements COM's *IPropertyPage* or *IPropertyPage2* interface.

    MFC's *COlePropertyPage* class makes creating OLE property pages a snap by implementing *IPropertyPage2* for you. You simply derive from *COlePropertyPage* and add a bit of infrastructure; MFC does the rest. (Of course, ControlWizard and Class-Wizard are happy to do the derivation for you and add the necessary infrastructure themselves.) Typically, you don't even have to override any virtual functions except for *DoDataExchange*, which links the controls in the property page to properties exposed by the ActiveX control. I'll describe exactly how this linkage is performed later in this chapter.

CConnectionPoint and COleConnPtContainer

ActiveX controls use COM's connectable object protocol to accept interface pointers from their containers for event firing. A connectable object is one that implements one or more *connection points*. Logically, a connection point is a receptacle that interfaces can be plugged into. Physically, a connection point is a COM object that implements the *IConnectionPoint* interface. To expose its connection points to clients, a connectable object implements COM's *IConnectionPointContainer* interface. Implementing *IConnectionPoint* and *IConnectionPointContainer* also means implementing a pair of enumerator interfaces named *IEnumConnectionPoints* and *IEnumConnections*. All this just so a control can fire events to its container.

The details of connectable object interfaces are beyond the scope of this discussion, but suffice it to say that implementing them is no picnic. Enter MFC, which provides default implementations of all four in classes such as *CConnectionPoint* and *COleConnPtContainer*. The implementations are generic enough that they can be used even outside the ActiveX control architecture, but it is ActiveX controls that benefit the most from their existence. For the most part, you don't even know these classes are there because they're tucked away deep inside *COleControl*.

COleControlContainer and *COleControlSite*

The bulk of MFC's support for ActiveX control containers is found inside the classes *COleControlContainer* and *COleControlSite*. The former implements *IOleContainer* and *IOleInPlaceFrame*, and the latter contributes stock implementations of *IOleClientSite*, *IOleControlSite*, *IOleInPlaceSite*, and other per-control interfaces required of ActiveX control containers. When you build a control container with MFC, you get a container that looks very much like the one in Figure 21-3 with three additional interfaces thrown in:

- *IBoundObjectSite*
- *INotifyDBEvents*
- *IRowsetNotify*

These interfaces are used to bind ActiveX controls to external data sources—specifically, RDO (Remote Data Object) and OLE DB data sources.

COleControlContainer and *COleControlSite* are complex classes, and they work in conjunction with a similarly complex (and undocumented) class named *COccManager*. Fortunately, it's rare to have to interact with any of these classes directly. As you'll see, simply checking a box in AppWizard or adding a statement to *InitInstance* is enough to endow any MFC application with the ability to host ActiveX controls. Five minutes with MFC can save you literally weeks of coding time.

BUILDING ACTIVEX CONTROLS

Armed with this knowledge of the ActiveX control architecture and the manner in which MFC encapsulates it, you're almost ready to build your first control. But first, you need to know more about the *process* of writing ActiveX controls with Visual C++ and MFC. The following sections provide additional information about the nature of ActiveX controls from an MFC control writer's perspective and describe some of the basic skills required to write a control—for example, how to add methods, properties, and events, and what impact these actions have on the underlying source code.

Running ControlWizard

The first step in writing an MFC ActiveX control is to create a new project and select MFC ActiveX ControlWizard as the project type. This runs ControlWizard, which asks a series of questions before generating the project's source code files.

The first series of questions is posed in ControlWizard's Step 1 dialog box, shown in Figure 21-4. By default, the OCX generated when this project is built will contain just one control. If you'd rather it implement more, enter a number in the How Many Controls Would You Like Your Project To Have box. ControlWizard will respond by including multiple control classes in the project. Another option is Would You Like The Controls In This Project To Have A Runtime License? If you answer yes, Control-Wizard builds in code that prevents the control from being instantiated in the absence of a valid run-time license. Implemented properly, this can be an effective means of preventing just anyone from using your control. But because ControlWizard's license-checking scheme is easily circumvented, enforcing run-time licensing requires extra effort on the part of the control's implementor. For details, see the section "Control Licensing" at the close of this chapter.

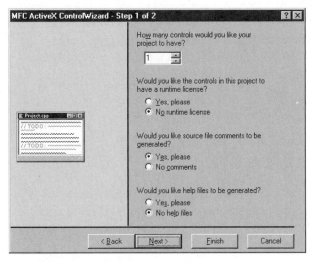

Figure 21-4. *ControlWizard's Step 1 dialog box.*

ControlWizard's Step 2 dialog box is shown in Figure 21-5. Clicking the Edit Names button displays a dialog box in which you can enter names for the classes ControlWizard will generate, the names of those classes' source code files, and ProgIDs for the control and its property page. If you'd like the control to wrap a built-in control type such as a slider control or a tree view control, choose a WNDCLASS name from the list attached to the Which Window Class, If Any, Should This Control Subclass box. The "Control Subclassing" section later in this chapter explains what this does to your source code and what implications it has for the code you write.

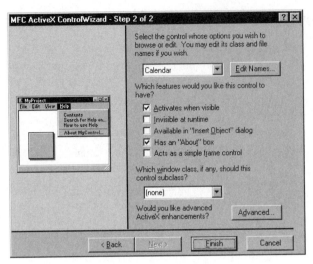

Figure 21-5. *ControlWizard's Step 2 dialog box.*

The options under Which Features Would You Like This Control To Have? can have profound effects on a control's appearance and behavior. The defaults are normally just fine, but it's hard to understand what these options really mean from the scant descriptions provided in the online help. Therefore, here's a brief synopsis of each one. The term *miscellaneous status bits* refers to a set of bit flags that communicate certain characteristics of the control to the control container. A container can acquire a control's miscellaneous status bits from the control itself or, if the control isn't running, from the registry.

- **Activates When Visible**—Sets a flag in the control's miscellaneous status bits informing the container that the control wants to be active whenever it's visible. Disabling this option gives the container the option of disabling the control, which it might do to conserve resources or speed start-up time. If you uncheck this box, you should check the Mouse Pointer Notifications When Inactive box described below if your control processes WM_MOUSEMOVE or WM_SETCURSOR messages.

- **Invisible At Runtime**—Sets a flag in the control's miscellaneous status bits indicating that the control wants to be visible in design mode but invisible in user mode. In other words, the control should be visible in a design-time environment such as the Visual C++ dialog editor, but invisible when the application that uses the control is running. One example of a control that might choose to exercise this option is a timer control that fires events at specified intervals. The control doesn't need to be seen at run time, but it should be visible at design time so that the user can display its property sheet.

■ **Available In "Insert Object" Dialog**—Because most ActiveX controls implement a functional superset of the interfaces required to act as object linking and embedding servers, most of them can, if asked, masquerade as object linking and embedding servers. When this option is selected, the control gets registered not only as an ActiveX control but also as an OLE server, which causes it to appear in the Insert Object dialog box found in Microsoft Word, Microsoft Excel, and other OLE containers. Checking this box is generally a bad idea because most OLE containers don't know how to interact with ActiveX controls. Except in isolated cases, the best strategy is to forget that this option even exists.

■ **Has An "About" Box**—If checked, adds a method named *AboutBox* to the control that displays an About dialog box. Select this option if you'd like developers using your control to be able to learn more about it and its creator from an About box. ControlWizard creates a simple dialog resource for you; it's up to you to add a professional touch.

■ **Acts As A Simple Frame Control**—Tells ControlWizard to add an *ISimpleFrameSite* interface to the control, and sets a flag in the miscellaneous status bits identifying this as a "simple frame" control. A simple frame control is one that hosts other controls but delegates much of the work to its own control container. Use this option for controls, such as group box controls, whose primary purpose is to provide a site for (and visual grouping of) other controls.

You can access still more options by clicking the Advanced button in the Step 2 dialog box, which displays the window shown in Figure 21-6. All are relatively recent additions to the ActiveX control specification (most come directly from OCX 96), and none are universally supported by control containers. Nevertheless, they're worth knowing about, if for no other reason than the fact that ControlWizard exposes them

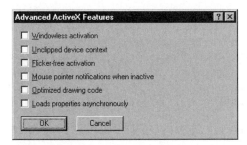

Figure 21-6. *ControlWizard's Advanced ActiveX Features dialog box.*

to you. Here's a brief summary of the options found in the Advanced ActiveX Features dialog box:

- **Windowless Activation**—Makes the control a windowless control. If the container doesn't support windowless activation, the control will be instantiated in a window as if it were a regular windowed control. Windowless controls are discussed at length later in this chapter.

- **Unclipped Device Context**—According to the documentation, this option, if selected, speeds redraws ever so slightly by preventing *COle-Control::OnPaint* from calling *CDC::IntersectClipRect* on the device context passed to the control to prevent the control from inadvertently painting outside its own window. Despite what the documentation says, this option has no effect whatsoever on the control's behavior in MFC 6.0.

- **Flicker-Free Activation**—Most ActiveX controls are activated when they're created and remain active indefinitely. If a container deactivates an active control, however, the container repaints the control. And if an inactive control becomes active, the control repaints itself. For controls that look the same whether active or inactive, this repainting is unnecessary and can cause unsightly flicker. The flicker-free activation option eliminates redrawing induced by state transitions in containers that support it.

- **Mouse Pointer Notifications When Inactive**—Allows containers to forward WM_SETCURSOR and WM_MOUSEMOVE messages to inactive controls via an MFC-provided implementation of *IPointerInactive*. This option is typically used with controls that don't use the Activates When Visible option but want to alter the appearance of the mouse cursor or respond to mouse movements even while inactive.

- **Optimized Drawing Code**—When *IViewObjectEx::Draw* is called to draw a windowless control, the control is responsible for leaving the device context in the same state in which it found it. Some containers free the control from this obligation, in which case the control can speed repainting by reducing the number of GDI calls. To take advantage of this feature in supportive containers, select this option and call *COleControl::IsOptimizedDraw* each time *OnDraw* is called. If *IsOptimizedDraw* returns nonzero, there's no need to clean up the device context.

- **Loads Properties Asynchronously**—Indicates that this control supports datapath properties. Unlike standard control properties, datapath properties are downloaded asynchronously, typically from a URL. For controls designed to sit in Web pages, implementing properties that encapsulate large volumes of data as datapath properties can improve performance dramatically. MFC makes implementing datapath properties relatively easy, but (in my opinion, anyway) controls designed for the Internet should be written with the Active Template Library, not with MFC. For more information about implementing datapath properties in MFC, see the article "Internet First Steps: ActiveX Controls" in the online documentation.

When you select any of the advanced options—with the exception of Loads Properties Asynchronously—ControlWizard overrides a *COleControl* function named *GetControlFlags* in the derived control class and selectively sets or clears bit flags in the control flags that the function returns. For example, selecting Flicker-Free Activation ORs a *noFlickerActivate* flag into the return value. Some options prompt Control-Wizard to make more extensive modifications to the source code. For example, selecting Optimized Drawing Code adds *canOptimizeDraw* to the control flags and inserts a call to *IsOptimizedDraw* into *OnDraw*. MFC calls *GetControlFlags* at various times to find out about relevant characteristics of the control.

When ControlWizard is done, you're left with an ActiveX control project that will actually compile into a do-nothing ActiveX control—one that has no methods, properties, or events, and does no drawing other than erase its background and draw a simple ellipse, but one that satisfies all the criteria for an ActiveX control. That project includes these key elements:

- A *COleControlModule*-derived class representing the control's OCX.

- A *COleControl*-derived class representing the control. ControlWizard overrides *OnDraw*, *DoPropExchange*, and other virtual functions in the derived class, so you don't have to. The control class also includes essential infrastructure such as a COM class factory and dispinterfaces for methods, properties, and events.

- A *COlePropertyPage*-derived class and a dialog resource representing the control's property page.

- An ODL file that ClassWizard will later modify as methods, properties, and events are added and from which the control's type library will be generated.

- A toolbar button bitmap that will represent the control on toolbars in design-time environments such as Visual Basic.

ControlWizard does nothing that you couldn't do by hand, but it provides a welcome jump start on writing an ActiveX control. I'm not a big fan of code-generating wizards, and there's much more I wish ControlWizard would do, but all things considered, it's a tool that would be hard to live without.

Implementing *OnDraw*

When a control needs repainting, MFC calls its *OnDraw* function. *OnDraw* is a virtual function inherited from *COleControl*. It's prototyped like this:

```
virtual void OnDraw (CDC* pDC, const CRect& rcBounds,
    const CRect& rcInvalid)
```

pDC points to the device context in which the control should paint itself. *rcBounds* describes the rectangle in which painting should be performed. *rcInvalid* describes the portion of the control rectangle (*rcBounds*) that is invalid; it could be identical to *rcBounds*, or it could be smaller. Use it to optimize drawing performance the same way you'd use *GetClipBox* in a conventional MFC application.

OnDraw can be called for three reasons:

- A windowed control receives a WM_PAINT message.

- *IViewObjectEx::Draw* is called on an inactive control (or one that's about to become inactive) to retrieve a metafile for the control container. If you'd like to draw the control differently when it's inactive, override *COle-Control::OnDrawMetafile*. The default implementation calls *OnDraw*.

- *IViewObjectEx::Draw* is called on a windowless control to ask it to paint itself into the container's window.

Regardless of why it's called, *OnDraw*'s job is to draw the control. The device context is provided for you in the parameter list, and you can use *CDC* output functions to do the drawing. Just be careful to abide by the following rules:

- Assume nothing about the state of the device context passed in *OnDraw*'s parameter list. You shouldn't assume, for example, that a black pen or a white brush is selected in. Prepare the device context as if its initial attributes were all wrong.

- Leave the device context in the same state you found it in, which means not only selecting out the GDI objects you selected in, but also preserving the drawing mode, text color, and other attributes of the device context. As an alternative, you can check the Optimized Drawing Code box in ControlWizard to advertise the control's intent *not* to preserve the state of the device context. But because many containers don't support this option, you must call *COleControl::IsOptimizedDraw* inside *OnDraw* to find out whether it's OK.

- Limit your drawing to the rectangular area described by the *rcBounds* parameter included in *OnDraw*'s parameter list. For a windowed control, *rcBounds*' upper left corner will be (0,0). For a windowless control, these coordinates can be nonzero because they describe an area inside the container's window.

■   Begin *OnDraw* by erasing the control's background—the rectangle described by *rcBounds*. This is typically accomplished by creating a brush of the desired color and calling *CDC::FillRect*. If the control is windowless, you can effect a transparent background by skipping this step.

These rules exist primarily for the benefit of windowless controls, but it's important to heed them when writing controls that are designed to work equally well whether they're windowed or windowless. To determine at run time whether a control is windowed or windowless, check the control's *m_bInPlaceSiteWndless* data member. A nonzero value means the control is windowless.

Using Ambient Properties

Ambient properties allow a control to query its container for pertinent characteristics of the environment in which the control is running. Because ambient properties are Automation properties implemented by the container, they are read by calling *IDispatch::Invoke* on the container. *COleControl* simplifies the retrieval of ambient property values by supplying wrapper functions that call *IDispatch::Invoke* for you. *COleControl::AmbientBackColor*, for example, returns the ambient background color. The table on the following page lists several of the ambient properties that are available, their dispatch IDs, and the corresponding *COleControl* member functions. To read ambient properties for which property-specific retrieval functions don't exist, you can call *GetAmbientProperty* and pass in the property's dispatch ID.

The following code, which would probably be found in a control's *OnDraw* function, queries the container for the ambient background color and paints the control background the same color:

```
CBrush brush (TranslateColor (AmbientBackColor ()));
pdc->FillRect (rcBounds, &brush);
```

Notice the use of *COleControl::TranslateColor* to convert the OLE_COLOR color value returned by *AmbientBackColor* into a Windows COLORREF value. OLE_COLOR is ActiveX's native color data type.

If your *OnDraw* implementation relies on one or more ambient properties, you should override *COleControl::OnAmbientPropertyChange* in the derived control class. This function is called when the container notifies the control that one or more ambient properties have changed. Overriding it allows the control to respond immediately to changes in the environment surrounding it. A typical response is to repaint the control by calling *InvalidateControl*:

```
void CMyControl::OnAmbientPropertyChange (DISPID dispid)
{
    InvalidateControl (); // Repaint.
}
```

AMBIENT PROPERTIES

Property Name	Dispatch ID	COleControl Retrieval Function
BackColor	DISPID_AMBIENT_BACKCOLOR	AmbientBackColor
DisplayName	DISPID_AMBIENT_ DISPLAYNAME	AmbientDisplayName
Font	DISPID_AMBIENT_ FONT	AmbientFont
ForeColor	DISPID_AMBIENT_ FORECOLOR	AmbientForeColor
LocaleID	DISPID_AMBIENT_ LOCALEID	AmbientLocaleID
MessageReflect	DISPID_AMBIENT_MESSAGEREFLECT	GetAmbientProperty
ScaleUnits	DISPID_AMBIENT_SCALEUNITS	AmbientScaleUnits
TextAlign	DISPID_AMBIENT_TEXTALIGN	AmbientTextAlign
UserMode	DISPID_AMBIENT_USERMODE	AmbientUserMode
UIDead	DISPID_AMBIENT_UIDEAD	AmbientUIDead
ShowGrabHandles	DISPID_AMBIENT-_SHOWGRABHANDLES	AmbientShow-GrabHandles
ShowHatching	DISPID_AMBIENT_SHOWHATCHING	AmbientShowHatching
DisplayAsDefaultButton	DISPID_AMBIENT_DISPLAYASDEFAULT	GetAmbientProperty
SupportsMnemonics	DISPID_AMBIENT-_SUPPORTSMNEMONICS	GetAmbientProperty
AutoClip	DISPID_AMBIENT_AUTOCLIP	GetAmbientProperty
Appearance	DISPID_AMBIENT_APPEARANCE	GetAmbientProperty
Palette	DISPID_AMBIENT_PALETTE	GetAmbientProperty
TransferPriority	DISPID_AMBIENT_TRANSFERPRIORITY	GetAmbientProperty

The *dispid* parameter holds the dispatch ID of the ambient property that changed, or DISPID_UNKNOWN if two or more properties have changed. A smart control could check this parameter and refrain from calling *InvalidateControl* unnecessarily.

Adding Methods

Adding a custom method to an ActiveX control is just like adding a method to an Automation server. The procedure, which was described in Chapter 20, involves going to ClassWizard's Automation page, selecting the control class in the Class Name box, clicking Add Method, filling in the Add Method dialog box, and then filling in the empty function body created by ClassWizard.

Adding a stock method is even easier. You once again click the Add Method button, but rather than enter a method name, you choose one from the drop-down list attached to the External Name box. *COleControl* provides the method implementation, so there's literally nothing more to do. You can call a stock method on your own control by calling the corresponding *COleControl* member function. The stock methods supported by *COleControl* and the member functions used to call them are listed in the following table.

STOCK METHODS IMPLEMENTED BY *COLECONTROL*

Method Name	Dispatch ID	Call with
DoClick	DISPID_DOCLICK	*DoClick*
Refresh	DISPID_REFRESH	*Refresh*

When you add a custom method to a control, ClassWizard does the same thing it does when you add a method to an Automation server: It adds the method and its dispatch ID to the project's ODL file, adds a function declaration and body to the control class's H and CPP files, and adds a DISP_FUNCTION statement to the dispatch map.

Stock methods are treated in a slightly different way. ClassWizard still updates the ODL file, but because the function implementation is provided by *COleControl*, no function is added to your source code. Furthermore, rather than add a DISP-_FUNCTION statement to the dispatch map, ClassWizard adds a DISP_STOCKFUNC statement. The following dispatch map declares two methods—a custom method named *Foo* and the stock method *Refresh*:

```
BEGIN_DISPATCH_MAP (CMyControl, COleControl)
    DISP_FUNCTION (CMyControl, "Foo", Foo, VT_EMPTY, VTS_NONE)
    DISP_STOCKFUNC_REFRESH ()
END_DISPATCH_MAP ()
```

DISP_STOCKFUNC_REFRESH is defined in Afxctl.h. It maps the Automation method named *Refresh* to *COleControl::Refresh*. A related macro named DISP_STOCKFUNC-_DOCLICK adds the stock method *DoClick* to an ActiveX control.

Adding Properties

Adding a custom property to an ActiveX control is just like adding a property to an MFC Automation server. ActiveX controls support member variable properties and get/set properties just like Automation servers do, so you can add either type.

You add a stock property by choosing the property name from the list that drops down from the Add Property dialog box's External Name box. *COleControl* supports most, but not all, of the stock properties defined in the ActiveX control specification. The table on the next page lists the ones that it supports.

STOCK PROPERTIES IMPLEMENTED BY *COLECONTROL*

Property Name	Dispatch ID	Retrieve with	Notification Function
Appearance	DISPID_APPEARANCE	GetAppearance	OnAppearanceChanged
BackColor	DISPID_BACKCOLOR	GetBackColor	OnBackColorChanged
BorderStyle	DISPID_BORDERSTYLE	GetBorderStyle	OnBorderStyleChanged
Caption	DISPID_CAPTION	GetText or InternalGetText	OnTextChanged
Enabled	DISPID_ENABLED	GetEnabled	OnEnabledChanged
Font	DISPID_FONT	GetFont or InternalGetFont	OnFontChanged
ForeColor	DISPID_FORECOLOR	GetForeColor	OnForeColorChanged
hWnd	DISPID_HWND	GetHwnd	N/A
ReadyState	DISPID_READYSTATE	GetReadyState	N/A
Text	DISPID_TEXT	GetText or InternalGetText	OnTextChanged

To retrieve the value of a stock property that your control implements, call the corresponding *COleControl* get function. (*COleControl* also provides functions for setting stock property values, but they're rarely used.) To find out when the value of a stock property changes, override the corresponding notification function in your derived class. Generally, it's a good idea to repaint the control any time a stock property changes if the control indeed uses stock properties. *COleControl* provides default notification functions that repaint the control by calling *InvalidateControl*, so unless you want to do more than simply repaint the control when a stock property value changes, there's no need to write a custom notification function.

Under the hood, adding a custom property to a control modifies the control's source code files as if a property had been added to an Automation server. Stock properties are handled differently. In addition to declaring the property in the ODL file, ClassWizard adds a DISP_STOCKPROP statement to the control's dispatch map. The following dispatch map declares a custom member variable property named *SoundAlarm* and the stock property *BackColor*:

```
BEGIN_DISPATCH_MAP (CMyControl, COleControl)
    DISP_PROPERTY_EX (CMyControl, "SoundAlarm", m_bSoundAlarm, VT_BOOL)
    DISP_STOCKPROP_BACKCOLOR ()
END_DISPATCH_MAP ()
```

DISP_STOCKPROP_BACKCOLOR is one of several stock property macros defined in Afxctl.h. It associates the property with a pair of *COleControl* functions named *GetBackColor* and *SetBackColor*. Similar macros are defined for the other stock properties that *COleControl* supports.

Making Properties Persistent

After adding a custom property to a control, the very next thing you should do is add a statement to the control's *DoPropExchange* function making that property persistent. A persistent property is one whose value is saved to some storage medium (usually a disk file) and later read back. When a Visual C++ programmer drops an ActiveX control into a dialog and modifies the control's properties, the control is eventually asked to serialize its property values. The dialog editor saves those values in the project's RC file so that they will "stick." The saved values are reapplied when the control is re-created. Controls implement persistence interfaces such as *IPersistPropertyBag* for this reason.

To make an MFC control's properties persistent, you don't have to fuss with low-level COM interfaces. Instead, you override the *DoPropExchange* function that a control inherits from *COleControl* and add statements to it—one per property. The statements are actually calls to PX functions. MFC provides one PX function for each possible property type, as listed in the following table.

PX FUNCTIONS FOR SERIALIZING CONTROL PROPERTIES

Function	Description
PX_Blob	Serializes a block of binary data
PX_Bool	Serializes a BOOL property
PX_Color	Serializes an OLE_COLOR property
PX_Currency	Serializes a CURRENCY property
PX_DataPath	Serializes a *CDataPathProperty* property
PX_Double	Serializes a double-precision floating point property
PX_Float	Serializes a single-precision floating point property
PX_Font	Serializes a *CFontHolder* property
PX_IUnknown	Serializes properties held by another object
PX_Long	Serializes a signed 32-bit integer property
PX_Picture	Serializes a *CPictureHolder* property
PX_Short	Serializes a signed 16-bit integer property
PX_String	Serializes a *CString* property
PX_ULong	Serializes an unsigned 32-bit integer property
PX_UShort	Serializes an unsigned 16-bit integer property

If your control implements a custom member variable property of type BOOL named *SoundAlarm*, the following statement in the control's *DoPropExchange* function makes the property persistable:

```
PX_Bool (pPX, _T ("SoundAlarm"), m_bSoundAlarm, TRUE);
```

pPX is a pointer to a *CPropExchange* object; it's provided to you in *DoPropExchange*'s parameter list. *SoundAlarm* is the property name, and *m_bSoundAlarm* is the variable that stores the property's value. The fourth parameter specifies the property's default value. It is automatically assigned to *m_bSoundAlarm* when the control is created.

If *SoundAlarm* were a get/set property instead of a member variable property, you'd need to retrieve the property value yourself before calling *PX_Bool*:

```
BOOL bSoundAlarm = GetSoundAlarm ();
PX_Bool (pPX, _T ("SoundAlarm"), bSoundAlarm);
```

In this case, you would use the form of *PX_Bool* that doesn't accept a fourth parameter. Custom get/set properties don't require explicit initialization because they are initialized implicitly by their get functions.

Which brings up a question. Given that custom properties are initialized either inside *DoPropExchange* or by their get functions, how (and when) do stock properties get initialized? It turns out that MFC initializes them for you using commonsense values. A control's default *BackColor* property, for example, is set equal to the container's ambient *BackColor* property when the control is created. The actual initialization is performed by *COleControl::ResetStockProps*, so if you want to initialize stock properties yourself, you can override this function and initialize the property values manually after calling the base class implementation of *ResetStockProps*.

When you create a control project with ControlWizard, *DoPropExchange* is overridden in the derived control class automatically. Your job is to add one statement to it for each custom property that you add to the control. There's no wizard that does this for you, so you must do it by hand. Also, you don't need to modify *DoPropExchange* when you add stock properties because MFC serializes stock properties for you. This serialization is performed by the *COleControl::DoPropExchange* function. That's why ControlWizard inserts a call to the base class when it overrides *DoPropExchange* in a derived control class.

Customizing a Control's Property Sheet

One other detail you must attend to when adding properties to an ActiveX control is to make sure that all those properties, whether stock or custom, are accessible through the control's property sheet. The property sheet is displayed by the container, usually at the request of a user. For example, when a Visual C++ programmer drops an ActiveX control into a dialog, right-clicks the control, and selects Properties from the context menu, the dialog editor displays the control's property sheet.

To make its properties accessible through a property sheet, a control implements one or more property pages and makes them available through its *ISpecifyPropertyPages* interface. To display the control's property sheet, the container asks the control for a list of CLSIDs by calling its *ISpecifyPropertyPages::GetPages* method. Each CLSID corresponds to one property page. The container passes the CLSIDs to *::OleCreate-PropertyFrame* or *::OleCreatePropertyFrameIndirect*, which instantiates the property page objects and inserts them into an empty property sheet. Sometimes the container will insert property pages of its own. That's why a control's property sheet will have extra pages in some containers but not in others.

MFC simplifies matters by implementing *ISpecifyPropertyPages* for you. It even gives you a free implementation of property page objects in the form of *COlePropertyPage*. ControlWizard adds an empty dialog resource representing a property page to the project for you; your job is to add controls to that page and link those controls to properties of the ActiveX control. You accomplish the first task with the dialog editor. You connect a control on the page to an ActiveX control property by using ClassWizard's Add Variable button to add a member variable to the property page class and specifying the Automation name of the ActiveX control property in the Add Member Variable dialog box's Optional Property Name field. (You'll see what I mean when you build a control later in this chapter.)

Under the hood, ClassWizard links a dialog control to an ActiveX control property by modifying the derived *COlePropertyPage* class's *DoDataExchange* function. The *DDP_Check* and *DDX_Check* statements in the following *DoDataExchange* function link the check box whose ID is IDC_CHECKBOX to an ActiveX control property named *SoundAlarm*:

```
void CMyOlePropertyPage::DoDataExchange(CDataExchange* pDX)
{
    DDP_Check (pDX, IDC_CHECKBOX, m_bSoundAlarm, _T ("SoundAlarm"));
    DDX_Check (pDX, IDC_CHECKBOX, m_bSoundAlarm);
    DDP_PostProcessing (pDX);
}
```

DDP functions work hand in hand with their DDX counterparts to transfer data between property page controls and ActiveX control properties.

Adding Pages to a Control's Property Sheet

When ControlWizard creates an ActiveX control project, it includes just one property page. You can add extra pages by modifying the control's property page map, which is found in the derived control class's CPP file. Here's what a typical property page map looks like:

```
BEGIN_PROPPAGEIDS (CMyControl, 1)
    PROPPAGEID (CMyControlPropPage::guid)
END_PROPPAGEIDS (CMyControl)
```

The 1 in BEGIN_PROPPAGEIDS' second parameter tells MFC's implementation of *ISpecifyPropertyPages* that this control has just one property page; the PROPPAGEID statement specifies that page's CLSID. (*CMyControlPropPage::guid* is a static variable declared by the IMPLEMENT_OLECREATE_EX macro that ControlWizard includes in the property page class's CPP file.)

Adding a property page is as simple as incrementing the BEGIN_PROPPAGEIDS count from 1 to 2 and adding a PROPPAGEID statement specifying the page's CLSID. The big question is, Where does that property page (and its CLSID) come from?

There are two possible answers. The first is a stock property page. The system provides three stock property pages that ActiveX controls can use as they see fit: a color page for color properties, a picture page for picture properties, and a font page for font properties. Their CLSIDs are CLSID_CColorPropPage, CLSID_CPicture-PropPage, and CLSID_CFontPropPage, respectively. The most useful of these is the stock color page (shown in Figure 21-7), which provides a standard user interface for editing any color properties implemented by your control. The following property page map includes a color page as well as the default property page:

```
BEGIN_PROPPAGEIDS (CMyControl, 2)
    PROPPAGEID (CMyOlePropertyPage::guid)
    PROPPAGEID (CLSID_CColorPropPage)
END_PROPPAGEIDS (CMyControl)
```

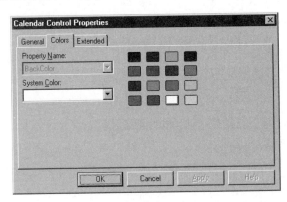

Figure 21-7. *The stock color property page.*

The second possibility is that the PROPPAGEID statement you add to the property page map identifies a custom property page that you created yourself. Although the process for creating a custom property page and wiring it into the control isn't difficult, it isn't automatic either. The basic procedure is to add a new dialog resource to the project, derive a class from *COlePropertyPage* and associate it with the dialog resource, add the page to the property page map, edit the control's string table resource, and make a couple of manual changes to the derived property page class. I won't provide a blow-by-blow here because the Visual C++ documentation already includes one. See "ActiveX controls, adding property pages" in the online help for details.

Adding Events

Thanks to ClassWizard, adding a custom event to an ActiveX control built with MFC is no more difficult than adding a method or a property. Here's how you add a custom event:

1. Invoke ClassWizard, and go to the ActiveX Events page. (See Figure 21-8.)

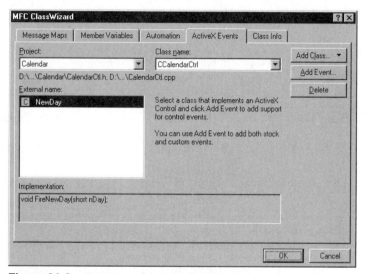

Figure 21-8. *ClassWizard's ActiveX Events page.*

2. Click the Add Event button.

3. In the Add Event dialog box (shown in Figure 21-9), enter the event's name (External Name), the name of the member function that you'd like to call to fire the event (Internal Name), and, optionally, the arguments that accompany the event. Because an event is an Automation method implemented by a container, events can have parameter lists.

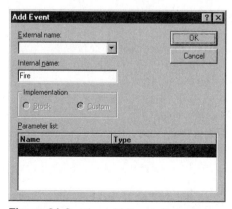

Figure 21-9. *The Add Event dialog box.*

For each custom event that you add to a control, ClassWizard adds a member function to the control class that you can use to fire events of that type. By default, the function name is *Fire* followed by the event name, but you can enter any name you like in the Add Event dialog box. These custom event-firing functions do little more than call *COleControl::FireEvent*, which uses a form of *COleDispatchDriver-::InvokeHelper* to call Automation methods on the container's *IDispatch* pointer.

Adding a stock event is as simple as selecting an event name from the list attached to the Add Event dialog box's External Name box. The following table lists the stock events you can choose from, their dispatch IDs, and the *COleControl* member functions used to fire them.

STOCK EVENTS IMPLEMENTED BY *COLECONTROL*

Event Name	Dispatch ID	Fire with
Click	DISPID_CLICK	*FireClick*
DblClick	DISPID_DBLCLICK	*FireDblClick*
Error	DISPID_ERROREVENT	*FireError*
KeyDown	DISPID_KEYDOWN	*FireKeyDown*
KeyPress	DISPID_KEYPRESS	*FireKeyPress*
KeyUp	DISPID_KEYUP	*FireKeyUp*
MouseDown	DISPID_MOUSEDOWN	*FireMouseDown*
MouseMove	DISPID_MOUSEMOVE	*FireMouseMove*
MouseUp	DISPID_MOUSEUP	*FireMouseUp*
ReadyStateChange	DISPID_READYSTATECHANGE	*FireReadyStateChange*

The *Fire* functions in this table are inline functions that call *FireEvent* with the corresponding event's dispatch ID. With the exception of *FireReadyStateChange* and *FireError*, these functions are rarely used directly because when you add a *Click*, *DblClick*, *KeyDown*, *KeyUp*, *KeyPress*, *MouseDown*, *MouseUp*, or *MouseMove* event to a control, MFC automatically fires the corresponding event for you when a keyboard or mouse event occurs.

Technically speaking, a COM interface that's implemented by a control container to allow a control to fire events is known as an *event interface*. Event interfaces are defined just like regular interfaces in both the Interface Definition Language (IDL) and the Object Description Language (ODL), but they're marked with the special *source* attribute. In addition to adding *Fire* functions for the custom events that you add to a control, ClassWizard also declares events in the project's ODL file. In ODL, an event is simply a method that belongs to an event interface. Here's how the event interface is defined in the ODL file for a control named MyControl that fires *PriceChanged* events:

```
[ uuid(D0C70155-41AA-11D2-AC8B-006008A8274D),
```

```
      helpstring("Event interface for MyControl Control") ]
dispinterface _DMyControlEvents
{
    properties:
        //  Event interface has no properties
    methods:
        [id(1)] void PriceChanged(CURRENCY price);
};

//  Class information for CMyControl

[ uuid(D0C70156-41AA-11D2-AC8B-006008A8274D),
  helpstring("MyControl Control"), control ]
coclass MyControl
{
    [default] dispinterface _DMyControl;
    [default, source] dispinterface _DMyControlEvents;
};
```

The *dispinterface* block defines the interface itself; *coclass* identifies the interfaces that the control supports. In this example, *_DMyControl* is the *IDispatch* interface through which the control's methods and properties are accessed, and *_DMyControl-Events* is the *IDispatch* interface for events. The leading underscore in the interface names is a convention COM programmers often use to denote internal interfaces. The capital D following the underscore indicates that these are dispinterfaces rather than conventional COM interfaces.

Event Maps

Besides adding *Fire* functions and modifying the control's ODL file when events are added, ClassWizard also adds one entry per event (stock or custom) to the control's event map. An *event map* is a table that begins with BEGIN_EVENT_MAP and ends with END_EVENT_MAP. Statements in between describe to MFC what events the control is capable of firing and what functions are called to fire them. An EVENT-_CUSTOM macro declares a custom event, and EVENT_STOCK macros declare stock events. The following event map declares a custom event named *PriceChanged* and the stock event *Click*:

```
BEGIN_EVENT_MAP(CMyControlCtrl, COleControl)
    EVENT_CUSTOM("PriceChanged", FirePriceChanged, VTS_CY)
    EVENT_STOCK_CLICK()
END_EVENT_MAP()
```

MFC uses event maps to determine whether to fire stock events at certain junctures in a control's lifetime. For example, *COleControl*'s WM_LBUTTONUP handler fires a *Click* event if the event map contains an EVENT_STOCK_CLICK entry. MFC currently doesn't use the EVENT_CUSTOM entries found in a control's event map.

Building an ActiveX Control

Now that you understand the basics of the ActiveX control architecture and MFC's support for the same, it's time to write an ActiveX control. The control that you'll build is the calendar control featured in Figure 21-1. It supports the following methods, properties, and events:

Name	Description
Methods	
GetDate	Returns the calendar's current date
SetDate	Sets the calendar's current date
Properties	
BackColor	Controls the calendar's background color
RedSundays	Determines whether Sundays are highlighted in red
Events	
NewDay	Fired when a new date is selected

Because Calendar is a full-blown ActiveX control, it can be used in Web pages and in applications written in ActiveX-aware languages such as Visual Basic and Visual C++. Following is a step-by-step account of how to build it.

1. Create a new MFC ActiveX ControlWizard project named Calendar. Accept the default options in ControlWizard's Step 1 and Step 2 dialog boxes.

2. Add three int member variables named *m_nYear*, *m_nMonth*, and *m_nDay* to *CCalendarCtrl*. *CCalendarCtrl* is the class that represents the control. The member variables that you added will store the control's current date.

3. Add the following code to *CCalendarCtrl*'s constructor to initialize the member variables:

```
CTime time = CTime::GetCurrentTime ();
m_nYear = time.GetYear ();
m_nMonth = time.GetMonth ();
m_nDay = time.GetDay ();
```

4. Add the following variable declaration to the *CCalendarCtrl* in CalendarCtrl.h:

```
static const int m_nDaysPerMonth[];
```

Then add these lines to CalendarCtrl.cpp to initialize the *m_nDaysPerMonth* array with the number of days in each month:

```
const int CCalendarCtrl::m_nDaysPerMonth[] = {
    31,        // January
    28,        // February
    31,        // March
    30,        // April
    31,        // May
    30,        // June
    31,        // July
    31,        // August
    30,        // September
    31,        // October
    30,        // November
    31,        // December
};
```

5. Add the following protected member function to *CCalendarCtrl*:

```
BOOL CCalendarCtrl::LeapYear(int nYear)
{
    return (nYear % 4 == 0) ^ (nYear % 400 == 0) ^
        (nYear % 100 == 0);
}
```

This function returns a nonzero value if *nYear* is a leap year, or 0 if it isn't. The rule is that *nYear* is a leap year if it's evenly divisible by 4, *unless* it's divisible by 100 but not by 400.

6. Add a *BackColor* property to the control by clicking the Add Property button on ClassWizard's Automation page and selecting *BackColor* from the External Name list in the Add Property dialog box. (See Figure 21-10.)

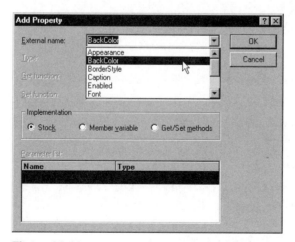

Figure 21-10. *Adding the BackColor property.*

7. Modify the property page map in CalendarCtrl.cpp as shown below to add a stock color page to the control's property sheet. Users will use this property page to customize the control's background color:

```
BEGIN_PROPPAGEIDS (CCalendarCtrl, 2)
    PROPPAGEID (CCalendarCtrl::guid)
    PROPPAGEID (CLSID_CColorPropPage)
END_PROPPAGEIDS (CCalendarCtrl)
```

8. Fill in the Add Property dialog box as shown in Figure 21-11 to add a custom member variable property named *RedSundays*. In response, ClassWizard will add a member variable named *m_redSundays* (which you can then change to *m_bRedSundays*) and a notification function named *OnRed-SundaysChanged* to the control class. Follow up by adding the following statement to the notification function so that the control will automatically repaint when the property value changes:

```
InvalidateControl ();
```

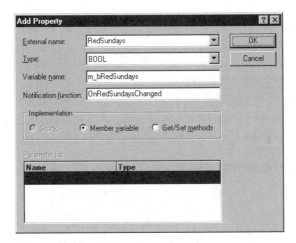

Figure 21-11. *Adding the RedSundays property.*

9. Add the following statement to *CCalendarCtrl::DoPropExchange* to make *RedSundays* persistent and to assign it a default value equal to TRUE:

```
PX_Bool (pPX, _T ("RedSundays"), m_bRedSundays, TRUE);
```

10. Switch to ResourceView, and add a checkbox control to the dialog resource whose ID is IDD_PROPPAGE_CALENDAR. (See Figure 21-12.) This is the resource that represents the control's property page. Assign the check box the ID IDC_REDSUNDAYS and the text "Show Sundays in &red."

Figure 21-12. *The modified property page.*

11. On ClassWizard's Member Variables page, select the property page's class name (*CCalendarPropPage*) in the Class Name box, click the Add Variable button, and fill in the Add Member Variable dialog box as shown in Figure 21-13. This will connect the check box control to the property named *RedSundays*.

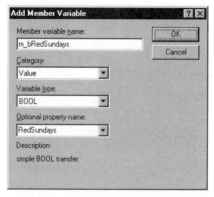

Figure 21-13. *Associating the check box with RedSundays.*

12. Implement the control's *OnDraw* function. See the CalendarCtrl.cpp listing in Figure 21-18 beginning on page 1259 for the finished code. Notice that *OnDraw* uses *GetBackColor* to retrieve the value of the *BackColor* property and then uses that value to paint the control's background. Also notice that it checks the value of *m_bRedSundays* and sets the text color to red before drawing a date corresponding to a Sunday if *m_bRedSundays* is nonzero. This explains how the two properties that you added affect the control's appearance.

13. Add methods named *GetDate* and *SetDate*. To add a method, click the Add Method button on ClassWizard's Automation page. Pick DATE as *GetDate*'s return type (as in Figure 21-14) and BOOL as *SetDate*'s return type. Include three parameters in *SetDate*'s parameter list: a short named *nYear*, a short named *nMonth*, and a short named *nDay* (as in Figure 21-15). See Figure 21-18 for the method implementations.

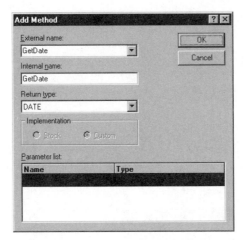

Figure 21-14. *Adding the GetDate method.*

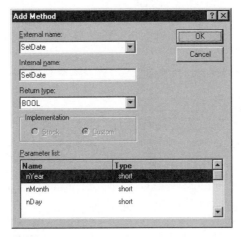

Figure 21-15. *Adding the SetDate method.*

14. Add a *NewDay* event to the control by clicking the Add Event button on ClassWizard's ActiveX Events page and filling in the Add Event dialog box as shown in Figure 21-16.

15. Add a WM_LBUTTONDOWN handler to the control class that sets the current date to the date that was clicked on the calendar. You add a message handler to a control the same way you add a message handler to a conventional MFC application. Refer to Figure 21-18 for the implementation of *OnLButtonDown*. Notice the call to *FireNewDay* near the end of the function.

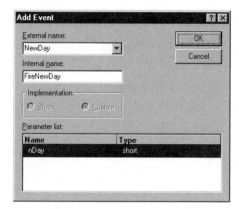

Figure 21-16 *Adding the NewDay event.*

16. In ResourceView, customize the control's toolbar button bitmap to look like the one shown in Figure 21-17. You'll find the button bitmap under the project's list of bitmap resources. The bitmap's resource ID is IDB_CALENDAR.

Figure 21-17. *The calendar control's toolbar button bitmap.*

17. Build the control.

With that, you've just built your first ActiveX control. It probably didn't seem very complicated, but rest assured that's only because of the thousands of lines of code MFC supplied to implement all those COM interfaces. Selected portions of the finished source code appear in Figure 21-18.

CalendarCtl.h

```
#if !defined(
    AFX_CALENDARCTL_H__68932D29_CFE2_11D2_9282_00C04F8ECF0C__INCLUDED_)
#define AFX_CALENDARCTL_H__68932D29_CFE2_11D2_9282_00C04F8ECF0C__INCLUDED_

#if _MSC_VER > 1000
#pragma once
#endif // _MSC_VER > 1000

// CalendarCtl.h : Declaration of the CCalendarCtrl ActiveX Control class.
```

Figure 21-18. *The calendar control's source code.*

(continued)

Figure 21-18 *continued*

```
//////////////////////////////////////////////////////////////////////////
// CCalendarCtrl : See CalendarCtl.cpp for implementation.

class CCalendarCtrl : public COleControl
{
    DECLARE_DYNCREATE(CCalendarCtrl)

// Constructor
public:
    CCalendarCtrl();

// Overrides
    // ClassWizard generated virtual function overrides
    //{{AFX_VIRTUAL(CCalendarCtrl)
    public:
    virtual void OnDraw(CDC* pdc, const CRect& rcBounds,
        const CRect& rcInvalid);
    virtual void DoPropExchange(CPropExchange* pPX);
    virtual void OnResetState();
    //}}AFX_VIRTUAL

// Implementation
protected:
    BOOL LeapYear(int nYear);
    static const int m_nDaysPerMonth[];
    int m_nDay;
    int m_nMonth;
    int m_nYear;
    ~CCalendarCtrl();

    DECLARE_OLECREATE_EX(CCalendarCtrl)       // Class factory and guid
    DECLARE_OLETYPELIB(CCalendarCtrl)         // GetTypeInfo
    DECLARE_PROPPAGEIDS(CCalendarCtrl)        // Property page IDs
    DECLARE_OLECTLTYPE(CCalendarCtrl)         // Type name and misc status

// Message maps
    //{{AFX_MSG(CCalendarCtrl)
    afx_msg void OnLButtonDown(UINT nFlags, CPoint point);
    //}}AFX_MSG
    DECLARE_MESSAGE_MAP()

// Dispatch maps
    //{{AFX_DISPATCH(CCalendarCtrl)
    BOOL m_bRedSundays;
    afx_msg void OnRedSundaysChanged();
    afx_msg DATE GetDate();
```

```
    afx_msg BOOL SetDate(short nYear, short nMonth, short nDay);
    //}}AFX_DISPATCH
    DECLARE_DISPATCH_MAP()

    afx_msg void AboutBox();

// Event maps
    //{{AFX_EVENT(CCalendarCtrl)
    void FireNewDay(short nDay)
        {FireEvent(eventidNewDay,EVENT_PARAM(VTS_I2), nDay);}
    //}}AFX_EVENT
    DECLARE_EVENT_MAP()

// Dispatch and event IDs
public:
    enum {
    //{{AFX_DISP_ID(CCalendarCtrl)
    dispidRedSundays = 1L,
    dispidGetDate = 2L,
    dispidSetDate = 3L,
    eventidNewDay = 1L,
    //}}AFX_DISP_ID
    };
};

//{{AFX_INSERT_LOCATION}}
// Microsoft Visual C++ will insert additional declarations
// immediately before the previous line.

#endif
// !defined(
//     AFX_CALENDARCTL_H__68932D29_CFE2_11D2_9282_00C04F8ECF0C__INCLUDED)
```

CalendarCtl.cpp

```
// CalendarCtl.cpp : Implementation of the
// CCalendarCtrl ActiveX Control class.

#include "stdafx.h"
#include "Calendar.h"
#include "CalendarCtl.h"
#include "CalendarPpg.h"

#ifdef _DEBUG
#define new DEBUG_NEW
#undef THIS_FILE
static char THIS_FILE[] = __FILE__;
#endif
```

(continued)

Figure 21-18 *continued*

```
IMPLEMENT_DYNCREATE(CCalendarCtrl, COleControl)

const int CCalendarCtrl::m_nDaysPerMonth[] = {
    31,         // January
    28,         // February
    31,         // March
    30,         // April
    31,         // May
    30,         // June
    31,         // July
    31,         // August
    30,         // September
    31,         // October
    30,         // November
    31,         // December
};

/////////////////////////////////////////////////////////////////////////////
// Message map

BEGIN_MESSAGE_MAP(CCalendarCtrl, COleControl)
    //{{AFX_MSG_MAP(CCalendarCtrl)
    ON_WM_LBUTTONDOWN()
    //}}AFX_MSG_MAP
    ON_OLEVERB(AFX_IDS_VERB_PROPERTIES, OnProperties)
END_MESSAGE_MAP()

/////////////////////////////////////////////////////////////////////////////
// Dispatch map

BEGIN_DISPATCH_MAP(CCalendarCtrl, COleControl)
    //{{AFX_DISPATCH_MAP(CCalendarCtrl)
    DISP_PROPERTY_NOTIFY(CCalendarCtrl, "RedSundays", m_bRedSundays,
        OnRedSundaysChanged, VT_BOOL)
    DISP_FUNCTION(CCalendarCtrl, "GetDate", GetDate, VT_DATE, VTS_NONE)
    DISP_FUNCTION(CCalendarCtrl, "SetDate", SetDate, VT_BOOL,
        VTS_I2 VTS_I2 VTS_I2)
    DISP_STOCKPROP_BACKCOLOR()
    //}}AFX_DISPATCH_MAP
    DISP_FUNCTION_ID(CCalendarCtrl, "AboutBox", DISPID_ABOUTBOX,
        AboutBox, VT_EMPTY, VTS_NONE)
END_DISPATCH_MAP()

/////////////////////////////////////////////////////////////////////////////
// Event map
```

```
BEGIN_EVENT_MAP(CCalendarCtrl, COleControl)
    //{{AFX_EVENT_MAP(CCalendarCtrl)
    EVENT_CUSTOM("NewDay", FireNewDay, VTS_I2)
    //}}AFX_EVENT_MAP
END_EVENT_MAP()


/////////////////////////////////////////////////////////////////////////
// Property pages

// TODO: Add more property pages as needed.
// Remember to increase the count!
BEGIN_PROPPAGEIDS(CCalendarCtrl, 2)
    PROPPAGEID(CCalendarPropPage::guid)
    PROPPAGEID (CLSID_CColorPropPage)
END_PROPPAGEIDS(CCalendarCtrl)


/////////////////////////////////////////////////////////////////////////
// Initialize class factory and guid

IMPLEMENT_OLECREATE_EX(CCalendarCtrl, "CALENDAR.CalendarCtrl.1",
    0xed780d6b, 0xcc9f, 0x11d2, 0x92, 0x82, 0, 0xc0, 0x4f, 0x8e, 0xcf, 0xc)


/////////////////////////////////////////////////////////////////////////
// Type library ID and version

IMPLEMENT_OLETYPELIB(CCalendarCtrl, _tlid, _wVerMajor, _wVerMinor)


/////////////////////////////////////////////////////////////////////////
// Interface IDs

const IID BASED_CODE IID_DCalendar =
        { 0x68932d1a, 0xcfe2, 0x11d2,
            { 0x92, 0x82, 0, 0xc0, 0x4f, 0x8e, 0xcf, 0xc } };
const IID BASED_CODE IID_DCalendarEvents =
        { 0x68932d1b, 0xcfe2, 0x11d2,
            { 0x92, 0x82, 0, 0xc0, 0x4f, 0x8e, 0xcf, 0xc } };


/////////////////////////////////////////////////////////////////////////
// Control type information

static const DWORD BASED_CODE _dwCalendarOleMisc =
    OLEMISC_ACTIVATEWHENVISIBLE |
    OLEMISC_SETCLIENTSITEFIRST |
    OLEMISC_INSIDEOUT |
    OLEMISC_CANTLINKINSIDE |
    OLEMISC_RECOMPOSEONRESIZE;
```

(continued)

Figure 21-18 *continued*

```
IMPLEMENT_OLECTLTYPE(CCalendarCtrl, IDS_CALENDAR, _dwCalendarOleMisc)

/////////////////////////////////////////////////////////////////////////////
// CCalendarCtrl::CCalendarCtrlFactory::UpdateRegistry -
// Adds or removes system registry entries for CCalendarCtrl

BOOL CCalendarCtrl::CCalendarCtrlFactory::UpdateRegistry(BOOL bRegister)
{
    // TODO: Verify that your control follows apartment-model
    // threading rules. Refer to MFC TechNote 64 for more information.
    // If your control does not conform to the apartment-model rules, then
    // you must modify the code below, changing the 6th parameter from
    // afxRegApartmentThreading to 0.

    if (bRegister)
        return AfxOleRegisterControlClass(
            AfxGetInstanceHandle(),
            m_clsid,
            m_lpszProgID,
            IDS_CALENDAR,
            IDB_CALENDAR,
            afxRegApartmentThreading,
            _dwCalendarOleMisc,
            _tlid,
            _wVerMajor,
            _wVerMinor);
    else
        return AfxOleUnregisterClass(m_clsid, m_lpszProgID);
}


/////////////////////////////////////////////////////////////////////////////
// CCalendarCtrl::CCalendarCtrl - Constructor

CCalendarCtrl::CCalendarCtrl()
{
    InitializeIIDs(&IID_DCalendar, &IID_DCalendarEvents);

    CTime time = CTime::GetCurrentTime ();
    m_nYear = time.GetYear ();
    m_nMonth = time.GetMonth ();
    m_nDay = time.GetDay ();
}


/////////////////////////////////////////////////////////////////////////////
// CCalendarCtrl::~CCalendarCtrl - Destructor
```

```
CCalendarCtrl::~CCalendarCtrl()
{
    // TODO: Cleanup your control's instance data here.
}

///////////////////////////////////////////////////////////////////////////
// CCalendarCtrl::OnDraw - Drawing function

void CCalendarCtrl::OnDraw(
        CDC* pdc, const CRect& rcBounds, const CRect& rcInvalid)
{
    //
    // Paint the control's background.
    //
    CBrush brush (TranslateColor (GetBackColor ()));
    pdc->FillRect (rcBounds, &brush);

    //
    // Compute the number of days in the month, which day of the week
    // the first of the month falls on, and other information needed to
    // draw the calendar.
    //
    int nNumberOfDays = m_nDaysPerMonth[m_nMonth - 1];
    if (m_nMonth == 2 && LeapYear (m_nYear))
        nNumberOfDays++;

    CTime time (m_nYear, m_nMonth, 1, 12, 0, 0);
    int nFirstDayOfMonth = time.GetDayOfWeek ();
    int nNumberOfRows = (nNumberOfDays + nFirstDayOfMonth + 5) / 7;

    int nCellWidth = rcBounds.Width () / 7;
    int nCellHeight = rcBounds.Height () / nNumberOfRows;

    int cx = rcBounds.left;
    int cy = rcBounds.top;

    //
    // Draw the calendar rectangle.
    //
    CPen* pOldPen = (CPen*) pdc->SelectStockObject (BLACK_PEN);
    CBrush* pOldBrush = (CBrush*) pdc->SelectStockObject (NULL_BRUSH);

    pdc->Rectangle (rcBounds.left, rcBounds.top,
        rcBounds.left + (7 * nCellWidth),
        rcBounds.top + (nNumberOfRows * nCellHeight));
```

(continued)

Figure 21-18 *continued*

```
    //
    // Draw rectangles representing the days of the month.
    //
    CFont font;
    font.CreatePointFont (80, _T ("MS Sans Serif"));
    CFont* pOldFont = pdc->SelectObject (&font);

    COLORREF clrOldTextColor = pdc->SetTextColor (RGB (0, 0, 0));
    int nOldBkMode = pdc->SetBkMode (TRANSPARENT);

    for (int i=0; i<nNumberOfDays; i++) {
        int nGridIndex = i + nFirstDayOfMonth - 1;
        int x = ((nGridIndex % 7) * nCellWidth) + cx;
        int y = ((nGridIndex / 7) * nCellHeight) + cy;
        CRect rect (x, y, x + nCellWidth, y + nCellHeight);

        if (i != m_nDay - 1) {
            pdc->Draw3dRect (rect, RGB (255, 255, 255),
                RGB (128, 128, 128));
            pdc->SetTextColor (RGB (0, 0, 0));
        }
        else {
            pdc->SelectStockObject (NULL_PEN);
            pdc->SelectStockObject (GRAY_BRUSH);
            pdc->Rectangle (rect);
            pdc->Draw3dRect (rect, RGB (128, 128, 128),
                RGB (255, 255, 255));
            pdc->SetTextColor (RGB (255, 255, 255));
        }

        CString string;
        string.Format (_T ("%d"), i + 1);
        rect.DeflateRect (nCellWidth / 8, nCellHeight / 8);

        if (m_bRedSundays && nGridIndex % 7 == 0)
            pdc->SetTextColor (RGB (255, 0, 0));

        pdc->DrawText (string, rect, DT_SINGLELINE | DT_LEFT | DT_TOP);
    }

    //
    // Clean up and exit.
    //
    pdc->SetBkMode (nOldBkMode);
    pdc->SetTextColor (clrOldTextColor);
```

```
    pdc->SelectObject (pOldFont);
    pdc->SelectObject (pOldBrush);
    pdc->SelectObject (pOldPen);
}

//////////////////////////////////////////////////////////////////////////
// CCalendarCtrl::DoPropExchange - Persistence support

void CCalendarCtrl::DoPropExchange(CPropExchange* pPX)
{
    ExchangeVersion(pPX, MAKELONG(_wVerMinor, _wVerMajor));
    COleControl::DoPropExchange(pPX);
    PX_Bool (pPX, _T ("RedSundays"), m_bRedSundays, TRUE);
}

//////////////////////////////////////////////////////////////////////////
// CCalendarCtrl::OnResetState - Reset control to default state

void CCalendarCtrl::OnResetState()
{
    COleControl::OnResetState(); // Resets defaults found in DoPropExchange

    // TODO: Reset any other control state here.
}

//////////////////////////////////////////////////////////////////////////
// CCalendarCtrl::AboutBox - Display an "About" box to the user

void CCalendarCtrl::AboutBox()
{
    CDialog dlgAbout(IDD_ABOUTBOX_CALENDAR);
    dlgAbout.DoModal();
}

//////////////////////////////////////////////////////////////////////////
// CCalendarCtrl message handlers

BOOL CCalendarCtrl::LeapYear(int nYear)
{
    return (nYear % 4 == 0) ^ (nYear % 400 == 0) ^ (nYear % 100 == 0);
}

void CCalendarCtrl::OnRedSundaysChanged()
{
    InvalidateControl ();
    SetModifiedFlag();
```

(continued)

Figure 21-18 *continued*

```
}

DATE CCalendarCtrl::GetDate()
{
    COleDateTime date (m_nYear, m_nMonth, m_nDay, 12, 0, 0);
    return (DATE) date;
}

BOOL CCalendarCtrl::SetDate(short nYear, short nMonth, short nDay)
{
    //
    // Make sure the input date is valid.
    //
    if (nYear < 1970 || nYear > 2037)
        return FALSE;

    if (nMonth < 1 || nMonth > 12)
        return FALSE;

    int nNumberOfDays = m_nDaysPerMonth[m_nMonth - 1];
    if (nMonth == 2 && LeapYear (nYear))
        nNumberOfDays++;

    if (nDay < 1 || nDay > nNumberOfDays)
        return FALSE;

    //
    // Update the date, repaint the control, and fire a NewDay event.
    //
    m_nYear = nYear;
    m_nMonth = nMonth;
    m_nDay = nDay;
    InvalidateControl ();
    return TRUE;
}

void CCalendarCtrl::OnLButtonDown(UINT nFlags, CPoint point)
{
    int nNumberOfDays = m_nDaysPerMonth[m_nMonth - 1];
    if (m_nMonth == 2 && LeapYear (m_nYear))
        nNumberOfDays++;

    CTime time (m_nYear, m_nMonth, 1, 12, 0, 0);
    int nFirstDayOfMonth = time.GetDayOfWeek ();
    int nNumberOfRows = (nNumberOfDays + nFirstDayOfMonth + 5) / 7;
```

```
    CRect rcClient;
    GetClientRect (&rcClient);
    int nCellWidth = rcClient.Width () / 7;
    int nCellHeight = rcClient.Height () / nNumberOfRows;

    for (int i=0; i<nNumberOfDays; i++) {
        int nGridIndex = i + nFirstDayOfMonth - 1;
        int x = rcClient.left + (nGridIndex % 7) * nCellWidth;
        int y = rcClient.top + (nGridIndex / 7) * nCellHeight;
        CRect rect (x, y, x + nCellWidth, y + nCellHeight);

        if (rect.PtInRect (point)) {
            m_nDay = i + 1;
            FireNewDay (m_nDay);
            InvalidateControl ();
        }
    }
    COleControl::OnLButtonDown(nFlags, point);
}
```

Testing and Debugging an ActiveX Control

Now that you've built the control, you'll want to test it, too. Visual C++ comes with the perfect tool for testing ActiveX controls: the ActiveX Control Test Container. You can start it from Visual C++'s Tools menu or by launching Tstcon32.exe. Once the ActiveX Control Test Container is running, go to its Edit menu, select the Insert New Control command, and select Calendar Control from the Insert Control dialog box to insert your control into the test container, as shown in Figure 21-19.

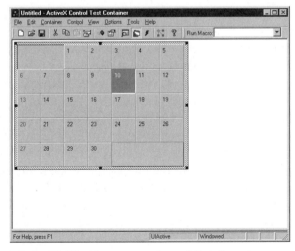

Figure 21-19. *The ActiveX Control Test Container.*

Initially, the control's background will probably be white because MFC's implementation of the stock property *BackColor* defaults to the container's ambient background color. This presents a wonderful opportunity to test the *BackColor* property you added to the control. With the control selected in the test container window, select Properties from the Edit menu. The control's property sheet will be displayed. (See Figure 21-20.) Go to the Colors page, and select light gray as the background color. Then click Apply. The control should turn light gray. Go back to the property sheet's General page and toggle Show Sundays In Red on and off a time or two. The control should repaint itself each time you click the Apply button. Remember the *OnRedSundaysChanged* notification function in which you inserted a call to *InvalidateControl?* It's that call that causes the control to update when the property value changes.

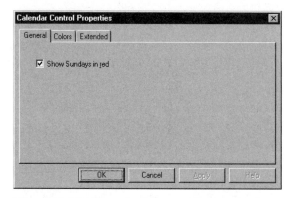

Figure 21-20. *The calendar control's property sheet.*

You can test a control's methods in the ActiveX Control Test Container, too. To try it, select the Invoke Methods command from the Control menu. The Invoke Methods dialog box, pictured in Figure 21-21, knows which methods the control implements because it read the control's type information. (That type information was generated from the control's ODL file and linked into the control's OCX as a binary resource.) To call a method, select the method by name in the Method Name box, enter parameter values (if applicable) in the Parameters box, and click the Invoke button. The method's return value will appear in the Return Value box. Incidentally, properties show up in the Invoke Methods dialog box with PropGet and PropPut labels attached to them. A PropGet method reads a property value, and a PropPut method writes it.

The ActiveX Control Test Container also lets you test a control's events. To demonstrate, choose the Logging command from the Options menu and make sure Log To Output Window is selected. Then click a few dates in the calendar. A *NewDay* event should appear in the output window with each click, as in Figure 21-22. The event is fired because you included a call to *FireNewDay* in the control's *OnLButtonDown* function.

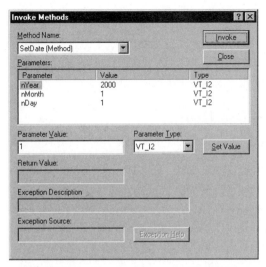

Figure 21-21. *The ActiveX Control Test Container's Invoke Methods dialog box.*

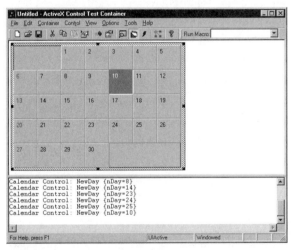

Figure 21-22. *Events are reported in the ActiveX Control Test Container's output window.*

If your control uses any of the container's ambient properties, you can customize those properties to see how the control reacts. To change an ambient property, use the Ambient Properties command in the Container menu.

What happens if your control doesn't behave as expected and you need to debug it? Fortunately, you can do that, too. Suppose you want to set a breakpoint in your code, see it hit, and single-step through the code. It's easy. Just open the control project in Visual C++ and set the breakpoint. Then go to the Build menu and select Start Debug-Go. When Visual C++ asks you for an executable file name, click the arrow next to the edit control and select ActiveX Control Test Container. Insert the control into the container and do something to cause the breakpoint to be hit. That should pop you into the Visual C++ debugger with the arrow on the instruction at the breakpoint. The same debugging facilities that Visual C++ places at your disposal for debugging regular MFC applications are available for debugging controls, too.

Registering an ActiveX Control

Like any COM object, an ActiveX control can't be used unless it is registered on the host system. Registering an ActiveX control means adding entries to the registry identifying the control's CLSID, the DLL that houses the control, and other information. When you build an ActiveX control with Visual C++, the control is automatically registered as part of the build process. If you give the control to another user, that user will need to register it on his or her system before it can be used. Here are two ways to register a control on another system.

The first way is to provide a setup program that registers the control programmatically. Because an OCX is a self-registering in-proc COM server, the setup program can load the OCX as if it were an ordinary DLL, find the address of its *DllRegisterServer* function, and call the function. *DllRegisterServer*, in turn, will register any and all of the controls in the OCX. The following code demonstrates how this is done if the OCX is named Calendar.ocx:

```
HINSTANCE hOcx = ::LoadLibrary (_T ("Calendar.ocx"));
if (hOcx != NULL) {
    FARPROC lpfn = ::GetProcAddress (hOcx, _T ("DllRegisterServer"));
    if (lpfn != NULL)
        (*lpfn) ();     // Register the control(s).
    ::FreeLibrary (hOcx);
}
```

To implement an uninstall feature, use the same code but change the second parameter passed to *::GetProcAddress* from "DllRegisterServer" to "DllUnregisterServer."

To register an ActiveX control on someone else's system without writing a setup program, use the Regsvr32 utility that comes with Visual C++. If Calendar.ocx is in the current directory, typing the following command into a command prompt window will register the OCX's controls:

```
Regsvr32 Calendar.ocx
```

By the same token, passing a /U switch to Regsvr32 unregisters the controls in an OCX:

```
Regsvr32 /U Calendar.ocx
```

Regsvr32 isn't a tool you should foist on end users, but it's a handy utility to have when testing and debugging a control prior to deployment.

USING ACTIVEX CONTROLS
IN MFC APPLICATIONS

Now you know how to write ActiveX controls. But what about control containers? Not just any window can host an ActiveX control; to do it, someone must implement the requisite COM interfaces. Fortunately, MFC will provide those interfaces for you. All you have to do is check a box in AppWizard and insert the control into the project. The control will then appear in the dialog editor's control toolbar, where it can be inserted into any MFC dialog.

Here are the steps required to use an ActiveX control in an MFC application:

1. In AppWizard's Step 2 dialog box (for dialog-based applications) or Step 3 dialog box (for nondialog-based applications), check the ActiveX Controls box, as shown in Figure 21-23.

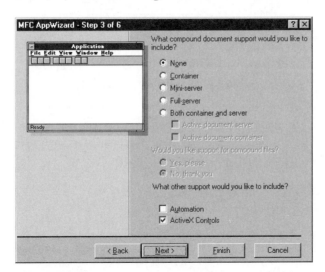

Figure 21-23. *Checking AppWizard's ActiveX Controls box makes any MFC dialog an ActiveX control container.*

2. When AppWizard is done, use Visual C++'s Project-Add To Project-Components And Controls command to insert the control into the project. This command displays the Components And Controls Gallery dialog box. The Registered ActiveX Controls folder contains a list of all the ActiveX controls installed on this system. (See Figure 21-24.)

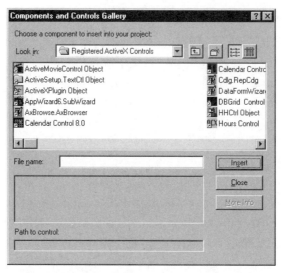

Figure 21-24. *The Components And Controls Gallery dialog box showing a list of registered ActiveX controls.*

3. When the Confirm Classes dialog box (shown in Figure 21-25) appears, either edit the class name and file names or accept the defaults. Visual C++ will create a wrapper class that the container can use to interact with the control. Member functions in the wrapper class will provide access to the control's methods and properties. Visual C++ gets the information it needs to build the wrapper class from the control's type library.

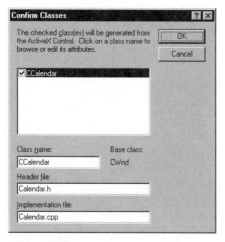

Figure 21-25. *The Confirm Classes dialog box.*

4. Close the Components And Controls Gallery dialog box.

If you now switch to ResourceView and open a dialog resource, the dialog editor's controls toolbar will contain a button representing the control. Adding the control to a dialog is a simple matter of clicking the button and drawing the control into the dialog. You can display the control's property sheet by right-clicking the control and selecting Properties from the context menu. Any changes you make to the control's properties will be serialized into the project's RC file and reapplied when the dialog is displayed.

Calling an ActiveX Control's Methods

Can it really be that easy? You bet. But that's not all. You can program the control—call its methods and read and write its properties programmatically—using the wrapper class generated when the control was added to the project. First, though, you must instantiate the wrapper class and connect it to a running control. Here's how to do it:

1. Go to ClassWizard's Member variables page, and select the ActiveX control's ID in the Control IDs box.

2. Click the Add Variable button, and choose the wrapper class's name (for example, *CCalendar*) in the Variable Type box. Enter a name for the instantiated class in the Member Variable Name box, too.

3. Click OK.

After that, you can call a control method or access a control property by calling the corresponding member function on the object whose name you entered in the Member Variable Name box. For a calendar control object named *m_ctlCalendar*, the following statement calls the control's *SetDate* method to set the date to January 1, 2000:

```
m_ctlCalendar.SetDate (2000, 1, 1);
```

The next statement sets the control's background color to light gray:

```
m_ctlCalendar.SetBackColor (OLE_COLOR (RGB (192, 192, 192)));
```

It works because ClassWizard added a *DDX_Control* statement to the dialog's *DoDataExchange* function that connects *m_ctlCalendar* to the running ActiveX control. You could add this statement yourself, but regardless of how you choose to do it, the fact remains that accessing the control from your program's source code is now no more difficult than calling a C++ member function.

Processing Events

You might want to do one more thing with an ActiveX control in an MFC application: process events. In Chapter 1, you learned that MFC uses message maps to correlate messages to member functions. Similarly, it uses *event sink maps* to correlate events fired by ActiveX controls to member functions. Here's a simple event sink map that connects *NewDay* events fired by our calendar control to a *CMyDialog* member function named *OnNewDay*:

```
BEGIN_EVENTSINK_MAP (CMyDialog, CDialog)
    ON_EVENT (CMyDialog, IDC_CALENDAR, 1, OnNewDay, VTS_I2)
END_EVENTSINK_MAP ()
```

The second parameter passed to ON_EVENT is the control ID. The third is the event's dispatch ID. The fourth is the member function that's called when the event is fired, and the final parameter specifies the types of parameters included in the event's parameter list—in this case, a 16-bit integer (VTS_I2). An event sink map can hold any number of ON_EVENT entries, making it a simple matter for an MFC container to respond to all manner of control events.

How do you write event sink maps? You don't have to write them by hand because ClassWizard will write them for you. To write an event handler, go to ClassWizard's Message Maps page, select the class that hosts the control in the Class Name box, and select the control's ID in the Object IDs box. You'll see a list of events that the control is capable of firing in the Messages box. (See Figure 21-26.) Select an event, and click the Add Function button. Enter a name for the member function you want to be called when the event is fired, and ClassWizard will add the member function to the class and an entry to the event sink map. When an event of that type is fired, the member function will be called just as if it were an ordinary message handler.

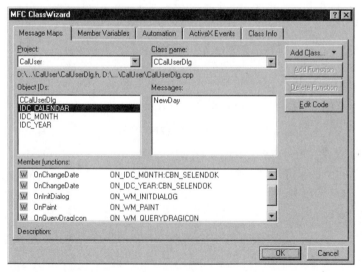

Figure 21-26. *Adding an event handler with ClassWizard.*

The CalUser Application

The CalUser application shown in Figure 21-1 on page 1226 is a dialog-based MFC application that hosts the MFC calendar control. Selecting a new month or year changes the calendar by calling its *SetDate* method. Clicking a square in the calendar pops up a message box that echoes the date that was clicked. The message box is displayed by an event handler named *OnNewDay* that's called each time the control fires a *NewDay* event. Relevant portions of CalUser's source code are reproduced in Figure 21-27.

CalUserDlg.h

```
// CalUserDlg.h : header file
//
//{{AFX_INCLUDES()
#include "calendar.h"
//}}AFX_INCLUDES

#if !defined(
    AFX_CALUSERDLG_H__85FDD589_470B_11D2_AC96_006008A8274D__INCLUDED_)
#define AFX_CALUSERDLG_H__85FDD589_470B_11D2_AC96_006008A8274D__INCLUDED_

#if _MSC_VER > 1000
#pragma once
#endif // _MSC_VER > 1000


/////////////////////////////////////////////////////////////////////////////
// CCalUserDlg dialog

class CCalUserDlg : public CDialog
{
// Construction
public:
    CCalUserDlg(CWnd* pParent = NULL);    // standard constructor

// Dialog Data
    //{{AFX_DATA(CCalUserDlg)
    enum { IDD = IDD_CALUSER_DIALOG };
    CComboBox     m_ctlYear;
    CComboBox     m_ctlMonth;
    CCalendar     m_ctlCalendar;
    //}}AFX_DATA

    // ClassWizard generated virtual function overrides
    //{{AFX_VIRTUAL(CCalUserDlg)
```

Figure 21-27. *The CalUser application.*   *(continued)*

Figure 21-27 *continued*

```
    protected:
    virtual void DoDataExchange(CDataExchange* pDX);      // DDX/DDV support
    //}}AFX_VIRTUAL

// Implementation
protected:
    static const CString m_strMonths[];
    void InitListOfYears ();
    void InitListOfMonths ();
    HICON m_hIcon;

    // Generated message map functions
    //{{AFX_MSG(CCalUserDlg)
    virtual BOOL OnInitDialog();
    afx_msg void OnPaint();
    afx_msg HCURSOR OnQueryDragIcon();
    afx_msg void OnChangeDate();
    afx_msg void OnNewDay(short nDay);
    DECLARE_EVENTSINK_MAP()
    //}}AFX_MSG
    DECLARE_MESSAGE_MAP()
};

//{{AFX_INSERT_LOCATION}}
// Microsoft Visual C++ will insert additional declarations
// immediately before the previous line.

#endif
// !defined(
//     AFX_CALUSERDLG_H__85FDD589_470B_11D2_AC96_006008A8274D__INCLUDED_)
```

CalUserDlg.cpp

```
// CalUserDlg.cpp : implementation file
//

#include "stdafx.h"
#include "CalUser.h"
#include "CalUserDlg.h"

#ifdef _DEBUG
#define new DEBUG_NEW
#undef THIS_FILE
static char THIS_FILE[] = __FILE__;
#endif
```

```
/////////////////////////////////////////////////////////////////////////////
// CCalUserDlg dialog

CCalUserDlg::CCalUserDlg(CWnd* pParent /*=NULL*/)
    : CDialog(CCalUserDlg::IDD, pParent)
{
    //{{AFX_DATA_INIT(CCalUserDlg)
    //}}AFX_DATA_INIT
    // Note that LoadIcon does not require a subsequent
    // DestroyIcon in Win32
    m_hIcon = AfxGetApp()->LoadIcon(IDR_MAINFRAME);
}

void CCalUserDlg::DoDataExchange(CDataExchange* pDX)
{
    CDialog::DoDataExchange(pDX);
    //{{AFX_DATA_MAP(CCalUserDlg)
    DDX_Control(pDX, IDC_YEAR, m_ctlYear);
    DDX_Control(pDX, IDC_MONTH, m_ctlMonth);
    DDX_Control(pDX, IDC_CALENDAR, m_ctlCalendar);
    //}}AFX_DATA_MAP
}

BEGIN_MESSAGE_MAP(CCalUserDlg, CDialog)
    //{{AFX_MSG_MAP(CCalUserDlg)
    ON_WM_PAINT()
    ON_WM_QUERYDRAGICON()
    ON_CBN_SELENDOK(IDC_MONTH, OnChangeDate)
    ON_CBN_SELENDOK(IDC_YEAR, OnChangeDate)
    //}}AFX_MSG_MAP
END_MESSAGE_MAP()

const CString CCalUserDlg::m_strMonths[] = {
    _T ("January"),
    _T ("February"),
    _T ("March"),
    _T ("April"),
    _T ("May"),
    _T ("June"),
    _T ("July"),
    _T ("August"),
    _T ("September"),
    _T ("October"),
    _T ("November"),
    _T ("December")
};
```

(continued)

Figure 21-27 *continued*

```
///////////////////////////////////////////////////////////////////////////
// CCalUserDlg message handlers

BOOL CCalUserDlg::OnInitDialog()
{
    CDialog::OnInitDialog();

    SetIcon(m_hIcon, TRUE);          // Set big icon
    SetIcon(m_hIcon, FALSE);         // Set small icon

    //
    // Initialize the Month control.
    //
    COleDateTime date = m_ctlCalendar.GetDate ();
    int nMonth = date.GetMonth ();
    int nYear = date.GetYear ();

    InitListOfMonths ();
    m_ctlMonth.SetCurSel (nMonth - 1);

    //
    // Initialize the Year control.
    //
    InitListOfYears ();
    m_ctlYear.SetCurSel (nYear - 1970);

    return TRUE;
}

void CCalUserDlg::OnPaint()
{
    if (IsIconic())
    {
        CPaintDC dc(this); // device context for painting

        SendMessage(WM_ICONERASEBKGND, (WPARAM) dc.GetSafeHdc(), 0);

        // Center icon in client rectangle
        int cxIcon = GetSystemMetrics(SM_CXICON);
        int cyIcon = GetSystemMetrics(SM_CYICON);
        CRect rect;
        GetClientRect(&rect);
        int x = (rect.Width() - cxIcon + 1) / 2;
        int y = (rect.Height() - cyIcon + 1) / 2;
```

```
            // Draw the icon
            dc.DrawIcon(x, y, m_hIcon);
        }
        else
        {
            CDialog::OnPaint();
        }
}

HCURSOR CCalUserDlg::OnQueryDragIcon()
{
        return (HCURSOR) m_hIcon;
}

void CCalUserDlg::InitListOfMonths()
{
        for (int i=0; i<12; i++)
            m_ctlMonth.AddString (m_strMonths[i]);
}

void CCalUserDlg::InitListOfYears()
{
        for (int i=1970; i<=2037; i++) {
            CString string;
            string.Format (_T ("%d"), i);
            m_ctlYear.AddString (string);
        }
}

void CCalUserDlg::OnChangeDate()
{
        int nMonth = m_ctlMonth.GetCurSel () + 1;
        int nYear = GetDlgItemInt (IDC_YEAR);
        ASSERT (nYear != 0);
        m_ctlCalendar.SetDate (nYear, nMonth, 1);
}

BEGIN_EVENTSINK_MAP(CCalUserDlg, CDialog)
    //{{AFX_EVENTSINK_MAP(CCalUserDlg)
    ON_EVENT(CCalUserDlg, IDC_CALENDAR, 1 /* NewDay */, OnNewDay, VTS_I2)
    //}}AFX_EVENTSINK_MAP
END_EVENTSINK_MAP()

void CCalUserDlg::OnNewDay(short nDay)
{
        static const CString strDays[] = {
            _T ("Sunday"),
```

(continued)

Figure 21-27 *continued*

```
        _T ("Monday"),
        _T ("Tuesday"),
        _T ("Wednesday"),
        _T ("Thursday"),
        _T ("Friday"),
        _T ("Saturday"),
    };

    COleDateTime date = m_ctlCalendar.GetDate ();
    int nMonth = date.GetMonth ();
    int nYear = date.GetYear ();

    CTime time (nYear, nMonth, nDay, 12, 0, 0);
    int nDayOfWeek = time.GetDayOfWeek () - 1;

    CString string;
    string.Format (_T ("%s, %s %d, %d"), strDays[nDayOfWeek],
        m_strMonths[nMonth - 1], nDay, nYear);

    MessageBox (string);
}
```

Using ActiveX Controls in Nondialog Windows

MFC and ClassWizard make it wonderfully easy to use ActiveX controls in dialogs, but what about nondialog windows? It turns out that MFC allows any *CWnd* object to host ActiveX controls. You can create ActiveX controls just about anywhere in an MFC application, but outside of dialog windows, you have to do some manual coding to make it happen.

Here's how to add the MFC calendar control to a view:

1. Insert the control into the project. Name the wrapper class *CCalendar*.

2. Add a *CCalendar* member variable named *m_ctlCalendar* to the view.

3. Add the following statement to the view's *OnCreate* handler:

    ```
    m_ctlCalendar.Create (NULL, WS_VISIBLE,
        CRect (0, 0, 400, 300), this, IDC_CALENDAR);
    ```

When the view is created, the calendar control will be created in the view's upper left corner and assigned the control ID IDC_CALENDAR. Most of the work is done by *CCalendar::Create*, which calls the *CreateControl* function *CCalendar* inherits from *CWnd. CWnd::CreateControl* indirectly calls *COleControlSite::CreateControl*, which creates an ActiveX control and wires it up to its container.

So far, so good. But what if you want the view to process control events, too? This is where it gets tricky. ClassWizard will add event handlers to dialogs, but not to nondialogs. So you code the event sink map by hand. That wouldn't be too bad if it weren't for the fact that an event's parameter list has to be coded into the ON_EVENT statement in the form of VTS flags. Some programmers get around this by doing the following:

1. Add a dummy dialog to the application.

2. Insert the ActiveX control into the dialog.

3. Use ClassWizard to write event handlers into the dialog.

4. Copy the event sink map from the dialog to the view.

5. Delete the dummy dialog.

I didn't say it was pretty. But it works. If you use this technique, don't forget to copy the DECLARE_EVENTSINK_MAP statement from the dialog's header file to the view's header file. DECLARE_EVENTSINK_MAP declares an event sink map just as DECLARE-_MESSAGE_MAP declares a message map.

All this assumes, of course, that you checked AppWizard's ActiveX Controls box when you created the project. If you didn't, you can add container support to the application after the fact by adding an

```
AfxEnableControlContainer ();
```

statement to *InitInstance*.

Using ActiveX Controls in Web Pages

One of the reasons ActiveX controls exist is to make Web content more interactive. An <OBJECT> tag in an HTML page denotes an ActiveX control. The control's methods and properties are accessible from within the HTML code, and events can be processed as well. The following HTML page displays this chapter's calendar control and responds to *NewDay* events by popping up a message box announcing which date was clicked:

```
<HTML>
<BODY>
<OBJECT
    CLASSID="CLSID:ED780D6B-CC9F-11D2-9282-00C04F8ECF0C"
    WIDTH=400
    HEIGHT=300
    ID="Calendar"
>
<PARAM NAME="BackColor" VALUE=12632256>
```

(continued)

```
</OBJECT>
</BODY>
<SCRIPT LANGUAGE=VBScript>
Sub Calendar_NewDay(day)
    dt = Calendar.GetDate
    yr = DatePart ("yyyy", dt)
    mon = DatePart ("m", dt)
    MsgBox (CStr (mon) + "/" + CStr (day) + "/" + CStr (yr))
End Sub
</SCRIPT>
</HTML>
```

You can try out these statements by typing them into an HTML file and opening the file with Internet Explorer. You'll have to modify the CLSID in the <OBJECT> tag if you create the control yourself because your control's CLSID will differ from mine. And remember that for the page to display properly, the control must be installed on your system. (In real life, the <OBJECT> tag would include a CODEBASE attribute and a URL telling Internet Explorer where to find the control if it's not already installed.) Notice the WIDTH and HEIGHT statements that specify the size of the control and the PARAM statement that sets the control's background color to light gray. The VBScript code in the SCRIPT block is called whenever a *NewDay* event is fired. It calls the control's *GetDate* method and displays the resultant date.

ADVANCED TOPICS

No chapter can possibly cover everything there is to know about ActiveX controls. You've learned the essentials, but there are some additional issues that every control developer should be aware of. The following sections present three such issues.

Windowless Controls

Although ActiveX controls have existed in one form or another since 1994, 1996 was the year they came of age. OCX 94 defined the baseline control architecture; OCX 96 introduced a number of enhancements designed to allow controls to run faster and more efficiently and consume fewer resources while doing so. One of those enhancements was the windowless control.

OCX 94–style controls are always created with windows of their own. This is consistent with the behavior of Windows controls, which also have their own windows. That's fine when you're hosting just one or two controls, but if a container creates tens, perhaps hundreds, of ActiveX controls, giving each a window of its own introduces an appreciable amount of overhead in terms of resource requirements and instantiation time.

It turns out that most controls don't really need windows of their own if their containers are willing to help out by performing a few small chores such as simulating the input focus and forwarding mouse messages. This interaction between the control and the container—the physical mechanisms that permit a windowless ActiveX control to borrow a portion of its container's window—was standardized in OCX 96.

Here, in a nutshell, is how it works. A windowless control implements the COM interface *IOleInPlaceObjectWindowless*; a container that supports windowless controls implements *IOleInPlaceSiteWindowless*. When a windowless control is created, it has no window, which means it can't receive mouse or keyboard input. Therefore, the container forwards mouse messages and, if the control has the conceptual input focus, keyboard messages to the control by calling its *IOleInPlaceObject-Windowless::OnWindowMessage* method. Another *IOleInPlaceObjectWindowless* method named *GetDropTarget* permits the container to get a pointer to the control's *IDropTarget* interface if the control is an OLE drop target. (Recall from Chapter 19 that registering as an OLE drop target requires a *CWnd* pointer or a window handle.) To draw a windowless control, the container calls the control's *IViewObjectEx::Draw* method and passes in a device context for the container window. A windowless control receives no WM_PAINT messages, so it's up to the container to tell the control when to draw.

Clearly, the container shoulders an extra burden when it supports windowless controls, but the control also has to do certain things differently, too. For example, if it wants to repaint itself, a windowless control can't just call *Invalidate* because it has no window to invalidate. Nor can it get a device context by calling *GetDC*. So instead it calls *IOleInPlaceSiteWindowless::InvalidateRect* on its container to invalidate itself, or *IOleInPlaceSiteWindowless::GetDC* to get a device context. There's more, but you probably get the picture.

Obviously, windowlessness requires extra effort on the part of both the control and the control container. The good news is that *COleControl* supports both windowed and windowless controls, and it abstracts the differences between them so that you write to one programming model and the control will work either way. Many *COleControl* functions behave differently in a windowed control than they do in a windowless control. *COleControl::InvalidateControl*, for example, calls *CWnd-::Invalidate* if the control is windowed or *IOleInPlaceSiteWindowless::InvalidateRect* if it isn't. *COleControl::GetClientRect* calls *CWnd::GetClientRect* for a windowed control, but for a nonwindowed control, it obtains the control rectangle from the control's *m_rcPos* data member.

Another example demonstrating how *COleControl* masks the differences between windowed and windowless controls relates to the message map. When a container forwards a message to a windowless control via *IOleInPlaceObjectWindowless-::OnWindowMessage*, *COleControl* routes the message through the message map. This means that if you register an *OnLButtonDown* handler in a control's message map, the handler will be called when a windowed control receives a WM_LBUTTONDOWN message or when a windowless control receives a pseudo-WM_LBUTTONDOWN message. In fact, *COleControl* does such a good job making windowless controls behave just like windowed controls that you almost have to deliberately set out to write *COleControl* code that won't work in windowless controls. Even so, you'll want to avoid these three common mistakes:

- Don't use *Invalidate* to force a repaint; use *InvalidateControl* instead.

- Don't trap messages directly; use the message map.

- Don't rely on window-oriented messages such as WM_CREATE and WM_DESTROY; windowless controls don't receive them.

Another common problem is using the *rcBounds* parameter passed to *OnDraw* or the rectangle returned by *GetClientRect* and forgetting that the upper left corner might not be (0,0) for a windowless control. The following code, which computes the center point of the control, is fine in a windowed control, but flawed in a windowless control:

```
CRect rect;
GetClientRect (&rect);
int x = rect.Width () / 2;
int y = rect.Height () / 2;
```

Why is this code in error? Because if *rect*'s upper left corner is anywhere other than (0,0), the calculation must take that into account. Here's the corrected code:

```
CRect rect;
GetClientRect (&rect);
int x = rect.left + (rect.Width () / 2);
int y = rect.top + (rect.Height () / 2);
```

Windows programmers have been conditioned to treat client rectangles as if the upper left corner coordinates are always (0,0). You must break this habit if you want to write windowless controls that work.

Don't forget that a control created using ControlWizard's default options is strictly a windowed control. To enable the windowless option, check the Windowless Activation box in ControlWizard's Advanced ActiveX Features dialog box. You can convert a windowed control to a windowless control after the fact by overriding *GetControlFlags* in the derived control class and implementing it like this:

```
DWORD CMyControl::GetControlFlags ()
{
    return COleControl::GetControlFlags () | windowlessActivate;
}
```

If *GetControlFlags* is already overridden, simply add *windowlessActivate* to the list of control flags.

What happens if you build a windowless control and it's instantiated in a container that doesn't support windowless controls? An MFC control will simply fall back and run in a window. Which brings up an interesting point: even though MFC has supported windowless controls for a while now, the test container that ships with Visual C++ didn't support windowless controls prior to version 6.0. Don't make the mistake I once did and attempt to test a windowless control's windowless behavior in the Visual C++ 5.0 test container, because the control will always be created in a window. You can selectively enable and disable windowless support in version 6.0's test container using the Options command in the Container menu.

Control Subclassing

One of the questions that ControlWizard asks you before creating an ActiveX control project is, Which Window Class, If Any, Should This Control Subclass? (See Figure 21-5 on page 1238.) The default is none, but if you select a WNDCLASS name, ControlWizard will create an ActiveX control that wraps a Windows control. This makes it relatively easy to write ActiveX controls that look and act like tree view controls, slider controls, and other built-in control types.

• Subclassing a control seems simple, but there's more to it than meets the eye. When a "subclassing" control is created, MFC automatically creates the corresponding Windows control. To do that, MFC must know the control's type—that is, its WNDCLASS. ControlWizard makes the WNDCLASS name you selected in the Which Window Class, If Any, Should This Control Subclass box known to MFC by overriding *COleControl::PreCreateWindow* and copying the class name to CREATESTRUCT's *lpszClass* data member. Programmers frequently modify ControlWizard's implementation to apply default styles to the Windows control, as shown here:

```
BOOL CMyControl::PreCreateWindow (CREATESTRUCT& cs)
{
    cs.lpszClass = _T ("SysTreeView32"); // Tree view control
    // Apply default control styles here.
    return COleControl::PreCreateWindow (cs);
}
```

Furthermore, at certain points in an ActiveX control's lifetime, MFC needs to know whether the control has subclassed a Windows control. Consequently, a subclassing control must override *COleControl::IsSubclassedControl* and return TRUE:

```
BOOL CMyControl::IsSubclassedControl()
{
    return TRUE;
}
```

ControlWizard writes this function for you if you check the Which Window Class, If Any, Should This Control Subclass box.

When a subclassing control is created, MFC silently creates a "reflector" window that bounces notification messages emitted by the Windows control back to the ActiveX control. The message IDs change en route: WM_COMMAND becomes OCM_COMMAND, WM_NOTIFY becomes OCM_NOTIFY, and so on. To process these messages in your control, you must modify the derived control class's message map to direct OCM messages to the appropriate handling functions. The following code demonstrates how an ActiveX control that subclasses a push button control might turn button clicks into *Click* events by processing BN_CLICKED notifications:

```
BEGIN_MESSAGE_MAP (CMyControl, COleControl)
    ON_MESSAGE (OCM_COMMAND, OnOcmCommand)
END_MESSAGE_MAP ()
    :
    :

LRESULT CMyControl::OnOcmCommand (WPARAM wParam, LPARAM lParam)
{
    WORD wNotifyCode = HIWORD (wParam);
    if (wNotifyCode == BN_CLICKED)
        FireClick ();
    return 0;
}
```

ControlWizard adds an empty *OnOcmCommand* handler similar to this one to the control class, but if you want to process other types of OCM messages, you must add the handlers and message map entries yourself.

It's also your job to add any methods, properties, and events you would like the control to have. They're added to a subclassing control the same way they're added to a regular control. If you need to access the Windows control from the ActiveX control's method implementations, you can get to it through the *m_hWnd* data member. To illustrate, the following code fragment adds strings to a list box that has been subclassed by an ActiveX control:

```
static const CString strMonthsOfTheYear[] = {
    _T ("January"),  _T ("February"), _T ("March"),
    _T ("April"),    _T ("May"),      _T ("June"),
    _T ("July"),     _T ("August"),   _T ("September"),
    _T ("October"),  _T ("November"), _T ("December")
};

for (int i=0; i<12; i++)
    ::SendMessage (m_hWnd, LB_ADDSTRING, 0,
        (LPARAM) (LPCTSTR) strMonthsOfTheYear[i]);
```

Subclassing Windows controls has a dark side; it has to do with painting. ControlWizard writes an *OnDraw* function that looks like this:

```
void CMyControl::OnDraw(CDC* pdc, const CRect& rcBounds,
```

```
    const CRect& rcInvalid)
{
    DoSuperclassPaint(pdc, rcBounds);
}
```

DoSuperclassPaint is a *COleControl* function that paints a subclassed control by simulating a WM_PAINT message. It works fine as long as the ActiveX control is active. But if the control goes inactive, the Windows control it wraps is asked to paint itself into a metafile device context. Some controls don't render well into a metafile, which leaves you to write the code that paints an inactive control by overriding *OnDraw-Metafile*. That can be quite a lot of work. As a rule, subclassing Windows common controls works better than subclassing classic controls—list boxes, combo boxes, and so on—because the common controls' internal painting logic is more metafile-friendly.

You can mostly avoid this problem by checking ControlWizard's Activates When Visible box. If the container honors your request (remember, however, that this isn't guaranteed), the control will be active whenever it's visible on the screen. This means the control's metafile will never be seen. And if it's never seen, it doesn't matter how good (or bad) it looks.

Incidentally, a similar set of issues arises when writing ActiveX controls that create child controls. Rather than open a new can of worms, I'll refer you to an excellent discussion of this matter in the "Converting a VBX and Subclassing Windows Controls" chapter of Adam Denning's *ActiveX Controls Inside Out* (1997, Microsoft Press).

Control Licensing

Most COM objects in the world today are accompanied by class factories that implement COM's *IClassFactory* interface. Anyone who has the DLL or EXE (or OCX) that houses such an object can create object instances by calling *IClassFactory-::CreateInstance* or a wrapper function such as *::CoCreateInstance*. This is exactly what happens under the hood when a container instantiates an ActiveX control.

If you check the Yes, Please box in response to the question Would You Like The Controls In This Project To Have A Runtime License? in ControlWizard's Step 1 dialog box, ControlWizard inserts a special class factory that implements *IClassFactory2* instead of *IClassFactory*. *IClassFactory2* adds licensing methods to *IClassFactory* and affords the control's implementor veto power over instantiation requests. Exercised properly, this feature can be used to restrict the use of an ActiveX control to individuals (or applications) who are legally authorized to use it.

Here's how licensing works in an MFC ActiveX control. When the licensing option is selected, ControlWizard overrides a pair of virtual functions named *VerifyUserLicense* and *GetLicenseKey* in the control's embedded class factory class. Exactly when these functions are called depends on the context in which the control is being used. Here's what happens when you drop a licensed control into a dialog in Visual C++'s dialog editor.

1. *VerifyUserLicense* is called. Its job is to verify that the control is licensed for use in a design-time environment. Returning 0 prevents the control from being instantiated; a nonzero return allows instantiation to proceed.

2. If *VerifyUserLicense* returns a nonzero value, *GetLicenseKey* is called. Its job is to return a licensing string that Visual C++ can embed in the compiled executable. This string becomes the control's run-time license.

Now suppose you compile and run the application. When the application is executed and the container attempts to instantiate the ActiveX control, a different series of events ensues:

1. The MFC-provided class factory's *VerifyLicenseKey* function is called and passed the licensing string embedded in the control container. Its job: to check the string and determine whether it represents a valid run-time license.

2. *VerifyLicenseKey* calls *GetLicenseKey* to retrieve the run-time licensing string from the control and compares that string to the one supplied by the container. If the strings don't match, *VerifyLicenseKey* returns 0 and the class factory will refuse to create the control. If the strings match, instantiation proceeds as normal.

VerifyLicenseKey is a third virtual function that plays a role in licensing. ControlWizard doesn't override it because the default implementation compares the strings and does the right thing, but you can override it manually if you want to implement a custom run-time verification algorithm.

These semantics might vary somewhat from container to container, but the result is the same. In effect, the control supports two separate licenses: a design-time license and a run-time license. At first, this dichotomy might seem odd, but it makes terrific sense when you think about it. If a developer uses your control in an application, you can make sure that he or she has the right to do so. But once the application is built, you probably don't want to force individual users to be licensed, too. Design-time licenses and run-time licenses are treated separately for precisely this reason.

The licensing scheme implemented by ControlWizard is exceedingly weak, so if you really want to build a licensed control, you must do some work yourself. Here's how ControlWizard implements *VerifyUserLicense* and *GetLicenseKey*:

```
static const TCHAR BASED_CODE _szLicFileName[] = _T("License.lic");
static const WCHAR BASED_CODE _szLicString[] = L"Copyright (c) 1999 ";
```

```
BOOL CMyControl::CMyClassFactory::VerifyUserLicense()
{
    return AfxVerifyLicFile(AfxGetInstanceHandle(), _szLicFileName,
        _szLicString);
}

BOOL CMyControl::CMyClassFactory::GetLicenseKey(DWORD dwReserved,
    BSTR FAR* pbstrKey)
{
    if (pbstrKey == NULL)
        return FALSE;

    *pbstrKey = SysAllocString(_szLicString);
    return (*pbstrKey != NULL);
}
```

AfxVerifyLicFile is an MFC helper function that scans the first *n* characters in the file
whose name is specified in the second parameter for the string passed in the third,
where *n* is the string length. Visual C++ places a text file named License.lic in the
same folder as the control's OCX. Inside that file is the text string "Copyright (c) 1999."
If the file is present and it begins with the expected string, *AfxVerifyLicFile* returns a
nonzero value, allowing the control to be instantiated. Otherwise, it returns 0. In other
words, the control's design-time license amounts to a simple text file that anyone could
create with Notepad.

There are endless ways to modify ControlWizard's code to strengthen the licensing policy. You could, for example, have *VerifyUserLicense* display a dialog box
prompting the developer to enter a password. Or you could have it check the registry for an entry created by the control's setup program. However you choose to do it,
keep in mind that determined users will be able to circumvent just about any scheme
you come up with, and many will steer clear of copy-protected products, period, if
at all possible. For these reasons, most ActiveX control writers have opted not to license their controls. You be the judge.

Index

Note: Italicized page references indicate figures, tables, or program listings.

Index

Index

Index

Index

Index

Index

JEFF PROSISE

Jeff Prosise makes his living programming Windows and teaching others how to do the same. Soon after receiving a B.S. in mechanical engineering from the University of Tennessee in 1982, he purchased his first PC and embarked upon a hobby that would eventually become his career.

Today Jeff spends his working hours writing books about programming and articles for *PC Magazine* and *Microsoft Systems Journal,* teaching MFC programming and COM programming classes through David Solomon Expert Seminars, providing consulting services for companies who write Windows software, and developing software of his own. He speaks at programming conferences around the world and takes time out whenever possible to enjoy his three children—Adam, Amy, and Abigail. He considers himself one of the luckiest people alive not only because he has been blessed with good health and a wonderful family, but also because he can earn a living by doing what he enjoys the most.

You can contact Jeff by sending e-mail to *jeffpro@msn.com* or by visiting his Web site at *www.prosise.com.*

The manuscript for this book was prepared using Microsoft Word 97. Pages were composed by Microsoft Press using Adobe PageMaker 6.52 for Windows, with text in Garamond and display type in Helvetica Black. Composed pages were delivered to the printer as electronic prepress files.

Cover Graphic Designer

Tim Girvin Design, Inc.

Cover Illustrator

Glenn Mitsui

Interior Graphic Artist

Joel Panchot

Compositors

Barb Runyan

Carl Diltz

Principal Proofreader/Copy Editor

Patricia Masserman

Indexer

Hugh Maddocks

The *definitive guide* to the **Win32 API**

U.S.A. **$59.99**
U.K. £56.49 [V.A.T. included]
Canada $86.99
ISBN 1-57231-995-X

"Look it up in Petzold" remains the decisive last word in answering questions about Microsoft® Windows® development. And in PROGRAMMING WINDOWS, Fifth Edition, the esteemed Windows Pioneer Award winner revises his classic text with authoritative coverage of the latest versions of the Windows operating system—once again drilling down to the essential API heart of Win32® programming. Packed as always with definitive examples, this newest Petzold delivers the ultimate sourcebook and tutorial for Windows programmers at all levels working with Windows 95, Windows 98, or Windows NT.® No aspiring or experienced developer can afford to be without it.

Microsoft®

mspress.microsoft.com

32-bit
behavior
modification

Inside the Microsoft Windows 98 Registry

Tapping into the Power of the Registry for Microsoft Windows 98

Günter Born

The Registry in any 32-bit version of Microsoft®
Windows®—Windows 95, Windows 98,
Windows NT® 4.0, or Windows 2000—determines
default behavior for many parts of the Windows
environment. Knowing how to successfully manipulate the Registry is crucial to seamlessly
integrating new applications—and you'll find the
answers you need in INSIDE THE MICROSOFT
WINDOWS 98 REGISTRY. This book-and-CD set
covers Registry concepts and features, baseline
tools such as Registry Editor, and customizing
properties and settings. Extend the functionality of
various Windows shells by modifying Registry files.
and get your 32-bit house in order with INSIDE THE
MICROSOFT WINDOWS 98 REGISTRY.

Microsoft®

mspress.microsoft.com

A view of the future:

Internet business
built on
Windows NT

U.S.A. **$44.99**
U.K. £41.99 [V.A.T. included]
Canada $64.99
ISBN 1-57231-852-X

The Internet is a major driving force in the computer industry today. By harnessing it with the services of Microsoft® Windows NT,® you are equipped to develop the next generation of business server applications. INSIDE MICROSOFT WINDOWS NT INTERNET DEVELOPMENT delivers an authoritative overview of the complex issues involved in building these business applications, and it explains why Active Server greatly simplifies their development. Content is reinforced by partial case study information drawn from the author's projects and clients, with sample code on CD-ROM illustrating how the various technologies are applied. Major sections of the book are devoted to Microsoft Transaction Server and Active Server Pages. Code samples are drawn from a variety of development languages.

mspress.microsoft.com

MICROSOFT LICENSE AGREEMENT

Book Companion CD

IMPORTANT—READ CAREFULLY: This Microsoft End-User License Agreement ("EULA") is a legal agreement between you (either an individual or an entity) and Microsoft Corporation for the Microsoft product identified above, which includes computer software and may include associated media, printed materials, and "online" or electronic documentation ("SOFTWARE PRODUCT"). Any component included within the SOFTWARE PRODUCT that is accompanied by a separate End-User License Agreement shall be governed by such agreement and not the terms set forth below. By installing, copying, or otherwise using the SOFTWARE PRODUCT, you agree to be bound by the terms of this EULA. If you do not agree to the terms of this EULA, you are not authorized to install, copy, or otherwise use the SOFTWARE PRODUCT; you may, however, return the SOFTWARE PRODUCT, along with all printed materials and other items that form a part of the Microsoft product that includes the SOFTWARE PRODUCT, to the place you obtained them for a full refund.

SOFTWARE PRODUCT LICENSE

The SOFTWARE PRODUCT is protected by United States copyright laws and international copyright treaties, as well as other intellectual property laws and treaties. The SOFTWARE PRODUCT is licensed, not sold.

1. **GRANT OF LICENSE.** This EULA grants you the following rights:

   a. **Software Product.** You may install and use one copy of the SOFTWARE PRODUCT on a single computer. The primary user of the computer on which the SOFTWARE PRODUCT is installed may make a second copy for his or her exclusive use on a portable computer.

   b. **Storage/Network Use.** You may also store or install a copy of the SOFTWARE PRODUCT on a storage device, such as a network server, used only to install or run the SOFTWARE PRODUCT on your other computers over an internal network; however, you must acquire and dedicate a license for each separate computer on which the SOFTWARE PRODUCT is installed or run from the storage device. A license for the SOFTWARE PRODUCT may not be shared or used concurrently on different computers.

   c. **License Pak.** If you have acquired this EULA in a Microsoft License Pak, you may make the number of additional copies of the computer software portion of the SOFTWARE PRODUCT authorized on the printed copy of this EULA, and you may use each copy in the manner specified above. You are also entitled to make a corresponding number of secondary copies for portable computer use as specified above.

   d. **Sample Code.** Solely with respect to portions, if any, of the SOFTWARE PRODUCT that are identified within the SOFTWARE PRODUCT as sample code (the "SAMPLE CODE"):

      i. **Use and Modification.** Microsoft grants you the right to use and modify the source code version of the SAMPLE CODE, *provided* you comply with subsection (d)(iii) below. You may not distribute the SAMPLE CODE, or any modified version of the SAMPLE CODE, in source code form.

      ii. **Redistributable Files.** Provided you comply with subsection (d)(iii) below, Microsoft grants you a nonexclusive, royalty-free right to reproduce and distribute the object code version of the SAMPLE CODE and of any modified SAMPLE CODE, other than SAMPLE CODE, or any modified version thereof, designated as not redistributable in the Readme file that forms a part of the SOFTWARE PRODUCT (the "Non-Redistributable Sample Code"). All SAMPLE CODE other than the Non-Redistributable Sample Code is collectively referred to as the "REDISTRIBUTABLES."

      iii. **Redistribution Requirements.** If you redistribute the REDISTRIBUTABLES, you agree to: (i) distribute the REDISTRIBUTABLES in object code form only in conjunction with and as a part of your software application product; (ii) not use Microsoft's name, logo, or trademarks to market your software application product; (iii) include a valid copyright notice on your software application product; (iv) indemnify, hold harmless, and defend Microsoft from and against any claims or lawsuits, including attorney's fees, that arise or result from the use or distribution of your software application product; and (v) not permit further distribution of the REDISTRIBUTABLES by your end user. Contact Microsoft for the applicable royalties due and other licensing terms for all other uses and/or distribution of the REDISTRIBUTABLES.

2. **DESCRIPTION OF OTHER RIGHTS AND LIMITATIONS.**

   - **Limitations on Reverse Engineering, Decompilation, and Disassembly.** You may not reverse engineer, decompile, or disassemble the SOFTWARE PRODUCT, except and only to the extent that such activity is expressly permitted by applicable law notwithstanding this limitation.

   - **Separation of Components.** The SOFTWARE PRODUCT is licensed as a single product. Its component parts may not be separated for use on more than one computer.

   - **Rental.** You may not rent, lease, or lend the SOFTWARE PRODUCT.

   - **Support Services.** Microsoft may, but is not obligated to, provide you with support services related to the SOFTWARE PRODUCT ("Support Services"). Use of Support Services is governed by the Microsoft policies and programs described in the user manual, in "online" documentation, and/or other Microsoft-provided materials. Any supplemental software code provided to you as part of the Support Services shall be considered part of the SOFTWARE PRODUCT and subject to the terms and conditions of this EULA. With respect to technical information you provide to Microsoft as part of the Support Services, Microsoft may use such information for its business purposes, including for product support and development. Microsoft will not utilize such technical information in a form that personally identifies you.

- **Software Transfer.** You may permanently transfer all of your rights under this EULA, provided you retain no copies, you transfer all of the SOFTWARE PRODUCT (including all component parts, the media and printed materials, any upgrades, this EULA, and, if applicable, the Certificate of Authenticity), **and** the recipient agrees to the terms of this EULA.

- **Termination.** Without prejudice to any other rights, Microsoft may terminate this EULA if you fail to comply with the terms and conditions of this EULA. In such event, you must destroy all copies of the SOFTWARE PRODUCT and all of its component parts.

3. **COPYRIGHT.** All title and copyrights in and to the SOFTWARE PRODUCT (including but not limited to any images, photographs, animations, video, audio, music, text, SAMPLE CODE, REDISTRIBUTABLES, and "applets" incorporated into the SOFTWARE PRODUCT) and any copies of the SOFTWARE PRODUCT are owned by Microsoft or its suppliers. The SOFTWARE PRODUCT is protected by copyright laws and international treaty provisions. Therefore, you must treat the SOFTWARE PRODUCT like any other copyrighted material **except** that you may install the SOFTWARE PRODUCT on a single computer provided you keep the original solely for backup or archival purposes. You may not copy the printed materials accompanying the SOFTWARE PRODUCT.

4. **U.S. GOVERNMENT RESTRICTED RIGHTS.** The SOFTWARE PRODUCT and documentation are provided with RESTRICTED RIGHTS. Use, duplication, or disclosure by the Government is subject to restrictions as set forth in subparagraph (c)(1)(ii) of the Rights in Technical Data and Computer Software clause at DFARS 252.227-7013 or subparagraphs (c)(1) and (2) of the Commercial Computer Software—Restricted Rights at 48 CFR 52.227-19, as applicable. Manufacturer is Microsoft Corporation/One Microsoft Way/Redmond, WA 98052-6399.

5. **EXPORT RESTRICTIONS.** You agree that you will not export or re-export the SOFTWARE PRODUCT, any part thereof, or any process or service that is the direct product of the SOFTWARE PRODUCT (the foregoing collectively referred to as the "Restricted Components"), to any country, person, entity, or end user subject to U.S. export restrictions. You specifically agree not to export or re-export any of the Restricted Components (i) to any country to which the U.S. has embargoed or restricted the export of goods or services, which currently include, but are not necessarily limited to, Cuba, Iran, Iraq, Libya, North Korea, Sudan, and Syria, or to any national of any such country, wherever located, who intends to transmit or transport the Restricted Components back to such country; (ii) to any end user who you know or have reason to know will utilize the Restricted Components in the design, development, or production of nuclear, chemical, or biological weapons; or (iii) to any end user who has been prohibited from participating in U.S. export transactions by any federal agency of the U.S. government. You warrant and represent that neither the BXA nor any other U.S. federal agency has suspended, revoked, or denied your export privileges.

DISCLAIMER OF WARRANTY

NO WARRANTIES OR CONDITIONS. MICROSOFT EXPRESSLY DISCLAIMS ANY WARRANTY OR CONDITION FOR THE SOFTWARE PRODUCT. THE SOFTWARE PRODUCT AND ANY RELATED DOCUMENTATION IS PROVIDED "AS IS" WITHOUT WARRANTY OR CONDITION OF ANY KIND, EITHER EXPRESS OR IMPLIED, INCLUDING, WITHOUT LIMITATION, THE IMPLIED WARRANTIES OF MERCHANTABILITY, FITNESS FOR A PARTICULAR PURPOSE, OR NONINFRINGEMENT. THE ENTIRE RISK ARISING OUT OF USE OR PERFORMANCE OF THE SOFTWARE PRODUCT REMAINS WITH YOU.

LIMITATION OF LIABILITY. TO THE MAXIMUM EXTENT PERMITTED BY APPLICABLE LAW, IN NO EVENT SHALL MICROSOFT OR ITS SUPPLIERS BE LIABLE FOR ANY SPECIAL, INCIDENTAL, INDIRECT, OR CONSEQUENTIAL DAMAGES WHATSOEVER (INCLUDING, WITHOUT LIMITATION, DAMAGES FOR LOSS OF BUSINESS PROFITS, BUSINESS INTERRUPTION, LOSS OF BUSINESS INFORMATION, OR ANY OTHER PECUNIARY LOSS) ARISING OUT OF THE USE OF OR INABILITY TO USE THE SOFTWARE PRODUCT OR THE PROVISION OF OR FAILURE TO PROVIDE SUPPORT SERVICES, EVEN IF MICROSOFT HAS BEEN ADVISED OF THE POSSIBILITY OF SUCH DAMAGES. IN ANY CASE, MICROSOFT'S ENTIRE LIABILITY UNDER ANY PROVISION OF THIS EULA SHALL BE LIMITED TO THE GREATER OF THE AMOUNT ACTUALLY PAID BY YOU FOR THE SOFTWARE PRODUCT OR US$5.00; PROVIDED, HOWEVER, IF YOU HAVE ENTERED INTO A MICROSOFT SUPPORT SERVICES AGREEMENT, MICROSOFT'S ENTIRE LIABILITY REGARDING SUPPORT SERVICES SHALL BE GOVERNED BY THE TERMS OF THAT AGREEMENT. BECAUSE SOME STATES AND JURISDICTIONS DO NOT ALLOW THE EXCLUSION OR LIMITATION OF LIABILITY, THE ABOVE LIMITATION MAY NOT APPLY TO YOU.

MISCELLANEOUS

This EULA is governed by the laws of the State of Washington USA, except and only to the extent that applicable law mandates governing law of a different jurisdiction.

Should you have any questions concerning this EULA, or if you desire to contact Microsoft for any reason, please contact the Microsoft subsidiary serving your country, or write: Microsoft Sales Information Center/One Microsoft Way/Redmond, WA 98052-6399.

Register Today!

Return this
*Programming Windows® with MFC,
Second Edition*

registration card today

Microsoft®*Press*
mspress.microsoft.com

OWNER REGISTRATION CARD   **1-57231-695-0**

*Programming Windows® with MFC,
Second Edition*

FIRST NAME   MIDDLE INITIAL   LAST NAME

INSTITUTION OR COMPANY NAME

ADDRESS

CITY   STATE   ZIP

(   )

E-MAIL ADDRESS   PHONE NUMBER

U.S. and Canada addresses only. Fill in information above and mail postage-free.
Please mail only the bottom half of this page.

For information about Microsoft Press®
products, visit our Web site at
mspress.microsoft.com

Microsoft Press